ISBN 978-1-330-93696-2
PIBN 10123621

This book is a reproduction of an important historical work. Forgotten Books uses state-of-the-art technology to digitally reconstruct the work, preserving the original format whilst repairing imperfections present in the aged copy. In rare cases, an imperfection in the original, such as a blemish or missing page, may be replicated in our edition. We do, however, repair the vast majority of imperfections successfully; any imperfections that remain are intentionally left to preserve the state of such historical works.

1 MONTH OF
FREE
READING

at
www.ForgottenBooks.com

By purchasing this book you are eligible for one month membership to ForgottenBooks.com, giving you unlimited access to our entire collection of over 1,000,000 titles via our web site and mobile apps.

To claim your free month visit:
www.forgottenbooks.com/free123621

English
Français
Deutsche
Italiano
Español
Português

www.forgottenbooks.com

Mythology Photography **Fiction**
Fishing Christianity **Art** Cooking
Essays Buddhism Freemasonry
Medicine **Biology** Music **Ancient
Egypt** Evolution Carpentry Physics
Dance Geology **Mathematics** Fitness
Shakespeare **Folklore** Yoga Marketing
Confidence Immortality Biographies
Poetry **Psychology** Witchcraft
Electronics Chemistry History **Law**
Accounting **Philosophy** Anthropology
Alchemy Drama Quantum Mechanics
Atheism Sexual Health **Ancient History**
Entrepreneurship Languages Sport
Paleontology Needlework Islam
Metaphysics Investment Archaeology
Parenting Statistics Criminology
Motivational

A TREATISE

ON

THE LAW OF FIRE INSURANCE,

ADAPTED TO THE PRESENT STATE OF THE LAW,

ENGLISH AND AMERICAN,

WITH

COPIOUS NOTES AND ILLUSTRATIONS.

By H. G. WOOD,

AUTHOR OF "THE LAW OF NUISANCES," "THE LAW OF MASTER
AND SERVANT," ETC., ETC.

BANKS & BROTHERS, LAW PUBLISHERS,
NEW YORK: No. 144 NASSAU STREET,
ALBANY, N. Y.: 473 AND 475 BROADWAY.
1878.

B39165

KF
1196
W87

CHARLES VAN BENTHUYSEN & SONS,
Printers, Stereotypers and Binders,
Albany, N. Y.

PREFACE.

The preparation of this work was undertaken at the suggestion of several members of the profession, who assured me that there was room for a work covering the topic in its practical aspects, and adapted to the present state of the cases. I have attempted to perform this service, and discharge the duty incident thereto, fully; and if I have failed to do so, the result is not due to any lack of effort on my part. In my division of topics, I have selected as leading ones, those that I regarded as of the most practical utility, and in reference to which, investigation is most likely to occur. I have, in many instances, in the citation of cases, referred as well to the original reports as to Bennett's Fire Insurance Cases, as I thought this would often be found convenient; particularly to those who have Mr. BENNETT's excellent reports. I have also referred to the American Reports, as they have found their way into the libraries of so many lawyers, both in this country and England, as to be entitled to recognition as a distinctive series. In numerous instances, when their importance seemed to warrant it, I have given, in the form of notes, all that portion of leading cases bearing upon difficult and important topics, believing that this will often prove of great service to members of the profession who are not so fortunate as to possess a full set of the reports of all the States. This method has not decreased my labors, or diminished the body of the text, as it will be seen that the work is a very large one, and that it contains more than a third more matter than the average modern text-books. The law controlling many features of insurance contracts, has been essentially modified in the last three years. Particularly is this the case in reference to the powers and functions of agents, implied waiver, estoppel, and the scope of the risk. I have endeavored to give the very latest and freshest cases upon these points, and, as will be seen, have been able to give the gist of many important cases considerably in advance of their publication in the reports. I have labored faithfully to give the very latest phase of the law covering each topic, and to present to the profession a work, that will lighten their burdens in a small degree, and aid them somewhat, at least, in their investigation of questions arising under the topics treated. I have endeavored to bring together the main body of the cases, and eliminate their doctrines. Of course, there are many that have been purposely omitted, because they do not express the law as now held ; while, doubtless, many others have been omitted through inadvertence, although I have endeavored to make the latter class very small. Hoping that the work may be found useful, and may tend, in a measure, to lighten the burdens of those members of the profession having occasion to investigate the questions discussed, I submit it to their criticism.

H. G. WOOD.

ALBANY, *January 22nd*, 1878.

TABLE OF CONTENTS.

CHAPTER I.

FIRE INSURANCE.

CHAPTER II.

THE POLICY.

CHAPTER III.

THE APPLICATION — WARRANTIES — REPRESENTATIONS — CONCEALMENT AND MISREPRESENTATION.

CHAPTER IV.

PROMISSORY WARRANTIES.

CHAPTER V.

WARRANTIES AND REPRESENTATIONS.

CHAPTER VI.

MISREPRESENTATION AND CONCEALMENT.

CHAPTER VII.

ALTERATION OR CHANGE OF RISK.

CHAPTER VIII.

WHO MAY BE INSURED—INSURABLE INTEREST.

CHAPTER IX.

ALIENATION.

CHAPTER X.

ASSIGNMENT OF POLICIES.

CHAPTER XI.

OTHER INSURANCE—DOUBLE INSURANCE.

CHAPTER XII.

AGENTS.

CHAPTER XIII.

NOTICE AND PROOFS OF LOSS.

CHAPTER XIV.

LIMITATION OF ACTION.

CHAPTER XV.

ADJUSTMENT OF THE LOSS.

CHAPTER XVI.

SUBROGATION.

CHAPTER XVII.

REFORMATION OF POLICIES.

CHAPTER XVIII.

COURT AND JURY—QUESTIONS FOR.

CHAPTER XIX.

REMEDIES UPON POLICIES.

CHAPTER XX.

WAIVER.

CHAPTER XXI.

ESTOPPEL.

CHAPTER XXII.

EVIDENCE.

CHAPTER XXIII.

MUTUAL INSURANCE.

TABLE OF CASES.

A

THE LAW OF FIRE INSURANCE.

CHAPTER I.

FIRE INSURANCE.

1

Who may be insurers.

SECTION 1. Any person, by the common law, may be an insurer, and may enter into a valid contract to indemnify another against loss from any cause, unless prohibited from so doing by some positive law, or because it contravenes public policy. Thus, an individual, for a legal consideration, may contract to indemnify another against the loss of a debt, from the dishonesty or negligence of a servant, from fire, from accident, from the perils of the sea, or indeed from any cause, when the contract is not prohibited by positive law, or when it is not *malum in se*.[1] Indeed, formerly the business of insurance was done by individuals or firms, and the contract was by parol, the assured trusting to the integrity of the insurer to carry out in good faith the terms and conditions of his agreement. And that this was generally done, is evidenced by the fact, that, until within the last century, very little litigation, growing out of insurance contracts, was indulged in. But at the present time the business of insurance is generally, indeed we may say entirely, done by corporations, created and formed for that purpose, who assume the position of insurers, while those contracting with them for indemnity take the place of the assured. Insurance companies exist for many purposes, generally confined to a particular class of casualties, as life insurance, marine, accident, fire, etc., although they sometimes unite the whole in a single company. The same general principles control in reference to the liability of the insurers, and the rights of the assured, against whatever casualty indemnity is contracted for, except so far as the same are modified by the subject-matter, peculiar usages and customs, and the contracts themselves. In this work we propose to deal only with contracts of fire insurance, although cases arising under other branches of insurance will often be cited, to sustain a principle common to all. An

---

[1] Park on Insurance, p. 5; Angell on Insurance, 43.

insurance company can enter into a valid contract to insure only against such casualties as it is authorized to insure against, by its a charter, or the articles of association under which it is formed. Thus, corporation, authorized by its charter to insure against casualties from fire, alone, cannot enter into a valid contract of insurance against "the perils of the sea," against "accident," or other casualties, but is restricted to the class of hazards against which, by the law under which it exists, it is authorized to transact the business of an insurer. Therefore it follows that the contracts of such companies are only valid and binding upon the corporation when they are *inter vires*, and are absolutely void when they are *ultra vires*, or in excess of the powers of the corporation. The question, as to whether a contract of insurance is *inter vires* or otherwise, may often arise under policies; and, in determining this question, the charter or articles of association, and the general laws applicable thereto, are the only touch-stones by which the question of authority can be tested and ascertained. How far the charter of a company can be regarded as modifying the terms or conditions of the contract of insurance, or as imposing conditions upon the assured, depends largely upon the circumstance whether it is a *public* or *private* statute. If, in terms, it is made a public act, the assured is bound to know its terms and provisions, and ignorance thereof will not excuse him;[1] but, if it is a private act, he is not bound to know its provisions, and is not affected thereby, except they are specially referred to and made a part of the policy, or are specially recited in the policy itself. It may often be important, in determining the liability of an insurer, to keep this distinction in mind. As in cases where the charter of a company provides that the application, survey, etc., made by the assured, shall be a part of the policy, the question whether they are so or not may depend' entirely upon the question whether the act creating the company is public or private. If the former, the assured is bound to know its provisions, and the contract embraces not only the policy, but the papers made a part thereof by the law creating the company. If, however, it is a private statute, the policy alone expresses the contract, and the application, survey, etc., are no part of the contract, unless expressly referred to and adopted as such ; or, as is required in some States, unless they are embodied in the policy itself. These general remarks will be fully illustrated under proper heads in succeeding chapters. There are two classes of companies—

---

[1] *Ill. etc., Ins. Co.* v. *Marseilles Mfg. Co.*, 6 Ill. 236.

stock and mutual. The former take the entire risk, and assume the entire liability, and the assured is not bound to know the condition of their charters; while in the latter, the assured becomes a member of the company, and liable to contribute to the payment of all its losses, his own included, and is bound to know, not only the conditions of its charter, but also of its by-laws.[1]

Contract one of indemnity.

Sec. 2. Fire insurance is a contract entered into between the parties thereto, by which one party—the insurer—undertakes, for a certain consideration, to make good to the other party—the insured—such loss or damage as he may sustain from an injury to, or destruction of, certain property specifically provided for in the contract, by fire, to an extent not exceeding the amount stipulated in the contract itself.[2]

---

[1] *Satterthwaite* v. *Ins. Co.*, 14 Penn. St. 393; *Rhinehart* v. *Allegany, etc., Ins. Co.*, 1 Penn. 332; *Liscomb* v. *Boston, etc., Ins. Co.*, 9 Met. (Mass.) 205; *Abbott* v. *Hampden, etc., Ins. Co.*, 31 Me. 252; *Susquehanna Ins. Co.* v. *Perriène*, 7 W. & S. (Penn.) 348; *Mitchell* v. *Lyoming Ins. Co.*, 51 Penn. St. 402; *F. Ins. Co.* v. *Mayor, etc.*, 8 Barb. (N. Y.) 450; *Diehl* v. *Adams Co., etc., Ins. Co.*, 59 Penn. St. 443. But he is not bound by any by-law that conflicts with the charter. *Great Falls, etc., Ins. Co.* v. *Harvey*, 45 N. H. 292. Nor is he a member of the company unless he gives a deposit note. If the company accepts a gross sum *in cash* for his premium, he stands in the same relation that he would to a stock company, unless the charter provides otherwise. *Ill. Ins. Co.* v. *Stanton*, 57 Ill. 354.

[2] "Insurance is a contract by which a person, in consideration of a gross sum, or of a periodical payment, undertakes to pay a larger sum on the happening of a particular event," Smith's Common Law, 299; "a contract whereby, for a stipulated consideration, one party undertakes to *indemnify* the other against certain risks," 1 Phillips on Insurance, sec. 1; "by our law, it is regarded as a guarantee or contract of *indemnity*." Addison on Contracts, Phil. Am. Edn. 553. "A wager," says COLERIDGE (afterwards judge), in his argument in *Paterson* v. *Powell*, 9 Bing. 322, "is a contract for the payment of an absolute value; *but a policy of insurance is essentially a contract of indemnity; for every policy of insurance must insure some thing or person from some risk to which that thing or person is liable.* That is, *must indemnify* the assured from the consequences attendant on the happening of that risk; *and the risk insured against ought to be one in which the party insured has an interest.*"
Mr. PHILLIPS, in his very excellent work upon Insurance, vol. 1, sec. 4, says: "As to the essential part of this contract, it does not differ from a bond of indemnity, or a guaranty of a debt, since the obligor takes upon him certain risks to which the obligee or creditor would otherwise be exposed. The only difference is in name, and the form of the instrument."
"The contract of insurance," says ELLSWORTH, J., in *Glendale Mfg. Co.* v. *Protection Ins. Co.*, 21 Conn. 31, "is a contract of indemity, upon the terms and conditions specified in the policy of insurance, * * The insurer undertakes for a comparatively small premium to guarrantee the insured against loss or damage upon *the exact terms and conditions agreed upon,* and no other." POTHIER, in his "Contrat d'Assurance," No. 4, calls it a species of contract of sale, the assured being the vendors, and the assurer the vender, and the thing sold *is the risk attached to the thing insured.* And different authors have given various, and entirely different definitions of the term and the nature of the contract, some describing it as a partnership, others as a mandate, and still others as a contract of letting and hiring; and it may justly be said that by a process of subtle reasoning, either one of these definitions may be quite plausibly sustained; but, what.

The consideration received therefor is denominated the premium, and the instrument that evidences the contract is denominated the policy. The term policy seems to have been derived from the Italian word *poliza*, which signifies a schedule and security, and has been adopted into our legal nomenclature by various statutes, and indicates a contract or security against loss or damage from casualties named therein. The system of fire insurance now existing, is of comparatively modern origin, and a legitimate outgrowth of marine insurance, and in many respects, indeed, in all respects so far as applicable, is governed by the same general principles—the distinction, so far as there is any, arising from the difference in the contract, the nature of the risks, and certain special usages and customs that have grown up and identified themselves with marine insurance. This species of insurance was received with great disfavor, in early days, upon the ground 'that it encouraged carelessness on the part of property owners, and induced such a relaxation of care and diligence in the protection of property as operated disastrously to the public generally. It appears from POTHIER[1] that it was not introduced into Paris until 1754, when a marine insurance company obtained permission to make insurances against fire. But that author informs us that it was but little resorted to at the time when he wrote. But in England it was in use at a much earlier date, and Mr. MARSHALL, in his Treatise upon Insurance,[2] informs us that it was in use there considerably over a century before he wrote, which was in 1802, and that, notwithstanding the heavy stamp duties imposed on such insurances, it had been brought into very general use. Indeed, he says, " I might almost have said, *into universal use*, particularly in London and other cities and large towns." And at the present time, in this country, a man is regarded as exceedingly improvident and reckless, if he neglects to protect him-

---

ever may be the recognized nature of the contract elsewhere, by our law, it is regarded as a contract of indemnity, by which one party, for a legal consideration, undertakes to indemnify the other against loss from casualties within the scope of the risk assumed. But there are instances in which the contract assumes a different character, and becomes something more than a mere indemnity, as will be seen by reference to matters hereafter stated in the text. It is believed, however, that the class of cases in which the effect of policies has been so extended, are wide departures from principle, and that the interests of both the insured and the insurer would be better protected by a strict adherence to the doctrine that such contracts *are mere contracts of indemnity, personal in their character, and not available except to the insured himself or those holding the contract by proper assignment.*

[1] Contrats d'Assurance, 3.

[2] Page 681.

self, by an insurance upon his property against loss or damage
by fire. Thus it will be seen that, in spite of the burdens imposed
upon insurance companies of this class by the government; in
spite of the hostility of wiseacres who seemed to think that the
whole world would be destroyed by fire, if this species of insurance
was encouraged, it has now come to be regarded [1] as one of the most
efficient aids to business, and a beneficent institution that is indispensable to the healthy growth of cities and towns, and the development
of industrial interest. Few people would be inclined to risk the capital essential for the erection, maintenance and equipment of large
manufacturing establishments, and the bringing together of the large
amount of stock and property essential to keep them in operation, unless the protection afforded by these institutions could be made available. Indeed, the credit, required in the prosecution of nearly all
mercantile, manufacturing or other business where the capital employed

---

[1] As illustrative of the views entertained in reference to these institutions in the
early part of the present century, I copy the remarks of Mr. MARSHALL in his
Treatise upon Insurance, p. 681. He says: "I do not find, however, that this
species of insurance is much in use in other countries. It was not till the year
1754 that it came into use at Paris. In that year, one of the companies instituted
there for marine insurances, obtained from the government permission to make
insurances against fire. But they have never, as Pothier informs us, become
general even at Paris. In Holland, though insurance against fire is not altogether
unknown, few people seek its protection; perhaps because the people of that
country can rely so much on their own caution, that they think it unnecessary to
pay for any greater security. Indeed I have heard it confidently asserted, by
persons well acquainted with the cities both of London and Amsterdam, that after
making all fair allowances, there is, upon an average, more property destroyed
by fire in the former in one year, than in the latter in seven.

"It cannot be denied that this species of insurance affords great comfort to individuals, and often preserves whole families from poverty and ruin. And yet it
has been much doubted, by wise and intelligent persons, whether, in a general
and national point of view, the benefits resulting from it are not more than coun-
terbalanced by the mischiefs it occasions. Not to mention the carelessness and
inattention which security naturally creates; every person who has any concern
in any of the fire offices, or who has attended the courts of Westminster for any
length of time, must own, that insurance has been the original cause of many fires
in London, with all their train of mischievous consequences.

"On the other hand, the advocates for this species of insurance, though they admit it to have been sometimes the cause of intentional fires; yet they insist, that,
even as a national concern, the benefits vastly outweigh the mischiefs which proceed from it. And when we recollect the precautions used by the different insurance companies, to prevent the spreading of fires, by providing a number of fire
engines, which are kept in constant repair, and fit for immediate use, not only in
all parts of the metropolis, but in every other considerable town in the kingdom;
—by keeping in constant pay, a number of engineers and firemen, expert in extinguishing fires, and porters for the removal of goods;—by employing a number
of these in patrolling the streets at all hours of the night, in constant readiness to
fly to the spot from whence any alarm of fire may proceed. When we recollect
that the courage, promptitude, and address of these people often stop the progress
of the most dangerous fires, and thereby rescue many valuable lives, and im-
mense property from destruction — when these benefits, I say, are fairly considered, it is impossible to deny that they generally outweigh all the disadvantages that can be put in the opposite scale."

by the owners is exposed to the hazards of fire, could not be obtained without, and is almost universally made dependent upon, the proper protection of the creditor, against this species of hazard and loss, by proper insurance. So that to-day, after more than a century of bitter opposition, both from the government and the people, these institutions, instead of being regarded as of doubtful and dangerous tendency, have come to be recognized not only as beneficent, but really *indispensable*, and no greater calamity could befall any civilized country, than to be deprived of the advantages which these companies afford. Therefore they should be, as they are, regarded with favor by the courts, and afforded all the protection in the prosecution of their business, that is accorded to individuals.[1] The contract is largely, one resting upon the integrity of the insurer. Indeed it may be said to be the main reliance of the assured.

Applying the strict rules of law, the instances are, perhaps, few, if proper objections are taken, in which a recovery could be had upon ordinary policies. But it is a refreshing fact, that generally, these companies conduct their business with a fair regard to the rules of morality and fair dealing and do not resist losses when the case is free from suspicion, upon merely technical or legal grounds. To do otherwise, tends to destroy their credit among business men, and so impair their business that the loss to them is more serious than losses under their policies. BLACKBURN, J., in a recent case before him,[2] in which the insurer availed himself of his own neglect in omitting to stamp a policy, very aptly said : " When the history of this case is published it will frighten foreign houses from English business, and the statute will thus turn out impolitic, as well as harsh. And there appears to have been no desire to *cheat* in this case; there was merely a mistake resulting in a loss to the revenue of some four or five shillings ; however, the loss would be the same if the loss were a three-pence only. The legislature has enacted that the whole benefit of the insurance shall be lost in such a case. The penalty is wholly disproportionate, and the principle impolitic as well as immoral, *for it holds out inducements to mean men to take mean advantages*, and makes those who pass the law, guilty of the immorality of it." In an earlier English case [3] BULLER, J., says : "The

---

[1] For a history of the origin and development of insurance, see *"Beekman's History of Inventions,"* Tit. *Insurance,* also Anderson's History of Commerce, vol. 2, p. 102.

[2] *Sassoon* v. *Harris*, L. T., January 22, 1876, p. 216.

[3] *Wolff* v. *Hardcastle*, 1 B. & P. 3.

time was when no underwriter would have dreamed of making such an objection. If the solicitor had suggested a loophole by which he might escape *he would have spurned the idea.* He would have said: Is it not a fair policy? Have I not received the premium? And shall I not now, when the loss has happened, pay the money? This would have been his answer and he would immediately have ordered his broker to settle the loss." In the case first named, immediately after BLACKBURN, J., had delivered his judgment, the insurer sent for the plaintiff and adjusted the loss. The instances are rare in which a respectable insurance company will take a mean advantage of a policy holder, even though the law may warrant it; but, in cases free from suspicion or real, substantial defenses, will pay the loss although upon technical or trivial grounds the law would shield them from liability.

Nature of the contract—leading characteristics of.

SEC. 3. The contract is *usually*, although, as will be seen hereafter, not necessarily, evidenced by a written or printed instrument, called a policy, and when a policy has been issued and *accepted* by the insured, he becomes bound by all its terms and conditions, unless they are contrary to the express provisions of the statute, or are in defiance of the principles of a sound public policy. "The parties," say the court, in a New York case,[1] "may insert what conditions they please in a policy, provided there be nothing in them contrary to the criminal law, or public policy." But, it must be remembered that, in order to be obligatory upon the assured, the conditions *must be assented to by him;* and, while the acceptance of a policy with conditions written or printed therein is *prima facie* evidence of his assent thereto, yet, he is not thereby in all cases estopped from showing that he never *in fact* gave his assent to them. Thus, where the policy refers to papers *dehors* the policy itself, as to an application or survey, and adopts it as a part of the contract, the insured may show that he never executed such papers, or authorized their execution,[2] or that the matters therein stated are erroneous or incorrect, and were written by the agent of the insurer, to whom a *correct* statement was made,[3] or that he signed the

---

[1] *Beadle* v. *The Chenango, etc., Ins. Co.,* 3 Hill (N. Y.) 161.

[2] *Denny* v. *Conway, etc., Ins. Co.,* 13 Grey (Mass.) 492.

[3] An exception is made in favor of the assured, where he correctly states the nature, character, extent and incidents of the risk, to the insurer or his agent, when insurance is applied for, and in such cases, even though the policy contains provisions inconsistent with the real condition and incidents of the risk, he may, at least in those states where courts of law also have equity powers, show the knowledge of the insurer, as to the true condition of the risk before the policy

papers in blank and correctly stated the nature of the answers that should be made, and the agent of the insurer erroneously or fraudulently wrote incorrect or untruthful answers.[1] But, where the conditions are written or printed upon the *face* of the policy, the assured, by accepting it, becomes bound thereby, and is estopped from denying that he assented thereto,[2] and if the policy does not *in fact* express the

---

issued, to defeat the operation of such inconsistent conditions. *Ins. Co.* v. *Wilkinson*, 13 Wall. (U. S.) 222; *Benedict* v. *Ocean Ins. Co.*, 31 N. Y. 389; 4 Bennett's F. I. C. 462; *Citizen's Mut. Ins. Co.* v. *Sortwell*, 8 Allen (Mass.) 217; *Ins. Co.* v. *Keyser*, 32 N. H. 313; *Goit* v *National, etc., Ins. Co.*, 25 Barb. (N. Y.) 189; *Clark* v. *Manufacturers' Ins. Co.*, 8 How. (U. S.) 235; 2 Bennett's F. I. C. 529; *Wilson* v. *Conway F. Ins. Co.*, 4 R. I. 141; *Moore* v. *Atlantic Mut. Ins. Co.*, 56 Mo. 343; *Marshall* v. *Columbian Ins. Co.*, 27 N. H. 157. Thus, where an application contained a question, "what incumbrances, liens and mortgages are upon the property?" and the answer was "none," it was held competent for the assured to show that the application was filled up by the agent of the insurer, and that he signed it without reading it, the agent assuring him that it was all right; and that the agent made no inquiries of him as to incumbrances, and that nothing was said in reference thereto. *Geib v. International Ins. Co.*, 1 Dill. (U. S. C. C.) 443; *Howard Ins. Co.* v. *Bruner*, 23 Penn. St. 50. See also, *Roth* v. *City Ins. Co.*, 6 McLean (U. S.) 324; *Ins. Co.* v. *Mahone*, 21 Wall. (U. S.) 152; *May* v. *Buckeye, etc., Ins. Co.*, 25 Wis. 291; *Aurora F. Ins. Co.* v. *Eddy*, 55 Ill. 213. So where the *title* of the property was misstated, as, where the application described the property as "his house," and in fact the assured had only an equitable estate therein, which the agent who drew up the application knew. *Hough* v. *City F. Ins. Co.*, 29 Conn. 10. See also, *Peck* v. *New London, etc., Ins. Co.*, 22 id. 584; *Commercial Ins. Co.* v. *Ives*, 56 Ill. 402; *James River Ins. Co.* v. *Merritt*, 47 Ala. 287. See especially, *Wood* v. *Dwarris*, 11 Exchq. 493; *Sommers* v. *Athenæum F. Ins. Co.*, 9 Lower Canada, 61. Evidence may be given to explain the meaning of terms used in a policy, where they are ambiguous, or have acquired a meaning *different* from that in which they are usually employed. *Coit* v. *Com'l Ins. Co.*, 7 John. (N. Y.) 385; *Gracie* v. *Marine Ins. Co.*, 8 Cr. (U. S.) 75; *Wade* v. *Walter*, 3 Camp. 163; *Gray* v. *Harper*, 1 Story (U. S. C. C.) 574. Or to show the meaning of *foreign* words. *Sleight* v. *Hartshorne*, 1 John. (N. Y.) 149. But if the language is plain and unambiguous, parol evidence is not admissible to show that a different meaning was intended from that ordinarily accorded to the language used *In order to admit of explanatory evidence, the meaning must be doubtful*, and this applies equally to evidence of an usage or custom. *Brackett* v. *Royal Exchange Ins. Co.*, 2 Cr. & J. 244; *Schooner Reeside*, 2 Sum. (U. S.) 567. Generally it may be said that *deceit, misrepresentation, fraud or mistake* in the execution of the contract, may be shown *in a court of equity*, and the policy be reformed to embrace the real contract entered into by the parties. *Moliere* v. *Penn. F. Ins. Co.*, 5 Rawle (Penn.) 342; *Alston* v. *Mechanics', etc., Fire Ins. Co.*, 4 Hill (N. Y.) 329; *Motteaux* v. *London Assurance Co.*, 1 Atk. 545; *Drew* v. *Whetten*, 8 Wend. (N. Y.) 166; *Graves* v. *Boston, etc., Ins. Co.*, 2 Cr. (U.S.) 418. But, where the policy expressly and in explicit terms sets forth the conditions upon which it is issued, and there is no ground for misconception or mistake on the part of the assured, as to the conditions of the contract, he cannot show any knowledge or understanding on the part of the assured to change the effect of the contract, but must resort to a court of equity for its reformation, when all such matters can be shown. *Dow* v. *Whetten*, 8 Wend. (N. Y.) 160.

[1] *Ins. Co.* v. *Mahone*, 21 Wall. (U. S.) 152; *Ins. Co.* v. *Wilkinson*, 13 id. 222; *May* v. *Buckeye Ins. Co.*, 25 Wis. 291; *McBride* v. *Republic Ins. Co.*, 30 id. 562; *Sommers* v. *Athenæum F. Ins. Co., ante*; *Geib* v. *Ins. Co., ante*.

[2] *Denny* v. *Conway, etc., Ins. Co., ante*; *Com'l Ins. Co.* v. *Ives*, 56 Ill. 402; *Illinois* v. *Mut. F. Ins. Co.* v. *O'Niell*, 13, Ill. 89; *Schimdt* v. *Peoria, etc., Ins. Co.*, 41 Ill. 295; *Lippincott* v. *Louisiana Ins. Co.*, 2 La. 399; *Eistner* v. *Equitable Ins.*

contract actually made, his only remedy is to seek its reformation.[1]
So, where an application or other papers are referred to and made a
part of the contract, if they were executed by an agent of the insured,
he is bound by their contents, and cannot set up his personal ignorance,
to obviate or excuse erroneous statements therein. The rule, *qui facit
per alium facit per se*, applies in such cases and estops him from setting
up his own ignorance of the contents of such papers.[2]

Contract need not be in writing.

SEC. 4. A contract of insurance, or an agreement to insure, need
not necessarily be in writing as at common law ; merely verbal contracts of this character are valid and binding, and are not within the
statute of frauds.[3] The policy is the evidence of the contract, and
not, in all cases, necessarily the contract itself.

Co., 1 Dis. (Ohio) 412; *Tibbetts* v. *Hamilton, etc., Ins. Co.*, 3 Allen (Mass.) 569 ;
Ashworth v. *Builders', etc., Ins. Co.*, 112 Mass. 422; *Conway Tool Co.* v. *Hudson
River Ins. Co.*, 12 Cush. (Mass.) 144 ; *Ætna Ins. Co.* v. *Burns*, (Ky.) 5 Ins. L. J.
69 ; *Madison Ins. Co.* v. *Fellows*, 1 Disney (Ohio) 217 ; *Hartford F. Ins. Co.* v.
Webster, 69 Ill. 392 ; *Baker* v. *Home Ins. Co.*, 4 T. & C. (N. Y.) 582 ; *Ins. Co.* v.
Lyman, 15 Wall. (U. S.) 664 ; *New York Ins. Co.* v. *Thomas*, 3 John. Cas. (N. Y.)
1 ; *Lamont* v. *Hudson R. Ins. Co.*, 17 N. Y. 199 ; *Alston* v. *Mechanics', etc., Ins.
Co.*, 4 Hill (N. Y.) 329 ; *Kentucky, etc., Ins. Co.* v. *Southard*, 8 B. Mon. (Ky.) 634.

[1] *Madison Ins. Co.* v. *Fellows*, 1 Dis. (Ohio) 217.   See chapter on Reformation of
Policies, *post.*

[2] *Goddard* v. *Monitor Ins. Co.*, 108 Mass. 56.

[3] *Commercial Mut. Ins. Co.* v. *Union, etc., Ins. Co.*, 19 How. (U. S.) 318; *Mobile
Marine Ins. Co.* v. *McMillan*, 31 Ala. 711; and in *First Baptist Church* v. *Brooklyn*, 19 N. Y. 305, parol contracts insuring property against injury from fire
were held valid. See also, *Wood* v. *Rutland, etc., Ins. Co.*, 31 Vt. 562. Where
there is no stamp act, contracts of insurance need not necessarily be in writing.
West Mass. Ins. Co. v. *Duffy*, 2 Kan. 347 ; *Morgan* v. *Mather*, 2 Ves. Jr. 18 ; *Ellis* v.
Albany City F. Ins. Co., 50 N. Y. 402 ; *American Horse Ins. Co.* v. *Patterson*, 28 Ind.
17 ; *Angel* v. *Hartford F. Ins. Co.*, 59 N. Y. 171; 17 Am. Rep. 122 ; *Anderson* v.
Excelsior Ins. Co., 27 N. Y. 216 ; *Franklin Ins. Co.* v. *Hewitt*, 3 B. Mon. (Ky.)
231 ; *Sanborn* v. *Firemen's Ins. Co.*, 16 Gray (Mass.) 448 ; *Hamilton* v. *Lycoming
Ins. Co.*, 5 Barr. (Penn.) 339 ; *Kennebec Co.* v. *Augusta Ins. Co.*, 6 Gray
(Mass.) 448 ; *McCullough* v. *The Eagle Ins. Co.*, 1 Pick. (Mass.) 280. No
written instrument is necessary to create or uphold a contract of insurance.
Kohn v. *Ins. Co. of North America*, 1 Wash. C. C. (U. S.) 93 ; *Blanchard*
v. *Waite*, 28 Me. 51 ; *Emerigon* on Ins. 26 ; *Duer* on Ins. 60. In *No. Western
Ins. Co.* v. *Ætna Ins. Co.*, 26 Wis. 78, a parol contract to insure a cargo was
enforced, and it was held, that the written policy usually employed, was only
controlling so far as it could be applied to the contract made, and that evidence
was properly admitted to show that a different contract was made, as in the
absence of statutes to the contrary, such a contract, like any other, is valid
at common law ; hence, when no policy has been issued the contract may be
proved by parol, or by letters, or any means that establish a binding obligation.
McCulloch v. *The Eagle Ins. Co.*, 1 Pick. 278 ; *Tayloe* v. *Merchant's Fire Ins. Co.*,
9 How. (U. S.) 390. In *Ide* v. *Phenix Ins. Co.*, 2 Biss. (U. S.) 333, the defendant's
agent made a contract with the plaintiff to insure certain property, but before a
policy was issued a loss occurred and the company was held responsible.
Henning v. *U. S. Ins. Co.*, 47 Mo. 425 ; 4 Am. Rep. 332 ; *E. Carver Co.* v. *Manufacturer's Ins. Co.*, 6 Gray (Mass.) 214 ; *Palm* v. *Medina Ins. Co.*, 20 Ohio, 529 ; *Kennebec Co.* v. *Augusta, etc., Ins. Co.*, 6 Gray (Mass.) 204 ; *Warren* v. *Ocean Ins. Co.*,

It is, however, when accepted by the insured, evidence of such
high character, that parol evidence is not admissible to control or

---

16 Me. 439; *Northrup* v. *The Mississippi Ins. Co.*, 47 Mo. 435; 4 Am. Rep. 337. But
when the act of incorporation of the company, or the general law, prohibits the
making of such contracts by parol, or requires them to be made in a certain
manner, parol contracts would be void. *Henning* v. *U. S. Ins. Co., ante; Train* v.
Holland Purchase Ins. Co., 62 N. Y. 598. So, where the statute requires a
contract of insurance to be in writing, no valid legal contract can be made by
parol, and in such cases, equity will not relieve a party unless his acts were in
reliance upon the contract and induced by it. Thus, in Georgia, where by statute all such contracts are required to be in writing, it was held, that the parol
consent of an agent of an insurance company to the removal of goods already
covered by a policy of the company, and an agreement to indorse such consent
on the policy, did not estop the company from setting up that the contract was
not in writing, in defense, and that the case was not a proper one for the interference of a court of equity. *Simonton* v. *Liverpool, etc., Ins. Co.*, 51 Ga. 76;
Croghan v. *Underwriter's Agency*, 53 Ga. 109. In *Cockerell* v. *Cincinnati Ins.
Co.*, 16 Ohio, 148, it was held, that a valid contract of insurance or any waiver
of its conditions could only exist in writing, but this doctrine has since been
overruled by *Dayton Ins. Co.* v. *Kelly*, 24 Ohio St. 345; in which it was held,
that a parol contract for insurance is valid.

In *Fisk* v. *Cottinett*, 44 N. Y. 538, F. entered into verbal negotiations with the
agent of an insurance company for a policy of fire insurance. The agent was
authorized "to bind the company during the correspondence," but, through his
neglect, the company did not receive and act upon the application of F., until a
loss by fire had occurred. *Held*, that the company was liable, a parol contract
being valid and not within the statute of frauds. *Kelly* v. *Commonwealth Ins.
Co.*, 10 Bosw. (N.Y.) 82; *Commercial etc., Ins. Co.* v. *Union, etc., Ins. Co.*, 19 How.
(U. S.) 318; *New England, etc., Ins. Co.* v. *Robinson*, 25 Ind. 536. "Whatever
doubts may formerly have existed in reference thereto, it is now certain that
oral contracts of insurance are valid and binding." GROVER, J., in *Ellis* v. *Albany
City Ins. Co., ante*. In reference to life insurance, such contracts have been held
valid. Thus, in *Cooper* v. *Pacific Mut. Life Ins. Co.*, 7 Nev. 116, a wife made
application to the agent of an insurance company for a policy on the life of her husband, and paid fifty dollars in accordance with the company's rules, which was to
be applied to the first year's premium provided the risk should be taken; and in
due time a policy was made out and forwarded to the agent for delivery; but
before it was delivered the husband died, whereupon the agent, though tendered
the balance of the premium, refused to deliver it. *Held*, that there was a valid
contract for a policy; that upon the taking of the risk, the fifty dollars became the
property of the company, and the assured became entitled to the policy; and that
such a contract was as available to sustain an action for the amount of the insurance as if the policy had been delivered. *City of Davenport* v. *Peoria Ins. Co.*,
17 Iowa, 276; *Bragdon* v. *Appleton Mutual Ins. Co.*, 47 Me. 259; *Andrews* v. *Essex
Ins. Co.*, 3 Mason (U. S.) 6; *McCulloch* v. *Eagle Ins. Co.*, 1 Pick. (Mass.) 278;
Palm v. *Medina Ins. Co.*, 20 Ohio, 529. Payment of the premium is not essential
as a condition precedent to a valid verbal agreement to insure. *Audubon*
v. *Excelsior Ins. Co.*, 27 N. Y. 216; *Trustees* v. *Brooklyn Fire Ins. Co.*, 19 id.
305; *Flint* v. *Ohio Insurance Co.*, 8 Ohio, 501; *Kelly* v. *The Com. Ins. Co.*, 10
Bosw. (N. Y.) 82; *Baxter* v. *Massasoit Ins. Co.*, 13 Allen, 320. In case of an oral
agreement, preliminary to a written policy, the obligation of the agreement
continues until a valid and binding policy is either tendered or delivered. *Kelley*
v. *The Com. Ins. Co., supra; Commercial Ins. Co.* v. *Halleck*, 28 N. J. 645.
In England, by statute 25 Geo. 3, chapter 42, an insurance was not valid
unless the name of the party insured appeared *in* the policy; and by a later
statute, 35 Geo. 3, chapter 63, were required to be engrossed, printed, or written,
consequently a verbal contract of insurance is not valid. *Cox* v. *Perry*, 1 T. R.
464; *Reid* v. *Allen*, 4 Exchq. 326; and where such contracts require to be stamped
it has been held, that a parol contract to insure would be invalid. *West Mass.
Ins. Co.* v. *Duffy*, 2 Kan. 347; *Morgan* v. *Mather*, 2 Ves. Jr. 18; but there seems
to be no validity in such a doctrine unless the stamp act expressly prohibits the

vary its terms,[1] but in all cases, where there is a written order or application for insurance referred to and adopted as a part thereof, they form a part of the contract, although not set forth in the policy, and will control the provisions of the policy itself, in matters in which there is a variance between them.[2]

So, too, it has been held, that where a note is taken for the whole or part of a premium, it is also to be treated as a part of the contract, if it contains any provisions that in anywise affect the construction, operation or validity of the policy. Where a policy refers to the *application*, "for a more full and particular description and forming a part of this policy," and declares that the policy is made and accepted in reference to the terms and conditions therein contained, and thereto annexed, which are declared to be a part of the contract by force of such reference, the application is made a part of the contract.[3]

A parol agreement to insure is valid and binding when all the essential elements of the contract have been agreed upon, and the minds of the parties have met. Thus, where the plaintiff completed an application for an insurance upon his life, which was forwarded to the company and accepted, and a policy sent to the agent, Oct. 25th, but prior to its reception by the agent the assured died, and the agent immediately returned the policy, it being shown that the first

---

making of contracts by parol, and a contrary doctrine was held in *Fisk* v. *Cottinett, ante,* and the argument adduced by HUNT, J., in support of this view is conclusive. A policy of insurance which has not been executed, will not support an action ; *but if there be a valid agreement to insure and to issue a policy,* an action may be brought upon such agreement. *Peoria, etc., Ins. Co.* v. *Walser,* 22 Ind. 73.

[1] See note 3, *ante,* p. 8.

[2] *Marshall* v. *Columbian, etc., Ins. Co.,* 27 N. H. 157 ; *Fourdinier* v. *Hartford F. Ins. Co.,* 15 U. C. (C. P.) 403 ; *Routledge* v. *Burrell,* 1 H. Bl. 254 ; *Ins. Co.* v. *Miller,* 39 Ind. 475 ; *Shoemaker* v. *Glens Falls Ins. Co.,* 60 Barb. (N. Y.) 84 ; *Philbrook* v. *N. E. M. & F. Ins. Co.,* 37 Me. 137 ; *Le Roy* v. *Market F. Ins Co.,* 37 N. Y. 90 ; id. 45 N. Y. 89 ; *Roberts* v. *Chenango, etc., Ins. Co.,* 3 Hill (N. Y.) 501 ; *Eagan* v. *Mut. Ins. Co.,* 5 Den. (N. Y.) 326 ; *Brown* v. *Cattaraugus, etc., Ins. Co.,* 18 N. Y. 385.

[3] In *Shoemaker* v. *Glens Falls Ins. Co.,* 60 Barb. (N. Y.) 184, the court held that where the conditions annexed to a policy required that applications for insurance should be in writing, and that any misrepresentation, concealment, suppression or omission of facts or circumstances known to the assured, increasing the hazard, should avoid the policy. The defendant, in an application for insurance upon premises covered by a mortgage, falsely stated that there was no incumbrance thereon ; and at the foot of such application, covenanted and agreed that "the foregoing statement is a just, full and true exposition of all the facts and circumstances in regard to the condition, situation, value and risk of the property to be insured, so far as the same are known to the applicant and are material to the risk," the covenant was a *warranty ;* and that whatever is expressly embraced in a policy, or in any condition or collateral instrument annexed thereto, and made expressly a part of the contract, is a warranty, in respect to the facts specified therein, or clearly referred to. This rule applies to all substantial statements which relate to the risk, and not to matters merely stated incidentally.

year's premium was agreed to be taken in one year's advertising in the insured's paper, it was held that the contract was valid and bind. ing upon the company, although the policy was never delivered.[1]

Where it is provided that a policy shall not attach until the premium is paid, the provision may be waived by the company, and as to whether it has done so or not, is a question of fact for the jury.[2] Where there is a valid agreement to insure, an action may be brought on such agreement, although no policy has been issued.[3]

VALIN[4] and POTHIER[5] both lay down the doctrine that, in insurances, the writing is only required as proof of the contract, and that in case it is denied, recourse may be had to the *serment decisiore*. But while their positions are undoubtedly correct, that the writing—with us the policy—is only necessary as proof of the contract, yet, if it is accepted by the insured, understandingly, there is no question but that it is evidence of such high character, that it cannot be contradicted or varied by parol or by other written documents, unless they form a part of the contract, in which case they control the policy in matters in which there is a variance between them.[6]

EMERIGON, in his excellent work upon Insurance, p. 26, in commenting upon the force and effect of a written contract of insurance, says: "I agree to the general rule that the writing is extrinsic to the substance of agreements. They are reduced to writing for the purpose of

---

[1] *Kentucky Mu. Ins. Co.* v. *Jenks*, 5 Ind. 96.

[2] *Kentucky Mu. Ins. Co.* v. *Jenks, ante;* Angell on Insurance, 343.

[3] *Peoria M. & F. Ins. Co.* v. *Walner*, 22 Ind. 73. In *N. E. Fire & Marine Ins. Co.* v. *Robinson*, 25 Ind. 536, the plaintiff made an application to the agent of a foreign insurance company to insure a building against fire. The proposition was accepted by the company, and a parol contract was thereupon made with the agent for an insurance of $1,000, for one year. It was also agreed with the agent that the policy was to be delivered when called for, and the premium was to be paid in five days. Before the expiration of that time, and before the payment of the premium, the building was destroyed by fire. The plaintiff thereupon tendered the premium and demanded a policy, which was refused. The court held that under this state of facts, the insurance was complete and binding, and that a policy was not essential as the foundation of an action, and that the plaintiff was not obliged to allege or show a compliance with the conditions, as the refusal of the company to issue a policy on demand was a waiver of the conditions precedent. It was also held that, unless specially restrained by its charter, a company may make a valid insurance by parol. See also, *Am. Horse Ins. Co.* v. *Patterson*, 28 Ind. 17.

[4] Art. 2, h. t., p. 27.

[5] Contrat d'Assurance, 99.

[6] *New York Gas-Light Co.* v. *Mechanics' Fire Ins. Co.*, 2 Hall (N. Y.) 108 ; *New York* v. *Brooklyn Fire Ins. Co.*, 4 Keyes (N. Y.) 465 ; *Ashworth* v. *Builders' Fire Ins. Co.*, 112 Mass. 422 ; *Hartford Fire Ins. Co.* v. *Webster*, 69 Ill. 392 ; *Madison Ins. Co.* v. *Fellows*, 1 Dis. (Ohio), 217 ; *Jenkins* v. *Quincy, etc., Ins. Co.*, 7 Gray (Mass.) 370 ; see Chapter on "EVIDENCE," *post.*

more easily preserving their proof. *Finut scripturæ sut quod actum est facilius probari possit.* The Guidon,'" he adds, "informs us, that formerly insurances were made without writing; they were termed, in confidence, because the person stipulating for insurance did not make his bargain in writing, but trusted to the good faith and honesty of his insurer." Mr. DUER, in his work upon Insurance,[2] admits that upon the principles of the common law, an unwritten or parol contract of insurance is valid and binding, but insists that, inasmuch as by general usage such contracts have been made in writing, this usage ought to be regarded as evidence of the legal necessity of a written contract. But the author, perhaps, had forgotten that the practice of reducing insurance contracts to writing, grew up under the Statute of 25 George 3, compelling it, and that prior to such statute such contracts were commonly made by parol, and the very fact that a statute requiring such contracts to be in writing was passed, evidences the fact that the practice, if not the custom, was to make such contracts by parol, which is fatal to his theory that, by universal custom, such contracts can only be legally made in writing; as that which is done by compulsion of a statute, cannot be evidence of a usage or custom, and all the early writers agree that, until statutes and ordinances were established, prohibiting the making of such contracts otherwise than in writing, the almost universal practice was to leave them resting in parol;[3] therefore, so far as any actual usage or custom is concerned, it would seem to have been entirely the reverse of that stated by Mr. DUER. Mr. PHILLIPS, in his work on Insurance, p. 9, says: "It does not appear why, *under the common law,* a valid oral insurance may not be made against loss by fire, or the ordinary perils of the sea, if it were upon a *real* interest, for a good consideration, and made in terms sufficiently explicit." Without stopping to refer to other authors for authority upon this question, it is safe to say that, in all cases where such contracts are not by statute required to be in writing, a parol contract of insurance is valid and binding,[4] as well as a parol contract to insure.[5]

---

[1] Ch. 1, Art. 2, p. 223.

[2] J. Duer on Insurance, vol. 1, p. 60.

[3] Emerigon, 26; Valin, Art. 2, h. t., p. 27; Pothier, Contrat d'Assurance, 99; Marshall,

[4] *Trustees First Baptist Church* v. *Brooklyn*, 19 N. Y. 305; *Mobile Ins. Co.* v. *McMillan*, 31 Ala. 711; *Angel* v. *Hartford F. Ins. Co., ante; Relief Fire Ins. Co.* v. *Shaw*, recently decided by the United States Supreme Court, and reported in

[5] In *Angel* v. *Hartford Ins. Co.*, 59 N. Y. 171; 17 Am. Rep. 322, the plaintiff entered into an agreement with the agent of the defendant company to insure his

Contract must be complete.

Sec. 5. In order to make a valid contract of insurance several things must concur. *First, the subject-matter to which the policy is to at-*

Albany Law Journal, vol. 15. p. 474, the doctrine of the text was fully recognized even in a case where the charter of the company required all contracts to be in writing. Bradley, J., in delivering the opinion of the court, said : "The principal question in this case is, whether a parol contract of insurance, made on behalf of the plaintiff in error by its agent, in the city of Boston, was valid. That a contract of insurance can be made by parol, unless prohibited by statute, or other positive regulation, has been too often decided to leave it an open question. That it is not usually made in this way, is no evidence that it cannot be so made. To avoid misunderstandings in a contract of such importance and complexity, it is undoubtedly desirable that it should always be in writing ; and such is the requirement of many codes of commercial law. But the very existence of the requirement shows that it was deemed necessary to make it. The question came before the Supreme Judicial Court of Massachusetts in 1860, on a contract made under circumstances very nearly similar to those of the present case ; and it was adjudged that a parol contract of insurance can be made. *Sanborn* v. *Firemen's Ins Co.*, 16 Gray, 448. The court, in that case, says : 'No principle of the common law seems to require that this contract, any more than other simple contracts made by competent parties upon a sufficient consideration, should be evidenced by a writing. No statute of Massachusetts contains such a requirement. Upon principle, therefore, we can find no authority in courts to refuse to enforce an agreement which the parties have made, if sufficiently proved by oral testimony.' This decision, being directly in point, and being made by the highest court of the State where the present contract was made, is entitled to the highest consideration. The Court of Appeals of New York held the same doctrine in 1859, in the case of *The Trustees of the First Baptist Church* v. *Brooklyn Fire Ins. Co.*, 19 N. Y. 305. Judge Comstock, delivering the opinion of the court, after briefly and accurately stating the history of policies of insurance, in regard to this point, says : 'The contract, as I have said, had its origin in mercantile law and usage. It has, however, become so thoroughly incorporated into our municipal system, that a distinction which denies the power and capacity of entering into agreements in the nature of insurances, except in particular modes and forms, rests upon no foundation. The common law, with certain exceptions, having regard to age, mental soundness, etc., concedes to every person the general capacity of entering into contracts. This capacity relates to all subjects alike, concerning which contracts may be lawfully made, and it exists under no restraints in the mode of contracting, except those which are imposed by legislative authority. There is nothing in the nature of insurance which requires written evidence of the contract. To deny, therefore, that parol agreements to insure are valid, would be simply to

---

building for $1,000, for three years, for the sum of $30, and to make out and deliver a policy, the premium to be paid when the policy was delivered. The agent did not make out the policy, and the premises having been destroyed by fire, the plaintiff tendered the premium and demanded a policy. The defendant refused to execute or deliver the policy, and action was brought to recover for the breach of the contract *to insure*, and the court held that the measure of the recovery was the actual loss not exceeding the sum agreed to be insured. Grover, J., in delivering the opinion of the court, said : "The counsel for the appellant is mistaken in supposing that the action was based upon a parol contract of insurance for three years. There was not sufficient evidence to show that Carpenter was authorized to make such a contract by the defendant. It was alleged in the complaint, and the testimony tended to prove, that a preliminary contract was made by which it was agreed that the defendant should insure the plaintiff upon the property against damage by fire, for a sum and at a rate agreed upon, for the term of three years from the time of making the contract, and that a policy of insurance should shortly thereafter be made out, to take effect from that time, and delivered to the plaintiff by Carpenter, at which time it was agreed the premium should be paid. It was proved that Carpenter was the agent of the defendant, with authority to negotiate contracts of insurance in its behalf, agree

taoh, must exist; Second, the risk insured against; Third, the amount of the indemnity must be definitely fixed; Fourth, the duration of the risk; and Fifth, the premium or consideration to be paid therefor must be agreed upon, and paid, or exist as a valid legal charge against the party insured where payment in advance is not a part of the condition upon which the policy is to attach. The absence of either or any of these requisites is fatal, in cases where a parol contract of insurance is relied upon.[1] In order to make a contract of insurance, or an agreement to insure, binding and obligatory, these elements must concur, otherwise it will have

---

affirm the incapacity of parties to contract where no such incapacity exists, according to any known rule of reason or of law.' *Kelly* v. *Commonwealth Ins. Co.*, 10 Bosw. 82. We have been referred to the case of *Cockerill* v. *Insurance Co.*, 16 Ohio, 148, in which it is held that a parol contract of insurance is not recognized as valid by the commercial law, but must be expressed in a written policy. We have also been referred to Duer on Insurance, p. 60, and to Miller on Insurance, p. 30; which are to the same purport as the Ohio case. On examination of the books on maritime law, on which these authorities rely, we find that the requirement of a written policy, though almost if not quite universal in maritime codes, is always by positive regulation; and we find those regulations as far back as the subject of insurance is discussed or legislated upon. But while this is true, the considerations referred to by Judge COMSTOCK, in the New York case last cited, are unanswerable. And the numerous cases in which a parol contract for a policy of insurance has been sustained, are conclusive that there is nothing in the nature of the subject which renders it insusceptible of a parol agreement. And while a statutory regulation requiring a writing may be very expedient, in the absence of such a statute it cannot be held that a parol insurance is void." Not only is a parol contract *for* insurance, but a parol acceptance of a *proposal for insurance* is a valid contract, in the absence of any statute prohibiting it. *Com'l Mut. Ins. Co.* v. *Union, etc., Ins. Co.*, 19 How. (U. S.) 318; *Kohne* v. *Ins Co.*, 1 Wash. C. C. (U. S.) 93. And though the charter of the company requires the contract to be in writing, equity will enforce a parol contract to insure. *Constant* v. *Alleghany Ins. Co.*, 3 Wall. Jr. (U. S.) C. C. 87.

upon the rate of premium, the term of insurance, and, in short, to agree upon all the terms of the contract. That he was furnished with policies executed in blank by the president and secretary of the defendant, with authority to fill up and deliver the same to any party with whom he made a contract. This authorized him to make a preliminary contract, binding upon the defendant, to be consummated by filling up, and delivering a policy pursuant thereto. The case comes directly within the principle upon which *Ellis* v. *The Albany City Fire Ins. Co.*, 50 N. Y. 402; S. C., 10 Am. Rep. 495, was decided by this court. The question whether such an agent was authorized to bind his principal by such a contract was fully considered in that case. The only distinction between that and the present is, that in that case, the premium was paid to the agent at the time of making the contract, and had been paid to the company, while in this, credit was given therefor until the policy should be delivered. This has no effect upon the validity of the contract. *Trustees, etc.,* v. *The Brooklyn Fire Ins. Co.*, 19 N. Y. 305; *Audubon* v. *The Excelsior Insurance Co.*, 27 id. 216. A recovery of the amount insured was proper in the action for the breach of the contract. *Ellis* v. *The Albany Fire Insurance Co.*, and cases cited, *supra*. The private instructions given by the defendant to Carpenter, by which he was to regulate his conduct in the transaction of the business, were not known to the plaintiff, or her agent, and could not therefore affect the rights of the parties."

[1] *Tyler* v. *New Amsterdam, etc., Ins. Co.*, 4 Robt. (N. Y.) 151; *First Baptist Church* v. *Brooklyn Ins. Co.*, 28 N. Y. 153; *McCulloch* v. *Eagle Ins. Co.*, 1 Pick. (Mass.) 278.

no validity, because indefinite, uncertain and vague,[1] the minds of the parties have not met, and no agreement exists.[2]

---

[1] *First Baptist Church* v. *Brooklyn Ins. Co.*, *ante.* In *Strohn* v. *The Hartford F. Ins. Co.*, 37 Wis. 625; 19 Am. Rep. 777, the plaintiff claimed to recover under a parol contract to insure under the following circumstances. He called upon the agent of the defendant for insurance upon tobacco, three several times, and upon these three several contracts he claimed a recovery. The facts, as well as the rule adopted, will be found in the opinion of COLE, J., which I give, because it will often be found useful to the profession. He said: "The court below non-suited the plaintiffs upon the ground that, as there was no time fixed for the expiration of the policy or continuance of the risk, no complete contract of insurance was entered into between the parties. The correctness of this view of the case is the main question before us; for, if sustained, it ends the cause. The complaint states three separate parol agreements for insurance, made by H. N. Comstock for the benefit of himself and the plaintiffs, with O. J. Dearborn as agent of the defendant company. These agreements, as set out in the complaint, are explicit and definite as to the amount insured, the continuance of the risk, and the rate of premium to be paid. And did the proof in regard to the contract come up to and sustain these allegations, there would be no doubt as to the plaintiff's right to recover under the former decision. *Strohn* v. *The Hartford Ins. Co.*, 33 Wis. 650. But it seems to us that the proof fails to show a valid contract of insurance. The verbal arrangement relied on to show a contract was in substance this: Comstock, who effected the insurance, if any contract was made, testified that in the spring of 1872 he contemplated establishing a tobacco warehouse for the storage of tobacco, and, when ready to receive it, and when he had received some, he went to Dearborn in relation to insurance. He told Dearborn that he had received some tobacco in his warehouse, and had advertised to receive and store tobacco for other parties, and keep it insured and sell it, or hold it subject to the order of the owners, as the case might be, and that he wanted to effect some insurance. He says that Dearborn told him that an open policy would be best; the amount perhaps would be increasing or diminishing as time passed along, and he thought it would not be best to issue an ordinary policy of insurance, specifying the amount for a specified time, but that the witness had better have what was called, in insurance parlance, an open policy, allowing the amount to be increased or diminished as witness thought proper. Before the conversation closed, the witness said to Dearborn: 'Insure me $400. * * Insure $400 on tobacco in my warehouse, belonging to me, and held by me in store for others. * * Finally he said he would give me $400 insurance in the Hartford in that way. * * Finally he said he would give me $400 upon any tobacco I had then in the warehouse; I asked him what per cent.? He said 1¾. I said, 'All right; how about the premium being paid?' Well, he said he didn't know how much it would be, because we didn't either of us know how long the insurance would continue on that amount; and he said, 'I will call on you when I want the premium; you can pay me when I call for it.' I said 'All right.' This is all that was said in regard to the first contract, made on the 23d of April. On the 3d of May, the witness testified that he went to Dearborn, and said to him 'that I wanted $1,500 more insurance on tobacco in the rink or warehouse; he said, 'Put it in the same open policy as the other;' and I said, 'That will be satisfactory to me, with the same premium, yes, sir.' I asked him if that was all right. He said, 'Yes, make it the same as the other.' The conversation in regard to the third agreement was substantially the same as that in respect to the second, except the witness did not remember whether at that interview any thing was said about the payment of premium; but he testified that Dearborn said 'he would make the entries and issue a policy in proper time, or he would give me a policy; or would make out the papers.' In the conversation, when any thing was said about payment of the premium, the witness said that Dearborn told him he would call upon him for it when he wanted it; witness tendered no money, but said he would pay it if Dearborn wanted it. 'His excuse was, that he did not know exactly how much to take, and he would not take it just then.' And the witness closed his

[2] *McCulloch* v. *The Eagle Fire Ins. Co.*, *ante.*

2

Elements requisite to establish completed agreement.

SEC. 6. In this class of contracts, as in all others, the contract must be definite and certain, and the parties must have agreed upon all its

---

testimony with the statement that ' there was nothing said between me and Dearborn as to how long this insurance should run.' This is really all the evidence in relation to the several contracts set out in the complaint; and, it seems to us, it fails to show that the negotiations resulted in a valid agreement, or that the parties came to an understanding upon all the material conditions of the contract. The amount of premium to be paid, and the continuance of the risk, are not agreed upon, nor is there any stipulation in the agreement from which these important elements of the contract could be fixed and determined. The rate of premium and continuance of policy are certainly important terms in a contract of insurance. Perhaps a contract which either party could terminate at any time by a notice to the other, might be a valid contract, as intimated by COMSTOCK, J., in *Trustees of the Baptist Church* v. *Brooklyn Fire Ins. Co.*, 19 N. Y. 305, until the notice was given. However this may be, the general rule is, that to constitute a valid contract of insurance, the minds of the parties must meet as to the premises insured, and the risk; as to the amount insured; as to the time the risk should continue; and as to the premium. Same case in 28 N. Y. 153. Where parties verbally agreed upon all the terms of the insurance except the rate of premium, and a previous insurance was referred to in the conversation, upon the same kind of property in the same place as the property sought to be insured, nothing being said about any change of rate, it was held to be a fair inference of fact that the rate was to be the same as that paid for the previous risk, and that the minds of the parties met upon that amount. *Audubon* v. *Excelsior Ins. Co.*, 27 N. Y. 216. In *Kennebec Co.* v. *Augusta Ins. Co.*, 6 Gray, 204, where, under an open policy of insurance on property on board a vessel from New Orleans to Boston, the cotton was insured for the voyage, and also, in addition, against fire from the time of its deposit in a warehouse until it was shipped, the objection was taken that the agreement fixed no certain time when the risk was to commence or terminate. But the court held that the risk commenced the day the cotton was first put in store by the plaintiffs at New Orleans, and that the termination of the whole risk, which included both the hazard of fire on shore and the perils of the sea on the voyage to be performed, was to be upon the safe arrival of the cotton at Boston, the place of its ultimate destination. In marine insurance, where a cargo is insured for a particular voyage, the policy ' to continue on the property until landed' (*Mansur* v. *New England M. M. Ins. Co.*, 12 Gray, 520), there is no difficulty in determining when the risk terminates. In *Walker* v. *Metropolitan Ins. Co.*, 56 Me. 371, where the evidence showed an application for a builder's risk, and a permanent yearly risk for a given amount, and that, though no specific premium was agreed upon, yet it was understood that the amount of premium should be deducted from the sum due the plaintiff from the defendants, the court said enough was done to make a complete contract of insurance. But all these cases, and others of the same character which might be cited, are manifestly in their features distinguishable from the one before us. Here Comstock says the rate of premium was to be 1¾ per cent. ; yet this, it is admitted, had reference to the annual rate. But the more serious defect in the contract is, that no time was fixed for the continuance of the risk. Suppose a bill in equity had been filed, as is sometimes done, to specifically enforce the performance of the contract to issue a policy. How could the court determine the essential elements of the contract which it was called upon to enforce? How long was the risk to continue, one month, two months, six months, or a year? All is uncertain and indefinite upon that point. Again, suppose the company had brought an action to recover the premium due on the contract: how much could it have claimed and recovered? It seems to us it is impossible to say. The property was destroyed on the 21st of May, and it is assumed that this was the termination of the risk. But suppose the property had been destroyed a month later, or not destroyed at all, what then would have been its termination? These tests clearly show, as it appears to us, that while the parties negotiated about insurance, still they did not agree upon all the terms, and that no contract was ever completed so as to become binding upon them. For this was a case in which the duration of the risk might and

essential terms. If anything has been left open, no contract exists, because the minds of the parties have not met, and there is not an *agreement* that can be enforced by either party, and both parties must be bound, the one to insure, and the other to pay the premium.[1]

The contract must be complete and perfect. All its elements must be agreed upon, and if anything is left open or undetermined, so that the minds of the parties have not met, no contract exists, and consequently no liability for a loss occurring.[2] As where the rate of premium is left undetermined,[3] or the time when the policy

---

should have been fixed. It was not one where the period was left indefinite, as it is in a voyage policy. It is true, the parties speak of the policy as an "open policy." Precisely what meaning they attached to these words is not readily perceived. Mr. MAY, in his work on Insurance, defines an open policy to be one in which the sum to be paid as an indemnity, in case of loss, is not fixed, but is left open to be proved by the claimant in case of loss, or is to be determined by the parties. § 30; Angell on Fire and Life Insurance, § 253. In *Watson* v. *Swann,* 103 E. C. L. 755, such a policy is spoken of as a "running policy;" but we do not understand that such policies *leave the duration of the risk indefinite.* There are elements by which the continuance of the policy can be ascertained. * * The continuance of the risk is an important element in determining the rate of premium; and how can the company fix its rates when that factor is left entirely indeterminate? *A parol contract of insurance indefinite as to time, and as to rate of premium,* is, as it appears to us, incapable of enforcement."

[1] *Train* v. *Holland Purchase Ins. Co.,* 62 N. Y. 598.

[2] *Real Estate Mu. Ins. Co.* v. *Roessle,* 1 Gray (Mass.) 336; *Mutual Life Ins. Co.* v. *Young,* 2 Sawyer (U. S.) 325; *Hughes* v. *Mercantile Mut. Ins. Co.,* 55 N. Y. 265.

[3] In *Orient Mut. Ins. Co.* v. *Wright,* 23 How. (U. S.) 401, the court held that where the insurer imposed a condition precedent to its liability under the policy, *such condition must be complied with, before a binding contract exists,* and that if the assured refuses to comply with such condition, no contract exists. Therefore, where the policy covers a shifting risk, and the policy in terms, provides that the rate shall be fixed at the time of indorsement, the assured cannot recover if he refuses to pay the rate so fixed, because a new contract arises under each indorsement, and, if the assured refuses to pay the rate fixed, the minds of the parties have not met, and no contract exists. *Hartshorn* v. *Shoe and Leather Ins. Co.,* 15 Gray (Mass.) 240; *Sun Mut. Ins. Co.* v. *Wright,* 23 How. (U. S.) 412. In *First Baptist Church* v. *Brooklyn F. Ins. Co.,* 28 N. Y. 153, an attempt was made to charge the defendants for a loss, upon the ground that they had agreed to renew the policy until notice to the contrary should be given. But it appearing that, prior to the loss, the defendants refused to renew the policy unless an increased rate of premium was paid, which was acceded to by the plaintiffs, it was held, that the variation of the contract in this respect, annulled the contract for indefinite renewal, and that a new assent of the parties thereto must be shown. *Sun Mut. Ins. Co.* v. *Wright,* 23 id. 412. In *Christie* v. *North British Ins. Co.,* 3 C. C. (Sc.) 360, the plaintiff averred and offered to prove, that his assignor, one Stead, applied to the Phenix Insurance Co., for insurance on his wire mill to the amount of £2,000, £3,000 to be placed elsewhere; that the risk not being one for which there was a known rate, the determination of the rate was referred to the directors in London; and that he also applied to the defendant company for insurance upon the same risk, to the amount of £3,000, and delivered an order therefor, to the secretary. That the secretary agreed to take the risk *at the same rate that should be fixed by the Phenix Co., and to make out and deliver a policy as soon as that was ascertained.* That Stead offered on two occasions to deposit a sum sufficient to cover the premiums, but the secretary declined to receive it, as being unnecessary, and that afterwards a person employed by the office surveyed the

shall attach,[1] or the apportionment of the risk has not been agreed
upon,[2] or if the insured retains control over the premium note or any
papers, the delivery of which is a condition precedent,[3] or if anything
remains to be done by the insured as a condition precedent, as the
payment of the premium,[4] or if the duration of the risk is not agreed
upon,[5] or if any condition precedent has not been complied with,[6] and
if, upon the whole evidence, it is left in doubt whether a binding contract was really made, a recovery will not be permitted, as the assured
takes the burden of establishing all the elements requisite to make a
completed agreement.   The *aggregatio mentium* must be fully estab-

---

premises, and the Phenix and defendant company exchanged notes of the terms
of insurance; that the defendant company made an entry of the insurance in its
order book, and in its ledger, the number of the intended policy and its date, the
columns for the intended premium being left blank.   That prior to the loss, on
the 30th of May, there had been two meetings of the directors of the defendant
company, and that although no premium had been paid, or policy issued, the
Phenix Co. paid its proportion of the loss.   It was held, upon these facts, that
there was no completed contract, and no liability on the defendants' part for the
loss   "If," said Lord Justice CLERK, "the premium in this case had been agreed
on, the insurance would have been effected, although no policy was delivered;
but the premises cannot be held to have been insured, *the premium never having
been determined on, and never having been fixed by the Phenix office.*   The pursu-
ers (plaintiffs) rest very much on Stead having been told by the Secretary that
he might hold himself insured; but, without inquiring whether this may warrant
a claim in another form of action, *it clearly cannot establish a contract of insurance with the company,* which is the ground of the present process, nor can the
subsequent action of the Phenix Co. affect the question with the North British."
As to the latter point, relative to the action of the Phenix Co., see *Buffum* v.
Fayette Ins. Co., 3 Allen (Mass.) 366; 4 Bennett's F. I. C. 582.   In *Train* v.
Holland Purchase Ins. Co., 3 T. & C. (N. Y.) 777, where a policy of insurance
was never delivered and accepted, nor received by the insured until after the
loss, and no premium paid or rate agreed upon, and the court held that the contract was never consummated between the parties, that the delivery of the policy
to the insured without payment of the premium, and after the premises insured
had been destroyed by fire, was unauthorized and the insurance void by the
terms of the policy.   The complaint alleged that the premium upon a policy of
insurance was paid, and the answer denied that the plaintiff was insured by the
defendant, and alleged that the policy was not delivered: *Held,* that this was
sufficient to make an issue upon the question whether the premium was paid.

[1] *Mutual Life Ins. Co.* v. *Young, ante.*

[2] *Sandford* v. *Trust F. Ins. Co.,* 11 Paige Ch. (N. Y.) 547.

[3] *Thayer* v. *Middlesex Mut. Ins. Co.,* 10 Pick. (Mass.) 326; *Belleville Mut. Ins.
Co.* v. *Van Winkle,* 12 N. J. Eq. 333.

[4] *Buffum* v. *Fayette Mut. F. Ins. Co.,* 3 Allen (Mass.) 360; *Bremer* v. *Chelsea
Mut. Fire Ins. Co.,* 14 Gray (Mass.) 203; *Mulvey* v. *Shawmut Mut. Ins. Co.,* 4
Allen (Mass.) 116; *Walker* v. *Provincial Insurance Co.,* 7 Grant's Ch. (Ont.) 137;
Wallingford v. *Home Ins. Co.,* 30 Mo. 46.

[5] *Strohn* v. *Hartford Fire Ins. Co.,* 37 Wis. 625.

[6] *Graham* v. *Barras,* 5 Barn. & Adol. 101; *Rose* v. *Medical Invalid Life Asso-
ciation Soc.,* 11 C. C. S. 151; *Walker* v. *Provincial Ins. Co.,* 7 Grant's Ch. 137;
Chase v. *Hamilton Ins. Co., ante; Winneshiek Ins. Co.* v. *Holzgrafe, ante,
Phlato* v. *Merchants', etc., Ins. Co.,* 38 Mo. 248; *Wallingford* v. *Home, etc., Ins.
Co.,* 30 Mo. 46; *Rogers* v. *Charter Oak Life Ins. Co.,* 41 Conn. 97; *Schaeffer* v.
Baltimore Marine Ins. Co., 33 Md. 109; *Myers* v. *Keystone, etc., Ins. Co.,* 27
Penn. St. 268.

lished, and nothing must remain to be done but to deliver the policy. *The details of the contract must be fixed*, and if the agreement or understanding of the parties in reference thereto are not mutual; that is, if one party understands the matter one way, and the other another, the minds of the parties have not met, and no contract exists that can be enforced either at law or in equity.[1]

Where an agreement to insure was entered into, and the president of the company made a memorandum thereof upon the application-book of the company, but the assured gave notice to the company that he desired to have the risk differently apportioned, and the premium was not paid, and no policy made because of such notice, it was held that no contract existed, and the premises having been burned before the apportionment of the risk was determined, no recovery for the loss could be had.[2] So, where the risk is not substantially as represented, as where the application was for insurance upon a stone house, when in fact it was part stone and part wood.[3] So where the plaintiff applied for insurance upon " his house," and the agent knowing that he resided the previous year in a house on the Cornwall road, and supposing that he still resided there, and that that was the house intended to be covered by the insurance, made the policy to cover that house. In fact, the plaintiff had removed to another house, which he then owned, and the latter house was the one which he desired to have insured. In an action to reform the policy it was held that there was no contract to reform, because the parties labored under a mutual mistake and their minds had not met.[4]

---

[1] In *Hughes* v. *Mercantile, etc., Ins. Co.*, 55 N. Y. 265, the policy covered " a bark called the Empress, or by whatever other name or names the vessel is or shall be called." The plaintiff claimed to recover upon the policy for the loss of the bark St. Mary, but the court held that, unless the insurer intended to take the risk upon that bark, no recovery could be had, because the minds of the parties had not met, and therefore no contract existed. *Watt* v. *Ritchie*, F. D. (Sc.) 43; *Chase* v. *Hamilton Ins. Co., ante; Mead* v. *Westchester, etc., Ins. Co., post.*

[2] *Sandford* v. *Trust Fire Ins. Co.*, 11 Paige Ch. (N. Y.) 547.

[3] *Chase* v. *Hamilton*, 20 N. Y. 52.

[4] In *Mead* v. *Westchester, etc., Ins. Co.*, 64 N. Y. 454, RAPALLO, J. said : " The power of courts of equity to reform written instruments is one in the exercise of which great caution should be observed. To justify the court in changing the language of the instrument sought to be reformed (except in case of fraud), it must be established that both parties agreed to something different from what is expressed in the writing, and the proof upon this point should be so clear and convincing as to leave no room for doubt. Losing sight of these cardinal principles, in the administration of this peculiar remedy, would lead to the assumption of a power which no court possesses, of making an agreement between parties to which they have not both assented. We think that the General Term were right in holding that the proofs in the present case failed to come up to the required standard. It is reasonably clear that the plaintiffs intended to obtain an insurance upon the

Both parties must be bound; the one to insure, and the other to pay therefor. If the contract is not so far perfected that the insurer, upon delivery of the policy, could maintain an action for the premium, no perfect agreement exists, and the insurer is not liable.[1] Thus, if the

building which was afterwards burned. But the question is, whether it is shown that the defendant intended to insure that building. The policy was issued on the 1st of July, 1871, to Thomas Foley, on his own application, loss, if any, payable to Mead and Taft, the plaintiffs. The property insured was described in the policy as 'his two-story frame dwelling, situate,' etc. The policy was issued by Mr. Dales, the agent of the defendant. It appeared in evidence that Foley had occupied this dwelling-house for four years prior to the 1st of April, 1871; and that the furniture therein had been insured by Mr. Dales on the application of Foley. Foley owned the adjoining building, which had also been insured by Mr. Dales, in the office of the Home Insurance Company, for $2,000, and this policy was outstanding when the insurance now in question was effected. In April, 1871, Foley removed from the dwelling-house into this building, but Dales testified that he supposed that Foley owned the dwelling-house also, though, in fact, he did not. Dales had on his books the descriptions of both buildings. The dwelling-house was described as a 'two-story frame dwelling, situate,' etc., and the adjoining building as a 'two and a-half-story frame building, and the additions attached, occupied as a dwelling and paint shop, with stable in the basement,' situate, etc. The established rate of premium upon this building, and that which was then being paid thereon, was two and a-half per cent. per annum; that upon the dwelling adjoining was one and a-half per cent. These were the circumstances existing at the time of the application for the policy in question. The application was made in writing by Foley to Mr. Dales, and was in the following words: 'I would like you to make me out a policy of $800 on my house, in favor Mead & Taft, in case of loss, in the cheapest company.' Thereupon, Mr. Dales made out a policy for $800 on the dwelling-house, charging premium at the rate of one and a-half per cent., which policy he delivered to one of the plaintiffs, who paid the premium. The adjoining building, in which the paint shop was kept, was afterwards burned, and the object of this action is to have the policy reformed so as to describe that building.

"The only direct evidence to establish that the defendant intended to insure the building which was afterwards burned is the testimony of Mr. Dales, who, on his direct-examination, was asked: 'To what property *do* you understand this letter of Foley's referred?' To which he answered: 'To the property which he occupied, which has since been burned, and described in my book.' On his cross-examination he was asked: 'At the time of issuing this policy, and before it was issued, did you not suppose the application referred to the building Foley formerley occupied? A. I was in doubt about it; the simple question was, if it was on the building in which he lived, it was two and a-half per cent., and if on the one he formerly occupied, one and a-half per cent. Question. You issued it for one and a-half, which was it on? Answer. My idea was on the one he formerly occupied.' The purport of this evidence, taken as a whole, is, we think, that at the time of the trial, and in view of the facts which had then been developed, the witness was satisfied that Foley intended by his letter, to refer to the building in which the paint shop was; but that, at the time of issuing the policy the witness concluded that the dwelling-house was the one desired to be insured, *and that he intentionally made out the policy to cover this building, charging the lesser rate of premium. These facts do not justify the reformation of the instrument.* * * We cannot make a contract for the defendant which it did not in fact, make, even though the failure to make the insurance which the plaintiffs desired was owing to the plaintiffs' misapprehension of the application." See also, *Hughes* v. *Merchants' Ins. Co.*, 55 N. Y. 265 ; *First Baptist Church* v. *Brooklyn Fire Ins. Co.*, 28 id. 161 ; *Ledyard* v. *Hartford Fire Ins. Co.*, 24 Wis. 496 ; *Kent* v. *Manchester*, 29 Barb. (N. Y.) 595 ; *Goddard* v. *Monitor Ins. Co.*, 108 Mass. 56 ; *Watt* v. *Ritchie*, Faculty Dec. (Sc.) 43.

[1] *Wood* v. *Poughkeepsie, etc., Ins. Co.*, 32 N. Y. 619.

policy *is* not accepted, and the assured is not bound to pay for it, no contract exists, and the assured cannot, *after* a loss, by signifying his acceptance, and offering to pay the premium, convert the policy into an operative contract, if he has retained it an unreasonable period before signifying his acceptance.[1] The evidence of a contract must be conclusively established,[2] and the circumstance that a contract in writing was contemplated and has not been executed, is entitled to great weight in determining whether a complete and perfect contract has been made,[3] but such evidence is not conclusive, and is entitled to weight in proportion only to the length of time that has elapsed since the contract is claimed to have been made ; and the distance between the insurer and the insured, the facilities for communication, and all the circumstances surrounding the transaction, are competent to explain or excuse delay.[4]

---

[1] *Wood* v. *Poughkeepsie, etc., Ins. Co., ante.* In *Tarleton* v. *Stainforth,* 5 T. R. 695, the agreement under which the plaintiffs were insured, contained a stipulation that they would pay half yearly, on the 10th of June and on the 10th of December, the sum of £7 10s., and that they would, *as long as the managers agreed to accept the same,* make their payments within fifteen days after the day limited. The insurers were held not liable because they and the assured had not agreed for the next half year when the loss happened, and because it would be unjust that the assured should have the interval to consider whether or not he would insure for the next half year ; if no loss happened during the fifteen days, he might not insure, but in the event of a loss during that period he would insure after it happened. In order to make the insurers liable, as on a contract, both the contracting parties must be bound ; whereas, according to the construction claimed by the assured, only the insurers were bound for the fifteen days. One object of the insurers was to have the policy continued ; and to induce the assured to pay the premium at an early period within the fifteen days, he was to be at his own risk between the time when the former insurance expired, and the beginning of the new insurance. In a subsequent case, which was tried before Lord ELENBOROUGH (*Salvin* v. *Jones,* 6 East R. 571), it was decided that where the rate of premium was altered by the insurers, and notice thereof given to the assured, and a refusal on his part to pay the increased premium, then a loss having happened within the fifteen days, and tender of the increased premium having been made after the loss, and within the fifteen days, the insurers were not bound to accept the premium ; and that, by the former refusal and actual non-payment of the premium at the time of the loss, the insurance was determined, and no sum recoverable for the loss. But in case there is no notice to determine the policy, or to increase the premium, or in case the original policy was for a special period without any power of renewal (conditional or absolute), then the insurance is considered as continuing for that special period, or from year to year. *Wood* v. *Poughkeepsie Ins. Co., ante.*

[2] *McCann* v. *Ætna Ins. Co.,* 3 Neb. 198 ; *Nevill* v. *Merchants', etc., Ins. Co.,* 19 Ohio, 452.

[3] *Real Estate Mut. F. Ins. Co.* v. *Roessle,* 1 Gray (Mass.) 454 ; HOAR, J., in *Sanborn* v. *Fireman's Ins. Co.,* 16 id. 454.

[4] *Insurance Co.* v. *Johnson,* 23 Penn. St. 72 ; *Belleville Mut. Ins. Co.* v. *Van Winkle,* 12 N. J. Eq. 333 ; *Ins. Co.* v. *Colt,* 20 Wall. (U. S.) 560 ; *Tayloe* v. *Merchants' Ins. Co.,* 9 How. (U. S.) 390. In *Ide* v. *Phœnix Ins. Co. of Hartford,* 2 Biss. (U. S.) 333, the plaintiff applied to the agent of the defendants for an insurance on his house for $1,000 for three years, and the agent agreed to insure it for a certain sum, which sum plaintiff immediately paid to the agent. The agent had not

Failure to notify assured of rejection of application.

SEC. 7. The question as to whether a failure on the part of the insurer to notify the assured of the rejection of his application can be construed as an acceptance thereof, is largely dependent upon the circumstances of each case.

An interesting question under this head came before the Supreme Court of Pennsylvania,[1] which resulted in an equal division of the court, one member being absent. A., the agent, secretary and director of a mutual insurance company, took the application for insurance, premium note, and note of hand for cash premium, of B., promising to notify him if the application was rejected, and, in that case, to return the note of hand. A by-law of the company required the approval of two directors to every application. B.'s application was rejected by two directors, of whom A. was one. B. received no notice of the rejection of his application until after the premises were burned, seven months after application was made. The court below had held that the plaintiff could recover against the company upon the agreement to insure, and, the court being divided, that judgment was affirmed. *Ordinarily, a proposal not answered remains a proposal for a reasonable time, and then is regarded as withdrawn.*[2]

In the case last cited it was held that a proposal is not to be presumed to be accepted from a delay of near six months to refund the premium paid, and to notify the applicant that his offer has been rejected. The reason is, that *delay cannot, of itself, make a contract.* The applicant has in his own hands the power of correcting the delay; and both parties are interested in the acceptance of the proposal, *and both are expected to attend to it with reasonable diligence.* But *a neglect or delay that has properly a tendency to mislead another, and which is incompatible with honesty, may be charged as a ground of liability.* In the Somerset case, there was not only a delay and neglect for nearly seven months

---

the policy ready then, but promised to give it to the plaintiff in a few hours. The policy was demanded of the agent several times, but was never delivered. During the term for which the insurance was sought to be effected, the house burned down accidentally. Notice of the loss was promptly given to the agent of defendants, who said that "the loss was all right," and that "the company would pay," etc. This action being brought for a recovery of the amount of insurance, *held*, that the parol contract for insurance upon complainant's house was valid, and could be enforced without a policy; that the failure to issue a policy by the company after the payment of the premium could not be taken advantage of by it in a court of equity; that the action of the company's local agent amounted to a waiver of the provisions in their policies as to strict proofs and suit within one year.

[1] *Somerset Co. Mut. Ins. Co.* v. *May*, 2 Weekly Notes of Cases (Penn.) 43.

[2] *Insurance Company* v. *Johnston*, 23 Penn. St. 72.

to refund the premium and give notice that the application was rejected, but there was an express promise to notify the plaintiff if the application was rejected, and this promise was made by the secretary of the company, who was also one of its directors. The company put the plaintiff off his guard, and it would seem reasonable that it should therefore be liable.

When company is left discretionary with agent.

SEC. 8. The fact that the company in which the insurance shall be placed is left discretionary with the agent, is not material, provided he has, in fact, decided in what companies to place the risk before a loss occurs, and an entry in his register is conclusive upon the company in which he determines to place the risk.[1] If the liability of the company once attaches, it continues until legally discharged, either by the act of the assured, or of the insurer, and if a discharge therefrom is claimed, the burden of establishing it is upon the company.[2]

As to powers of agent to bind company.

SEC. 9. The fact that the agent, with whom the contract was made, had no power to make out policies, but only to issue those sent him by the company, upon applications sent to it by him, does not, necessarily, evidence a want of authority on his part to make a valid contract for insurance. If he has authority to effect insurance,[3] his contracts therefor will be binding upon the company,[4] and the court will, in the absence of an express provision in the contract to the contrary, take judicial notice of the usage to make such contracts date from the date of the application.[5]

Distinction between contracts for, and of insurance.

SEC. 10. A contract *for* insurance is one thing, and a contract *of* insurance is another. Even where a statute provides that policies of insurance shall be valid only when made in writing and attested by

---

[1] *Ellis* v. *Albany City Fire Ins. Co.*, 50 N. Y. 402, was an action on an alleged contract of insurance. McC. was agent for several companies, including defendant. Plaintiff applied for insurance upon a quantity of cotton; the amount to be insured and the premium was agreed upon, and McC. agreed to insure as requested. Plaintiff left it with McC. to decide in what companies, and how much in each the insurance should be. He decided to place $6,100 with the defendant, and entered the contract to that effect in his register, received the premium and credited the amount to the defendant. It was held, that this was in substance a contract to issue a policy for the amount so placed, and was binding upon the defendant.

[2] *Ellis* v. *Albany City Fire Insurance Company, ante.*

[3] *Sanborn* v. *Fireman's Ins. Co.*, 16 Gray (Mass.) 44-48.

[4] *Post* v. *Ætna Ins. Co.*, 43 Barb. (N. Y.) 361.

[5] GROVER, J., in *Ellis* v. *Albany City Ins. Co., ante.*

the signature of the president and secretary, yet a valid contract to insure can be made by parol, and the company will be liable thereon.[1]

So, where the charter of an insurance company provided that all contracts, bargains, agreements, policies and other instruments should be in writing, under the seal of the corporation, and attested by the signature of certain officers, it was held that this did not prevent the making of a valid contract *for* insurance by parol, and that the charter only related to *executed* contracts.[2]

The fact, that the charter of the company requires that all contracts, bargains or agreements and policies shall be in writing, is held not to relate to a preliminary contract *for* insurance, but only to executed contracts *of* insurance. Hence, while in the case of companies where charters contain such a provision, a contract *of insurance* would be invalid, yet an executory contract *for* insurance, is held valid and binding. In a quite recent case heard in the Supreme Court of the United States, this question was quite carefully considered.[3] In that case the charter of the defendant company authorized its officers to make insurance against fire, and for that purpose to execute such " *contracts, bargains, agreements, policies and other instruments* " *as were necessary ; and declared that every such contract, bargain, agreement and policy should be in writing, or in print, under the seal of the corporation, signed by the president and attested by the secretary or proper officer.* The court held that the requirement of the charter had reference only to *executed* contracts or *policies of insurance, by which the company is legally bound to indemnify against loss,* and not to those initial or preliminary arrangements which necessarily precede the execution of the formal instrument by the officers of the company. It is not essential to the validity of these initial contracts that they should be attested by the officers and seal of the company.[4] FIELD, J., who delivered the opinion, in speaking of another point in the case, said: " There is no suggestion that the preliminary contract in this case was not made in perfect good faith on both sides, with full knowledge by the agent of the condition, char-

---

[1] *Commercial Ins. Co.* v. *Union Mutual Ins. Co.,* 19 How. (U. S.) 318 ; *Jones* v. *Provincial Ins. Co.,* 16 Up. Can., Q. B. 477.

[2] *Insurance Co.* v. *Colt,* 20 Wall. (U. S.) 560 ; *Security Fire Ins. Co.* v. *Kentucky Marine & Fire Ins. Co.,* 7 Bush (Ky.) 81 ; *N. E. Ins. Co.* v. *Robinson,* 25 Ind. 536 ; *Sanborn* v. *Fireman's Ins. Co.,* 16 Gray (Mass.) 448 ; *Mills* v. *Albton Ins. Co.,* 6 S. & D. 409.

[3] *Franklin Ins. Co.* v. *Colt,* 20 Wall. (U. S.)

[4] The case of *Security Fire Ins. Co. of N. Y.* v. *Kentucky Marine and Fire Ins. Co.,* 7 Bush (Ky.) 81 ; 3 Am. Rep. 301, relating to parol contracts for insurance, was approved.

acter and value of the property insured. The credit allowed for the payment of the premium was an indulgence which the agent was authorized by general usage to give. Its allowance did not impair the preliminary contract; that, being valid, could have been enforced in a court of equity against the company; and having been enforced by the procurement of a policy, an action could have been maintained upon the instrument; or the court, in enforcing the execution of the contract, might have entered a decree for the amount of the insurance. But no resort to a court of equity for specific performance was necessary in this case, by reason of the action of the agent in filling up the blank policy, which was duly attested, as he should have done immediately after the preliminary arrangement with the assured. The agent was authorized to do, after the fire, that which he had previously stipulated to do on behalf of the company. * * * * The filling up of the policy was a voluntary specific performance of the preliminary agreement. And when filled up, the policy was, by express stipulation, to be held by the agent, in his safe, for the assured, and no actual manual transfer was, under these circumstances, essential to perfect the latter's title. It then became his property, and upon a refusal of the defendant to surrender it, two courses were open to him: either to proceed by action to recover the possession of the policy, or to sue upon the policy to recover for the loss; and in the latter case to prove its contents upon failure of the company to produce the instrument on the trial.[1]

---

[1] In support of these positions the following cases will be found confirmatory: *Kohne* v. *Ins. Co.*, 1 Wash. C. C. 93; *Sheldon* v. *Conn. Mut. Ins. Co.*, 25 Conn. 207; *Lightbody* v. *N. American Ins. Co.*, 23 Wend. 18; *City of Davenport* v. *Peoria Marine and Fire Ins. Co.*, 17 Iowa, 277. In *Sanborn* v. *Fireman's Ins. Co.*, 16 Gray (Mass.) 454, the court in a similar case adopted the same rule. HOAR, J., in a very able opinion in commenting upon this question, pertinently says: "We cannot think that a provision in the charter of an insurance company authorizing contracts authenticated by the signature of a particular officer, and without any words of restriction, should generally be construed to limit the power of the company, and to prevent them from making contracts within the ordinary scope of their chartered powers. On the contrary, the phraseology of these statutes respecting the execution of policies should be regarded as consisting simply of enabling words, not restraining the power which they confer to make contracts, of which the policies are the evidence." *Commercial, etc., Ins. Co.* v. *Union, etc., Ins. Co.*, 19 How. (U. S.) 321. And the learned judge discussed another important question in reference to the powers of an agent, whose authority is limited to 'issuing policies' made out by the company. Upon this question he said: "The objection that the agent had only power to issue policies, and not otherwise to make contracts binding on the defendants, comes within the same rule of construction. His power of attorney authorized him 'to effect insurance,' and 'for this purpose to survey risks, fix the rate of premium and issue policies of insurance signed by the president, etc.' We are of opinion that this gave him authority to make the preliminary contract, as well as to issue the policy. He was not a special agent, employed merely to receive and transmit proposals to his principal, but had power to do whatever the company could do in effecting insurance."

A contract of insurance may be changed by parol,[1] or by indorsement upon the policy,[2] and the parties thereto may thus be changed,[3] or the subject-matter of the risk;[4] and such change effected by any person whom the company places in a position of apparent authority, will, *prima facie*, be binding upon it, as an agent authorized to make contracts of insurance,[5] a clerk or person acting as secretary in the office of the company,[6] or any person whom the company permits to act for it in such a manner as to indicate authority to act in such respects.[7]

An agent authorized to negotiate contracts of insurance, and to fill up and issue policies, has authority to bind the company by a parol contract to insure, and to give credit for the premium, and in an action upon such a contract, the plaintiff is entitled to recover as damages, the amount of his loss, not exceeding the sum agreed to be insured.[8] Such a contract is valid and binding upon the company,[9] and is not within the statute of frauds.[10]

---

[1] *Payne* v. *Marine Ins. Co.*, 5 W. & S. (Penn.) 122 ; *Kennebec Co.* v. *Augusta Ins., etc., Co.*, 6 Gray (Mass.) 204 ; *Warren* v. *Ocean Ins. Co.*, 16 Me. 439 ; *Cummings* v. *Arnold*, 3 Metc. (Mass.) 486 ; *Bunce* v. *Beck*, 43 Mo. 266 ; WAGNER, J., *Henning* v. *U. S. Ins. Co.*, 47 Mo. 425.

[2] *Salonnes* v. *The Rutgers Fire Ins. Co.*, 2 Keyes (N. Y.) 416 ; *Northrup* v. *The Miss. Valley Ins. Co.*, 47 Mo. 435.

[3] In *Salomes* v. *The Rutgers Fire Ins. Co.*, ante, the policy was, by the mistake of the insurer, made in the name of the husband, instead of that of the wife, who owned the property. Afterwards the insurers were notified of the mistake, and were requested to make the loss, if any, payable to the mortgagee. An endorsement was made by the secretary upon the policy, making the loss payable to the mortgagee ; and the court held, that this amounted to a new contract with the wife, by which the policy was made to cover her interest in the property. In *Benjamin* v. *Saratoga Co. Mut. Ins. Co.*, 17 N. Y. 415, a policy of insurance was issued to plaintiff as agent of the owners. Plaintiff had an interest in the property as mortgagee, of which he informed the insurers. Afterwards he obtained title by foreclosure. He notified the insurers of this, and of the fact that he had agreed to convey to a third person. They consented that the policy should remain valid till the vendee's title was perfected. It was held that this agreement was equivalent to issuing a new policy to plaintiff.

[4] *Northrup* v. *The Miss. Valley Ins. Co.*, ante.

[5] *Pechner* v. *Phenix Ins. Co.*, 65 N. Y. 194 ; *Clark* v. *Manufacturers' Ins. Co.*, 8 How. (U. S.) 235 ; *Gloucester Manf. Co.* v. *Howard Fire Ins. Co.*, 5 Gray (Mass.) 497 ; *Hotchkiss* v. *Germania Fire Ins. Co.*, 5 Hun (N. Y.) 90 ; *Goit* v. *Ins. Co.*, ante ; *Perkins* v. *Washington Ins. Co.* ante ; *Baubie* v. *Ætna Ins. Co.*, 2 Dill. (U. S. C. C.) 156 ; *Washington Fire Ins. Co.* v. *Davidson*, 30 Md. 91 ; *N. E. F. & M. Ins. Co.* v. *Schettler*, 38 Ill. 166 ; *Viele* v. *Germania Ins. Co.* 26 Iowa, 9.

[6] *Salomes* v. *The Rutgers Ins. Co.*, 3 Keyes (N. Y.) 416 ; *Conover* v. *Mut. Ins. Co* 1 N. Y. 290 ; *Northrup* v. *The Miss. Valley Ins. Co.*, ante.

[7] *Henning* v. *U. S. Ins. Co.*, ante.

[8] *Angell* v. *The Hartford Fire Ins. Co.*, 59 N. Y. 171 ; *Ellis* v. *Albany Ins. Co.*, 50 N. Y. 402.

[9] *Audubon* v. *Excelsior Ins. Co.*, 27 N. Y. 216.

[10] *Dresser* v *Dresser*, 48 Barb. (N. Y.) 330, affi'd in Ct. of Appeals ; *Fisk* v. *Cuttenett*, 44 N. Y. 538 ; *First Baptist Church* v. *Brooklyn Fire Ins. Co.*, 19 N. Y. 305.

Agreements to insure will be enforced in equity.

SEC. 11. The distinction between a contract of insurance and a contract *to* insure, is, that the one is executed, and the other executory, and in the one case the action is upon the contract for the loss or damage sustained under the risk, while, in the other, the action is for a breach of the contract, for not insuring, and the measure of recovery is the loss sustained,[1] so that the effect is the same in either case.

Parol contracts to insure, will be enforced in equity, even though the charter of the company requires all its contracts to be in writing;[2] the courts holding, in such cases, that there is a broad dis-

---

[1] *Angell* v. *Hartford Ins. Co.*, 59 N. Y. 171; 17 Am. Rep. 322; *Shearman* v. *The Niagara Fire Ins. Co.*, 46 N. Y. 530; *Kelly* v. *Com. Ins. Co.*, 10 Bos. (N. Y.) 82; *Baxter* v. *Massasoit Ins. Co.*, 13 Allen (Mass.) 320; *Hamilton* v. *Lycoming Ins. Co.*, 5 Penn. St. 339; *Ellis* v. *Albany Fire Ins. Co.*, 50 N. Y. 402; *Palm* v. *Medina Ins. Co.*, 20 Ohio, 529; *Suydam* v. *Columbus Ins. Co.*, 18 id. 659; *Audubon* v. *Excelsior Ins. Co.*, 27 N. Y. 216; *Perkins* v. *Washington Ins. Co.*, 4 Cow. (N. Y.) 605; *Bragdon* v. *Appleton, etc., Ins. Co.*, 42 Me. 259; *Pratt* v. *N. Y. Cent. Ins. Co.*, 64 Barb. (N. Y.) 589; *Andrews* v. *Essex F. & M. Ins. Co.*, 3 Mas. (U. S.) 6; *Davenport* v. *Peoria M. & F. Ins. Co.*, 17 Iowa, 276; *Union Mut. Ins. Co.* v. *Com. Ins. Co.*, 19 How. (U. S.) 318; *Sanborn* v. *Fireman's Ins. Co.*, 16 Gray (Mass.) 448; *Carpenter* v. *Ins. Co.*, 4 Sandf. Ch. (N. Y.) 408; *Post* v. *Ætna Ins. Co.*, 43 Barb. (N. Y.) 361.

[2] In *Security Ins. Co.* v. *Kentucky Marine F. Ins. Co.*, 7 Bush (Ky.) 81, this question was carefully considered, ROBERTSON saying: "In the summer of the year 1865, McFerran, Manifee & Co., owning a large quantity of cotton purchased in Georgia, for resale in New York—to be shipped from Columbus in barges down the Chattahooche to Appalachicola, in Florida, and to be thence transhipped in the Mary Lucretia and Metropolis, ships, to the city of New York — procured from the appellee an oral contract for insurance against the perils of navigation, which the appellant re-insured to the appellee; and to fill up the uninsured gap between the landing and transhipment of the cotton at Appalachicola, the owners also obtained from the appellee, on the 10th of October, 1865, an oral contract for insurance against fire risks *' on cotton at Appalachicola awaiting shipment per Mary Lucretia and Metropolis.'* On the same day the appellant made with the appellee a similar contract of re-insurance of the same cotton against the same risk. And, on the 17th of October, 1865, the appellant's agent, Muir, made in his book B, kept by him as evidence of insurances, an entry of the insurance and re-insurance, described as insuring against a *'fire risk on cotton at Appalachicola awaiting shipment.'* There is neither proof nor sufficient presumption that, at the date of the entry in book B, owners or insurers knew that the cotton had reached Appalachicola; but, as afterward appeared, some of it (46 bales) had been consumed by fire at the wharf at Appalachicola on the 6th of October, 1865. On satisfactory proof, the appellee adjusted the loss and paid the owners its portion of the liability according to its contract of insurance, and thereafter brought this suit against the appellant for a specific execution of its contract of re-insurance and for indemnity in damages, and finally recovered a judgment, which by this appeal the appellant seeks to reverse on the following grounds, on which the action was unsuccessfully defended:

1. There was no retrospective insurance or re-insurance against fire beyond the date of the contract.

2. An oral contract for insurance was not, according to the common law, binding and enforceable.

3. If such a contract was valid at common law, the appellee's charter modified that law in that respect by requiring a written memorial signed by the president; and, consequently, as the alleged insurance was not binding, the re-insurance

tinction between an *executory* and an *executed* contract, and that the
charter provisions can only be held to apply to the latter.   That is,

was not obligatory, because it only insured the original insurer against an enforceable liability.

Simple insurance, *prima facie*, implies the existence of the thing insured
at the date of the contract. But when, as in marine policies, the thing being distant and its *status* unknown to either party, an insurance *'lost or not lost'* may
bind the insurer for a loss occuring before the date of the contract. Such a provision is quite usual in fire as well as marine insurances, and without these express
words circumstances may sufficiently imply the same intent. 1 Arnould on Ins.
25; Phill. on Ins. § 925; *Gen. Int. Ins. Co.* v. *Ruggles*, 12 Wheat. 403. The
marine insurance and re-insurance in this case were expressly retrospective, and
the evident purpose of the owners and of the appellee was to protect the cotton
from fire from the landing to the transhipment of it at Appalachicola. The
testimony is conclusive to that effect. This authorizes the presumption that the
insurance was co-extensively comprehensive; and the testimony, when carefully
analyzed, preponderates decidedly that way, and does not conflict with the necessary construction of the entry in book B. Although a policy, as an executed
contract of insurance, is defined to be documentary and authenticated by the
underwriter's signature, yet a contract to issue a policy as an executory agreement
to insure may be binding without any written memorial of it. No statute of
frauds applies, and the common law does not require writing. This has been often
adjudged; but for the purpose of mere authority now the cases of *Tayloe* v. *Merchants' Ins. Co.*, 9 How. 390; and of *Commercial Ins. Co.* v. *Union Mutual Ins. Co.*,
19 id. 318, are deemed sufficient. And in the case in 9 Howard the Supreme Court
decided, as many other courts have also decided, not only that such an oral contract for a policy might be specifically enforced, but that a court of equity having
jurisdiction for specific enforcement would, to avoid unnecessary circuity, adjudge
the damages just as if a policy had been executed, and an action had been brought
on it for the loss of the thing thereby insured. In our judgment the appellee's
charter does not require such executory contract to be in writing. *If it does,
it is an anomaly, for we know of no other American charter that does so require.*
The seventh section of the appellee's charter recognizes the power of the corporation to insure all kinds of property against fire and marine risks, and *to do
all things respecting insurance which an individual might lawfully do,* 'and all
other thing necessary and proper to promote these objects.' As the common law
allows an unincorporated citizen to make contracts of insurance, and does not
require written memorials of executory agreements to insure, and the object of an
act of incorporation is only to give legal individuality to a multitude of persons,
and to limit the natural rights and powers, this seventh section certainly concedes
the right of this corporation to make initial contracts for insurance without any
writing; and we cannot presume that the thirteenth section was intended to curtail that right by providing 'that all policies or contracts of insurance which may
be made or entered into by the said corporation shall be subscribed by the president or president *pro tem.*, and signed and attested by the secretary, and being
so signed and attested shall be binding and obligatory on the said corporation
without the seal thereof, according to the tenor, extent, and meaning of such policies or contracts.' Even according to its literal interpretation this section does not
require all contracts of insurance to be in writing, but only dispenses with the
corporate seal for authenticating such as are in writing whenever signed and
attested as prescribed, and *which cannot be done as to oral contracts.* It applies
to the authentication of written contracts, and does not purport to change the
common law as to what contracts shall be written. If such a repeal of the
common law had been intended, why did not the section expressly require that
all contracts, executory as well as executed, for instance, shall be in writing?
'All policies or contracts of insurance' imports executed insurances, and not
executory contracts for policies or *for* insuranse. Such initial contracts for insurance by policy are generally made by agents and neither could be conveniently
nor, so far as we know, ever have been, signed by the president and secretary. The policy only, *in whatever form,* is so signed. The fair inference is, that
the object of the thirteenth section was to enlarge the common-law rights of the
corporation and not to curtail them, and consequently the whole aim of that

that a contract *of* insurance must be in writing, but that a contract *to* insure, may be by parol.[1]

---

section was to dispense with the corporate seal in cases in which it was previously necessary for authenticating corporate acts in writing; and such has been the judicial construction of the like provisions in charters in other States. A general statute of Massachusetts, applicable to all insurance companies, provides that all policies of insurance made by such companies *shall* be subscribed, etc., and be as obligatory as if certified by the common seal. The Supreme Court of that State construed that enactment as intended only to dispense with the corporate seal, and not as requiring writing not required by the common law, and that an oral contract to issue a policy was valid and enforceable. And this was affirmed by the Supreme Court of the United States in the case in 19 How. *supra*. The slight difference in the language of the 13th section and in that of the Massachusetts act is not, in our opinion, such as to require a different interpretation of the object of the two provisions. In most of the States, as well as in the Supreme Court of the United States, executory oral contracts to insure have been specifically enforced in equity, although executed contracts must be in writing. See Sandf. 408; 4 Cow. 646; 17 Iowa, 278; 20 Ohio, 529. And in a case published in 1 Am. Law Reg. (N. S.) p. 116, Justice Grier adjudged in the western district of Pennsylvania, that equity would enforce an oral agreement *for* insurance even though the insurer's charter required that 'all policies, bargains, contracts, and the agreements for insurance *shall be in writing or in print*, and signed by the president and attested by the secretary.' This is a peculiar case, which may be somewhat questionable, as the charter expressly required writing in policies and all other contracts *for* insurance. But his notion was that there was no purpose to repeal the common law, but that the legislative object was to require writing in policies and all other executed contracts *ejusdem generis*. However this may be, we are satisfied that the 13th section of the appellee's charter *not expressly requiring writing* does not modify the common law as to oral contracts *for* insurance. And we are also satisfied that Muir, as appellant's agent, had implied authority to re-insure against fire out of Kentucky as well as in it. The consequence is, that the appellee was entitled to judgment; and the appellant, re-insuring the fire risk taken by the appellee for the owner must be liable as for a fire and not a mere risk. The judgment, conforming to the fire standard by which the appellee's liability was adjusted, does not therefore appear too high; the amount does exceed the legal liability according to the law and the facts of the case." *Commercial Union Ins. Co. v. Union, etc., Ins. Co.*, 19 How. (U. S.) 318; *Sanborn v. Fireman's Ins. Co.*, 16 Gray (Mass.) 448; *Henning v. U. S. Ins. Co.*, 2 Dill. (U. S.) C. C. 26. It has been held in Missouri, in *Henning v. U. S. Ins. Co.*, 47 Mo. 425, that where the charter requires the contract to be in writing, a parol contract to insure, or of insurance was invalid, and where, by law, as in Georgia, all contracts of insurance are required to be in writing, it has been held that an agreement to renew a policy when it expired, made by parol, is inoperative, even though the insurance is paid. *Croghan v. N. Y. Underwriters' Agency*, 53 Ga. 109. And in Arkansas it has been held that, where the charter requires the policy to be sealed, a policy not under seal cannot be enforced. *Lindauer v. Delaware Mut. Safety Ins. Co.*, 13 Ark. 461. See also, *Franklin F. Ins. Co. v. Taylor*, 52 Miss. 441; *Phenix Ins. Co. v. Hoffheimer*, 46 id. 657; *Franklin Ins. Co. v. Colt, ante*.

Commercial[1] Union Ins. Co. v. Union, etc., Ins. Co., 19 How. (U. S.) 318. In *Relief Ins. Co. v. Shaw*, recently decided in the United States Supreme Court, reported in vol. 15, p. 474, of the *Albany Law Journal*, Bradley, J., in passing upon this question, says: "It is contended, however, that the present case is subject to, and is to be governed by, certain express regulations which take it out of the general rule of the common law. The charter of the defendant company is referred to as restraining its power to enter into contracts of insurance in any other manner than by a written instrument. The company was formed in 1856, under the general fire insurance companies' act of New York, passed in 1853, by which any association proposing to be organized under its provisions, was required to file a copy of its charter in the office of the comptroller, and therein 'set forth the name of the company, the place where its business should be located, the

Equity will compel performance, and enforce payment of loss.

SEC. 12. Where a bill for specific performance is brought, the court will not only decree performance by a delivery of the policy, but will

---

mode and manner in which the corporate powers granted by the act are to be exercised, etc.' The company in this case filed such a charter, by the first article of which it was declared as follows: 'The name of this company shall be the Relief Fire Insurance Company. The principal office for the transaction of its business shall be in the city of New York. Its purpose and business shall be by instrument under seal or otherwise to make insurance on dwelling-houses, stores, and all other kinds of buildings, and upon household furniture, and other property against loss or damage by fire, etc.' By article V. it is declared that 'the president or other officer appointed by the board of directors, for the purposes aforesaid, shall be authorized in the name and behalf of the company, and in and by policy of insurance in writing to be signed by the president or other officer and the secretary of the company, to make contracts of insurance with any person or persons, or body politic or corporate, against loss or damage by fire, etc.' It is insisted that these articles are the company's law of existence, and that it would be *ultra vires* for it to make parol contracts of insurance. But it is manifest that the article last quoted is merely affirmative as to what may be done by the officers in the usual course, and contains no negative clause that an insurance made otherwise than by a written policy shall be void. And the clause in the first article which declares that the company's 'purpose and business shall be by instrument under seal or otherwise, to make insurance,' admits of a wider construction than that contended for. The words, 'by instrument under seal or otherwise,' may as well mean 'by sealed instrument, or otherwise,' as to mean 'by instrument — either under seal or otherwise.' The substantial power given by law to an association organized under it, is to make insurance against loss and damage by fire. The mode and form in which it shall make its contracts is not prescribed as an essential part of its being or mode of action. The expressions referred to are not of that character. They indicate, in language chosen by the company itself, and not by the legislature, the ordinary mode of conducting its business. After having, by its officers and agents, made a parol contract of insurance and induced the insured party acting in good faith to rely on its engagements, it cannot be permitted to shelter itself behind any such ambiguous expression in its charter and claim to have a special statute of frauds for its own benefit. Substantially similar provisions to those now relied on were contained in the charter of the Fireman's Insurance Company in the case of Sanborn, in 16 Gray; but the court held that they were merely enabling in their character, and not restrictive of the general power to effect contracts in any lawful and convenient mode. 'We cannot think,' said Judge HOAR, delivering the opinion of the court, 'that a provision in the charter of an insurance company, authorizing contracts authenticated by the signature of a particular officer, and without any words of restriction, should generally be construed to limit the powers of the company, and to prevent them from making contracts within the ordinary scope of their chartered powers. On the contrary, the phraseology of those statutes respecting the execution of policies should be regarded as consisting simply of enabling words, not restraining the power which they confer to make contracts, of which the policies are the evidence.' 16 Gray, 454. Substantially the same views were expressed by the Court of Appeals of New York in the case of *First Baptist Church* v. *Brooklyn Fire Ins. Co.*, 19 N. Y. 309–311. But, besides all this, it is not perceived how the insured can be affected by these verbal minutiæ in the charter of the company without their being brought to his knowledge. The charter is a document on file in the office of the comptroller of New York in the city of Albany. A person dealing with the company in Massachusetts cannot be expected to know its precise terms. It holds itself out to be an insurance company, authorized to take risks against losses by fire, and by its officers and agents assumes to act in the same manner as other insurance companies do. However it may expose itself to be questioned by the government which created it, for exceeding the precise limits of the powers granted, it is estopped from eluding its obligations, incurred toward those who, in ignorance of these limits, contract with it in good faith, and upon the basis of the powers

also adjudicate and compel the payment of the loss;[1] and the fact that the party has a remedy at law, will not be sufficient to oust the court of its jurisdiction, as the party has a right to have the contract enforced by a delivery of the policy, and the court having jurisdiction for one purpose, will, to prevent circuity of actions, compel a payment of the loss under the policy.[2] In such cases, the assured has his election of remedies. He may proceed at law upon the contract to insure,[3] or in

---

assumed by its recognized agents to exist. It is contended, however, that there is a statute of Massachusetts which, in effect, requires that all contracts of insurance shall be in writing, namely: chapter 196, section 1, of the acts of Massachusetts for 1864, which provides as follows: 'In all insurance against loss by fire hereafter made by companies chartered or doing business in this Commonwealth, the conditions of insurance shall be stated in the body of the policy, and neither the application of the insured nor the by-laws of the company shall be considered as a warranty or a part of the contract, except so far as they are incorporated in full into the policy and appear on its face before the signatures of its officers.' It is evident that the object of this statute was, not to prohibit parol contracts of insurance, but to prohibit the practice of referring to a set of conditions not contained and set out in the policy, but embodied in some other paper or document. The statute was passed for the benefit of the insured, in order that they might not be entrapped by conditions to which their attention might never be called, and which they might inadvertently overlook and disregard if they were not embraced in their policies. It applies in terms only to policies, that is, to written contracts of insurance; and has no application whatever to parol insurances. It does not prohibit them nor affect them in any way. Other points were taken by the plaintiff in error, to the effect that there was no evidence that the agent ever had authority to make other than a written contract, or that a completed oral contract was ever made as stated in the declaration, or that the insurance company ever authorized its agent to delegate to another the power to make insurance. An examination of the bill of exceptions shows that it does not contain all the evidence which was adduced. Whether the omitted portions would furnish any light on these points we are unable to say. But we think that the evidence which is spread upon the record was sufficient to go to the jury, and we see no error in the charge of the court in this behalf. The agent who acted in this case had been accredited as the general agent of the company in the Commonwealth of Massachusetts from the beginning of 1870, and had during all that time been transacting the business of the company as such agent in the city of Boston. His mode of doing business was not materially different from that of other agents or companies. He had during all that period been assisted by a clerk or clerks who attended to the business in his absence, which the company must have known. These and other facts sufficiently shown by the evidence entirely justify the charge of the court, and the finding of the Jury is conclusive."

[1] *Lightbody* v. *N. American Ins. Co.*, 23 Wend. (N. Y.) 18; *Hallock* v. *Com. Ins. Co.*, 26 N. J 268; *Carpenter* v. *Mut. Ins. Co.*, 4 Sandf. Ch. (N. Y.) 408; *Union Mut. Ins. Co.* v. *Com. Ins. Co.*, 2 Curtis (U. S.) 254; *Perkins* v. *Washington Ins. Co.*, 4 Cow. (N. Y.) 645; *Suydam* v. *Columbus Ins. Co.*, 18 Ohio, 659.

[2] *Jones* v. *Provincial Ins. Co.*, 16 U. C. Q. B. 477; *Ellis* v. *Albany City F. Ins. Co.*, 50 N. Y. 402.

[3] *Jones* v. *Provincial Ins. Co.*, ante.; *Commercial Union Ins. Co.* v. *The Union Ins. Co.* 19 How. (U. S.) 321; *Trustees, etc.,* v. *Brooklyn F. Ins. Co.*, 19 N. Y. 205; *Andrews* v. *Essex F. M. Ins. Co.*, 3 Mas. (U. S.) 6; *Tayloe* v. *Merchants' F. Ins. Co.*, 9 How. (U. S.) 390. In *Ellis* v. *Albany City F. Ins. Co.* ante. GROVER, J., said: "Whatever doubts may formerly have existed as to the validity of parol contracts of insurance, made by insurance companies authorized by their charters to make insurance by issuing policies, it is now settled that they are valid. It is equally well settled that parol contracts of such companies to effect an insurance

equity to compel a delivery of the policy, *and* a payment of the loss. Generally, it is believed that the safest and best remedy is to be found in a court of equity.[1]   An agreement by parol to insure, and that the risk shall attach pending the application, is good,[2] or a parol agreement to make a policy by a person authorized to do so, is binding upon the company, and a court of equity will compel a specific performance of the contract,[3] and where a definite time is agreed upon, within which it shall be issued, no demand therefor is necessary.[4]

by issuing policies, are valid, and will be enforced by compelling specific performance by the company, or in an action for a breach of the agreement; *in either of which a recovery for a loss of the property agreed to be insured will be awarded to the plaintiff.*" *Kentucky Mut. Ins. Co.* v. *Jenks*, 5 Ind. 96; *Ide* v. *Phenix Ins. Co.*, 2 Biss. (U. S.) 333; *Mills* v. *Albion Ins. Co.*, 4 C. C. (Sc.) 575; *Angel* v. *Hartford F. Ins. Co.*, 59 N. Y. 171; *Shearman* v. *Niagara Fire Ins. Co.*, 46 N. Y. 530; *Kelly* v. *Com. Ins. Co.*, 10 Bos. (N. Y.) 82; *Baxter* v. *Massasoit Ins. Co.*, 13 Allen (Mass.) 320; *Hamilton* v. *Lycoming Ins. Co.*, 5 Penn. St. 339; *Braydon* v. *Appleton, etc., Ins. Co.*, 42 Me. 259; *Davenport* v. *Peoria, etc., Ins. Co.*, 17 Iowa, 276; *Audubon* v. *Excelsior Ins. Co.*, 27 N. Y. 216.

[1] *Jones* v. *Provincial Ins. Co., ante*; *Dunning* v. *Phenix Ins. Co.*, 68 Ill. 414; *Gerrish* v. *German Ins. Co.*, 55 N. H. 355; *Kelly* v. *Com. Ins. Co.*, 10 Bos. (N. Y.) 82.

[2] In *Audubon* v. *Excelsior Ins. Co.*, 27 (N. Y.) 216, the court held that a verbal agreement to insure property against fire is valid, where all the terms have been agreed upon except the rate of premium, where a former rate had been fixed, and nothing was said about any change therein, is valid and binding, the presumption being that the same rate would continue, and the company under such a contract was held liable for a loss occurring the next day after the contract was made, and before the policy had been delivered. In *Franklin Ins. Co.* v. *Hewitt*, 3 B. Mon. (Ky.) the defendant company agreed to deliver the plaintiff a policy covering certain property, the terms and conditions of the insurance being agreed upon, but it sent a policy varying from the contract, and a loss occurring within the insurance contracted for, but which was not covered by the policy, it was held that a recovery might be had *according to the contract agreed upon*, it being shown that they had never seen the policy until after the loss, and were not aware of the variance between the policy and the contract. In *Davenport* v. *Peoria Ins. Co.*, 17 Iowa, 276, an agreement for insurance was entered into through the defendant's agent, and on the next day a policy was delivered and received by the plaintiff, dated as of the previous day. Before the policy was delivered a loss occurred, and the company was held liable therefor, although the charter of the company provided that all policies should be subscribed by the president and signed and sealed by the secretary, and that the premium was not paid until the policy was delivered. In *Goodall* v. *N. E. F. Ins. Co.*, 25 N. H. 169, the secretary of the defendant company delivered to the plaintiff a memorandum, stating that the directors consented to continue in force a policy previously issued to him by the company, and that it might cover certain property not embraced in the previous policy, and it was held that this certificate was evidence of a valid contract of insurance, upon which the defendants were liable. See also, *State, etc., Ins. Co.* v. *Porter*, 3 Grant's Cases (Penn.) 123, and *Eureka Ins. Co.* v. *Robinson*, 56 Penn. St. 256, in which it was held that in such cases it will be presumed that the contract entered into is that ordinarily and usually expressed in the form of policy employed by the company at the time when the contract was made, and that the declaration may set forth the contract in accordance with such form. But if any special contract differing therefrom was made, it should be specially set forth. *Davenport* v. *Peoria Ins. Co., ante.*

[3] *Kelly* v. *Commonwealth Ins. Co.*, 10 Bos. (N. Y.) 82; *Commercial Mut. Marine Ins. Co.* v. *Union Mut. Ins. Co.*, 19 How. (U. S.) 318; *N. England, etc., Ins. Co.* v.

[4] *West'n Mass. Ins. Co.* v. *Duffy*, 2 Kan. 347.

SEC. 13. A contract of insurance, or *to* insure, is established by the same class of proof required to establish any other contract. If there has been any correspondence between the parties, relative to the matter, it is competent evidence either to prove or disprove the fact that a contract was made, but is not always conclusive. The burden of establishing it is upon the assured, and he must satisfy the jury that a complete and perfect contract was made ;[1] that an agreement was entered into,

---

Robinson, 25 Ind. 536 ; 5 Bennett's F. I. C. 62 ; *Union, etc., Ins. Co.* v. *Commercial, etc., Ins. Co.* 2 Curtis (U. S.) 524. But in all such cases, in order to entitle the party to specific performance by issuance of a policy, a valid contract must be established, and the party must show that he has complied with all the conditions thereof. Thus, where the plaintiff did not establish a contract entered into with an authorized agent of the company, and payment of the premium, the relief was denied ; *Deming* v. *Phœnix Ins. Co.*, 68 Ill. 414 ; but payment of the premium, as well as other conditions, may be waived as a condition precedent, but the burden is on the party applying for relief to establish the waiver. *Davenport* v. *Peoria Ins. Co., ante.* In *Gerrish, etc.,* v. *German Ins. Co.*, 55 N. H. 355 ; 5 Bennett's F. I. C. 726, the plaintiff made a contract with the defendants' agent to insure a quantity of wool for $3,500, for one year, commencing Sept. 30th, 1873, at noon, and the agent agreed to procure and deliver a policy therefor. Oct. 1st, 1873, the wool was destroyed by fire. No policy had been delivered. The plaintiff made preliminary proofs, and demanded a policy and payment of the loss, which was refused. A bill in equity was brought to compel a delivery of the policy, and for payment of the loss, and the court held that he was entitled to a decree of specific performance, compelling a delivery of the policy, and to prevent circuity of action, to compel a payment of the loss.

[1] *Strohn* v. *Hartford F. Ins. Co.*, 37 Wis. 625 ; 19 Am. Rep. 777; 5 Bennett's F. I. C. 491 ; *McCullough* v. *Eagle Ins. Co.*, 1 Pick. (Mass.) 280 ; *Trustees, etc.,* v. *Brooklyn F. Ins. Co.*, 19 N. Y. 305. In *Ide* v. *Phenix Ins. Co.*, 2 Biss. (U. S.) 333 ; 5 Bennett's F. I. C. 318, the agent was familiar with the property, and offered to insure it for three years for a certain premium, which was paid to him by the plaintiff. The policy was not made, but the insured called for it frequently, and failing to get it, soon after left the State. Before the agent had remitted the premium to the company, the property was burned. The agent appropriated the money to his own use, and never reported the risk. The loss was promptly reported to the agent, who promised that it should be paid at various times between the autumn of 1864 and 1866. In 1866, the agent notified the assured that the company would not pay the loss. The court held that the contract was binding upon the defendants, and that the fact that proofs of loss were not made, or the action brought within a year, was not fatal to a recovery, as the acts of the agent amounted to a waiver of compliance with the conditions. In *Banbie* v. *Ætna Ins. Co.*, 2 Dill. (U. S. C. C.) 156 ; 5 Bennett's F. I. C. 526, the defendants' agent, who was supplied with policies signed in blank, entered into a contract with the plaintiff to insure certain property for him to the amount of $4,000, for six months, and issued a policy to him therefor, and renewed it for six months after the policy expired. An agreement, however, between the plaintiff and the agent was shown, by which the agent agreed to renew every six months, and draw for the premium. He did not do so, however, and the property was burned. The court held that the contract was binding upon the company, and that the plaintiff could not be affected by any private instructions given the agent, or by any secret limitations upon his powers. See also, *Taylor* v. *Germania Ins. Co.*, 2 Dill. (U. S. C. C.) 282 ; 5 Bennett's F. I. C. 454 ; also, *Hotchkiss* v. *Germania Ins. Co.*, 5 Hun (N. Y.) 90, in which, under a very similar state of facts, a similar doctrine was held. See *Sanborn* v. *Fireman's Ins. Co.*, 16 Gray (Mass.) 448. As bearing upon the effect of secret instructions to the agent, the case of *Citizen's Mut. F. Ins. Co.* v. *Sortwell*, 8 Allen (Mass.) 217, is a strong one. In that case the directors issued instructions to their agents

and that nothing essential to the contract was left open for future determination,[1] and the proof must be clear that such a contract was made, or an action will not be upheld upon it at law, nor will it be enforced in equity.[2] If the premium is not fixed, and there is anything to show that the amount was in dispute, so that the presumption as to former or customary rates does not apply, no contract exists;[3] or if any essential details of the contract are not agreed upon,[4] as if the apportionment of the risk is not determined,[5] or if the risk is not as described by the assured,[6] or if the policy has not been accepted, or its

---

that distilleries were not insurable. The agent, however, in defiance thereof, issued a policy to the plaintiff upon his distillery, and received a premium note from him therefor. The court held that the policy was obligatory, notwithstanding the instructions, and formed a good consideration for the note. See also, *Franklin F. Ins. Co.* v. *Massey*, 33 Penn. St. 221, where the agent was directed to cancel a policy, but neglected to do so, and the company was held responsible for a loss occurring thereafter.

[1] *Strohn* v. *Hartford F. Ins. Co.*, *ante; Neville* v. *Merchants', etc., Ins. Co.*, 19 Ohio, 452; *Eliasen* v. *Hurshaw*, 4 Wheat. (U. S.) 228; *Ocean Ins. Co.* v. *Carrington*, 3 Conn. 357; *Hallock* v. *Ins. Co.*, 27 N. J. 268; *Belleville Mut. Ins. Co.* v. *Van Winkle*, 12 N. J. Eq. 333.

[2] *Neville* v. *Merchants', etc., Ins. Co.*, 19 Ohio, 452. In *Perkins* v. *Washington Ins. Co.*, 4 Cow. (N. Y.) 645; 1 Ben. F. Ins. C. 148, the defendants' agent was authorized to receive applications for insurance, and, with the premium, forward them to the insurer, when, if the company was satisfied with the risk, and recognized the rate of premium, a policy was to be issued binding *as of the time of the agreement.* The agent received a premium *at the established rate* of the plaintiff, under an agreement to insure his goods, but before the application was forwarded by him, a loss occurred, and the defendants claimed that, as they had not *assented to the premium,* no perfected contract existed. But the court held that, as the rate was the *usual* rate charged by the company, it could not arbitrarily object thereto, or reject the risk *after a loss.* WOODWORTH, J., in a very able opinion, discussed the relative rights of the assured and the insurer, in such cases, and clearly illustrated the rule, that a court of equity would, in all cases, enforce a contract entered into by the insurer's agent, within his apparent power, when there was no fraud on the part of the assured, *and a loss had intervened,* which was evidently the only ground which induced the action of the company. The court decreed payment of the amount of the loss. See also, to same effect, *Woodbury Savings Bank* v. *Charter Oak Ins. Co ,* 31 Conn. 518; *Leeds* v. *The Mechanics' Ins. Co.*, 8 N. Y. 351; *Hallock* v. *Commercial Union Ins. Co.*, 26 N. J. 268; *Lightbody* v. *N. American Ins. Co.*, *ante,* as to powers of an agent to bind the company by such contracts.

[3] *Orient Mut. Ins. Co.* v. *Wright*, 23 How. (U. S.) 401; *First Baptist Church* v. *Brooklyn F. Ins. Co.*, 28 N. Y. 153. In *Christie* v. *N. British Ins. Co.*, 3 C. C. (Sc.) 360, Lord Justice CLERKE said: "If the premium in this case had been agreed on, the insurance would have been effected, although no policy was delivered; but the premises here cannot be held to have been insured, the premium never having been determined on, *and never having been fixed by the Phœnix office.*"

[4] *Phlato* v. *Merchants', etc., Ins. Co.*, 38 Mo. 248; *Mut. Life Ins. Co.* v. *Young*, 5 Ins. L. J. 17; *Winnisheik Ins. Co.* v. *Holzgrafe*, 53 Ill. 516; *Bidwell* v. *St. Louis Floating Dock Ins. Co.*, 4 Mo. 42.

[5] *Sandford* v. *Trust F. Ins. Co.*, 11 Paige Ch. (N. Y.) 547.

[6] *Chase* v. *Hamilton*, 20 N. Y. 52; *Watt* v. *Ritchie F. D.*, (Sc.) 43; *Mead* v. *Westchester Ins. Co.*, 64 N. Y. 453; *Goddard* v. *Monitor Ins. Co.*, 108 Mass. 56; 5 Bennett's F. I. C. 377.

terms assented to ;[1] if the duration of the risk is not agreed on,[2] if the premium has not been paid, when payment thereof is a condition pre-cedent,[3] or if the assured has once refused to receive the policy, he cannot afterwards insist upon its delivery without the insurer's consent.[4]

It is competent for the company, when the evidence is doubtful as to whether a contract by parol has in fact been entered into, to prove that it was the usual course of business *of other insurance companies, acting through their agents in that place, to receive propositions for insur-ance by parol, and that when accepted, the transaction was entered and recorded on their books as an agreement between the parties for insurance, upon the terms and conditions* of the policies in use by such companies, *a policy to issue at any time on request, and that the parties contracted in reference to such usage.*[5]

All conditions precedent must be complied with.

SEC. 14. In order to make a perfected contract binding upon the par-ties, all conditions precedent must be complied with. Thus, the plain-tiff applied March 16, 1849, for $1,500 insurance upon his factory, etc., in the defendant company. The defendant's secretary accepted the offer at three per cent., to which complainant assented by letter; but it mis-carried; and, subsequently, complainant saw the secretary, mentioned the fact that he had sent the letter, requested a policy, and offered to pay the premium. The secretary replied that he did not know then how much the balance would be; that complainant might send it at any time, and also assured complainant that his property was then insured; that he would make out his policy and send it right away. It was made April 18th, and on the 20th the secretary enclosed a premium note to complainant, requesting him to sign and remit it with $7.20 cash, promising to send the policy. The note was one of the usual printed blanks, requiring complainant to procure a surety for its pay-ment. The letter and note were deposited in the post-office at Belle-

---

[1] *Wood* v. *Poughkeepsie Ins. Co.,* 32 N. Y. 619 ; 5 Bennett's F. I. C. 60 ; *Linda-ner* v. *Del. Mut. Ins. Co.,* 13 Ark. 461 ; *Rose* v. *Medical, etc., Association Soc.* 20 Scot's Jurist. 534 ; *Real Estate, etc., Ins. Co.* v. *Roessle,* 1 Gray (Mass.) 335.

[2] *Strohn* v. *Ins. Co., ante; Tyler* v. *New Amsterdam Ins. Co.,* 4 Rob.(N. Y.) 151.

[3] *Train* v. *Holland Purchase Ins. Co.,* 62 N. Y. 598 ; *Berthoud* v. *Atlantic Marine & F. Ins. Co.,* 13 La. 539 ; *St. Louis Mut. Life Ins. Co.* v. *Kennedy,* 6 Bush (Ky.) 450 ; *Walker* v. *Provincial Ins. Co.,* 7 Grant's Ch. (Canada) 137 ; *Hieman* v. *Phœnix Mut. Life Ins. Co.,* 17 Minn. 153 ; *Hardie* v. *St. Louis Mut. Ins. Co.,* 26 La. An. 242 ; *Collins* v. *Ins. Co.,* 7 Phila. (Penn.) 201 ; *Myers* v. *Keystone Mut. Life Ins. Co.,* 27 Penn. St. 268 ; *Rogers* v. *Charter Oak Ins. Co.,* 41 Conn. 97.

[4] *Schwartz* v. *Germania Life Ins. Co.,* 18 Minn. 448 ; *Ocean Ins. Co.* v. *Carring-ton,* 3 Conn. 357.

[5] *Ætna Ins. Co.* v. *N. W. Iron Co.,* 21 Wis. 458.

ville, April 21st; and on the 22d, before the note could be returned, the premises were consumed by fire. Complainant tendered the note and the money after the fire, but they were refused. The court held that there was not a completed contract, because the act of incorporation provided that "Every person who shall become a member by effecting insurance shall, before he receives the policy, deposit his premium note for such a sum as may be determined by the directors;" and that there was no contract until the deposit of the note.[1]

Plaintiff must establish contract. Binding receipts.

SEC. 15. So, too, the plaintiff must conclusively establish the fact that a contract was made, and if the matter is left in doubt, the insurer is entitled to the benefit of it.[2] So long as the *locus penitentiæ* exists, that is, so long as the matter is in a situation that either party can recede from or withdraw his offer, no perfected contract exists. Thus, it has been held that if the offer is made by mail, and is withdrawn *before* the other party has posted his acceptance of the terms, although *he does not receive* the letter withdrawing the offer until after the acceptance is mailed;[3] or if the letter of acceptance is in the hands of the agent of the assured at the time of the loss, and is not seasonably forwarded, the insurer cannot be held chargeable for the loss.[4]

But this doctrine has been somewhat impugned by a later case in the United States Court,[5] and by several cases in the courts of other States,[6] and the doctrine as established by the later cases would seem to be, that the *locus penitentiæ* is lost, if an acceptance of the offer is posted

---

[1] *Belleville Mut. Ins. Co.* v. *Van Winkle*, 12 N. J. Eq. 333.

[2] *McCann* v. *Ætna Ins. Co.*, 3 Neb. 198.

[3] In *McCulloch* v. *The Eagle Ins. Co.*, 1 Pick. (Mass.) 277, the question as to what constitutes a perfected agreement, arose upon the following state of facts: "On the 29th of December, 1820, the plaintiff, who lived in Kennebunk, in Maine, wrote to the defendants requesting to know on what terms they would insure $2,500 on his brig Hesper, and cargo, from Martinico to the United States. The defendants, on the first of January, 1821, sent an answer, saying they would take the risk at two and a half per cent. This letter was received by the plaintiff the 3rd of January, on which day he wrote a reply requesting the defendants to fill a policy on the terms proposed by them. The defendants, on the 2d of January, wrote again to the plaintiff, declining to take the risk, but the plaintiff had sent his letter of the 3rd before he received the last letter of the defendants. All the letters were sent by mail, and were duly received by the parties respectively. The vessel was afterwards lost on the voyage." The court held that there was no perfected contract between the parties, and that the plaintiff could not recover for a loss occurring thereunder.

[4] *Thayer* v. *Middlesex Mut. Fire Ins. Co.*, 10 Pick. (Mass.) 326 ; 1 B. F. Ins. Cas. 329.

[5] *Tayloe* v. *The Merchants', etc., Ins. Co.*, 19 How. (U. S.) 390.

[6] *Hamilton* v. *Lycoming Ins. Co.*, 5 Penn. St. 339 ; *Hallock* v. *Commercial, etc., Ins. Co., ante.*

before the letter withdrawing the terms *is received*, even though it was posted *before* the letter of acceptance is mailed. It is perhaps questionable, however, whether the latter doctrine can hold, if the insurer by his letter of withdrawal has placed himself in a position *that he could not enforce the contract by compelling the acceptance of a policy made according to the contract*, and it would seem that such would be the position of the parties. The question may perhaps be regarded as an open one, and its solution must depend largely upon the circumstances of each case.[1]

If the evidence is conflicting, and it is not clear that a contract was, in fact, made, a bill for specific performance will be dismissed,[2] and no recovery can be had at law.[3] The proof may be by parol, but

[1] It is proper to say that the weight of authority is opposed to the doctrine expressed in *McCulloch* v. *Eagle Ins. Co.*, *ante*, and the *locus penitentiæ* is regarded as ended when the offer or acceptance has passed beyond the control of the party so that he cannot recall it. Therefore, when he *mails* an offer or acceptance, he cannot recall it, after the other party has *accepted his terms*, by himself having *mailed* a notice thereof *before* any notice of a recall of the terms has been received by him, although it may be on its way, by due course of mail. This question was discussed in *Adams* v. *Lindell*, 1 B. & Ald. 681, and what would seem to be the true doctrine was announced. In that case the defendants, on Sept. 2d, by mail, offered to sell the defendants a quantity of wool. Their letter containing the offer was as follows: " We now offer you 800 tods of wether fleeces, of a good fair quality, of our country wool, at 35s. 6d. per tod, to be delivered at Leicester, and to be paid for by two months' bill in two months, and to be weighed up by your agent within fourteen days, *receiving your answer in course of post*." This letter was *misdirected*, and in consequence did not reach the plaintiff until the evening of Sept. 5th. On that evening the plaintiff wrote and mailed an *acceptance* of the wool on the terms proposed, and the answer did not reach the defendant until Sept. 9th. On the 8th of Sept. not having heard from the plaintiffs, the defendants *sold* the wool. The court, at *nisi prius*, told the jury that, as the delay in the receipt of the offer was due to the negligence of the defendants in directing the letter, they must take it; that the acceptance was sent by due course of post, and that the defendants were liable for the loss sustained. Upon a rule for a new trial, the ruling was sustained, the court saying in reply to the argument of the defendant's counsel, that there was no contract *until the acceptance was actually received by the defendants*: " If that were so, no contract would ever be completed by post; for, if the defendants were not bound by their offer when accepted by the plaintiffs, till the answer was received, then the plaintiffs ought not to be bound, till after they had received the notification that the defendant had received their answer *and assented to it;* and so it might go on *ad infinitum. For the defendants must be considered in law as making, during every instant of time their letter was traveling, the same identical offer to the plaintiffs;* and then the contract is completed by the acceptance of it by the latter." While the letter is under the control of the party, as if it is in the hands of an agent, it may be recalled, but when it is placed in the public post, it cannot be, unless the other party is notified in person, or by telegraph, before his receipt of the letter *and the acceptance of the terms offered*, that the offer is recalled. Nor then, can he recall an acceptance of an offer, when a loss has intervened *before* the acceptance, or recall. *Holbrook* v. *Commercial Union Ins. Co., ante; Hamilton* v. *Lycoming Ins. Co., ante.*

[2] *Suydam* v. *Columbus Ins. Co.*, 18 Ohio, 459; *Dinning* v. *Phenix Ins. Co.*, 68 Ill. 414.

[3] *Strohn* v. *Hartford Ins. Co., ante; Hartford Fire Ins. Co.* v. *Wilcox*, 57 Ill. 180; 5 Bennett's F. I. C. 321.

must be full and clear,[1] and proof of a mere offer on the one hand without acceptance on the other, or of an incomplete contract, that is, when anything is left open for future adjustment, either as to the amount of the risk, the premium to be paid, or the duration of the risk, no contract obligation exists.[2] The fact that an application has been made for insurance, and a long time has elapsed, and the rejection of the risk has not been signified, does not warrant a presumption of its acceptance. In such cases there must be an actual acceptance, or there is no contract.[3]

But, where the insurer or his agent has done or said anything that induces the assured to believe that the risk is accepted, the insurer will be estopped from denying its acceptance. Thus, in a Canada case,[4] the plaintiff applied for insurance, and the agent who took the application gave him a binding receipt for twenty-one days, pending the approval of the company. The receipt was given October 27th, and on the 1st of December, the property was destroyed by fire. No policy had been issued, but prior to the fire the plaintiff had applied to the agent for the policy, and the agent, relying upon the fact that the application had not been rejected, told the plaintiff that the risk was accepted. The company, however, *after the loss*, insisted that the risk had not been accepted, but the court held that the insurer, in view of what the agent had told the plaintiff, and the confidence thereby induced in the plaintiff, was estopped from denying its acceptance of the risk.

Where a permanent risk exists, and a policy is outstanding upon the property, and a builder's risk is applied for which is granted by parol, it is good, even though the amount to be paid therefor is left open and indefinite. But this is rather in the nature of a license, than of a contract for insurance, and, even though nothing was paid therefor, if the insurers assented to carry the risk, with the increase of risk incident to the change in its character, they would be estopped from setting up the increase of hazard in avoidance of liability.[5]

---

[1] *Mills* v. *Albion Ins. Co.*, 6 S. & D. 409; *N. W. Ins. Co.* v. *Ætna Ins. Co.*, 23 Wis. 160; *N. E. Ins. Co.* v. *Robinson*, 25 Ind. 536; *Kelly* v. *Com. Ins. Co.* 10 Bos. (N. Y.) 82.

[2] *Strohn* v. *Hartford Fire Ins. Co., ante; Kelly* v. *Com. Ins. Co., ante; McCulloch* v. *Eagle Ins. Co., ante; Tyler* v. *New Amsterdam, etc., Ins. Co., ante; Trustees, etc.,* v. *Brooklyn Fire Ins. Co.*, 28 N. Y. 153, also 19 N. Y. 305; *Audubon* v. *Excelsior Ins. Co.*, 27 N. Y. 216.

[3] *Ins. Co.* v. *Johnson*, 23 Penn. St. 72.

[4] *Penley* v. *Beacon Ins. Co.*, 7 Grant's Ch. (Ont.) 130.

[5] *Walker* v. *Metropolitan Ins. Co.*, 47 Me. 361.

In an action upon an oral contract of insurance, the fact that the agent's book in which he enters risks, does not contain an entry of the risk in suit, does not tend to show that no such contract was made, and the book is not admissible as evidence upon that point.[1]

Policy may be renewed by parol.

SEC. 16. A contract of insurance may be made or modified by parol; consequently, a renewal of a policy may be modified by parol so as to express a different contract from that expressed by the policy. Thus, in a New York case,[2] the plaintiff procured an insurance on stock, on the first floor of 39 Centre street, in New York city. Subsequently, the plaintiff removed the goods to an upper story of the same building and the same number; after the removal of the goods, the policy was renewed. Previous to the renewal of the policy, the defendant's agent called upon the plaintiff, and then knew by actual observation, and was also informed by the plaintiff, that the insured property was moved "up stairs." The renewal receipt described the premises as 39 Centre street, N. Y., and omitted the words "first floor," and purported to renew and keep on foot the original policy. A loss having occurred, the defendant company denied all liability, because the goods were removed from the *first* floor, as described in the policy, to an upper story of the same number, but the court held, *that, as the company had notice of the change of location before the policy was renewed, it would be presumed that they intended, by the contract of renewal, to modify the original contract so as to make it operative to cover the goods where they knew they were, and not to impose upon the assured by inducing him to believe that his property was insured, when in fact it was not.*[3]

---

[1] *Sanborn* v. *Fireman's Ins. Co.*, 16 Gray (Mass.) 448. It is sufficient if a contract is established, and the fact that no record of the risk exists upon any of the company's books, will not defeat the claim. *Warren* v. *Ocean Ins. Co.*, 16 Me. 439.

[2] *Ludwig* v. *The Jersey City Ins. Co.*, 48 N. Y. 379; *Baubie* v. *Ætna Ins. Co.*, 2 Dill. (U. S. C. C.) 156.

[3] HUNT, C., in delivering the opinion of the court, said: "An insurance against loss by fire may be made by parol as well as by writing. *Fish* v. *Cottenet*, 44 N. Y. 538. A written contract of insurance may be modified by parol without the passage of any new consideration to support it. *Trustees First Baptist Church* v. *Brooklyn Fire Ins. Co.*, 19 N. Y. 305; *Blanchard* v. *Trim*, 38 id. 225. Every renewal of a policy constitutes a new contract, and the old contract may be modified in any of its parts at the pleasure of the parties. A contract is to be construed to mean: 1. What its terms plainly express; or, 2. What the promisor intended the promisee to understand that it meant. *Botsford* v *McLean*, May, 1870. Here the insurance had expired, or was about to expire. No loss had been incurred, and no liability existed. Both parties wished the contract to be extended. The plaintiff desired an insurance upon his goods in the upper stories of the building. He had none in the lower story. The company wished to insure him on his goods where they were, not where they were not. Knowing exactly

Burden extends to showing authority of the agent.

SEC. 17. The burden is upon the person seeking to enforce a parol contract of insurance, to establish not only the making of a contract, but also the authority of the agent to make it; and if any waiver is relied upon, both the waiver and the authority of the agent to make it; and it has been held that mere general expressions, that do not clearly and necessarily import an assent or agreement, are not sufficient to establish either an agreement or a waiver. Thus, where the defendants' solicitor, simply empowered to solicit renewals, called at the plaintiff's place of business just before a policy, issued by his principals upon the plaintiff's property, expired, to renew it, and the plaintiff being absent, the solicitor was told, by the plaintiff's clerk, that the policy could be renewed, and that if he would carry the risk and send him the bill, he would pay upon presentation, to which the solicitor replied, " all right," and went away, and the policy was not renewed, nor the premium paid, or offered to be, until after a loss, it was held that this was not sufficient evidence either of an agreement to renew, or of the waiver, or of the authority of the solicitor to waive the premium, and the bill to

---

where they were, they receive the compensation for one year's insurance and deliver him the contract before us. I doubt not that they intended to give him a valid insurance, and intended him to believe that he had received such. To suppose otherwise would be to impute to them a fraudulent disposition, which there is nothing in the case to justify. The parties supposed that the paper delivered reached the case, and intended that it should. We can accomplish this intent by such a construction of the writing. It is as if the defendant had indorsed upon the policy a memorandum that the location of the goods had been changed, or as if notice of that fact had been verbally given and assented to. The contract would then have been for an insurance upon goods on the first floor, modified as to the floor or story. The modification is established in two modes: 1, by the new paper, which, referring to the policy, describes also the goods as being simply in store No. 39 Centre street; and, 2, by the fact that the defendant knew perfectly where the goods were, and insured them there, or intended the plaintiff to suppose that it did so insure them. *Botsford* v. *McLean, supra.* If the plaintiff had said to the defendant at its office, I have removed my goods to the third story, I wish to continue the insurance for one year, and had paid it thirty dollars, which it had received, it would certainly have been liable in case of a loss. The reference to the first story in the original policy would have been deemed to have been modified by the notice and the acceptance of the premium. The plaintiff has lost nothing by taking a receipt which, so far as it goes, sustains his view of the case. The only support of this defense is the position that, when it gave the renewal receipt, the defendant did not intend to make any further insurance. This cannot be sustained without an imputation on its honesty. It knew when it took the premium that something was expected of it. Men do not pay moneys to insurance companies gratuitously, without expectation of benefit or return. It knew, also, that the plaintiff had no property on the first floor to be protected. The only possible alternative is the case claimed by the plaintiff, to wit: that the original contract was understood and intended to be modified by applying the policy to the goods on the upper stories. *Salomes* v. *The Rutger Fire Ins. Co.*, 3 Keyes, 416; *Mayor* v. *Exchange Fire Ins. Co.*, id. 436; *Plumb* v. *Cattaraugus Co.*, 18 N. Y. 392."

compel the making of the policy was dismissed.[1] If there is *any* doubt, the plaintiff is not entitled to have a specific performance,[2] and in any event, in order to recover, he must comply with the requirements of the policy, as to notice and proofs of loss.[3]

Application, and acceptance of risk by mail.

Sec. 18. When application is made for insurance by mail, and the agent taking the application has no authority to bind the company during the pendency of the application, or there is nothing in the application itself that binds the company in the *interim of time*, the risk does not attach *until it is actually accepted by the company. But as soon as the risk is accepted, and acceptance is signified by the posting of a notice thereof, the contract is complete ;*[4] and has relation back to the time when the appli-*

---

[1] *Hamilton* v. *Home Ins. Co.*, 6 Biss. (U. S.) 9. See also, *Neville* v. *The Merchants', etc., Ins. Co.*, 19 Ohio, 452.

[2] *Neville* v. *Ins. Co., ante; McCann* v. *Ætna Ins. Co.*, 3 Neb. 198.

[3] *Hoff* v. *Ins. Co.*, 4 John. (N. Y.) 132 ; *Columbian Ins. Co.* v. *Lacorina*, 2 Pet. (U. S.) 53

[4] In *Tayloe* v. *Merchants' F. Ins. Co.*, 9 How. (U. S.) 390, the complainant applied to the defendants' agent for $8,000 insurance upon his dwelling-house for one year. The agent was requested to fill up the application for him, and state the reason that prevented the plaintiff from signing it, and to send the company's answer to him. The agent did as requested, Nov. 25th. The company replied that the risk would be taken at 70 cents premium ; and the agent, on receipt of the company's reply, giving their terms, stated : "Should you desire to effect the insurance, send your check for $57, to my order, and the business is concluded." This was mailed to the plaintiff on the 2d day of Dec., but being *misdirected*, did not reach the plaintiff until the 20th of Dec. Upon the 21st of Dec. the plaintiff sent his check for $57 to the agent, but the letter was not received by the agent until Dec. 31st. On the 22d day of Dec. a part of the premises were destroyed by fire, and the agent refused to effect the insurance upon the ground that the acceptance came too late. The court held that the liability of the defendants was fixed by the acceptance of their terms by the plaintiff, and that the offer, under the circumstances stated, giving the terms, was intended and was to be deemed a valid undertaking, on the part of the company ; that they would be bound by the terms of the offer, if an answer should be given, in due course of mail, accepting them, *which could not be withdrawn*, unless the withdrawal reached the party before his acceptance of the terms had been posted. In reference to the delay in transmission, the court held that the plaintiff had a right to regard it as a *continuing* offer, until the letter signifying the offer reached him, and was in due time accepted or rejected by him. *Hallock* v. *Ins. Co.*, 26 N. J. 268 ; *Eliasan* v. *Hurshaw*, 4 Wheat. (U. S.) 228 ; *Lungstrass* v. *German Ins. Co.*, 48 Mo. 201 ; *Mactier* v. *Frith*, 6 Wend. (N. Y.) 104 ; *Perkins* v. *Washington Ins. Co.*, 4 Cow. (N. Y.) 645 ; *Hallock* v. *Com. Ins. Co.*, 27 N. J. 268 ; *Ocean Ins. Co.* v. *Carrington*, 3 Conn. 357 ; *Ins. Co.* v. *Colt*, 20 Wall. (U. S.) 560 ; *Audubon* v. *Excelsior Ins. Co.*, 27 N. Y. 216. In *Fried* v. *Royal Ins. Co.*, 50 N. Y. 243, the plaintiff applied for $5,000 insurance upon the life of her husband. The application was made, the rate of premium was fixed, and paid by the plaintiff to the defendants' agent, and a receipt taken therefor. The proposal was duly forwarded and accepted by the company, and a policy forwarded to the agent to be executed and delivered. The agent executed the policy, but refused to deliver it, because he had ascertained that the health of the assured had failed. When the next premium became due, she tendered the premium to the agent, who refused to receive it. The assured died before another premium became due, and proofs of death were duly made, and an action brought to recover on the policy. The court held that a binding

cation was made, or the time designated in the application—if any—when the risk should commence, and covers a loss occurring before the acceptance.[1]

As to whether the company is bound for a loss occurring "pending the application," depends, 1st, upon the question whether the agent had power to so bind the company, and 2d, whether he so contracted with the applicant. If he had no power to bind the company, the fact that the premium had been paid to him and had not been refunded when the loss occurred, and the application had been pending six months and neither been accepted or rejected, does not charge the company for the loss.[2] So where an agent is authorized to bind the company pending advisement, the contract ceases to be operative after notice of its rejection has been mailed to him and has reached the post-office where he gets his mail, and the fact *that he did not get it until after a loss*, will not render the company liable, if his failure to get it resulted from his failure to go to the post-office seasonably.[3] *When the company has acted upon the application, and finally rejected it, and has mailed or sent a notice of its rejection by the usual mode, its liability under a binding receipt is ended, after the lapse of a reasonable time for the receipt of such notice by the agent, even though he in fact never receives it,*[4] and the fact that the receipt provides that the party is "to be considered insured" for a specified time, as twenty-one days, does not aid the applicant, if his application has been rejected before the lapse of such period and notice thereof properly sent to the agent. In such case the insurance ceases within a reasonable time after notice of the rejection of the risk is sent, even though the period stated in the receipt has not expired. *Such a receipt is not an absolute contract for insurance for the period named, but an insurance pending the application, not to exceed such period,* and if negotiations

---

contract existed, and that the plaintiff was entitled to recover the loss. A similar doctrine was held in *Cooper* v. *Pacific Mut. Ins. Co.*, 7 Nev. 116. In that case the plaintiff entered into a contract with the defendants' agent to insure her husband's life, made an application therefor, and paid him $50, to apply on the first year's premium, *in case the company should conclude to issue a policy.* The application was sent, and a policy was issued and forwarded to the agent for delivery. It did not reach the agent until after the husband's death. The court held that by the acceptance of the risk, the contract became a valid contract *as of the date of the application,* and that she was entitled to recover the amount insured. *Callaghan* v. *Atlantic Ins. Co.*, 1 Edwards' Ch. (N. Y.) 64; *Rhodes* v. *Railway Pass. Ins. Co.*, 5 Lans. (N. Y.) 71; *Whitaker* v. *Farmers', etc., Ins. Co.*, 29 Barb. (N. Y.) 312; *Post* v. *Ætna Ins. Co.*, 43 id. 351.

[1] *Lightbody* v. *N. American Ins. Co.*, 23 Wend. (N. Y.) 18; *Kohn* v. *Ins. Co.*, 1 Wash. C. C. (U. S.) 93; *Genl. Int. Ins. Co.* v. *Ruggles,* 1 Wheat. (U. S.) 408.

[2] *Ins. Co.* v. *Johnson,* 23 Penn. St. 72.

[3] *Henry* v. *Agricultural Ins. Co.*, 11 Grant's Ch. (Ont.) 125; *Fish* v. *Cottinett,* 44 N. Y. 533.

[4] *Henry* v. *Ins. Co., ante.*

are sooner terminated by the rejection of the risk, the receipt becomes inoperative.[1]

Liability may exist where property is destroyed when contract is made.

SEC. 19. Where the property has *been actually destroyed by fire, when the application is made and the contract entered into,* and the contract is *antedated,* or is to take effect at a period earlier than the date of the application, *if both parties are ignorant of the loss, the contract is valid, and the insurers are liable therefor.*[2] But, if the applicant for insurance *knew* of the loss, before his application was posted, although not until after it was drawn, a policy, although issued thereon, would be void, because in that case his conduct is fraudulent, and he has been guilty of a fraudulent concealment of a material fact.[3] In all cases, the important question is: " *What was the contract, and when did it commence?* "[4] If the loss occurred *after* the contract was made, and *after* the risk attached, the insurer is liable,[5] but if the loss occurred *before* the risk attached, by the terms of the contract, the contract is void, and the insured is entitled to a return of the premium paid.[6] But, if it is evident from the language of the policy that the insurers intended to make themselves liable for the risk, even though a loss had occurred *before* the contract was made, the policy will be valid, and the loss recoverable. Thus, in an Arkansas case,[7] on May 1, 1868, the insured took from the insurer an open, or what is sometimes called a running policy, to continue for one year, insuring goods "lost or not lost; shipments to be reported and indorsed." It was proven that the insured had not reported all their risks; that one shipment was insured in another

---

[1] *Walker* v. *Provincial Ins. Co.,* 7 Grant's Ch. (Ont.) 137.

[2] *Mead* v. *Davidson,* 3 Ad. & El. 303 ; Bunyon on Fire Insurance, 53 ; *Genl. Mut. Ins. Co.* v. *Ruggles, ante.*

[3] *Fitzherbert* v. *Mather,* 1 T. R. 12.

[4] Bunyon on Fire Insurance, 53.

[5] In *Davenport* v. *Peoria, etc., Ins. Co.,* the plaintiff applied to the defendants' agent for insurance. All the terms of the contract were agreed upon, and the agent, *if matters were found as represented,* agreed to issue a policy, to take effect from noon of that day (March 20th). He examined the risk that day, and gave notice that it was accepted. That night—no policy having been issued—the building was burned. The next day the agent and the plaintiff, both *knowing* that the building had been destroyed, issued a policy in conformity with the contract, and the court held that the policy was valid. *Genl. Int. Ins. Co.* v. *Ruggles,* 12 Wheat. (U. S.) 408 ; *Perkins* v. *Washington Ins. Co.,* 4 Cow. (N. Y.) 645 ; *Walker* v. *Met'n, etc., Ins. Co.,* 56 Me. 371 ; *Bragdon* v. *Appleton M. & F. Ins. Co.,* 42 Me. 259.

[6] This is upon the ground that nothing existed to which the risk could attach, and consequently the contract, without the fault of the parties, became inoperative. *Franklin* v. *Long,* 7 G. & J. (Md.) 407 ; *Strickland* v. *Turner,* 7 Exchq. 208.

[7] *Arkansas Ins. Co.* v. *Bostick,* 27 Ark. 539.

company, not by the procurement, however, of the insured, but by the consignors of that shipment. April 1, 1869, the insured ordered tobacco from Louisville for Fort Smith. They received the invoice April 11th, and reported the shipment on the 12th, to the insurers' agent, who sent the application to the insurers' secretary, who rejected it on the 14th, because he had heard the tobacco had been burned on the 10th. It appeared that the insured was asked by the insurers' agent whether the risk should be indorsed from Louisville or from Memphis only, and he replied he would be satisfied to have it taken from Memphis, and it was so indorsed upon the policy. She reached Memphis in safety, entered the Arkansas river, struck a snag forty miles below Little Rock, sank, and was burned to the water's edge. *It was held that the insurers could make themselves responsible for a loss that had already happened, even though it were total; and that their intention so to do was evidenced by the words " lost or not lost," found in the policy;* that under such a policy the contract was not completed until the desire to insure was made, and until made, the contract was inchoate; that when the desire to insure was made to insurers' acting and accredited agent, and the premium agreed upon and charged to the insured, then the contract became complete. The failure to report all shipments to the insurers did not work a forfeiture of the policy, because there was no agreement between the parties that the insured should report them; and a failure to perform an implied duty does not avoid a contract; and as the contract itself did not fix a penalty for the failure to report them, the law will not arbitrarily say the failure *ipso facto* created a forfeiture.

Acceptance of risk binds the company; what constitutes.

SEC. 20. When the risk is accepted upon the terms designated in the application, whether the same is made by writing or parol, the contract is complete,[1] and neither can recede therefrom, and whether a policy has been executed or not, *the risk attaches at the date of the application, or at the time designated therein,* and the insurer is liable for any loss that occurred after the time when the risk, by the contract, commenced, even though it occurred *before* its acceptance thereof;[2] and if

---

[1] *Bently* v. *The Columbia Ins. Co.*, 17 N. Y. 421.

[2] *Keim* v. *Home Mut. Ins. Co.*, 42 Mo. 38; 5 Bennett's F. I. C. 128; *American Horse Ins. Co.* v. *Patterson*, 28 Ind. 17; *Lightbody* v. *N. American Ins. Co., ante; Xenos* v. *Wickham*, L. R. Q. H. L. 296; *Baldwin* v. *Choteau Ins. Co.*, 56 Mo. 151; 17 Am. Rep. 671; *Whittaker* v. *The Farmers' Union Ins. Co.*, 29 Barb. (N. Y.) 312; *Commercial Mut. Marine Ins. Co.* v. *Union, etc., Ins. Co.*, 19 How. (U. S.) 318; *Hubbard* v. *Hartford Fire Ins. Co.*, 33 Iowa, 325; *Hallock* v. *Com., etc., Ins. Co.*, 26 N. J. 268. In

the risk is accepted and a policy is issued which, by mistake, does not conform to the contract, either as to the time when the risk attaches or otherwise, a court of equity will compel its correction, and the real contract entered into by the parties will be enforced.[1] The person seeking insurance is under no obligation to inform the company of a loss transpiring *after* the application is made, but before its acceptance is signified. Thus, in a New York case,[2] the plaintiff, on the 28th of March, applied to the defendant's agent for insurance, and agreed upon the premium, and took his receipt acknowledging payment of the premium, and stating that the policy was to take effect from noon of that day. The premium was not, however, in fact paid, it being agreed that the plaintiff might send it at his convenience. On the 7th of April, the property was destroyed by fire, and the plaintiff, immediately after the fire, sent the premium to the agent, who, without being informed of the loss, at once forwarded the premium and application to the defendant company, and the company, without any knowledge of the loss, accepted the risk, and forwarded a policy for the plaintiff, to the agent, but subsequently, upon being

---

New England Ins. Co. v. *Robinson*, 25 Ind. 536, the plaintiff applied for insurance. An application was made, forwarded to the company, and the risk accepted. It was agreed between the plaintiff and the agent that the policy should be delivered when called for, and that the premium should be paid within five days. Before the five days expired, the building was burned. The court held that the contract was complete from the acceptance of the risk. It has been held that where the plaintiff had made oral application for insurance, and the defendant filled out an application and premium note, and sent them on the 15th of January, providing that the policy should take effect January 16th, with a statement that, if signed and returned to them, a policy would be made; and plaintiff kept them until the 28th, when he signed and handed them to the postmaster, who was his agent for procuring the insurance, to be forwarded, but the postmaster retained them until February 13, before mailing them, and a fire occurred upon the 31st of January; that there was no complete contract *before the fire*, as the plaintiff, during all the time that the papers were in the hands of his agent, the postmaster, had the right to recall them. The case proceeds upon the ground that the *locus penitentiæ* still existed. Had the papers been deposited by the plaintiff in the mail, there is no question but that the court would have held that the risk attached, although nothing is said by the court upon that point. *Thayer* v. *Middlesex, etc., Ins. Co.*, 10 Pick. (Mass.) 326. That such is the rule elsewhere, see *Hamilton* v. *Lycoming Ins. Co.*, 5 Penn. St. 339; *Tayloe* v. *Merchants', etc., Ins. Co.*, 9 How. (U. S.) 396, and cases cited *ante* in this note.

[1] *Flint* v. *Ohio Ins. Co.*, 8 Ohio, 501.

[2] *Whittaker* v. *The Farmers' Union Ins. Co.*, 29 Barb. (N. Y.) 312. In *Keim* v. *Ins. Co.*, 42 Mo. 38; 5 Bennett's F. I. C. 128, an application for insurance was made and accepted, February 9th, and the policy was made out at once, but the premium was not paid nor the policy taken until March 14th, following. *At the time when the assured paid the premium and took the policy, the premises, insured were burning, as the assured knew, but of which fact the insurer was ignorant.* The court held that the insurer was liable, and that, as the contract was complete *before* the loss, the assured could not be charged with fraud in omitting to inform the assured of the condition of the property *at the time he took the policy.*

informed of the loss, directed him not to deliver it. The court held, however, that the defendant was liable for the loss; that by the acceptance of the risk, and the premium, and the execution and delivery of the policy to the agent, the contract was complete and perfect, and by relation extended back to March 28th, and covered the loss in question, and that the plaintiff was entitled to a specific performance, by the delivery of the policy to him, and the payment of the amount of the loss, and that the fact that he did not inform the defendant of the loss, under the circumstances detailed, did not excuse the liability of the defendant, because he was under no obligation, *legal* or *moral*, to inform them of the destruction of the building. If the risk is accepted, and a policy made in accordance with the terms of the application, but is not delivered because the premium has not been paid, and after holding the policy several weeks, without any demand for the premium, and a loss occurs, and *after* the loss, but without informing the insurer thereof, the assured pays the premium and takes the policy, the company is liable for the loss, as much as though the premium had been paid, and the policy had been delivered on the day it bore date. Thus, in a Missouri case,[1] the plaintiff applied for insurance upon certain property on the 10th of January, 1871. The application was accepted, the terms agreed on, and the policy was made out and signed the same day, being in force from noon of that day. The policy, however, was retained by the company until the 27th of March, when the plaintiff paid the premium and took the policy. The property was destroyed by fire the day before, March 26th, which the plaintiff knew, but of which the defendant was ignorant. The court held that the plaintiff was under no obligation to voluntarily inform the defendant of the loss, and that, by the acceptance of the premium and delivery of the policy, the contract related back to the time when the application was filed and the policy was issued, although the property covered thereby had, in the meantime, been destroyed by fire. WAGNER, J., after a careful review of the case, said: "There can be no doubt but that the policy would have been delivered to the plaintiff and been regarded by the defendant as binding from noon on the 10th day of January, 1871, if the house had not been burned on the 26th day of March. And if it had been delivered, it would have been valid from the time it was made to take effect. *If it would have been valid if no fire took place, I cannot see how the fact that a fire happened invalidated it.*

---

[1] *Baldwin* v. *Choteau Ins. Co., ante.*

There could be no justice in allowing the company to construe it into a contract when it was to its advantage, and to repudiate it when it was disadvantageous. *When the defendant accepted the premium and delivered the policy, the agreement to insure was complete and ratified as of the* 10*th day of January,* 1871. *The plaintiff had a right to rely on his agreement, and was not bound to voluntarily inform the defendants of the fire.*" The same doctrine has been held in the United States Supreme Court, in a case which is often referred to, and may be said to be a leading case upon the points covered by it.[1] In that case an application was made by the plaintiff company for re-insurance upon a certain risk, upon Saturday, upon certain terms, which were declined, and other terms demanded, and on Monday, these last mentioned terms were accepted by the plaintiff, and assented to by the president of the defendant company, but Monday being a holiday, a policy was not made, and on that night, before anything more was done, the property was destroyed by fire. On the next day, the plaintiffs tendered their note for the premium and demanded a policy, which the defendants refused to execute or deliver. But the court held that *when the parties agreed upon the terms, the contract was complete and executed,* and that the plaintiffs were entitled to the indemnity contracted for. The doctrine of these cases is expressive of the American law upon this subject, and is believed to be in full accord with the English rule.[2]

When notice of acceptance is placed in the mail, the risk attaches.

SEC. 21. In order to bind the insurers, it is not necessary that the acceptance should be *known* by the assured. It is enough, *if the risk has been, in fact, accepted,* and notice thereof, or a policy in pursuance of the agreement has been mailed, either to the assured, or the agent through whom the insurance was sought, even though it was never received;[3]

---

[1] *Commercial Mut. Marine Ins. Co.* v. *Union, etc., Ins. Co., ante.*

[2] *Mackie* v. *European Assurance Co.,* 21 L. T. (N. S.) 102; *Pattison* v. *Mills,* 1 Dow. & C. 342; *Lishman* v. *Northern, etc., Ins. Co.,* L. R. 10 C. P. 179; *Gledstanes* v. *Royal, etc., Assurance Co.,* 5 B. & S. 797; *Laidlaw* v. *Liverpool & London Ins. Co.,* 13 Grant's Ch. (Ont.) 337.

[3] *Hallock* v. *Ins. Co., ante.* In *Lungstrass* v. *German Ins. Co.,* 48 Mo. 201, the company's agent applied for insurance upon his own property, and a policy was sent him, but not being satisfied with its terms, he returned it for a reduction of the rate of premium. The reduction was made and the policy returned to him Nov. 6th. On the morning of the 7th the property was burned, and the company claimed that they were not liable because he had not signified his acceptance of the policy, or paid the premium. It appeared that on the 6th of Nov., upon receipt of the policy, he charged himself with the premium in the company's account, and it being shown that the practice was to return his accounts only

4

but the mere making of a policy which is still retained by the insurers, does not amount to an acceptance. So long as the policy is retained, the *locus penitentiæ* exists, but when the insurer does an act that clearly indicates that all deliberation is over, and the terms of the contract, as well as the risks are accepted, as, by the posting of a notice of his

---

once a month, the court held that his acceptance of the policy was sufficiently signified, and the premium paid.

In *Tayloe* v. *Merchants Ins. Co.*, 9 How. (U. S.) 390, a party wrote to the defendant company accepting their terms of insurance as made known to him in a previous letter. After his letter was posted, and before it was received by the company, the property was destroyed by fire; and the company refused to issue the policy, on the ground that the contract of insurance was not complete at the time of the loss. The by-laws provided, that no insurance should be considered as made or binding, until the premium was actually paid. Their agent wrote to insured, "Should you desire to effect the insurance, send me your check, payable to my order, for the amount of the premium, and the business is concluded," and it was held that the putting a letter directed to the agent in the post-office, with the check inclosed, was a payment within the provision of the by-laws. In the same case the by-laws of the company required the assured, as soon as possible after a loss, to give in a particular account thereof under oath. The assured gave in his particular account eleven months after the loss, on receipt of which the secretary wrote him that the company declined to pay the claim as therein made by him and that under the circumstances of the case, they did not waive any grounds of defense whatever, but would avail themselves of all and any that by law they might. It was held that the company, by refusing to issue a policy, and denying the contract, had waived their right to require the particular account within a reasonable time. In *Chase* v. *Hamilton Mut. Ins. Co.*, 22 Barb. (N. Y.) 527, the insurer wrote their agent, through whom application for insurance had been made, that the risk would be taken at two per cent., and if the plaintiff wished the insurance, to send a new application, adding, "If that be sent we will forward policies." The agent showed the plaintiff so much of this letter only as related to the rate of premium, and the rent day, November 1, the plaintiff paid to the agent the balance on the premium demanded, beyond the amount previously paid on the temporary policy, and received a receipt to that effect. On the night of November 2, the property was destroyed by fire without any fault of the plaintiff. On November 4, the agent, by letter, bearing date November 1, forwarded to the defendant the amount of the plaintiff's premium. The defendants immediately replied, declining to issue the policy, proposing to place the amount received to the credit of the agent. *Held*, that the contract was fully completed between the parties when the plaintiff accepted the defendant's terms and paid the premium to their agent, that the defendants were bound to issue a policy to the plaintiff and were liable for the loss to the amount insured, and that as no time was fixed by the company within which the proposition was to be accepted and the money sent, the law fixes a reasonable time, and that under the circumstances the time employed was a reasonable time; also, that it made no difference, that the money was not sent by the agent until after the loss, as it was paid before the loss. In a recent case in Massachusetts (*Myers* v. *London, Liv. and Globe Ins. Co.*, 121 Mass. 338), the plaintiff contracted with the defendants' agent for insurance upon his dwelling, the amount, rate and duration of risk being agreed upon. The agent was authorized to bind the company "during correspondence only." The plaintiff directed the agent to inform him when the policy came, and he would call and pay for it, and the agent agreed to do so. The policy was made and sent, and the agent notified the plaintiff thereof by letter, and requested him to call for it; which the plaintiff did several times, but failed to find the agent in. The agent kept the policy until a few days before the fire and then cancelled it. The court held, that the evidence *did not disclose an oral contract for insurance on the day the contract was made, but for a policy to be issued and delivered to him on payment of the premium*; citing, *Markey* v. *Mut. Ben. Ins. Co.*, 118 Mass. 178.

acceptance, or of a policy, the agreement is complete and the risk and liability incident thereto attaches,[1] *and cannot be withdrawn, even though*

---

[1] *Xenos* v. *Wickham*, L. R. 2 H. L. Cas. 324; *Tayloe* v. *Merchants' Ins. Co.*, ante; *Hamilton* v. *Lycoming*, etc., *Ins. Co.*, 5 Penn. St. 339; *Mactier* v. *Frith*, 6 Wend. (N. Y.) 104; *Hallock* v. *Ins. Co.*, post. In a case recently decided in the Supreme Court of the United States, not yet reported, the doctrine stated in the text was fully sustained. *Eames* v. *Home Ins. Co. of N. York*, 15 Albany Law Journal, 31. In that case the plaintiffs owned a flouring mill in Staunton, Ill., which had previously been insured by the defendants, the application and insurance having been made through one Beach, a local agent. Beach had no authority to take risks on extra hazardous property, in which class the mill in question belonged; but one Ducat, the defendant's general agent, at Chicago, had such authority. Oct. 12th, 1872, the plaintiffs applied to Beach for insurance, and he sent the application to Ducat with the following letter:

"Dear Sir—I inclose application for insurance which you have carried for two years, and was not renewed in Feb. because I charged five and one-half (you were carrying it at five per cent). They now want to insure again. The other large mill in Staunton has lately burned, which is, I suppose, the reason. I have not learned the particulars, but some think the owners burned it."

Ducat replied Oct. 14th, saying, that the rate on this risk would not be less than six and one-half per cent., which plaintiffs probably would not pay. After some further correspondence, Beach informed the plaintiffs that six and one-half was the lowest rate. The same letter inclosed an application in another company for additional insurance at six per cent. This application was filled out and returned to Beach with a letter as follows:

"*Mr. James Beach, Bunkerhill, Ill.:*   "Staunton, *Oct.* 25, 1872.

"Dear Sir—I believe I have answered all the questions necessary, and to the best of my knowledge six and one-half per cent. is pretty heavy, but I guess we will have to stand it, as I do not know where we can do better at present.

"Yours, etc.,   EAMES & COOLEY."

"On the 28th of October, Beach mailed a letter to Ducat, asking him to send a 'ticket of insurance for the amount applied for on the mill.' On the 29th, the order for insurance was countermanded by Beach, by telegraph, the mill having been burned in the interval. Ducat was on the point of sending the policy of insurance when the telegram from Beach was received. The question was, whether there was an insurance effected. The court, reversing the decision below, decide that there was, saying: Supposing this to be the meaning of the correspondence, the next question is, whether it had the effect of creating a contract. Eames had put in an application for insurance. It was made out in the regular form. The property was fully described; the amount of insurance was named, and the rate of premium at five and one-half per cent. was proposed to be paid. Everything was satisfactory to the general agent, except the rate of premium. No question was made about anything else. The whole subsequent correspondence related to that alone. The agent required six and one-half per cent. instead of five and one-half; and finally, as we construe the letter of Eames, he (Eames) agreed to, and accepted this modification. Supposing all the parties to be acting in good faith, as they were bound to act, had he not a right to suppose that the agreement was concluded, and that the risk was taken by the defendant? We do not well see how this conclusion can be avoided. He had not paid the premium, it is true; but it is shown that this was not required until the policy was made out and delivered. It had not been required of Cooley in 1870, and yet the policy in that case, when issued, was made to run from the date of the application, some two weeks prior to its issue, and, of course, covered the risk during that antecedent period. If parties could not be made secure until all the formal documents were executed and delivered, especially where the insuring company is situated in a different State, the beneficial effect of this benign contract of insurance would often be defeated and rendered unavailable. As said by Mr. Justice Field in the case of *The Insurance Company* v. *Colt*, 20 Wall. 567, 'it would be impracticable (for a company) to carry on its business in other cities and States, or at least the business would be attended with great

notice of such acceptance has never reached the assured. By its accept-
ance, without qualification or condition, and a posting of a notice thereof,

embarrassment and inconvenience, if such preliminary arrangements required
for their validity and efficacy the formalities essential to the executed contract.
The law,' he continues, 'distinguishes between the preliminary contract to make
insurance or issue a policy and the executed contract or policy. And we are not
aware that in any case, either by usage or the by-law of any company, or by
any judicial decision, it has ever been held essential to the validity of these
initial contracts that they should be attested by the officers and seal of the company. Any usage or decision to that effect would break up, or greatly impair
the business of insurance as transacted by agents of insurance companies.' In
regard to another question raised in the case the court says: But it is objected,
in the next place, that the contract, if one was made, was not complete and precise in its terms; that it did not state the period of time during which the risk
was to continue, and did not state what kind of a policy (of two or three different kinds which the Home Company used) Eames wished to have. It does
appear that the application, which was signed on the 12th of October, did not (as
is usually done) call for a statement of the period of insurance. It was one of
the company's own printed blanks, and the probability is that the reason this
item was not inserted was the almost universal practice of taking ordinary insurance against fire for a year. Nothing else seems to have been in the minds of
the parties. The former insurance on the property had been for that period.
The bill states that Eames applied to Beach for a contract of insurance and policy
on the mill *for a year,* and this is not denied in the answer; the application to
the other companies, the Phœnix and the Hartford, seem to have been for a year.
Mr. Beach in his testimony, when asked by the counsel of defendant whether
anything had been said as to the length of time the complainants wanted insurance in the Home, promptly answered, 'If I mistake not, the application states
'for one year;'' and was only convinced to the contrary after an inspection of the
document. The premium is constantly spoken of by the witnesses and in the
letters as so much per cent. absolutely, six and one-half per cent., without
adding 'per annum;' and yet we know that a year's premium was meant. It
may be said that this is the usual mode of speaking when rate per annum is
intended. This is undoubtedly true when an ordinary policy for a year is the
subject of discussion. But when insurance for a fractional part of a year, or any
unusual period, is proposed or spoken of, it is not the customary mode of speaking. It is then usual to add the words 'per annum,' in order to avoid mistake.
We think it perfectly manifest from all the evidence taken together, that the parties meant and intended an insurance for a year, and had nothing else in their
minds. This is the inference to be drawn from all their conduct, conversations
and correspondence; and we should be sticking in the bark to ignore it. There
is no difficulty as to the time when the risk was to commence. It was the practice of the defendant, as it is of most if not all other companies, to ante-date the
policy to the time of making the application, which, in this case, was on the 12th
day of October, 1872. This practice is more beneficial to the companies than
to the insured. They are not liable until the contract is completed, and if a
loss occurs before its completion they have nothing to pay; and yet they get
the benefit of the premium for this period whenever the contract is completed.
As to the plea that the contract does not specify what kind of a policy was desired,
it does not appear that the complainants had any knowledge or notice that the
defendant issued different kinds of policies. As Eames justly said, he supposed
(as he had a right to suppose) that they would get the same kind of policy which
had been issued on the property before. If no preliminary contract would be
valid unless it specified minutely the terms to be contained in the policy to be
issued, no such contract could ever be made, or would ever be of any use. The
very reason for sustaining such contracts is, that the parties may have the benefit
of them during that incipient period when the papers are being perfected and
transmitted. It is sufficient if one party proposes to be insured, and the other
party agrees to insure, and the subject, the period, the amount and the rate of
insurance is ascertained or understood, and the premium paid if demanded. It
will be presumed that they contemplate such form of policy, containing such con_

the bargain is closed beyond recall. Thus, in a New Jersey case,[1] the insurers made out a policy and mailed it to their agent to be delivered to the plaintiff. Before the policy was received by him, and before the plaintiff *knew* of the acceptance of the risk, the insurer telegraphed notice of the withdrawal of its acceptance of the risk, and directed the agent to return the policy, *because the premises had previously been burned.* The plaintiff called upon the agent, tendered the premium, and demanded the policy. The agent accepted the money, but refused to deliver the policy. The court held that the insurer was liable for the loss. The question was ably discussed by Vredenburgh, J., and the portion of his opinion pertinent to this point is given in the subjoined note.[2]

---

ditions and limitations, as are usual in such cases, or have been used before between the parties. This is the sense and reason of the thing, and any contrary requirement should be expressly notified to the party to be affected by it."

[1] *Hallock* v. *The Com. Ins. Co.,* 26 N. Y. 268; 4 Bennett's F. I. C. 195.

[2] He said : " The case shows that the plaintiff, when he made his application, offered Breck the premium, who said he would consider it as paid, but would leave it with the plaintiff, who was his banker, till the policy arrived, when he would call and get it. Would it have made the payment more real if the plaintiff had handed Breck the money, and Breck had deposited it with his banker ? The money was, in legal effect, paid to Breck, and by him placed on deposit. It was, in contemplation of law, an actual payment to the company, as much so as if Breck had transmitted the money, as well as the application, to the company. But if not an actual payment, the defendants are estopped from saying that it is not. They must be considered as doing what Breck did, viz., saying to the plaintiff, on the 2d of March, when he tendered them the money, we will consider it as paid. *N. Y. Central Ins. Co.* v. *National Protection Ins. Co.,* 20 Barb. (N. Y.) 474; 1 Ben. F. I. C. 96. Secondly. The defendants insist that the application, having been made on the 2d of March, and no action having been taken by the defendants until the 13th, we cannot consider the plaintiff as still continuing his offer to the defendants; that we are bound to consider it as withdrawn. But why so ? There is no pretense of any express withdrawal. The question and the answer can never, in any case, be simultaneous ; the question must always remain for some length of time with the one to whom it is put, and abide the answer. In every negotiation, whether by telegraph, by letter, or by word of mouth, the application and the answer can never be at the same precise instant. The application must wait upon the answer. If the application is considered to be withdrawn as soon as made, no two minds ever could meet upon any proposition. The *aggregatio mentium* never could take place. In all cases, the application is construed to stand until the contrary appears; until it is either withdrawn or answered. Pothier Traite du Contrat du Vente, p. 1, § 2, art. 3, No. 32; *Mactier* v. *Frith,* 6 Wend. (N. Y.) 103. But here the plaintiff avers the application to be still standing. The defendants treat it as still before them on the 13th of March, by accepting it, and making out the policy. We must therefore treat it as the parties treat it, as still at noon on the 13th of March a standing and valid offer by the plaintiff to the defendants. Thirdly. The defendants contend that the policy never was delivered, so as to make it a living contract. But it appears, by the case, that the contract to insure was complete before they mailed the policy to Breck. Their telegraphic dispatch, dated on the 15th of March, says, 'Risk not taken when burnt; return policy when received.' This necessarily implies that the risk was taken, but after the fire. Breck had no authority to insure. After the proposals were accepted by the company, they made out the policies, and sent them to Breck to deliver ; so that it appears, by the case, that before they mailed the policy to Breck, they must have received the premium and accepted the risk.

Whenever the insurer has done an act, amounting to an actual agreement to undertake the risk, liability attaches, and he cannot recede

---

and thus completed the contract to insure. If the case had gone no further, and no policy had ever been made out, it is well settled that the plaintiff could have sued them upon this contract at law or forced from them a policy in equity. *Perkins* v. *Washington Ins. Co.*, 4 Cow. 660; 1 Ben. F. I. C., 148; *Hamilton* v. *Lycoming Ins. Co.*, 5 Penn. St. 339; 2 Ben. F. I. C. 542; Angell on Fire Ins. §§ 84, 47; *Union Mut.* v. *Commercial Mut.*, Law Reporter, March, 1856, p. 610. Under these circumstances, a policy drawn up and signed by the proper officers wants no further delivery. It is a vital policy as soon as signed, becomes instantly the property of the insured, and is held by the insurer for his use. Ang. on Fire Ins. §§ 31, 33; *Pinn* v. *Reid*, 6 Man. & Grang. 1; 2 Ben. F. I. C. 542; *Kohne* v. *Ins. Co.*, 1 Wash. C. C. R. 93. But here were further acts of delivery of the policy. It was, on the 13th of March, mailed and sent to Breck, to deliver to the plaintiff. This was sending it to the plaintiff by Breck. Breck and the mail were only the vehicles to carry it to him. It was the same thing as if mailed or sent directly to the plaintiff. The defendants suggest, in answer, that Breck was their agent, and that, by sending it to him, they did not part with the possession of the policy, and that they only gave authority to Breck to deliver, which they could and did revoke before actual delivery. But when they mailed the policy to Breck to deliver, they did not constitute him their agent to receive or keep it for them, nor to retain it as their agent. He was, in that regard, no agent of theirs; he had nothing further to do for them. By sending him the policy to deliver, they made Breck trustee for the plaintiff; they made it a deposit with Breck to the credit of the plaintiff. It was a delivery to Breck to deliver to the plaintiff, which was a good delivery to the plaintiff. Shep. Touch. 58. This is not a question of the authority or acts of an agent; but whether the defendants by sending the policy to Breck to deliver, did an overt act intended to signify that the policy should have a present vitality. This certainly was such an act. Without any further interference on their part, it would have resulted in actual delivery to the plaintiff. It was intended to signify to the plaintiff not only that the policy was a present contract, but to effect an actual delivery of it to him. *Kentucky Mut. Ins. Co.* v. *Jenks*, 5 Porter R. (Ind.) 96; 5 Penn. St. 339; 9 How. (U. S.) 390. Suppose the defendants had retained the policy, and had merely told Breck to tell the plaintiff that they held the policy subject to the plaintiff's order, would they not have been deemed as holding the policy for the plaintiff? The defendants next suggest that the plaintiff was ignorant of their acceptance of the risk, of their making out and mailing the policy to Breck until after they had countermanded its delivery, and that the *aggregatio mentium* could not take place until after the acceptance of the proposition by the defendants came to the plaintiff's knowledge, and that before that the defendants had changed their own minds, so that in fact it never did take place, and that consequently there was no legal delivery of this policy. This involves the more general question, does a contract arise when an overt act is done intended to signify the acceptance of a specific proposition, or not until that overt act comes to the knowledge of the proposer? This question may arise upon every mode of negotiating a contract, whether the parties be in each other's presence or not. First comes the mental resolve to accept the proposition; but the law can only recognize an overt act. Whether that act be a word spoken, a telegraphic sign, or a letter mailed, some interval of time, more or less appreciable, must intervene between the doing of the act and its coming to the knowledge of the party to whom it is addressed. In the meantime, what is the condition of affairs? is it a contract or no contract? If the bidder does not see the auctioneer's hammer fall; if the article written for and sent never arrives; if the verbal answer, when the parties are in each other's presence, is in a foreign tongue, or by sudden noise or distraction is not heard; if the telegraphic circuit is broken; if the mail miscarries; if the word spoken or the letter sent is overtaken, and countermanded by the electric current, is there no contract? In the progress of the negotiation, at what precise point of time does mind meet mind, does the contract spring into life? Upon this subject, with respect to negotiations conducted by written communications, there has been some variety of decision; but it appears to me that the weight of authority, as well as reason and necessity, admit of but one solution.

therefrom so as to exempt himself from liability for a loss that has occurred pending his deliberation ;[1] and a loss may be recovered under a policy, even though *both* parties, at the time of its execution, knew

---

The meeting of two minds, the *aggregatio mentium* necessary to the constitution of every contract, must take place *eo instanti* with the doing of any overt act intended to signify to the other party the acceptance of the proposition, without regard to when that act comes to the knowledge of the other party ; everything else must be question of proof, or of the binding force of the contract by matters subsequent. The overt act may be as various as the form and nature of contracts. It may be by the fall of the hammer, by words spoken, by letter, by telegraph, by remitting the article sent for, by mutual signing or by delivery of the paper, and the delivery may be an act intended to signify that the instrument shall have a present vitality. Whatever the form, the act done is the irrevocable evidence of the *aggregatio mentium :* at that instant the bargain is struck. The acceptor can no more overtake and countermand by telegraph his letter mailed, than he can his words of acceptance after they have issued from his lips on their way to the hearer. If the two minds do not meet *eo instanti* with the act signifying acceptance, when can they, in the nature of things, ever approach each other more closely ? The defendants say, when the act of acceptance comes to the knowledge of the other party. But this knowledge would be a fact without any force, unless we suppose in the proposer a power still of electing not to accept the acceptance. But if we do this, it is apparent that the negotiation is yet precisely in the same stage of development it was in when the first proposition was waiting upon the first answer. The notion that there is no contract until the acceptance comes to the knowledge of the other party, proceeds upon the ground, in the first place, that the proposal has been withdrawn or lost its force, which is against the intent of the parties and the necessities of the case ; and in the second place, upon the ground that the answer is conditional, whereas we suppose it to be absolute. We suppose the acceptor to say not simply I agree, but to say I agree if you do, which requires an answer from the proposer ; so that the minds do not meet till he answers. But in the meantime the acceptor may have changed his mind, and for the same reason as before, there is no bargain until this last answer comes to the knowledge of the other party ; and so, upon this theory, it must go on *ad iufinitum* without the possibility of the *aggregatio mentium* ever taking place. There is in fact no difference between the acceptance of a proposition by word of mouth, and a letter stating an acceptance. In the one case it is articulate sounds carried by the air ; in the other, written signs, carried by the mail or by telegraph. The vital question is, was the intention manifested by any overt act, not by what kind of messenger it was sent. The bargain, if ever struck at all, must be *eo instantia* with such overt act. Mailing a letter containing an acceptance, or the instrument itself intended for the other party, is certainly such an act. *Adams* v. *Lindsell,* 1 Barn. & Ald. 681 ; *Dunlop* v. *Higgins,* 1 House of Lords Cases, 381 ; *Duncan* v. *Topham,* 8 C. B. 225 ; *Potter* v. *Saunders,* 6 Hare, 1 ; *Tayloe* v. *Merchants' Ins. Co.,* 9 How. 390 ; *Hamilton* v. *Lycoming Ins. Co.,* 5 Barr, 339 ; *Vasser* v. *Camp,* 14 Barb. 341 ; *Mactier* v. *Frith,* 6 Wend. 103 ; *Kentucky Mut. Ins. Co.* v. *Jenks,* 5 Porter's R. (Ind.) 96. This last case, in all its essential features, is identical with the one before us. The only English case sustaining the defendants in their view, that I have seen, is that of *Cooke* v. *Oxley,* 3 Term R. 653, which, it will be perceived by the above references, has been effectually overruled in their courts. In the State of New York, the case of *Mactier* v. *Frith,* 1 Paige, 434, was reversed in their court of errors by a very large vote (6 Wend. 111), and the doctrine sustained as contended for by the plaintiff. The only other American case on this side of the question is that of *McCulloch* v. *The Eagle Ins. Co.,* 1 Pick. 278. This last is against the whole current of authorities both in England and in this country, and appears to me requires for the creation of a contract a fact without significance, or a condition that would render its creation impossible.''

[1] *Xenos* v. *Wickham, ante ; Mead* v. *Davidson,* 3 Ad. & El. 303 ; *Parry* v. *The GreatShip Co.,* 10 Jur. (U. S.) 295 ; *Motteaux* v. *The London Assurance,* 1 Atk. 544 ; *The Earl of March* v. *Pigot,* 5 Burr. 2802.

that it had occurred, *if the agreement* had been entered into before the loss;[1] and so for a loss occurring before application was made, if it was not known to *either* party.[2]

When policy is conditionally delivered.

SEC. 22. Retention of the policy by the assured is evidence of his acceptance thereof, even though it is sent to him with other papers, as a survey, which he is requested to sign and return, which he does not do, but retains both. If, however, the policy is delivered upon the express condition that the paper sent for his signature shall be signed and returned to the company, the policy will not be binding unless the condition is complied with.[3]

When conditions precedent are imposed on assured, contract takes effect, when.

SEC. 23. If the terms are agreed upon, but the assured is required to do some act before it takes effect, it becomes effectual immediately upon his giving notice to the insurer of his compliance with the conditions. Thus, in a Pennsylvania case,[4] the plaintiff applied for insurance on an academy, and paid the required proportion of the premium, and executed his note for the residue, and had a survey made. The secretary of the company wrote the agent to require the plaintiff to substitute earthenware collars instead of sheet iron, and to require him to have the trustees, who held the title, assent to the insurance, and, when these were done, he would send a policy. The plaintiff performed and complied with all these conditions, and the plaintiff requested the defendant's agent to call for the trustees' consent, which he promised to do but neglected, and the building was burned before he got it. The court held that the contract was complete the moment the plaintiff gave notice that he had complied with the conditions, and that the defendants were liable for the loss.[5]

When company substitutes policies in other companies obtained before, but not delivered until after loss, liability for loss remains.

SEC. 24. When an agent of an insurer sends an application to him for insurance, and the insurer to whom application is made, and whose binding receipt the applicant holds, sends policies in another company or in other companies therefor, in place of its own policy, it is not thereby discharged from liability to the assured, for a loss occurring

---

[1] *Mead* v. *Davidson, ante; Arkansas Ins. Co.* v. *Bostick,* 27 Ark. 539.

[2] *The Earl of March* v. *Pigot, ante.*

[3] *Le Roy* v. *Park Ins. Co.,* 39 N. Y. 56.

[4] *Hamilton* v. *Lycoming Ins. Co.,* 5 Penn. St. 339.

[5] See also, *E. Carver Co.* v. *Manufacturers' Ins. Co.,* 6 Gray (Mass.) 214.

after such policies are made, but before their delivery to him, even though he, *after* the loss, relying upon it that they afforded indemnity to the amount insured therein, accepts such policies and surrenders the binding receipt issued to him by the company, to whom application was made, and in which insurance was expected to be obtained.[1]

---

[1] In *Dayton Ins. Co.* v. *Kelly*, 24 Ohio St. 345 ; 19 Am. Rep. 612, it appeared that " J. R. Young, the secretary of the defendant below (an incorporated insurance company), was authorized by the company to negotiate contracts for insurance, to sign and issue certificates like the one sued upon, to appoint agents to solicit risks, and to receive applications for policies, and to authorize such agents to deliver to applicants for policies, the above-named certificates, and to collect premiums for insurance. Charles F. Gunckel was appointed such agent by the secretary, and was supplied with certificates duly signed by the secretary, with authority to countersign, till blanks, and to deliver the same to applicants upon the receipt of premiums. Gunckel was also agent for several other insurance companies, among which were the Ætna, the Home of New York, and the Hamilton. About the 30th of November, 1867, Gunckel, being such agent, solicited a risk from the plaintiff, and agreed with him to postpone the payment of the premium for ninety days from the date of insurance ; and at the same time prepared an application for a policy, which contained the usual interrogations, respecting the proposed risk. The ninth interrogatory was as follows : ' Insurance — what amount is now insured on the property ? In what offices (state particularly), and on whose account ?' To this interrogatory there was no answer given. The fact was, however, that the plaintiff had previously obtained a policy from the Enterprise Insurance Company, for $2,000, on the same property. This application was signed by the plaintiff, and delivered to Gunckel with the understanding, that upon call by the plaintiff for insurance, Gunckel should address and forward the application to such company as he might select. On the 5th of December following, the plaintiff, by letter to Gunckel, requested insurance to the amount of $5,000. Same day, upon receipt of plaintiff's letter, Gunckel remitted to plaintiff a certificate signed by Secretary Young, a copy of which is set out in the petition, having first, however, erased the words, ' or should the risk be not accepted, and the above sum of money refunded to applicant, then this receipt is void, and of no effect;' and at same time forwarded the plaintiff's application to the home office of the defendant, with information that a certificate for insurance had been issued to the plaintiff. The erasure by Gunckel was without authority from defendant. The plaintiff, however, received the certificate in good faith, and without any knowledge of the circumstances of the erasure. Upon the receipt of the plaintiff's application at the home office of the defendant, the officers in charge procured from the German Insurance Company a policy in favor of the plaintiff for $2,000, from the Cooper Ins. Company a like policy for $2,000, and from the Central Company one for $1,000 ; and forwarded the same to Gunckel to be delivered to the plaintiff in lieu of their own policy for $5,000. Each of these policies contained a condition, that ' if the assured shall have or shall hereafter make any other insurance on the property hereby insured, without the consent of this company written hereon,' then this policy shall be void. At the time the German, Cooper and Central Companies delivered the policies to the defendant, they respectively charged the defendant with the amount of the premium thereon, and the defendant charged Gunckel with the amount of premium on the plaintiff's risk. The printed policies of the defendant, referred to in the instrument upon which the suit was brought, contained the following conditions : ' Provided, further, that in case the assured shall have already any other insurance against loss by fire, on the property hereby insured, not notified to this company, and mentioned in or indorsed upon this policy, or if the said assured, or his assigns, shall hereafter effect any insurance on the same property, and shall not, with all reasonable diligence, and before any loss by fire occurs, give notice thereof to this company, and have same indorsed on this policy, or otherwise acknowledged by them in writing, this policy shall cease and be of no effect.' And also a further condition, that ' no insurance shall be considered as binding until the actual payment of the pre-

In such case, the assured may maintain an action against such company for his loss. But it seems that in such case when a policy is

---

mium.' On the 13th of same month, 'the plaintiff made application, by letter, to Gunckel, for further insurance, on the same description of property, to the amount of $10,000; and at same time informed him that he (plaintiff) had obtained other insurance on same property, from the agency of Landis & Son, to the amount of $13,000, including $7,000 applied for on that day. The amount of insurance thus notified to Gunckel included also the policy for $2,000, from the Enterprise Company. which had been obtained before the execution of the instrument sued on. On the next day, December 14, Gunckel indorsed on the policies, then in his hands, from the German, Cooper and Central Companies, the amount of insurance in other companies, which was thus notified to him. Neither the German, the Cooper, nor the Central Company assented to or was notified of any insurance on the property effected by plaintiff after the date of their respective policies. On the 18th day of same month, the property insured was destroyed by fire; and on the next day, Gunckel, having full knowledge of the loss, delivered the German, Cooper and Central policies to the plaintiff, who, in consideration thereof, and in the belief that they were valid and binding policies upon the companies by whom they had been issued, surrendered the instrument sued on to Gunckel to be canceled, and at the same time executed to Gunckel his note for the amount of the insurance premium as per agreement. This note was afterward paid, and the payment accounted for by Gunckel. The loss was notified to the companies interested, including the German, Cooper and Central, and proof thereof duly made. The German, Cooper and Central Companies repudiated the plaintiff's claim on the ground that their policies were avoided by reason of subsequent insurance, without notice to them, and without their consent. Proof of loss was afterward, and about three months after the fire, made as against the defendant. McILVAINE. J., said : 1. The court instructed the jury, among other things, as follows : 'In regard to the issues made by the first and seventh defenses, if it was proved that the contract upon which suit was brought was signed by J. R. Young, as secretary of the defendant, and if Charles F. Gunckel was agent of the defendant, the contract would have the effect of binding the company, though not signed by the president of the company.' The defenses referred to were based on the provisions of defendant's charter, the ninth section of which provides as follows (49 Ohio L. 191): 'That all policies or contracts of insurance, that may be made or entered into by said company, may be made either under or without the seal thereof, and shall be subscribed by the president, or by such other officer as may be designated for that purpose by the board of directors, and attested by the secretary ; and being so subscribed and attested, shall be obligatory upon said company according to the tenor, intent and meaning of this act, and of such policies or contracts.' This charge assumed, as was averred in the answer and not denied in the reply, that the contract sued on was not subscribed by the president, and that the secretary had not been designated by the board of directors as an officer for the purpose of subscribing 'policies or contracts of insurance,' as required by the ninth section. It must be admitted that the charter gave to the company all the powers that it possessed. It undoubtedly gave the power to make contracts of insurance, and the ninth section prescribed a form for the preservation of the evidence of its contracts, which is made obligatory on the company. If this form constitutes the only mode by which the company can obligate itself, of course any other mode would no more create a binding contract of insurance than if the corporation had never existed. The question therefore arises, is the form thus prescribed the only one in which the defendant can enter into a binding contract of insurance ? It will be observed that the ninth section does not, *in totidem verbis*, confer upon the company the power to make contracts of insurance. If there were no express grant of such power to be found elsewhere in the charter, I admit that it would be implied from the provisions of this section ; and in that case, the form therein prescribed would be exclusive. But if the grant of power to contract be found elsewhere in the charter, then our inquiry will be confined to the question, whether the form prescribed in the ninth section was intended as a limitation upon the power to contract, or merely as prescribing the manner of executing its policies. Insur-

obtained *without the knowledge of the assured*, he may ratify the act of the person procuring it, *even after a loss*, and by such ratification, by

---

ance against fire was the sole object and purpose for which the defendant was incorporated. And the first section of its charter declares that it shall be capable 'generally to do and perform all things relative to the object of the association.' This grant is certainly broad enough to confer the power to make contracts relative to insurance — power to negotiate and agree upon all the terms and conditions of the risk. Indeed, the very terms of the ninth section seem to imply that negotiations have ended in a complete contract before the execution of the formal instrument is required. Having found in the first section of the charter a grant of power to contract for insurance, we do not feel authorized to so construe the ninth section as to render null and of no effect all contracts made within the scope of the power there conferred, unless and until the president or other designated officer has subscribed the 'policy or contract of insurance.' On the other hand, we feel justified in holding that the terms, 'policies or contracts of insurance,' as here used, were intended to embrace the final instruments — such as are technically called policies of insurance, and do not include intermediary contracts of insurance, or contracts for policies. 2. The court further charged: 'That if the jury find that Gunckel was the agent of the defendant and that he made the alteration in the receipt or contract before it was delivered to Kelly, and that he did not do so by Kelly's procurement or assent or knowledge, then the alteration does not affect the liability of the defendant, but would be liable upon what remained of the contract.' We find no error in this instruction. The testimony shows that the secretary of the company was authorized to negotiate contracts for insurance, and also to appoint agents to solicit applications, etc. It also shows that the secretary had supplied Gunckel, as agent of the company, with these receipts or certificates, duly signed by himself, with authority to deliver them to applicants. We think the company, therefore, and not the applicant, should bear the consequences of Gunckel's erasure, although he was acting in violation of his duty to the company in making it. The company held Gunckel out to the world clothed with the *apparent* authority to bind it, by the delivery of such contracts; and that, too, with an erasure of part, such as was made in this instance. The plaintiff was justified in believing he was authorized to do so, for he had no means of knowing but that the paper was in the precise form in which it was when issued by the secretary. The *appearance* of authority extended as well to the *document erased* as to the *document entire*. 3. The court instructed the jury in relation to the condition in the contract concerning other insurance, as follows: 'That even if the jury should find that Kelly did not notify Gunckel of the insurance in the Enterprise Company of November 27th, 1867, on or before the 5th day of December, A.D. 1867, yet if he wrote to Gunckel on the 13th December, informing him of all the insurance, and Gunckel was the agent of the defendant, that such notice, if received before the loss, would be a good compliance upon the part of Kelly, with his obligation to give notice to the company of all other insurance, and that it would be sufficient as to the Enterprise insurance, and sufficient as to the $7,000 applied for on that day to Landis & Son, although such $7,000 was not issued until the 14th of December. That it was not necessary that any indorsement of either prior or subsequent insurance should be made upon the contract sued upon or recited in the same.' If, under the contract, the plaintiff was required to give notice of *prior insurance*, we doubt whether this instruction, in so far as it relates to that subject, could be sustained. The contract was for insurance according to the 'tenor and conditions of the printed policies' of the defendant. The conditions, in relation to other insurance contained in the printed policy, were as follows: 'Provided, further, that in case the assured shall have already any other insurance against loss by fire on the property hereby insured, not notified to this company, and mentioned in or indorsed upon this policy, or if the said assured, or his assigns, shall hereafter effect any insurance on the same property, and shall not, with all reasonable diligence, and before any loss by fire occurs, give notice thereof to this company, and have same indorsed on this policy, or otherwise acknowledged by them in writing, this policy shall cease and be of no effect.' A fair and reasonable construction of this contract would require notice of prior insurance to be given at the time of

relation, it becomes an operative contract of insurance from its date.[1]
In an English case,[2] the plaintiff applied to an agent of the defend-

---

making application for insurance. The object of notice is to enable the insurer to act prudently and intelligently in relation to the risk; yet, notwithstanding the reference to the condition in the printed policy, it was competent for the defendant to waive the condition, and we think it was waived, in so far as it related to the notice of prior insurance. The risk was taken upon an application which formed part of the contract. The interrogatory in the application for insurance, in relation to prior insurance, was not answered. The acceptance of the risk upon such an application is a waiver of any notice which a truthful answer to the interrogatory would have disclosed. 21 Ohio St. 176; 6 Gray, 85. As to notice of subsequent insurance, the charge of the court was right. Notice to Gunckel was notice to the defendant. We are not prepared to say that the notice to Gunckel would have been sufficient, if he had been the agent of the defendant merely for the purpose of soliciting applications and collecting premiums. Confessedly his authority in relation to this risk was much more extensive. He was, in fact, intrusted with the German, Cooper, Central policies, for the purpose of delivering them, in lieu of the defendant's own policy, and lifting the instrument sued on. Had he been intrusted with a policy of the defendant, for delivery, in performance of the contract, there can be no doubt that notice to him and indorsement by him of subsequent insurance thereon would have bound the company. He, in fact, indorsed the subsequent insurance upon the policies in his possession, and, in our opinion, he thereby assented, as the agent of the defendant, to all the subsequent insurance of which he had notice. We also think the court below was right in charging the jury 'that it was not necessary that any indorsement of either prior or subsequent insurance should be made upon the contract sued upon, or recited in the same.' The parties contemplated and contracted for a 'regular policy,' but the instrument sued on is not such policy. We understand, as did the court below, that the meaning of the parties was, that prior, as well as subsequent, insurance should be mentioned in or indorsed upon the regular policy, when or after it should be issued. Such recitals or indorsements would be a full compliance with the contract in this respect. No such policy having been issued, there was no failure to comply with this condition. The court also instructed the jury: 'That, if the company charged the amount of the premium to Gunckel, and Gunckel received the note of Kelly for the same, which was subsequently paid, that was a good and sufficient compliance with the contract upon Kelly's part, and the contract is binding, although said note was not given until after the fire.' The facts assumed in this charge, in connection with the fact admitted in the defendant's answer, viz., that Gunckel was the agent of the company, 'to solicit applications and to collect premiums, when insurance was effected,' amount to a waiver of the condition in their 'printed policies;' 'that no insurance, whether original or continued, shall be considered as binding until the actual payment of the premium.' It is very doubtful whether such condition in the policy contracted for, attaches to a contract for intermediary insurance (10 Bos. (N. Y.) 83); but whether it does or not, the charging of the premium to such agent, and the agent's agreement to give time for its payment, and the subsequent payment to the company, constitutes a waiver of prepayment."

[1] In *Excelsior Ins. Co.* v. *Royal Ins. Co.*, 55 N. Y. 543, Mrs. C. was the owner of a mortgage interest in a certain building in the city of Rochester. Her husband as her agent applied to one McC., the agent of plaintiffs, for insurance on her mortgage interest. McC. issued two policies, for each plaintiff, for $3,500 each. When McC. made his daily reports to the home offices, the plaintiffs each directed him to cancel the policies. This McC. neglected to do, but applied to defendants' agents for re-insurance. Defendants' agents as they claim, and as plaintiffs deny, refused to re-insure, but they did issue a new policy to Mrs. C. for the amount of the other two. Mrs. C. did not authorize McC. to get the insurance with defendants. She held the plaintiffs' policy at that time. Shortly after this, the building was burned, and Mrs. C. then paid defendants' agents the premiums for their insurance, and they accepted it, as they claim, under protest and

[2] *Mackie* v. *European Assurance Co.*, 21 L. T. (N. S.) 102.

ant, who was authorized to accept or reject risks for insurance, supposing that he was also agent for another company in which he had formerly been insured, but the agent sent him a receipt for the premium in the defendant company. The plaintiff thereupon wrote the agent that he did not want to change, *if the old office was willing to take the insurance*, as he knew nothing about the defendant company, and should require to be satisfied of its respectability and standing, before he consented to the change. Before anything more was done, and within five days thereafter, the premises were burned, and the plaintiff having brought an action upon the policy to recover the loss, the court held that it amounted to an acceptance of the policy, and made it a completed contract from the day of its date.

When company is not agreed on.

SEC. 25. The fact that the *company or companies* in which the risk is to be placed are not agreed upon, but is left for the agent himself to determine, does not affect the question, *if the agent in fact selects the companies, and enters the risk in their books.* Thus, in a New York

---

as plaintiffs claim voluntarily. The defendants' policy was not delivered to Mrs. C. until after the fire; it was held by McC., Mrs. C. assigned her interest in said policy to plaintiffs, and they brought this action to recover of defendants, first, on ground that defendant is a re-insurer, and second, as assignees of Mrs. C. There was a verdict for plaintiffs in court below for full amount of the policies. The court held that defendants cannot be held to be re-insurers, their policy does not purport on its face to be a contract of re-insurance. It is made in Mrs. C.'s name. The defendant was not informed that a re-insurance had been applied for. The application sent to the home office was for an ordinary policy. If defendant was chargeable with the knowledge of its agent not communicated to it, it cannot be void from the evidence that defendants' agent understood that the policy issued was for a re-insurance. That although defendants' policy, had it been issued to take up those of plaintiffs, might be void, because plaintiffs' policies were not canceled. Defendant waived such right, by receiving the premiums from Mrs. C. after the fire, and when its agents knew plaintiffs' policies were still in existence. That plaintiffs are entitled to recover as assignees of Mrs. C. That although McC. was not the agent of Mrs. C., and had no authority from her to procure the insurance from defendant, she afterward ratified his acts, paid the premium, and thus rendered the policy valid *ab initio*. That such ratification was sufficient, although made after the fire. That there being no request to submit the question, whether the premium was paid to defendants' agent under protest, to the jury, the finding of the court is conclusive that it was not so paid. That if the plaintiffs had purchased defendants' policy of Mrs. C., unconnected with their liability upon their own policies, it would be doubtful whether such purchase would have been valid. But, in this case, the purchase was undoubtedly valid. Defendants' policy contained a clause that, in case of other insurance on the same property, defendants should only be liable to pay its ratable proportion, according to the terms of its policy. *Held*, that under this clause defendant's policy, the plaintiffs' policies being in existence at the time of the fire, plaintiff could only recover, as assignees of Mrs. C., one half of defendants' policy.

In *Miltenberger* v. *Beacom*, 9 Penn. St. 198, it was held that one for whose benefit insurance had been effected, without his authority, might, *even after a loss*, adopt the act of such person, and by relation, such adoption extended back to the issuing of the policy, and rendered it an operative security.

case,[1] the plaintiff called upon the defendant s agent in January, 1866, to insure $26,000, upon a quantity of cotton, and paid the premium thereon. No company was designated in which the risk was to be placed, and the agent was also agent for several other companies. No policy was made out, but the agent entered $6,100 of the risk in the book of the defendant, reported the risk to them and forwarded the premium. In February, 1866, the property was damaged by fire, *and after the loss*, the agent made out and delivered a policy in the defendant company to the plaintiff, and in an action upon the policy to recover the loss, the court, upon these facts, directed a verdict for the plaintiff, which was sustained by the Court of Appeals.[2]

---

[1] *Ellis* v. *Albany City Fire Ins. Co.*, 50 N. Y. 402.

[2] GROVER, J., in delivering the opinion of the court, upon this question, said : "The inquiry in this case is whether an agreement to issue a fire policy upon the cotton, for the loss of which this action was brought, was made by the defendant. It was proved that C. F. McCoy, a resident of Augusta, Georgia, in 1865 was engaged in the insurance business as agent for several insurance companies, incorporated by different States ; that in November of that year the defendant appointed him its agent, giving him a power of attorney, the material part of which in this case was as follows : 'Be it known, that C. F. McCoy, of Augusta, State of Georgia, is hereby duly appointed and constituted an agent of the Albany City Fire Insurance Company, at Augusta, during the pleasure of said company. As agent, he is authorized and empowered to receive proposals for insurance against loss or damage by fire, and to make insurance by policies of the said Albany City Fire Insurance Company, to be countersigned by the said C. F. McCoy, and to renew the same, to assent to assignments and transfers.' That at the same time defendant delivered to McCoy a quantity of blank policies of insurance, signed by its president and secretary. The question in this case is whether this authorized McCoy to make a contract binding upon the defendant for the issue of a policy of insurance. In determining this question the prevailing usage in transacting such business must be regarded ; as it is an elementary principle that the delegation of an authority to transact any business includes an authority to transact it in the usual way, and to do the acts usual in its accomplishment. It must also be kept in mind that he was clothed with full authority to make all necessary surveys to determine the risk, its duration and the rate of premium, without any reference to a consultation with the company or any of its officers ; in short, to negotiate and conclude all the terms of the contract, and to consummate it by filling up and countersigning the policy. This necessarily includes power to make a preliminary contract for the issuing of a policy ; as it is manifest that no policy could ever be issued in the absence of such a contract. The question is whether this preliminary contract is binding upon the company. In other words, whether, when made, and the premium therefor paid by the assured, the company is bound, before the policy is actually filled up, countersigned and delivered. It is clear that if binding upon the company at all for the shortest period of time, it will so continue until, by some act of the assured or in some other way, it is discharged therefrom ; mere lapse of time, short of the running of the statute of limitations, will not have this effect. The usage of making agreements for insurance and paying the premiums, providing for the issuing of policies thereafter, to be dated at and in force from the time of making the agreement, is so general that judicial notice must be taken of it. It would, upon principle, follow that an unrestricted authority to negotiate a contract of insurance by issuing a policy, included authority to make a valid preliminary contract for such issue. In *Post* v. *Ætna Insurance Co.*, 43 Barb. 361, it was shown that the agent was intrusted with blank policies and certificates of renewal, executed by the officers of the company, which provided that they should not be operative until countersigned

SEC. 26. When the insurer has previously insured *the same property, or other property of the same kind, in the same locality, there being no*

---

by the agent. The agent was shown to have transacted business for some time for the defendant. It was held that the possession and use of these papers by the agent showed that he was authorized to make a preliminary agreement for the renewal of a policy by issuing a certificate, although a parol agreement, renewing the same, would be unauthorized. This is a direct authority for the power of the agent in the present case to make a like agreement for the issuing of a policy. The possession of blank policies and certificates of renewal by an agent, providing that they shall be effective only when countersigned by such agent, imports nothing more than what is expressed in the power of attorney in the present case ; that is, an authority to bind the company by filling up, countersigning and delivering the policy or certificate ; and so it was regarded by the court, as the validity of the contract was placed upon the ground that it was necessary that such agreement should precede the issuing of the paper, and that the company was responsible for the failure of the agent to perform what he had undertaken to do by such agreement. In *Sanborn* v. *Fireman's Insurance Company*, 16 Gray, 448, this question was considered. The court remarked : 'The objection that the agent had only power to issue policies, and not otherwise to make contracts binding on the defendant, comes within the same rule of construction. His power of attorney authorized him to effect insurance, and, for this purpose, to survey risks, fix the rate of premium and issue policies of insurance, signed by the president. etc. We are of opinion that this gave him authority to make the preliminary contract as well as to issue the policy. He was not a special agent employed merely to receive and transmit proposals to his principal, but had power to do whatever the company could do in effecting insurance ; and it appeared by the evidence of the defendant that he was furnished with policies signed in blank, to be filled up and issued at his discretion. It will be seen that the court declared the authority to make the preliminary contract from the full power given to negotiate the contract, and fill up and issue the policy in his discretion, and not from a construction giving the agent power to bind the company by parol contracts of insurance. In this view, the case sustains the position contended for by the plaintiff in the present case. It is not claimed that McCoy could bind the defendant by a parol contract of insurance. That is not the question ; but it is whether, having agreed upon the terms of an insurance and to issue a policy therefor, the company is liable for his failure to perform such contract. My conclusion is that it is. It may be said that this construction would enable McCoy to perpetrate a fraud upon the company by making preliminary contracts when its design was only to become bound by writing. This, to a certain extent, may be true ; but it furnishes no reason for depriving third persons of the benefit of contracts entered into with him as its agent, who relied thereon for indemnity from a loss from the peril embraced in the contract, by a construction of the papers more strict and rigid than is fairly required by their import. It is an elementary rule that the principal must bear a loss sustained by the misconduct of his agent, acting within the scope of his authority, rather than a third person who has fairly dealt with him as such. Assuming that McCoy was authorized to bind the defendant by a contract to issue a policy, the defendant insists that no such contract was in fact made. The undisputed evidence showed that, in the fall of 1865, McCoy was the agent of several insurance companies ; that the plaintiff had about 112 bales of cotton at Howard's landing, upon the Chattahooche river ; that he applied to McCoy for insurance upon this cotton while there, and for further insurance while on its transit from that place to Appalachicola, and, also, for insurance upon the same after its arrival at the latter place until placed on shipboard for Liverpool ; that the amount to be insured was agreed upon, and the premium determined by McCoy, who agreed to insure the same as requested ; that the plaintiff left it to McCoy to determine in what companies he would place the insurance, and the amount in each respectively ; that McCoy, among other companies, determined to place $6,100 of the amount to be insured in the defendant's company, and entered the contract to that effect in the register kept by him, received the premium thereon, and credited the amount to

change in the nature of the risk notified to the insurer, a mere order for insurance, and an agreement to insure, without any of the terms being spoken of or discussed, would be good, *as a contract to insure the same property, for the same sum, for the same time, and at the same rate,* the presumption being, from the fact that the insurer promised to insure without making any change in his rates or conditions, and that the insured signified no change, that the contract was to be the same as the previous. *If any changes are made by the insurer, but the property is of the same class, and in the same locality, although the amount of insurance and the term are different, and no rate is named, the presumption is that the same rate is to continue,* and the contract will be regarded as complete [1]

May be complete contract when rate is not agreed upon.

SEC. 27. The fact that no rate of premium is agreed upon, does not necessarily defeat the contract, *if customary rates for the same class of property exist,* and if the contract is complete except as to the premium, and there is an understanding that the insurance was effected, *and the contract is otherwise complete, the premium will be presumed to be at the customary rates,* and an acceptance by an agent of a certain sum as the premium, or *the fixing of a certain sum as the premium,* will render the contract complete. This doctrine was well illustrated in a Maine case,[2] in which the plaintiff entered into a contract to insure $3,500 on

---

the defendant; and, before any loss accrued, reported the risk taken, and paid the premium to the defendant. This was a contract by McCoy to insure the above amount in the defendant's company; and as he could only effect this by issuing a policy, a contract (as was held in *Post* v. *The Ætna Company, supra*) to issue such policy. This contract being valid against the defendant, it follows that all exceptions taken to rulings of the judge, as to the competency of evidence given for the purpose of showing a subsequent ratification, are unavailable.' "

[1] In *Audubon* v. *Excelsior Ins. Co.*, 27 N. Y. 216, the plaintiffs were in the habit of sending plates of their work to a bindery on Spruce street, New York, to be bound, and of procuring insurance upon them for the brief period they remained at the bindery. Some two months prior to the loss, they sent sets of their work to the bindery, and procured a policy of $1,000 thereon for one month. Afterwards they sent five additional sets of their work to the bindery, and sent to the defendant for insurance upon them for one month. The secretary was informed what the plaintiffs required, and of all matters sufficient to embrace the contract, except as to the rate of premium. Reference was made to the former policy on other sets, and the secretary said he would send the policy Monday. This occurred on Saturday afternoon. A loss having occurred on Sunday, before a policy was issued, the defendants denied their liability; but the court held that the contract was complete, and that the risk attached Saturday afternoon, and consequently that the defendants were responsible for the loss. The court held that the fact that the defendant had insured the same description of property, at the same place, just prior to this occasion, the fair inference was, that the same rate of premium would continue, and the fact that nothing was said about the premium, *under these circumstances,* did not leave the contract incomplete.

[2] *Walker* v. *Metropolitan Ins. Co.*, 56 Me. 371.

a building owned by him, upon a builder's risk, and requested him to continue the insurance when the builder's risk expired, which the agent agreed to do, and entered the risk in his blotter. After the builder's risk expired, the risk was continued as a permanent yearly risk, commencing July 1st, 1866. No specific premium was agreed upon, but the plaintiff had a claim against the company, and the agent was directed to take the amount from such claim, to which the agent assented, and in settling the claim, *after the loss sued for*, he retained a certain sum as premium upon the policy. No policy, however, had, in fact, been made, but the practice was shown to be to make them subsequent to the taking of the risk, and to regard them as attaching at the time of their entry in the blotter. The defendant refused to recognize the act of the agent, and directed him to pay the amount retained as premium, and insisted that, as no premium had been fixed, and no policy made *at the time of the loss*, no valid contract existed. But the court held that, if the plaintiff and the defendant's agent understood that an insurance was, in fact, effected, the pre-payment of the premium was unnecessary, as the company might waive that, and that, if no premium was fixed, it must be presumed *that it was to be at the customary rates*, and the fixing of a sum by the agent, as the premium, *even after a loss*, and assented to by the plaintiff, would, the contract being otherwise complete, render the contract complete and operative.

Acknowledgment of receipt of premium in policy. Pre-payment of premium not always essential. May be waived, even after policy is made.

SEC. 28. In all cases where, by the terms of the contract itself, pre-payment of the premium is a condition precedent, unless such condition is waived, full performance must be shown, or the risk does not attach,[1] and a part payment thereof, *unless credit is given for the balance*, will not render the contract obligatory.[2] The question as to whether a waiver exists in a given case, is one of fact, to be determined by the jury in view of all the facts and circumstances. A waiver may be implied from the acts of the agent, and if he has so dealt with the assured in reference thereto, as fairly to induce a belief, on his part, that the condition is waived, *and the premium has not been called for*, after a loss, the company cannot insist that the risk never attached

[1] *Sandford* v. *The Trust F. Ins. Co.*, 11 Paige Ch. (N. Y.) 547; *Bergesen* v. *The Builders' Ins. Co.*, 38 Cal. 541.

[2] *Barnes* v. *Piedmont, etc., F. Ins. Co.*, 74 N. C. 22

5

because the premium was unpaid.[1] It has been held, that when the insurer, by his conduct or course of dealing, has fairly induced a belief in the mind of the assured that a forfeiture or condition will not be insisted upon, as, where it prints upon its policy, "every policy non-forfeiting," or where it has *habitually* waived forfeitures under similar circumstances *with the assured*, and others, to his knowledge, it is estopped thereby from insisting upon the same.[2]

But, so far as evidence of the practice of the agent, to give credit to others is concerned, it is hardly believed that evidence thereof of itself, can establish a waiver, and that it is inadmissible to establish a waiver, unless connected with other proof to establish it. *If it is also shown, or offered to be shown, that the agent has previously given credit for premiums to the plaintiff*, then evidence of his practice in that respect in reference to others, may be shown, and the circumstance that the policy is in his possession,[3] *in connection with such evidence, tends to establish a credit for the premium.*[4] So it has been held that the mere fact that the policy is sent to the assured, by the agent, even though the condition therein as to pre-payment is express, is of itself evidence that a short credit is given,[5] unless the agent indi-

---

[1] *Hallock* v. *Com. Ins. Co.*, *ante; First Baptist Church* v. *Brooklyn Ins. Co.*, *ante; Boehen* v. *Williamsburgh F. Ins. Co.*, 35 N. Y. 131.

[2] *Home Life Ins. Co.* v. *Pierce*, 75 Ill. 426 ; *Helme* v. *Philadelphia Life Ins. Co.*, 67 Penn. St. 107; *Contra*, see *Wood* v. *Poughkeepsie Ins. Co.*, 32 N. Y. 619.

[3] *Teutonia Ins. Co.* v. *Anderson*, 77 Ill. 382 ; *Madison Ins. Co.* v. *Fellows*, 1 Dis. (Ohio), 217 ; *New York Central Ins. Co.* v. *National Pro. Ins. Co.*, 20 Barb. (N. Y.) 468 ; *Hemenway* v. *Bradford*, 14 Mass. 121 ; *Troy Fire Ins. Co.* v. *Carpenter*, 4 Wis. 20 ; *Baker* v. *Union Mut. Life Ins. Co.*, 43 N. Y. 283 ; *Illinois Central Ins. Co.* v. *Wolf*, 37 Ill. 354 ; *Teutonia Ins. Co.* v. *Mueller*, 77 id. 22 ; *Provident Ins. Co.* v. *Fernell*, 49 id. 180 ; *Marsh* v. *N. W. Ins. Co.*, 3 Biss. (U. S.) 351 ; *Michael* v. *Mut. Ins. Co.*, 10 La. An. 737 ; *Barnum* v. *Childs*, 1 Sandf. (N. Y.) 58 ; *Goit* v. *National Protection Ins. Co.*, 25 Barb. (N. Y.) 189.

[4] See opinion of Davis, J., in *Wood* v. *Poughkeepsie Ins. Co.*, 32 N. Y. 627; see also, *Sheldon* v. *Atlantic F. Ins. Co.*, 26 N. Y. 460.

[5] *Boehen* v. *Williamsburgh Ins. Co.*, *ante*. In *Miller* v. *Life Ins. Co.*, 12 Wall. (U. S.) 285, the application provided that the policy shall not be binding until the premium shall have been received by the company or some authorized agent in the lifetime of the person whose life is insured. The premium was to be part cash and part notes. Insured told the agent to call on his partner for the cash, and to send the policy to him. The notes were sent to the insured, who executed and returned them to the agent. In the letter inclosing them, the company's agent wrote : "The cash payment we will get of Scott when the time arrives." The policy recited the consideration, but upon the margin, noted that agents were not authorized to waive, alter or change any of the provisions of the policy. The receipt which accompanied the policy contained a notice : "Agents must not deliver policies till the premium is received, as no policy is in force till paid for." The policy was delivered, together with the receipt, but Scott never paid the cash part of the premium. The agent notified the insured that Scott refused to pay the premium, and the insured promised the agent to get the money and send it along in a few days. The insured became sick. The agent wrote to him, inclos_

cates a contrary intention. It is held in numerous cases that, where the policy contains a condition requiring pre-payment of the premium as a condition precedent, *and also a receipt for the premium, that a delivery of the policy to the assured estops the company from setting up the forfeiture for non-payment of the premium, because the receipt is absolute evidence of payment.*[1]

In the case last referred to, BEASLEY, C.J., in passing upon this question, says: " *This policy, executed by the president and secretary of the company, contains a formal acknowledgment of the payment of the premium in question, and in my opinion, this should prevent the defendants from averring or showing non-payment for the purpose of denying that the contract ever had any legal existence.* What does this receipt, in connection with its delivery, import, if it does not mean *that the payment of the premium is conclusively admitted to the extent that such payment is necessary to give validity to the contract ?* Unless this be the meaning, it serves no legal office, for it does not mean that the money has been actually received. It is true that there is an express declaration that the policy is to have no effect until the premium shall have been paid; but in this same instrument is an equally express declaration, *that the act upon which the contract is to become efficacious has been done.* Such an acknowledgment appears to be analogous and equivalent to the acknowledgment of the receipt of a valuable consideration in a conveyance operative by force of the statute of uses, being always considered as conclusive for the purpose of giving a legal force to the transaction. *This policy purports to have an effect immediately on delivery, founded on a paid up consideration. It does not seem competent for the promisor to prove that the acknowledgment is not true, and that the contract never had any existence.* I think that, when the assured received this policy, *he had a right to presume, either that the agent had settled the premium with the company, or that they, by their receipt, intended to relinquish the clause requiring pre-payment.* The usual legal rule is, that a receipt is only *prima facie* evidence of payment, and may be explained; *but this rule does not apply where the question involved is not only as to the fact of payment, but as to the existence of rights*

---

ing the two premium notes, and requested a return of the policy. The insured died before this letter reached him. It was held that the agents had power to waive the payment of the premium, and to deliver the policy without exacting the cash premium ; *and that delivering the policy, without requiring payment of premium, raised a presumption that credit was intended ; and where a credit is intended, the policy is valid, though the premium be never paid.*

[1] *Provident Ins. Co.* v. *Fernell*, 49 Ill. 180 ; *Basch* v. *Humbold, etc., Ins. Co.,* 35 N. J. 429 ; 5 Bennett's F. I. C. 421.

springing out of the contract. With a view of defeating such right, the party giving the receipt cannot contradict it. An acknowledgment of an act done, contained in a written contract, and which is requisite to put it in force, is as conclusive against the party making it as any other part of the contract, and cannot be contradicted or waived by parol. "[1]

Indeed, this rule is so strict that it has been held that an action to recover a portion of the unearned premium might be maintained by the policy holder, *even when the premium was paid by a promissory note, and the note had not been paid,*[2] and that an action in favor of the company against the assured, unless an obligation in writing exists against him, cannot be maintained therefor[3] *A delivery of the policy, with such a receipt, is conclusive upon the insurer, and the fact of payment cannot be denied by the insurer in an action to enforce the policy.*[4] The possession of the policy is of itself conclusive evidence of payment.[5] It is also held that this rule holds good in the case of renewal receipts.[6]

There is no conflict of authority as to the power of a stock insurance company to waive the condition of a policy, as to pre-payment of premium, and such waiver may be made by an agent of the company, having either apparent or actual authority to do so, and may be shown by any act or circumstance that tends to show an intention or purpose to dispense with it. The cases upon this point are numerous.[7]

---

[1]3 Kent's Com. 3d ed. 260; *Hodgson* v. *Marine Ins. Co.*, 5 Cr. (U. S.) 100; *Prince of Wales Life Assurance Co.* v. *Harding*, El. Bl. & El. 183; *Consolidated Fire Ins. Co.* v. *Cashaw*, 41 Md. 59; *Anderson* v. *Thornton*, 8 Exchq. 425; *Dalzell* v. *Muir*, 1 Camp. 532.

[2] *Hemmingway* v. *Bradford*, 14 Mass. 121; *Dalzell* v. *Muir* 1 Camp. 532.

[3] *Airy* v. *Bland*, Park. 27; see also, Marshall on Ins. 334; Park. on Ins. 26.

[4] *Madison Ins. Co.* v. *Fellows*, ante; *Prince of Wales Life Ass'n* v. *Harding*, El. Bl. & El. 183; *Consolidated F. Ins. Co.* v. *Cashaw*, ante; *Michael* v. *Mu. Ins. Co.*, ante.

[5] *Troy F. Ins. Co.* v. *Carpenter*, 4 Wis. 20; *Dalzell* v. *Muir*, 1 Camp. 532; *De Ganimede* v. *Pigon*, 4 Taunt. 246; see also cases in previous note; see, holding a contrary doctrine, *Ins. Co. of Penn.* v. *Smith*, 3 Whart. (Penn.) 520; *Sheldon* v. *Atlantic F. Ins. Co.*, 26 N. Y. 400.

[6]*Prince of Wales Life Ass'n* v. *Harding*, ante.

[7] *Bersche* v. *Globe Mut. Ins. Co.*, 31 Mo. 546; *Ins. Co.* v. *Stockblower*, 26 Penn. St. 199; *Heaton* v. *Manhattan Fire Ins. Co.*, 7 R. I. 502; *Keenan* v. *Dubuque Mut. Fire Ins. Co.*, 13 Iowa, 375; *Mitchell* v. *Lycoming Ins. Co.*, 51 Penn. St. 402; *Rathburn* v. *City Fire Ins. Co.*, 31 Conn. 194; *Tuttle* v. *Robinson*, 33 N. H. 104; *Hallock* v. *Commercial Union Ins. Co.*, 26 N. J.; ante; *Buckley* v. *Garrett*, 48 Penn. St. 204; *Bragdon* v. *Appleton Mut. Ins. Co.*, 42 Me. 259; *Perkins* v. *Washington Ins. Co.*, ante; *Lungstrauss* v. *German Ins. Co.*, 48 Mo. 201; *Bouton* v. *American Mut. Life Ins. Co.*, 25 Conn. 542; *Fourdray* v. *Dart*, 26 Conn. 376; *Chase* v. *Hamilton Ins. Co.*, 22 Barb. (N. Y.) 527. In *Mowry* v. *Home Life Ins. Co.*, 9 R. I. 346, the defendants executed a receipt for the premium, on a policy, and delivered it to their agent, who delivered it to the assured, and took his note for

Such waiver may be shown by parol;[1] and a delivery of the policy, without requiring pre-payment, is *prima facie* evidence of such waiver;[2] but this may be overcome by proof that no waiver was intended, or

---

the amount of the premium. In an action upon the policy, the defendants claimed that it had been forfeited by non-payment of the premium. The court, however, held, that in the absence of notice to, or knowledge by the assured, that the agent was not authorized to give credit for the premium, the taking of the note operated as a payment. But, where the agent accepts in payment of a premium due the company in money, articles of personal property, without special authority from the company, it is held a fraud and not binding upon the company, *Hoffman* v. *Hancock Mut. Life Ins. Co.*, 92 U. S. 161; but an agreement on the part of the company, made by the president, to charge the premiums to the assured as they become due, is a valid and binding agreement. *Missouri Life Ins. Co.* v. *Dunklee*, 16 Kan. 168; and the agent has the right to pay the premium to the company, and take the notes of the assured, payable to himself therefor. *Home Ins. Co.* v. *Curtis*, 32 Mich. 402. In a recent case before the Court of Appeals in New York, *Marcus* v. *St. Louis Ins. Co.*, not yet reported, reversing the case as reported in 7 Hun (N. Y.) 5, it was held that where a life insurance policy contained a provision forfeiting the policy for the non-payment of premiums when due, a general agent, who represented the company, issuing the policy, before a premium became due, had authority to extend the time of payment, and to waive the forfeiture, and that another clause in the policy that "agents are not authorized to make, alter, or discharge contracts," did not apply to such general agents. Reaffirming the doctrine of *Sheldon* v. *Atlantic Fire Ins. Co.*, 26 N. Y. 460; *Wood* v. *Poughkeepsie Ins. Co.*, 32 id. 619. The doctrine of this case conflicts with that of *Mentz* v. *Lancaster Fire Ins. Co.*, 79 Penn. St. 475, in which it was held that a *general* agent has no power to waive *any* conditions in a policy. The premium must be paid as provided in the policy, unless payment according to its terms is waived, and the burden of establishing a waiver is upon the insured. Thus, in *Bradley* v. *Potomac Ins. Co.*, 32 Md. 108, the Potomac Fire Insurance Company issued its policy of insurance to B., stipulating therein that the company would pay all loss to the property insured, resulting from fire, and not exceeding the amount specified, during one year from the date of the policy. There were further provisions in the policy, expressly providing that the company should not be held liable under the policy, until the premium in full was actually paid, and that, if the premium was not paid within fifteen days from the date of the policy, it should be null and void. A loss by fire occurred to the property covered by the insurance, after the delivery of the policy, but before the premium was paid, and before the expiration of the "fifteen days." The insured, while the fifteen days were still unexpired, tendered the amount of the premium and claimed indemnity for the loss. The court held that actual payment of the premium, not only within the "fifteen days," *but before loss*, was necessary to render the company liable under the policy, and that the holder, not having fulfilled the conditions, could not recover for the loss. In Massachusetts, it is held that where, by the by-laws of a mutual insurance company, the policy is not to be binding until the premium is paid, that a policy made, but not delivered, will not be operative, even though the treasurer of the company agrees that if anything happens, he would see the premium paid, or that he would take it upon himself to keep the policy good, *Buffum* v. *Fayette, Mut. Ins. Co.*, 3 Allen (Mass.) 360; but this was placed upon the ground that the treasurer had no authority to waive the condition. If the waiver had been made by a proper officer, it would doubtless have been held good, *Priest* v. *Citizen's, etc., Ins. Co.*, 3 Allen (Mass.) 602; and such waiver may be either express or by implication. *Underhill* v. *Agawam Ins. Co.*, 6 Cush. (Mass.) 440; but it is held that, if the matter affected by the waiver is *of the substance of the contract*, the officers of a mutual company have no power to waive them. *Hale* v. *Mechanic's Ins. Co.*, 6 Gray (Mass.) 169; *Bremer* v. *Chelsea Ins. Co.*, 14 id. 203.

[1] *Pino* v. *Merchants' Ins. Co.*, 19 La. An. 214.

[2] Davis, J., in *Wood* v. *Poughkeepsie Ins. Co.*, 32 N. Y. 619.

understood by the assured, as, that the policy was merely delivered for examination, with a distinct notice that, if satisfactory, the premium was to be paid at once.[1] But if the policy is sent for examination, with a statement, "Should you decline the policy, please return it by return mail; if you retain it, please send me the amount of premium," it has been held that a credit was given, and pre-payment waived.[2] The delivery of a policy, before the premium is paid, does not necessarily make the policy operative, and if there is no credit given for the premium, and the policy specially provides that the policy shall not attach until the premium is paid, and that unless paid within a certain time, the policy shall be null and void, the insured will not be liable for a loss occurring within the number of days from the date of the policy specified therein, *even though within that time, but after the loss*, the premium is tendered to the insurer. In such a case there is nothing to which the policy can attach, and the party has, at his peril, neglected to make the policy operative, by complying with the terms of the policy as to the payment of the premium.[3] But a delivery of the policy without exacting the pre-payment of the premium, is *prima facie* evidence of a waiver thereof, and imposes the burden upon the insurer of show-

---

[1] *Wood* v. *Poughkeepsie Ins. Co., ante; Goit* v. *National, etc., Ins. Co.,* 25 Barb. (N. Y.) 189 ; *Boehen* v. *Williamsburgh F. Ins. Co., ante.*

[2] *Sheldon* v. *Atlantic Ins. Co., ante.*

[3] In *Bradley* v. *Potomac F. Ins. Co.,* 32 Md. 108, by a policy dated the 11th of November, 1867, and executed by the company and delivered to the insured on that day, it was declared that the company, in consideration of $150, to be actually paid to it by the insured, within fifteen days from the date of the policy, did insure B. against loss or damage by fire to the amount of $4,000, on his property therein described; and in the clause that followed the description of the property, it was set forth that the company promised and agreed to make good unto the insured, his executors, etc., all such immediate loss or damage, not exceeding, etc., as should happen by fire to the property described, during one year, to wit: from the 11th of November, 1867 (at 12 o'clock at noon), until the 11th day of November, 1868 (at 12 o'clock at noon), the said loss or damage to be estimated, etc. By a condition in the policy it was provided that the company should not be held liable under the policy, or under any renewal thereof, until the premium in full therefor was actually paid ; and by a further condition it was mutually agreed that, if the premium on the policy was not paid within fifteen days from its date, the policy should be null and void ; and it was further agreed that the policy was made and accepted in reference to the terms and conditions therein set forth. A portion of the property insured was totally destroyed by fire, and the balance damaged by fire and water, within fifteen days of the execution and delivery of the policy. Proper preliminary proof of the loss was furnished to the company. After the fire, and within fifteen days from the date of the policy, the premium was tendered to the company by the insured, but not accepted. An action was brought to recover on the policy. *Held,* that the actual payment of the premium within fifteen days from the date of the policy was a condition precedent to the attaching of the risk, and as the property was destroyed before the tender of payment within the time limited, there was nothing upon which the risk could attach, and the company, therefore, was not liable for the loss.

ing that, *in fact*, no credit was given or intended, and that the condition was not waived,[1] and where a credit is given for the premium, at the time of making the contract, or when the policy is delivered, it is equally obligatory as though the premium was paid.[2]

If no mode of payment is prescribed in the contract, of course it is incumbent upon the assured to offer to pay in such money as is recognized as legal tender, although an offer to pay in current bank bills would be good, if not objected to upon that ground. But, if the assured is seeking to enforce performance of a contract, prudence would suggest a tender of money that is recognized as a legal tender. But, where the company or agent accept payment in a different mode, they are bound thereby, and are estopped from afterwards setting up a failure to pay "in money," in avoidance of liability. A check, bill of exchange, draft, or note even, accepted in payment, if good, and paid upon presentation, is an operative and sufficient payment.[3] But it has been held, that the receipt by an agent of articles of personal property, in payment of a premium, without special authority from the company, is a fraud upon it, by which it is not bound, and that the assured can claim no benefit from such a payment. He is bound to ascertain whether the agent has authority to receive payment in that way.[4] But it has been held, that where an agent accepts the note of the assured, payable to himself even, the insurer is bound thereby,

---

[1] Opinion of DAVIS, J., in *Wood* v. *Poughkeepsie Ins. Co.*, 32 N. Y. 619; *Boehen* v. *Williamsburgh Ins. Co.*, 35 N. Y. 131; *Bodine* v. *Excelsior Ins. Co.*, 51 id. 117; 10 Am. Rep. 566; *Sheldon* v. *Atlantic, etc., Ins. Co.*, 26 id. 460; *Goit* v. *The Nat. Protection Ins. Co.*, 25 Barb. (N. Y.) 189; *Trustees, etc.*, v. *Brooklyn, etc., Ins. Co.*, 19 N. Y. 305.

[2] Thus in *Church* v. *Lafayette F Ins. Co.*, 13 Alb. Law Jour. 446, an action was brought upon a policy upon a house. It appeared that plaintiff had dealt with the defendant company for many years, and was in the habit of getting policies without paying for them at the time; that on September 6th, he applied to the secretary of the company for insurance for the coming year, and asked a reduction of rates which was refused, that the plaintiff then said, "Very well, I must have it insured." The next day defendant made out the policy to plaintiff, insuring him from September 6. On September 9, plaintiff asked the secretary if he had taken the building, and he replied that he had at the old price. On the 16th of October plaintiff applied at the company's office to a clerk in charge, for insurance upon another building, and stated to the clerk that he would pay for both together, to which the clerk replied, "Very well." Subsequently the house was burned; and, thereafter, plaintiff tendered the premiums upon both policies; but that for the policy upon the burned house was refused, the secretary stating that the company was not liable because the house was unoccupied when burned. The other premium for the other policy from its original date was received by the company a few days afterwards. It was held that it was for the Jury to determine whether or not a waiver of payment was made when the policy upon the burned house was taken out, and a nonsuit was error. *Bowman* v. *Agricultural Ins. Co.*, 59 N. Y. 521.

[3] *Tayloe* v. *Merchants' Ins. Co.*, *ante*; *Mowry* v. *Home Life Ins. Co.*, 9 R. I. 346.

[4] *Hoffman* v. *Hancock Mut. Life Ins. Co.*, 92 U. S. 161.

as the assured is not bound to know that such an act is in excess of his authority, and unless he knows, or has notice to that effect, the note operates as a payment.[1] So it has been held, that an agreement by the president of an insurance, to charge the premiums to the assured, upon the company's book as they matured, is valid and binding upon the company;[2] and generally, it may be said that a payment of premiums made to an officer or duly authorized agent of an insurance company, in any of the ordinary modes adopted in business, will be binding upon the company in the absence of notice or knowledge on the part of the assured, that such officer or agent is not authorized to accept payment in such way.[3]

Usage to collect premium when policy is delivered. Effect of.

Sec. 29. In an action upon an agreement to insure, it is competent for the plaintiff to prove a usage that, when there has been a verbal agreement for insurance, and the terms agreed upon, the contract is deemed valid, and the premium not due until the policy is delivered.[4] But in such a case, in order to make the contract operative, it would be the duty of the assured to be ready to receive the policy and pay the premium within a reasonable time.[5]

When the insurer does any act that indicates that a credit is given, knowing that the insured desires it, it is a waiver of any forfeiture that might otherwise arise from payment according to the letter of the policy. Thus, where the policy provided that, when a premium note was taken for a cash premium, any default in its payment should operate to suspend the company's liability until it should be paid; the assured gave such a note and, immediately after it was due, having another policy which he desired canceled, and the unearned premium thereon applied to this note, and not knowing how much would be due the company, he proposed by letter, to pay, asking for a statement of the amount, whereupon the company at once applied upon the note the amount in their hands, and directed him, by letter, to remit the balance, which he did by first mail; but a loss occurred before the remittance was mailed, and it was held that the forfeiture was waived.[6]

---

[1] *Marcus* v. *St. Louis Co.* (N. Y. Ct. of Appeals, not yet reported). See also, *Mowry* v. *Home Life Ins. Co.*, 9 R. I. 346 ; *Home Ins. Co.* v. *Curtis*, 32 Mich. 402.

[2] *Missouri Life Ins. Co.* v. *Dunkler*, 16 Kansas, 168.

[3] See note 7, *ante*, page 68.

[4] *Baxter* v. *Massasoit Ins. Co.*, 13 Allen (Mass.) 320.

[5] Hoar, J., in *Baxter* v. *Massasoit Ins. Co.*, *ante*.

[6] *Sims* v. *State Ins. Co.*, 47 Mo. 311.

The power of an agent to waive *any* provision of a policy, whether it be a condition precedent or subsequent, is to be ascertained from his apparent authority, and not necessarily from the authority actually possessed by him. If the principal clothes him with apparent, although not with real authority, to act for him in such respects, he is bound thereby. The assured is not, *at his peril*, bound to ascertain what the *actual* authority of the agent is, but has a right to rely upon his apparent power, and if the company permitted the agent to act in such a manner as to induce the assured to believe that he had authority to bind it, touching the particular matter in controversy, the company is thereby estopped from setting up want of authority in the agent [1]

Payment of premium not essential; unless required in case of contracts to insure.

SEC. 30. It is not essential, unless expressly required by the agent, that the premium should be paid at the time when the contract is entered into, in order to constitute a valid contract to insure. It is enough if the premium is paid when the policy is made, or even if not paid at all, if the agent has given a credit therefor.[2] The rule is, that in the case of a mere oral contract of insurance, supported by a sufficient consideration, which is to take effect forthwith, although it may be entered into contemporaneously with an agreement by the insurers to deliver, and the assured to accept subsequently, as a substitute therefor, a written policy by the former in the form usually adopted by them, becomes binding and remains in force until the delivery or tender of such policy. Until then, the condition usually inserted in such policies, requiring pre-payment of the premium to make them binding, unless expressly adopted by the parties in such oral contract, forms no part of the contract of insurance between them. A mere demand of the premium, without insisting upon it or tendering a valid policy, does not terminate the oral insurance; and the insured may recover thereon for a loss, although after it occurred, and while the insurers were ignorant of it, he paid them the premium, and received from them a written policy which was not binding on them, by reason of not being countersigned by one of their officers as was required in the body of it.[3]

---

[1] See AGENTS, *post*.

[2] *Audubon* v. *Excelsior Ins. Co., ante; Hallock* v. *Comm'l Union Ins. Co., ante; Post* v. *Ætna Ins. Co.*, 43 Barb. (N. Y.) 351; *Whittaker* v. *Farmers' Union Ins. Co.*, 29 id. 312.

[3] *Kelly* v. *Commonwealth Ins. Co.*, 10 Bos. (N. Y.) 82. In *Davenport* v. *Peoria, etc., Ins. Co.*, 17 Iowa, 276, the court held, that under an oral contract to insure, it is not necessary, unless specially provided otherwise that the premium should

The premium is not payable until the policy issues, then the assured must accept the same and pay the premium.[1] In nearly all the cases where actions have been brought upon such contracts, it will be seen that the premiums were not paid until *after* the loss, when the premium was tendered and a policy demanded;[2] and under such circumstances, specific performance has often been decreed in courts of equity;[3] and actions for a breach of the contract sustained in courts of law.[4] The fact that the policies contain a condition that the risk shall not attach until the premium is paid, does not affect the question, because the assured cannot be presumed to know the conditions of a paper he has never seen, and, unless expressly adopted in the oral contract, they form no part of it, and the premium is not due until a valid policy is executed and tendered to the assured. In a leading case upon this question,[5] a defective policy was executed and delivered to the plaintiff after a loss had occured, when the premium was paid. The plaintiff, admitting that the policy was invalid, brought an action upon the oral agreement to insure, and joined therewith a count upon the defective policy. The defendants denied their liability for the loss, either under the oral contract or the policy—under the oral contract, because the premium was not paid until after the loss, when the policy required it to be paid before the risk attached. The action was upheld, and a recovery permitted under the oral contract, and as the doctrine of the case is important, I give the opinion of Robertson, J., entire, in the subjoined note.[6]

---

be paid. Where an application for insurance is made and accepted, and the policy is made out in duplicate, and the name of the assured, as such, put down on the books of the insurance company, the contract is complete; and unless the company have required payment of the premium, or given notice that they will not be bound until the premium is paid, there is a waiver of such payment. Proof of such a waiver is no violation of the rule prohibiting parol evidence to vary or contradict a written contract. *Pino* v. *Merchants' etc., Ins. Co.*, 19 La. An. 214.

[1] Denio, J., in *Audubon* v. *Excelsior Ins. Co.*, 27 N. Y. 216. 4 Bennett's F. I. C. 696 ; *Davenport* v. *Peoria, etc., Ins. Co., ante ; Hamilton* v. *Lycoming, etc., Ins. Co.*, 5 Penn. St. 339 ; *Kohne* v. *Ins. Co. of N. America*, 1 Wash. (U. S. C. C.) 93 ; *Ellis* v. *Albany F. Ins. Co.*, 50 N. Y. 402 ; *Sanborn* v. *Fireman's Ins. Co.*, 16 Gray (Mass.) 443 ; *N. E. Ins. Co.* v. *Robinson*, 25 Ind. 536 ; *Baldwin* v. *Choteau Ins. Co., ante ; Loring* v. *Proctor*, 26 Me. 18 ; *Hallock* v. *Commercial Ins. Co., ante.*

[2] See cases cited in the last note.

[3] *Ellis* v. *Albany F. Ins. Co., ante ; Palm* v. *Medina Ins. Co.*, 20 Ohio, 529 ; *Andrews* v. *Ins. Co.*, 3 Mas. (U. S.) 6 ; *Tayloe* v. *Merchants' Ins. Co., ante.*

[4] *Kelly* v. *Com. Ins. Co.*, 10 Bos. (N. Y.) 82 ; *Shearman* v. *Niagara Fire Ins. Co.*, 46 N. Y. 530 ; *Audubon* v. *Excelsior Ins. Co., ante ; Pratt* v. *N. Y. Cent. Ins. Co.*, 641 Barb. (N. Y.) 589.

[5] *Kelly* v. *Commonwealth Ins. Co.*, 10 Bos. (N. Y.) 82 ; 3 Bennett's F. I. C. 641.

[6] He said: "Under the evidence and charge to the jury in this case, the only embarrassment grows out of that part of the complaint which states a cause of

In the case of mutual insurance companies, whose charter provides that the premium shall be paid before the risk attaches, as

---

action arising out of the execution of the policy, of which a copy is annexed. The testimony of Kelly, one of the plaintiffs, by itself, shows clearly the making of an independent oral contract to insure, irrespective of an agreement to deliver a policy. The question of the reliability of such testimony, and the making of such contract, were fairly left to the jury, as matters of fact. The only questions to be considered in regard to such contract are those raised by the requests to charge, to wit: Whether, as the parties contemplated the making of a policy in a certain form, the same conditions were grafted on such contract as would be contained in such form, and whether the tender of a policy in such form and demand of the premium, and the refusal of the latter, would not terminate the oral contract. I apprehend no such construction can be given to the original contract: otherwise if the policy had failed to be returned from Philadelphia before the beginning of the risk the plaintiffs would have been without insurance altogether. It certainly became binding the moment it was made, and the utmost effect that can be given to the additional promise to execute a policy in a certain form is that, upon the tender of that policy, and a demand of the premium, the oral contract should cease. But, in this case, no such policy was ever prepared; the only one prepared was one that declared it to be only obligatory when ratified by the agent for the defendants. Unless the defendants waived that condition when tendering it, if they ever made such tender, they could not escape from the continuing obligation of the oral contract. In regard to that branch of the case, the charge of the court as well as its refusal to charge, is unimpeachable. So, too, the refusal to charge that Campbell was not the agent of the defendants, in regard to any material fact, is warranted by the facts. The only important point of his agency was his receipt of the policy. There was evidence that Hewson, the acknowledged agent of the defendants, employed Campbell to deliver the policy, and receive the premium. His delivery of it was, therefore, theirs, as he did not make it until he received the premium. There was no pretense that the delivery to Campbell was as the agent of the plaintiffs; indeed, the defendants contended to the contrary. In regard to the premium, it was actually paid before the policy was delivered, and its pre-payment formed no part of the oral contract to insure. It was not necessary, therefore, to establish either its waiver, or any authority to waive it. What the parties intended in regard thereto is wholly immaterial, if such intent was not conveyed in the language by which the contract was formed. The payment of the premium, after the fire, did not affect the agreement between the parties; by the oral contract credit was given to the plaintiffs for it, at least until a proper policy should be tendered, and such premium demanded. The conflicting testimony of the plaintiffs, Kelly, and Campbell's clerk (Crary) left it uncertain whether the premium was ever demanded, and the actual payment corresponded in time with Kelly's last promise to pay it; Campbell, at all events, in demanding the premium, for which he was the agent of the defendants, never dealt with the plaintiffs as though desirous of ending the oral contract, since he sent to them several times for it. I do not see how, if the defendants chose to carry out their agreement to execute a policy, by receiving the premium, its times of payment, whether before or after the fire, could make any difference. The only point remaining in the requests to instruct, except that as to the interview between one of the plaintiffs and a temporary representative of Campbell, is the refusal of the court to instruct the jury that the policy in question was inoperative, because it was not countersigned by the agent of the defendants. The complaint clearly contains two causes of action, although, perhaps, not distinctly enumerated as such. The statement of the second cause, growing out of the written policy, would necessarily have been insufficient to maintain a legal action, without the allegation of waiver of the countersigning of such policy by the agent for the defendants. In the absence of that, it might have been sustained as an action to compel the countersigning, and then to recover on such countersigned policy, which are causes of action that may be joined. *Bunten* v. *Orient Ins. Company*, 8 Bosw. 448. But the summons is merely for a money demand on contract, and there is no demand for relief, except damages. The complaint concedes the insufficiency of the policy, unless properly delivered and the signa-

also in cases where the assured is notified that such pre-payment is a
condition precedent to a binding contract, the premium must be paid

---

ture of the agent waived ; while the answer virtually admits its efficiency, if both
those contingencies occurred. The request, therefore, to charge absolutely that
'the policy was ineffective and inoperative, for the reason that it was not countersigned by the agent,' was too broad and general, without the qualification,
unless such signature by such agent was waived. A change in the form requested
would have been, in substance, that nothing could atone for the absence of the
signature. The defendants had a right to ask that the jury might be instructed,
that unless the plaintiffs proved the waiver, they could not recover, because that
was the issue ; but not merely and absolutely that a policy in the same form,
unsigned by the agent, was not binding, because no such issue was involved.
Notwithstanding the change in the form of pleading, juries are confined in their
findings to the issues actually made by them. Indeed, the court, by charging
that the plaintiffs were entitled to recover, 'if the policy was delivered to them,
nothing remaining to be done, the defendants being competent to *waive any provision in their policy that it should not take effect unless certain things were done,'*
or, 'if it was handed to them *as intended to be an effectual agreement binding on
the defendants,'* virtually conceded the effect of the conditions as to countersigning and pre-payment of premium, and every other provision to render it inoperative, contained in it. It virtually said the converse ; that if anything remained
to be done, required by the policy to be done to make it binding, or if it was not
intended to be an effectual agreement binding on the defendants, it was not so.
Not much stress was laid, in the argument, upon this, and no great reliance was
probably placed upon it at the trial. The only remaining point as to which an
instruction was requested was, the conversation between one of the plaintiffs and
Brewster, a temporary representative of Campbell ; this was to the effect that
what was said or done by the former to the latter was not a tender of the premium
to the defendants. In the view I have taken of this case, it was not necessary
for the plaintiffs to tender any premium ; it was not alleged in the complaint, and
the plaintiffs' case did not depend upon it. As to the exception taken to the
admission of the conversation, it was properly overruled. The evidence shows
that Campbell, being employed as a sub-agent by Hewson, to deliver the policy
and receive the premium, and interested to earn his commissions as a broker,
sent to Kelly to notify him the policy was ready ; the latter went to the office of
the former to procure a change in the policy, and found Campbell unwell in an
adjoining office, who employed a friend (Brewster) to receive Kelly's communication ; he did so, wrote a memorandum of it and put it in the policy, where it was
seen by Campbell. It was sent by him to Hewson, but went to Kelly by mistake.
Kelly had a right to show that he had not refused, but only delayed, with the
defendants' assent, to pay the premium ; that he went to Campbells's office to
give his reason for such delay, and that such reason was communicated to Campbell. When they delivered him the policy and returned the memorandum, which
return, he had reason to believe, was virtually a denial of his request, he promised to pay the original premium, and paid it at the time. The taking down of
such conversation by Brewster, and the making of such memorandum and inclosing it to Campbell, were features in the dealings between the parties, to show
that there never had been any intention to abandon the contract of insurance
with the plaintiffs. *The defendants, at that time, could have sued him for the premium and recovered; there was no reason why they should not be equally held for
the insurance, unless, upon a tender of the policy and a peremptory demand by them
for the premium, the plaintiffs had refused to pay it.* The evidence was admitted
in the first place, subject to be stricken out, if not connected with the defendants.
The court instructed the jury that it was immaterial. No application was made
to strike it out, but simply a request to pass upon its effect, while the defendants
themselves introduced Brewster and Campbell to testify as to such conversation.
Under such circumstances the exceptions should not prevail. * * From all
the circumstances it appears that the jury had a right to find that a valid oral
contract to insure was made, *determinable on the execution and delivery of a written
contract;* that such delivery and the vigorous demand of the premium, so as to
terminate the oral contract, was delayed until after the fire ; that the premium

when the application is made, unless waived, or liability will not be created either upon an agreement to insure or a contract of insurance.[1] The fact that the by-laws and regulations of the company require that the premium shall be prepaid, does not affect this species of contract, but only relates to executed contracts of insurance. And if they did relate to executory contracts, they would not apply, unless the assured was shown to have had notice of the fact, nor even then, if the agent or the company, without receiving the premium, accepted the risk and executed a policy. In such case, the insurer would be regarded as having *waived* performance of this condition, and, upon payment of, or an offer to pay, the premium within a reasonable time after the acceptance of the risk, or after a policy was made, the contract would be obligatory.[2] But if the assured has notice that "no contract for insurance is to be regarded as binding, until the premium is paid," he must pay the premium, or receive credit therefor, or the contract is not binding, even though a policy is made but not delivered.[3] The company or an agent may waive this condition, and if the agreement is entered into without anything being said as to the payment of the premium,[4]

---

was then paid, and an imperfect policy delivered, intended to have been made perfect by the defendants, on payment of the premium. *It is clear that for such premium the defendants intended to have taken the risk; they had a right to stop the credit for the premium and the oral contract by presenting a perfect policy and demanding the former.* They did not exercise the right, and when a loss has occurred they seek to evade it." The verdict for the plaintiff was upheld. See also, opinion of DENIO, J., in *Audubon* v. *Excelsior Ins. Co., ante,* in which he says, "It is true that in this case the consideration was not paid, *but the owners of the property were ready to pay it when the policy should be delivered. In the meantime it was a debt against the owners for which credit was given until the delivery of the policy.*" See also, to same effect, *Pratt* v. *N. Y. Central Ins. Co., ante.* Also a much stronger case than either of the others, *Societe De Bienfasence, etc.,* v. *Morris,* 24 La. An. 347.

[1] *Baxter* v. *Massasoit Ins. Co.,* 13 Allen (Mass.), 326; *Flint* v. *Ohio Ins. Co.,* 8 Ohio, 50; *Buffum* v. *Fayette Ins. Co.,* 3 Allen (Mass.) 360.

[2] *Hallock* v. *Comm'l Union Ins. Co., ante; Excelsior Fire Ins. Co.* v. *Royal Ins. Co., ante; Callaghan* v. *Atlantic Ins. Co.,* 1 Edwards' Ch. (N. Y.) 64; *Keim* v. *Home Ins. Co.,* 42 Mo. 38.

[3] *Flint* v. *Ohio Ins. Co.,* 8 Ohio, 501.

[4] In *Post* v. *Ætna Ins. Co.,* 43 Barb. (N. Y.) 351, the plaintiff had an interview with defendant's agent February 27th, who then inquired whether plaintiff desired to have this and another insurance on the same property, in another company, renewed when they should expire, both being to expire at the same time, to which plaintiff replied that he required them to be renewed for sixty days. In the afternoon of March 24th, the agent was asked by plaintiff whether he had renewed these policies. The agent inquired when they expired, and the plaintiff told him they had expired that day, and the agent stated he would go right over and do it. This conversation occurred, not in the agent's place of business, but in a neighboring store. Nothing was said about the premium, but the evidence disclosed the fact that this agent had previously renewed several insurances for the plaintiff in the same way. The agent was a banker, and plaintiff kept his bank account with him, and he had on former occasions debited plaintiff in account with the

or if the agent waives the condition and gives credit, the contract is obligatory. Thus, in a New York case,[1] the plaintiff, on March 28th, applied to the defendant's agent for insurance. The risk was accepted by him, and he delivered a receipt to the plaintiff for the premium, although it was not in fact paid, and agreed that the policy should take effect from noon of that day. As to the premium, the agent agreed that the plaintiff might send it to him when convenient. The property was destroyed April 7th. Insured sent the premium to the agent immediately after the fire, said nothing about the loss, and the agent, not having heard of it, sent the premium and application to defendants, who, without any notice of the loss, made and sent a policy to the agent to be delivered to the plaintiff; but subsequently, on hearing of the loss, directed him not to deliver it. It was held that the defendant could not be permitted to say that the policy would have been valid from March 28th, *if no fire had occurred*, and also to insist that it was not valid, *because of the fire April 7th ;* that the plaintiff was under no legal or moral obligation to inform the defendant of the fire before or at the time the premium was paid; that he was entitled to have his application acted upon after the fire in precisely the same manner as if no fire had occurred.[2]

If an agent has power to bind the company until the application is accepted or rejected by it, the assured is not bound to call for the

---

necessary amount of premium, without any check for it. It was held, the evidence was sufficient to establish a contract to renew the insurance for sixty days, notwithstanding all policies and renewal certificates, supplied by the company to the agent, declared they should not be valid till countersigned by the agent. *Kein* v. *Home Mut. Ins. Co.*, 42 Mo. 38.

[1] *Whittaker* v. *Merchants' Union Ins. Co., ante.*

[2] In *Excelsior Ins. Co.* v. *Royal Ins. Co.*, 55 N. Y. 343, the plaintiffs' agent having executed their policy, insuring certain buildings, machinery and fixtures, was ordered by them to cancel it. Whereupon he instructed his clerk to make application to defendants' agents to reinsure the risk. They made a policy in the name of the owner covering the risk described in plaintiffs' policy, and delivered it to the clerk of plaintiffs' agent, who made an unsuccessful effort to find the owner, and to deliver it. The premises were consumed two days after defendants' policy was issued. The day after the fire occurred defendants' agents received the premium. The owner made proof of loss and sent them to the plaintiffs, claiming that the policy made by the defendant was without authority from her, and that the plaintiffs' agent in procuring it had no authority so to do. The court held that this was not a contract to reinsure, but one of original insurance, and upon which the plaintiffs, as assignee of the owner, were entitled to recover. In *N. Y. Central Ins. Co.* v. *Nat. Protection Ins. Co.*, 20 Barb. (N. Y.) 468, the agent of the insurer was told that the money was in the bank ready for him, and he said "let it lie, and when I want it I will draw for it." *Held*, a waiver. *Walker* v. *Metropolitan Ins. Co., ante ; Boehen* v. *Williamsburgh City Fire Ins. Co.*, 35 N. Y. 84; *Sheldon* v. *Atlantic, etc., Ins. Co.*, 26 N. Y. 460; *Lycoming Ins. Co.* v. *Schellerberger*, 44 Penn. St. 259; *Blanchard* v. *Waite*, 26 Me. 18; S. C. 28 Me. 51.

policy, nor to pay the premium unless required, but may hold the company for any loss sustained, *even though the agent never informed the company of the application*, until he is notified of the acceptance or rejection of his application, unless the loss occurs *after* the lapse of the period during which the policy was to run.[1] But if he is notified

---

[1] In *Fish* v. *Cottinett*. 44 N. Y. 538, the defendant company, of which Cottinett was president (The Liverpool, London and Globe), by letter dated February 12, 1862, appointed Harry Wilbur of Batavia, its agent, with power to receive proposals for insurance against loss and damage by fire, in Batavia and vicinity; to fix rates of premium, to receive money, subject to such instructions as might from time to time be given to him. Written instructions were also sent as follows: "Your appointment as agent, gives you the power of binding the company during the pleasure of its general agent or board of directors, to an amount not exceeding $10,000 upon alternate buildings or their contents. You are hereby instructed to avoid all specially hazardous risks and decline them; should any be offered you, from parties of the highest character, you will forward the application, with your comments thereon, and may bind the company during the correspondence.   *   *   On accepting a risk, you will fill up the application, and, when desired, issue your certificate of insurance, which should be returned upon receipt of policy.   *   *   *   All remittances are to be made on the first day of each month." The company did not intrust Wilbur with blank policies, to be filled up and signed by him. Upon his application to the company to do so, its general agent wrote to him, on the 12th day of November, 1863: "We send by early mail policies, as per application. I am fully satisfied that you can do quite as large a business by having policies issued here as if written by you. The delay of one day is trifling, when the insured are as fully protected when you take the risk as if the policy was delivered." Under his appointment, Wilbur opened an agency and transacted business for the company, from February, 1862, until after January, 1864, at Batavia. In 1864, further instructions were sent the agent, containing the following directions, among others: "Remittance must be made up and forwarded to Albany on the first of each month, including every item to that date,   *   *   whether the premium be collected or not.   *   *   Risks may be taken for the following amounts, viz.: On hazardous and non-hazardous, $20,000; extra hazardous, $10,000; specially hazardous, $5,000; to be increased only by special permission." In June, 1863, the plaintiff, being the owner of the brewery buildings and property mentioned in the complaint, sold and conveyed them to one Boyle and one Smith, who gave to him their mortgage thereon, to secure the payment of $8,000 being part of the purchase money thereof. The brewery buildings, in the business of insurance, are stated as specially hazardous. On or about the 20th day of October, 1864, the plaintiff applied to Wilbur, as agent, to insure him upon the brewery buildings, as mortgagee, against loss and damage by fire, to the amount of $5,000. And it was then verbally agreed, between the plaintiff and Wilbur, who assumed to act in behalf and in the name of the company, from that time forth, and for the space of one year therefrom, would insure the plaintiff, upon the brewery buildings, against loss and damage by fire, in the sum of $5,000, and would deliver to the plaintiff its policy of insurance accordingly; and that the plaintiff would, when requested (its then payment being waived), pay to the company two and a half per cent. upon that sum, as the premium for insurance. On the 24th day of October, 1864, the plaintiff became the owner, in fee, of the brewery buildings and property. On that day he called upon Wilbur, and informed him of the fact that he had become the owner of the property, and that if the policy had not been made out, he wished it made to him as owner, instead of mortgagee. Wilbur told him that it should be so made over. The plaintiff, after this, frequently called upon Wilbur, to get the policy, and Wilbur, upon each and every of said occasions, told the plaintiff that the policy had not yet come, but that it would come; that he need not give himself any trouble about it; and that he was just as much insured as if he had the policy. The plaintiff acted in good faith, and relied upon the agreements and upon the statements of Wilbur. On

that the policy is made, and is called upon to complete the contract, a neglect to pay the premium is an abandonment of the contract and all rights under it.[1]

Agent to whom policy is sent, bound to deliver.

SEC. 31. When an application for insurance is sent through an agent of the insurer's, and the risk is accepted, and a policy is sent to him for delivery to the assured, the contract is complete, as of the date of the application, and the agent is bound to deliver it, *unless he has discovered that the insured has been guilty of such fraud in the procurement of the company's acceptance of the risk, as would operate as a full defense to the insurer in an action upon the policy,* in which case, of course, no contract exists. *The fact that a loss has occurred, or any circumstance transpiring after the contract is made,* will not excuse a non-delivery of the policy, or destroy the right of the insurer to enforce its delivery,[2] and a delivery thereof to the agent of the company, *or sending it to him by mail,* is a delivery to the assured, and its delivery by the agent to the assured is a good delivery, *even though he has previously been directed by his principal not to deliver it.*[3] So it seems that a policy bearing date on the day that the premium is paid, *takes effect by relation from that*

---

the 24th day of January, 1865, the buildings were destroyed by fire, and the plaintiff thereby sustained loss to an amount exceeding $5,000. No policy of insurance upon the buildings was ever delivered by the company to the plaintiff; nor was the premium ever demanded or paid. Wilbur never communicated to the company the application of the plaintiff for insurance, nor the agreement made with him. Immediately after the loss by fire, the plaintiff made and delivered to the company proper proofs of the loss. Upon these facts, it was held that the plaintiff was entitled to recover.

[1] *Sandford* v. *The Trust F. Ins. Co.,* 11 Paige Ch. (N. Y.) 547.

[2] *Fried* v. *Royal Ins. Co.,* 50 N. Y. 243; *Cooper* v. *Pacific Ins. Co.,* 7 Nev. 116; *Kentucky Mut. Ins. Co.* v. *Jenks,* 5 Ind. 96; *Kohne* v. *Ins. Co. of N. America,* 1 Wash. C. C. (U. S.) 93; *Mactiers* v. *Frith,* 6 Wend. (N. Y.) 103; *Tayloe* v. *Merchants' Ins. Co., ante.* The doctrine of the text was well illustrated in *Hallock* v. *Com. Union Ins. Co,* 26 N. J. 268; also, 27 N. J. 645. In that case the defendants' agent was authorized to accept proposals and premiums for insurance, but not to make contracts therefor. The proposals were received by him, forwarded to the company, and policies, if issued thereon, returned to him for delivery. The plaintiff applied to the agent for insurance, March 12th, and an application was made, under which, if accepted, the insurance was to commence at noon of that day. The amount of premium was fixed, and the plaintiff offered to pay it, but the agent told him that he could keep it, and he would call for it. The plaintiff was a banker, with whom the agent kept an account. The application was not acted upon until March 13th, when a policy was made and sent to the agent for delivery. Ten hours prior to the making of the policy the property was destroyed by fire, and the defendants telegraphed the agent *not to deliver the policy.* The plaintiff tendered the premium, which the agent accepted, but refused to deliver the policy. The court held that the contract was complete when the risk was accepted, and that even though the assured was not aware of the acceptance, and that the defendants, *after a loss,* could not recede from the contract, and the agent was bound to deliver the policy.

[3] *Hallock* v. *Ins. Co.,* 26 N. J. 268.

day, although not delivered until several days afterwards, *and where the premium has been previously paid, although the assured had been informed of the insurer's intention of revoking the agent's authority, a delivery of the policy by such agent is binding upon the company even after his authority is revoked.*[1] The doctrine of the case last cited does not go the extreme length stated in the text, but it is evident that the doctrine stated in the text is correct, because, as previously stated, the policy, *immediately upon being executed, becomes the property of the assured*, hence any person who withholds it from him is a wrong-doer, and liable in trover for its conversion.[2]

The simple test is, whether the *aggregatio mentum* exists. If so, and nothing remains to be done but to deliver the policy; the contract is complete, as well *before* as *after* the policy is made. The policy is merely evidence of the contract, and, before its execution, delivery and acceptance, the contract may be proved by parol, and if a contract *in fact* is established, the insurer is liable for a loss under it happening after the time when the risk attached.[3]

As soon as the policy is executed and all conditions precedent are performed, it instantly becomes the property of the assured.[4] But the burden is upon the assured to establish his right to the policy, by

---

[1] *Lightbody* v. *N. America Ins. Co.*, 23 Wend. (N. Y.) 18.

[2] *Hallock* v. *Ins. Co., ante; Ellis* v. *Albany Ins. Co., ante.*

[3] *Whittaker* v. *Farmers' Ins. Co.*, 29 Barb. (N. Y.) 312; *Pinly* v. *Beacon Ins. Co.*, 7 Grant's Ch. (Ont.) 130; *Kein* v. *Home, etc., Ins. Co., ante; Hallock* v. *Commercial Ins. Co.*, 26 N. J. 268; 27 id. 645; *Arkansas Ins. Co.* v. *Bostick*, 27 Ark. 539. In *Kentucky, etc., Ins. Co.* v. *Jenks*, 5 Ind. 96, the application was made by the husband for a policy upon his life, payable to his wife. The application was made Sept. 27, 1850, and the company's approval thereof was duly entered on their books; and October 2d, 1850, a policy was issued and forwarded to their agent. It was agreed that the premium should be credited against the assured's bill against the company for advertising. The assured was taken sick Sept. 29th, 1850, and died Oct. 4th, 1850, and the agent returned the policy to the company. The court held that the contract was complete, and that the defendants were liable thereon. The ground upon which the ruling is predicated is, that the proposal is a continuing offer up to the time of its acceptance or rejection, and that, *when accepted*, and nothing remains to be done as a condition precedent by the assured, the risk attaches and the insurer by its own act cannot relieve itself from liability. *Walker* v. *Met'n Ins. Co.* 56 Me. 571; *Marland* v. *Royal Ins. Co.*, 73 Penn. St. 393; *Hamilton* v. *Lycoming Ins. Co., ante; Kein* v. *Home Mut. F. & M Ins. Co., ante; Hubbard* v. *Hartford Ins. Co.*, 33 Iowa, 325; *Palm* v. *Medina Ins. Co.*, 20 Ohio 529; *Cooper* v. *Pacific Mut. Ins. Co.*, 7 Nev. 116; *Baldwin* v. *Chateau Ins. Co.*, 56 Mo. 151; *Audubon* v. *Excelsior Ins. Co.*, 27 N. Y. 216; *Fried* v. *Royal Ins. Co.*, 50 N. Y. 243; *Tayloe* v. *Merchants' Ins. Co., ante; Ins. Co.* v. *Colt, ante; Ins. Co.* v. *Wright*, 1 Wall. (U. S.) 456; *Hartshorne* v. *Union, etc., Ins. Co.*, 36 N. Y. 172; *Pattison* v. *Mills*, 1 Dow & C. 342; *Lishman* v. *Northern, etc., Ins. Co.*, L. R. 8 C. P. 216; *American Horse Ins. Co.* v. *Patterson*, 28 Ind. 17; *Blanchard* v. *Waite*, 28 Me. 51; *Hyde* v. *Ins. Co.* 10 La. 543; *Willets* v. *Sun Mut. Ins. Co.*, 45 N. Y. 45; *Warren* v. *Ocean Ins. Co.*, 16 Me. 439.

[4] GROVER, J., in *Ellis* v. *Albany F. Ins. Co., ante; Hallock* v. *Ins. Co., ante.*

6

showing performance or offer of performance of all conditions precedent, within a reasonable time.

The insurer, in such cases, is regarded as holding the policy in trust
for the assured, and is bound to deliver it upon demand, and failing
to do so, is liable in trover therefor.[1]

The policy is not binding, when not delivered to assured, as to matters in which it varies from the actual contract.

SEC. 32. When a valid contract for insurance is made, the policy is
not binding upon the assured, *if it varies from the real contract entered
into, unless he, with knowledge of its provisions, has accepted it.* If the
policy is made and retained by the insurer, or its agent, until *after* a
loss, the assured never having seen it, the real contract will prevail,
and the policy is not evidence, even, of the contract entered into; and
this is so, even though the policy has expired, and has been renewed
by a receipt which expressly refers to the policy for the terms of insurance. Thus, in an English case,[2] the plaintiffs entered into a valid
contract, with the agent of the defendants, for insurance upon a vessel,
and took from him an agreement for a policy. The agreement contained no exception suspending the policy while the vessel should be
at sea. The agent sent the order to the defendants, who made a
policy, and sent it to the agent. The policy contained a provision
exempting the insurer from liability while the vessel was at sea. The
policy was not called for by the plaintiff, nor was it ever seen by him,
but was retained by the agent. When the policy expired, it was
renewed, the receipt referring to the policy for the terms of the contract, but the renewal receipt, like the policy, was retained by the
agent. A loss having occurred while the vessel was at sea, the defendants denied their liability, under the policy, for the loss, insisting that
the policy, and not the agreement, expressed the contract. But the
court held that, under the circumstances; the plaintiffs had a right to
rely upon it that the policy would be made in conformity with the
agreement, and that the memorandum delivered by the agent, and
not the policy, must be regarded as the contract.

Insurer bound to make policy conform to agreement. Warranties not agreed upon, cannot be enforced.

SEC. 33. *When a valid agreement to insure is made, and the terms are
agreed upon, the insurer cannot insert additional terms not then entered*

---

[1] *Hamilton* v. *Lycoming Ins. Co.*, 5 Penn. St. 337; 2 Bennett's F. I. C. 542;
Bragdon v. *Appleton, etc.*, F. Ins. Co., 42 Me. 259; *Hallock* v. *Ins. Co.*, ante; *Davenport* v. *Peoria, etc.*, Ins. Co., ante; *Goodall* v. *N. E. Mut. F. Co.*, 25 N. H. 169.

[2] *Pattison* v. *Mills*, 2 Bli. (N. S.) 519.

into. Thus, in a late English case,[1] the plaintiff entered into an agreement with the defendants on the 11th of March, to insure his vessel.
On the 16th of March she was lost, and on the 17th, without saying
anything about her loss, he demanded a policy in pursuance of the
agreement. Then, for the first time, the defendants required to be
informed of the amount insured upon her hull, and inserted in the
policy, " warranted not insured for more than £2,700 after March
20th." In fact there was a policy for £500, outstanding, which expired
that day, and there was an agreement that unless notice was given in
ten days, of an intention to discontinue, it should be considered as
renewed and in force for another term. No notice having been given,
the defendant insisted that the warranty was broken. The court held
that the warrant was utterly inoperative, *as it was no part of the con-*
tract entered into, and that the insurers were bound by the contract as
made March 11th. The court also held that, even though the policy
as made, was operative, there was no breach of warranty, for after a
total loss on the 16th of March, before the £500 policy expired, there
was not, and could not be any renewal thereof under the agreement.

In another English case,[2] the insurer's agent made an insurance upon
a vessel and took from the agent an agreement for a policy. There
was no exception in it suspending the policy while the vessel should
be at sea. The agent transmitted the order for the policy to his principals, who sent a policy to him, which contained a clause exempting
insurer from claim while the vessel should be at sea. It was not
demanded by, nor was it delivered or shown to the insured, who
renewed the policy through the same agent at the end of the year.
The memorandum of renewal referred to the specific policy then in
the agent's office in Glasgow. It was neither demanded by, delivered
nor shown to the insured; and soon after she was destroyed by fire at
sea. *It was held the memorandum delivered to the insured was the contract*
between the parties ; that the policy was not the contract, because it did not
conform to the original agreement, and because the insured was never
informed as to the exemption, and therefore never adopted the policy ; also
that the renewal had reference to the original agreement, and the
insurers *were bound to execute it conformably to the stipulation of the*
original agreement.

[1] *Lishman* v. *Northern Maritime Ins. Co.,* L. R. 8 ; C. P. 216.
[2] *Pattison* v. *Mills, ante.*

SEC. 34. Where a valid contract to insure is made by parol, the insurer cannot, *after a loss*, refuse to execute the policy because, *in fact*, the property covered by the contract cost less than the amount they had agreed to insure, *unless positive fraud, such as would avoid the policy if made, can be shown on the part of the assured, in reference to his representations as to value.* Thus, in a Canada case,[1] the plaintiff contracted with the defendants to issue a policy to him upon a building for a certain sum. The policy was not made out at the time, nor was it made when the loss occurred, but a valid contract *to insure* existed. The defendants, in an action brought to compel a specific performance of the contract, defended upon the ground that the *real value* of the property was much less than they had been led to believe. But the court held that this constituted no defense.

SEC. 35. As to all matters not entering into the *essence* of the contract, but which merely relate to the forms to be observed, when there is no essential departure from the terms of the charter or the articles of association, the officers may waive strict performance, and a contract, essentially, although not strictly conforming to the charter requirments, will be upheld. Thus, in an English case,[2] the registered deed of settlement provided that the common seal should "not be affixed to any policies, except by order of three directors, signed by them, and countersigned by the managers." Another section provided that "every policy shall be given under the hand of not less than three of the directors, and sealed with the common seal." A policy was issued, executed and sealed, signed by three directors, *one of whom was the manager; no previous order had been given, signed by three directors*, as required, and upon this ground, the company insisted that the policy was inoperative and void. But the court held *that the mere omission of a formality, or an immaterial variation from the forms prescribed by the deed, would not vitiate a policy.* So, too, it has been held that, where a policy contains a provision that it shall not be valid *unless countersigned by the agent;* a policy delivered by the agent, without being countersigned by him, *is nevertheless a valid and operative contract.*[3] The rule may be said

[1] *Laidlaw v. Liverpool & London Ins. Co.*, 13 Grant's Ch. 337.

[2] *Prince of Wales Life Ass'n v. Harding*, El. B. C. & El. 183; *Kelly v. Com. Ins. Co.*, 10 Bos. (N. Y.) 82.

[3] *Myers v. Keystone, etc., Ins. Co.*: 27 Penn. St. 268; *Norton v. Phœnix, etc., Ins. Co.*, 36 Conn. 503; *Hibernia Ins. Co. v. O'Connor*, 29 Mich. 241.

to be *that in all cases where there has been a substantial, although not a literal compliance with directions as to form, or the method of execution, the contract is valid, unless the omission shows that certain matters, essential to the making of the contract itself, were omitted to be done.* In the cases previously referred to, the provisions were obviously intended as a method of obtaining the judgment of the directors, in the one case, as to the propriety of entering into the contract, *and this was obtained by their execution of the contract.* In the other case, the purpose is to obtain the judgment of the agent, as to whether anything has occurred between the receipt of the application and the making of the policy, rendering it inexpedient to enter into the contract, and this is secured by his delivery of the contract, intending it as a valid contract of insurance.[1]

If the circumstances attending the delivery of the policy are such as show that it was the intention of the parties to treat a policy not countersigned, *as an executed agreement, and to dispense with that condition,* the policy will be operative, as, where the agent receives the premium and delivers the policy, omitting to countersign it through mistake,[2] but the burden is upon the assured to show that the condition was waived, and mere possession of the policy is not enough to establish the fact,[3] but if they were delivered *as completed instruments;* as if the premium had been paid, the company is thereby estopped from setting up such omission in avoidance of the policy,[4] unless the act of incorporation itself provides that the policy shall not be valid unless countersigned, and in that case, if the premium has been paid, the company will be compelled to issue a valid policy, and in all cases where such a defect exists it would seem to be the better course to proceed for a specific performance of the contract.[5]

But, in any event, if a valid and binding contract was entered into, no defect in the execution of the policy would shield the company

[1] *Hibernia Ins. Co.* v. *O'Connor, ante. Contra,* see *Kelly* v. *Com. Ins. Co., ante.*

[2] *Myers* v. *Keystone, etc., Ins. Co.,* 27 Penn. St. 268 ; *Norton* v. *Phenix, etc., Ins. Co.,* 36 Conn. 503.

[3] *Prall* v. *Mut. Protection, etc.. Ins. Co.,* 5 Daly (N. Y. C. P.) 298 ; *Badger* v. *American Popular, etc., Ins. Co.,* 103 Mass. 244.

[4] *Hibernia Ins. Co.* v. *O'Conner,* 29 Mich. 241.

[5] *Perry* v. *Newcastle Fire Ins. Co.,* 8 U. C. (Q. B.) 363. In *Lynn* v. *Burgoyne,* 13 B. Mon. (Ky.) 400, it was held that if it is stipulated in the policy that "it shall not be valid until countersigned by A.," a policy which is not thus countersigned is not valid. But, in such a case, if it is shown that A. delivered the policy, *intending it as an operative instrument,* it is clear that the ultimate liability of the company cannot thus be defeated.

from ultimate liability.   The remedy of the party would be to seek its reformation so as to represent a valid and operative instrument, and the very fact that a policy was issued, however defective, affords ample proof of the intention of the insurer to issue a valid policy, as it will not be presumed that it intended to issue an invalid or inoperative policy, but the reverse.[1]

---

[1] See Chapter on Reformation of Policies, *post*.

CHAPTER II.

THE POLICY.

Kinds of.

SEC. 36. As has been seen, a contract of insurance to insure, as well as the renewal of a policy about to expire, or that has already expired, may be by parol,[1] and is equally as valid and binding as though it was in writing, unless by statute, it is required to be in writing, or executed in a particular manner. But, generally, contracts of this nature are evidenced by a writing, called a policy, executed by the proper officers of the company from which it issues. The person whose interest is insured under the policy, is the assured or insured, and the person or company taking the risk, is the insurer. Policies are either wager or interest, open or valued.

Wager policies.

SEC. 37. Wager policies are those covering a risk, *interest or no interest,* and which do not, in any measure, depend upon the pecuniary

---

[1] In *Ludwig* v. *Jersey City Ins. Co.*, 48 N. Y. 379, the plaintiff's policy being about to expire, he applied to the defendants' agent to renew it. The policy insured his stock of goods at 29 Centre street, upon the first floor. Before the renewal was made they were removed to an upper floor, at the same number, and the plaintiff so informed the agent, and the agent also knew the fact from personal observation, as he called to see the plaintiff *after* his removal, and before the contract for renewal was made. The renewal receipt professed to renew the prior policy, but in the memorandum of location simply said, "Premises 39 Centre street, city of New York," omitting the words of the policy "contained in the first story." A loss having occurred, the defendants insisted that they were not liable because the goods were not, at the time of the loss, in the place where they were described to be, in the policy. But the court held that, as the defendants *knew* of the change of location before the contract was made, the presumption was that they intended to make a valid insurance, and to change the terms of the policy so as to cover the goods where they *knew* them to be when the contract was made, and where they knew the assured desired to have the policy cover them, and that the change, in this respect, might be shown by parol. See also, *Trustees, etc.*, v. *Brooklyn Fire Ins. Co., ante.*

interest of the assured for their validity, but which are operative in the hands of a person who is a stranger to the title, or to *any* proprietary interest in the subject-matter insured. At common law, these policies, as applied to marine risks, have been recognized as valid, although a contrary doctrine has been held;[1] but the weight of authority is to the effect that, at common law, such policies are valid *as applied to marine risks*.[2] But this doctrine has never been applied to *fire insurance*, and it is not believed that even though the stat. 19 George 2, c. 37, had not virtually put an end to such contracts, before questions of fire insurance had been much considered by the courts, that the doctrine would have been held applicable to them. The extreme jealousy with which such contracts were regarded, by both the courts and the people, and the dangerous tendencies which they were believed to involve, would undoubtedly have prevented the courts from applying the doctrine to this class of contracts.[3] In any event, there is no warrant from the common law for wager policies of *fire* insurance. Partaking strongly of the nature of gambling contracts, they are generally discouraged, and are inoperative in those States where gambling contracts are prohibited by statute;[4] but unless specially prohibited, it must, in order to fall within the provisions of a statute against gaming, amount to a mere wager or bet,[5] and is always a question of legal construction.

---

[1] In *Godart* v. *Garnett*, 2 Vernon, 269, heard in 1692, a bill was filed to compel the surrender of a policy, upon the ground that the assured had no interest in the subject-matter of the risk. The assured had loaned £300 upon bottomry upon the ship, and insured her for £450. The court directed the policy to be delivered up for cancellation, remarking, "The law is settled, that if a man has no interest and insures, the insurance is void, although it be expressed in the policy, *interested or not interested*; and the reason the law goes upon is, that insurances are made for the encouragement of trade, and not that persons unconcerned in trade, not interested in the ship, should profit by them." See the report of this case in Marshall on Insurance, 99.

[2] *Harman* v. *Van Hutton*, 2 Vernon, 717; *De Paiba* v. *Ludlow*, 1 Com. Rep. 361; *Good* v. *Elliott*, 3 T. R. 693; *Assinedo* v. *Cambridge*, 10 Mod. 77; *Dean* v. *Dicker*, 2 Str. 1250; *Goss* v. *Wither*, Burr. 695; *Crawford* v. *Hunter*, 8 T. R. 23; *St. John* v. *American Mut. Life Assurance Co.*, 2 Duer (N. Y.) 419; *Miller* v. *Eagle, etc., Ins. Co.*, 2 E. D. S. (N. Y. C. P.) 268; *Juhel* v. *Church*, 2 John. Cas. (N. Y.) 333; *Abbott* v. *Sebor*, 3 id. 39; *Buchanan* v. *Ocean Ins. Co.*, 6 Cow. (N. Y.) 318; *Clendining* v. *Church*, 3 Caines (N. Y.) 141.

[3] In Pennsylvania this species of contract has been held void as being opposed to public policy, even as to marine risks. *Pritchet* v. *Ins. Co. of N. America*, 3 Yeates (Penn.) 461; *Callamore* v. *Day*, 2 Vt. 144; *Lord* v. *Dall*, 12 Mass. 115; *Hoit* v. *Hodge*, 6 N. H. 104; but in New York such contracts were held valid before prohibited by statute, as applied to marine risks, *Jubel* v. *Church*, 2 John. Cas. (N. Y.) 333.

[4] *Paterson* v. *Powell*, 9 Bing. 339; *St. John* v. *American Mut. Life Ins. Co.*, 13 N. Y. 31.

[5] *Dalton* v. *National Loan Fund Life Association*, 22 Barb. N. Y. 9; *Delonguemere* v. *Phœnix Ins. Co.*, 18 John. (N. Y.) 127; *Potapsco Ins. Co.* v. *Coutler*, 3 Peters (U. S.) 397; *Pleasants* v. *Maryland Ins. Co.*, 8 Cr. (U. S.) 55; *Kane* v. *Columbian Ins. Co.*, 8 John. (N. Y.) 229; *French* v. *Ins. Co.*, 16 Pick. (Mass.) 439.

Interest or no interest.

SEC. 38. The words, "interest or no interest," used in a policy, do not necessarily convert it into a wager policy; the true test is, *whether, at the time the policy issued, and at the time of the loss, the person to whom it was issued, or who claims under it, had an interest, legal or equitable, in the property insured, to the extent of the sum insured, or in trust for the real owner.* A partial interest in the property insured, bearing a small proportion to the sums insured, *if the policy is valued,* does not save the policy from being a wager policy, unless the assured stands in such a relation to the property, that as to all the balance of the sum insured, he stands as a trustee for the owner. Otherwise, valued policies would be a mere cover for this species of gaming.[1]

Interest policies.

SEC. 39. All policies of *fire insurance* are interest policies, and in order to be valid, must be predicated upon an interest of the insured in the property covered.[2]

Open policies. Blanket policies, floating policies, etc.

SEC. 40. Open policies are those in which the value of the loss is not fixed, but is left open to be determined by the value of the property actually lost, or in which the subject-matter of the risk is indeterminate, changing, fluctuating, or contingent. Policies of the class last named, where the risk is constantly changing, cannot, in the nature of things, be valued. Often—indeed, generally—the property covered by such policies was not owned or possessed, by the assured, at the time when the policy issued, or, perhaps, was not in existence, and for this reason, are called floating policies. Thus, a policy issued to a merchant upon a stock of goods of a particular class, as dry goods, covers not merely the goods then on hand and owned by the assured, *but goods of that class which he has on hand at the time of the loss.* The goods which the insurer is called upon to pay for, in case of a loss, may not have been in existence when the contract was made. At that time, even the materials of which they are composed, may not have existed, and *necessarily* the value of the loss is left open for adjustment, according to the value of the goods actually destroyed. It may be said that *in all cases where the policy contemplates that the risk is shifting, fluctuating, varying, and is applied to a class of*

---

[1] Marshall on Insurance, 109; *Lewis* v. *Rucker,* 2 Burr. 1171; *Kent* v. *Bird,* Cowp. 583; *Alsop* v. *Com. Ins. Co.,* 1 Sum. (U. S.) 451; *Clark* v. *The Ocean Ins. Co.,* 20 Pick. (Mass.) 287; *Robinson* v. *Ins. Co.,* 1 Met. (Mass.) 143.

[2] See chapter on INSURABLE INTEREST.

property, rather than to any particular article or thing, the policy is
necessarily open, and all policies which, in terms, leave the value of
the loss—in case of total loss—to adjustment, according to the value at
the time of loss, are also open. Such policies are sometimes called
blanket policies, among insurers, being intended as a species of catch-
all, to use a homely phrase, and indemnify the assured from loss upon
a certain class of property, in which he may have an insurable interest
at the time of loss, wherever situated, which is not otherwise covered
by insurance. They are called blanket policies, because they are
spread over property indiscriminately, and frequently over risks
already fully covered by insurance, but which are fluctuating, and
extended, at times, so that one day the policy may attach, and another
day be useless. This species of policies are especially adapted to risks
taken for merchants, manufacturers, carriers, railroad companies, etc.,
and all classes of risks where the policy is not intended to cover specific
property, but rather property of the class named.

Valued policies.

SEC. 41. Valued policies are those in which both the property insured
and the loss are valued, and which bind the insurer to pay the whole
sum insured, in case of a total loss. They may be said to be policies,
in which the insurer himself, at the time of making the policy, assesses
the damages in case of a total loss, unless fraud, inducing an over-valuation on the part of the assured, is established. As a matter of
course, these policies can only be applied to articles *specifically* insured,
where the risk is fixed, and no diminution, increase or change therein
is contemplated. Indeed, a policy is never strictly valued unless
applied to specific articles, without the right of substitution, express
or implied. Therefore, except as applied to fixed property, such as
buildings, machinery, and fixtures, or specific articles, naming them,
and not extending to others of the same class in lieu thereof, a policy
is not, and cannot be treated as a valued policy, even though so
appearing to be upon its face. It often happens that a policy may
be mixed; that is, both an open and a valued policy—valued as
to one class of property, and open as to another. Thus, for example, a policy is issued to A. as follows: "$500 upon his dwelling-
house, frame, slate roof, etc., valued at $500, and $500 upon his
household furniture therein." Now, so far as the policy relates to
the building, it is valued, and in case of a total loss, the sum insured
must be paid; but, although *all* the household furniture is destroyed,
the insurer is bound to pay no more than the *value* of the furniture

destroyed, and the same is true as to policies covering a building and fixed machinery, and also stock and materials. As to the former, it may be valued, and as to the latter, open.[1] In order to constitute a valued policy, the policy must contain words that show an *intention,* on the part of the assured, to value the loss, and this is usually accomplished by using the words, "valued at," although such words are not indispensable. *If there is anything in the policy that clearly indicates an intention, on the part of the insurer, to value the risk and the loss, in whatever words expressed,* the policy is valued, otherwise it is open.   Thus, a policy expressed to be "on 380 kegs of tobacco, worth $9,600," is a valued policy.[2] So, "on goods valued at £1,400," although no particular goods are stated, but in such case, in order to recover the entire sum, all the goods insured must have been lost.[3] So, where the policy recites that the amount insured is not more than one-half, two-thirds, three-fourths, etc., of the value of the property insured,[4] *and indeed in all cases* where, from the language used, it is evident that the policy was intended *as a valued policy;* that is, that the sum named was intended as a valuation of the loss, it is to be so treated without reference to the words or form of expression employed.   No particular form of expression is necessary ; the *intention* of the parties, gathered from the whole instrument, must determine the matter;[5] but if the written portion of the policy is inconsistent with the printed, the writing must control, although if possible to give effect to the whole instrument it will be done.[6] Although the words, "valued at," are used, the policy may still be an open one, if, from other written portions of the policy, it is evident that the valuation did not apply to the property insured, but simply to furnish a standard by which the value of the property in foreign money was to be estimated in our money.   As where the policy contained these words, "the said goods and merchandise are valued at," and immediately following the words, "18 francs, valued at $4 and

---

[1] *Cushman* v. *Northwestern Ins. Co.,* 34 Me. 487 ; *Riley* v. *Hartford Ins. Co.,* 2 Conn. 368.

[2] *Harris* v. *Eagle Ins. Co.,* 5 John. (N. Y.) 368.

[3] *Francis* v. *Natusch,* 6 Tryw. 401.

[4] *Brown* v. *Quincy, etc., F. Ins. Co.,* 105 Mass. 396; 7 Am. Rep. 538; *Nichols* v. *Fayette Mut. F. Ins. Co.,* 1 Allen (Mass.) 63 ; 4 Bennett's F. I. C. 520 ; *Phillips* v. *Merrimack Ins. Co.,* 10 Cush. (Mass.) 350 : *Borden* v. *Hingham Ins. Co.,* 18 Pick. (Mass.) 523 ; *Fuller* v. *Boston, etc., Ins. Co. ; Luce* v. *Dorchester, etc., F. Ins. Co.,* 105 Mass. 297 ; 7 Am. Rep. 522.

[5] *Fuller* v. *Boston, etc., Ins. Co., ante.*

[6] *Cushman* v. *N. W. Ins. Co., ante.*

44 cents," it was held that the policy was not valued.[1] When the policy is, in fact, valued, and no fraud, on the part of the assured, is established, the insurer is estopped from proving that the property was less valuable than that agreed upon,[2] and *e converso*, the assured is estopped from proving that it is more valuable.[3] In the case of a partial loss the value of the property destroyed is to be estimated at the rate specified for the whole property, of the same class, if the valuation is such that the value of a parcel thereof can be estimated. The rule in such cases, was well illustrated in an early case in New York,[4] previously referred to. In that case, the policy insured $20,000 upon the plaintiff's tobacco, manufactured and unmanufactured, described and distributed in the policy as follows:

"Ten thousand dollars upon his merchandise and utensils, specified on the back hereof, and contained in his two story frame building, occupied by the assured as a tobacco manufactory."   *   *

"Ten thousand dollars upon his merchandise and other property, as specified on the back hereof, contained, etc."

The memorandum upon the back of the policy, among other things insured, specified 380 kegs of manufactured tobacco, *worth* $9,500. A loss occurred under the policy, and, among other things, 157 kegs of this tobacco was destroyed. The plaintiff claimed to be compensated at the same rate for the tobacco destroyed as specified in the memorandum to be the value of the whole, whereas the defendants claimed that, the loss being partial, they were only liable to pay for it at its first cost, and a verdict was taken for the plaintiff at the rate of compensation claimed by him, which was sustained upon appeal, THOMPSON, J., in a very able opinion, reviewing the principles applicable in such cases. He said: "Which of these rules ought to govern, must, it appears to me, depend upon the question, whether this is to be deemed an open or valued policy. We find in the books but few cases in which the subject of insurance against loss by fire has come under consideration; and none which throw any light upon the present question. The rules applicable to marine insurance, so far as the

---

[1] *Ogden* v. *Columbia Ins. Co.*, 10 John. (N. Y.) 273.

[2] *Phœnix Ins. Co.* v. *McLean*, 100 Mass. 475; *Fuller* v. *Boston Mut. F. Ins. Co.*, *ante*; *Ins. Co. of N. America* v. *McDowell*, 50 Ill. 120; *Laurent* v. *Chatham F. Ins. Co.*, 1 Hall (N. Y.) 41; *Lycoming Ins. Co.* v. *Mitchell*, 49 Penn. St. 372; *Trull* v. *Roxbury, etc., Ins. Co.*, 3 Cush. (Mass.) 263; *Peoria F. Mut. Ins. Co.* v. *Lewis*, 18 Ill. 553.

[3] *Holmes* v. *Charlestown, etc., Ins. Co.*, 10 Met. (Mass.) 211.

[4] *Harris* v. *Eagle F. Ins. Co.*, 5 John. (N. Y.) 368; 1 Bennett's F. I. C. 85.

analogy between the two cases will hold, ought to govern us. And according to those rules, this must, I think, be considered a valued policy, so far as relates to the kegs of tobacco. The case states, that among the articles insured there were 380 kegs manufactured tobacco, worth $9,600; this was the rate at which the tobacco was estimated, in making up the $20,000, the amount of the insurance. The premium was paid according to this valuation; and the 157 kegs, which were lost, are expressly stated *to be of the same kind and quality* as the whole 380 kegs. We have, therefore, an infallible rule by which to estimate the several and distinct value of each keg of tobacco. But it was said on the argument, that admitting this to be a valued policy, it would make no difference, for it was only in case of a total loss that there was any distinction between an open and a valued policy; that in case of a partial loss, the like inquiry into the true amount of such loss is to be made, whether the policy be of the one sort or the other. This is undoubtedly true, when ascertaining the extent of damage which the particular subject has sustained, and when there was not an absolute destruction of the subject. But where there is an actual total loss of any article, distinctly valued in the policy, that valuation, I apprehend, must govern in all cases. The valuation in a policy is in the nature of liquidated damages, to save the necessity of proving them. In case of a total loss of the subject, by allowing the value to be inserted in the policy, the underwriter agrees that it shall be taken as there stated. This valuation is always considered as the fair amount of the prime cost, or at least that which the parties have agreed to adopt as such. If, in the valuation of an article manufactured by the assured, he has chosen to estimate his labor and supposed profits, and to pay a premium therefor, I see no objection against it. It furnishes no evidence of a fraudulent intention to over-value.

In France, where almost all policies are valued, if the goods be of the growth or manufacture of the assured, the *current price* is always adopted as the value. 2 Marsh. 533. The effect of a *valuation* is only fixing conclusively the *prime cost*: if it be an open policy, the prime cost must be proved; if a valued policy, it is agreed.

In a case before him,[1] Lord MANSFIELD, throughout, speaks of the prime cost and valuation as meaning the same thing. In speaking of the general nature of the contract of insurance, he says: 'The insurer engages, so far as the *prime cost* or *value* in the policy, that the thing

---

[1] *Lewis* v. *Rucker*, 2 Burr. 1167.

shall come safe. If the goods be *totally* lost, he must pay the prime cost, that is, the value of the thing he insured at the outset. If part of the cargo, capable of a several and distinct valuation, at the outset, be *totally* lost, as if there be *one hundred* hogsheads of sugar, and *ten* happen to be lost, the insurer must pay the prime cost (or valuation) of those ten hogsheads. But where an entire individual, as one hogshead, happens to be spoiled, no measure can be taken from the prime cost to ascertain the quantity of such damage.'

To apply these rules to the case before us. The parties have agreed, in order to save the necessity of particular proof in case of loss, that the valuation in the policy shall be considered the prime cost of the tobacco. That is, that the prime cost of 380 kegs of tobacco shall be estimated at $9,600 ; *each keg is, therefore, capable of a several and distinct valuation.* There has been a total loss of 157 kegs of this tobacco, and, according to Lord MANSFIELD's doctrine, the underwriters must pay the prime cost, or valuation, of the 157 kegs. Had the 380 kegs been totally destroyed, would there have been any doubt but that the defendants must have paid the $9,600 ? I see no reason why a different rule should prevail where there has been a total loss of any number of the kegs, each one being of equal weight and quality. There is much greater certainty and simplicity in this mode of calculation, than to go into an inquiry as to the value of the raw material, and the expense of manufacturing it. There is no pretense that there has been any fraud or over-valuation." [1]

An open policy may be converted into a valued one by an indorsement thereon ;[2] but an indorsement upon a prior open policy of a subsequent valued policy upon the same risk, does not convert the prior open policy into a valued one.[3]

What are not valued policies.

SEC. 42. The intention of the parties is to be ascertained, and will control in determining whether the policy is open or valued. As has been previously stated, when the property is valued in the policy, as where the sum insured is represented as being a certain proportion of the real value, the policy is valued, but if, after stating the value of the property, there is anything to show that the insurer did not intend *to value the loss,* as, when the property is valued in the application which is

---

[1] To same effect see *Howes* v. *Union Ins. Co.,* 16 La. An. 235.

[2] *Howes* v. *Union, etc., Ins. Co., ante.*

[3] *Millaudon* v. *Western M. & F. Ins. Co.,* 9 La. 27 ; 1 Bennett's F. I. C. 502.

made a part of the policy, at $1,200, and the amount insured is $800, but the policy expressly stipulates that "in no event liable beyond the sum insured, *nor beyon l three-fourths of the actual cash value of the property insured, at the time of loss or damage, nor beyon l such sum as will enable the assured to replace or restore the property damaged,*" the policy is not valued, although the property is valued, *because the loss is left open to be determined by the value thereof whenever it may occur.*[1] So, where the policy provides that an over valuation shall avoid it, and that the insurer shall only be liable for the cash value, and the assured in his application valued the property at a certain sum, the policy is not valued, because the insurer is at liberty to go into proof to show that the valuation is excessive, and thus is liable — if at all — for no more than the actual value.[2]

The fact that the property is insured at a certain sum, does not render the policy a valued one. In order to make it so, there must be enough in the policy to show an intention and agreement to make it so.[3]

Conclusive, although over-valued.

SEC. 43. When a valuation is made by the insurer, he is, in the absence of fraud, estopped from disputing it, and is liable for the value fixed, *although the real value of the loss is less than the sum insured.*[4] In such cases the insured is required to make no proof as to value. His case is made when he establishes a total loss of the property,[5] and a substantial interest in a subject corresponding to, and satisfying the description mentioned in the policy.[6]

Gross over-valuation is presumptive evidence of fraud, but of itself

---

[1] *Brown* v. *Quincy, etc., Fire Ins. Co.,* 105 Mass. 396 ; 7 Am. Rep. 538.

[2] *Cox* v. *Ætna Ins. Co.,* 29 Ind. 586.

[3] *Cox* v. *Charleston Ins. Co. ; Wallace* v. *Ins. Co.,* 4 La. 289.

[4] *Wilson* v. *Woodie,* Faculty Decisions, 1781 to 1787. p. 207 ; *Forbes* v. *Manuf. Ins. Co.,* 1 Gray (Mass.) 371 ; *Aiken* v. *Ins. Co.,* 16 Martin (La.) 640 ; *Lovering* v. *Mercantile Ins. Co.,* 12 Pick. (Mass.) 348 ; *Clark* v. *Ocean Ins. Co.,* 16 Pick. (Mass.) 289 ; *Sturm* v. *Atlantic, etc., Ins. Co.,* 6 Jones & Spen. (N. Y.) 281 ; *Rhand* v. *Robb,* Faculty Dec. 1801 to 1807, p. 433 ; *Whitney* v. *American Ins. Co.,* 3 Cow. (N. Y.) 210 ; *Davy* v. *Hallett,* 3 Cai. (N. Y.) 16 ; *Fuller* v. *Boston, etc., Ins. Co.,* 4 Met. (Mass.) 206 ; *Cushman* v. *N. W. Ins. Co., ante; Pritchet* v. *Ins. Co. of N. America,* 3 Yates (Penn.) 458 ; *Cole* v. *Louisiana Ins. Co.,* 14 Martin (La.) 165. If the insurer agrees to a valuation in the policy, it is estopped from denying it. *Gardner* v. *Columbian Ins. Co.,* 2 Cr. (C. C. U. S.) 473 ; *Alsop* v. *Commercial Ins. Co.,* 1 Sum. (U. S.) 451 ; *Carson* v. *Marine Ins. Co.,* 2 Wash. C. C. (U. S.) 468 ; *Marine Ins. Co.* v. *Hodgson,* 6 id. 206 ; *Patapsco Ins. Co.* v. *Coulter,* 3 Pet. (U. S.) 222 ; *Griswold* v. *Union, etc., Ins. Co.,* 3 Blatch. (U. S.) C. C. 231, and can only be attacked on the ground of fraud. *Howland* v. *Ins. Co.,* 2 Cr. C. C. (U. S.) 471.

[5] *Bentaloe* v. *Pratt,* 1 Wash. C. C. (U. S.) 58 ; *Nichols* v. *Fayette, etc., Ins. Co., ante.*

[6] *Atlantic Ins. Co.* v. *Lamar,* 1 Sandf. Ch. (N. Y.) 91.

7

is not sufficient. The insurer takes the burthen of establishing fraud, and the plaintiff makes a *prima facie* case by the production of the policy.[1] *When the valuation is fixed in the policy, a stipulation in the application that is not incorporated in the policy that the valuation shall not be conclusive, does not defeat the valuation, or open the question of value to proof.*[2] Thus, in the case last referred to, a policy was issued to the assured upon his dwelling-house for $400, " being," as stated in the policy, " not more than three-fourths of the value of the property as stated by the applicant." The assured, in the application, covenanted that the estimated valuation should not be conclusive. A loss having occurred, the defendants offered to show *that at the time of loss* the value of the property was much less than the sum insured. This evidence, as well as the offer of the application in evidence, was rejected, the court holding that the insurers were bound by the valuation stated in the policy. Gray, J., said : " The building insured has been totally destroyed by fire. The policy states that the amount insured is not more than three-fourths of the value of the property, as stated by the applicant. The amount insured is $400, and the value stated by the applicant is $800. The valuation thus agreed on by the parties is conclusive, in the absence of fraud.[3] The restriction, in the subsequent proviso, to three-fourths of the actual value of the property at the time of the loss, applies only to the whole amount of insurance when there is an additional policy upon the property. The case is thus distinguished from that of *Brown* v. *Quincy Ins. Co.*[4] The covenant in the application, that the estimated valuation shall not be conclusive upon the company, is not embodied or stated in the policy, and cannot, therefore, be deemed a part of the contract.[5] Where the loss is valued, the fact that by a subsequent printed provision in the policy it is provided that the loss or damage should " be estimated according to the true and actual cash value at the time such loss or damage shall happen," does not strip the policy of its character as a valued policy. Thus, in a case heard by the Supreme Court of Maine[6] this question was ably and elaborately discussed, and the doctrine as

---

[1] *Sturm* v. *Atlantic, etc., Ins. Co.,* 6 J. & S. (N. Y. Superior Ct.) 281.

[2] *Luce* v. *Dorchester, etc., Ins. Co.,* 105 Mass. 297; 7 Am. Rep. 522.

[3] *Borden* v. *Hingham Ins. Co.,* 18 Pick. 523; *Fuller* v. *Boston, Ins. Co.,* 4 Metc. (Mass.) 206 ; *Phillips* v. *Merrimack Ins. Co.,* 10 Cush. (Mass.) 350 , *Phœnix Ins. Co.* v. *McLoon,* 100 Mass. 475.

[4] 105 Mass. 532.

[5] Stat. 1864, ch. 196; *Eastern R. R. Co.* v. *Relief Ins. Co.,* 98 Mass. 420.

[6] *Cushman* v. *N. A. Ins. Co.,* 34 Me. 487 ; Bennett's F. I. C. 490.

stated in the text established. In that case, the assured took a lease of a cotton factory for one year at a rental of $2,171.01, and paid the rent in advance in repairs and improvements upon the mill. The defendants issued a policy to him, the written portion of which was as follows; " to the amount of $2,000, namely, on the building and fixed machinery of the cotton mill, $1,700; on moveable machinery therein, $150; on stock raw and wrought, $150; said Cushman, being the lessee of said mill for one year from November 1st, 1850, and having paid the rent therefor, of $2,171.01, *which interest, diminishing day by day in proportion for the whole rent for a year, is hereby insured.*" A subsequent printed provision provided that " the said loss or damage to be estimated according to the actual cash value of the property at the time such loss or damage shall happen." The mill was destroyed by fire Nov. 23, 1850, with all the machinery, and nearly all the stock. The defendants offered to prove that the value of the repairs and improvements actually made upon the mill by the plaintiff, and estimated in the policy at $2,171.01, was fifty per cent. less than that sum. The plaintiff consented that the defendants might show, if they could, that the plaintiff, when applying for the policy and before it was issued, represented to the defendants in any way, except by exhibiting his lease to them, that he had paid rent to the amount of $2,171.01, also that defendants might prove, if they could, that there was fraudulent collusion between the plaintiff and his lessor in computing the amount of the bills. For any other purpose, the plaintiff objected to the testimony. The judge ruled the evidence to be inadmissible, beyond the purposes thus assented to by the plaintiff. Whereupon the defendants declined to introduce it. The defendants then contended that the plaintiff was bound to prove the extent and value of his interest in the property destroyed. The judge ruled that, as to the $1,700 upon the building and fixed machinery, and as to the $150 on the movable machinery, the policy was a valued one. The plaintiff thereupon waived all claim as to the $150 upon the stock. The defendants charged that in some material particulars the survey and representations of the plaintiff were false and fraudulent. These charges were negatived by the verdict. The jury returned a verdict for the plaintiff, assessing the damage, including interest, at $1,872.12, with a special finding that the loss in the movable machinery was $151.79, which is included in the same verdict.

TENNEY, J., said: " Is the policy in this case in any respect a valued policy ? A contract for insurance, like others, is to be construed upon an examination of the whole instrument, and therefrom the intention of the parties is to be ascertained. No particular form of words is required to give effect to the intention when discovered. It is proper to see what property was the subject of the policy. The plaintiff held a lease for the term of one year of the mill described, with all the privileges and appurtenances thereto belonging. The whole machinery of the mill both fixed and movable was evidently intended to be embraced. He had at the time of the insurance, stock, raw and wrought, and it is apparent that he expected that such would continue to be in the mill, though it might change from time to time.

The defendants make insurance for the plaintiff against loss or damage by fire to the amount of $2,000; $1,700 of which is on the mill and fixed machinery, and $150 on the movable machinery; the balance of the $2,000 was on the raw and wrought stock. The property last referred to is fully specified, and the policy so far was clearly open. But to prevent any question as to the portions before specified, the policy states that ' the said Cushman being the lessee of said mill for one year from November 1, 1850, and having paid the rent therefor of $2,171.01, which interest, diminishing day by day in proportion to the whole for the year, is hereby insured.' By natural, and also by the most strict grammatical construction, the ' interest ' here referred to was that which the plaintiff acquired by his lease. The raw and wrought stock could not have been the ' interest,' without a forced construction; and this is not insisted on by the defendants' counsel. No other interest or right of any kind is previously mentioned in the policy, and the plaintiff is not shown to have any other right. The sum of $2,000, and its subdivisions cannot be regarded as the interest insured, for that is the amount of the value upon which the insurance of the ' interest ' is made.

The lease was effectual between the parties thereto; and in an open policy neither the plaintiff nor defendants would be benefited in any degree by the insertion therein particularly of the rent paid by the assured to his lessor; it was wholly immaterial and unnecessary. Again, if the policy was open, there was no occasion that it should recite that the interest should diminish ' day by day,' etc. This would be only one element in the computation of the value of the loss, and one so obvious, especially if the policy was near its expiration, or had run any considerable time, that it could not be expected to be over-looked. The price paid by the plaintiff for the lease, a few days before the policy was executed, may be presumed to have been in his opinion the value of that interest, as he paid the consideration therefor in advance. And the defendants, when they executed the policy, which recited the price of the interest, must be understood as assenting to that as the value agreed upon.

It is objected that the clause in the policy, which is in the following words, is inconsistent with the construction contended for by the plaintiff, namely: 'The said loss or damage to be estimated according to the true and actual cash value of the said property, at the time such loss or damage shall happen.' We cannot suppose that this clause in the printed part of the policy was designed to annul the meaning of previous matter, which was *written* in the blank. But effect must be given to every part of the instrument if possible. And it is believed that this may be done in the policy now before us, without doing violence to any provision found therein. The policy, so far as it was intended to cover the stock, was such as to require proof of the amount of loss or damage of that portion of the property. And although it was agreed that the loss or damage should be estimated according to the actual value at the time of the loss or damage, still the parties could fix upon a rule to determine this value. And if they had agreed that the actual value of the rent for any given period during the year should be the same as for a like period at its commencement, such agreement would not be repugnant to the meaning of the clause we are considering. They did fix upon a basis by which the cash value should be determined, and the value would vary daily by the application of the rule, and was not inconsistent with other parts of the policy.

It is insisted for the defendants that the evidence offered, and rejected, excepting for the purpose of showing a fraud in the plaintiff, should have gone to the jury without restriction. If the representation of the value of the plaintiff's interest in the mill and machinery was made without fraud, it is not easy to perceive on what principle the evidence offered was competent. The defendants were so satisfied with the plaintiff's estimation, that they adopted it, and had the benefit of the premium. And they could not change the value by proving simply that others would have fixed upon a different estimation. *To allow them to introduce the evidence offered for other purposes than to prove a fraud, would be a permission to vary a written contract by parol testimony.*"

In Massachusetts,[1] a doctrine somewhat opposed to this has been

---

[1] *Brown* v. *Quincy Mut. F. Ins. Co.*, 105 Mass. 396.

held. In that case, the application valued the property at $1,200, and the policy covered $800, " being," as expressed in the policy, "not more than three-fourths of the value of the property described in the application." A subsequent clause in the policy provided that " this company shall in no event be liable beyond the sum insured, *nor beyond three-fourths of the actual cash value of the property insured at the time of the loss or damage, nor beyond such sum as will enable the insured to replace or restore the property lost or damaged.*" In this case, the court held that the latter condition in the policy controlled the valuation in the application, and left the question of damage open to proof. When the policy recites that the amount insured is not more than three-fourths the value of the property covered, it is a valued policy;[1] and, if the application is made a part of the policy, a valuation therein is as effectual to make the policy a valued one as though stated in the policy itself.[2]

When portion of property not at risk at time of loss.

SEC. 44. If, however, any part of the property insured under a valued policy is saved, or is not at risk at the time of the loss, the insurer is entitled to ratable deduction from the sum insured.[3] It is incumbent upon the assured, also, to show that the property lost was covered by the policy. That is, that it was the identical property insured, *or of the same class, and equal value,* if the policy contemplates a shifting risk. Where the policy covers a variety of property, under one head, as merchandise, and the valuation is general and applied to the bulk, if only a part of the property is lost, the question of value is open, because there is no standard by which its value can be ascertained.[4] Thus, in one case, where the policy was valued, the court ordered the assured to discover what goods he had on hand, and referred the case to a master to ascertain their value;[5] but this was a proceeding in equity, in a court of law the question would be for the jury.[6]

---

[1] *Nichols* v. *Fayette, etc., Ins. Co.,* 1 Allen (Mass.) 63; *Borden* v. *Hingham Ins. Co.,* 18 Pick. (Mass.) 523; *Fuller* v. *Boston Ins. Co.,* 4 Metc. (Mass.) 206; *Holmes* v. *Charlestown Ins. Co.,* 10 id. 211; *Phillips* v. *Merrimack Ins. Co.,* 10 Cush. (Mass.) 350.

[2] *Nichols* v. *Fayettee Ins. Co., ante; Phœnix Ins. Co.* v. *McLoon,* 100 Mass. 475.

[3] *Wolcott* v. *Eagle Ins. Co.,* 4 Pick. (Mass.) 429; *Patrick* v. *Eames,* 3 Camp. 441; *Tobin* v. *Hanford,* 17 C. B. (N. S.) 528; *La Pyrpe* v. *Farr,* 2 Vernon, 716; *Richmond* v. *Carstairs,* 2 N. & M. 562. The difference between the agreed value, and the damaged value, is the measure of recovery. *Natches Ins. Co.* v. *Bruckner,* 5 Miss. 63; *Le Pyrpe* v. *Farr,* 2 Vern. 716.

[4] *Rickman* v. *Carstairs, ante.* See cases cited in preceding note.

[5] *La Pyrpe* v. *Farr, ante.*

[6] *Forbes* v. *Aspinall,* 13 East, 323; *Tobin* v. *Hanford, ante.*

Valuation fixed by company.

SEC. 45. When the company fixes the valuation of the property insured, in the absence of fraud, concealment, or misrepresentation, on the part of the assured, it is treated as a valuation by mutual agreement, and the best evidence of the real value of the property.[1]

In a Massachusetts case,[2] the defendant company was authorized, by its charter, to insure only for three-fourths the value of the property, but the court held that, where the officers of the company deliberately placed a valuation upon property, they were thereby estopped from setting up that the property was insured for *more* than three-fourths its value. But the rule would, of course, be different, if there was any fraud, collusion, misrepresentation, or fraud on the part of the assured. In such cases, the valuation fixed by the company is taken as the best evidence of the value of the property.[3]

SHAW, C.J., in a leading case upon this point,[4] in commenting upon the effect of a valuation of the property, said : "In determining what amount shall be insured, the company necessarily determine the value of the building, or rather they fix a valuation over which it shall not be rated, for the purpose of insurance. Being limited to insure not exceeding three-fourths of the value, in determining the sum to be insured they, by necessary consequence, fix a valuation at such a sum, that the sum insured shall not exceed three-fourths of it. The result is, that as the valuation is thus proposed on the one side, and after the proposition is considered and modified, it is acceded to on the other, and the amount insured, and the rate of premium, assessments and

---

[1] In *Farmers' Mut. Ins. Co.*, Ins. L. J., Nov. 1873, a policy was issued to G. B. Forney, upon his dwelling-house. The company intended to adopt the principle that every member insured should stand his own insurer to the extent of one-fourth of any loss which should occur. The by-laws prohibited more than three-fourths of the actual cash value of any building being insured, but in case of a partial loss the insured might claim the whole amount, provided it did not exceed the sum insured. To remedy this the directors passed a resolution that only three-fourths of any actual loss should be paid. *Held*, that in the agreement that "in case any loss should occur to our respective properties by fire, we will only claim and receive three-fourths of the amount of the actual loss, provided three-fourths of the amount as aforesaid does not amount to more than three-fourths of the sum insured," the insertion of the proviso was unwarranted by the resolutions, and is not limited in case of a total loss to three-fourths of the amount insured. The agreement was not to apply when three-fourths of the actual loss should exceed three-fourths of the sum insured, and in case of a total loss the insured is entitled to receive the whole amount of his insurance, which is three-fourths of the actual cash value, and is not limited to three-fourths of the amount of the policy.

[2] *Fuller* v. *Boston Mut. Ins. Co.*, 4 Met. (Mass.) 206.

[3] *Borden* v. *Hingham Mut. Fire Ins. Co.*, 18 Pick. (Mass.) 523.

[4] *Fuller . Boston, etc., Co., ante.*

liability established on the same basis, *it is*, in the highest sense, *a valuation by mutual agreement.*"[1]

"No rule of law," says GRAY, J.,[2] "is better settled by authority, than that by which, when the assured has some interest at risk, *and there is no fraud*, a valuation of the subject insured in the policy is held conclusive upon the parties at law and in equity.[3] And none is better founded in reason."

Shifting risk—Floating Policies.

SEC. 46. As all insurers are presumed to be familiar with the usages and incidents of a risk, the contract is always construed with reference thereto.[4] Therefore, when the stock of a manufacturer is insured, although nothing is said in the policy in reference thereto, yet, it being understood that the stock insured is to be manufactured and sold, and replaced by other stock, the policy covers the stock on hand at the time of loss, although no part of it was on hand when the policy was made. It is not the identical stock on hand when the insurance was made, but stock similar in kind, and pertaining to the business that may be on hand when a loss occurs, that is covered by the policy.[5] A policy covering merchandise, in a store, does not cover any special or particular property, *but property comprising such a stock as may be on hand when a loss occurs*, although nothing is said in the policy con-

---

[1] See also, *Phillips* v. *Merrimack, etc., Ins. Co.*, 10 Cush. (Mass.) 350.

[2] *Phenix Ins. Co.* v. *McLean*, 100 Mass. 476.

[3] *Hodgson* v. *Marine Ins. Co.*, 5 Cr. (U. S.) 100; *Alsop* v. *Commercial Ins. Co.*, 1 Sum. (U. S.) 451; *Irving* v. *Manning*, 6 B. & C. 391; *Barker* v. *Janson*, L. R. 3 C. P. 303; *Coolidge* v. *Gloucester Ins. Co.*, 15 Mass. 341; *Robinson* v. *Manuf. Ins. Co.*, 1 Met. (Mass.) 147; *Fuller* v. *Boston Ins. Co.*, 4 id. 206.

[4] *Livingston* v. *Maryland Ins. Co.*, 7 Cr. (U. S.) 506; *Citizens' Ins. Co.* v. *McLaughlin*, 53 Penn. St. 485; *De Forest* v. *Fulton F. Ins. Co.*, 1 Hall (N. Y.) 84; *Hancox* v. *Fishing Ins. Co.*, 3 Sum. (U. S.) 132; *Macy* v. *Whaling Ins. Co.*, 9 Met. (Mass.) 354; *Fulton F. Ins. Co.* v. *Milner*, 23 Ala. 420; *Glendale Woolen Co.* v. *Protection Ins. Co.*, 21 Conn. 19.

[5] In *New York Gas-Light Co.* v. *Mechanics' Fire Ins. Co.*, 2 Hall (N. Y.) 108, the policy covered fixtures and gas meters belonging to and rented by the assured, placed or to be placed in the buildings, stores, or dwellings of subscribers, for seven years. It was held that the liability of the insurer was not limited to the property in the buildings at the time when the insurance was made, but to all such property placed and remaining in the places covered by the policy *at the time of the loss*. *Wood* v. *Rutland, etc., Ins. Co.*, 31 Vt. Insurance against fire for a term of five years was effected on farm buildings, including a granary, and "grain therein, or in stack." In the application for the policy, the land on which the buildings stood was particularly described. *Held*, that grain sown and stacked on land afterwards bought by the assured was covered by the policy. *Sawyer* v. *Dodge Co. Mut. Ins. Co.*, 37 Wis. 504. In *Whitwell* v. *Putnam Fire Ins. Co.*, 6 Lans. (N. Y.) 166, the policy covered "merchandise, liquors, etc.," held by the assured for sale, and it was held that the policy attached to all goods of that class subsequently purchased, in lieu of that on hand when the insurance was made.

cerning the matter. This is implied *from the nature of the risk, and the usages of the business covered by the policy.*[1]

In a New York case,[2] the property insured consisted of a stock of goods in a "retail store," and it was held that the policy covered any goods, a part of such stock, whether on hand at the time when the policy was issued, or subsequently purchased, PRATT, J., said: "It was manifestly the *intention* of the parties to the policy, in this case, *that it should cover to the amount of the insurance any goods of the character and description specified in the policy, which, from time to time during its continuance, might be in the store. A policy for a long period upon*

---

[1] In *Peoria, etc. Ins. Co.* v. *Anapaw*, 51 Ill. 283, the policy covered a stock of tobacco and cigars on storage. Subsequently the assured procured an insurance upon his own goods of the same kind, in the same building, and while that policy was in force he purchased the stock on storage and took an assignment of the policy, duly assented to by the insurer. The policy upon his own stock prohibited other insurance, and the point was raised, that the policy assigned amounted to other insurance. The court held that a policy upon a stock of goods, which is being constantly sold and replenished, covers as well the new purchase as the stock on hand at the date of the policy. But that in order that goods subsequently purchased shall become a part of the stock in trade so as to be covered by the insurance thereon, *it is not enough that other goods are purchased, but it must appear they became a part of the stock, from which sales were to be made as from the general stock; of which it may be claimed the new purchases became a part.* PARRIS, J., in *Lane* v. *Maine, etc., Ins. Co.,* 12 Me. 44; 1 Bennett's F. I. C. 482, discussed this question. He said, "as to the goods" (being a stock of a merchant), "we are clear that the policy was intended to cover *whatever goods the plaintiff might have in his store at any time during the continuance of the risk, not exceeding the amount actually insured.* A construction limiting the policy to the goods actually in the store, at the time the insurance was effected, would defeat the very object of the insured, and so it must have been understood by the insurer. The plaintiff's business was trade, the vending of goods from his store. According to the construction put upon this policy by the company, the plaintiff has no security except upon the goods actually in the store when the policy was issued, and when those were disposed of, their liability was at an end. We cannot listen for a moment to such a suggestion. A policy of insurance being a contract of indemnity, must receive such a construction of the words employed in it as will make the protection it affords coextensive, if possible, with the risks of the assured. *Dow* v. *The Hope Ins. Co.,* 1 Hall, 166. The risk of the assured was to continue six years, and the assurers assumed that risk to the amount of $200, on the goods in the store. Both parties must have understood this to mean on goods which may be in the store at any time during the continuance of the policy. If the assured had goods to an amount exceeding $200, the undertaking of the company was limited to that amount. If, by sale, the quantity was reduced below that sum in value, the insurers were so far benefited as their risk was diminished below that paid for by the premiums, and if the whole were sold, the insurers were benefited to a still greater degree by a suspension of the risk. And it was a mere suspension, for upon filling up again the risk revived; and we see no difference in principle between the case where the quantity is diminished by a partial sale, and then replenished, and where the whole is sold and an entire new stock purchased. In either case there is a risk, limited in amount by the contract, which has been assumed by the insurer, and for which the insured has paid the stipulated premium. We are clear that it is a continuing risk, to the amount specified, upon such goods as the insured may have in the store, within the term covered by the policy, and not confined to such as were there at the time of assuming the risk."

[2] *Draper* v. *Hudson River F. Ins. Co.,* 17 N. Y. 424; 4 Bennett's F. I. C. 266.

goods in a retail shop, applies to the goods successively in the store from time to time.[1] Any other construction of a policy upon a stock in trade, continually changing, would render it worthless as an indemnity. It is a primary principle in the construction of the contract, to give it the effect, as an indemnity, which the parties to it designed."

A policy which insures property of a certain description, "manufactured and in process of manufacture," and which provides that the company shall not be liable for "loss for property owned by any other party, unless the interest of such party is stated on this policy," does not cover any other than the property of the insured, and does not extend to the goods of others, being manufactured by him, even though he is, by contract, liable to them for their loss or destruction.[2] But, under a policy insuring the property of the assured generally, with no restriction as to interest, a recovery can be had when an *insurable interest* exists in the property destroyed, although the assured has not the legal title therein.

It is not essential that the article covered should be *in esse*, at the time when the policy is made, if the policy covers a special or general class of property, in order to render it operative; it is simply necessary that goods of the class insured belonging to the assured, or held by him in trust, *should have been included in the loss*, within the provisions of the policy. Thus, a policy issued to a railway company upon its rolling stock, wherever situated, covers not merely rolling stock on hand at the time when the policy was made, but all rolling stock *owned* by it *at the time of the loss*, although it was manufactured *after* the policy was issued, and if the policy covers all rolling stock *in use* by said company, at the time of the loss, it covers all rolling stock, its own or the property of other companies destroyed upon its line, which is there for the purposes of the assured.[3] So policies may be issued, and

[1] *Lane* v. *Maine, etc., Ins. Co., ante; Sawyer* v. *Dodge Co., etc., Ins. Co.,* 47 Wis. 503; *Peoria, etc., Ins. Co.* v. *Anapaw,* 51 Ill. 283. In *British American Ins. Co.* v. *Joseph,* 9 L. C. Rep. 448; Mem. in 4 Bennett's F. I. C. 161, a policy upon a certain quantity of coal was held to cover coal afterwards deposited on the premises as well as that there at the time when the insurance was made. In *Mills* v. *Farmers' Ins. Co.,* 37 Iowa, 400, the policy covered live stock, and it was held that the fact that the horse killed was purchased *after* the insurance was made, was of no account. That where property was insured as a *class,* the policy covered property of that class, whether on hand at the time when the policy issued or not. That it is only when property is *specifically* insured that the policy is restricted to particular articles. *Hooper* v. *H. R. Ins. Co.,* 17 N. Y. 424; *Worthington* v. *Bearse,* 12 Allen (Mass.) 382.
[2] *Getchell* v. *Ætna Ins. Co.,* 14 Allen (Mass.) 325; *Waters* v. *Monarch Ins. Co.,* 5 El. & Bl. 870; *London, etc., R. R. Co.* v. *Gye,* 1 El. & El. 652.
[3] Where a policy to a railroad company covered freight cars owned or used by the assured, the freight cars of other railroad companies, in use by it at the time

often are, to indemnify the assured against possible loss to the property of another, by reason of the use of the property of the assured for certain purposes, for which injury the assured would be liable to such third person ; and in such cases it is only necessary to show an injury to, or the destruction of the property of third persons by the use of the property of the assured, *for which the assured is liable,* and the loss to the assured thereby.[1] Whether there can be a recovery upon such a policy before the loss has been paid by the assured, or whether the assured would be at liberty to settle for the loss without notice to the insurer, or whether he must submit to an action in favor of the person whose property was injured, and cite the insurer in to defend the action, are questions the solution of which must largely depend upon the terms of the policy itself. If the policy is silent upon these questions, prudence would suggest immediate notice to the insurer of the loss, and an inquiry as to the course which the insurer desires the assured to pursue in settling the losses. In all cases where the policy, either expressly or by implication, shows that the risk *is shifting,* and applies to no particular articles of property, *but to a class of property*, it attaches, if at the time of an alleged loss, articles of that class belonging to the assured are included therein. To illustrate the distinction between a shifting and a fixed risk: A policy issued to a railroad company "upon its rolling stock, to wit: ten locomotive engines, numbered respectively, 1, 2, 3, etc., and named respectively, No. 1, 'Abraham Lincoln,' etc. ; forty passenger cars, numbered respectively, 1, 2, 3, etc.," is a fixed risk, and only attaches to the specific property named in the policy, and does not apply to *other* rolling stock used in place of that named. But a policy issued to a railroad company, "upon its rolling stock of every kind and description, used by it upon its railway, wherever situate upon said railway, etc.," is a shifting risk, and does not apply to specific articles of rolling stock, but covers all rolling stock owned by the assured, and injured by the casualties insured against, anywhere upon its line, whether the same was owned by it at the time when the insurance was made or not. So a policy issued to a merchant "upon his stock of groceries and general merchandise," attaches to no particular stock, but to all goods of that class *which the assured may have on hand at the time of loss*, and this, although the policy

---

of the fire, are covered by the policy. *Com.* v. *Hide and Leather Ins. Co.* 112 Mass. 141 ; *Vt. and Mass. R. R. Co.* v. *Fitchburgh R. R. Co.*, 14 Allen (Mass.) 462 ; *Eastern R. R. Co.* v. *Relief F. Ins. Co.*, 98 Mass. 420.

[1] *Eastern R. R. Co.* v. *Relief F. Ins. Co.*, Mass.

itself is silent upon the point, because the insurer, *knowing* the purposes for which the stock is kept by the assured, is presumed to have intended to issue the policy to cover *a class* of property, rather than *certain specific articles*, or a specific stock.[1] *In all cases*, the nature of the property, the uses to which it is devoted, and the intention of the parties, to be gathered therefrom, in connection with the language of the policy, is to determine whether property acquired by the assured subsequently to the issue of the policy, is covered thereby.[2]

Places within the description, and property covered by.

SEC. 47. A policy is inoperative, except as to goods kept in the *place* designated in the policy. Locality is an important element in the contract, *and when the location of the risk is such as not to fall within the terms of the policy*, as where it is described as being at one number of a building, when, in fact, it is in another, *the policy is inoperative*, although purely a mistake, and the policy cannot be reformed, without showing that the contract was, in fact, to insure it in such other building.[3] Therefore, it often becomes a material question whether the property destroyed, at the time of the loss, was upon the premises, or in the location designated in the policy, and to determine the question extrinsic evidence may be resorted to. Thus, where a policy covered a lot of timber described as being in a certain ship yard, the insurers insisted that they were not liable for timber destroyed outside the boundaries of the ship yard proper. But the court held that evidence was admissible to show whether the parties intended to limit the policy to a ship yard, bounded by exact lines, or to a yard, *as in fact used by the assured in conducting their business*. And that, upon this question,

[1] *Crosby* v. *Franklin Ins. Co.*, 5 Gray (Mass.) 504; *Modinger* v. *Mechanics' F. Ins. Co.*, 2 Hall (N. Y.) 490; *Wall* v. *Howard Ins. Co.*, 14 Barb. (N. Y.) 383; *Bigler* v. *N. Y. Ins. Co.*, 20 id. 635; *Franklin Ins. Co.* v. *Drake*, 2. B. Mon. (Ky.) 51; *Peoria, etc., Ins. Co.* v. *Lewis*, 18 Ill. 553; *Clarke* v. *Fireman's Ins. Co.*, 18 La. 431; *Clary* v. *Protection Ins. Co.*, 1 Ohio, 227.

[2] *Mills* v. *Farmers' Ins. Co.*, 37 Iowa, 400. In *Sawyer* v. *Dodge Co., etc., Ins. Co.*, 37 Wis. 503, the policy covered a building and "$300 on his grain therein *or in stack.*" on section 19, town 13, range 15, in the town of Chester. Subsequent to the issue of the policy, the assured purchased another small farm in section 17 in the town of Chester, and grain *stacked thereon* was destroyed by fire, and the court held that it was a loss within the policy, the court holding that it was the intention of the insurer to cover his grain in stack, and that, as the policy did not locate the *stacks*, it would cover his grain *stacked* anywhere upon premises owned by him in the town of Chester, whether he owned the premises when the policy was issued or not, and, perhaps, under the rule that in cases where there is ambiguity or doubt as to what was intended, the benefit of the doubt is to be given to the assured, the doctrine can be sustained. *Peterson* v. *Mississippi Valley Ins. Co.*, 24 Iowa, 494. See, also, *Everett* v. *Continental Ins. Co.*, 21 Minn. 85.

[3] *Severance* v. *Continental Ins. Co.*, 5 Biss. (U. S.) 156.

evidence of an usage among the owners of ship yards, in New York, to keep timber upon the streets in the vicinity of their yards, was admissible.[1] In all cases in determining whether the loss is within the policy, so far as location is concerned, the nature of the property, the uses to which it is devoted, and the evident *intention* of the parties, to be gathered from the language used in connection with the nature of the property and its use, is to control, unless the locality is specifically defined. Thus, in a Massachusetts case,[2] a policy was issued to the plaintiff upon " their road furniture, consisting of locomotives, cars, etc., on the line of their road and in actual use." Some wharf owners had constructed a track the whole length of the wharf, connecting the Charlestown Branch Railroad with the plaintiff's road for the purpose of transporting ice. The cars, for the loss of which this action was brought, were drawn over the plaintiff's road and the Charlestown road, and left, one night, at the extreme end of the track, some four hundred and forty feet from the Charlestown road, near a shed used by the occupants of the wharf to store shavings and saw dust. A fire originating in this shed destroyed the cars, and the insurers insisted that they were not liable, because the cars, at the time of the loss, were not upon the plaintiff's road. But the court held that, if the plaintiffs had adopted this track, for all practical purposes, as a part of its line, the fact that the track was owned by the wharf owners would not defeat the liability of the insurers, and that the loss of the cars there, was a loss within the policy.

But, in a case where the policy provided that " all the property hereby insured is on premises used or occupied by the assured,"[3] it was held that the policy could not be construed to cover the property on premises occupied by the plaintiff at the time of the loss, *but which were not occupied by it at the time when the policy was issued.*

A policy does not cover property unless it is in the place designated in the policy at the time of loss, and this rule is strictly enforced in favor of the insurer, and its entire justice is apparent. Thus, the assured in his application—which was made a part of the policy— stated that the property was in the building in the rear of 82 Eddy street, used as a furnace, and, in point of fact, the property, at the time of the loss, was in a store-house which could not be properly described as in the rear of 82 Eddy street, but in the rear of 82 *and* 84 of that

[1] *Webb* v. *Nat. Ins. Co.*, 2 Sandf. (N. Y.) 397.
[2] *Fitchburgh R. R. Co.* v. *Charlestown, etc., Ins. Co.*, 7 Gray (Mass.) 64.
[3] *Providence, etc., R. R. Co.* v. *Yonkers F. Ins. Co.*, 10 R. I. 74.

street. Under this state of facts, the court held that the insurers were not liable for the loss.[1] If property is insured *as being in a certain building*, the policy only covers the goods *in that building*, and if the building is torn down, and a new one erected in its place, the policy does not, in the absence of the consent of the insurer to the change, attach to the goods in the *new building*. *Place and location is of the essence of the risk*, and the insurers cannot be deprived of the privilege of judging for themselves *how and where* they will take risks. Thus, in a Pennsylvania case[2] a firm took out a policy upon merchandise "contained in a new frame barn, wagon and wareroom," situated on an alley and occupied for a warehouse, and subsequently assigned their interest in the policy and property insured. Their assignees erected a brick addition to their store-room upon the front of the lot, on the rear of which the frame barn was erected, extending it back to the alley, and requiring a removal of *part of* the barn. A loss having occurred, the court held that no recovery could be had for goods lost in .the brick addition, and if at all, *only for those in the remnant of the frame barn and wareroom as originally erected and insured*, and that the fact that the plaintiffs took out and had paid for a carpenter's risk, which purported to be, as appeared by indorsement by the insurer upon the policy " for additional risk in extending store-room," could not be construed as a consent to the change, or as a consent to cover the goods in the new building. "It is quite extraordinary," said STRONG, J., " that under a policy of insurance upon merchandise in a building particularly described, a recovery has been permitted for a loss in another building erected in part upon the site of the one in which the goods were insured."

Where goods are described as being "contained in" a certain building, the words describing the location are treated as the statement of a fact relating to the risk,[3] and as amounting to a stipulation that they shall remain there.[4] But in a case recently decided in the Supreme Court of Iowa this is made to depend *upon the nature and uses of the property*.[5] Thus, in that case, a policy was issued upon

---

[1] *Eddy St. Foundry* v. *Camden, etc., Ins. Co.*, 1 Cliff. (U. S.) 300 ; see also *Providence, etc., R. R. Co.* v. *Yonkers Ins. Co.*, 10 R. I. 74 ; *Liebenstein* v. *Ætna Ins. Co.*, 45 Ill. 303 ; *Boynton* v. *Clinton, etc., Ins. Co.*, 16 Barb. (N. Y.) 254 ; *Lycoming Ins. Co.* v. *Updegroff*, 40 Penn. St. 311.

[2] *Lycoming Ins. Co.* v. *Updegraff*, 40 Penn. St. 311 ; 4 Bennett's F. I. C. 565.

[3] *Wall* v. *East River Ins. Co.*, 7 N. Y. 370.

[4] *Houghton* v. *Manuf. F. Ins. Co.*, 8 Met. (Mass.) 254 ; *Boynton* v. *Clinton, etc.,* *Ins. Co.*, 16 Barb. (N. Y.) 254.

[5] *McCluer* v. *The Girard F. & M. Ins. Co.*, 48 Iowa, 349.

"a phæton" "contained in a frame barn." It was burned while in a carriagemaker's shop for repairs. The court held that it was a loss within the policy, holding that from the very nature of the property and the uses to which it was devoted, location was not of the essence of the risk, and, taken in connection with the *nature and uses of the property insured*, amounted only to a warranty *that the phæton would be contained in the barn and would remain there except when absent for temporary purposes.* "In the case at bar," said ADAMS, J., "there is nothing to indicate that it was the intention to insure the contents of the barn as such. *Each policy must be construed according to the intention of the parties as manifested by all its terms.* We are of the opinion, therefore, that while the words, 'contained in a barn,' describing it, are words relating to the risk and constitute a warranty that the carriage would continue to be contained in the barn, *they mean only that the barn described was their place of deposit when not absent therefrom for temporary purposes incident to the ordinary uses and enjoyment of the property.*" But the doctrine of this case is believed to be at variance with a long line of authorities, and to extend the effect of a policy by implication to an unwarranted length. *It converts an ordinary policy into a floating contract, and that, too, in defiance of the language of the contract and the ordinary rules of construction.* Upon the principle upon which this case proceeded, a policy upon "a horse kept in a brick stable in the rear of his dwelling" would cover the horse in any stable in which he might be placed during the life of the policy. A policy upon machinery "in the frame woolen mill, etc.," if removed to another building, *because the building in which it was then used had become unfit for its use there*, would still be covered. The doctrine is forced, inconsistent with principle, and wholly unsustained by authority, and courts will be slow to abandon the time-honored doctrine previously expressed, that *location is of the essence of the risk*, and, in the absence of words covering the property, by fair construction, outside of the locality designated, must be treated as only covering it when at the place named. It is true that it was in the contemplation of the parties that the phæton would not be kept constantly in the barn during the entire life of the risk, but it is equally clear from the words of limitation used, "contained in," that the insurer intended to take only the risk of the destruction of the phæton when in the identical barn in which it was described as being when the risk was taken. No special or general usage was shown, peculiar to such risks, bringing it within the rule of Younger v. Royal Exchange Assurance Co., referred to in another section. The language of the policy is specific and susceptible of but one interpretation. It is equivalent to an agreement that, during the life of the policy the insurer will indemnify the assured against the destruction by fire, of the phæton, *in the barn described*, but not e sewhere. The court say that the words "contained in," amount to a warranty that the phæton shall be kept in the barn except ' when absent for temporary purposes." Under this ruling, if the assured employed the phæton for the entire year in making a journey through the country, it being a purpose for which such vehicles are employed, the insure would be liable for its destruction by fire, in any barn or other building in which it might be placed, during the temporary rests made by the assured in his journey, without any reference to the difference in hazard that might thus exist. We are inclined to the opinion that there is neither reason or authority for saying, in view of the words of limitation used, that the parties contemplated any other risk to the property than such as it was subjected to in the place described.[1]

The language of the policy must first be regarded, and if it definitely fixes the location of the risk, the policy does not attach if the property is destroyed outside the locality designated. As when the property is described as being "upon premises occupied by the assured," the policy relates to premises occupied by the assured *at the issuance of the policy*, and not to *any* premises which may subsequently be occupied by the assured during the life of the policy.[2] The rule is, that the language of the policy is first to be looked to, and if, by the well settled rule of construction, the intention of the parties is not clear, then extrinsic evidence may be resorted to;[3] but if the language is plain and unambiguous, it must control, and extrinsic evidence is not admissible to control its construction.[4]

Permission to remove goods, effect of.

SEC. 48. The fact that permission to remove goods has been given, will not relieve the company from liability for a loss occurring, *even though the goods are not removed*. Permission to remove, does not obligate the assured to remove them, but leaves it optional with him to do

---

[1] *Contra* and holding a doctrine as stated in the text, see *Annapolis R. R. Co.* v. *Balt. Ins. Co.*, 32 Md. 37; *Providence, etc., R. R. Co.* v. *Young*, 10 R. I. 74; *Lewis* v. *Springfield F. & M. Ins. Co.*, 10 Gray (Mass.) 159; *Lycoming Ins. Co.* v. *Updegraff*, 40 Penn. St. 311; *Boynton* v. *Clinton, etc., Ins. Co.*, 16 Barb. (N. Y.) 258; *Hartford Fire Ins. Co.* v. *Farrish*, 73 Ill. 176.

[2] *Providence, etc., R. R. Co.* v. *Yonkers F. Ins. Co.*, 10 R. I. 74.

[3] *Savage* v. *Howard Ins. Co.*, 44 How. Pr. (N. Y.) 4

[4] *Hough* v. *People's Ins. Co.*, 32 Md. 398

so.[1] Where, however, such permission has been given and the removal has been effected to such an extent that property enough has been removed to exceed the value of the insurance, *the policy will not cover a loss at the original location,* because the parties will not be presumed to have contemplated but one risk.[2] The property may be removed from the premises to avoid the peril insured against, when the danger is such that a man of ordinary prudence would not permit them to remain, and the insurer is answerable, under the policy, for the damages sustained thereby.[3] Particularly is this the case when the policy provides that the assured shall labor for their protection.[4] A removal made without permission, except as previously stated, avoids the policy.[5]

Misdescription, effect of.

SEC. 49. In order to render the policy invalid, upon the ground of misdescription, it must be so radically defective, *that of and by itself* it cannot be applied to the subject-matter to which the assured intended that it should apply. If, by any reasonable construction, or the aid of such proof of extraneous matter, as is permitted by the rules of evidence, it can be applied to the subject-matter actually intended, it will be so applied. The maxim, "*certum est quod, certum reddi potest,*" comes in aid of the assured, whenever there is enough in the policy itself, to enable the courts to apply it. Therefore, where the description is simply defective, *and not totally wrong,* the policy is not inoperative; but if it is totally defective, and there is not enough in the description, so that it can be certainly applied, the policy is inoperative.[6] A mere erroneous description, does not prevent the policy

---

[1] In *Kunzee* v. *American Ex. Ins. Co.,* 41 N. Y. 412, the plaintiff, the holder of a policy of fire insurance, upon his goods in a certain store, being desirous of removing the goods to another store, and of having the policy cover the goods when so removed, applies to the defendant, the insurance company, by whom the policy was issued, "to have it transferred to cover the goods in the new building," stating that the goods were to be moved that day, and the company accordingly, by their secretary, indorsed on the policy and signed a memorandum, that it was "transferred to cover similar property" in the new building. It was held, a fire having the next day destroyed the goods before their removal, that the defendants were still liable for the loss.

[2] *McClure* v. *Lancashire Ins. Co.,* 9 Ir. Jurist (N. S.) 63.

[3] *Haltzman* v. *Franklin Fire Ins. Co.,* 4 Cr. (U. S. C. C.) 205; *Case* v. *Hartford Fire Ins. Co.,* 13 Ill. 676.

[4] *Tallman* v. *Home, etc., Ins. Co.,* 16 La. An. 426; *Peoria M. & F. Ins. Co.* v. *Wilson,* 5 Minn. 53.

[5] *Simonton* v. *Liv., Lon. & Globe Ins. Co.,* 51 Ga. 76; *Croghan* v. *Underwriters' Agency,* 53 id. 109.

[6] *Bryce* v. *Lorrillard Ins. Co.,* 55 N. Y. 240; *Ionides* v. *Pacific Fire Ins. Co.,* L. R. 6 Q. B. 674; *Everett* v. *Ins. Co., ante.*

8

from attaching, if there is enough to point, with reasonable certainty, to the subject-matter intended to be covered. The maxim, *falsa demonstratio non nocet*, applies in such cases, as well as to other written instruments, and the description, so far as it is false, is rejected, and applies to no subject at all, and, so far as it is true, is applied to carry out and effectuate the real purpose and intention of the parties.[1]

---

[1] In *Heath* v. *Franklin Ins. Co.*, 1 Cush. (Mass.) 257, the policy covered a building "on the corner of Charles street and Western avenue. A cabinet-maker's shop is in the building." In point of fact, there was no cabinet-shop there, and the insurers insisted that their policy did not cover the building destroyed, although it was on the corner of the streets named. In passing upon this question, DEWEY, J., said: "In the policy itself and on the face of it, there is nothing to create any ambiguity, as to the description of the building. But, upon proof of the circumstances, and the actual state of things in reference to the two buildings, the ambiguity arises. The plaintiff, however, insists that, upon the proper reading of the description in the policy, it may well be taken to apply to the western building; and this would very clearly be so if the words, 'situate at the corner of Charles street and the Western avenue,' are to be taken as referring to the 'adjoining building,' and not to the building insured. But this, we think, cannot be maintained. The case does not seem to be one in which any grammatical rule, referring the words 'situate,' etc., to the next antecedent, can properly be applied. Such a rule is not one of general application, especially to cases like the present, where the words are used in a continuous description of various distinct and independent circumstances, applicable to the building insured, and which, from their very nature, are distinct and independent descriptions. The object of each and all these different descriptions is to set forth fully all the essential circumstances relating to the property insured. Among these circumstances the most prominent is the location of the building to be insured. We might well expect, as a part of the description contained in the policy, a statement of the location of the particular building which was the subject of it; and it is much more natural and probable that the location of the building to be insured should be given, than the location of a building not insured, and which was only introduced incidentally to disclose the manner of the connection of the building insured with an adjacent building. We cannot doubt that a proper reading of the policy requires that the words 'situate at the corner of Charles street and the Western avenue' should be applied to the building insured, rather than to the adjoining building. Having settled this point, we are then to look at the whole description, and see whether it can, upon any sound principle, apply to the western building. And in reference to this inquiry it will be seen that the recital in the policy, as we have just held, varies from the description which would embrace the western house, in the most material particular, namely, the house insured is described as situate at the corner of Charles street and the Western avenue; but that is the location of the eastern house, and not the western. That part of the description, therefore, being inappropriate, the application of the policy to the western house must be shown by other parts of the same description. We do not doubt the propriety of rejecting a particular description, which is clearly false, in order to give effect to other descriptive words, when such words are sufficient to define the object intended to be described. In such a case, the false description may be rejected as surplusage. But the difficulty here is, that we are called upon to reject that particular part of the description which is the most leading. Again, if we reject this description, we have no other elements of description sufficient to embrace any particular house as within the policy. Striking out the words, 'situate at the corner of Charles street and the Western avenue,' we have no locality and no particular house insured. The matter stands thus as to the western house. Rejecting this particular in the description as false, and giving full force and effect to all the other parts of it, the description is then so substantially defective that it cannot be held to apply to the particular house which the plaintiff insists was insured. This view of the case precludes the plaintiff from recovering damages for any loss which he may

This must be understood, however, as only applying to cases when, after rejecting the false description, there is enough left of that which is true, to describe the property, intended to be covered, with reason. able certainty.[1] The application of this rule is well illustrated in a New York case,[2] in which the testator devised to his wife, during her life, "the farm which I now occupy," and it was claimed that he intended to devise the whole of his real estate, which included a farm of about 90 acres, at that time in the occupancy of a tenant, and that he gave such instructions to the attorney who drew the will; and the plaintiff offered to show these facts, but the court held that the evidence was inadmissible, because there was no latent ambiguity, but a mistake merely, which could not be corrected by evidence outside the instrument itself. In the English case,[3] last referred to, the testator devised to the defendant, " all those two cottages or tenements, the one occupied by my son, John Hubbard, the other occupied by my grand. daughter." The building which the defendant claimed passed to him, under the will, was divided into four parts or tenements, having no communication with each other; one tenement, in which was occupied by John Hubbard, and another by the testator's grandaughter, one by

---

have sustained in the destruction of the western house by fire. It was suggested, that the policy might be construed to embrace the whole block, that is to say, the two buildings, and thus avoid the difficulty in the variance of the description as to situation. But we think that this cannot have been the true intention of the policy, the description clearly referring to one building, and that a building 'connected by doors with the adjoining building.' The next inquiry is, whether this policy must totally fail for uncertainty in the description, or whether it may be held to attach to the eastern building, which, it was in evidence, had sustained some small damage by fire. The fact that the parties intended to cause a policy to be made as to one of these two buildings will hardly be doubted; and, having decided that the western house was not covered by the policy, it might seem to result as a matter of course that the policy attached to the eastern house. But such is not necessarily the consequence, as the description may be equally uncertain as to both. In such case, the policy must wholly fail. But the fact that the policy was intended for the one house or the other may have some influence ; and if there be not only a preponderance of evidence resulting from the description and the actual state of things, in favor of one building rather than the other, *but sufficient evidence after rejecting the false description to identify the particular building*, we may well conclude that such building is covered by the policy, and was designed to be so by the parties. In looking at the policy, we find all the leading descriptions, and particularly that of location, to be directly applicable. The only description that is inapplicable and which appears by the evidence not to be true, is the recital, 'a cabinet-maker's shop is in the building.' * * * The rules of law fully authorize the rejection of any false description, *if what remains* be sufficient to clearly designate the object intended to be described. * * * We are of the opinion that the recital, 'a cabinet-maker's shop is in the building,' may be rejected as erroneous, and that the policy will then attach to the eastern building."

[1] PATTESON, J., in *Hubbard* v. *Hubbard*, 15 Q. B. 241.

[2] *Jackson* v. *Sill*, 11 John. (N. Y.) 201.

[3] *Hubbard* v. *Hubbard, ante.*

the defendant, and the other by another tenant. The defendant claimed that the testator intended to devise to him the *whole* building, and offered to show that such was the intention of the testator, but the court rejected the evidence. "Can the legal maxim," said WIGHT-MAN, J., "that a false demonstration does not prejudice, apply to this case ? I think not. *The maxim applies only to cases in which the false demonstration is superadded to that which was sufficiently certain before.* In the present case, if the demonstration said to be false, were rejected, the terms of the devise would be: 'I do hereby give to.my son, David Hubbard, two cottages, etc.,' leaving it uncertain, which or where." Thus, it will be seen, that in all cases where, after rejecting all the description that is false, if there is not enough left that is true, to point, with reasonable certainty, to the premises inte, ded to be covered by the policy, the policy is inoperative, and the error cannot be corrected by parol evidence, either in an action upon the policy, or to reform it.[1]

Location of goods.   When within description.

SEC. 50. Goods insured as being in a certain building, are covered, although at the time of the loss they are in a part of the building not occupied by the assured when the policy was made. Thus, a policy was issued upon " goods contained in a third story of building 18 and 19 Harvard Place, Boston. To be void, if said property shall be moved without necessity." Prior to the loss, the goods were removed into other rooms in the *same* story of the building, where they were destroyed by fire. It was held they were covered by the policy.[2] But

---

[1] *Bryce* v. *Lorrillard Ins. Co. ante.* In *Ionides* v. *Pacific Fire Ins. Co., ante,* the plaintiff's clerk applied for insurance upon hides on board the Socrates. Five ships were named in the register, one name immediately following the other, and the first *Socrates* and the other *Socrate* The manager asked the clerk which ship he meant, and he replied, "the Socrates." The hides were really shipped on the Socrate, and were lost, and it was held that they were not covered by the policy. In *American Central Ins. Co.* v. *McLanathan,* 11 Kansas, 533, the plaintiff took out a policy for $2,000 on his two-story frame dwelling, occupied by him, situate on southwest corner of Second and Vine streets, Leavenworth, Kansas, and $300 on frame barn in rear of same. The agent of insurer knew the premises for which insured sought insurance ; that they were situated on the southwest corner of Elm and Second streets, and that neither party intended to cover property on the corner of Vine and Second streets. Held, not a case of an entire misdescription, for insured did not occupy the buildings on the corner of Second and Vine streets, and therefore it was unnecessary to have the instrument reformed, because, if either from the face of the instrument or from extrinsic facts, the true and the false description could be made to appear, that which was false must be rejected .(citing 1 Greenl. Ev. sec. 301). Held, also, no repugnance appeared on the face of the instrument. Applying it to the subject insured, the true and the false description appeared, and that which was false must be rejected.

[2] *West* v. *Old Colony Ins. Co.,* 9 Allen (Mass.) 316.

where goods are insured is being " in the store part of the building," if removed to *another* part of the building, they cease to be covered.[1]

When change of locality does not defeat policy.

SEC. 51. Where a policy covers goods in a certain building, or upon the floor of a certain building, or at a certain number of a certain street, it covers them anywhere in the building, or upon the floor, or at the number designated, although they are not kept in the same part of the building, or in the same room or rooms upon the floor, in which they were kept when the policy issued, and that, even though the policy provides that it shall be void if the goods are removed to any other place without necessity.[2] But where the policy specifically designates the locality of the property, it is not covered by the policy, if moved away from such locality; as if insured as being in a certain building, if moved into another adjoining,[3] or if upon a certain floor if moved to another.[4] But if the property still remains where it comes within the general application of the terms employed, it is covered by the policy, although not where it was when the policy issued.[5] Thus, in a recent case in Massachusetts,[6] it was held that a policy upon goods described as being in a certain building, covered the goods *in any part of the building*, although at the time when the policy issued the goods were all in one store in the building, and a plan referred to in the policy shew that the building was divided into *several* stores. But in this case it was evident that the plan was referred to, not to locate the place in the building where the goods were kept, but merely to show the relative situation of the building itself. If the purpose

---

[1] *Boynton* v. *Clinton, etc., Ins. Co.,* 16 Barb. (N. Y.) 254. The Baltimore Fire Insurance Co. issued a policy of insurance to a railway company, insuring " two Murphy & Allison passenger cars, *contained in* car house No. 1, and engine J. H. Nicholson, *contained in* engine house No. 2." One of the cars and the engine, described in the policy, having been subsequently damaged by fire while making a regular trip on the line of the railway, in an action on the policy, *held* that the words " contained in " were designed to restrict the risk to the property, while actually inside of the car and engine-houses, specified in the policy; and that the railway company could not recover for the loss. *The Annapolis, etc., R. R. Co.* v. *Baltimore Fire Ins. Co.* 112.

[2] *West* v. *Old Colony Ins. Co.,* 9 Allen (Mass.) 316.

[3] In *Moadinger* v. *Mechanics' F. Ins. Co.,* 2 Hall (N. Y.) 496; 1 Bennett's F. I. C. 285, the plaintiff had a policy upon his stock in trade as a baker in a " frame dwelling-house and bake-house, front and rear." He had a quantity of flour stored for use in his bakery, *in a shed* leading from the bake-house to the dwelling. It was held that this was not covered by the policy.

[4] *Storer* v. *Elliott Ins. Co.,* 45 Me. 175.

[5] *West* v. *Old Colony Ins. Co., ante.*

[6] *Fair* v. *Manhattan Ins. Co.,* 112 Mass. 320.

had been to designate the precise location of the goods insured, the rule would have been otherwise.

A policy upon property described only "as property in" a certain building, will not cover property specified in the policy as not insurable, unless by special agreement;[1] but a policy issued to a railroad company upon "any property upon which they may be liable, in freight, buildings or yards" of the corporation, covers merchandise belonging to other parties *for which the corporation is liable as common carriers*, even though other common carriers are, by contract, liable to indemnify the corporation against all loss upon the property.[2]

Property not belonging to the class insured.

Sec. 52. In an English case,[3] the plaintiff insured his "stock in trade, household furniture, *linen*, wearing apparel and plate." He was not a linen draper, but followed the business of a coach plater and cow keeper. A fire occurred during the life of the policy, and a large quantity of linen drapery goods which he had just previously to the fire, but *after* the policy was made, purchased "on speculation," were burned. He claimed to recover under the policy, for the loss of these linen goods, but the court held that they were not covered by the policy. "I am clearly of the opinion," said Lord Ellenborough, "that the word *linen*, in the policy, does not include articles of this description. Here we may apply *noscitur a sociis*. The preceding words are "household furniture," and the latter "wearing apparel." The *linen must be household linen or apparel*.

Concealed property not covered, when purpose is unlawful.

Sec. 53. So, a policy upon "stock, *wearing apparel and household furniture* in a grocery store and dwelling-house" does not cover linen, sheets and shirts, smuggled into the country for clandestine sale, nor a watch.[4] In this case, the facts were, that the plaintiff procured a policy upon property described in the policy as stated, *supra*. The company sent their surveyor to look at the property intended to be covered. The stock was very small; there was but little furniture, and that was of a cheap kind; the wearing apparel that was shown, was of the poorest kind. No irish linen, or sheets, or shirts, were shown to the surveyor, or spoken of. The store was a grocery in

---

[1] *Com.* v. *Hide & Leather Ins. Co.*, 112 Mass. 136.

[2] *Com.* v. *Hide & Leather Insurance Co., ante.*

[3] *Watchorn* v. *Langford,* 3 Camp. 422; 1 Bennett's F. I. C. 91.

[4] *Clary* v. *Protection Ins. Co.*, 1 Ohio, 227; 1 Bennett's F. I. C. 432.

which it was usual to keep liquors, wooden ware, slops, and gross arti
cles of most varieties. Among other things, compensation was claimed
for about 350 yards of irish linen, a watch, nineteen pairs of fine linen
sheets, thirty-eight fine linen shirts, and a quantity of diaper, which
had been smuggled into the country from Ireland. These articles had
never been used, though once washed because soiled in the passage.
They were stowed away in the garret, and were not used in the house
or kept in the store for sale. The judge charged the jury that "such
articles of linen sheets and shirts as were actually laid in with a view
to the use of the family, if exhibited at the preliminary inspection,
were within the policy; so were such as had been laid in for sale or
traffic in the usual way in the store; but such as were concealed, *and
intended for secret sale,* or for other use, were not embraced within the
policy," also that "the watch is of the description of articles usually
denominated memorandum articles, and is not included in the policy,"
and this ruling was sustained upon appeal.[1]

Property of same class, although not in use, covered by policy, when.

SEC. 54. The fact that property insured, is not, at the time of the
loss, *in actual use,* does not defeat the policy as to that, *if it is intended
for the uses contemplated by the policy.* Thus, it has been held that furniture stowed away in the garret, because there was no room for it in
other parts of the house, although not used in the garret, but which
was intended for use as needed, is covered by a policy covering household furniture,[2] and the same rule would hold in reference to merchandise or other property. The test is, not whether the property is in
actual use for the purposes contemplated, at the time of the loss, but
*whether it was bona fide intended by the assured to be so used as necessity
required, and was really a part of the class described in the policy, in view
of the nature of the property insured, and the uses for which it was
intended.*

What policy covers by implication. Stock in trade, etc.

SEC. 55. "All goods placed or to be placed in the building for seven
years," covers all goods placed there before the date of the policy, as
well as those afterwards placed there.[3] So a policy on a mechanic's
"stock in trade" covers all the fixtures, tools, etc., used by him, in
prosecuting his business.[4] So it *covers all articles incident to, or neces-*

---

[1] *Burgess* v. *Alliance Ins. Co.,* 10 Allen (Mass.) 221.
[2] *Clarke* v. *Fireman's Ins. Co.,* 18 La. 431.
[3] *New York Gas-Light Co.* v. *Mechanics' Fire Ins. Co.,* 2 Hall (N. Y. S. C.) 108.
[4] *Moadinger* v. *Mechanics' Fire Ins. Co.,* 2 Hall (N. Y.) 490.

sarily used in the prosecution of the business,[1] and such a policy is not confined to the identical articles on hand when the policy issued, *but articles of the same class on hand at the time of the loss.*[2] A policy may also be extended to cover goods not strictly within the premises named, if a usage is shown to exist in regard to contiguous places as within the description. Thus, on " stock of ship timber in a ship-yard," held to embrace and cover timber lying on the sidewalks near the yard, a usage being shown to regard the street as a part of the yard.[3] A policy on a "steam saw-mill" covers not merely the building, but also all the fixtures and machinery therein.[4]

A policy can only be construed to cover property naturally embraced under the term used, or such property as usage has made incident to it as an addition to the ordinary meaning of the term. Thus, a policy on a "ship on the stocks" does not embrace timber lying in the vicinity in the yard, although prepared for and intended to be used in the construction of the ship, nor, unless attached.to the keel.[5]

A policy upon an unfinished house does not cover timber to be put into it, lying in another adjoining building,[6] nor, under the doctrine established in the preceding case, would such timber have been covered by the policy if it had been piled in the unfinished building, and in no wise annexed to it. Until connected with the building, such timber remains materials, and is, in no sense, any part of the building.[7]

---

[1] *Spratley* v. *Hartford Ins. Co.,* 1 Dil. U. S. (C. C.) 392 ; *Phœnix Fire Ins. Co·* v. *Favorite,* 49 Ill. 259 ; *Lichenstein* v. *Baltic F. Ins. Co.,* 45 id. 301 ; *Crosby* v. *Franklin Ins. Co.,* 5 Gray (Mass.) 540 ; *Seavey* v. *Central, etc., Ins. Co.,* 111 Mass. 540 ; *Moadinger* v. *Mechanics' Ins. Co.,* 2 Hall (N. Y.) 490.

[2] *Crombie* v. *Portsmouth F. Ins. Co.,* 26 N. H. 389.

[3] *Webb* v. *National Fire Ins. Co.,* 2 Sandf. (N. Y.) 447.

[4] *Bigler* v. *N. Y. Central Ins. Co.,* 20 Barb. (N. Y.) 635.

[5] *Hood* v. *Manhattan Ins. Co.,* 11 N. Y. 532 ; 5 Penn. 183 ; 3 G. & J. (Md.) 468.

[6] *Ellmaker* v. *Franklin Ins. Co.,* 5 Penn. St. 183.

[7] In *Hood* v. *Manhattan Ins. Co., ante,* JOHNSON, J., said: " The inquiry is, at what point in the process of building the vessel, will such timbers cease to be materials for the barque, and become a part of the barque? The answer, I think, is, When they have entered into the structure which, when completed, will be a barque. This construction accords with the ordinary use of language upon such subjects. If a man had entered this ship-yard and asked to be shown the barque building for Howes, Godfrey & Co., he would have been shown the structure upon the keel, irrespective of how far the work had progressed, as being the barque ; and it would have occurred to no one to point out materials not annexed to the keel, although completely prepared for that use, as being the barque. It is true that, in a technical sense, neither the keel, with the incomplete structure thereon, nor any of the materials intended for the vessel, is a barque ; but in the ordinary use of language, the former would be so spoken of, and the others, though the work on them was all done, would not. It is in this ordinary sense that the language of parties is to be interpreted. I do not think it necessary to place any reliance upon the words ' on the stocks near said ship,' nor upon the expression of

A policy on "fixtures and gas metres, belonging to and rented by the company, placed or to be placed in the buildings, stores or dwell-

---

a 'privilege to build another vessel along side;' for though these words perhaps confirm the view which I have taken, indicating as they do an estimate of the amount of risk with reference to the precise locality to be occupied by the subject insured, yet the broader ground is more satisfactory, that the language used, in its ordinary acceptation, embraces the structure which, when completed, will be the barque, and does not embrace materials which are not become a part of the structure, by being fixed to or in it. The decision below is objectionable in another aspect. If it be upheld, it follows that timber so far completed becomes thereupon part of the vessel, and consequently loses its character of 'materials,' and could not be insured under that name. It frequently happens that one man owns the keel and employs another, the ship-builder, to furnish materials and finish the ship. Such materials, though completely finished, remain the property of the builder until they actually become a part of the structure of the ship. *Johnson* v. *Hunt*, 11 Wend. 135; *Merritt* v. *Johnson*, 7 John. R. 473; *Andrews* v. *Durant*, 1 Kern. 35. In such a case, upon a loss by fire, the ship-owner could not recover upon a policy on the 'ship building,' for lack of interest; nor the ship-builder upon a policy on 'materials,' because the property has lost the character of 'materals,' and become a part of the 'ship building.' This consequence must follow, unless courts are at liberty to hold property to be properly described as 'materials' and not as 'parts of a ship,' or as 'parts of a ship' and not as 'materials,' according as one or the other description is necessary to give indemnity to the assured. The construction given accords with the law regulating the change of property when the owner and builder are different persons; that the common use of language is in harmony with it, and that the test of liability is simple and easy of application, recommend as fit to be adopted. The case of *Mason* v. *Franklin Fire Ins. Co.*, 12 Gill & John. 468, presents substantially the same question, and was decided in the same way by the Court of Appeals in Maryland. *Ellmaker* v. *Franklin Ins. Co.*, 5 Barr, 183, is analogous, and was decided on the same principle in Pennsylvania. The plaintiff should have been nonsuited, and the judgment must be reversed and a new trial ordered; costs to abide the event." PARKER, J. said: "Although it is said that policies of insurance are to be construed liberally for the insured (1 Story's R. 360; 2 Sumner's R. 380; 5 Cranch, 335), yet, where the words are not ambiguous, and the expression of the intent of the parties is full, I know of no reason why they should be excepted from the general rules of law applicable to the construction of all contracts. In deciding, therefore, whether the property in question is covered by the insurance, the language of the transfer is to be construed in its usual and popular sense, there being nothing to take it out of that general rule. The question to be decided is not, whether the property in question is covered by the first or the second policy. If it is excluded from the first, it does not necessarily follow that it is included in the second. But the question is whether it is within the first policy, on which this action is brought; that is to say, whether the 462 sticks of timber burned were a part of the barque then building for Howes, Godfrey & Co. The sticks were cut and ready to be framed, but they had not been framed. They did not constitute frames. They not only had never been annexed to the barque, but they were not ready to become a part of it, for they could not be annexed to the barque till they had been framed. They were sticks of timber cut to be used in the construction of the barque, but had never been so used in fact. These sticks were scattered about the ship-yard, and a part of them lay on the opposite side of the ship in which the fire broke out. It is true, the proof shows that these sticks, being cut for the frame of the barque, were useless for any other purpose. But I do not see how that fact tends to show that they were part of the barque. It only shows that in getting them ready to make them a part of the barque, they had been rendered unfit for any other use. That may be a misfortune to the owners, if they are not covered by the subsequent insurance on 'lumber and building materials,' but it is not an argument tending to show that they were part of the barque. If it were necessary, however, to the decision of this case to decide which policy covered the sticks of timber in question, I should have no hesitation in saying that they continued to be 'building materials' at the time

ings of subscribers, for seven years," was held to cover all fixtures and metres placed *after* the policy issued, as well as those placed before, and that though the number and value of them was largely increased, the insurers were liable for a loss on any, to the extent of the amount insured.[1]

A policy on "merchandise," without describing it, covers all articles kept for sale, including books and stationery, furniture, and all species of goods in which the assured deals, whether incident to any particular class of merchants or not.[2]

Where a policy covers " *the stock of the assured or held by him in trust,*" it will cover stock intrusted to him for the purposes of manufacture.[3] So goods helds by him in pawn.[4]

The profits of a business are insurable, but in order to be covered by a policy they must be insured *qua* profits.[5]

A policy issued upon different classes of property, and divided into several sums and valuations; as, " $500 on building, $500 on machinery,

---

they were destroyed. The insured party seems to have taken a similar view of this question, and to have selected appropriate words, when, in his preliminary proofs, he called the property ' timber and lumber,' and described it as ' 462 pieces of timber ready to be put into the frame of the barque.' The property to be insured was a barque on the stocks, building, that is to say, being built for Howes, Godfrey & Co. Now, it was only the barque on the stocks which was insured. The sticks scattered around the yard, though they had been ready to be annexed, were not on the stocks. I suppose the term ' on the stocks ' is descriptive of the whole property insured ; and that it would do violence to the language of the contract to make it extend to property, only part of which was on the stocks. The description of the barque as being near the ship, and the privilege being given to build another vessel along side of it, shows that it referred to what was on the stocks alone. Such language was not applicable to property scattered all over the yard. Any other rule of construction than that I have adopted would lead to great uncertainty and confusion. If the sticks become part of the vessel before being actually incorporated in it by annexation, when did they become so ? At what point did they cease to be ' building materials' and become ' a barque !' When the timber was cut in the forest ? It may have been so selected and cut as to be fit for no other vessel. Or was it when the sticks were brought to the yard ? or when the work was commenced on them to fit them for the barque ? or when they were ready to be framed ? or when they were framed and ready to be annexed ? If all this would make the sticks a barque, which I deny, it is one step more than had been taken in this case, for the sticks had not been framed. It is apparent that as soon as we leave the safe rule, which requires actual annexation, there is no point of preparation at which the thing changes its entire character. If it were the building of a house instead of a ship, none of the materials furnished would lose their character as personal property and become part of the realty, until actually annexed. Ferard on Fix. 9, note *a*. ' *Ubi eadem ratio, ibi idem jus.*' "

[1] *N. Y. Gas Light Co.* v. *Mechanics' F. Ins. Co.,* 2 Hall (N. Y.) 108 ; 1 Bennett's F. I. C. 279.

[2] *Siter* v. *Morris,* 13 Penn. St. 218.

[3] *Stillwell* v. *Staples,* 19 N. Y. 401.

[4] *Rafel* v. *Nashville, etc., Ins. Co.,* 7 La. An. 244.

[5] *In re Wright* v. *Pole,* 1 Ad. & El. 621.

and $1,500 on stock therein," if renewed by a receipt which simply states that the policy is renewed for $2,500, is thus changed, so that the distribution of the risk ceases, and it becomes a policy for $2,500 upon all the property.[1]

A policy upon "property," kept in a certain building, covers articles kept for use as well as for sale ; but a policy upon "merchandise" only covers property kept for sale, and excludes that kept for use.[2] Thus, a policy upon " a jeweler's stock in trade," was held not to cover blankets, purchased with the consent of the insurer, to protect the store from a fire burning in an adjoining building.[3] And even where certain classes of property are incident to the business insured, yet, if the policy specifically designates the classes of property covered, all other is excluded. Thus, where a policy was issued "on stock in trade, *consisting of* corn, seed, hay, straw, fixtures and utensils in business," no other kind of property, except that designated, is covered by the policy, even though it was *in fact* a part of the stock in trade at the time when the policy was issued.[4] So, where a policy was issued upon "jewelry and clothing, being stock in trade," it was held that it did not cover musical or surgical instruments, guns, pistols, books, etc., although they were a part of the assured's stock in trade, because the classes of property insured were specifically designated, and no other classes could be included.[5] So a policy upon a " stock of hair, *wrought, raw, and in process*, as a retail store," does not extend to fancy goods *made of other materials*, although they are such as are usually kept in a retail hair store.[6] Thus it will be seen that the question whether a particular class of property is covered by a policy not naming it, will depend, *first*, upon whether it is impliedly excluded by the language of the policy ; and *second*, whether it belongs to the class insured, either as a natural incident thereof, or by usage. *If the property insured is*

[1] *Driggs* v. *Albany Ins. Co.*, 10 Barb. (N. Y.) 440.

[2] *Burgess* v. *Alliance Ins. Co.*, 10 Allen (Mass.) 221. In *Kent* v. *London, etc., Ins. Co.*, 26 Ind. 294, the term "merchandise," in a policy of insurance against loss, etc., by fire, on grain and other merchandise, in each of two warehouses, which were kept by the assured, who were grain merchants, for the purpose of receiving and storing grain, was held not to include a platform scale, bedded in the floor of one of the warehouses, or belting, or a corn-sheller, or a beam-scale, which things had been dispensed with in the business, but which had not been offered for sale ; or tools, implements, or articles of property purchased for use in the warehouses, as being necessary or convenient in the business, and which were used as occasion required.

[3] *Welles* v. *Boston Ins. Co.*, 6 Pick. (Mass.) 182.

[4] *Joel* v. *Harvey*, 5 W. R. 488.

[5] *Raifel* v. *Nashville, etc., Ins. Co.*, 7 La. An. 244.

[6] *Medina* v. *Builders' Ins. Co.*, 120 Mass. 225.

specifically designated, all other is excluded, even though usually of the same tribe of that insured. If, however, the policy is general in its description of the property, it may be shown that a certain species of property is *usually* included in the same class, and so covered by the policy.[1]

So, if the classification is evidently intended to enlarge, rather than to restrict the risk, as if the word including is used instead of the words " consisting of," the classification does not exclude other articles not enumerated.   Thus, where a policy covered " a stock of ship timber, *including* planks, futtocks, knees, locust standards, staves blocks, falls, clamps, screws, augers and tools contained in the yards and buildings, etc.; " it was held that locust capstans, partly prepared, were embraced in the risk.[2] The naming of particular articles, as covered by the policy, does not exclude all others, when such is not the obvious intent, and natural construction of the language used. When the policy covers a " stock in trade *consisting* of" none other than articles belonging in one or the other of the classes named are covered, because the obvious intent of the parties is to particularly define the risk; but when the policy covers a " stock in trade, *including, etc.*," the obvious intent of the parties is to enlarge the scope of the risk beyond what would otherwise be included therein.

Under a policy which insures a certain sum " on all or either" of certain buildings, the insured are liable for the full amount of a loss, not exceeding the sum insured, occasioned by the burning of either or any of the buildings.[3]

Silver forks, spoons, knives, etc., are not covered by a policy insuring "silver plate."[4]

When a policy covers a particular business, or class of property, as

---

[1] In *Crosby* v. *Franklin Ins. Co.*, 5 Gray (Mass.) 504, a doctrine apparently in conflict with this, was held. In that case, the policy was for a certain sum "on their stock of watches, watch trimmings, etc.," and the court held that the word *stock* included the *general stock*, and was not limited to watches, watch trimmings and material. The doctrine of this case is in conflict with the case cited *supra* from the 120th Mass. ; and is also in conflict with the current of authority. The word "stock," when employed generally, as a "jeweler's stock," a "stock of groceries," "druggist's stock," etc., includes all articles *usually* kept as a part thereof; but, when the word "stock " is defined by the insurer, and limited to a certain *class* of goods, as was done in this case, there is no rule of law that will permit a *different* construction to be placed thereon. In such a case, the court, by permitting evidence as to what is "usually" a part of such stocks, permits an addition to be made to the contract, which is in contravention of that actually made by the parties. *Medina* v. *Builders' Ins. Co., ante ; Rafel* v. *Nashville, etc., Ins. Co., ante ; Joel* v. *Harvey, ante.*

[2] *Webb* v. *National F. Ins. Co.*, 2 Sandf. (N. Y.) 497.

[3] *Com.* v. *Hide and Leather Ins. Co.*, 112 Mass. 136.

[4] *Hanover F. Ins. Co.* v. *Mannasson,* 29 Mich. 316.

"a starch manufactory,"[1] it covers *all fixtures, machinery, implements, tools, etc., necessary or incident to the business.* A policy covering an "engine and machinery for the manufacture of tin ware," covers all the implements used in connection with the machinery, as a part thereof, even though not attached to it. Thus, under a such a policy, it was held that it covered 600 dies, used to give form to various articles manufactured, although a single pair of t ese dies only could be used at one time, and when not in use, they were taken out and kept upon shelves.[2] A policy upon the stock of a mechanic includes all the tools and implements used by him in his business. Thus, a policy upon the assured's "stock in trade as a baker, and upon household furniture contained in a frame dwelling and bake house," was held to cover *all the implements necessary for carrying on the business,* as pans, sieves, bread troughs, etc.[3] So a policy upon "articles used in packing hogs, cattle, etc.," was held to cover coal used upon the premises, necessary to be used in the process, and reasonable in quantity, for the business done.[4] A policy upon "stock in trade, being mostly chamber furniture in sets,

---

[1] *Peoria, etc., Ins. Co.,* v. *Lewis,* 18 Ill. 553. In *Liebenstein* v. *Ætna Ins. Co.,* 45 Ill. 303, insurance was effected on "chair lumber and such other stock as is usually used in a chair manufactory, contained in the chair factory situated on Superior street, Chicago." The establishment consisted of a main building, and also an engine-house standing ten feet in the rear of the main building, and connected with it by a platform, and by the belting passing from the engine to the machinery in the main building. A fire caught in the engine-house, and consumed a portion of the chair material which had been placed therein. *Held,* that the material in the engine-house fell within the description of the property insured as "contained in the chair factory." In *Mark* v. *Ætna Ins. Co.,* 29 Ind. 390, an open or running policy stipulated not to cover a loss accruing from any disaster by explosion or otherwise, "which occurrence might be known to the applicant, the public, or the company, at the time of such application being made, whether such property was known to be involved thereby or not, without such contingency is expressly provided for in writing on this policy," was *held* not to cover the loss of a package of money sent by the assured by express, and without his knowledge placed on a steamboat, which, at the time of the application, had exploded its boiler, and sunk, the explosion being known to the public and the insured. In *Home Ins. Co.* v. *Favorite,* 46 Ill. 263, the policy covered goods held in trust or on commission, and it was held that this included goods held on storage, but it was also held that whether a policy "on hogs and cattle, salt, cooperage, boxes, *and articles used in packing the same,*" covered coal on the insured premises, was a question of fact for the jury, and depended for its solution upon the question whether it was necessary or incident to the business of packing. Insurance was effected upon property "contained in the two-story frame building occupied by the assured as a chair manufactory, situated on Superior street." The factory comprised a main building of two stories, and a two-story building ten feet distant, used for an engine and dry-house. The main building was called the chair factory, where the work was carried on. *Held,* that the insurance covered only the property in the main building. *Liebenstein* v. *Ætna Ins. Co.,* 45 Ill. 303.

[2] *Leavy* v. *Central, etc., Ins. Co.,* 111 Mass. 540.

[3] *Moadinger* v. *Mechanics', etc., Ins. Co.,* 2 Hall (N. Y.) 490.

[4] *Phœnix Ins. Co.* v. *Favorite et al.,* 49 Ill. 259; *Home Ins. Co.* v. *Same,* 49 id. 263.

and other articles usually kept by furniture dealers," was held to cover
varnish and oils necessary for use in such business, to the extent that
they are usually kept by such dealers, as well as all other articles *usually*
kept by persons engaged in that business.[1]   So a policy covering
" blacksmith and carriage maker's stock, manufactured and in process
of manufacture," covers raw or unmanufactured stock used in the
business.[2]

Intention of parties must be gathered from the policy.

SEC. 56.   *When the policy is specific as to the subject-matter of the risk,
it cannot be extended by implication, nor is evidence admissible to show that
the parties intended to have it cover matters not specified.*   Thus, where a
policy covered "oil mill occupied for crushing linseed and grinding
dye wood, £1,000; on fixed machinery and millwright works, including all the standing and growing gear therein, £1,000; one engine-
house adjoining the mill, £200; one steam engine therein, £300; one
logwood warehouse in which chopping dyewood is performed, £200;
one warehouse on the other side of the mill, £300."   The assured
claimed that the policy covered the machinery and gear in the logwood house, and offered to show that the parties intended that the
policy should so cover, but the court held that, as the policy was
specific as to the subject-matter of the risk, it could not be construed
to cover any risk not named, and that the *intention* of the parties must
be gathered from the policy, and could not be shown by evidence
aliunde.[3]   In an Illinois case,[4] the policy covered chair lumber, contained "in the two-story frame building occupied by the insured as a
chair manufactory, situated on the north side of Superior street;"
there was an engine-house near this building, connected with it by
a platform, and used as a part of the plaintiff's factory, and a considerable quantity of chair lumber was stored therein.   The plaintiff
insisted that it was the intention of the parties to embrace the chair
lumber therein, in the risk, and that the policy should be construed
as covering it, but the court held that the intention of the insurers
must be gathered from the policy, and that, as the risk therein was
restricted to the lumber in the two-story frame building, the insurer
was only liable for the lumber lost therein.[5]

[1] *Haley* v. *Dorchester, etc., Ins. Co.,* 12 Gray (Mass.) 545.
[2] *Spratley* v. *Hartford Ins. Co.,* 1 Dil. U. S. (C. C.) 392.
[3] *Hare* v. *Barstow,* 8 Jur. 928.
[4] *Liebenstein* v. *Ætna Ins. Co.,* 45 Ill. 303.
[5] See *Annapolis R. R. Co.* v. *Baltimore F. Ins. Co.,* 32 Md. 37 ; *Lycoming Ins.
Co.* v. *Updegraff,* 40 Penn. St. 311.

A policy "on stock in trade," consisting of corn, seed, hay, straw, fixtures and utensils in business, does not cover hops and matting, although they were in fact a part of the stock in trade when the insurance was made, and were usually kept by persons engaged in that business.[1]

Neither a watch, nor other articles of jewelry, although used for personal adornment, are comprehended under, or covered by a policy upon household furniture or wearing apparel.[2]

Construction of policies.

SEC. 57. The legal maxim *benignae faciende sunt interpretationes propter implicitatem laicorum ut res magis valeat quam pereat; et verba intentione, non e contra, debent insevire*, is as applicable in the interpretation of policies of insurance as of other written instruments, and the courts are inclined to construe them liberally, and so as to carry out and effectuate the real, true intention of the parties thereto.[3]

Every part of the instrument will be made operative and effective, if possible, but, if it is evident that one part of the instrument expresses *the real intent* of the parties, and another part of it *is inconsistent therewith*, the part which is inconsistent with the intention of the parties must be rejected and yield to that part of it which will effectuate their real purpose. Thus, where the written and printed portions of a policy conflict, effect is given to the *written* portion of it, because, being incorporated into the contract *at the time when it was made*, it is presumed that it expresses the actual agreement made, and that the parties intended thereby to override that portion of the contract expressed in type, which is inconsistent therewith.[4] The maxim, *quando res non valit ut ago, valeat quantum valere potest* applies, and the courts will look to the *intent* of the parties and effectuate it in some form, if possible, and, if necessary to do so, will reject that which is inconsistent.[5] But, if there is no *real* inconsistency, and

---

[1] *Joel* v. *Harvey*, 5 W. R. 488.

[2] *Clary* v. *Protection Ins. Co., ante* ; 2 Johns. (N. Y.) 261.

[3] *Riggin* v. *Patapsco Ins. Co.*, 7 H. & J. (Md.) 279 ; *Crauisllat* v. *Bull*, 8 Yeates (Penn.) 375.

[4] *Nicoll* v. *American Ins. Co.*, 3 W. & M. (U. S.) 529.

[5] *Maugher* v. *Holyoke, etc., Ins. Co.*, 1 Holmes (U. S. C. C.) 289. In *Bowman* v. *Pacific Ins. Co.*, 27 Mo. 15, the policy contained stipulations that "if there shall be kept or stored therein any articles denominated hazardous or extra hazardous, or included in the memorandum of special rates, so long as the same shall be appropriated, these presents shall cease ;" also: "No greater amount than 25 lbs. of gunpowder shall be placed at any time in the building described in this policy." Insured kept from four to six pounds of powder in his store. Gunpowder was included in the memorandum of special rates. It was held that

the evident intent of the parties can be effectuated by interpreting the instrument as a whole, that is, by retaining both the written and printed portions thereof, effect will be given to the whole.[1] One of the golden rules of interpretation was well expressed by Lord HALE.[2] : " *The judges,*" said he, " *ought to be curious and subtle to invent reasons and means to make acts effectual according to the just intent of the parties; they will not therefore cavil about the propriety of words, when the intent of the parties appears, but will rather apply the words to fullfil the intent, than destroy the intent, by reason of the insufficiency of the words.*" The language of a policy is to be construed according to its natural meaning, its ordinary and usual signification, except where such construction would render the words used, senseless, or it is evident from the general scope and intent of the instrument that the words were used in some other sense. *In all cases the words of a policy are to be taken most strongly against the insurer.* The maxim *verba chartarum fortius accipintur contra proferentum,* is rigidly enforced in all cases where other rules of construction fail. This is upon the theory that, as the insurer makes the policy, and selects his own language, he is presumed to have employed that which expresses his real intention and the actual contract entered into, and has left nothing to be inferred or supplied by reference to extraneous matters.[3] But this does not permit either party to show how they understood the contract. The court is to construe the instrument *from the language used,* and so far as there is any inconsistency, give to it a construction most favorable to the assured. It was well said by the court in a Kentucky case,[4] " there is no principle of law which allows the understanding of one of the parties to determine the meaning of the contract. The rule is sometimes applied in cases of ambiguity, that words are to be construed most strongly against the party using them. That is founded upon a principle of common honesty and good faith, that, when a promise or stipulation is susceptible of two meanings, it should be construed and effectuated in that sense *in which the party making it knew, or had reason to believe it*

---

the two clauses will harmonize if one be understood as modifying the other; the general was to be controlled by the special clause, for, to give a preponderating importance to the general provision would interpolate a material qualification upon the special clause; that keeping less than 25 lbs. of powder did not affect the right of the insured to recover.

[1] *Stacey* v. *Franklin Fire Ins. Co.,* 2 W. & S. (Penn.) 44.

[2] *Crossing* v. *Scudamore,* 2 Lev. 9.

[3] *Palmer* v. *Warren Ins. Co.,* 1 Story (U. S.) 360 ; *Nicoll* v. *The American Ins. Co., ante; Ins. Co.* v. *Wright,* 1 Wall. (U. S.) 529.

[4] *Montgomery* v. *Fireman's Ins. Co.,* 16 B. Mon. (Ky.) 427.

was understood and received by the other party." Thus, in a case in New York,[1] the defendants issued a policy to the plaintiff upon "a stock of goods" in a certain building. Subsequently the goods were removed to another building, and the insurer indorsed thereon, "*This policy is transferred to the frame building* owned by Marco on the east side of Whitehall street." The defendants claimed that thereby the policy was applied to the *frame building*, and did not cover the stock. But the court held that the indorsement must be construed in view of the circumstances, and according to the *intent* of the parties, and as the plaintiff had a right to understand it.

All the stipulations in a policy, both printed and written, are to be given effect, if it can be done without defeating the written stipulations. If it cannot be done, then the written stipulation is to prevail.[2] If the words written in the policy, have received a judicial construction, and also a peculiar commercial construction by usage, variant with such judicial construction, the judicial construction is to control,[3] but if no judicial construction has been given to them, and by usage they have acquired any meaning variant from that in which they are ordinarily used, such meaning by usage may be shown, unless from the whole instrument it is evident that they were used in their ordinary sense.[4] Thus, in the case cited from Massachusetts, to an inquiry in an application for insurance upon a manufactory, "are there casks of water in each loft kept *constantly* full?" the answer was, "there are casks of water in each room, kept constantly full," and the court held that evidence was admissible to show that, in the general use of language among manufacturers, the whole of a loft or story, appropriated to a particular department, was called "one room," although the same was divided by partitions with doors; and that the meaning of the word "room," and whether there was any such general use of language, were questions for the jury and not for the court; also, *that if such use of the word "room" was general among manufacturers, it need not be known and general among insurers, in order to effect a contract of insurance upon manufacturing property;* for the insurers

[1] *Marco* v. *Liv., Lon. & Globe Ins. Co.*, 35 N. Y. 664.

[2] *Goss* v. *Citizen's Ins. Co.*, 18 La. An. 97; *Bargett* v. *Orient Ins. Co.*, 3 Bos. (N. Y.) 385. In *Lettiner* v. *Granite Ins. Co.*, 5 Duer (N. Y.) 394, the court say that no part of the words of a policy are to be rejected as insensible or inoperative, if a rational or intelligible meaning can be given to them consistent with the general design and object of the whole instrument.

[3] *Bargett* v. *Orient, etc., Ins. Co.*, 3 Bos. (N. Y.) 385.

[4] *Daniels* v. *Hud. Riv. Ins. Co.*, 12 Cush. (Mass.) 416; *Mobile, etc., Ins. Co.* v. *McMillan*, 27 Ala. 77.

9

must be presumed to have so understood it, when they insured such property." [1]

Conditions in policies. Classification of hazards, effect of.

Sec. 58. As has previously been stated, it is competent for the insurer to prescribe the terms and conditions upon which he will assume a risk, and, so long as those conditions are not in violation of law, or contrary to public policy, they are binding and obligatory upon the assured, and any violation thereof by him, releases the insurer from liability, whether the loss resulted from such violation or not. [2] Thus, the insurer may decide what risks are *hazardous, extra-hazardous or specially hazardous*, and what are not so, and if they are named and specified in the policy, and prohibited therein, a violation of the condition avoids the policy, even though in fact such articles or use are not hazardous. The question is not open, whether the hazards of the risk are increased thereby or not. The insurer, by electing to regard it so, and having so declared it in the policy, has precluded all inquiry in that direction, and, if the keeping of ice or water upon the premises was specified as hazardous, the keeping of either, without permission, would avoid the policy as much as the keeping of gunpowder or nitro-glycerine. [3] The insurer having con-

---

[1] In *Whitmarsh* v. *Conway Ins. Co.*, 16 Gray (Mass.) 657, it was held that evidence of a well-settled custom, by which the words of a policy covering "store fixtures" are applied *to all furniture in the store*, whether fixed or movable, necessary or convenient for use in the course of trade, was admissible. "If," said Chapman, J., "the term *store fixtures* is a term of trade, commonly used among traders and insurers, and is used in such a signification as to include any or all the articles mentioned as such in the report, those were insured by this policy. The parol evidence on this subject was proper and admissible."
See chapter on Evidence.

[2] *Wood* v. *Hartford Ins. Co.*, 13 Conn. 533.

[3] Mr. Marshall, in his work on Insurance, 249, says : "It is quite immaterial for what purpose or with what view it is made ; or whether the assured had any view at all in making it ; unless there has been a literal compliance, the assured can derive no benefit from the policy." On p. 251, he says : "It is also immaterial to what cause the non-compliance is attributable, *for if it be not in fact complied with, although perhaps for the best reasons*, the policy is void." In *Faulkner* v. *Central F. Ins. Co.*, 1 Kerr (N. B.) 279, the plaintiff took out a policy upon goods, which contained a provision that, if there should at any time be more than twenty-five pounds' weight of gunpowder, on the premises insured, or where any goods are insured, such insurance should be void, and no benefit derived therefrom. To an action for a loss under the policy, the defendant plead a breach of this condition, and the plaintiff replied *that the powder was put there without his privity, because a vessel in which it was intended to ship it had sailed without it ;* and that *he had used every exertion to find another conveyance without success.* Also that *it in no wise increased the risk, because before the fire which destroyed the building reached it, the powder was all removed and thrown into the harbor, so that no loss or damage was thereby occasioned to the goods.* The court held that the replication was bad, and the policy avoided. "This is," said Chipman, C.J., "in delivering the opinion of the court, "a positive and unqualified condition inserted

tracted upon that basis, the assured is estopped from denying that they are hazardous.[1] But, under the rule that the written portion of a policy is to have effect over the printed, if the language used in describing the property insured is such as to import a license to keep any of the articles denominated hazardous, extra hazardous, or specially hazardous, the keeping of such articles, or the use of the premises for such purposes, does not avoid the policy. Thus, where a policy covers "a stock of dry goods and groceries, *such as are usually kept in country stores*," or simply "groceries," the term carries with it a license to keep for sale any article *usually* kept in country stores of that class, or such as are usually embraced in a stock of groceries, even though it involves the keeping of many articles coming under the head of *hazardous*, etc.[2] But where the policy covers a stock of "*merchandise, hazardous and not hazardous*," no such license can be imported, even though it be shown that the keeping of "extra hazardous" goods is usual in such stores as was kept by the plaintiff,[3] nor where the term is restricted, as ' a stock of *family* groceries,"[4] nor even though the insurer *knew* that the plaintiff kept such goods, and the application called for insurance " upon a stock such as is usually kept in a country store."[5] A license cannot be implied, unless the language of the policy clearly warrants it, and, although the defendant *knew* that the assured kept "hazardous" or "extra hazardous" articles, yet, *if they are excluded by the terms of the policy, and the description of the stock does not embrace them*, they cannot be kept without defeating the policy.[6] If the policy covers goods

---

by the parties to prevent the introduction of gunpowders, * * * and it seems by the parties to have been regarded as a necessary clause, and we cannot but give effect to the words of a contract which seems clearly to manifest the intent of the parties, which they have used. I think, therefore, according to the meaning of the parties, *to be collected from the express words of the contract, that on the introduction of this gunpowder the policy became void.*"

[1] *Pindar* v. *Continental Ins. Co.*, 38 N. Y. 364.

[2] *Niagara Ins. Co.* v. *DeGraff*, 12 Mich. 124 ; *Girard F. Ins. Co.* v. *Stephenson*, 44 Penn. St. 298 ; *Citizens' Ins. Co.* v. *McLaughlin*, 54 id. 485 ; *Archer* v. *The Merchants', etc., Ins. Co.*, 43 Mo. 434 ; *Franklin Ins. Co.* v. *Updegraff*, 50 Penn. St. 350 ; *Pindar* v. *Kings Co. Ins. Co.*, 36 N. Y. 648 ; *Harper* v. *N. Y. City Ins. Co.*, 22 id. 441 ; *Rafferty* v. *New Brunswick Ins. Co.*, 3 Har. (N. J.) 480 ; *Leggett* v. *Ins. Co.*, 10 Rich. (S. C.) 292 ; *Langdon* v. *N. Y. Equitable Ins. Co.*, 1 Hall (N. Y.) 226 ; *Mayor* v. *Hamilton Ins. Co.*, 10 Bos. (N. Y.) 537.

[3] *Pindar* v. *The Continental Ins. Co.*, 38 N. Y. 364.

[4] *People's Ins. Co.* v. *Kuhn* (Tenn.) 1 Cent'l Law Jour. 214.

[5] *Pindar* v. *Continental Ins. Co.*, 47 N. Y. 114.

[6] In *Richards* v. *Protection Ins. Co.*, 30 Me. 273 ; 3 Bennett's F. I. C. 76, a classification of hazards was annexed to the policy and referred to in the body of it. The classification exhibited certain sorts of goods to be "not hazardous," others

"hazardous, extra hazardous and specially hazardous," *any goods coming* under either of those heads, *or any goods not enumerated, may be kept.* So if the policy covers a building "privileged to be used for *extra hazardous* purposes," although it is then being used for a particular purpose coming within the list of special hazards, *and such purpose is embraced in the privilege,* the building may be devoted to any "*specially hazardous purpose.*"[1] In a Connecticut case that has measurably come to be regarded as a leading case upon this question,[2] the policy covered a paper mill, and contained a clause that the policy should become void if devoted to a use denominated hazardous or extra hazardous. Paper mills and grist mills were embraced in the class of hazardous uses. After the insurance was effected, the plaintiff took out the rag picker, and put in a pair of millstones for grinding grain, the building and machinery in all other respects, remaining the same. The court held that the policy was not thereby avoided.

The language of the condition must be looked at, and in many instances where there seems to be apparent conflict, there will be no conflict in fact; the difference in results arising from a difference in the employment of terms to express the condition. Thus, in a New Brunswick case cited, and the facts and doctrine stated in a previous note,[3] the condition was, "*if at any time*" there should be more than twenty-five pounds of gunpowder upon the premises, the policy should be void, and in this case, under this condition, the policy was held avoided by the breach, *although it in no wise increased the risk or contributed to the loss,* because the condition was absolute, and was susceptible of but one construction; but, in a case in Maine,[4] where a policy covering a stock of dry goods, con-

---

to be "hazardous," and "extra hazardous." Among the hazardous articles were "oil, glass and tallow." The policy covered "a stock in trade, consisting of 'non-hazardous' merchandise." The plaintiff kept articles embraced in the list of "hazardous" articles, as, oil, tallow candles, glass, etc. The court held that the policy was thereby avoided. "The description of the property insured, in the body of the policy," said SHIPLEY, C.J., "when the rate of premium is thereby affected, operates as a warranty that the property is of the character and class described, *and that the property is all, and not partly, of that character and class.* Such a warranty is in the nature of a condition precedent, and performance of it must be shown by the person insured before he can recover upon the policy." *Duncan v. Sun F. Ins. Co.,* 6 Wend. (N. Y.) 488; 1 Bennett's F. I. C. 340; *Fowler v. Ætna F. Ins. Co.,* 6 Cow. (N. Y.) 672; 1 Bennett's F. I. C. 179; *Wood v. Hartford F. Ins. Co.,* 13 Conn. 533; 2 Bennett's F. I. C. 24. See Chap. on "Warranties."

[1] *Reynolds v. Commerce Ins. Co.,* 47 N. Y. 597.

[2] *Wood v. Hartford F. Ins. Co.,* 13 Conn. 533; 2 Ben. F. I. C. 24.

[3] *Faulkner v. Central F. Ins. Co.,* note 3, page 130.

[4] *Moore v. Protection Ins. Co.,* 29 Me. 97; 2 Ben. F. I. C. 758.

tained a condition that the policy should be void " in case the prem-ises shall, at any time after the making and during the continuance of this insurance, *be appropriated, applied or used, to or for the purpose of carrying on, or exercising therein, any trade, business or vocation,* denomi-nated hazardous or extra hazardous, or specified in the memorandum of special rates, * * or for the purpose of keeping or storing therein any of the articles, goods or merchandise, in the same terms and conditions, denominated hazardous or extra hazardous, etc. ; " it was held that the keeping of a hazardous article for sale, *among other goods,* was not an infraction of the policy, because, by a fair construc-tion of the condition, it was merely a protection *against appropriating the store for a depository of such goods as a sole or principal business.*[1] " The restriction," said TENNEY, J., " does not extend to the keeping of a single article denominated hazardous or extra hazardous, as a part of the dry goods stock in trade, *provided the store was not appro-priated, applied or used for purposes not intended by the language of the policy.* These purposes were of a general nature, and distinguished from that of keeping a stock of dry goods for sale. It is not pretended that the store was used *for carrying on a business unauthorized by the policy,* and if the plaintiffs had, or kept in their stock, a hazardous article, *it is by no means the same thing as appropriating, applying or using the store for keeping or storing therein goods and merchandise which was hazardous.*" In Massachusetts[2] a doctrine similar to that adopted in the Maine case, was held, thus, in the case last cited, the policy covered machinery in a silk factory, which contained a provision that it should be of no effect " while the premises shall be used for storing 'cotton in bales,' ' rags' or ' wool,' or for a ' cotton mill,' ' woolen mill,' or other manufacturing establishment or trade, requiring the use of heat; " it was held, that the policy was not avoided by the use of one room for weaving a few pieces of stuff from woolen and linen thread and cotton spun elsewhere, and kept in the room, because such use could not be said to amount to a *use* of the building for any of the prohibited purposes, and, generally, it may be said, that while condi-tions of a policy form a part of the contract,[2] yet, in all cases, if the

[1] To the same effect see *Langdon* v. *N. Y. Equitable Ins. Co.*, 1 Hall (N. Y.) 226, and S. C. Aff'd, 6 Wend. (N. Y.) 628.
[2] *Vogel* v. *People's, etc., Ins. Co.*, 9 Gray (Mass.) 23.
[2] *Desilver* v. *State Ins. Co.*, 38 Penn. St. 130; *Rafael* v. *Nashville Ins. Co.*, 7 La. An. 344; *Jube* v. *Brooklyn Ins. Co.*, 28 Barb. (N. Y.) 412; *Lynn* v. *Burgoyne*, 16 B. Mon. (Ky.) 400; *Corter* v. *Hulmboldt, etc., Ins. Co.*, 12 Iowa, 287; *Brown* v. *Savannah, etc., Ins. Co.*, 24 Ga. 97; *Ripley* v. *Ætna Ins. Co.*, 30 N. Y. 136; *Diehl* v. *Adam & Co. Ins. Co.*, 58 Penn. St. 443.

condition is susceptible of a construction consistent with the use alleged as a breach, it will be so construed, because it is the business of the. insurer to use language that leaves no doubt as to the meaning of the condition, and failing to do so, the benefit of the doubt will be given to the assured.[1]

The assured, by accepting a policy describing the goods or premises insured as "non-hazardous," is thereby treated as warranting that they are so. Therefore it becomes a condition precedent, and, in order to recover, he must show that the warranty was true, and that the property was *entirely* "non-hazardous." If it was only *partly so,* the warranty is violated;[2] unless, as previously stated, the language of the policy is such as not to exclude all such goods.[3] It has been held that, where a policy was issued upon "a stock of dry goods," the keeping of cotton in bales, for the purposes of sale as a part of the stock, although classed as "hazardous," was not a violation of a condition that the building should not be applied, appropriated or used for the keeping or storing of goods of a hazardous character, nor of a condition that the risk should not be increased.[4] The court holding, that the intent of the parties was to be gathered, from the language used in connection with the subject-matter of the risk, and that it must be construed according to the natural import of the words used in connection with the nature of the risk and its incidents, and that the keeping of articles denominated hazardous as a part of the stock could not be said to be a "storing" of hazardous goods, or an appropriation of the premises to a hazardous purpose, or to amount to an increase of the risk within the meaning of the policy.[5] So, too, it has been held that keeping or using articles classed as "hazardous" upon the premises, for the purpose of making necessary repairs, such as paints, oils and turpentine,[6] or the heating of tar,[7] or the prosecution of a hazardous trade, as a carpenter making repairs,[8] or the use of hazardous articles in the prosecution of the business of the insured, as

---

[1] *Rafferty* v. *New Brunswick Ins. Co.,* 3 Harrison (N. J.) 480.

[2] *Burritt* v. *Saratoga, etc., Ins. Co.,* 5 Hill (N. Y.) 188; *Richards* v. *Protection Ins. Co., ante; Rawson* v. *Watson,* Camp. 787; *Wood* v. *Hartford Ins. Co., ante.*

[3] *Langdon* v. *N. Y. Equitable Ins. Co., ante; Moore* v. *Protection Ins. Co., ante.*

[4] *Moore* v. *Protection Ins. Co., ante.*

[5] *Langdon* v. *Equitable Ins. Co., ante.*

[6] *O'Neil* v. *Buffalo Fire Ins. Co.,* 3 N. Y. 122; 2 Ben. F. I. C. 103.

[7] *Dobson* v. *Sotheby,* 1 M. & M. 90.

[8] *Lounsberry* v. *Protection Ins. Co.,* 3 Conn. 459.

described in the policy.[1] But, in such case, the hazard must be an incident of the business, or the policy is thereby avoided. Thus, where a policy was issued upon "merchandise, hazardous and non-hazardous, cabinet-ware included," it was held that the use of the premises for putting together and finishing chairs, avoided the policy, *because it was not an incident of the business,*[2] and as the insurer is presumed to be familiar with the usual incidents of a business, and the methods and articles connected with its prosecution; he is presumed to contract with reference thereto, *and the description of the business is construed as carrying with it a license to do that which is incident to the business, although it conflicts with the printed conditions of the policy.*[3]

When a policy expressly prohibits the keeping of certain articles, and there is nothing in the written portion of the policy to overcome the same by the keeping of such articles, or any of them, the policy is invalidated, although it appears that the prohibited articles are such as are usually kept by persons keeping a similar stock with that insured. Thus, where a stock of goods in a country store was insured, but the policy *did not describe it as such a stock as is usually kept in a country store,* and the keeping of turpentine and other articles was prohibited, it was held that the keeping of such articles avoided the policy, and that it was not competent for the assured to show that such articles were usually a part of such stocks, or that the insurers were informed of the character of the stock, and requested to issue a policy similar in all respects with one sent them, covering the *same* stock, and describing the goods as "such as are usually kept in a country store."[4]

"The first offer," said RAPALLO, J., "was to prove that before the issue of the policy in suit, a policy issued by the Kings County Fire Insurance Company to the plaintiff's assignor on his stock, 'such as is usually kept in country stores,' contained in the store in question, was mailed to the defendants, with a request to issue their policy on the stock in the same store to the amount of $3,000, in the language of and just like the Kings county policy, and that the wording should

---

[1] *Harper* v. *Albany, etc., Ins. Co.,* 17 N. Y. 194.

[2] *Appleby* v. *Astor Fire Ins. Co.,* 54 N. Y. 253.

[3] *Brown* v. *Kings Co. Fire Ins. Co.,* 31 How. (N. Y.) 508 ; *Mayor, etc.,* v. *Hamilton Ins. Co.* 10 Bos. (N. Y.) 537 ; *Grant* v. *Howard Ins. Co.,* 5 Hill (N. Y.) 10 ; *Billings* v. *Tolland Ins. Co.,* 20 Conn. 139 ; *Moore* v. *Protection Ins. Co., ante* ; *Merchants', etc., Ins. Co.* v. *Washington, etc., Ins. Co.,* 1 Handy (Ohio) 181 ; *Leggett* v. *Ætna Ins. Co.,* 10 Rich. (S. C.) 202.

[4] *Pindar* v. *Resolute Fire Ins. Co.,* 47 N. Y. 114.

be followed exactly as in that policy; and that in response to that request the defendant sent to the plaintiff's assignor the policy in suit.

" This evidence must have been offered for the purpose of laying the foundation of a claim or argument on the part of the plaintiff, that by sending the policy in response to this application, the defendant assented to and assumed to comply with the request made of it, and that it therefore treated the language of the policy sent, as synonymous with that of the Kings county policy. In other words, that the facts offered to be proved, amounted to an admission by the defendant that both policies meant the same thing. For no other purpose can the evidence have been relevant. The evidence was properly rejected for two reasons. First, because the facts offered to be proved would not, if established, have justified or sustained an inference or finding by the jury that the policy sent was intended as a compliance with the request made by the plaintiff's assignor. The wording of the Kings county policy was sufficient, as was held in the case of Pindar v. The Kings County Insurance Company,[1] to cover any and every description of goods usually kept in country stores, embracing extra hazardous, as well as hazardous, if proved to be usually kept in such stores. The request was to follow exactly the wording of that policy. So far from doing, or attempting to do so, the defendant sent a policy worded in an entirely different manner, not at all resembling the policy sent as a precedent, but on the contrary expressly restricting the insurance to the two classes of goods defined as not hazardous and hazardous. This was in effect a refusal to grant as comprehensive a policy as the one applied for, and must have been so understood by any person of ordinary intelligence on a comparison of the two policies.

But in the second place, had the offer been to prove by oral evidence that the parties to the contract intended the policy in suit to be co-extensive with the Kings county policy, such evidence would have been wholly inadmissible. Evidence of surrounding circumstances, and other parol evidence is in some cases admissible to show the meaning of language employed in a contract, or the sense in which it has been used, but never to show the intent of the parties as contradistinguished from what the words express; and when the language of an instrument has a settled legal construction, parol evidence is not admissible to contradict that construction. Where the policy, as in this case, expressly declares that only goods not hazardous and haz-

---

[1] 36 N. Y. R. 648.

ardous are insured, and that the keeping of extra hazardous, or specially hazardous goods on the premises shall avoid the policy, and such language has a settled meaning, parol evidence tending to show a different understanding or agreement, preceding or cotemporaneous with the issuing of the policy, is inadmissible. All such understandings are merged in the written instrument, and neither party can be permitted to prove that the instrument does not mean what it says.

The evidence was not admissible for the purpose of showing notice to the defendant that the plaintiff's assignor kept in the store such merchandise as was usually kept in country stores, and that consequently it insured the goods in the store as it was. That notice was not material, so long as the defendant did not accept the risk as offered, or insert in the policy its permission to keep the prohibited goods.[1] The policy gave notice to the insured, in plain language, that so long as the prohibited goods were upon the premises the policy was not operative, and that if he desired to avail himself of the insurance, he must remove them. If he was not content to submit to those conditions, he should have rejected the policy. The second and only other offer of proof not passed upon on the former appeal, was, that neither the assured or the plaintiff discovered the difference between the wording of this policy and that of the Kings County Insurance Company until after the fire. This fact could not change the construction of the instrument. The failure of the insured to read the policy could not enlarge the liability which it imposed upon the defendant. The evidence was, therefore, clearly immaterial for the purposes of this action. The fact offered to be proved, explains the conduct of the assured in relying upon a policy so illy adapted to his protection, and adds another to the often recurring instances, in which the object for which insurance sought, is frustrated by the neglect of the assured to acquaint himself with the provisions of his policy. So long as insurance companies are permitted to deal with the public as they do, by issuing policies encumbered with an infinite variety of complicated printed conditions and stipulations which the courts are bound to enforce as constituting essential parts of the contract, there is no safety in accepting a policy without the most rigid scrutiny of its contents. It is true that this degree of care is not usual with the mass of mankind, and through their caution, insurers often escape the liability which they were supposed to have assumed, and it would be exceedingly desirable, if prac-

---

[1] *Barrett* v. *The Union Mut. Ins. Co.*, 7 Cush. 175, 180 ; *Lee* v. *Howard Co.*, 3 Gray (Mass.) 583, 592.

ticable, some system should be devised by which a simpler and more uniform description of policy should be adopted. * * *But as the law now stands, there is no restriction upon the insertion in policies of any conditions, not unlawful in themselves, and they must be construed and enforced by the courts in the same manner as other private contracts whose provisions are understood and assented to by the parties.*[1]

But where there is anything in the written portion of the policy, or in the description of the property itself, that shows that any articles, within the prohibited class, are permitted to be kept, the force of the printed clause is overcome.[2]

---

[1] In Massachusetts it is held that where the policy stipulates against the keeping or storing of certain hazardous articles named, the keeping of them as a part of the stock, although usually kept as a part of such stocks, avoids the policy when the words describing the risk do not of themselves import a license. Thus, where a policy covered a general stock of "dry goods, groceries, hardware, crockery, glass and wooden ware, brittania and tin ware, stoves of various kinds, and various other wares and merchandise," and also provided that a use of the premises for the purpose of keeping or storing any of the articles denominated "hazardous," among which "rags" were named, it was held that the keeping of "rags" as a part of this stock, avoided the policy. See also, to same effect, *Lee* v. *Howard Ins. Co.*, 3 Gray (Mass.) 592 ; *Witherell* v. *City Fire Ins. Co.*, 16 Gray (Mass.) 276. The case of *Whitmarsh* v. *Conway Fire Ins. Co.*, 16 Gray, 359 ; 4 Ben. F. I. C. 482, holds, that *if the description of the stock is such as to embrace the prohibited articles, or if evidence is given showing that the prohibited articles usually formed a part of such a stock*, the policy is not avoided by keeping them, and distinguished this case from those previously named upon that ground. See also, *Elliott* v. *Hamilton, etc., Ins. Co.*, 13 Gray (Mass.) 139.

[2] In *Reynolds* v. *Commerce Ins. Co.*, 47 N. Y. 597, an action was brought upon a policy, whereby the defendant insured the plaintiff in the sum of $5,500 "on the brick and frame buildings situate on the south side of West Thirty-ninth street, extending from the Eleventh avenue to the North river, this city, known as the New York abbatoirs, and numbered from 1 to 43, inclusive, on plan of same, for the amount specified on each," viz.: The amount insured on Nos. 23, 24, 25, 26, 27, 28 and 29 was $900. By the terms of the policy, the premises were "privileged to be occupied as hide, fat melting, slaughter and packing houses, and stores and dwellings, and for other extra hazardous purposes." According to the classification of hazards in and by the policy, the division and distribution of risks was as follows, viz. : Into "first class," including "not hazardous," "hazardous No. 1," and "extra hazardous No. 1 ;" and into "second class," including "hazardous No. 2," "extra hazardous No. 2," "extra hazardous No, 3," and "specially hazardous." Each of the above subdivisions of hazard contains a specific designation of the "trades, occupation and merchandise," intended to be comprehended therein. The clause in the policy in relation to "specially hazardous" risks contained the following provision, viz.: "The following trades, occupations and merchandise add to the rate of the building and its contents fifty cents or more per $100, and to be covered must be specially written in the policy ;" and after mentioning a number of particular trades and articles of merchandise, winds up with the clause, "and all work-shops, manufacturing establishments, trades and mills not above enumerated as hazardous or extra hazardous." Distilleries are not included in the specification of risks contained in either of the designations of hazards in the policy under the heads "hazardous" or "extra hazardous." A fire broke out in the general premises in question, extending from Nos. 23 to 29, inclusive, by which Nos. 24 and 25 were entirely destroyed, and the others damaged and partially destroyed. The fire originated in Nos. 24 and 25. Nos. 24 and 25 were then occupied as a distillery and rectifying establishment. In the body of the policy, following the description of the premises

A verdict having been rendered for the plaintiff, it was sustained upon appeal.[1]

---

insured, was the following clause: "If the above mentioned premises, at any time during the period for which this policy would otherwise continue in force, shall be used for the purpose of carrying on therein any trade or occupation, or for storing or keeping therein any articles, goods or merchandise denominated hazardous or extra hazardous or specially hazardous in the second class of the classes of hazards annexed to this policy, except as herein specially provided for, or hereafter agreed to by this corporation, in writing, upon this policy, from thenceforth so long as the same shall be so used, this policy shall be of no force or effect." The policy sued upon was a renewal of a previous policy covering the same premises; and the first policy was in the same words with the second policy, except that the former was dated May 4, 1864, and the buildings Nos. 41 and 42 were therein noted as being vacant. At the close of the plaintiff's case the defendant's counsel moved for a dismissal of the complaint, on the ground that it appeared by the plaintiff's own evidence that, at the time of the fire, there was a change in the use and occupation of the premises insured, affecting and increasing the risk. The court denied the motion, and the defendant's counsel excepted. At the close of the case on both sides, the court directed the jury to find a verdict upon the following question, viz.: Did Mr. Lang, the agent or representative of the plaintiff, say that he thought that a change had occurred in the business carried on in the premises, and refer the defendant to the Merchants' Insurance Company for information on that subject at the time the renewal was asked for?

[1] CHURCH, C.J., in a very able opinion, said: "It is an elementary rule that where there is an inconsistency in the written portion of a policy, and indeed of any contract, the written is to be preferred to the printed, as the attention of the parties is supposed to be more directly drawn to such parts as are written than to the printed, which are used in all cases. 2 Par. on Contracts, 516; 1 Arnould on Insurance, 80. The privileged uses specified are 'specially hazarduos," as defined in the classification of hazards annexed to the policy. They are not enumerated, but are included in the general words of 'all workshops, manufacturing establishments, trades and mills, not above enumerated as hazardous or extra hazardous.' The words in the policy, 'or *other* extra hazardous purposes,' must be taken to mean purposes of the same class as those before specified, and the term 'extra hazardous' must yield to .the specifications accordingly. If the language had been, *and other like purposes*, the right of the plaintiff to use the premises for any purpose enumerated as specially hazardous would have been unquestioned. No other construction could have been given. The language used is certainly capable of the same construction, and such is the construction which persons receiving a policy would ordinarily put upon it. It is the same as though every occupation enumerated as specially hazardous had been specified, and then the general words, 'and other *extra* hazardous purposes,' used. In such a case it is clear that the term 'extra hazardous' would be construed with reference to the specification preceding them, upon the principle that general words yield to particular recitals. 2 Par. 501, note a. I think this principle applies to this policy, and that the plaintiff had a right to use the premises for any special hazardous purpose. Insurance companies are not restricted in the right to insert such terms and conditions in their policies as they see fit, and it is the duty of courts to construe them according to established legal principles. If persons receiving policies neglect to examine these conditions, they must take the consequences, but legal principles and public policy demand that equivocal language, especially if calculated to mislead the assured, shall be construed most strongly against those using the language and issuing the policies. It is a general rule, that in cases of doubt arising from the ambiguity of the language, the construction is to be favorable to the grantee. 10 N. H. 305 Chancellor KENT says the true principle is 'to give the contract the sense in which the person making the promise believed the other party to have accepted it, if he in fact did so understand and accept it,' and this of course must be determined by the language used and the surrounding circumstances. 2 Kent's Comm. 557. The words , other extra hazardous purposes ' would naturally be understood to include other

Sec. 59. *It is the duty of the insurer to clothe the contract in language so plain and clear, that the insured cannot be mistaken or misled as to the*

---

like purposes, and we must presume that both parties so understood it. The special finding of fact by the jury has an important bearing upon the question. That finding is, that the plaintiff's agent informed the company at the time the renewal or new policy was applied for, that he thought that a change had occurred in the business carried on in the premises, and referred them to the Merchants' Insurance Company for information on that subject. The Merchants' Insurance Company had, it seems, recently insured the property, and caused a survey to be made, and if the defendant had made the inquiry, it would have led to a knowledge of the real facts. The statment of the agent, therefore, that he thought a change of business had taken place, and a reference to where the fact could be ascertained, was equally effective as a notice of the very change that had been made. In such a case, whatever is notice enough to excite attention, and put a party upon his guard and call for inquiry, is notice of everything to which such inquiry might have led. When a person has sufficient information to lead him to a fact, he shall be deemed conversant with it. 2 Kent's Comm. 631, note 1; 3 Myl. and Keen, 719. It is unnecessary, however, to go beyond actual notice that a change had taken place which the finding established. This knowledge is a circumstance proper to be considered in determining the intention of the defendant in the language employed, and it does not conflict with the rule that parol evidence is inadmissible to vary the terms of written instruments. We may resort to surrounding circumstances in all cases of doubtful construction and *patent* ambiguity. If the words are clear and unambiguous, a contrary intention derived from outside circumstances is of no avail. A new contract cannot be made by showing that the intention was to make one different from that expressed. But to ascertain what the contract is in case of ambiguous language, a resort may be had to the circumstances surrounding the author at the time. So his knowledge or ignorance of certain facts are competent to determine what he meant by the language used. As in a devise to Mary B., for life, with remainder to her three daughters, Mary, Elizabeth and Ann. At the date of the will Mary B., had two legitimate daughters, Mary and Ann, living, and one illegitimate, named Elizabeth. It was held that evidence was admissible to show that Mary B., formerly had a legimate daughter named Elizabeth, who died some years before the date of the will, and that the testator did not know of her death, or of the birth of an illegitimate daughter. 12 A. and E. 431. So where a testator divised a farm in A. in possession of T. H. to T. R., and he had two farms in A., in possession of T. H., it was held that if one of the farms was subject to a trust, or if the testator supposed it was and treated it as such, the other farm would pass by the devise, as he was presumed to have intended the farm devised for the personal use of T. R. 12 Eng. Law and Equity, 52. Mr. Parsons, in his work on Contracts, lays down the rule in such cases as follows: 'If the meaning of the instrument, by itself, is affected with uncertainty, the intention of the parties may be ascertained by extrinsic testimony, and this intention will be taken as the meaning of the parties expressed in the instrument, if it be a meanig, which may be distinctly derived from a fair and rational interpretation of the words actually used.' This intention, however, it should be observed, is to be ascertained, except in cases of *latent* ambiguity, by a development of the circumstances under which the instrument was made. Mere declarations are not admissible for the purpose, but the knowledge of facts by the party is competent, and notice that a change had been made is as potent upon the question of intention, as if the defendant knew that these buildings were actually used distilleries. I think they are chargeable with that knowledge; but they certainly knew that a change had taken place. We are to place ourselves, as nearly as may be, in the position of the author of the instrument, and consider the facts surrounding him, with his knowledge or ignorance of facts, and with his belief of the existence or non-existence of certain facts, and, in that position, we may often see clearly the meaning of language, which, without these aids, would be unintelligible or doubtful. The old policy which had expired contained the same language as this one permitting, specifically, several specially hazardous uses; and with a knowledge that a

burdens or duties thereby imposed upon him. Having the power to impose conditions, and being the party who draws the contract, he must see to it that all conditions are plain, easily understood, and free from ambiguity. In the language of the court in an English case,[1] it "*ought to be so framed that he who runs, can read. It ought to be framed with such deliberate care that no form of expression by which on the one hand, the party assured can be caught, or by which, on the other, the company can be cheated, shall be found on its face.*" Failing to employ a clear and definite form of expression, the benefit of all doubts will be resolved in favor of the assured. The courts will not permit the assured to be misled, or cheated, where there is any sort of justification, from the language used, for the interpretation placed by him upon the instrument. A contract drawn by one party, who makes his own terms, and imposes his own conditions, will not be tolerated as a snare to the unwary, and if the words employed, of themselves, or in connection with other language used in the instrument, or in reference to the subject-matter to which they relate, are susceptible of the interpretation given them by the assured, although in fact intended otherwise by the insurer, the policy will be construed to favor the assured.[2]

---

change had taken place in the use of some of them, we must presume an intention on the part of the defendants to provide for them in this policy, and as those uses expressly permitted, belonged to the highest grade of hazards, and the language employed is capable of a construction permitting all other like uses, we are bound to presume that the defendant intended such a construction, otherwise it must have acted in bad faith, which is never presumed. We are to suppose, if the language will permit it, that the defendant intended to protect the property of the assured according to the change which it knew had taken place. The distinction between this and the *Pindar case* is, that in that case the language was held to be unambiguous, and, although the policy was claimed to be different from that called for, yet, having been issued, delivered and accepted, and sued upon the assured was bound by its terms, and that extrinsic evidence of circumstances, or otherwise, was incompetent to change it. Such is the established law, but it does not apply to a case where the language is capable of different constructions. The defendant was defeated upon the issue of fact made in the court below, and that finding is conclusive upon this court, whether right or wrong, and the effect of it, upon what the defendant intended by the language used, is adverse to the construction put upon it by it. This construction of the contract renders the testimony offered, that distilleries are more hazardous than the establishments specified, immaterial. The assured having the right to use the premises for any specially hazardous purpose, it was not competent to prove any distinction of hazard in these premises."

[1] *Anderson* v. *Fitzgerald,* 4 H. L. Cas. 484.

[2] *Hoffman* v. *Ætna Ins. Co.,* 32 N. Y. 405; *Reynolds* v. *Commerce Ins. Co.,* 47 id. 597; *Chandler* v. *St. Paul F. & M. Ins. Co.,* 21 Minn. 85; 18 Am. Rep. 385; *Blackett* v. *Assurance Co.,* 2 C. & J. 244; *Merrick* v. *Germania Fire Ins. Co.,* 54 Penn. St. 277; *Braunstein* v. *Accidental Death Ins. Co.,* 1 B & S. 782; *Catlin* v. *Springfield Fire Ins. Co.,* 1 Sum. (N. S.) 434; *Bartlett* v. *Union M. & F. Ins. Co.,* 46 Me. 500; *The Mayor of N. Y.* v. *Hamilton Fire Ins. Co.,* 39 N. Y. 45; *Phillips* v. *Putnam Ins. Co.,* 28 Wis. 472; *Wilson* v. *Conway Fire Ins. Co.,* 4 R. I. 141; *Palmer* v, *Warren Ins. Co.,* 1 Story (U. S.) 360.

The courts will not favor cunningly devised policies which are intended to enable the company to reap the advantage and yet escape the risk, and, where there has been a fair contract, and a substantial compliance with its terms, it will be enforced, although there may be some trifling or technical laches.[1] And in construing conditions, it is proper, for the purpose of determining whether the insurer has misled the insured, to look at the *place* in the policy where the condition is printed, and the kind of type, as compared with the rest of the policy,[2] and, for the purpose of arriving at the real intention of the parties, reference may be had to matters *dehors* the policy, as to the location, situation and purposes of the risk, the uses to which it was devoted, the usages, if any, incident thereto, or, indeed, to any attending facts and circumstances that tend to show the real purpose and intention of the parties.[3]

---

[1] *Kentucky Mut. Ins. Co.* v. *Jenks*, 5 Ind. 96 ; *Ind. Mut. F. Ins. Co. v. Conner*, id. 170.

[2] *Kingsley* v. *Mut. F. Ins. Co.*, *ante*.

[3] In *Mauger* v. *Holyoke Ins. Co.*, 1 Holmes (U. S.) 287, the assured took out a policy of insurance to the amount of $2,000, "on their new lithographic printing press, contained in the fourth story of brick building situate No. 13 Banker street, Boston, Mass. It is understood that $300 of the amount shall attach on hand presses." Just before this insurance was effected, in April, 1872, the assured had purchased a new lithographic press worth $3,500, and of a smaller size than the one purchased afterwards and referred to in the policy. Permission was given July 3 for removal to fourth and fifth stories of stone and brick building corner of Milk and Devonshire streets, Boston. In June, 1873, the assured procured insurance to the amount of $4,000 "on their lithographic presses and ink-mill, with shafting and belting connected therewith, contained in the fourth and fifth stories of stone building 57 Milk street, corner of Devonshire street." At this time the assured had *two* lithographic presses and several hand presses. The press upon which the defendants' policy was issued was purchased in October, 1872, and was insured by the defendants in November, 1872, for one year in the sum of $4,300, as follows: "On their Hugh & Kimbler's No. 6 steam lithographic press, size 30x40, situate in chambers of granite and brick building, situate No. 57 Milk street, corner of Devonshire street," payable, in case of loss, to the plaintiff. The policy, by its terms, required the defendants to pay three-fourths of the value of the property in sixty days after proofs of loss had been made, unless the amount was to be reduced under the following provision of the policy: "In case of any other contract of insurance upon the property hereby insured, *whether such contract be valid or not*, as against the parties thereto, or either of them, the insured shall not, in case of loss or damage, be entitled to recover of this company any greater portion of the loss or damage sustained than the amount herein insured shall bear to the whole amount insured on said property." As previously stated, the assured, at the time of the loss, in November, 1872, had *three* lithographic presses at 57 Milk street, besides shafting and belting. The defendant contended that *all* the policies attached to the press specifically insured by its policy, and that the clause relating to double insurance applied in the adjustment of the loss. The court held that there was no double insurance, and that, in determining the question as to the *intention* of the parties, facts and circumstances *dehors* the policy might be shown. "Explaining the policies in this case," said SHEPLEY, J., "in the light of attending facts and circumstances at the time they were effected, the attention of the parties is arrived at without difficulty. The first policy was clearly on the *new* lithographic press,

Courts will not go outside the policy to ascertain its meaning, or the intention of the parties, *when it can be reasonably construed without,*[1] but that matters outside the policy may be resorted to for the purpose of arriving at the real intention of the parties, when there is any ambiguity in the policy, is established by numerous respectable authorities.[2] Thus, in a case in the Circuit Court of the United States,[3] the policy provided that the assured should keep a force pump on the premises. The court held that this included power to operate it, but no particular power. "If," said CURTIS, J, "the warranty was of a force pump in a dwelling-house at all times ready for use, I should hold it satisfied by the existence of a force pump *in a condition to be worked,*" because, referring to the subject-mattter of the contract, no inference could be drawn that *power* was to be provided therefor. 'Considering," he added, "the nature of the works and the notorious and uniform usage to have such a pump in such a position *driven by power,*" it must be presumed that the parties contracted in reference thereto, and that power was included in the warranty. "*Policies are to be construed largely according to the intention of the parties, and for the indemnity of the assured, and the advancement of trade.*[4] *Facts and circumstances dehors the instrument, may be proved in order to discover the intention of the parties.*" The doctrine that, unless excluded by the fair interpretation of the words employed in the policy, reference will be had to the nature of the risks, its condition, situation and attending circumstances at the time when the policy was made, as well as to the ordi-

---

definitely described and located. The policy of June 28th was on the *two* lithographic presses then in the chambers, 57 Milk street, and was not intended to apply, *and did not apply*, to any *steam* lithographic presses to be subsequently placed therein. It was not a *floating* policy on a stock of merchandise in a store, bought for sale, and with the intention of replacing it as sold and keeping the stock good; but on specific machinery, intended for permanent use in the location described. It was not expected or intended to embrace, and the literal meaning of the words used does not embrace, any presses not then in the building. It could only embrace such presses subsequently placed in the building, if explained by facts and circumstances *dehors* the policy, and the facts and circumstances do not thus explain it or aid such a construction. The policy is specifically upon the third steam lithographic press, not in the building when the other insurances were effected, and not within the description in those policies. There was, therefore, no double insurance." *Stacey* v. *Franklin F. Ins. Co.*, 2 W. & S. (Penn.) 506, is a case involving similar questions, and holding a similar doctrine. See also *Younger* v. *Royal Exchange Ins. Co.*, 1 Burr. 341; *May* v. *Buckeye, etc., Ins. Co.*, 25 Wis. 291; 5 Ben. F. I. C. 295; *Bond* v. *Gonsales, post.*

[1] *Baltimore Ins. Co.* v. *Loney*, 20 Md. 36; *Astor* v. *Union Ins. Co.*, 7 Cow. (N. Y.) 202; *Murray* v. *Hatch*, 6 Mass. 465; *Levy* v. *Merrill*, 4 Me. 480.

[2] *Finney* v. *Bradford*, 8 Met. (Mass.) 348; *Sayles* v. *N. W. Ins. Co.*, 2 Curtis (U. S. C. C.) 610; *Stacey* v. *Franklin Fire Ins. Co., ante.*

[3] *Sayles* v. *N. W. Ins. Co., ante.*

[4] ROGERS, J., in *Stacey* v. *Franklin Ins. Co., ante.*

nary incidents or usages relating to the risk, was well expressed and illustrated in an early English case.[1]

In that case, the policy covered the " body, tackle, apparel, ordnance, munition, artillery boat and other furniture of and in the said ship." The vessel sailed and arrived in Canton river, China, where she was to stay *to clean and refit*, and for other purposes. Upon her arrival there, the sails, yards, tackle, cables, rigging apparel, and other furniture, were, by the captains orders, taken out of her and put into a ware-house built for that purpose, on a small sand bar, in order that the articles named might be kept dry and be preserved until the ship should be *heeled and cleaned*. While in the warehouse, *for this purpose*, they were destroyed by fire, and the insurers insisted that it was not a loss covered by the policy, as the articles were not destroyed *in the ship*. It was found that the course pursued by the captain was *necessary, prudent* and *usual*, and the court held that the loss was covered by the policy, and the rules established were *that, that may be done which is usually done in reference to such risks, and that the ends or purposes for which the subject-matter of the risk is employed, may be obtained by any of the usual means or methods employed in such business or with such risks.* " The insurer," said Lord MANSFIELD, " in estimating the price at which he is willing to indemnify the trader, against all risks, must have under his consideration, *the nature of the voyage to be performed, and the usual course and manner of doing it. Everything done in the usual course, must have been foreseen and in contemplation at the time he engaged.* He took the risk upon the supposition *that, what was usual or necessary would be done.* It is absurd to suppose that the usual means of obtaining it, are meant to be excluded." " It is certain," said LEE, C.J., in the same case, " that in the construction of policies, the *strictum jus* or *apex juris* is not to be laid hold on ; but they are to be construed largely for the benefit of trade. * * * *The construction should be according to the course of trade.*"[2]

Thus, where a policy contains repugnant, or conflicting conditions, the course pursued by the assured in attempting to comply with the requirements of the contract, will be sustained, *if the instrument is susceptible of such an interpretation*, although, in fact, contrary to the intention and meaning of the insurer. As, where the policy contained a condition, that " no suit for the recovery of any claim under this policy, shall be commenced after the end of one year after any

---

[1] *Younger* v. *Royal Exchange Assurance Co.*, 1 Burr. 341.

[2] *Bond* v. *Gonsales*, 2 Salk. 445 ; *McCluer* v. *Girard, etc., Ins. Co.*, 43 Iowa, 398.

claim shall occur, and in case such suit shall be commenced after the end of one year next after such loss or damage shall have occurred, the lapse of time shall be conclusive evidence against the validity of the claim," and also a condition that the company should not be liable to pay the loss until sixty days *after* the giving of notice, and proofs of loss were furnished, and an action was not commenced within one year after the loss occurred, but was commenced within one year after the lapse of sixty days from the filing of proof of loss, it was held that the action was seasonably commenced, because the terms of the condition were antagonistical, and the insured was justified in understanding that an action commenced within one year from the time *when the claim arose*, to wit: sixty days after proofs were furnished, was in conformity with the requirements of the policy. A similar doctrine has been held in several cases under similar provisions.[1]

In such cases, under such conditions, a claim against the company does not arise from the mere happening of the loss. No claim exists until all the conditions subsequent have been complied with ; that is, until notice has been given, and proofs of loss duly furnished. These are essential elements to perfect the claim, and until so perfected no legal claim exists.[2]

---

[1] *Mix* v. *Andes Ins. Co.*, 9 Hun (N. Y.) 397 ; *Mayor, etc.*, v. *Hamilton Ins. Co.*, 39 N. Y. 45 . *Ames* v. *N. Y. Union Ins. Co.*, 14 N. Y. 253 ; *Haward* v. *Franklin M. & F. Ins. Co.*, 9 How. Pr. (N. Y.) 45.

[2] YOUNG, J., in *Chandler* v. *St. Paul F. & M. Ins. Co.*, *ante.* In *Mix* v. *Andes Ins. Co.*, 9 Hun (N. Y.) 397, TALCOTT, J., said : "The condition of the policy on which the defendant relies for a defense in the action is as follows : ' It is, furthermore, hereby expressly provided, that no suit or action against said company for the recovery of any claim upon, under, or by virtue of the policy, shall be sustainable in any court of law or chancery, unless such suit or action shall be commenced within the 'term of twelve months next after any loss or damage shall occur ; and in case any such suit or action shall be commenced against said company after the expiration of twelve months next after such loss or damage shall have occurred, the lapse of time shall be taken and deemed as conclusive evidence against the validity of the claim thereby so attempted to be enforced.' The Court of Appeals has expressly decided in several cases, that such a condition in a policy of insurance is valid and binding, and that an action must fail unless commenced within the time limited. *Ripley* v. *The Ætna Ins. Co.*, 30 N. Y. 136 ; *Roach* v. *The N. Y. & Erie Ins. Co.*, 30 id. 546. But the same court has also held that according to the true and just interpretation of such a condition, the time therein specified within which an action must be commenced does not begin to run until the cause of action shall have accrued. *The Mayor of N. Y.* v. *The Hamilton Ins. Co.*, 39 N. Y. 45. In the case cited, the condition was like the one in the policy under consideration, limiting the time for the commencement of the action to a certain period after the loss or damage shall occur. But it was also provided that payment of losses should be made by the company within sixty days from the adjustment of the preliminary proofs of loss by the parties. In the case at bar the policy provides as follows : No. 11. ' Until proofs, declarations and certificates are produced, and examination submitted to, if required, the loss shall not be deemed payable.' No. 12. ' Payment of losses shall be made sixty days after the loss has been ascertained and proved.' According to the decision in the case last cited, the cause of action did not accrue on the policy in question, until sixty days after the preliminary proofs of loss had been served upon the

Insurers may impose any lawful conditions upon the insured, as a basis upon which the risk will be carried, but they must use language that leaves no doubt as to the meaning of the condition. If there is any doubt or ambiguity in the expressions employed, they will be construed most strongly against the insurer. This is upon the principle that a person who draws a contract must draw it with such certainty of expression, that the other party, following the ordinary and usual sense of the words employed, or the meaning which the party obviously intended to give them, in connection with the subject-matter to which they relate, will not be misled thereby, and if there is any ambiguity, the party is not bound to inquire of the other party what was intended, but is fully justified in following the ordinary and usual interpretation of the words used. But, if in connection with other parts of the contract, it is evident that the insurer intended to extend their meaning, and the insured acts upon that theory, the insurer is estopped from setting up in defence, that the insured has violated the conditions of the contract because he has acted upon the enlarged sense of the language employed, which was fully justified by the language used and the subject-matter to which it related.[1] Thus, in the case last referred to, the policy contained a provision as follows: "The above premises are privileged to be occupied as hide, fat-melting, slaughter and packing houses, and stores and dwellings, *and for other extra hazardous purposes.*" In the classification of hazards annexed to the policy, the occupations specially priviliged were not embraced in the *extra hazardous* class, but came within a general clause under the head of *specially hazardous.* The insured let a portion of the building for a distillery and rectifying establishment, which also came under the specially hazardous class, and the insurers claimed that this use was not warranted by the terms of the policy, and consequently that

---

defendant. The fire by which the insured property was destroyed occurred on the 7th day of July, in the year 1872. But the proofs of loss were not delivered to the defendant until the 24th day of August, 1872, at which date the loss upon the policy was settled and agreed upon by the defendant at the sum of $4,571.43. Consequently, according to the just interpretation of the condition, by which the time for commencing an action on the policy was limited to twelve months, that time did not commence to run until sixty days after the said 24th day of August, in the year 1872. The suit was actually commenced by service of the summons and complaint, upon the duly appointed agent of the defendant, appointed to receive service of process in the State of New York according to the laws thereof, on the 11th day of September in the year 1873, and within twelve months from the time within which the cause of action accrued. See also, *Ames* v. *The N. Y. Union Ins. Co.,* 14 N. Y. 254."

[1] *Reynolds* v. *Commercial F. Ins. Co.,* 47 N. Y. 597. The opinion of CHURCH, C. J., in this case will be found very instructive upon the question of construction of contracts.

they were not liable for the loss. But the court held that the words "hazardous" or "extra hazardous" must be taken to mean *purposes of the same class as those before specified, and that the assured had a right to use the premises for any specially hazardous purpose. If the insurer expressly puts a construction upon certain terms employed, and there is no doubt as to the meaning, the insured is bound thereby,*[1] but if he employs language in such a connection as to leave a doubt, the benefit of the doubt will be given to the assured.[2]

Words claimed to create condition must be set forth in proper place.

SEC. 60. Words purporting to be a condition upon which the policy was issued, must be set forth in such a place, and in such manner in the policy as leaves no doubt that they were so intended, and words inserted promiscuously therein, having no connection with other conditions of the policy, although the word condition is used, will not be treated as a condition of the policy. Thus where the words, "on condition that the applicants take all risk from cotton waste," inserted between the statement of the sum insured on the property, and the description of its location, were held not to constitute either a condition or exception, so as to throw the burden of proof upon the insured to show that the fire was *not* occasioned by the cotton waste, or so as to render it necessary to negative such fact in the declaration.[3] Such words, used in such a connection in the policy, are nothing more than a proviso, signifying the intention of the insurers not to be liable for a fire originating from such cause, and being inoperative either as a condition or exception, if the insurer seeks to avoid liability upon that ground, he takes the burden of showing that the loss originated from the cause to which the proviso relates.[4]

Most favorable construction in favor of assured will be made.

SEC. 61. In case repugnant or inconsistent statements appear in the policy, that statement will be given effect that is most favorable to the assured. Thus, where the application was made a part of the policy, and the application contained a clause, "if it shall hereafter appear that any fraudulent concealment or *designedly* untrue statement be contained therein, then all the money which shall have been paid on account of the policy shall be forfeited, and the policy shall be abso-

[1] *Pindar* v. *Continental Ins. Co.*, 38 N. Y. 366.
[2] *Reynolds* v. *Commerce Ins. Co., ante.*
[3] *Kingsley* v. *N. E. Mut. F. Ins. Co.*, 8 Cush. (Mass.) 393.
[4] METCALF, J., in *Kingsley* v. *N. E. Mut. F. Ins. Co., ante.*

lutely void," but the policy itself contained a provision that, "if any statement contained in the declaration (application) *is untrue*, the policy shall be void," the court held that, in order to avoid the policy because of an untrue statement in the application, the insurer must show that it was *designedly* untrue, because the insured was entitled to the most favorable construction that the contract would bear. In a Massachusetts case,[1] the by-laws of a Mutual Insurance Company provided that all the statements of the assured in his application should be warranties; but in the application itself, which was made a part of the policy, the insured agreed that the "application contains a correct description of the property, so far as it regards the condition, situation, value and risk of the same, and that any misrepresentation or suppression of *material* facts shall destroy his claim for damage or loss." Under these repugnant conditions, the court held that the insured was bound by the statements in the application *only so far as they were material to the risk*, and that the question of materiality was for the jury.

Written stipulations, effect of, upon printed.

Sec. 62. Where one stipulation is printed, and the other *written*, although repugnant, the *written* stipulation will prevail,[2] although both will be upheld, if possible.[3] And while, where both conditions are *printed*, the last will generally overcome the first, yet, where one is *written* and the other *printed*, the written condition will be given effect without any reference to their position in the policy.[4] Thus, where the printed portion of the policy provides that if other insurance is obtained without the consent of the company indorsed on the policy, the policy shall be void, the words, "other insurance permitted without notice until required," written in the policy, overcome the printed condition, and operate as a license to the assured to procure other insurance without the consent of the insurer,[5] and such permission upon the *face* of the policy is a compliance with a condition requiring permission to be *indorsed* upon the policy.[6]

---

[1] *Elliott* v. *Hamilton Ins. Co.*, 13 Gray (Mass.) 137.

[2] *Niagara Ins. Co.* v. *De Graff*, 12 Mich. 124 ; *Bargett* v. *Orient Mut. Ins. Co.*, 3 Bos. (N. Y.) 385 ; *Coster* v. *Phœnix Ins. Co.*, 2 Wash. C. C. (U. S.) 51 ; *Consolidated F. Ins. Co.* v. *Cushaw*, 41 Md. 59 ; *Schroeder* v. *Stock, etc., Ins. Co.*, 46 Mo. 174 ; *Frederick Co. Mut. Ins. Co.* v. *Deford*, 38 Md. 414 ; *Blake* v. *Exchange Mut. Ins. Co.*, 12 Gray, 265.

[3] *Stokes* v. *Cox*, 1 H. & N. 533.

[4] *Leeds* v. *Mechanics' Ins. Co.*, 8 N. Y. 351 ; *Hernandez* v. *Sun Mut. Ins. Co.*, 6 Blatch. (U. S.) 317 ; *Forbes* v. *American Mut. Life Ins. Co*, 15 Gray (Mass.) 249.

[5] *Blake* v. *Exchange Ins. Co.*, 12 Gray (Mass.) 265.

[6] *Ames* v. *N. Y. Union Ins. Co.*, 14 N. Y. 253.

Repugnant stipulations as to the subject-matter of the risk.

SEC. 63. Where the written portion of the policy describes the property insured as of a certain class, and the property *as described* embraces a class of articles ranked in the policy as hazardous, extra hazardous, or specially hazardous, or which, by the printed terms of the policy, are prohibited, as if the goods are described as a stock, "such as is usually kept in a country store,"[1] and the printed portion of the policy *prohibits* the keeping of certain articles *usually* kept in a country store, the written portion of the policy overcomes the force of the printed stipulations, and the keeping of such articles does not operate as a breach of the conditions of the policy. Thus, where a policy covered property described as a stock such as is usually kept in a general retail store, and the keeping of gunpowder was prohibited by the printed portion of the policy, it was held that, if gunpowder formed a part of the stock *usually* kept in a "general retail store," the keeping of gunpowder was not a violation of the conditions of the policy.[2] So as to other articles, as "whale oil, friction matches, earthenware, etc.,"[3] "alcohol and other spirituous liquors,"[4] "spirits of turpentine,"[5] it may always be shown that such articles are *usually* kept as a part of the stock of the *class* insured, and if proved, the printed prohibitory clause is overcome by the written description of the class of property insured.[6] So where a building is insured for the prosecution of a certain trade,[7] or if machinery and stock in a certain trade is insured, the policy is treated as licensing the using or keeping in a reasonable way, all such articles as are essential to the business, or as are usually used in the

[1] *Franklin F. Ins. Co.* v. *Updergaff*, 43 Penn. St. 350; *Pindar* v. *Kings Co. Ins. Co.*, 36 N. Y. 648; *Whitmarsh* v. *Conway F. Ins. Co.*, 16 Gray (Mass.) 359; *Elliott* v. *Hamilton Mut. Ins. Co.*, 13 id. 139; *Phœnix Ins. Co.* v. *Taylor*, 5 Minn. 492.

[2] *Phœnix Ins. Co.* v. *Taylor*, 5 Minn. 492; *Duncan* v. *Sun F. Ins. Co.*, 6 Wend. (N. Y.) 488. In *Peoria F. & Mut. Ins. Co.* v. *Hall*, 12 Mich. 202, the policy prohibited the keeping of gunpowder. The insured was permitted to show that the agent issuing the policy *knew* that gunpowder formed a part of the stock kept by the insured, and that he intended to continue to keep it. The policy prohibited its keeping. The court held that the company were estopped from setting up a breach of such condition in defense, as the knowledge of the agent must be treated as the knowledge of the company, and it must be presumed that they intended to issue a valid policy, and therefore *waived* the condition.

[3] *Whitmarsh* v. *Conway F. Ins. Co.*, 16 Gray (Mass.) 359.

[4] *Niagara F. Ins. Co.* v. *De Graff*, 12 Mich. 124.

[5] *Pindar* v. *County Ins. Co.*, 36 N. Y. 648.

[6] *Steinbach* v. *Lafayette F. Ins. Co.*, 54 N. Y. 90; *Peoria F. & Mut. Ins. Co.* v. *Hall*, 12 Mich. 202; *Pindar* v. *Kings Co. Ins. Co.*, ante; *Viele* v. *Germania Ins. Co.*, 26 Iowa, 9.

[7] *Archer* v. *Merchants'*, etc., *Ins. Co.*, 43 Mo. 434; *Citizens' Ins. Co.* v. *McLaughlin*, 53 Penn. St. 485.

prosecution of the business in any of its details, although such use or keeping is expressly prohibited by the printed portion of the policy. Of course, if the insurer, in writing upon the policy, inserts a prohibition, it is operative, and overcomes the force of the implied license; but in the absence of such written prohibition, the written description of the uses or class of property described carries with it a license to use or keep any and all articles, the use or keeping of which is a *usual* incident of the business.[1]

---

[1] In *Harper* v. *Albany Mut. Ins. Co.*, 17 N. Y. 194, and *Harper* v. *N. Y. City Ins. Co.*, 22 N. Y. 441, the keeping or use of camphene was prohibited; but, as the policy covered a printer's stock and materials, and it being shown that camphene was necessary to clean the type, and was *usually* employed by printers for that purpose, the prohibition was held not to apply. In *Hall* v. *N. Y. Ins. Co.*, 58 N. Y. 292, the use of "kerosene" was prohibited; but, as the policy covered a photographer's stock, *materials*, etc., and, it being shown that kerosene was usually employed in the business, for heating paper and other purposes, it was held that the prohibition did not apply, even though gas could have been equally well used for that purpose. This principle was well illustrated in *Steinbach* v. *La Fayette Fire Ins. Co.*, 54 N. Y. 90. In that case an action was brought to recover for a loss sustained under a policy issued by the defendants. It insured plaintiff "on his stock of fancy goods, toys and other articles in his line of business, contained in the three-story brick building situated on the south-east corner of Baltimore street and Tripolett's alley, and now in his occupancy as a German jobber and importer." It was also written in the policy that plaintiff was "privileged to keep fire-crackers on sale." The insurance was for $5,000; premium, twenty dollars. It was provided in the policy that if the premises should be "used for the purpose of carrying on therein any trade or occupation, or for storing or keeping therein articles, goods or merchandise denominated hazardous, or extra hazardous, or specially hazardous in the second class of hazards annexed to the policy, except as herein specially provided for, or hereinafter agreed to by this corporation in writing upon this policy, from thenceforth so long as the same shall be so used, this policy shall be of no effect;" and it was declared that the policy was "made and accepted in reference to the terms and conditions herein contained and hereto annexed, which are hereby declared to be a part of this contract." Among the second class of hazards classed as "hazardous No. 2," are enumerated "fire-crackers in packages," which add to the rate of premium ten cents per $100. "Fire-works" classed as "specially hazardous," add fifty cents or more to the rate. Upon the trial a witness, on the part of plaintiff, was asked: "Are fire-works usually kept in Baltimore by persons in the same line of business as Mr. Steinbach?" Objected to. The objection was overruled, and defendant's counsel excepted. Defendant's counsel asked his witnesses various questions, in substance, as to whether fire-works were a part of the line of business of a German jobber and importer dealing in fancy goods, toys, etc. These were objected to by plaintiff. Objection sustained, and defendant excepted. The defendant's counsel requested the court to charge: "1. That the fact of the insured being privileged to keep fire-crackers on sale is strong evidence that the insured was not permitted by his contract to keep them without such privilege." The court refused to charge in the terms of the request, but did charge: "If you come to the conclusion that fire-works were in the line of Mr. Steinbach's business, then it is no evidence at all. If you come to the other conclusion, it would be strong evidence." The defendant excepted to the judge's refusal to charge as requested. The defendant's counsel also requested the court to charge the jury: "2. That fire-works were not insured by the policy, if fire-crackers were not covered without the privilege. 3. The fact of the fire-crackers being privileged is strong evidence, on the part of the defendant, that fire-works were not insured. 4. Under the evidence fire-works are not a part of the stock in the line of business of a German jobber and importer. 5. It is evidence to the jury on the question whether fire-works were intended to be insured to consider the rate of premium

So too, where the prohibition is not total, as, where in one clause of
the policy the use or storing of petroleum, rock or earth oil, is prohib-

---

paid in the policy.   7. Under the evidence in this case fire-works were not included in the line of business of the plaintiff as a German jobber and importer."
The court refused so to charge, and the jury found a verdict for plaintiff of $4,596.52.
Upon appeal the ruling of the court was sustained, REYNOLDS, C., saying :
"The plaintiff was insured for one year against fire, on his stock of fancy goods,
toys and other articles in his line of business, in his store in the city of Baltimore,
in his occupancy as a German jobber and importer, and he was privileged to keep
fire-crackers on sale.   It was provided in the policy that if the premises should
be used for the purpose of carrying on therein any trade or occupation, or of
storing or keeping therein articles, goods or merchandise denominated hazardous
or extra hazardous or specially hazardous, in the second class of hazards annexed
to the policy, except as therein specially provided for, or thereinafter agreed to
by the defendant, in writing upon the policy, then so long as the same shall be so
used the policy was to be of no effect.   The policy of insurance was accepted by
the plaintiff with the condition last referred to, and the privilege to keep ' fire-
crackers on sale ' was specially written in the policy, and added ten cents more of
premium to the $100.   ' Fire-works ' are claimed as 'specially hazardous,' and
added fifty cents or more per $100 to the rate of insurance, and, it is claimed,
that to be covered by the insurance, must have been specially written in the
policy which, in this case, was not done.   The rule which prevails in the interpretation of contracts of insurance is or should be the same as in all other written
contracts of whatever nature.   The intent is to be ascertained and observed, and,
if it clearly appears by the writing, the contract must have effect according to its
terms.   In this case, without evidence *aliunde*, it would be difficult, if not impossible, to say what articles in fact were intended to be insured.   The court cannot
judicially take notice of the precise commodities which make up a stock of fancy
goods, toys and other articles in that line of business, nor can it be declared, as a
legal proposition, what precise things pertain to the occupancy of a building in
the city of Baltimore as a ' German jobber and importer.'   In the prosecution
of his business the plaintiff did keep ' fire-works,' and the loss was occasioned by
their accidental ignition, and it appears to have been absolutely necessary, in order
to settle the dispute between the parties, to ascertain whether the keeping of
' fire-works ' for sale were ' in the line of the plaintiff's business.'   If not, it is
very clear they were not insured against, because they were not specially ' written in the policy,' and the fact that the privilege to keep ' fire-crackers on sale ' was
specially written in the policy, affords a very strong argument in favor of the defendant that ' fire-works ' were not insured against, for there was no special writing
in regard to them, unless included in the written words ' in the line of the business '
of the plaintiff.   I do not understand it was claimed by the counsel for the defendant, on the trial, that the plaintiff was not at liberty to show that keeping ' fire-
works ' for sale was in the line of the plaintiff's business.   It was in fact shown,
without objection, that he had always kept them as a part of his stock in trade,
and had some on hand when the insurance was effected.   Evidence was also given,
on the part of the plaintiff, tending to show that similar dealers usually kept fire-
works as a part of their stock in trade.   Evidence on the part of defendant was
given tending to show the contrary, but it was not very conclusive.   If, therefore, as a matter of fact, the keeping of fire-works was in the line of the plaintiff's business, the cases are quite too numerous and familiar to need citation,
that ' fire-works ' were embraced in the written description of the property covered by the policy.   The question seems to have been fairly submitted to the jury
by the learned judge at the circuit, and their verdict for the plaintiff is conclusive
as to the fact.   We find no error of law which seems to require a new trial."
JOHNSON, C., said : "The judge's charge in this case was not excepted to, nor was
there any motion for a nonsuit.   The questions for review are presented by exceptions to the rulings in the admission or rejection of evidence, and upon requests
to charge presented by the defendant ; but no question was presented as to the
non-liability of the defendant for any particular part of the loss, if it was liable
at all, upon the policy.   Under the condition in the policy, suspending its operation so long as the premises should be used for the purpose of carrying on therein

ited, and in another clause the lighting of the premises by certain
inflammable substances, among which "kerosene" is not included, the
assured does not, by the use of kerosene for illuminating purposes,

---

any trade or occupation, or for storing or keeping therein, any articles, goods or
merchandise, denominated hazardous or extra hazardous or specially hazardous,
in the second class of the classes of hazards annexed to the policy, except as
therein specially provided for or thereafter agreed to by the corporation in writing
upon the policy, it is the settled law of this State, that any such article is specially
provided for, if it as matter of fact, enters into and forms a part of the kind or
line of business specified in the written part of the policy in the description of
the risk assumed. The insurers being bound to know the nature and kind of
articles belonging to the business and occupations against the risks of which they
undertake to insure, the specification of the business is a sufficient special provision for all the articles belonging to it under the condition in the policy, even
though some of those articles belong to the second class of hazards mentioned in
the condition. *Harper v. Albany Mut. Ins. Co.*, 17 N. Y. 194; *Harper v. N. Y.
City Ins. Co.*, 32 N. Y. 441. The defendant's exceptions to the question by the
plaintiff, whether fire-works are usually kept in Baltimore, by persons in the same
line of business as the plaintiff, and his exception to the exclusion of various
questions put by him, whether fire-works are a part of the line of business of
German jobbers and importers dealing in toys, fancy goods, etc. ; whether, when
they are kept by German jobbers and importers dealing in fancy goods, they are
in or out of their line of business, present the principal question of evidence
involved. The plaintiff sought to show what was the fact in respect to keeping
fire-works in Baltimore, by dealers in the same line of business with him, while
the defendant's question involved the element of opinion on the part of the witnesses, as to the propriety of considering fire-works as forming part of the line of
business of German jobbers and importers. That was of no sort of consequence,
the material point being, whether, in fact, the persons known in trade under the
designation mentioned, did usually and generally, as matter of fact, keep fire-
works. Accordingly the judge at the trial ruled that the opinion of witnesses
could not be substituted for facts, and while excluding the questions under consideration, instructed the defendant's counsel that he was at liberty to ask if the
persons whom the witness knew in Baltimore, carrying on the kind of business
that the plaintiff did, usually kept fire-works. This the defendant's counsel
declined to ask, and yet this was exactly material in the case. The question, what
things were in the line of business the plaintiff was carrying on, was not one to
be answered by opinions of experts, but by an investigation of facts, and the
judge was, therefore, correct in excluding evidence of opinion on that point, on
the part of the witnesses. Several requests to charge, were founded on the fact
that there was written on the policy a privilege to keep fire-crackers on sale.
One was that fire-works were not insured by the policy, if fire-crackers were not
covered without the privilege. The others were in substance that a privilege for
fire-crackers, was strong evidence that it was necessary to warrant the plaintiff to
keep them and also that fire-works were not insured. The judge refused so to
charge and rightly, because if keeping fire-works was part of the plaintiff's
business described in the policy, the expression of a privilege for fire-crackers,
whether necessary or not, was immaterial, and was equally so if, as the defendant
contended, keeping fire-works was not part of the plaintiff's business. The
request that the jury might consider the rate of premium paid, as bearing upon
the question whether fire-works were intended to be insured, was properly
refused. The company was not tied down to its printed rates, and the question
was not whether it had charged premium enough for fire-works, *but whether having
insured the plaintiff's business, fire-works were not covered us a part of it.*" The
court adverted to *Steinbach* v. *Ins. Co.*, 13 Wall. (U. S.) 183, in which a contrary doctrine was held and expressly disapproved it, JOHNSON, J., saying: "The New
York cases do not seem to have been adverted to, *nor the case itself much considered*, and should not be justified under these circumstances in abandoning a
settled line of decisions in our own State in order to conform to it." See also, *Citizen's Ins. Co.* v. *McLaughlin*, 49 Penn. St. 485 ; *Archer* v. *Merchants', etc., Ins.
Co.*, 43 Mo. 434.

violate the conditions of the policy, because by expressly stating what substances *shall not* be used for that purpose, the assured has a right to understand that all other substances *not named may be used.*[1] In the case last referred to, which was an action upon a policy issued upon the plaintiff's paper mill, and contained provisions or conditions as stated in the text, the defendant insisted that the first condition prohibited the use of kerosene *for any purpose*, and that its use by the plaintiff for illuminating purposes avoided the policy, but the court held that inasmuch as the defendants had expressly named the substances that *should not* be used for lighting purposes, the assured was justified in using any substance *not named*, for that purpose, or which did not come under the terms of such prohibition, and that the previous clause prohibiting the use or storing of petroleum, rock oil, etc., must be regarded as applicable only to their use or storage *for other purposes.*

It is not competent to show by parol that words written in a policy, and which have received a judicial interpretation, have acquired by the usage of trade a peculiar commercial meaning, variant from that which the courts have adjudged to be their true meaning.[2] The policy must be so construed, if practicable, that effect may be given to the written words in it, according to their meaning in such contracts as settled by judicial decisions; when giving to them that meaning, they conflict with some customary provision found in the printed part of the policy, the latter must be rejected, and the written words allowed to prevail.[3] The construction of a policy depends upon the ordinary

---

[1] *Buchanan* v. *Exchange Fire Ins. Co.*, 61 N. Y. 26.

[2] *Winthrop* v. *Union Ins. Co.*, 2 Wash. C. C. (U. S.) 7; *Hare* v. *Barstow*, 8 Jur. 928.

[3] *Bargett* v. *Orient, etc., Ins. Co.*, 3 Bos. (N. Y.) 385. In *Robertson* v. *French*, 4 East, 134, Lord ELLENBOROUGH very pertinently said: "In the course of the argument it seems to have been assumed that some peculiar rules of construction apply to the terms of a policy of assurance, which are not equally applicable to the terms of other instruments and in all other cases. It is, therefore, proper to state, under this head, that the same rule of construction which applies to other instruments, applies equally to this, * * viz., *that it is to be construed according to its sense and meaning, as collected, in the first place, from the terms used in it, which terms are themselves to be understood in their plain, ordinary and popular sense, unless they have generally, in respect to the subject-matter, as by the known usage of trade, or the like, acquired a peculiar sense, distinct from the popular sense of the same words ; or unless the context evidently points out that they must, in the particular instance, and in order to effectuate the immediate intention of the parties to the contract, be understood in some other and peculiar sense.* The only difference between policies of assurance and other instruments in this respect, is, that the greater part of the *printed language* of them, *being invariable and uniform*, has acquired, from use and practice, *a known and definite meaning*, and that the words superadded in writing (subject, indeed, always to be governed, in point of construction, by the language and terms with which they are accompanied), are entitled, nevertheless, *if there should be any reasonable doubt upon the*

or usual meaning of the words used, rather than upon the presumed intention of the parties. If there is any ambiguity, it will be taken most strongly against the company, following the maxim: " *Verba chartarum fortius accepiuntur contra proferentum.*"[1] " If," said Lord St. Leonards, in the case last cited, " there be any ambiguity in it, it must be taken according to law, more strongly against the person who prepared it." In another part of the opinion, he says: " The courts, observing how very often companies of this nature have been subjected to frauds, will carefully guard them against fraud, and will give effect to any part of the contract which has this object. *   * But, however severe the terms, *there should be no ambiguity in the instrument itself.*" Questions of construction, as well as the effect thereof between the parties, when there is no ambiguity, are for the court; but when a question arises as to the meaning of any term employed in the instrument, of a technical kind, or requiring the explanation of mercantile usage, the jury are to determine the sense in which it was intended to be used.[2] In cases of a conflict between the written and printed portions of the policy, *if possible*, a construction will be adopted that will reconcile both.[3] Where the language is plain and free from doubt, full effect will be given every condition, however harshly or severely it may affect the assured. It is not a question of strict justice, or morality, or honest dealing between the parties, but of construction; and if there is no ambiguity, the court has no other alternative, except to hold the assured up to the rigid exactions of the condition. And this is so, even though the assured was not, in fact, aware of the terms of the condition, or had no reason to anticipate it, or would not have accepted the policy had he been aware of the burden imposed upon him. The courts cannot shield parties from the consequences of their own negligence. They must, at their peril, examine contracts to which they are parties, and failing to do so, in the absence of fraud, on the part of the other party, or mistake in making a writing that does not express the contract entered into, there is no redress. Thus,

---

sense and meaning of the whole, to have a greater effect attributed to them than to the printed words, inasmuch as the written words are the *immediate language and terms selected by the parties themselves for the expression of their meaning*, and the printed words *are a general formula, adapted equally to their case and that of all other contracting parties upon similar occasions and subjects.*"   *Wilson* v. *Hampden Ins. Co.* 4 R. I. 159 ; 4 Bennett's F. I. C. 128.

[1] *Anderson* v. *Fitzgerald*, 4 H. L. Cas. 484 ; 24 Eng. Law & Eq. 11.

[2] Arnould on Ins. 3d ed. 1068 ; *Hutchins* v. *Bowker*, 5 M. & W. 547.

[3] *Stokes* v. *Cox*, 1 H. & N. 533.

in a recent English case,[1] there was an insurance upon a ship, but against fire only, and the policy, which was prepared upon a form applicable to the insurance of a house, contained the following clause : "The company is not responsible for or liable to pay any loss or damage occasioned by or through any explosion, and if more than 20 pounds' weight of gunpowder shall be upon the premises at the time when any loss happens, such loss will not be made good." A fire occurred, and the ship, a steamer, was destroyed, and a plea that at the time of the fire there was a larger quantity of gunpowder than 20 pounds on board—in fact, as the jury found, a package of 100 pounds as freight—was held good. It was contended that it was usual for steamers of this character to carry gunpowder as freight, and that the condition was inapplicable to the subject-matter of the insurance, and should be struck out, or that the words "in use," excluding freight, should be inserted, or that the company should not be relieved from their responsibility without proof of fraud, the policy being a "contrat aléatoire," to be carried out in good faith, and without a further proof that the fire had extended by reason of the excess of gunpowder carried ; also that the word "premises" must be considered to have been used in their popular sense of buildings, in opposition to their legal sense of the thing previously expressed, and could not be applied to a ship. But the court thought otherwise, and held that the policy was avoided.

The presumed practice of other offices will not be allowed to alter a policy.

SEC. 64. Another English case,[2] which is often cited, covers the law applicable to the construction of a specially worded policy, and may be considered to prove that the terms of such an instrument cannot be extended or altered to cover a loss, because, by the usage of the insurance offices, no additional charge would have been made for the privilege of more extensive terms. The policy was for £10,000 for three months, "for the hull of the steamship Indian Empire, with her tackle, furniture and stores on board belonging, lying in the Victoria Docks, London, with liberty to go into dry dock, and light the boiler fires once or twice during the currency of this policy." Adjoining the Victoria Docks there was a graving dock, not strictly a dry dock, although available as such, but the entrance was too small to admit the ship ; she was therefore moved two miles up the river to another dry dock,

[1] *The Beacon F. O.* v. *Gibb*, 9 Jur. N. S. 185, P. C. C.
[2] *Pearson* v. *Commercial Union Ins. Co.* 15 C. B. (N. S.) 304

and the lower part of her paddle-wheels removed to allow her admission. The repairs being complete at the end of two months, she was towed down the stream to within 500 or 700 yards of the Victoria Docks for the purpose of having the parts of the paddle-wheels, which had been removed, replaced there. The utmost despatch was used, and in ten days the work was nearly complete, when she was burned at her moorings. It was proved that the premium would have been the same with the principal London offices, whether the ship lay in the river or in the docks, but that in the Victoria Docks there were very careful precautions taken against fire—watchmen at all hours, and a numerous fire brigade, with an ample supply of water, and all the usual appliances for putting out fires; while in the river there were only three floating engines, between the arrival of the first of which and the breaking out of the fire nearly an hour had, in fact, elapsed. It was also proved that the work might as well have been done in the dock as in the river, but that the expense would have been much greater. The court held that the policy protected the vessel while in the Victoria Docks, or any dry dock, whether in the river or not, and notwithstanding that the latter might be at some distance from the former, and also while in transition, but that the risk was limited to the transit, and did not extend to the time during which the ship stopped in the river not for the purpose of that transit. This judgment was affirmed in the Exchequer Chamber.

Provisos to avoid the policy generally construed as rendering them voidable.

SEC. 65. It is also to be noted that provisions declaring policies void in certain events have been generally construed as rendering them not absolutely void, but voidable at the election of the insurers, and that such right of avoidance was subject to waiver, either by express agreement or by necessary implication arising from the acts of the parties.[1] If a company receives a renewal premium, after notice of the infringement of a condition, it would not be allowed to rest upon that condition, and repudiate its liabilities in the event of a loss;[2] but an agent cannot revive a void policy without some authority for the act.[3]

Alterations by indorsement.

SEC. 66. When an alteration is required in a policy, it may be made by indorsement, if it is such as is provided for by the conditions of the policy.

---

[1] *Armstrong* v. *Turquand*, 9 Ir. Ch. L. R. 32.

[2] *Wing* v. *Harvey*, 5 De Gex, M. & G. 265.

[3] *British Industry Life Ass. Co.* v. *Ward*, 17 C. B. 644; Bunyon on Fire Insurance, 59–61.

Policy construed according to its terms.

SEC. 67. The policy must be construed according to its terms, and the evident intent of the parties, to be gathered from the language used, and the court cannot extend the risk beyond what is fairly within the terms of the policy. New conditions cannot be added by the court, but the rights of the parties must stand upon the contract as made. This was well illustrated in a recent English case,[1] in which a time policy against fire was effected on a steamship. The policy described it as then "lying in the Victoria docks," but gave it "liberty to go into dry dock, and light the boiler fires once or twice during the currency of this policy." The only dry dock into which the ship could go was Lungley's dock, at some distance up the river. To go there it was necessary to remove the paddle-wheels; they were removed in the Victoria docks, and the ship was then towed up to Lungley's dock. The necessary repairs there having been completed, the ship was brought out and moored in the river, preparatory to replacing the paddle-wheels. This operation could have been perfectly performed in the Victoria docks, but it was found that in such case it was customary, as the more economical course, to replace the paddle-wheels while the ship lay in the river. Before the wheels had been replaced the ship was burnt. The court held that the policy covered the ship while in the Victoria docks, and while passing from them to the dry dock, and while directly returning from the dry dock to the Victoria docks; but did not cover the vessel while moored in the river for a collateral purpose. Lord CHELMSFORD said: "An insurance against fire necessarily has regard to the locality of the subject insured." Lord O'HAGAN said: "To construe the policy as allowing the vessel to remain in the river while the paddle-wheels were replaced, would be to add a new condition to the policy, which cannot be done."

A policy of insurance is to be construed as a whole, and particular clauses are not to be wrested from their context, so as to destroy the unity of the contract, and create conflict where there should be agreement; but one part is to be elucidated by another, so as to reconcile them, if possible, to one common intent or design, and so as to carry out the *intention* of both parties, *as gathered from the whole instrument*, and this is to be done accurately, without severity on the one hand or liberality upon the other, but so as to carry into effect the real purpose and understanding of the parties.[2] But all conditions

[1] *Pearson v. Com. Ins. Co.*, L. R. 1 App. Cas. 498.
[2] *Merchants' Ins. Co.* v. *Davenport*, 17 Gratt. (Va.) 138; *Phœnix Ins. Co.* v. *Slaughter*, 12 Wall. (U. S.) 404.

involving forfeitures, as well as all exemptions, will be construed strictly, and most favorably to the assured,[1] and so as not to impeach the good faith of either party, for in construing a contract, reference is to be had to the presumption that it was entered into in good faith by the parties, to effectuate the evident purpose for which it was made.[2]

When policy takes effect.

SEC. 68. A policy takes effect on the day of its date, although the premium is not paid until several days after, unless otherwise agreed by the parties,[3] or upon the completion of the contract. If a policy is not issued in the first instance, when an application is made according to the rules of the company, and when it is agreed between the agent and the person applying that the making of the application shall operate as a protection until it has been acted upon, a recovery may be had for a loss happening before the application reaches the company, although the company rejects the risk.[4]

Policy suspended may re-attach.

SEC. 69. Where a policy issues to a merchant, or to a person in any business where the risk is shifting; that is, where property, as a class, rather than specific articles, are insured, and the business, including the property, is sold during the life of the policy, the policy not being assigned, *and, while the policy is still in force, the assured buys back the business*, before a loss under the policy, the insurer is liable for a loss occurring *after such re-purchase*. In such cases, the policy not attaching to any particular articles of property, but to such articles within the class insured, as the assured may own *in the place insured, at the time of loss*, while by a total alienation of the business, the policy is suspended, yet, upon the re-purchase of the stock by the assured, it is revived, and becomes operative as to such goods of the same class, as he may have at the place named in the policy at the time of loss.[5]

There would seem to be no question however, but that, if the insurer stipulated against an alienation of the property — which of course would relate to a conveyance of the business insured — the policy, upon such *cesser* of interest, would be avoided. This, however, is an open question, and has never been directly decided. BIGELOW, J., in

---

[1] *Liverpool, etc., Ins. Co.* v. *Verdier*, 33 Mich. 138.

[2] *Ins. Co.* v. *Slaughter*, 12 Wall. (U. S.) 404.

[3] *Lightbody* v. *N. American Ins. Co.*, 23 Wend. (N. Y.) 18.

[4] *Palm* v. *Medina Co. M. F. Ins. Co.*, 9 West. L. J. 337; 20 Ohio St. 529.

[5] *Lane* v. *Maine Mut. Ins. Co.*, 12 Me. 44. See also, *Hooker* v. *Hud. Riv. Ins. Co.*, 17 N. Y. 424; *Worthington* v. *Bearse*, 12 Allen (Mass.) 382.

a case before the Massachusetts Supreme Court,[1] and referred to by Mr. Bennett in a note to Hooper v. Hudson River Ins. Co.,[2] intimated such a doctrine. But there are arguments quite plausible against it. Thus, a policy covering a shifting risk as "a stock of dry goods," "a stock of groceries," etc., imports a license to sell, and does not cover any particular articles, *but property of a class which the assured may own at the time of loss*, and the ordinary provision against alienation is overcome by the implied license to sell. But can the license thus implied be extended beyond sales in the ordinary modes employed in the business insured? *Does it cover a sale of the business, as well as of the goods?* It would seem that it would not, but the case of Lane v. Ins. Co., cited *ante*, seems to establish a different rule, although this particular question was not discussed. At least, the question is an open one, and upon principle, as well as upon fair construction, it would seem that a sale of the property and the business, would defeat the policy.

When policy is exhausted.

SEC. 70. A policy can only be made operative to the extent of the sum insured. When that sum has been paid, whether in partial or a total loss, the contract is ended. Thus, if a policy upon property is issued to the amount of $10,000, and there is a loss of $5,000, which is paid, the policy only remains for $5,000, and if there is a subsequent loss to more than that amount, $5,000 is the limit of recovery, and upon payment of that sum, the policy is quieted, and the contract fully met.[3] And if the insurer rebuilds, the policy is not thereby terminated, but still remains as an indemnity for the difference between the cost of rebuilding, and the sum insured.[4]

Detached—meaning of, in policy.

SEC. 71. The word "detached," when employed in a policy, is to be interpreted in its ordinary and usual sense, and means, not connected with, not attached to, standing apart from; and it is not competent to show that, by special usage among insurance companies or men, it is used to designate buildings standing twenty-five feet, or any other distance, from other buildings, *unless it is also shown that the insured knew or had notice of the sense in which it was employed.*[5]

---

[1] *Worthington* v. *Bearse*, 12 Allen (Mass.) 382.
[2] 17 N. Y. 424; 4 Ben. F. I. C. 268.
[3] *Crombie* v. *Portsmouth F. Ins. Co.*, 26 N. H. 389.
[4] *Trull* v. *Roxbury, etc., Ins. Co.*, 3 Cush. (Mass.) 263.
[5] *Hill* v. *Hibernia Ins. Co.* 10 Hun (N. Y.) 26.

When a word has a well established meaning, and is ordinarily used in that sense, it is not competent to show that it has acquired a special meaning in a particular branch of business, *unless it is also shown that the person to be affected by such special meaning knew that it was employed to express a special meaning in the class of contracts into which he was entering.*[1]

Machinery. What is, is question for court.

Sec. 72. As to what constitutes *machinery* under a policy of insurance, is a question of law for the court, and not a question of fact for the jury.[2] A policy covering " machinery " will be construed to cover all instruments used, or intended to be operated exclusively by machinery in the business of the assured, and which are so operated from time to time in the regular and ordinary prosecution of the business described or referred to in the policy, although such instruments are not a part of any particular machine, but are used in connection with the machinery as occasion requires, in the prosecution of the business. Thus, where the plaintiffs procured a policy upon " their engine and machinery * * for the manufacture of tin-ware, sheet-iron, japanned ware, and fancy plated ware," it was held that the policy covered dies (642 in number) which were used to give form to various utensils manufactured in the prosecution of the business, although such dies were not a part of any particular machine, and when not in use were deposited upon shelves apart from the machines or presses in which they were used.[3] So the wheels of a polishing machine, although detached therefrom, are treated as machinery within the meaning of the term, and generally it may be said that any implement or contrivance used in connection with machinery, although not a part of it, in the prosecution of the business, is covered by a policy upon machinery used in that business.[4]

" In trust," how construed in policy.

Sec. 73. A policy upon property, "his own and in trust or on commission," is not limited merely to the proprietary interest of the assured, but enures to the benefit of the consignor. The words " in trust," are to be construed according to their meaning by commercial usage, and " whatever," says Ames, J.,[5] "the consignees might recover on such poli-

---

[1] *Walls* v. *Bailey,* 49 N. Y. 464. Barnard, J., in *Hill* v. *Hibernia Ins. Co.,* 10 Hun (N. Y.) 29.

[2] *Buchanan* v. *Exchange Ins. Co.,* 61 (N. Y.) 26.

[3] *Seavey* v. *Central M. F. Ins. Co.,* 111 Mass. 540.

[4] *Pierce* v. *George,* 108 Mass. 78.

[5] *Johnson* v. *Campbell,* 120 Mass. 449.

cies, *in excess of their own claims,* they would hold in trust for the consignors.[1] It follows, therefore, that the consignors were in fact insured, and there is nothing in the contract that imports that the insurance was to be effected in their name, or that the policy should be in their possession or control. * * *We see nothing in the evidence to sustain the position that the consignees were confined to the goods themselves, as the means of recovering their advances.* To the owners of those goods they stood in the relation of creditors, and if from any cause, without their fault, the proceeds of the goods proved insufficient to repay their advances, they would have a valid claim against the consignors for the àmount found deficient on settlement." Thus, it will be seen that the consignee may insure the goods of the consignor, not only to protect his own interest therein, but also the interests of the consignors, and that he is only the trustee of the consignor *for the balance of the insurance money, if any, remaining in his hands after he is himself reimbursed for advances and charges upon the property.*

From — until.

SEC. 74. A policy from one day certain *until* another certain day, as from February 14, 1867 *until* August 14, 1868, includes a loss occurring at any time during the 14th of August.[2]

Immediate—forthwith.

SEC. 75. The words "immediate" or "forthwith," employed in the condition of a policy, means *a reasonable time in view of the circumstances,*[3] as where the policy provides that "*immediate* notice of loss shall be given," it is construed to mean that notice shall be given within a reasonable time in view of the circumstances.[4]

Contiguous.

SEC. 76. The word "contiguous," when employed in the condition of a policy, is to be construed according to its usual and ordinary meaning, and the insurer will not be permitted to show that among insurance men it has acquired a peculiar meaning. Thus, in a New York case,[5] one condition of the policy was " the generating or evaporating

---

[1] *Waters* v. *Monarch Assurance Co.,* 5 El. & Bl. 870 ; *DeForest* v. *Fulton Fire Ins. Co.,* 1 Hall (N. Y.) 84 ; *Stilwell* v. *Staples,* 19 N. Y. 401.

[2] *Duwees* v. *Manhattan Ins. Co.,* 34 N. J. 244.

[3] *Cashan* v. *N. W., etc., Ins. Co.,* 5 Biss. (U. S.) 476 ; *Edwards* v. *Lycoming Ins. Co.,* 75 Penn. St. 878.

[4] *Cashan* v. *Ins. Co., ante.*

[5] *Arkell* v. *Commerce Ins. Co.,* 7 Hun (N. Y.) 454, aff'd Court of Appeals, April, 1877.

within the building *or contiguous thereto* of any substance for a burning gas, or the use of gasoline for lighting is prohibited, unless by special agreement, indorsed in this policy." The owners of the building insured, erected, at a distance at least fifty feet from the building, works for the purpose of manufacturing gas from gasoline, which gas was conducted to the building in pipes and other apparatus, and used for the purpose of lighting. The court held that this was not a violation of the condition mentioned. Fifty feet from the building was not contiguous, and the use of gas made from gasoline was not prohibited.

Contained in.

SEC. 77. When a policy describes the property as "*contained in*" a certain building, it is only at risk while in that building, and when elsewhere it is not covered by the policy. Thus, a policy covering two locomotives, "contained in car-house No. 1, and an engine, J. H. Nicholson, in engine-house No. 2," was held not to cover the engines except when in the respective buildings named. The words "contained in" were held to operate not as descriptive terms, but as a limitation of the risk.[1] But, where a number of buildings are used for the same purpose, by the same person, in the same enclosure, and together are called "*a mill*" or "*factory*," and the term applies to *all* collectively, a policy that describes the property as "contained in his factory" or "in his mill," will cover the property *in either or all of* the buildings.[2]

Deliver in.

SEC. 78. When a policy provides that in case of loss, the assured shall *deliver in* proofs of the same, or that he shall "*deliver in* a statement of the construction, etc.," of the building, it is held that the words bind the assured to perform the condition to which they relate *in writing*, but they do not impose upon the assured the burden of delivering them in person, but only by any of the ordinary and usual modes.[3]

Survey.

SEC. 79. The term survey, when used alone in a policy, is treated as including the application.[4] But in Massachusetts it is held to relate only to the description of the risk, and does not embrace the application.[5]

---

[1] *Annapolis, etc., R. R. Co.* v. *The Baltimore Fire Ins. Co.*, 32 Md. 37; 5 Bennett's F. I. C. 258.

[2] *Lichenstein* v. *Baltic, etc., Ins. Co.*, 45 Ill. 301; 5 Bennett's F. I. C. 115.

[3] *Davis* v. *The Scottish, etc., Ins. Co.*, 16 U. C. (C. P.) 176.

[4] *May* v. *Buckeye, etc., Ins. Co.*, 25 Wis. 291; *Glendale Manuf. Co.* v. *Protection Ins. Co.*, 21 Conn. 19.

[5] *Denny* v. *Conway, etc., Ins. Co.*, 13 Gray (Mass.) 497.

Sec. 80. The terms "hazardous," "extra hazardous," "specially hazardous," and "not hazardous," are well-understood technical terms in the business of insurance, having a distinct meaning. Although what goods are included in each designation may not be so known as to dispense with actual proof, the terms themselves are distinct, and known to be so; so that an insurance upon goods "hazardous" does not include goods "extra hazardous" or "specially hazardous;" and an insurance on goods "extra hazardous" does not include goods "specially hazardous." "Extra hazardous" and "specially hazardous" are not subdivisions or classifications of goods under the more general term "hazardous," but distinct classes of goods,[1] and when employed in a policy, and not limited in their application, are to be construed in their ordinary sense; but when the policy expressly classifies and defines the meaning placed upon the term by the insurer, as, where it contains a list of occupations or uses regarded as coming within the terms, *all others are excluded*, as where a policy prohibited the carrying on of any trade or business upon the premises, hazardous or extra hazardous, and also contained a list of trades under each head, regarded as coming within the respective classes; and also against storing goods, hazardous or extra hazardous, also enumerated, and the trade of a grocer was not among them, it was held that the business did not come within either class, and that no trades not enumerated would be regarded as coming under either head, for the "expression of one, was the exclusion of the other."[2] This rule is applied under various heads in insurance. Thus, when a policy limits its liability by excepting certain causes, against which it does not insure, *it is liable for all other causes of loss within the peril insured against*, for, having stated the particular perils for which it will not be liable, all other causes are excluded.[3] In an English case,[4] the policy covered plate glass "against damage from any cause except *fire, breakage during removal, alteration or repairs of premises*." A fire occurred upon adjoining premises, and slightly injured the rear of those in which the windows were situated. While the plaintiff was engaged, with others, in removing his stock to a safe place, a mob,

[1] *Pindar* v. *Continental Ins. Co.*, 38 N. Y. 364.
[2] *N. Y. Equitable Ins. Co.* v. *Langdon*, 6 Wend. (N. Y.) 623; *Pim* v. *Reid*, 6 M. & G. 1.
[3] *Insurance Co.* v. *Transportation Co.*, 12 Wall. (U. S.) 194; *Marsden* v. *City, etc., Assurance Co.*, L. R. 1, C. P. 232.
[4] *Marsden* v. *City, etc., Assurance Co., ante.*

attracted by the fire, broke down the shutters and broke in the windows for the purposes of plunder. It was held that the company were liable, *because the loss did not come within the exceptions.*

Occupied—Vacant.

SEC. 81. By the term *occupied,* in a policy, is meant a substantial use, for the purposes contemplated in the policy. Thus, where a dwelling-house and barn were insured under a policy which provided that "if the buildings shall be vacated, etc.," the policy should be void, it was held that, where the house was only used by the insured and his servants for the purpose of taking their meals when engaged in working a contiguous farm, and the barn was only used for storing hay and farming tools, the buildings were vacant within the meaning of the term.[1] "Occupancy," said COLT, J., "as applied to such buildings, implies an actual use of the house as a dwelling place, and such use of the barn *as is ordinarily incident to a barn belonging to an occupied house, or at least something more than its use for mere storage.*"

Keeping—storing.

SEC. 82. When a policy provides that the *keeping or storing* of certain articles shall avoid the policy, the words refer to an *habitual* and not a temporary or occasional presence of such article, or the occasional use of the premises for such purposes. Thus, in a Maryland case,[2] the policy prohibited the keeping of hazardous articles of any class, but permission was given to keep one barrel of benzine, and varnish in tin cans. A barrel of benzine was taken into the store in a wooden barrel and immediately emptied into a tin can, and the court held that this was not a keeping within the meaning of the condition.[3] A mere temporary deposit of such articles does not avoid the policy.[4]

Where a policy provides that the premises shall not be used for certain specified or hazardous purposes, the condition is construed to apply only to their *habitual* use for such purposes, and an occasional or accidental use for such purposes does not avoid the policy. Thus, a building insured as a granary, with a kiln for drying corn, was upon one occasion used *for drying bark,* and the court held that, although the policy provided that it should be forfeited if the trades carried on

---

[1] *Ashworth* v. *Builders' Ins. Co.,* 112 Mass. 422; Am. Rep. ; 5 Bennett's F. I. C. 497.

[2] *Maryland Fire Ins. Co.* v. *Whitford,* 31 Md. 219.

[3] See also *Hynds* v. *Schenectady Ins. Co.,* 11 N. Y. 554; *The City Fire Ins. Co.* v. *Corlies,* 21 Wend. (N. Y.) 367.

[4] *Hynds* v. *Schenectady Ins. Co., ante; Williams* v. *Fireman's Fire Ins. Co.,* 54 N. Y. 569.

therein were not correctly described, or if any alteration therein material to the risk should be made, without notice to the insurer, the policy
was not avoided, because the use for the drying of bark upon this single occasion, was not "carrying on a trade" other than that for which
the premises were insured, and, that although the premises were
destroyed while they were being so used, the insurers were liable.[1] So,
in a case where the policy described the property "where no fire is
kept and no hazardous goods are deposited," and upon one occasion a
fire was kindled in the building for the purpose of heating tar, with
which to repair the roof, it was held that the policy was not avoided,
*because the description of the ·use of the premises must be held to relate to
their habitual, rather than to an occasional or accidental use for a prohibited
purpose.*[2] So, where the policy prohibits the use of the premises for *a
hazardous business*, the use of hazardous articles therein for *heating or
lighting* the building, does not come within the condition. Thus, under
a policy containing such a provision, it was held that the use of gasoline for *lighting* the premises, was not *a hazardous business* within the
meaning of the condition.[3] So, where the keeping or use of certain
articles, as petroleum, is prohibited, it is held to refer to its use for
commercial purposes, and not to its use *for lighting the premises*, unless
its use for such purpose is expressly and in terms prohibited,[4] particularly where such article is customarily used for that purpose in the
community where the risk is situated.[5]

Policy covers entire building.

SEC. 83. A policy upon a building describing it as a dwelling-house,
covers the *entire building*, although a part of it is occupied for other
purposes. Thus, an application for a policy of insurance on a "dwelling-house and wood-house," described as "occupied for the usual purposes," covers a building, built at one time, with a single frame and
roof, and designed for one building, for a carriage-house and wood-
house, of which the wood-room constitutes two-thirds, and is separated
from the carriage-room by a loose partition extending to the eaves on

---

[1] *Shaw* v. *Robberds,* 6 Ad. & El. 75 ; 1 Bennett's F. I. C. 621 ; *Loud* v. *Citizens'
Ins. Co.,* 2 Gray (Mass.) 221 ; *Williams* v. *N. E. Ins. Co.,* 31 Me. 219 ; *Billings*
v. *Tolland Ins. Co., ante.*

[2] *Dobson* v. *Sotheby,* M. &. M. 90 ; 1 Bennett's F. I. C. 199 ; *Maryland, etc., Ins.
Co. v. Whitford,* 31 Md. 219 ; *Ins. Co.* v. *McDowell,* 50 Ill. 120 ; *Watson* v. *Farm
Building Association,* 9 Hun (N. Y.) 415 ; *Hartford Ins. Co.* v. *Harmer,* 2 Ohio
St. 452.

[3] *Coatsville Shoe Co.* v. *Ins. Co.,* 80 Penn. St. 176.

[4] *Morse* v. *Buffalo, etc., Ins. Co.,* 30 Wis. 534.

[5] *Morse* v. *Buffalo Ins. Co., ante.*

one side, and half way to the roof on the other; and does not exclude evidence that the whole building was called by the tenants and neighbors the wood-house, and a hog-pen and hen-house, from three and a half to six feet high, covered with boards, with a partition of boards between them, are not a building, within the meaning of an application for insurance which represents that there are no buildings not disclosed within a certain distance; and evidence that they increased the risk is inadmissible.[1] *A policy of insurance upon a building covers every part of it, everything that in any measure forms an essential element of it,* and this extends to and includes the foundation walls.[2] So it has been held that a policy upon a house covers the back buildings, although separated therefrom,[3] but it only covers the building *as such,* and does not cover the materials of which it is composed; therefore, if from any cause outside of the peril insured against, as by wind, explosion, earthquake, *or any cause,* the building falls in pieces, or so much of it, that it ceases to be a building, and afterwards a fire breaks out and destroys the materials, the loss is not one under the the policy.[4] But a cellar in a house is not regarded as a story thereof.[5]

Open policy on merchandise covers merchandise kept for sale only.

SEC. 84. An open policy upon "merchandise" only covers articles kept for sale, and does not extend to property kept upon the premises for use; but a policy upon "property," not specifying particularly what kind of property, will cover property of all kinds, whether kept for use or sale.[6]

Construction of pro rata clause in policies of re-insurance.

SEC. 85. When property is re-insured in part, and the policy of re-insurance contains a condition that the re-insurer shall pay the

---

[1] *White* v. *Mutual, etc., Assurance Co.,* 8 Gray (Mass.) 566.

[2] *Ervin* v. *N. Y. Central Ins. Co.,* T. & C. (N. Y.) 213.

[3] *Workman* v. *Louisiana Ins. Co.,* 2 La. (U. S.) 507.

[4] In *Nave* v. *Home Mut. Ins. Co.,* 37 Me. 430; 5 Ben. F. I. C. 88, the building insured was used as a warehouse, and being overloaded, or from some other cause without the agency of fire, it fell down and became a mass of rubbish. *After its fall,* a fire broke out and the materials were consumed. The court held that it was not a loss within the policy. "The subject insured," said HOLMES, J., "had ceased to be such, and became a mere congerie of materials before the fire occurred, *and by reason of a cause not insured against in the policy.* The maxim *causa proxima non remota spectatur,* has no application to such a case. If the fire had been the immediate cause of the destruction and the loss, then the remote causes of the fire might have been immaterial. The cause of the loss * * was not the fire, *but the fall.* That a fire sprung up afterwards in the rubbish and destroyed the fallen materials, was wholly another matter. *The materials were not insured. The building insured, no longer existed as such, and it ceased to exist by reason of a peril not insured against.*"

[5] *Benedict* v. *Ocean Ins. Co.,* 31 N. Y. 389.

[6] *Burgess* v. *Alliance Ins. Co.,* 10 Allen (Mass.) 221.

"loss, if any, *pro rata*, and at the same time with the re-insured," the re-insurer cannot be held to pay more than its *pro rata* share of the loss, *but actual payment of its share of the loss* by the re-insured, is not a condition precedent to payment by the re-insurer. The re-insurer must pay his share of the loss, whether the re-insured has paid, or has the ability to pay, its proportion of the loss or not. The re-insurer has no concern with the claim against the re-insured, except so far as to determine whether a valid claim exists against it therefor. The insolvency or inability of the re-insured to meet the loss, does not operate to defeat a recovery.[1] This was well illustrated in a recent New York case,[2] which was an action upon a policy of re-insurance, issued by defendant to the North American Insurance Co., of which company plaintiff is the receiver. The plaintiff's company issued a policy to K. & Co. for $5,000 upon a stock of goods. On the same day the defendant re-insured said company for $2,500 on the risk; the policy of re-insurance contained this clause: "Loss, if any, payable *pro rata* and at the same time with the re-insured." The property insured was destroyed by fire, and the loss adjusted at $4,407.62. The North American Insurance Company became insolvent, and the plaintiff, as receiver, declared dividends of forty-four per cent. on all claims against the company, and that per cent. is all that had been or would be paid to the original assured upon their policy. The plaintiff claimed to be entitled to recover one-half the amount of the loss, and the defendant claimed that it was only liable to pay one-half the amount actually paid to K. & Co. The court held that the defendant, by virtue of the first part of the clause, "Loss, if any, payable *pro rata* at the same time with the re-insured," was not bound to pay the full amount re-insured, but only one-half the loss; that by the latter part actual payment by the re-insured upon its policy was not required to precede or accompany payment by the defendant, but it merely fixed the time for payment, to wit., *the same time as was fixed for payment by the re-insured;* that the extent of the liability of the defendant was not affected by the insolvency of the re-assured, nor by the latter's inability to fulfill its contract with the original insured.[3]

---

[1] *Hone* v. *Mut. Safety Ins. Co.*, 1 Sandf. (N. Y.) 137; Affd. 2 N. Y. 235; *Blackstone* v. *Alemania Ins. Co.*, 56 N. Y. 105; *Eagle Ins. Co.* v. *La Fayette Ins. Co.*, 9 Ind. 443.

[2] *Blackstone* v. *Alemania Ins. Co.*, ante.

[3] A similar doctrine was held in *Consolidated, etc., Ins. Co.* v. *Cashaw*, 41 Md. 59, in which the insurers obtained re-insurance, "loss, if any, payable to them at same time and in same manner as they pay." A loss happened; and the insurers,

Sec. 86. It is not in all cases, where the legal title is not vested in the insurer, that the policy will be void because he represented the property as his. When the policy provides that, if the title is not absolute, it must be so stated in the policy, or it shall be void, the question is, first, *whether the insured had really an insurable interest in the property, and second, whether, if the property is destroyed, the entire loss falls upon him.* This was well illustrated in a Connecticut case,[1] in which the application described the property as "his house." The policy contained a condition that, "if the interest in the property is less than absolute, it must be so represented to the company, and expressed in the policy in writing; *otherwise the insurance shall be void.*" The legal title to the property was in another party, with whom the insured had, at the time of the application, made a parol contract for its purchase, for a price agreed upon, which the insured had agreed absolutely to pay, and a part of which he had paid, and the insured had entered into possession as purchaser, and had made valuable improvements on the property. Upon the claim of the insurance company, in a suit on the policy, that the insurance was void by reason of the omission of the insured to state in his application the condition of the title, the court charged the jury that the plaintiff was to be regarded as the owner of the property if he had the equitable title, and his interest was such that the loss would fall on him if the property was destroyed.

The court also charged the jury that *that is to be regarded as an absolute interest which is so completely vested in the party owning it, that he cannot be deprived of it without his consent.*

The plaintiff offered parol evidence to show that he stated to one H., an agent of the defendants, the exact facts as to the state of his title, and that H. filled out the application in his own language. It was held that the evidence was not inadmissible, on the ground that the parol statement was merged in the written one, since, so far as the latter varied from the former, it was the defendants' own mistake, of which they ought not to be allowed to take advantage, and which ought not to debar the plaintiff from showing that the statement which he actually made was in accordance with the truth. That it was also

---

being insolvent, paid to the assured only a dividend on the amount insured, *Held,* that the re-insurers were nevertheless liable for the whole amount of their insurance.

[1] *Hough* v. *City F. Ins. Co.*, 29 Conn. 10.

admissible as showing that the parties, upon the statement of the facts, agreed to consider and describe the property as the property of the plaintiff. And further, that, as the interest of the plaintiff was *in fact absolute*, the condition of the policy, which required a statement of it in writing only where not absolute, did not apply. The defendants claimed that H. was their agent only for certain definite purposes, and that he had no authority as such to fill out applications for parties applying for insurance. The defendants had recognized him in their policies as their agent, but there was no written evidence of the extent of his authority. Upon all the evidence, the court submitted the question as to the extent of his authority, wholly as one of fact to the jury, and it was held that this course was correct.

But, where the insured has neither a legal or equitable estate in the property insured, although the title is such that his creditors might compel an application of it upon his debts, as where he has conveyed the property to a third person without any consideration for the purpose of defrauding his creditors, a statement that the property is his, would be such a misstatement as would avoid the policy. Thus, where the plaintiff was insured in a mutual company by a policy which contained an express condition that the provisions of the by-laws should be a part of the contract of insurance. The by-laws provided that the written application for insurance should be a part of the policy, and should be held to be a warranty on the part of the insured, and that the policy should be void unless the true title and interest of the insured were stated in the application, and all incumbrances on the property disclosed, and unless the applicant should make a true statement of all facts inquired for in the application. The application contained the following inquiry : " Whose is the property insured, and is it incumbered, and for how much ? state the true title and interest." To this the plaintiff had replied : " Owned by me ; incumbered to several ; about $6,000." There were, in fact, mortgages on the property to the amount of $13,000, and the plaintiff had conveyed all his remaining interest to his brother by an absolute deed, both the deed and the mortgages appearing on the public records. The mortgages, however, beyond the $6,000, and the deed to the plaintiff's brother, were given without consideration, and for the purpose of defrauding creditors, and the brother had agreed to reconvey the title whenever requested. It was held that the answer of the plaintiff was to be taken as a warranty. That the conveyances being good between the parties, the the property was to be considered as incumbered beyond the amount stated by the plaintiff, and the plaintiff as having no title or insurable interest. That there could, therefore, be no recovery on the policy.

The court also held that the representation of the plaintiff with regard to the ownership of the property by him, was not relieved by the fact that the deed to his brother was made and placed on record without the knowledge of the latter, and that on being informed of the fact the grantee at first refused to receive it, and afterwards only agreed that the title might remain in him to be reconveyed whenever the plaintiff should desire; the deed being good between the parties, and the right to a reconveyance being one which a court of equity would not enforce.[1]

In a Michigan case,[2] the plaintiff brought an action upon a fire policy upon a barn situated on a farm. The insured, in his application, stated, in answer to a question, that he was owner of the buildings to be insured, and of the farm. The defense was that the answer was false. The evidence showed that the legal title to the farm was in his wife; that just before her marriage with the plaintiff her father bought the farm for her, paying $2,000 in cash, she giving back to the vendor a mortgage for $4,000 for the balance of the purchase price; that it was arranged between her, her father and the plaintiff, that the latter and his wife should go upon the farm, cultivate and improve it, care for and support the family, and pay off the incumbrance, and that she was thereupon, on request, to convey the farm to the plaintiff. At the time of the application he was carrying out this arrangement, had moved at once after the marriage upon the place, cultivated and improved it and made repairs, and paid the most of the incumbrance, and was proceeding in good faith to perform his part of the verbal arrangement. It was urged on behalf of the company that the arrangement between plaintiff, his wife and her father, did not amount to any contract, but left the plaintiff to go on or not, as he chose, and that therefore he had no equitable claim upon the property. The court held that the whole circumstance went to show an undertaking on the part of the insured to perform the verbal arrangement, and a part performance thereof in good faith on his part, which had gone so far that he could not retire from it without great loss, and that the ruling that he was upon the facts equitable owner was correct, and that as such he was entitled to insure, and that such ownership was sufficient to support the statement in the application.

---

[1] *Treadway* v. *Hamilton, etc., Ins. Co.*, 29 Conn. 68.
[2] *Farmers' Mut. Fire Ins. Co.* v. *Fogleman*, 2 Mich. Lawyer, 201.

A statement in an application, that the assured is the *owner* of the property, *is simply a warranty that he has an insurable interest* therein, and unless the species of title is expressly stated, it cannot be construed as a warranty that he has an absolute title thereto.[1] Unless the assured states *the kind of title* he has in the property, in his application, he is simply bound to show an insurable interest therein. Thus, where the application contained an inquiry whether the title was by warranty deed or bond, and the assured wrote " W. D.," it was held that this could not be construed as a warranty that the assured had a title in fee, and that if such a title as established an insurable interest in the assured existed, the warranty was met.[2]

It is a matter of no concern to the insurer *how* the assured acquired title to the property, the question is, whether at the time the insurance was entered into, and at the time of loss, he had a legal or equitable interest therein; if so, the fact that he acquired it by fraud, will not defeat the policy. There must a property interest exist however, and it follows that, if by reason of fraud, the sale or conveyance to him *is absolutely void*, he has no insurable interest in the property *because he has no title thereto*, but if the sale to him is merely voidable, on account of fraud, he has an insurable interest therein.[3]

A person who is called upon to state whether he is "the sole and unconditional owner" of the property, may properly reply in the affirmative, even though there is a mortgage outstanding thereon. The mortgagor *is the owner* of the property, until the title has passed to the mortgagee by proper proceedings of foreclosure. The ownership of the mortgagor is absolute, and depends upon no condition, and therefore may be said to be unconditional. His title is liable to and may be defeated upon the happening of certain events; but his ownership, until such events have been availed of to defeat his title or divest him thereof, is none the less unconditional.[4]

---

[1] *Rockford Ins Co.* v. *Nelson,* 65 Ill. 415.

[2] *Rockford Ins. Co.* v. *Nelson,* 65 Ill. 415.

[3] *Phœnix Ins. Co.* v. *Mitchell,* 67 Ill. 48.

[4] BECK, J., in *Hubbard* v. *Hartford Fire Ins. Co.,* 33 Iowa, 364; 11 Am. Rep. 125. A policy contained the condition that, "if the interest of the assured in the property be any other than the entire, unconditional and sole ownership of the property, for the use and benefit of the assured, it must be so represented to the company, and so expressed in the written part of this policy, otherwise the policy shall be void.". It was held, that under this condition the failure to represent and have so expressed in the written part of the policy, the fact that incumbrances by way of mortgage existed upon the insured building at the time of the insurance did not avoid the policy. *Clay F. & M. Stock Ins. Co.* v. *Beck,* 43 Md. 64; *Conover* v. *Mut. Ins. Co.,* 3 Den. (N. Y.) 254; 1 N. Y. 290; *Rollins* v. *Columbian,*

Where a policy provides that, "if the interest of the assured in the property, whether as owner, factor, agent, mortgagee, lessee, or otherwise, is not truly stated in this policy, this policy shall be void," an *assignee* of the mortgage properly describes his interest by representing it as that of mortgagee.[1] Thus, in the case last referred to, the policy contained such a condition. It appeared that the assured was the *assignee* of the motgagees, and his interest in the policy was described as mortgagee, which the insurers insisted was a misdescription of his interest in the property. The court held otherwise. GRAY, J., in passing upon the question, said : "It is admitted that Little & Stanton are the assured in this policy, and that the plaintiff is only the person to whom any sum recoverable under it is to be paid.[2] Upon the facts agreed by the parties, two questions have been argued; 1st. Whether Little & Stanton had an insurable interest; 2d. Whether, if they had, that interest is well described in the policy. 1. In the present state of the law, there can be no doubt that, at the time of procuring this policy, Little & Stanton, although they had no legal title in the property, had an equitable right and an insurable interest therein. The mortgage stood as security for the payment of the mortgage notes, and the assured, having themselves indorsed those notes at the time of assigning the mortgage, would be entitled in equity, upon being charged on those notes and paying the amount thereof, to have the mortgage reassigned to them, to secure reimbursement from the original makers of the notes and mortgage.[3] In Gordan v. Massachusetts Ins. Co.,[4] one who had made an absolute bill of sale of a vessel, and taken back an agreement in writing from the purchasers to apply the proceeds of the vessel to the payment of certain notes and obligations due from him and indorsed by them, was held to have retained an insurable interest in the vessel. In Strong v. Manufacturers' Ins. Co.,[5] it was held that a mortgagor of real estate, whose equity of redemption had been seized and sold on execution,

---

etc., Ins. Co., 25 N. H. 206 ; *Shepherd* v. *Union, etc., Ins. Co.,* 38 id. 232 ; *Pollard* v. *Somerset, etc., Ins. Co.,* 42 Mo. 221 ; *Norcross* v. *Ins. Co.,* 17 Penn. St. 429 ; *Williams* v. *Roger Williams Ins. Co.,* 107 Mass. 377 ; 9 Am. Rep. 41.

[1] *Williams* v. *Roger Williams Ins. Co., ante.*

[2] *Loring* v. *Manufacturers' Ins. Co.,* 8 Gray (Mass.) 28 ; *Bates* v. *Equitable Ins. Co.,* 10 Wall. (U. S.) 33.

[3] *Eastman* v. *Foster,* 8 Metc. 19 ; *Bryant* v. *Damon,* 6 Gray (Mass.) 564 ; *Rice* v. *Dewey,* 13 id. 47 ; *New Bedford Institution for Savings* v. *Fairhaven Bank,* 9 Allen (Mass.) 175 ; *Matthews* v. *Aikin,* 1 N. Y. 595.

[4] 2 Pick. 249.

[5] 10 Pick. 40.

had still, so long as the time of redeeming from such sale had not expired, an insurable interest in the premises. And it is now well established that even one who has no title, legal or equitable, in the property, and no present possession or right of possession thereof, yet has an insurable interest therein, if he will derive benefit from its continuing to exist, or will suffer loss by its destruction.[1] We are also of opinion that the interest of the assured was sufficiently described in the policy. In the absence of any specific inquiry by the insurers, or express stipulation in the policy, no particular description of the nature of the insurable interest would have been necessary.[2] By a familiar rule of construction, the provisions requiring a statement of the nature of the interest of the assured, being inserted by the insurers for their own benefit, are to be strictly construed against them. The second of the provisions relied on merely required that, if the interest of the assured was any other than the entire, unconditional and sole ownership of the property for the use and benefit of the assured, it should be so represented and expressed; and the description of the assured in the policy as 'mortgagees' clearly represented and expressed that they had not such entire, unconditional and sole ownership. The first provision required that the interest of the assured in the property, whether as owner, trustee, consignee, factor, agent, mortgagee, lessee, or otherwise, should be truly stated in the policy, and the statement that they were mortgagees truly stated to which of these classes their interest belonged. This provision does not call for a distinction between legal and equitable title, but only for a true statement of the nature of the insurable interest; and that interest was the same, whether the title of the assured was legal or equitable.[3] The description, therefore, satisfied the terms of both of the provisions of the policy."

Where the policy provides that " if the interest in property to be insured be a leasehold interest, or other interest not absolute, *it must be so represented to the company and expressed in the policy in writing*, otherwise the insurance shall be void," the owner of the equity of redemption in premises may properly be described as owner.[4] Thus, in the

[1] *Putnam* v. *Mercantile Ins. Co.*, 5 Metc. (Mass.) 386; *Eastern R. R. Co.* v. *Relief Ins. Co.*, 98 Mass. 420, 423, and other cases there cited; *Springfield Ins. Co.* v. *Brown*, 43 N. Y. 389.
[2] *Strong* v. *Manufacturers' Ins. Co.*, 10 Pick. (Mass.) 40; *King* v. *State Ins. Co.*, 7 Cush. (Mass.) 1, 13; *Springfield Ins. Co.* v. *Brown*, 43 N. Y. 389.
[3] *Swift* v. *Vermont Ins. Co.*, 18 Vt. 305; *Hough* v. *City Ins. Co.*, 29 Conn. 10; *Gaylord* v. *Lamar Ins. Co.*, 40 Mo. 13.
[4] *Washington Fire Ins. Co.* v. *Kelly*, 32 Md. 421; 3 Am. Rep. 149.

case last cited, a policy was issued upon the conditions that if the interest of the assured in the property was a leasehold interest, or other interest not absolute, the company should be so informed at the time of contracting the insurance, or the policy would be void; and that a sale or conveyance of the property, or an assignment of any interest in the policy without the consent of the company, would render the policy void. The insured at the time the insurance was negotiated, was the owner of an equity of redemption only, with possession of the property insured; but no mention of that fact was made. Subsequently, the insured entered into a contract for the sale of the property under which he received a part of the purchase-money, but continued in possession and held insurance policies for the benefit of the vendee. A total loss, by fire, of the property, afteward occurred; and, in an action on the policy by the assignee of the assured, it was held that there was no misdescription of interest.

Where a policy contains such a condition, as to the statement of the interest of the assured, and at the time of its issue, the interest of the assured was misdescribed in the policy; but before its renewal, he became possessed of such an interest in the property, as is described in the policy, the breach is cured, *for by the renewal, the policy is to be treated as written on the day of renewal*, and the interest being correctly expressed at that time, there is no breach of the condition.[1]

---

[1] In *Noyes* v. *The Hartford F. Ins. Co.*, 54 N. Y. 668, the policy contained this clause: "If the assured is not the sole and unconditional owner of the property insured, or if said property be a building or buildings of the land on which said building or buildings stand, by a sole and unconditional ownership and title, and is not so expressed in the written portion of the policy," then the same should be void. The original paper was issued December 28, 1866, for twenty days; it was renewed January 17, 1867, for twenty days more. The plaintiffs were partners in the cotton-growing business. On the 15th January, 1866, they made an agreement with one Flournoy to operate his plantation in Arkansas for one year. Plaintiffs were to furnish supplies and stock to the amount of $10,000; the implements and stock on the plantation were to remain and be used, and whatever more was required plaintiffs were to furnish. Flournoy was to supervise and attend to the work on the plantation, and was to make all permanent improvements. The crop of cotton was to be delivered to plaintiffs at the river bank to be transported to market and sold. The proceeds were to be used: 1st, To reimburse plaintiffs for all advances, and the balance of the net proceeds to be divided equally between their firm and Flournoy. At the expiration of one year, the stock and implements were also to be equally divided. In pursuance of this agreement, plaintiffs repaired the gin-house and put in a new gin and press and mule power. The cotton was picked and a portion sent to market. On the 18th January, 1867, while a portion was in the gin-house, a fire occurred, consuming it and its contents. Plaintiffs recovered below for loss on cotton, $2,812.50; on account of the mule power, under the head of repairs to the gin-house, $425, and for gin and press, $600. Held, that by the terms of the agreement, plaintiffs were not necessarily the sole and unconditional owners of the cotton, but that they were either partners or tenants in common with Flournoy in carrying on the plantation. But it appearing that plaintiffs had expended more than the whole

So, a person in possession of premises under a contract of purchase, under which only a part of the purchase-money has been paid, may properly describe his interest as that of "owner," and the condition of the policy as to statement of interest is not broken.[1]

Possession of real or personal property claiming it as owner, is *prima facie* evidence of title, and all presumptions are made in its support, and if the insurer sets up want of title in the assured, he takes the burden of establishing, not only that the assured had no title in the property, but also, that he had no insurable interest therein.[2] The issuance of a policy to a person is *prima facie* evidence of his title to the premises, and unless questioned, is conclusive.[3]

A statement by the insured that he is a mortgagee in possession, without stating that he is in possession under a first mortgage, and that there are other subsequent mortgages upon the property, will not avoid the policy, particularly where their interest is greater than the amount of the policy. The company by accepting a general answer to an interrogatory as to whether the property is incumbered, without making any question as to the *amount* thereof, is treated as waiving any objection to the answer on the ground of insufficiency, and cannot subsequently, in an action upon the policy, set up the insufficiency of such answer as a defense.[4]

This doctrine was well expressed by Lord MANSFIELD, in a celebrated case,[5] where the defendant who had issued a policy of £10,000 to the plaintiff upon a fort, in the East Indies, insuring it against capture for one year, resisted payment, upon the ground that the plaintiff had not fully informed him of the weakness of the fort

---

crop of cotton was worth, and as therefore they were entitled, under the contract, to the entire proceeds, and Flournoy had no interest therein, within the spirit and meaning of the policy, they were the sole and unconditional owners and entitled to recover the loss. But that as to the gin and press, they were a portion of the stock in which Flournoy had, under the agreement, an equal interest with their firm ; that the policy was to be treated as written on the day of its renewal, and the year having then expired, Flournoy was then tenant in common with them ; that they were therefore, not the sole owners, and were not entitled to recover ; that the mule power was not part of the gin-house, and could in no way be classed as repairs thereto, and was not covered by the policy, but if it was, it was simply as a portion of the stock, and did not belong solely to plaintiffs, and they could not recover therefor.

[1] *Lorrilard Fire Ins. Co.* v. *McCulloch*, 21 Ohio St. 176 ; 8 Am. Rep. 52.

[2] *Franklin Ins. Co.* v. *Chicago Ice Co.*, 36 Md. 102 ; 11 Am. Rep. 169.

[3] *Fowler* v. *N. Y. Ins. Co.*, 23 Barb. (N. Y.) 156 ; *Levan* v. *Liv., Lon. & Globe Ins. Co.*, 52 Mass. 704 ; *Nichols* v. *Fayette Ins. Co.*, 1 Allen (Mass.) 63.

[4] *Nichols et al.* v. *Fayette Mut. Ins. Co.*, 1 Allen (Mass.) 63 ; *Wyman* v. *People's Equitable Ins. Co.* 1 id. 301 ; *Liberty Hall Association* v. *Housatonic M. F. Ins. Co.*, 7 Gray (Mass.) 261.

[5] *Carter* v. *Bochm*, 3 Burr. 1905.

and the dangers to which it was subjected. It appeared that no questions were asked in reference to the fort, or the dangers to which it was exposed, and that eminent jurist, in passing upon the validity of the defense, said : " If the objection that he was not told is sufficient to vacate it, he took the premium *knowing the policy to be void*, in order to *gain*, if the alternative turned out one way, and to make *no satisfaction* if it turned out the other. He drew the governor into a false confidence, that if the worst should happen, he had provided against total ruin, *knowing* at the same time that the indemnity to which he trusted was void. There was not a word said to him of the affairs of India, or the state of the war there, or the condition of Fort Maulborough. *If he thought that omission an objection at the time, he ought not to have signed the policy with a secret reserve in his own mind to make it void. If he dispensed with the information, and did not think this silence an objection then, he cannot take it up now after the event.'* It must be remembered, however, that there is a wide distinction between a case where no information was asked, or given, in reference to the risk, and one where the assured is called upon for information, but fails to disclose matters *material to the risk.*

When forfeiture is waived.

SEC. 87. Whenever the insurer, *with knowledge* of any act of the assured that works a forfeiture, does any act that shows that he recognizes his liability under the policy as an outstanding obligation ; as, when he accepts a premium for a renewal of the policy, or for any increase of risk, the forfeiture is waived, and the policy remains operative.[1]

---

[1] In *N. Berwick Co.* v. *N. E. F. & M. Ins. Co.*, 52 Me. 336 ; 4 Bennett's F. Ins. Cas., 790, in answer to an interrogatory, "During what hours is the factory worked?" the assured replied, "usually from 6¼ A. M. to 12½ P. M., and 1 to 7 in summer; from 6¾ A. M. to 12½ P. M., and 1 to 7 P. M. in winter; short time now." After August 1st the mill was run all night, and October 19 the plaintiff applied to the defendants' agent for permission to run nights. October 29 the agent informed the plaintiffs that the insurers would give permission on payment of ⅜ per cent. additional premium for three months. These terms were acceded to and the premium paid, and permission given, dated and taking effect from November 1st. A loss having occurred after such consent was given, the company insisted that they were not liable therefor, as the policy was avoided by running all night, without consent, from August to November. But the court held, that the acceptance of the additional premium, *with knowledge of the forfeiture* on the part of the insurers' agent, was a waiver of the forfeiture, and reinstated the policy. APPLETON, C.J., said: "The defendants insist that the answer to the seventeenth interrogatory is a warranty on the part of the plaintiffs that their factory is not to be run nights, and that having been broken by running from August 1 to 19th of October, the policy thereby became void; and that thus they are absolved from all legal obligation. The defendants were not harmed by the running of the mill all night between the 1st of August and the 24th of October,

But where the additional premium is received, or other act relied upon to reinstate the policy is done, *without knowledge of the forfeiture by the insurer, the act cannot have that effect.*

In a Vermont case,[1] the plaintiffs procured an insurance upon their factory in Bennington, Vt. An application was made by them in writing, which formed a part of the policy, and in which the plaintiffs described the risk and gave the number of stoves used. But they

---

when their agent stated to the plaintiffs the extra premium he should require for such running. From the answer to the seventeenth interrogatory, it may fairly be inferred that it was expected that at times the mill would be run nights. Whether such running, unattended with loss, would render the plaintiffs' policy void, it is neither necessary to consider nor to determine. A forfeiture is to be construed strictly. Its enforcement is not to be favored. It may be waived by the acts and conduct of the party whose right it is to exact it. The renewal of a policy, after the existence of facts which would authorize the insurer to insist upon a forfeiture would be deemed a waiver. Thus the forfeiture, by reason of a misrepresentation or concealment, may be waived by the insurers ; *as by receiving a new premium on a fire policy, after the misrepresentation is known.* 1 Phil. on Insurance, § 668 ; *Allen* v. *Vermont Mut. Fire Ins. Co.*, 12 Vermont, 366. *So the act of receiving an additional premium for the variation of a risk must, in the absence of fraud or concealment, be regarded as having the same effect.* It would be a gross fraud to receive a premium for the continuance of a policy or the variation of a risk, with the intention of avoiding the insurance, if the risk provided for should occur, and of retaining the premium in case it should not. The agent of the defendants testified he knew the plaintiffs had been running their mill nights when he gave his permission of November 1, 1861. In his letter to the defendants of November 2, he writes : 'They had been working night and day for some time. They wrote me a few days ago for a permit to work day and night, and agreed to keep a watchman.' The extra premium for permission to run the mill nights was received by the defendants after the loss, and without objection. No complaint appears to have been made on their part of any concealment or misrepresentation on the part of the plaintiffs or of their agent. Nor is this all. The defendants, by their power of attorney under seal, appointed John P. Slade, of Fall River, their agent ; 'and, as such agent, he is authorized and empowered to receive proposals for insurance against loss or damage by fire, and *to make* insurances by policies of said New England Fire and Marine Insurance Company of Hartford ; *to renew* the same, or *to vary the risk,* according to the rules and instructions he shall from time to time receive from the said company. And all policies of insurance against loss or damage by fire, *issued by* said agent, shall be to *all intents* valid and binding upon the said New England Fire and Marine Insurance Company of Hartford.' There is no proof that the agent has violated any rules or regulations he may have received from the defendants. His authority is most ample. He may issue policies. He may renew them. He may vary the risk. His *acts* are 'to all intents valid and binding' on the defendants. Notice to him must be deemed notice to the company. The insured had a right to rely on his acts. Indeed, it has been held that a general agent may waive, under some circumstances, a condition in the policy that no insurance shall be considered as binding till actual payment. *Sheldon* v. *Atlantic F. & M. Ins. Co.*, 26 N. Y. 460, *ante.* Much more would he be deemed to have such right, when powers as ample as in the present case are conferred. In the policy on the personal property there is found no limitation as to the time plaintiffs were to run their mill. The plaintiffs might therefore, so far as regards this risk, run their mill the maximum of time. The two policies have no connection. Each must be construed by itself. The instructions in this respect were correct. There was no increase of risk within the meaning of the policy—for the plaintiffs were under no restrictions by its terms as to the time they might run their mill."

[1] *Allen, Safford & Co.* v. *Vermont Mut. Fire Ins. Co.*, 12 Vt. 336 ; 2 Bennett's F. I. C. 13.

12

omitted to state that an apparatus for manufacturing sizing was used in the building in which fire was used, and which was employed once and sometimes twice a week. It appeared that, prior to the loss, but *after* the policy was issued, the defendant company sent their agent to Bennington to examine the factories as to their safety and internal construction, and, that, *after* the agent had discharged this duty, the defendant made a call upon the plaintiffs for an assessment of $44 upon the policy, and the plaintiffs insisted that, even though the policy was void in its inception, yet, that the acceptance of such sum, *after* the agent had performed this mission, operated as a waiver of the forfeiture, and rendered the policy valid and operative. The plaintiffs had a verdict under the charge of the trial judge, but upon appeal it was set aside, BENNETT, J., announcing the doctrine applicable in such cases, thus: He said—" This case involves several important questions, and some of them are not without considerable difficulty. It has been argued at great length and with much ability; but, from the shortness of the time allowed us for an examination, we are not prepared, at this time, to come to a conclusion on all the questions which the case presents. There is, however, one point upon which the court are all satisfied that the defendants must have a new trial, and we are, therefore, induced to decide the case on that single point, leaving all other questions open. It seems, after this policy had been executed, and after the company had sustained a loss on some other factory insured by them at Bennington, the company passed a vote directing that a member of the company should be appointed to go and examine the loss at Bennington, and also examine the factories as to their safety and internal construction; and Thomas Reed was, on the second day of February, 1836, appointed to perform this duty. It appears, also, that evidence was given to the jury tending to prove that, in pursuance of said vote, an agent of the company visited Bennington and examined the factories there, and that subsequently the company received of the plaintiffs an installment of $44 on the policy in question. On this part of the case, the jury were told that if they found that the agent of the company went *in pursuance of the vote of the company to the factory in question*, and the company afterwards received the installment, the defendants were liable on the policy of insurance, although they should find that the sizing apparatus was material to the risk, and had been omitted in the application. This was evidently incorrect.

The vote of the company did not contemplate that the agent

THE POLICY.

should examine the factories ' as to their safety and internal construction ' with a view of comparing them with the applications, in order to
enable the company to decide whether any of the policies were fraudulent. The object seemed to be to make a general examination of
them, and there is no evidence that the agent even knew what the
representation was, as specified in the application, upon which the
policy in question was executed. *There is no evidence that the agent
ever saw, or had any knowledge of the existence of, the sizing apparatus.
The jury were not, by the instructions given them, required to find such
knowledge.* The court say, if the agent, in pursuance of the vote of the
company, went to the factory in question, and the company afterwards
received the installment, it is sufficient. It is not necessary to decide
whether, if this policy was obtained through the fraudulent suppression of what was material to the risk, it was competent for the company to waive the objection by subsequent matter, so as to render
valid the policy. *If the agent had been clothed with power to examine as
to the validity of the policy, it is clear that the reception of a subsequent
installment could not operate as a waiver of such suppression, unless the
agent had knowledge, at the time of the payment, of the fact suppressed.
This knowledge, the jury should, at least, have been told they must find,
before they could give any effect to the reception of the installment."* On this
ground, the judgment of the county court was reversed, and the cause
remanded for a new trial.

Conditions. Company estopped from setting up breach of, when.

SEC. 88. It is well settled by the weight of authority, that, where a
policy is issued containing conditions *inconsistent with the facts, and the
agent knew the facts when the policy was issued, the conditions are waived so
far as they conflict with the facts known to the agent;* [1] *and this is peculiarly
the case where the agent fills up the application erroneously, when the facts
were correctly stated to him by the assured. In such cases, the doctrine of
estoppel has a very just application, as, if it was not permitted to apply,
an innocent party would be made to suffer.* [2] But it is possible that this

[1] *Ætna Ins. Co.* v. *Maguire,* 51 Ill. 342; *Miner* v. *Ins. Co.,* 27 Wis. 693; *Mechler*
v. *Ins. Co.,* 38 id. 665; *Winans* v. *Ins. Co.,* 38 id. 342.

[2] *Rowley* v. *Empire Ins. Co.,* 36 N. Y. 550; *Bodine* v. *Ins. Co.,* 51 N. Y. 117;
N. W. Mut. Life Ins. Co. v. *The Germania Fire Ins. Co.,* 40 Wis. 446; *Meadow-
craft* v. *Ins. Co.,* 61 Penn. St. 91; *Mechler* v. *Ins. Co., ante; New England, etc.,
Ins. Co.* v. *Schettler,* 38 Ill. 166; *Lycoming, etc., Ins. Co.* v. *Sailer,* 67 Penn. St.
108; *Miller* v. *Ins. Co.,* 31 Iowa, 116; *Aurora Ins. Co.* v. *Eddy, ante; Ætna Ins.
Co.* v. *Olmstead,* 21 Mich. 246; *Ins. Co.* v. *Lyons,* 38 Tex. 271; *Reaper Ins. Co.*
v. *Jones,* 62 Ill. 458; *Masters* v. *Madison, etc., Ins. Co.,* 11 Barb. (N. Y.) 624; *Ins.
Co.* v. *Wilkinson,* 13 Wall. (U. S.) 222; *American, etc., Ins. Co.* v. *McLanathan,* 11

is subject to the qualification that, where the policy expressly provides
that the agent shall be considered the agent of the assured, and not
the agent of the insurers under any circumstances, the assured is liable for the mistakes of the agent.[1] But we have taken occasion to
question the correctness of this rule, *except where the assured, at the time
when the application was made, knew of this provision of the policy.* And
it seems to be subject to still another exception that, where the agent
is required by the assured to fill up the application, he cannot, under
any circumstances, be regarded as the agent of the insured.[2] Indeed
in some of the cases it has been held that, even where the assured
pays the agent for making an examination of the property, and filling
up the application, he is still to be treated as the agent of the insurer.[3]

Vacant Premises.

SEC. 89. When the policy specially provides that in case the premises
" shall be left unoccupied," [4] " or shall remain unoccupied," [5] or shall

---

Kan. 549; *Franklin* v. *Ins. Co.*, 42 Mo. 457; *Woodbury Savings Bank* v. *Ins. Co.*,
31 Conn. 517; *Ætna Ins. Co.* v. *Maguire, ante; N. A. Ins. Co.* v. *Throop*, 22
Mich. 159; *Malleable Iron Works* v. *Ins. Co.*, 25 Conn. 465; *Beebe* v. *Ins. Co.*, 25
id. 51; *Clark* v. *Ins. Co.*, 40 N. H. 333; *Combs* v. *Ins. Co.*, 43 Mo. 148; *Cheek* v.
Ins. Co., 1 Cent. L. J. 465; *Harris* v. *Ins. Co.*, 18 Ohio, 116; *Campbell* v. *Ins. Co.*,
37 N. H. 35, *ante; Guardian Life Ins. Co.* v. *Hogan*, 80 Ill. 35; *Roberts* v. *Continental Ins. Co.*, 41 Wis. 321.

[1] *Rohrback* v. *Ins. Co., ante.*

[2] *Sprague* v. *Holland Purchase Ins. Co., ante.*

[3] *Patten* v. *Merchants', etc., Ins. Co.*, 40 N. H. 375. In *Clark* v. *Union Mut.
Ins. Co.*, 40 id. 333, the assured applied to the defendant's agent for insurance,
and, as he was unable to describe the premises, he told the agent that, if he
would go and examine them he would pay him for doing so. The court held that
the agent still remained the agent of the insurer, and that, too, notwithstanding
the by-laws, made a part of the policy, provided that the agent taking the application should be the agent of the assured.

[4] In *Paine* v. *Agricultural Ins. Co.*, 5 T. & C. (N. Y.) 619, where a policy of
insurance against fire, upon a dwelling-house, contained a provision that if the
house should be "left unoccupied, without giving immediate notice to the company, the policy should cease and be of no force or effect," it was held that the
absence of the one who resided in the house, without notice to the company, for
six weeks, although he frequently returned and looked after the house, and the
furniture and goods all remained therein, would avoid the policy. Occupation of
a dwelling-house, according to the view of the court, *is living in it, not mere
supervision over it,* and while a person need not live in it every moment, *there must
not be a cessation of occupancy for any considerable portion of time.* In this case,
a person living near by visited the house frequently and maintained a general
oversight and care over it, but this was held not to take the case out of the operation of the forfeiting clause. The following authorities were relied upon to sustain
the decision: *Wustman* v. *City Fire Ins. Co.*, 15 Wis. 138; *Harrison* v. *City Fire
Ins. Co.*, 9 Allen (Mass.) 231; *Keith* v. *Quincy Mut. Fire Ins. Co.*, 10 id. 228.
But if there is no express stipulation that the premises shall not be left vacant,
the policy will not be void. *Camwell* v. *Merchants and Farmers' Mut. Fire Ins.
Co.*, 12 Cush. (Mass.) 167.

[5] *Keith* v. *Quincy Mut. F. Ins. Co.*, 10 Allen (Mass.) 228.

"become vacant,"¹ or "unoccupied,"² or shall be vacated,³ or "shall become vacant *or* unoccupied,"⁴ or "shall be vacant or unoccupied when insured."⁵ *A practical occupancy consistent with the purposes or uses for which it was insured, is intended, and an occupancy that measur-ably lessens the vigilance and care that would be incident to its use for such purposes,* is not an occupancy within the meaning of the term as thus employed. *The intent of the parties in respect to occupancy is to be gathered from the usual and ordinary use of the premises for the purposes to which they are devoted.*⁶

---

¹ *Cummins* v. *Agricultural Ins. Co.*, 5 Hun (N. Y.) 554; *Cane* v. *Niagara Ins. Co.*, 3 T. & C. (N. Y.) 33, affd. 60 N. Y. 619.

² *Ætna Ins. Co.* v. *Burns*, 5 Ins. L. J. 69; *Wustman* v. *City Fire Ins. Co.*, 15 Wis. 138.

³ *Hartford Fire Ins. Co.* v. *Walsh*, 54 Ill. 164; *Ashworth* v. *Builders' Mut. F. Ins. Co.*, 112 Mass. 422.

⁴ *American Ins. Co.* v. *Padfield*, 8 Chicago Leg. News 138.

⁵ *Thayer* v. *Agricultural Ins. Co.*, 5 Hun (N. Y.) 556.

⁶ In *Whitney* v. *Black River Ins. Co.*, 9 Hun (N. Y.) 39, LEARNED, P.J., in a very able opinion, elucidates and applies this doctrine, in the case of a saw mill, and his opinion is so valuable upon this point that I give it entire. He says: "Three defenses are set up in the answer: non-occupation of the mill; increase of risk, after the issue of the policy, by using a planing mill; excessive valuation at the time of obtaining the policy. Of the last there seems to be no evidence. The testimony as to the price paid for the premises might have aided the referee in determining the value; but there is no finding on this point. The clause in the policy on which the second defense depends, is, 'If the above mentioned premises shall be occupied or used so as to increase the risk.' The policy was issued May 28, 1872. There had been a planing machine on the premises, connected with the saw-mill, before December, 1871, and it was there when the policy was issued. There was no change afterwards. The planing machine had been used before. Goodno, the defendant's agent, had been on the premises before the policy was issued; he had a general knowledge of insurable property at Morley (where these premises were), including the mill. There was no concealment of the machine. The defense set up is not false representation, or a warranty as to the mode of use of the building. It is, that after the policy was obtained, the risk was increased. This must mean that, by some act of the plaintiff, the risk became greater than it was at the time of insurance. Several cases are cited by the defendants showing that where there is a warranty as to the present or the future use of the premises, and such warranty is broken, the insured cannot recover. *Mead* v. *North. Ins. Co.*, 7 N. Y. 530; *Wall* v. *E. R. M. Ins. Co.*, 7 id. 370 In a later case (*Smith* v. *H. M. and T. F. Ins. Co.*, 32 N Y. 399), it was held that the description of the premises was a warranty of their present, not of their future use. But it is not necessary to consider what the warranty is. The defense is not made to depend upon it, but upon an actual increase of the existing risk. If the use of the planer was a breach of the warranty contained in the description of the premises then, as was said in the case last cited, the warranty would have been broken *in presenti*. But the defendants do not claim this; they assert only that, by a subsequent act, the risk was increased, contrary to the condition of the policy. The defendants evidently appreciated this, because they asked leave to set up an amended answer containing allegations of fraudulent misrepresentation as to the condition of the property in respect to this planer; and leave was refused. The third defense is, that the premises were 'vacant and unoccupied,' from April 1 to May 16, 1873. The referee finds that the mill had been used as a custom mill and to saw the owner's lumber; that in the winter of 1873 one man did most of the sawing; that the gang broke down in February, 1873; that some work was

Where the policy provides that "if the premises shall be vacated, in whole or in part," the policy shall be void, the condition is binding upon the assured, and if they are left "vacant," within the meaning of the term, for any time, *and are burned while so vacated*, no recovery can be had upon the policy.[1]

---

done by the English gate until April seventh, when a portion of the belts were taken to the plaintiff's store, and no more sawing was done until the last days of April, when the belts were taken back and two to four days of sawing was done; that no more use was made of saws or machinery till the fire; that the plaintiff's men were occasionally at work about the mill handling lumber, and a few sales of lumber were made from the mill after April seventh. At the time of the fire there were about 100 logs remaining at the mill yard, and about 160 standard logs about 100 rods above the mill, intended to be cut at the mill. The referee finds that the premises did not become vacant and unoccupied. *The words 'vacant and unoccupied' must be construed with reference to the kind of structure or building on the premises.* 'Occupation of a dwelling-house is living in it.' *Paine* v. *Ag. Ins. Co.*, 5 N. Y. S. C. R. 619. But people do not live in a saw-mill. In *Keith* v. *Quincy Fire Ins. Co.*, 10 Allen, 231, the plaintiff closed up a trip-hammer shop, the property insured, and it was held to be vacant. A shop of that kind, ordinarily, has people working in it on every working day. A saw-mill is different. If a custom mill it must depend on the logs brought to it for business. In any case, when driven by water power, it must rely on the supply of water, and must be idle when that fails. Nor does it appear to me that the intent of the owner is of any use in determining the question of mere vacancy of the building. A house is none the less vacant because the owner intends to occupy it again. And, in like manner, if a saw-mill can properly be said to be vacant and unoccupied in any case, then, if for want of water it lies idle a week, it is vacant, although the owner is ready to resume work as soon as he can. I cannot think that such should be taken to have been the meaning of the parties. Of course the policy is the contract between the parties. But still, in construing this contract, it is just to notice that this condition, on which the defendants rely, is contained in those two or more, finely (almost microscopically) printed pages which follow the written part of the insurance policies, and which, probably, no insured person ever reads. It is especially necessary, therefore, that the written part should control the printed; and it seems to be hardly possible to apply the words, 'vacant and unoccupied,' with the meaning which they ordinarily have, to a saw-mill like this, driven by water power. If a few days of non-user of the saw-mill are to be construed to avoid the policy, that construction seems incon-sistent with the contingencies of use, which must have been contemplated by the parties who had knowledge of the nature of the property. Perhaps there might be such entire abandonment of the mill as would be, in respect to such property, equivalent to the closing and leaving unoccupied of a dwelling-house. But I think that such abandonment was not proved; that the referee correctly decided that this defense was not made out. The defendants, while examining one of their own witnesses, offered to show that plaintiff had endeavored to prevent him from testifying. The plaintiff objected, but subsequently this testimony was admitted, so that the defendants are not injured. Evidence of arrears due from the property, to maintain the dam, was excluded. This was not error. A lien on the property did not tend to show an overvaluation. The defendants insist that proofs of an arrangement made by the plaintiff for logs to stock the mill was improperly received to show absence of intent to abandon. They say that there is no question of intent, but only a question of practical vacancy and non-occupation. I think, as above stated, that this view is correct whenever the words 'vacant and unoccupied' can accurately be applied as to a house or shop. But in regard to such property as a saw-mill, as already stated, if these words can be applied at all, it seems to me they can only be used as expressing an abandonment; and to this the intent of the owner is material."

[1] *Franklin Savings Institution* v. *Central, etc., Ins. Co.*, 119 Mass. 240.

Where a policy provides that, in case the premises shall be "vacated," immediate notice thereof shall be given or the policy shall be void, a substantial occupancy is referred to, and intended; and a person who removes his family from a dwelling-house, cannot save a policy with such a clause, *by leaving some of his furniture or goods in the house. The house is vacant when it ceases to be occupied as a dwelling, by some person or persons who reside there either permanently or temporarily.*[1]

In a Massachusetts case,[2] a policy upon a trip-hammer shop, and the machinery therein, contained a provision that the policy should be void if the building remained unoccupied for the period of thirty days without notice. During the life of the policy, and for more than thirty days prior to the loss, the shop remained unoccupied for the purposes of carrying on the business of the shop, or for any purpose, but the tools and machinery were there, and the plaintiff's son went through the shop every day to see that everything was right. But the court held that the shop was "vacant and unoccupied" within the meaning of the term, and could only be said to be occupied when employed for some *practical* use. Lord, J., in the lower court, charged the jury upon this point, as follows: "It is not sufficient," said he, "to constitute occupancy, that the tools remained in the shop, and that the plaintiff's son went through the shop almost every day to look around and see if things were right, *but some practical use must have been made of the building;* and if it thus remained without any practical use for the space of thirty days, it was, within the meaning of the policy, an unoccupied building;" and this ruling was fully sustained upon appeal. In a more recent case in the same State,[3] the rule as applied to a dwelling and barn, was held to be as stated in the text. "Occupancy," said Colt, J., "as applied to such buildings, implies an actual use of the house *as a dwelling place, and such use of the barn as is ordinarily incident to a barn belonging to an occupied house,* or at least, something more than a use of it for mere storage. *The insurer has a right, by the terms of the policy, to the care and supervision* which is involved in such an occupancy."[4]

---

[1] *Sleeper* v. *Ins. Co.*, 56 N. H. 401; *Am. Ins. Co.* v. *Paddlefield*, 78 Ill. 167. In *Chamberlain* v. *Ins. Co.*, 55 N. H. 249, it was held, under the statute providing that a policy should not be forfeited in consequence of any *mistake* of the assured, that a neglect to give notice that a building was unoccupied for the space of nine months, was *such a mistake* as was contemplated by the statute, and that the policy was not thereby avoided; but this case, so far as this point is concerned, was directly overruled by the case cited from the 56th N. H., *ante*.

[2] *Keith* v. *Quincy Ins. Co.*, *ante*.

[3] *Ashworth* v. *Builders'*, etc., *Ins. Co.*, 112 Mass. 423; 17 Am. Rep. 117.

[4] In this case (*Ashworth* v. *Builders' Ins. Co.*, *ante*), the action was for a loss under a policy upon a dwelling-house, and upon a barn described as "near by"

Where a policy contains a provision that "if the premises shall be occupied or used so as to increase the risk, or shall become vacant and unoccupied, *or the risk increased by any other means within the control of the assured*," etc., the policy shall become void; if the premises are vacated, the assured must show that they became so without fault on his part, *and by reason of causes not under his control*, as, if the term of the tenant expired, that he had used reasonable efforts to secure another, and, failing in such proof, his policy is avoided.[1]

Dwellings—warranties in presenti and continuing.

Sec. 90. The fact that a building is described in the application as a "dwelling," does not imply that it is occupied; and the question whether the failure of the insured to disclose the fact that it was

---

the house. The application signed by the plaintiff, in answer to the question, "How are the premises occupied?" contained the answer, "For farming purposes by the assured." The proof of loss contained the statement that at the time of the fire the buildings were unoccupied. The policy contained the following provisions: "If the buildings insured shall be vacated and remain so more than thirty days without the consent of this company, * * this policy shall be void." "Buildings unoccupied are not covered by this policy, unless insured as such." The plaintiff in opening his case stated that he should prove that the application was made to the company through the company's agent at Palmer, and that the policy was issued upon it; that the buildings were situated upon a farm owned and carried on by him; that the farm did not extend down to the road named in the policy, but that a lane a half mile in length ran from the road to the house and barn; that the lane was made for communication with the road, and led no further than to the house; that the house had no other communication with any road; that the description in the policy of the house and barn was correct, unless the statement that it was situated on the road was incorrect; that he owned and occupied as his dwelling place, at the time of his application and the issuing of the policy, another house and barn, which were situated on another farm and directly on the road named in the policy, but that he should prove that these were insured elsewhere at the time of the taking out of this policy; that he informed the agent of the defendants, when he made his application, that the house and barn situated on the lane were the buildings he wished to insure; that the agent assented and inquired the nearest public road to them, and on being told by plaintiff the road named in the policy, the agent wrote the description contained in the policy; that at the time of taking out the policy, and up to the time of the fire, the buildings were occupied only as follows: "When the plaintiff was engaged in carrying on the farm contiguous to the buildings, he and his servants took their meals in the house, and the barn was used for the usual purposes of a farm-barn for storing hay and farming tools, but cattle were not kept in it; that, at the time the application was made and the policy was issued, he told the agent the nature of his occupation of both house and barn, and the agent issued the policy, knowing all the facts; that the agent assented to them, and wrote all the written parts of the application and policy; that in about two months after the policy was issued, the buildings were destroyed by an accidental fire, and that due notice and proof of loss were given. The defendant contended that on the proof of such of the above facts as were competent, the plaintiff could not maintain this action, and the court so ruled, and a verdict was thereupon rendered for the defendant, and the case was reported by the presiding judge to the Supreme Court, where the ruling was sustained.

[1] *American Ins. Co.* v. *Zaengers*, 63 Ill. 464; *Kelly* v. *Worcester, etc., Ins. Co.*, 97 Mass. 284.

unoccupied was a fraudulent concealment of a material fact, is a question for the jury, and their finding is conclusive.[1]

---

[1] In *Hill* v. *Hibernia Ins. Co.*, 10 Hun (N. Y.) 26, the defendant issued to the plaintiff a policy of insurance on the 5th of January, 1874, to expire in one year. The subject of the insurance was "the two-story frame dwelling, composition roof, standing detached on the west side of Bennett avenue, about 125 feet north of Duryea avenue, East New York, Long Island." The house was entirely destroyed on the 17th of June, 1874. At the time of the insurance this house was unoccupied, and so continued until the fire. The house stood about seven feet from another house. Upon the trial the defendant offered to show that the words "standing detached" in a policy meant, "amongst insurance men generally," that the subject of the insurance should be at least twenty-five feet from external exposure. This offer was rejected, and the plaintiff had a verdict. The defendant made two principal objections to the recovery: First. That the word "dwelling" in the policy imports a warranty that the building was then occupied as a dwelling, and being broken, the policy was void. Second. That it was error to exclude the evidence as to the special meaning of the words "standing detached." BARNARD, P.J., said: "If the policy is made out different from the application, the policy should conform to it. Carroll, defendants' agent, does not deny that there was a written application, but says that Bond left it—importing that Bond drew it. No matter who drew it, the evidence is conclusive, that the written paper contained a statement that the house was unoccupied. Bond says Carroll drew it from what he stated, and that the fact of the house being unoccupied was a part of it. Carroll says, I don't remember Bond telling me so, but 'he left a written memorandum of what he wanted.' In filling out the policy, Carroll was defendants' agent, and his error in filling out the policy should not destroy the policy. *Rowley* v. *The Empire Ins. Co.*, 36 N. Y. 550. As to the second objection taken by defendants, there are two reasons why it should not prevail: First. There is no ambiguity in the words 'standing detached.' Second. There is no offer to prove that the particular meaning claimed for the words was known to the assured. When the usage is as to a particular trade or profession, a party to be bound by it 'must be shown to have knowledge or notice of its existence.' *Walls* v. *Baily*, 49 N. Y. 464." GILBERT, J., said: "The defense in this case seems to be entirely destitute of merit. The company received a verbal notice of the loss immediately after the fire, and nine days after the fire proofs of loss were served, which also contained a formal written notice of the loss. All these were received and retained without objection, and the company put its refusal to pay the loss upon other grounds than a non-compliance with the conditions of the policy in relation to these matters. Such conduct is a waiver of the strict performance of such conditions. The building insured is described in the policy as a dwelling as and '*standing detached.*' This is the language of the insurer. No survey or statement, showing whether the building was occupied or not, or the distance between it and adjacent buildings was required of the assured or furnished by him. The insurance was effected through a broker, who had been engaged in that business twenty years. He testified that he informed the insurer before he effected the insurance that the building was vacant, and that he was willing to pay an extra premium on that account. We think that the use of the word 'dwelling' does not imply that the building is occupied, but if it does, the use of it by the insurer alone does not create a warranty by the assured. The question whether the fact that the building was vacant was fraudulently suppressed by the assured, was fairly submitted to the jury, and their conclusion upon it is fully supported by the evidence. The defendants having knowingly insured a vacant building, the condition, that if the building should afterwards become vacant or unoccupied, without their assent indorsed on the policy, affords them no shield. That condition by its terms, applies only to an insurance upon an occupied dwelling, which is vacated after the insurance was effected. The building did stand detached. It was seven feet from any other building. The attempt to show that the phrase 'standing detached' meant that it was distant twenty-five feet, or thereabouts, from any other building, was properly rejected. The phrase is not in the slightest degree ambiguous, and extrinsic proof was not admissible to give it a meaning different from its plain import. A new contract cannot be made in that way. *Reynolds* v. *Commerce Ins. Co.*, 47 N. Y. 605."

Where the application describes the property as occupied for a certain purpose, and the application is made a part of the policy, the statement is a warranty that the building *is so occupied at the time when the contract was made*, and if untrue, although the real occupancy was less hazardous than that described, the policy is void. Thus, the application for insurance described the property to be insured as situated in a building occupied by the applicant as a tavern barn. By the terms of the policy, loss or damage was to be paid only "after due notice and proof thereof made by the insured in conformity to the by-laws and conditions annexed to the policy;" and the policy also stated that it was made and accepted subject to the terms, by-laws, and conditions of the company, which were to be resorted to to explain and ascertain the rights and liabilities of the parties. One of the conditions annexed to the policy was, that as a part of the preliminary proofs, there should be a statement that there had been no alteration or occupation of the premises not assented to by the company, which increased the hazard of the property. It was held that the terms of the policy in connection with the terms of the conditions controlled the construction of the contract of insurance, and bound the insured by an agreement that the premises should not be occupied so as to increase the risk after the insurance. Also, that an occupation of a part of the barn as a livery stable was such a change in the use of the premises as was material to the risk, and entitled the company to notice; and that it was immaterial that the person keeping the livery stable was a mere tenant at will of the insured, and subject to be removed at pleasure.[1]

Where there is a provision in a policy of insurance of "a dwelling-house," that if the building be used for carrying "on any specially hazardous trade or occupation," the policy shall be of no force and effect," and classifying "all workshops, manufacturing establishments, trades and mills" with certain exceptions as "specially hazardous," is equivalent to a stipulation or warranty that the building shall not be so used, to the knowledge of the policyholder, and the truth or fulfillment of this covenant is a condition precedent to his right to recover on the policy, and if the holder of such policy of insurance knowingly permits a part of such building to be used as a workshop for any of the purposes specified as hazardous, even though he continues to reside therein, and calls it "a dwelling-house," such use constitutes a breach of the covenant, and entails a forfeiture of the policy.[2]

---

[1] *Hobley* v. *Dana*, 17 Barb. (N. Y.) 111.
[2] *Gasner* v. *Metropolitan Ins. Co.*, 13 Minn. 483.

In a Connecticut case,[1] a survey embraced in the application contained the following interrogatory: "How are the several stories occupied?" which the applicant had answered as follows: "Unoccupied, but to be occupied by a tenant." "When a policy is issued upon a survey and description of the property, such a survey and description shall be deemed to be a part of the policy, and a warranty on the part of the assured." The court held that the answer was not to be considered as a stipulation that the house should be occupied by a tenant, but as a reservation on the part of the applicant, of the right to have it so occupied, and to avoid the inference that it was to remain unoccupied. The plaintiff, however, offered evidence to prove that he had made all reasonable effort to let the premises, from the time of the insurance in January down to the time of the fire, in September following, but without success; and the court instructed the jury that even if the answer was a stipulation that the house should be occupied by a tenant, yet as no time was specified when such occupancy was to commence, the warranty would not be broken if such occupancy was procured within a reasonable time, and left it to them as a question of fact upon the evidence whether the stipulation was broken by a non-occupation beyond a reasonable time, and the court held that this construction was correct.

Unlawful use of buildings—effect upon insurance.

SEC. 91. The fact that the insured permits a building to be temporarily used for an unlawful purpose, that does not materially increase the risk, as a building insured as a shoe factory to be used for drawing a lottery upon a single occasion;[2] or where the building, without the knowledge or consent of the insured, is used by a tenant for an unlawful purpose, as a building insured and rented as a hotel, when it is in fact used as a house of ill fame,[3] the policy is not thereby rendered void, but if the policy specially provides that, in case the building shall be used for any *unlawful* purpose, the policy shall be void, it will become so, when habitually devoted to an unlawful use, whether *with* or *without* the knowledge or consent of the insured, as for the sale of intoxicating liquors in States where such traffic is prohibited;[4] and in *all* cases, where the building is let for an unlawful use with the knowl-

---

[1] *Hough* v. *City Fire Ins. Co.*, 29 Conn. 10.

[2] *Boardman* v. *Merrimack Mut. F. Ins. Co.*, 8 Cush. (Mass.) 386.

[3] *Hall* v. *People's Mut. F. Ins. Co.*, 6 Gray (Mass.) 185.

[4] As keeping hotel therein without a license, *Campbell* v. *Charter Oak Ins. Co.*, 10 Allen (Mass.) 213; selling liquors, *Kelly* v. *Home Ins. Co.*, 97 Mass. 288.

edge of the assured, unless he truly disclose the use to which it is to be devoted, the policy will be void, as where he lets a dwelling-house to be used as a house of ill fame.[1] All prohibitory clauses and conditions in a policy are to be reasonably construed so as to execute the actual intent of the parties, rather than the strict letter of the policy. Thus, where, by a clause in the policy, it was provided that "smoking shall be strictly prohibited in or about the buildings," it was held that the mere fact that there had been smoking upon the premises, without the knowledge or consent of the insured, and contrary to his instructions, did not invalidate the policy. All that can be required in such cases is, that the act should be prohibited by the assured, and reasonable precautions adopted to prevent it.[2] If a building covered by insurance is *knowingly* devoted to unlawful uses by the assured, as, if a building insured as a hotel is kept as a hotel without a license, when a license is made necessary by law, the policy is thereby avoided if the policy provides that "all unlawful business or trade is prohibited."[3] So too, if prohibited articles are kept or used therein, as if burning fluid is used as an illuminator, when its use for that purpose is specially prohibited.[4]

Contingent interests not covered unless so expressed.

SEC. 92. A contingent interest of the insured in the property of others, will not be presumed to be covered by a policy, unless words appropriate to express such intention are used, when the insured has property of his own to which the policy is applicable. Thus, a railroad company procured a policy of insurance upon "all the wood and logs cut and piled along the line of their railroad, from Winchendon, Mass., to Peterboro, N. H." At the time of taking out the policy, as well as at the time of the fire, the plaintiff had wood cut and piled along the line of its road, upon its own premises and in its woodsheds, but it never owned any logs. A quantity of wood and logs piled upon the land of the owner, along the line of the plaintiff's road, were, by sparks from its engines, ignited and destroyed, which the plaintiff claimed were covered by the policy, and notice of the loss was duly given. The defendant claimed that the policy only applied to property *owned* by the plaintiff, and this view was sustained by the court.

[1] *Com.* v. *Harrington*, 3 Pick. (Mass.) 36. METCALF, J., in *Boardman* v. *Merrimack Ins. Co.*, 8 Cush. (Mass.) 594.
[2] *The Aurora F. Ins. Co.* v. *Eddy*, 55 Ill. 213.
[3] *Campbell* v. *Charter Oak Ins. Co.*, 10 Allen (Mass.) 213.
[4] *Campbell* v. *Charter Oak Ins. Co., ante; Cerf* v. *Home Ins. Co.*, 44 Cal. 346.

AMES, J.,[1] in discussing the question, said : "There is nothing upon the face of the policy to indicate that it was intended to cover any-thing more than the plaintiff's own property; *prima facie*, they were insured as owners simply. It is true that railroad companies are liable for fires kindled by their locomotive engines, and that to enable them to protect themselves against the risk, they are held to have an insur-able interest in the property of others exposed to danger from that cause, but this special and contingent interest is different from that of an owner. Whether it can be insured in the same form of words, as if the assured were the exclusive owner, it is not necessary to decide. *But where the assured is the owner of property such as is described in the contract, we must assume, in the absence of any indication to the contrary, that he was insured as the owner of that property.* If the parties meant anything more than that, they should have expressed their intention in appropriate language."

By what law governed.

SEC. 93. A contract of insurance is to be governed by the law of the place where its execution was completed, and it became a binding and operative contract, and not necessarily by the law of the place where dated.[2]

Assignment of policy.

SEC. 94. Although a policy provides that an assignment thereof, without the consent of the company, shall render it void, yet this only applies to an assignment *before* a loss under it. After a loss, it may

---

[1] *Monadnock R. R. Co.* v. *Manufacturers' Ins. Co.*, 113 Mass. 77.

[2] A question of interest in respect to fire insurance contracts arose in the case of *Todd* v. *State Ins. Co. of Missouri*, recently decided by the Lancaster, Penn., Common Pleas, and reported in 3 Weekly Notes of Cases, 330. The defendant, a Missouri corporation, and having general agents in New York, through such agents insured certain real and personal property situated in New Jersey. The policy of insurance purported to be signed by the president, and attested by the secretary of the company, at Hannibal, Missouri. It contained, however, a condition that "this policy shall not be valid unless countersigned by the duly authorized agents at New York city." It was so countersigned, and the premium was paid to the agents in New York. The question was by what law the contract was to be governed. The court held that it was by the law of New York, following the doctrine enunciated by Lord ELDON in *Male* v. *Roberts*, 3 Esp. 163, that "the law of the country where the contract arose must govern the contract." The same rule is followed in *Coe* v. *United States*, 6 Peters, 172; *Duncan* v. *United States*, 7 id. 435; *Pomeroy* v. *Manhattan Life Ins. Co.*, 40 Ill. 398; *Kennebec Co.* v. *Augusta Ins. Co.*, 6 Gray, 208; *Hubner* v. *Eagle Ins. Co.*, 10 id. 131; *Daniels* v. *Hudson River Fire Ins. Co.*, 12 Cush. 416. In a recent case in Massachusetts (*Thwing* v. *Gt. Western Ins. Co.*, 111 Mass. 93), a policy was issued by the defend-ant company in New York, and dated there, but it was delivered in Boston, and the premium note was there executed, and it was held that the contract must be governed by the law of Massachusetts. See also, *Hubner* v. *Eagle Ins. Co.*, 10 Gray (Mass.) 131.

be assigned, like any other obligation, against a third person, and such assignment does not destroy the insurer's liability. The contract while the risk is active, is personal, and the parties' contract, in reference to the *delectus personæ* of each other, therefore the obligation cannot be changed without the insurer's consent, but, when liability actually attaches under the policy, the entire relation is changed, and the relation of insurer and insured is changed to that of debtor and creditor, and the *delectus personæ* of the contract is no longer material.[1] And a clause in the policy that the policy shall not be assigned *after* loss, is null and void, because it seeks to prevent the assignment of a chose in action.[2] Nor is it rendered void by a general assignment for the benefit of creditors, as such an assignment only includes such policies as the insured could legally assign, and, if he still retains an insurable interest in the property, he will be entitled to recover thereon notwithstanding the general assignment.[3]

Mistakes in policies, when may be explained by parol.

SEC. 95. When there is a latent ambiguity in a policy, parol evidence is admissible to explain it. Thus, where the insured had a policy upon " hay and grain," which was described as being in a barn upon the plaintiff's premises, but he had two barns on the place, and the policy did not state *which barn* was covered by the policy, parol evidence was held admissible to show which barn was intended to be insured.[4] But when the policy is specific as to the property covered, parol evidence is never admissible to prove that by mistake it was made to

---

[1] In *Franklin* v. *National Ins. Co.*, 43 Mo. 491, a policy of insurance was issued to John Franklin, payable to P. H. French. After loss, French assigned to the Union Savings Association, and the latter assigned to John Franklin. In an action on the policy by Franklin as assignee of French, it was held that French as payee of the policy had a sufficient interest in the contract to sustain the validity of the policy. It is to be regarded in the same light as if assigned at its inception to French with the consent of the company. *Miller* v. *The Hamilton F. Ins. Co.*, 17 N. Y. 609 ; *Walters* v. *Washington Ins. Co.*, 1 Cole, 404 ; *Courtney* v. *N. Y. City Ins. Co.*, 28 Barb. (N. Y.) 116 ; *Carter* v. *Hulmboldt Ins. Co.*, 12 Iowa, 287 ; *Brichtu* v. *New York, etc., Ins. Co.*, 2 Hall (N. Y.) 372 ; *Pennebaker* v. *Tomlinson*, 1 Tenn. Ch. 598 ; *West Branch Ins. Co.* v. *Halfenstein*, 40 Penn. St. 289 ; *Goit* v. *National Ins. Co.*, 25 Barb. (N. Y.) 189 ; *Carroll* v. *Charter Oak Ins. Co.*, 38 id. 402.

[2] *West Branch Ins. Co.* v. *Halfenstein*, 40 Penn. St. 284 ; *Carroll* v. *Charter Oak Ins. Co.*, 1 Abb. Dec. Ct. of App. (N. Y.) 316 ; *Mershon* v. *National Ins. Co.*, 34 Iowa, 87 ; *Courtney* v. *N. Y. City Ins. Co.*, 28 Barb. (N. Y.) 116 ; *Bradley* v. *Priexto*, 3 Ves. 324. But in *Dey* v. *Poughkeepsie Ins. Co.*, 28 Barb. (N. Y.) 623, where the policy expressly provided that an assignment "*before or after a loss*" should avoid it, it was held that the condition was valid; but the doctrine of this case has been repeatedly repudiated by the courts of New York in later cases.

[3] *Lazarus* v. *Com. Ins. Co.*, 19 Pick. (Mass.) 81.

[4] *Bowman* v. *Agricultural Ins. Co.*, 59 N. Y. 521.

cover other property than that intended.[1] The only remedy if any, in such a case, is in an action to reform the policy.[2]

Requirements of policy, as to notice or consent, must be complied with.

SEC. 96. If a policy provides that any change in the risk shall be made, or that "subsequent to the making of the application any new fact shall exist, either by a change of any fact disclosed in the application, the erection or alteration of any building, etc., by the assured or others, or any change not made, not named in the application, and specifically permitted · in the policy," the policy shall be void; the alteration of a building, or any material change therein, made without consent, will invalidate the policy.[3] And, in the case of a mutual company, the officers of the company cannot waive express stipulations of their policies or by-laws which relate to the *substance* of the contract, although they may waive such as merely relate to collateral matters, as proofs of loss, etc.[4] But as to all matters relating *to the substance of the contract*, the officers of the company are powerless to waive the rules established in reference thereto, however much the same might be sanctioned by strict equity.[5] In all such cases the consent must be obtained in the mode, and from the person designated as authorized to give it; and an agent, authorized merely to take applications, receive cash premiums and issue " a binder" therefor, has no authority to give such consent, nor is he a proper person to whom to give notice of any

---

[1] *Holmes* v. *Charlestown, etc., Ins. Co.*, 10 Met. (Mass.) 211 ; *Emer* v. *Washington Ins. Co.*, 16 Pick. (Mass.) 502 ; *Miller* v. *Travers*, 8 Bing. 244.

[2] HUBBARD, J., in *Holmes* v. *Charlestown, etc., Ins. Co.*, 10 Met. (Mass.) 216.

[3] *Evans* v. *Trimountain M. F. Ins. Co.*, 9 Allen (Mass.) 329.

[4] *Muley* v. *Shawmut Ins. Co.*, 4 Allen (Mass.) 116 ; *Priest* v. *Citizen's Ins. Co.*, 3 id. 602 ; *Buffum* v. *Fayette Ins. Co.*, 3 id. 360 ; *Brewer* v. *Chelsea Ins. Co.*, 14 Gray (Mass.) 203.

[5] *Worcester Bank* v. *Hartford Ins. Co.*, 11 Cush, (Mass.) 265 ; *Loring* v. *Manufacturers' Ins. Co.*, 8 Gray (Mass.) 28 ; *Pendar* v. *American Ins. Co.*, 12 Cush. (Mass.) 469. In *Evans* v. *Trimountain Ins. Co.*, *ante*, this doctrine, in a case of great hardship to the plaintiff, was well illustrated. Thus, the plaintiff took out a policy for $800, in the defendant company, containing a provision identical with that previously stated in the text. Being desirous of altering the house, the policy was taken to the office for that purpose. The secretary indorsed a written permission upon the policy, as follows : " Boston, February 25th, 1864. Permission is hereby given to the within insured to occupy the dwelling insured by policy No. 1084, by mechanics, for the purpose of making such improvements and alterations as he may think necessary. The risk continues on said property and the policy is not vitiated." The secretary and the director to whom application for consent was made being under the impression that the president must sign the contract, retained the policy for the purpose of procuring the president's signature thereto, but neglected to obtain it, and the building was afterwards burned. In fact, the secretary was the person to sign · the consent. The court held that no recovery could be had, because the consent of the company to the alterations was not indorsed upon the policy.

change, notice of which is required to be given the company.[1]   Thus where, as in the case last cited, immediate notice was required to be given *to the company* in case the premises were vacated, it was held that notice to an agent whose powers were limited, as previously stated, was not a compliance with the requirements of the policy.[2]   But where the agent is clothed with power to make and execute contracts of insurance, notice to him, and his assent to changes in the risk, is binding upon the company, unless otherwise specially provided in the policy, because within the scope of his apparent power.[3]

Must be consequence of ignition.   Injury by heat without ignition, not covered.

SEC. 97. Where fire is employed as an agent, either for the ordinary purposes of heating the building, for the purposes of manufacture, or as an instrument of art, the insurer is not liable for the consequences thereof, *so long as the fire itself is confined within the limit of the agencies employed*, as, from the effects of smoke or heat evolved thereby, or escaping therefrom, from any cause whether intentional or accidental. In order to bring such consequences within the risk, there must be actual ignition outside of the agencies employed, not *purposely* caused by the assured, and these, as a consequence of such ignition, *dehors* the agencies.[4]

In the case referred to, the plaintiff was the owner of a sugar manufactory, seven or eight stories high. On the ground floor were pans for boiling the sugar, and a stove to heat them. A chimney or flue extended to the top of the building, and registers were inserted therein upon each floor, with an aperture into the rooms to introduce heat as desired. The upper floors were used for drying the sugar. One morning the fire being lighted as usual, below, the servant, whose duty it was to have opened the register, forgot to do so, and as a consequence the smoke, sparks and heat from the stove were entirely intercepted, and, instead of escaping through the top of the flue, were forced into the rooms where the sugar was drying, and from the combined effects of the smoke, sparks and heat, the sugar was damaged to the extent of several thousand pounds. The flames were confined within the stove and flue, and no actual ignition took place outside thereof. It was held that the loss was not covered by the policy. "There was," said GIBBS, C.J., "no more fire than always exists when

---

[1] *Harrison* v. *City F. Ins. Co.*, 9 Allen (Mass.) 231.

[2] *Snow* v. *Perry*, 9 Pick. (Mass.) 542 ; *Lobdell* v. *Baker*, 1 Met. (Mass.) 201.

[3] See chapter on "AGENTS."

[4] In *Austin* v. *Drew*, 4 Camp. 361.

the manufacture is going on. *Nothing was consumed by fire.* The plaintiff's loss arose from the negligent management of the machinery. The sugars were chiefly damaged by the heat, and what produced that heat? Not any fire against which the company insures, but the fire for heating the pans which continued all the time to burn without any excess. The servant forgot to open the register by which the smoke ought to have escaped, and the heat to have been tempered." At this point a juryman interposed: "If my servant by negligence sets my house a fire, and it is burnt down, I expect, my lord, to be paid by the insurance office." "And so you would, sir," replied the Chief Justice, "but *then there would be a fire*, whereas, *here, there has been none.* If there is a fire, it is no answer that it was occasioned by the negligence or misconduct of servants; but in this case there was no fire except in the stove and flue, as there ought to have been, *and the loss was occasioned by the confinement of heat. Had the fire been brought out of the flue and anything had been burnt,* the company would have been liable. But can this be said where the fire was never at all excessive, and was always confined within its proper limits? This is not a fire within the meaning of the policy, nor a loss for which the company undertakes. They might as well be sued for the damage done to drawing-room furniture by a smoky chimney." The doctrine of this case has been considerably misconceived, both by the courts and by text-writers, and some absurdity and conflict of doctrine has been the result. This, in a measure, and perhaps entirely, has resulted from discrepancies in the report of the case by different reporters, and from a misconception of the doctrine or a misapplication of it by text-writers. For these discrepancies the reader is referred to the following reports and text-books.[1] The case as given above is, however, believed to be correct, and corresponds with the report of it as given in Holt. N. P. 126, and the doctrine evolved therefrom is, in the main, sustained both by Marshall, vol. 2, 3d ed., 790, and by Beaumont, 37, and is the doctrine held by all the better class of both English and American cases.[2]

---

[1] *Austin* v. *Drew*, 6 Taunt. 436 ; 2 Marshall on Ins. 130 ; Ellis on Ins. 25 ; Beaumont on Ins. 37 ; Hughes on Ins. 507–511.

[2] In *Millaudon* v. *New Orleans Ins. Co.*, 4 La. An. 15, the policy covered sugar, in the plaintiff's sugar manufactory. The boiler used in the manufacture thereof exploded, and seriously damaged the sugar. The boiler exploded from excessive heat. *Held*, that the loss was not within the policy. *Kenniston* v. *Ins. Co.*, 14 N. H. 341 ; *Perrin's Admrs.* v. *Protection Ins. Co.*, 11 Ohio, 146 ; *Grim* v. *Phenix Ins. Co.*, 13 John. (N. Y.) 451 ; *Jameson* v. *Royal Ins. Co.*, 7 Irish L. R. 126 ; *Geisick* v. *Crescent, etc., Ins. Co.*, 19 La. An. 297 ; *Babcock* v. *Montgomery, etc., Ins. Co.*, 6 Barb. (N. Y.) 637.

13

SEC. 98. *There must be an accident by fire,* to lay the foundation of a claim.   By this it is not meant that the property itself must have been on fire, *but that there must have been either an ignition of the property itself, or of other substances or property near to it, which was the proximate cause of the loss.* ` Fire must have been the proximate cause of the loss.`   This rule does not require that the property itself should have been burned *by the fire, or even injured directly by fire at all,* but simply, that *fire* must have been the proximate cause of the injury.   Thus, an injury to buildings by lightning, when actual ignition does not transpire, is not within the loss covered by ordinary policies;[1] and the same is

---

[1] In *Babcock* v. *Montgomery Ins. Co.,* 6 Barb. N. Y. 637, the court reviewed the questions involved in this class of cases, in a very thorough and able manner.   In that case the building was rent and torn to pieces by lightning, but without being burnt, and the question was, whether the insurer was liable as for a loss by fire.   The court held that there was no liability.   PRATT, J., said: "This action was brought upon a policy of insurance against loss by fire.   The word fire, in contracts of this kind, should be construed in its ordinary signification.   6 Bac. Abr. 658.   It should not be confined to any technical and restricted meaning which might be applied to it upon a scientific analysis of its nature and properties, nor should it receive that general and extended signification which by a kind of figure of speech is sometimes applied to the term ; but it should be construed in its ordinary popular sense.   Nor is the damage, for which fire insurance companies are liable, to be confined to loss by actual burning or consuming ; but they are liable for all losses which are the immediate consequences of fire or burning.   *City Fire Ins. Co.* v. *Corlies,* 21 Wend. 367.   Thus, goods injured by being removed to save them from fire, or by water in extinguishing a fire, are within the provisions of the policy.   So other cases might be mentioned, where the insurers are liable for damages which can be traced directly to fire as the immediate cause of the loss, and yet the insured article itself be in no danger of being burned or consumed.   But giving to the plaintiff in this cause the benefit of the most liberal rule yet established by legal adjudication, I am wholly unable to arrive at the conclusion that the damage done to the plaintiff's house was a loss within the provisions of the policy.

"*First.* The plaintiff has the *onus probandi* upon himself.   In order to entitle him to a recovery he must prove that the loss was occasioned by fire ; and as the building was not consumed nor set on fire, he must be able to show that electricity of sufficient intensity to rend a building, is fire, in the popular and ordinary signification of the term.   It is not sufficient to show that fire is one of its constituent principles.   He must be able to demonstrate that the rending and destruction of the building were the result of that particular principle.   That I think cannot be done in the present state of the science of electricity.   It can neither be proved that fire, in its ordinary signification, is a constituent element in electricity ; nor, if that be so, that its mechanical or rending effects are the consequences of such fire.   Of the actual nature of what we call electricity, but little is pretended to be known with certainty.   It is even a disputed point among scientific men, who have made it the subject of their investigation, whether it be 'an actual fluid, or merely a property of other matter.   Ed. Ency. tit. Electricity.   The only real knowledge which we possess, in relation to it, is a knowledge of its properties derived from observation of its effects.   We find that under certain conditions it exhibits phenomena, or effects, which are the most wonderful as well as the most powerful within the observation of man.   These phenomena are divided, by writers upon the science, into three classes, the mechanical and the chemical and the magnetical ; and some writers add a fourth, termed the physiological.   Ed. Enc. tit. Electricity ; Sturgeon's Lectures on Elec. 124.   When the *fluid* (if we may be allowed the expression) is excited to a high degree of intensity, the mechanical

true of a building or property destroyed by an explosion from gun-powder,[1] steam boilers,[2] or from any cause when actual ignition does

effects of an electric discharge are manifested by perforating or rending any non-conducting substance against which such discharge may be directed. Excited to a high degree of intensity, its chemical effects are also manifested by fusing metals, and igniting combustible substances. These effects belong to different classes of phenomena, and are, for aught we know, entirely distinct in their character. I have not been able to find any writer, nor was our attention on the argument directed to any author, who insists that the mechanical effects of electricity are produced by its calorific properties, except M. Arago. His theory was that the explosive effects of lightning were caused by its heating properties upon the water and moisture contained in the subject of the explosion. But this theory has not been generally adopted. See Lardner's Lectures, subject Electricity. Whilst it is admitted that nothing is absolutely known of the method by which heat is evolved in electric phenomena, the theory which is the most generally adopted makes it the result, and not the cause, of the mechanical action. Ed. Enc. tit. Heat. Mr. Sturgeon, an able and lucid lecturer upon the subject of electricity, suggests the existence of two separate fluids which pervade all matter —the electric and the calorific; that heat is evolved, and ignition produced, by the mechanical action of the electric fluid upon the calorific. Stur. Lec. p. 162. Without assenting to any of the numerous theories which have resulted from speculations upon the subject by men of science, I only allude to them to show that nothing is known with sufficient certainty to form a basis for legal adjudication. I may remark, in passing, that it is with a considerable degree of diffidence that I dissent from the positions taken by the learned jurist, Judge Willard, who has written an opinion upon the points involved in this case, and which was cited upon the argument. If I understand the position taken by him, it is that if the lightning had not torn the building to pieces it would have set it on fire, and hence he deduces an argument in favor of holding the company liable. In the first place, I am unable to find any evidence that there was any such alternative in the case. The phenomena of nature are constant: like causes produce like effects; and there is no evidence that the electric fluid which demolished the house was, under the existing circumstances, capable of setting it on fire, or exhibiting any different phenomena from those which it did exhibit. In the second place, if it were so, it would not alter the case. The contract of the insurers was to indemnify the insured against loss by fire. It by no means follows that they are liable for the damage done by violence to the insured property because the agent by which the violence was effected might have set it on fire. A heated ball or bombshell may injure the building against which it is hurled. It would not do to hold the insurers liable, because, if the force which caused it to perforate the wall had been less, or the resistance greater, it might have lodged in the walls and set them on fire.

"*Secondly*. If it could be demonstrated that the mechanical action of lightning is the result of its calorific properties, it by no means follows that the damage is occasioned by fire. The terms caloric and fire admit of very different significations. One is the cause and the other the effect. That which is termed caloric seems to pervade every material substance. It may be evolved from a snowball or a piece of ice. Fire, on the other hand, is not an elementary principle, but is the effect produced by the application of heat, or caloric, to combustible substances. Walker says that in the popular acceptation of the word, 'fire is the effect of combustion.' It is therefore equivalent to ignition or burning. Unless, therefore, there be actual ignition, and the loss be the effect of such ignition, the insurers are not liable. Not that the identical property to which the damage occurred should be consumed, or even ignited, but there must be a fire or burning which is the proximate cause of the loss. It is immaterial how intense the heat may be; unless it be the effect of ignition, it is not within the terms of the policy. The heat of the sun often contracts timber, from which losses occur; but they would

[1] *Taunton* v. *The Royal Ins. Co.*, 2 H. & M. 235; *Everett* v. *The London Assurance Co.*, 19 C. B. (N. S.) 126.
[2] *Millaudon* v. *New Orleans Ins. Co.*, 4 La. An. 15

not transpire, unless the explosion itself was occasioned by an *accidental* burning, or fire.[1] The rule where an explosion is occasioned by

---

not be considered losses by fire. *Ellis on Fire Ins.* 273 ; *Steph. N. P.* 1079 ; 11 *Petersd. Ab.* 18. Hence in the case of *Austin* v. *Drewe*, 6 Taunt. 436 ; 4 Camp. 360, it was ruled in the case of an insurance upon the stock of a sugar house, that damage to the stock by the heat of the usual fires in consequence of the accidental mismanagement of the dampers, was not within the policy against loss by fire. *Gibbs*, Ch.J. ruled, and his ruling was sustained by the court, that if there was a fire it was no answer to say that it was occasioned by negligence or misconduct of servants ; but in this case there was no fire, except in the stove where it ought to be, and the loss was occasioned by the confinement of the heat, and not by fire.

"*Thirdly.* The terms of the policy exclude the idea that it was intended to cover damage by lightning when there was no ignition. The words of the policy are that the company will be liable for fire by lightning. 1st. If the company intended to insure against all damage by lightning, it seems strange that they should have used that form of expression—that they had not used the phrase directly, ' damage or loss by lightning.' If the word fire includes in itself lightning, then one of those words was entirely superfluous. It seems obvious to me, therefore, when the parties to the contract make use of the term 'fire by lightning,' they use the term lightning not as fire itself, but as an agent capable, under certain circumstances, of causing fire. 2d. The use of the same expression, in the books, strengthens this position ; for the parties will be deemed to use the term in its legal acceptation. Ellis on Fire Insurance, page 25, says 'that it is sometimes expressly stated to remove any doubt, though little could exist, that losses occasioned by fire from lightning will be made good.' Kent, in a note to his Commentaries, third volume, edition 1836, says that it has been usually held that losses by fire from lightning are within the policy. It is hardly probable that two writers so correct in the use of language would put in the word fire where it would be utterly superfluous if they did not mean to convey the idea of ignition or burning by it. Lord Ellenborough said, in *Gordon* v. *Remington*, 1 Camp. 123, ' Fire is expressly mentioned in the policy as one of the perils against which the underwriters undertake to indemnify the assured, and if the ship is destroyed by fire it is of no consequence whether this was occasioned by a common accident, or by lightning, or by an act done in duty to the state.' 1 *Phil. on Ins.* 632. And in the Traite des Assurances Terrestres, by De Querault, cited by Judge Willard, I infer it is used in the same sense. I have not had access to the work, but in the citation by the learned judge, the term lightning is evidently spoken of as the cause of fire, and not fire itself. ' La compagnie assure contra l'incendie m me contre celui provenant du fue du ciel,' as I translate it, reads, ' The company insures against burning (conflagration) even against that which proceeds from lightning.' So also Pothier, in his Traite du Contract d'assurance, chapter 1, under the head of fire, says, ' Les assurers en sant tenus, lorsque c' est par un cas fortuit comme par le feu du ciel ou dans un combat que le feu a pres au vaisseau.' ' The insurers are liable when the vessel takes fire by accident, as by lightning, or in battle.' In marine policies losses by fire and by perils of the sea are usually specially mentioned as losses for which the insurers will be liable. Among the former is uniformly classed burning or fire by lightning ; and among the latter, damage by lightning. Phillips on Insurance, speaking of marine policies, under the head ' loss by fire' (vol. 1, p.631), says, ' That the insurers are answerable for the loss when the property is consumed by lightning or takes fire in an engagement with another vessel ;' citing Pothier. And under the head, perils of the sea (p. 635), he enumerates ' losses by the winds, waves, lightning, rockshoals,' etc. See 2 Bac. Ab. 661. 3d. The practice of other companies, to the by-laws or proposals of some sixteen of which we were referred upon the argument, instead of weakening, strengthens the view which we have taken of

---

[1] *Scripture* v. *Lowell, etc., Ins. Co.*, 10 Cush. (Mass.) 356 ; *Hayward* v. *London, etc., Ins. Co.*, 7 Bos. (N. Y.) 385 ; *Waters* v. *Louisville Ins. Co.*, 1 McLean (U. S.) 275 ; *Greenwald* v. *Ins. Co.*, 3 Phila. (Penn.) 52 ; *Citizen's Ins. Co.* v. *Glasgow*, 9 Mo. 406 ; *Perrin* v. *Protection Ins. Co.*, 11 Ohio, 147.

fire, is thus formulated by CUSHING, J.[1] "*Where*," said he, "*the effects produced are the immediate results of the action of a burning substance in contact with a building, it is immaterial whether these results manifest themselves in the form of combustion or explosion, or of both combined. In either case, the damage occurring is by the action of fire and covered by the ordinary terms of a policy against loss by fire.*" In this case, the plaintiff was in the possession of a building occupied by a tenant. The tenant's son carried a cask of gunpowder into the attic without the plaintiff's knowledge or consent, *and fired it with a match.* The gunpowder took fire, exploded, set fire to a bed and clothing, charred and stained some of the woodwork, and blew off the roof of the house. The court held that the *whole* damage was within the policy insuring " against loss or damage by fire."[2] This rule does not include dam-

---

the construction of the present policy. Doubtful terms in a written instrument are to be construed according to the ordinary usages of trade. The practice and usage of so many companies restricting their liability to losses occasioned by actual burning by lightning shows that the general usage is not to be liable for damage by lightning, unless accompanied by burning. A fair construction of those policies would not require that the property should be actually consumed, to entitle the assured to indemnity, but that the lightning should cause a fire which fire should be the proximate cause of the loss; the same as a loss by fire in ordinary cases. If that view be correct, I do not see as the terms of the policies in those cases differ, substantially, from that under consideration. Losses from burning by lightning, and losses from fire by lightning, it seems to me, are equivalent terms, and should be construed as imposing upon the parties the same rights and liabilities. We are, therefore, of opinion, that the damage which the plaintiff has sustained is not within the provisions of the policy, and that the defendants are not liable in this action." *Kenniston* v. *Merrimack Ins. Co.*, 14 N. H. 341.

[1] *Scripture* v. *Lowell, etc., Ins. Co.*, 10 Cush. (Mass.) 356.

[2] *Duncan* v. *Sun Insurance Co.*, 6 Wend. (N. Y.) 488; *Grim* v. *Phœnix Insurance Co.*, 13 John. (N. Y.) 451. In *Waters* v. *Merchants' Louisville Insurance Co.*, 11 Pet. (U. S.) 213; 1 Bennett's Fire Insurance Cas., 615. STORY, J., in a very able opinion, reviewed the cases and laid down the rule applicable in such cases. He said : " As we understand the first question, it assumes that the fire was directly and immediately caused by the barratry of the master and crew as the efficient agents ; or, in other words, that the fire was communicated and occasioned by the direct act and agency of the master and crew, intentionally done from a barratrous purpose. In this view of it, we have no hesitation to say that a loss by fire caused by the barratry of the master or crew is not a loss within the policy. Such a loss is properly a loss attributable to the barratry as its proximate cause, as it concurs as the efficient agent, with the element *eo instanti*, when the jury is produced. If the master or crew should barratrously bore holes in the bottom of the vessel, and the latter should thereby be filled with water and sink, the loss would properly be deemed a loss by barratry, and not by a peril of the seas or of rivers, though the flow of the water should co-operate in producing the sinking. The second question raises a different point, whether a loss by fire remotely caused by the negligence, carelessness, or unskillfulness of the master and crew of the vessel, is a loss within the true intent and meaning of the policy. By unskillfulness, as here stated, we do not understand in this instance a general unskillfulness, such as would be a breach of the implied warranty of competent skill to navigate and conduct the vessel, but only unskillfulness in the particular circumstances remotely connected with the loss. In this sense it is equivalent to negligence or carelessness in the execution of duty, and

ages resulting from a mere explosion, "not involving ignition and combustion of the agent of explosion, such as the case of steam or

---

not to incapacity. This question has undergone many discussions in the courts of England and America, and has given rise to opposing judgments in the two countries. As applied to policies against fire on land, the doctrine has for a great length of time prevailed that losses occasioned by the mere fault or negligence of the assured or his servants, unaffected by fraud or design, are within the protection of the policies, and as such recoverable from the underwriters. It is not certain upon what precise grounds this doctrine was originally settled. It may have been from the rules of interpretation applied to such policies containing special exceptions, and not excepting this; or it may have been, and more probably was founded upon a more general ground, that as the terms of the policy covered risks by fire generally, no exception ought to be introduced by construction except that of fraud of the assured, which upon the principles of public policy and morals was always to be implied. It is probable, too, that the consideration had great weight that otherwise such policies would practically be of little importance, since, comparatively speaking, few losses of this sort would occur which could not be traced back to some carelessness, neglect, or inattention of the members of the family. Be the origin of it, however, what it may, the doctrine is now firmly established both in England and America. We had occasion to consider and decide the point at the last term, in the case of *The Columbian Insurance Company of Alexandria* v. *Lawrence*, 10 Pet. 517, 518, which was a policy against the risk of fire on land. The argument addressed to us on that occasion endeavored to establish the proposition, that there was no real distinction between policies against fire on land and at sea, and that in each case the same risks were included, and that as the risk of loss by fire occasioned by negligence was not included in a marine policy, unless that of barratry was also contained in the same policy, it followed that as the latter risk was not taken on a land policy no recovery could be had. In reply to that argument the court made the comments which have been alluded to at the bar, and the correctness of which it becomes now necessary to decide.

"It is certainly somewhat remarkable that the question now before us should never have been directly presented in the American or English courts, namely, whether, in a marine policy (as this may well enough be called), where the risk of fire is taken, and the risk of barratry is not (as is the predicament of the present case) a loss by fire remotely caused by negligence, is a loss within the policy. But it is scarcely a matter of less surprise, considering the great length of time during which policies against both risks have been in constant use among merchants, that the question of a loss by negligence in a policy against both risks should not have arisen in either country until a comparatively recent period. If we look to the question upon mere principle, without reference to authority, it is difficult to escape from the conclusion that a loss by a peril insured against, and occasioned by negligence, is a loss within a marine policy, unless there be some other language in it which repels that conclusion. Such a loss is within the words, and it is incumbent upon those who seek to make any exception from the words to show that it is not within the intent of the policy. There is nothing unreasonable, unjust, or inconsistent with public policy, in allowing the insured to insure himself against all losses from any perils not occasioned by his own personal fraud. It was well observed by Mr. Justice BAYLEY, in delivering the opinion of the court in *Busk* v. *The Royal Exchange Assurance Co.*, 2 Barn. & Ald. 79, after referring to the general risks in the policy, that 'the object of the assured certainly was to protect himself against all the risks incident to a marine adventure. The underwriter being therefore liable, *prima facie*, by the express terms of the policy, it lies upon him to discharge himself. Does he do so by showing that the fire arose from the negligence of the master and mariners?' 'If, indeed, the negligence of the master would exonerate the underwriter from responsibility in case of a loss by fire, it would also in cases of a loss by capture or perils of the sea. And it would, therefore, constitute a good defense in an action upon a policy, to show that the captain had misconducted himself in the navigation of the ship, or that he had not resisted an enemy to the utmost of his power.' There is great force in this reasoning, and the practical inconvenience of carving out such an

any other substance acting by expansion, without combustion.[1] It
likewise excludes all damage occasioned but *remotely or consequentially*

---

implied exception from the general peril in the policy, furnishes a strong ground
against it ; and it is to be remembered that the exception is to be created by construction of the court, and is not found in the terms of the policy. The reasons of
public policy, and the presumption of intention in the parties to make such an
exception, ought to be very clear and unequivocal to justify the court in such a
course. So far from any such policy or presumption being clear and unequivocal, it may be affirmed that they lean the other way. The practical inconvenience
of creating such an exception would be very great. Lord TENTERDEN alluded to
it in *Walker* v. *Maitland*, 5 Barn. & Ald. 174. 'No decision (said he) can be
cited, where in such a case (the loss by a peril of the sea), the underwriters have
been held to be excused in consequence of the loss having been remotely occasioned by the negligence of the crew. I am afraid of laying down any such rule.
It will introduce an infinite number of questions as to the *quantum* of care, which,
if used, might have prevented the loss. Suppose, for instance, the master were
to send a man to the masthead to look out, and he falls asleep, in consequence of
which the vessel runs upon a rock or is taken by the enemy ; in that case it might
be argued, as here, that the loss was imputable to the negligence of one of the
crew, and that the underwriters are not liable. These, and a variety of other
such questions, would be introduced in case our opinion were in favor of the
underwriters.' His lordship might have stated the argument from inconvenience,
even in a more general form. If negligence of the master or crew were under
such circumstances a good defense, it would be perfectly competent and proper
to examine on the trial any single transaction of the whole voyage ; whether
there was due diligence in all respects in hoisting or taking in sail, in steering
the course, in trimming the ship, in selecting the route, in stopping in port, in
hastening or retarding the operations of the voyage, for all these might be
remotely connected with the loss. If there had been more diligence, or less
negligence, the peril might have been avoided or escaped, or never encountered
at all. Under such circumstances the chance of a recovery upon a policy for any
loss, from any peril insured against, would of itself be a risk of no inconsiderable
hazard.

"This is not all ; we must interpret this instrument according to the known
principles of the common law. It is a well established principle of that law that
in all cases of loss we are to attribute it to the proximate cause, and not to any
remote cause : *Causa proxima non remota spectatur*, and this has become a maxim,
not only to govern other cases, but (as will be presently shown) to govern cases
arising under policies of insurance. If this maxim is to be applied, it disposes
of the whole argument in the present case, and why it should not be so applied
we are unable to see any reason. Let us now look to the authorities upon the
point. In *Busk* v. *The Royal Exchange Assurance Company*, 2 Barn. & Ald. 73,
the very point came before the court. The policy covered the risk by fire, and
the question made was, whether the fact that the loss of the ship by fire, occasioned by the negligence of the crew, was a good defense. The court held that
it was not. In that case the policy also included the risk of barratry ; and it is
now said that the decision of the court turned wholly upon that consideration, the
court being of opinion that in a policy where the underwriter takes the superior
risk of barratry, there is no ground to infer that he does not mean to take the
inferior risk of negligence ; it is certainly true that the court do rely in their
judgment upon this circumstance ; and it certainly does fortify it. But there is
no reason to say that the court wholly relied upon it, and that it constituted the
exclusive ground of the judgment ; on the contrary, Mr. Justice Bayley, in
delivering the opinion, takes pains, in the earlier part of that opinion, to state,
and to rely upon the maxim already stated. He said : 'In our law, at least, there
is no authority which says that the underwriters are not liable for a loss, the
proximate cause of which is one of the enumerated risks, but the remote cause
of which may be traced to the misconduct of the master and mariners.' 'It is

---

[1] *Perrin's Admr.* v. *Protection Ins. Co.*, 11 Ohio, 146 ; *Caballero* v. *Home Mut.
Ins. Co.*, 15 La. An. 217.

through the agency of gunpowder, such as injury done to a house by falling fragments in the blasting of rocks, or the shattering of a house by the stroke of a cannon ball; in which examples the shock of a projectile, and not ignition or combustion, is the proximate cause of the damage." [1]

Where, however, the explosion is caused by fire, *the damage must be traceable directly to the fire as the proximate cause, and not merely as the result of the explosion.* The fire must be shown to be the *causa proxima* and not the *causa remota.* If the injury is entirely due to concussion,

---

certainly a strong argument against the objection now raised for the first time, that in the great variety of cases upon marine policies, which have been the subjects of litigation in courts of justice (the facts of many of which must have presented a ground for such a defense), no such point has ever been made.' In *Walker* v. *Maitland*, 5 Barn. & Ald. 173, a similar question was presented, where the maxim was still more strongly indicated as the general, though not as the exclusive ground of the judgment; the case of *Bishop* v. *Pentland*, 7 Barn. & Cress. 219, turned exclusively upon the very ground of the maxim, and not a single judge relied upon the policy as containing the risk of barratry. Indeed, it does not appear that the risk of barratry was, in that case, in the policy. Mr. Justice Bayley, on that occasion, put the former cases as having been expressly decided upon this maxim. His language was: 'The cases of *Busk* v. *The Royal Exchange Assurance Company*, and *Walker* v. *Maitland*, establish as a principle that the underwriters are liable for a loss, the proximate cause of which is one of the enumerated risks, though the remote cause may be traced to the negligence of the master and mariners.' Then came the case of *The Patapsco Insurance Company* v. *Coulter*, 3 Pet. 222, where the loss was by fire, and barratry was also insured against. The court on that occasion held that in such a policy, a loss which was remotely caused by the master or the crew was a risk taken in the policy, and the doctrine in the English cases already cited was approved. It is true that the court laid great stress on the fact that barratry was insured against, but it may also be stated that this ground was not exclusively relied on, for the court expressly refer to and adopt the doctrine of the English cases, that the proximate and not the remote cause of a loss is to be looked to. It is known to those of us who constituted a part of the court at that time, that a majority of the judges were then of opinion for the plaintiff upon this last general ground, independently of the other. It was under these circumstances that the case of *The Columbian Insurance Company of Alexandria* v. *Lawrence*, 10 Pet. 507, came on for argument; and the court then thought that in marine policies, whether containing the risk of barratry or not, a loss whose proximate cause was a peril insured against is within the protection of the policy, notwithstanding it might have been occasioned remotely by the negligence of the master and mariners. We see no reason to change that opinion, and, on the contrary, upon the present argument, we are confirmed in it. The third and fourth questions are completely answered by the reasoning already stated. Those pleas contain no legal defense to the action in the form and manner in which they are pleaded, and are not sufficient to bar a recovery by the plaintiff. Some suggestion was made at the bar whether the explosion, as stated in the pleas, was a loss by fire or by explosion merely. We are of opinion that, as the explosion was caused by fire, the latter was the proximate cause of the loss. The fifth plea turns upon a different ground. It is that the taking of gunpowder on board was an increase of the risk. If the taking of the gunpowder on board was not justified by the usage of the trade, and therefore was not contemplated as a risk by the policy, there might be great reason to contend that, if it increased the risk, the loss was not covered by the policy. But in our opinion the facts are too defectively stated in the fifth plea to raise the question."

[1] CUSHING, J., in *Scripture* v. *Lowell, etc., Ins. Co., ante.*

the fact that it was caused by fire does not make the fire the proximate
cause, but the *cause of the cause*, and consequently the *causa remota*
instead of the *causa proxima*. "It were infinite for the law," says
Lord Bacon,[1] to consider the *causes of causes*, and their impulsion one
of another; therefore it contenteth itself *with the immediate cause*, and
judgeth of acts by that, without looking to any further degree." "If
that were not so," said Byles, J.,[2] "and a ship was in the neighborhood of Etna or Vesuvius, and was violently shaken by an eruption,
that would be damage by fire; or if a gun were fired off, loaded with
small shot, among crockery, that would be damage by fire; or it might
be said, that if the heat of the sun was too great, that would be damage by fire." The question as to the liability of an insurer against
"loss or damage by fire," for damage resulting from an explosion
caused by fire, was raised in an English case.[3] In that case, an action
was brought to recover for damages from what is called the Enith
explosion, which occurred in 1864, in the gunpowder magazines of
Messrs. Hall, at Euith, as was supposed from some accident on board
a barge moored against the bank, and loading gunpowder at the time.
Not only were the magazines destroyed, but great destruction was
occasioned to the buildings in the neighborhood, and even at a considerable distance walls were thrown down, windows driven in and glass
broken, and furniture injured in a great many instances. Upon these,
a variety of claims were preferred against the offices, but one (a) was
alone litigated, and seems to have been selected on account of the
particular phraseology of the policy, which it was imagined was more
extensive in operation than the usual expression "loss or damage by
fire" alone. The variation was slight, and was treated as unimportant by the court; the words were, that the insurers should make good
"*such loss or damage as might be occasioned by fire*" to the property of
the assured. The conditions of the policy set out in the case as
material, were the 5th, which provided "that losses by lightning"
would be made good when the property insured was actually set on
fire thereby, and burnt in consequence thereof; and the 8th, which
negatived all responsibility "where more than 25 pounds weight of
gunpowder was deposited or kept on the premises." It was argued on
the part of the plaintiff, that under the words "occasioned by fire,"
the injury was not confined to a fire on the premises, but included
every injury occasioned by fire in any way and at any distance. That

[1] Bac. Max. Reg. 1.
[2] *Everett* v. *The London Assurance*, 19 C. B. (N. S.) 126.
[3] *Everett* v. *The London Assurance, ante.*

the condition negativing the liability of the company when more than 25 lbs. of gunpowder were kept on the premises, showed that the parties contemplated the possibility of losses by explosion of gunpowder; that in the case of injury by water to a house done by putting out a fire in an adjoining house, it was the common practice of insurance offices to treat the damage as one arising from fire, and that if the injury was done by an explosion of gas in the next house, the loss would be made good. That the only difference was, that here the explosion was at a greater distance; that it did not follow that this injury was not contemplated by the policy, because an explosion of this kind was not the ordinary incident of all fires; that whenever a fire takes place, a disturbance of the air follows, only the more rapid and violent when gunpowder or gas suddenly ignites, and that the company must be liable here, when the loss arises from the ignition of the particular article—gunpowder. That in a recent scientific treatise by Professor Tindal, it had been shown that fire was the motion of the particles of the air when heated, and that this concussion of the air was nothing more than a movement of the particles, similar in fact to fire itself. In reply, it was contended that the loss in question was not within the meaning of the policy or the intention of the parties, as a damage by fire. That the atmospheric disturbance was the *causa proxima*, and fire only the *causa remota*, which would not be looked to in construing the rights of the parties; that, were it otherwise, injury occasioned to buildings by an earthquake, which was usually attributed to the action of subterranean fire; or upon the shattering of window glass by the salvos of artillery at a review, would be damage by fire. It was also urged that there must be actual ignition, or the action of fire upon the property. The court was unanimously in favor of the defendants, considering, per ERLE, C.J., that the decision depended entirely upon the question—"What was the meaning of the parties under the contract?" That the true construction was, that the words in which it was contained did not apply to the damage in question, and this view was fortified by the conditions of the policy. Per WILLES, J.: "In these insurance cases we are bound to look to the immediate cause. In this instance, it cannot be said that the loss was occasioned by fire, it was occasioned by a concussion caused by fire, and we must therefore go to the cause of causes before we arrive at the origin of the loss; but then this is not what was contemplated by the parties to the policy."[1]

. [1] In *Caballero* v. *Home, etc., Ins. Co.*, 15 La. An. 217, a fire broke out in a building about 200 feet away, in which a quantity of gunpowder was stored, which

But the damage in such cases is so intimately connected with the risk, that it is held that an insurance company may, at its option, pay a loss arising therefrom, and an injunction at the suit of a stockholder of the company to restrain the officers from paying such a claim will not be granted.[1]

Of course it is competent for the insurer to stipulate against liability for loss either by explosion or a fire resulting therefrom, and in such cases, where the proximate cause of the loss is an explosion, no liability exists.[2] Thus where the policy contained a provi-

---

exploded and caused the walls of the plaintiff's building to crack, and did other damage to the building to the amount of nearly $1,000, but the fire did not reach the building. Held not a loss within the policy.

[1] *Taunton* v. *Royal Ins. Co.*, *ante*.

[2] *U. S. Ins. Co.* v. *Foot*, 22 Ohio St. 340; 10 Am. Rep. 735; *Hayward* v. *Liverpool and London Ins. Co.*, 3 Keyes (N. Y.) 456; *Insurance Co.* v. *Tweed*, 7 Wall. (U. S.) 44; *Montgomery* v. *Fireman's Ins. Co.*, 16 B. Mon. (Ky.) 427; *Roe* v. *Columbus Ins. Co.*, 17 Mo. 301; *McAllister* v. *Tenn. Fire and Mar. Ins. Co.*, 17 id, 306; *Stanley* v. *Western Ins. Co.*, L. R. 3 Ex. 71. In *St. John* v. *Amer. Mut. Fire and Mar. Ins. Co.*, 11 N. Y. 516; 3 Bennett's Fire Ins. Cas., 761, the policy contained a clause providing that "this company will be liable for loss on property *burnt* by lightning, *but not for any loss or damage by fire happening by means of an invasion, riot or civil commotion, of any military or usurped power, nor for any loss occasioned by the explosion of a steam boiler, or explosions arising from any other cause, unless specially specified in the policy.*" The proofs of loss were properly made, and in them the fire and the manner in which it originated are stated and described as follows : "That on the 4th day of February, 1850, a fire occurred in the said building, Nos. 5 and 7 Hague street, whereby great and immediate loss and damage were sustained by deponents, by the injury done to their property insured as aforesaid. That the said fire originated on the said 4th day of February, 1850, and was immediately preceded by an explosion of a steam-boiler on the said premises, whereby the walls of the said building were mostly thrown down, and the fire which was used in the furnace of the steam-boiler and in stoves in various parts of the said building was communicated to the frame and woodwork of said building, and the materials and machinery contained therein." At the close of the plaintiffs' case the counsel for the defendants moved the court to dismiss the complaint, on the ground that it appeared from the evidence that the insured property was brought into contact with the fire solely by means of the explosion of the boiler, and that thus the loss, so far as the same was caused by fire, was occasioned directly by such explosion of the boiler ; and that, by the express conditions of the policy, the defendants were not liable for loss so occasioned. The justice granted the motion, and ordered judgment dismissing the complaint, and the counsel for the plaintiffs excepted. This judgment was affirmed by the superior court at general term ; and the plaintiffs appealed, and the judgment was affirmed upon appeal. DENIO, J., said : "As the sole peril insured against by this policy of insurance was loss or damage by fire, we should naturally expect, in examining exceptions contained in the contract, to find pointed out some circumstances under which the insurers would not hold themselves liable, though a loss by fire should take place. Hence a loss occasioned by invasion, insurrection, riot, and the 'like, has usually been found excepted in such policies; and, although in this, and perhaps in policies generally, the exception in this respect is in terms of losses by fire, the clause would be equally definite and intelligible if those words were omitted in the clause stating the exception. When, therefore, this policy proceeds to declare that the defendants will not be liable for any loss 'occasioned by the explosion of a steam-boiler,' it refers, *prima facie*, to such a loss as by the prior provisions of the contract the defendants would be bound to indemnify against, and not to one

sion exempting the company from liability for losses occasioned "by lightning or explosion of any kind unless fire ensues," and then

---

which would not be embraced in the general terms of the policy, and as to which there was no occasion to introduce an exception. The most usual consequence of the explosion of a steam-boiler is the breaking and rending the building in which it is contained and the movable property therein; and if this were the only consequence to be apprehended from such an occurrence, the exception introduced into this policy would be quite unnecessary, and we may presume it would not have been inserted. It would not be a loss or damage by fire, unless there was combustion, and then only to the extent of the damage properly attributable to the combustion. *Millaudon* v. *New Orleans Ins. Co.*, 4 Rob. La. R. 15. In one sense, it is true, the explosion is the consequence of fire, as steam is created by the application of heat; but it is understood that where fire is applied by design, as in culinary and several manufacturing processes, and a loss occurs in consequence of overheating or other misapplication of fire to the subject upon which it was intended to operate, and the injury is limited to that particular subject, such damage is not considered a loss by fire within the meaning of this class of contracts. Beaumont on Ins. 37, and *seq.* But another very usual concomitant of the explosion of a steam-boiler is, that the place in which it is situated is set on fire. Though this is not universally the case, it is sufficiently common to constitute a subject of consideration in entering into contracts for insurance. As the furnace is required to be in immediate proximity to the boiler, and as the explosion usually overturns and displaces everything in its vicinity, the danger of a loss by burning is very imminent. I think, therefore, we must understand by the assertion that the company will not be liable for any loss occasioned by the explosion of a steam-boiler, that the defendants contracted for an exemption, not from responsibility for such losses as they would not be bound to make good if no such clause had been inserted, but for those which, by the preceding terms of the policy, they had agreed to indemnify against, and which were very likely to be caused by an explosion. It is true, as argued by the plaintiffs' counsel, that the language would have been more distinct and certain if the words, by fire, had been inserted, as in the earlier member of the sentence, where losses by invasion, etc., are excepted; but where we see that the comprehensive words, 'any loss,' are used in the place of 'any loss or damage by fire,' we cannot, upon any authorized rules of interpretation, hold that a restricted meaning was intended.

"It is also true, as was insisted at the bar, that where the proximate cause of a loss, either in a marine or a fire policy, is one of the perils expressly insured against, the insurer cannot escape responsibility by showing that the property was brought within that peril by a cause not mentioned in the contract. The familiar example of a loss attributable to the negligence of the servants of the assured has recently been before this court, and we have recognized the principle to be as stated by the plaintiffs' counsel. *Matthews* v. *The Howard Ins. Co.*, 11 N. Y. 9. If, therefore, there had been nothing said in this policy respecting a steam-boiler, this loss, having been occasioned by fire as its proximate cause, would have rested on the insurers, though it had been shown, as it might have been, that the fire was kindled by means of the explosion. But this principle does not, I think, aid the plaintiffs. The doctrine is, that the courts will not go back to the remote cause where the immediate one belongs to the class insured against. Hence, as before remarked, the negligence of servants does not relieve the insurers. But suppose, by the very terms of a policy against fire, the parties agree that the insurers shall not be answerable for losses occasioned by the negligence of the servants of the assured, and it is found that a dwelling insured had been burned by the neglect of some necessary precaution which should have been taken by the housekeeper of the assured. It would clearly be a loss within the very terms of the exception, and the insurers would be discharged. The case is the same here. The parties knowing that fires were liable to be kindled by the explosion of a steam-boiler, and that by the general terms of the policy the insurers would be liable for a fire thus originating, agreed that for such losses the party would be his own insurer. The loss is within the terms of the exception, according to its popular meaning as well as its grammatical construction, and I do not see anything in the nature of the case which would warrant us in

for the loss or damage by fire only; the plaintiffs were engaged in
the business of rectifying spirits.   There was a small lamp standing

---

indulging in a criticism which should give the language a different meaning.
There is, as was mentioned on the argument, a possible case where the language
in question would not be entirely unmeaning upon the construction contended
for by the defendants' counsel.   An explosion may be caused by a fire exterior
to the boiler or furnace, and the building and movables may be injured by the
force of the steam. though no combustion takes place, and it may be true that the
insurer would be protected from answering for that loss by the exception in question.   But this theory requires a set of circumstances so unlikely to happen, that
I cannot think that the contract was framed with any view to them.   We shall, I
am persuaded, be more likely to construe the contract according to the intention
of the parties by adopting that interpretation which is most natural and obvious,
rather than to suppose possible cases, very unlikely to happen, and which it is
improbable the parties had in view.   I am of opinion, therefore, that the judgment of the superior court should be affirmed.   JOHNSON, J.   "The question in
this case is, whether the loss sustained by the plaintiffs by the burning of their
property. under the circumstances of this case. was a loss occasioned by the
explosion of a steam-boiler.   If it was, the defendants have expressly stipulated
that they shall not be charged with it.   Several interpretations of the clause in
question offer themselves for consideration.   In the first place, it may be that the
clause was introduced to exclude the mere injury by explosion without fire ; and
that although such an injury is not by law to be borne by an insurer against fire,
yet that the insurers thought it wise to guard against the possibility of its being
considered a loss by fire.   That such a loss has been sought to be recovered as a
loss by fire, though unsuccessfully (*Millaudon* v. *New Orleans Ins. Co.*, 4 La.
Rep. 15), and that the clause in question immediately follows a stipulation in
respect to liability for property burnt by lightning, which undeniably is merely a
statement of the exact measure of the liability which the law imposes in the absence
of any stipulation, are grounds for taking the view suggested of the clause in question.   Another interpretation suggested applies the exception to damage produced
by explosion, when the explosion is caused by a fire which itself comes within the
perils insured against ; as in case a fire should occur in the engine-room, and its
heat should cause the boiler to explode.   Upon the interpretation suggested, the
damage occasioned by the explosion would not be recoverable against the company.   Still another interpretation applies the exception to any loss by fire
occasioned by the explosion, and so exempts the company from responsibility for
the loss in this case.   This interpretation was adopted by the Superior Court,
upon the ground that every stipulation in a contract should be so expounded as
to give it some operation, and that this clause could have none unless it was so
construed.   Though the principle of exposition on which that court proceeded is
sound, we have already seen that the clause is capable of meaning, without
recourse to the particular interpretation put upon it in that court.   Neither of
these proposed interpretations is entirely satisfactory.   The general peril against
which the defendants undertook to indemnify the plaintiffs was 'immediate loss
or damage by fire.'   That was the subject-matter, and the only one about which
the contract was made.   All the defendants' relations with the plaintiffs grow out
of that one subject-matter, and any qualifications of their liability, contained in
the contract, presumptively relate to the indemnity which they have contracted
to afford to the plaintiffs, and to cases which but for those qualifications would or
might be covered by the contract for indemnity.   The language used, construing
it with reference to the subject-matter, is equivalent to a declaration on the part
of the insurers that they are not to be held responsible for any loss, whether it
comes within the general peril of fire or not; and without undertaking to consider whether it does or not, if such loss happen to be occasioned by the explosion
of a steam-boiler.   This is, I think, the fair sense of the language employed.
The prominent intention is to exclude the risk from the explosion of steam-boilers—
not the risk merely of the exploding force, but all risk.   That peril the insured
were content to bear.   Among the risks consequent upon an explosion, the most
prominent, next to the direct destruction by the explosive force, is the hazard
from the fire of the furnaces and other fires in the building being thrown about

in the building which was brought there by a person engaged in repairing the machinery. The vapor from the works filled the room

---

among combustible matter. So patent is it, that no one can contemplate the event of an explosion without recognizing this risk as one of the most obvious and important hazards attending upon such an event. Only one casualty happened to the premises and occasioned the destruction of property which the defendants are called upon to answer for. That was the explosion of the boiler. The burning was the direct and natural consequence of the explosion of the boiler, although it did not necessarily follow that fire would take place. It was as direct a consequence as the falling of the walls would have been in case the explosion had broken but a single timber, and the walls had not fallen for some hours. In such case it might be argued that the explosion broke but one timber, which brought the great weight upon some other, which giving way produced the catastrophe, and that therefore the fall of the whole was not a direct consequence of the explosion. The answer in both cases is, that the resulting destruction followed from the original casualty, without the intervention of any new cause, and followed from the nature and condition of the subject at the time of the casualty. The breaking of the beam in the supposed case, and the scattering of the coals from the stoves in the actual case, are the direct and immediate consequences of the explosion of the boiler; the fall and the fire are the natural consequences, due to no new casualty, but resulting from obvious natural forces, operating under the circumstances produced by the original exploding force. The whole loss in both cases is the immediate consequence of the explosion of the boiler. It was urged upon the argument that as fire was the actual means of destruction of the property in question, the court could not look back beyond the fire, upon the familiar principle, *causa proxima non remota spectatur*. It is undoubtedly true, that if the policy contained no exception this loss would clearly have been a loss by fire. There would be no occasion to consider how the fire happened, the parties not having contracted for indemnity against fire occurring only in particular ways, but generally against fire. The existence of the exception renders the inquiry necessary to enable us to say whether the loss is within its terms, and the meaning of those terms we have already considered. It was also argued, that if the parties had intended to except loss by fire occasioned by the explosion of a steam-boiler, those words should have been used; but that would have narrowed the exception to losses by fire only, whereas the language now used is broad enough to cover all losses so occasioned, whether by fire or explosive force, or in any other way in which losses by the excepted peril could be produced. The judgment should be affirmed." PARKER, J. "In this policy of insurance against fire was an exception in the following words : 'This company will be liable for losses on property burnt by lightning, but not for any loss or damage by fire happening by means of any invasion, insurrection, riot, or civil commotion, or of any military or usurped power, nor for any loss occasioned by the explosion of a steam-boiler, or explosions arising from any other cause, unless specially specified in this policy.' It is a question of law whether the facts of the case, which are undisputed, are covered by this exception of the policy. The policy must be so construed, if practicable, as to give effect to all its parts and make them severally consistent with each other. The insurance being against damage by fire alone, the exception of loss occasioned by the explosion of a steam-boiler would be needless and entirely inappropriate to the subject of the contract, unless it had some reference to damage done by fire. I think this clause was inserted with reference to the agency of fire, not in burning after the explosion, but in causing the explosion itself. All explosions of steam-boilers are referable to the action of fire. Without fire there could be no steam and no explosion ; and I think it was to save all doubt as to the question whether the destruction consequent upon an explosion was caused by fire, that the exception was inserted. That doubt may have been suggested by *Waters* v. *Merchants' Lous. Ins. Co.*, 11 Peters, 213, and *Millaudon* v. *The N. O. Ins. Co.*, 4 Louis. R. 15. The insured premises, having on them a steam-engine and boiler, were much more exposed to injury than they would have been without them ; but by making an exception, which threw upon the insured the risk of injury from explosion, the premises could be insured at the same premium as other premises on which there were no engine and boiler. The

where the lamp was, and coming in contact with the flame of the lamp, an instantaneous explosion ensued. The roof was blown off, and the principal part of the walls of the building were blown down, and the machinery was greatly injured. Soon after the explosion a fire ensued from the flame coming in contact with the spirits in the rear of the building. The damage caused by the explosion was considerable, while that caused by the fire way comparatively small. The court directed the jury to find the damage done by the explosion, and also that done by the fire, separately, and rendered judgment upon the verdict for the damage done by the fire alone; and, upon appeal, the judgment was sustained.[1] "There was," said PECKHAM, J., "no fire prior to this explosion. *The burning lamp was not a fire,* within the policy. The machinery was not on fire, within the meaning of the term, until after the explosion. The *explosion* here *was the principal* and *the fire the incident.* In such a case, there can be no doubt that the defendant is not liable for the damage caused by the explosion. Where, however, the explosion is the incident, and the fire the principal, a different question would be presented. Had the building been on fire, and in the course of a general conflagration there had been an explosion which had injured the machinery, which was rapidly consuming, different views and considerations might well

---

ordinary risk was thus cast upon the insurer, the extraordinary risk upon the insured. I do not think the parties to the contract had in view at the time it was made any other fire than that which, by its heat, caused the explosion. But they provided in express terms, that the insurers should not be liable for any loss occasioned by the explosion of a steam-boiler. This is a full and complete protection against loss of every description which might be occasioned by such explosion. Such explosion might occasion loss in different ways. It did so in this case; and because fire happened to be one of the means of destruction, it does not take that portion of the loss out of the exception and bring it within the general terms of the policy. The burning was as much a consequence of the explosion as the breaking and destruction from expansion. All were 'occasioned' by the explosion. The explosion was caused by fire, but, with all its immediate consequences, it was excepted from the operation of the policy. The injury by fire is plainly within the exception, as the injury would have been if the property had been destroyed by water in consequence of the breaking of the water-pipes by the explosion. As to the extent to which consequential damage may be traced and charged to the moving cause, I suppose the same rule applies to the exception as to the policy itself. In an action on the policy for loss by fire, the insured would be indemnified not only for goods actually burned, but also for those wet and soiled, for furniture cracked and warped. and under some circumstances, for goods stolen and lost by the removal of goods. The construction I have put on the extent of the exception is certainly not broader. The fire was an immediate consequence of the explosion, and the loss of property by fire, as well as by breaking and displacement, was clearly occasioned by it. The plaintiff could not recover for any damage caused by the explosion; and I think he had no more claim for that done by burning than for that portion broken and crushed by the concussion. The judgment of the superior court should be affirmed."

[1] *Briggs* v. *North American, etc., Ins. Co.,* 53 N. Y. 447.

obtain." The rule, as held in this case, is that *in all cases where the policy contains an exemption from liability for damages caused by an explosion, in order to entitle the insured to recover, where an explosion ensues, an accidental fire must have been the proximate, and the explosion the remote cause of the loss.*[1] This has been held to be the case even

---

[1] In *United States Life, F. & M. Ins. Co.* v. *Foote*, 22 Ohio St. 340 ; 10 Am. Rep. 735, McILLVANE, J., said : "The testimony shows that, at the time of taking out the policy, and until the time of the fire, the plaintiffs were engaged in the business of rectifying whiskey, and manufacturing fine spirits by the use of steam, in the building occupied by them as a liquor store, and in which the insured stock of merchandise, consisting principally of liquors. etc., was kept. The size of the building was sixty by one hundred and eighty feet, and was four stories high. There was communication between the stories through open stairways and hatches, The business of rectifying was carried on in the basement story, where the stills—large metallic vessels—were located The upper stories were chiefly used for storage of liquors and cooperage. The process of rectifying was conducted as follows : The raw spirits or liquor was conveyed by means of pipes, called leaders, from tubs situate in the upper stories to the stills below ; when the stills were thus charged, the liquor therein was converted into vapor by means of steam which passed through the stills in copper pipes, called worms ; the vapor thus evolved was conducted by other pipes to a condenser, where it was reduced to a liquid state. The vapor evolved in the process of rectification is an inflammable substance. It readily mixes with the atmosphere, and when so mixed, in certain proportions, is explosive, and when such mixture is brought in contact with flame it explodes. On the morning of the fire a large still was being charged through a leader about two inches in diameter, which passed into the still through a *vacuum valve* (an aperture in the still near its top), the diameter of which was about four inches. At the same time steam was passing through the worm, converting the liquor in the still into vapor, which escaped through the vacuum valve into the still room, and thence no doubt into other parts of the building. The process of thus charging the still, accompanied with the discharge of vapor, had continued for some time—perhaps an hour—preceding the fire. During the progress of this process, two jets of gas were burning in the still-room, one at a distance of three or four feet from the vacuum valve, and the other in another part of the room. There was no other fire or flame in the room or in the building at the time. Such being the circumstances, an explosion took place in the still-room. A sudden and violent combustion of the vapor, accompanied with a noise —described by one witness as being like the crack of a gun ; by another, as if a bundle of iron had been thrown on the pavement ; by another, as a crash, and by another, as a gush of fire ; and at the same instant the flame was driven through a doorway into another building, whereby a witness was badly burned. Immediately after the explosion, a flame was discovered escaping from the still through the vacuum valve, and at the same time, the building was discovered to be on fire throughout the several stories. From these facts and circumstances, we think, it was clearly shown that the fire, by which the building and stock of merchandise insured were consumed, was occasioned by, and resulted from, an explosion of spirit vapor mixed with atmosphere, and that the explosion was caused by the mixture coming in contact with the burning gas-jet.

" 1. The first question that we notice particularly is this : Was the explosion, which in fact occurred, such, in degree of violence, as was contemplated by the parties to the policy? The word 'explosion' is variously used in ordinary speech, and is not one that admits of exact definition. Its general characteristics may be described, but the exact facts which constitute what we call by that name, are not susceptible of such statement as will always distinguish the occurrences. It must be conceded that every combustion of an explosive substance, whereby other property is ignited and consumed, would not be an explosion within the ordinary meaning of the term. It is not used as the synonym of combustion. An explosion may be described generally, as a sudden and rapid combustion, causing violent expansion of the air, and accompanied by a report. But the rapidity of

when the explosion and the fire originating therefrom occurred outside the premises of the assured, *if the fire resulting could be traced directly*

---

the combustion, the violence of the expansion, and the vehemence of the report, vary in intensity as often as the occurrences multiply. Hence, an explosion is an idea of degrees, and the true meaning of the word, in each particular case, must be settled, not by any fixed standard, or accurate measurement, but by the common experience and notions of men in matters of that sort. In this case, although the building was not rent asunder, or the property therein broken to pieces, there was a sudden flash of flame, a rush of air, and a report like the 'crack of a gun,' which certainly brings the occurrence within the common meaning of the word, as used in many instances. 'Any explosion whatever' is the phrase used in the condition to the policy, and it is qualified by the context only to the extent that it must be an 'explosion' of some 'explosive substance,' and of sufficient force as to result in loss or damage to the property insured. And these characteristics we have found to exist in the occurrence that resulted in the loss of this property.

"2. It is claimed that the fire which destroyed the property insured did not result from the explosion, but, on the contrary, that the explosion was incident to and caused by the fire, which, if there had been no explosion, would have accomplished the whole loss and damage ; or, at least, that such inferences may be drawn from the facts in the case as fairly and legitimately as contrary inferences. The proof unquestionably shows that the origin of the fire and the explosion were simultaneous. It may be true, in a strictly scientific sense, that all explosions caused by combustion are preceded by a fire. The scientist may demonstrate, in a case where gunpowder is destroyed by fire, or in any case where the explosion is caused by or accompanies combustion, that ignition and combustion precede the explosion ; but the common mind has no conception of such combustion, as a fact independent of the explosion where they occur in such rapid succession that no appreciable space of time intervenes. The terms of this policy must be taken in their ordinary sense ; and we are satisfied that the proof shows, according to the ordinary sense and understanding of men in reference to such matters, that the explosion occasioned the fire which destroyed the property insured ; or, in other words, that the loss resulted from an explosion within the true intent and meaning of this policy. It is true that the explosion was caused by a burning gas-jet, but that was not such fire as was contemplated by the parties as the peril insured against. The gas-jet, though burning, was not a destructive force, against the immediate effects of which the policy was intended as a protection ; although it was a possible means of putting such destructive force in motion, it was no more the peril insured against than a friction match in the pocket of an incendiary. The conclusions to which we thus arrive are mere inferences from other facts — facts, however, about which there was no conflict in the testimony— yet they are so manifestly true that we think it was error of law, under our statute, to reverse the judgment rendered thereon at the special term of the Superior Court, upon the strength of contrary inferences drawn from the same facts by the reviewing court.

"3. The next question arises upon the terms of the policy, and is one of construction purely : Was it intended, by the provisions of the seventh condition, to exempt from the risks assumed by the policy, losses *by fire* occasioned by an explosion? It is claimed that the clause exempting losses by explosion taken alone, or construed in connection with other clauses in the condition, does not show such intention. It is true that the words 'by fire,' or their equivalent, are omitted in this clause, though expressed in some of the former clauses. The foundation point, however, in construing this condition, is found in the general undertaking of the policy. It will be observed that the underwriter undertook to insure against loss and damage *by fire* only ; but, nevertheless, against loss and damage by fire generally, and the maxim, *causa proxima, non remota, spectatur,* applies. Now, we think, without doubting, that the purpose of inserting this condition was to relax the vigor of this maxim, and exempt from the general risk of the policy certain losses, which would otherwise fall within its scope and meaning. The first clause of the condition provides that 'this company is not liable for loss or damage by lightning or tornado, unless expressly mentioned or insured

14

to the explosion as the proximate cause, and no near cause had intervened
between the fact accomplished and the cause.   Thus, in a case decided by

---

against.' If this were the whole of the clause, and it were not understood that
the loss and damage referred to, were such as might result from *fire occasioned by
lightning or tornado,* it would be utterly meaningless and nugatory, for the reason
that the underwriter had not undertaken to insure against lightning or tornado.
So far the construction is plain enough, but a difficulty arises from the conclusion
of the clause, to wit, 'but will be responsible for loss or damage to property consumed by fire occasioned by lightning.' The exception to the rule of exemption
from loss by lightning appears to be as broad as the rule itself. But I apprehend
that a case might arise in which effect and operation could be given to all the
terms of this clause, including those which are implied as well as those expressed.
At all events, it is perfectly clear that loss and damage by lightning and tornado
are not within the expressed risks of the policy, unless a fire supervenes; nor is
there anything in the policy from which such risks can be implied. The condition continues : 'Nor will the company be responsible for any loss or damage to
property consumed by fire happening by reason of, or occasioned by, any invasion, insurrection, riot, or civil commotion, or any military or usurped power.'
The exemptions here provided for are expressly limited to losses within the terms
of the general risk of the policy. But if such limitation had not been expressed,
it would have been implied. The next clause is as follows : 'Nor when the loss
is occasioned or superinduced by the fraud, dishonesty, or criminal conduct of the
insured.' There is no pretext for holding that the loss here contemplated is other
than loss by fire, although no such qualification is expressed. Then follows the
clause in question, which, to all intents and purposes, is framed like the preceding one : 'Nor to any loss or damage occasioned by, or resulting from, any explosion whatever, whether of steam, gunpowder, camphene, coal oil, gas, nitroglyc-
erine, or any explosive article or substance, unless expressly insured against and
special premium paid therefor.' Unless there is something in the subject-matter
of this clause that indicates that the words 'by fire' were omitted, for the purpose of showing a design to adhere to, and continue the general risk in case an
explosion should result in a fire, we think that they, or their equivalent, should
be supplied by implication or construction. Is such purpose indicated by any
fair use of the terms employed? That a loss, other than by combustion, resulting
from an explosion, when the explosion itself is caused by a destructive fire already
in progress, comes within the general risk of a policy against fire only, is a doctrine not only reasonable in itself, but is sustained by authority. *Waters* v. *La.
Mer. Ins. Co.,* 11 Pet. 225; *Scripture* v. *Low. Mut. Fire Ins. Co.,* 10 Cush. 357;
Millaudon v. *N. O. Ins. Co.,* 4 La. Ann. 15. And it is quite clear that a loss by
fire, which is occasioned by an explosion, is within the like risk. Now, the express
terms of this clause are, 'any loss or damage occasioned by, or resulting from,
any explosion whatever.' These terms are certainly comprehensive enough to
include both descriptions of loss — whether loss by the explosive force, or loss by
superinduced combustion. And that such is their legal effect has been directly
decided in the case of *Stanley* v. *Western Ins. Co.,* Law Rep. 1868; 3 Excheq. 71.
It is not necessary at this time to either approve or disapprove, to the whole
extent, the doctrine in *Stanley's case,* as in this case no damage was sustained
from the explosion without the intervention of a fire, nor, indeed, was the explosion caused by a fire within the meaning of the policy. But we can find no good
reason for doubting that loss and damage *by fire,* resulting from an explosion, was
intended to be exempted by this condition from the general risk of the policy, and
are of opinion, therefore, that this clause properly construed should read, 'nor
any loss or damage *by fire* occasioned by, or resulting from, any explosion whatever.'

"4. It is claimed by defendants in error, that the peril by which the property
insured was destroyed, was within the exception to the seventh condition; that
is, it was 'expressly insured against, and special premium paid therefor;' or, in
other words, was excepted out of the exception. The reasoning by which this
proposition is sought to be maintained is thus stated : 'The body of the policy
covered loss by fire on liquors, etc., with the privilege of rectifying and manufacturing fine spirits by steam not generated in the building. The property

the United States Supreme Court,[1] the plaintiff held a policy upon a quantity of cotton stored in a warehouse. The policy contained a stipulation, among other things exempting the insurer from "any loss or damage that may happen by means of any * * * explosion * * *." An explosion occurred in a warehouse directly across the street, some fifty feet distant, which threw down the walls of the

---

insured was whisky, as well in the process of rectification and manufacture as manufactured—whisky in the still; as well as spirits in the barrel—the whisky vapor itself, while passing through the columns to the cooler, or wherever else it might make its way. If it was in this form *an explosive substance or article*, such as is intended by the language of the condition, or if, in the process of manufac_ ture allowed by the policy, it was likely to become such by escape and mingling with the air in the building, then the insurance was upon it, as an agent known to be explosive under certain circumstances likely to happen, and with the express assent of the company to the carrying on of that process, in the course of which its explosive nature would naturally and probably be developed.' The principle sought, by this argument, to be applied, is announced in *Harper* v. *New York City Ins. Co.*, 22 N. Y. 441; *Fitton* v. *Accidental Death Ins. Co.*, 17 Com. Bench N. S. 112. In the case of *Harper* v. *N. York City Ins. Co.*, the condition exempted the company from liability *for loss occasioned by camphene*. The fire was occasioned by a workman's throwing a lighted match into a pan upon the floor containing camphene. The risk was upon a printing stock, privileged for a printing office, camphene not being expressly enumerated. But it was shown that that article was a usual part of such a stock, and its use was therefore authorized. For this reason alone, because it was impliedly insured, it was held that the exception did not apply. The following extract from the opinion expresses its doctrine : 'A policy can be so framed as to allow the presence of a dangerous article, and even so as to insure its value, while, at the same time, it might exempt the insurer from loss if occasioned by the presence or use of the article. But I think it would need very great precision of language to express such an intention. When camphene or any hazardous fluid is insured, and its use is plainly admitted, the dangers arising from that source are so obviously within the risk undertaken, that effect should be given to the policy accordingly, unless a different intention is very plainly declared.' In answer to this claim, we say : 1. That the spirit vapor, having escaped from its confinement and passed into the still-room, where it became mixed with atmosphere so as to form an explosive substance, under circumstances that precluded all possibility of reclaiming and utilizing it, was no longer a part of the stock of merchandise insured, and was not under the protection of the policy. 2. If, from the nature of the property insured, the parties, at the time the risk was taken, might reasonably have anticipated the peril by which it was afterward destroyed, it is reasonable to suppose that such peril was in contemplation at the time, and that they contracted in reference to it. Hence, if the general risk of the policy was expressed in terms broad enough to include the peril, it must be presumed that they intended to do so ; and, on the other hand, if an exception to the risk was made in terms which fairly and plainly took such particular peril out of the general risk, it must be presumed that they intended to exempt such particular peril from the risk. Again, if it be claimed that there was an exception to such exemption, whereby the particular peril was saved from the exemption and left under the general risk, it is reasonable that the terms of exception should be at least as explicit as the terms of exemption. How is it in this case? The risk was against all loss by fire. The exception from the risk was 'any loss or damage occasioned by an explosion of steam, gunpowder,' etc. The exception to this exemption was 'unless expressly insured against, and special premium paid therefor.' Therefore, it only remains to be said, that no loss or damage occasioned by an explosion of any of these substances named was expressly insured against, nor was any special premium paid for any such special risk."

[1] *Insurance Co.* v. *Tweed*, 7 Wall. (U. S.) 44.

warehouse in which the explosion occurred, and scattered the cotton and other combustible materials in the street, and an extensive conflagration ensued, in which the plaintiff's warehouse was consumed. The fire was not communicated directly to it from the building in which the explosion occurred, but from another building fired by the explosion. The court held that, *if the fire happened or took place by means of the explosion*, the insurers were not liable; and to ascertain that fact it was important to ascertain *whether any near cause had intervened between the explosion and the fire that consumed the warehouse*, that was of itself sufficient to stand as the cause of the misfortune. The fact that the fire did not reach the plaintiff's warehouse directly from the building fired by the explosion, or that the wind carried the flames there, supplied no near force sufficient to stand as the *cause* of the burning, and the loss must therefore be attributed to the explosion as the proximate cause. But it is believed that the doctrine of this case is really untenable, and not fairly within the spirit or intention of the policy or the parties thereto. It is evident that the exemption was only intended or expected to apply to cases of an explosion in the building itself, and not to fires occurring by reason of explosions elsewhere. Again, applying the rule advanced in the case, a whole city might be consumed, and yet the insurers who had taken the precaution to insert such clauses in their policies, would escape liability in case the fire originated from an explosion, unless some *extraordinary cause* intervened that, in the language of the court, "would stand for a new cause." This rule is very proper as applied to the building in which the explosion occurred, but to apply it to other buildings consumed by reason of the ignition of buildings standing apart therefrom, is not only contrary to the evident intent of the parties and a fair construction of the instrument, but is also unjust, unreasonable and unwarranted, and is in defiance of the rule that exemptions in a policy of insurance will be construed according to the evident intention of the parties, and most favorably for the assured. The better doctrine is that exemptions in a policy, as well as conditions, will be strictly construed, and will not be operative to protect the insurer, unless the case is brought strictly within the *letter* of the exemption. This principle was well illustrated by a novel case which came before the Connecticut Supreme Court.[1] In that case, goods stored in a town occupied by the United States forces during the war, were insured against fire by a policy exempting the insurers from liability for damage by fire, arising by

[1] *Bacon* v. *The Ætna Ins. Co.*, 40 Conn. 575.

means of any invasion, insurrection, riot or civil commotion, or of any
military or usurped power.   The town, being attacked by a superior
force of the enemy, was abandoned by the troops, who, by order of
their commanding officer, set fire to a building containing military
stores, to prevent their falling into the hands of the enemy.   The fire
spread to the building containing the insured goods, destroying them.
The court held: 1. That the fire which destroyed the plaintiffs' goods
did not happen or take place by means of the attack by the rebels on
the city, nor by means of invasion or insurrection, riot or civil commotion, within the meaning of the proviso in the policy.   The attack by
the rebels furnished a motive to the setting on fire of the city hall, but
was not the proximate cause of the fire.   2. That the terms "military
or usurped power," in the proviso, do not include the lawful acts of
the military authorities of the government, but relate to organized
unlawful force, acting in hostility to the government or in subversion
thereof.   A fire caused by the lawful orders of the officer in command
of the military forces of the United States would not, therefore, be
within the exception.   3. That the defendants were liable for the loss.
The court further laid down the rule *that it is the duty of an insurance
company, seeking to limit the operation of its contract of insurance by special
provisos or exceptions, to make such limitations in clear terms, and not leave
the insured in a condition to be misled.   The insured may reasonably be
held entitled to rely on a construction favorable to himself where the terms
will rationally permit it.* [1]

Destruction of buildings to arrest fire.

SEC. 99.   When a fire is raging in the vicinity of a building or property insured, its destruction by explosion or otherwise, by the muni-

---

[1] In *Commercial Ins. Co.* v. *Robinson,* 64 Ill. 265, the policy stipulated against
liability for "*damages by fire caused* by means of an invasion, insurrection, riot,
civil commotion, or military or usurped power, nor from any loss caused by the
explosion of gunpowder, camphene or any explosive substance, *or explosion of
any kind.*"   Under this peculiar wording of the restriction as to liability, inasmuch as the last clause of exemption did not provide that the insurer should
not be liable for *a fire* resulting from "an explosion of any kind," it was held
that, as the fire was not caused by the explosion of gunpowder or camphene, the
insurers were liable.   In *Boatman's Ins. Co.* v. *Parker,* 23 Ohio St. 85, where the
policy stipulated, "not liable for damages occasioned *by the explosion of a steam
boiler, nor for damages resulting from such explosion, nor explosions caused by gunpowder, gas or other explosive substances,*" it was held that the insurers were
liable for a loss by fire occasioned by an emission of gas from oil in the process
of distillation, which settled near the floor and came in contact with the fire under
the stills.   The fire extended into the receiving-house, where gas and oil were
ignited and the explosion occurred, and the ignited oil being thus spattered over
the works, they were consumed.   But in *United States, etc., Ins. Co.* v. *Foote,* 22
Ohio St. 340, a contrary doctrine was held.   See statement of case, *ante.*

cipal authorities, to prevent the spread of the conflagration, is held to
be a loss by fire within the terms of a policy;[1] so injuries to goods by

---

[1] In *City Fire Ins. Co.* v. *Corlies*, 21 Wend. (N. Y.) 367, BRONSON, J., in passing
upon this question, said : " The building containing the goods was destroyed by
order of the mayor of the city, for the purpose of arresting the progress of a conflagration. Are the insurers answerable for this voluntary destruction of the
property? This question has been presented in a double form,—the one supposing that the mayor acted with, and the other that he acted without, authority.
1. Let us first assume that the mayor acted illegally. If the fire had been
kindled by an incendiary, it is not denied that the insurers would be answerable.
Why are they not then answerable, if the mayor acted without authority? The
act, though not done for a wicked purpose, was as illegal as though it had been
the work of a felon. The answer attempted is, that although the mayor had no
authority, yet as he acted *colore officii*, this is a case of loss happening by means
of usurped power, which is expressly excepted by the policy. It is impossible
to maintain that a mere excess of jurisdiction by a lawful magistrate is the exercise of an usurped power within the meaning of this contract. That is not what
the insurers had in mind when they made the exception. It was an usurpation
of the power of government against which they intended to protect themselves.
Such was the interpretation given to the same words in a policy as early as the
year 1767. *Drinkwater* v. *The London Assur. Co.*, 2 Wils. 363; *ante*, 12. The
property insured was destroyed by a mob, which arose on account of the high
price of provisions; and the insurers were held liable, notwithstanding a proviso
in the policy that they would not answer for a destruction by 'usurped power.'
BATHURST, J., said those words, according to the true import thereof and the
meaning of the parties, could only mean an invasion of the kingdom by foreign
enemies, to give laws and usurp the government, or an internal armed force in
rebellion, assuming the power of government, by making laws, and punishing for
not obeying those laws. WILMOT, C.J., said, the words meant invasion from
abroad, or an internal rebellion, when armies are employed to support it; when
the laws are dormant and silent, and firing of towns is unavoidable. In *Lang-
dale* v. *Mason*, 2 Marsh. Ins. 791; *ante*, 16, it was said by Lord MANSFIELD, that
these words were ambiguous, but they had been the subject of judicial determination; that they must mean rebellion conducted by authority—determined
rebellion, with generals who could give orders. And he added: 'Usurped
power takes in rebellion, acting under usurped authority.' Whatever doubt
there may have been originally about the meaning of the words 'usurped
power,' in a policy, their legal import had been settled long before this contract
was made; and we cannot assume that these parties used the words in any other
than their legal sense. 2. But the mayor acted under lawful authority; there
was no usurpation of any kind. Whether he had the concurrence of two aldermen as the statute provides, or not, there can be no doubt of his common-law
power, as the chief magistrate of the city, to destroy buildings, in a case of necessity, to prevent the spreading of a fire. Indeed the same thing may be done by any
magistrate, or even by a citizen without official authority. *The Mayor of N. Y.* v.
Lord, 17 Wend. 285. If the mayor acted by lawful authority, it is then said that
the property was destroyed for the benefit of the city, and that the corporation
(not the insurers) must bear the loss. This case does not fall within the statute
charging certain losses on the city, because it does not appear that the mayor
had 'the consent and concurrence of any two aldermen,' 2 R. L. 367, § 81; and
for the further reason, that the property would have been consumed by fire, if
its destruction had not been ordered by the magistrate. *The Mayor of N. Y.* v.
Lord, 17 Wend. 285. It is said that the coporation is liable at the common law
for the acts of the mayor; but no authority was cited in support of the position,
and I am not prepared to say that, in a case like this, the doctrine can be maintained. The inclination of my mind is strongly the other way. But suppose the
city is liable, I do not see how that fact can affect this contract. If the insurers
pay the loss, they may, perhaps, have an action against the corporation of the
city, in the name of the assured, to recover back the money. *Mason* v. *Sainsbury*,
8 Doug. 61; *ante*, 19. But however that may be, the fact that the assured may
have a remedy against the city, cannot change or qualify the undertaking of the

water used in endeavoring to extinguish a fire.[1] So it has been held that an injury to a building by the fall upon it of the wall of a build- ing destroyed by fire, although not occurring until three days after the fire, is covered by a policy insuring against a loss by fire.[2]

Loss by theft—proximate cause.

SEC. 100. So where goods are stolen from a burning building, or while they are being removed therefrom, the loss is within the policy if they were stolen on account of the fire,[3] upon the principle that

insurers." *Gordon* v. *Remington,* 1 Camp. 133 ; *Waters* v. *Merch., etc., Ins. Co.,* 11 Pet. (U. S.) 225. In *Greenwald* v. *The Ins. Co.,* 3 Phila. (Penn.) 323, the property insured, a stock of mechandise in a frame store building, was situated in the town of Americus, Georgia, in which there are no means of extinguishing a fire by the use of water. It appears that the fire in question did not originate on the premises insured, but it had reached them and they were burning when the citizens assembled, with the view to extinguish the fire and prevent its spreading further, applied gunpowder to them and blew them up. 'Had this measure,' said SHARSWOOD, J., 'been resorted to before the fire had actually begun its work of destruction on the property insured, it might be a question whether the under- writers would be liable.' *Hilliers* v. *Alleghany Mutual Insurance Company,* 3 Barr, 470, might be an authority in this case. But here, altogether apart from the fire caused from the explosion, the proximate loss was a fire not caused by an explosion. The case is like the destruction of goods by water applied to extin- guish the flames which had caught them or the building in which they are stored. If left to themselves they would have been inevitably destroyed by the fire ; it would last as long as it had fuel to feed on. It is certainly very much against the true interests of insurers to raise objections founded on the honest efforts of the insured or others, to prevent the spread of fires, much more to frame clauses meant to make the right of recovery depend upon what is or is not done by strangers or others present at the fire. Life indeed as well as property is often in peril, but where it is not, men might be disposed under such circumstances, out of regard to the insured, to stand still and let property perish. rather than imperil by interfering with his claim for indemnity against the insurers. It would be a novel clause to introduce into a policy that in case of fire, the insur- ance should be void, if any water were applied to extinguish it. Quite as novel would it be were it provided that if there were no water nothing else should be done. Yet the defendants in this case have told us, that the clause, that the insurers should not be liable for an explosion by gunpowder, was meant to guard against the very thing which had been done. Had the citizens of Americus, instead of resorting to gunpowder, have succeeded in any other way in separat- ing the building in question from those contiguous to it, we would probably have been told that it was destruction by a mob, against which there is a pro- vision in most policies, if not in this. We construe this clause differently, and more for the interests of the underwriters when we say, that fire *originating* from an explosion of gunpowder was what was meant to be guarded against, and not an honest effort, even if it was injudicious, on the part of those present to stop the flames." *Greenwald* v. *Ins. Co.,* 3 Phila. (Penn.) 323.

[1] *Witherell* v. *Maine Ins. Co.* 49 Me. 200 ; *Geisick* v. *Crescent. etc., Ins. Co.,* 19 La. An. 297 ; *Hilliers* v. *Alleghany Ins. Co.,* 3 Penn. St. 470 ; *Thompson* v. *Mon- treal Ins. Co.,* 6 U. C. Q. B. 319 ; *Independent, etc., Ins. Co.* v. *Agnew,* 34 Penn. St. 96 ; *Whitehurst* v. *Fayetteville, etc., Ins. Co.,* 6 Jones L. (N. C.) 352.

[2] *Johnson* v. *West Scotland Ins. Co.,* 7 C. C. (Sc.) 52.

[3] *Newmark* v. *Liverpool, etc., Ins. Co.,* 30 Mo. 160 ; *American Ins. Co.* v. *Bryan,* 26 Wend. (N. Y.) 563 ; *White* v. *Republic Ins. Co.,* 57 Me. 91 ; 2 Am. Rep. 22 ; *Witherell* v. *Maine Ins. Co.,* 49 Me. 200 ; *Hillier* v. *Alleghany Ins. Co.,* 3 Penn. St. 470 ; *Whitehurst* v. *Fayetteville, etc., Ins. Co.,* 6 Jones (N. C.) 352 ; *Tallman* v. *Home Ins. Co.,* 16 La. An. 426 ; *Lewis* v. *Springfield F. & M. Ins. Co.,* 10 Gray (Mass.) 159 ; *Thompson* v. *Ins. Co.,* 6 U. C. (Q. B.) 319.

when goods are damaged *ex necessitate* to preserve them, the insurer is liable for the damage.[1] It is immaterial whether the goods were burned or stolen, while being removed, or after they are removed, so far as the liability of the insurers is concerned; if the existing circumstances are such that their continuance in the building would create a total loss, it remains a total loss until the property is beneficially restored to the assured, and, if the goods would have been destroyed by the fire, if they had not been removed, the loss by theft or water is a natural consequence of the peril insured against.[2]

The insurer is liable for a loss happening to the property insured, from the peril insured against, when the peril covered by the policy is the proximate cause of the loss. He is only relieved from liability when the peril insured against is the *remote* cause of the loss, or the loss results from the fault of the insured, or when from his *laches* or *fraud* the contract is avoided.[3] When the insurance is against loss by fire, the insurer is liable for any damage done to the property by reason of a fire, even though the property itself was not burned, or in anywise injured by fire, *if the fire was the proximate cause of such damage, and the damage arose in consequence of efforts reasonably made by the assured or others, in view of the imminence of the peril, to preserve the property from conflagration,* which must be judged of from the peculiar circumstances of each case.[4] But, as it is competent for the insurer to impose such

---

[1] *Case* v. *Hartford F. Ins. Co.*, 13 Ill. 676; *Witherell* v. *Maine Ins. Co.*, 49 Me. 200; *Leiber* v. *Liverpool, London & Globe Ins. Co.*, 6 Bush (Tenn.) 639; *American Ins. Co.* v. *Bryan*, 26 Wend. (N. Y.) 563; *Tilton* v. *Hamilton Ins. Co.*, 1 Bos. (N. Y.) 367; *Independent Ins. Co.* v. *Agnew*, ante. The rule in such cases was well illustrated in *Gordon* v. *Remington*, 1 Camp. 123, where, upon the ship being chased by a privateer, *to prevent her capture*, her guns were discharged down her hatchways which set her on fire, and the court held it a loss within the policy. So, in *City Ins. Co.* v. *Corliss*, and *Greenwald* v. *Ins. Co.*, ante, where the blowing up of buildings, *to prevent the spread of a conflagration*, was held a loss within the policy.

[2] *Tilton* v. *Hamilton Ins. Co.*, ante; *Bondrett* v. *Hentigg*, Holt (N. P.) 149; *Hahn* v. *Corbett*, 2 Bing. 205. In *Independent Ins. Co.* v. *Agnew*, 34 Penn. St. 96, the premises were discovered to be on fire, and the goods were considerably injured by water, and many of them were stolen. It was held that the insurers were liable for the goods stolen.

[3] *White* v. *Republic F. Ins. Co.*, 57 Me. 91; 2 Am. Rep. 22.

[4] In *White* v. *Republic F. Ins. Co.*, ante, it appeared that on the night of the conflagration of July 4, 1866, at Portland, the plaintiff, apprehensive that the building known as Ware's block, on the northerly side of Federal street, the third story of which was occupied by him for the manufacture of brushes, would be destroyed by fire, removed his stock, consisting of bristles and manufactured brushes, and his tools from the building. The block was not destroyed or injured by the fire; and the plaintiff brought an action to recover the damages thus done to his stock and tools, and for the expense incurred in removing them. "The important and interesting question," said DICKENSON, J., "is raised, whether the plaintiff's loss is covered by the policy. In general, the assured is entitled to

conditions as he pleases, he may, of course, stipulate against liability for
theft either *during* or *after* a fire, and, in such case, no liability attaches

---

indemnity, unless the loss happens from the qualities or defects of the subject
insured, his own fault, or some peril for which he is answerable. 1 Phillips on
Ins. 639. It is argued by the learned counsel for the defendants, that this is not
a loss by fire; that fire was not the proximate cause of the damage; and that
therefore the loss is not covered by the policy. While it has been held that a loss
by lightning without combustion is not a loss by fire, it has also been held that
the loss of a building by being blown up by gunpowder, and demolished to stop
a conflagration, is within the terms of a fire policy. *Babcock* v. *Montgomery Co.
Mut. Ins. Co.*, 6 Barb. 637; *Keniston* v. *Merrimack Co. Mut. Ins. Co.*, 14 N. H.
341; *City Ins. Co.* v. *Corlies*, 21 Wend. 367. Damage done to goods by having
water thrown upon them in extinguishing a fire, and a loss of goods by theft after
they have been removed from a fire, are covered by the policy. *Hillier* v. *Alleghany Ins. Co.*, 3 Penn. 470; *Witherell* v. *Maine Ins. Co.*, 49 Me. 200. A bolt
may be loosened, or a timber started, in a storm, without causing any loss until
the subsequent action of the water or climate, or the greater strain of a different
cargo has so augmented the injury, as to cause the loss of the vessel; and yet
such a loss is a loss by the storm. *Stephenson* v. *Piscataquis Ins. Co.*, 54 Me. 76.
So if, after a storm has subsided, the boat is lost by reason of the disabled condition of the ship, in consequence of damage done during the storm, it is a
loss by the storm. *Potter* v. *Ocean Ins. Co.*, 3 Sum. 27. In these and like cases
the direct proximate cause of the damage or loss is not to be found in the fire,
or the storm but in the water, the removal of the goods, the action of the climate,
or strain of the cargo, or the disabled state of the ship. If courts were required
to hold that no loss is caused by a policy of insurance unless the peril insured
against is directly operating upon the subject insured at the time of the ultimate
catastrophe, they would deny the right to recover in many cases where it has
long been recognized by courts of the highest authority. The legal maxim, *causa
proxima spectatur*, is by no means of unusual application in its strict technical
sense. If a loss from demolishing a building with gunpowder to stay the progress of a conflagration comes within the terms of a fire policy, ought not the
damage and expense of removing such building to be recoverable, if the object
in view could be as speedily and successfully accomplished? In such cases is not
the fire, the impending conflagration, the existing operating cause alike of the
destruction of the building or of its removal from danger? Is the assured entitled to recover damages for one of the effects of the same procuring cause, and
not for the other? If by reason of the immobility of real estate and the necessity
of speedy action on such occasions, it becomes necessary to demolish a building,
at the cost of the underwriters, to prevent it and other property from being
destroyed by fire, does not the analogy of the law require that they should also
be chargeable for the damage and expense of saving personal property from
destruction by removing it to a place of safety? Is not the producing cause of
both results the same? So if the underwriters are liable for damage done to
goods by having water thrown upon the building in which they are stored, to
extinguish the fire, ought they not, also, to be liable for damage done to goods, in
time of imminent peril, by throwing water upon the building containing them to
prevent it and them from destruction, though actual ignition has not taken place?
In both cases, technically speaking, the water and not the fire is the direct proximate cause of the damage. It is neither the policy of the law nor public policy
to make it for the interest of the assured, in case of fire, to postpone the use of
the means for extinguishing the fire, and the removal of the goods, until the
building containing them is actually on fire. In many, if not most, cases, such
delay would be tantamount to consigning both goods and building to destruction.
Would the interest of insurance companies or the public morals be subserved by
the establishment of such a policy?

"The question presented is one of considerable difficulty, and one upon which
the authorities are at variance. While the supreme court of Illinois, in a case
like the one at bar, have held that the underwriters are liable for the damage to
the goods and the expense of removing them, the court in Pennsylvania have
denied them liability. *Case* v. *Hartford Ins. Co.*, 13 Ill. 676; *Hillier* v. *Alleghany*

for goods stolen.[1]   The general rule embraces all losses by an injury to
the goods by water, while endeavoring to extinguish a fire;[2] by theft

Ins. Co., 3 Penn. 470.   We think the liability of the underwriters, in these and
similar cases, depends very much upon the imminence of the peril, and the rea-
sonableness of the means used to effect the removal.   The necessity for removal
is analogous to the necessity that justifies the sale of a disabled vessel, by the
water.   It is not to be determined by the result alone, but by all the circumstances existing at the time of the fire.   The necessity for removal need not be
actual, that is, the building may not have been actually burned, since this may
have been prevented by a change in the direction or force of the wind, the more
skillful or efficient management of the fire-engines, or the sudden happening of a
shower, or a like unforeseen event.   But the imminence of the peril must be
apparent, and such as would prompt a prudent uninsured person to remove the
goods; it must be such as to inspire a conviction that to refrain from removing
the goods would be the violation of a manifest moral duty; the damage and
expense of removal, too, must be such as might reasonably be incurred under the
circumstances of the occasion.   Angel on Fire Ins. § 117.   When such a case
exists, we think it the better opinion to hold that the underwriters are chargeable
for the damage and expense of removing the goods, as this result seems most in
accordance with reason, the analogies of the law, and public policy.   Such, also,
is the conclusion of Mr. Phillips, the learned commentator on the law of insurance.   "It seems," he says, "to be the better doctrine, and the one most closely
analogous to the jurisprudence on the subject of insurance generally, that the
underwriters are liable for such damage and expense, reasonably and expedi-
ently incurred, as being directly occasioned by the peril insured against." 1
Phillips' Ins. 645, 646.   The doctrine we maintain on this subject is applicable to
a large class of cases, recognized by the law of insurance, and is found in that
well-established principal of the law of insurance, that insurance against, or an
exception of a peril, besides the consequences immediately following it, may
include, also, a loss or expense arising on account of it, although what is insured
against, or excepted, does not actually occur, provided the peril insured against,
or excepted, does not actually occur, provided the peril insured against, or excepted, is the efficient acting or imminent cause or occasion of the loss or expense.
1 Phillips' Ins. § 1131.   The proximity of the fire to the building occupied by the
plaintiff, its rapid progress, terrible intensity and fearful ravages, leave no reason
to doubt but the goods were removed through a reasonable apprehension that
they would be destroyed by fire if suffered to remain.   Their situation, too, in the
third story, requiring earlier attention, rendered their condition more hazardous
than if they had been on the first floor.   A prudent uninsured person could
scarcely have omitted the precaution taken by the plaintiff.   In removing the
goods, the plaintiff was bound to exercise that reasonable degree of care which
was suited to the circumstances of the occasion: and, when we consider the situation of the goods, the imminence of the peril, and the terror and consternation
naturally excited by the progress and fury of the conflagration, we are not prepared to say that he did not exercise such care." *Brady* v. *N. W. Ins. Co.*, 11
Mich. 425; *Case* v. *Hartford Ins. Co.*, 13 Ill. 676.

   In *Hillier* v. *Alleghany Ins. Co., ante*, it was held that the company was not
liable for damage resulting from a removal where there was reasonable ground
of danger, and the fire was then raging in the same block with that from which
the goods were removed.   But the doctrine of this case, it is believed, does not
express the true rule in such cases, and the question is made to depend upon the
circumstance whether the goods were removed *ex necessitate* to prevent them
from being destroyed, and there was reasonable ground to apprehend such
danger.   A loss by theft, breakage, or other cause, is recoverable.   *Witherell* v.
Maine Ins. Co., ante; Case v. *Hartford, etc., Ins. Co., ante.*   In *Tilton* v. *Hamilton F. Ins. Co., ante*, it appeared that the value of the goods saved amounted to

---

[1] *Webb* v. *Protection Ins. Co.*, 14 Mo. 3; *Fernandez* v. *Merchants', etc., Ins. Co.*,
17 La. An. 131; *Liverpool, Lon. & Globe Ins. Co.* v. *Creighton*, 51 Ga. 95; *Leiber*
v. *L., L. & G. Ins. Co.*, 6 Bush. (Ky.) 639.

[2] *Witherell* v. *Maine Ins. Co.*, 49 Me. 200; *Hillier* v. *Alleghany Ins. Co.*, 3 Penn.
St. 470.

during the progress of the fire while the goods are being, or even after they are removed;[1] by the blowing up of the building, to stay the progress of a conflagration,[2] or from any cause which is traceable directly to an accidental *fire*, as injuries from smoke or cinders,[3] the fall of burning buildings, or of the walls of buildings destroyed by fire.[4] In every case, of course the liability of the insurer is to be determined by the contract itself, and the circumstances of the case, and it is a question of fact for the jury, whether the damage is the proximate result of the peril insured against.[5]

The *proximate* cause of the loss determines the liability of the insurer, in cases where exceptions to its liability are made. Thus, where a canal boat was insured by policy exempting the insurers from liability if the boat should be "prevented or detained by ice" from finishing her trip. In a storm the boat was broken away from the tug which was towing her, and stranded. Ice formed round her during the night, and she remained frozen in for some days, until a

---

$9,488.66. When the store was closed the evening previous, the value of the stock amounted to $12,948.01. The fire was discovered about midnight, and before it reached the stock in question it was removed across the street, piled up on the sidewalk by persons acting in behalf of insurance companies generally, who were stationed in charge of them; was subsequently removed to another building one hundred feet distant, locked up, and the key retained by one of the insurance agents until it was delivered the following day to the insured. Several hundred persons assisted in removing the goods, and there was a great deal of confusion, and much opportunity for some of the goods to have been stolen. It was held, it was immaterial whether the goods were burned, or abstracted, or stolen while they were being removed out of the reach of the fire, for where existing circumstances, by their continuance, would create a total loss, the loss continues total, although those circumstances may have wholly changed, if the property is not beneficially restored to the insured; that if the goods were removed from a building actually on fire, and they would have been destroyed by that fire had they remained in it, the loss was a natural consequence of the peril insured against. *Case* v. *Hartford Ins. Co.*, 13 Ill. 676; Angell on Fire Insurance, sec. 17.

[1] *Hillier* v. *Alleghany Ins. Co., ante; Witherell* v. *Maine Ins. Co., ante; White* v. *Republic Ins. Co., ante.*

[2] *Greenwald* v. *Ins. Co. ante; City Fire Ins. Co.* v. *Corlies, ante.*

[3] *Geisick* v. *Crescent Mut. Ins. Co.*, 19 La. An. 297; *Thompson* v. *Montreal Ins. Co.*, 6 U. C. (Q. B.) 319.

[4] *Johnson* v. *West of Scotland Ins. Co.* 7 Ct. of Sessions Cases (Sc.) 52.

[5] *Webb* v. *Rome, etc., R. R Co.*, 49 N. Y. 420; *Kellogg* v. *Chicago, etc., R. R. Co.*, 26 Wis. 224; *Penn'a R. R. Co.* v. *Hope*, 80 Penn. St. 393; *Lent* v. *R. R. Co.*, 49 Ill. 349; *Higgins* v. *Dewey*, 107 Mass. 494. In *Ryan* v. *N. Y. C. R. R. Co.*, 35 N. Y. 210, and in *Kerr* v. *Penn'a R. R. Co.*, 62 Penn. St. 353, a contrary doctrine was held, but the doctrine of those cases has been repudiated by the courts of those States in later cases. "The question always is," said Mr. Justice STRONG in *Milwaukee, etc., R. R. Co.* v. *Kellogg*, 94 U. S. 475, "was there an unbroken connection between the wrongful act and the injury, a continuous operation? Did the facts constitute a continuous succession of events, so linked together as to make a natural whole; or was there some new and independent cause intervening between the wrong and the injury?"

thaw came, when she was cast against another boat, and lost. It was held that the storm, and not the ice, was the proximate cause of the loss, and, therefore, that the insurers were liable.[1] So where a policy was issued exempting the insurers from liability from loss by fire caused by invasion, riot, etc., or for a loss caused by explosion, it was held that this did not exempt the company from liability *for a fire* caused by explosion.[2] Where the terms of a policy declare that the company shall not be liable for any loss or damage " by fire, which shall arise by any explosion," an exception is created to the general language of the policy, and the company is not liable for a loss caused by a fire arising from an explosion of a steam-engine, or from any other article which was included among the things covered by the policy.[3] The proximate cause of the fire controls in such cases, and, even though an explosion results, it is not necessarily the case that no recovery can be had. The question is, whether the explosion was the proximate cause of the fire. This principle was well illustrated in an English case.[4] In that case, by an insurance policy, plate-glass in the plaintiff's shop-front was insured against damage " originating from any cause whatsoever, except fire, breakage during removal, altera-tion, or repair of the premises," none of the glass being " horizontally placed or movable." A fire broke out on premises adjoining the plain-tiff's, and slightly damaged the rear of his shop, but did not approach the part where the glass was. While the plaintiff was removing his stock to a place of safety, a mob, attracted by the fire, broke the

[1] *Brown* v. *St. Nicholas Ins. Co.*, 61 N. Y. 332.

[2] *Commercial Ins. Co.* v. *Robinson*, 64 Ill. 265.

[3] *St. John* v. *American, etc., Ins. Co.*, 11 N. Y. 516 ; *Hayward* v. *London, etc., Ins. Co.*, 7 Bos. (N. Y.) 385 ; 1 Duer (N. Y.) 371 ; *Harper* v *N. Y. City Ins. Co.*, 1 Bos. (N.Y.) 520, affirmed 22 N.Y. 441. But a contrary doctrine was held in *Boatman's F. & M. Ins. Co.* v. *Parker*, 23 Ohio St. 85, in which property was insured against fire by a policy exempting the insurers from liability " for damages occasioned by the explosion of a steam-boiler, or for damages by fire resulting from such explosion, or explosions caused by gunpowder, gas, or other explosive substances," and it was held that the insurers were liable for damage by *fire* resulting from an explosion of gas. In *Insurance Co.* v. *Tweed,* 7 Wall. (U. S.) 44, cotton in building A. was insured against fire ; fire happening " by means of any invasion, riot, explosion, or hurricane," being excepted. An explosion occurred in build-ing B., across the street, which threw down the walls of building A., and pro-duced an extensive fire in which building A. was destroyed. The fire was not communicated directly from building B. to building A., but it was communicated first to a third building, C., and from thence to building A. The wind was blow-ing in a direction to favor the fire spreading from building C. to building A. *Held,* that the explosion was the proximate cause of the fire which destroyed the cotton, and that the insurers were not liable. *Evans* v. *Columbian Ins. Co.,* 44 N. Y. 146; *McAllister* v. *Ins. Co.,* 17 Mo. 306 ; *Stanley* v. *Western Ins. Co.,* L. R. 3 Ex. 71 ; *Strang* v. *Sun Mut. Ins. Co.,* 31 N. Y. 103.

[4] *Marsden* v *City, etc., Ins. Co.,* L. R. 1 C. P. 232.

window for the purposes of plunder. It was held that the proximate cause of the damage was the lawless act of the mob, and that the damage was not within the exception.

Negligence of assured producing loss, effect of.

SEC. 101. Mere negligence on the part of the assured or of his servants or agents, will not defeat a recovery for a loss happening as a consequence thereof. In order to have that effect, his negligence must amount to recklessness or willful misconduct,[1] or, as it is sometimes expressed, "such as evinces a corrupt design.[2] There must be *mala fides*, and while gross negligence may be evidence thereof, it does not necessarily of itself amount to fraud or bad faith. "Gross negligence," says Lord KENYON, C.J.,[3] "'may be evidence of *mala fides*, but is not the same thing. We have shaken off the last remnant of the contrary doctrine." It must be such conduct as evinces fraud, or design.[4]

But in Pennsylvania it has been held that where the act of the assured is reckless, although not willful, it is such as excuses the insur-

---

[1] *Johnson* v. *Berkshire M. F. Ins. Co.*, 4 Allen (Mass.), 388 ; *Chandler* v. *Worcester, etc., F. Ins. Co.*, 3 Cush. (Mass.) 328 ; *Williams* v. *N. E. Mut. F. Ins. Co.*, 31 Me. 219 ; *Huckins* v. *Ins. Co.*, 31 N. H. 238 ; *Waters* v. *Merchant's, etc.. Ins. Co.*, 11 Pet. (U. S.) 213 ; *Sherwood* v. *General Mut. Ins. Co.*, 14 How. (U. S.) 351 ; *Busk* v. *Royal Exchange Ins. Co.*, 2 B. & Ald. 73 ; *Shaw* v. *Robberds*, 6 Ad. & El. 75 ; *Dixon* v. *Sadler*, 5 M. & W. 405 ; *Gove* v. *Farmers' Ins. Co.*, 48 N. H. 41 ; 2 Am. Rep. 168 ; *Young* v. *Washington, etc., Ins. Co.*, 14 Barb. (N. Y.) 545 ; *Gates* v. *Madison, etc., Ins. Co.*, *ante* ; *Daniels* v. *Hud. R. Ins. Co.*, 12 Cush. (Mass.) 416 ; *Waters* v. *Merchants', etc.. Ins. Co.*, 11 Pet. (U. S.) 213 ; *Campbell* v. *Monmouth Ins. Co.*, 59 Me. 430 ; *St. Louis Ins. Co.* v. *Glasgow*, 8 Mo. 713 ; *Kane* v. *Hibernia Ins. Co.*, 38 N. J. 441 ; 20 Am. Rep. 409 ; *Catlin* v. *Springfield F. & M. Ins. Co.*, 1 Sum. (U. S.) 434 ; *Columbian Ins. Co.* v. *Lawrence*, 10 Pet. (U. S.) 507 ; *Sandford* v. *Ins. Co.*, 12 Cush. (Mass.) 541 ; *Maryland F. Ins. Co.* v. *Whitford*, 31 Md. 219 ; *Mickey* v. *Burlington Ins. Co.*, 35 Iowa, 174. In *Troy F. Ins. Co.* v. *Carpenter*, 4 Wis. 20, the policy stipulated that, "whenever any alteration shall be made that increases the hazard, so as to increase the premium, the policy shall be void, unless an additional premium shall be given according to the rate of exposure, and insurers are not liable for any loss in consequence of repairing, finishing or building additions." A stove was put in the building for the purpose of drying plastering that had lately been put on, and the insurers claimed that the fire resulted from the negligence of the assured's servants. The court held, however, that, unless the use of the stove was a breach of the conditions of the policy against increase of risk. the *negligence of his servants, however great in degree*, was no defense. See also *Busk* v. *Royal Ex. Ass. Co.*, 2 B. & A. 73 ; *Walker* v. *Maitland*, 5 id. 171. Proof of mere negligence is not admissibe. *Henderson* v. *Western M. & F. Ins. Co.*, 10 Rob. (La.) 164. And the same rule prevails in reference to marine risks. Unless the negligence of the assured, or of the master and crew, is so wilful as to amount to barratry, the insurer is liable. *Dixon* v. *Sadler*, 5 M. & W. 405 ; *Carruthers* v. *Gray*, 3 Camp. 142 ; *Busk* v. *Royal Ex. Ass. Co.*, 2 B. & A. 73 ; *Redman* v. *Wilson*, 14 M. & W. 476.

[2] *Hyndes* v. *Schenectady, etc., Ins. Co.*, 16 Barb. (N. Y.) 119.

[3] *Goodman* v. *Harvey*, 4 Ad. & El. 876. If the negligence of the assured was not *wilfull* or so *gross* as to amount to fraud, the insurer is liable for. *Lycoming Ins. Co.* v. *Barringer*, 73 Ill. 230.

[4] *Columbian Ins. Co.* v. *Lawrence*, 10 Peters (U. S.) 507.

ers. Thus, when the owner of a steamboat, who was also master, while racing with another boat, took a barrel of turpentine, put it in front of the furnace and used it on the wood and coal to increase the steam, and as a consequence the boat was destroyed; although the jury specially found that the conduct of the master was not willful, yet the court held his misconduct was such as excused the insurers.[1] In a New York case[2] a fire was communicated to the building covered by the policy, by the burning of a building being erected by the assured on an adjoining lot. The policy did not prohibit rebuilding. The court held that the negligence or misconduct was not such as to debar him from a recovery for the loss; but seems to have put the case upon the ground that there was no evidence but that the assured exercised reasonable care to prevent the accident.[3]

Imprudence on the part of the assured does not excuse the insurer.[4]

---

[1] *Citizen's Ins. Co.* v. *Marsh*, 41 Penn. St. 386; see also, *Himley* v. *Stewart*, 1 Brev. (S. C.) 209; *Morel* v. *Mississippi, etc., Ins. Co.*, 4 Bush (Ky.) 585.

[2] *Young* v. *Washington Co. Mut. Ins. Co.*, 14 Barb. (N. Y.) 545.

[3] *Young* v. *Ins. Co.*, 14 Barb. (N. Y.) 545; *Stebbins* v. *Globe Ins. Co.*, 2 Hall (N. Y.) 632. But that the question does not depend upon such a condition, see *Champlin* v. *Railway Pass. Ass. Co.*, 6 Lans. (N. Y.) 71; *Brown* v. *Kings Co. F. Ins. Co.*, 31 How. Pr. (N. Y.) 508.

[4] *Sperry* v. *Del. Ins. Co.*, 2 Wash. (U. S.) C. C. 243. In *Johnson* v. *Berkshire Mut. Fire Ins. Co.*, 4 Allen (Mass.) 388, in the afternoon of a hot day in a dry season in August, during the time covered by the policy, the plaintiff and his son were unloading hay from a wagon, and placing it in a shed adjoining the barn, and while so engaged were annoyed by bees whose nest was in a hollow place under the door, and the plaintiff finding that no hot water could readily be had, undertook to smoke them out by thrusting a wisp of straw into their hole and lighting it with a match. A fresh breeze was blowing at the time; the building was very old and covered on the outside with whitewood boards. The barn adjoining was full of hay, and some hay was stored in the loft of the shed. After withdrawing the straw, and while attempting to extinguish it, the fire spread with great rapidity on the outside of the shed, and destroyed the property. It was admitted that there was no fraudulent intent. Upon this state of facts it was held that the plaintiff was entitled to recover. "In the present case," said MER-RICK, J., "there is nothing in the facts found to show either a fraudulent intent or any willfulness on the part of the plaintiff. In the Irish courts, the negligence or carelessness of the assured, or his servants, is held not to constitute a defense. In England, *Shaw* v. *Robberds*, ante; *Jameson* v. *Royal Ins. Co.*, 7 Irish L. R. 126; so also in New Hampshire, *Huckins* v. *People's Mut. Fire Ins. Co.*, 31 N. H. 38, and in a more recent case, *Gove* v. *Farmers', etc., Ins. Co.*, 48 N. H. 41; 2 Am. Rep. 168; in Missouri, *Mueller* v. *Putnam Fire Ins. Co.*, 45 Mo. 84; in North Carolina, *Whitehurst* v. *Fayetteville, etc., Ins. Co.*, 7 Jones (N. C.) 352; in Kansas, *Kansas Ins. Co.* v. *Berry*, 8 Kan. 159; in Iowa, *Mickey* v. *Burlington Ins. Co.*, 35 Iowa, 174; in Ohio, *Sherlock* v. *Globe Ins. Co.*, 1 Cin. Sup. Ct. 198; *Perrin* v. *Protection Ins. Co.*, 11 Ohio St. 147; *Germania Ins. Co.* v. *Sherlock*, 25 id. 33; in Louisiana, *Henderson* v. *Western M. & F. Ins. Co.*, 10 Rob. 164; in Maine, *Williams* v. *N. E. Mut. Fire Ins. Co.*, 31 Me. 219; in New York, *Gates* v. *Madison Co. Ins. Co.*, 5 N. Y. 469; *Brown* v. *Kings Co. Fire Ins. Co.*, 31 How. Pr. (N. Y.) 508; *Champlin* v. *Railway Passenger Assurance Co.*, 6 Lans. (N. Y.) 71; *Arctic Fire Ins. Co.* v. *Austin*, 6 T. & C. (N. Y.) 63; in Kentucky, *Fireman's Ins. Co.* v. *Powell*, 13 B. Mon. (Ky.) 311; in Maryland, *Maryland Fire Ins. Co.* v. *Whiteford*, 31 Md. 219; in Wisconsin, *Troy Fire Ins. Co.* v. *Carpenter*, 4 Wis.

Negligence tha⁺ erɤuses the insured must be willful or fraudulent,[1] must be such as exhibits fraud or design,[2] and mere negligence or misconduct, although gross, will not prevent a recovery.[3] Thus, in

---

20; *Schneider* v. *Provident, etc., Ins. Co.*, 24 Wis. 28; and in Pennsylvania the doctrine of *Citizen's Ins. Co.* v. *Marsh*, has been virtually repudiated in a later case, *Phœnix Fire Ins. Co.* v. *Cochran*, 51 Penn. St. 143.

[1] *Firemen's Ins. Co.* v. *Powell*, 13 B. Mon. (Ky.) 311.

[2] *Henderson* v. *Western M. & F. Ins. Co.*, 10 Rob. (La.) 164; *Williams* v. *N. E. Mut. F. Ins. Co.*, 31 Me. 219; *Columbian Ins. Co.* v. *Lawrence, ante.*

[3] *Muellers* v. *Putnam Ins. Co.*, 45 Mo. 84; *Fireman's Ins. Co.* v. *Powell*, 13 B. Mon. (Ky.) 311. A loss resulting from the *negligence* of the assured is not a loss by design. *Design* imports plans, schemes and intention carried into effect. *Catlin* v. *Springfield F. Ins. Co.*, 1 Sum. (U. S.) 434. In *Gove* v. *Farmers', etc., Ins. Co.*, 48 N. H. 41; 2 Am. Rep. 168, the plaintiff's buildings, which were insured, were intentionally set on fire by his wife who was insane. The plaintiff left her alone, and the defendants claimed that this was such negligence on his part, as excused them from liability. But the court held otherwise, NESMITH, J., upon this question, remarking: "The doctrine now appears to be well settled by the authorities, that a loss by fire on land, occasioned by the mere fault and negligence of the insured party, his servants or agents, without fraud or design, is a loss protected by the policies, and as such recoverable from the underwriters. Judge Story, in *Waters* v. *The Merchants' Louisville Ins. Co.*, 11 Pet. 213; *Sherwood* v. *General Mutual Ins. Co.*, 14 How. 351; 3 *Kent's Com.* 374, and notes; *Ruck* v. *Royal Exchange Co.*; Angell on Ins. §§ 124, 125, and 122; 2 Barn. & Ald. 73; *Dixon* v. *Sadler*, 5 M. & W. 405; 8 id. 894; *Shaw* v. *Robarts*, 6 A. & E. 75. Generally, *negligence* is not *design*. *Catlin* v. *The Springfield Fire Ins. Co.*, 1 Sum. 434. The court in the State of New York, say that before this ground of defense can be made available, there must be evidence of such a degree of negligence as will evince a corrupt design. *Hyndes* v. *Schenectady County Mut. Ins. Co.*, 16 Barb. 119. There are cases of gross neglect which are, in law, deemed equivalent to a fraudulent purpose or design, founded on the consideration of doing nothing, when the slightest care on the part of the insured would prevent a great injury. Judge Shaw supposes the case where the insured, in his own house, sees the burning coals in the fire-place roll down on his wooden floor, and does not brush them up. This would be nonfeasance, and evidence of a culpable recklessness and indifference to the rights of others. He also supposes the insured premises to take fire, and the flames beginning to kindle in a small spot, which a cup of water might put out, and the insured has the water at hand but neglects to put it out. This, also, would be culpable negligence, manifesting a willingness differing little in character from a fraudulent and criminal purpose to commit injury to others. *Chandler* v. *Worcester Mut. Fire Ins. Co.*, 3 Cush. 328; 31 Me. 219; *Huckins* v. *Insurance Co.*, 31 N. H. 238; Angell on Ins. § 130. It would be fair to infer a fraudulent intent in the insured, as would be indicated in a forbearance to use all reasonable exertions to save his property from the ravages of fire, when ample preventive means and ability are at hand. Evidence of this kind of negligence will tend to discharge underwriters and insurers from their liability in case of loss. There are some cases where it has been held that the insured is entitled to indemnity, though the loss occur from the gross carelessness of his servant, the proximate cause being only looked to, and fraud being absent. *Gates* v. *Madison County Mut. Fire Ins. Co.*, 1 Seld. 469; approved and followed in *Matthews* v. *Howard Ins. Co.*, 1 Kern. 9; 1 Duer, 371. From the aforesaid cases we may derive a knowledge of some of the leading principles applicable to questions of indemnity by fire insurance companies, where negligence is imputed to the insured, his agents or servants. One remaining duty is to inquire how far any of the aforesaid rules will govern the case before us. The defense suggested by the defendants is, that the plaintiff, the husband of his insane wife, and part owner of the property, alleged to be insured by the defendants, left his wife alone on the day of the fire for some time, it does not appear how long, and that she *intentionally* set her

the case last referred to, the defendant requested the court to instruct the jury, that "if the fire originated from the *gross carelessness or gross misconduct* of the assured, they could not recover, but the court refused the instruction, and the refusal was sustained upon appeal, the court remarking that 'the word gross is sometimes treated as equivalent to fraud, and should not be used without properly explaining its import; and negligence is one of the risks assumed by the insurer.'" In a Kansas case,[1] the defendant requested the court to charge the jury "that the defendants need not prove beyond a reasonable doubt that the fire was intentional on the part of the insured, and if the jury believe from the evidence that the plaintiff willfully, negligently or carelessly allowed the property to be destroyed by fire, so as to procure the insurance thereon, or that any portion of the stock was removed before the fire, they must find for the defendant." The court held that the instruction, as a whole, was improper, and, therefore, that a refusal so to instruct the jury was not error. *A fraudulent purpose, a corrupt design, may be inferred from the negligence of the assured; but,*

---

husband's buildings on fire. The case finds the wife was insane at the time of committing the act. It appears to us, it would be a misnomer of terms that she, being admitted to be in this state, could so far control her reasoning powers as to be able to plan or design the act done by her beforehand, in such a manner as to render herself responsible as a moral agent. The word *insane* implies unsoundness or derangement of mind or intellect, not a mere temporary or slight delirium which might be occasioned by fever or accident; and we cannot attach moral accountability to a wrongful act admitted to be done by an *insane* person. Then, the question recurs, if the wife be admitted to be insane when the fire was set by her, was the husband guilty of negligence in leaving her alone? On this point, the case finds that she had frequently been left alone two or three hours at a time before this day. It does not appear that she had set fires or destroyed her own or others' property on these occasions when left alone; or that her husband or friends had any previous warning of any proclivity on her part to commit excesses of any kind by inflicting injury either upon person or property. The fact that when before left alone on other occasions, the wife had not committed any wrong or violence, furnished an argument in her favor as well as her husband. The husband cannot be held to anything more than the exercise of ordinary care and prudence in his conduct towards his wife and others interested in her welfare. It is doubtless a safe general rule, as tested by experience, to commit the subjects of derangement to an assylum, or to skillful medical treatment, at an early stage of their disease; but, because this course is not adoped in every instance, we think the inference of gross negligence is not to be imputed to the friends of such patients as prefer to travel another path. The friends of the insane must be allowed some indulgence and discretion, if they prefer to watch over the incipient stages of the diseased subject at home, and to use their efforts to arrest the progress of the malady there. They may not have the pecuniary ability to support the unfortunate friend at an asylum, or away from home. Such considerations must weigh materially in cases of this kind, and will serve to rebut the presumption of the existence of that degree of negligence which is deemed equivalent to a fraudulent purpose or design in him who is the responsible keeper of insane persons. We cannot see in this case evidence of the existence, either of design or of that degree of negligence or carelessness, which will constitute a legal defense for the defendants."

[1] *Kansas Ins. Co.* v. *Berry*, 8 Kan. 159.

in all cases, in order to defeat a recovery, the negligence must be of such a *character as to warrant the inference.*[1] SHAW, C.J., in a Massachusetts case,[2] said : "The general rule unquestionably is, in case of insurance against fire, that the carelessness and negligence of the agents and servants of the assured, constitute no defense. Whether the same rule will apply equally to a case where a loss has occurred, by means which the assured by ordinary care could have prevented, is a different question. Some of the cases countenance the distinction.[3] But it is not necessary to decide this question. *The defendants offered to prove gross misconduct on the part of the assured.* The question then is, whether there can be any misconduct, however gross, not amounting to a fraudulent intent to hurt the building, which will deprive the assured of his right to recover. We think there may be. *By an intent to burn a building, we understand a purpose manifested and followed by some act done, tending to carry that act into effect, but not including a mere misfeasance. Suppose the assured, in his own house, sees the burning coals in the fire-place roll down on the wooden floor, and does not brush them up.* This would be mere non-feasance. It would not prove an intent to burn the building, *but it would show a culpable recklessness and indifference to the rights of others.* Suppose the premises insured should take fire, and the flames begin to kindle in a small spot, which a cup of water would put out, and the assured has the water at hand, but neglects to put it on. This is mere non-feasance, yet no one would doubt that it is culpable negligence, in violation of the maxim *sic uteri tuo ut alienum non lædas.* To what extent such negligence must go in order to amount to gross misconduct, it is difficult, by any definitive or abstract rule of law, independently of circumstances to designate. The doctrine of the civil law, that *crassa negligentia* was, of itself, proof of fraud, or equivalent to fraudulent purpose or design, was no doubt founded in the consideration that, although such negligence consists in doing nothing, and is therefore a non-feasance, yet *the doing of nothing, when the slightest care or attention would prevent a great injury, manifests a willingness, differing little in character from a fraudulent and criminal purpose to commit such injury.* Whether the facts relied on to show gross negligence and gross misconduct, of which evidence was offered, would have proved any of these supposed cases, or any like case, we have no means of knowing; but as they might have done so, the court

---

[1] Lord KENYON, C.J., in *Goodman* v. *Harvey,* 4 Ad. & El. 876.

[2] *Chandler* v. *Worcester, etc., Ins. Co.,* 3 Cush. (Mass.) 328.

[3] *Lyon* v. *Mills,* 5 East. 428 ; *Pipon* v. *Cope,* 1 Camp. 434.

15

are of opinion that the proof should have been admitted, and proper instructions given in reference to it." It is true that the court says that negligence or misconduct, *not amounting to an intent to burn the building*, may be sufficient to excuse the insurer, but it will be noticed that, while in the cases used by way of illustration, there was no act done by the insured which originally caused the fire, yet *he omitted to do that which good faith required that he should do, and which evinced an intent on his part to permit the premises to burn when good faith and common honesty required that he should have used his best efforts to prevent the loss;* and it is submitted that this is such conduct as would warrant the jury in finding a fraudulent purpose or design to defraud the insurers, which, within the rule, would relieve them from liability. No definite rule can be given that will afford a test of liability or exemption therefrom on the part of the insurer in all cases. Necessarily, the question in each case is for the jury, and while mere negligence on the one hand, nor gross negligence or misconduct on the other, as a matter of law, does not excuse the insurer from liability, *yet the negligence or misconduct of the insured may be such as to warrant the jury in finding a fraudulent purpose or design, on the part of the assured, to defraud the insurer, which will operate to excuse the insurer from liability; hence, negligence, on the part of the assured, may be shown as tending to establish fraud or design on his part, but not as of itself, a legal excuse of the liability of the insurer.*[1] The question is for the jury, whether in view of all the facts, the negligence or misconduct of the assured was such as to evince a fraudulent purpose or design.[2]

In a New York case[3] it was held that the contributory negligence which excuses the defendant from liability for injury caused in part by his negligence *must be the personal act of the party injured,* otherwise as to him all contributing thereto are joint wrong-doers. Accordingly where the owner of corn shipped it by a boat over which he had no control, and it was lost in consequence of a collision between such boat and defendant's boat, caused by the defendant's negligence; it was held that the negligence of those in charge of the boat carrying the corn would not excuse the defendant from liability from such loss. This rule operates to protect the assured in all instances where the loss originates from the carelessness, gross misconduct or fraudulent acts

---

[1] Lord KENYON, C.J., *Goodman* v. *Harvey, ante; Chandler* v. *Worcester, etc., Ins. Co., ante; Citizen's Ins. Co.* v. *Marsh, ante; Johnson* v. *Berkshire, etc., Ins. Co., ante.*

[2] See cases cited in previous note.

[3] *Arctic Fire Ins. Co.* v. *Austin,* 6 T. & C. (N. Y.) 63.

of his servants or agents, without the direction or assent of the master, express or implied.[1] Of course, the insurer may stipulate against loss arising from the negligence of the assured or his agents, or there may be express warranties or conditions in the policy that will control the question of liability in a given case; therefore, in determining the question of the insurer's liability, or exemption in a given case, the language of the policy must be looked to. Thus, in a Canada case,[2] the policy covering the cargo of a vessel contained a clause exempting the company from liability for "loss caused by the negligence of the master or crew in navigating the vessel." The vessel was stranded, and it was held that, if the stranding was caused by the negligence of the master or crew in navigating the vessel, the insurer was discharged. In all such cases the question of liability or exemption must turn upon the question, whether the negligence of the assured or his servants or agents was the *proximate* cause of the loss, for if it was only the *remote* cause, liability exists.[3]

In a Maine case,[4] the policy stipulated against liability for losses resulting from the *gross* negligence of the assured, and the courts held that, in order to avoid liability, the insured must exercise such want of diligence as even careless men (*dissoluti honimes*) are wont to exercise,[5] thus adopting Mr. May's[6] definition of the term.

Of course gross misconduct, amounting to fraud,[7] or a willful burn-

---

[1]*Perrin* v. *Protection Ins. Co.*, 11 Ohio, 147; *St. Louis Ins. Co.* v. *Glasgow*, 8 Mo. 173; *Phœnix F. Ins. Co.* v. *Cochran*, 51 Penn. St. 143; *Gates* v. *Madison Co. Mut. Ins. Co.*, ante. In *Mickey* v. *Burlington Ins. Co.*, 35 Iowa, 174, the plaintiff's wife set up a bed over a stovepipe-hole. The stove and pipe in the lower room had not been removed, and subsequently, forgetting that she had placed the bed there, she built a fire in the stove, and the bed catching fire, the house was consumed. The court held the insurers liable. *Germania Ins. Co.* v. *Sherlock*, 25 Ohio St. 33; *Waters* v. *Merchants'*, etc., *Ins. Co.*, 11 Pet. (U. S.) 213; *Williams* v. *N. E. F. Ins. Co.*, 31 Me. 219; *Redman* v. *Wilson*, 14 M. & W. 476; *Busk* v. *Royal Ins. Co.*, ante; *Sturm* v. *Atlantic Mut. Ins. Co.*, 2 J. & S. (N. Y. Superior Ct.) 281; *Dixon* v. *Sadler*, 5 M. & W. 405; *Troy F. Ins. Co.* v. *Carpenter*, 4 Wis. 20; *Sperry* v. *Del. Ins. Co.*, ante; *Maryland F. Ins. Co.* v. *Whiteford*, 31 Md. 219; *Henderson* v. *Western M. & F. Ins. Co.*, 10 Rob. (La.) 164.

[2]*Gillispie* v. *British*, etc., *Assurance Co.*, 7 U. C., Q. B. 108; *Campbell* v. *Monmouth*, etc., *Ins. Co.*, 59 Me. 430. See also, *City of Worcester* v. *Worcester Fire Ins. Co.*, 9 Gray (Mass.)

[3]*Rice* v. *Homer*, 12 Mass. 230; *Scripture* v. *Lowell M. F. Ins. Co.*, 10 Cush. (Mass.) 356; *Hahn* v. *Corbett*, 2 Bing. 205; *American Ins. Co.* v. *Ins. Co.*, 7 Penn. St. 233.

[4] *Campbell* v. *Monmouth*, etc., *Ins. Co.*, 59 Me. 430; 5 Ben. F. I. C. 395.

[5] Hein Elem Jur. lib. 3 tit. 14, sec. 787.

[6] May on Ins. 495. See also, *Lycoming Ins. Co.* v. *Barringer*, 73 Ill. 230, where the court say "gross negligence" as used in a policy of insurance, "indicates the want of that diligence which even *careless* men are accustomed to exercise."

[7] *Citizens' Ins. Co.* v. *Marsh*, 41 Penn. St. 386; *Himley* v. *Stewart*, 1 Brev. (Sc.) 209; *Morel* v. *Miss. Valley Life Ins. Co.*, 9 Bush (Ky.) 535.

ing of the premises by the assured, excuses the insurer from liability.[1] But proof of negligence, does not establish design. In order to establish that, there must be a purpose and intent to burn the property insured.[2] A mere omission to exercise due care in preventing the property from being destroyed,[3] does not establish a fraudulent purpose, nor the fact that he was careless, and did not do that which a prudent person would do,[4] or that he was very careless,[5] or that the loss resulted from the willful negligence, misconduct, or fraudulent acts of his servants or agents.[6] In order to avoid liability, design, or acts amounting to it, *on the part of the assured*, must be established.[7]

But, whether the proof must be such as to establish the fact beyond a reasonable doubt, or whether a mere preponderance of evidence is sufficient, is a question upon which there is much diversity of opinion, and much conflict of authority; and in view of this, an author would be arrogating quite too much, to attempt to lay down a rule applicable to the question. There are a multitude of very respectable authorities holding the affirmative of the proposition,[8] and an equally respect-

---

[1] *Fireman's Ins. Co.* v. *Powell*, 13 B. Mon. (Ky.) 311.

[2] *Catlin* v. *Springfield F. & M. Ins. Co., ante; Atlantic Ins. Co.* v. *Sturm*, 63 N. Y. 77.

[3] *West* v. *Reid*, 2 Hare, 249; *Gove* v. *Fireman's, etc., Ins. Co.*, 48 N. H. 41.

[4] *Mickey* v. *Burlington Ins. Co., ante.*

[5] In *Maryland Ins. Co.* v. *Whitford*, 31 Md. 219, the policy permitted the assured "to keep one barrel of benzine or turpentine in tin cans, and one-half barrel of varnish, for use." Insured were not in the habit of allowing barrels of benzine or turpentine to remain on their premises for a time longer than necessary to empty them. A barrel of benzine was carried into the store, a syphon inserted into the bunghole, and the process of emptying into a tin can commenced. The weather being moist, the liquid vaporized rapidly. A workman with a lamp, searching for a leak, approached within six feet of the barrel, an explosion resulted and started the fire which consumed the premises. It was held that the insurers were liable for the loss. See also, *Scripture* v. *Lowell Ins. Co., ante.*

[6] *Lowell* v. *Scripture, ante; Fireman's Ins. Co.* v. *Powell*, 13 B. Mon. (Ky.) 311; *Gates* v. *Madison Co., etc., Ins. Co., ante; Sperry* v. *Del. Ins. Co.*, 2 Wash. (U. S. C. C.) 243; *Phœnix Fire Ins. Co.* v. *Cochran*, 51 Penn. St. 143; *Gove* v. *Farmers' Ins. Co., ante; St. Louis Ins. Co.* v. *Glasgow*, 8 Mo. 713; *Sherlock* v. *Globe Ins. Co.*, 1 Cin. (Ohio) 193. Thus, in *Dixon* v. *Sadler, ante*, the defendant plead that the "loss arose wholly from the *wrongful, negligent and improper conduct of the master and even by* wilfully, wrongfully and negligently, etc." The court held that this was no defense.

[7] *Catlin* v. *Springfield Fire Ins. Co., ante; Kane* v. *Hibernia, etc., Ins. Co.*, 38 N. J. 441; 20 Am. Rep. 409.

[8] *Kane* v. *Hibernia Ins. Co.*, 38 N. J. 441; 20 Am. Rep. 409; *Chalmers* v. *Shackell*, 6 C. & P. 475; *Thurtell* v. *Beaumont*, 1 Bing. 339; *Woodbeck* v. *Keller*, 6 Cow. (N. Y.) 118; *Hopkins* v. *Smith*, 3 Barb. (N. Y.) 559; *Clark* v. *Dibble*, 16 Wend. (N. Y.) 601; *Shultz* v. *Pacific Ins. Co.*, 2 Ins. L. J. 495 (Florida); *Coulter* v. *Stuart*, 2 Yerg. (Tenn.) 225; *Steinman* v. *McWilliams*, 6 Penn. St. 170; *Lanter* v. *McEwen*, 8 Blackf. (Ind.) 495; *McConnell* v. *Del. M. & F. Ins. Co.*, 18 Ill. 228; *Butman* v. *Hobbs*, 35 Me. 227; *Thayer* v. *Boyle*, 30 id. 475; *Fountain* v *West*, 23 Iowa, 9; *Ellis* v. *Lindley*, 38 id. 461; *Tucker* v. *Call*, 45 Ind. 31.

able, and more modern class of cases, holding that a preponderance of evidence is sufficient.[1] Thus, it will be seen that the tendency of the modern cases, in this country, is in support of the doctrine that the jury may find the defense of willful burning, from a prepon_derance of evidence. Whether there is an adequate reason for the departure of the courts from the former doctrine, in view of the con_flict involved, and the fact that no particular principle, but rather the application of mere arbitrary rules, is involved, is a matter with which an author can hardly be expected to deal.

Where a policy of fire insurance is assigned as collateral to a mort_gage, with the consent of the company, the assignee takes it subject to all the conditions thereof, and no recovery can be had, merely in con_sequence of the equities of the assignee, if the assignor has lost the right to recover by violating the terms of the contract; and in an action by the assignor of the policy for the use of the assignee, evidence to show that plaintiff set the building on fire is admissible.[2]

Right to recover back premium.

Sec. 102. Where a policy fails to attach, by reason of an innocent mistake of the parties, the insured is entitled to a return of the premium paid,[3] but not if the failure results from the fraud or misrepresentation of the assured.[4]

And it has been held that the assured is entitled to have the premium returned, where the failure of the policy to attach arose from a misrepresentation without fraud.[5] So where the policy is declared void upon principles of public policy,[6] or for breach of warranty where there is no fraud,[7] but if the risk has once attached and is defeated by subsequent acts of the assured, the premium is treated as earned,[8]

---

[1] *Blaeser* v. *Milwaukee, etc., Ins. Co.*, 37 Wis. 31; 19 Am. Rep. 747; *Ellis* v. *Buzzell*, 60 Me. 209; 11 Am. Rep. 204; *Knowles* v. *Scribner*, 57 id. 497; *Roths-child* v. *American, etc., Ins. Co.*, 62 Mo. 356; *Matthews* v. *Huntly*, 9 N. H. 150; *Gordon* v. *Parmalee*, 15 Gray (Mass.) 413; *Kincade* v. *Bradshaw*, 3 Hawk (N. C) 63; *Marshall* v. *Marine Ins. Co.*, 43 Mo. 586; *Washington Ins. Co.* v. *Wilson*, 7 Wis. 169; *Schmidt* v. *N. Y. Union, etc., Ins. Co.*, 1 Gray (Mass.) 529; *Scott* v. *Home Ins. Co.*, 1 id. 105.

[2] *The Illinois, etc., Ins. Co.* v. *Fix*, 53 Ill. 151; 5 Am. Rep. 38.

[3] *Gray* v. *Sims*, 3 Wash. (U. S. C. C.) 276; *Penson* v. *Lee*, 2 B. & P. 330; *Wad-dington* v. *U. S. Ins. Co.*, 17 John. (N. Y.) 23; *Clark* v. *Manufacturers' Ins. Co.*, 2 W. & M. (U. S.) 472.

[4] *Friesmuth* v. *Agawam, etc., Ins. Co.*, 10 Cush. (Mass.) 588.

[5] *Faise* v. *Parkinson*, 4 Taunt. 640; *Hentig* v. *Staniforth*, 5 M. & S. 122.

[6] *Mount* v. *Waite*, 7 John. (N. Y.) 334.

[7] *Delavigne* v. *U. S. Ins. Co.*, 1 John. Ch. (N.Y.) 310; *Huntig* v. *Staniforth*, ante.

[8] *Furtado* v. *Rogers*, 3 B. & P. 191; *Moses* v. *Pratt*, 4 Camp. 297.

or if the assured was guilty of fraud in procuring the policy,[1] as if the assured fraudulently conceals facts material to the risk,[2] or fraudulently misrepresents the risk,[3] or if the assured had no insurable interest,[4] the assured is not entitled to a return of any part of the premium. So, if there is a total loss, although the policy has a long term to run, the premium for the entire term is treated as earned. If a building falls to pieces before the term is ended, or if from any cause outside of the peril insured against, and over which the assured has no control it ceases o exist as a building, and there is nothing at risk, or if from any cause, *without the action or fault of the assured*, the risk fails, the assured is entitled to a return of the unearned premium.

When assignment policy creates a new contract.

SEC. 103. When a policy in a mutual company is assigned to a mortgagee, with the consent of the insurer, and a new premium note is given by the mortgagee, and he becomes liable for all future assessments thereon, and agrees that the policy shall continue to be a lien upon the property, *the policy becomes a new contract* between the insurer and the mortgagee, and the misconduct of the mortgagor, or a subsequent breach of any of the conditions of the policy, does not defeat the mortgagee's right to recover thereon;[5] and in all cases where the title to property passes, and the policy is assigned to the vendee with the consent of the insurer, the policy is treated as a new contract with the vendee.

Indorsement passes title in proceeds of policy.

SEC. 104. An indorsement, " pay the within in case of loss to A. B." on a policy, and assented to by the insurers, passes the legal interest in the proceeds of the policy to the payee named therein, and he may sue for a loss under the policy in his own name.[6]

The words " for value received pay the within in case of loss to A," do not operate as an assignment of the policy to a purchaser of the property covered by it, and cannot have that effect, even though so intended by the parties, and although the assent of the company is duly obtained, unless it is also shown that the company *knew* that the

---

[1] *Schwartz* v. *U. S. Ins. Co.*, 3 Wash. (U. S. C. C.) 170.

[2] *Hoyt* v. *Gilman*, 8 Mass. 335.

[3] *Friesmuth* v. *Agawam, etc., Ins. Co.*, 10 Cush. (Mass.) 587.

[4] *McCulloch* v. *Royal, etc., Assurance Co.*, 3 Camp. 406 ; *Lowrey* v. *Bordieu*, 2 Doug. 468 ; *Boehm* v. *Bell*, 8 T. R. 154.

[5] *Foster* v. *Equitable Ins. Co.*, 2 Allen (Mass.) 216.

[6] *Barrett* v. *Union Mut. Fire Ins. Co.*, 7 Cush. (Mass.) 175.

property had been sold to the person to whom it was so made payable, and was intended as an assignment.[1]

Policy not countersigned by agent.

SEC. 105. The fact that a policy provides that it shall have no validity, unless countersigned by an agent, will not prevent a recovery where the policy was delivered to the assured as a perfect policy. The company is thereby estopped from denying the validity of the instrument.[2]

Right to cancel — reservation of — when cancellation takes effect.

SEC. 106. When the policy provides that the assured may, at any time, surrender his policy for cancellation, and that thereupon he shall be entitled to a ratable portion of the unearned premium; and that the insurer may, any time, at its option cancel it, on giving notice to that effect, and paying a ratable proportion of the premium for the unexpired term; *payment of the unearned premium* is essential to absolve the company from liability under the policy, and, although the policy has been surrendered to the company, yet, *if the unearned premium has not been paid until after a loss*, the company is liable for the loss, and this, even though the assured, *after the loss, but in ignorance of it*, accepts the balance of premium due him for the unexpired term.[3]

In order to cancel a policy so as to extinguish the liability of the insurer, not only must notice be given that the policy *is* cancelled, but a noticeable proportion of the premium must be refunded or tendered to the assured, and until this is done, the policy remains on foot. Notice that the policy *will* be cancelled at a future time, is not enough, neither is an offer to pay if the assured will call at the office of the company, or of the agent. It is not the duty of the assured to seek the insurer, *but the insurer must seek the assured and pay or tender to him the amount of unearned premium; and his liability remains until this is done.*[4] *The policy is not cancelled until the unearned premium is actually received by the assured or his agent*; and, if after he receives notice to return the policy for cancellation, he sends it to the insurer,

---

[1] *Fogg* v. *Middlesex, etc., Ins. Co.*, 10 Cush. (Mass.) 337.

[2] *Hibernia Ins. Co.* v. *O'Connor*, 29 Mich. 241.

[3] *Hollingsworth* v. *Germania Ins. Co.*, 15 Ga. 291; 12 Am. Rep. 579.

[4] *Van Valkenburgh* v. *The Lenox F. Ins. Co.*, 51 N. Y. 465; *Ins. Co.* v. *Webster*, 6 Wall. (N. Y.) 129; *Columbia Ins. Co.* v. *Stone*, 3 Allen (Mass.) 385; *Peoria F. & M. Ins. Co.* v. *Botts*, 47 Ill. 516; *Hathorn* v. *Germania Ins. Co.*, 55 Barb. (N. Y.) 28; *Lyman* v. *State Mut. Ins. Co.*, 14 Allen (Mass.) 329; 5 Bennett's F. I. C. 106; *Wilkins* v. *Tobacco Ins. Co.*, 1 Cin. S. C. (Ohio) 349; *Ætna Ins. Co.* v. *Maguire*, 51 Ill. 342; *McLean* v. *Republic F. Ins. Co.*, 3 Lans. (N. Y.) 421.

but before he receives the return premium, a loss occurs, the insurer *is liable therefor*.[1] If, however, the assured is indebted to the company for the premium, or a sufficient portion thereof to cover the unearned premium, notice alone, according to the terms of the policy, effects the rescission.[2] And where the policy requires notice of the cancellation to be given in a certain manner, or of a certain time, the policy cannot be cancelled until such notice is given.[3] The fact that the assured was notified that his policy was cancelled, and requested the agent to hold the risk until a certain time, which was done, does not operate as a cancellation of the policy *upon the expiration of such time, unless the return premium has been paid or tendered to him*.[4] Payment or tender thereof, or a waiver of payment by the assured must be shown by the insurer, or the policy remains in force.[5] The fact that the unearned premium was credited to the assured upon the company's books and subject to his order,[6] or that it was sent to the agent through whom the insurance was effected, or to the broker or person procuring it for the assured,[7] does not release the insurer from liability. *Actual payment to the assured, or some person authorized to act for him, must be shown.* Neither does the fact that the assured gave his note for the premium, absolve the insurers from refunding in money the premium unearned,[8] nor does an acceptance by the assured of the unearned premium *after a loss* unknown to either party and a surrender of the policy,[9] nor, would the acceptance of the premium and a surrender of the policy *after a loss* release the insurers, even though both parties *knew* of the loss ; for, *from the time of the loss the insurer became an absolute debtor for the sum lost to the extent of the sum insured*, from which liability he could not discharge himself by part payment.[10] Nor is the insurer relieved from liability, because a person having no authority to do so, as a broker or person through whom the insurance was effected, has, without the *knowledge* of the assured, surrendered the policy, and

[1] *Hollingsworth* v. *Germania F. Ins. Co.*, 45 Ga. 294 ; 12 Am. Rep. 579.

[2] *Bergeson* v. *The Builders' Ins. Co.*, 38 Cal. 541 ; 5 Bennett's F. I. C. 253.

[3] *Landis* v. *Home, etc., Ins. Co.*, 56 Mo. 591.

[4] *Hathorn* v. *Germania Ins. Co., ante ; Goit* v. *National Protection Ins. Co.*, 25 Barb. (N. Y.) 189.

[5] *Ætna Ins. Co.* v. *Maguire, ante.*

[6] *Van Valkenburgh* v. *Lenox F. Ins. Co.*, 51 N. Y. 465.

[7] *Van Valkenburgh* v. *Lenox F. Ins. Co., ante.*

[8] *Home Ins. Co.* v. *Curtis* (Mich.), 5 Ins. J. 120.

[9] *Van Valkenburgh* v. *Lenox F. Ins. Co., ante.*

[10] *Van Valkenburgh* v. *Lenox F. Ins. Co., ante.*

placed the risk elsewhere. Thus in a New York case,[1] the insurers directed their agent to cancel the policy unless the assured would pay an additional premium, of which the agent gave notice to the broker through whom the insurance was effected. The assured refused to pay the increased rate, and the broker requested the agent to wait until he could get the risk placed elsewhere. The vessel was destroyed by fire March 1st, *and the broker not knowing of the loss* procured a policy upon the same risk, for the same amount, and took it to the office of the assured, and, *without the knowledge of the assured*, took out the policy in the defendant company, and substituted the new policy in its place. The policy in the defendant company was marked cancelled and returned by him to the agent. It was held that the policy was not thereby cancelled, and that the defendant was liable for the loss.[2]

In the case of a mutual company, the policy cannot be canceled by it without a return of the premium note,[3] unless the assured is still liable thereon for assessments.[4] Nor can it be canceled without notice to the assured.[5]

Right to cancel when property is threatened with destruction.

SEC. 107. The reservation of a right to cancel a policy on a return of the unearned premium, does not warrant the company in cancelling the same while a conflagration threatening the destruction of the insured property is in existence, *unless the assured is neglecting to employ such means as a reasonably prudent man would employ to prevent the destruction of the property.*[6] The question as to the right of the company to rescind, is not one depending upon the *intention* of the insurer, *but the actual position of the property as to threatened danger of destruction from the casualty insured against at the time when the cancellation is attempted.* The insurer cannot be permitted to cancel a policy *instanter*, except in case of fraud on the part of the assured, or acts or omissions that amount to fraud on his part, but must give the assured a reasonable opportunity to secure protection by insurance elsewhere.[7]

[1] *McLean v. Republic Ins. Co., ante.* See *Standard Oil Co.* v. *Triumph Ins Co.,* 6 T. & C. (N. Y.) 300, *contra.*

[2] *McLean v. Republic Ins. Co., ante.*

[3] *Ætna Ins. Co.* v. *Webster,* 6 Wall. (U. S.) 129 ; *Landis* v. *Home, etc., Ins. Co., ante.*

[4] *Emmott* v. *Slater Mut. Ins. Co.,* 7 R. I. 562 ; *Coles* v. *Iowa State Mut. Ins. Co.,* 18 Iowa, 425.

[5] *Latoix* v. *Germania, etc., Ins. Co.,* 27 La. An. 113.

[6] *Home Ins. Co.* v. *Heck,* 65 Ill. 111.

[7] *Home Ins. Co.* v. *Heck,* 65 Ill. 111.

When policy expires when hour is not fixed.

SEC. 108. When a policy is made to cover a risk from a certain day to a certain day, without fixing the precise time when it ceases to be operative, it will be construed as covering the risk during the entire day of the last day named. Thus, where goods were insured against fire by a policy in which the insurance was expressed to be "from the 14th February, 1868, until the 14th August, 1868, and for so long after as the said assured should pay the sum of $225 at the time above mentioned." The goods were destroyed by fire on the night of the 14th August, 1868, the insurance not having been renewed. It was held that the insurance continued during the whole of the 14th of August, and the loss was, therefore, covered by it.[1] But this question will seldom, arise as the policy usually fixes the precise time when the risk terminates.

Void policy may be revived.

SEC. 109. When a policy has become void, by a breach of any of its conditions, it may be revived and set on foot again as an operative instrument, by an act from which the consent of the insurer may be fairly implied.[2] Thus, where the property covered by the policy is

[1] *Isaacs* v. *The Royal Ins. Co.*, 22 L. J. Q. B. 681.
[2] CHURCH, C.J., in *Shearman* v. *Niagara F. Ins. Co.*, 46 N. Y, 526; 7 Am. Rep. 380; *Keeler* v. *Niagara F. Ins. Co.*, 16 Wis. 523. In *Howell* v. *Knickerbocker Life Ins. Co.*, 44 N. Y. 276, it was held that evidence as to an agreement made *at the time* when a policy is issued, that it should not become void by non-payment of premium *at the precise time* when it became due, was not admissible, but that an agreement made *subsequently* to the issue of the policy might be shown, and was binding upon the parties *because they had a right to modify the policy by a subsequent parol agreement.* *Wolfe* v. *Security F. Ins. Co.*, 39 N. Y. 51; *Hooper* v. *Hudson River F. Ins. Co.*, 17 id. 424. This question was raised in *Buckley* v. *Garrett*, 47 Penn. St. 270, and a similar doctrine held to that stated in the text. In that case it was held that, while a transfer from one tenant in common to a co-tenant, or from one partner to another, is within the prohibition of a policy of insurance which declares that alienation by sale or otherwise shall forfeit the policy. Yet a provision that it should become void upon a sale or transfer of property insured, unless it was also transferred to the purchaser, and the transfer accepted by the president or secretary of the company, within twenty days after the sale or transfer, or before a fire, the assignment to be indorsed on, or annexed to the policy, does not apply to a case where the assured had parted with his interest in the policy by an assignment approved by the company; and the policy is not avoided by such assignment. Also, that where the policy was to continue so long as the yearly payments stipulated therein were made, and after its assignment approved by the insurance company, one of the partners of the firm insured sold and transferred his interest in the property insured to his co-partner who continued for several years thereafter to make the yearly payments required by the policy to the treasurer, the authorized agent to receive them, but no notice of sale of the partnership interest was regularly given or any transfer of the policy executed to the purchaser, it is not thereby necessarily made void; but the facts were evidence to be submitted to the jury upon the question whether the state of the policy was known to the company; if so, their receipt of the annual premiums for years after the assignment tended to show an acquiescence in the alienation, and therefore a waiver of the forfeiture and consequent estoppel. "Hence," say the court, "it was error to instruct the jury that the transfer

transferred, and the policy is assigned to the vendee *before* the con_
sent of the insurer is obtained thereto, although the policy is thereby
rendered void, yet, by subsequently assenting to such transfer, the
policy is revived, and becomes an operative instrument in the hand
of the vendee.[1]

---

by one of the partners to the other having made the policy void, the payment of
the annual installment to the treasurer and acceptance by him would not render
it valid, and that under the evidence the plaintiff was not entitled to recover."

[1] In *Shearman* v. *Niagara Fire Ins. Co.*, 46 N. Y. 526; 7 Am. Rep. 380, this
question was directly raised and decided as stated in the text. In that case the
property was conveyed March 4, and on the 21st of March the vendor renewed
the policy, and on the 15th of the next April transferred the policy to the vendee,
and on the same day the company's agent, by an indorsement on the policy, *consented* to the transfer. Thus it will be seen that on March 4th the policy became
void by a conveyance of the property, was renewed by the vendor while it was
void and when he had no interest in the property, and was a dead instrument
when transferred to the plaintiff. Yet, the court correctly held, that the consent
of the company's agent to its transfer to the plaintiff revived the policy, as a
valid and operative contract on the part of the defendant. "Assuming," said
CHURCH, C.J., "that when Lewis J. Shearman transferred the property he
retained no insurable interest, I cannot assent to the position, that the policy
thereby became a wager policy, and void in the sense that it was an illegal contract, and that it could not be revived and restored to life by the act of the
defendant. It was void, not for any vice or illegality in the contract itself, but
for the reason that there was nothing upon which it could operate. *Howard* v.
Albany Ins. Co., 3 Denio, 301. The parties, it is true, agreed that in a certain
contingency it should be void; and if a loss had occurred during that period, no
action could have been maintained upon the policy, but the happening of the
contingency did not impress upon the contract the character of illegality, so that
no subsequent agreement could restore it. It is claimed, however, by the counsel for the appellant, that, when the renewal was obtained, the transfer had been
made, and that this renewal constituted a new policy, which was void and illegal
within the principle before stated. I do not think so. The renewal simply
revived the original policy, and continued it with all the virtue which it would
have had, for any purpose, if it had not expired. Besides, Lewis J. Shearman
had an insurable interest remaining, as lessee and owner of the equity of redemption, which may be deemed sufficient to obviate this objection. The important
question is, whether the forfeiture was waived and the policy revived by the
consent of the defendant to the transfer of it to the plaintiff. In the case of an
insurance upon goods, it has been held by this court, that a request that the company would consent to an assignment of the policy was a sufficient notice to them
that the party making it had acquired, or was about to acquire, some interest in
the goods insured, and was a compliance with the condition of the policy on that
subject. *Hooper* v. *Hudson River Fire Ins. Co.*, 17 N. Y. 424; *Wolfe* v. *The
Security Fire Ins. Co.*, 39 id. 49. An assignment of the policy would be useless
for any purpose, unless the assignee had some interest in the subject insured.
This interest may be as owner or incumbrancer, but whatever it is, the underwriters, by consenting to the assignment, agree to become answerable to the
assignee, to the extent of whatever interest he has, and if the whole interest is
transferred, the consent is equivalent to an agreement with the condition of the policy as a subsisting operative contract. I see no reason why the
same rule should not apply to a policy upon real as well as personal property, but
it is unnecessary in this case to determine that the request to assign was a sufficient notice of the transfer of the property, because it expressly appears that the
agent was informed of the fact at the time the request was made. It is objected
that the agent was not informed of the time of the transfer, nor that the renewal
was subsequent to the transfer, but this is not material. It is enough that the
plaintiff requested that he should be substituted as the insured, on the ground
that the property had been transferred to him, and the company consented to it.

Mortgagee cannot retain money for loss under assigned policy, unless debt is due.

SEC. 110. Where a mortgagor assigns a policy of insurance upon the mortgaged property to the mortgagee, or when the insurance is made payable to the mortgagee in case of loss, *the mortgagee has no right, upon receipt of the money to apply it in reduction of the mortgage, unless the mortgage debt is due,* but is bound to pay it over to the mortgagor; but he may insist that the money shall be applied to a restoration of the premises to their former condition, so that the security shall not be lessened by the fire.[1] Thus, in the case last referred to, the defendant held a mortgage upon certain premises, also a policy of insurance obtained in the name of the mortgagor, but made "payable in case of loss" to the defendant. The plaintiff held a second mortgage upon the same premises. A partial loss occurred under the policy *before any part of the defendant's mortgage became due,* and the sum of $780 was paid to it under the policy. The mortgagor having restored the property to a condition as good as that in which it was before the fire, the defendant paid over to the mortgagor the money received under the policy. Subsequently the mortgage matured, and not being paid, the premises were sold by the defendant under the mortgage, and the sum of $136.60 received therefor, above the amount of its mortgage, which was paid over to the plaintiff upon his mortgage debt. The plaintiff then brought a bill in equity to compel the defendant to apply the sum of $780, received by it under the policy, upon its mortgage, but the court held that the defendant was not bound so to apply the money, "*and could not have done it without the consent of the mortgagor.*"

Promise to pay loss when not liable therefor—effect of.

SEC. 111. Although a policy does not in fact cover a certain loss, yet if the insurer recognizes his liability, and promises to pay the loss if the insured will do certain things, *if the insured does the acts required of him by the insurer,* liability for the loss is fixed, and the insurer cannot

---

It is of no importance whether his conveyance was recent or remote, nor whether they knew that the policy was void at the time of the renewal by reason of the transfer before that time. They might have insisted upon the forfeiture if they had so elected, at whatever time it was made. They knew that the policy was void when the request was made, and they chose to revive it, and thereby consented to insure the property in the hands of the plaintiff as effectually as if they had given a new policy to him. The retention of the premium received on the renewal was a good consideration for this agreement. No other construction can be given to the transaction. The condition requiring consent is important to underwriters, to enable them to determine the character and standing of the insured; and when they agree to a transfer of a policy to a particular person, knowing that he owns the subject insured, the whole purpose of the provision is complied with, and they have no interest to know how or why he acquired it."

[1] *Gordon* v. *Ware Savings Bank,* 115 Mass. 588.

escape therefrom upon the ground that the loss is not within the perils insured against. Thus, where the defendants[1] insured a cargo, and the boat was frozen in at the mouth of the Potomac river on her pas_ sage, and a large quantity of cider, a part of the cargo, was frozen, and the defendant promised the plaintiff that, if he would go to Wash_ ington and sell the cider to the best advantage, they would pay the deficiency, it was held that, although the loss was not covered by the policy, yet, as the insurers had recognized their liability therefor, and in consideration of the insured doing certain acts requested by them, their liability was fixed, and they could not escape payment upon the ground that there was no original liability. Although a mere promise to pay, where no liability to pay existed, would be a *undum partum*, and not enforceable, yet where there is a consideration for the promise, as the doing of something which the promisor requests to have done, or the omission to do some act at his request and upon the faith of the promise, the promise is enforceable and cannot be avoided upon the ground of lack of mutuality.[2]

Misstatement as to incumbrances, or neglect to state.

SEC. 112. When the policy requires that the insured shall truly state all incumbrances existing upon the property at the time of insurance, and also contains a condition that any concealment or misrepresentation shall make such insurance void, a failure to disclose all the incumbrances upon the property, is such a concealment within the meaning of the condition, as invalidates the policy,[3] and it is immaterial whether

---

[1] *Willett* v. *Sun Mut. Ins. Co.*, 45 N. Y. 45; 6 Am. Rep. 31.

[2] *L'Amoreaux* v. *Gould*, 7 N. Y. 349; *Train* v. *Gold*, 5 Pick. (Mass.) 380; *Hilton* v. *Southwick*, 17 Me. 303.

[3] In the case of *Beck* v. *Hibernia Ins. Co. of Ohio*, 44 Md. 95, the policy in question, which insured certain buildings therein particularly described, against loss or damage by fire, provided that the conditions thereunto annexed should form part of the instrument, and were to be resorted to in order to explain the rights and obligations of the parties to it. By one of the conditions it required every applicant for insurance in the company to state any incumbrance that might exist on the property to be insured; and by another, it declared that "if any person insuring any building or goods in this office shall make any misrepresentation or concealment, such insurance shall be void." Prior to, and at the time the policy was issued, there were two mortgages on the insured buildings, the existence of which was never communicated to the insurance company or its agent. A loss occurring, this action was brought upon the policy, The court held that the failure to disclose the existence of the mortgages avoided the policy and defeated the action. See as sustaining the decision, *Bowman* v. *Franklin Fire Ins. Co.*, 40 Md. 620; *Hutchins* v. *Cleveland Mut. Ins. Co.*, 11 Ohio St. 477; *Gehagan* v. *Un. Mut. Ins. Co.*, 43 N. H. 176; *Patten* v. *Mer. & Farm. Ins. Co.*, 38 id. 338; *Bowditch Mut. Fire Ins. Co.* v. *Winslow*, 3 Gray (Mass.) 415; *Same* v. *Same*, 8 id. 38; *Penn. Ins. Co.* v. *Gottsman*, 48 Penn. St. 151; *Campbell* v. *New England Mut. Life Ins. Co.*, 98 Mass. 403. But see *Hoffman* v. *Ætna Fire Ins. Co.*, 32 N. Y. 451; *Peck* v. *New London Mut. Ins. Co.*, 22 Conn. 575; *Jacobs* v. *Eagle Ins. Co.*, 7 Allen (Mass.) 132.

the policy contains such a provision or not, if a written application is
made which is referred to and made a part of the policy, and the
insured omits to state all the incumbrances, or falsely states the same,
for in such a case the statements of the assured amount to warranties,
and must be strictly true,[1] and it would seem that this would be the
case, even though the application is not made a part of the contract,
because it is a concealment or misrepresentation of a *material* fact.[2] At
least, such would be the result, if the jury should find as a fact that
such concealment or misrepresentation was intentional and fraudulent,[3]
or was material to the risk,[4] and, *the fact that specific inquiries in reference thereto are made in the application, implies that the insurer regards it
as material, and the insurer has a right to judge for himself what is material, and to prescribe the terms on which he will assume the risk,* it is not
competent for the court to say that the insurer misjudged as to the
materiality of the facts,[5] and, whether the facts are material in fact
or not, a suppression or misstatement thereof will avoid the policy.
The courts can only construe and enforce the contract which the parties have made. It cannot make a new contract for them, or add to
or detract from it.[6]

---

[1] *Eagan* v. *Mut. Ins. Co.*, 5 Den. (N. Y.) 326 ; *Cooper* v. *Farmers' Ins. Co.*, 50
Penn. St. 299 ; *Jacobs* v. *Eagle Mut. Fire Ins. Co.*, 7 Allen (Mass.) 132.

[2] *Shoemaker* v. *Glen's Falls Ins. Co.*, 60 Barb. (N. Y.) 84.

[3] *Cumberland Valley, etc., Ins. Co.* v. *Mitchell*, 48 Penn. St. 374.

[4] *Draper* v. *Charter Oak Ins. Co.*, 2 Allen (Mass.) 569.

[5] *Draper* v. *Charter Oak Ins. Co., ante; Davenport* v. *N. E. Mut. Fire Ins. Co.*,
6 Cush. (Mass.) 340; *Shoemaker* v. *Glen's Falls Ins. Co., ante; Patten* v. *Merchants', etc., Ins. Co.*, 38 N. H. 338. The very fact that inquiry is made respecting it, makes it material, and this pplies to every fact inquired about. *Fitch* v.
Am. Popular Life Ins. Co., 59 N. Y. 557; *Campbell* v. *N. E. Mut. Ins. Co.*, 98
Mass. 381 ; *Day* v. *Mut. Benefit Life Ins. Co.*, 1 McArthur (U. S.) 91 ; *Miller*
v. *Same*, 31 Iowa, 216.

[6] *Patten* v. *Merchants', etc., Ins. Co., ante; Wilson* v. *Canada Fire Ins. Co.*, 4
R. I. 141; *Shoemaker* v. *Glen's Falls Ins. Co., ante; Dennison* v. *Thomaston Mut.
Fire Ins. Co.*, 20 Me. 125; *Pennsylvania Ins. Co.* v. *Gottsman*, 48 Penn. St. 151;
Hayward v. *Mut. Fire Ins. Co.*, 10 Cush. (Mass.) 444. And even if the mortgage
was invalid at the time when the insurance was made, if it subsequently became
operative, the policy is void. *Packard* v. *Agawam Mut. Fire Ins. Co.*, 2 Gray
(Mass.) 334; *Murphy* v. *People's, etc., Ins. Co.*, 7 Allen (Mass.) 239. In *Patten*
v. *Merchants', etc., Ins. Co.*, 38 N. H. 338, the plaintiff applied for insurance in
the defendant company, and signed a written application therefor. A question,
and the answer made thereto in the application, was as follows : " Is the property
incumbered by mortgage or otherwise ? Ans. No." There was, in fact, a mortgage of $5,000 on the property. The court held that this was the concealment of
a material fact that avoided the policy. In *Davenport* v. *N. E. Mut. Fire Ins.
Co.*, 6 Cush. (Mass.) 340, under a similar state of facts, the court held the policy
void upon the ground that the failure to disclose the existence of a mortgage was
the concealment of a material fact. FLETCHER, J., in passing upon the question,
said : " It is manifest that the defendants deemed this information material, and
they put the direct question, and it was a proper and a practical question, *and it*

Proceeds of policy after death of assured. Rights of widow and of heirs to.

SEC. 113. Where a policy is made to the insurer, "his executors, administrators or assigns," and the building is burned after the death of the insured, *and after an assignment of the building to the widow as dower*, the proceeds of the policy belong to the widow, *to the extent of her interest*, with remainder to the heirs.[1]

Materials of which building composed, not insured.

SEC. 114. An insurance upon a building is an insurance *upon the building as such, and not upon the materials of which it is composed*, and if a building, from defect of construction or other cause, falls down, so as to cease to have a distinctive character as such, and subsequently the materials take fire and are destroyed, the insurer is not liable therefor.[2]

But it has been held that, where a policy covered goods in a build_ing, and one of the end walls gave way, and half of the store, and the whole of the adjoining building fell, *and before there was time to remove the goods not displaced or injured by the fall*, the insurer is liable for the loss of such goods.[3] In this case, the court laid great stress upon the fact that the fire *instantly* followed the fall, and destroyed the goods, *before there was time to remove them*. An exception in a policy that "if a building shall fall, *except as the* result of fire, all insurance by this company shall cease and determine," is to be construed according to the ordinary meaning of the words, and so long as the building remains standing, no matter how dilapidated it may become, or how depreciated in value, the policy remains operative.[4]

Assured must show the loss to be one not excepted against.

SEC. 115. Where a policy contains exceptions to the liability of the insurer, as, where it is provided that it shall not be liable for a fire ocurring in a certain way, or from a particular cause, it is the duty of the

---

was material that the plaintiff should answer it truly. The plaintiff having given an untrue answer, *whether by accident, mistake, or design, it matters not, to a direct, plain and practical question, he cannot now be heard to say it was immaterial.*" In *Shoemaker v. Glen's Falls Ins. Co., ante*, the policy was held void because the plaintiff stated that the premises were free from incumbrances, when in fact they were not, the court holding that it was the concealment of a material fact. *Towne v. Fitchburyh, etc., Ins. Co.*, 7 Allen (Mass.) 51 ; *Bowditch Mut. Fire Ins. Co. v. Winslow*, 8 Gray (Mass.) 38 ; *Fales v. Conway, etc., Mut. Ins. Co.*, 7 Allen (Mass.) 46.

[1] *Wyman v. Wyman*, 26 N. Y. 253 ; *Hudnall v. Burkle*, (Sup. Ct. of Tenn.) 11 Pacific L. Rep. 27.

[2] *Nave v. Home, etc., Ins. Co.*, 37 Mo. 430.

[3] *Lewis v. Springfield F. & M. Ins. Co.*, 10 Gray (Mass.) 159.

[4] *Fireman's, etc., Ins. Co. v. Congregation Rodeph Sholom*, 80 Ill. 558.

insured to show that the loss sought to be recovered for, did not occur in any of the modes or from any of the causes covered by the exceptions. Thus, where a policy upon a theatre, contained a condition that the policy should not cover a loss or damage by fire which might orginate "in the theatre proper," it was held that, in order to entitle the plaintiff to recover, he must show that the fire did not so originate.[1] In such a case, the fact that the fire was communicated to the rest of the building from "the theatre proper," will not prevent a recovery, *unless the fire originated there;* thus, where "the theatre proper" was set on fire by causes originating *outside thereof*, as from the heating of the bricks in a flue in the walls, from a fire used in a furnace connecting with such flue, used in a shop adjoining the theatre, it was held that this was not a fire originating in the theatre proper, within the meaning of the condition.[2]

Distance from other buildings.

SEC. 116. When the policy makes the application a part thereof, and in the application the insured is required to state the "distance of the building insured from other buildings within a hundred feet, and how the other buildings are occupied;" and also contains a clause by which the assured "covenants and agrees, etc., that the foregoing is a correct statement and description of all the facts inquired for, or material to the risk;" the insured is bound to state all the buildings within one hundred feet, and the character of their occupancy, and a failure to do so avoids the policy.[3]

But unless the application calls for a description of the risk, and its relative situation as to other buildings, none need be given, but if a description is called for, it must be true as to all matters material to the risk. Thus, where an application called for a statement of all the buildings within ten rods of the one insured, and the distance from each; it was held that an omission to state all the buildings within that distance, was a fraudulent concealment, which rendered the policy inoperative;[4] and if the application is made a part of the policy,

---

[1] *Sohier* v. *Norwich F. Ins. Co.*, 11 Allen (Mass.) 336.

[2] *Sohier* v. *Norwich F. Ins. Co.*, ante.

[3] *Tebbetts* v. *Hamilton, etc., Ins. Co.*, 1 Allen (Mass.) 305; *Hardy* v. *Un. Mut. Fire Ins. Co.*, 3 id. 217.

[4] *Wilson* v. *Herkimer Co. Mut. Ins. Co.*, 6 N. Y. 53; *Calvert* v. *Hamilton, etc., Ins. Co.*, 1 Allen (Mass.) 308; *Burritt* v. *Saratoga, etc., Ins. Co.*, 5 Hill (N. Y.) 188; *Chaffee* v. *Cattaraugus, etc., Ins. Co.*, 18 N. Y. 376; *Brown* v. *Same*, 18 N. Y. 385; *Day* v. *Conway Ins. Co.*, 52 Me. 60; *Tebbetts* v. *Hamilton, etc., Ins. Co.*, 1 Allen (Mass.) 305; *Jennings* v. *Chenango Co. Mut. Ins. Co.*, 7 Hill (N. Y.) 122.

it is immaterial whether the matter is material to the risk or not.[1] The answers amount to a warranty that the facts are as stated.[2] In such cases, the description of the surroundings of the risk, is a warranty that must be substantially true.[3] But even though the assured misstates the relative situation of surrounding buildings in the application, but subsequently discovers the mistake, and informs the insurer or his agent thereof, and is told that it will make no difference, the breach is waived, and the company is estopped from setting up such misdescription in avoidance of liability.[4] When the application calls for a statement of the relative situation of other buildings, and he answers: "Dwelling about four feet distant one side, about fifteen feet to a small dwelling and store-house," and there in fact other buildings, a few feet further from the building insured, *not disclosed,* it is held that this is not a fraudulent concealment, for, if the insurer desired further information, it was his duty to have sought it, and the assured could not be presumed to know that it was material for him to state all the buildings within a certain distance, unless so informed in the application.[5]

So, where an application calls for a statement of all *buildings* within a certain distance, the inquiry has reference to buildings of a permanent character, and does not call for temporary structures not properly coming within the term. Thus, where in answer to an inquiry, " are there other buildings within four rods ? the assured answered, " no other buildings within four rods," and there were in fact within that

---

[1] *Hardy* v. *Union, etc., Ins. Co.,* 4 Allen (Mass.) 217; *Anderson* v. *Fitzgerald,* 4 H. L. Cas. 484; *Cazenove* v. *British Assurance Co.,* 6 C. B. (N. S.) 487.

[2] *Murdock* v. *Chenango Ins. Co.,* 2 N. Y. 310; *Frost* v. *Saratoga, etc., Ins. Co.,* 5 Den. (N. Y.) 154; *Kennedy* v. *St. Lawrence, etc., Ins. Co.,* 10 Barb. (N. Y.) 285; *Farmers' Ins. & Loan Co.* v. *Snyder,* 16 Wend. (N. Y.) 481.

[3] *Burritt* v. *Ins. Co., ante,* and cases cited in last note. In *Chaffee* v. *Cattaraugus, etc., Ins. Co., ante,* in answer to an inquiry as to the situation of the risk, relative to other buildings within ten rods, the assured replied: "In the middle of a block, of three stories; one clothing store; one grocery; one hardware and stove store; one tin shop; mansion house across the street, about six rods; cabinet shop, three rods; harness shop, five rods; grocery and dwelling-house, five rods; wagon shop and blacksmith shop, about eight rods; new building, to be used for tin shop, about three rods; one store-house and one barn, about four rods," and the assured stated that "all exposures within ten rods are mentioned;" and the application was made a part of the policy; it was held that the fact that there were other buildings within ten rods was a breach of warranty that avoided the policy.

[4] *Farmers' etc., Ins. Co.* v. *Chestnut,* 50 Ill. 111; *Atlantic Ins. Co.* v. *Wright,* 22 id. 474.

[5] *Allen* v. *Charlestown, etc., Ins. Co.* 5 Gray (Mass.) 387; *Hall* v. *People's Mut. F. Ins. Co.,* 6 Gray (Mass.) 185; *Gates* v. *Madison Co. Mut. Ins. Co., ante; Peoria, etc., Ins. Co.* v. *Perkins.* 16 Mich. 380; *Girard F. & M. Ins. Co.* v. *Stephenson,* 37 Penn. St. 290; *Susquehanna Ins. Co.* v. *Perrine,* 7 W. & S. (Penn.) 348.

distance a hog-house and hen-house three and a half feet high in the rear, and six feet in front, covered with boards, neither shingled or battened, it was held that *they were not buildings*, and the omission to state their existence was not a fraudulent concealment.[1] At least, it seems that the existence of such temporary structure will not be regarded as avoiding the policy *unless it is found to have materially increased the risk.* Thus, in a case,[2] the assured was required to state *all* the buildings within 150 feet. There was a rough structure forty-five feet long, and eighteen feet high, within fifty feet of the property insured, used by the carpenters engaged to erect the building insured, of which nothing was said. The court held that this could not be regarded as a *building* within the meaning of the term, and that the question as to whether or not the omission to state its existence would avoid the policy, must depend upon whether by its use, it materially increased the risk.[3] In another case,[4] the policy described the premises as "a house bounded in the rear by a stone building covered with tin, and by a yard;" in which yard there was being erected a first class store, which would and did communicate with the building insured. The court held that the policy was valid, although there was between the house and stone building, a brick building covered with shingles, communicating with both by doors; there being no proof that the omission to mention in the description the communicating doors was fraudulent, and it being proved that the loss was not caused by the connecting buildings.[5]

Adjoining premises, when changes in do not affect liability of insurer.

SEC. 117. Unless specially provided for in the policy, the assured is not bound to inform the insurer of any changes in adjoining premises, however much the risk may be thereby enhanced. By not making this a condition of the policy, the insurer accepts all the risk incident to such changes.[6] If, however, there has been any misrepresentation or concealment of important facts *existing at the time when the insurance was entered into*, the rule would be otherwise. The statements of the

---

[1] *White* v. *Mutual Fire Ins. Co.*, 8 Gray (Mass.) 566.

[2] *Richmondville Seminary* v. *Hamilton, etc., Ins. Co.*, 14 Gray (Mass.) 459.

[3] See also, *Clark* v. *Union Mut. Ins. Co.*, 40 N. H. 333.

[4] *Casey* v. *Goldsmid*, 4 L. C. 107.

[5] *Sayles* v. *N. W. Ins. Co.*, 2 Curtis (U. S.) 610; *Hall* v. *People's, etc., Ins. Co.*, 6 Gray (Mass.) 185; *Dennison* v. *Thomaston, etc., Ins. Co.*, 20 Me. 125.

[6] *Miller* v. *Western Farmers', etc., Ins. Co.*, 1 Handy (Ohio) 209; 5 Bennett's F. I. C. 16; *Gates* v. *Madison Co. Mut. Ins. Co.*, 5 N. Y. 467; *Stebbins* v. *Globe Ins. Co.*, 2 Hall (N. Y.) 632.

assured as to the *surroundings* of the risk cannot be regarded as a promissory warranty that the same surroundings shall continue, but only as to the condition of the premises *when insured*. If the insurer desires to impose the burden upon the assured, to see that no changes are made, it must be provided for in the policy.[1] If, however, the policy contains a provision against an increase of risk, *it relates to an increase within the control of the assured*, and if he erects a building upon adjoining premises, materially increasing the risk, or converts an adjoining building owned by him to a more hazardous use, the policy will be avoided thereby; *but it is for the jury to say whether the risk is thereby in fact increased.*[2] But he is not responsible for any increase of risk resulting from the acts of adjoining owners.[3] Nor is he deemed as violating the terms of the policy, *if the conditions as to increase of risk relate entirely to any alteration of the building insured or the business carried on therein*, by himself erecting a building upon adjoining premises,[4] nor upon the same premises, as a barn[5] or any other building.[6]

Application must be true at time policy issues, as well as when application is made.

SEC. 118. The statements of the assured, relative to the location, situation and condition of the risk, must not only be true at the time when the application was made, but also at the time when the policy issues, so far as relates to any chnages therein essentially affecting the risk, within the control of the assured. Thus, where an application was made in California, October 30th, for insurance upon a dwelling, and a full and particular description of the same was given, which application was forwarded to the insurer in London, who, on the 7th day of the succeeding April, made a policy thereon covering "brick building used as a dwelling-house store (described in the paper attached to this policy)." The paper attached gave a minute description of a *two-storied* house. The description was, in fact, accurate up to the succeeding March, *when a new story was added to the house*, without the knowledge or consent of the insurers. The court held that the descrip-

---

[1] *Miller v. Ins. Co., ante.*

[2] *Howard v. Ky. & Louisville Ins. Co.*, 13 B. Mon. (Ky.) 289; *Boatwright v. Ætna Ins. Co.* 1 Strob. (S. C.) 281; *Stebbins v. Globe Ins. Co.*, 2 Hall) N. Y.) 632; *Stetson v. The Mass. F. Ins. Co.*, 4 Mass. 330.

[3] *Howard v. Ky. & Louisville Ins. Co., ante; Stebbins v. Globe Ins. Co., ante.*

[4] *Gates v. Madison, etc., Ins. Co., ante.*

[5] *Gates v. Madison, etc., Ins. Co., ante; Stebbins v. Globe Ins. Co., ante; Stetson A. Mass. F. Ins. Co., ante.*

[6] *Stebbins v. Globe Ins. Co., ante.*

tion of the house was a warranty, not only that the house was as described in the application at the time of its execution, but also a warranty that the assured would not voluntarily do anything to make the building vary from such description, and that the addition of a new story thereto, was a breach of such warranty. "It would," said CAMPBELL, C.J., "seem revolting, if, as soon as the insurers had sent off their description, to be shown to an insurance office or private underwriter, they might have added several stories to the house, and removed from it all the described safeguards against fire, and that, although the description misdescribed the state of the premises at the date of the policy, a fire afterwards happening, an indemnity might be claimed, for which the underwriter had received no adequate consideration. * * *We are of the opinion that the description in the policy amounts to a warranty that the assured would not, during the time specified in the policy, voluntarily do anything to make the condition of the building vary from this description, so as thereby to increase the risk, or liability of the underwriter."[1]

When policy requires facts, subsequent to issue of policy, to be noticed.

SEC. 119. Where either the policy, or the by-laws, when made a part of the policy, require that notice of all alterations in the risk, or alteration or erection of any building which increases the risk, or which it would have been necessary to state had it existed at the time when the insurance was first made, shall be given and the consent of the company obtained or the policy shall be void, imposes the burden upon the assured of exercising the same degree of strictness in disclosing new facts as in disclosing facts existing at the time of making the application.[2]

Prohibited uses—when policy avoided by acts of tenants.

SEC. 120. Where the policy prohibits the *use* of a building for certain purposes, the policy becomes void if devoted to such uses by a tenant without the knowledge or consent of the assured;[3] or where it provides that certain articles shall be kept in a certain way, as ashes, the policy is avoided if they are kept in a different way, even though the act is done by a servant without the assured's knowledge or direc-

---

[1] *Sillem* v. *Thornton*, 1 El. & Bl. 868.

[2] *Calvert* v. *Hamilton Mut. Ins. Co.*, 1 Allen (Mass.) 308.

[3] *Kelly* v. *Worcester Ins. Co.*, 97 Mass. 284. But a contrary doctrine is held in Rhode Island, and in such a case, a plea that the use was without the knowledge or consent of the insured, is held a good answer. *Hoxie* v. *Providence Mut. Ins. Co.*, 6 R. I. 517.

tion.[1] But where the language of the policy is such as to indicate that it refers only to an unlawful or prohibited use by the assent or privity of the assured, and a contrary construction would in any measure be forced; the use of the premises in that way must be shown to have been with the owner's privity.[1]

Where the policy specially provides that, if the building is used for an unlawful purpose, the policy shall be void, if devoted to such use *by a tenant, even without the knowledge of the assured*, the policy is thereby invalidated;[3] and a policy upon property kept and sold contrary to law, is invalid, as the law will not give effect to a contract made to protect traffic which it has prohibited,[4] as upon a stock of liquors kept for sale in violation of law.[5] A policy effected by a mortgagor out of possession, which prohibits the use of the premises in a certain way or for certain purposes, is invalidated by the use of the premises in that way, either by the mortgagor or any person in possession of the premises under him.[6] Thus, in the case last referred to, the mortgagor took out a policy, containing a prohibition as to certain hazardous trades, among which was that of a "sail maker," or the depositing or keeping therein of certain hazardous articles, among which was "confectionary." The mortgagee in possession, let the store to a tenant, who sublet the loft to a sail maker, who, about two weeks before the fire, moved his stock and tools into the building, although he had not at the time of the loss commenced work therein. The dwelling was let to several persons, one of whom occupied it as a barber's shop, and also kept "confectionary" in small quantities, in glass jars on his counters and shelves. The fire did not originate either in the barber's shop or in the sail maker's rooms, but the court held that the policy was invalidated by their use for those purposes, although such use did not contribute to produce the loss. The use was directly contrary to the terms of the policy, and rendered it void.[7]

---

[1] *Worcester* v. *Worcester Ins. Co.*, 9 Gray (Mass.) 27 ; *Howard* v. *Baltimore, etc., Ins. Co.*, 16 Md. 377 ; *Mead* v. *N. W. Ins. Co.*, 14 N. Y. 533 ; *Fire Ass. of Phila.* v. *Williamson*, 26 Penn. St. 196.

[2] *Cunard* v. *Hyde*, El., Bl. & El. 670 ; *Wilson* v. *Rankin*, 34 L. J. (N. S.) Q. B. 62

[3] *Kelly* v. *Worcester Ins. Co.*, 97 Mass. 284 ; *contra*, see *Hoxie* v. *Providence Ins. Co.*, 6 R. I. 517.

[4] *Kelly* v. *Home, etc., Ins. Co.*, 97 Mass. 288 ; *Richardson* v. *Marine Ins. Co.*, 6 Mass. 111 ; *Breed* v. *Eaton*, 10 Mass. 21 ; *Clark* v. *Protection Ins. Co.*, 1 Story (U. S.) 109.

[5] *Kelly* v. *Home, etc., Ins. Co.*, ante.

[6] *Witherell* v. *City F. Ins. Co.*, 16 Gray (Mass.) 276.

[7] *Lee* v. *Howard Ins. Co.*, 3 Gray (Mass.) 383 ; *Macomber* v. *Howard F. Ins. Co.*, 7 Gray (Mass.) 257.

SEC. 121. If a person seeks to bind an insurance company under a policy procured by an agent, he must himself be bound by what the agent did in procuring it, and he cannot be permitted to repudiate the agent's acts in obtaining the policy and still claim that the insurers are liable on their part. The whole contract must stand, or none of it. The acceptance of a policy procured by an agent, is evidence of the ratification of the agent's acts, and the insured will not be permitted to show that he never read the policy, for the purpose of showing that he never *in fact* ratified the agent's acts.[1] He is bound by the representations made by such agent in reference to the property, and if such agent makes a written application, although it is not signed, which is referred to and made a part of the policy, the assured, by accepting the policy, ratifies the agent's acts, and is estopped from denying his authority to make such application.[2] Thus, in the case last referred to, the plaintiff authorized one Robly, through whom they had previously procured insurance upon the same property, to procure insurance for them in some good stock company, telling him that the property was situated as before. When the previous insurance was obtained by him for them, there were two mortgages upon the property, and they were still outstanding when the insurance in the defendant company was obtained, but were not mentioned in the application made by Robly. The court held that the insured was bound by the application made by Robly, and was estopped from denying his authority to make it.

SEC. 122. When a person has been induced by the fraud of an insurance company or its agent to accept a policy with conditions therein which such officers or agent *knew* would relieve the company from all liability for a loss under the policy, the assured cannot, upon proof of these facts, enforce the policy, but must seek his remedy either through a reformation of the policy, or by an action against the insurer for fraud.[3] The court held, that where an application was made which incorrectly described the property, and was, in terms, made a part of the policy, the fact that the agent or officers of the company *knew* the real situation of the property, did not affect the question; that

[1] *Monitor Mut. Ins. Co.* v. *Buffum*, 115 Mass. 343. See also, *Grace* v. *Adams*, 100 Mass. 515, in support of the general doctrine that a party must be bound himself, if he would bind the other party to a contract.

[2] *Draper* v. *Charter Oak Ins. Co.*, 2 Allen (Mass.) 569.

[3] *Tebbetts* v. *Hamilton Mut. Ins. Co.*, 3 Allen (Mass.) 569.

the insurer had a right to rely upon the application rather than upon their own knowledge of the facts. But if the application had been filled up by an agent of the company, and the erroneous statements were made by him according to the better class of cases, the plaintiff might have enforced the policy.[1]

Assured may cancel policies although other policies provide they shall only be liable pro rata.

SEC. 123. Where several policies are outstanding upon the same property, and it is a condition of either of said policies that, in case of loss, the insurer shall only be liable for a *pro rata* part thereof, in the absence of a condition requiring a specific amount of insurance to be kept up, it is competent for the insured to cancel any of said policies, and in case, by any act of his, either of the policies become void, the other insurers will be liable for the loss, and cannot insist that they shall only be liable for such a sum as they would have been liable for if *all* the policies had been kept on foot.[2]

When liability has attached under policy, payment of loss upon one class of property does not defeat claim for loss on another, though receipted in full.

SEC. 124. Where the liability of an insurer has attached under a policy by a total loss of the property covered, the acceptance of a sum insured upon one class of property will not release the company from liability for property of another class *separately valued*, even though upon the payment of such sum a receipt is given, expressed to be " in full satisfaction for the loss," and the policy is cancelled. Thus, in a New York case,[3] an action was brought to recover the amount of a policy of insurance for $1,500—$500 on dwelling-house; $600 on barn; and $400 on the produce therein. The barn and its contents were destroyed by fire. Defendant did not dispute the liability of $400 on produce,

---

[1] In *Reaper City Ins Co.* v. *Jones, Sup. Ct. of Ill.,* 5 W. Ins. Rev. 683, one clause in the policy sued on made it void if gunpowder was kept in the house without written permission, and it was further declared, that nothing less than a distinct agreement indorsed on the policy should be construed as a waiver of any condition or restriction. The assured, at the time of loss, had on hand a few pounds of gunpowder, kept with the knowledge and express permission of the agent of the company. The agent did not call the attention of the assured to the particular condition of the policy. Held, that the company can waive such a condition, it being for the benefit of the company. The company received the payment of the premiums with a determination to resist payment if loss occurs. The company was chargeable with the act of their agent in giving permission to keep powder; such conditions, printed in the smallest type and read with great difficulty, are but traps when attention is not called to them. With knowledge of the fact on the part of agents, and when no notice is given of the stringent character of the condition, but specific authority is granted to continue to keep the articles, the company waives the forfeiture.

[2] *Hand* v. *Williamsburgh Fire Ins. Co.,* 57 N. Y. 41.

[3] *Redfield* v. *Holland Purchase Ins. Co.*

and paid this amount, and received a writing declaring that it was received in full satisfaction for the loss, and " cancelling $1,500 on said policy." The court held that the writing was not a technical release, and the payment formed no consideration for the discharge of the defendant from liability as to the barn, and that it did not preclude plaintiff from recovering the insurance thereon.

Right of insurer to recover back money paid for loss.

SEC. 125. Although fraud vitiates all contracts, so that an adjustment of a loss obtained by fraud, would be void, yet this proceeds upon the ground that the parties have treated without suspicion, and does not apply to a case where fraud is set up by an insurer, as a reason why the loss should not be paid to an innocent holder of the policy, and, as a result, without fraud, misrepresentation or conceal-ment on the part of the policy-holder, the loss is compromised, the insurer is thereby estopped from recovering back the money that has been paid under such compromise, on the ground that subsequent thereto it had discovered that the loss was fraudulent.[1] But *if, at the time of the compromise*, the policy-holder *had known* of the fraud, and had designedly concealed the facts, or if he was personally implicated in the original fraud, the rule would be different, and a recovery might be had.[2]

Property described without words limiting the risk as to locality.

SEC. 126. When no words of limitation are used the policy covers the risk, wherever the property may be, as where the policy covers " $300 on his granary and his wagon-house ; $300 on his grain *therein, or* in stack," described as being on sections 17, 19, 20. When the policy was issued the plaintiff owned a tract of land, consisting of 380 acres, lying in each of the sections named, but not embracing *all* the land in those sections. After the issue of the policy, he purchased twenty acres more in section 17, but not adjoining his other land. He raised and stacked wheat on this piece of land, and it was burned, and the court held that it was covered by the policy, *because the assured was not limited to stacks on any particular portion of the sections named.*[3] Under such a policy, the assured clearly had a right to deposit his grain at any place upon either or all the sections. To that extent it

---

[1] *Barlow et al.* v. *Ocean Ins. Co.*, 4 Met. (Mass.) 270 ; *Hage* v. *Hage*, 1 Watts (Penn.) 216 ; *Haigh* v. *Brooks*, 10 Ad. & El. 309 ; *Union Bank* v. *Geary*, 5 Peters, (U. S.) 99 ; *Holcombe* v. *Stimpson*, 8 Vt. 141.

[2] HUBBARD, J., *Barlow* v. *Ocean Ins. Co.*, *ante.*

[3] *Sawyer* v. *Dodge Co. Mut. Ins. Co.*, 37 Wis. 503.

was a floating policy. In an Iowa case,[1] the policy described the property as follows : " On his dwelling-house $400 ; grain in the stack or crib, $600; hay in stack, $320; seven horses, $750; cattle, $275; *situated* in section 22, town 99, range 7 west." There was also a provision against increase of risk. While the assured was engaged in hauling his grain to market he stopped at a hotel for the night, and put his team in a hotel barn, which was burned during the night, together with one of the horses. It was found that the danger from fire in the hotel barn was greater than it was on the farm of the assured. The insurers insisted that they were not liable, for the reason that the property was not destroyed on the farm, and also because, by placing the horses in the hotel barn, the assured had violated the condition as to increase of risk. But the court held that the word " *situate*," used in the policy, was merely one of description, used to identify the risk, and was not a word of limitation, confining the liability of the insurers to a loss occurring on the premises named, and that the defendant was liable for the loss.

When a policy contains language clearly indicating an intention on the part of the insurer to stand liable for any loss that the assured may sustain from fire upon his premises, the risk is not restricted to premises then owned or occupied by the assured, if, from the nature of the business and the uses to which the property insured is devoted, it is evident that the parties did not intend any such restriction. Thus, in a Massachusetts case,[2] the plaintiffs took out a policy on their road furniture, consisting of locomotive engines and cars of all descriptions and snow plows on the line of their road and in actual use; but not on machine or repair shops. The owners of a wharf in Charlestown laid a track the whole length of the wharf, which connected the Charlestown Branch Railroad with the Fitchburg Railroad, for the purpose of conveniently shipping and receiving ice. The cars for which this action was brought, were drawn over the Fitchburg and Charlstown Branch Railroads and left over night on the track at the extreme end of the wharf, four hundred and forty feet from the line of the Charlestown Branch, near a shed used by the occupants of the wharf to store shavings and sawdust. A fire originated in the shed and consumed the cars. The insurers claimed that they were not liable, because the cars were not destroyed on a part of the line of the assured's road proper, or which was owned by or in its possession when the policy was issued. The

---

[1] *Peterson v. Miss. Valley Ins. Co.*, 24 Iowa, 494.
[2] *Fitchburgh R. R. Co. v. Charleston, etc., Ins. Co.*, 7 Gray (Mass.) 64.

court held, however, that the defendants were liable, holding that, in construing the policy, they must look not only at the words of the policy, but also to their evident intent as evinced by the nature of the property and its uses; and that, in view of all the circumstances, if the cars were destroyed upon a track which had been adopted by it as a part of its line, it was a loss within the policy. The same prin-ciple was adopted in a New York case.[1] In that case, the plaintiffs, as trustees of a railroad, made insurance "on any property belonging to the said Trust Company as trustees and lessees as aforesaid, for which they may be liable; it matters not of what the property may consist or what it may be, provided it is on premises owned or occupied by said trustees, and situate on their railroad premises in the city of Racine, Wis." The railroad company had purchased, and the plaintiffs as mortgagees and trustees owned, certain wharf prop-erty fronting on Root river. The cars came to the river, and the wharf was used for the transferring of freight between boats and cars. Plaintiffs owned a dredgeboat, to keep the water a sufficient depth in front of the wharf, and while made fast to the wharf, it was consumed by fire. It was held, the boat was in plaintiff's possession annexed to the railroad premises, and was therefore upon the prop-erty of the plaintiffs within the meaning of the policy.

Policies in blank or to whom it may concern.

SEC. 127. While an insurable interest is essential to uphold a policy, and, while generally the party insured is named in the policy, yet, this is by no means indispensable, and a policy may be issued in blank, covering the interests of any person having an insurable interest in the property, or, as is generally the case, "to whom it may concern."[2] And in such case, unless the policy stipulates against an alienation of the property, the policy applies to the benefits of the person who may own the property at the time of the loss.[3]

In such cases, the person having the title to the property at the time of loss, although not having an interest therein when the policy issued, may, by adoption of the contract, avail himself of its advantages, and extrinsic evidence is admissible to show who was, in fact, concerned[4]

---

[1] *Farmers' Loan & Trust Co.* v. *Harmony F. & M. Ins. Co.*, 41 N. Y. 619.

[2] *Turner* v. *Burrows*, 8 Wend. (N. Y.) 144; *Burgher* v. *Columbian Ins. Co.*, 17 Barb. (N. Y.) 274.

[3] *Turner* v. *Burrows*, *ante.*

[4] *Newson* v. *Douglass*, 7 H. & J. (Md.) 417. In *Black* v. *Columbian Ins. Co.*, 42 N. Y. 393, a policy was issued as follows: "To H. C. & Co., on account of A. B. & Co., on property consigned to H. C. & Co. by regular invoice and bill of lading.

But, in order to avail himself of the policy, *he must show not only his interest therein at the time of loss, but also that the interest acquired by him was within the contemplation of the parties procuring the insurance.* Thus, it would be presumed that a person taking out such a policy upon a cargo of merchandise, had in contemplation the interest of any person who might subsequently purchase the same, or an interest therein from him before the voyage was ended, and the policy would enure to such person's benefit, but, if the cargo should be seized and sold to satisfy a debt against the assured, the policy would not enure to the benefit of the purchaser, because neither he nor his interest was within the contemplation of the parties when the policy was taken out.[1] But, if such a policy contains a stipulation against alienation, it is restricted to those in interest *at the time when the contract was made.*[2] The inten. tion of the parties must control, and the fact that the words "for the benefit of whom it may concern," are not used, is not decisive. The policy must be construed according to the evident intention of the parties, as gathered from the language employed and the circumstances under which it was procured, and if it appears that it was the intention of the insurer to insure for the benefits of any person in interest, *although not named therein,* the rights of the parties will not be defeated, because the usual and customary words are not employed to express such intent.[3]

Risks applicable hereto to be reported to this company for indorsement on the policy, as soon as known to the insured." Gold was shipped by L. S. & Co., by bill of lading in their name. The invoice was by U. B. of San Francisco, addressed to U. B. & Co. at New York, the heading of which was, "Shipped by A. B. & Co., to be delivered to H. C. & Co." They called the attention of insurer's president to the bill of lading and invoice. He said it made no difference, and directed the insured to an entry clerk who made the indorsement, and the premium was afterwards paid. It was held that the consignment and bill of lading were nominally to U. B., but really to the insured; that the acts and words of the company's president were properly received, to show how the defendants led insured to construe or understand the contract. In *Irving* v. *Excelsior Ins. Co.,* 1 Bos. (N. Y.) 507, the plaintiff stated in his preliminary proofs of loss that the firm of Irving, Clark & Co., of which he was the principal member, manufactured the goods insured; that he had furnished all the capital to the firm, was its sole creditor, and that his interest in it would cover all the assets of the firm. It appeared that Clark and the plaintiff had abandoned all intention of a copartnership, and that Clark was to be paid for his services. *Held,* the facts as stated in the preliminary proofs were conclusive; that if the evidence of Clark and the plaintiff did not harmonize with the statements in the preliminary proofs, it must be rejected; but that the plaintiff was the substantial owner of the property insured; hence the policy was effectual, though made to the plaintiff individually.

[1] *Waring* v. *Indemnity Ins. Co.,* 45 N. Y. 606; *Newson* v. *Douglass, ante.*

[2] *Minturn* v. *Manufacturers Ins. Co.,* 10 Gray (Mass.) 501.

[3] *Duncan* v. *Sun Mutual Ins. Co.,* 12 La. An. 486; 4 Ben. F. I. C. 191.

SEC. 128. Where a policy is issued in the name of an agent, for an unnamed principal, *no one but the person for whom the agent acted at the time of insurance*, can avail himself of the advantages of the policy.[1] A third person, not in the contemplation of the parties at the time, cannot avail himself thereof.[2] In order that a stranger to the contract, may avail himself of it, the language thereof must be such as to embrace and cover his interests.[3] A policy taken out by an agent without any previous authority, may be made available by the principal by a notification of the act, *even after a loss*,[4] and it seems that, even where a policy is taken out by a third person, not in any sense an agent of the assured, either the principal or an agent having authority in the premises, may adopt the policy by notifying the act of such person in its procurement.[5] Where an agent, or other person, procures insurance to be made for the benefit of another, to cover such other persons interest in the property, and the insurance was paid for by the person for whose benefit it was made, the person procuring it cannot compel the payment of the loss to him.[6]

Joint owners.

SEC. 129. A policy of one joint owner upon joint property, covers only his interest therein, and does not embrace the interest of his co-owner. In order to extend to other interests, the language of the policy must be such as clearly to embrace them.[7] If the assured acts for others as well as himself, he must make known the relation in which he stands.[8] Thus, in a New York case,[9] A. took out a policy in his own name to cover the interests of A. and B. in an adventure in which *three* persons were interested. The court held that the interests of A. and B. were covered, but not the interest of C. therein.[10] When a policy is taken out in the name of partners, or other joint

[1] *Graves* v. *Boston, etc., Ins. Co.*, 2 Cr. (U. S.) 215; *Russell* v. *N. E., etc., Ins. Co.*, 4 Mass. 82.

[2] *Waring* v. *Indemnity Ins. Co., ante; Newson* v. *Douglass, ante*.

[3] *Burgher* v. *Columbian Ins. Co., ante; Pacific Ins. Co.* v. *Catlett*, 4 Wend. (N. Y.) 75.

[4] *Finney* v. *Fairhaven Ins. Co.*, 5 Met. (Mass.) 192; *Farmers, etc., Ins. Co.* v. *Marshall*, 29 Vt. 23.

[5] *Mound City Life Ins. Co.* v. *Huth*, 49 Ala. 529.

[6] *Pritchett* v. *Ins. Co.*, 27 La. An. 525.

[7] *Burgher* v. *Columbian Ins. Co.*, 17 Barb. (N. Y.) 274.

[8] *Dumas* v. *Jones*, 4 Mass. 647; *Tappan* v. *Atkinson*, 2 id. 365.

[9] *Pacific Ins. Co.* v. *Catlett*, 4 Wend. (N. Y.) 75.

[10] See *Turner* v. *Burrows*, 5 Wend. (N. Y.) 144.

owners of property, the death of one does not defeat the policy, but the survivor may recover for the loss of all property owned by the firm, or by himself and his co-owner, at the time of such co-owner's death, but not for any property purchased by him *subsequent thereto, unless they were purchased for the benefit of the estate or heirs of such deceased co-owner, as well as for himself, and under authority to that end.*[1]

Rebuilding, right of, how acquired. Election to rebuild must be made according to policy. Con_ verts policy into building contract. Effect of impossibility of performance. Measure of recovery for failure to perform or defective performance.

SEC. 130. The insurer, unless provision is made therefor in the policy, is bound to pay the loss in money, and cannot reinstate the building or replace the property destroyed, by other, in kind and value.[2] Immediately upon the happening of the loss, the loss of the assured, to the extent of the amount insured, becomes a debt against the com_ pany, which it is bound to discharge in the same manner as other debts are discharged. But if the insurer, as he may, stipulates to pay the loss in a particular way, he is only bound to pay in that mode; and if he stipulates to reinstate the building, or replace the property in value or kind, he must be permitted to do so; and if the assured refuses to receive indemnity for his loss, in the mode provided, he can recover nothing upon the policy. Thus, where a policy provided that the insurer, in case of loss or damage to the building, might rebuild or repair the building if he elected so to do within thirty days after loss, *and the assured* immediately after loss commenced rebuilding, but before the thirty days had elapsed the insurer gave notice of an intention to rebuild, which the assured refused to permit them to do, it was held that he could maintain no action upon the policy for the loss.[3] The right to reinstate the property must be exercised in the

---

[1] In *Wood* v. *Rutland, etc., Ins. Co.*, 31 Vt. 552, it was held that the survivor could not maintain an action upon the policy *in his own name* to recover more than his own interest, *unless the insurers had promised to pay him after the loss*, but that he must be joined with the administrator or executor in the suit.

[2] *Com. Ins. Co.* v. *Sennett*, 37 Penn. St. 205. In *Wallace* v. *Ins. Co.*, 37 Penn. St. 205; 1 Ben. F. I. C. 412, PORTER, J., says, in reference to the claim of insurers to rebuild when the policy is silent upon that question, "No usage is found to sanction such a pretension. There is no law which authorizes it. The contract makes no mention of it, on the contrary, it stipulates that the loss shall be paid in money. It is true that rebuilding might in some cases be an indemnity for the loss. It would perhaps have been so in this instance; but then, *it was not the indemnity the insured paid for*, and we are at a loss to conceive how, on policies where such a right is not expressly confirmed, it could be supposed one of the parties had a right to change the agreement, and substitute one mode of performance for another."

[3] *Beals* v. *Home Ins. Co.*, 36 N. Y. 522; *N. Y. F. Ins. Co.* v. *Delavan*, 8 Paige Ch. (N. Y.) 418.

mode and noticed within the time prescribed in the policy, or it is
lost, and if *after* such right has lapsed, by a failure to make its election
within the time prescribed, it goes on and rebuilds or repairs the premises, non-compliance with the policy, in respect to notice, etc., not
having been waived by the assured—he is bound to pay the loss to
the assured in money, notwithstanding the reinstatement of the
property by it, and is entitled to no deduction from the amount of
the loss in consequence of such new building or repairs.[1]

Thus, in the case last cited, the policy contained a reservation of a
right to reinstate the property within thirty days after loss. Notice
of loss was served by the assured upon the local agent May 6th, and
notice of an intention to repair was not given until the *middle* of June.
The insurers after giving such notice, went on and made repairs to the
amount of about $150. The assured never assented to the making of
such repairs, and in an action upon the policy, to recover for the loss,
it was held by the court, that no deduction could be made from the
amount of the actual loss, for the repairs made by the assured, and a
verdict for $385.75 was sustained.

SCOTT, J., in passing upon the relative rights of the parties under
the circumstances detailed, among other things, said: "The defense
relied on is, that the company elected to, and did, repair the property
insured after the injury occasioned by the fire. The policy contained
a clause, that it should be optional with the company to repair, rebuild
or replace the property, loss or damage with other like kind, within a
reasonable time, by giving notice of its intention so to do, within thirty
days after the receipt of proof of loss. It is in proof that the company did elect to repair the property insured, and did do work upon
it, for which it paid the carpenter who did the work the sum of $150.
There is great conflict in the evidence as to the fact whether the
building, after the work was completed by the company, was in as
good condition as before the fire. The building was an old one, and
the weight of evidence seems to be that it was so nearly destroyed by
the fire, that the work and materials used in making the repairs were
a useless expenditure.

The appellee insists that the company did not make its election to
repair the property within the thirty days, the period fixed by the
provisions of the policy in which the company had the right to make
such election. The repairs that were made by the company were not
made with the express, or even the implied consent of the assured. It

[1] *North American Ins. Co.* v. *Hope*, 53 Ill. 75 ; 11 Am. Rep. 48.

is in evidence that he protested when he was first notified that the company intended to repair the property against any work being expended thereon, and placed his objections on two grounds : First, that the building was so badly injured that it could not be repaired to any advantage ; and, Second, that the company did not make its election within thirty days. It is therefore a material inquiry, whether the company did make its election to repair the property, within thirty days after the receipt of proof of loss, and so notified the assured.

The right of the company to replace or repair the property insured, in case of loss, is created by the provisions of the policy, and if the company does not make its election in apt time, and give the assured notice, the right to so build or repair does not exist. And, in the event that the company does such work outside of the terms of the policy, without the consent of the assured, it will be in its own wrong, and no deduction can be made from the amount of the loss on account of such work. If the election to replace or repair the property is not made within the period fixed by the express terms of the policy, and notice given, the right of action becomes complete in the assured, and no subsequent election on the part of the company, not assented to by the assured, will divest that right of action.

The proofs of loss, in this instant, were furnished to the local agent on the 6th day of May, and the evidence establishes the fact, that the notice to repair the property was not given until about the middle of June, a period of more than thirty days having elapsed.

It is insisted that it is not a sufficient compliance with the terms of the policy, to deliver the proofs of loss to the local agent, and that the time in this instance would not begin to run until such proofs were delivered to the general agent of the company at Chicago. We find no such condition in the policy. In the absence of any provision to the contrary, the delivery of proofs of loss to the local agent will be taken and considered as a delivery to the company, for all the purposes of the policy, and if the local agent fails to forward the same to the home office, or to the office of the general agent, as required by the usage of the business, that negligence cannot be charged to the assured.[1] The objection that the proofs of loss, when presented on the 6th day of May, were not in conformity to the conditions of the policy, does not aid the cause of the appellant. Only a general objection was made by the agent when the proofs were presented, and no

---

[1] *Heron* v. *Peoria Marine and Fire Ins. Co.*, 28 Ill. 235.

specific defect was suggested or pointed out. The rule is, that if the proofs of loss are insufficient when presented, it is the duty of the company, or agent, to give notice to the assured of the specific defect, and if the company or agent fail to point out wherein the proofs are defective, such proof, notwithstanding a general objection, will be deemed sufficient.[1]

The proofs of loss were not, in fact, forwarded to the office of the general agent at Chicago until the 25th day of May, but that was the fault of the local agent, and not of the assured, and the company can derive no benefit from the negligence of its own agent. The assured ought not to be prejudiced or delayed in the collection of his loss by reason of any negligence of the local agent to discharge his full duty to the company. We are of opinion that the notice of election on the part of the company to repair the property on which the loss occurred was not given in apt time. It does not appear that the assured ever consented that the company might make the repairs, and without such consent, if the election to repair was not made in the proper time, the company had no right to do the work. The expenditure of work and materials in making the repairs, was the voluntary and unauthorized act of the company, and no deduction can be made from the amount of the loss occasioned by the fire, on account of such work."[2]

Thus it will be seen that notice of an intention to rebuild must be given *within the time prescribed in the policy*, and if no time is fixed within which notice shall be given, the election must be made within a *reasonable* time, and as to what is a reasonable time, is question for the jury to determine in view of all the circumstances.[3]

In determining what *is* a reasonable time, reference is to be had to the time when notice and proofs of loss were received,[4] and whether negotiations for a settlement of the loss have been pending.[5]

If, after having made his election, the insurer fails to proceed with the work *with reasonable dispatch*, liability attaches for damages resulting from such *unreasonable* delay;[6] but it has been held in

---

[1] *The Great Western Ins. Co.* v. *Staaden*, 26 Ill. 365.

[2] See contra as to right to allowance for repairs made. *Parker* v. *Eagle Ins. Co.*, 9 Gray (Mass.) 152.

[3] *Haskins* v. *Hamilton, etc., Ins. Co.*, 5 Gray (Mass.) 432; *Sutherland* v. *Society of the Sun F. Ins. Co.*, 14 Court of Sessions (Sc.) U. S. 77.

[4] *Sutherland* v. *Society of the Sun F. Ins. Co.*, *ante*; *Ins. Co. of N. America* v. *Hope*, *ante*.

[5] *Sutherland* v. *Society of the Sun F. Ins. Co.*, *ante*.

[6] *Home Ins. Co.* v. *Thompson*, 1 N. C. (E. & Ap.) 247.

Massachusetts that in such a case, the assured is not bound to sue for damages, but may sue upon the policy for the loss.[1] But in New York it is held that, in case of defective repairs, the insurer is bound to make the defect good.[2]

When the insurer attempts to rebuild or repair the property, but fails to complete his work, or performs it defectively, he is liable for the *actual damage* and is not entitled to any deduction for a difference between old and new. That is, the fact that the building he has erected is *new*, while the one destroyed was old, is not to be considered by the jury, but the difference between the value of the building as erected and what its value would have been if properly erected, is the measure of recovery.[3] But in such a case, *even though the insurer is proceeding improperly, or with unreasonable delay*, a court of equity will not interfere to restrain the completion of the work, but will leave the assured to his remedy for damages.[4]

It has been held in New York[5] that, when an insurer, under such a

---

[1] *Haskins* v. *Hamilton Ins. Co.*, 5 Gray (Mass.) 432.

[2] *Ryder* v. *Com. Ins. Co.*, 52 Barb. (N. Y.) 447; also see *Parker* v. *Eagle Ins. Co.*, 9 Gray (Mass.) 152, where the insurer commenced to repair, but did not complete them, and it was held that the assured was entitled to recover *the difference between the value of the repairs made, and what the value would have been if the repairs had been fully completed.* See *Times F. Ins. Co.* v. *Hawke*, 5 H. & N. 935.

[3] *Brinley* v. *National Ins. Co.*, 11 Met. (Mass.) 195; *Parker* v. *Eagle Ins. Co.*, 9 Gray (Mass.) 152.

[4] *Home Ins. Co.* v. *Thompson, ante.*

[5] *Morrell* v. *Irving Ins. Co.*, 33 N. Y. 429, which being a leading and important case, I give entire. In that case, the defendant insured the plaintiff against loss or damage by fire, to the amount of $3,000, on a certain three-story brick build-ing in the city of Brooklyn, for one year from March 20th, 1856. The policy contained a condition that, "in case of loss or damage to the property insured, it shall be optional with the company to replace the article lost or damaged, with others of the same kind and quality, and to rebuild or repair the build-ing or buildings within a reasonable time, giving notice of their intention to do so, within twenty days after having received the preliminary proofs of loss required by the ninth article of these conditions." The building was destroyed by fire January 6th, 1857. The action was upon the policy to recover the $3,000 and interest. The plaintiff made the proof necessary to entitle him to recover. The defendant then read in evidence a policy of insurance upon the same build-ing made by the Excelsior Fire Insurance Company for $2,000, containing the like condition. The plaintiff also put in evidence a joint notice of both companies to the plaintiff, dated January 27th, 1857, that they were prepared to rebuild the said building, and requested the plaintiff to furnish them with the plans and specifications of the same. The defendant then gave evidence tending to show that plans were furnished by the plaintiff to a builder employed by the compa-nies; that the work of rebuilding was commenced in February, and was com-pleted within a reasonable time, according to the plans furnished, and that the building was thereupon occupied by the plaintiff. The plaintiff gave evidence tending to prove that plans and specifications were furnished, and that the build-ing was not properly constructed according to the plans and specifications, and that there had not been a substantial compliance with the stipulation to rebuild. The defendant gave further evidence upon this question tending to prove full per-formance of the work. It should be stated that the defendant, after putting in

17

clause in the policy, signifies his intention to rebuild, *and enters upon performance*, the insurance contract is thereby converted into a building

---

their evidence in chief, moved to dismiss the complaint, on the ground that the the action should have been brought upon the condition or covenant to rebuild, and not upon the policy. The motion was denied, and the defendant excepted. At the close of the evidence the motion was renewed, on the ground that it was shown that the two companies elected to rebuild, and made a joint contract to rebuild, and did jointly rebuild, and therefore the suit should be jointly against both companies. This motion was denied, and the defendant excepted. The court, after stating the case and some facts not in dispute, stated that the company undertook to rebuild and did construct a building upon the same lot, and that the question is, whether they have substantially complied with the condition of the policy touching the rebuilding. That it was the right of the parties to the contract to change it in regard to the form of the structure and the material of which it was composed. And if the company have put up such a structure as Morrell required, it is a sufficient performance of the condition, and the plaintiff cannot recover. "To make out the defense," said the judge, "the jury must be satisfied from the evidence that the new building, in respect to form, material and goodness of workmanship, is substantially like the building destroyed, as the same were described in the plans and information given to the company by Morrell." "That if the jury are of the opinion that the company have failed to fulfill the condition and reconstruct the building in the manner which I have before specified, then the plaintiff is entitled to recover the amount of the loss, without reference to the value of the building which the company have put upon the premises." The counsel for the defendant excepted in the language of the case: "1st. To so much of the charge as submitted to the jury the question in this case whether the defendants rebuilt as the building was before the fire. 2d. As to the measure of damages submitted." There were some requests to charge, some of which were complied with, and others not; and, as to some, the court refused to charge otherwise than as it had already charged. The verdict was for the plaintiff, $3,315. Judgment was entered upon the verdict, and upon appeal to the general term it was affirmed, and thereupon the defendant appealed to this court. MARVIN, J., said : "It is well-settled law in this State, that he woo undertakes to build a house for another, or to perform any work, to be paid for when the house is completed, or the other work done, cannot recover any portion of the stipulated price or value of the work, until he has substantially performed the contract on his part. *Smith* v. *Brady*, 17 N. Y. R. 173, and cases therein cited. It is also well-settled law that when one contracts with another to build for him a house, or do other work, and agrees to pay portions of the consideration in instalments as the work progresses, and does so pay, or pays the whole consideration in advance of the performance of the work, he can maintain no action for money had and received, though the contract has been broken and remains unperformed unless the contract has been wholly rescinded. His action must be upon the contract, and his damages must be for the breach or breaches of the contract. The amount of damages will not depend upon the amount of money he had paid, but the damages will be the amount of loss sustained by a failure to perform the contract. In other words, what it will cost to procure a full completion of the contract, including, if the case calls for it, any special loss by reason of delays, etc. In the present case, the first of the above principles has been applied, and the defendant has been placed in the position of one who has contracted to construct a building in a certain manner, and for which he is to be paid after the work is done, and who claims that he has performed the contract, and seeks, by action, to recover the consideration, and is met with the issue that he had not performed the condition precedent, upon the performance of which his right of action depends. This issue being decided against the defendant, it is held that he is to have nothing on account of the house actually built, but is to pay to the plaintiff the entire sum specified in the policy as indemnity to the plaintiff for the loss of his building. I am not satisfied that this rule should be applied to the case. It is important to determine, with some precision, what the case is—what the contract was between the parties. It is said that the contract was, on the part of the defendant, that in consideration of a sum presently paid, it would indemnify (the contract is insure)

contract, and the assured is entitled to recover for non-performance, precisely the same as against any other contractor, *without any refer-*

---

the plaintiff to the amount of $3,000 for any loss he should sustain by fire on a certain building ; and the defendant promised and agreed to make good to the plaintiff, etc., all such loss or damage not exceeding in amount the sum insured, as shall happen by fire to the property specified. But this was not the entire contract. One of its terms and conditions was that in case of any loss or damage to the property insured, it should be optional with the company to rebuild or repair the building within a reasonable time, giving notice to do so within twenty days after receiving the preliminary proofs of loss. What construction should be given to this provision? What relation was established by it between the parties? The agreement is not exactly that the defendant shall do one of two things, one of which being performed satisfied the contract. There is no absolute contract that the defendant, upon the happening of a certain event, should pay a sum of money or rebuild the house. But the agreement was that the defendant should pay an amount of money equal to the loss, not exceeding $3,000. Call it an indemnity for the loss, and the question will not be changed, for the company might within twenty days after proof of the loss, elect or decide to rebuild the building, and give notice of such election or decision. In other words, the defendant had the right, by the contract, to elect to rebuild, and in that way indemnify the plaintiff by rebuilding. When the election to rebuild was made and notified to the plaintiff, what was the relation between the parties? The building had been destroyed by fire. The amount of the loss may or it may not have been known. There may have been dispute between the parties touching the amount of the loss. The insured could only claim $3,000, though the loss may have been greater. He could only recover his actual loss as an indemnity, but the actual amount of the loss may have been, and often is, a matter of dispute and difficulty requiring a lawsuit to settle it. The insured may claim a much greater sum than the insurer is willing to pay, and for the purpose of avoiding the difficulties and litigation likely to arrive from such disputes, the insurer secures, by the contract, a right to indemnify the insured by rebuilding the destroyed building instead of paying money, the amount of which is uncertain, and the insured agrees to accept indemnity in this way in lieu of any amount of money. All necessity for ascertaining the amount of the loss ceases when the insurer undertakes the restoration of the property. It seems to me that when the insurer elects to rebuild, and gives notice of such election, the contract at once is that the insurer will rebuild absolutely in consideration of the premises, and the defendant's agreement is that the insurer may do so, in satisfaction of the demand, uncertain in amount, which he claims of the insurer. This becomes the absolute agreement between the parties, by virtue of the agreement originally made, and which, prior to the election, was subject to certain contingencies, terms, and conditions ; and it seems to me that after such election and notice, the relation between the parties is simply that of a contractor to build, who had received the entire consideration in advance, and a party for whom the building is to be erected and who has made full payment, therefore, in advance of the work. Such, I think, is the fair construction of the contract. This provision was intended to obviate difficulties, some of which have been suggested. In this view no action could be maintained for the purpose of recovering the $3,000, or such portion of it as should be equivalent to the loss. There can be no inquiry as to the amount of the loss. The action will be upon the contract to rebuild, and the amount of the damages to be recovered upon a breach of the contract, will be determined as in other actions for the breach of building contracts, and such amount may exceed the $3,000. The defendant agreed that it would build the house, and it has been paid for its agreement and must perform the agreement or pay the damages. The peculiar language used in this provision has not escaped attention. "It shall be optional with the insurance company to replace and to rebuild," the insurance company "giving notice of their intention to do so." It may be said that the language is not sufficient to make a present contract to rebuild after the election and notice. That although the defendant had the optional right to rebuild and elected to rebuild, and gave notice of intention to do so, still it was not bound to go on and build, but it might stop and

ence to the sum insured.   While this case cannot perhaps be regarded
as an authority for the doctrine that the insurer, upon signifying his

---

leave the insured to his remedy for a moneyed indemnity.   This is not, in my
opinion, the fair construction of the provision, nor was such the intention of the
parties to the contract.   The option was with the defendant, and it was to give
notice of its election.   The language as to the notice may not have been very hap-
pily chosen in using the word "intention" instead of the words *election, option,*
or *choice;* but there can be no difficulty about the meaning.   The right to rebuild,
and the obligation to rebuild, depended upon an election to rebuild, and the
notice was simply to inform the other party that such election had been made.
The parties so understood the language.   The notice actually given in this case
said nothing about intention.   Its language is : " We hereby give you notice that
we are prepared to rebuild said building," and this was treated as sufficient, and
both parties acted upon it.   It seems to me very clear that, after the election and
notice, there existed a contract between the parties for the rebuilding of the
building destroyed, and the contract to make good in money the loss no longer
existed between the parties.   If I am right in the view taken of the contract, the
position that the contract for indemnity in money remained in force until the
house was actually rebuilt, must fail.   This position would seem to regard the
provision as an *accord* not valid as a *satisfaction* until executed, whereas I regard
it as a part of the *original agreement* by which this provision might, upon the happening of a certain contingency, be substituted by the election of one of the parties for and in the place of the provision to indemnify in money, and it is the
agreement of both parties, and both are bound by it.   It is, I submit, an error
to suppose that this was a conditional agreement by which, when performed,
the previous agreement to pay in money was satisfied, and if not performed,
then such money agreement remained in force.   I have read carefully the dissenting opinion of Justice EMOTT in the court below ; and though I am not able
to concur fully in his construction of the contract, I have no difficulty in adopting
his argument against the rule of damages enunciated at the circuit.   Assuming
that the agreement to indemnify in money was not entirely superseded by the
agreement to rebuild, what would the rights of the parties be upon a failure or
partial failure to rebuild ?   The defendant had the right to satisfy the claim for
the loss by rebuilding.   Suppose the loss to have been $3,000, and the insurer
expends $2,000 judiciously and profitably towards the rebuilding of the house,
and then stops, and the insured takes up the work and completes the house by
expending $1,000 ?   Has not this claim for damages been partially satisfied ?   I
certainly think so ; and this is the position of Justice EMOTT.   He applies to the
case the same principles applicable to an action against a contractor for a breach
of the contract to build, and refuses to apply the strict rule against a contractor
who seeks to recover the price, and is met with the objection that the work has
not been completed according to the contract.   But the learned justice limits the
recovery to a sum not exceeding the amount that would have produced indemnity
had the agreement to rebuild never existed, and in this we differ.   It seems to
me that this rule will be very difficult in practice.   The indemnity in money can
never exceed the amount of the risk specified in the policy.   Suppose the risk
taken to be $3,000, and the insurer elects to rebuild and actually expends, neces-
sarily and properly, $3,000, and the building is not completed, may he stop and
leave the building to be completed by the insured at, say, the cost of an additional $1,000 ?   This must be so if the insured in such case is only entitled to an
indemnity, measured by the sum of money specified in the policy ; for the $3,000,
having been judiciously expended, is worth so much to him.   The learned justice, however, lays down the rule, that the plaintiff is entitled to recover such an
amount not exceeding the amount of the insurance as will be necessary to make
the building erected equal in all respects, and similar to the one burned.   The
result of this rule would be, in the case above supposed, that the plaintiff could
recover the additional $1,000 expended by him though the defendant had expended
already the full amount insured, and this is precisely what I claim.   But suppose
the insurer expends $1,000, and it costs $3,000 to complete the building, the
insured, by the rule laid down, will recover $3,000.   Will he not in such a case
realize for indemnity $4,000 ?   Certainly he will.   Or suppose the insurer expends

election to rebuild, thereby assumes the character and position of a
contractor for that purpose, yet it tends strongly in that direction, and

---

$2,000, and the insured $3,000, to complete the building, the latter will recover
the $3,000 and thus realize $5,000. He is to recover such an amount as will be
necessary to complete the building, not, however, exceeding the amount of the
insurance. Under such a rule, an insurer who has elected to rebuild, and has
performed a part of the work and discovers that he has a hard bargain and cannot complete the work for the amount of the insurance, will at once abandon the
work or may do so, being liable only for the payment of the amount insured.
Under such a rule the amount of the loss will always come up for litigation and
adjustment, and, as I understand, the principal object of the provision we are
considering, is to permit the insurer to obviate all disputes and litigation touching
the amount of the loss by replacing the articles lost or damaged, or by repairing
and rebuilding the building destroyed. By adopting the construction for which
I contend, we have a simple rule which excludes any inquiry as to the amount of
the loss, and the inquiry will be, has the insured replaced the articles or rebuilt
the building in the manner agreed, and if not, the damages will be as in other
cases of the breach, by the builder, of his agreement to build.

It is supposed that, in a case like the present, difficulties exist touching parties to the action. I think that the supposed difficulties will disappear upon a
brief examination of the law applicable to such cases. The plaintiff held two
policies upon the same building, one issued by the defendant, taking a risk of
$3,000, the other issued by the Excelsior Fire Insurance Company taking a risk
of $2,000. Each policy contained the same provisions or condition touching the
optional right to rebuild. In this case both of the companies elected to rebuild,
and they united in one notice that they were prepared to rebuild. The case does
not contain, as it should, the policies. But they were, of course, both *valid*, and,
in contemplation of law, constituted one policy, so far as the amount of loss was
concerned. That is to say, the insured could not recover the amount of his loss
of each insurer, supposing it had been less than the smallest risk. All he is entitled to from all the insurers is one indemnity. If he recovers this of one of the
insurers, such insurer may recover of the other, by way of contribution, his
proper proportion. It is very common in this country to provide in fire policies,
that in case of two or more insurances upon the same property, each insurer shall
be liable only for a ratable proportion of the loss. See Par. Mer. L. 516, 517.
Whether it was provided in the present case that each company should only be
liable for its ratable proportion of the loss does not appear, but I think this will
be seen not to be material. Though the plaintiff could not have maintained a
joint action against the companies upon these policies if there had been no election
to rebuild, but could have maintained separate actions, recovering from the
defendant three-fifth of the loss not exceeding $3,000, and from the other company
two-fifths not exceeding $2,000, it does not follow that, upon an election by both
companies to rebuild, he could not maintain a joint action against both, upon the
agreement to rebuild, I think he could maintain such action, and that the action
in this case should properly have been against both companies. When they
jointly elected to rebuild, they jointly agreed to rebuild, and were jointly liable
in an action for a breach of their agreement. I have no doubt the action would
have been well brought against both companies. They would not be permitted
to allege that they had not jointly contracted with the plaintiff. I am not prepared to say that the action was not well brought against the defendant alone. I
think the plaintiff might well treat the election to rebuild as the election of
each insurer, and for a breach of the building agreement maintain his action
against either company, and recover full damages, or perhaps a separate action
against each for full damages, collecting the damages, however, but once.
I think these positions follow from the legal relations and rights of all the parties.
The two companies were bound to pay the loss rateably if so stipulated in the
policies, and if not so stipulated, the whole loss should be paid by one, then the
other would be liable for contribution. When one of the companies should elect
to rebuild, it would come under obligation to the insured to make full indemnity
by rebuilding; and if there were a provision in the policy that it should only be
liable to pay a ratable proportion of the loss, such provision would be superseded

has support from the English cases, and there can be no question but
that the doctrine is apparently reasonable and consistent with principle.
A policy containing a clause of that character is not a contract to pay a
sum of money to the assured, in case of loss, not exceeding the sum
named in the policy, but a contract to pay the loss, not exceeding such
sum, *in money*, or *to replace the property in kind and value*. Which of these
it will do, it is optional with the insurer to choose, *and when he has
made his election the contract becomes one to pay money if he so elects, or
to reinstate the property if he elects to do that, without any reference to the
expense of doing so*. When he has made his election in the mode indicated in the contract, *the contract becomes precisely what he elects to make
it, and the rights of the parties are thereby fixed*. The insurer cannot
recede from his election without the consent of the assured. The
maxim, *quod semel placuit in electionibus amplius displicer non potest*,
applies, and the insurer is bound thereby, whatever may be the consequences as to expense.[1] This view was fully sustained by the last
cited case. In that case, the defendants executed a policy insuring
the plaintiff's premises against fire, reserving to themselves the right
of reinstatement in preference to the payment of claims. The premises were destroyed by fire, and the defendants elected to reinstate
them, but did not do so *because the reinstatement, after the loss, was prohibited by the commissioners of sewers*, and the structure was by them
ordered to be taken down *as being in a dangerous condition*, which dangerous condition *was not occasioned by the fire*. In an action to recover
the damages, it was held that the assured was entitled to recover the
damages he had sustained by reason of the failure of the insurer to
reinstate the building. Lord CAMPBELL, C.J., said : " *The case stands*

---

by the agreement to rebuild. If only one of the insurers should elect to rebuild,
and should perform the building contract, it would be entitled to contribution
from the other company, not a proportion of the amount expended in building,
but a ratable proportion in money of the actual loss. So also if the party undertaking to rebuild should fail to perform the contract, and the insured could
recover and collect damages for the breach of the agreement, such party should
recover of the other insurer a rateable proportion of the loss. Such insurer
would, by the payment of the damages recovered by the insured, have satisfied
the demand for the loss. The insured would be fully indemnified, and the insurer
who paid nothing and did nothing would be liable for contribution. In my opinion, the insured, in a case like the present, may have his action against both
insurers jointly, or against either separately, and recover his full damages for the
breach of the building contract, and leave the two insurers to an adjustment of
their rights between themselves according to well-settled rules of law applicable
to different insurers of the same property. The judgment should be reversed,
and there should be a new trial. DENIO, C.J., read an opinion to the same effect,
DAVIES, WRIGHT, ROSEKRANS, and BALCOM, JS., concurred. SELDEN and EMOTT,
JS., dissented.

[1] CROMPTON, J., in *Brown v. Royal Ins. Co.*, 1 E. & E. 856 ; 4 Ben. F. I. C. 371.

as if the policy had been simply to reinstate the premises, in case of fire; because, where a contract provides for an election, the party making the election is in the same position as if he had originally contracted to do the act which he has elected to do. The premises, then, having suffered this damage by fire, and the defendant not having reinstated them, do these pleas furnish an excuse for not reinstating? I am of opinion that they do not. The defendants undertook to do *what was lawful at the time*, and has continued to be lawful. That being so, the fact that performance has become impossible is no legal excuse for their not performing it, and they are liable in damages. That is the doctrine to be deduced from a class of cases to which I referred [1] in Hall *v.* Wright.[2] If any one undertakes to do a particular, lawful act, and does not do it, *it is no excuse that he cannot do it if the law has not since rendered it unlawful.* There was nothing unlawful in this contract; and if it is impossible for the defendants to perform it, *they must pay for that impossibility.*" [3]

In Illinois, it has been held that an election by the insurer to rebuild, and notice thereof to the assured, *does not convert the contract into a building contract,* and that, in case of their failure to rebuild within a reasonable time, the assured is merely entitled to recover the amount of his actual loss, not exceeding the sum insured with interest thereon,

---

[1] The cases referred to by the learned judge are *Hall* v. *Wright*, 1 El. Bl. & El. 746; *Parradine* v. *Jane*, Aleyn, 27; *Hadley* v. *Clark*, 8 T. R. 267. See also, similar in principle, cases decided in the courts of this country, *Harmony* v. *Bingham*, 12 N. Y. 99; *Adams* v. *Nichols*, 19 Pick. (Mass.) 275; *School District* v. *Dauchy*, 25 Conn. 530; *Trustees, etc.*, v. *Bennett*, 27 N. J. 514; *Tompkins* v. *Dudley*, 25 N. Y. 272. See very able note of Hon. THEO. W. DWIGHT to *Morrell* v. *Irving Ins. Co.*, ante, in 3 Am. Law Reg. (N. S.) 415.

[2] 1 El. Bl. & El. 746, 758.

[3] See, similar in its facts, *Brady* v. *N. W. Ins. Co.*, 11 Mich. 425, in which a policy was issued on a wooden building in Detroit for $2,000, containing a condition that, "the insurers shall have the right to rebuild or repair within a reasonable time after damage or loss." Subsequently to the making of the contract, a city ordinance was passed which prohibited, without the consent of the proper authorities, any rebuilding or repairs upon wooden buildings within the limits of the city. The roof of the building insured being completely burned away, insurers offered to repair it, but the authorities refused their consent. Before the fire the building was worth $4,000; it was now not worth $100. The contract of insurance was renewed after the adoption of the city ordinances. It was held by the court that, by renewing the policy, the parties consented to be bound by the laws and ordinances existing at that time, and contracted with reference to them; whether the city authorities would permit the building to be repaired was a risk assurer assumed, for it was optional with insurers whether they would or would not repair; and, if for any cause they could not exercise that option, they must bear the loss, hence *the amount that the plaintiff was entitled to recover would be the sum insured,* because the value immediately preceding the fire exceeded that sum. It will be seen that in this case the court restrict the recovery *to the sum insured.*

and the rental value of the ground during the delay.[1] But in this case, the charter of the company provided, that the company might rebuild, *provided no more than the sum insured was expended therein.*

When the insurer elects to reinstate the property, and gives notice thereof to the assured, it is held that *he is not excused from doing so, because performance has become impossible.*[2] Nor will he be excused from paying the entire amount of the loss.[3] An election to rebuild operates as a waiver of all defenses except fraud or mistake.[4]

In any event where a policy contains a provision that the insurer may, if he elects to do so, rebuild or repair the property, the service of a notice of an intention to rebuild, if it does not operate as an absolute contract to do so, so that the insured may sue for a breach thereof, yet it does bind the insurer to rebuild within a reasonable time, or upon failure to do so, the insured may sue for and recover the amount of the policy and interest, and the fair rental value of the land during the time of the delay caused by the act of the company, upon the ground that, during the period, the insured is prevented from building, and thus deprived of the beneficial use of the ground,[5] he is entitled to indemnity. The right is a condition *subsequent*, and the assured, in his declaration, need not negative the performance of it.[6]

Renewals.

Sec. 131. When a policy of insurance is renewed, the renewal stands upon the same ground as the original policy, and subject to the same defenses. Not only is the policy, but all the elements upon which it was predicated, are continued in force, and it is treated as having been made upon the same grounds, representations and considerations that dictated the issue of the policy,[7] and if any change is agreed upon or intended, it must be expressed in the renewal receipt, or it cannot be relied upon without a reformation of the receipt, as a renewal receipt is a contract and receipt, and is only open to parol proof, except so far as it fills the office of a receipt. So far as it relates to the continuance of the policy, it is a contract, not a new contract of

---

[1] *Home Mut. Ins. Co.* v. *Garfield,* 60 Ill. 124. See also, *Brady* v. *N. W. Ins. Co., ante.*

[2] *Brown* v. *Royal Ins. Co., ante; Brady* v. *N. W. Ins. Co., ante.*

[3] *Brady* v. *N. W. Ins. Co., ante.*

[4] *Bersche* v. *Globe Mut. Ins. Co.,* 31 Mo. 546.

[5] *Home Mut. Ins. Co.* v. *Garfield,* 60 Ill. 124; 14 Am. Rep. 27.

[6] *Ætna Ins. Co.* v. *Phelps,* 27 Ill. 71; 4 Ben. F. I. C. 581.

[7] *State, etc., Ins. Co.* v. *Porter,* 3 Grant's Cas. (Penn.) 123; *Witherell* v. *Maine Ins. Co.,* 49 Me. 200; *Lancey* v. *Phœnix F. Ins. Co.,* 56 Me. 562.

insurance, but a contract for continuing in force the former contract, and under such contract the original contract is kept on foot, and in case of loss, is the basis of the action, in connection with the contract of renewal, and the matter is not changed, because the renewal is procured by an assignee of the policy, as the parties are not thereby changed.[1] But it so far a new contract, that any change in the law, relating either to the risk or the liability of the parties, made after the issue of the policy and before the renewal, enters into and becomes a part of the renewed policy.[2]

When it is intended to change the original contract, it must be expressed in the renewal receipt, and if any change is made therein it will prevail over the original policy. Thus, where the risk was distributed in the policy as follows: $1,800 on grist mill, and $700 on machinery, but upon renewal the receipt was in general terms for the sum of $2,500, it was held that it was the intention of the parties that the insurance should thereafter be without any distribution of the risk, and should apply generally to the machinery and building.[3]

A policy under seal, renewed by a receipt, *not* under seal, becomes a simple contract, and assumpsit, and not covenant, is the proper remedy.[4]

Void policy not vitalized by consent of insurer to transfer.

SEC. 132. A policy, void in its inception, either by reason of a want of insurable interest in, or fraud on the part of the original holder, or for any cause, is not vitalized and rendered valid and operative by a subsequent assignment thereof with the assent of the company. In order to render such a policy valid, something must be shown which establishes a new valid contract between the parties,[5] or which amounts to a waiver, with knowledge of the facts rendering the policy invalid.[6]

Cancellation without authority.

SEC. 133. Where a policy is assigned by the insured to another as security for a debt or other obligation, the company has no authority to cancel such policy and issue a new one to the assignee, *without the consent of the assured*, and the fact that it was done at the request of the agent of the assured, will not relieve the company from liability to

---

[1] *New England, etc., Ins. Co.* v. *Wetmore*, 32 Ill. 221.

[2] *Brady* v. *N. Western Ins. Co.*, 11 Mich. 425.

[3] *Driggs* v. *Albany Ins. Co.*, 10 Barb. (N. Y.) 440; 3 Ben. F. I. C. 183.

[4] *Lucciani* v. *American F. Ins. Co.*, 2 Whart. (Penn.) 167; 1 Ben. F. I. C. 626.

[5] *Eastman* v. *Carroll Co. Ins. Co.*, 45 Me. 307.

[6] *Shearman* v. *Niagara F. Ins. Co.*, 46 N. Y.

the assured, *unless he is affected with notice or knowledge of such change,*[1] and the retention of the policy by the person to whom it was assigned for a long time — in this case, seven months — does not, as a matter of law, constitute an acceptance of the new policy by the assured.

Equitable lien upon insurance money.

SEC. 134. Where the owner of real estate has contracted with another to sell him a lot of ground, and permits him to go on and erect a building thereon, under a contract that he shall procure the buildings to be insured for the benefit of the vendor, and the vendee procures insurance thereon *in his own name*, and without any reference in the policy to the interest of the vendor therein, the vendor, in case of loss, by notice to the insurers of his equitable interest therein, makes them his trustees of the fund to the extent of his interest therein, and either he or his assignee of the contract, may recover the same of the insurers, even though they, after such notice, have paid the loss to the vendee.[2]

---

[1] *Bennett* v. *City Ins. Co.*, 115 Mass. 241.

[2] This question arose and was passed upon in *Cromwell* v. *The Brooklyn F. Ins. Co.*, 44 N. Y. 52. The opinion of EARL, C., contains a statement of the facts in the case. He said: "Chesley held a written contract for the purchase from Beach of the lot in question, and under the contract took possession of the lot. He then made the parol agreement with Eichenlaube, to sell the lot to him, and build a house upon it for the sum of $1,600. In pursuance of this agreement, he went on and built the house, and completed it in April, 1854. Not being able then to procure his title, and Eichenlaube being desirous to take possession, it was arranged that he should take possession, and pay the taxes and interest, and keep the house insured for the benefit of Chesley, and that Chesley should give the deed as soon as he could get the title from Beach. The original parol agreement was not repudiated or abandoned, but simply modified as to the time and manner of performance. There was clearly such a part performance of this agreement, as to take it out of the statute of frauds, and make it enforceable in a court of equity. As between Chesley and Beach, the former was the equitable owner of the lot, and, as such, had rights and interests therein. He agreed to perfect his title to this lot, and convey the same to Eichenlaube, and that created between them the relation of vendor and vendee, and according to well settled principles of law, Chesley had an equitable lien upon the lot for the balance of the purchase-money due from Eichenlaube, occupying the relation to Eichenlaube of equitable mortgagee. If Eichenlaube had procured the insurance for his own benefit without any agreement to insure for the benefit of Chesley, the latter could not have claimed any benefit from the insurance. A contract of insurance against fire, as a general rule, is a mere personal contract between the assured and the underwriter, to indemnify the former against the loss he may sustain, and in case a mortgagor effects an insurance upon the mortgaged premises, the mortgagee can claim no benefit from it, unless he can base his claim upon some agreement. But where the assured has agreed to insure for the protection and indemnity of another person having an interest in the subject of the insurance, then such third person has an equitable lien, in case of loss, upon the money due upon the policy to the extent of such interest. These are principles of law well settled. *Carter* v. *Rockett*, 8 Paige, 437; *Thomas, Administrator,* v. *Van Keft,* 6 Gill. & Johnson, 372; *Providence Co. Bank* v. *Benson,* 24 Pick. 204; *Nichols* v. *Baxter,* 5 R. I. 311; *Ellis* v. *Krentsinger,* 27 Mo. 311. In this case, Eichenlaube had agreed to insure for the benefit of Chesley. He did, at first procure an

Where the insurance is to be paid for by the mortgagor and the money
paid therefor exists as a valid charge against him in favor of the mort-

---

insurance in his name, which by the terms of the policy was payable to Chesley.
When that policy expired the company refused, for some reason, to renew it.
Eichenlaube then took out another policy in his own name, which contained no
specification that the loss, if any, was payable to Chesley or the plaintiff. But in
the absence of any proof to the contrary, it must be inferred that he made the
insurance in pursuance of his agreement, and for the benefit of his vendor. And
such, undoubtedly, would have been the legal inference, no matter what may
have been his secret intention when he effected the insurance, provided he did it
while in possession of the premises, and while the agreement between him and
Chesley was binding, either in law or equity. It is claimed, however, that the
plaintiff could not have the benefit of this insurance, because he was in default in
the performance of the agreement to convey the lot on his part. The proof does
not show such default, and the judge who tried this case has not found it. The
plaintiff was bound to convey the lot as soon as he could procure the title from
Beach. He made efforts from time to time to get the title from Beach, and
as soon as he got it, he offered to convey it to Eichenlaube. There does not
appear to have been any want of good faith on the part of the plaintiff. It is
true that Eichenlaube several times demanded his deed, but he never in any
way repudiated or put an end to the agreement, and he retained the undisputed
possession of the lot, thus reaping the fruits of the agreement. Under such circumstances it cannot well be claimed that the plaintiff was in default, and that
the agreement was not equitably binding at the time of the fire. The plaintiff
notified the company of his equitable claim to the insurance money before payment to Eichenlaube. After such notice, the company made the payment at its
peril, just as much so as if there had been a regular assignment of the money to
the plaintiff, and it had paid it to Eichenlaube after notice of such assignment.
While both plaintiff and Fichenlaube were claiming the money, it would doubtless
have been unwise for the company to have paid it to either. But it could have
waited for suit by one of the claimants and then have paid the money into court
and been relieved from all responsibility under section 122 of the Code. These
are all the questions raised in the case which I deem it important to consider and
I have reached the conclusion that the judgment should be affirmed with costs.

LEONARD, C., who also delivered an opinion in the case, said: "Cromwell, as
assignee of the contract between Chesley and Eichenlaube, became entitled to
its performance. Part of that agreement was, that Eichenlaube should keep the
premises to which the contract related, insured for the benefit of Chesley. At
the time of the fire, Eichenlaube had a policy with the defendants covering the
premises, in his own name and for his own benefit, but none for the benefit of
Chesley or Cromwell. Cromwell recovered judgment against Eichenlaube, upon
the contract assigned to him by Chesley, for an amount greater than the sum
insured The judgment was good evidence in this case, to prove that the contract
with Eichenlaube was in full force, and that the obligation to insure still rested
on him. As between Cromwell and Eichenlaube there can be no doubt of the
right of Cromwell in equity to receive the insurance money upon the happening
of a loss. That right arises from Eichenlaube's contract to insure for the benefit
of Chesley, and the fact that he had not paid the sum due under the contract.
Had there been no judgment, Cromwell must have proven in this action that there
was a sum due to him on the contract with Chesley. The judgment established
that fact without other proof, as Eichenlaube, the defendant in that action, was
the only party interested in contesting the amount due. The plaintiff in due season notified the insurance company of his equitable claim to be paid the amount
due under the policy of Eichenlaube, by reason of the loss against which the
company had insured. The company have not denied their policy, nor their loss,
nor their liability to pay the amount. On the contrary, admitting their liability,
the company have paid the loss to Eichenlaube, and insist that such payment is a
full discharge of their liability. The company thereby refused to recognize the
right of Cromwell to charge them as a trustee of the fund due upon the policy.
The company assumed the hazard of resisting the equity claimed by the plaintiff.
If the company erred in their interpretation of the law, their payment to Eichen-

gagee, the mortgagor is entitled to the benefit of the insurance, although effected in the name of the mortgagee. The test of his right in this respect is, whether, by agreement between him and the mortgagee, he is liable for the premium paid.[1]

---

laube is no discharge of their liability for the loss arising under their policy. The case of *Carter* v. *Rockett*, 8 Paige, 437, is against the construction of the law assumed and acted upon by the company. That case is a full authority for the claim made by Cromwell. This claim does not operate as an assignment of the policy, against which the company, by a condition of that instrument, stipulated. *They become by reason of the facts, and the notice given by Cromwell, trustees of a fund which they were equitably bound to pay to the party justly entitled. The party entitled in this case was the plaintiff, and the payment to Eichenlaube is no discharge.*"

[1] In *Waring* v. *Loder*, 53 N. Y. 581, this question arose, and was decided as stated in the text. ANDREWS, J., in delivering the opinion of the court, said: "The Lycoming Insurance Company, in respect to the right to enforce the judgment against the defendant Loder for the deficiency on the foreclosure sale, stands in the place of Waring, their assignor. The assignee of a judgment takes it subject to the equities of the judgment debtor, and if the judgment could not have been enforced by Waring at the time of the assignment, the company hold it subject to the same disability. *Douglass* v. *White*, 3 Barb. Ch. 621. The insurance in the Lycoming Insurance Company was effected by Minor, the mortgagee, under the authority contained in the mortgage. This is conclusively established, as against the plaintiff, by the record in the foreclosure suit. The complaint alleges that the premium paid is a part of the indebtedness secured by the mortgage. It was included in the amount reported by the referee to be due, and the judgment for the deficiency is increased by the amount of the cost of the insurance. The import of the transaction is, that the insurance was additional collateral security for the mortgage debt, furnished by the mortgagor at his expense, and procured by the mortgagee, acting as his agent and by his authority. The general rule, that the proceeds of collateral securities in the hands of the creditor are to be applied, when received by him, in the reduction of the debt (SHAW, J., in *King* v. *The State Mut. Ins. Co.*, 7 Cush. 1), would require that the insurance money, when collected by the plaintiff, should be applied upon the judgment, and, if sufficient to pay it, should extinguish it. Nor do we see any ground for taking this case out of the operation of the rule. The mortgagee, it is true, owed no duty to the mortgagor to insure the property, and he could, in the absence of any agreement with the mortgagor, have insured the debt simply, so that the mortgagor in case of loss could have claimed no benefit from the insurance. But the mortgagor had an insurable interest. When the mortgage was given he had the legal title to the land on which the insured building stood. When he sold the land, he had still an interest in the preservation of the property, in order that his debt might be paid out of it, the land as between him and his grantee being primarily charged with its payment. And this was, we think, an insurable interest within the cases. *Crawford* v. *Hunter*, 2 B. & P. (N. R.) 269; *Herkimer* v. *Rice*, 27 N. Y. 163. The authority given in the mortgage was an authority to the mortgagee to procure an insurance for the benefit of both parties. This is its fair interpretation. It was immaterial to the mortgagor whether the insurance was in his name or in the name of the mortgagee, if the avails of it in case of loss should apply in reduction of the debt. The mortgagee had no interest to procure an insurance limited to his own protection merely, where the expense was to be paid by the other party and was secured on the land. It has been held in several cases that insurance procured by a mortgagee upon the request or at the expense of the mortgagor is held by the mortgagee for the protection of both interests, and the implied obligation arising is, that the insurance money when paid to the former shall apply upon the mortgage debt. *Holbrook* v. *American Ins. Co.*, 1 Curtis, 193; PRATT, J., in *Buffalo Steam Engine Works* v. *Sun Mut. Ins. Co.*, 17 N. Y. 406; *Clinton* v. *Hope Ins. Co.*, 45 id. 467. The loss by fire occurred intermediate the commencement of the foreclosure and the rendition of the judgment. The plaintiff received from the underwriter, after the judgment was entered, an amount sufficient to pay it, and upon the

The same rule prevails in case of an agreement between the vendor and vendee of land where no deed has been executed.[1]

---

receipt the law giving effect to the contract between the mortgagor and the mort-gagee applied it in payment of the debt. The plaintiff then had no further claim under the judgment. It was extinguished, and he had nothing to assign to the underwriter. It is immaterial, so far as the plaintiff's rights are concerned, that the assignment of the judgment was made a condition of the payment, by the company, of the loss on the policy. The company and the plaintiff could not by their agreement qualify the effect of the receipt, by the mortgagee, of the insurance money, as between the plaintiff and defendant. It becomes unnecessary to consider whether the underwriter was, by the form of the contract of insurance, entitled to be subrogated (in the absence of any agreement between the mort-gagor and mortgagee) to the mortgage security and to the claim against the mortgagor, or whether the company could have defended an action to recover for the loss, on the ground that the right of subrogation had been defeated by the act of the assured. *Kernochan* v. *New York Bowery F. Ins. Co.,* 17 N. Y. 428. Those questions are between other parties. The plaintiff received the insurance money, and the defendant by his contract with the mortgagee is entitled to have it applied upon the judgment."

[1] In *Wood* v. *N. Western Ins. Co.,* 46 N. Y. 422, a policy was issued containing the following restrictions and conditions: "Camphene, spirit gas or burning fluid, phos-gene or any other inflammable liquid, when used in stores, warehouses, shops or manufactories as a light, subjects the goods therein to an additional charge, and per-mission for such use must be indorsed in writing on the policy. A claim against this company by the assignee or mortgagee, or other person or persons holding this policy as collateral security, shall not be payable until payment of such portion of the debt shall have been enforced, as can be collected out of the original security to which this policy may be held as collateral, and this company shall then only be held liable to pay such sum, not exceeding the sum insured, as cannot be collected out of such primary security." The policy was renewed annually; the last renewal was in December, 1865. The premiums were, with the knowledge and assent of Campbell'f agent, deducted from the payments made by him on the contract. On the 29th November, 1866, the property was destroyed by fire. After the fire, Campbell, who had not performed the contract, declined to make further pay-ments, and at his request plaintiff took the property, and the contract was can-celed. The value of the machinery destroyed was $2,200; the total loss $3,800. The referee gave judgment for the amount of the policy and interest.

FOLGER, J., said: "It appears by the findings of the referee, that Campbell, the vendee of the property insured, by the contract of sale, agreed to pay the expense of insuring the factory and saw-mill; that the plaintiff did insure the property, and pay the premiums therefor, and charge the same to Campbell; and that by so much was lessened the amount paid by him on the purchase-price. It appears from the testimony, that though Campbell did not know of this, yet that his brother, who acted for him with the plaintiff in adjusting, from time to time the payments and indorsing them on the contract, did settle the dealings which included these items of expense for insurance; so that the premiums of insurance were in fact paid by Campbell, under an agreement so to do. It fol-lows, then, that the insurance was really one for the benefit of Campbell. *Hol-brook* v. *Am. Ins. Co.,* 1 Curtis C. C. 193, and cases cited. In such case, the defendants had no right of subrogation, even if they issued the policy, without notice of the contract of sale. *Benjamin* v. *Saratoga Ins. Co.,* 17 N. Y. 415; *Kernochan* v. *N. Y. Bowery Ins. Co.,* id. 428. Though the plaintiff's especial insurable interest was that of vendor, holding an equitable lien on the property for the security of the purchase-money, yet he held also the legal title, and this made it competent for him to cover, not only his especial interest in the property, but the property itself. *Holbrook* v. *Am. Ins. Co., supra;* see also, *Tyler* v. *Ætna Ins. Co.,* 12 Wend. 507; S. C., 16 id. 385; 1 Phillips on Ins. 347, sub-sect. 640; Angell on Ins., §§ 67, 185, 186, and note. And this insurable interest existed in the machinery as well as in the buildings; for though there was a contract of sale, it was executory. The title had not passed, and though Campbell went into possession about two years after the policy was issued, he had no right to remove

Conditons in policy must be strictly complied with unless waived.

SEC. 135. All the provisions of a policy, relating to the risk, are conditions precedent, and, unless waived, must be strictly complied with, such as promissory warranties,[1] or conditions relating to increase or alteration of risk;[2] to the giving of notice, and presenting proofs of loss;[3] the production of builders, citizens or magistrates certificate of loss;[4] as to the giving notice of other insurance;[5] and indeed, each and every condition of the policy must be fully and strictly performed, before an action can be maintained for a loss under the policy. When the policy requires pre-payment of the premium as a condition precedent to the vitalizing of the policy, unless pre-payment is waived, the policy does not attach until payment is made. As to what constitutes a waiver, or giving of credit for the premium, or a payment of the same, see Sec. 28, page 65.

Sending premium by mail.

SEC. 136. When the by-laws of a mutual company provide that the policy shall be void, if the policy-holder shall neglect, for the period of thirty days, to pay his premium note or any assessment thereon, when requested to do so by mail or otherwise, a policy becomes void, unless payment is made within that time, *after notice is duly mailed to him postpaid and properly directed, whether the insured received the notice or not*[6] upon the ground that, where by an agreement between the parties the mails are to be trusted for any purpose, all that the parties are required to do under the contract, is to place the matter in the mails in such a way that, so far as any *laches* on their part is concerned, there is no reason why it should not reach the other party.[7]

---

the machinery without the consent of Wood. There was never such a delivery of it to Campbell as gave him title. Wood still retained on it a lien for purchase-money, and a right, on non-payment to resume exclusive possession. He had, then, an insurable interest in it. *Clinton* v. *Hope Ins. Co.*, decided in this court 4th April, 1871; see also, *Burt* v. *Dutcher*, 34 N. Y. 493; *Tallman* v. *Atlantic Ins. Co.*, 3 Keyes, 87.

[1] *Murdock* v. *Chenango Co.*, etc., *Ins. Co.*, 2 N. Y. 210; *Couch* v. *City F. Ins. Co.*, 38 Conn. 181; *Coolidge* v. *Blake*, 15 Mass. 429; *Thatcher* v. *Bellows*, 13 id. 111.

[2] *Diehl* v. *Adams*, etc., *Ins. Co.*, 58 Penn. St. 443; *Appleby* v. *Fireman's Ins. Co.*, 54 N. Y. 253; *Harris* v. *Columbian Ins. Co.*, 4 Ohio St. 285; *Gardiner* v. *Piscatiqua*, etc., *Ins. Co.*, 38 Me. 439; *Lynan* v. *State*, etc., *Ins. Co.*, 14 Allen (Mass.) 327; *Francis* v. *Somerville*, etc., *Ins. Co.*, 25 N. J. 78.

[3] *Bottaile* v. *Merchants' Ins. Co.*, 3 Rob. (La.) 384. See chapter on PROOFS OF LOSS.

[4] *Worsley* v. *Wood*, 6 T. R. 710. See chapter on PROOFS OF LOSS.

[5] See chapter on OTHER INSURANCE.

[6] *Lathrop* v. *Greenfield*, etc., *Ins. Co.*, 2 Allen (Mass.) 82.

[7] *Shed* v. *Brett*, 1 Pick. (Mass.) 401; *Kington* v. *Kington*, 11 M. & W. 233; *Warwick* v. *Noakes*, 1 Peake, 67; *Hawkins* v. *Rutt*, id. 186.

CHAPTER III.

THE APPLICATION — WARRANTIES — REPRESENTATIONS — CONCEALMENT
AND MISREPRESENTATION.

Application, when a part of policy. Other papers, when part of contract. When only representations.

Sec. 137. When the policy refers to the application or other papers connected with the risk, and adopts them as a part of the contract of insurance, all the statements of the assured contained therein relative to the situation, use, care or character of the property, are warranties on his part [1] that must be strictly complied with, *whether material to the risk or not*, and herein lies the principal distinction between a warranty and a representation.[2] But in order to form a part of the contract, the policy must not only *refer to, but must, either in express terms or by necessary implication, adopt such documents as a part of the contract*,[3] and a mere reference thereto does not make the paper or papers referred to a part of the contract, nor its statements warranties.[4] But it seems that, when the policy refers to papers, *dehors* the policy, and makes them, in terms, the basis of future action in every respect, or a guide as to what is to be, or may be done; they are to be treated as a part of the contract, although, in *express terms*, not so provided.[5] So, where a paper

---

[1] GROVER, J., in *First Nat'l Bank* v. *Ins. Co. of N. America*, 50 N. Y. 47; *Le Roy* v. *The Market Ins. Co.*, 39 N. Y. 91, also 45 N. Y. 80; *Ripley* v. *Ætna Ins. Co.*, 30 N. Y. 136; *Garcelon* v. *Hampden, etc., Ins. Co.*, 50 Me. 580; *Draper* v. *Charter Oak Ins. Co.*, 2 Allen (Mass.) 569; *Tibbetts* v. *Hamilton, etc., Ins. Co.*, 1 Allen (Mass.) 305; *Bersche* v. *St. Louis, etc., Ins. Co.*, 31 Mo. 555; *Bartholomew* v. *Merchants' Ins. Co.*, 25 Iowa, 507; *Olmstead* v. *Iowa, etc., Ins. Co.*, 24 id. 503; *Battles* v. *York*, 41 Me. 208; *Brown* v. *Peoples' Ins. Co.*, 11 Cush. (Mass.) 280; *Treadway* v. *Hamilton Ins. Co.*, 29 Conn. 68; *Richardson* v. *Maine Ins. Co.*, 46 Me. 394; *Gahagan* v. *Union, etc., Ins. Co.*, 43 N. H. 176; *Lawrence* v. *St. Marks, etc., Ins. Co.*, 43 Barb. (N. Y.) 479; *Kelsey* v. *Universal Ins. Co.*, 35 Conn. 225. The application in such cases must truly represent the risk, and must be true in all respects, whether material or not. *Marshall* v. *Columbian, etc., Ins. Co.*, 27 N. H. 157. But the part of it relating to the risk, its situation, etc., is not, in the absence of words or circumstances making it so, a warranty that the risk shall remain as described. Thus, where, in the application, the assured in answer to a question whether the lamps
An application on file in another office, may be incorporated into a policy by proper words, but a mere reference thereto, and stating where it may be found, does not have that effect. *Com. Ins. Co.* v. *Monninger*, 18 Ind. 352.

[2] *Newcastle F. Ins. Co.* v. *MacMorran*, 3 Dow. 255; Ben. F. I. C. 45.

[3] *The Farmers' Ins. Co.* v. *Snyder*, 16 Wend. (N. Y.) 48; *Conn. Ins. Co.* v. *Monninger*, 18 Ind. 352; *Delonguemare* v. *Tradesmen's Ins. Co.*, 2 Hall (N. Y. S. C.) 589; *Sheldon* v. *Hartford Ins. Co., post*; *Jefferson Ins. Co.* v. *Cotheal*, 7 Wend. (N. Y.) 72; *Wall* v. *Howard Ins. Co.*, 14 Barb. (N. Y.) 338.

[4] *Jennings* v. *Chenango Ins. Co.*, 2 Den. (N. Y.) 75; *First Nat'l Bank* v. *Ins. Co. of N. America, ante*; *Le Roy* v. *Market Ins. Co.*, 39 N. Y. 90, also 40 N. Y. 80, In *Com. Ins. Co.* v. *Monninger*, 18 Ind. 352, the policy referred to the application and the place where it might be found, but the court held that this did not make the application a part of the contract. *Wall* v. *Howard Ins. Co.*, 14 Barb. (N. Y.) 383; *Denny* v. *Conway F. Ins. Co.*, 13 Gray (Mass.) 492; *Columbia Ins. Co.* v. *Cooper*, 50 Penn. St. 331.

[5] In *Simreal* v. *Dubuque Ins. Co.*, 18 Iowa, 319, by the terms of a policy, the assured undertook to pay "assessments, made pursuant to the articles of association and by-laws," and the company agreed to pay and settle any losses that might arise under the policy, "according to the provisions of said articles," and it was held that the articles of association and by-laws were to be regarded as a part of the policy, as much as though written therein.
In *Sheldon* v. *Hartford F. Ins. Co.*, 22 Conn. 235, reference was made in the policy to a survey, in these words: "Reference is had to survey No. 83, on file in the office of the Protection Insurance Company." The survey consisted of answers given by the insured, to questions proposed by the insurers. Some of the questions were intended to draw forth a minute description of the premises to be insured, and others, to enable the insurers to estimate the degree and extent of

is annexed to the policy by the insurer, it is to be treated as a part of the contract, although not referred to in the policy.[1] Thus, where the policy is printed on one half, and the conditions on the other half of the sheet, the conditions are to be treated as a part of the policy, although not referred to therein.[2] So, where the policy is, in terms, made subject to the terms and conditions of the application and survey, they are to be construed together, as forming the contract.[3] So where the policy is, in terms, founded upon the application.[4]

the risk. It was held that the reference in the policy, to the survey, was not merely for a fuller description and identification of the premises to be insured, than was contained in the body of the policy, but was a proper reference, for the purpose of incorporating all the survey, as much as any part of it, into the policy, and that all the answers, applicable to the subject-matter, were obligatory on the insured. It was also held, that the policy and the survey constituted the entire contract between the parties, and that, as there was no imperfection or ambiguity in its language, evidence of parol representations, made prior to the issuing of the policy, could not be received, to explain and qualify the contract. But when one of the interrogatories was: "Is there a watchman in the mill during the night?" to which the answer was: "There is a watchman nights," the court were inclined to consider the answer not as a warranty, but as a representation material to the risk, to be substantially kept and performed. See also, relating to the last proposition, *Sayles* v. *N. W. Ins. Co.*, 2 Curtis (U. S. C. C.) 610; *Bulkley* v. *Protection Ins. Co.*, 2 Paine (U. S.) 82; *Gloucester Mf'g Co.* v. *Howard F. Ins. Co.*, 5 Gray (Mass.) 497.

[1] *Murdock* v. *Chenango County Mut. Ins. Co.*, 2 N. Y. 210.

[2] *Duncan* v. *Sun F. Ins. Co.*, 6 Wend. (N. Y.) 488. In such cases the juxtaposition of the papers is a sufficient indication of the intent of the parties to incorporate them into the contract, *at least prima facie*, even though no words are used to that effect. *Emerson* v. *Murray*, 4 N. H. 171; *Stocking* v. *Fairchild*, 5 Pick. (Mass.) 181. In *Roberts* v. *Chenango Co., etc., Ins. Co.*, 3 Hill (N. Y.) 501, the policy was printed on one side of the sheet, and on the other side was a printed statement, headed "Conditions of Insurance," but no express reference was made thereto in the body of the policy. The court held that the "conditions" were a part of the policy; Cowen, J., saying: "There can be no doubt of the intent, that both should be taken together. The assured accepts the policy with what purports to be conditions on the same sheet, or *any* sheet *physically attached. There is in such case, no need of an express reference by the policy, to the conditions in order to fix the meaning. The juxtaposition of the papers is a sufficient expression*, at least *prima facie*. That may be rebutted by parol evidence, as by showing that the two were thus connected by mistake, but no attempt was made to disannex them at the trial, and for aught I see, the legal effect was conceded."

[3] *Le Roy* v. *Market Fire Ins. Co.*, 36 N. Y. 90. The proposal for insurance if adopted by the policy as a part thereof, is to be regarded as though incorporated into the policy itself. *Duncan* v. *Sun Mut. Ins. Co.*, 6 Wend. (N. Y.) 488. And all the statements therein are warranties that must be strictly or literally true. *Chase* v. *Hamilton Ins. Co.*, 20 N. Y. 52. Thus, where the policy stated "reference being had to the application, for a more particular description, and the conditions annexed, as forming a part of this policy," makes the conditions and application as much a part of it as though they were written in its body; and statements in the application as to the situation and uses of the premises are to be regarded as express warranties, and parol evidence cannot be admitted to modify such application; and the policy is void if a warranty is untrue, though the loss happens in a mode not affected by the falsity. *Jennings* v. *Chenango Co. Mut. Ins. Co.*, 2 Den. 75; *Gates* v. *Madison Co. Mut. Ins. Co.*, 5 N. Y. 469; *Bur-*

[4] *Brown* v. *Cattaraugus, etc., Ins. Co.*, 18 N. Y. 385.

18

So too, where there is a written application for a policy, and it is referred to therein as the basis of the insurance, the application is as much a part of the contract as the policy, and *both together*, and neither alone, forms the actual contract between the parties.[1] But where the application is not made a part of it, and the policy *varies* from the application, or a written order for insurance, in proceeding for its reformation, the application or order will be considered as containing the actual contract between the parties. But in all respects where there is no material variance between the application and the policy, the policy will be regarded as alone the proper evidence of the contract, and the application or order can only be resorted to so far as a variance between them exists.[2]

In Massachusetts, by statute, all conditions of insurance are required to be stated in the body of the policy,[3] but it is held, that this requirement is met, by an express reference to a schedule or details of regulations printed upon another sheet or page of the policy, but that the fact that regulations and conditions are printed upon the policy, does not make them a part thereof *unless referred to in the body of the policy and the substance thereof is printed in the body of the policy.*[4] But this doctrine is predicated upon the ground of statute requirement, and is not expressive of the common law rule. In New Hampshire, by statute it is provided that no policy of insurance shall be avoided by reason of any mistake or misrepresentation, unless

ritt v. *Saratoga Co. Mut. Fire Ins. Co.*, 5 Hill, 188 ; *Duncan* v. *Sun Fire Ins. Co.*, 6 Wend. 488. An application signed by the insured, and referred to in the policy, "as forming a part thereof," is thereby incorporated into the policy. *Smith* v. *Empire Ins. Co.*, 25 Barb. (N. Y.) 497 ; *Chaffee* v. *Cattaraugus Ins. Co.*, 18 N. Y. 376 ; *Murdock* v. *Chenango, etc., Ins. Co.*, 2 id. 210 ; *Snyder* v. *Farmers' Loan Ins. Co.*, 13 Wend. (N. Y.) 92 ; *Burritt* v. *Saratoga Ins. Co.*, 5 Hill (N. Y.) 188. It was held in *Eagan* v. *Ins. Co.*, 2 Den. (N. Y.) 326, that the mere words "for a more *particular description and forming a part of this policy*," made the application a part of the contract. But if the policy merely refers to the application "for a more particular description," *only that portion describing the risk*, becomes a part thereof. *Owens* v. *Holland P. Ins. Co.*, 56 N. Y. 565 ; *Wall* v. *Howard*, 14 Barb. (N. Y.) 383 ; aff'd Ct. of Appeals, 17 N. Y. 197 ; *Delonguemere* v. *Tradesman's Ins. Co.*, 2 Hall (N. Y.) 589 ; *Stebbins* v. *Globe Ins. Co.*, 2 id. 632. *So all papers annexed to and delivered with the policy*, are *prima facie* a part thereof. *Jube* v. *Brooklyn F. Ins. Co.*, 28 Barb. (N. Y.) 412 ; *Murdock* v. *Chenango, etc., Ins. Co.*, ante ; *N. Y. Central Ins. Co.* v. *National Protection Ins. Co.*, 20 id. 468 ; *Roberts* v. *Chenango, etc., Ins. Co.*, 3 Hill (N. Y.) 501 ; *Sexton* v. *Montgomery, etc., Ins. Co.*, 9 Barb. (N. Y.) 191 ; *Allen* v. *Hudson R. Ins. Co.*, 19 id. 442. But in determining whether they are so or not, must depend upon the *manner* of their annexation and the evident intention of the parties. *Murdock* v. *Chenango Ins. Co.*, ante.

[1] *Philbrook* v. *N. E. Mutual F. Ins. Co.*, 37 Me. 137.
[2] *Delaware Ins. Co.* v. *Hogan*, 2 Wash. (U. S.) 4.
[3] Statutes of 1864, Chap. 196.
[4] *Mulloney* v. *National Ins. Co.*, 118 Mass. 393.

fraudulent;[1] and in Georgia, the whole contract is required to be in writing.

Stipulation in application does not make it part of policy. Owens v. Holland Purchase Ins. Co.

SEC. 138. The policy must adopt the application as a part of the contract, and, failing to do so, it does not become so, although the application in terms so provides. Indeed, it has been held that, although it is expressly stipulated in the application "that the fore-going valuation, description and survey are true and correct," and that the assured "submits them as his warranty," yet, the application is not thereby made a part of the policy, nor are the statements therein warranties, except so far as they are expressly referred to in the policy. Thus, in a quite recent case before the Court of Appeals in New York,[2] an action was brought upon a policy issued by the defendant company, upon the plaintiff's dwelling-house, farm build-ings, stock, furniture, etc. In the application, the value of the dwell-ing-house and wood-shed attached, was stated to be $1,000, and the value of the land and buildings $14,000, and that the premises were unincumbered to the extent of $8,000. The application contained a clause as follows: "And the applicant hereby covenants and agrees that the foregoing valuation, description and survey, are true and correct, *and they are submitted as his warranty and a basis for the desired insurance.*" The only reference to the application in the policy, was a statement that the company insured the plaintiff "against loss or damage by fire or lightning, to the amount of $4,500, upon the follow-ing property *as described in application and survey bearing even date herewith.*" The defendants claimed that the *value* of the property had been overstated in the application, and, consequently, that there was a breach of warranty on the part of the assured which discharged their liability. The referee found that the value of the land and buildings was not less than $10,000, nor more than $12,000. The court held that the statements in the application did not amount to warranties although so declared therein, and that, the policy not having made the application a part of it, it could only be regarded as having so much of it as it specially referred to, and that only embraced *the description* and not the *valuation* of the premises. The doctrine of this case is in consonance with the doctrine of the English courts. Thus, where the policy without adopting the application or proposal, singles

---

[1] Gen. Statute, ch. 157, sec. 2.

[2] *Owens* v. *Holland Purchase Ins. Co.*, 56 N. Y. 565; *Weed* v. *Schenectady Ins. Co.*, 7 Lans. N. Y. 452.

out particular statements therein to constitute their warranties, and
then generally provides that "if anything so warranted shall not be
true, or if anything material in the statement shall not have been
truly stated, or has been misrepresented or concealed, and has not
been fully or fairly disclosed and communicated to the company ; or
if any fraud has been practiced upon the company, or any false statement made to it in or about the obtaining or effecting the insurance,
the policy shall be void," it is held that the statements in the proposal
are not to be treated as warranties, but as mere representations.[1] Nor,
indeed, is every statement in a proposal for insurance to be treated as
a warranty, although incorporated into the policy. In order to constitute a warranty, it must amount to more than mere words of description, *and must be an affirmative statement of certain facts, or a state of
facts*, and not mere descriptive matter not understood or intended by
the parties as a warranty.[2]

Description of risk a warranty, except when insurer knows it is erroneous ·

SEC. 139. The description of the risk amounts to a warranty *that the
risk is as described*, but not necessarily that it shall remain so. Thus,
where the property is described as a frame house filled in with brick,
the policy is void, *unless* the house is in fact filled in with brick,[3] and it
has been held that in such cases where the falsity of the application
was *known* to the agent who drew it, the company were not estopped
from relying upon its falsity in defense ;[4] but this is hardly expressive
of the rule as generally held. The tendency of the later and better
class of cases is, that, *when the insurer knows the falsity of the warranty
when the contract is made*, he cannot avail himself thereof as a defense

[1]*Budd* v. *Fairwaner*, 8 Bing. 48; *Anderson* v. *Fitzgerald*. 4 H. L. Cas. 484;
Stokes v. *Cox*, 1 H. & N. 533.

[2]*Budd* v. *Fairwaner, ante; Stokes* v. *Cox, ante.*

[3] *Fowler* v. *Ætna Ins. Co.*, 6 Cow. (N. Y.) 673. But it seems that it is competent
to show by builders that a house in part constructed of brick, and in part of
wood, is regarded as a brick building,   *Mead* v. *N. W. Ins. Co.*, 7 N. Y. 530.
A warranty, if broken, whether material or not, defeats the policy ; it is never to
be created by construction, but must necessarily result from the nature of the
contract, or must appear on the face of the policy, or in its body ; *and the printed
proposals annexed to the policy are not exceptions to the rule, for they are incorporated in it by reference. Jefferson Ins. Co.* v. *Cotheal*, 7 Wend. (N. Y.) 73.

[4] *Kennedy* v. *St. Lawrence, etc., Ins. Co.*, 10 Barb. (N. Y.) 285 ; *Chase* v. *Hamilton Ins. Co., ante; Brown* v. *Cattaraugus, etc., Ins. Co.*, 18 N. Y. 385, being the
condition on which the policy is made, it must be strictly true, even though immaterial to the risk ; *and though knowledge on the part of the insurers of the falsity of
a mere representation will be ground for relief, such knowledge in the case of a warranty will not.   State Mut. Fire Ins. Co.* v. *Arthur*, 30 Penn. St. 315.

to an action upon the policy;[1] and it seems to be now very well settled that an untrue or fraudulent statement on the part of the applicant, of a fact material to the risk, does not avoid the policy, when *either the company or its agent was informed of and knew the real facts at the time when the contract was made or the premium paid.*[2] And especially is this the case when the agent fills up the application, and *knowing* the real facts, mistakes them either fraudulently or through

---

[1] *Sherman* v. *Madison Ins. Co.*, 39 Wis. 104; *Roberts* v. *Continental Ins. Co.*, 41 Ind. 321; *Continental Ins. Co.* v. *Kasey*, 25 Gratt. (Va.) 268; 18 Am. Rep. 681; *Ætna Ins. Co.* v. *Olmstead*, 21 Mich. 246; *Guardian Life Ins. Co.* v. *Hogan*, 80 Ill. 35; *Witherell* v. *Maine Ins. Co.*, 49 Me. 200; *McFarland* v. *Peabody Ins. Co.*, 6 W. Va. 425; *Campbell* v. *Merchant's Ins. Co.*, 40 N. H. 333; *Cumberland, etc., Ins. Co.* v. *Schel*, 29 Penn. St. 31; *James River Ins. Co.* v. *Merritt*, 49 Ala. 387; *Campbell* v. *Farmers', etc., Ins. Co.*, 37 N. H. 35; *People's Ins. Co.* v. *Spencer*, 53 Penn. St. 353; *Franklin* v. *Atlantic Ins. Co.*, 42 Mo. 456; *Hartford Protection Ins. Co.* v. *Harmer*, 2 Ohio St. 452; *Atlantic Ins. Co.* v. *Wright*, 22 Ill. 462; *Ayres* v. *Hartford Ins. Co.*, 17 Iowa, 176; *Aurora F. Ins. Co.* v. *Eddy*, 55 Ill. 213; *Ayres* v. *Hartford Ins. Co.*, 21 Iowa, 185; *Howard, etc., Ins. Co.* v. *Cornick*, 24 Ill. 455; *Andes Ins. Co.* v. *Shipman*, 77 Ill. 189; *Rockford* v. *Nelson*, 65 id. 415; or recognizes the validity of the contract after knowledge of its breach, *Frost* v. *Saratoga Mut. Ins. Co.*, 5 Den. (N. Y.) 154; *Mershon* v. *National Ins. Co.*, 34 Iowa, 87; *Keenan* v. *Missouri, etc., Ins. Co.*, 12 Iowa, 126; *Viall* v. *Genesee, etc., Ins. Co.*, 19 Barb. (N. Y.) 440; *Lycoming Ins. Co.* v. *Stockbower*, 26 Penn. St. 199.

[2] *Miller* v. *Mut. etc., Ins. Co.*, 31 Iowa, 216; *Aurora Ins. Co.* v. *Eddy*, 55 Ill. 213; *Ins. Co.* v. *Wilkinson*, 13 Wall. (U. S.) 222. In *Eames* v. *Home Ins. Co.*, recently decided in U. S. Sup. Ct., 94 U. S. 384, defendant objected that the application did not correctly set forth the title of plaintiff in the property insured, or the nature of the incumbrances therein. The court say : As to the objection that the application in this case does not truly set forth the title of the complainants, and the amount and nature of the incumbrances on the property, and the amount of insurance in other companies, it is sufficient to say that the evidence abundantly shows that all the facts were fully and frankly communicated to Beach, the agent of the company, and were indeed known to him before; and that he wrote down the answers according to his view of their bearing and legal effect, Eames relying entirely on his experience in such matters. There is no reason to suppose that either Eames or Beach did not act in entire good faith in the transaction. And, indeed, it cannot be pretended that the facts were not substantially as represented in the application. The complainants are represented to be the owners of the property which is stated to be subject to a mortgage for $6,000. The fact was that they had purchased the property for $12,000, and had paid $6,200 of the purchase-money, the vendor having a lien for the balance of $5,800, but no deed had ever been given. So that, in truth, the complainants did not hold the legal title, although they had an equitable one; and had not given a mortgage, although the vendor's lien was equivalent to one. In another answer, however, explaining the mortgagee's interest, it is stated expressly to be a "lien on mill to secure payment of sale." As the exact facts were communicated to the agent, and he took the responsibility of stating them in the way he did, leading the applicant to suppose that it was all right, we think it would be great injustice to turn him out of court now for this inexact method of statement. According to the views expressed by this court in the case of *Insurance Co.* v. *Wilkinson*, 13 Wall. 222, and other more recent cases, the defendant was concluded by the act of its agent. The reference to collateral insurances in other companies is subject to the same consideration. The insurances were being applied for through this very agent who wrote the answers, and who knew the whole facts, and between whom and the general agent they had been referred to in their correspondence. The defense on this ground is utterly destitute of equitable consideration.

mistake,[1] and when the agent of the insurer fills up the application, he cannot be treated as the agent of the assured, although the *policy* so provides, because as the application *precedes* the policy, the assured cannot be presumed to know what its conditions or provisions are, and to hold that by such a stipulation *unknown* to the assured, at the time when the application was made, and when he relied upon it that the agent, acting for the insurer, knew how the facts should be stated, what should be stated, and what was material, etc., the insurer could make *its* agent the agent of the assured, so as to make him responsible for the agent's *laches*, would not only enable the insurer to perpetrate the most outrageous frauds upon its patrons, but would also enable the insurer to saddle the assured with burdens which he never anticipated, and by a species of chicanery that is never tolerated by the law, to deprive him of the benefits of all legal presumptions as to the apparent powers of agents.[2] It would certainly require an extraordinary stretch of legal principles to hold that a person dealing with an agent having *apparently* full authority to act for his principal in the matters to which the contract related, could, *by notice given after the contract is made, that the agent was not an agent of the insurer at all, as to the matter, but really the agent of the assured, depriving the assured of the benefits of the contract. In order to be efficacious, such notice must be given before the negotiations are completed.*[3] It will be presumed, however, that the assured *knew* of the application and its contents, and he takes the burden of showing the contrary.[4] So where an application is filled out by an agent of the insurer and signed by the assured in blank, or without reading the application, it will be presumed that he authorized its making and *knew* its contents, but he may show the contrary if he can.[5]

---

[1] *Roberts* v. *Continental Ins. Co.*, *ante*; *Andes Ins. Co.* v. *Shipman*, *ante*; *Pitney* v. *Glen's Falls Ins. Co.*, 65 N. Y. 6; *Planters' Mut. Ins. Co.* v. *Deford*, 38 Md. 382; *Roth* v. *City F. Ins. Co.*, 6 McLean (U. S.) 324; *Commercial Ins. Co.* v. *Ives*, 56 Ill. 402; *Ins. Co.* v. *Malone*, 21 Wall (U. S.) 152; *Ins. Co.* v. *Wilkinson*, 13 Id. 222; *Hough* v. *City F. Ins. Co.*, 29 Conn. 10; *Gieb* v. *International Ins. Co.*, 1 Dil. (U. S. C. C.) 443; *McBride* v. *Republic F. Ins. Co.*, 30 Wis. 562; *Peck* v. *New London, etc., Ins. Co.*, 22 Conn. 484.

[2] *Insurance Co.* v. *Wilkinson*, 13 Wal. (U. S.) 222; *Roth* v. *City Ins. Co.*, 6 McLean (U. S.) 324.

[3] See CHAPTER ON AGENTS.

[4] *Hartford Life, etc., Ins. Co.* v. *Gray*, 80 Ill. 28.

[5] *Hartford Life, etc., Co.* v. *Gray*, 80 Ill. 28.

Examination of the risk by the insurer or its agent.

SEC. 140. When the insurer examines the premises before insurance, a misdescription thereof will not avoid the policy.[1] So, where the insurer *knew that there was other insurance*, that such insurance does not operate a breach of the condition of the policy against other insurance, and the same rule applies to each and every condition of the contract, the rule being that a person has no right to rely upon the *truth* of a statement, which he *knows* to be false.[2]

When knowledge of agent is not knowledge of insurer.

SEC. 141. It will generally be found that, in cases where a contrary doctrine has been held, the question turned upon the fact that the agent was possessed of only special powers of which the insured was, or ought to have been, aware. If a *general* agent *knows* the real condition of the risk when the contract is entered into by him, no misdescription, or misstatement thereof in the application, or in the policy, will avoid it.[3]

In many instances the doctrine is predicated upon the fact that the charter or general laws provided how a condition should be waived; and in such cases, of course, a waiver could not be made otherwise than as the law provided.[4]

Waiver by agent. Mechler v. Phenix Ins. Co.

SEC. 142. This was well illustrated in a Wisconsin case,[5] the plaintiff and his brother entered into a contract for the sale and conveyance of a certain piece of land in the village of Reedsburg, Sauk county, for $1,600, payable in one year from the date of the instrument, with interest at ten per cent. Under this contract they took possession of the land, and erected a brewery building and fixtures, and put in the personal property insured. In October, 1872, the plaintiff contracted with Florian Mechler for a sale and conveyance to the latter of all the plaintiff's interest in said real property under the contract, as well as in the personal property, for $6,600, Florian covenanting meanwhile

---

[1] *Benedict* v. *Ocean Ins. Co.,* 31 N. Y. 389; *Continental Ins. Co.* v. *Kasey,* 25 Gratt. (Va.) 268; 18 Am. Rep. 681; *Wood* v. *Rutland, etc., Ins. Co.; Emery* v. *Piscataqua, etc., Ins. Co.,* 52 Me. 332; *Cumberland Valley, etc., Ins. Co.* v. *Schell,* 29 Penn. St. 31; *Clark* v. *Manufacturers' Ins. Co.,* 8 How. (U. S.) 235; *Beal* v. *Park Ins. Co.,* 16 Wis. 241.

[2] *Sherman* v. *Madison, etc., Ins. Co., ante.*

[3] *Guardian Life Ins. Co.* v. *Hogan,* 80 Ill. 35; *Roberts* v. *Continental Ins. Co.,* 41 Wis. 321. In *Roth* v. *City F. Ins. Co.,* 6 McLean (U. S.) 324, it was held that, where the agent of the insurer made the survey, and was as well acquainted with the situation of the risk as the assured, the insurer could not avail itself of a misdescription of the risk in defense.

[4] *Buffum* v. *Bowditch, etc., Ins. Co.,* 10 Cush. (Mass.) 540.

[5] *Mechler* v. *Phenix Ins. Co.,* 38 Wis. 665; 5 Ben. F. I. C. 807.

to keep the property insured. Florian Mechler then took exclusive
possession of the property, and was in possession when the policy was
issued and when the loss occurred. At the date of the application for
said policy, no part of the principal sum of $1,600 had been paid on
the contract; and it appears that about $6,000 were due from Florian
Mechler to the plaintiff on the contract between them. The application of Florian Mechler for said policy contained the following questions and answers:—

Q. "Ownership and value of the building and machinery; title
owned in fee simple by the applicant, or are either or both held by
lease? Is there any other person interested in the property, or any
part of it? If so, state fully the nature of such interest."

Ans. "Applicant has bond for deed; his brother owns the legal
title."

Q. "What is the cash value of the buildings above the foundations,
aside from the land? What is the cash value of the machinery and
fixtures? What is the cash value of the stock?"

Ans. "Average $4,000 — machinery and stock $4,000."

Q. "Incumbrance. Is the property incumbered by mortgage or
otherwise, and if so, to what amount and to whom?"

Ans. "The whole, together with the real estate, which is worth
$3,000, is incumbered about $6,000."

Q. "Other insurance, what amount on building?"

A. "$2,000 in Hartford Ins. Co."

The policy provided that the application should be considered a
part of the contract and a warranty by the assured; that any false
representation by him of the condition, situation, or occupancy of the
property, any omission of facts material to the risk, any over-valuation, and any misrepresentation, in the written application or otherwise, should avoid it; that if any change should take place in the
title or possession, whether by legal process, judicial decree, or voluntary transfer or conveyance, or if the interest of the assured in the
property were not truly stated in the policy, it should be void; and
that in case of a renewal of the policy, it should be considered as continued under the original representations. It also provided that any
loss under it should be payable to the plaintiff, as his interest in the
premises should appear. In February, 1874, Joseph Mackey, to whom
the interest of S. Mackey & Co. in the contract of the latter with the
Mechlers had been transferred, commenced an action to foreclose the
rights of the latter under that contract; and on the 19th of March fol-

lowing, took a judgment by which the rights of the defendants therein were to be forever barred, unless they should pay said Mackey $1,717.47 within ninety days. On the 16th of May following, the plaintiff procured a renewal of the policy, and paid the premium therefor. The land was never redeemed from this foreclosure. On the 12th of June, 1874, a few days before the time for redemption expired, the property insured was wholly destroyed by fire. At that time over $6,000 were due to the plaintiff from Florian Mechler, on the contract between them. The answer alleged intentional misrepresentations by Florian Mechler, in his application, first, in respect to the value of the building, which is alleged not to have exceeded $2,400; secondly, as to the state of the legal title to the realty; thirdly, as to the incumbrances, the lien of S. Mackey & Co. being concealed. It also averred that the foreclosure of the Mackey contract was had and suffered at the instigation and in the interest of the plaintiff herein, and that he had made arrangements with Joseph Mackey to purchase the property of him again, after the equity of redemption should be extinguished, for the sum due him, and thus to cut off the interest of Florian Mechler. It also set up the change which had taken place in the title before the renewal; averred that such renewal was procured by plaintiff without the privity or consent of Florian; and insisted that the renewal was not binding on defendant. On the trial, plaintiff testified that the building was worth, when burned and when insured, from $2,400 to $2,500. The person who took the original application for the policy, as defendant's agent, testified that it was in his handwriting; that he knew at the time the state of the title to the land, and the fact that the Mackey contract had not been paid up, but that something over $1,600 was due on it, though he did not know the exact amount; that he could not account for the statement about the title, unless it was a blunder of his; that he also knew of the contract between the Mechlers, but did not know how much was due plaintiff thereon; that he had no recollection whether the $6,000 named in the application was inclusive or exclusive of the amount due Mackey; that he should say that the $6,000 must have been Florian Mechler's statement of the amount due, though he had no recollection about it; that he also knew the building, and had looked it all over about the time he took the application; that he thought he didn't know anything about the value of the building, but took the applicants' statement for that, though he did not recollect it; that he was well acquainted with the value of property in that neighborhood; that he never interfered with the valuation of property by the parties, but if he thought they wanted too much insurance, would not give it to them, because he would think that they had over-estimated the value; that he used his own judgment as to the amount of insurance; and that he did not mean to insure this building for over one-half or two-thirds of its value. Florian Mechler testified that he signed the application after the agent made it out; that he informed the agent that he had bought his brother out, and owed him $6,300; that the fact of Mr. Mackey having a claim for $1,600 was mentioned; that nothing was said about the plaintiff having a deed of the property; that he told the agent that the whole property—land, building and contents—was worth something over $7,000, but nothing was said about the value of the building separately. He further testified that he did not get the policy renewed, nor request any one to have it renewed. The person who acted as defendant's agent at the time of the renewal of the policy, testified that he spoke to the plaintiff about the renewal at the time; and that he then knew that Mackey's claim had been foreclosed. The court refused instructions asked by the defendant, substantially as follows: That the application in evidence was the statement of the assured, and an agreement on his part that the statements therein were true; that the valuation of the property in the application was material to the risk, and an over-valuation rendered the policy void; that if the oral evidence in regard to the valuation was equally balanced, then the application itself created a preponderance of evidence in favor of the supposition that the assured gave the value as therein stated; and that if Florian Mechler did not procure the renewal, the policy was not renewed. The jury were instructed: 1. *That if at the time the application was made defendant's agent knew of his own knowledge, or was credibly informed by the applicant, in regard to any of the questions stated therein, whether in relation to the title, incumbrances, value, or any other circumstance, and himself filled up the application, then any mistakes therein were mistakes of the defendant, and not of the assured, and would not avoid the policy. 2. That if at the time of the renewal of the policy the agent knew of any change which had taken place in regard to the title to the premises, such renewal was a waiver of the conditions of the policy relative to such changes in the title. 3. That, notwithstanding the judgment of foreclosure, in evidence, Florian Mechler and the plaintiff had an insurable interest in the premises, until the time for redemption had expired.* 4. That Florian Mechler was bound to keep the premises insured for plaintiff's protection, and, if he failed to do so, plaintiff had a right to renew the policy. 5. That by the terms of the contract between the Mechlers, unless it

were terminated by a foreclosure or surrender thereof, Florian would
be entitled to a conveyance of the premises from the plaintiff, upon
complying with its conditions, whether plaintiff acquired the legal
title before or after the Mackey foreclosure had become absolute, and
this would uphold the insurable interest of Florian in the premises.
6. *That any erroneous representations of the assured would not vitiate the
policy, unless relied upon in issuing it.* 7. *That, prima facie, all the statements in the application were to be regarded as having been made by the
applicant; but if the jury should find, from the oral evidence, that he
made no statement to the agent about the value, except as to all the property
(including the land, building, etc., etc.), and that such value was not intentionally misstated or materially over-estimated, and that the agent relying
upon his own judgment as to the value of the property, or as to how much
risk he would take upon it, made the insertions in relation to the value of
the property found in the application, the fact that the value was stated too
high by the agent would not defeat the policy.*

A verdict was rendered for the plaintiff for the amount claimed,
which was upheld on appeal.[1]

Policy must clearly show that statements in application are to be treated as warranties.

SEC. 143. Nothing stated in the application can be construed as a warranty, unless it is clearly made so by the terms of the policy, *or by some
direct reference therein,*[2] nor unless it is clearly intended as a warranty.
Thus, in an application for insurance upon a manufacturing establishment, certain questions were asked and answered as follows: "Are
there casks kept in each loft constantly supplied with water?" Answer,
"There are, in *each room*, casks kept constantly full." This answer was
not literally true, but there were casks kept in each loft, constantly
full, and this was what the assured meant in his answer, and the court
held that evidence was admissible to show that in the general use of
language among manufacturers the whole of a loft or story appropriated to a particular department, although the same is divided by partitions with doors, and that the meaning of the word "room," and whether
there was any such general use of language, was for the jury, and not
for the court. In this case, SHAW, C.J., pertinently said: "There is
undoubtedly some difficulty in determining, by any simple and certain

[1] *May* v. *Ins. Co.*, 25 Wis. 291; *McBride* v. *Ins. Co.*, 30 id. 562; *Devine* v. *Ins.
Co.*, 32 id. 471; *Parker* v. *Ins. Co*, 34 id. 363. See also, *Beal* v. *Ins. Co.*, 16 id.
241; *Keeler* v. *Ins. Co.*, id. 523; *Miner* v. *Ins. Co.*, 27 id. 693; *Wright* v. *Ins. Co.*,
36 id. 522; *Winans* v. *Ins. Co.*, 38 id. 342.

[2] *Daniels* v. *Hudson R., etc., Ins. Co.*, 12 Cush. (Mass.) 416.

test, what proposition in a contract of insurance constitute warranties, and what, representations. One general rule is, that a warranty must be embraced in the policy itself. *If, by any words of reference*, the stipulation in another instrument, such as the proposal or application, can be construed a warranty, it must be such as to make it, *in legal effect*, a part of the policy. In a recent case, it was said that ' the proposal or declaration for insurance, when forming a part of the policy, amounts to a condition or warranty, which must be strictly true, or complied with, and upon the truth of which, whether a misstatement be intentional or not, the validity of the whole instrument depends.'

---

[1] *Vose* v. *Eagle Life & Health Ins. Co.*, 6 Cush. (Mass.) 47. A survey or application, though referred to in the body of the policy *as more particularly describing the building containing the goods insured*, is not such a constituent part of the policy as to operate as a warranty; *it is a mere representation, and if substantially correct the policy is valid, although one of the conditions attached to the policy be, that if the assured shall make any misrepresentation the insurance shall be void.* To give the effect of a warranty to an application referred to in a policy, *it should be referred to in such manner as to show that it was intended by the parties that it should have such effect.* *Farmers' Ins. Co.* v. *Snyder*, 16 Wend. (N. Y.) 481; *Burritt* v *The Saratoga Co. Mut. F. Ins. Co.*, 5 Hill (N. Y.) 188. A warranty, whether express or implied, is in the nature of a condition precedent, and must be strictly complied with or the policy is void; but this is not so as to a representation; in respect to them, the rule is, that the policy is valid unless the representation is false or mistaken in a matter material to the risk; and whether there has been such a misrepresentation as will avoid the policy, is a question for the jury. *The description of the property insured in a policy is a warranty that the property is as described;* and if untrue in substance, the policy is void, though the misdescription arise from mistake, and there be no fraud. *Fowler* v. *Ætna F. Ins. Co.*, 6 Cow. (N. Y.) 673. Stipulations in policies are considered *express warranties*, and it is not requisite that the circumstance or act warranted should be material to the risk. An express warranty in this respect is distinguished from a representation. *Duncan* v. *Sun F. Ins. Co.*, 6 Wend. (N. Y.) 488. Such a warranty is a condition or contingency, and, unless performed, there is no contract. This rule prevails as well in the case of a warranty applying to matters subsequent as to matters precedent. *Fowler* v. *Ætna Ins. Co.*, 6 Cow. (N. Y.) 673. An application *describing* a building, is not a warranty *unless inserted in the policy;* and a reference in the policy to the application will not be sufficient to give it the effect of a warranty, the relaxation of the rule on this subject not extending beyond the proposals of underwriters usually attached to policies, in reference to which it is expressly declared that the policies are made and accepted, or when by express words the application is adopted, and thus imported into the policy. *Jefferson Ins. Co.* v. *Cotheal*, 7 Wend. (N. Y.) 72. Although the description of premises in the application may vary very considerably from the actual state of the property at the time of the loss, *if the variance was not fraudulently intended, and does not in fact affect the rate of insurance or change the actual risk,* the policy will not be avoided; *it is only where there is fraud, or where the underwriter has been misled,* that the policy is affected by a false representation. *When required,* however, by the conditions of insurance, *the insured is bound to make a true and full representation concerning all matters brought to his notice, and any concealment will avoid the policy; and it is not necessary to show that any fraud was intended.* *Burritt* v. *The Saratoga Co. Mut. F. Ins. Co.*, 5 Hill (N. Y.) 188. A description of buildings to be insured, filed with the insurers, and referred to in the policy in general terms as a report of the situation of the premises, is not to be considered as incorporated into the policy, or as amounting to a warranty that the premises insured shall conform in all respects to the description referred to. Buildings represented as finished, must correspond substantially with such

But no rule is laid down in that case, for determining how or in what mode such statements contained in the application, or in answer to interrogatories, shall be embraced or incorporated into the policy so as to form a part thereof. The distinction is most essential, as indicated in a definition of a warranty in the case last cited; and as stated by the counsel for the defendants in the prayer for instruction, if any statement of fact, however unimportant it may have been regarded by both parties to the contract, is a warranty, and if it happens to be untrue, it avoids the policy; if it be construed a representation, and is untrue, it does not avoid the contract if not willful or if not material. To illustrate this, the application, in answer to an interrogatory, is this: 'Ashes are taken up and removed in iron hods;' whereas it should turn out in evidence that ashes were taken up and removed in copper hods, perhaps a set recently obtained, and unknown to the owner. If this was a warranty, the policy is gone, but if a representation, it would not, we presume, affect the policy, because not willful or designed to deceive; but more especially because it would be utterly immaterial, and would not have influenced the mind of either party in making the contract, or in filling its terms. Hence it is, we suppose, that the leaning of all courts is to hold such a stipulation to be a representation rather than a warranty, in all cases where there is any room for construction; because such construction will, in general, best carry into effect the real intent and purpose which the parties have in view in making their contract.[1] In the present case the only clause in the policy having any bear-

---

representation, for a material misrepresentation avoids the policy. *Delonguemare v. The Tradesmen's Ins. Co.*, 2 Hill (N. Y.) 589. Instructions for an insurance, unless inserted in the instrument or policy, do not amount to a warranty. *Snyder v. Farmers' Ins. Co.*, 13 Wend. (N. Y.) 92; *Stebbins v. The Globe Ins. Co.*, 2 Hall (N. Y.) 632. And as a policy speaks its own language, and is to be construed by its terms plainly expressed in it, it cannot be varied by parol proof as to the representations made. *The New York Gas Light Co. v. The Mech. F. Ins. Co.*, 2 Hill (N. Y.) 108; *Thompson v. Ketchum*, 8 John. (N. Y.) 189; *Snyder v. Farmers' Ins. Co.*, 13 Wend. 92; *Delonguenare v. The Tradesmen's Ins. Co.*, 2 Hill (N. Y.) 589; *Dow v. Whetten*, 8 Wend. (N. Y.) 166.

[1] In *Pim v. Reid*, 6 Scott, 982, the policy was made subject to the following condition: "In the insurance of goods, wares or merchandise, the building or place in which the same are deposited is to be described, the quality and description of such goods, also whether any hazardous trade is carried on, or any hazardous articles deposited therein; and if any person or persons shall insure his or their buildings or goods, and shall cause the same to be described otherwise than as they really are, to the prejudice of the company, or shall misrepresent or omit to communicate any circumstance which is material to be made known to the company, in order to enable them to judge of the risk *they have undertaken or are required to undertake*, such insurance shall be of no force;" it was held that this condition applied only to misrepresentations or omissions to communicate circumstances *existing at the time of effecting the policy, and that the insurance was not avoided by the carrying on a more hazardous trade upon the premises, or the placing hazardous goods thereon, pending the current year of the insurance.* So where an

ing upon the question is this : 'And this policy is made and accepted
in reference to the terms and conditions hereto annexed, which are to
be used and resorted to in order to explain the rights and obligations
of the parties hereto, in all other cases not herein otherwise specially
provided for.' Here is no reference whatever to the application or the
answers accompanying it; the only reference is to the conditions
annexed to the policy. In looking at these conditions, second clause
of article first, the provision is that 'if any person insuring any building
or goods in this office, shall make any misrepresentation or concealment, or,' etc.—mentioning several other cases, all of which would tend
to increase the risk—'such insurance shall be void, and of no effect.'
But further, the clause in this policy has none of the characteristics
of a warranty, because it is not, in its own terms, or by reference to the
terms or conditions annexed, an absolute stipulation for the truth of
any existing fact, or for the adoption of any precise course of conduct
for the future, making the truth of such fact or a compliance with such
stipulation, a condition precedent to the validity of the contract, or
the right of the assured to recover on it. The policy is made in reference to the terms and conditions annexed; but these are referred to,
not as conditions precedent, but ' to be used and resorted to in order to
explain the rights and obligations of the parties hereto, in cases not
herein otherwise specially provided for.' They are not to control or

---

application in which the applicant agrees that it is " a correct description of the
property, so far as regards the condition, situation, value and risk on the same,"
and that " the misrepresentation or suppression of material facts shall destroy
his claim for damage or loss," is not a warranty of the truth of the answers to
interrogatories in it, except so far as they are material to the risk ; although the
by-laws, to which the insurance is expressly made subject, provide that the
application shall be held to be a part of the policy and "a warranty on the part
of the assured," and that "unless the applicant shall make a correct description
and statement of all facts inquired for in the application, and also of all other
facts material in reference to the insurance, or to the risk, the policy shall be
void." And the materiality of any answer is to be determined by the jury.
Elliott v. *Hamilton, etc., Ins. Co.*, 13 Gray (Mass.) 139. In a recent case before
the supreme court of Nevada, it was held that an instruction to the jury that the
mere failure of the insured to disclose material facts known to the insurer or
unknown to the insured would not prevent a recovery, was pertinent and not
erroneous. *Gerhauser* v. *North British & M. Ins. Co.*, 7 Nev. 174. Where, however, a policy provides that a false description by the assured, or the omitting to
make known any fact or feature in the risk which increases the hazard of the
same, renders the policy void, and that the statement of the assured shall be a
warranty on his part, the omission by the assured in answer to inquiries to mention the existence of a building adjoining the one insured, both in his description
of the latter and in his statement as to what buildings were near it, is a breach
of warranty that avoids the policy. Thus, where the building insured was a
" wooden four-story paper-mill," and the adjoining building was a bleach-house,
connected with it by a shed-roof building, it was held that it made no difference
whether the bleach-house was a part of the mill or not, as in either case it should
have been mentioned. *Day* v. *Conway Ins. Co.*, 5 Me. 60.

alter any express provision in the contract, or become parts of the policy, but they are statements in a collateral document which both parties agree to, as an authoritative exposition of what they both understand as to the facts, on the assumption and truth of which they contract, and the relations in which they stand to each other. The court are of opinion, therefore, that the statements in this application were not warranties, and could have no greater effect than that of representations, and that the judge was right in giving such instruction to the jury." [1]

It may be said that, when the policy, in express terms, incorporates the application or other papers as a part of it, [2] or refers thereto for a more particular description of the subject insured and the grounds upon which the policy was issued, [3] the application, or other papers referred to, are a part of the policy, and are to be construed in connection with each other, [4] and the application and survey, or other

---

[1] Where specific descriptions of the property are required by the terms of an insurance office, which are referred to and incorporated as part of the conditions of the policy, the suppression of an *immaterial* fact will not invalidate the policy. *Whitehurst* v. *Fayetteville, etc., Ins. Co.*, 6 Jones (N. C.) 352. Representations made *by their own agent*, as to the situation and nature of the interest insured, are binding upon the company, and they cannot defend by showing an error in such representations. *Atlantic Ins. Co.* v. *Wright*, 22 Ill. 462. The materiality of the disclosure or concealment by which a policy is to be rendered void, is a question of fact, which must be submitted to the jury; and a prayer omitting to request this is, for this reason, defective. A condition that it shall be void if the party insuring his buildings or goods "shall cause the same to be described in the policy otherwise than as they really are, so as the same be charged at a lower premium than is herein proposed," *relates to a misdescription of the property*, and not to the character of the title or interest in it. *Franklin Ins. Co* v. *Coates*, 14 Md. 285. An express condition in the body of a policy, that the application contains a just, full and true exposition of all the facts and circumstances in regard to the condition, situation, value and risk of the property, so far as the same are known to the insured and material to the risk, will authorize the company to resist payment of a loss, on the ground that the application contained material misrepresentations in those respects. *Barre Boot Co.* v. *Milford, etc., Ins. Co.*, 7 Allen (Mass.) 42. An application for insurance on a stock of goods represented that it was "all of goods usually kept in a country store," and that there was no "cotton or woolen waste or rags kept in or near the property to be insured." The by-laws, to which the insurance was expressly made subject, provided that no building in which cotton or woolen waste, or oily rags were allowed to remain at night should be insured; and that all cotton, woolen, hempen or oily waste, or rags, should be destroyed or removed every evening. Held, that the keeping of clean, white cotton rags, if usually forming part of the stock of "a country store," did not avoid the policy. *Elliott* v. *Hamilton Ins. Co.*, 13 Gray (Mass.) 139.

[2] *Phillbrook* v. *N. E. Mut. Fire Ins. Co.*, 37 Me. 137; *Fourdenier* v. *Hartford Fire Ins. Co.*, 15 Upper Canada (C. P.) 403; *Routledge* v. *Burrell*, 1 H. Bl. 254; *Sheldon* v. *Hartford Fire Ins. Co.*, 22 Conn. 275; *Shoemaker* v. *Glen's Falls Ins. Co.*, 60 Barb. (N. Y.) 84; *Cox* v. *Ætna Ins. Co.*, 29 Ind. 586.

[3] *Shoemaker* v. *Glen's Falls Ins. Co., ante; Mut. Benefit Life Ins. Co.* v. *Miller*, 39 Ind. 475.

[4] *Maryland Ins. Co.* v. *Bossiere*, 9 G. & J. (Md.) 121.

papers referred to, will, in such cases, control the construction of the policy itself.[1] Thus, where a policy stipulated that if the interest of the assured was not absolute, the policy should be void unless the interest of the assured was truly represented therein, and the assured had mortgaged the premises, which was not stated in the policy, but which was correctly stated in the application, and the application was referred to as a part of the policy, it was held that the application and policy were to be construed together as one instrument, and the interest of the assured being correctly stated in the application, the condition was complied with.[2]

Application may be in part adopted.

SEC. 144. As to whether the whole application, or only a portion thereof specially referred to, forms a part of the policy, will depend upon the *intention* of the parties, to be gathered from the language used. When the application is only specially referred to, as for purposes of description, use, etc., and nothing more is said, only the portion embraced within the reference, will be treated as a part of the contract.[3] In the case of a mutual insurance company, the assured is bound to take notice of the charter, and the by-laws made under it,[4] but they are not treated as a part of the contract unless referred to as a part of the policy,[5] or printed thereon.[6]

Application made after policy is executed, not a part thereof.

SEC. 145. If a survey or application did not exist at the time when the policy is sued, it does not form a part thereof, although one was subsequently executed.[7] Nor is an application or survey referred to in the

---

[1] *Norris* v. *Insurance Co. of N. America*, 3 Yates (Penn.) 84; *Fourdenier* v. *Hartford Fire Ins. Co., ante.*

[2] *Fourdenier* v. *Hartford Ins. Co., ante.*

[3] *First National Bank* v. *Insurance Co. of N. America, ante; Trench* v. *Chenango Co. Mut. Ins. Co.,* 7 Hill (N. Y.) 122; *Com. Ins. Co.* v. *Monninger,* 18 Ind. 352. In *Owens* v. *Holland Purchase Ins Co.,* 56 N. Y. 565, the valuation of the property was excessive. The application concluded as follows: "The applicant hereby covenants and agrees that the foregoing valuation, description and survey are true and correct, *and they are submitted as his warranty and the basis of the desired insurance.*" The only reference to the application contained in the policy was "on the following property, as described in the application;" and the court held, that this only adopted the application so far as the description of the property was concerned, and that there was no warranty as to value.

[4] *Simreal* v. *Dubuque, etc., Ins. Co.,* 18 Iowa, 319; *Illinois, etc., Ins. Co.* v. *Marseilles Mfg. Co.,* 6 Ill. 236.

[5] *Marshall* v. *Columbian, etc., Ins. Co.,* 27 N. H. 157.

[6] *Simreal* v. *Dubuque, etc., Ins. Co., ante.*

[7] *Le Roy* v. *Park Ins. Co.,* 39 N. Y. 36; *Newman* v. *Springfield F. & M. Ins. Co.,* 17 Minn. 123.

policy as a part thereof, to be treated as a part of the policy; unless it was made by the insured or by some person authorized by him to make it, or having been made by a third person, he, with full knowledge thereof, ratified it. Thus, where the policy was made "in reference to a survey on file in this office." It appeared that the insured made no survey, nor was there any evidence that he had knowledge that any had been made in his name, but the insurers produced a survey that was made by the president of another company, who delivered it to the defendant company and procured the policy and renewal thereon. The court held that the application and survey could not be regarded as a part of the contract, as the assured could not be regarded as assenting to the conditions of an instrument, of the existence of which he had no knowledge.[1]

---

[1] *Denny* v. *Conway, etc., Ins. Co.*, 13 Gray (Mass.) 492. In this case the facts were that Henry A. Denny, President of the Worcester Manufacturers' Mutual Ins. Co., applied to the defendant for insurance upon the plaintiff's factory, in Barre, Mass. The application was headed, "Manufacturer's Mutual Fire Ins. Co. The application of ——, for insurance." Among other written answers to questions in the application were these: "There is one stationary ladder from the ground to the roof, and another soon to be erected." "A watch is kept constantly in the building;" and was signed only thus: "I certify that the above is a correct survey of the mill as made by myself. HENRY A. DENNY, President Worcester Manufacturers' Mutual Ins. Co."

There was also a letter annexed to the defendants' answer, from Henry A. Denny, as follows: "Office of the Mechanics' Mut. F. Ins. Co. Worcester, Dec. 24th, 1855," which was addressed to the defendant's secretary, saying: "Do you wish to renew policy No. 1,262, on the woolen mill of E. Denny, of Barre, at same rate? I have recently examined the premises. We shall renew our policy at the same rate; whole amount of insurance, $30,000." The policy was renewed. Upon the face of the policy were these words: "$25,000 insured on same elsewhere." In the body of the policy, it was "agreed and declared that this policy is made and accepted in reference to the survey on file at this office, and the conditions hereto annexed, which are to be used and resorted to, in order to explain the rights and obligations of the parties hereto, in all cases not herein otherwise specially provided for." There was another condition in the policy. as follows: "Applications for insurance, must specify the construction and materials of the buildings to be insured, or containing the property to be insured; by whom occupied, whether as a private dwelling, or how otherwise; its situation, with respect to contiguous buildings, and their construction and materials; whether any manufactory is carried on within or about it. * * * And if any survey, plan or description of the property herein insured, is referred to in this policy, such survey, plan or description shall be deemed and taken to be a warranty on the part of the assured." The defendants set up in defense to the action, that no watch was kept in the building, that there were no ladders, such as was described in the application, nor any other ladder affixed to said building, and that there was no other insurance upon the property, and claimed that the policy was forfeited by reason of the breach of the warranties in the application in these respects. The defendant offered evidence to prove these several grounds of defense, but as the application, on its face, purported to have been made by a third person, and there was no offer to show that the plaintiff directed the making of the application, or knew its contents, the offer was rejected, and a verdict was rendered for the plaintiff, for the amount of the policy, which was sustained upon appeal, BIGELOW, J., saying: "This paper did not, on its face, purport to have been made by the plaintiff, or in his behalf, nor was it signed by him. *It was* a description of the property by a third person; nor was there any evidence that its contents were

Application not binding unless made by assured or his authority.

SEC. 146. The fact that a survey, application, or other documents are referred to in the policy, and that the policy is made upon the faith

---

assented to, or even known by the plaintiff. The defendants, however, sought to hold him responsible for the statements and stipulations-contained in it, by reason of a clause in the policy, to the effect that the contract of insurance was made and accepted in reference to a 'survey' on file in the office of the defendants, which was to be resorted to in order to explain the rights and obligations of the parties under the contract. The argument was, and it is now again urged, that the plaintiff having accepted a policy which referred to a survey, is shown to have had constructive notice of the existence of such survey; that he is bound by the stipulations and representations contained in it, and in seeking to enforce the contract, is estopped to deny that they were made by him or by his authority. Admitting the soundness and force of this argument, and that the plaintiff is bound by the survey, so far as he has recognized and adopted it, by accepting the policy, the question still remains to be determined to what extent such recognition and adoption go. And the answer of this question depends on the proper and legitimate meaning of the word 'survey,' because it was of this, and this only, that the plaintiff had notice by the terms of his policy. Upon this point we think there can be no doubt. In its strict signification, as well as in the broader meaning which it may be supposed to have as applied to the subject matter, it can be taken to import only a plan, and the description of the present existing state, condition and mode of use of the property. It cannot, by any reasonable construction, be held to signify that any statements or representations of a promissory or executory nature were embraced within it, relating to any contemplated alteration or improvement in the property, or to the mode in which the premises were to be occupied during the continuance of the policy. In this sense, the word appears to be used in the conditions of insurance attached to the policy and forming a part of the contract. The terms 'survey, plan and description' are there used as being nearly synonymous. Such being the true import of the word 'survey,' we can have no difficulty in ascertaining the extent to which the plaintiff is bound by the representations and stipulations contained in the paper which the defendants offered in evidence at the trial. So far as they are of an executory nature, or relate to the use or occupation of the premises, subsequently to the date of the policy, it is clear that the plaintiff is not bound by them. He has neither recognized or adopted them, nor is he estopped from showing that they are not obligatory upon him. The defendants, therefore, cannot sustain their first ground of defense by proof that no watchman was constantly kept in the mill, or that ladders were not erected on the buildings. Those were stipulations by which he was not bound. The condition in the certificates of renewal, 'that the application upon which said policy was originally predicated shall continue valid and in full force,' cannot enlarge the the effect of the original reference in the policy. 2d. As to the second ground of defense, based on the alleged misrepresentation concerning the amount of insurance on the property when the policy was issued, it is sufficient to say that there was no evidence, at the trial, that any representation on the subject were ever made or authorized by the plaintiff. It was suggested, at the argument of the case, on the questions raised at the trial, and presented by the report of the judge, that the facts in evidence disclosed an additional ground of defense. The policy on its face contains the express stipulation or warranty that twenty-five thousand dollars were insured on the property elsewhere, and it appeared at the trial that the amount actually insured was much less than this sum. It is quite probable that this would have been a sufficient answer to the plaintiff's claim, if it had been seasonably insisted on. But we think it is quite too late for the defendants to avail themselves of it. No such ground of defense was distinctly stated in their answer, nor was it suggested at the trial. They cannot be permitted, in this stage of a cause, to start a new objection to the plaintiff's right to recover, which was within their knowledge at the time of the trial, and of which they did not seek to avail themselves, when the plaintiff had an opportunity to meet it." See, similar in principle and quite similar in its facts, *Commercial Ins. Co.* v. *Ives*, 56 Ill. 402.

thereof, when the insured has not made or authorized any such papers to be made, does not debar him from a recovery, nor estop him from showing that they are not obligatory upon him. But a statement upon the face of the policy, that there is other insurance upon the property to a certain amount, when, in fact, there is no such insurance, is a statement independent of the papers referred to, and a condition of the policy itself, which is obligatory upon the insured, even though he did not himself represent, or authorize any one else to represent to the insurer that there was any such insurance.[1] Such words, upon the face of the policy, may be said to constitute a warranty that at the time when the insurance was effected, such other insurance, to the amount named, existed.[2] A misrepresentation or concealment by a person who is authorized by the assured to obtain the insurance (unless such person is the agent of the insurer) is as binding upon him as though made by himself, because, by clothing such person with authority to procure the insurance, he is treated as having clothed him with power to do any act necessary to consummate that end.[3]

When renewal is, and when not, subject to application.

SEC. 147. When a policy is renewed, the renewal remains subject to the conditions expressed in the policy, and the representations or warranties in the survey or application. But if the renewal covers other or different property, or if *any* change is made in the risk, as to amounts, or the class of property insured, the renewal is not subject to the application or survey, at least so far as such change of risk necessarily changes the effect of the assured's statements therein.[4] If there are no words of reference to the application or survey in the policy, they form no part thereof, even though the policy provides that "if an application or survey is referred to, it shall be considered a part of the contract and a warranty on the part of the assured." The fact that an application or survey exists does not, under such a policy, become a part thereof. If the insurer desires to make them so, he must comply with the terms of the policy and *refer* to them, and failing to do so, cannot claim that, by implication, they are to be treated as a part of the contract. Nothing can be imported into the contract, which is not clearly within the evident intent of the parties to be gathered from the language used.[5]

---

[1] *Denny* v. *Conway, etc., Ins. Co., ante.*

[2] *Forbush* v. *West'n Mass. Ins. Co.,* 4 Gray (Mass.) 343.

[3] *Carpenter* v. *American Ins. Co,,* 1 Story (U. S.) 57,

[4] *Eddy Street Foundry* v. *Farmers' Mut. F. Ins. Co.,* 5 R. I. 426.

[5] *Weed* v. *Schenectady Ins. Co.,* 7 Lans. (N. Y.) 452.

Policy cannot be burdened with new restrictions.

SEC. 148. Neither can a policy be made subject to any conditions except such as are stated in the contract; therefore, if an insurance company decides to impose certain new restrictions or conditions upon its policy-holders, it cannot, by a mere notice to that effect, make outstanding policies subject thereto. Such restrictions or conditions can only apply to policies in which such restrictions or conditions are contained.[1]

Indorsements on policy, part thereof. When language of policy prevails over application.

SEC. 149. Every indorsement upon a policy, in any wise relating to the risk, forms a part of the contract, and is to be construed in connection therewith, if its purpose and intent clearly appear.[2] But where there is a discrepancy between the condition in a policy, and that contained in papers referred to and made a part of it, the condition expressed in the policy will prevail, and the conditions stated in the papers referred to will be treated as surplusage, completely overcome by the terms of the policy itself.[3] Thus, in the case referred to in the last note, the policy contained the words: "And due notice thereof as aforesaid," referring to notice of the loss. No previous mention in the policy had been made in reference to notice, but the act of incorporation provided that notice should be "given at the office in writing within thirty days," and one of the by-laws printed upon the policy provided that the insured should "forthwith give notice thereof as required by the act of incorporation,' etc. The court held that the word "aforesaid," as used in the policy, in connection with the requirements as to notice, could not be treated as referring to the act of incorporation or the by-laws, and that all the plaintiff was required to do, was to give "*due notice*" as required in the body of the policy, the conditions in that respect contained in the papers referred to being overridden by the conditions expressly stated in the policy itself.

[1] *Ins. Co.* v. *Connor*, 17 Penn. St. 136.

[2] In *McLaughlin* v. *At. Mut. Ins. Co.*, 57 Me. 170, the body of a policy on a cargo of molasses provided that the company were "not liable for leakage on molasses, unless occasioned by stranding or collision." The margin contained the following memoranda: "On molasses . . . if by shifting of cargo owing to stress of weather, any casks become stove or broken, and the staves started by each other, so as to lose their entire contents, and the same amount to fifteen per cent. on the quantity laden (being five per cent. over ordinary leakage), the said excess of five per cent. or over on the quantity shipped to be paid for by the company; but this company not liable for leakage arising from causes other than as above mentioned." Held, 1. That the company were not liable for any loss by leakage unless occasioned by stranding; nor, 2. For any loss by shifting of the cargo unless it amounts to fifteen per cent. of the whole quantity laden. Such memoranda upon the margin of a policy are a part of the contract of insurance.

[3] *Kingsley* v. *N. E. Mut. F. Ins. Co.*, 8 Cush. (Mass.) 393.

WARRANTIES. 293

What is embraced in mutual policy. Misstatements as to title or incumbrances—what are.

SEC. 150. In the case of mutual insurance companies generally, the application, premium note and policy together, constitute the contract,[1] and the contract is strictly construed.[2] But, while the contract, as expressed in the policy, is construed strictly, yet the courts are inclined to be more liberal as regards omissions or misrepresentations, and hold that they are not fatal to a recovery, unless material.[3]

The fact that the by-laws of a mutual insurance company are referred to and made a part of the policy, does not necessarily make the statements in the application, warranties, even though the by-laws provide that it shall be so held. If the application is to be made a part of the policy, it must be so declared in the body of the policy itself.[4] Thus, in the case last referred to, the application contained a clause to the effect that the applicant agreed that it contained a correct description of the property so far as regards the condition, situation, value and risk on the same, and that the misrepresentation or suppression of material facts should destroy his claim for damage or loss, and the by-laws to which the insurance was expressly made subject, provided that the application should be held to be a part of the policy and "a warranty on the part of the assured;" yet the court held that the answers of the assured, in the application, were not warranties, except so far as they were material to the risk, and that the question of materiality is for the jury. The by-laws of the company required the applicant to state incumbrances, if any, on the property. He stated them to be *about* $3,000. They, in fact, amounted to $4,000, and it was held that the policy was avoided.[5] And this is the case even though the policy covers other property that is not incumbered, if the contract is entire.[6]

Where the policy provides that the interest of the assured shall be truly stated, a statement that it belongs to the assured, when, in fact, it was partly owned by another, invalidates the policy,[7] or that it is unincumbered, when, in fact, it has been sold for taxes,[8]

---

[1] *Schultz* v. *Hawkeye Ins. Co.*, 42 Iowa, 239 ; *Murdock* v. *Chenango Co. Ins. Co.*, 2 N. Y. 221.

[2] *Burritt* v, *Saratoga County, etc., Ins. Co.*, 5 Hill (N. Y.) 188.

[3] *Hardy* v. *Union, etc., Fire Ins. Co.*, 4 Allen (Mass.) 217.

[4] *Elliott* v. *Hamilton Mut. F. Ins. Co.*, 13 Gray (Mass.) 136.

[5] *Hayward* v. *N. E. Ins. Co.*, 10 Cush. (Mass.) 444.

[6] *Friesmuth* v. *Agawam, etc., Ins. Co.*, 10 id. 588.

[7] *Wilbur* v. *Bowditch, etc., Ins. Co.*, 10 Cush. (Mass.) 446.

[8] *Wilbur* v. *Ins. Co.*, 10 Cush. (Mass.) 444.

and this is so, even though the assured did not intend to deceive the insurer, and was not aware of the falsity of his answers.[1]

When the assured stated that the property was his, but that it was incumbered, and, in fact, two mortgages were outstanding thereon, executed by the former owner, and the former owner's equity of redemption had been sold thereon, it was held no misdescription of the title of the assured, as he still had a legal right to redeem the premises, and thus an insurable interest therein.[2]

In a New York case,[3] the conditions annexed to a policy of insurance, and forming a part thereof, required that applications for insurance should specify the nature of the applicant's title, if less than a fee simple; and that any misstatement or concealment should render the insurance void. B., in an application for insurance, represented that he owned the property by virtue of an article of agreement with C. The agreement, as proved, was for the sale of a village lot by C. to B., without any exception or reservation, for a specified sum to be paid by B. The dwelling-house was on the lot, at the date of the agreement, and when the insurance was applied for. There was no proof that B. represented, in his application, that he owned the dwelling-house as a chattel not affixed to the soil. The court very properly held that the contract of insurance related solely to the interest which B. had in the building, as the vendee in possession of the soil on which it stood; and that the judge on the trial, properly overruled B.'s offer to prove that the building was a chattel not affixed to the free-hold, and that, at the time of the insurance, he was the owner of it, and continued to be the owner up to the time of the fire. It was also, held, that the statement in the application, respecting the nature of B.'s title, was a warranty; and it being untrue, the policy did not take effect. That the insurers did not insure the building as a chattel, and the agreement of the parties precluded all inquiry as to whether B. had any other insurable interest than that warranted; or as to whether the thing warranted was material to the risk. Where a party states, in his application for insurance, that he is the owner of the property, by virtue of an article of agreement with another, he cannot be allowed to show, in an action on the policy, that at the time of making the application he told the agent of the insurer that he owned the building, having purchased it before he

---

[1] *Wilbur* v. *Ins. Co.*, *ante.*

[2] *Buffum* v. *Bowditch, etc., Ins. Co.*, 10 Cush. (Mass.) 540.

[3] *Birmingham* v. *The Empire Ins. Co.*, 42 Barb. (N. Y.) 262.

took the contract for the land; it being an offer to contradict the written application by parol. Where articles of the agreement for the sale and purchase of land provide that, in case the purchaser shall be in default in making his payments, the vendor shall have the right to declare the contract void, and may take possession of the premises; and the purchaser being in default, the vendor notified him to sur_ render the possession, and he complied with the demand and removed from the premises, these proceedings terminated B.'s insurable inter_ est in the building, under the contract, and the contract became void.

Interest need not be stated unless required. When required, must be truly stated.

SEC. 151. Unless the policy requires that the interest of the assured shall be disclosed, a failure to disclose the nature of his interest, or of the existence of a lien or incumbrance thereon, is not a fraudulent concealment, and the policy is operative if the assured in fact has an insurable interest therein.[1] But if there is a warranty, or a representation amounting to a warranty, that there are no liens or incumbrances upon the property, the statements in reference thereto must be literally true, whether such representations were given in answer to an inquiry or not.[2] Where the policy provides that, unless the interest of the assured if less than absolute, is truly stated in the policy, the policy shall be void, if there is anything in the policy itself that shows that there are liens or incumbrances upon the property, although only by inference, the policy is valid. As, where the title is stated to be in fee simple, and yet the loss, if any, is made payable to a third person, this is held a statement of a lien or incumbrance upon the property that qualifies the title, and upholds the policy.[3] When a

---

[1] *West Rockingham, etc., Ins. Co.* v. *Sheets,* 26 Gratt. (Va.) 854.

[2] *W. Rockingham, etc., Ins. Co.* v. *Sheets, ante.* The insurer is not chargeable with notice of the state of the assured's title as it appears of record, *Mutual Ins. Co.* v. *Deale,* 18 Md. 26, but may rely on the correctness of the assured's statement. *Fales* v. *Conway, etc., Ins. Co.,* 7 Allen (Mass.) 46; *Phillips* v. *Knox Co. Mut. Ins. Co.,* 20 Ohio, 174; *Leathers* v. *Ins. Co.,* 24 N. H. 259. But if the insurer does not call for an accurate statement of title, an incorrect statement thereof, not material to the risk, will not avoid the policy, *Wyman* v. *Peoples' Ins. Co.,* 1 Allen (Mass.) 301, nor will the policy be avoided if the statement as to title is, in any sense, true. As where a person who has entered upon premises under a contract of purchase, erects a house, pays the purchase-money, *and, before a conveyance has been made,* represents the title to be in him. *Chase* v. *Hamilton, etc., Ins. Co.,* 22 Barb. (N. Y.) 527.

[3] In *Home Mut. Ins. Co.* v. *Garfield,* 60 Ill. 124; 14 Am. Rep. 27, the policy provided that if the title of the assured was less than absolute, it should be so stated, in the policy, otherwise it should be void. The insured stated that his title was in fee simple. The policy was payable to one Reynolds, who had a mortgage thereon. The existence of the mortgage was known to the agent and to the vice-president of the company, and the court held that there was no concealment of the true title to the property, and that the policy was valid. See Sec. 86, page 168.

written application for insurance is made, and any of the questions are left unanswered, the issue of a policy thereon is treated as a waiver of the information called for by the inquiry, and the insurer is afterwards estopped from setting-up such neglect to answer, as a concealment of material facts, and a ground of defense against a loss under the policy. Thus, in an Ohio case,[1] the plaintiff being in possession of premises, under a contract of purchase, having paid only part of the purchase-money, the rest not being due, obtained a policy of fire insurance on the premises, and in his written application, which was made a part of the policy, answered the questions propounded as follows: Question. "Is the property owned and operated by the applicant?" Answer. "Yes." Question. "Is any other person interested in the property—if so, state the interest?" Answer. "No." Question. "Incumbrance—is there any on the property?" Answer. "Held by contract." The policy contained a provision that the insured thereby covenanted that the application contained "a just, full and true exposition of all the facts and circumstances in regard to the condition, situation and value of the property to be insured, as far as the same are known to the applicant, and material to the risk," and that the same is made a condition of the insurance, and a warranty on the part of the insured. The court held that, as the plaintiff had an insurable interest in the policy, and as his answers to the inquiries, so far as made, were substantially true, the fact that he did not answer the inquiries fully, could not be set up to defeat his rights under the policy, because the defendant, by issuing the policy without calling for fuller answers, thereby waived further information. "It seems to us," said WELCH, J., "sufficient to say that the receipt of the application and the issuance of the policy thereupon, was a waiver of the questions in so far as they remained unanswered, and that the policy cannot, therefore, be avoided by the company on the ground that the answers are not full. The objection should have been made at the time of the receipt of the premium, and the issuance of the policy, or not at all. Had further answers been insisted upon at that time, the applicant would doubtless have given them. To receive this premium, and issue the policy upon the answers as given, and afterward avoid the policy, on the ground that the answers were not full, would be to practice a virtual fraud upon the insured.

But are the answers false? We think not. Taken together, and construed as a whole, they are substantially true. To the question

---

[1] *Lorrillard Ins. Co. v. McCulloch,* 26 Ohio St. 52; 8 Am. Rep. 52.

whether he owned the property, the assured answers, " yes ; " to the question whether any person has an interest in it, he answers, " no ; " and to the question whether there are any incumbrances upon it, he answers that it is " held by contract."

It is contended that, even admitting the interest of the defendant to be an insurable interest, and that the title of a purchase by mere contract is sufficient to justify a warranty of ownership, yet these answers are false, because they do not disclose the fact that there was a *lien* for unpaid purchase-money, but, on the contrary, allege that no other person has an interest in the property. The three answers, it is said, can only be reconciled and sustained as true, upon the theory that the purchase-money had been all paid, and that the equitable title of the defendant was thus made complete. We do not so understand the answers. The answer which sets forth that the property was " held by contract," is made in response to the question whether there was any " incumbrances " upon the property. We think it was fairly to be inferred from this answer, made in this connection, that there was such an incumbrance as usually exists in such cases, namely, a *lien* in favor of the vendor for purchase-money. Substantially, the answers amount to this : " The property is held by contract of purchase merely, and is subject to no incumbrance except what that description of ownership implies ; I am the owner of that title ; I am the sole owner." Understood in this sense, the answers are substantially in accordance with the facts of the case." [1]

---

[1] A condition in a policy that the application contains a full exposition of all the facts in regard to the condition, situation, value and risk of the property, is not violated by a failure to disclose the fact that an agreement had been made by the applicant to convey it, and that the greater part of the consideration money had been paid therefor. *Davis* v. *Quincy, etc., Ins. Co.*, 10 Allen (Mass.) 113. But if an application is expressly made a part of the policy, and the policy is also made subject to the conditions and limitations expressed in the by-laws annexed, and these by-laws provide that the policy shall be void if the application shall not express *the true title of the assured to the property and his interest therein,* an answer that the applicant owns the property to be insured, in reply to a direct inquiry in the application upon that subject, when, in fact, he only holds a bond for a deed, will avoid the policy. So an answer in such application, that the property is incumbered " for $1,000 with other property," in reply to the question, " Is it incumbered by mortgage or otherwise ; if so, for what sum?" will avoid the policy, if in fact there is a mortgage for $1,400 upon the property insured and other property. *Fales* v. *Conway, etc., Ins. Co.*, 7 Allen (Mass.) 46. But it seems that, if the assured really has such an interest or property in the subject-matter of the risk, that, calling it " his own," or " his," or " my," etc., can in any sense be construed as consistent with the truth, the policy will be upheld, although the absolute title did not vest in the assured. See pp.
and cases cited. The test is, whether the assured had an insurable interest and stood in such a relation to the property that it could in any light be regarded as his. But this rule does not apply when the application calls for a statement of the *true* title of the assured to the premises ; as where a person holding a bond

Void in part, void in toto. Exceptions.

SEC. 152. When application is made for insurance at the same time and in the same application, upon two separate and distinct pieces of property, as upon a store and the goods therein, and the statements of the insured in reference to the ownership of the building is false, the contract is regarded as entire, and the policy is wholly void.,[1] but, if the transaction is severable, as if two policies are issued, one upon the building and the other upon the goods, and separate premiums are paid therefor, the policy upon the goods will stand, unless it is found that the defendants' false statement was material to the risk upon the goods.[2]

When the warranty, as to the title or interest of the assured in the real estate, fails, and the policy covers in part personal property, the whole policy is void,[3] unless the contract is severable, and a separate valuation is placed upon each.[4] But it seems that where the contract is entire, and a gross premium is agreed upon, the fact that a separate valuation is made and specified in the policy will not prevent the failure of the entire policy on account of fraud as to either.[5] But, when the fraud is not original, that is, does not leave the whole contract at its inception, when there is a separate valuation, fraud as to one, resulting from the act of the party subsequent to the issue of the policy, will only render it void as to that portion to which the fraud, or breach of the conditions of the policy applies. As where two pieces of real estate are covered by the same policy, but separately valued, and the policy provides that alienation of the property without consent, shall avoid the policy, and one piece is conveyed without consent, the policy will still remain good as to the other piece not conveyed.[6] In the language of FLETCHER, J., in the case last referred

---

for a deed, in reply to a direct inquiry, he replies, "the applicant owns the property." *Fales* v. *Conway Ins. Co.*, 7 Allen (Mass.) 46. So where a tenant by curtesy represents the property as his. *Leathers* v. *Ins. Co.*, 24 N. H. 259. In all cases, the language of the contract must be looked to, and the statement of title must be such as, in view of the language used, it is false, or the policy will be upheld. *Chase* v. *Hamilton Ins. Co.*, 22 Barb. (N. Y.) 527; *Lawrence* v. *St. Marks Ins. Co.*, 48 id. 479.

[1] *Lovejoy* v. *Augusta Ins. Co.*, 45 Me. 472.

[2] *Lovejoy* v. *Augusta, etc., Ins. Co., ante.*

[3] *Gottsman* v. *Penn. Ins. Co.*, 56 Penn. St. 419; *Smith* v. *Empire Ins. Co.*, 25 Barb. (N. Y.) 84; *Gould* v. *York Ins. Co.*, 47 Me. 402; *Draper* v. *Charter Oak Ins. Co.*, 2 Allen (Mass.) 569; *Treadway* v. *Hamilton Ins. Co.*, 29 Conn. 68.

[4] *Koontz* v. *Hamilton Ins. Co.*, 42 Mo. 126; *Trench* v. *Chenango Co. Ins. Co.*, 7 Hill (N. Y.) 49; *Clark* v. *N. E. Mut. F. Ins. Co.*, 6 Cush. (Mass.) 342.

[5] *Brown* v. *People's Mut. Ins. Co.*, 11 Cush. (Mass.) 280; *Gottsman* v. *Penn. Ins. Co., ante.*

[6] *Clark* v. *N. E. Mut. Fire Ins. Co.*, 6 Cush. (Mass.) 342.

to, "the policy shall be void as to the property thus alienated, but not as to other property separately insured, not alienated." There is a marked distinction between fraud in the *inception* of such contracts, and fraud that arises subsequent to the making of the contract, and does not affect the consideration upon which it rests. In the one instance the fraud *leavens* the whole contract, while in the other, it only affects it in reference to that to which the fraudulent acts relate, made the subject of a warranty in the contract itself.

Concealment or misrepresentation as to matters known to the insurer.

Sec. 153. Where the matter in relation to which the concealment is alleged, is a matter of common report or knowledge, *and is known to the insurer at the time when the contract is entered into,* he cannot complain that the assured did not disclose the information. *If he had the knowledge from any source, or if he ought to have possessed it,* the parties were *pari passu,* and the contract is obligatory.[1]

Where an application stated that the stock upon which insurance was sought, was "all of goods usually kept in a country store," and that there was no "cotton or woolen waste or rags kept in or near the property," and the by-laws provided that no building in which cotton or woolen waste or oily rags were allowed to remain at night should be insured, and that all cotten, woolen hempen or oily waste or rags should be destroyed or removed every evening; it was held, that the keeping of clean white rags, *if usually forming a part of the stock of a country store* did not avoid that policy.[2]

When the insurers *know* the situation of the building before insurance, they are estopped from setting up a misstatement in reference thereto in the application.[3] So if, *after knowledge* of a breach of a condition in a policy,[4] either as to a sale or transfer of the premises,[5] or as to the keeping of hazardous goods,[6] or the character of the risk,[7] or of fraud in obtaining the policy,[8] *the insurer recognizes the policy as*

---

[1] In *Gerhauser* v. *North British F. & Ins. Co.,* 7 Nev. 78. it was held that the failure to disclose facts *known* to the insurer, or unknown to the insured, would not invalidate the policy.

[2] *Elliott* v. *Hamilton Ins. Co.,* 13 Gray (Mass.) 139.

[3] *Frost* v. *Saratoga, etc., Ins. Co., ante; Phœnix Ins. Co.* v. *Lawrence,* 4 Met. (Ky.) 9 ; *Delonguemare* v. *Tradesmen's Ins. Co.,* 2 Hall (N. Y.) 587 ; *Moore* v. *Protection Ins. Co.,* 29 Me. 92 ; *McFee* v. *S. C. Ins. Co.,* 2 McC. (S. C.) 503.

[4] *Gilliat* v. *Pawtucket, etc., Ins. Co.,* 8 R. I. 282 ; *Mershan* v. *National, etc., Ins. Co.,* 34 Iowa, 87 ; *Sherman* v. *Niagara F. Ins. Co.,* 46 N. Y.

[5] *Gilliat* v. *Pawtucket Ins. Co., ante.*

[6] *Keenan* v. *Missouri Ins. Co., ante.*

[7] *McFee* v. *S. C. Ins. Co.,* 2 McCord (S. C.) 503.

[8] *Armstrong* v. *Turquand,* 9 Ir. (C. L.) 32.

a valid instrument by any mode that tends to throw the assured off his guard as to its validity, he is bound thereby and the policy is thereby rendered valid and operative, although it contains a provision that for the causes named, it shall be void.

Oral application.

SEC. 154. An oral application for insurance, although referred to in the policy, does not thereby become a warranty. The verbal statements made by the assured are merely *representations*, which, if not fraudulent *and material to the risk*, do not avoid the policy.[1] Nothing can be incorporated into, or be said to be a part of a written contract, except it is in writing; and the danger of permitting such a doctrine to gain a foothold, is readily perceived. Lord MANSFIELD, in the case last cited, said: "It would be of very dangerous consequences to add a conversation that passed at the time, as part of the *written* agreement." In all cases, however, when verbal representations are made, *material to the risk*, they may be shown for the purpose of establishing fraud on the part of the assured. But even though such statements are false, *if they were honestly made*, the policy is not avoided. *They must be both false and fraudulent* to have that effect.[2]

---

[1] In *Liddle* v. *Market, etc., Ins. Co.*, 29 N. Y. 184, one of the conditions annexed to a policy on property in Brooklyn was, that insurance on property out of New York and Brooklyn were to be made upon the written representations of the applicant; that insurances once made might be renewed, and that all insurances, original or renewed, should be considered as made under the original representation, in so far as it might not be varied by a new representation in writing, which it should be incumbent on the assured to make in all cases where the risk had been changed either within itself or by the surrounding buildings. And that if, at or before the time of renewing any policy where the risk had been increased by the erection of buildings, or by the use of the premises insured or the neighboring premises, the assured should fail to give information thereof, the policy and renewal should be void. There was no representation made when the policy was issued, the risk being taken on the report of the company's surveyor. It was held, that there was nothing in the contract that bound the assured to given written notice to the company, at the time his policy was renewed, of the erection of a bakery, by which the risk was increased; that the omission to give notice of the fact in written form was no breach of any warranty; and that the stipulation for notice, at or before renewal, of an increased risk occasioned by the use of neighboring premises, was satisfied by an oral communication of the fact to the company. Also, that the first clause of the condition, requiring the assured, upon a change of risk as specified therein, to make a new representation in writing, had no application to an insurance on property in the city of Brooklyn, where the insurance was effected, nor upon any written representations of the insured, but upon a survey by the company itself; the company in the latter case, assuming the risk upon its own survey, without any representations of the assured. Also, that if the true construction of the condition of the policy required the assured to give information in writing of the erection of the bakery, the company might waive a strict compliance, they having power to waive any condition of the contract in their favor. *Kimball* v. *Ætna Ins. Co.*, 9 Allen (Mass.) 540; *Vandervoort* v. *Smith*, 2 Cai. (N. Y.) 155; *Suckley* v. *Delafield*, 2 id. 222; *Pawson* v. *Watson*, Cowp. 785.

[2] *Pawson* v. *Watson, ante.*

No statement of the assured, not embraced in the policy, or in papers that are referred to therein, and made a part of it, either expressly or by fair implication, amounts to a warranty,[1] all other statements, whether oral or written, are mere representations or collateral statements such as are essential to, or required by the insurer, to enable him to form a just estimate as to the nature and character of the risk, and which are not required to be strictly correct, but are sufficient if substantially true.[2]

Statements relating to incumbrances.

SEC. 155. In an application for insurance in writing which, by agreement, formed a part of the policy, the insured stated that the premises were free from incumbrance, except a certain mortgage. It appeared that, in fact, at the time when the application was made, the premises were subject to a prior mortgage, but that the mortgagee in the mortgage referred to in the application, was to apply the payments to extinguish the prior mortgage, and had placed his notes and mortgage in the hands of the holder of the first mortgage for that purpose, and that the second mortgage was afterwards increased to the amount of the first, it was held that the statement amounted to a warranty, and being untrue, avoided the policy.[3]

When the insurer, in answer to a question in the application, whether the premises are encumbered, and for how much, states generally that they are, without stating to whom, or for how much, the company, by issuing a policy, are treated as waiving a specific answer and the whole amount of incumbrance is immaterial.[4] Neither is the policy avoided because a mortgage upon the property appears of record, if it was in fact paid, at the time when insurance was applied for, although not discharged of record. In such a case no incumbrance *in fact* exists, and the warranty is met.[5]

So where an application, which, by reference was made part of the policy, contained certain interrogatories and answers, and among them the following: " Do you own the land ? Is it unincumbered by mortgages or otherwise ? " " Yes." Previously to the issuing of the policy, the insured had executed a mortgage deed to a third

---

[1] *Owens* v. *Holland Purchase Ins. Co., ante.*

[2] *Daniels* v. *H. R. Ins. Co., ante; Warnwrig* v. *Bland,* 1 M. & W. 32.

[3] *Battles* v. *York Mut. Fire Ins. Co.,* 41 Me. 208 ; *Smith* v. *Empire Ins. Co.,* 25 Barb. (N. Y.) 497 ; *Gottsman* v. *Penn. Ins. Co.,* 56 Penn. St. 210.

[4] *Nichols* v. *Fayette, etc., Ins. Co.,* 1 Allen (Mass.) 63.

[5] *Hawks* v. *Dodge Co. Ins. Co.,* 11 Wis. 188.

person, to secure a large sum of money, which deed was then held by such person, and shortly thereafter duly recorded. It was held, that the unrecorded mortgage was an incumbrance, within the meaning and object of the inquiry, and that the insured not having disclosed in his answer the existence of such mortgage, the policy was void.[1]

It is of no importance whether the concealment or misstatement relates to the entire absence of incumbrances, or *as to the amount thereof*. If the amount of the incumbrances is stated at a *less* sum than is actually due the policy, is void, but if it is overstated, the insurer cannot complain, as the object of the inquiry is to ascertain the value of the insurable interest of the assured, and no injury is done if its value is underrated, but only when it is set at a larger value than in fact exists. Thus, if there is a mortgage upon the premises for $4,000, and it is stated at about $3,000, the misstatement is material and the policy is void[2] under the facts detailed in the text. BIGELOW, J., said : "It seems to us too clear to admit of a doubt, that the answer given by the plaintiff, in his application to the inquiry respecting incumbrances, was *materially* false, making all due allowances for the loose manner in which such documents are often prepared, and giving the plaintiff the full benefit of the word "about" as if nulifying and limiting his answer, it cannot in any view be deemed to be *substantially* true. To hold so wide a deviation from the fact to be immaterial, would be to defeat the very purpose which the questions and answers in the application were intended to accomplish, and render them but a vain and idle ceremony. We are, therefore, of the opinion, that the representation as to the amount of the incumbrance upon the property was a material one, which the plaintiff was bound to make *substantially* true, and that having failed to do so, he cannot recover upon his policy."

If there is doubt as to whether statements are intended as warranties, will be treated as representations merely.

SEC. 156. When it is doubtful from the words used whether certain statements made by the insured, relative to the subject-matter insured, are to be regarded as warranties or representations, the benefit of the doubt will be given to the assured, and they will be treated as representations merely,[3] and while in construing the language used, the ordinary meaning of the words is to be first resorted to, yet, if from the

---

[1] *Hutchins* v. *Cleaveland, etc., Ins. Co.*, 11 Ohio St. 477.
[2] In *Hayward* v. *Mut. F. Ins. Co.*, 10 Cush. (Mass.) 444.
[3] *Wilson* v. *Conway Fire Ins. Co.*, 4 R. I. 141.

connection in which they are used, the subject matter to which they are applicable, or the general tenor of the instrument it is evident that they were used in a different sense, which is readily ascertainable, the sense in which they were used, will prevail.[1]

Defect in plan of insured premises.

Sec. 157. If an application is expressly made a part of the policy, and a warranty on the part of the insured, and contains a clause inserted after the printed questions by which the applicant " covenants and agrees with said company that the foregoing is a correct statement and description of all the facts inquired for or material in reference to this insurance," and the by-laws, which are also expressly made a part of the policy, provide that " unless the applicant for insurance shall make a correct description and statement of all facts required, or inquired for in the application, and also all other facts material in reference to the insurance, or to the risk, the policy issued thereon shall be void," the applicant must be held to warrant *that all facts inquired for are correctly given, whether material or not ; and the omission to mention several buildings within one hundred feet of the property insured, in reply to a question, "What is the distance of said building from other buildings within one hundred feet, and how are such other buildings constructed and occupied ? Annex a ground plan to the application,"* will avoid the policy.[2]

---

[1] *Wilson* v. *Hampden Ins. Co.*, 4 R. I. 157.

[2] *Tebbetts* v. *Hamilton, etc., Ins. Co.*, 1 Allen (Mass.) 305. In an application referred to in the policy, the inquiry in relation to the premises was : " How bounded, and distance from other buildings, if less than ten rods, and for what purpose occupied, and by whom ? " The answer stated the nearest buildings in every direction, but did not state all the buildings within ten rods. It was held that such answer was not a warranty that there were no other buildings within that distance than those mentioned ; and that as the applicant answered the inquiry as he understood it, and the insurers accepted the application and issued a policy, they could not, after a loss, defend on the ground that the answer was a warranty which was broken. *Gates* v. *Madison County Mut. Ins. Co.*, 2 N. Y. 43 ; *Masters* v. *Madison County Mut. F. Ins. Co.*, 11 Barb. (N. Y.) 624. But, where the inquiry called for the distance from each other building, if less than ten rods, and the answer enumerated only a part of those within that distance, it was held that the policy was avoided by such omission. *Burritt* v. *Saratoga County Mut. Ins. Co.*, 5 Hill (N. Y.) 188. So, where, in answer to a similar inquiry, and to one as to what the premises were occupied for, the application simply stated that the building was a grist-mill, and bounded by space on all sides, whereas mechanical operations were carried on in the mill, and there was another building within ten rods. It was held that either of these omissions, though the facts were known to the company's agent at the time of issuing the policy, vitiated it. *Jennings* v. *Chenango County Mut. Ins. Co.*, 2 Den. (N. Y.) 75 ; *Gates* v. *Madison County Mut. Ins. Co.*, 2 N. Y. 43 ; S. C., 5 N. Y. 469 ; *Wilson* v. *Herkimer County Mut. Ins. Co.*, 6 N. Y. 53. So where the application was in the form of answers to printed interrogatories furnished by the insurers. One of them asked the "relative situation of the property to be insured as to other buildings ; distance to each within ten rods ; " and the printed form concluded with the statement : " All of the exposures within ten rods are

When assured attempts to answer inquiries, must do so with substantial accuracy, although he does not pretend to state accurately.

SEC. 158. While the use of an expression in the application that indicates that the answer is not intended to express the *exact* amount of the incumbrances, will excuse a misstatement as to immaterial sums; that is when the variance is so small as not too material to the risk, yet it does not excuse the insured from stating the amount of the incumbrances with *substantial accuracy*.[1] It is not enough that the statement is correct as to the amount appearing due upon *the face* of the mortgage; the amount due, *including accrued interest,* must be stated with *substantial correctness.* Thus, where in an application for insurance, the insured stated that there were two mortgages amounting to "$2,700, in all. First of $1,150, and 2nd mortgage $1,550," and it appeared that, in addition to the amount appearing to be due upon the first mortgage, there was also due, the sum of $300, accrued interest, making the whole amount due thereon $1,450, and the actual amount of incumbrances upon the property $3,000, instead of $2,700, as stated, the variance was held material and the policy void. DEWEY, J., remarking: "We do not suppose *entire precision* is requisite in such a statement, or that the omission to state *a small amount* of accumulated interest would avoid the policy. But this was not such a case. The interest having accumulated to the amount of $300, *became a substantial part of the incumbrance*, and it is difficult to see why, *to that extent* this statement, as to existing incumbrances on the property, was not false."[2]

Insurer may rely on statements of insured. Not bound to make inquiries of others.

SEC. 159. The insurer has a right to rely upon the statements of the assured, and is not bound to make any inquiry beyond that made of the assured himself. He need not inquire whether the interest upon the mortgage debt is payable yearly or otherwise, or whether it has been paid at all. *The assured must at his peril state with substantial accuracy the amount due upon the mortgage, including interest.*[3] If the insurance

---

mentioned." It was held that the application constituted a warranty that no other building than those named existed within ten rods, and that, whether it increased the risk, or was material thereto or not, was not open to inquiry. *It was for the insurers to determine whether a building within that distance constituted an exposure. Chaffee* v. *Cattaraugus County Mut. Ins. Co.*, 18 N. Y. 376; *Brown* v. *Cattaraugus County Mut. Ins. Co.*, id. 385.

In *Brown* v. *People*, 11 Cush., there were two mortgages, amounting to $4,700. The applicant stated the incumbrances to be "about $4,000." The court held that this was a material misstatement and not excused by the qualifying word. *Hayward* v. *Ins. Co.*, *ante*.

[2] *Jacobs* v. *Eagle, etc., Ins. Co.*, 11 Cush. (Mass.) 132.

[3] *Murphy* v. *People's, etc., Ins. Co.*, 7 Allen (Mass.) 239.

is in favor of a mortgagee, and he holds prior mortgages upon the property and omits to state the fact in answer to an inquiry in reference to incumbrances in the application, the policy is void. Indeed it would seem that under *any* circumstances, a mortgagee who should procure insurance upon premises to secure his interest therein under a particular mortgage, without disclosing the fact that he held *other* mortgages upon the same premises, whether prior or subsequent, would be a fraudulent concealment.[1] The insurer cannot show in excuse of his statement, that it occurred by mistake,[2] was unintentional[3] or even that he did not know the contents of the application or the provisions of the policy, as he could neither read or write,[4] nor, if the policy provides that the company will not be bound by a statement made to an agent, can he show that he stated the amount of the incumbrance to the agent, who omitted to state it in the application.[5] But, in the absence of such notice of a limitation of the agent's authority notice to, or the knowledge of the agent of an incumbrance will be notice to, or the knowledge of the company.[6] In such cases it is the duty of the agent to report the fact to the company, and his neglect to do so, will not defeat the right of the insured to recover upon the policy.[7]

So where the company's agent fills up the application, and without making any inquiry of the insured, or reading or explaining to him the requirements of the company in that respect, it has been held, very properly, that the company must be treated as having waived any right to have a correct disclosure of the amount of incumbrance upon the property.[8]

By incumbrance is meant *any valid lien upon the property, created by the act of the insured, or of others preceding him in title, or by operation of law, which substantially lessens the value of the interest of the assured therein,* and this applies to mortgages,[9] mechanics' liens,[10] judgments

---

[1] *Smith* v. *Columbia Ins. Co.,* 17 Penn. St. 253.

[2] *Cooper* v. *Farmer's Ins. Co.,* 50 Penn. St. 299.

[3] *Lochner* v. *Home Mut. Ins. Co.,* 17 Mo. 247.

[4] *Fuller* v. *Madison Ins. Co.,* 36 Wis. 599.

[5] *Lochner* v. *Home Mut. F. Ins. Co., ante; Rabback* v. *Germania Ins. Co.,* 62 N. Y. 613.

[6] *Masters* v. *Madison Ins. Co.,* 11 Barb. (N. Y.) 624; *Owen* v. *Farmer's Ins. Co.,* 57 Barb. (N. Y.) 518.

[7] *Ins. Co. of N. America* v. *McDowell,* 50 Ill. 120.

[8] *Geib* v. *International Ins. Co., ante.*

[9] *Van Buren* v. *St. Joseph, etc., Ins. Co.,* 28 Mich. 398; *Hutchins* v. *Cleaveland, etc., Ins. Co.,* 11 Ohio St. 477.

[10] *Cumberland, etc., Ins. Co.* v. *Mitchell,* 48 Penn. St. 374

20

in States where they operate as a lien,[1] attachments upon writs or levies under execution, or any contract, or legal proceeding that operates as a *valid lien upon the property, and lessens the value of the interest of the assured therein,*[2] *provided, however, that in all cases the lien must be legal and valid, and there must, in fact, be something due thereon. The mere fact that a mortgage appears of record, is not enough; it must also appear that it represents some indebtedness, either on the part of the assured or the person who executed the same.*[3] If it was given to secure a surety upon a note or other obligation, in order to make it an incumbrance, it is not enough to show that the note or obligation is still outstanding; it must be shown that the mortgagee has paid the debt or perfected his right to enforce the mortgage,[4] and so in the case of a mechanic's lien, an attachment or other process, it must appear *as a fact that an indebtedness exists, and that it exists as a valid claim upon the property, whereby the value of the interest of the assured therein is materially lessened.*[5] An unrecorded mortgage is an incumbrance, because it can be enforced as against the assured whether recorded or not.[6] So a mortgage executed before the assured acquired title to the property, is an incumbrance, because, upon the vesting of the title in the assured, the mortgage attaches.[7]

Statements made in application not called for by questions, not warranties.

SEC. 160. Although the policy refers to and makes the application a part thereof, yet only statements made strictly in answer to the inquiries contained therein can be regarded as warranties. *All other matters stated therein, not called for by the questions, or the policy, are merely representations, and need only be substantially true;*[8] and this is the case also, where the policy only refers to the application for special purposes, as in reference to the description or value of the premises. In such case only the answers relating to those matters are adopted as a

---

[1] *Bowman* v. *Franklin F. Ins. Co.*, 40 Md. 620.

[2] *Bowman* v. *Franklin Ins. Co., ante; Brown* v. *Com. Mut. Ins. Co.*, 41 Penn. St. 187.

[3] *Hawkes* v. *Dodge Co. Ins. Co.*, 11 Wis. 188.

[4] *Viall* v. *Genesee Mut. Ins. Co.*, 19 Barb. (N. Y.) 440.

[5] *Hawkes* v. *Dodge Co. Ins. Co.*, 11 Wis. 188; *Brown* v. *Com. Ins. Co.*, 41 Penn. St. 187.

[6] *Hutchins* v. *Cleaveland, etc., Ins. Co., ante.*

[7] *Packard* v. *Agawam F. Ins. Co.*, 2 Gray (Mass.) 334.

[8] *Hartford Protection Ins. Co.* v. *Harmer.* 2 Ohio St. 452; 3 Bennett's F. I. C. 643.

part of the contract, and all other matters in the application are merely representations.[1]

---

[1] In *Hartford Protection Ins. Co. v. Harmer, ante*, it appeared that one of the policies was issued upon a written application, drawn up by the agent of the company and signed by the defendant in error, by his agent, Wilson James. We make no question that it was the paper of the defendant, and that he is legally responsible for its contents. This paper is headed "Survey." ("To be signed by the applicant.") The balance of it consists of questions and answers, thirteen in number, most of them having relation to the character of the structures, materials of which they are composed, distance from other buildings, etc. The 8th and 13th are as follows: "Ashes. How are they disposed of?" Answer: "Thrown out." "What incumbrance, if any, is now on said property?" Answer: "None; attachment on goods released by bond." In relation to the ashes, the evidence tended to prove, that for some time before the policy was underwritten some of the ashes had been taken by the family of the defendant's clerk, who occupied the store building, and placed in a box in the kitchen, for the purpose of breaking water to wash with; and what was not wanted for this purpose was thrown out. That the uniform practice had been, to wet them thoroughly when they were placed into the box for this purpose, until the evening before the fire, to which allusion has been made, when some were put in it by his wife, who forgot to wet them; and in the night the box was found to be on fire, and some part of the woodwork of the room adjacent to it. As to incumbrances, it was proved that the goods, and lots upon which the buildings were situated, had been taken by a writ of attachment, at the suit of a creditor, the agent of the company acting as one of the attorneys, which was pending at the time the policy was underwritten; the goods having been previously released by bond, but the lien still remaining upon the lots. The agent testified "that he knew of the existence of the said proceeding in attachment, at the time said survey was made out, and made the entry, attachment on goods released by bond, from his own knowledge; that, at the time, he did not think of the fact that the attachment on the lots was still existing, and not released, or he would have entered it, or have communicated the fact to James, and with his consent have entered it." Following a general reference to the property insured, on the face of the policy the following language is used: "For a more particular description of said premises, see survey No. 74, furnished by the insured, which is hereby made a part of this policy." It is also declared "that this policy is made and accepted in reference to the conditions hereto annexed, which are to be used and resorted to in order to explain the rights and obligations of the parties hereto, in all cases not herein specially provided for." The 1st, 4th, and 17th conditions are as follows: 1st Condition. "Applications for insurance should be in writing, and specify the construction and materials of the building to be insured, or containing the property to be insured; by whom occupied; whether as a private dwelling, or how otherwise; its situation with respect to contiguous dwellings, and their construction and materials; and whether any manufactory is carried on within or about it; and in relation to the insurance on goods," etc. 4th Condition. "A false description, by the assured, of a building, or of its contents * * shall render absolutely void a policy issued upon such description. But the office will be responsible for surveys and valuations made by its agents." 17th Condition. "When a policy is made and issued upon a survey and description of certain property, such survey and description shall be taken and deemed to be a part and portion of such policy, and warranty on the part of the assured." Upon this state of the facts, counsel for the plaintiff in error contended that the 8th and 13th questions and answers constituted a part of the contract between the parties, and warranty on the part of the assured. That the answers were not true, and therefore the policy had never attached, and was void. But the court instructed the jury, in substance, that only so much of the written application *as related to the situation and description of the property insured*, was, by the policy, made a warranty; and that the answers to the questions referred to were to be treated as representations which the parties had made material, and therefore their materiality was not a question for the jury. That if the representation as to the ashes was *substantially* untrue; if the habit was to deposit the ashes in the building insured, the policy was void, whether the repre-

Thus where the insured *omits* to answer the inquiry in reference to incumbrances, and a policy is issued without objection, the company is treated as waiving any information upon the subject and cannot afterwards set up the omission of the insured as a fraudulent concealment of a material fact.[1] Thus, where the insured, in answer to an inquiry in the application, wrote: "Incumbered to the amount of $——," it was held that the insurer, by issuing a policy without requiring a specific answer to the inquiry, waived the benefit of any condition in the policy avoiding it for any concealment or misrepresentation in that respect, and were thereby estopped from setting up such omission in avoidance of its liability, under the policy.[2]

Equivocal or doubtful answers.

SEC. 161. While the assured is bound to disclose all material matters relating to the risk, whether usual or extraordinary, if inquiries are put to him relative thereto, yet, if he leaves any question unanswered, or if his answer is equivocal, and it is evident that it does not fully meet the inquiry, and the insurer issues a policy without requiring a definite answer in reference to the matter, he is treated as having waived more definite information, and cannot afterwards set up the failure of the assured to give a full answer to the inquiry, to defeat the policy. If he was not satisfied to take the risk without full replies to his inquiries, he should have sought further information before the contract was completed, and cannot afterwards repudiate his liability

---

sentation was made intentionally or by mistake, *and whether the applicant knew what was done with the ashes or not ; but if the ashes were generally and usually thrown out, and only deposited in the building occasionally, or for special or extraordinary purposes, or accidentally, it would not avoid the policy.* That the attachment proceeding showed an incumbrance on the building insured ; *but that, if the agent of the company knew, at the time he issued the policy, of the existence of this incumbrance, the policy was not void on that account, because he was not misled by it ;* and this ruling was freely sustained upon appeal. In *Owens v. Holland Purchase Ins. Co.*, 56 N. Y. 565, an action was brought upon a policy. The application contained a valuation of the lands and buildings, which was excessive, and concluded as follows : "The applicant hereby covenants and agrees that the foregoing valuation, description and survey are true and correct, and they are submitted as his warranty and the basis of the desired insurance." The only reference in the policy to the application was a statement that the insurance was "on the following property, as described in application." It was held that this only adopted that portion of the application describing the property, and that there was no warranty as to value. In an application for insurance, no part can be regarded as a warranty, unless made so by the contract of insurance. The parts not adopted and made the basis of the contract, so as to constitute warranties, are to be treated as representations not prejudicing the rights of the insured, unless they are material to the risk, are untrue, and were not made in good faith.

[1] *Geib* v. *International Ins. Co.*, 1 Dill (C. C. U. S.) 443.

[2] *Bursche* v. *St. Louis, etc., Ins. Co.*, 31 Mo. 555.

because full answers were not given. By entering into the contract, under such circumstances, *he waives further information.*[1]

" A fair and reasonable construction of the contract " said McILVAINE, J.,[2] " would require notice of prior insurance to be given at the time of making the application. * * *The object of the notice is to enable the insurer to act prudently and intelligently in relation to the risk; yet, not-* withstanding the reference to the condition in the printed policy, *it was competent for the insurer to waive the condition, and we think it was waived in so far as it related to the notice of prior insurance.* The risk was taken upon an application that formed a part of the policy. The interrogatory in the application for insurance, in relation to prior insurance, was not answered. *The acceptance of the risk upon such an application is a waiver of any notice which a truthful answer to the interrogatory would have disclosed.*"[3] The rule may be said to be that, *in all cases where the answer of the assured professes to be, and prima facie is, a full and complete answer to the inquiry, if anything material to the risk is omitted which the inquiry called for, it is fatal to the policy, whether omitted through the fraud or mistake of the assured; but if it is not prima facie a complete answer to the inquiry, and upon its face puts the insurer upon further inquiry, and he issues a policy without eliciting or seeking to elicit further information in reference thereto, he waives a fuller answer, and cannot avoid liability upon the ground that the assured has concealed material facts.* He assents to take the risk with imperfect knowledge

---

[1] In *Dohn* v. *Farmers'* etc., *Ins. Co.*, 5 Lans. (N. Y.) 275, the policy required the assured to state the nature of his title, and whether there were incumbrances. He made no reply to the question. *Held*, a reply was waived by the issue of a policy. In *Dayton Ins. Co.* v. *Kelly*, 24 Ohio St. 345 ; 15 Am. Rep., there was an inquiry relating to prior insurance, which was not answered. It was held a waiver of any information upon that point, 612. In *Roth* v. *City Fire Ins. Co.*, 6 McLean (U. S.) 324, the assured failed to answer an inquiry calling for information as to the materials of which the building was composed, and it was held that information on that point was waived, and could not be set up as a fraudulent concealment. In *Haley* v. *Dorchester Ins. Co.*, 12 Gray (Mass.) 545, the assured was asked to state " who occupies the building ? " In *Dodge Co. Mut. Ins. Co.*, 12 Wis. 337, the application called for statement of the way the barn was occupied. In *Liberty Hall Assn.* v. *Housatonic, etc., Ins. Co.*, 7 Gray (Mass.) 261, the question " how many tenants ? " and in all these cases the questions not being answered, it was held that issuing the policy on defective application was a waiver of defects.

[2] *Dayton Ins. Co.* v. *Kelly, ante.*

[3] *Hall* v. *People's Ins. Co.*, 6 Gray (Mass.) 185 ; 21 Ohio St. 176 ; *Liberty Hall Association* v. *Housatonic Ins. Co.*, 7 Gray (Mass.) 261 ; *Nichols* v. *Fayette Mut. Fire Ins. Co.*, 1 Allen (Mass.) 63 ; *Allen* v. *Charlestown Ins. Co.*, 5 Gray (Mass.) 384 ; *Haley* v. *Dorchester Mut. Fire Ins. Co.*, 12 id. 545 ; *Dodge Co. Mut. Ins. Co.* v. *Rogers*, 12 Wis. 337.

thereof, and he thereby assumes all the consequences incident to his negligence in that respect.[1]

SEC. 162. When a policy is issued upon a verbal application, without any representations in reference thereto, *all information relative to the risk, except such as is unusual and extraordinary,* is waived, and the policy is valid, even though it contain a clause or stipulation that "the insured covenants that the representations given in the application for this insurance contain a just, full and true exposition of all facts and circumstances in respect to the condition, situation, value and risk of the property insured,"[2] and, although the policy professes to be made upon the faith or representations made by the insured, yet, it is valid, even though no representations whatever were made in reference to the risk, and the lack thereof is not a matter of defense. The insurer cannot charge the assured with *laches,* induced by its own conduct.[3]

Thus, where in an application for insurance on goods, the assured stated, in answers to questions, that the building in which they were, was occupied by one tenant; the condition of the policy required a description of the building the goods were in, but none of its occupancy, which was specially required when insurance was desired on a building, it was held, that the assured was not obliged to state the occupancy ; that his statement of it did not amount to a warranty, but only to a representation, the falsity of which was immaterial if the loss was not occasioned by the nature of the occupancy.[4]

When matters in application are not warranties.

SEC. 163. When an application is imported into the policy, it is to be construed in connection therewith, and in the absence of anything in the contract excusing strict compliance, *all* the statements therein, however immaterial, are warranties ; but even though the policy expressly states that such statements are to be treated as warranties, yet, if the application contains explanations or declarations inserted

---

[1] *Harmer* v. *Protection Ins. Co., ante ; Haly* v. *Dorchester Ins. Co.,* 12 Gray (Mass.) 545 ; *Com.* v. *Hide & Leather Ins. Co.,* 112 Mass. 136 ; *Dayton* v. *Ins. Co.,* 24 Ohio St. 345 ; *Dodge Co., etc., Ins. Co.* v. *Rogers,* 12 Wis. 337.

[2] *Com.* v. *Hide and Leather Ins. Co.,* 112 Mass. 136.

[3] *Com.* v. *Hide and Leather Ins. Co., ante ; Bahringer* v. *Empire Mut. Life Ins. Co.,* 2 T. & C. (N. Y.) 610.

[4] *Howard, etc., Ins. Co.* v. *McCormick,* 24 Ill. 554 ; *Hartford Protection Ins. Co.,* v. *Harmer,* 2 Ohio St. 452 ; *Benham* v. *Life Ins. Co.,* 16 Jur. 691.

therein by the insurer, which qualify the effect of such statements, or indicate that a warranty in the strict legal sense *was not intended*, such explanations or qualifications in the application will control. Thus, in a New York case,[1] in an application and policy, the statements of the insured were declared to be warranties and the basis of the contract; but, in the printed form of application furnished by the company under the head of "explanation," it was stated, in substance, that all that was required was good faith, that the assurance could be jeopardized only by dishonesty or inexcusable carelessness; and that, if the application was made in good faith and the conditions fulfilled, premiums paid, etc., the assured might confidently rely upon the payment of the assurance ; and to the policy was annexed a notice to the holder that the payment would be contested only in case of fraud. In an action upon the policy, it was held that the warranty was simply that the statements were made in good faith, and in order to sustain a defense based thereon it was necessary to show not only that the statements were untrue, but that they were known to be so, and were made with a fraudulent intent.

"This document," said RAPALLO, J., "which the applicant is required to sign, concludes with a declaration that his answers to the questions and the written statements in the preceding statement, declaration *or warranty*, together with the statement made to the examining physicians and signed, are *warranties* correct and true, and that there is not concealed, withheld or unmentioned therein any circumstance in relation to the past or present state of the health, habits of life, condition or intentions of the applicant, nor any fact concerning his relatives or ancestry with which the company ought to be made acquainted (without specifying what is the nature of such last mentioned facts) ; also that the statements, etc., shall be the basis and form part of the contract or policy, and if not in all respects true and correct, the policy shall be void. This application was signed by Fitch, the questions being wholly or in part answered by means of the stipulated hieroglyphics, and a policy was thereupon issued on his life in favor of the plaintiff as assured for $3,000. This policy contains a declaration on the part of the company that it is issued in *entire unconditional honest good faith* and with the *just intent* of scrupulously fulfilling all the conditions and engagements of the contract with absolute certainty, and then proceeds to state that *fraud or intentional misrepresentation* violates the

---

[1] *Fitch v. American, etc., Life Ins. Co.*, 59 N. Y. 557.

policy, and that the statements and declarations made in the application are warranties and in all respects true, and do not suppress or omit any fact relative to the insured affecting the interest of the company, or which, whether material or not, would tend to influence the company in taking the risk. To this policy is annexed a notice to the policy-holders of the conditions of the insurance, one of which is that proofs of the loss may be presented at any time, but that *as the payment will be contested only in case of fraud*, it is agreed and provided in order that the facts may be fresh and attainable, that no action on the policy shall be sustainable unless commenced within twelve months after the decease of the insured. It seems to us, looking at all these papers together and considering the character of the minute inquiries made of the applicant, the extravagance of supposing as to many of them that any one could undertake to answer them categorically as required and warrant the answers, or at most do more than express an opinion concerning the subject of them; coupled with the repeated professions of good faith on the part of the company and exhortations to like good faith on the part of the applicant, and the declarations that if the application is made in *good faith* equal to that professed by the company, and the conditions fulfilled, premiums paid, etc., the assured may confidently rely upon *the prompt payment of the assurance by the company as one of the most certain of human events;* that the assurance can be jeopardized only by dishonesty or inexcusable carelessness on the part of the applicant; that *the sole object* is to protect *the honest* from the effects of misstatements by having everything so plain that *a misstatement can be made by intention only;* that *fraud or intentional misrepresentation violates* the *policy,* and that *the payment will be contested only in case of fraud;* the true construction of the papers is that the policy is to be void only in case of intentional and fraudulent misrepresentation or suppression of facts by the applicant, and that although the term warranty is used, yet its legal effect is so modified by the explanations and declarations by which it is accompanied, that it imports no more than an assurance that the statements are made honestly, in good faith, and are believed by the applicant to be correct and true. These explanations and declarations are so inconsistent with the legal effect of a warranty, in the strict legal sense of the term, that both cannot stand together; and to hold the applicant to the strict rules applicable to warranties, would be to entrap him into an agreement which he never intended to make. The statement that payment of the loss will be contested only in case

of fraud, is one easily comprehended by every man of ordinary understanding; and, together with the other plain declarations, explanations and assurances contained in the papers, must have been intended,
and were calculated, to inspire confidence in applicants for insurance
and to induce them to believe that an unintentional and honest mistake or omission on their part, in traveling through the maze of complicated questions put to them, would not be taken advantage of by
the company. *Where a warranty is understandingly and clearly given
by an insured, no matter how immaterial the fact warranted may be, he
will be held strictly to his contract. But when thrown off his guard and
induced to enter into such a contract by declarations of the insurer, such as
appear in this case to have been contained in the papers prepared by the
defendant and evidencing the contract, the declaration in the same papers
that the statements are warranties and the basis of the contract, etc., must
be so construed if possible, as to harmonize with the explanations and declarations of the insurer; and if this is not possible they should be rejected.*
Under this view of the contract it was necessary, in order to sustain the defense, to show not only that the statements were untrue,
but that they were known by the insured so to be, and that they and
the alleged omissions were made intentionally and with a fraudulent
design; and to entitle the defendant to the nonsuit asked, it was necessary that this fraud should be so conclusively proved that there was
no question for the jury."

Where the matter is stated merely by way of description, and is
not material to the risk, it is not to be treated as importing a condition or warranty. Thus, where the assured in the application stated
that the building was tenanted, it was held that the fact that it was
casually vacant, owing to the difficulty of getting a tenant, or by a
bona fide intention to sell, would not work a forfeiture of the policy.[1]

All statements in policy relating to risk are warranties.

SEC. 164. All the conditions set forth in the policy are warranties,
and must be strictly and literally complied with; but they will be construed liberally, and will not be extended by implication beyond the
usual scope of the language used. Thus, where the policy provided
that the risk should not be increased by the assured, it was held that
this was a protection against the erection of a building by him upon
his premises that enhanced the risk;[2] but where the assured owns

---

[1] *Schultz* v. *Merchants' Ins. Co.*, 57 Mo. 331; 5 Ben. F. I. C. 562.
[2] *Murdock* v. *Chenango, etc., Ins. Co.*, 2 N. Y. 210.

adjoining premises, that are described in his application as " vacant," he may build upon *such* lot without avciding the policy. In such cases the insurers are charged with notice, because such is the usual course, that a vacant lot will be built upon whenever the owner sees fit to do so, and if it would avoid the increase of risk thereby, it must expressly stipulate against it.[1] In the case last cited, the right to recover where the assured had built upon an adjoining lot, was made to depend upon the circumstance that the loss did not result from such erection; but this distinction was repudiated in the former case, and a right of recovery held to depend upon no such condition, but to exist as an absolute right.

Where an application states that the premises are occupied by A., this is not a warranty that A. shall continue to occupy them, but is fully met if he *in fact* occupied them when the application was made, although he left them the very next day;[2] and this is so, although A. was a very careful and prudent man, and the tenant who succeeds him is very careless.[3] Unless the policy stipulates against the premises becoming unoccupied, the policy is not avoided by their non-occupancy.[4] When the applicant undertakes to set forth the occupancy of a building, he must state it fully. Thus, if he describes it as " his store," and it turns out that, in fact, his store is in a building occupied as a tavern, and taverns are classed as hazardous, his neglect to state the fact is such a fraudulent concealment of a material fact as will avoid the policy,[5] and he is also debarred from recovery for a loss if he uses, or permits the premises to be used for a purpose that is more hazardous than that for which it was used when insured. Thus, where a barn was insured as a " tavern barn," and there was a condition against increase of risk, it was held that the use of the barn as a " livery stable " was a violation of the condition that invalidated the policy.[6] In all cases, it may be said that, where the policy prohibits certain uses of the property, or the keeping of certain articles, there is a prospective or promissory warranty on the part of the assured that the premises shall not be devoted to such uses, or that such articles shall not be kept; and its breach, whether by the assured

---

[1] *Young* v. *Washington Co. Mut. Ins. Co.*, 14 Barb. (N. Y.) 545; *Stebbins* v. *Globe Ins. Co.*, 2 Hall (N. Y.) 602.

[2] *O'Neil* v. *Buffalo F. Ins. Co.*, 3 N. Y. 122.

[3] *Gates* v. *Madison Co. Ins. Co.*, 5 N. Y. 469.

[4] *O'Neil* v. *Buffalo Ins. Co.*, *ante.*

[5] *Prudhomme* v. *Salamander, etc., Ins. Co.*, 27 La. An. 695.

[6] *Hobly* v. *Dana*, 17 Barb. (N. Y.) 111.

himself or by his tenants, with or without his consent, avoids the policy.[1] So where the assured represents that certain things will be done, or where the policy states that certain things are to be done, as that a chimney of a certain character is to be erected, or that certain safeguards are to be employed, this is a promissory warranty on the part of the assured that must be performed within a reasonable time, if no time is fixed.[2] So where the application or the policy states that a "watch is kept on the premises nights," this is construed, in view of the purposes for which the premises are employed, as a promissory warranty that a suitable watch will be kept while the premises are devoted to such use; and whether it has been substantially kept, or rather, whether a watch suitable, in view of the risk, has been kept, is a question for the jury.[3] So where the policy provides that if the premises are devoted to certain uses, or certain articles are kept or used, an additional premium must be paid; as, if camphene is used for lights, the habitual use of the premises for such purposes, or the keeping or use of such articles for any purpose, violates the conditions of the policy and invalidates it.[4] But where the policy merely prohibits the keeping of certain articles for sale, and then provides that certain kinds of illuminators shall not be used, any illuminator except those expressly prohibited may be used, although embraced in the list of hazardous articles, unless, from the description of the risk, a license to do those things, or keep or use such articles, can be implied.[5]

---

[1] *Mead* v. *North Western Ins. Co.*, 7 N. Y. 530. As to the assured's responsibility for the acts of tenants, see *Duncan* v. *Sun Mut. Ins. Co.*, 6 Wend. (N. Y.) 488.

[2] *Murdock* v. *Chenango Ins. Co., ante.*

[3] *Hovey* v. *Am. Mut. Ins. Co.*, 2 Duer (N. Y.) 554; *Glendale Woolen Co.* v. *Protection Ins. Co.*, 21 Conn. 19; *May* v. *Buckeye Ins. Co.*, 25 Wis. 291

[4] *Westfall* v. *Hudson R. Ins. Co.*, 12 N. Y. 289; *Stelliner* v. *Granite Ins. Co.*, 5 Duer (N. Y.) 594.

[5] *Wall* v. *Howard Ins. Co.*, 14 Barb. (N. Y.) 383; aff'd Ct. of Appeals, 17 N. Y. 197. In *Gates* v. *Madison Co., etc., Ins. Co.*, 5 N. Y. 469, it was held that where a policy contains such a condition, an habitual, and not a casual use is referred to, and that a mere temporary use for such prohibited purpose. See also, *Sand* v. *Citizen's Ins. Co.*, 2 Gray (Mass.) 221; *Shaw* v. *Robberds*, 6 Ad. & El. 75; *Dobson* v. *Sotheby*, 1 M. & M. 90. So where the alleged breach arose from making repairs. Thus, a provision prohibiting the use of the premises for the purpose of carrying on or exercising any trade, etc., and, among others, "house building or repairing," is to be understood as referring to a use of the premises for carrying on the trade of building or repairing houses, and is not broken by making repairs to the building itself. *Grant* v. *Howard Ins. Co.*, 5 Hill (N. Y.) 10. So where the conditions specified certain trades as hazardous, and houses building or repairing were mentioned as insurable only at special rates, and oils and turpentine were classed among articles hazardous. The policy, by its terms, was to become void if the building should be used for any trade or purpose denominated hazardous, or specified in the special rates of insurance annexed, or for the purpose of storing hazardous articles. It was held that the insurers were liable for a loss, although at the time of the loss the dwelling insured was repairing

A warranty is to be construed in reference to the subject-matter to which it relates, *and the knowledge of the insurer* as to the condition of the property. Thus, where a policy upon a building *in the course of construction*, contained a clause " water tanks to be well supplied with water at all times," it is complied with, if the tanks at the commencement of the risk are reasonably advanced towards completion, compared with the then state of the buildings, and their construction is afterwards continued with reasonable dispatch until the time of the fire.[1]

If it be doubtful from the words of a policy whether certain statements made by the insured relative to the subject of insurance are to be regarded as warranties or representations, they will be regarded as representations merely.[2]

and painting, and for that purpose oils and turpentine were introduced. Ordinary repairs on a building insured are covered by such a policy, the object of the restraining clause being only to prevent the habitual use of the building for the specified trade or purpose, and the habitual deposit, in store, of the specified articles. *O'Neil* v. *Buffalo F. Ins. Co.*, 3 N. Y. 122. The things required to be done, by the conditions, are conditions precedent, and excuses for non-performance are not, in general, admissible. Notice of loss given thirty-eight days after the fire, is not given "forthwith," within a requirement to that effect in the conditions, and affords no ground of recovery. *Inman* v. *Western F. Ins. Co.*, 12 Wend. (N. Y.) 452; *McEvers* v. *Lawrence*, Hoffm. Ch. (N. Y.) 172. So where gunpowder was prohibited, putting it in a building for the purpose of blowing it up to stop the spread of a fire, was held not a storing. *City F. Ins. Co.* v. *Corlies*, 21 Wend. (N. Y.) 367; see also, *Hynds* v. *Schenectady Ins. Co.*, 11 N. Y. 554.

[1] *Gloucester Manuf. Co.* v. *Howard Fire Ins. Co.*, 5 Gray (Mass.) 497.

[2] Thus, in *Wilson* v. *Conway Fire Ins. Co.*, 4 R. I. 141, where the written application for a policy contained, amongst others, the following questions and answers: " Are the works operated on account of the proprietors, or are they rented ? Ans. By the proprietor. Are they immediately superintended by one of the proprietors? If not, by whom ? Ans. Yes;" which answers were both untrue. It was held that evidence was inadmissible to show that these misstatements were under the circumstances immaterial to the risk ; since, whether they were to be regarded as warranted or not, they were, being asked and answered, made by the parties material as representations, and so their truth made a condition of the policy, whether they were in fact material or not. In *Wilson* v. *Hampden Ins. Co.*, 4 R. I. 159, which was an action for a loss growing out of the burning of the same property as the previous case, the court held that in construing the answers to the interrogatories in an application, although the proper meaning of the words used is to be first resorted to, yet the meaning attached by the applicant to them, clearly ascertainable from the connection in which he uses them, is to prevail over their proper meaning. Inaccuracies in the answers to such interrogatories, caused by the ambiguity of the interrogatories, taken in their connection with each other, are to be charged to the account of the insurers who prepared the applications. Where the applicant for insurance on a cotton mill and machinery, to previous questions had answered that the buildings and machinery, with certain specified exceptions, belonged to one person, himself, and that certain machinery, not to be insured in the policy, belonged to one A. H., and that "the works" were not operated by the proprietors but were rented, and in reply to the question, "Are they (the works) immediately superintended by one of the proprietors?" answers "Yes;" the answer is sufficiently verified by the fact, that "the works" were superintended by the tenant A. H., in common parlance, a "proprietor," as distinguished from his employees, and who actually owned a part of the machinery run in the works, whether the meaning intended to be conveyed, or actually conveyed by the answer, under the circumstances, be considered.

CHAPTER IV.

PROMISSORY WARRANTIES.

Promissory warranties, what are.

SEC. 165. Promissory warranties, or an agreement or assurance by the insured that certain things shall be done, must be strictly and literally performed, or rather *actually* performed. It has been held in several cases, that such warranties are met by a substantial compliance;[1] but it seems to be pretty well settled that the compliance must be strict and literal. Thus, in a New York case,[2] where the application or survey was referred to and made a part of the policy, it was held that an answer made by the applicant to an inquiry, "Is there a watchman kept in the building during the night?" that "there is a watchman nights," was a promissory warranty on the part of the assured that a watch should be kept there every night during the life of the policy, and that such warranty was broken by a failure to keep a watch there from twelve o'clock Saturday night until twelve o'clock Sunday night, and the policy thereby avoided. And it was held that evidence of a custom on the part of similar establishments in the

---

[1] *Percival* v. *Maine Ins. Co.*, 33 Me. 242; *Hovey* v. *Am. Mut. Ins. Co.*, 2 Duer (N. Y.) 554; *Parker* v. *Bridgeport Ins. Co.*, 10 Gray (Mass.) 202; *Crocker* v. *Peoples' Mut. Ins. Co.*, 8 Cush. (Mass.) 79.

[2] *Ripley* v. *Ætna Ins. Co.*, 30 N. Y. 136.

vicinity, not to have a watchman during such period, was not admissible to control the warranty.[1]

The parties make their own contract, and the only office of the courts is to construe and effectuate the contract made. It cannot add to, or detract from it, but must carry out the evident purpose and intention of the parties, clearly expressed in the contract, however great may be the hardship to either party, and it is not for the court to say that this condition or that shall not be enforced, or be regarded as operative, because not material to the risk; it is enough that they agreed upon it, however foolish, improvident, or immaterial.[2] But in order to make a representation a warranty, it must be made so by the terms of the policy itself, or by some direct reference therein to the representation, or to papers in which it is contained, which are adopted as a part of the policy,[3] as the survey,[4] the application,[5] or any other documents referred to in the policy, as the charter of the company, by-laws, etc., and made a part of it.[6] This must also be regarded as subject to the qualification that there is nothing in the policy, or the documents referred to, that shows that the statements made were to be regarded rather as representations than as warranties.[7] Thus, in the

---

[1] *First National Bank* v. *Ins. Co. of North America*, 50 N. Y. 48. See, as to effect of custom upon the construction of conditions, *Citizen's Ins. Co.* v. *McLaughlin*, 53 Penn. St. 485. In *First National Bank* v. *Ins. Co.*, 5 Lans. (N. Y.) 203; aff'd 50 N. Y. 48, it was held that, where by a policy of insurance, the owner of a mill was required to keep a watchman on the premises nights, the condition must be strictly performed, and the fact that the sheriff had levied upon the property and locked up the building, and taken away the key, did not excuse the omission, and that the warranty was not satisfied by the presence of the sheriff, during the night, who did not undertake the duty of watchman, in a shed two rods from the building, although he entered and examined the mill twice during the night. In *N. Y. Belting Co.* v. *Washington F. Ins. Co.*, 10 Bos. (N. Y.) 428; *Sayles* v. *N. W. Ins. Co.*, 2 Curtis (U. S.) 610; *Gloucester Manuf. Co.* v. *Howard F. Ins. Co.*, 5 Gray (Mass.) 497; *Crocker* v. *Peoples' F. Ins. Co.*, 8 Cush. (Mass.) 79; *Lee* v. *Howard Ins. Co.*, 3 Gray (Mass.) 583; *Lawless* v. *Tenn. F. Ins. Co.*, Hunts' Mer. Mag. Feb. 7, 1853, 205; *Glen* v. *Lewis*, 8 Excheq. 607; *Aurora F. Ins. Co.* v, *Eddy*, 49 Ill. 106; *Percival* v. *Maine, etc., Ins. Co.*, 33 Me. 242; 3 Ben. F. I. C. 314; *Hovey* v. *American Ins. Co.*, 2 Duer (N. Y.) 554.

[2] *State Mut. Fire Ins. Co.* v. *Arthur*, 30 Penn. St. 315.

[3] *Daniels* v. *Hudson River, etc., Ins. Co.*, 12 Cush. (Mass.) 416; *Wilson* v. *Conway Fire Ins. Co.*, 4 R. I. 141; *Wall* v. *Howard Ins. Co.*, 14 Barb. (N. Y.) 383.

[4] *Jennings* v. *Chenango Ins. Co.*, 2 Den. (N. Y.) 75; *Farmers' Ins. Co.* v. *Snyder*, 16 Wend. (N. Y.) 481; *Ripley* v. *Ætna etc., Ins. Co.*, 30 N. Y. 136.

[5] *Garcelon* v. *Hampden, etc., Ins. Co.*, 50 Me. 580; *Draper* v. *Charter Oak Ins. Co.*, 2 Allen (Mass.) 564; *Ripley* v. *Ætna, etc., Ins. Co.*, ante; *Kennedy* v. *St. Lawrence Co., etc., Ins. Co.*, 10 Barb. (N. Y.) 285; *Tebbetts* v. *Hamilton, etc., Ins. Co.*, 1 Allen (Mass.) 385; see same case, 3 Allen, 569; *Kentucky Ins. Co.* v. *Southard*, 8 B. Mon. (Ky.) 634; 2 Benn. F. I. C. 765; *Delonguemare* v. *Tradesmen's Ins. Co.*, ante; *Jefferson* v. *Cotheal*, ante.

[6] *Commonwealth Ins. Co.* v. *Monninger*, 18 Ind. 352; *Suneral* v. *Dubuque, etc., Ins. Co.*, 18 Iowa, 319.

[7] *Houghton* v. *Manufacturers', etc., Ins. Co.*, 8 Met. (Mass.) 114.

Case referred to in the last note, the application and the answers made thereto were termed *representations* in the policy, and the court held that, inasmuch as the contract undertook to fix the character of the application and answers therein given, the character so given thereto in the policy, should be adopted, and the application and answers should be treated as representations and not as warranties. But this is, of course, subject to the qualification that the policy does not, in direct terms, provide that such *representations* are to be treated as warranties, as in such a case they would be treated as made warranties by the agreement of the parties. In a Maine case,[1] a doctrine similar to that held in the Massachusetts case, was adopted. In that case, the applicant covenanted in his application that it contained " a just, full and true exposition of all the facts and circumstances in regard to. the condition, situation, value, and risk of the property to be insured, so far as the same are known to the applicant, *and are material to the risk*, and the policy declared the application a part of the policy, and that it is made and accepted *upon the representation of the assured in his application*. The court held that, from the language used in the policy, it was doubtful whether the answers of the assured could be regarded as warranties, but that in any view, taken in connection with the application, they must be treated as qualified by the statement therein, " so far as material to the risk," and could not be available as avoiding the policy, unless they were, in fact, shown to be material, thus putting them upon the same ground as mere representations, and establishing the doctrine that a warranty will not be raised when the language used in the contract itself leaves it doubtful whether the answers were so intended or treated by the parties.

Failure to keep warranty avoids policy.

SEC. 166. Where the assured, expressly or by fair implication, promises to do a specific act in reference to the risk, a failure to do it will avoid the policy, and if it relates to some change in the building, or its use, and no time is named in which it shall be done, he will be required to do it in a *reasonable* time; and as to what is a reasonable time, is a question for the jury in reference to the materiality of the change, its character, and the evident expectation of the parties from the circumstances existing at the time when the application was made. Thus, where the insured in his application, which was made a part of the policy, stated that there was one stove in the building, and that

---

[1] *Garcelon v. Hampden, etc., Ins. Co.*

the pipe passed through the window, but that a stove chimney would be built and the pipe pass into it at the side; it was held that this amounted to a warranty that a chimney should be built *within a reasonable time*, a violation of which would avoid the policy. And where, after the insurance, no chimney was built, but the stove was removed to another part of the building, and the pipe passed through a stone fixed in the roof, and the secretary of the company indorsed upon the policy "consent is given that the within policy remain good notwithstanding the stove has been removed;" it was held that this did not waive compliance with the terms of the warranty.[1]

Warranty construed in reference to risk, and beneficially to insured.

SEC. 167. No particular form of words is necessary; it is enough if the language is such, as applied to the risk, to indicate that it was the intention of the parties that a certain thing should be done, or a certain state of things continue,[2] and the language must be such as to leave no doubt that a continuing warranty was intended. As in case of doubt, it will be treated either as a mere representation or a warranty *in presenti*.[3] *In no case will the courts extend the warranty beyond its apparent scope.* Nothing will be implied, but the rights of the parties will be determined by the language used. A warranty will neither be extended or created by construction; it must clearly appear either in express terms or as a *necessary* result from the nature of the contract.[4] The rule is, that *representations in a policy are construed to be warranties when it is apparent that they had in themselves, or in the view of the parties, a tendency to induce the company to enter into the contract on terms more advantageous to the insured than without them.*[5]

The contract must embrace everything relied upon by the assured, and nothing can be imported into it by parol. There can be no warranty except as to matters *stated and written or printed in the contract,*

---

[1] *Murdock* v. *Chenango, etc., Ins. Co.,* 2 N. Y. 210.

[2] *Stout* v. *City F. Ins. Co.,* 12 Iowa, 371; *Jennings* v. *Chenango Ins. Co.,* 2 Den. (N. Y.) 75; *Wilson* v. *Conway Ins Co.,* 4 R. I. 141; *Bornadaih* v. *Hunter,* 5 M. & G. 639; *Murdock* v. *Chenango Ins. Co.,* 2 N. Y. 210; *Glendale Woolen Co.* v. *Protection Ins. Co.,* 21 Conn. 19; *Sayles* v. *N. W. Ins. Co.,* 2 Curtis (U. S.) 610.

[3] *Sheldon* v. *Hartford F. Ins. Co.,* 22 Conn. 235; *Lindsey* v. *Union Ins. Co.,* 3 R. I. 157; *Delongusmare* v. *Tradesman's Ins. Co.,* 2 Hall (N. Y.) 489; *Frisbie* v. *Fayette Ins. Co.,* 27 Penn. St. 325; *Wall* v. *Howard Ins. Co.,* 14 Barb. (N. Y.) 483; *Garcelon* v. *Hampton F. Ins. Co.,* 50 Me. 580; *Jefferson Ins. Co.* v. *Cotheal,* 7 Wend. (N. Y.) 72; *Lycoming Ins. Co.* v. *Mitchell,* 48 Penn. St. 367.

[4] *Jefferson Ins. Co.* v. *Cotheal, ante.*

[5] *Frisbie* v. *Fayette Ins. Co., ante.*

but representations may be either in writing or by parol. If, however, written representations are made, parol representations are excluded, the writing is presumed to embrace all that were made, or that were required by the insurer, but, if no written application exists and parol representations were made, in reliance upon which the policy was issued, they may be proved.[1]

Aurora Fire Ins. Co. v. Eddy—Smoking—Buckets filled with water—Stoves used in Building.

SEC. 168. *Warranties are to be construed according to the evident intent of the parties in view of the language used, the subject-matter to which they relate, and the matters naturally or usually incident thereto. Impossible matters are not within their provisions, neither are unusual matters, where a fixed and definite usage exists, nor unlawful acts, unless the stipulation is specific and imposes an absolute duty upon the assured, which excludes the idea that the warranty is limited in any of these respects.*[2] This rule, as well as the distinction between a warranty *in presenti* and a continuing warranty, as well as the true rule for construing warranties, is most excellently illustrated in an Illinois case.[3] In that case, there was a stipulation in the policy that the assured should keep eight buckets filled with water on the first floor and four in the basement, for use at all times in case of fire; also, that smoking was prohibited in or about the buildings. There was also a statement in the application that no stoves were used to heat the buildings. The defendant claimed that there was a breach of these warranties on the part of the plaintiff. The facts appear in the opinion of WALKER, J., which is so valuable as a guide to the true interpretation of contracts of this class that I give the main portions of it here. He said: "There was a stipulation in the policy that the assured should keep eight buckets filled with water on the first floor where the machinery was run, and four in the basement by the reservoir, ready for use in case of fire. In considering the case when previously before us, we held that a reasonable construction of this clause required that while, from freezing or unavoidable causes, a literal compliance with the warranty might have been impossible, and could not have been in the contemplation of the par-

---

[1] *Boardman* v. *N. H. Mut. F. Ins. Co.*, 20 N. H. 551; *Glendale Woolen Co.* v. *Protection Ins. Co.*, 21 Conn. 19; *Lycoming Ins. Co.* v. *Mitchell*, 48 Penn. St. 367; *Witherell* v. *Maine Ins. Co.*, 49 Me. 200; *Nicoll* v. *American Ins. Co.*, 5 W. & M. (U. S. C. C.) 529; *Snyder* v. *Farmer's Ins. Co.*, 13 Wend. (N. Y.) 92. See *Wainwright* v. *Bland*, 1 M. & W. 32.

[2] See very able opinion of LEARNED, P.J., in *Whitney* v. *Black River Ins. Co.*, 9 Hun (N. Y.) 36, as to effect of the character of the risk upon the construction of the policy.

[3] *Aurora F. Ins. Co.* v. *Eddy*, 50 Ill. 106.

ties, still, it was incumbent on the assured to show that the required number of buckets, in good and serviceable condition, were at the places designated in the agreement, ready for instant use. This being the requirement, it devolved upon the assured to prove that he had complied therewith. On that question, there was some contrariety in the evidence, which the jury were required to reconcile, or, if unable to do so, then to give weight to such as they believed to be true. In such cases, it is the province of the jury to carefully weigh the whole of the evidence, and to find according to its weight, and the presumption is, that they have done so, unless we see from the record that they misunderstood or disregarded the proof. The court will not disturb their finding on any question, unless it appears clearly to be unsupported. In this case, while we might have arrived at a different conclusion, we are not prepared to say that there were not the required number of buckets in their places, in good order and ready for instant use. The testimony on this question introduced by appellee is more positive and affirmative in its character than that of appellants. The witnesses of the latter, in the main, only say they did not see the buckets, but fail to state that they had searched for the buckets, or had their attention called to the matter. It is true, that two of them say they had, at one time, occasion to use some buckets but only found six. This may have been true, and the proper number still have been in the mill. Dodds, on his examination in chief, seems to be positive as to the want of buckets, but the value of this testimony is greatly impaired by his cross-examination, when he was not at all positive on the subject. On the other hand, appellee's witnesses all examined expressly to see if the buckets were there. At most, it seems to be no more than doubtful whether the buckets were all there; but it is by no means clear, nor is there a clear preponderance of evidence, that there was not the requisite number.

It is next urged that there was smoking allowed in the factory, contrary to the stipulation in the policy. It was agreed, that smoking should be strictly prohibited in and about the premises. Eddy swears he prohibited smoking in and about the building, and this was a literal compliance with his part of the agreement to prohibit smoking. In the case of The Insurance Co. of North America v. McDowell, 50 Ill. 121, it was stated, in answer to a question propounded to the assured, and which became a part of the conditions upon which the policy was issued, that smoking was not allowed. And it appears there had been smoking by some of the employees about the mill, but as soon as the attention of the assured was called to the fact that it was contrary to the terms of the policy, he forbid it, and put up a notice that it was not allowed. It was there held, that in such a case the assured only undertakes that he himself will not do the act, or allow others to do so, if by reasonable precaution he can prevent it. In this case appellee prohibited smoking, and there is no evidence that he had any notice that his orders had been disregarded, so as to require him to resort to other and more energetic steps for its prevention. He did not agree that, if there should be smoking in or about the buildings, the policy should be void. He, or any man who is at all qualified to transact the most ordinary business, would not enter into such an engagement, as strangers and others over whom he had no control were liable to smoke about the buildings. Had the evidence shown that his orders were disregarded, and that it had come to his knowledge, then a different question would have been presented for our consideration. But the jury were, under the evidence before them, warranted in finding appellee had used reasonable efforts to prevent smoking in or about the buildings.

It is next urged that there was a violation of the condition, that if the title to the property should be transferred or changed, the policy should be void. It appears that when the property was insured Eddy was only the owner of the equity of redemption, Town then holding a mortgage on the premises, and loss, if any, was payable to Town, as his interest might show. Subsequently, appellee conveyed the premises, with other property, to Brown, and he, at the same time, and as a part of the same transaction, gave back to appellee a defeasance. This arrangement was made to enable Eddy to take up his mortgage to Town, which was done, and to procure means for other purposes. That this conveyance and defeasance only constituted a mortgage, is so obvious that the citation of authorities to establish the proposition is wholly unnecessary.

The question is then presented whether the execution of a mortgage on the premises was such a change or transfer of the property as rendered the policy void. It was but an equity of redemption that was insured, and this transaction still left appellee as fully the owner of the equity of r demption as he was at the time the insurance was effected. This was not, therefore, any change or transfer of title in appellee, but the only change was, that a different person held the mortgage, and it was, perhaps, for a different amount. But appellee's title was the same. But even if this were not so, still, the execution of a mortgage on the insured premises has been held, in the case of the Commercial Ins. Co. v. Spanknable, 52 Ill. 53, not to be a sale, alienation, conveyance, transfer, or change of title, such as is prohibited by a similar clause in a policy, and that the right to insist upon such a forfeiture is *stricti juris;* that liberal intendments and enlarged constructions will not be indulged in favor of such forfeitures. They must be brought clearly within the forfeiting clause. This, then, disposes of that question.

It is also urged that, by erecting and putting into operation machinery for the manufacture of rope increased the hazard and avoided the policy. It appears that at the time the risk was taken appellee notified the agent that he intended to put in rope machinery, and he inquired whether it would affect the policy, and was informed it would not, as the term flax factory was broad enough to embrace it, and we have no doubt he was correct in his definition of the term flax factory. It is believed to be quite common in such establishments to manufacture rope. It is a usual part of the business, and for that reason we incline to the opinion that this was no breach of the condition. But if it was, still the agent of the company assured appellee that it would not be, and shall appellee be misled when he is procuring a policy, and induced to take one that he intends, and the agent of the company assures him is broad enough to cover rope works, when it does not, and shall appellants now be heard to say, it is true our agent misled appellee, and induced him to do an act that we knew would avoid his policy, and thus enable us to obtain the premium when we incurred no risk? A court of justice would never sanction such a fraud, and thus enable parties to obtain and enforce such an unjust advantage. The agent was acting within the scope of his authority, and was, when appellants authorized him to take policies, empowered to give a construction to the written portion of the policy, if no more, and the company must be held estopped by this declaration of their agent. The instruction given on behalf of appellee, on that question, was proper.

It is also urged that there was a breach of the warranty in the policy, that no stoves were used. The question was asked, ' How is the building warmed? If any stoves and pipes, how are they secured?' To this, it was answered, 'No stoves used.' Appellee agreed in the application, that if any untrue answer was given therein the insurance was to be void, and the policy of no effect. It is not contended that the buildings, or any part of them, were then warmed by a stove, but that one was subsequently used for the purpose, and that this representation was a continuing one, and was a warranty that a stove would not be used for warming purposes. In the case of Schmidt v. The Peoria Fire & Marine Ins. Co., 41 Ill. 295, a similar representation was held not to be a continuing warranty that there should be no fire in the tannery, except under the boiler, as represented, during the life of the policy, but only a representation of the condition of the property at the time the policy was issued. We will not give a forced construction to language to enable a party to enforce a forfeiture, but rather adhere to the natural import of the words used. In this case the questions and answers are in the present and not in the future tense. The use, then, of the stove was not a breach of the warranty. But if used recklessly it might be regarded as increasing the risk. Dodd testifies, that on the evening of the loss he made a fire and heated it red hot. But he says that the principal or foreman, or Eddy, was not there, and he says Ticknor, Turner or Eddy never directed him to make a fire in the stove, and he says 'the bosses' did not want him to make the fire, but he was asked to do so by the girls who worked in the factory, that they might warm their feet before going home. Hoborn also testified, that he had seen fire in the stove and that he had seen it red hot. Other witnesses, who had better opportunities of seeing and knowing the facts, speak of seeing fire in the stove, but do not speak of its being unusually hot; and it was for the jury to say, whether it was used in a grossly negligent manner, and they have found it was not, and seem not to have given much weight to the evidence of Dodd and Hoborn, and from the uncertainty they manifest in reference to other matters about which they testify, we are not prepared to say that it was entitled to receive more weight than was given to it."

Appellants asked, but the court refused to give, this instruction :

'The jury are instructed, that so far as relates to the question of buckets, the policy requires that the plaintiff must keep ' at all times ready for use in case of fire, four buckets of water' in the basement story and eight buckets on the middle floor; and the plaintiff must show affirmatively that he did substantially so keep said buckets of water, and if he has not proved these facts, the jury must find for the defendant.'

While this instruction may not be entirely incorrect, it was certainly calculated to mislead. What would amount to a substantial compliance with a contract, is very indefinite, and a question about which well founded differences might exist. This form of instruction was held to be erroneous when this case was previously before this court. We then but followed the decision on the same point in the case of Taylor v. Beck, 13 Ill. 336. The court below had already given an instruction, clear, definite, and free from misapprehension on this question. It was this:

If the jury believe from the evidence that buckets could not be kept in the mill filled with water all the time, in accordance with the literal provisions of the policy, because of freezing, then a literal compliance with the said provisions of the policy concerning buckets, was not required and could not have been in the contemplation of the parties when the policy was made, but all that was required by the plaintiff in order to comply with such stipulation was to have the required number of buckets in good and serviceable condition at the proper places ready for instant use.'

This is the construction we gave in the former opinion, on the previous trial. The instruction on this point, as well as all others, is free from objection. It presented the law of the case fairly to the jury.

It is objected that the court below permitted appellee to introduce evidence tending to prove a promise by the president and secretary of the company to pay the loss, after it had occurred. The evidence was proper for the consideration of the jury. It might reasonably be inferred from such evidence, that these officers had carefully examined the circumstances of the loss, and become convinced it was a fair one, and was properly payable. It would certainly be evidence to that, if to no greater extent, and it was clearly admissible.

After a careful examination of this record, we fail to perceive any error requiring a reversal of the judgment, and it must, therefore, be affirmed."

Rule in Ripley v. Ætna Ins. Co. Watchman. Duty to keep on Sundays.

SEC. 169. The distinction between a warranty subject to the qualifications stated in the previous rule, and one where such a construction is excluded by the language used, was well illustrated in a New York case,[1] in which in answer to a question in the application, whether there was a watch kept in the mill nights, the insured answerd "*there is a watchman* nights." The application was referred to and made a part of the policy, and the court held that this constituted a warranty that there should be a watchman in the building *every* night, and that,

---

[1] *Ripley* v. *Ætna Ins. Co.*, 30 N. Y. 136.

it being conceded that no watch was kept from twelve o'clock Saturday night until twelve o'clock Sunday night, the warranty was broken
and the company released from liability, even though the loss had no
connection with the breach. The court also held that the language
was so explicit as to exclude evidence of a custom of similar establishments *not* to keep a watch during that period. It is proper to say,
however, that there was at the time this decision was rendered, no
statute in New York prohibiting secular labor upon Sunday, so that
that question was not raised or passed upon by the courts. But in a
Connecticut case,[1] the question was presented under a policy issued
in and controlled by the laws of Massachusetts, and the point was
made that the keeping of a watchman between the hours of twelve
o'clock Saturday nights and twelve o'clock Sunday nights, was unlawful under the statutes of Massachusetts, but it will be seen by a reference to the opinion of the court that the statute was not proved, and
the court did not seem to be informed whether there was such a statute or not. It is true the court intimated that the existence of such a
statute would make no difference, as, even though the warranty
required the doing of an unlawful act, it was obligatory. But this
doctrine can hardly prevail. The courts are hardly inclined to uphold
a provision of a contract that requires the violation of a penal statute
by the other party, *particularly when the contract will bear a contrary
construction;* and a *contrary* and much more acceptable doctrine was
held in a Wisconsin case,[2] the *gist* of which is given elsewhere in this
work.

Custom of Trade. Incidents of business.

SEC. 170. An insurer is bound to know of the existence of customs
or usages incident to any business that he undertakes to insure,[3] as well
as all the risks usually incident thereto, and when he takes a risk,
he is presumed to contemplate all the perils connected with it, to the
minutest detail thereof, so far as the same are usually connected
therewith, in the prosecution of the business,[4] and even though the

---

[1] *Glendale Woolen Co.* v. *The Protection Ins. Co.*, 21 Conn. 19.

[2] *Prieger* v. *Exchange Ins. Co.*, 6 Wis. 86.

[3] *May* v. *Buckeye Ins. Co.*, 25 Wis., 291. In *Sims* v. *State Ins. Co.*, 47 Mo. 54 ; 4
Am. Rep. 311, the defendants insured a tobacco warehouse, and the assured stated
the use of the building to be a "tobacco pressing, no manufacturing." Hogsheads
were manufactured in a shed adjoining. The court held that it was for the jury to
say whether the manufacture of hogsheads was an incident of the business.

[4] In *United States, etc., Ins. Co.* v. *Kimberley*, 34 Md. 224 ; 6 Am. Rep. 325, a
policy was issued "on a four-story warehouse * * * first floor occupied by
machinery used for making barrels, with privilege of storing barrels on the

particulár business insured is not conducted in the usual manner, yet,
if the insurer sends an agent to examine the risk, he is presumed to
act upon the knowledge of such agent as to all matters apparent to
observation or which would have been ascertained upon reasonable
examination and inquiry, and he cannot defend against the policy
upon the ground that he was misled as to the risk in any matter
chargeable to the fault, ignorance or incapacity of the agent. As to
all the ordinary, apparent hazards he is presumed to act upon such
agent's knowledge and examination, and is estopped from setting up
false representations or fraudulent concealment of facts by the assured
relating thereto.[1] Thus, where the defendant took a risk on a sulphuric
acid manufactory, and machinery, and chemical apparatus connected
with the establishment, it was held that they must be presumed to
know the methods of the business and the incidents of the risk, and,
having sent an agent to examine the risk before taking it, they were
estopped from repudiating their liability upon the ground of fraud on
the part of the assured, as to matters which it was the business of the
agent to have seen and known.[2]

How extent of warranty is determined.

SEC. 171. In construing a warranty in an application, every part
of it relating to the matter to which the warranty pertains, must be
taken and construed together ; and the warranty, modified or enlarged
by every matter pertaining thereto, is to determine the rights and obli-

---

premises, and other merchandise not more hazardous." The policy contained a
clause requiring a true and accurate description of the use and occupation of the
premises, under the penalty of forfeiture. The policy further declared, in printed
words, that it was the intention of the parties that in case the insured premises
should be used or appropriated for the purpose of carrying on or exercising the
trade, business or vocation of (a large number of manufactures specified therein,
including) "cooper, carpenter, cabinetmaker," * * * "so long as the said
premises shall be wholly or in part appropriated or used for any or either of the
purposes aforesaid, these premises shall cease and be of no force or effect unless
otherwise specially agreed by this corporation, and such agreement shall be signed
in writing in or on the policy." The premises, at the time the insurance was
effected, were used for making and storing barrels as mentioned in the written
portion of the policy. Subsequently small circular saws and a work-bench were
introduced and boxes were manufactured, but this kind of work had ceased from
two to four months when a loss by fire occurred. The saws and work-bench had
remained in the building and a lathe had been put up the day preceding the fire,
for the purpose of making broom-handles and brush-blocks. In an action on
the policy, *held,* (1) that the description of the property was not a *continuing*
warranty, but a warranty *in presenti;* (2) that the policy was suspended during
the prohibited use of the premises, but was revived when the use ceased to
exist ; and (3) that there was no such "appropriation" of the premises, at the
time of the fire, to a prohibited use as was contemplated in the policy or as
prevented a recovery.

[1] *Washington, etc., Ins. Co.* v. *Davidson,* 30 Md. 91.

[2] *Washington, etc., Ins. Co.* v. *Davidson, ante.*

gation of the insurer.[1] Thus, in the case last referred to, the plaintiff, in answer to an inquiry, stated that he was the owner of the property, and that no other person had an interest therein; but in answer to a question as to incumbrances, he answered, "by contract." He was in possession under a contract for a deed, but the premises had not been conveyed to him. The insurer claimed that this constituted a breach of warranty as to title; but the court held that all his statements in reference to title must be taken together, and that the last answer qualified the first in such a way as to preclude the insurer from setting up a warranty of absolute ownership, or exclusive interest, and, as a whole, truthfully set forth his interest in the premises.

The *language* of the policy is to be looked to, and the *intention of the parties* is to be gathered from that, if possible, and the language is always to be construed *most liberally for the assured*. If it can be construed so as to prevent a forfeiture, it will be so construed; because forfeitures are *odious* to the law, and the insurer, selecting his own language, is presumed to use such as expresses his intention and excludes every use of the premises which he desires to exclude. Thus, where a policy provided that, if gunpowder, saltpetre, phosphorus, etc., were kept on the premises, or if camphene, burning fluid, refined coal or earth oils were kept for sale, stored or used on the premises *in quantities exceeding one barrel* at any one time, it was held that the keeping of *gunpowder* in quantities less than one barrel did not avoid the policy, because, by a fair construction of the policy, such was the expressed intention of the assured, although a contrary construction might be put upon it, and probably, *in fact*, was what the insurer intended.[2]

The conditions or statements in a policy may constitute both an affirmative and promissory warranty, as where the policy describes the building as "occupied for stores below, the upper portion to remain unoccupied during the continuance of this policy," the portion relating to the lower part of the building is an affirmative warranty that is met, if true when the policy was made, but that portion of it relating to the upper stories is a promissory warranty that is broken, if *at any time* during the life of the policy, the upper portion of the building is occupied.[3] In all cases, if the description merely relates to the present condition of the property, *and there is nothing in the policy to indicate*

[1] *McCulloch* v. *Norwood*, 58 N. Y. 563.

[2] *Ins. Co.* v. *Slaughter*, 12 Wall. (U. S.) 404.

[3] *Stout* v. *City F. Ins. Co.*, 12 Iowa, 371; 4 Ben. F. I. C. 556.

that the state of things then existing is to remain as described, the warranty is merely affirmative, and is met, if true when made; but if from the language of the policy *and the usages of the business* insured, or which is carried on upon the premises, it is evident that the parties contracted in reliance upon a continuance of the state of things described. *That the usages and incidents of the business* are to be considered in determining this question, has been held in numerous cases. In policies in which it is stated, " a night watch kept," it is held that this amounts to a warranty that a *suitable* watch shall be kept, according to the usuages of such business during the life of the policy, so long as the property is devoted to such uses.[1] So when the building is described as a barn, "no fire is kept and no hazardous goods deposited," while there is a warranty that the building shall not be devoted to a more hazardous purpose, yet a temporary hazardous use, essential to the repair of it, does not avoid the policy, because it is an *incident* of the risk,[2] and the same is true even as to express conditions in the policy, when the description of the business is such that, taken in connection *with its usual incidents* it imports a license to do certain prohibited things. *Generally*, it may be said that *a description relating to the occupancy of a building is a warranty in presenti, and does not amount to a warranty that such occupancy shall continue during the life of the policy*,[3] or that a certain state of things shall continue,[4] but it does import a warranty that the hazards of the risk shall not be materially increased, but any change not producing such a result, is not a breach of warranty.[5]

---

[1] *May* v. *Buckeye Mut. Ins. Co.*, 25 Wis. 291; *Prieger* v. *Exchange, etc., Ins. Co.*, 6 id. 89.

[2] *Dobson* v. *Sotheby*, M. & M. 90; *Catlin* v. *Springfield Ins. Co.*, 1 Sum. (U. S.) 434; *Billings* v. *Tolland Ins. Co.*; *Land* v. *Citizen's Ins. Co.*; *Shaw* v. *Robberds*, Ad. & El.; *Williams* v. *N. E., etc., Ins. Co.*, 31 Me. 219.

[3] *O'Niel* v. *Buffalo F. Ins. Co.*, 3 N. Y. 122; *Frisbie* v. *Fayette, etc., Ins. Co.*, 27 Penn. St. 325; *United States F. & M. Ins. Co.* v. *Kimberly*, 34 Md. 224; *Prieger* v. *Exchange Ins. Co., ante*; *May* v. *Buckeye Ins. Co., ante*; *Maher* v. *Hibernian Ins. Co.*, 6 Hun (N. Y.) 353; *Smith* v. *Mechanic's, etc., Ins. Co.*, 32 N. Y. 399.

[4] *Schmidt* v. *Peoria, etc., Ins. Co.*, 41 Ill. 295; *Cumberland Valley, etc., Protection Co.* v. *Schell*, 29 Penn. St. 31; *Catlin* v. *Springfield F. M. Ins. Co., ante*.

[5] *Whitehead* v. *Price*, 5 Tryw. 825. In *Mayall* v. *Mitford*, 6 Ad. & El. 670, the policy covered cotton mills, warranted brick built. The policy stated that they were warmed and worked by steam, lighted by gas, and worked by day only. Plea: the steam engine, upright and horizontal shafts, parts of said mills were, without leave of insurers, worked by night, and not by day only. Replications: that the engine, upright and horizontal shafts, were not part of said mills, and were not, without leave of insurers, worked by night, and not by day only. The jury found the issues upon that plea for the defendants. Motion for judgment *non obstante veredicto*. It was held that the plaintiff was entitled to judgment,

Sec. 172. When the policy provides that a watchman shall be kept nights, it is construed as binding the assured to keep a watchman on the premises *every* night, until the usual hours for resuming work in the morning;[1] but unless the language is specific, and requires the watchman to be kept *constantly* on the premises, the question as to whether the warranty has been broken by a temporary absence of the watchman from the premises, is for the jury, and, as bearing upon the question, the usage of other similar establishments in this respect is admissible;[2] but in order to make evidence of a usage in this respect admissible, it must either be so general that the courts will presume that the insurer had notice of its existence, or it must be shown that he in fact had knowledge thereof, so that it will be presumed that the parties contracted in reference to it. "For this purpose," said Mullen, J.,[3] "the custom must be established, and not casual,—uniform, and not varying,—general, and not personal, *and known to the parties.*" The court fell into an error, which resulted from the wrong use of terms. There is a wide distinction between an usage and a custom. Long usage makes custom, but it is not every usage that amounts to a custom, but only such usages as have become so fixed and permanent in connection with a particular business as to have become an incident thereof *and a law thereunto.* When an usage has ripened into a custom, no proof except of the existence of the custom is necessary, because the law presumes all persons to be aware of it; but an usage simply, must not only be shown to exist, but also it must be shown that the parties *knew* of its existence. At common law, custom is *immemorial usage—usage so long continued that its origin cannot be discovered.* If its inception can be shown, upon the ground that thereby the person by whose particular will it was originated

---

notwithstanding the verdict, for the plea was bad, because working a part of the machinery at night was not working the mills at night. In *Aurora F. Ins. Co.* v. *Eddy,* 55 Ill. 213, the application—made a part of the policy—stated that no stoves were used in the building. A stove was subsequently put into the building to heat it, and the court held that this was not a breach of the warranty. That the language did not amount to a promise on the part of the assured *that no stoves should be used therein.*

[1] *Crocker* v. *People's Ins. Co.,* 8 Cush. (Mass.) 79; 3 Bennett's F. I. C. 234; *Ripley* v. *Ætna Ins. Co.,* 29 Barb. (N. Y.) 552; *Glendale Woolen Co.* v. *Protection Ins. Co.,* 21 Conn. 19; 3 Bennett's F. I. C. 213.

[2] *Crocker* v. *People's Ins. Co., ante,* the policy contained this clause, "a machine shop; a watchman kept on the premises." There was no watchman at the time of the fire, and had been none for some ten days prior to the fire. *May* v. *Buckeye Ins. Co.,* 25 Wis. 291. But see *Glendale Woolen Co.* v. *Protection Ins. Co., ante,* for instances when evidence of usage will not be permitted.

[3] *Ripley* v. *Ætna Ins. Co.,* 30 N. Y. 136; 3 Benn. F. I. C. 223.

is thereby ascertained, it cannot be treated as a custom, *because a custom, being a law, cannot have its origin in the impotent act of any particular individual, but in the will of the whole.*[1] Thus, a distinction of a very important and decisive character exists between an usage and a custom, and this distinction must not be lost sight of in the construction of policies of insurance, even though the courts, by confusing terms, sometimes seem to fail to observe the distinction. When a custom is shown, *it is as much a part of a contract in reference to which it relates as a statute is, because it is a part of the law pertaining to those matters*, and, unless specially excepted against in the contract, will control its interpretation.

Where the warranty is, "a watch kept," the assured is treated as contracting to keep a *suitable* watch, and it is for the jury to say whether or not there has been substantial compliance with the warranty, and in determining that fact, it is competent to show that such a watch was kept as is usually kept in similar establishments.[2] If the warranty is to keep a watch "at all times when the business is not in operation," a temporary absence of the watchman during such periods, avoids the policy, even though the watchman is prevented by officers of the law from discharging his duties.[3] And a warranty to keep "a

---

[1] *Simpson* v. *Wells*, L. R., 7 Q. B. 214; *Rex* v. *Joliffe*, 2 B. & C. 54; *Master Pilots, etc.*, v. *Bradley*, 2 E. & B. 428 n.

[2] *Crocker* v. *People's Mut. Ins. Co., ante.* In *Parker* v. *Bridgeport Ins. Co.*, 10 Gray (Mass.) 30, in a policy upon a saw-mill, the assured covenanted "that a representation given in the application for this insurance contains a just, full and true exposition of all the facts and circumstances in regard to the condition, situation, value and risk of the property insured, so far as the same are known to the assured and material to the risk; and that if any material fact or circumstance shall not have been fully represented, the risk hereupon shall cease and determine, and the policy be null and void." The applicant, to a question, "Is a watch kept upon the premises during the night? Is any other duty required of the watchman than watching for the safety of the premises?" answered, "A good watch kept; men usually at work; watchmen work at the saws"; and answered in the negative this question: "Is the building left alone at any time after the watchman goes off duty in the morning till he returns to his charge in the evening?" In fact, no watch was ever kept on the premises after twelve o'clock on Saturday night, or at all on Sunday night, other than the workmen sleeping there, who were instructed to, and habitually did, examine the mill with reference to fires before going to bed; and the fire occurred on Sunday night, when no one was on the premises. It was held, that the term "good watch" must be interpreted to mean "suitable" or "proper watch"; and that it was for the jury to decide whether the watch kept was a suitable and proper one, and whether the risk was affected by the watch actually kept, as compared with the one stipulated for.

[3] In *First National Bank of Ballston* v. *Ins. Co. of N. America*, 50 N. Y. 45, it appeared that, in a survey, which was referred to and made a part of a policy upon a paper mill, this inquiry was made, "Watchman: Is one kept in the mill or on the premises during the night and at all times when the mill is not in operation, or when the workmen are not present?" Answer: "Yes." On the day previous to the destruction of the property by fire, the personal property in the mill was levied upon by the sheriff, by virtue of an execution against the assured.

watchman nights," includes Sunday nights, even though by statute labor upon that day is prohibited.[1] The question as to whether the warranty has been complied with, is exclusively for the jury.[2]

When a policy requires a watchman to be kept on the premises, the insured is not required to keep one there constantly, but only at such times and during such periods as men of ordinary care and skill in such business, employ one, and in this respect the usage of similar establishments is admissible.[3]

The sheriff excluded the employees from the mill, took the keys and locked up the building. The deputy sheriff and one of the trustees of the assured remained in the office of the mill, about two rods from it, during the night, up to the time of the discovery of the fire, which occurred about 4 A. M., but they did not keep watch. In an action upon the policy, it was held, that the question and answer in the survey constituted a warranty, that the levy did not excuse from the obligation to perform it; that the deputy sheriff and trustee were not to be regarded as watchmen within the meaning of the policy, and that there being a breach of the warranty, plaintiff was properly nonsuited. GROVER, J., saying, "Failure to comply with a warranty will bar a recovery in case of loss, whether the loss was caused by such failure or not. *Cases, supra.* In the present case the survey is made part of the policy. In the survey the following inquiry is made: 'Watchman: Is one kept in the mill or on the premises during the night and at all times when the mill is not in operation or when the workmen are not present? Ans. Yes.' This statement was promissory, but the rights and duties of the parties were the same under it as though it had been affirmative. *Ripley v. The Ætna Ins. Co., supra.* The proof was, that upon the day previous to the destruction of the property by fire, the sheriff levied an execution against the assured upon the personal property in the mill, and excluded their employees therefrom, took the keys and locked up the building. The counsel for the appellant insists that this act of the sheriff, being an act that it was his legal duty to perform, must be regarded as the act of the law, and cites authorities showing that when performance of a contract becomes impossible by the act of God or the law, performance will be excused. The answer to this, in the present case, is that it was the default of the assured in not paying the judgment that caused the issuing and levy of the execution. The levy does not, therefore, excuse it from the obligation to perform the warranty. The counsel further insists, that as the deputy sheriff and one of the trustees of the assured remained in the office of the company, a building about two rods from the mill, during the night and until the discovery of the fire, they should be regarded as watchmen within the meaning of the policy. But the testimony failed to show that they were such, or even so regarded themselves. That shows that they looked through the building twice in the evening, the last time about eleven o'clock, and then went into the office, laid down and dozed until about four o'clock, when the deputy sheriff turned over and discovered the mill in flames, the fire being so extensive as to render all attempts to save the building and property hopeless. It is clear that these persons never undertook with the assured to act as watchmen, and consequently incurred no liability to it for negligence in the performance of the duties of such employment. In case of a recovery in the action, the defendant would have no right by subrogation to any remedy against them on that ground. This shows that they were not watchmen within the meaning of the term."

[1] *Glendale Woolen Co.* v. *Protection Ins. Co., ante; Ripley* v. *Ætna Ins. Co., ante.* But see *May* v. *Buckeye Ins. Co.,* 25 Wis. 291, where it is held that the law will not presume that the parties contemplated an *unlawful* act.

[2] *Crocker* v. *People's Ins. Co., ante; Hovey* v. *American Ins. Co.,* 2 Duer (N. Y.) 554; *Sheldon* v. *Hartford Ins. Co.,* 22 Conn. 553; 3 Bennett's F. I. C, 551; *Houghton* v. *Ins. Co.,* 8 Met. (Mass.) 114.

[3] In *Crocker* v. *The People's Mut. Fire Ins. Co.,* 8 Cush. (Mass.) 79, the plaintiff procured insurance upon his machine-shop, and the policy contained a provision as

SEC. 173. In all cases, when a strict and literal compliance with the terms of a warranty is known to be impossible, it is presumed that a substantial compliance therewith was intended, and if there is a substantial compliance, the warranty is met, as when the policy requires water to be kept in the building, the requirement need only be substantially complied with. Thus, where the policy stipulated that the "insured is to keep eight buckets filled with water on the first floor, where *the machinery is run, and four in the basement by the reservoir, ready for use at all times," it was held that this stipulation was to be construed reasonably, *and in view of natural or unavoidable causes—such as freezing weather—and that, while a literal compliance might not be possible, yet the assured must show that he kept the buckets at all times, as required by the policy, in a good and serviceable condition at the places designated, ready for instant use.* So a warranty in this respect is to be construed according to the intent and evident understanding of the parties, as applied to the condition of the risk, its uses and purposes.

Force pump or other appliances, rule as to.

SEC. 174. The same rule applies where the assured, by the terms of the policy, is required to have a force-pump or other appliances for extinguishing fires upon the premises. In such cases, the warranty is construed as requiring him to have the appliances there in condition for use at all times; but even though the warranty is in express terms

---

follows : "Machine shop, watchman to be kept on the premises." The plaintiff employed a watchman on the 14th of November to watch one-fourth the night, leaving the shop at about half-past seven in the evening. On the 28th of November the watchman was hired for one-half the night, leaving the shop at half-past ten in the evening, and on December 28th at about one o'clock in the morning, a fire broke out and the building was destroyed. The defendant resisted payment upon the ground that plaintiffs had broken this condition of the policy. .The plaintiff was permitted to show the usage in this respect, by different similar establishments. The court charged the jury that, under .this condition of the policy, "some watchman must have been kept on the premises in order to comply with this clause. It must not have been a pretense merely, or only a colorable keeping of a watchman. *But if in good faith, and without fraud,* a watchman was kept upon the premises, and such a watchman, and for such a portion of the time or at such specified hours as, *in the exercise of ordinary care and prudence,* was deemed sufficient for the safety of the building, that would be a compliance with the provision of the policy, and that, in order to determine whether or not a watchman was kept on the premises *in good faith and in the exercise of ordinary care and prudence,* the jury might refer to the evidence in the case as to what was common and usual in regard to keeping watchmen in other similar establishments," and upon appeal this ruling was sustained. "What is common and usual," said SHAW, C.J., "under given circumstances, is evidence tending to show what is reasonable."

[1] *Aurora Fire Ins. Co.* v. *Eddy,* 49 Ill. 106 ; *Garrett* v. *Provincial Ins. Co.,* 20 Upper Canada, Q. B. 200.

that the pump shall be "at all times ready for use," yet, if it is ready for use when the fire occurs, the fact that it becomes disabled *during the fire*, does not operate as a breach.[1] Such a warranty will be reasonably construed, and will not be extended beyond its terms. But as a force-pump would be useless without power to operate it, it will be construed to include such power, but not to include any particular power. But even this depends upon extrinsic matters, and will be construed in reference to the subject-matter of the risk. This was well illustrated by CURTIS, J., in the case last cited. He said: "If this warranty were of a force-pump in a *dwelling-house* at all times ready for use, I should hold it satisfied by the existence of a force-pump in a condition to be worked, * * considering the nature of the works, and the uniform and notorious usage to have such a pump in such a position *driven by power*." A warranty of this kind, however, is held not to require the assured to have hose for use in connection with the pump.[2]

Gloucester Manufacturing Co. v. Howard Fire Ins. Co.

SEC. 175. This was well illustrated in a Massachusetts case.[3] In that case the policy contained this stipulation: "water tanks to be well supplied with water at all times." An indorsement upon the policy converted it into an insurance upon buildings "in course of construction," and the court held that the warranty in reference to the water tanks and water, was to be construed in reference to the condition of the risk, and that, while in the course of construction, the assured was not required to have them supplied with water in the same manner and to the same extent that would be required in the case of finished buildings.

Warranties conditions precedent. Affirmative, unless clearly otherwise intended. Instances of application of rule.

SEC. 176. A warranty, *affirmative* or *promissory, is in the nature of a condition precedent*. An affirmative warranty is the positive and unqualified statement of a fact *as then existing*, and for the truth of which the assured vouches to the insurer, and which is satisfied, if the fact is as stated at the time when the contract is entered into. They are sometimes denominated warranties *in presenti*. That is, warranties that a certain state of facts exists in relation to the risk *at the time when they are made*.

---

[1] *Sayles* v. *N. W. Ins. Co.*, 2 Curtis (U. S.) 610.

[2] *Peoria, etc., Ins. Co.* v. *Lewis*, 18 Ill. 553; mem. of case in 4 Bennett's F. I. C. 187.

[3] *Gloucester Manuf. Co.* v. *Howard Fire Ins. Co.*, 5 Gray (Mass.) 497.

All warranties are treated as affirmative, unless from the language used, and the subject-matter of the risk, a contrary construction is inevitable. Thus, the words "occupied as a dwelling,"[1] "as a hotel,"[2] as a paper mill,[3] merely relate to the *present* condition or use of the property, *and are not to be construed as warranties that they shall be used for no other purpose. But they are warranties that the premises shall be used for no other purposes materially increasing the risk.* In a policy "on a four-story warehouse, first floor occupied by machinery used for making barrels, with privilege of storing barrels on the premises," the warranty was held to relate only to the *present* use of the property, and was not a warranty that it should be used for no other purpose, and the premises having subsequently been used for making boxes, and a circular saw and work bench introduced into the building for that purpose, which use, however, had ceased before the fire, it was held that the policy was not thereby avoided.[4]

So, where the policy described the building as "a two-story framed building *used for winding and coloring yarn,* and for the storage of spun yarn, etc.," and the policy also contained a clause stating it "to be the true intent and meaning of the parties hereto, that in case the above mentioned premises shall, at any time after the making and during the time this policy would otherwise be in force, be appropriated, applied or used to, or for the purpose of carrying on or exercising therein any trade, business or vocation denominated hazardous, or extra hazardous, or specified in the memorandum of special rates in the terms and conditions annexed to this policy, or for the purpose either of depositing, storing or keeping therein any of the articles, goods or merchandise in the same terms or conditions denominated hazardous, or extra hazardous, or included in the memorandum of special rates, except as herein expressly provided for, or hereafter agreed to by this corporation, in writing, to be added to, or indorsed upon, this policy, then and from thenceforth so long as the same shall be so appropriated, applied or used, these presents shall cease and be of no force or effect."

---

[1] *Schultz* v. *Merchants' Ins. Co.,* 57 Mo. 331 ; *Cumberland, etc., Ins. Co.* v. *Schell,* 29 Penn. St. 31.

[2] *Catlin* v. *Springfield Fire Ins. Co.,* 1 Sum. (U. S.) 434.

[3] *Wood* v. *Ins. Co., ante; May* v. *Buckeye Ins. Co., ante.*

[4] *United States Ins. Co.* v. *Kimberly,* 34 Md. 224 ; 6 Am. Rep. 325 ; *Billings* v. *Tolland, etc., Ins. Co.,* 20 Conn. 139 ; *Smith* v. *Mechanics' & Traders' Ins. Co.,* 32 N. Y. 399 ; *O'Niel* v. *Buffalo Ins. Co.,* 3 N. Y. 122 ; *Blood* v. *Howard Fire Ins. Co., ante.*

Among the subjects enumerated in the memorandum of special rates contained in the conditions annexed to the policy are "wool mills, wheel-wrights and wool waste, and generally all mills and manufacturing establishments requiring the use of fire heat not before enumerated." In October, 1861, the manufacture of carpets having been tempo-rarily suspended under the pressure of the times, the insured placed in the building covered by the policy in suit, thirteen hand-looms for weaving woolen army blankets, which looms were in part made from materials before used in manufacturing carpets, and partly from new materials. On the 1st of November, 1861, defendant, for an additional premium at an enhanced rate, consented that building " C," one of the several constituting the carpet factory, be occupied for weaving, *full-ing* and storage purposes, and gave privilege " to run the mill nights for the term of three months." After this period the insured com-menced weaving army blankets by hand power in the building insured by defendants, and continued that business until the whole establish-ment was destroyed by fire, which occurred in January, 1862, and originated in another building. There was no evidence that the change in the use of the building increased the risk, and the plaintiff offered to show that the risk was in fact *decreased*, but the evidence was excluded. It was proved that the process of *fulling* was never used in the manufacture of carpets, but was a necessary part of the manufacture of blankets; and that it was not customary for carpet factories to be run nights. The court below nonsuited the plaintiff, but upon appeal the judgment was reversed and the warranty held to be merely a warranty *in presenti*, and that a change in the use did not avoid the policy unless it *materially* increased the risk.[1]

---

[1] *Smith* v. *Mechanics', etc., Ins. Co.*, 32 N. Y. 397, DAVIS, J., said : " The state-ment of the policy that the building insured was 'used for winding and coloring yarn, and for storage of spun yarn,' was undoubtedly a warranty of its then present use. *Jenkins* v. *Chenango Mut. Ins. Co.*, 2 Denio, 75 ; *Wall* v. *The East River Ins. Co.*, 3 Seld. 370. This is all that is settled by the above cases. But there is no pretense that the building in this case was not used at the time of the insurance precisely as stated, and, therefore, none for saying that the warranty was broken *in presenti*, as it was in the cases cited. The only question, there-fore, on this part of the policy is, whether it contains a warranty that the build-ing, during the continuance of the policy, should be used only 'for winding, coloring and storing yarn,' with the fixtures and machinery then in it. In *O'Neil* v. *The Buffalo Ins. Co.*, the premises were described as occupied by a certain individual as a private dwelling. The occupant moved from and ceased to occupy the house several weeks before the fire, and it stood vacant when burned. This court held that the description in the policy must be regarded as a warranty of the fact that the person named was the occupant at the date of the policy, and nothing more. 3 Comstock, 122. In *Catlin* v. *The Springfield Ins. Co.*, 1 Sum. 435, the policy was on a dwelling-house, 'at present occupied by one Joel Rogers as a dwelling-house, but to be occupied hereafter as a tavern, and privileged as

22

So where the policy described the building as " a two-story frame building, etc., occupied by the Hon. George J. Goodhue as a private

---

such,' it was held that there was no continuing warranty that the house should be occupied as a tavern or otherwise, and that the company were liable, although the building was destroyed while vacant, by foul means, which probably could not have occurred if it had been occupied. A distinction was made in the court below between the use of the word 'occupied' and the word 'used,' in the description of policy as to the effect upon the question of continuing warranty; but to my mind the suggestion is without force. Both relate to the present actual use of the property, and are, when so applied, synonymous in intent and meaning. If the courts do not find a warranty in the phrase *occupied* in a particular manner, it would be overstraining to find one in the words, *used* in a specified way. If an insurance company desire to protect itself by a warranty as to future or continued use in the same manner as when insured, it may always do so by language, the object and meaning of which will be understood by both parties; and the courts should not thus construe words which are fully satisfied as a description of a present use or condition, into a promissory warranty, unless the inference is natural and irresistible that such was the understanding and design of both parties. Where there is such a warranty as to future use, the designated use must continue, or the warranty will be broken, for courts have no right to say that the assured may abandon the particular use or occupancy, and allow the premises to lie vacant or idle; for the very act of requiring such a warranty is conclusive that the insurer considered the continuance of the designated use or occupancy material to the risk, and made the contract accordingly. In my opinion, there was no continuing warranty of future use in the clause of the policy under consideration. The view that the description was not designed as such continuing warranty, is strengthened by the fact that the company have retained in the policy the clause in regard to using or appropriating the property in any manner included in their tabular statement of hazardous, extra hazardous and special rates; and thus, by force of the well known maxim '*expressio unius est exclusio alterius*,' assented to changes not within the prohibition. Another question of the case is, whether the change of use of the building from the purposes named in the description to the use of the hand looms for weaving blankets, falls within the prohibition just referred to. In considering this question, it is to be remembered that the property was insured as a part of a manufactory of woolen fabrics—carpets made of wool—and is therefore properly within the designation 'wool mills,' as used in the list of special rates. Indeed, the factory is described by defendants as 'the mill' in the privilege given for running nights. It was insured at the special rates fixed by the company because of the kind of business carried on. In making the change, no new or additional business was superadded to that of manufacturing carpets. The latter was temporarily abandoned, and the making of blankets temporarily substituted. The same material was used, prepared substantially in the same manner, but brought to a differently constructed loom for the purpose of turning out a different fabric. But there was no change of the premises or of the business from something not 'hazardous or extra hazardous,' or not specified in the memorandum of special rates, to something coming within either. The wool mills remained wool mills, although they made blankets instead of carpets for the time being, and never by the change lost their character as a manufactory of woolen goods in which they were insured. In no just sense of the prohibitory clause above quoted, was there any change obnoxious to its provisions; for an establishment within the special rates, because it manufactured woolen goods of one kind, was no more within them because it made the same material into a different kind of goods. In my judgment, the policy was not forfeited by force of the clause relied upon by substituting the making of blankets for carpets in the manner described in the evidence, because it was no such change or different 'appropriation' as is contemplated by that clause. The question is, therefore, the same precisely as though the insured, instead of setting up hand looms for weaving blankets in the building named by defendants, had put there the same number of looms for weaving carpets. And as there was no continuing warranty that the particular use of the building stated in the policy should be continued while the policy run,

dwelling," it was held that this was merely descriptive of the present use of the building, and was not a warranty that it should continue to be occupied by the same tenant during the whole life of the policy.[1] "The description in the policy," said RUGGLES, J., "must be regarded as a warranty of the fact that he was the occupant, *at the date of the policy, and nothing more.* The description imports nothing more. The defendant insists that the description warrants not only that he (the tenant named) was the occupant at the date of the policy, but that he was to remain the occupant during the continuance of the risk. But the parties have not thought it proper to express themselves to that effect. * * If it had been the intention of the parties to make it a condition that he should remain the occupant during the term of the insurance, it would have been easy to say so, *and there is no good reason in the case for supposing that the parties intended what they have not expressed.*"

A policy often contains both an affirmative and a promissory warranty as to the risk. That is, a warranty may be in part affirmative, and in part promissory. Thus in an Iowa case,[2] the policy described the occupancy of the property thus : "Occupied for stores below, *the upper portion to remain unoccupied during the continuance of this policy.*' The court held that the former part of the statement was an *affirmative*, and the latter part a *promissory* warranty. The former merely affirmed that a certain state of facts *did* exist, the latter, not only that a certain state of facts did, *but should continue to exist.* The former was not broken by a change in the use, unless the use substituted was more hazardous, while in the latter case, an occupancy of the upper portion of the building for *any* purpose, was a breach of the warranty, and avoided the policy.

Where a policy stated that no stoves "are used in the building," it

---

the case ought to have gone to the jury on the question whether the risk was materially increased by the conduct of the assured without the consent of the company. The evidence which was offered to show that the change, in fact, diminished instead of increasing the risk, should have been allowed upon this question. I have not considered the force to be given (if any) to the consent of the company, that one of the buildings, constituting a part of the manufacturing establishment, might be used for a process wholly unknown in carpet making, but requisite to the manufacture of most other woolen goods, as implying that such goods might be made in the establishment as required that process. It is not necessary to the determination of this case, in its present aspect, that anything further should be done than to settle the construction of the clauses of the policy above considered."

[1] *O'Niel* v. *Buffalo F. Ins. Co.*, 3 N. Y. 122 ; 3 Bennett's F. C. I. 103.

[2] *Stout* v. *City Fire Ins. Co.*, 12 Iowa 374 ; 4 Bennett's F. I. C. 555. See also, *Carter* v *Humboldt, etc., F. Ins. Co.*, 17 id. 456.

was held a mere *in presenti* warranty, and that the use of a stove in the building, *subsequently*, did not avoid the policy.[1]

A warranty, being always expressed in the body of the policy, or in papers expressly referred to therein and made a part thereof, is a part of the contract, and a condition precedent, full performance of which is essential in order to entitle the assured to recover for a loss under the policy; and this applies equally to an affirmative or promissory warranty. The former must be shown to be literally true, and the latter to have been strictly performed, and that too, without any reference to the question whether they were material to the risk. The insurer is permitted to judge for himself upon what conditions he will assume a risk, *and what is material thereto*, and if he sees fit to insert immaterial conditions in the policy, the assured cannot defend against a breach thereof upon that ground. By inserting them in the policy, *the insurer has made them material*, and the assured is estopped from going into that inquiry. *They are conditions of the contract, and must be literally performed, even though the risk is thereby increased. The assured has no election, but must stand upon his performance of them.*[2]

Unless it is clear from the language used, that the parties intended a warranty to apply *to the future use* of the premises, it will be construed as a warranty *in presenti* merely. Thus, where the assured stated in his application, "clerk sleeps in the store," it was held that this merely referred to the *present* occupancy of the store, and could not be construed as a warranty that the same state of things would continue.[3] "Whether," says LOWRIE, J., " a statement shall be taken as a warranty, is a mere question of interpretation to be ascertained in policies of insurance just as in other contracts. * * Here it does not expressly appear that the clerk was to sleep in the store as a precaution against fire, and it is not otherwise obvious that that was the intention of sleeping there. * * It may be a mere license. 1 Sum. (U. S.) C. C. 435. We may illustrate the impossibility of the arbitrary construction contended for, by changing the sentence and making it read, "clerk cooks his victuals in the store." It would hardly be contended that he should continue to do so, for this would increase the risk. Or, let it read, "a tavern is kept in part of the house," this would not be regarded as a warranty that he should continue to do so,

---

[1] *Aurora F. Ins. Co.* v. *Eddy, ante.*
[2] Marshall on Ins. 249.
[3] *Frisbie* v. *Fayette Mut. Ins. Co.,* 27 Penn. St. 325 ; 4 Benn. F. I. C. 159.

for the by-laws show that the company regarded such a use of the house as adding to the risk. The rule seems to be that such represen. tations in, or a part of the policy, are construed to be warranties when it appears to the court that they have had, in themselves, or in the view of the parties, a tendency to induce the company to enter into the contract on terms more favorable to the insured, than without them. *If the court cannot say so*, then they are treated as representations, and it is left to the jury to say whether or not they are material mis. representations tending to mislead, and actually misleading the insurers. The rule perhaps may be more concisely stated thus. *Any statement or description, or any undertaking on the part of the assured, on the face of the policy, which relates to the risk, is a warranty, an express warranty, and a condition precedent.* It is not necessary that it should be stated to be a warranty, or that it should be so by construction. *It is enough that it appears upon the face of the policy and relates to the risk.*[1]

---

[1] In *Wood* v. *Ins. Co.*, 13 Conn. 533, the subject of insurance was described in the policy as " the one undivided half of the paper-mill which the insured owned at W., together with the half of the machinery, wheels, gearing," etc., and in a memorandum in the conditions annexed to the policy, paper-mills and grist-mills were mentioned among the articles which were to be insured at special rates of premium, in contradistinction to those which were not hazardous, hazardous or extra hazardous. In February, when the insurance was effected, the building in question was a paper-mill, and was used for no other purpose. In August following, its use as a paper-mill was discontinued, the rag-cutter and duster were removed, and a pair of millstones, for grinding grain, were put in their places, moved by the same gearing, and by the power of the same water-wheel, all the other machinery remaining as it was. By the use of the millstones, the risk was greater than it would have been if no use had been made of the premises, but not greater than if the paper-mill only had been in operation. In September, during the continuance of the risk, the premises were destroyed by fire, not caused by the millstones. In an action on the policy against the insurers, it was held that the description of the building as a paper-mill related to the risk; that it was a warranty, and that if the building was not a paper-mill at the time of the loss, the warranty was not complied with; that at the time of the loss it was a paper-mill, ready for use, and, consequently, the warranty was duly kept; and that the insurers were not absolved from their obligations by reason of any increased hazard resulting from the alterations in the mill.

CHAPTER V.

WARRANTIES AND REPRESENTATIONS.

Representations; what are; must be material.

SEC. 177. A representation precedes the contract; and, being only the inducement thereto, need only be true as to matters *material to the risk*, and that influence the insurer in taking or rejecting the risk, or in fixing the rate of premium therefor.[1] It is not, however, for the insurer, *but for the jury to say whether the representation is material.* The mere fact that the insurer insists that the risk would have been

---

[1] *Boardman* v. *N. H., etc., Ins. Co.,* 20 N. H. 551; *Price* v. *Phœnix, etc., Ins. Co.,* 17 Minn. 497; *Nicoll* v. *American Ins. Co.,* 3 W. & M. (U. S.); 2; *Williams* v. *N. E., etc., Ins. Co.,* 31 Me. 289; *Columbian Ins. Co.* v. *Lawrence,* 10 Pet. (U. S.) 507; see, also same case, 2 Pet. (U. S.) 25; *Stebbins* v. *Globe Ins. Co.,* 2 Hall (N. Y. S. C.) 632; *Barber* v. *Fletcher,* 1 Doug. 305; *Daniels* v. *Hudson River Ins. Co.,* 12 Cush. (Mass.) 416; *Dennison* v. *Thomaston, etc., Ins. Co.,* 20 Me. 125; *Delonguemere* v. *Tradesman's Ins. Co.,* 2 Hall (N. Y. S. C.) 589; *Harmer* v. *Protection Ins. Co.,* 2 Ohio St. 452; *Glendale Mf'g Co.* v. *Protection Ins. Co.,* 21 Conn. 19; *Peoria M. & F. Ins. Co.* v. *Perkins,* 16 Mich. 380; *Witherill* v. *Maine Ins. Co.,* 49 Me. 200; *Marshall* v. *Columbian Ins. Co.,* 27 N. H. 157; *Cumberland Valley, etc., Protection Co.* v. *Schell,* 29 Penn. St. 31; *Wall* v. *Howard Ins. Co.,* 14 Barb. (N. Y.) 383; *Carpenter* v. *American Ins. Co.,* 1 Story (U. S.) 57; *Roth* v. *City F. Ins. Co.,* 6 McLean (U. S.) 324; *Clark* v. *N. E. Mut. F. Ins. Co.,* 6 Cush. (Mass.) 342; *Gould* v. *York Co. Mut. F. Ins. Co.,* 47 Me. 403.

rejected, or the rate of premium would have been higher, if the real facts had been known to him, is not enough to weaken the validity of the policy. *The jury must find, as a matter of fact, that the representations were material, and in fact influenced the insurer in taking the risk at a lower rate of premium than he would have taken it for, if the real state of the risk had been known.*[1]

In arriving at a proper result, the jury may consider the evidence of insurance men as to the materiality of the statements, but that is only an *aid* to the result, and by no means decisive. *The jury must say, from all the facts and circumstances, whether the representations were material or not.*[2] But in a case where the facts are not in dispute, the question of materiality is for the court.[3]

The assured is not held to the strict or even literal truth of his representations. It is enough if they are *substantially* true.[4] "*It is enough*" says SUTHERLAND, J.,[5] "*if a representation be made without fraud, and be not false in any material point; or if it be substantially, although not literally true.*[6] Although," he adds, "the description may

---

[1] In *Clason* v. *Smith*, 3 Wash. (U. S. C. C.) 156, the assured represented to the insurer that they had no doubt that they could get the insurance in New York for 15 per cent. The defendants charged them 20 per cent. In fact, the assured had applied to several offices in New York, and 20 per cent. had been demanded. In an action upon the policy this misrepresentation was set up in defense. The court held that the representation was not material, as it did not influence the insurers to take 15 per cent., and that, as they charged and received the risk at 20 per cent., it must be presumed that they acted upon their own judgment rather than upon what the assured said. "While," say the court, "the statement could not be defended at the bar of conscience, the misrepresentation could have had no influence affecting the rate of premium, because upon their own judgment they demanded 20 per cent. instead of 15; nor ought it to have induced the acceptance of the risk at all, nor influenced the rate of premium, for the representation expressed nothing but an opinion that the insurance could be effected at that rate; *and the insurer could not have accepted it as a candid opinion, because the facts showed that it was not;* for, if it were, why leave New York and go to Philadelphia, and then pay 20 instead of 15 per cent. ?" *Hubbard* v. *Glover*, 3 Camp. 313.

[2] *Wainwright* v. *Bland*, 1 M. & W. 32; *McLanahan* v. *Universal Ins. Co.*, 1 Pet. (U. S.) 170; *McLaws* v. *United Kingdom, etc., Institution*, 23 C. C. S. (Sc.) 559; *Sexton* v. *Montgomery, etc., Ins. Co.*, 9 Barb. (N. Y.) 191; *Power* v. *City F. Ins. Co.*, 8 Phila. (Penn.) 566; *Mut. Ins. Co.* v. *Deah*, 18 Md. 26; *Life Ins. Co.* v. *Fransisco*, 17 Wall. (U. S.) 672; *Percival* v. *Maine Ins. Co.*, 33 Me. 242; *Parker* v. *Bridgeport Ins. Co.*, 10 Gray (Mass.) 302; *Boardman* v. *N. H., etc., Ins. Co.*, 21 N. H. 551; *Bulkley* v. *Protection Ins. Co.*, 2 Paine (U. S.) 82.

[3] *Curry* v. *Com. Ins. Co.*, 10 Pick. (Mass.) 535; *Fletcher* v. *Com. Ins. Co.*, 18 id. 419; 1. Ben. F. I. C. 556.

[4] *Nichol* v. *American Ins. Co.*, 3 W. & M. (U. S.) 527; *Edwards* v. *Footner*, 1 Camp. 530.

[5] *Jefferson Ins. Co.* v. *Cotheal*, 7 Wend. (N. Y.) 72; 1 Ben. F. I. C. 354.

[6] *Pawson* v. *Watson*, Camp. 787. The force of this proposition will perhaps be more readily grasped, from a brief statement of what has been held by the courts in various cases involving the question. Thus in *Delonguemare* v. *Tradesmen's Ins. Co., ante,* the building was represented as *completed;* held, complied with if

differ very considerably from the actual state of the property insured, *if such variation were not fraudulently intended, and did not in fact affect the rate of insurance, or change the actual risk, it can scarcely be deemed material.*" [1] The assured is not bound to state what his opinion is of the risk, but the bald, naked facts relating thereto.[2]

Where the misrepresentation alleged is of something that is independent of the property insured, the policy is not invalidated when the loss is not affected thereby; [3] nor when the application was made out by the insurer's agent, and, knowing the facts, he misstated them; [4] or when the facts were stated as they were, by his direction.[5] A representation may be made either in writing or by parol, and is equally fatal to a recovery in the one case as in the other, if false and material to the risk.[6]

If an answer to an interrogatory is false and relates to a material matter, it is fatal to a recovery under the policy.[7] The assured is bound to answer truly or not at all; and as to whether, in view

---

substantially finished. In *Collins* v. *Charlestown Mut. F. Ins. Co.*, 10 Gray (Mass.) 155, the building was represented as used for manufacturing lead pipe *only*. Reels, for winding pipe on, were also made in the building; held, no misrepresentation. In *Suckley* v. *Delafield*, 2 Caines (N. Y.) 222, it was represented that the ship would sail with ballast, she sailed with *one trunk and ten barrels of gunpowder*; held, a substantial compliance. In *Alexander* v. *Campbell*, 27 L. T. (N. S.) 462, the vessel was represented as having been *new metaled*, in fact new metal had only been put on where needed; held, the representation was met. In *Ins. Co. of N. America* v. *McDowell*, 50 Ill. 120, the assured represented that *no open lights* were used in *the mill*, in fact an open kerosene lamp was used in the counting-room; held, no misrepresentation. In *Lee* v. *Howard Ins. Co.*, 11 Cush. (Mass.) 324, the value of the goods was represented as being between $2,000 and $3,000. When the application was made there was not $2,000 worth of goods on hand; held, that the policy was not thereby avoided, if the assured in good faith intended and expected to keep that amount during the life of the policy. In *Irvin* v. *Sea Ins. Co.*, 23 Wend. (N. Y.) 380, it was represented "no spirits allowed on board." There were two kegs of four or five gallons each on board, but they were not on board for use, nor were they tapped during the voyage; held, not a misrepresentation. See also, *Wynne* v. *Liv., Lon. & Globe Ins. Co.*, 71 N. C. 121; *Dennison* v. *Thomaston, etc., Ins. Co.*, 20 Me. 125; *Allen* v. *Charlestown Ins. Co.*, 5 Gray (Mass.) 384.

[1] See also, *Daniels* v. *Hudson River Ins. Co.*, 12 Cush. (Mass.) 416; *Clason* v. *Smith, ante; Chase* v. *Washington Mut. Ins. Co.*, 12 Barb. (N. Y.) 695; *Williams* v. *N. E. Mut. F. Ins. Co., ante.*

[2] *Dennison* v. *Mut. Ins. Co.*, 20 Me. 125.

[3] *Howard F. & M. Ins. Co.* v. *Cornick*, 24 Ill. 455.

[4] *Michael* v. *Mut. Ins. Co.*, 10 La. An. 737; *Home Mut. F. Ins. Co.* v. *Garfield*, 60 Ill. 124; *Ayres* v. *Hartford F. Ins. Co.*, 17 Iowa, 176; *Pitney* v. *Glen's Falls Ins. Co.*, 65 N. Y. 6; *Viele* v. *Germania F. Ins. Co.*, 26 Iowa, 9; *Awles Ins. Co.* v. *Shipman*, 77 Ill. 189; *Reaper City Ins. Co.* v. *Jones*, 62 id. 458; *McBride* v. *Republic Ins. Co.*, 30 Wis. 562.

[5] *Rockford Ins. Co.* v. *Nelson*, 75 Ill. 548.

[6] *Wainwright* v. *Bland*, 1 M. & W. 32.

[7] *Burritt* v. *Saratoga, etc., Ins. Co.*, 5 Hill (N. Y.) 188; *Cumberland Valley, etc., Protection Co.* v. *Schell*, 27 Penn. St. 31.

of the language of the whole instrument, and the facts attending the risk, his answer is true, or relates to a material matter, is a question for the jury.[1] It is not necessary that the jury should find that the assured made the representation with *a fraudulent intent; for if it does not relate to a material matter, it does not defeat the policy, however fraudulent may have been the intent or purpose of the assured.*[2] The question is, whether it related to a matter so material that if it had not been made on the one hand, or if made on the other, the insurer would have been influenced to reject the risk or materially modify his contract.[3] *If the representation is material to the risk, although the result of accident or mistake, it avoids the policy.*[4]

The insurer takes the burden of establishing both the falsity of the statements and their materiality,[5] and this must be done by full proof, as the law will not presume fraud, but the reverse, and will not set aside a contract upon that ground, unless the fraud and materiality of the statement are fully established.[6]

Representations affecting the risk. Tests of materiality.

SEC. 178. Any representation of the assured, in reference to the property, that *is material to the risk, and influences the insurer either in taking or rejecting it,* and affects the rate of premium at which the risk is assumed, *if relied upon by the insurer,* and is untrue, avoids the policy,[7]

---

[1] *Cumberland, etc., Protection Co.* v. *Schell, ante; Crocker* v. *People's Ins. Co.,* 8 Cush. (Mass.) 79 ; *Parker* v. *Bridgeport Ins. Co.,* 10 Gray (Mass.) 302 ; *Bellatty* v. *Thomaston Ins. Co.,* 61 Me. 414 ; *Curtis* v. *Home Ins. Co.,* 1 Biss. (U. S.) 485.

[2] *Continental Ins. Co.* v. *Kasey,* 25 Gratt. (Va.) 268.

[3] *Hollowman* v. *Life Ins. Co.,* 1 Woods (U. S. C. C.) 674 ; *Columbian Ins. Co.* v. *Lawrence,* 2 Pet. (U. S.) 25 ; *Quin* v. *National Ass. Co.,* 1 J. & C. (Irish) 316. In *Columbian Ins. Co.* v. *Lawrence,* 10 Pet. (U. S.) 507, STORY, J., says, in reference to the effect of a *misdescription* of the risk, that " *if the misdescription were material to the risk, and would increase it, but yet would not reduce the premium, it would not avoid the policy.*" Thus holding that the test of materiality is the effect which the misrepresentation had in inducing the taking of the risk at a higher or lower rate of premium. This, however, while *one* of the tests, is not now regarded as the only one. See *Battles* v. *York, etc., Ins. Co., ante; Hollowman* v. *Life Ins. Co., ante; Battles* v. *York Co., etc., Ins. Co.,* 41 Me. 208 ; *Swift* v. *Mut. Life Ins. Co.,* 2 T. & C. (N. Y.) 302.

[4] *Carpenter* v. *American Ins. Co.,* 1 Story (U. S.) 57.

[5] *Cushman* v. *U. S. Life Ins. Co.,* 4 Hun (N. Y.) 783.

[6] *Pine* v. *Vanuxem,* 3 Yeates (Penn.) 30.

[7] The distinction between a representation and a warranty in an application for an insurance is, that in the one case the underwriter's action is induced or affected thereby, while a representation may or may not be fatal if false, in proportion as it is material or immaterial to the risk undertaken, *Commonwealth Ins. Co.* v. *Monninger,* 18 Ind. 352, and a warranty will be strictly construed. *Grant* v. *Lex. Ins. Co.,* 5 Ind. 23 ; *Pawson* v. *Watson,* Cowp. 601-784 ; *De Hahn* v. *Hartley,* 1 T. R. 343. Where the survey is in terms made a part of the policy, the statements therein are regarded as warranty. *Cox* v. *Ætna Ins. Co.,* 29 Ind. 586. ; *Columbian Ins. Co.* v. *Lawrence,* 2 Pet. (U. S.) 25.; *Sheldon* v. *Hartford Ins.*

and this applies to representations as to the title,[1] the character of the

---

Co., 22 Conn. 235 ; *Nicoll* v. *American Ins. Co.*, 3 W. & M. (U. S.) 529. In *Girard Fire and Marine Ins. Co.* v. *Stephenson*, 37 Penn. St. 292, the plaintiff, in conversation with the defendant's agent who took the application, stated that he expected to be from home much of the time, and that the carpenter's shop would be but little used, though he might want to use it, and that there would be no fire in it. This conversation *was not* reported to the company, and they issued the policy in ignorance of it.   The court held that it could not operate as a defense to the policy, though false, *because the insurers not knowing of. could not have been influenced by it.* Representations precede and are no part of the contract, but are merely collateral thereto.   They may induce the *making* of the contract, but are no part of, unless in terms incorporated into it.   When they are imported into the contract, they become warranties, and must be strictly true, otherwise they need only be *substantially* true, and have no effect, unless they relate to matters *material* to the risk.   *Higbee* v. *Guardian Ins. Co.*, 66 Barb. (N. Y.) 462; *Buford* v. *New York Life Ins. Co.*, 5 Oreg. 334 ; *Cox* v. *Ætna Ins. Co.*, 29 Ind. 586; *Lycoming Ins. Co.* v. *Mitchell*. 48 Penn. St, 362 ; *Daniels* v. *Hudson River Ins. Co.*, 12 Cush. (Mass.) 416 ; *Nicoll* v. *American Ins. Co.*, 3 W. & M. (U. S.) 529 ; *Wilson* v. *Conway Ins. Co.*, 4 R. I. 141 ; *Glendale Woolen Co.* v. *Protection Ins. Co.*, 21 Conn. 19 ; *State, etc., Ins. Co.* v. *Arthur*, 30 Penn. St. 315 ; *Wall* v. *Howard Ins. Co.*, 14 Barb. (N. Y.) 383.   But, if they are incorporated into the policy, they become warranties, and must be literally, strictly true.   *Battles* v. *York Mut. Ins. Co.*, 41 Me. 208 ; *Pennsylvania Ins. Co* v. *Gottman*, 48 Penn. St. 151 ; *Gould* v. *York, etc., Ins. Co.*, 47 Me. 403 ; *Gahagan* v. *Union, etc., Ins. Co.*, 48 N. H. 176 ; *Leathers* v. *Ins. Co.*, 24 id. 259.

[1] *Bellatty* v. *Thomaston Ins. Co.*, 61 Me. 414.   An application made to a mutual insurance company, in a printed form issued by them, by one of their agents, without knowledge of the person to be insured, for insurance on a building, stated that "the property to be insured" belonged to him, when, in fact, he owned the building only, and was a mere tenant at will of the land on which it stood.   A policy was issued thereon, expressly made subject to the lien of the company on the interest of the assured in any personal property or buildings insured and the land under such buildings, upon which lien the company expressed their intention to rely ; and to the by-laws, the conditions of which were declared to be part of the policy, and provided that the application should be a part of the policy and warranty on the part of the assured, that any policy should be void, "unless the true title and interest of the insured be expressed in the proposal or application ; that property held by lease, or standing on land so held, shall not be insured, unless specially described as such in the application ;" that, "in case the application is made through an agent, the applicant shall be held liable for the representation," and that "no insurance agent or broker forwarding applications to this office is authorized to bind the company in any case whatever."   The court held that the assured, by accepting the policy, adopted the representations of the agent ; that the failure to specify the nature of his interest avoided the policy ; and that parol evidence of the agent's knowledge of the actual facts was inadmissible.   *Kibbe* v. *Hamilton, etc., Ins. Co.*, 11 Gray (Mass.) 163.   Two partners, in an application for insurance on a building which was required to contain "a full, fair and substantially a true representation of all the facts and circumstances respecting the property, so far as they are within the knowledge of the assured and are material to the risk," stated that they owned the land on which it stood.   In fact, one of them, to whom the policy was made payable, owned it, and the other was charged on their books with half its cost.   The partnership was afterwards dissolved, and all that owner's interest in its assets transferred to his co-partner, to whom the insurers, with notice of the facts, agreed that the policy should "stand good."   It was held that the insurers were liable for a loss by a subsequent fire.   *Collins* v. *Charlestown, etc., Ins. Co.*, 10 Gray (Mass.) 155 ; *Phenix Ins. Co.* v. *Lawrence*, 4 Met. (Ky.) 9.   A lessee of land for a term of years, with the right to remove the buildings to be erected thereon at the termination of his term, effected an insurance of the buildings, as the owner thereof ; the policy contained a condition that, "if the interest in the property to be insured be a leasehold interest, or other interest not absolute, it must be so represented to the company and expressed in the policy in writing,

risk,[1] or as to any matter in relation to the risk stated by the assured.[2]

otherwise the insurance shall be void." It was held that the insured, being the absolute owner of the buildings, had a right to insure them as such, and was not bound to disclose the extent of his interest in the land. *Hope, etc., Ins. Co. v. Brolaskey,* 35 Penn. St. 282. If an application is expressly made a part of the policy, and the policy is also made subject to the conditions and limitations expressed in the by-laws annexed, and these by-laws provide that the policy shall be void if the application shall not contain a full, fair and substantially true representation of all the facts and circumstances respecting the property, so far as they are within the knowledge of the assured and material to the risk, and the premises are subject to two mortgages made by the insured, the mentioning of only one of them, in reply to a question in the application, "Is the property mortgaged or otherwise incumbered, and to what amount?" will avoid the policy. And the fact that the insured did not then recollect the other mortgage is immaterial. *Towne* v. *Fitchburg, etc., Ins. Co.,* 7 Allen (Mass.) 51. A policy was issued under the conditions and limitations expressed in the by-laws of the insurance company, one of which was that, when any property insured should be taken possession of by a mortgagee, the policy should be void, and the application, which was expressly made a part of the policy, contained an agreement that, if the answers did not give a full, just and true exposition of all the facts and circumstances in relation to the condition, situation, value and risk of the property to be insured, the policy should be void, the omission to disclose in the application the fact that possession of the premises to be insured had been taken under a second mortgage, and a subsequent retaking of possession under the same mortgage, without the consent of the underwriters, will avoid the policy. *Battles* v. *York, etc., Ins. Co.,* 41 Me. 208; *Smith* v. *Empire Ins. Co.,* 25 Barb. (N. Y.) 497. The policy will also be rendered invalid if, in reply to a question in the application calling for the amount of incumbrances, the answer was that there were two mortgages, for $2,700 in all, the first of which was for $1,150, and the second for $1,550, when in fact the first was for $1,150 as principal, and for accrued interest to the amount of $300 more. *Jacobs* v. *Eagle Ins. Co.,* 7 Allen (Mass.) 132; *Murphy* v. *People's, etc., Ins. Co.,* id. 239.

[1] In *Farmers', etc., Ins. Co.* v. *Snyder,* 16 Wend. (N. Y.) 481, the plaintiff described the building in his application, which was *not* made a part of the policy, as follows: "Thick stone partitions running lengthwise through the building to the roof." The stone partition, in fact, did not extend beyond the garret floor. The court held that the policy was valid, unless the fact that the stone partition did not extend higher than the garret floor was material to the risk, and that the jury were the sole judges of the fact. In *Boardman* v. *N. H. Mut. Ins. Co.,* 20 N. H. 551, the application stated that the store was occupied by tenants, including a cabinetmaker. The third story was vacant. There were carpenters' and joiners' shops in the first story. It was held not to be a warranty as to occupancy, and not to avoid the policy, unless the jury found that the difference in occupancy was material to the risk. *Stebbins* v. *Globe Ins. Co.,* 2 Hall (N. Y.) 632.

[2] *Hollowman* v. *Life Ins. Co.,* 1 Woods (U. S.) 671; *Continental Ins. Co.* v. *Kasey,* 25 Gratt. (Va.) 268; *Quin* v. *National Assurance Co.,* 1 J. & C. 316. Where representations material to the risk are shown to be false, the contract of insurance does not take effect. By reason of the fraud, the minds of the parties have not met, and no contract has ever existed, unless the insurer, *knowing* of the fraud, has waived it. *Taylor* v. *Ætna Ins. Co.,* 120 Mass. 254; *Towne* v. *Fitchburg, etc., R. R. Co.,* 7 Allen, (Mass.) 51; *Campbell* v. *N. E. Ins. Co.,* 98 Mass. 381. Where the insurer received the representations of its own agent as to the nature of the interest of the assured in the property, it cannot set up a misdescription to defeat the policy. *Atlantic Ins. Co.* v. *Wright,* 22 Ill. 462. It is not a material misdescription that a mill, situated in the corner of one section, is described as being in the adjoining corner of the next section just across a stream. *Prieger* v. *Exchange Ins. Co.,* 6 Wis. 86. A representation as to the contiguity of other buildings, in an application incorporated into the policy, is a warranty, and if the assured is required to state *all* the buildings within ten rods, a failure to do so will render the policy void, if the insurer so elects (*Huntley* v. *Perry,* 38 Barb. (N. Y.) 569); but if, in answer to an inquiry, What is the relative situation of other buildings? the answer was, "Two buildings with fifty feet;" the court

The utmost good faith is required, both on the part of the assured and the insurer, and the same rules of construction that are applied in ordinary contracts, are not always applicable in these cases. If they were, the consequences might be disastrous.[1]

The distinction, however, between a representation and a warranty, is marked, as in the one case it is sufficient if the statement is *substantially* true,[2] whereas a warranty must be *strictly* true *whether material to the risk or not*,[3] and whether it was made *bona fide* by the insurer,

---

held that this must be construed to mean *within* fifty feet, and that it was sufficient, although one was within *two* feet. *Allen* v. *Charlestown, etc., Ins. Co.,* 5 Gray (Mass.) 384. A false description of the interest of the assured in a policy, *when, by the charter of the company,* the insurer has a lien upon the property for payment of the premiums, invalidates the policy whether the assured knew that the charter gave such lien or not. *Pinkham* v. *Morany,* 40 Me. 587. So also, where the by-laws are made a part of the policy, and they require a true statement of title, although there was no intent to deceive. *Hayward* v. *N. E. Mut. F. Ins. Co.,* 10 Cush. (Mass.) 444; *Wilbur* v. *Bowditch Ins. Co.,* 10 id. 446. But the misstatement must be radical, if it is in effect correct, although not so technically, the policy is not avoided. Thus, where the by-law of a mutual company, to which the policy was made subject, provided that the policy should be void unless the true title of the assured was expressed in the proposal, the plaintiff called the property "his," but stated it was incumbered. In fact, *two* mortgages then existed on the estate, given by a former owner to third persons; and the former owner's equity of redemption had been sold on execution to another person before the plaintiff acquired his interest in the estate. The court held that, as the insured still had the right to redeem and make his title absolute, there was no essential misrepresentation of title. *Buffum* v. *Bowditch Ins. Co.,* 10 Cush. (Mass.) 540; *Chase* v. *Hamilton Ins. Co.,* 22 Barb. (N. Y.) 527.

[1] *Farmers' Mut. Fire Ins. Co.* v. *Marshall,* 29 Vt. 23.

[2] Mr. MARSHALL, in his excellent work upon Insurance, thus clearly and accurately defines the distinction between representations and warranties. "There is a material difference," he says, "between a representation and a warranty. A warranty being a condition upon which the contract is to take effect, is always a part of the written policy, *and must appear upon the face of it.*" This must be regarded as subject to the qualification, except in cases where the order for insurance or application is referred to in the policy and made a part of it, in which case the warranty may be shown by the order or application and need not be stated in the policy. "Whereas," he continued, "*a representation* is only matter of collateral information or intelligence on the subject insured, and makes no part of the policy. A warranty being in the nature of a condition precedent, *must be strictly and literally complied with,* but it is sufficient if *a representation is true in substance.* By a warranty, *whether material to the risk or not,* the insured states his claim of indemnity *upon the precise truth of it,* if it be affirmative, or upon the exact performance of it, if it be executory; but it is sufficient if a representation be made without fraud, and be not false in any material point; or if he *subtantially,* though not *literally,* performed a false warranty, avoids the policy as being a breach of a condition upon which it is to take effect, *and an insurer is not liable for any loss though it do not happen in consequence of the breach of the warranty.* A false representation *is no breach of the contract, but if material to the risk,* avoids the policy on the ground of *fraud,* or at least *because the* insurer has been misled by it." *Lycoming Ins. Co.* v. *Mitchell,* 48 Penn. St. 367; *Glendale Woolen Co.* v. *Protection Ins. Co.,* 21 Conn. 19; *Witherell* v. *Maine Ins. Co.,* 48 Me. 200; *State, etc., Ins. Co.* v. *Arthur,* 30 Penn. St. 315.

[3] *State Mut. Fire Ins. Co.* v. *Arthur,* 30 Penn. St. 315.

believing it to be true, or through ignorance or mistake, or fraudulently and with a purpose to deceive it.[1]

Fatal representation of interest.

SEC. 179. A false representation as to the *interest* of the assured in the property, is regarded as material, and such as, if substantially false, avoids the policy. In reference to such representations, MARSHALL, J.,[2] pertinently says: "The contract for insurance is one in which the underwriters generally act on the representation of the assured, and that representation ought consequently to be fair, and to omit nothing which it is material for the underwriters to know. It may not be necessary that the person requiring insurance should state every incumbrance on his property, which it might be required of him to state if it was offered for sale; but fair dealing requires that he should state everything *which might influence, and probably would influence*, the mind of the underwriter in forming or declining the contract. A building held under a lease for years, about to expire, might be generally spoken of as the building of the tenant, but no underwriter would be willing to insure it as if it was his, and an offer to insure it, stating that it belonged to him, would be a gross imposition. Generally speaking, insurances against fire are made in the confidence that the assured will use all the precautions required to avoid the calamity insured against *which would be suggested by his interest. The extent of this interest* must always influence the underwriter *in taking or rejecting the risk and estimating the premium. So far as it may influence him in this respect, it ought to be communicated to him.* Underwriters do not rely so much upon the principles, *as on the interest of the assured,* and it would seem, therefore, to be always material, that they should know how far this interest is engaged in guarding the property from loss." In this case, the plaintiffs represented the property to be theirs, when in fact their title was a leasehold interest in one-sixth of it, as mortgagees of one-half of two-thirds, and under an executory contract whose conditions had not been complied with for a moiety of the two-thirds, which, if complied with, would give them title to two-thirds as mortgagees. The court held that, as a matter of law, these facts did not sustain the representation of the plaintiffs, that they were the owners of the property, and, the

---

[1] *Richardson v. Maine Ins. Co.*, 46 Me. 394; *Bowditch, etc., Ins. Co.* v. *Winslow,* 8 Gray (Mass.) 38.

[2] *Columbian Ins. Co.* v. *Lawrence,* 2 Pet. (U. S.) 48; *Rohrback* v. *Germania F. Ins. Co.*, 62 N. Y. 47.

court below having directed the jury that this proof established such
an interest in the property in the plaintiffs, as they had described
in their offer for insurance, the judgment was reversed.[1]

As to occupancy.

SEC. 180. When the answers of the assured in the application, set
forth the manner of occupancy, it will not be construed as a promissory
warranty, but merely affirmative, and if true *in presenti*, the policy is
not avoided, because at a subsequent period during the life of the policy,
the premiums are used for another purpose not more hazardous.[2] Thus,
a statement that " the building is a dwelling occupied by a tenant," is
a warranty that at the time when the application was made, it was so
occupied, and if false, avoids the policy, but it is not a warranty that
it shall continue to be so occupied during the whole life of the policy,[3]

---

[1] The doctrine of this case, so far as it relates to the particular misrepresentation
as to title, was repudiated by the court upon re-argument. See 10 Pet. (U. S.) 507,
and is generally repudiated by the State courts throughout the country. See sec.
86, page 168, *et seq.* See also, *Strong* v. *Manufacturers' Ins. Co.*, 10 Pick. (Mass.)
40 ; 1 Ben. F. I. C. 326 ; *Curry* v. *Com. Ins. Co.* 10 id. 535.

[2] *New England Ins. Co.* v. *Wetmore*, 32 Ill. 221. Where the application
described the occupation as " a four-story warehouse. First floor occupied by
machinery used for making barrels, with privilege of storing barrels on the premises, it was held that this was only a warranty as to the present use of the premises, and that a subsequent change in the use, not more hazardous, or not within
prohibited uses, would not avoid the policy. *U. S. Fire, etc., Ins. Co.* v. *Kimberly,*
34 Md. 224. Where the insured in his application stated that the building was
" occupied for stores below, the upper portion to remain unoccupied during the
continuance of this policy," was construed as only a warranty *in presenti* in reference to the lower floor, but a *continuing* warranty as to the upper. *Stout* v.
City F. Ins. Co., 12 Iowa, 371. So, where the application described the building
as " a two-story frame building, used for winding and coloring yarn, and storing
spun yarn." Held, only a warranty *in presenti* as to occupancy. *Smith* v.
Mechanics', etc., Ins. Co., 32 N. Y. 399. So, where a kiln drying machine was
described as designed " for burning hard coal," it was held that this could not be
construed as a warranty that it should be used with hard coal, or that the insured
would not use other fuel therein if necessary. *Tillou* v. *Kingston Mut. Ins. Co.*,
7 Barb. (N. Y.) 570.

[3] *Cumberland, etc., Ins. Co.* v. *Douglass*, 58 Penn. St. 419. Unless the character
of the occupancy is known to be otherwise by the agent or company insuring.
Sarsfield v. *Metropolitan Ins. Co.*, 61 Barb. (N. Y.) 479. Where the application
stated that no lamps were used in the picking room of a factory, and it appeared
that at the time when the application was made, lamps had been suspended there
for years, and were occasionally used, it was held that the policy was void. *Clark*
v. *Manufacturers' Ins. Co.*, 2 W. & M. (U. S.) 472. In *Sarsfield* v. *Metropolitan
Ins. Co.*, 61 Barb. (N. Y.) 479, in an action upon a policy of insurance to recover
a loss by fire, the insurance was upon the plaintiff's "two-story frame dwelling-
house, situated," etc., and it was provided in the contract that if, at any time during the period covered by the policy, the premises " shall be used for the purpose
of carrying on therein any trade or occupation," etc., denominated hazardous or
extra-hazardous in the printed classes of hazards annexed to the policy, that " from
thenceforth, so long as the same shall be the case, this policy shall be of no force
or effect." Among the printed class of hazards annexed to the policy, and denominated extra-hazardous, were " billiard saloons and their contents," " lager beer
saloons," " restaurants," " bar rooms," etc. It appeared that at the time of the

and, unless occupied in a manner that increases the risk, the policy is not avoided. Thus, where the application stated that the building was occupied as a dwelling-house, but was hereafter to be occupied as a tavern, and the policy contained the same language, with the addi_ tion, "and to be privileged as such," it was held that this did not amount to a warranty that it should be used as a tavern.[1] So, where the application set forth that the premises were occupied by a tenant, naming him, it has been held that this is merely a warranty *in presenti*, and if true, the policy is not avoided, because such tenant ceases to occupy the premises, and another succeeds him during the life of the policy.[2] So, where the application states matter which is merely descriptive of the occupancy, unless from the whole tenor of the policy and papers referred to, show that it was intended as a warranty, it can_ not have that effect, as where in an application for insurance upon a stock of goods, the insured stated that the "clerk sleeps in the store," but upon the night when the fire occurred he was not there. It was held that this was merely descriptive of the general character of the occupancy, at the time when the application was made, and not a warranty that the clerk should continue to sleep there every night.[3]

As to method of use.

SEC. 181. So, where the policy stated that there was "no fire in or about the building, except one under a kettle, securely imbedded in masonry, used for heating water, and made perfectly secure against accident, it was held that this could not be regarded as referring to the future use of the building, and was merely descriptive of the manner of its use, as to fires, at the time when the policy was issued, and if true then, the policy was not avoided because other fires were used in the building subsequently during the life of the policy.[4] But if from the lan-

---

fire, one portion of the building was used as a billiard saloon, another portion as a restaurant or eating-house, and that a bar was kept there. It also appeared that one room in the second story was used as a billiard saloon at the time the contract was made. Held, that the description of the building as a dwelling-house in the policy, was a warranty by the insured that the building *was a dwelling-house, and used as such exclusively*, and that no trade or occupation was carried on there which was denominated hazardous or extra-hazardous in the printed list annexed to the policy. Held, also, that the use of the building for such purposes, at the time of the fire, rendered the policy of no force or effect at that time, and that plaintiff could not recover. Such statement is a warranty *in presenti*, and such use at the time when the contract was made *avoids the policy, unless the agent effecting the insurance knew the use to which the building is devoted.*

[1] *Catlin* v. *Springfield F. Ins. Co.*, 1 Sum. (U. S.) 434.

[2] *O'Neil* v. *Buffalo F. Ins. Co.*, 3 N. Y. 122.

[3] *Frisbie* v. *Fayette Ins. Co.*, 27 Penn. St. 325.

[4] *Schmidt* v. *Peoria M. & F. Ins. Co.*, 41 Ill. 295. In *Williams* v. *N. England Mut. F. Ins. Co.*, 31 Me. 219, the applicant, in answer to an inquiry, "how many

guage used, it is evident that the parties referred to the future as well
as present use of the building; the statement, either in the policy or
application, when made a part of the policy, will be treated as a continuous warranty, the violation of which will render the contract inoperative.   Thus, where the policy recited that "no fire is kept, and no
hazardous goods are deposited," it was held that the statement referred
to the *habitual* use of the premises, and not an occasional necessary use,
and they having been destroyed by the burning of a tar barrel upon
the premises while making repairs, the policy was not avoided, and
a recovery could be had.[1]

---

stoves are used in the building?" answered "none," and it was held that the use
of a stove for a few days in drying paint, did not avoid the policy, as the statement could only be regarded as referring to the habitual use of stoves, and was
not a warranty that none should be used if rendered necessary by a contingency.
In *Aurora Fire Ins. Co.* v. *Eddy*, 55 Ill. 213, a similar doctrine was held.   In
Mickey v. *Burlington Ins. Co.*, 35 Iowa, 174, the plaintiff, applying for a policy of
fire insurance, covenanted to keep his stoves and pipes well secured.   The pipe
of one stove passed through a hole in the floor of an upper room, and the wife,
when summer came, took down the pipe in the upper room, and to "secure" the
hole, set the bed over it.   Afterward, forgetting about the removal of the pipe
above, she kindled a fire in the stove below, and lost not only her bed, but the
house.   The court held that a recovery might be had.   It thus seems, that
although one may not take advantage of his own wrong, he may of his wife's
folly.

[1] *Dobson* v. *Sotheby*, 1 Moo. & M. 90.   In *Houghton* v. *Manufacturers' Mut. Fire
Ins. Co.*, 8 Met. (Mass.) 114, the policy covering a woolen mill, contained a provision as follows: "If the representations made in" the application of the assured
for insurance "do not contain a just, full and true exposition of all the facts and
circumstances in regard to the condition, situation, value and risk of the property
insured,.so far as the same are known to the said applicants, and are material to
the risk; or if the situation or circumstances affecting the risk thereupon shall
be so altered or changed, by or with the advice, agency or consent of the assured
or their agent, so as to increase the risk thereupon, without the consent of this company," (the underwriters) "this policy shall be void."   There were annexed to
the application of the assured, various questions by the underwriters, and a notice
that it was expected that the answers thereto, would meet the requirements of
the underwriter's office, one of which requirements was, that an examination
should be had of the insured premises, thirty minutes after work.   Among the
written answers of the assured to said questions were these : The factory is worked
from "5 o'clock A. M. to 8½ o'clock P. M.   Sometimes extra work will be done in
the night."   "No watch is kept in or about the building, but the mill is examined
thirty minutes after work."   The court held that the representations of the assured
were legally adopted and embodied in the policy, as part of the contract, to the
same effect as if they had been therein set forth at large, also, that although the
answers of the assured were representations rather than warranties, and were
therefore sufficient, if the statements therein, of the facts relied on as the basis of
the contract, were made in good faith, and were substantially true and correct,
as to existing circumstances, and were substantially complied with, so far as they
were executory; yet that, subject to this qualification, it was a condition precedent to the liability of the underwriters, that the answers should contain a just,
full and true exposition of all the facts and circumstances in regard to the condition, situation, value and risk of the property insured, *so far as known to the
assured, and material to the risk*, and that although the assured were themselves
the owners and occupants of the property insured, and made the application for
insurance, yet the question *whether they knew certain facts and circumstances
respecting it, which were omitted, or not accurately stated in their answers, was a*

Warranty not to be so construed as to require an unlawful act.

SEC. 182. But, even though the statements in reference to the use of the building are to be regarded as warranties, yet they are not to be so interpreted, as to require the insurer to do an *unlawful* act, in order to keep the same, and it will be presumed that, the occupancy or use of the premises as described, was only a warranty so far as it could be lawfully performed. Thus, where the application, which was made a part of the policy, described the building as a paper mill, one and a half stories high, are used for drying paper; that the premises were constantly worked, and no watch kept, except the people work_ing in the mill during the night, and the application declared that all the statements contained therein were a just, full and true exposition

---

question of fact to be left to a jury. It was also held that the representations made by the assured, as to certain usages and practices observed at the factory, concerning the modes of conducting their business, and the precautions taken to guard against fire, amounted to a stipulation *that such modes of conducting their business should substantially continue to be adopted, and such precautions substantially continue to be taken, during the term of insurance; and that a discontinuace thereof by the assured, or by those entrusted by them with the management of the property,* without the consent of the underwriters, *would render the policy void, by virtue of the proviso therein respecting an alteration or change in the situation or circumstances affecting the risk,* and that the answers of the assured were to be construed with reference to the requirements of the underwriters, as specified in the notice accompanying the questions; and that a mere literal conformity and compliance would not be sufficient. *The assured were bound, by their representation that the mill was examined thirty minutes after work, to make such examination thirty minutes after the extra work, as well as after the other work;* and that the question, what is a cessation of work at the factory, from which the thirty minutes are to be computed, is a question for the jury, under all the circumstances of each particular case. In *Bilbrough* v. *Metropolis Ins. Co.,* 5 Duer. (N. Y.) 587, the application which was made a part of the policy contained an inquiry: ' During what hours is the factory worked?" The answer was: "We run the cards, picker, drawing-frames and speeder, day and night, the rest only twelve hours daily. We only intend running nights until we get more cards, etc., which are making; shall not run nights over four months," it was held, that this statement of an intention to cease running when the cards were received, was equivalent to an agreement to that effect, the intervening period, at all events, not to exceed four months, and a subsequent renewal of night work avoided the policy. In answer to the printed interrogatories of the company, an applicant for insurance represented that the premises were a stone building of certain dimensions, roof of wood. After answering the question touching the distances and direction of adjacent buildings, etc., he answered in reply to the last question: " Are there any other material circumstances?" " No." In the notice given the company of a loss, the insured subsequently described the premises as a stone dwelling-house of certain dimensions, etc., with a one-story wood kitchen part attached thereto. Held, that as it did not appear whether this kitchen part attached to the house was a mere temporary structure, or how it was constructed and attached, and whether or not, it was a part and parcel of the house, the court could not say as the case appeared before them, that the referee was bound to find a false representation or description of the "stone dwelling-house." It was also held that whether the omission avoided the policy, under the provision in the by-laws making the policy void, unless the applicant makes a true representation of the property, so far as concerns the risk and value thereof, was a question of fact for the referee, and that if the answer in the negative of the insured, to the question as to the existence of "any other material circumstances," was a warranty, the referee had found, by his decision for the plaintiff, that it was not broken.

23

of all the facts and circumstances in regard to the condition, situation, value and risk of the property, so far as the same were material to the risk; and it appeared that the mill was not operated upon Sunday, it was held, that this did not avoid the policy, because it must be presumed that the parties did not contemplate an *unlawful* use of the property by the assured, but merely that it should be constantly used, so far as it could be done lawfully, during the usual customary working days and hours.[1] So where there is a general usage as to the time or manner in which a certain business is conducted, or a special custom established by the insured as to the time and manner in which his business is conducted, of which the company or its agent, through whom the insurance is procured, is aware the policy will be presumed to have been made in reference thereto, and will be construed in reference to such general or special custom.[2] Thus, where the assured in his application, in answer to the questions, "During what hours are the premises worked?" "From six A. M. to seven P. M." "How many hands are employed?" "*About twenty.*" "Have you a night watch always on duty?" "*We have.*" "Is the building left alone after the watchman goes off duty in the morning until he returns to his charge at evening?" "*It is not.*" "Is any duty required of him other than watching for the safety of the premises?" "*None.*" "Is there a force pump upon the premises expressly for putting out fire?" "*There is.*" "Is it a good pump, and in condition at all times for immediate use?" "*It is.*" "How often is it tried to know if it is in order?" "*Every two or three days*," and by the terms of the application covenanted that the statements contained therein were a just, full and true exposition of all the facts, etc., material to the risk, and it appeared that *in fact*, the mill was only run during a part of each year, *of which fact the agent was aware*, when he took the application; it was held, that *the usage of the plaintiff in the conduct of the business*, to run his mill only a part of each year, *known to the agent of the defendant at the time when the insurance was effected*, must be treated as qualifying the plaintiff's statements, to the extent that the pruden-

---

[1] *Prieger* v. *Exchange Mut. Ins. Co..* 6 Wis. 86.

[2] *May* v. *Buckeye Ins. Co.*, 25 Wis. 291. But unless the usage is general, so that knowledge thereof by the insurer can be presumed, it is held not to affect the contract. *Glendale Mf'g Co.* v. *Protection Ins. Co.*, 21 Conn. 19; *Stebbins* v. *Globe Ins. Co.*, 2 Hall (N. Y. S. C.) 632; *Hartford Protection Ins. Co.* v. *Harmer*, 2 Ohio St. 452; *Cobb* v. *Lime Rock F. & M. Ins. Co.*, 58 Me. 326; or if it leads to absurd results. *Lecomb* v. *Provincial Ins. Co.*, 10 Allen (Mass.) 305.

tial measures referred to in the application, were only adopted *during the season in which he usually run the mill.*[1]

Fluctuating uses — Permanent uses.

SEC. 183. It may fairly be stated as a proposition settled by the better class of recent cases, that all matters stated in reference to the occupancy of premises, the occupancy of which is fluctuating and subject to change, which merely purport to describe the present condition and occupancy thereof, are to be treated only as warranties *in presenti*, and do not amount to an engagement that it shall continue during the life of the policy, *and if true when made,* the policy is not avoided by any subsequent change in the use of the property that does not essentially increase the risk or is not within a class of prohibited uses.[2] But *when, by the usual course*

---

[1] As to the effect of knowledge by the agent of peculiarities of the business, as conducted by the assured, see *Ins. Co.* v. *Schetteler,* 38 Ill. 166 ; *Rowley* v. *Ins. Co.,* 36 N. Y. 550 ; *Columbian Ins. Co.* v. *Cooper,* 50 Penn. St. 331 ; *Viele* v. *Germania Ins. Co.,* 26 Iowa, 9. In *Carter & Co.* v. *Philadelphia Coal Co.,* 1 Week. Not. Cas. 384, the Supreme Court of Pennsylvania considered the question how far evidence of custom or usage is admissible to interpret a contract. The suit was brought to recover back certain commissions claimed by defendants, and allowed to them on a previous settlement. It appears that defendants, who did business at Philadelphia, managed the affairs of plaintiff company and sold coal for them ; that in doing so they employed S. & Co., as brokers, to make sales of coal to the P. & R. railroad company. Plaintiff company now claims that the employment of the brokers was unauthorized, and that the commissions to the amount paid to the brokers should be recovered back. Defendant offered to show that it was the usual and customary method of the Philadelphia coal trade to sell coal through the agency of brokers, to whom a commission was paid ; that defendants sold largely to the P. & R railroad company through S. & Co., and that the sales so effected could not have been made in any other way. This offer was rejected, and the court on appeal held that the rejection was error. The court said : "It is not necessary to prove all the elements of a custom necessary to make law ; the object here is to interpret a contract. The usages of a particular trade or business are presumed to be known to those engaged therein. They may, therefore, in the absence of any express stipulation inconsistent therewith, be supposed to have entered into the understanding of the parties in making the contract ; they furnish a most valuable aid in arriving at the mutual assent of the parties, and, when not contrary to law, are admissible in evidence. *Lewis* v. *Marshall,* 7 Mann. & Gr. 729 ; *United States* v. *Duval,* 1 Gil. (Ind.) 372 ; *Furniss* v. *Hone,* 8 Wend. 247 ; *Oatwater* v. *Nelson,* 29 Barb. 29 ; *Girard Fire and Marine Ins. Co.* v. *Stephenson,* 1 Wright, 293 ; *Helme* v. *The Philadelphia Life Ins. Co.,* 11 P. F. Smith, 107 ; *McMasters* v. *The Pennsylvania R. R. Co.,* 19 id. 374.

[2] *United States F. & M. Ins. Co.* v. *Kimberly,* 34 Md. 224 ; 6 Am. Rep. 326. A policy was issued "on a four-story warehouse, * * * first floor occupied by machinery used for making barrels, with privilege of storing barrels on the premises and other merchandise not more hazardous." The policy contained a clause requiring a true and accurate description of the use and occupation of the premises under penalty of forfeiture. The policy further declared, in printed words, that it was the intention of the parties that in case the insured premises should be used or appropriated for the purpose of carrying on or exercising the trade, business or vocation of (a large number of manufactures specified therein, including) "cooper, carpenter, cabinet-maker," * * * "so long as the said premises shall be wholly or in part appropriated or used for any or either of the purposes aforesaid, these premises shall cease and be of no force or effect unless

of business, the uses referred to is permanent and continuous, and from a fair interpretation of the whole contract it is evident that the parties contracted in reference to such continued use of the property by the insured, and he can fairly be held to have contracted to make no changes in the condition or use of the premises, the warranty will be deemed continuing, except so far as it may be affected by a general custom, a special custom of the insured *known to the insurer,* or as such use may be *unlawful* at particular periods.[1] It must be understood, however, that it is competent for the parties to contract for the use of the premises in a specific manner; and when they do so, the contract is obligatory and binding;[2] and in all cases, as to whether the applicant's statements in reference to the occupancy of the premises is to be regarded as a continuing warranty, or only *in presenti,* must be determined from the language used and the subject-matter to which it relates. This species of contracts are not uniform, nor are they required to be. Every insurer has a right to say upon what terms he will insure property, and the terms agreed upon, as expressed in the policy or contract, must control, except so far as they are qualified by general or special customs, or extraneous matter referred to in the policy.

Of course, the language of a policy may be such as to constitute the

---

otherwise specially agreed by this corporation, and such agreement be signed in writing in or on the policy." The premises, at the time the insurance was effected were used for making and storing barrels, as mentioned in the written portion of the policy. Subsequently, small circular saws and a work-bench were introduced and boxes were manufactured, but this kind of work had ceased from two to four months when a loss by fire occurred. The saws and work-bench had remained in the building, and a lathe had been put up the day preceding the fire, for the purpose of making broom handles and brush blocks. In an action on the policy, it was held that the description of property was not a *continuing* warranty, but a warranty *in presenti;* that the policy was suspended during the prohibited use of the premises, but was revived when the use ceased to exist; and that there was no such "appropriation" of the premises, *at the time of the fire,* to a prohibited use, as was contemplated in the policy or as prevented a recovery. As to effect of description of premises and uses to which devoted, and that it is to be regarded as merely a warranty *in presenti,* and that the premises will not be devoted to more hazardous uses, see *Maryland F. Ins. Co. v. Whiteford,* 31 Md. 221; *Smith v. Merchants' Ins. Co.,* 29 How. Pr. (N. Y.) 884; *N. E. F. & M. Ins. Co. v. Wetmore,* 32 Ill. 221; *Herrick v. Union, etc., Ins. Co.,* 48 Me. 588; *Lounsbury v. Protective Ins. Co.,* 8 Conn. 467; *Catlin v. Springfield F. Ins. Co.,* 1 Sum. (U. S.) 442; *Blood v. Howard F. Ins. Co.,* 12 Cush. (Mass.) 472; *Frisbie v. Fayette Mut. Ins. Co.,* 27 Penn. St. 325; *O'Neil v. Buffalo Ins. Co.,* 3 N. Y. 122; *Billings v. Tolland, etc., Ins. Co.,* 20 Conn. 139; *Hough v. City F. Ins. Co.,* 29 id. 10; *Boardman v. N. H. Mut. F. Ins. Co.,* 20 N. H. 551; *Hawkes v. Dodge Co. Mut. Ins. Co.,* 11 Wis. 188; *Annapolis R. R. Co. v. Baltimore Ins. Co.,* 32 Md. 37; *May v. Buckeye Ins. Co.,* 25 Wis. 291.

[1] *May v. Buckeye Ins. Co., ante.*

[2] *United States v. Kimberley,* 34 Md. 227; *Reynolds v. Commerce Ins. Co.,* 47 N. Y. 597; *Atlantic Dock Co. v. Libby,* 45 N. Y. 499; *Dittmer v. Germania Ins. Co.,* 23 La. An. 458; *Ins. Co. v. Slaughter,* 12 Wall. (U. S.) 404.

representations as to occupancy, a continuing warranty, and when such is the case, any change therein would invalidate the policy, but in order to have that effect, *the representation must be such as to leave no doubt as to the intention of the parties;* and, generally, the cases in which such an interpretation has been put upon the policy, it will be found that *it related to the use, or method of use of the property insured, when used for a specific purpose,* and not as a restriction of its use to a particular purpose, although such a restriction would be competent, but in order to have that effect, *it must be expressly stated, or be fairly inferrable from the language used, and no such inference will be made if there is any reasonable ground for a contrary construction;* but in *all* cases, the use will be treated as restricted to a use *not more hazardous,* than that to which the property was devoted when the policy issued. [1] Thus it has been held that, when the assured in his application stated that no lamps were used in the building, that this should be treated as a warranty *that none would be used therein* so long as the building was used for the purposes for which it was insured. [2]

An answer in an application to a question as to what are the facilities for extinguishing fires? being "a force pump and abundance of water," it was held that this could not be construed as a warranty, except *in presenti,* and did not amount to a warranty that the pump should at all times during the life of the policy be kept in repair. [3]

So a description of a building as an "occupied dwelling-house" is held not to amount to a warranty that it shall continue to be so occupied during the existence of the policy, but that the warranty is answered if the building was in fact so occupied when the application was made. [4] But if it is specially provided in the contract that if the building shall be used for any other purpose than that named, or that if it shall be used for a more hazardous purpose, the policy shall be void, a fulfillment of this covenant is a condition precedent to a recovery, and if any portion of the building is used for any other *more hazardous* business, the policy is avoided, as much as though the whole

---

[1] *May* v. *Buckeye Ins. Co., ante; Clark* v. *Ins. Co.,* 8 How. (U. S.) 235; *Glendale Woolen Co.* v. *Protection Ins. Co.,* 21 Conn. 19; *Barrett* v. *Ins. Co.,* 7 Cush. (Mass.) 175; *Roberts* v. *Ins. Co..* 3 Hill (N. Y.) 501; *Stout* v. *Ins. Co.,* 12 Iowa, 371.

[2] *Clarke* v. *Manufacturers' Ins. Co., ante.* The case of *Glendale Woolen Co.* v. *Protection Ins. Co.,* 21 Conn. 19, has sometimes been cited, and regarded as holding a different rule, but an examination of that case will disclose the fact that it fully sustains the doctrine of the text.

[3] *Gilliatt* v. *Pawtucket, etc., Ins. Co.,* 8 R. I. 282; but holding a contrary doctrine, see *Sayles* v. *N. A. Ins. Co.,* 2 Curtis (U. S. C. C.) 610.

[4] *Cumberland, etc., Ins. Co.* v. *Douglass,* 58 Penn. St. 419.

building was so occupied.   As if the building is insured as a dwelling-house, and the owner permits a portion of it to be occupied as a work-shop for currying hides, the policy is avoided, *even though the owner continues to reside in a portion of the building !* [1]   So where the occupancy was described as that of a grist mill, when in fact a part of the building was occupied as a carpenter's shop occasionally, the policy was held void. [2]

Rule as to incidental or ordinary uses — Billings v. Tolland Co. Mut. Ins. Co.— Dobson v. Sotheby — Shaw v. Robberds.

SEC. 184. In a Connecticut case,[3] where in a policy of insurance on sundry buildings, they were described as barns, to which this clause was added, "all the above described barns are used for hay, straw, grain unthreshed, stabling and shelter ; " and on the trial, after proof of a loss by fire, it appeared, that on the day preceding the night of the fire, the insured had caused about two bushels of lime and six or eight pails of water to be placed in a tub standing in a room generally used for keeping therein unthreshed corn, in one of the barns, for the pur-pose of preparing the lime for rolling in it some wheat, which he was about to sow upon his farm; that a short time previous to the fire, he had commenced the painting of his house, and his painter had mixed his paints in the same room, and at the time of the fire, there were in it an oil barrel, containing about a gallon of oil, a keg of white lead and a pot with about a pint of mixed paint ; that in another building, described in the policy as used in part for a cider-mill, the insured, before and after the execution of the policy, had been in the habit of repairing his farming utensils, and had also made in it a bee-hive, and planed some boards for a room in his house; but a day or two before the fire, the building had been cleared out, leaving nothing in it but some apples.   The court held, 1. That the clause relating to the use of the buildings insured, was not a warranty that they should be used in that manner, and in no other; but was inserted merely for the purpose of designating the buildings insured, and not to limit their use, or to deprive the insured of the enjoyment of his property in the same manner as buildings of that description are generally used and enjoyed ; 2. That the acts of the insured, so far as they were, or could have been, the cause of the loss, were in accordance with the ordinary use of such buildings by farmers.   Therefore, where the court, on the

[1] *Gasner* v. *Metropolitan Ins. Co.*, 13 Minn. 483.
[2] *Jennings* v. *Chenango Mut. Ins. Co.*, 2 Den. (N. Y.) 75.
[3] *Billings* v. *Tolland, etc., Ins. Co.*, 20 Conn. 139.

trial of the cause, instructed the jury, that if the buildings insured were, in the ordinary acceptation of the terms, of the description stated in the policy, and continued such to the time of the fire, and were only put to the ordinary use of such buildings, the policy remained in force; but that the insured had no right to change the nature and use of the buildings, and if he did, he would lose the benefit of the policy—that a single act or so, which did not belong to the ordinary and appropriate use of the buildings, would not change their nature and character, and would not vacate the policy, or prevent a recovery thereon, unless such acts were fraudulent, or grossly careless, and if grossly careless, were the cause of the loss—and the jury found for the plaintiff; it was held no misdirection.

WAITE, J., in commenting upon the effect of usage or the ordinary use of property in construing warranties or conditions in policies of insurance, said: "The acts done by the plaintiff are set forth in the motion, so that one can see what they were. and whether they were a departure *from the common and ordinary use of such buildings. We very well know that farmers in the State are in the habit of using their barns for a variety of purposes*, connected with their agricultural business, besides that of storing their hay, and stabling their cattle. Their barns are frequently used as a shelter for their wagons, plows, sleds, and other farming implements. When the plaintiff procured the insurance to be effected on the buildings, it is not to be presumed that he meant to deprive himself *of their common and ordinary use*, or that the defendants, by their policy, intended any such thing. *And excepting, so far as there is an express prohibition in relation to the use of them, the understanding of the parties undoubtedly was, that the common and ordinary use of them was to be continued in the same manner as if the policy had never been issued.*"

And in all cases, where the breach complained of is only such a use of the property as is consistent with its *ordinary* use, it cannot, in the absence of an *express warranty* or condition, be made available. Thus, in a leading English case,[1] the plaintiff procured an insurance upon an agricultural building under the erroneous name of a barn, but it appeared that the rate of premium would have been the same if it had been correctly described, and the policy recited, "no fire is kept and no hazardous goods deposited," and in repairing the roof, which required tarring, a fire was lighted in the building and a barrel of

---

[1] *Dobson v. Sotheby*, 1 Moo. & M. 90.

tar was brought in for the purpose of performing the necessary operation ; it was held that the policy was not thereby avoided, for the condition must be taken to relate to the *habitual* use of a fire, and not to
one rendered necessary in the ordinary course of making necessary
repairs, or for doing those things essential for the protection and preservation of the property. When there is no warranty, express or
implied, that the premises shall continue to be occupied during the
whole time of insurance, in the manner or for the purpose specified in
the policy, and the policy undertakes to recite what uses are prohibited, or will render the policy void, the temporary use of the premises
for any other purpose than that named in the policy, if not within the
prohibited class, and does not involve a change of business, will not
render the policy void, even though such use is more hazardous, and
is the proximate cause of the destruction of the property. Thus, in
an English case,[1] the plaintiff effected an insurance upon his premises,
describing them as a granary and a kiln for drying corn. He was in
the habit of using the kiln for drying corn, and for no other purpose.
While the policy was in force, a vessel laden with oak bark was sunk
near the plaintiff's premises, and the owner of the bark requested him
to allow him to dry the bark on his premises, which he did gratuitously, and the owner commenced drying it there. No notice of this
was given to the insurers. The fire used in drying the bark was no
greater than that used in drying corn, but on the third day, while the
bark was drying, the kiln and all the premises took fire and were consumed. Lord Chief Justice DENMAN directed the jury to say, 1st.
Whether drying corn and drying bark were different trades ? 2d.
Whether drying bark was more dangerous than drying corn ? And
3d. Whether the fire was occasioned by drying the bark ? The jury
found that they were different trades ; that drying bark was most dangerous, and that the fire was occasioned by drying the bark, whereupon he directed a verdict for the defendant, with leave to the plaintiff to move for leave to enter a verdict for the full sum if the court
should be of opinion, that, upon these facts, he was entitled thereto.
Upon a rule to show cause, the court held that the plaintiff was entitled to recover upon the ground that the description of the premises,
and their use, *was true when made ;* that the plaintiff had not warranted not to use the premises temporarily for any other purpose, and
that there was no condition of the policy which was thereby violated.

---

[1] *Shaw* v. *Robberds,* 6 Ad. & El. 75.

Lord DENMAN, C.J., in delivering the opinion, said : " The sixth con_ dition points at an alteration of business ; *at something permanent and habitual ;* and if the plaintiff had either dropped his business or corn drying and taken up that of bark drying, or added the latter to the former, no doubt the case could have been brought within that condi_ tion. *Perhaps if he had made any charge for drying the bark,* it might have been a question for the jury whether he had done so as a matter of business, and whether he had not thereby (although it was the first instance of bark drying), *made an alteration* within the meaning of that condition. But, according to the evidence, we are clearly of the opinion that no such question arose for the jury, *and that this single act of kindness was no breach of the condition,*" and a verdict was entered for the plaintiff for the full amount of the loss, so far as covered by the policy.[1] Warranties and conditions of a policy must be liberally construed so as to effectuate, as far as possible, the intention of the parties.[2]

---

[1] See, similar in its facts, and identical in its doctrine, *Loud* v. *Citizens' Ins. Co.*, 2 Gray (Mass.) 221.

[2] In the application for a policy, the assured stated that his stoves and pipes were well secured, and that he would engage to keep them so. After the policy was issued, the wife of the assured, intending to remove during the summer a stove, the pipe of which passed through the floor in an upper room, and thence into a chimney, took down the pipe in the upper room, and put a bed over the hole in the floor through which the pipe passed, but did not remove the stove and pipe below. A few days after, forgetting what she had done, she built a fire in the stove, which set fire to the bed, and burnt the house. Held, that the assured could recover on the policy. *Mickey* v. *Burlington Ins. Co.*, 35 Iowa, 174. A similar doctrine was held in *Loud* v. *Citizen's, etc., Ins. Co., ante,* the plaintiffs procured a policy upon lumber, etc., in their two stores on their wharf in Weymouth. In the application for insurance, which was expressly made a part of the policy, it was stated that the stores were used for storing lumber, etc., and that one room was used for a counting-room. It was also stated that the counting-room was warmed by a coal stove, funnel and stove well secured, and that no lights were used in the building evenings, all of which was true *at the time when the application was made and the policy issued.* Subsequent to the issue of the policy, a schooner, when near the wharf, got aground and filled with water. The beds and bedding on board having been brought on deck, and being wet with the rain, were, by the plaintiffs' permission, removed into the store in which the counting-room was. About midnight, one of the plaintiffs, at the request of the captain and crew, gave them permission to sleep in the counting-room, but expressly told them they must not make any fire, use any light, or even smoke. There was a stove in the counting-room, the funnel of which passed through the loft overhead, but was not then in a safe condition. The captain and crew disregarding the instructions of the plaintiff, kindled a fire, and very soon the building was in flames. The defendant claimed that it was not liable for the loss, because the plaintiffs had violated their warranty as to the condition of the funnel, and because they had put the building to hazardous uses without its consent. The court held that the warranty as to the condition of the funnel was only a warranty *in presenti,* and was not a continuing warranty, and that the use of the building for one night for the purpose of lodging strangers in distress, was not putting the building to hazardous uses, within the meaning of the condition of the policy.

SEC. 185. If a certain use of the premises is *prohibited*, and there is nothing in the language used from which a license to use the premises for any of such prohibited purposes can be inferred, the policy is avoided by such use. When the insurer annexes a list of hazardous uses, which are prohibited, the use of the premises for *any* of such purposes is fatal to a recovery for a loss under the policy; *as, in such cases, the assured is treated as warranting that the premises shall not be used for any of such prohibited uses during the life of the policy.*[1]

---

[1] In *Mead* v. *N. W. Ins. Co.*, 7 N. Y. 530, the policy *prohibited* the carrying on of certain hazardous trades, and the court very properly held that this amounted to a promissory warranty that no such trades should be carried on upon the premises during the life of the policy, and that the question whether such use was material to the risk, was not open. WELLES, J., said: "Upon the trial the defendants' counsel offered to prove by the witness Halliday, who occupied one of the buildings insured at the time of the fire, that he did business and kept articles in said building denominated hazardous and extra hazardous at the time of the fire. The evidence was objected to, and the objection sustained by the judge, to which the defendants' counsel excepted. In this, I think, there was error. The policies all provided that in case the premises insured should, at any time after the making and during the continuance thereof, be appropriated, applied, or used to or for the purpose of carrying on or exercising therein any trade, business, or vocation denominated hazardous or extra hazardous, or specified in the memorandum of special rates in the proposals annexed to the policy, or for the purpose of storing therein any of the articles, goods, or merchandise in the same proposals denominated hazardous or extra hazardous, or included in the memorandum of special rates, unless therein otherwise specially provided for, or thereafter agreed to by the company in writing, to be added to or indorsed upon the policy, then and from thenceforth so long as the same should be so appropriated, applied, or used, the policy should cease and be of no force or effect. The offer was nearly in the language of one of the above provisions to show its violation. The answers given by the respondent's counsel to this point are, first, that the fire did not originate in the store occupied by the witness; second, that no knowledge of the business carried on was shown in the respondent; third, that there was no proof that the business had been changed from the time the insurance was effected to the time of the fire; and fourth, that this point was not reserved by the appellants' counsel at the close of the case, and is not among the objections then raised. None of those answers are sufficient. The provision of the policy referred to amounted to a prospective or promissory warranty, and was as obligatory as if it had been retrospective or concurrent. It was, therefore, of no consequence that the fire was not produced by its violation or breach. *Murdock* v. *Chenango Co. Mut. Ins. Co.*, 2 Comst. 210. It is equally unimportant that the respondent was ignorant that such business was carried on. The question whether a warranty has been broken can never depend upon the knowledge or ignorance or intent of the party making it touching the acts or the fact constituting the breach. It was undoubtedly competent for the parties to contract in relation to the future business to be carried on in the building insured without reference to the previous business, and such was the case here. That the business prohibited had been carried on up to the time the policy was made was no excuse for a violation of the contract. And finally it was not necessary or proper for the counsel to do more than to except to the decision of the judge at the circuit overruling the evidence offered. He was, in fact, precluded from making the point in any other stage of the case by the exclusion of the evidence." *Kelly* v. *Home Ins. Co.*, 97 Mass. 288; *Davern* v. *Merchants' Ins. Co.*, 7 La. An. 344; *Lee* v. *Howard Ins. Co.*, 3 Gray (Mass.) 183. "Cabinet making" was prohibited. Held, that "finishing chairs" was within the prohibition, and was not excused because the policy covered cabinet ware.

But of course it is understood, that where hazardous or prohibited articles are included in the class of goods insured, so as to overcome the force of a general prohibition in reference thereto, yet when the

See also, *Appleby* v. *Astor F. Ins. Co.*, 54 N. Y. 253. So, where "hat bleaching" was included in the list of hazards, and the policy covered a stock of "millinery goods," it was held that "bleaching bonnets" was "hat bleaching" within the terms of the policy and avoided it. *Merrick* v. *Provincial Ins. Co.*, 14 U. C. (Q. B.) 439. In *Demers* v. *Manhattan Ins. Co.*, 35 N. J. 366, the policy covered a building "occupied as a country store," and contained a provision that "in case the premises shall, at any time during the period for which this policy would otherwise continue in force, be used for the purpose of carrying on therein any trade or vocation, or for storing and keeping therein any articles, goods, or merchandise denominated hazardous, extra hazardous, or specially hazardous, in the second class of the classes of hazards annexed, from thenceforth, so long as the same shall be so used, this policy shall be void." At the time the policy was taken, and from thence to the time the fire occurred, the premises were used in part as a stable. Among the extra hazardous risks that of a private stable was enumerated. This was held a violation of the contract, which was not cured by the fact that insurers' agent, who made the policy, knew at the time that the premises were used for the purpose prohibited. In *Mutthews* v. *Queen City Ins. Co.*, 2 Cin. S. C. (Ohio) 109, the policy specified planing-mills, saw-mills, and carpenter shops as "hazardous;" and the use of the premises for any hazardous trades, business. or vocations, *in the conditions mentioned*, were prohibited, unless, by agreement, indorsed upon the policy. The policy was on a planing-mill and saw-mill. The second story was used as a carpenter shop, a risk in the same class of hazards as planing and saw-mills, and it was held that using the second story as a carpenter shop was a breach of the conditions. The doctrine of this case is not, however, believed to express the true rule in such cases, and the later and better class of cases hold that, where a building is insured for a *hazardous* purpose, or rather a purpose denominated as hazardous in the list of hazards embraced in the policy, the use of the premises for any other purpose embraced in the same list of hazards, does not avoid the policy. *Reynolds* v. *Commerce Ins. Co.*, 47 N. Y. 597; *Smith* v. *Mechanics' & Traders' Ins. Co.*, 52 N. Y. 399. At least such is the true construction, *unless the risk is increased by such use.* *State Mut. F. Ins. Co.* v. *Arthur*, 30 Penn. St. 315; *Reynolds* v. *Commerce Ins. Co., ante.* The fact that the use of the premises for a prohibited purpose was without the knowledge of the assured, is held to constitute no defense. Thus, in *Hoxsie* v. *Prov. Mut. Ins. Co.*, 6 R. I. 517, the policy covered a building described as "a dwelling-house, the basement being of stone and wood." The charter provided: "No policy shall extend to any sugar-house, bake-house, distill-house, joiner shop, or other house, except on such terms only as shall be specially agreed on by the directors, unless expressly mentioned in the policy." The defendant pleaded that after the policy was assigned the premises were used and occupied as a joiners' shop, and that the risk was thereby increased. The plaintiff replied it was so used and occupied without the knowledge of the plaintiff. It was held that the plea was a good bar, and the replication no answer to it. In *Steinmitz* v. *Franklin F. Ins. Co.*, 6 Phila. (Penn.) 21, the policy contained a stipulation that "mills and manufactories," among other things, were extra hazardous, and, therefore, that no policy would be construed to extend to such a risk, unless liberty be given for the purpose and expressed thereon. The fifth story of the building was used for making of muslin window shades by nine or ten persons regularly employed in that business as the sole means of their livelihood, and it was held that this constituted a manufactory within the meaning of the condition, and was a bar to the plaintiff's action. See also, *Gassner* v. *Metropolitan Ins. Co.*, 13 Minn. 483, in which the policy provided that "the interest of the mortgagee shall not be invalidated by any act of the mortgagor; but the mortgagee shall notify the insurers of any change of ownership or increase of hazard *as soon as the same shall come to his knowledge*, and shall, on reasonable demand, pay an additional charge for the same." The building was insured as a dwelling-house, and all specially hazardous trades (among which was that of a currier) were prohibited. The owner used the premises for currying, and it was held that the policy was thereby avoided.

language of the prohibition is specific, and leaves no doubt as to the intention of the insurer, and the assured at least *ought* from the language used to have known that the prohibition applied, the meaning of the term used in describing the goods as "groceries" or "goods such as are usually kept in country stores," cannot be permitted to overcome the plain prohibitory words used. Thus, in a California case,[1] the plaintiff's assignor procured an insurance from the defendant upon his stock of goods and fixtures, in a store occupied by him in Sacramento. The goods were covered by two several policies in the defendant company, both of which contained a provision that if the "assured shall keep gunpowder, fire-works, nitro-glycerine, phosphorus, saltpetre, nitrate of soda, petroleum, naptha, gasoline, benzine, or benzine varnish, or *keep* or *use* camphene, spirit gas, or any burning fluid or chemical oils, without written permission in their policy, then, and in every such case, this policy shall be void. Kerosene oil, however may be used for lights in dwellings, and kept for sale in stores, in quantities not exceeding five barrels, to be drawn by daylight only." The insured and his clerk slept in the store, in a back-room adjoining the store-room proper. The store was lighted with gas in the evening, and at night the gas was turned off and a small lamp, filled with kerosene oil, was left burning on the counter in the store all night, to keep off burglars. The court held, as a matter of law, that the use of kerosene oil as an illuminater *in the store*, was expressly excluded by the language of the policy, and that the fact that the insured and his clerk slept in the room adjoining the store, did not constitute it a "dwelling," within the ordinary meaning of the term, and the verdict for the plaintiff, in the court below was reversed. In this case, the use of kerosene was expressly prohibited, except as stated in the policy, and WALLACE, J., well said, in the course of his opinion, "and in the face of this, it would be doing violence to the plain intention of the parties as shown in the language of the policy, to extend that privilege so as to embrace the case of a store, as such." But all conditions in a policy are strictly construed, and in favor of the assured, upon the ground, that inasmuch as the insurer fixes his own terms, if he intends to impose restrictions upon the insured, he must use such language as clearly discloses his intention, *and nothing can be claimed by implication.* If there is any doubt as to the meaning of the language employed, the benefit of the doubt is given to the insured.[2]

---

[1] *Cerf* v. *Home Ins. Co.,* 44 Cal. 320 ; 13 Am. Rep. 165.
[2] *Smith* v. *Mechanics' & Traders' Ins. Co.,* 32 N. Y. 399.

In a case recently decided by the Commission of Appeals,[1] the rule of strict construction was well illustrated, and REYNOLDS, C., in the course of his opinion, shew the utter absurdity of making construc_ tions, to uphold and extend conditions which the insurer has seen fit to impose.   In that case, the plaintiff procured a policy of insurance in the defendant company, upon his office furniture, fixtures and merchandise, hazardous and extra hazardous, contained in prem- ises occupied by him in New York City.   It was provided in the policy, that if the premises should be used for storing or keeping therein, any articles, goods or merchandise, denominated hazardous, or extra hazardous, or specially hazardous, except as specially provided for in the policy, so long as the same continued, the policy should be of no force.   It was also provided that the policy should be void if *petroleum*, rock oil, earth oil, benzole, benzine, or naptha shall be *stored* in said premises, without written permission therefor, endorsed on the policy.   There was also a further provision in the policy, that the following trades, occupations and merchandise add to the rate of the building and its contents fifty cents or more per $100, and to be covered, must be specially written in the policy: "burning fluid, camphene," also, that camphene, spirits, gas or burning fluid, or any similar inflammable fluid, *when used in stores, warehouses, shops, or manu- factories, as a light,* subjects the goods therein to an additional charge, etc.   There was also another provision in the policy, that in case *the risk should be increased by any means within the contract of the insured,* or by the occupation of the premises for more hazardous purposes, the policy should be void.   It appeared that the plaintiff did not keep any of the prohibited articles for sale, nor did he store them on his premises, or use them for lights in his store; but, being afflicted with a severe cutaneous disease, he used crude petreleum oil as a remedy therefor, and kept a small quantity thereof *for that purpose* in a jug, on a shelf in his store, and it was there at the time of the fire. The defendants insisted that the keeping of the oil for medicinal purposes, avoided the policy under the conditions named.   The court held that the keeping of the oil for the purpose named, was not a keeping or storing within the meaning of the condition of the policy, because it was not for mercantile or commercial purposes, or as a busi- ness,[2] and that, not being used or kept for any of the prohibited

[1] *Williams* v. *Fireman's Fund Ins. Co.,* 54 N. Y. 569 ; 13 Am. Rep. 620.

[2] *Hoffman* v. *Ætna Ins. Co.,* 32 N. Y. 405 ; *Reynolds* v. *Commerce Ins. Co. of N. Y.,* 47 id. 597 ; *Catton* v. *Springfield Ins. Co.,* 1 Sum. (U. S.) 434 ; *N. Y. Equit-*

purposes, *and, the jury having found that it did not materially increase
the risk,* the keeping and using of it as alleged, did not avoid the policy.
The court correctly holding that the insurer having imposed its own
conditions, must be regarded as having intended no other prohibition
than that clearly stated in the policy, and that if the keeping or use
of any such articles *for any purpose* was intended, it should have been
so stated in the policy, so that the insured could be upon his guard,
and properly protect his interests.   REYNOLDS, C., pertinently said:
" It is very clear that, when the policy was written, *no one understood*
that the keeping of petroleum oil for merely medicinal purposes would
render void the obligation of the defendant.   The provision against
' storing or keeeping' was obviously aimed at storing or keeping in a
mercantile sense, in considerable quantities, for the purposes of commercial traffic.   It was not intended to prohibit its use as a medicine.
It might as well be claimed that if the plaintiff went to his medical
advisor and had his shirt and drawers saturated with petroleum, with
the view to a peaceful repose of a night, and brought them to bed, on
the insured premises, or if, indeed, *he had taken a quantity internally
for that purpose,* it would have been 'a keeping or storing' within the
meaning of the policy."

Change of use does not avoid policy.

SEC. 186. The fact that a particular use, which is regarded as hazardous, is specially permitted, does not amount to a warranty or condition
that such use shall continue during the life of the policy; but the
assured may, in the absence of any express prohibition to the contrary,
devote the premises to any other use that does not increase the risk.[1]
Thus, in a Pennsylvania case,[2] a policy of insurance on a building had
this condition: "The following risks being considered more hazardous
than others, *buildings* intended to be occupied by persons carrying on
any of the undermentioned trades or business, or in which any large
quantities of the undermentioned goods are deposited, will be sub-

---

able Ins. Co. v. *Langdon,* 6 Wend. (N. Y) 623. In *Wood* v. *North Western Ins.
Co.,* 46 N. Y. 421, the policy contained a clause forbidding the use of "camphene,
spirit gas, phosgene," etc., or "any other inflammable liquid." The court held,
that a liquid not mentioned by name, to be covered by the clause, "any other
inflammable liquid," must be inflammable, as are those enumerated articles.
And where "kerosene" was not named, and there was no finding or proof of its
character in this regard, this court cannot take judicial notice of its qualities.
Judicial notice cannot be taken that the article of "kerosene" is in all cases explosive, the legislature having declared that there is a degree of purity to which it
may be brought at which it may safely be kept on sale in cities.

[1] *Reynolds* v. *Commerce Ins. Co., ante.*
[2] *Franklin Ins. Co.* v. *Brock,* 57 Penn. St. 184.

jected to an extra premium on that account. No policy, therefore, will be construed to extend to such a risk, unless liberty be given for the purpose, and expressed thereon." One of the specifications of such risks was, "mills and manufactories of any kind." With the consent of the company the tenant kept hay, straw, produce, etc. This he gave up and kept broom-corn, and made brooms by hand. The insurer claimed that this avoided the policy; but the court held that it did not come within the prohibition of "mills and manufactories;" also that a mill, within the meaning of the prohibition, is not merely a place where something might be ground, nor a manufactory merely where something may be made by hand or machinery, but what common usage recognizes as a mill or manufactory respectively.

Distinct contracts.

SEC. 187. When two *adjoining* houses of the same owner are insured by one company at the same time, but in two distinct policies, the policies are distinct contracts, and the assured can recover for damage by fire to one building, although the other building may have been used in a manner prohibited by the policy, and the fire originated in it.[1]

Rate of premium does not necessarily determine character of risk.

SEC. 188. A premium for insurance above the usual rate, is evidence *indicating*, though not proving, that a more than usual risk was assumed; but a jury should not infer that a concealed or misrepresented fact was to be at the risk of the insurers.[2]

Description of use, unless otherwise clearly intended, relates only to present use.

SEC. 189. Describing a building insured as a "storehouse," is descriptive only, and *not a warranty or representation that nothing should be done in it but keeping a store or a storehouse.*[3] A *storehouse* was insured, and keeping broom-corn was not specified as a hazardous risk. The assured had a right to keep broom-corn there. Keeping it did not prevent his recovery for damage to the building by fire, because the danger was greater by keeping it, or because the fire originated in it.[4]

Effect of list of hazards upon contract.

SEC. 190. A policy enumerating certain risks as hazardous, does not cover any of them, unless liberty be given to keep the articles mentioned

---

[1] *Franklin Ins. Co.* v. *Brock, ante.*
[2] *Franklin Ins. Co.* v. *Brock, ante.*
[3] *Franklin Ins. Co.* v. *Brock, ante.*
[4] *Franklin Ins. Co.* v. *Brock, ante.*

as hazardous; but if words in a policy are of doubtful signification, the meaning most favorable to the assured is to be adopted.[1] If the prohibited article was *commonly* used in the business at the time when the insurance was effected, the fact that another and less hazardous article *might have been employed* will not affect the right of the assured. It is presumed that the insurer knew the custom and necessities of the trade, and such custom enters into and forms a part of the contract and modifies the force of the conditions. If the insurer desires to obviate the use of articles generally employed in the business, he must expressly so provide in the policy.[2]

Implied license.

SEC. 191. In a recent case before the court of appeals of New York,[3] the policy covered a printing press, types, negatives "and their stock as photographers, including engravings and materials used in their business." The policy contained a clause prohibiting the keeping or use of kerosene in a building containing the property insured except by consent in writing. The plaintiffs used in their business, as photographers, a portable kerosene stove, such as was generally employed in the business, and while so using the stove, *and from its use*, the premises were fired and the loss incurred. It was proved that a portable gas lamp or stove might have been as well used in the business, but that a kerosene stove was customarily used. The company was held liable for the loss, GROVER, J., remarking: "When a policy is issued upon a stock of goods in a specified business, *the underwriter is presumed to know what goods are usually kept by those insured in that business.*[4] When a policy is issued, as in the present case, upon the

---

[1] *Franklin Ins. Co.* v. *Brock, ante.*

[2] *Steinback* v. *LaFayette F. Ins. Co.,* 54 N. Y. 98 ; *Harper* v. *The Albany Mut. Ins. Co.,* 17 id. 194 ; *Harper* v. *N. Y. City Ins. Co.,* 22 id. 441 ; *Bryant* v. *Poughkeepsie Ins. Co.,* 17 id. 200.

[3] *Hall* v. *Ins. Co. of N. America,* 58 N. Y. 292.

[4] *Steinback* v. *LaFayette F. Ins. Co.,* 54 N. Y. 98. In *Whitmarsh* v. *Conway Ins. Co.,* 16 Gray (Mass.) 359, the plaintiffs were merchants, and procured a policy of insurance upon "their stock in trade, consisting of the usual variety of a country store (except dry goods), and on their store fixtures, etc. ; * * * permission to keep and sell burning fluids and gunpowder, as per application." There were conditions annexed to the policy, providing that if the insured should keep or store any of the articles enumerated therein as hazardous or extra hazardous, "included in the memorandum of special rates or of risks prohibited, unless herein otherwise specially provided for, or hereafter agreed by this company in writing, and added to or indorsed upon this policy then and from thenceforth, so long as the same shall be so appropriated, etc. ; these presents shall cease, and be of no form or effect." There were five classes of hazards enumerated. Among the articles belonging to these classes, and enumerated as such, were "burning fluids," "earthen or glassware," "oil," and among a class not to

materials used in the business of photography, *it includes all such as are in ordinary use,* although some other things might be substituted therefor." In an earlier New York case,[1] the plaintiff procured an insurance upon his printing and book materials, machinery, etc., with privilege for a printing office, bindery and book store. The use of camphene was prohibited by the printed conditions of the policy. The premises were consumed, and the fire was shown to have originated from a lighted match thrown into a pan of camphene, which was kept on the premises for cleaning the ink rollers, plates, etc. The use of camphene for this purpose was not only shown to be general among printers, but also *necessary* for the purposes named. The court held that the use of camphene by printers being common, and its use necessary, the defendants must be treated as having taken the risk subject to this usage of the trade, and a recovery was upheld. Thus, it will be seen that mere general conditions will not prevail to avoid a policy because of a use of the premises in a particular manner, or because of the keeping or use of certain prohibited articles, when the use of such premises or of such articles are either *necessary or usual* in the business which the policy covers, provided such use is reasonable, in view of the business and its necessities.[2]

---

be insured at any rates, were "gunpowder," "friction matches and match shops." The application was expressly made a part of the policy, and in answer to an interrogatory, "Is there any other fact or circumstance affecting the risk?" the insured stated, "applicant wants permission to use and sell burning fluids, and also to retail gunpowder, to be sold only in the day-time." The plaintiffs kept in their store for sale, during the existence of the policy, as a part of their usual stock in trade, "whale oil, friction matches and earthern and glassware." In an action to recover a loss under the policy, the defendants set up this alleged breach of the conditions of the policy in defense. The plaintiffs offered to show that all these articles were usually kept in country stores, and so were embraced in the terms of the policy. But the court excluded the evidence, and thereupon the defendants had a verdict. Upon appeal, this verdict was set aside, the court holding that the evidence to show that such goods were usually kept in a country store was admissible, and if established, entitled the plaintiffs to a recovery. "If," said CHAPMAN J., "the plaintiffs can prove that oil, friction matches, earthenware and glassware, *in such quantities as they kept them,* compose a part of the usual variety of a country store, they have not violated the policy by keeping them," and he refers to the case, *Elliott* v. *Hamilton Mut. Ins. Co.,* 13 Gray (Mass.) 139, as an authority in support of this position. In that case an application was made for insurance on a stock represented as being "all of goods usually kept in a country store" and that there was no cotton or woolen waste or rags kept in or near the property to be insured. The by-laws to which the insurance was specially made subject, provided that no building in which cotton or woolen waste, or *oily* rags were allowed to remain at night, should be insured; and that all cotton, hempen, or *oily waste or rags,* should be destroyed or removed every evening. The court held that the keeping of clean, white cotton rags, if usually forming part of the stock of a country store, did not avoid the policy.

[1] *Harper* v. *New York Ins. Co.,* 22 N. Y. 441; *Harper* v. *Albany Mut. Ins. Co.,* 17 id. 194.

[2] *Whitmarsh* v. *Conway F. Ins. Co.,* 16 Gray (Mass.) 359; *Franklin Ins. Co.* v. *Updegraff,* 43 Penn. St. 350; *Steinback* v. *LaFayette Ins. Co.,* 54 N. Y. 90. See

In a case quite recently heard in the Commission of Appeals in New York,[1] the question came up in this form: The plaintiffs procured an insurance on their paper mill, in which kerosene oil was used for lights. The policy expressly provided that petroleum, rock and earth oils, benzine, benzole and naptha should not be stored or used on the premises, without written permission indorsed on the policy, and that refined coal, carbon and kerosene oils, when stored in *less* quantities than ten barrels, shall be classed as extra hazardous. The plaintiffs, at the time of the fire, had about forty gallons of kerosene oil in the mill, to be used for lighting the mill. EARL, C., in passing upon the question whether a verdict for the plaintiff was sustainable in view of these facts, said: "The quantity was reasonable for the use for which it was provided. This kerosene was not *stored* within the meaning of the policy, and hence there can be no claim that the provision against storing was violated. *But it was used,* and the question is, whether its use for lighting violated and avoided the policy. I am inclined to think that the prohibition of the use of rock and earth oils upon the premises includes kerosene. * * But I do not think that its use for lighting *was intended to be prohibited.* Other use was

Steinback v. *Royal F. Ins. Co.,* 13 Wall. (U. S.) 183, which is in conflict with the previous case. and which really is in conflict with all the better class of cases, as it was held that evidence was not admissible to show that the business of a "German jobber," as which the plaintiff was insured, included the sale of fire-works. The doctrine of this case is not generally accepted as expressive of the rule of law prevailing in such cases. *Harper* v. *N. Y. City F. Ins. Co., ante; Harper* v. *Albany Mut. Ins. Co., ante; Bryant* v. *Poughkeepsie Mut. Ins. Co.,* 17 N. Y. 200; *Elliott* v. *Hamilton Mut. Ins. Co.,* 13 Gray (Mass.) 139; *Niagara F. Ins. Co.* v. *De Graff,* 12 Mich. 124; *Hall* v. *Ins. Co. of North America,* 58 N. Y. 292; *Pindar* v. *Kings Co. Ins. Co.,* 36 N. Y. 648; *Duncan* v. *Sun F. Ins. Co.,* 6 Wend. (N. Y.) 488; *Viele* v. *Germania Ins. Co.,* 26 Iowa, 9. In *Archer* v. *Merchants' & Mfrs. Ins. Co.,* 43 Mo. 434, this rule was well illustrated. In that case, the plaintiff procured an insurance upon a wagonmaker's shop and materials. The policy prohibited the use of camphene, benzine, etc. The plaintiff had a paint shop in connection with his business, where the wagons were painted, and had a half barrel benzine in the shop for mixing the paints. A loss occurring, payment was resisted, upon the ground that the keeping of benzine was in violation of the conditions of the policy. But the court held that, if a paint shop was a common part of a wagonmaker's shop, and paints were used for manufacturing wagons, and were customarily kept in the building and used for that purpose, and benzine was customarily used for mixing paints, the printed conditions were plainly repugnant to the written clause, and were to be rejected. In Minnesota, *Phœnix Ins. Co.* v. *Taylor,* 5 Minn. 492, the same rule was adopted as to gunpowder. In that case, the plaintiff procured an insurance upon his stock, "dry goods, groceries," etc., such as are usually kept in a general retail store. The policy prohibited the storing of gunpowder, saltpeter or phosphorus. The plaintiff kept gunpowder for sale, and in an action to recover for a loss, the company set up this breach of the condition of the policy in defense. The court held that if gunpowder and the articles prohibited were *usually* kept in general retail stores, the printed conditions were repugnant to the written portions of the policy, and inoperative.

[1] *Buchanan* v. *Exchange Fire Ins. Co.,* 61 N. Y. 26.

intended. Kerosene is considered reasonably safe for lighting, and is in ordinary and general use for lighting buildings in all parts of the country outside of cities where gas is used, *and the policy must have been made in reference to this well-known fact.*" There was another clause in the policy which covered the subject of lighting, which provided that camphene, spirit gas or burning fluid, phosgene, or any other inflammable liquid, when used in stores, warehouses, manufactories, etc., which provided that the use of such articles for lighting purposes should subject the property to additional rates, and should avoid the policy, unless consent was indorsed on the policy. Kerosene was not named in the prohibited list, and EARL, C., said: "Construing, therefore, the two clauses of the policy together, I am of opinion that kerosene for lighting was not prohibited."

Thus it will be seen that the force of a warranty, or condition in a policy, is to be construed in view, not only of the entire language of the policy and other papers forming a part of the contract, *but also in view of the subject-matter to which it relates*, the necessities of the business, or of the insured, so far as relates to the warranty or condition, and the general or special usage affecting the same. This was well illustrated in a New York case,[1] in which a policy was issued providing that, if the premises should be used for the purpose of carrying on any trade, business or vocation denominated hazardous or extra hazardous, or specified in the memorandum of special rates, in the proposals annexed to the policy, or for the purpose of storing therein any articles of goods coming within the same conditions, that, during such time, the policy should be of no effect. Oil and turpentine, and house building or repairing, were specially declared to be in the hazardous class. The plaintiff, while having the house painted upon the inside, kept there for use in making such repairs a quantity of paints, oils and turpentine, and while the painters were at work there, and the aforesaid articles were there, the house was consumed by fire. The defendants resisted payment upon the ground that the policy was avoided by a breach of such conditions, but the court held that, in construing the conditions, *the subject* of the condition should be regarded, and that they should not be *strictly*, but *liberally* construed in favor of the insured, and that the policy must be held to relate to the *habitual* use of such articles upon the premises, and were not intended to, and did not prohibit their use for *necessary* repairs.

---

[1] *O'Neil* v. *Buffalo Ins. Co.*, 3 N. Y. 122.

As has previously been stated, a warranty in a contract of insurance may be qualified by proof of a general custom, or of a special custom *known to the insurer*, or by the language of the contract itself, and in construing the language used, the actual intention of the parties is to control, in view of the language used, the subject-matter to which it relates, *the knowledge of the insurer in reference to the matters to which the warranties relate*, and the law relating thereto, statutory or common. Thus, where a policy covers a building occupied as a country store, and insures the goods therein as a general stock of merchandise, such as is usually kept, etc.; although the policy specially provides that the keeping of any hazardous articles, enumerating them, shall avoid the policy; yet, if in point of fact, such articles are usually kept for sale in a country store, the condition in reference thereto is treated as qualified by the nature of the business and the language relating thereto, and the keeping of such articles for sale will not avoid the policy,[1] even though their sale is prohibited by law,[2] so where a

---

[1] In the *Niagara F. Ins. Co.*, v. *De Graff*, 12 Mich. 124, this question arose under a policy covering a stock of groceries. The goods were described in the application as a stock of dry goods, groceries, etc., and the sum insured was specifically divided, covering in part the dry goods, and in part the groceries. The policy had annexed to it a condition that if the premises were used for *storing, or keeping* therein certain hazardous articles, among which were enumerated alcohol and spiritous liquors, "except as herein specially provided for or hereafter agreed to by the corporation *in writing* upon this policy," the policy should be void, etc. Alcohol and spiritous liquors were kept as a part of the stock, and it was insisted by the defendants that the policy was thereby avoided; but the court below held, and so instructed the jury, that if such articles were included, the term "*groceries*" as used in the policy, then their being kept by the plaintiffs did not avoid, but was specially provided for in writing in the policy. The jury found that they were included in the term, and upon appeal the ruling was sustained; CAMPBELL J, saying, "The question arises whether the court rightly left it to the jury to say, as a matter of fact, whether the term groceries included spirituous liquors and alcohol. That it may include them in the absence of such a statute (a statute prohibiting their sale, *see next note*), is not denied, the recognized definitions embracing them clearly, so that it may be doubted whether it might not, in that case, require evidence of usage to exclude that meaning, if such articles existed in an insured stock of groceries. *New York Equitable Ins. Co.* v. *Langdon*, 6 Wend. (N. Y.) 623. There was evidence before the jury in the case before us, that these things did *in fact* form a part of the stock, and evidence tending to show a knowledge by the agent of that fact. * * * If the jury found (as they must have done) that the term groceries included the liquors in question, then the other instructions complained of, which held that, *by insuring such a stock the liquors were embraced*, although extra hazardous, were clearly correct. *By the use of a term including them*, they are specially provided for in writing in the policy. *Insuring a class of goods includes what is usually contained in it, whether extra hazardous or not.* Bryant v. *Poughkeepsie Mut. Ins. Co.*, 17 N. Y. 200; *Harper* v. *Albany Mut Ins. Co*, id. 194; *Harper* v. *N. Y. City Ins. Co.*, 22 id. 441; *Delonguemare* v. *The Tradesman's Ins. Co.*, 2 Hall (N. Y.) 589; *Moore* v. *Protection Ins. Co.*, 29 Me. 97.

[2] In *Insurance Co.* v. *De Graff, ante;* it was insisted by the defendants that the policy was avoided, if for no other reason, because the sale of the articles was prohibited by law; but the court held, and so instructed the jury, that if alcohol

business is insured, in which certain prohibited articles are commonly used, although the use of such articles is expressly prohibited; yet, as the insurer is presumed to know the usages of a business, and the articles usually employed therein by insuring property used in such business, or a building in which such business is conducted, the con_ditions in reference to such articles is qualified by such usage and the ordinary *known* necessities of the business, and is regarded as specially provided for in the policy by the terms used to designate the business.[1]

---

and spirituous liquors were included in the term "groceries," as used in the policy, then they were specially provided for in the policy, and that the fact that their sale was prohibited would not render their keeping a violation of the con_ditions of the policy, and the jury having so found, upon appeal, the ruling was sustained. CAMPBELL, J., in delivering the opinion of the court, remarks: "It was claimed on behalf of the plaintiff in error, that if these liquors can be allowed to be included in a policy, the policy will be, to all intents and purposes, insuring an illegal traffic; and several cases were cited involving marine policies on unlaw_ful voyages and lottery insurances, which have been held void on that ground. These cases are not at all parallel, because they rest upon the fact that, in each instance, it is made a necessary condition of the policy that the illegal act shall be done. The ship being insured for a certain voyage, that voyage is the only one upon which the insurance would apply, and the underwriter becomes thus directly a party to an illegal act. So, insuring a lottery ticket requires the lottery to be drawn in order to attach the insurance to the risk. If this policy were in express terms, a policy insuring the party selling liquors against loss by fine or forfeiture, it would be quite analogous. But this insurance attaches only to prop_erty, and the risks insured against are not the consequences of illegal acts, but of accident. Our statute does not in any way destroy or affect the right of prop_erty in spirituous liquors, or prevent title being transmitted, but renders sales unprofitable by preventing the vendor from availing himself of the ordinary advantages of a sale, and also affixes certain penalties; *Hibbard* v. *People*, 4 Mich. 125; *Bagg* v. *Jerome*, 7 id. 145. If the owner sees fit to retain his prop_erty without selling it, or to transmit it into another state or country, he can do so. By insuring his property, the insurance company has no concern with the use he may make of it, and as it is susceptible of lawful uses, no one can be held to contract concerning it in an illegal manner, unless the contract itself is for a distinctly illegal purpose. Collateral contracts, in which no illegal design enters, are not affected by an illegal transaction with which they may be remotely con_nected. In the case of *The Ocean Ins. Co.* v. *Polleys*, 13 Peters, 157, an insurance upon a ship known by the insurance company to be liable to forfeiture under the registry laws of the United States, was held valid, and a recovery was permitted for a loss while sailing under papers known to be illegal. The case of *Armstrong* v. *Toler*, 11 Wheat. 258, is still stronger. It is difficult to perceive how public policy can be violated by an insurance of any kind of property recognized to exist." The question is, not whether the goods are *hazardous*, but whether they are required in the ordinary course of the person's trade, and are embraced in the class of goods insured. In that case, unless expressly, and in terms pro_hibited, liberty to keep them in reasonable quantities will be implied. *Moore* v. *Protection Ins. Co.*, 29 Me. 97.

[1] Insurers are presumed to know the general usages of the business in which the property insured is employed, and the policy will be interpreted with refer_ence to such usages. *Grant* v. *Lexington F., etc., Ins. Co.*, 5 Ind. 23. In *Citizen's Ins. Co.* v. *McLaughlin* 53 Penn. St. 485; 6 Am. Law Reg. (N. S.) 374, the plaintiffs were the proprietors of a patent leather manufactory, and procured an insurance thereon in the defendant company. It was insured as "*a patent leather manu_factory*," and the building having been destroyed by fire, the company resisted payment upon the ground that *benzole* was kept or used in the building contrary to the provisions of the policy. The policy provided that benzole in quantities

and if they know the special usage of the insured and insure him without objection thereto, they are estopped from setting up such matter in defense in an action on the policy.

But, if the use of the premises for certain purposes, or the keeping

---

not exceeding five barrels in a small shed, entirely detached from the other buildings, situated on the rear end of the lot, about one hundred feet from the main building, *and nowhere else on said premises.* It was well known that benzole was an essential article in the prosecution of the business, and was *necessarily and universally used in such business.* The custom of the workmen was to carry an open bucket of it into the factory as often as wanted, to be used in reducing the composition called "sweet meat," an article used in the process of manufacture, and on the morning of the fire a workman carried an open bucket containing three or four gallons of benzole into the factory, and set it down upon the floor, when it almost instantly ignited, and communicating the flames to the building, it was wholly destroyed. It was shown by the testimony of a witness, that it was the custom in *twelve* similar factories in Newark, N. J., to take benzole into the buildings in an open bucket, as was done by the plaintiffs, and no evidence was introduced to show a contrary custom in Pittsburgh, where the plaintiff's factory was located. WOODARD, J., in delivering the opinion of the court, said : "The argument on behalf of the company is, that the policy both in letter and spirit meant to confine the benzole to the shed on the rear of the lot, and to exclude it from any other part of the premises; that carrying it from the shed in open buckets across the yard, and setting it down in a room with the door open, was an abuse of the privilege granted by the company, which, if it could have been anticipated, would have prevented their taking the risk; that such use of it was keeping it elsewhere than in the shed, and was, therefore, a palpable violation of the covenant.

The answer which the learned judge made to this argument was substantially as follows: You insured a patent-leather manufactory ; you knew, *for you were bound to know, that benzole was ordinarily used in such factories;* you stipulated that five barrels of it might be kept on hand near to the factory ; and the necessary presumption is that you meant it might be kept for use in that factory, as the article is ordinarily used in similar factories. If, therefore, it was kept in the place stipulated, *and used according to the custom of the trade, it was one of the risks covered by the policy.* The jury found the fact that the mode of using it was according to custom, and so recovery was had.

It appears to us that the argument was well answered. This business is not enumerated in the list of hazardous risks, and the company could not have expected it to be suspended, nor to be carried on in any other than the customary modes. They insured it. They took the risk, after having their attention drawn to the dangerous article, and after excluding it, as stored in bulk from the policy. But did they mean to exclude it from the factory as an element or agent in the conduct of the business ? To assume that they did, in the absence of language to that effect, would be to assume that they expected the business to stop, or to be carried on out of the usual mode. The words of the policy descriptive of the subject-matter of the insurance, are, "*the buildings of their tannery and patent-leather manufactory,*" and *it must be intended that these words included whatever, not expressly excepted, was necessary and essential in conducting such a business.* In the case of *Harper* v. *The City Ins. Co.,* 1 Bos. N. Y. Rep. 520, this was the doctrine applied to a printing establishment where the fire originated from the use of camphene, which was one of the hazardous articles enumerated by the policy, but it appeared that camphene was ordinarily used by printers for cleaning their types and plates, and was so used in that instance. On this ground it was treated as one of the risks covered by the policy. See also, *Girard Ins. Co.* v. *Stephenson,* 1 Wright (Penn.) 198.

We think there was no error in the admission of the testimony of F. T. Harden. He gave an intelligible account of the mode of using benzole in twelve factories at Newark, New Jersey, and said it was brought in and used from cans and buckets. If any other custom had been established at Pittsburgh it could have been shown ; but in the absence of all other evidence on the subject, this was competent to fix the usage of the business."

of certain articles is prohibited, and the use is not a usual incident of the business covered by the policy, which the plaintiff takes the burden of establishing, such use will avoid the policy, even though such use does not, in fact, enhance the risk or contribute to the loss. And it makes no difference that the insured himself did not assent to the prohibited use. It is enough, if the premises were devoted to such use by one who was lawfully in possession as a sheriff under an attachment or levy;[1] or a mortgagee before the equity of redemption has expired.[2] Thus, in the case first cited in the last note, the plaintiff procured insurance on his dwelling-house and store, in which there was a provision that if the premises were, during the life of the policy, appropriated to or used for any purpose denominated hazardous or extra-hazardous in the policy, it should be of no force or effect. In the list of hazardous trades was that of "sail-makers," and in the extra-hazardous class were included "confectionery and confectionery manufacturers," The property being mortgaged, the mortgagee took possession for the purposes of foreclosure, and let the premises to various persons, one of whom occupied a portion of the dwelling as a barber's shop, but also kept confectionery for sale in glass jars, on the counter and shelves, in small quantities. The loft of the store was let to a sail-maker about two weeks before the fire, who moved his tools and stock, of the value of about one hundred and fifty dollars, into the building, but had not commenced work there at the time of the loss, but intended to commence the day after the loss. The court held that no recovery could be had under the policy.[3]

When the conditions of a policy have been broken, by devoting the property to a use prohibited in the policy, the policy does not thereby become a dead instrument, but is merely rendered inoperative, is suspended during the period of such use, and at once revives when such use ceases. It is the uses to which the property was devoted *at the time when the loss occurred*, that is to determine the question whether or not a condition prohibiting certain uses has been broken, and the condition is to be construed strictly, and not extended by implication to cover matters that are not within its obvious meaning. In a recent case in Pennsylvania,[4] the policy provided that the risk of property insured

---

[1] *First National Bank* v. *Ins. Co.*, ante.

[2] *Witherell* v. *City F. Ins. Co.*, 16 Gray (Mass.) 276 ; *Macomber* v. *Howard Ins. Co.*, 7 id. 257.

[3] *Macomber v. Howard Fire Ins. Co.*, 7 Gray (Mass.) 257; *Lee* v. *Howard Fire Ins. Co.*, 3 id. 583.

[4] *Mut. F. Ins. Co.*, etc., v. *Coatesville Shoe Factory*, 80 Penn. St. 375.

should be determined by the rates annexed, and if the risk should be increased as contemplated by a by-law annexed, the rates should be evidence of the additional risk. The by-law provided that if the insured devoted any part of the insured building, or one located by him near it, "to a more hazardous business," the policy should be immediately void. The insured for light introduced gasoline, named as increasing the risk; he afterward removed it; subsequently, the building was burned. The court held the policy was not void, and that the absence of a stipulation to that effect, the validity of the policy depended on the state of the premises at the time of the loss, and that *lighting* with gasoline was not devoting the building to a more hazard-ous *business*.

Representations need only be substantially true.

SEC. 192. If the representations made by the insured are *substantially* true, the insurer cannot avoid his liability upon the policy because they are not *literally* so. It is enough, if the variance is not such as materially affects the risk. Thus, where the insured represented the building as finished, it was held sufficient if it was substantially finished.[1] Where the insured stated that there was a dwelling and cabinet shop within fifty feet, and in fact there was a cabinet shop within *two* feet, it was held not to avoid the policy.[2] Where the representation is a mere expression of an opinion, and the insurer ought to have known that it was no more than an expression of the judgment of the assured, unless fraudulent, the policy is not avoided, however erroneous his opinion may have been. Thus, where the assured, in describing the risk, stated that there was, on the east side of the building a small one-story shed, which could not endanger the build-ing if they should burn, but, in fact the fire was communicated to the building by the burning of the sheds, the insurer was held liable under the policy.[3] So, where the building is represented to be used for a certain purpose, the insurer is bound to know what is incident to such purpose or business, and cannot escape liability unless such use as is incident to the business is specially excepted. Thus, where the assured stated that the building was used for the manufacture of lead pipe only, but in fact, reels upon which to wind the pipe were also

---

[1] *Delonguemare* v. *Tradesman's Ins. Co.*, 2 Hall (N. Y.) 589; *Williams* v. *N. E. Mut. F. Ins. Co.*, 31 Me. 219; *Pawson* v. *Watson*, Cowp. 785; *Kentucky, etc., Ins. Co.*, v. *Southard*, 8 B. Mon. (Ky.) 634.

[2] *Allen v. Charlestown Ins. Co.*, 5 Gray (Mass.) 384.

[3] *Dennison* v. *Thomaston Ins. Co.*, 20 Me. 125.

made there; it was held that, as such use was incident to the manufacture of lead pipe, and necessary for carrying on the business, the
insurers were liable.[1] In an Illinois case,[2] the assured represented that

---

[1] *Collins* v. *Charlestown Ins. Co.*, 10 Gray (Mass.) 155. In *Sims* v. *State Ins.
Co.*, 47 Mo. 54; 4 Am. Rep. 311, the assured stated in his application that the
building was used for "tobacco-pressing, no manufacturing." In a shed adjoining, hogsheads were made in which to pack the tobacco, and the insurer claimed
that this avoided the policy, but the court held otherwise. BLISS, J., in delivering the opinion of the court, said: "The insurance was upon plaintiff's tobacco,
in a certain building in DeWitt, Carroll county. In the application for the insurance, and in answer to the question 'for what purpose the building was used,'
the plaintiff replied, 'tobacco-pressing; no manufacturing.' The evidence shows
that in a shed—an addition to the main building—the tobacco hogsheads were
manufactured. This, it is claimed, was a concealment of the uses to which the
building was put, was a breach of the warranty, and vitiated the policy. The
plaintiff sought to prove that the business of making the hogsheads in which the
tobacco was packed, was incident to and appertained to the business of pressing,
and by general custom was included, and understood to be included, in the term
'tobacco-pressing,' without being specially mentioned. If such were the fact
there was no false warranty, and it was no more necessary for the plaintiff to
state that branch of the business than any other. The officers of the company,
in issuing the policy, should be supposed to know all the incidents of the business
of the insured, and if there was any branch of it considered extra-hazardous, and
which they were unwilling to cover by their contract, it should have been specially provided against. The law upon this subject has been recently considered
by us in *Archer* v. *The Merchants' and Manufacturers' Ins. Co.*, 43 Mo. 434, and it
is quite unnecessary to review the general doctrine. Whether the preparation of
the hogsheads was such an incident to the business as to be included in it, was a
question of fact, and we have only to see if the subject was fairly presented to
the jury. The jury were instructed that the application was a warranty as to
the condition and occupancy of the premises, that, if false, would make void the
policy, and that the words quoted were an undertaking that there should be no
manufacturing in the premises. But they were also further instructed in these
words: 'No. 7. The jury will find for the plaintiff on the fourth ground of
defense set up in defendant's answer, if they find that the business of tobacco-
pressing only was carried on in the building in which the insured property was
contained, and that the only coopering done therein was that connected with,
appertaining to, and incident to the business of tobacco-pressing, although the
jury may believe that said use for setting up of hogsheads was an increase of the
risk.' Does this instruction present the question to the jury fairly? It seems to
me not. It fails to present to their mind the true issue. First, for obscurity;
the construction they might put upon it is, that the court supposes that there is a
class of coopering incident to the business, and they are to inquire whether the
coopering complained of belongs to that class. The court seems to take for
granted the main question in dispute. The sentence is obscure, and may bear
another interpretation, but it is so drawn that the jury, especially if inclined
against the defendant, might very easily interpret it as assuming the chief proposition. Second, it does not give the jury to understand what facts they are to
find in order to make any coopering incident to plaintiff's business. The inquiry
should be, whether it is so generally customary for those engaged in the business
of tobacco-pressing to prepare their own hogsheads, and in the building where
the business is conducted, that such preparation can properly be called an incident to the business. The existence of such a custom is an affirmative proposition, and must be affirmatively found. To illustrate: coopering is necessary for
the manufacture of flour, whisky, powder, etc., and in a loose sense, is incident
to the business. So box making is, in the same sense, incident to various kinds of
manufacturing; but the making of flour or whisky barrels, or powder kegs, or
boxes, cannot be said to be so incident to the manufacture of flour, whisky,

[2] *Ins. Co. of N. America* v. *McDowell*, 50 Ill. 120.

no open lights were used in the mill. It appeared, however, that one open kerosene lamp was used in the *office* of the mill, but not in the mill proper. The court held that this was a substantial compliance with the representation.[1]

Ashes, method of keeping.

SEC. 193. A representation in an application for insurance that ashes are kept in brick, iron or other safes or places of deposit, is met if they are kept in any other place equally safe;[2] and if the application is made a part of the policy, this would equally be the rule, unless the statement can be regarded as a *continuing* warranty. *If the ashes were kept as represented at the time when the application is made* the warranty is met, if no increase of risk is created by a change in the mode of keeping them, unless the warranty is clearly continuing.[3]

Breaches of contract must be plead, or specially relied on at the trial.

SEC. 194. In order to avail himself of a breach of warranty in a contract of insurance, or of the falsity of representations made by the assured, the particular matters relied on must either be set forth in the pleadings, or specially relied on at the trial, otherwise they will be regarded as having been waived, and points in reference to which no question of law is raised in the lower court, cannot be raised on appeal.[4] The question as to whether there has been a breach of warranty, or whether certain representations are false in a substantive matter, is wholly for the jury, and their finding, unless clearly contrary to the evidence, cannot be disturbed.[5]

---

powder or the articles to be packed in the boxes, as to be included in the general term applicable to such manufacture, unless by a general custom they are prepared in connection with and as a part of the business. If it be the custom among country millers to make their own flour barrels in the mill, then the term 'flour mill' or 'flour making' may be properly held to include the necessary coopering; but the existence of such custom should be clearly and distinctly put to the jury, and in no equivocal or ambiguous terms."

[1] In *Peoria M. & F. Ins. Co.* v. *Perkins*, 16 Mich. 380, the plaintiff, in answer to inquiries in the application: "For what purposes used?" replied, "It is used for stores." "How many?" "Two." The building was in fact occupied as a boot and shoe store by the plaintiff, also as a newsroom, tobacco store, etc., and the *upper* story as *sleeping* rooms. The court held that the representation was substantially correct.

[2] *Underhill* v. *Agawam Mut. F. Ins. Co.*, 6 Cush. (Mass.) 440.

[3] *Underhill* v. *Agawam Ins. Co.*, ante.

[4] *Boos* v. *The World Mut. Life Ins. Co.*, 64 N. Y. 236.

[5] *Boos* v. *The World Life Ins. Co.*, ante.

CHAPTER VI.

MISREPRESENTATION AND CONCEALMENT.

Concealment and misrepresentation defined.

SEC. 195. A misrepresentation is the statement of something as fact which is untrue, *and which the assured states, knowing it to be untrue, and with intent to deceive, or which he states positively as true, not knowing it to be true, and which has a tendency to mislead,* such fact being in either case material to the risk; and concealment is the designed and intentional withholding of any fact material to the risk, which the assured

in honesty and good faith ought to communicate; and any fact is
material, knowledge or ignorance of which would naturally influence the insurer in making the contract at all, or in estimating the
degree and character of the risk, or in fixing the rate of insurance.[1]
The insurer has a right to be informed of every circumstance which
may fairly influence him in taking or rejecting the risk, or fixing the
rate of premium therefor,[2] and it is settled beyond all question that the
suppression of a material fact relating to the risk, as well as a false
representation relating thereto, avoids the policy.[3] Therefore, while
it is for the jury to say, where there is any dispute as to the facts,
whether a misrepresentation or concealment relates to a fact material
to the risk,[4] yet, as a matter of law, where the facts were such as, if
the truth had been known, they would have influenced the insurer
in accepting or rejecting the risk, or in fixing a higher rate of premium therefor, the policy is void.[5] In determining this question, the
jury are to say, not necessarily whether the particular insurer would
have been influenced thereby, but whether a man of ordinary prudence, in business matters, would have been likely to have been influenced as stated.   It follows, then, that facts relating to the construction,
location, situation and uses of the risk are material, as well as its character and value.

Concealment of material facts. Need not be fraudulent.

SEC. 196. It is the duty of the assured to disclose to the insurer
every such fact, even though he does not know that it would have
the effect to influence his action in declining or accepting the risk, or
in fixing the terms upon which it would be taken.[6] The law implies

---

[1] *Daniels* v. *Hud. R. Ins. Co.*, 12 Cush. (Mass.) 416 ; *Houghton* v. *Manufacturers' Ins. Co.*, 8 Met. (Mass.) 114 ; *Locke* v. *N. American Ins. Co.*, 13 Mass. 97 ;
Clark v. *Union, etc., Ins. Co.*, 40 N. H. 333 ; *Girard F. and M. Ins. Co.* v. *Stephenson*, 37 Penn. St. 293 ; *Protection Ins. Co.* v. *Harmer*, 2 Ohio St. 452 ; *Washington, etc., Ins. Co.* v. *Merchants', etc., Ins. Co.*, 1 Handy (Ohio) 408 ; *Lexington
Ins. Co.* v. *Powers*, 1 Ohio, 324.

[2] As that attempts have been made, or that rumors exist that an attempt has
been made, to set fire to adjacent property, that would, if burned, seriously jeop-
ardize the property sought to be insured.   *Walden* v. *Louisiana Ins. Co.*, 12 La.
134 ; 1 Ben. F. I. C. 668.

[3] *Lindenau* v. *Desborough*, 3 C. & P. 350 ; *Wainwright* v. *Bland*, 1 M. & W. 32.

[4] *Fletcher* v. *Com. Ins. Co.*, 18 Pick. (Mass.) 419 ; *Columbian Ins. Co.* v. *Lawrence*, 10 Pet. (U. S.) 507.

[5] *Columbian Ins. Co.* v. *Lawrence, ante.*

[6] *McLanahan* v. *Universal Ins. Co.*, 1 Pet. (U. S.) 170 ; *Columbian Ins. Co.* v.
Lawrence, 10 id. 507 ; 2 id. 25 ; *Bunday* v. *Union Ins. Co.*, 2 Wash. C. C. (U. S.)
243 ; *Vale* v. *Phenix Ins. Co.*, 1 id. 283.   The same degree of diligence in disclosing matters affecting the risk, is not required in fire as in marine insurance, as the
parties are differently situated in reference to the risk, and the insurer, in the case

a contract between the parties, that everything material to the risk, if inquired about, shall be disclosed, and this, whether the party applying therefor *knows whether it is material or not*. It is not a question what the party supposed or believed in reference thereto, but simply whether *in fact it is material*, and if so, its suppression is a fraud, whatever may have been the supposition, knowledge or belief of the insured, and this rule applies with equal force to all species of insurance.[1] The maxim *caveat emptor* does not apply to this species of contracts. In the very nature of things, it rests largely in the confidence of the parties, and the insured is bound to exercise the utmost good faith, and the test by which to determine whether a fact should have been communicated to the insurer, *depends entirely upon whether it was material.*[2] The rules of fair dealing, equity, and that degree of integrity and good faith that should characterize all commercial transactions, alike require that the parties should contract *pari passu*. But as has previously been intimated, the suppression of a material fact, although it is in law regarded as a fraud which renders the contract void *ab initio*, yet does not always evidence or involve fraud in fact. It is equally fatal to the contract whether the concealment is fraudulently made, or is the result of ignorance, accident, inadvertence or mistake.[3] "The insured," said Lord MANSFIELD, in the case referred to from Park on Insurance, "is bound to represent to the underwriters, all the material circumstances relative to the ship and the voyage; and if he does not, though the omission is by accident or negligence, the underwriters are not liable." In order, however, that a suppression of a material fact should have the effect to avoid the contract, it must not only be material to the

---

of fire insurance, has better facilities for ascertaining the nature and extent of the hazard, than in cases of marine insurance, where in a large measure, the insurer must necessarily depend upon the good faith of the insured, in imparting information in reference thereto. Therefore, a higher degree of good faith is required in the one case than in the other, and in cases of marine insurance, the insured is bound to disclose all matters within his knowledge, material to the risk, whether inquiries are made of him, calling for such information or not, while in the case of fire insurance, the insured may be silent as to many matters —indeed, as to all matters open to observation when the insurer examines the property for himself before insuring. *Green* v. *Merchants' Ins. Co.*, 10 Pick. (Mass) 402 ; *Fish* v. *Cottinett*, 44 N. Y. 538. Particularly as to such matters as the insurer is presumed to know about. Thus, where a carpenter's shop was insured, it was held that an omission to state that it was heated by a stove was not a fraudulent concealment. *Girard, etc., Ins. Co.* v. *Stephenson*, 37 Penn. St. 293. See also, *Norris* v. *N. American Ins. Co.*, 3 Yeates (Penn.) 84 ; *Columbian Ins. Co.* v. *Lawrence, ante.*

[1] *Von Lindeau* v. *Desborough*, 3 C. & P. 353.

[2] *Columbian Ins. Co.* v. *Lawrence*, 10 Peters (U. S.) 507.

[3] *Ratcliffe* v. *Shoolbred*, Park on Ins. 181.

risk, but also of some fact *that is not equally within the knowledge of the insurer,* and that is not patent, or such as may fairly be regarded as probable.[1]

Not bound to disclose facts which insurer knows, or ought to know.

SEC. 197. Mr. MARSHALL, in his work on Insurance, p. 353, very tersely and aptly expresses the rules of law applicable to concealment. He says: "Either party may be innocently silent *as to many matters which are open to both, and upon which they may both exercise their judgments. Aliud est celare, aliud tacere: Neque enim id est celare quicquid reticeas; sed eum quod tu scias, id ignorare, emolumenti tui causa, velis eos, quorum intersit, id scire.*[2] This definition of concealment, restrained to the efficient motives and precise subject of any contract, will generally hold to make it void in favor of either party who is misled by his ignorance of the thing concealed. *The insured may be innocently silent as to what the underwriter knows as well as he, however he may have come by his knowledge: Scientia utrinque par pares contrahentes facit. The insured, therefore, needs not mention what the underwriter ought to know, what he takes upon himself the knowledge of, or what he waives being informed of.* The underwriter *needs not to be told what lessens the risk agreed upon, and is understood to be comprised within the express terms of the policy.* He needs not be told *what is the result of political speculations, or general intelligence.* For instance, he is bound to know every cause which may occasion natural perils, as the difficulty of the voyage, the variation of seasons, the probability of lightning, hurricanes, etc.; he is bound to know every cause which may occasion political perils, from the rupture of States, from war, and the various operations of war; he is bound to know the probability of safety from the continuance and return of peace, from the imbecility of the enemy, the weakness of their councils, or their want of strength. If an underwriter insure private ships of war from ports to ports, and from places to places anywhere, he needs not be told the secret enterprises upon which they are destined, because he knows that some expedition must be in view; and, from the nature of the case, he waives the information. If he insures for a certain term, he needs not be told

---

[1] *Pim* v. *Lewis,* 2 F. & F. 778; *People* v. *Liv., Lon. & Globe Ins. Co.,* 2 N. Y. (S. C.) 268; *Green* v. *Merchants' Ins. Co.,* 10 Pick. (Mass.) 402; *De Wolf* v. *N. Y. Fireman's Ins. Co.,* 20 John. (N. Y.) 214; *Friere* v. *Woodhouse,* Holt, N. P. 572; *Fish* v. *Liv., Lon. & Globe Ins. Co.,* 44 N. Y. 538; *Norris* v. *Ins. Co. of N. America,* 3 Yeates (Penn.) 84; *De Longuemare* v. *N. Y. F. Ins. Co.,* 10 John (N. Y.) 120; *Satterthwaite* v. *Ins. Co.,* 14 Penn. St. 343; *Gerhauser* v. *Ins. Co.,* 7 Nev. 174; *Lexington Ins. Co.* v. *Paver,* 16 Ohio 324.

[2] Cic. de off. l. 3, c. 12, 13.

any circumstance to shew that the risk may be over in less time; or, if he insure a voyage, with liberty of deviation, he needs not to be told what tends to shew that there will be no deviation. Neither is it necessary to communicate to the underwriters that the ship insured is foreign built, though this enabled her to sail without convoy, and without a license to do so, being within the exception in the stat. 38 G. III. c. 76, § 6, it being the business of the underwriter to obtain this information for himself.[1] Men argue differently, from natural phenomena and political appearances. They have different capacities, different degrees of knowledge, and different intelligence; but the means of information and judging upon those subjects are open to both. Each professes to act from his own sagacity, and therefore neither needs to communicate to the other. The reason of the rule which obliges the parties to a mutual disclosure of all material information, is to prevent fraud and promote good faith; but it is applicable to such facts only as vary the nature of the contract, which one party privately knows, and the other is ignorant of, and has no opportunity of knowing, nor any reason to suspect. The question, therefore, in cases of concealment, must always be, whether there was, under all the circumstances, at the time the policy was underwritten, a full and fair statement, or a concealment; fraudulent, if designed, or, though not designed, varying materially the object of the policy, and changing the risk understood to be run,[2] and in both cases avoiding the contract.

It is a rule that it is unnecessary to make any communication or disclosure of that which the insured undertakes for by a warranty, express or implied; and, therefore, it is not necessary that there should be any representation as to the state or condition of the ship previous to the effecting of the policy, because, in every contract of insurance, there is an implied warranty that the ship is sea-worthy. This was determined in the following case: An insurance was made on a ship and cargo from Madeira to Charlestown.[3] The ship being captured in her voyage to Charlestown, an action was brought on the policy, in which it appeared that the captain had wrote two letters from Madeira to the owner, stating that the ship had been very leaky on her voyage thither, and that the pipes of wine had been half covered with water. But, in answer to this, it was proved that the leak had been com-

[1] *Long* v. *Bolton*, 2 Bos. & Pul. 209.
[2] Per Lord MANSFIELD in *Carter* v. *Boehm*, 1 Bl. 594; 3 Bur. 1909.
[3] *Shoolbred* v. *Nutt* at N. P. Hil., 1872, MSS. case; Park, 229.

pletely stopped before the ship sailed from Madeira. It was insisted,
however, that the not disclosing of the two letters was a material concealment which avoided the policy.   Lord MANSFIELD told the jury
'that there was no necessity to communicate the letters to the underwriter, or to show the condition of the ship or cargo at the end of the
former voyage.   It is true,' said he, 'that there should be a representation of everything relating to the risk which the underwriter has
to run, except it be covered by a warranty.   But it is a condition, or
implied warranty, in every policy, that the ship is sea-worthy, and
therefore there is no necessity for a representation of that.   If she sail
without being so, the policy is void.   The letters might be material
evidence to shew that the ship was leaky in her outward voyage; and,
if nothing had been done to her at Madeira, there would have been
ground to suppose that she was not sea-worthy when she sailed from
thence.   But the fact now appears that the leak was stopped and she
was in good condition before she sailed from Madeira.'   Accordingly,
there was a verdict for the plaintiff.   EMERIGON[1] mentions a case
from which it may be inferred that, in some instances, the state of the
ship ought to be represented to the insurers, and that, in others, the
insurers will be presumed to know that the ship is not sea-worthy.
That was the case of a ship taken by a French privateer, after an
action in which she lost her main and mizen masts.   The captain of
the privateer brought the prize to an anchor, and immediately sent
orders to get her insured, which was done, but without mentioning
the state she was in.   The ship being retaken by the English, the
insurers objected to pay the loss, because the debilitated state of the
ship had not been stated to them   They were condemned, however,
to pay the full sum insured, upon the ground that they ought to have
presumed that a vessel captured after a battle must have been damaged.   The following case will shew that the insured is not bound to
disclose a circumstance made material by a foreign ordinance, which
may be known by either party, but which neither is bound to know,
and which neither in fact knows.   An insurance was made on a Por-
tuguese ship, warranted neutral, at and from Madeira to her port of
discharge in Jamaica, with liberty to touch at the Leeward islands.[2]
The ship was captured by a French privateer, and condemned in the
Court of Admiralty in France, on the ground of her having an English
supercargo on board, the French having lately made an ordinance to

---

[1] Vol. 1, p. 172.
[2] *Mayne* v. *Walter*, MSS. case ; Park, 195.

authorize this, similar to one made in 1756. In an action to recover this loss, it was insisted for the defendant that the plaintiff ought to have disclosed to him that the supercargo was English. But it was determined by Lord MANSFIELD and the court that, if neither party knew of its arbitrary ordinance, which was against the law of nations, neither was guilty of any fault. If the defendant knew of it, he ought to have inquired what supercargo was on board. But, in this case, both being ignorant of this ordinance, both were innocent; and, in such case, the underwriter must run all risks.

I shall conclude the present chapter with the following singular case, which, though not upon a marine policy, turned upon a question of concealment.

An insurance was made for a year, from the 16th of October, 1759, against the capture of Fort Marlborough, in the island of Sumatra, by an enemy, for the benefit of the governor, George Carter.[1] The governor's instructions for the insurance were dated the 22nd of September, 1759, and the policy was signed in May, 1760. The fort was taken by Count D'Estaigne within the year, viz., in April, 1760, and an action brought to recover the loss. On the trial it was objected that there was fraud on the part of the insured, by the concealment of circumstances which ought to have been disclosed; particularly the weakness of the fort, and the probability of its being attacked by the French. This was offered to be proved by two letters; one from the governor to R. Carter, his brother and agent; and the other to the India Company, from which it appeared that the French, being unable to relieve their friends on the coast, were the more likely to make an attack on this settlement, which they had designed to take by surprise the year before; and that the broker who effected the policy, on his cross-examination, said that *in his opinion*, these letters ought to have been produced or the contents disclosed; for if they had, the policy would not have been underwritten. In reply to this, it was shewn that the governor had £20,000 in effects in the fort, and only insured £10,000; that it did not appear that the French had any design to make the attack till the end of March; that the governor had acted as in full security down to February, and in that month turned his money into goods; and that, though his office was mercantile and not military, he was guilty of no fault in the defense of the place, which was not calculated to resist an European force, but only for defense against the natives. The plaintiff had a verdict. A new trial was

---

[1] *Carter* v. *Boehm*, 3 Burr. 1905.

25

moved for, on the ground that all the circumstances were not sufficiently disclosed to the underwriters. But the court, after time taken
to deliberate, were clearly of opinion that the plaintiff was entitled to
recover, and that the verdict ought to stand. Lord MANSFIELD, in
delivering the opinion of the court, said; "The contingency was,
whether Fort Marlborough would be attacked by an European power,
by sea, between October, 1759 and October 1760. If it was, it must
be taken, being incapable of resistance. The underwriter in London,
in May, 1760, could judge much better of the probability of this contingency, than Governor Carter could at Fort Marlborough in September, 1759. He knew the success of the operations of the war in
Europe, what naval forces the English and French had sent to the
East Indies, and whether the sea was open to any attempt from the
French. He knew, or might have known, every thing which was
known at Fort Marlborough in September, 1759, of the general state
of affairs in the East Indies, or of the particular condition of Fort
Marlborough, by the ship which brought the orders for the insurance.
Under these circumstances, he insures against the general contingency
of the place being attacked by an European power. If there had
been any design on foot or enterprise begun in September, 1759, it
would have varied the risk understood by the underwriter, on account
of his not being told of a particular design *then subsisting*. But the
governor had no notice of such a design, nor was there, in fact, any
such design. The attempt was made without premeditation, from the
sudden opportunity of a favorable occasion, by the connivance of the
Dutch, which tempted D'Estaigne to break his parol. As to the *first*
concealment, that he did not disclose the condition of the place; the
underwriters knew that the insurance was for the governor, who must
be acquainted with the state of the place, and who could not disclose
it consistently with his duty; but, by insuring, he apprehended at
least the probability of an attack. With this knowledge, and without asking a question, he underwrote, and by so doing, he took the
knowledge of the state of the place upon himself; though it was a
matter about which he might have been informed various ways: It was
not a matter within the private knowledge of the governor only. But,
independent of that, it is enough that the fort was in the condition in
which it ought to be, which was only to resist the natives; in like
manner as that a ship insured is presumed to be sea-worthy. The contingency insured against was, whether the place would be attacked
by an European force, and not whether it would be able to resist such

an attack, if the ships could get up the river. It was found that this was the contingency in the contemplation of the parties. The second concealment was, his not having disclosed that the French, not being able to relieve their friends on the coast, might make an attack on him. This was mere speculation dictated by fear, and not a fact in the case. It was a bold attempt for the conquered to attack the conqueror in his own dominion. The practicability of it depended on the English naval force in those seas, of which the underwriter could better judge at London in May, 1760, than the governor at Fort Marlborough in September, 1759. The third concealment was that he did not disclose the design of the French to attack the place the year before. That design rested merely in report; but taking it in the strongest light, it is the report of a design the year before; but then dropped. Another silence, not objected to was, that it appeared by the governor's letter to his agent, that he was apprehensive of a Dutch war; that he had good grounds for this apprehension appeared from the subsequent conduct of the Dutch, to whom the loss of the place was owing. The reason why the counsel did not object to this concealment was, because it must have arisen from political speculation, and general intelligence; and it is not necessary to disclose such things to an underwriter. With respect to the opinion of the broker, the jury were not bound to pay the least regard to it. It was mere opinion, after the event. If rightly formed, it could only be drawn from the same premises from which the court and jury were to determine the cause; and therefore improper and irrelevant in the mouth of a witness. With respect to the governor, there was no ground to impute fraud to him. By the same conveyance which brought his orders to insure, he wrote to the company every thing he knew or suspected. He desired nothing to be kept secret which he wrote to them or to his brother. The reason of the rule against concealments is, to prevent fraud and encourage good faith. If the defendant's objections were to prevail, in the present instance, the rule would be turned into an instrument of fraud. The underwriter, knowing that the governor apprehended danger, and that he must have some ground for his apprehension, being told nothing of either, signed the policy, without asking a question. If the objection, ' that he was not told' be sufficient to vacate it, he took the premium, *knowing* the policy to be void, in order to gain if the alternative turned one way, and make no satisfaction, if it turned out the other. There was not a word said to him of the affairs of India, or the state of the war there, or the condition of Fort Marlborough. If he thought that omission an objection at the time, he ought not to have signed the policy, with a secret reserve in his own mind to make it void. If he dispensed with the information, and did not think this silence an objection then, he cannot take it up now after the event."

Mere silence, especially as to some matter which the assured does not consider it important for the insurer to know, is not such a concealment. Aliud est celare aliud tacere. Every fact, untruly stated, or wrongfully suppressed, the knowledge or ignorance of which would naturally influence the judgment of the insurer in making the contract at all, or in estimating the degree and character of the risk, or in fixing the rate of premium, is material to the risk. If the facts, untruly stated, or purposely suppressed, are not of this character, it is not a misrepresentation or concealment within the meaning of the term.[1]

The assured is only bound to disclose such facts as *are material to the risk*, and, if inquired of, he must do this at his peril, and any failure in that respect will be fatal to his policy, even though it was the result of a mistake, and was not fraudulent or designed.[2] Mere rumors, without any known or reliable origin, need not be disclosed, but intelligence, in the ordinary and usual sense of the term, *when known*, should be disclosed, and two questions are always presented in such cases, to wit: were reliable rumors or reports in circulation, which if true, would be likely to influence the insurer in taking or rejecting the risk, or which would have caused him to fix a higher rate of premium for the risk; and secondly, were such rumors or reports *known* by the assured;[3] and the question of materiality is for the jury.[4] Where fraudulent concealment is relied upon, *the defendant must satisfy the jury either that the assured had knowledge, or the means of knowledge in his possession;*[5] and the mere fact that an agent of the assured possessed such knowledge, does not establish knowledge on the part of the assured.[6] When no inquiries are made, the *intention* of the assured

---

[1] SHAW C. J., in *Daniels* v. *Hudson River Ins. Co.*, Cush. (Mass.) 425.

[2] *Walden* v. *Louisiana Ins. Co.*, 12 La. 134; *Bowery Ins. Co.* v. *N. Y. F. Ins. Co.*, 17 Wend. (N. Y.) 359.

[3] *Durrell* v. *Bederly*, Holt (N. P.) 283; *Greenwell* v. *Nicholson*, 1 Jur. 285; *Boggs* v. *American Ins. Co.*, 30 Mo. 63; *Hartford Protection Ins. Co*, v. *Harmer*, 2 Ohio St. 452; *Gates* v. *Madison Co., etc., Ins. Co.*, 5 N. Y. 43.

[4] *Gates* v. *Madison Co., etc., Ins. Co., ante; Perkins* v. *Equitable Ins. Co.*, 4 Allen (N. B.) 562; *Huguenin* v. *Rayley*, 6 Taunt. 186; *Elton* v. *Larkin*, 8 Bing. 198; *Littledale* v. *Dixon*, 4 B. &. P. 151; *Franklin F. Ins. Co.* v. *Coates*, 14 Md. 285; *People* v. *Liverpool, etc., Ins. Co.*, 2 T. & C. (N. Y.) 268; *Syneers* v. *Glasgow Ins. Co.*, 19 Scotch Jur. 49.

[5] *Bates* v. *Hewitt*, 4 F. & F. 1028.

[6] *Clement* v. *Phœnix Ins. Co.*, 6 Blatch. (U. S. C. C.) 481.

becomes material, and in order to avoid the policy, they must find, not only that the matter *was material, but also that it was intentionally fraudulently concealed.*[1] If the insurer makes *any* inquiries, the assured has a right to suppose that he inquires as to all matters that he regards as material, and waives knowledge as to all other matters, *except it be in reference to unusual or extraordinary circumstances, in reference to which the assured has knowledge, but in reference to which there is nothing to put the insurer upon inquiry.*[2] It was well said by BRONSON, J., in the case last cited, that "*if a man is content to insure my house without taking the trouble to inquire of what materials it is composed, how it is situated in reference to other buildings, or to what uses it is applied, he has no ground of complaint that the hazard proves to be greater than he had anticipated, unless I am chargeable with some misrepresentation concerning the nature of the risk.*" In a case in the United States court,[3] WOOD-BURY, J., in discussing the question, says: "As to the ordinary risks connected with the property insured, *if no representations whatever are asked or given, the insurer must be supposed to assume them;* and if he acts anywhere concerning them, seems quite as negligent as the assured *who is silent when not requested to speak.*" The rule thus expressed, extended as it was in an Ohio case[4] by RAMSAY, J., may be said to be the rule generally applied in such cases. He said, in speaking of the rule expressed in these cases: "This, I confess, seems to me the true rule; perhaps with the qualification more distinctly indicated, * * *that the insured does not withhold information of such unusual and extraordinary circumstances of peril* to the property, *as could not with reasonable diligence be discovered by the insurer, or reasonably anticipated as a foundation for specific inquiries.*"

Where the insured, at the time of obtaining insurance, knows that the building has just previously been on fire, and *suspects*, but has no reliable reason therefor, that it was set, the question as to whether the concealment of such fact is *material*, is for the jury, *and, in deter-*

---

[1] *Foster v. Mentor, etc., Ins. Co.*, 3 El. & Bl. 48; *Gates v. Madison, etc., Ins. Co., ante; Clark v. Manufacturers' Ins. Co.*, 8 How. (U. S.) 235; *Holmes v. Charlestown, etc., Ins. Co.*, 10 Met. (Mass.) 211.

[2] *Hartford Protection Ins. Co. v. Harmer*, 2 Ohio St. 452; 3 Bennett's F. Ins. C. 643; *Gates v. Madison, etc., Ins. Co.*, 5 N. Y. 43; 3 Bennett's F. I. C. 288; *Clark v. Manufacturers' Ins. Co.*, 8 How. (U. S.) 235; 2 Bennett's F. I. C. 520; *Burritt v. The Saratoga Ins. Co.*, 5 Hill (N. Y.) 192; 2 Bennett's F. I. C. 276; *Com. v. Hide & Leather Ins. Co.*, 112 Mass. 136; 17 Am. Rep. 72; *Liberty Hall Ass'n v. Housatonic, etc., Ins. Co.*, 7 Gray (Mass.) 261; *Hall v. People's Ins. Co.*, 6 id. 185.

[3] *Clark v. Manufacturers' Ins. Co., ante.*

[4] *Hartford Protection Ins. Co. v. Harmer, ante.*

mining that question, it is proper for them to consider the grounds of the assured's suspicion, as well as the fact that they proved to be unfounded.[1]

Where the plaintiff, in seeking re-insurance of a risk, knowing that the owners of the propery had had difficulties about their losses, and were in bad repute among insurers, failed to disclose the fact, it was held a fraudulent concealment.[2] So, where there had been a rumored attempt to destroy the premises by an incendiary, of which the insurer had knowledge.[3] But, if there is no foundation *in fact* for the rumor, it has been held *not* to amount to a concealment of a *material fact.*[4]

Where the assured has attempted to procure insurance elsewhere upon a ship, but, on account of apprehensions of the loss of the vessel, the risk was refused, and he omitted to disclose the existence of such apprehensions, and the vessel was in fact lost, it was held a fatal concealment,[5] and it seems that, if he has *heard* of the loss, and neglects to disclose the fact, and the intelligence proves correct, a policy obtained without disclosing the fact is void,[6] and it seems that this is so, if the assured had no actual intelligence of a loss, but had reason to apprehend it,[7] or even if he had heard rumors of a loss, but did not believe them.[8]

---

[1] In *Harmer* v. *Protection Ins. Co.*, 2 Ohio St. 452 ; 3 Bennett's F. I. C. 643, the plaintiff procured insurance upon some buildings and tobacco stored therein. It appeared that, *just prior* to the procurement of the insurance, one of the buildings had been on fire, and the plaintiff *suspected that it was fired by an incendiary.* The plaintiff did not communicate this fact to the agent of the insurer, and, in fact, his suspicions were not well grounded, and it was proved that the building was accidentally fired. The court instructed the jury to refer to and be governed by *the true cause of the fire, and not by the belief of the assured,* in determining the materiality of the facts concealed. This ruling was sustained, RAMSAY, J., pertinently remarking : "So far as his belief was of any value as an admission of the true cause, it went to the jury for what it was worth, and the company had the full benefit of it, *and, if his belief corresponded with the true cause,* of course no injury was done them. *If it did not, of what importance was his belief or suspicion to them ? Before the duty of disclosure arises, the fact must be material to the risk*—that is, *it must increase the chances of loss. If it was not in truth material, could his erroneous suspicions make it so ?* It was not pretended that he *knew* the cause, or had received any *information, true or false, which he failed to communicate.* In such cases, the marine rule is, that the assured is not bound to communicate his own expectations and opinions and speculations upon facts," and this was held by the court to be the rule applicable to fire insurance.

[2] *Bowery F. Ins. Co.* v. *N. Y. F. Ins. Co.*, 17 Wend. (N. Y.) 359. See same in principle, *Leigh* v. *Adams*, 25 L. T. (U. S.) 566 ; *Costa* v. *Scandrer*, 2 P. W. (U. S.) 176.

[3] *Walden* v. *Louisiana Ins. Co.*, 12 La. 134 ; *American F. Ins. Co.* v. *Throop*, 22 Mich. 146.

[4] *Hartford Protection Ins. Co.* v. *Harmer, ante.*

[5] *Vale* v. *Phœnix Ins. Co.*, 1 Wash. C. C. (U. S.) 283.

[6] *Johnson* v. *Phœnix Ins. Co.*, 1 Wash. C. C. (U. S.) 378 ; *Moses* v. *Del. Ins. Co.*, 1 id. 385.

[7] *Moses* v. *Del. Ins. Co., ante; Hoyt* v. *Gilman*, 8 Mass. 336 ; *Bowker* v. *Smith*, F. C. (Sc.) 571.

[8] *Graham* v. *Ins. Co.*, 6 La. An. 432.

When the assured is required to give information upon a particular point, he must give it correctly, and he must not, upon any ground, withhold material information or knowledge that he has in reference thereto. By putting an inquiry to him, the insurers have made the matter material, and he cannot excuse himself for not stating *all* the facts, upon the ground that he did not suppose it was material. As, when inquiry is made as to the *present* value of the property, it should be stated *at its present value*, and not *at its expected value* at some future time.[1] In such cases, so far as the question of value is concerned, strict exactness is neither expected or required; but the insurer is entitled to have the *honest judgment* of the assured, and not a fanciful or knowingly false statement thereof. The mere fact that the property is over-valued does not of itself necessarily establish fraud on the part of the assured, so as to avoid the policy; but if the valuation is *knowingly* excessive, or if it is *grossly and enormously* excessive, it is a circumstance to be considered in determining whether it is fraudulent.[2] But where, from the character of the risk, it is evidently *the understanding of the parties* that the value will be fluctuating, and that the policy relates to the average value, rather than the value at any particular time, if the assured overstates the value of the property as *then* existing, but states it at a sum that he reasonably expects it soon will be, his statement thereof will not amount to an over-valuation, although his expectations were not realized.[3]

Assured not bound to communicate facts arising subsequently to issue of policy.

SEC. 198. The concealment of a fact transpiring or coming to the knowledge of the assured *after* the contract is made, even though before the policy is made or delivered, will not avoid the policy, unless provision is made therefor.[4] Thus, in an English case,[5] this question

---

[1] *Protection Ins. Co.* v. *Hall*, 15 B. Mon. (Ky.) 411; 3 Bennett's F. I. C. 777.

[2] *Protection Ins. Co.* v. *Hall, ante; Franklin F. Ins. Co.* v. *Vaughn*, 92 U. S. 516. See OVER-VALUATION.

[3] In *Lee* v. *The Howard Ins. Co.*, 11 Cush. (Mass.) 321, the policy contained a clause by which it was covenanted that the application was "a just, full and true exposition of all the facts and circumstances in regard to the condition, situation, *value* and risk of the property, so far as the same are known and are material to the risk." The application stated the value of the goods to be between $2,000 and $3,000. The value of the property was much less than $2,000 at the time when the policy was issued, and a loss having occurred, the insurer insisted that the policy was void because the warranty as to value was broken; but the court held that, *if the representation was made in good faith*, that the stock on hand, with that which was to be added and kept during the life of the policy, should range between those sums, the policy was not void.

[4] *Cory* v. *Patton*, L. R., 9 Q. B. 577; *Lishman* v. *N. Western Ins. Co.*, L. R., 10 C. P. 179; *Curry* v. *Conn. Ins. Co.*, 10 Pick. (Mass.) 535. In *Insurance Co.* v. *Lyman*,

[5] *Cory* v. *Patton, ante.*

was carefully considered. In that case it was held that where underwriters have, by initialing a slip, made a contract of assurance, which, although invalid at law and equity for want of statutory requisites, is, nevertheless, in practice, and, according to the usage of those engaged in marine insurance, a complete and final contract binding upon them in honor and good faith, whatever events may subsequently happen, the assured need not communicate to the underwriters facts which afterward come to his knowledge material to the risk insured against; *and the non-disclosures of such facts will not vitiate the policy of insurance afterward executed. And it makes no difference that, the insurance being negotiated by an agent of the assured, the slip was initialed subject to the ratification of the assured.*[1]

In a later English case,[2] a proposal for insurance on freight was made and accepted on the 11th of March. On the 16th the ship was lost. On the 17th the assured *with knowledge of the loss, but without communicating it to the insurers, demanded a stamped policy.* The insurers then, for the first time, required to be informed as to the amount of the insurance upon the hull, and inserted in the policy (which the assured accepted) the following warranty : "Hull warranted not insured for more than £2,700 after the 20th of March." The vessel was then insured for an additional £500 in an insurance club, by the rules of which all ships belonging to members were insured from the 20th of March in one year to the 20th of March in the following year, " and so on from year to year, unless ten days' notice to the contrary be given;" and in the absence of notice, the managers of the club were to renew each

---

15 Wall. (U. S.) 664, where a parol agreement to insure was made Dec. 31st, and the vessel was lost Jan. 8th, and the policy was not executed and delivered until Jan. 15th, and it appeared that the plaintiff knew that the vessel was lost before the policy was delivered but did not disclose the fact, and the policy only took effect from the day of its execution, it was held that no recovery could be had, and that the insured could not be permitted to vary the terms of the policy actually accepted by him by proving that this contract was in fact made on the 8th. The court said, however, that, if the plaintiff had gone to the insurers and communicated the loss, and demanded a policy covering the contract, he would then have been in a position to have enforced the parol contract. See also, *McLanahan* v. *Universal Ins. Co.*, 1 Pet. (U. S.) 170, where it was held that, even after the application is made, but before its acceptance, a loss occurs *known* to the assured, he is bound to use due diligence to inform the insurer before the contract is complete. Also see *Scangall* v. *Young*, F. C. (Sc.) 166. But if the contract is complete, and no change is made or assented to therein, the insured is not bound to communicate facts that come to his knowledge *after* it is completed, but before the contract is executed, by delivery of the policy. *Lishman* v. *N. Marine Ins. Co.*, L. R., 8 C. P. 216. *Mere sensations and apprehensions* need not be communicated, unless predicated to the knowledge of the assured, upon reasonable grounds. *Bell* v. *Bell*, 2 Camp. 475.

[1] *Hagadorn* v. *Oliverson*, 2 M. & S. 485.

[2] *Lishman* v. *N. Western Ins. Co.*, *ante.*

policy on its expiration. The court held, affirming the decision of the court below, that, notwithstanding those rules, the club policy was not a continuing policy beyond the 20th of March of the current year; and that the ship having been lost before that date, no new effective policy could have been made, and, consequently, the warranty was complied with; also, that the risk having been accepted by the insur_ers on the.11th of March, the addition on the 17th of a term for their benefit, and not affecting the risk, did not prevent the policy from being one drawn up in respect to the risk accepted on the 11th, and, therefore, upon the authority of Cory v. Patton,[1] the concealment of the loss was not a concealment of a material fact so as to avoid the policy. This case presents in, perhaps, the strongest possible form the affirmance of the principles first laid down in Cory v. Patton,[2] and since acted upon in several cases, that after the acceptance of the risk there is no obligation on the assured to communicate any information to the underwriter. In this case, after the acceptance of the risk, but before the execution of the policy, the ship was lost, and the fact became known to the assured; he nevertheless asked for and obtained the stamped policy. The court of common pleas held that the assured was entitled to recover, and the exchequer chamber has affirmed the decision. The weight of recent authority in favor of the plaintiff was felt to be so great that on this branch of the case it was scarcely argued that he would not be entitled to recover, but for one circumstance. That circumstance was, that, on issuing the policy, the defendants had, with the consent of the plaintiff, inserted the additional term of a modified warranty against double insurance; but this was held to make no difference, and indeed, the desperate nature of the argument shows how difficult it was felt to maintain the defense. For the future, therefore, the observations in Mead v. Davison[3] as to the non-communication of a loss which becomes known to the assured between the acceptance of the risk and the making of the policy, must be read in the light of the late decisions, and of the statute of 30 and 31 Vict. c. 23, which, by taking away the absolute inadmissibility in evidence of a slip, led the way to them.

This question has been considered in several American cases, and the same doctrine held,[4] and it is difficult to conceive how any other

[1] L. R., 7 Q. B. 304.

[2] 20 W. R. 364; L. R., 7 Q. B. 304.

[3] 3 A. & E. 303.

[4] *Whittaker* v. *The Farmers' Union Ins. Co.*, 29 Barb. (N. Y.) 312; *Kohne* v. *Ins. Co. of N. America*, 1 Wash. C. C. (U. S.) 93; *Baldwin* v. *Choteau Ins. Co.*,

doctrine could be regarded as tenable. *When the contract has been made, and all its terms agreed upon*, the rights of the parties under it are complete, and their duties and obligations thereunder are fixed. A policy issued in pursuance of the agreement relates back to the time of the agreement, and can only properly bear that date. *Everything to be done subsequent to the making of the contract, is simply to furnish the evidence by which the contract itself is to be proved.* The contract exists, the only defect is in the evidence of it; when that can be established, the parties' rights are as complete without as with the policy itself. The contract exists as soon as its terms are agreed upon, and the minds of the contracting parties have met.[1]

When that stage in the negotiations between the parties is reached, and nothing remains to be done but to execute what has been agreed upon, the contract is complete, and the courts will interpose to compel either a specific performance of the contract by compelling the execution of the policy,[2] or by upholding an action upon the contract for the loss, if the contract is *of* insurance,[3] or for a breach thereof if it is *for* insurance, and the company refuses to execute a policy.[4]

In a Missouri case,[5] the question arose in the same form as in the English cases previously commented on, except that this was a case of fire insurance. In this case an application for insurance was made and accepted February 9th, but the policy was not delivered, and five days after the contract was made the premises burned. *After* their destruction the plaintiff, *without disclosing the loss*, paid the premium and took the policy. One of the grounds upon which the defendants resisted payment of the loss was, that the plaintiff had fraudulently

---

56 Mo. 151; 13 Am. Rep. 671; *Commercial Mut. Marine Ins. Co. v. Union Mut. Marine Ins. Co.*, 19 How. (U. S.) 318; *Keim v. Home. Mut. F. & M. Ins. Co.*, 42 Mo. 38.

[1] *American Horse Ins. Co. v. Patterson*, 28 Ind. 17; *Lightbody v. No. Mo. Ins. Co.*, 23 Wend. (N. Y.) 18; *Xenas v. Wickham*, L. R., 2 H. L. 296; *Hallock v. Com. Ins. Co.*, 26 N. J. L. 268; *Flint v. Ohio Ins. Co.*, 8 Ohio, 501; *Tyler v. New Amsterdam Ins. Co.*, 4 Robt. (N. Y.) 151; *Ellis v. Albany City Ins. Co.*, 50 N. Y. 402; *Com. Mut. Marine Ins. Co. v. Union Mut. Marine Ins. Co., ante; Trustees, etc., v. Brooklyn F. Ins. Co.*, 19 N. Y. 305; *Mobile Marine, etc., Ins. Co. v. McMillan*, 31 Ala. 711; *Kelly v. Commonwealth Ins. Co.*, 10 Bos. (N. Y.) 82; *N. E., etc., Ins. Co. v. Robinson*, 25 Ind. 536; *West. Mass. Ins. Co. v. Duffy*, 2 Kan. 347; *Audubon v. Excelsior Ins. Co.*, 27 N. Y. 216.

[2] *Kentucky Mut. Ins. Co. v. Jenks*, 5 Ind. 96; *Commercial Mut. Marine Ins. Co. v. Union Mut. Marine Ins. Co.*, 19 How. (U. S.) 318.

[3] *Mobile Marine, etc., Ins. Co. v. McMillan*, 31 Ala. 711; *West. Mass. Ins. Co. v. Duffy*, 2 Kan. 347; *First Baptist Church v. Brooklyn Ins. Co.*, 19 N. Y. 305.

[4] *Angell v. Hartford F. Ins. Co.*, 56 N. Y. 171; 17 Am. Rep. 322; *Audubon v. Excelsior Ins. Co.*, 27 N. Y. 216.

[5] *Keim v. Home Mut. F. Ins. Co.*, 42 Mo. 38.

concealed the fact of the loss; but the court held that, as the contract itself was complete on the 9th of February, the plaintiff was under no obligation, legal or moral, to disclose the fact of a loss occurring subsequent thereto. Many cases similar in principle have arisen in our courts, and the doctrine is firmly established.[1]

It follows from the doctrine of these cases, that *where a valid contract for insurance has been made,* for the breach of which an action could be brought, although the policy has not been made or the premium paid, the non-communication of the fact that the buildings have been destroyed, or of any other fact arising *material to the risk*, does not destroy or detract from the validity of the policy subsequently obtained.[2] The rule as to concealment only applies to facts existing when the contract is made.[3]

Must be material facts. Test of materiality.

SEC. 199. The rule applicable to the concealment of facts, is the same that applies in the case of representations. *Whenever the facts are such that if known to the insurer they would have or might have a real influence upon him, either in accepting or rejecting the risk, or in determining the rate of premium to be charged therefor, it is deemed a concealment of material facts, if a higher rate of premium would have been charged if such facts had been known.*[4] Facts that if known, would have induced the taking of the risk at a less rate, are not within the rule, because it is of no importance to the insurer that the risk *is less* than he had supposed. That is to his advantage. The insured alone suffers from the non-communication of such facts, and no principle of fair dealing or commercial integrity is violated by their non-communication. But where the facts are such that if known, the insurer would be influenced thereby to fix a higher rate of premium, or, in accepting or rejecting the risk, every principle of honesty and fair dealing requires that the facts should be disclosed, and from whatever cause a failure to disclose them arises, the law treats their suppression as a fraud;[5] and the legal effect is determined by the *materiality* of the matters stated or sup-

[1] *Baldwin* v. *Choteau Ins. Co.*, 56 Mo. 151; 17 Am. Rep. 671; *Angell* v. *Hartford Fire Ins. Co.*, 59 N. Y. 171; 17 Am. Rep. 322; *Commercial Mut. Marine Ins. Co.* v. *Union Mut. Marine Ins. Co.*, 19 How. (N. Y.) 318; *Whittaker* v. *Farmers', etc., Ins. Co.*, 29 Barb. (N. Y.) 312.

[2] *Kernochan* v. *Bowery Ins. Co.*, 17 N. Y. 428; *Norwich F. Ins. Co.* v. *Boomer*, 52 Ill. 442; *Clapp* v. *Union, etc., Ins. Co.*, 27 N. H. 143; *Delahy* v. *Memphis Ins. Co.*, 8 Humph (Tenn.) 684.

[3] *Curry* v. *Com. Ins. Co.*, ante.

[4] *Boggs* v. *American Ins. Co.*, 30 Mo. 63.

[5] *Columbian Ins. Co.* v. *Lawrence*, 2 Pit. (U. S.) 25.

pressed,[1] and the question is one for the jury, it being left for them to say whether *in fact* the insurer was influenced thereby in taking the risk or fixing the rate of premium therefor;[2] and their finding is conclusive.[3]

STORY, J., in a leading American case,[4] gave the rule applicable to representations or concealments thus: "Whenever the nature of this interest would have or might have a *real* influence upon the underwriter, *either not to underwrite at all, or not to underwrite except at a higher premium, it must be deemed material to the risk,* and if so, the misrepresentation or concealment of it will avoid the policy. One of the tests, and certainly a *decisive test,* whether a misrepresentation *is material to the risk,* is to ascertain whether, *if the true state of the property or title had been known, it would have enhanced the premium.* If it would, then the misrepresentation or concealment is fatal to the policy." It must be a concealment of such facts as affect the risk to such an extent, that the risk taken is different from that which the insurer understood he was taking, and induces him to enter into a contract different from that which he supposed he was entering into.[5] The distinction between a false representation, and a concealment of matters relating to the risk is, that in the one case, the contract is induced by facts

[1] *Kohn* v. *Ins. Co. of N. America,* 6 Binn. (Penn.) 219; *Ins. Co.* v. *Lyman,* 15 Wall (U. S.) 664; *Bowery Ins. Co.* v. *N. Y. Ins. Co.,* 17 Wend. (N. Y.) 359; *N. A. Ins. Co.* v. *Throop,* 22 Mich. 146; *Ritt* v. *Washington Ins. Co.,* 41 Barb. (N. Y.) 353.

[2] *Maryland Ins. Co.* v. *Ruden,* 6 Cr. (U. S.) 338. In *Sussex County Ins. Co.* v. *Woodruff,* 26 N. J. 541, the insured did not disclose the nature of his interest in the premises. The policy covered his "woolen manufactory and machinery therein." He was simply mortgagee. The court held that the question was exclusively for the jury, whether the concealment of his interest was material or not. A similar question arose in *Franklin Ins. Co.* v. *Coates,* 14 Md. 285, and a similar doctrine held. In that case, the assured procured a policy "on their lumber." Their real interest was that of material men for lumber supplied the builders. The court held that it was for the jury to say whether the concealment of their real interest in the property was material. See also, *Perkins* v. *Equitable Ins. Co.,* 4 Allen (N. B.) 562; *Gates* v. *Madison County Mut. Ins. Co.,* 2 N. Y. 43; *Littledale* v. *Dixon,* 4 B. & P. 151.

[3] In an early case in Massachusetts, *Curry* v. *Com. Ins. Co.,* 10 Pick. 535, the defendants, under a policy, set up the concealment of the following facts in defense. It appeared that the plaintiff had been instrumental in securing the arrest of an escaped convict, who, while being returned to prison, uttered threats of revenge by setting buildings on fire, in case he should ever find out who had informed against him. The court below left the question as to the materiality of these facts to the jury, and they having found a verdict for the plaintiff, upon appeal, in passing upon this question, WILDE, J., said: "As to the other objections, that respecting the alleged concealment, and that of the supposed increase of risk, by the addition to the house—these seem to depend *on facts which have been settled by the jury,* and we are of opinion that the evidence well supports the verdict. The instructions of the judge to the jury were perfectly correct on both points."

[4] *Columbian Ins. Co.* v. *Lawrence,* 10 Peters (U. S.) 516.

[5] *Hodges* v. *Marine Ins. Co.,* 5 Cr. (U. S.) 100.

stated, while in the other, it is by facts suppressed, and the same rules apply in either case.

Concealment of misrepresentation of interest. Incendiary threats. Rumors of, etc.

SEC. 200. The concealment of facts relating to the *interest* of the assured iu the property,[1] or relating to peculiar hazards to which the property is exposed, as incendiary threats to destroy it, or rumored attempts to do so,[2] or threats, or attempts to burn adjacent buildings, the burning of which would necessarily endanger the property of the insured, if material to the risk, avoid the policy.[3] So, if the property is located in the vicinity of buildings, in which, to the knowledge of the insured, extra hazardous trades are prosecuted, or uses which materially enhance the risk, as a petroleum store-house, oil refinery, oil-cloth manufactory, powder mill, cabinet shop, steam saw mill, or other similar establishments, there would seem to be no question that ordinarily, within the principle applicable to the concealment of *material* facts, the policy would be void. Proximity to what establishments would bring the insured within this rule, cannot be stated, but it is believed to be safe to say, that if any trade or business is carried on in the immediate neighborhood of the property of the insured, that *materially* affects the risk, in the respects previously stated, a concealment of such facts would render the policy inoperative and void.[4]

---

[1] *Sussex Co. Ins. Co.* v. *Woodruff, ante; Franklin Ins. Co.* v. *Coates,* 14 Md. 285; *Columbian Ins. Co.* v. *Lawrence,* 10 Peters (U. S.) 507; *Catron* v. *Tenn. M. & F. Ins. Co.,* 6 Humph. (Tenn.) 176; *Cousins* v. *Nantes,* 3 Taunt. 513.

[2] In *North American F. Ins. Co.* v. *Throop,* 22 Mich., inquiries were made of the plaintiff whether incendiary attempts had been made to fire the property, to which he answered, no; but the evidence shows that such attempts had been made, of which he had notice. The court instructed the jury that such attempts to fire the building might not be material to the risk. Upon appeal this was held error, the court holding that, as matter of law, such attempts were material, and that if such threats had been made and the plaintiff failed to disclose them, he could not recover. The effect of neglecting to disclose incendiary threats or attempts to burn the property is necessarily material.

[3] In *Bufe* v. *Turner,* 6 Taunt. 328, a fire broke out on Saturday, in a boat builder's shop, near the plaintiff's premises, and was apparently extinguished at about eight o'clock that evening. It was thought necessary to watch the premises, however, and on Monday the fire broke out again, and consumed a warehouse next but one to the premises that first took fire. On the Saturday evening, *when the fire was apparently out,* after the ordinary mart had been started, the owner of the warehouse sent instructions for its insurance by an extraordinary conveyance, but failed to communicate the fact of the fire which had occurred. It was held on general principles, and without reference to the rules and conditions of the company, that this concealment rendered the policy void.

[4] Bunyon on Fire Insurance, 65. In *McFarland* v. *Peabody Ins. Co.,* 6 W. Va. 425, an application was made for insurance upon the plaintiff's building, and a diagram was made showing the situation of other buildings in reference thereto. There was a building contiguous to the plaintiff's used for painting barrels, and in which benzine was kept and used, and it was held that a failure by the plaintiff to communicate such facts to the insurer rendered the policy void, such fact being material to the risk.

Incendiary threats.

SEC. 201. In order to avoid the policy upon the ground of *incendiary threats*, the danger must be real and substantial, and such as materially enhances the risk, and which a person of ordinary prudence would not regard as mere idle talk or reports.[1] The fact that the property is in a section of country where desperate measures for the gratification of private revenge are sometimes resorted to, and that the assured is very unpopular, or that those having the custody of the property are so, need not be disclosed, as the insurers are presumed to know the condition of society in communities in which they insure property,[2] and it is a well-settled rule that a party is not bound to communicate facts which the law presumes the other party knows,[3] and if the insurer *knew* the facts, which he complains were concealed, from *any* source, at the time he made the contract, a fraudulent concealment cannot be predicated thereon, as, where the insurers had previously directed a policy upon the same risk to be canceled, because of incendiary threats to destroy it, it was held that the fact that the insured did not state the fact, was not a concealment of a material fact;[4] at least the point was made by the defendant in the last named case, and the court did not deem it of sufficient importance to notice it in their opinion. If inquiries are made, even in reference to matters about which the insurer has knowledge, he is bound to disclose all material facts.[5]

Interest need not be particularly stated, unless called for.

SEC. 202. In the absence of anything in the contract calling therefor, it is not obligatory upon the insured to state his interest in the property insured;[6] the existence of a mortgage;[7] that he holds only as lessee;[8] that the property has been levied upon and is held by assured as attaching creditor;[9] that litigation is pending concerning the title of the property;[10] that the property has been set off on execution,[11] or

[1] *McBride* v. *Republic Ins. Co.*, 30 Wis. 562.

[2] *Keith* v. *Globe Ins. Co.*, 52 Ill. 518.

[3] *Norris* v. *Ins. Co. of N. America*, 3 Yeates (Penn.) 84; *Delonguemare* v. *N. Y. F. Ins. Co.*, 10 John. (N. Y.) 120.

[4] *Fish* v. *Cottinett*, 44 N. Y. 538.

[5] *Green* v. *Merchants' Ins. Co.*, 10 Pick. (Mass.) 402.

[6] *Turner* v. *Burrows*, 5 Wend. (N. Y.) 541.

[7] *Keenochan* v. *N. Y.*, etc., *Ins. Co.*, 17 N. Y. 428; *Delahy* v. *Memphis Ins. Co.*, 8 Humph. (Tenn.) 684: *Cumberland*, etc., *Ins. Co.* v. *Mitchell*, 48 Penn. St. 374.

[8] *Fletcher* v. *Com. Ins. Co.*, 18 Pick. (Mass.) 419.

[9] *Columbia Ins. Co.* v. *Cooper*, 50 Penn. St. 331.

[10] *Hill* v. *LaFayette Ins. Co.*, 2 Mich. 465.

[11] *Clapp* v. *Union*, etc., *Ins. Co.*, 27 N. H. 143.

that the assured holds it as mortgagee.[1] It is enough *if an insurable interest exists*, unless the policy requires the real title to be stated.[2]

May be waived.

SEC. 203. While, however, upon general principles, irrespective of any provisions or conditions in the application or the policy issued thereon, the fraudulent concealment of material facts renders the policy void, yet the insurer may, by his conduct, waive all such considerations and do that which will estop him from setting up such concealment as a ground for avoiding his liability under the contract. As, where the facts are *known* to him as well as to the assured,[3] or where they are a matter of general knowledge, of which he is bound to take notice.[4]

---

[1] *Norwich F. Ins. Co.* v. *Boomer*, 52 Ill. 442.

[2] *Fletcher* v. *Com. Ins. Co.*, ante; *Gilbert* v. *N. American Ins. Co.*, 23 Wend. (N. Y.) 13 ; *Ins. Co.* v. *Marselles Manuf. Co.*, 6 Ill. 236.

[3] *Green* v. *Merchants' Ins. Co.*, 10 Pick. (Mass.) 402. In an application which provided that questions not answered should be construed most favorably to the risk, the applicant left unanswered a question whether there was any livery stable in the vicinity. In an action on the policy, of which this application was made part, the jury were instructed that, if there was a livery stable in the vicinity at the time of the application, they were to determine what was the meaning of the question and of the word "vicinity," and whether there was a livery stable in that vicinity, having reference to the situation of the building in which the property insured was situated, the situation of other buildings, and the locality, as ascertained from the contract and evidence. It was held that the defendants had no ground of exception. *Haley* v. *Dorchester, etc., Ins. Co.*, 12 Gray (Mass.) 545. In the same case it was also held that, in an application made part of a policy on property in the second story of a large building, and providing that the description therein given shall be a full and true description of the property to be insured, and of all circumstances in relation thereto, material to the risk, and that the questions not answered shall be construed most favorably to the risk, an omission in answer to the question, "Who occupies it?" to state the occupation and occupants of all the rooms, does not avoid the policy, if the jury are satisfied that those not disclosed make the risk less hazardous than it would have been if the whole building had been occupied as stated in the answer. A policy issued on an oral promise, innocently made, that the premises insured would be occupied, is not avoided by the non-fulfillment of such promise. *Kimball* v. *Ætna Ins. Co.*, 9 Allen (Mass.) 540. The concealment of the fact that a ship, upon which a policy of insurance is effected, is in command of a master who sails her at halves, manning and victualling her and paying her port charges, does not avoid the policy. *Russ* v. *Waldo, etc., Ins. Co.*, 52 Maine, 187. A policy issued by an agent is not void for failing to state that the interest of the insured was that of mortgagee, when his title was fully known to the agent, and no written application was made, although a condition of the policy was that, if the property was held by any other than an absolute title, "it must be represented to the company, and expressed in the policy in writing; otherwise, the insurance as to such property to be void." The insured may recover upon such a policy, in case of loss, to the extent of his interest in the property. *Emery* v. *Piscataqua, etc., Ins. Co.*, 52 Maine, 322. A mortgagee of a part of certain buildings may recover the amount of his loss, although his policy covered his interest as mortgagee of the whole property. *Fox* v. *Phœnix, etc., Ins. Co.*, 52 Maine, 333. From the answer to a question in an application, that the factory insured is "worked usually" certain specified hours in the day time "in the summer," and certain specified hours "in the winter—short time now," it may be inferred that it was expected at times the factory would be run nights. *North Berwick Co.* v. *New England, etc., Ins. Co.*, 52 Maine, 336.

[4] *Norris* v. *Ins. Co. of N. America*, 3 Yeates (Penn.) 84.

Neither can they set up such matter in defense when they issue the
policy upon the knowledge of their agent, and not upon information
derived from the assured,[1] unless the information, the concealment of
which is complained of, was peculiarly within the knowledge of the
assured, and not known to the agent, or likely to be discovered by the
person sent by them to examine the premises.[2] If the insurer chooses
to send its own agents to examine the risk and ascertain its nature
and extent, it cannot complain of the concealment of any matter which
a person of reasonable prudence, by the exercise of reasonable diligence would be likely to discover.[3] So, if the policy is issued upon
the knowledge of the agent, without any application in writing by the
insured, or inquiries made of him in reference thereto, the insurer
cannot complain that it has been misled or deceived by the assured,
and must submit to the consequences of its own folly. By pursuing
such a course, the insurer is thrown off his guard, and has a right to
presume that the agent can determine the nature of the risk to the
satisfaction of his principal. But, if there are facts or circumstances

---

[1] *Continental Ins. Co.* v. *Kasey,* 25 Gratt. (Va.). This question was considered
in *Morrison* v. *The Universal Marine Ins. Co.,* L. R. 8 Exchq. 40, in which the
plaintiff's insurance broker effected an insurance with the defendants on the chartered freight of the plaintiff's ship Cambria, without disclosing to the defendants
certain information in his possession, which it was material that they should know.
(October 10.) In so doing he acted in good faith, supposing, from inquiries that
he had made, that the information was incorrect. After initialing the slip, but
before executing the policy, the defendants (October 13) became possessed of the
information which the broker had not disclosed; and they afterward executed and
delivered out the policy without any protest or any notice that they would treat it
as void. (October 14 or 15.) Upon receiving news of the loss of the vessel, they
gave notice to the plaintiff that they did not consider the policy binding on them.
(October 20.) On the trial of an action upon the policy, the judge directed the
jury, in substance, that the defendants were bound to make their election within
a reasonable time after they became aware of the concealment, and left it to them,
without expressing any opinion, whether the defendants had elected to go on with
the policy. Held (CLEASBY, B., dissenting), a misdirection, on the ground (by
MARTIN, B.), that if the conduct of the defendants in delivering out the policy
would induce the plaintiff to suppose that he had a valid policy, they were
estopped from denying it (by BRAMWELL, B.); that delivering out the policy with
knowledge of the concealment was *prima facie* an election, and threw on the
defendants the burden of showing circumstances to explain it. The information
not disclosed by the broker had appeared in *Lloyd's List,* which is a daily newspaper containing hundreds of entries relating to shipping in all parts of the
world, and circulating among ship-owners, underwriters, and insurance brokers;
the defendants were in fact subscribers to this newspaper. Held, that the broker
was not entitled to assume a knowledge by the underwriters of the contents of
Lloyd's List.

[2] *Safford* v. *Vt. Mut. Ins. Co.*

[3] *Continental Ins. Co.* v. *Kasey,* 25 Gratt. (Va.) 268; or if the company was
bound to examine the risk and did not, *Satterthwaite* v. *Ins. Co., ante;* or if the
concealment relates to a matter which the insurer is presumed to know, *Norris* v.
Ins. Co. of N. America, ante; or which by fair inquiry or reasonable diligence it
would have known, *Friere* v. *Woodhouse, ante;* or when the agent of the company
knew the facts, *Gerhauser* v. *Ins. Co.* 7 Nev. 174.

material to the risk, which the agent would not be likely to discover from a reasonably careful examination of the property, the insured is bound to communicate such facts.[1]

Concealment cannot be charged, when the matter is covered by a warranty.

SEC. 204. The rule does not apply to the *concealment* of facts that are covered by a warranty, express or implied. In all such cases the policy can only be avoided by establishing a breach of the warranty itself,[2] although in such a case, if a *false representation* is made, the policy is void.[3]

Rule when insurer knew the facts.

SEC. 205. Whether there has been a fraudulent concealment or mis-representation in a matter material to the risk, is essentially a question of fact for the jury;[4] and, even though the misrepresentation or conceal-ment is material, yet if the insurer *or its agent* had knowledge *of the true state of the matter*, from *any* source, *at the time when the contract was entered into*, the policy will not be thereby avoided, as a warranty can-not be held to cover matters which the other party *knows* do not and *cannot* exist.[5] And even though the by-laws of the company, or the policy, provides that the agent of the insurer, or the person who takes the application or survey, shall be the agent of the insured in respect thereto, yet he is to be considered as the agent of the insurer also, and the insurer is bound by his acts. Consequently if he, in filling up the application, without any fraud or fault on the part of the assured, misstates the facts, the insurer is estopped from setting up such mis-statements or omissions in defense to an action for a loss under the policy.[6]

---

[1] *Hartford Protection Ins. Co*, v. *Harmer*, 20 Ohio St. 452; *Clement* v. *Phœnix Ins. Co.*, 6 Blatch. (U. S.) 481; of course the assured cannot be required to com-municate facts not known to him, *Greenwell* v. *Nicholson*, 1 Jur. 285; mere rumors having no settled foundation need not be disclosed, *Durrell* v. *Bederly*, Holt N. P. 283; the names nor pursuits of tenants need be disclosed unless called for, *Lyon* v. *Commercial Ins. Co.*, 2 Rob. (La.) 266; in any event the fact concealed must have been *material* to the risk. *Gates* v. *Madison, etc., Ins. Co.*, 2 N. Y. 43; *Protection Ins. Co.* v. *Hall*, 15 B. Mon. (Ky.) 411.

[2] *Bulkley* v. *Protection Ins. Co.*, 2 Paine (U. S.) 82; *De Wolf* v. *Fireman's Ins. Co.*, 20 John. (N. Y.) 214; *Silloway* v. *Neptune Ins. Co.*, 12 Gray (Mass.) 73; *Popleston* v. *Kitchen*, 3 Wash. (U. S. C. C.) 138; *Walden* v. *N. Y. Fire Ins. Co.*, 12 John. (N. Y.) 128; *Gates* v. *Madison, etc., Ins. Co.*, ante.

[3] *Bulkley* v. *Protection Ins. Co.*, ante.

[4] *Clark* v. *Union Ins. Co.*, 40 N. H. 333; *Hartford Protective Ins. Co.* v. *Harmer*, 2 Ohio St. 452; *Mutual Ins. Co.* v. *Deale*, 18 Md. 26.

[5] *Patten* v. *Merchants' Ins. Co.*, 40 N. H. 375.

[6] *Clark* v. *Union Ins. Co.*, 40 N. H. 333. In *Bartholomew* v. *Merchants' Ins. Co.*, 25 Iowa, 507, the court say that, if the insured knew the provisions of the appli-cation, and had reason to know that the authority of the agent was limited to the

But the knowledge of the insurer of the agent must be shown by the insured, and must be of a fact then existing. The fact that he is

---

taking and forwarding of the application, and that such application is the basis upon which the risk is taken, he is bound to see that his statements and representations are correct. But if there is nothing to put him upon inquiry as to the agent's authority, and the agent furnishes and undertakes to fill up an application, and if in so doing he was correctly informed respecting an incumbrance on the property, and if the applicant was misled by the acts and conduct of the agent into supposing that the agent had taken down his answers truly, and that the application was correct, and if, through the fault of the agent, he did not know the contrary, the company, having received the premium, cannot successfully set up the existence of the incumbrance as a defense to an action on the policy. *Ames* v. *N. Y. Union Ins. Co.*, 14 N. Y. 253; *Alexander* v. *Germania Ins. Co.*, 5 T. & C. (N. Y.) 208; *Rowley* v. *Empire Ins. Co.*, 36 N. Y. 550. In *Combs* v. *Hannibal Savings and Ins. Co.*, 43 Mo. 148, an application for a policy of insurance contained questions and answers, by which it appeared that the title to the property was represented to be an unencumbered fee simple. A loss having occurred, the plaintiffs proved that R., the defendant's soliciting agent, had at the time full knowledge of the true state of the title, that he filled up the application in his own language, and assured the plaintiffs that it was all right; that they, believing it to be so, signed without knowing the contents as to title; and it was held, that, under the circumstances, the fact that the plaintiffs' title was only an encumbered eqiutable one, constituted no defense. In *Bidwell* v. *N. Western Ins. Co.*, 24 N. Y. 302, insurance was effected "upon the whole body," etc., of a ship, "warranted" by the insured to be "free from all liens." Evidence was offered to show that the insured interest was the equity of redemption of the insured party, and that the insurers at the time of application for and making of the policy knew such to be the interest of the insured, and that it was subject to two prior mortgages. Held, that this evidence was admissible. and if satisfactory, the existence of the mortgages was not a breach of the warranty. In *Hodgkins* v. *Montgomery, etc., Ins. Co.* 34 Barb. (N. Y.) 213, it was held that where the agent of the insurers writes out the application which the assured signs, no misstatement in the written application is fatal, if the assured disclosed the facts truly to the agent. In this case, the conditions in the policy provided that "when applications were filled out by the agent of the company, the company would be bound by the survey, that if the applicant should mistake his interest in the property, the policy should be void;" the applicant was in possession under a contract to buy, but having paid only a part of the price was not entitled to a deed; he showed his contract and stated the facts to the agent, who wrote in the application signed by the plaintiff that the applicant owned the premises. Held, that he had not misstated his interest. In *Peoria Ins. Co.* v. *Hall*, 12 Mich. 202, where by the provisions of the policy, it was provided that the keeping of gunpowder on the insured premises, "without written permission in the policy," should render the policy void. Held, that if the insurance agent knew that it was kept, and to be kept, the keeping of it would not render the policy void, whether the permission was indorsed, or intended to be indorsed on the policy or not. In the case of *Roberts* v. *The Continental Ins. Co.*, decided by the Supreme Court of Wisconsin, on the 20th of March, 1877, and not yet reported, it was held that if the agent of an insurance company, empowered to take risks and issue policies, knows, when he issues a policy, that there is other insurance upon the property, his failure to write the company's consent thereto in the instrument will not defeat an action thereon, although the policy itself declares that it shall be void in case the assured "shall have or shall hereafter make any other insurance upon the property without the consent of the company written herein;" and also declares that "the use of general terms, or anything less than a distinct, specific agreement, clearly expressed and indorsed upon the policy, shall not be construed as a waiver of any printed or written restriction therein." The Supreme Court of Pennsylvania, in a recent case, *Lycoming Fire Ins. Co.* v. *Woodworth et al.*, not yet reported, pass upon some interesting points arising in an action upon a fire insurance policy. The company named, through one Miller, who was represented as agent or surveyor, contracted for a policy of insurance with the defendants in suit. In the

aware of changes made *after* the policy is issued, does not aid the insured if such changes operate as a breach of the contract. Thus, where a condition of a policy was, "unoccupied premises must be insured as such, or the policy is void," and when the premises are insured as occupied, "the policy becomes void when the occupant per_sonally vacates the premises, unless immediate notice be given to the company and additional premium paid." The policy was silent as to the occupancy of the building insured, but the agent who issued the policy knew the building was then occupied. The occupant moved out, no notice was given to the company, and afterwards the building was destroyed by a fire of unknown origin. It was held that the com_pany was not liable for the loss.[1]

But the doctrine is well established that an agent, authorized to make contracts of insurance, has authority to waive conditions in the policy, and that his knowledge of the *real and true state of the risk is the knowledge of the company*. This doctrine has been recognized by a large number of authorities, and is consistent with the principles under_lying the relation of principal and agent. Thus, in a recent case in New York,[2] the policy contained a provision that, "if the premises *are at the time of insuring*, or during the life of this policy, become vacant, unoccupied, or not in use, and remain thus for over ten days, whether by removal of the owner or occupant, or for any cause without this company's consent indorsed thereon, this insurance shall be void and of no effect." The agent who effected the insurance *knew* that the house was vacant before the contract was consummated, and the court held that they were thereby estopped from setting up the fact that they were vacant to defeat their liability upon the policy. MILLER, P.J., in passing upon this question, pertinently said: "The company had notice of the insurance from Barns; received the premium, and is not, I think, in a position to claim that Barns had no authority to waive the condition as to vacant buildings. Concede that Barns acted beyond

---

court below, the company denied the right of the agent to make such contract, as was claimed to be made in this case, for them. Miller was called to define his power, and it was held that he was both agent and surveyor. The Supreme Court say that while it is true that one insuring in a company formed on the mu-tual plan is bound to inform himself of the rules and regulations of such company, it is also true that, as to those outside of it, such a company occupies no other or better position than one organized on the stock plan. As to one dealing for insurance, the company is bound by the representations of its agent in the act of making the contract, for it cannot assume the advantages of his act and avoid the disadvantages. After enjoying the benefits of insurance, a member of the com-pany is estopped from alleging fraud in bar of payment of assessments.

[1] *Wustrum* v. *City F. Ins. Co.*, 15 Wis. 138.

[2] *Cone* v. *Niagara F. Ins. Co.*, 5 T. & C. (N. Y.) 33; affd. 60 N. Y. 619.

the territory assigned to him, yet as the defendant sanctioned what he had done, and reaped the fruits of the transaction, it has no ground for complaint, and is estopped from denying his authority. As he was authorized and did not exceed his powers, it would be doing violence to the cases which hold that the agent may waive conditions of this character, now to decide that the company is exonerated from liability. Whatever may have been the course of decisions in other States, the whole tendency of the courts here has been to sanction the right of the agent to waive strict conditions in the policy where there has been no fraud, and the insured has acted in good faith in dealing with the agent, and it appears to me that such a tendency is in accordance with the adjudicated cases which uphold the spirit and substance of a contract without giving to either party the advantage of mere technical rules, so long as no principle of law is violated.[1]

---

[1] *North Berwick Ins. Co.* v. *N. E. F. & M. Ins. Co.*, 52 Me. 482; *Carrugi* v. *Atlantic, etc., Ins. Co.*, 40 Ga. 135; *Coombs* v. *Hannibal, etc., Ins. Co.*, 43 Mo. 148. In *Murphy* v. *Southern Life Ins. Co.*, the Supreme Court of Tennessee has recently held, that where a local agent of a life insurance company waived the forfeiture of a policy arising from the payment of only a portion of an annual premium when due, the waiver was binding on the company, although he was acting in excess of his special authority and in violation of his instructions, such waiver being within the apparent scope of his employment as agent. This case was distinguished from *Bouton* v. *The American Mut. Life Ins. Co.*, 25 Conn. 342, where the court denied the authority of the agent to waive payment of premium in advance before the policy took effect, because there was no other evidence than the terms of the policy as to his agency. In *Marky* v. *Mut. Benefit Life Ins. Co.*, 103 Mass. 78, it was held that the authority of an insurance agent must be determined by the nature of his business and the apparent scope of his employment. The general tendency of the cases is that officers and agents of insurance companies may waive the usual condition that the premium must be paid before the policy shall be effectual, as well as any other condition in the contract, and if the assured is allowed to act upon the confidence of such waiver, the insurer is estopped from denying the fulfillment of the condition. See *Baptist Church* v. *Brooklyn F. Ins. Co.*, 19 N. Y. 305. In *Alexander* v. *Germania F. Ins. Co.*, 5 T. & C. (N. Y.) 208, the defendant issued a policy of insurance to plaintiff on a house in Suffolk county for one year. The house shortly thereafter burned down. It had been occupied as a dwelling by a Mrs. Mowbray until about a month before the insurance was effected, but at the time of the insurance was unoccupied, and remained so until the fire. The application was taken by Henry Brewster, who for three years had solicited business, filled out applications, received premiums, taken surveys, and made descriptions of buildings for defendant. Mr. Brewster, knowing the house was unoccupied, applied to plaintiff to insure it. After some hesitation, plaintiff consented. Brewster made out the application, wrote all the answers which were written to the questions proposed; plaintiff signed it, and it was sent to the defendant, and upon it the policy in question was issued. In this application there is contained the following question: "Occupation—For what is the building used, and how many tenants are there?" To this the answer written by Brewster was "dwelling." It was held that the agents knowledge of the fact that the house was vacant, estopped the defendants. BARNARD, P.J., said: "It is now claimed that the policy thus issued is void, for the reason that plaintiff, by the application, made a warranty as to the occupation, which was broken when made, and thereby the policy was of no effect. This presents two questions for examination: What was the warranty in question? What effect had the knowledge of Brewster that the house was unoccupied, upon the defendant? The

Misdescription, when policy avoided by. When not.

SEC. 206. In order to avoid the policy for a misdescription as to the situation, condition or location of the property insured, it must be an actual material misdescription. If it is correct in *substance*, although not literally so, and does not materially change the risk, the policy will stand.[1]

---

question of warranty would not be free from doubt if the application had been filled out by plaintiff. The insured premises had been a dwelling until a few weeks before the fire—was a dwelling-house in ordinary and accurate language at the time of issuing of policy, having no tenant, and was expected to be tenanted as a dwelling in the near future. A general question as to mode of occupation might be answered as it was answered, "dwelling." All doubt is removed as to the question when the additional fact is considered that Brewster solicited and filled up the application himself. He was defendant's agent acting within the scope of his authority. He was told nothing by plaintiff, but wrote the company answer to the question with a full personal knowledge of the facts. Brewster cannot be held to have intended to deceive either his own principal or the plaintiff. In view of these facts and of the fact that that part of the question as to number of tenants is unanswered, the legal intendment must be that the company have only a covenant that the building was a dwelling-house and when used thereafter should be used as a dwelling. Assuming that the legal construction of the question and answer to be that the house was, at the date of the application, actually occupied as a dwelling, Brewster knew the fact to be otherwise, and prepared the application for plaintiff to sign. As has been already stated, ordinary men would make the answer in question in reference to an unoccupied dwelling-house. The defendant ought to be estopped by the knowledge of its agent when the acts and declarations of the agent induced the contract of insurance. This seems to be the doctrine of the Court of Appeals on this subject. *Ames v. N. Y. Union Ins. Co.*, 14 N. Y. 253; *Rowley v. Empire Ins. Co.*, 36 id. 550." A contrary doctrine is held in Massachusetts where the policy in express terms provides that "every insurance agent, broker, or other person, forwarding applications or receiving premiums, is the agent of the applicant and not of the company." It has been held that a misstatement of the title, in the application, although the true state of the title was known to the agent, avoids the policy. *Abbott* v. *Shawmut, etc., Ins. Co.*, 3 Allen (Mass.) 213; *Tebbetts* v. *Hamilton Ins. Co.*, 3 Allen (Mass.) 569.

[1] In *Friedlander*, v. *London Ass. Co.*, 1 M. & Rob. 171, the goods insured were described in the policy to be in the dwelling-house of the insured; the insured had only one room, as a lodger, in which the goods were: Held correctly described within the condition, that "the houses, buildings, or other places where goods are deposited and kept, shall be truly and accurately described;" such condition relating to the construction of the house, and not to the interest of the parties in it. In *Meadowcraft* v. *The Standard F. Ins. Co.*, 60 Penn. St. 84, the plaintiff procured an insurance on machinery, consisting of cards, pickers, etc., "contained in the first story of a four-story and basement brick building," etc. The pickers were in a one-story building, the floor on a level with the first story, built with bricks, joining into the main building, entering from it through a frame building adjoining, and then through a large iron door, "as if going from the house into the kitchen." There were no pickers except in the one-story room. It was held that the picker-room was part of the first story in which the goods were insured. The insurance agent who effected the insurance, knew the location of the pickers, and there was no misrepresentation to him. It was held that the company were bound by his acts; that the primary object was to insure the property described, its precise location was subordinate, and in the absence of misrepresentation as to location, the presumption is that the parties treated that as of less importance, and that declarations of the principal agent of the company to the agent who effected the insurance, that the company would not insure the pickers, would have no effect against the written policy. In *Dobson* v. *Sothbey*, M. & M. 9, an agricultural building was described in a policy as a barn, though it was not strictly

But where there is a material misdescription of the premises, although resulting from inadvertance, yet a policy issued under such erroneous description is void. Thus, where an application for insurance described the building as a "stone dwelling-house." It appeared in proof that the building was in fact a stone building with a wooden kitchen attached. Held, 1. That the application could not be deemed confined to the stone building, exclusive of the wooden one. A dwelling-house is an entire thing. It includes the building and such attachments as are usually occupied by the family for the ordinary purposes of the house. A kitchen constructed like the one proved, clearly constitutes a part of the dwelling-house. A policy of insurance upon a dwelling-house, when that is the only description of the subject of insurance, must attach to the whole, or it will not to any part of it, and consequently that there was no valid contract of insurance.[1]

Falsa demonstratio non nocet. Bryce v. Lorillard Ins. Co.

SEC. 207. If, either from the face of the instrument or from extrinsic facts, the true and the false description can be made to appear, that which is false must be rejected.[2] Thus, a policy was issued to the plaintiff upon a building situate "upon the corner of Charles street and Western avenue. A cabinetmaker's shop is in the building." The building was located as stated, but there was no cabinetmaker's shop in it, and the court held that the words "a cabinetmaker's shop is in the building" might be rejected, and then the policy would attach to the building intended to be insured.[3] But, if the misdescription is entire, so that, after casting out all that is false, there is not enough left to clearly point out the risk, the maxim *falso demonstratio non nocet* cannot be invoked and the policy is void. Thus, where a policy on merchandise was described as being in section lettered "C," Patterson stores, South Front, below Pine street, Philadelphia, when in fact the goods were in section "A," both at the time of insurance and of the

---

so. It was held by Lord TENTERDEN, not to be such a misdescription as would vacate the policy, as the building, had it been rather more correctly described, would have paid the same rate of insurance. In *Benedict* v. *Ocean Ins. Co.*, 31 N. Y. 389, the building in which the goods were was described as a five-story brick building. In fact, the building was five stories and a cellar or basement in addition, in which was kept a part of the goods destroyed. The court held that there was no such misdescription or concealment as avoided the policy. In *Gerhauser* v. *N. British Ins. Co.*, 7 Nev. 174, the building was described as a *brick* building. In fact, one of the walls had previously settled, and had been replaced with wood, but this was held not to amount to a misdescription.

[1] *Chase* v. *Hamilton Ins. Co.*, 20 N. Y. 52.
[2] *Loomis* v. *Jackson*, 19 John. (N. Y.) 449.
[3] *Heath* v. *Franklin Ins. Co.*, 1 Cush. (Mass.) 257.

loss, it was held that the policy was void, and there was no risk to which it could attach.[1]

In the last case cited, FOLGER, J., in a very able opinion, reviewed the principles, as well as the authorities, relating to the question, and his review of the subject is so able and thorough that I incorporate it as a part of the text. He says: "The claim of the plaintiff, that the contract of insurance was erroneous through mistake, and should have been reformed, is not tenable. The mistake which will warrant a court of equity to reform a contract in writing must be one made by both parties to the agreement, so that the intentions of neither are expressed in it; or it must be the mistake of one party, by which his intentions have failed of correct expression, and there must be fraud in the other party in taking advantage of that mistake and obtaining a contract with the knowledge that the one dealing with him is in error in regard to what are its terms. The findings show that the defendant made just the contract which it, from the first, intended to make, and just the one which it understood the plaintiff's assignor meant to make. Whatever may have been the intention of the insured or his agent, there is nothing in the findings, nor in the evidence, which shows or has a tendency to show that defendant or its agent purposed anything else than to insure property in section C of the Patterson stores. Such being the case, it is not in the power of the court to reform the instrument, for thereby violence will be done to the intentions of the defendant. Nor is there fraud in the defendant or its agent. Nor is there evidence which would warrant such finding. The case cited by the plaintiff[2] is not analogous to this. That was the case of a mistake in the attempt by the vendor to perform, by the execution of a conveyance, a pre-existing contract for the sale of land. The assignee of the vendee, knowing that the conveyance did not contain an exception stipulated for in the contract, and that the vendor was in an error in omitting it, still accepted the deed and refused to correct the mistake, intending to reap the profit of it. The conveyance was there reformed, on the ground of the fraud of the assignee of the contract, and on the ground that it was an erroneous performance of a contract, as to the terms of which there was no dispute. These two conditions cannot be predicated of the contract in the case in hand. Nor is this case like unto Coles v. Bowers.[3]

---

[1]*Bryce* v. *Lorrillard Ins. Co.*, 55 N. Y. 240.
[2]*Welles* v. *Yates*, 44 N. Y. 525.
[3] 10 Paige, 534.

There the chancellor refused to enforce a contract for the purchase
of land resting in parol, on the ground that the vendee did not understand and intend it as the vendors did. The vendors were seeking
to enforce a contract, as they claimed it to be, against one who denied
the making of that contract, and averred that he made another and a
different one. Specific performance was refused, because the doubt
was so great whether both parties understood alike the agreement to
be implied from defendant's bid. To allow this contract of insurance
to be reformed and then enforced would be to do just what the court
there refused to do ; for here as there, the defendant did not understand the terms of it, as they are claimed by the plaintiff to have
been, and to impose upon them in those terms would be to make a
contract for them which they did not intend to enter into. The
policy of insurance is, then, to be taken as the contract of the parties.
It was, then, a contract to insure property 'contained in letter C,
Patterson stores, South Front, below Pine street, Philadelphia.' And
that description of the place of deposit of the property, written into
the policy in accordance with the application of the insured, was a
warranty by him of its particular location, and the truth of that warranty became a condition precedent to any liability to him from the
defendant. And it was a warranty and a condition precedent, not to
be avoided by the fact that the truth of the description was not essential to the risk, nor an inducement to the defendant to enter into the
contract. This rule is so well established in the law of insurance, as
that it must be adhered to, though it may work hardship in a particular case. Nor does it depend upon its feeedom from a suscepti-
bility to a double interpretation, that a description is a warranty.
Whatever is expressed, whether with perspicuity or obscurity, that is
what is warranted. Other rules then come in to assist in the discovery
of what the language means. If there be latent ambiguity, that may
be removed by testimony. And here there is latent ambiguity. The
language used is the language of the parties. It does assert, and
therefore warrant, that the property is 'contained in letter C, Patterson stores,' etc. The phrase 'letter C,' taken by itself, has a
meaning. But, by reason of collateral matter and extrinsic circumstances, an ambiguity arises. It had an especial or technical meaning to those engaged in the business of putting property on storage in
the Pennsylvania warehouse, and to those who solicited and who wrote
insurance upon it. When the testimony gives that meaning, it indicates but one thing—that part of the Patterson stores, which is desig-

nated to owners of property, and to insurers of it, as the section or division C thereof.

It is impossible to say, in the light of all the circumstances disclosed by the pleadings and the testimony, that letter C. of the Patterson stores is not section C. thereof, and that a deicription of property, as that '*contained in letter C., Patterson stores*,' does not mean property deposited in that division of that warehouse known and designated as letter C. It is impossible to say that it does mean property mentioned in a book C. of the proprietors of that building as plaintiff contends.

The doctrine maintained in The Western Insurance Co. v. Cropper,[1] and Franklin Fire Insurance Co. v. Updegraff,[2] will not aid the plaintiff. Those cases hold that if the clauses of a policy be obscure, it is the fault of the insurer, for he it is who has penned the language; so that if it be capable of two interpretations, that must be adopted which is most favorable to the insured. There is not room here for but one interpretation. 'Letter C., Patterson stores,' has but one meaning. The latent ambiguity prevents that being seen on the bare reading of the phrase. When that ambiguity is done away with by the testimony, there is no difficulty in interpreting the words and reaching their sense. The plaintiff invokes the aid of the maxim, '*falso demonstratio non nocet*.' It may be conceded that there is a false description of the location of the property. But that is not enough to bring into operation the rule embodied in that maxim. There must be in the description so much that is true, as that, casting out that which is false, there is still enough left to clearly point out the place in which is the property. Indeed, an authoritative definition states and qualifies the rule more narrowly than this, viz.: 'As soon as there is an adequate and sufficient definition, with convenient certainty of what is intended to pass by the particular instrument, a *subsequent* erroneous addition will not vitiate it.' (Broom's Leg. Max. 464, 605.) But it needs not so to restrict in the case in hand. The phrase, 'letter C.' as meaning the place of storage of this property, is a false showing. If that phrase is rejected, then the whole description is contained in the words, 'Patterson stores, South Front, below Pine street, Philadelphia.' These words do, as far as they go in meaning, tell the truth as to the situation of the property. They do not, though, tell the whole truth, nor the whole essential truth. The word 'Philadelphia,' alone, would tell the truth, but not the whole of it. To be

---

[1] 22 Penn. St. 351.
[2] 43 id. 351.

made certain as to the exact place of deposit of the property, for the purposes of this contract, it needed not only to know what city it was, and on what street therein, but in what building on that street. And if that building was so constructed as to be of many divisions, practically separate, each from the other for safety from fire, and treated as distinct in making contracts of insurance, certainty of description needed some expression of what division it was in. This was the office of the phrase, 'letter C.' If that phrase be rejected, and no other truthful phrase be inserted, the description fails to show just where in the Patterson stores the property was placed. That phrase, though false, might harm, for it pointed the description to the wrong place, and some equivalent for it was needed to complete a truthful description.

The evidence taken against the objection of the plaintiff was competent. It was to show that this part of the description, though wrong, was harmful, and therefore not to be rejected. It was to show that though there was a warehouse known as the Patterson stores, it was one made up of several divisions, as distinct, for the purposes of storage of property and of the insurance of it against fire, as the dwelling-houses in a block; and that to know the place of the property, needed the naming of the section of the building in which it was, as much as if the risk had been on household goods. Their situation would not have been pointed out short of the expression in the description of the number of the house in the block. We are of the opinion that the defendant established a strictly legal defense to the action of the plaintiff. As we sit here to declare the law, and not to propound a code of morals, we must sustain it."

Ionides v. Pacific F. & M. Ins. Co.

SEC. 208. In a late Engish case ' the plaintiff's clerk applied for insurance on a lot of hides, on board the *Socrates*. There were two ships named in the register, one named *Socrate* and the other *Socrates*. The defendants' manager directed the clerk's attention to this fact, and asked him if it was the Socrates. The clerk replied that he thought it was, and the policy was so made. The hides were in fact, shipped upon the *Socrate*, and were lost. In an action to recover for the loss, the court held that the misdescription was entire and fatal to a recovery.

---

¹ *Ionides* v. *Pacific F. & M. Ins. Co.*, L. R. 6 Q. B. 674.

SEC. 209. In a late case in Kansas,[1] it was held that, where the misdescription is not entire, and there is enough left after rejecting the false description to fix the *situs* of the property, the policy can be enforced without being reformed. Thus, in that case, the policy covered a 'two story frame dwelling, *occupied by him*, situate on southwest corner of Second and Vine streets, Leavenworth, Kansas,' and ' on frame barn in rear of same.' The premises were, in fact, situate upon the south-west corner of *Elm* and Second streets, as the agent who wrote the policy knew. The court held that this was not a case of entire misdescription, because the insured did not occupy the buildings on the south-west corner of Vine and Second streets, either at the time of the insurance or of the loss, and from these extrinsic facts the true *situs* of the property could be ascertained.

Policy can only attach according to it terms.

SEC. 210. When the policy covers property, described as being in a certain place, the risk only exists while the property is in such place, and does not cover the same property in another place. The policy can only be held to *cover the property while kept in the place described*, unless otherwise provided in the policy.[2]

The policy can only attach according to its terms, and if the insurance is desired to cover it in different locations, it must so appear in the policy itself, and when it so appears, the risk continues wherever the property may be within the limits imposed. Thus in one case[3]

---

[1] *American Central Ins. Co.* v. *McLanathan*, 11 Kan. 533.

[2] In *Annapolis R. R. Co.* v. *Baltimore F. Ins. Co.*, 32 Md. 37, a policy taken out by the plaintiff described a portion of the property insured as follows : " $2,250 on two Murphy & Allison passenger cars, say $1,125 on each, one of them being used as a baggage and passenger car, *contained in* the car-house marked No. 1 ; and $3,000 on locomotive engine J. H. Nicholson, *contained in* the engine-house marked No. 2." After the insurance one of the Murphy & Allison cars was entirely destroyed, and the engine greatly damaged by fire, while on the line of the railroad making a regular trip. Upon an action brought by the railroad company against the insurance company for the injury thus done to the car and engine, it was held, that the words "*contained in*' were not intended merely to describe the car and engine covered by the policy, but were designed to limit the risk of the insurance company to the time during which the car and engine were actually in the car and engine-houses, and that, having been injured when out of the car and engine-houses, no recovery could be had on the policy. In *North American Fire Insurance Company* v. *Throop*, p. 146, 22 Mich., it was held, that a policy of insurance on "the stock, lumber and goods manufactured and in process of manufacture in said building," will not cover property in the yard adjoinining the building ; also, when the insurer writes out the application from the oral statement of the applicant, the latter, in a controversy arising thereon, may introduce parol evidence to show that he stated the facts truly, and that the conduct of the insurer was such as led him to believe that such as were omitted were immatarial.

[3] *The Farmer'*, etc., *Trust Co.* v. *The Harmony, etc., Ins. Co.*, 51 Barb. (N. Y.) 84.

the plaintiffs, as trustees of a railroad company, effected a policy of insurance with the defendants " on any property belonging to the said trust company, as trustees and lessees as aforesaid, and on any property for which they may be liable, it matters not of what the property may consist, nor where it may be, provided the property is on premises owned or occupied by the said trustees, and situated on their railroad premises in the city of Racine, Wisconsin." It was held, that a dredge-boat belonging to the plaintiffs, in their employ in the city of Racine, and attached to their wharf where the road terminated, was thereby in the plaintiffs' possession and annexed to the railroad premises, and therefore covered by the policy.

Where a stock of goods of a certain class, as dry goods, are insured, the policy will not cover goods afterwards bought by the insured and not embraced in that class; neither will an insurance upon household furniture, linen, wearing apparel, etc., cover furniture linen, or wearing apparel subsequently bought and kept for sale.[1]

General rule.

SEC. 211. It is a first principle of the law of insurance, that when a thing is warranted to be of a particular nature or description, it must be exactly such as it is represented to be, otherwise the policy is void; therefore where a mill was insured as being of one class, and turned out to have been of another at the time it was insured, it was held that an action on a policy could not be sustained, as, whether the misrepresentation was in a material point or not, or whether the risk was equally great in the one class as in the other, was wholly immaterial; the only question being, whether the *building was de facto that which was insured.* But even in a case of warranty, it is a good answer that the mistake or misrepresentation is attributable solely to the insurers themselves or their agent;[2] but it is held otherwise in New York, if the policy makes the agent the agent of the insured. Thus, in Alexander v. Germania Ins. Co.,[3] the owner of an unoccupied dwelling-house, at the solicitation of defendant's agent, took out

---

[1] In *Watchorn* v. *Langford*, 3 Camp. 422, the plaintiff, a coach-plater and cow-keeper, insured his stock in trade, *household furniture, linen, wearing apparel and plate.* Subsequently, he purchased a large stock of linen drapery goods on speculation. A fire occurring, he claimed to recover therefor. Lord ELLEN-BOROUGH said: " I am clearly of opinion that the word *linen* in the policy does not include articles of this description. Here we may apply ' *noscitur a sociis.*' The preceding words are ' *household furniture,*' and the succeeding, ' *wearing apparel.*' The *linen* must be *household linen or apparel.*"

[2] *Newcastle F. Ins. Co.* v. *MacMorran,* 3 Dow. 255; *Benedict* v. *Ocean Ins. Co.,* 1 Daly (N. Y. C. P.) 9; aff'd, 31 N. Y. 389.

[3] 5 T. & C. 208; 2 Hun, 655.

a policy of insurance thereon in defendant's company. The application was filled out by the agent, who knew all the circumstances, including the fact that the house was unoccupied. One of the questions in the application was, " For what is the building used ?" to which the answer was, "Dwelling." The application also provided that the statements should be warranties, and further, "*that any person other than the assured, who may have procured this insurance to be taken, shall be deemed to be the agent of the assured, and not of the company, under any circumstances whatever.*" The building having been burned, the defendant alleged breach of warranty, in that it was unoccupied when insured. It was held, reversing the judgment below, that the statement that the building was occupied as a dwelling was a warranty, and the breach thereof avoided the policy; that the agent's knowledge did not bind the company; that the provision making the person procuring the insurance the agent of the assured, was operative, and estopped the plaintiff from claiming that the company was bound by the knowledge of the agent.[1]

In a New York case,[2] the application described the building upon which insurance was sought, as a stone dwelling, and omitted to state that there was a frame addition thereto, used as a kitchen, and the court held that this was such a misdescription as invalidated the policy; but in a recent case in Massachusetts,[3] the policy described the property insured as "contained in three-story granite building." The front of the building was granite, one end and the rear of brick, the other end granite up one story, and brick above that, and the roof of slate. The plaintiff's store ran through the three-story block, *and then through a one-story building, having a sky-light in its tinned roof, and then into a three-story brick building;* the sides of the entire store were flush, and were the whole way from front to rear, one side and the rear of brick, the other side, for most of the way and perhaps all, of lathing and plaster, and the front of granite. The referee having found, as a matter of fact, that such a building might ordinarily and legally *be described in an insurance policy as a granite building*, the court held that there was no misdescription.[4] These cases demonstrate that,

---

[1] See also, *Rohrback* v. *Germania Ins. Co.*, 62 N. Y. But, where the insurer requires the application to be filled out by its agent, the company is bound by his errors or fraud. *Sprague* v. *Holland Pat. Ins. Co., post.*

[2] *Chase* v. *Hamilton*, 20 N. Y. 52.

[3] *Medina* v. *Builders', etc. Ins. Co.*, 120 Mass. 225.

[4] See also *Cox* v. *Ætna Ins. Co.*, 29 Ind. 583, where, in answer to a question : " Are the outside walls wood or brick ?" the assured replied " brick," when in fact they were part wood. It was held that this fact of itself did not avoid the policy.

in all cases where a misdescription is alleged, the question is, whether the description is such as is ordinarily or usually applied to the class of property insured, and whether the insurer *knew*, or had reason to know, that the description was not to be taken literally. In the New York case, the court went to an unwarranted length in invalidating the policy, because it appeared that the defendant's agent *knew* that there was a wooden addition to the building, and, under the rule as now held, that, of itself, would have estopped the defendants from setting up the misdescription in defense.[1] But where the description is *radically* erroneous, the policy is void. As, where the goods covered by the policy were described as being "contained in a two-story frame house *filled in with brick*," and in point of fact, the house was *not* filled in with brick, the policy was held void.[2]

Oral misrepresentations. Distinction when they apply to future, rather than present facts.

Sec. 212. A statement of an opinion, by the insurer, as to the future use or condition of the property, cannot be construed as a warranty that such use of condition shall exist. It is to be treated as a mere representation that does not avoid the policy, unless fraudulently made. Thus, where the insurer stated orally that a dwelling-house, then vacant, would be occupied, that he had a man in view who was

---

[1] *Emery* v. *Piscataqua Ins. Co.*, 52 Me. 322. In *Columbia Ins. Co.* v. *Cooper*, 50 Penn. St. 331, where an applicant for insurance on machinery in a mill, when inquired of as to incumbrances upon the property, answered that there were none, adding, however, that there were judgments on the land, but he did not think them liens on the property insured, in which opinion the agent concurred, and transmitted the application to the company with the answer that there were no incumbrances, it was held that such mistaken answer was not a covenant ; that the assured might prove the circumstances under which the answer was sent by the testimony of the agent ; and that the assured was not responsible for the mistake of the agent, notwithstanding a stipulation in the policy that if any agent should assume to violate its conditions, such violation should be construed to be the act of the assured, and render the policy void. It was also held that the fact that a small portion of the property insured belonged to a tenant of the assured, upon which the latter had a lien as landlord ; that he was not guilty of fraud in not disclosing such tenant's interest when making his application for insurance. *Where a party applies to the agent of a company for insurance, and at the same time mentions that he already has other insurance on the same property, and the agent neglects to enter the fact in writing on the policy, the assured will not suffer by reason of such neglect.* Id.; *N. E. Fire, etc., Co.* v. *Schettler*, 38 Ill. 166. If a local agent of an insurance company, who took an application for insurance, *was informed by the assured of the true condition of the ownership of the property, and failed correctly to take down the facts stated, and the policy was received by the assured in ignorance of any misstatement or omission, and if the agent had the power to pass upon, and did pass upon, the risk, and issue the policy without forwarding the application or submitting the matter to the company, the company cannot defeat a recovery, on the ground that the agent did not correctly state in the policy the facts concerning the title or interest of the assured.* *Ayres* v. *Home Ins. Co.*, 21 Iowa, 185. The rule is, that where the agent *knows* the facts, and that there is no *intention* on the part of the insured to deceive or defraud the insurer, the misstatement of facts by the agent will not avoid the policy.

[2] *Fowler* v. *Ætna Ins. Co.*, 6 Cow. (N. Y.) 673.

going to occupy it, upon the faith of which the policy was renewed, it was held that this, if it could have any effect upon the contract, being oral, could not be construed as a promissory warranty that the house should be occupied, but only as an expression of an opinion that it would be.[1]

Oral statements or representations made by the assured, unless embodied in the policy itself in reference to the future use or condition of the property, cannot be shown to alter or vary it, or to control its application or effect,[2] unless they are shown to have been fraudulent and made to mislead the defendant and induce the taking of the risk, or to take it at a lower premium than they otherwise would have done.[3]

But an oral misrepresentation as to a *present fact*, as to the title, situation, use or condition of the property *material to the risk*, may be shown to avoid the contract. Not to alter or vary it, but to show that, by reason of the fraud, it never had any vitality as an operative contract.[4] "If," says GRAY, J.,[5] "representations, whether oral or written, *concerning facts existing when the policy is signed, are false, it never has any existence as a contract, unless it contains in itself, terms which expressly, or by necessary implication waive or supersede the previous representation. If the representations are positive, and not of mere opinion or belief, it matters not whether they are made at or before the time of the execution of the policy, nor whether they are expressed in the present or future tense, if they relate to what the state of facts is, or will be, when the policy is executed and the risk of the underwriter begins.* If the facts are there materially different from the representations, *the whole foundation of the contract fails, the risk does not attach, the policy never becomes a contract between the parties.* Representations of facts existing at the time

---

[1] *Kimball* v. *Ætna Ins. Co.*, 9 Allen (Mass.) 540 ; *Herrick* v. *Union, etc., Ins. Co.*, 48 Me. 558 ; *Carter* v. *Boehem*, 3 Burr. 1911 ; *Pawson* v. *Watson*, Cowp. 785 ; *Whitney* v. *Haven*, 13 Mass. 172 ; *Bryant* v. *Ocean Ins. Co.*, 22 Pick. (Mass.) 200 ; *Rice* v. *N. E. Ins. Co.*, 4 id. 442 ; *Higginson* v. *Dall*, 13 Mass. 99.

[2] *Weston* v. *Emes*, 1 Taunt. 115 ; *Edwards* v. *Footeur*, 1 Camp. 530 ; *Alston* v. *Mechanics' Ins. Co.*, 4 Hill (N. Y.) 329, reversing the judgment given in the same case in 1 Hill (N. Y.) 510, where a contrary doctrine was held. *Allegre* v. *Maryland Ins. Co.*, 2 G. & J. (Md.) 136 ; *Undelock* v. *Chenango Ins. Co.*, 2 N. Y. 221 ; *Flinn* v. *Headlam*, 9 B. & C. 693 ; *Flinn* v. *Tobin*, M. & M. 367.

[3] SHAW, C.J., in *Bryant* v. *Ocean Ins. Co.*, *ante*; *Kimball* v. *Ætna Ins. Co.*, 9 Allen (Mass.) 551.

[4] *Alsop* v. *Coit*, 12 Mass. 40 ; *Dennistoun* v. *Lillie*, 3 Bligh, 202 ; *Vanderheuvel* v. *Church*, 2 John. Cas. 173, n ; *Van Tungeln* v. *Dubois*, 2 Camp. 151 ; *Feise* v. *Parkinson*, 4 Taunt. 640 ; *Bowden* v. *Vaughn*, 10 East, 415 ; *Pawson* v. *Watson*, Cowp. 786.

[5] *Kimball* v. *Ætna Ins. Co.*, 9 Allen (Mass.) 542.

of the execution of the policy need not be inserted in it, *for they are not necessary parts of it*, but, as is sometimes said, collateral to it. *They are its foundation ; and if the foundation does not exist, the superstructure does not arise.* Falsehood in such representations, is not shown to vary or add to the contract or to terminate a contract which has once been made ; *but to show that no contract has ever existed.*

But a representation as to some fact which does not exist when the policy is made, *but which is to exist thereafter*, is a part of the contract itself, and if the insurer relies upon, and intends to secure its enforcement, *he must incorporate it in the policy as a part of the contract, or be able to show that it was fraudulently made, with the view and purpose of inducing an acceptance of the risk, or its taking, at a lower rate of premium.* It cannot be shown as *a part of the contract*, nor as a defense thereto, *except it is tainted with the vice of fraud, and relates to a matter material to the risk.*[1] The mere fact that the condition of things to which the representation relates, does not transpire, does not operate as proof that it was fraudulently made ; *fraud in fact*, must be established. The insurer takes the burden of showing that it was not honestly made, in good faith, or with an expectation that it would transpire. Human expectations, seemingly well founded, fail, and because they do so the person indulging them, cannot, therefrom, be charged with dishonesty.[2]

Rule in Pawson v. Watson.

SEC. 213. In an English case[3] it was represented to one of the underwriters that the vessel sought to be insured — the Julius Cæsar — "mounts 12 guns and 20 men," but to the defendant it was only generally represented as "a ship of force." There were neither guns or men on board at the time of the insurance, and at the time of her capture she had less than twelve carriage guns, and less than twenty able men, *but so many swivels and boys as to be stronger than if she had that number.* The question was, whether the instructions shown to the first underwriter, were to be considered as warranties, the same as though inserted in the policy, or as representations that would only avoid the policy if fraudulent. Lord MANSFIELD instructed the jury that "it was a collateral representation, and if the party had considered it as a warranty, they should have had it inserted in the policy,

---

[1] Lord MANSFIELD, in *Carter* v. *Boehem, ante;* GRAY, J., in *Kimball* v. *Ætna Ins. Co.*, 9 Allen (Mass.) 543 ; Lord MANSFIELD, in *Pawson* v. *Watson*, 2 Cowp. 785.

[2] *Kimball* v. *Ætna Ins. Co., ante.*

[3] *Pawson* v. *Watson*, Cowp. 785.

also, that if the instructions were to be considered in the light of fraudulent misrepresentation, *they must be both material and fraudulent.*" A verdict having been rendered for the plaintiff, upon a rule to show cause, the verdict was upheld. Lord MANSFIELD, in a masterly opinion, reviewed the questions involved in all their aspects, and, as his opinion is a leading case upon these questions, and may often be useful, I give the main portion of it here. He said: " There is no distinction better known to those who are at all conversant in the law of insurance, than *that* which exists between a *warranty* or condition which makes part of a written policy, and a *representation* of the state of the case. Where it is a part of the written policy, it must be performed : as, if there be a warranty of convoy, there must be a *convoy.* Nothing tantamount will do or answer the purpose. It must be strictly performed, as being part of the agreement; for there it might be said, the party would not have insured without convoy. But as, by the law of merchants, all dealings must be fair and honest, fraud infects and vitiates every mercantile contract. Therefore, if there is fraud in a representation, it will avoid the policy, as a fraud, but not as a part of the agreement. If, in a life policy, a man warrants another to be in good health, when he knows at the same time he is ill of a fever, that will not avoid the policy ; because by the warranty he takes the risk upon himself. But if there is no warranty, and he says, ' the man is in good health,' when in fact he knows him to be ill, it is *false.* So it is, if he does not know whether he is well or ill ; for it is equally false to undertake to say that which he knows nothing at all of, as to say *that* is true, which he knows is not true. But if he only says, ' he believes the man to be in good health,' knowing nothing about it, nor having any reason to believe the contrary, there, though the person is not in good health, it will not avoid the policy, because the underwriter *then* takes the risk upon himself. So that there cannot be a clearer distinction, than that which exists between a warranty which makes part of the written policy, and a collateral representation, which, if false in a point of materiality, makes the policy void ; but if not material, it can hardly ever be fraudulent. So far from the usage being to consider instructions as a part of the policy, parol instructions were never entered in a book, nor written instructions kept, till many years ago, upon the occasion of several actions brought by the insured upon policies, where the brokers had represented many things they ought not to have represented, in consequence of which, the plaintiffs were cast; I advised the insured to bring an

27

action against the brokers, which they did, and recovered in several instances; and I have repeatedly, at Guildhall, cautioned and recommended it to the brokers, to enter all representations made by them in a book. That advice has been followed in London; but it appeared lately, at the trial of a cause, that, at Bristol, to this hour, they make no entry in their books, nor keep any instructions.

The question then is, 'whether, in this policy, the party insuring has *warranted* that the ship should *positively* and *literally* have *twelve carriage guns* and *twenty men?*' That is, 'whether the instructions given in evidence, are a part of the policy?' Now, I will take it by degrees. The two first underwriters before the court are Watson and Snell. Says Watson, 'it is part of my agreement, that the ship shall sail with twelve guns and twenty men; and it is so stipulated, that nothing under that number will do. Ten guns, with swivels, will not do.' The *answer* to this is, 'read your agreement; read your policy.' There is no such thing to be found there. It is replied, yes, but in fact there is, for the instructions upon which the policy was made, contain that express stipulation. The answer to that is, that there never were any instructions shown to Watson, nor were any asked for by him. What color then has *he* to say, that those instructions are any part of his agreement. It is said, he insured upon the credit of the first underwriter. A *representation* to the first underwriter has nothing to do with that which is the agreement, or the terms of the policy. No man, who underwrites a policy, subscribes, by the act of underwriting, to terms which he knows nothing of. But he reads the agreement, and is governed by that. Matters of intelligence, such as that a ship is or is not missing, are things in which a man is guided by the name of a first underwriter, who is a good man, and which another will therefore give faith and credit to; but not to a collateral agreement, which he can know nothing of. The absurdity is too glaring; it cannot be. By extension of an equitable relief in cases of fraud, if a man is a knave with respect to the first underwriter, and makes a *false representation* to him in a point that is *material,* as where having notice of a ship being lost, he says she was safe, that shall affect the policy with regard to all the subsequent underwriters, who are presumed to follow the first. How then do Watson and Snell underwrite the ship in question? Without knowing whether she had any force at all. *That* proves the risk was equal to a ship of no force at all; and the premium was a vast one—eight guineas. So much, therefore, for those two cases. The third case is that of Ewer, who saw the instructions, with the representations which they contained. Did the number of guns induce him to underwrite the policy? If it did, he would have said, 'put them into the policy; warrant that the ship shall depart with twelve guns and twenty men.' Whereas, he does no such thing, but takes the *same premium* which Watson and Snell did, who had *no* notice of her having any force. What does that prove? That he is paid and receives a premium, as if it were a ship of no force at all. The representation amounts to no more than this: 'I tell you what the force will be, because it is so much the better for you.' There is no fraud in it, because it is a representation only of what, in the then state of the ship, they thought would be the truth. And in real truth the ship sailed with a *larger* force; for she had *nine* carriage guns besides six swivels. The underwriters, therefore, had the advantage by the difference. There was no stipulation about what the weight of metal should be. All the witnesses say, 'she had more force than if she had had twelve carriage guns, both in point of strength, of convenience, and for the purpose of resistance.' The supercargo in particular says, 'he insured the *same ship*, and the *same voyage*, for the *same premium*, without saying a syllable about the force.' Why then it was a matter proper for the jury to say, whether the representation was false? or whether it was in fact an insurance, as of a ship without force? They have determined, and I think very rightly, that it was an insurance without force. Ewer makes an objection that the representation ought to be considered as inserted in the policy; but the answer to that is, he has determined whether it should be inserted in the policy or not, by not inserting it himself. There is a great difference, whether it shall be considered as a fraud. But it would be very dangerous to permit all collateral representations to be put into the policy." [1]

Actual fraud need not be shown.

SEC. 214. But where the conduct of the assured, either by acts of omission or commission, are such as influence the insurer in either or any of these respects, it in law is fraudulent, even though the insured did not know that his conduct was of that character, or did not intend to mislead the insurer. [2] It is not essential that the conduct of the assured in these regards should be such as indicate bad faith on his part. The matter does not depend so much upon the question as to

---

[1] See also, *Bize* v. *Fletcher*, 1 Doug. 285; *MacDowell* v. *Frazer*, 1 id. 261; *Weston* v. *Ennes*, 1 Taunt, 115; *Flinn* v. *Headlam*, 9 B. & C. 693.

[2] *Carpenter* v. *Am. Ins. Co.*, 1 Story (U. S.) 57.

whether the act is *fraudulent*, as, whether it is a violation of an implied contract on his part, to reveal everything material to the risk, or to state everything truly, that he undertakes to state, that influences the underwriter in taking or rejecting it, or in fixing a higher or lower premium. Where the assured does not undertake to state the matter charged to be false, as a matter of positive knowledge on his part; *as, if he states it as his opinion or belief*, if untrue, the policy will not be avoided. The insurer is thereby put upon his inquiry, and if he chooses to enter into the contract without more definite or positive information, he cannot charge the consequences upon the assured. He is treated as having waived more definite information, and can only avoid the policy, if the assured, *knowing the facts, misstated or suppressed them, or states a fact as of positive knowledge, when he did not know whether it was true or false.*[1] If he says "I believe," "I have been

---

[1] *Evans* v. *Edwards*, 13 C. B. 77; *Liberty Hall Ass'n* v. *Housatonic, etc., Ins. Co.*, 7 Gray (Mass.) 261. In *Clark* v. *Hamilton Ins. Co.*, 9 id. 148, a failure to disclose repeated incendiary attempts to burn the property was held not such a suppression of facts as avoided the policy, when such attempts were made after the policy was issued, although the policy provided that all changes increasing the risk should be communicated. In *Haley* v. *Dorchester Mut. F. Ins. Co.*, 12 Gray (Mass.) 545, an action was brought upon a policy, by which the plaintiff was insured " against loss or damage by fire, under the conditions and limitations expressed in the by-laws" of the defendants, annexed to the policy, on his "stock in trade, being mostly chamber furniture in sets, and other articles usually kept by furniture dealers, contained in second story of the building known as Gerrish Market, in the city of Boston, on Portland street, corner of Sudbury street." Among the by-laws annexed was the following : " Unless the applicant for insurance shall make a true representation in writing of the property on which he requests insurance, and of his title and interest therein, of its situation, and of all other matters materially affecting the risk, also all incumbrances, the policy shall be void." "All applications shall be approved by two directors, and no director shall approve an application for insurance on property in which he is in any way interested." The application was for insurance "on household furniture in the second story of the Gerrish Market, being my stock in trade, mostly chamber furniture in sets;" and provided that "all the questions must be answered," and that "the answers to the following interrogatories shall form the basis of the contract for insurance, and the applicant warrants them to be entirely true, and will be bound by them." "Is cotton waste, or any explosive or highly inflammable matter kept near or in the premises on which this insurance is applied for?" Answer. "Not to my knowledge." "Are there any other circumstances material to the risk, if so, what are they? If there be a livery or steam engine in the vicinity, state how near the risk." Answer. "There is a small steam engine in the fourth story." "Who owns the building to be insured, or which contains the property to be insured?" Answer. "Market-stall men; Self; White & Co., polishers; Barnard & Dillingham, painters; Sanborn, Carter & Bazin, bookbinders, and one ornamental do." And the said applicant hereby covenants and agrees with the said company, the description herein given is a full and true description of the property to be insured, and of all circumstances in relation thereto, material to the risk, and that the estimated valuation shall not be conclusive upon the company; but in case of loss, the true value at the time of loss may be inquired into and ascertained; the questions not answered above shall be construed most favorably to the risk; and that said applicant shall be bound by the provisions of the constitution and by-laws annexed to the policy, and all laws of the Commonwealth of Massachusetts in relation to the premises, as a part of this contract for insurance." It appeared that the Gerrish Market building was a very large

informed," "I have reason to suppose," etc., he cannot be held chargeable for the truth of the fact stated, but only for the *bona* or *mala fides*

building, in which a great variety of business was carried on under a great number of tenants; that, from the time of the application for insurance to that of the fire, the premises occupied by the plaintiff consisted of a large hall or salesroom and three rooms adjoining, a paint room, varnish room and store or packing room; the furniture was made at another establishment or manufactory, sent up to the salesroom "in the white," or unpainted, and varnished, painted and trimmed in the rooms adjoining the salesroom; and a quantity of varnish, oils and paints were kept in the premises, for use in finishing the furniture. There was no evidence of any intention on the part of the plaintiffs to conceal or neglect to make inquiries about the occupation. The whole stock was consumed by fire on the 12th of April, 1856. There was evidence tending to show that it was usual for furniture dealers in Boston to keep varnish as part of their stock, and that varnish was a highly combustible matter. The plaintiff introduced evidence, tending to show that varnish kept in casks was not a combustible or highly inflammable material, and also that some furniture dealers sold furniture "in the white," to other dealers, to be painted, varnished and sold by them.

The defendants objected that the policy covered only the stock of furniture finished, and did not extend to the paints and varnish, or any other articles; and introduced evidence that several of the answers in the application were not true, and that some questions were not fully answered, and others not answered at all. The judge ruled "that the contract of insurance covered the furniture of a furniture dealer, and such other articles as were proved to be usually kept by furniture dealers and necessary to the pursuit of the plaintiff's business; and that it was not confined to household furniture, mostly chamber furniture in sets, as the defendants contended, but might include the other articles usually kept by furniture dealers, as stated in the body of the policy; that, in order to recover for the varnish and oil destroyed, the plaintiff must show that such articles were usually kept by furniture dealers; that the jury were to inquire to what amount they were usually kept; and that the plaintiff would not be entitled to recover more in value than the usual amount, taking into consideration the nature and extent of the plaintiff's business and the quantity of furniture on hand; that the declarations, representations and statements in the application, so far as they related to the risk, if untrue, whether from design, ignorance or mistake, it would be fatal to a recovery by the plaintiff; that they were to be read fairly, and not captiously; that, so far as no answers were given to questions in the application, they might find that the company waived such answers, but that the company must have the benefit of the provision in the contract that such omission should be construed most favorably to the risk; and, if there was any material concealment, or concealment of a material fact, it would avoid the policy; that, as the answers given to specific questions, the meaning of the language as to both was to be determined by common use and acceptation, and by all the other provisions of the contract touching the same subject-matter, and by the different answers themselves; that, if a misstatement could have no possible relation to the risk, it would not affect the policy; that the clause as to explosive substances would not be violated in having on hand so much varnish and oil as were necessary in carrying on the business of a furniture dealer, and in such quantities as were usually kept, under the former limitations; and that the jury, in determining whether this question was answered truly, might refer to the answers made to another question as to the occupation of the building; and that, as to the answer relating to the livery stables, the jury were to inquire whether it was proved that there was a livery stable in the vicinity at the time of the application (the plaintiff contending that the evidence did not apply to that time, but to a subsequent period); and that, if it was so proved, they were to determine what was the meaning of the question, and of the 'vicinity,' and whether there was a livery stable in that vicinity, having reference to the situation of the building in which the property was situated, the situation of other buildings, and the locality, as ascertained from the contract and evidence." As to the question in regard to the occupation of the building, there being evidence tending to show that, at the time of the application, there were occupants in one or two rooms of

of the statement made by him.[1] The insured is not bound to state *every* fact material to the risk. He must not *misrepresent* or *designedly* conceal any material fact. He must, in good faith, answer all inquiries put to him, and having done that, *unless the fact not communicated could not with reasonable diligence be discovered by the insurer, or anticipated as a ground of specific inquiry, it is* not a concealment that invalidates the policy.[2]

But it should be remembered that *a broad distinction exists between statements made in answer to inquiries put by the insurer, and those stated by the insurer voluntarily and not in response to inquiries by the insurer. In the one case the answers are made material by the act of the assured, whether they are so in fact or not, while in the other case, even though the statements are made a part of the policy, they are not efficacious as warranties unless material in fact.*[3]

No distinction between effect of concealment and misrepresentation of facts.

Sec. 215. The effect of a concealment and of a misrepresentation of facts relating to the risk are the same, and their effect upon the rights of the parties are tested by the same rules, to wit: *whether they relate to matters material to the risk, or influence the insurer either in taking or declining the risk, or in fixing a less rate of premium than he would otherwise have charged therefor.*[4] The concealment or representation of untrue matters *that are not material to the risk* does not avoid the policy, because they do not influence the insurer in the respects previously named. Thus, if the assured states the situation and occupancy of the premises to be more hazardous than it in fact is, the insurer cannot complain because he has not been damnified thereby. *He would have taken the risk if the true facts in reference to those matters had been known to him.*[5]

---

the building not named in the answer, besides the general instructions given, the Jury were also instructed "that, if there were such occupants, not mentioned in the answer, the omission would not necessarily avoid the policy, if the jury were satisfied that, by such occupation, the risk was less hazardous than it would have been if the occupation and occupants were all such as stated in the answer; and that the purpose of the inquiry was to be borne in mind."

[1] Arnould on Ins. 300; *Dennistoun v. Lillie*, 3 Bligh, P. C. 202; *Lexington Ins. Co. v. Powers*, 16 Ohio, 324.

[2] *Hartford Protection Ins. Co. v. Harmer*, 2 Ohio St. 452.

[3] *Wilson v. Conway F. Ins. Co.*, 4 R. I. 141; *Dennison v. Thomaston, etc., Ins. Co.*, 20 Me. 125; *Frisbie v. Fayetteville Ins. Co.*, 27 Penn. St. 325; *Waldron v. N. Y. Fireman's Ins. Co.*, 12 John. (N. Y.) 128; *Boardman v. N. H. Ins. Co.*, 20 N. H. 551; *Wall v. Howard Ins. Co.*, 14 Barb. (N. Y.) 383; *Farmers' Ins. Co. v. Snyder*, 16 Wend. (N. Y.) 681; *Clark v. Hamilton Ins. Co.*, 9 Gray (Mass.) 148.

[4] *Columbian Ins. Co. v. Lawrence*, 10 Pet. (U. S.)   ; *Boggs v. American Ins. Co.*, 30 Mo. 63; *Hartford Protection Ins. Co. v. Harner*, 2 Ohio St. 452.

[5] *Haley v. Dorchester Mut. F. Ins. Co.*, 12 Gray (Mass.) 545.

SEC. 216. But, as to *all* matters inquired about by the insurer, as preliminary to the contract, he must, *at his peril*, answer truly.[1]

Failure to disclose proximity of other buildings.

SEC. 217. Thus, if required to state *all* the buildings within ten rods, or any other distance, an omission to state *all* of them, although it occurred by mistake, will avoid the policy,[2] but this does not require that the insured should state the existence of erections for temporary purposes not coming fairly within the term buildings, unless used for hazardous purposes. Thus, in answer to an inquiry, " What is the distance and direction from each other and from other buildings within a hundred and fifty feet, and for what purpose are said buildings occupied ? " it was held that the omission of the assured to state the existence of a temporary structure of rough timber, 45 feet by 12, and about 18 feet high, within the distance named, made for the use of the carpenters employed to erect the building insured, did not invalidate the policy, unless the jury found that it was used for purposes that materially enhanced the risk.[3] The presiding judge at the trial instructed the jury " that, if there was upon the premises of the plaintiff, and within one hundred and fifty feet of the building insured, *a carpenter shop, adapted and used for that purpose*, which shop was shown to belong to a more hazardous class, and one which would have required a greater premium to be paid for insuring the seminary building ; and the existence of said shop was not disclosed to the insurers in the answers in the application, but wholly omitted therefrom ; such omission would invalidate the policy." A verdict under this ruling was rendered for the plaintiff, which was sustained upon appeal.

Failure to disclose true state of the title.

SEC. 218. Where the application calls for the true state of the title of the assured in the property, a failure to set it forth truly, whether the misstatement resulted from design or mistake, will avoid the policy.[4] Thus, where a deed was executed by A. to B., absolute in form, to indemnify B. against loss from certain liabilities that he had

---

[1] *Jacobs* v. *Eagle, etc., Ins. Co.*, 7 Allen (Mass.) 172 ; *Handy* v. *Union Ins. Co.*, 4 id. 217 ; *Huntley* v. *Perry*, 38 Barb. (N. Y.) 569.

[2] *Huntley* v. *Perry*, 38 Barb. (N. Y.) 569 ; *Day* v. *Conway Ins. Co.*, 52 Me. 60.

[3] *Richmondville, etc., Seminary* v. *Hamilton Ins. Co.*, 14 Gray (Mass.) 489.

[4] *Hutchins* v. *Cleveland, etc., Ins. Co.*, 11 Ohio St. 477 ; *Reynolds* v. *State, etc., Ins. Co.*, 2 Grant's Cas. (Penn.) 326 ; *Mutual Ass. Co.* v. *Mahon*, 5 Call (Va.) 517 ; *Birmingham* v. *Empire Fire Ins. Co.*, 42 Barb. (N. Y.) 457.

assumed for A., and he executed to B. an agreement to reconvey the premises to him when released from such liabilities, and B. procured an insurance upon the buildings in his own name ; and the policy contained a condition that property held in trust, to include that held as collateral security, must be so insured ; it was held that the policy was void, because he did not set forth the fact that he held the property in trust.[1]

The insurer is bound to take notice of extent of risk.

SEC. 219. Where the description in a policy *and the purposes to which the building is dedicated* indicate the nature of the articles to be kept there, and the business to be prosecuted, the fact that such business or such articles are hazardous or extra hazardous will not invalidate the policy.[2] Thus, where a policy was issued upon a stock of drugs, chemicals and other medicines, hazardous and extra hazardous, it was held that the policy was not invalidated by anything done by the plaintiff incident to the business, however hazardous such act might be, as the placing of five gallons of a highly explosive mixture called ointment upon a stove to warm, by means of which the property was burned. In such cases, the act being incident to the business, the insurer is presumed to have been acquainted with the business, and to have contracted in reference to *all* its hazards, and if he desires or intends to make any exceptions, they must be clearly and definitely stated in the policy ;[3] and, even though the particular use is not an usual incident of the business, yet, if it is a use that the insured has practiced, or that a previous occupant of the building has practiced, *to the knowledge of the insurer*, and nothing has been said or done by the insured to indicate that any change in that respect will be made, the insurer is presumed to have anticipated and contracted with reference to such special use, and the insured may show the facts to sustain the policy.[4] In New York v. Hamilton Ins. Co., 39 N. Y. 45, an action was brought to recover upon a policy issued on the building known as the " crystal palace," the policy described it as " the one lately owned by the association for the exhibition of the industry of all nations," and the defendants were aware that it had been used exclusively for the purpose of exhibitions. The court very properly held that the defend-

[1] *Day* v. *Charter Oak Ins. Co.*, 51 Me. 91.

[2] *New York* v. *Brooklyn Fire Ins. Co.*, 41 Barb. (N. Y.) 231 ; *Smith* v. *The Mechanics', etc., Ins. Co.*, 32 N. Y. 399.

[3] *Brown* v. *Kings County Fire Ins. Co.*, 31 How. Pr. (N. Y.) 508 ; *New York* v. *Hamilton Fire Ins. Co.*, 39 N. Y. 45.

[4] *New York* v. *Exchange Fire Ins. Co.*, 9 Bos. (N. Y.) 424.

ants must be deemed to have been acquainted, when they issued the policy, with the use to which it was appropriated—*the nature of the objects exhibited, and the means employed to exhibit them*, and to have intended to include the proper management of such business in their risk; and that the keeping of a restaurant, with liquors and cigars, supplied with a kitchen with ovens, are a part of the necessary concomitants of an exhibition, and pass under the insurance.

Misrepresentation of value. Over-valuation.

SEC. 220. A misrepresentation of the value of the property to be insured, when the policy is valued, is material to the risk, and avoids the policy,[1] but it must be a fraudulent or intentional misstatement thereof, and not a mere error of judgment. In order to establish fraud in such a case, the mere fact that the property is worth less than the amount stated, is not sufficient; it must either be shown that the insured *knew* that it was worth less, or the actual value of the property must *be so much less* than that stated, as to warrant a presumption that the error was intentional, rather than an error of judgment, and in this, the burden is upon the insurer to establish the fraud.[2] In order to make misrepresentations as to value material, the policy must be valued, or the representation must be incorporated into the policy as a warranty. If the insurer, by the terms of the policy, is only liable for the *actual cash value* of the property, the amount of insurance, or the real value of the property, is not material.[3] So, too, the misstatement must relate to the *present* value of the property. If it relates to the value of property then on hand, and other which it is *bona fide* the intention and expectation of the insured to add thereto, as, in the case of merchandise, the amount and value of which is constantly changing, the policy is not avoided.[4] If the representation as to value is made in answer to an inquiry by the insurer in the application, and the application is made a part of the policy, it becomes a warranty, and the policy is

---

[1] *Lycoming Ins. Co.* v. *Rubin,* 8 Chi. Legal News, 150. In *Carpenter* v. *American Ins. Co.,* 1 Story (U. S.) 57, the plaintiff represented that there was other insurance to the amount of $15,000 on the property. The insurers declining to take the risk, he then represented that about $10,000 had been expended in additions to the property after the other insurance was made. In fact, only $700 had been added, and it was held that the policy was void, although the plaintiff honestly supposed that his statement was true.

[2] *Cushman* v. *U. S. Life Ins. Co.,* 4 Hun (N. Y.) 783; *Continental Ins. Co.* v. *Kasey,* 25 Gratt. (Va.) 268; *Hodgson* v. *Marine Ins. Co.,* 5 Cranch. (U. S.) 100; *Franklin F. Ins. Co.* v. *Vaughan,* 92 U. S. 516.

[3] *Aurora F. Ins. Co.* v. *Johnson,* 46 Ind. 315.

[4] *Lee* v. *Howard Ins. Co.,* 11 Cush. (Mass.) 324.

avoided if the value is less than that named.[1] If the parties *agree*
upon the valuation, and there is no material concealment or representation as to value, by the assured, however excessive the valuation
may be, the policy is valid.[2]

The question as to whether a policy containing a condition that the
policy shall be void, if the insured shall cause the property to be
insured for more than its value, imposes upon the insurer the necessity of ascertaining, at his peril, with *substantial certainty* the actual
cash value of the premises, or only applies in case of an intentional
over-valuation or a fraudulent concealment, is one upon which there is
some conflict. But whatever may be the number of decisions, holding
the one way or the other, there can be no doubt that, in conformity
with the ordinary rules of construction applied to insurance contracts,
and the ordinary principles of justice and fair dealing upon which
they are supposed to be predicated, *a policy cannot be held void for the
breach of such a condition, unless the over-valuation is intentional and
fraudulent, and not a fair expression of the honest judgment of the insurer,*[3]

---

[1] *Bobbitt* v. *Liverpool, etc., Ins. Co.*, 66 N. C. 70.

[2] *Hodgson* v. *Marine Ins. Co., ante.*

[3] *Fuller* v. *Boston Mut. F. Ins. Co.*, 4 Met. (Mass.) 206. In the case of *Field* v.
Insurance Company of North America, 6 Bissell (U. S.) 121, the Circuit Court for
the Northern District of Illinois held that a provision in a policy "that if the
assured shall cause the property to be insured for more than its value, the policy
shall be void," only avoids the policy in case of intentional over-valuation, or
fraudulent concealment, and that the burden of proof is on the insurance company to show that the over-valuation was intentional. In this case the agent of
the company who took the application for insurance was requested to examine
the property before the policy was issued. The court say, that "value is always,
to a considerable extent, a matter of opinion and judgment, and it would not be
right to hold a policy void for over-valuation, when it was clear, from the proof,
that there was no intention to deceive, and when there was room for an honest
difference of opinion." It has been held, however, that a false statement of the
cash value of property upon which insurance was asked, although not fraudulent,
would avoid a policy. *Cushman* v. *N. W. Ins. Co.*, 34 Me. 487 ; *Haven* v. *Gray*,
12 Mass. 75 ; *Akin* v. *Mississippi etc., Ins. Co.*, 4 Martin (La.) 661. In *Stewart*
v. *Phenix Fire Ins. Co.*, 3 Alb. Law Journal, 119, the insurance was based on a
representation made to another company, as to the condition and situation of the
building insured. The representation was made in 1857, and the policy was
issued in 1860. Upon the trial the defendant relied on two matters stated in the
representation, one as to the value of the building, and the other that the representations made as to the quantity of grain in the mill was untrue in 1860, when
the policy was issued. The evidence on the part of the defendants as to the
falsity of the representation, was mainly confined to the condition of the property
in 1860. Held, that the statement of the value of the building in 1857, was not
the statement of a fact as then existing, *but the mere opinion of the party as to his
estimate of value, and is not such a statement as would avoid the policy even if
the insured was in error, without proof that such misstatement was intentional, and
for a fraudulent purpose. The expression of an opinion, if honestly entertained
and communicated, is not a misrepresentation, however erroneous it may prove.* It
is not unusual for a man to value his own property higher than others, and it
would be a harsh rule to hold that his policy was void, because he formed such
an estimate of his property, without showing any facts from which it might be

and the fact that the property is considerably over-valued does not, of itself, establish such fraud upon the part of the assured as avoids the policy.[1] A fraudulent intent, or intentional purpose to deceive, must be shown, or circumstances that warrant such an inference, and the burden is upon the insurer to establish both the fact of over-valuation and of fraud.[2]

---

inferred that it was done with a fraudulent intent. The representations, if at all material, were made in 1857. There is no proof that the insured did anything in 1860 to re-affirm those representations as true then. On the contrary, the insurance was made on this paper as in the custody of another company, and not furnished by the assured, and although the policy refers to that statement it can only be shown to be false at the time it was made.

[1] *Miner* v. *Tagert*, 3 Binn. (Penn.) 204.

[2] *Field* v. *Ins. Co. of N. America, ante.* In *Gerhauser* v. *N. British Ins. Co.*, 7 Nev. 174, the plaintiff placed his loss at $6,000. The jury found it to be only $3,000, and the court held that a recovery could be had, unless there was a willful intent to defraud. In *Unger* v. *People's F. Ins. Co.*, 4 Daly (N. Y. C. P.) 96, the insurer stated his loss to be $9,989.03. The jury found it to be only $6,500. Held, not such evidence of an attempt to defraud as discharged the insurers from liability. In *Moore* v. *Protection Ins. Co.*, 29 Me. 97, the plaintiff stated his loss at $2,800. The jury found it to be $1,853, and the court upheld the verdict for that sum. See also, *Jones* v. *Mechanics' F. Ins. Co.*, 36 N. J. 29; *Britton* v. *Royal Ins. Co.*, 4 F. & F. 905; *Franklin F. Ins. Co.* v. *Updegraff*, 43 Penn. St. 350. In *Marchesseau* v. *Merchants' Ins. Co.*, 1 Rob. (La.) 438, the loss was stated at $15,549. The jury found it to be only $8,000, and the court held that this did not establish fraud *per se.* In *Planters', etc., Ins. Co.,* v. *Deford*, 38 Md. 382, the plaintiff claimed for 338 more hides than were shown to have been destroyed. The court held that this would not defeat a recovery unless *an intent to defraud* was shown. See also, *Bonham* v. *Iowa Central Ins. Co.*, 25 Iowa, 328; *Clark* v. *Phenix Ins. Co.*, 36 Cal. 168; *Hoffman* v. *Western, etc., Ins. Co.*, 1 La. An. 216; *Wolfe* v. *Goodhue F. Ins. Co.*, 43 Barb. (N. Y.) 406; *Protection Ins. Co.* v. *Hall*, 15 B. Mon. (Ky.) 411; *Sims* v. *State Ins. Co.*, 47 Mo. 54; *Franklin Ins. Co.* v. *Culver*, 6 Ind. 137; *Hickman* v. *L. I. Ins. Co.*, Edm. Sel. Cas. (N. Y.) 374; *Williams* v. *Phenix Ins. Co.*, 61 Me. 67, but *contra* see *Wall* v. *Howard Ins. Co.*, 51 Me. 32, where the plaintiff, in his sworn statement, placed his loss at $2,400, and the jury found it to be only $1,040, and the court held that the difference was so great as to raise a presumption of an *attempt* to defraud the insurers, which released them from liability. So in *Catron* v. *Tenn. Ins. Co.*, 6 Humph. (Tenn.) 176, the actual value of the property was $8,000. The insured stated it in his proofs of loss to be $12,000, and the court held this to be, as a matter of law, a fraudulent over-valuation. See also, *Regnier* v. *Louisiana Ins. Co.*, 12 La. (O. S.) 336; *Dickson* v. *Equitable Ins. Co.*, 18 U. C. (Q. B.) 246. In *Phenix Ins. Co.* v. *Munday*, 5 Cold. (Tenn.) 547, the insured stated his loss at $15,989.18. The jury found it to be $12,043. Held fraudulent. It should be stated that, the fact that a *largely excessive valuation is made*, unless satisfactorily explained, has a strong tendency to establish fraud, but the question is for the jury, and, except as appears from the last cases cited, their finding is conclusive. The over-valuation must be intentional. *Laidlaw* v. *The Liverpool and London Ins. Co.*, 13 Grant's Ch. (Ont.) 377; *Cox* v. *Ætna Ins. Co.*, 29 Ind. 586; *Bonham* v. *Iowa, etc., Ins. Co., ante;* *Riach* v. *Niagara, etc., Ins. Co.*, 21 U. C. (C. P.) 464; *Williams* v. *Phenix F. Ins. Co.*, 67 Penn. St. 373; *Am. Ins. Co.* v. *Gilbert*, 27 Mich. 429. Over-valuation may be shown as tending to establish willful burning. *Ins. Co. of N. America* v. *McDowell*, 50 Ill. 120. If the jury find that the assured could not reasonably think the property was worth the sum insured, the over-valuation is fatal. *Newton* v. *Gore Dist., etc., Ins. Co.*, 33 U. C. (Q. B.) 93. It must appear that the over valuation did not result from accident or mistake, but was intentional and fraudulent. *Park* v. *Phenix Ins. Co.*, 19 U. C. (Q. B.) 110; *Lycoming Ins. Co.* v. *Rubin*, 79 Ill. 402.

This doctrine has been denied, however, by the courts of several States in this country, and in England, and the doctrine held that, in cases where the policy provides that "an over-valuation or misrepresentation shall make the policy void," any substantial over-valuation, *whether fraudulent or not,* avoids the policy. Thus, in a recent English case,[1] the insurers under such a policy alleged over-valuation in defense, and the court submitted the question to the jury to say whether the valuation was excessive, and if so, whether it was made with a fraudulent intent; also, whether it was material to the risk. The jury found the valuation excessive, but that it was not made with a fraudulent intent; they also found that the real value of the property was material to the risk, and found for the defendants. The Court of Queen's Bench upheld the verdict. In a comparatively recent case in Michigan,[2] the court held that the question of over-valuation is for the court, and should not be submitted to the jury, upon the ground that the statement of value is to be treated as a warranty, so that a *substantial* over-valuation operates a breach of it and avoids the policy. But, *quere,* is it not for the jury to say whether there was an over-valuation in fact? How is value determined? Is it not a matter of judgment and opinion wholly, except, it may be, in special instances? How is the value of real estate to be estimated? What is the standard by which to ascertain the value of a building? Is it what this man or that says it is worth? Is it what it would cost to build another of the same style and materials? The ascertainment of any of these facts is a mere matter of judgment. Has not the insured the same right to exercise his judgment, if he exercises it honestly, that his neighbors on the jury have? When the insurers propound this inquiry, upon what basis and by what standard is it to be presumed they expect the insured to estimate the value? Is it reasonable to suppose that they expect him to estimate the value of the materials composing it; the cost of labor to build it, or rather to give his *honest judgment and opinion upon the question?* Suppose the question in the application to be, "What, in your honest judgment and opinion, is the value of the

---

[1] *Ionides* v. *Pender*, L. R., 9 Q. B. 531. In *Bobbitt* v. *Liverpool, London and Globe Ins. Co.*, 66 N. C. 70, the insured was asked to state the cash value of the property to be insured. He stated $30,000, and that it would be increased to $50,000; that the average value was $30,000. The court held that this was the statement of a fact, and, if untrue, would, under a condition to that effect, avoid the policy. The Supreme Court of Illinois also held that a false representation of the value of stock on hand at the time the policy issues releases the insurer. *Lycoming Ins. Co.* v. *Ruben*, 8 Chicago Leg. News, 150.

[2] *American Ins. Co.* v. *Gilbert*, 27 Mich. 429.

property?" Would it not be held that, in order to avoid the policy, the insurer must show that the value was not given according to the honest judgment and opinion of the insured? Most certainly. And it is difficult to conceive how the introduction of the words "judgment or opinion" into the question can affect the rights of the parties at all, for, in nearly *all* instances, the question of value is well known to be a mere matter of opinion. Particularly is this so as to buildings and real estate generally, and all the insurer expects or has a right to expect in answer to a question of the value thereof is simply the honest judgment and opinion of the assured, and it is absurd to hold the assured responsible for an error of judgment *honestly* made, simply because his neighbors differ with him in that respect. A doctrine that held the insurer up to a strictly exact valuation would be extremely unjust, and would result in vitiating one-half the policies issued, for, under the rule, the difference of *one cent* is as disastrous as a difference of a large amount.

The rule as adopted by the better class of cases, and sustained by the weight of authority is, that in order to avoid a policy for over-valuation, *it must be intentional and fraudulent, and an over-valuation, the result of an honest error of judgment, or of a mistake,* will not have that effect.[1] It is true that the question in the cases referred to has

---

[1] *Ins. Co.* v. *Weides,* 14 Wall. (U. S.) 375; *Grenier* v. *Monarch Fire, etc., Ins. Co.,* 7 L. C. Jur. 100. In *Rice* v. *Provincial Ins. Co.,* 7 U. C. (C. P.) 548, the plaintiff claimed his loss to be £600, on his building. The jury found the actual damage on the building to be £200, and £200 upon machinery. The verdict being for the plaintiff, it was upheld upon the ground that the whole question turned upon the *bona* or *mala fides* of the insured in making the valuation, and the verdict repelled all presumptions of bad faith. In a late case heard and decided in the Supreme Court of the United States, this question was ably considered. *Franklin F. Ins. Co.* v. *Vaughn,* 92 U. S. 516. In that case the plaintiff bought a lot of goods at auction and left them with the vendor for sale. The purchase-money therefor was not all paid, and the plaintiff arranged that the balance due, $3,150, should be paid out of the avails of the first sales. He procured an insurance thereon in the defendant company for $2,500, representing that they were unincumbered. He also stated their value to be $12,000. There had been about $2,000 worth sold when the loss occurred, and the insurers claimed that the value of the goods destroyed did not exceed $6,000, consequently that there was an over-valuation that avoided the policy. The jury found the value of the goods destroyed to be $7,204, making the value of the goods at the time of their destruction about $9,200, taking the price at which the goods were sold as the test. The court below charged the jury that in order to defeat the policy the over-valuation must have been *knowingly* or fraudulently made, and that the fact that the purchase-money had not all been paid, and was to be paid out of the avails of the first sales, was not an incumbrance within the conditions of the policy. A verdict was rendered for the plaintiff which was sustained upon appeal, HUNT, J., saying: "The value of the goods was to be estimated by the applicant. He gave this estimate at $12,000, *and there is not the slightest evidence that such was not his honest estimate of their value.* Insurance agents as well as most persons know with what partiality most men estimate their property, and how much more valuable they esteem it when their own, than when it is their neighbor's.

generally arisen, when the over-valuation was made after a loss, but the principle is the same, as in either case the over-valuation, by the terms of the policy, relieved the company from liability.[1] If the

---

They do not object to this principle when the premiums are received. It is only when losses occur that they seek to apply the more rigid test of *actual* value. *The value of stock is not always, nor usually what it costs.* Such goods are often bought in the country to be sold at retail, and at a profit. *What may be expected to be obtained for them under such circumstances, may reasonably be considered their value.* And that the owner and purchaser should estimate them *at much more than he gave for them,* and should hope and expect to make large gains and profits upon their sale, *was no doubt understood by the agent making the insurance.* The counsel for the defendant concedes that it is not *every* over-valuation which will avoid a policy, but he objects to the charge of the judge, that to produce this result the over-valuation must be 'grossly, enormously,' in excess of the truth. It is hardly just to the judge that the charge should rest on this statement. The judge undoubtedly said : '*If the valuation was grossly, enormously in excess of the value of the goods, then the burden is cast on the plaintiff of showing that he acted honestly and in good faith in making the valuation, and that it was not made for any fraudulent purpose or with any fraudulent intention, but was an honest and unintentional error.*' He did not say, however, that nothing less than this would have that effect. He said, also, 'The law exacts the utmost good faith in contracts of insurance, both on the part of the insured and the insurer, *and a knowing and willful over-valuation of property by the insured, with a view and purpose of obtaining insurance thereon for a greater sum than could otherwise be obtained,* is a fraud upon the insurance company that avoids the policy. *It is a question of good faith and honest intention on the part of the assured,* and though he may have put a valuation on his property greatly in excess of its cash value, in the market, *yet, if he did so in the honest belief that the property was worth the valuation put upon it, and the excessive valuation was made in good faith and was not intended to mislead or defraud the insurance company, then such over-valuation was not a fraud that will defeat a recovery,*" and this ruling was fully sustained by the court. In the case of *Mobile Fire Dep. Ins. Co.* v. *Miller,* decided on the 5th ult., by the Supreme Court of Georgia (see vol. xv, p. 44, 7 Alb. Law Journal), the facts were these : Miller took out a policy of insurance in the company named, October 27, 1874, for $5,000. He stated in answer to questions in the application that his goods were inventoried last, in April previous, and amounted to $13,000. It was specially agreed in the policy that the answers to these questions should be considered as warranties, and if not true the policy should be void. On the trial it appeared that the last inventory of the goods was, in fact, made on October 4th, just previous to the insurance, and that the goods amounted to $7,600 at that time—but that Miller had afterward purchased $11,000 worth of goods from parties in Savannah. and had them on hand at the time of the insurance. The court held that the variation did not avoid the policy, saying that it is not any and every variation from the representations contained in the application, that will constitute a breach of the covenant of warranty and avoid the policy. The varia. tion must be such as to change the nature, or extent, or character of the risk, in order to avoid the policy. The court further said that whether the variation claimed in this case changed the nature, or extent, or character of the defendant's risk, or whether it was material or done willfully, or fraudulently, were questions of fact to be determined by the jury from the evidence, and not questions of law for the court to decide. We recognize the principle that by the terms of the policy a willful attempt at fraud by the insured, by false swearing, or otherwise, would void the policy, but inasmuch as the entire charge is not set out in the record, we will presume that the court made the proper explanation of the charge upon which error is assigned. The court also held that evidence that the agent of the defendant knew before, and at the time of issuing the policy that gunpow. der and kerosene were to be kept by the insured, in the house, was admissible in this case. The omission to insert the permission in the policy was the fault of the defendant's agent, as shown by his own testimony.

[1] *Franklin Ins. Co.* v. *Vaughn, ante.*

lnsnred *knowingly* and *falsely* over-values the property;[1] willfully mis-states it;[2] or fraudulently,[3] the insurer is discharged from liability, and the same is true of a *mere attempt to defraud, although not carried into effect*.[4]

Any fraud *or attempt at fraud*, is fatal to a recovery.[5]

When a valuation of the assured property is made in good faith by the insurer, and without fraud on the part of the assured, it is conclusive upon both parties, and neither can be permitted to show that it was *in fact*, more or less;[6] and this is so, even though there is a considerable over-valuation of the property.[7] The valuation fixed in the policy, in the absence of fraud, is conclusive upon the insurer and insured;[8] but if there is anything in the policy that shows that such valuation is not intended to be conclusive, it is open to proof of actual value, as when the policy provides that the company "shall in no case be liable beyond three-fourths of the actual cash value of the property insured, *at the time of the loss or damage, nor beyond such sum as will enable the insured to replace or restore the property lost or damaged*.'[9]

Question of materiality, compliance, etc., for the jury.

SEC. 221. It is for the jury to say whether the facts concealed or misstated weie material to the risk,[10] and the burden is upon the insurer to establish the materiality of the representation and its falsity.[11]

---

[1] *Geib* v. *International Ins. Co.*, 1 Dill. (U. S. C. C.) 441; *Grenier* v. *Monarch Ins. Co.*, 7 L. C. Jur. 100.

[2] *Britton* v. *Royal Ins. Co.*, 4 F. & F. 905.

[3] *Hercules Ins. Co.* v. *Hunter*, 15 C. C. (Sc.) 800; *Catron* v. *Tenn. Ins. Co.*, 6 Humph. (Tenn.) 176; *Haigh* v. *De La Cour*, 3 Camp. 319.

[4] In *Phœnix Ins. Co.* v. *Munday*, 5 Cold. (Tenn.) 547, the court refused to charge the jury that the plaintiff could not recover if he had attempted to defraud the insurer, and the refusal was held erroneous.

[5] *Geib* v. *International Ins. Co.*, *ante*; *Chapman* v. *Pale*, 22 L. T. (U. S.) 306; *Wall* v. *Howard Ins. Co.*, 51 Me. 32.

[6] *Holmes* v. *Charlestown Ins. Co.*, 10 Met. (Mass.) 216; *Fuller* v. *Boston, etc., Ins. Co.*, 4 id. 206; *Borden* v. *Hingham, etc., Ins. Co.*, 10 Pick. (Mass.) 523.

[7] *Fuller* v. *Boston, etc., Ins. Co.*, *ante*.

[8] *Luce* v. *Dorchester Ins. Co.*, 105 Mass. 297; *Fuller* v. *Boston Ins. Co.*, 4 Met. (Mass.) 206.

[9] *Brown* v. *Quincy Mut. F. Ins. Co.*, 105 Mass. 396.

[10] *Boardman* v. *N. H. Ins. Co.*, 20 N. H. 551; *McLanaghan* v. *Universal Ins. Co.*, 1 Pet. (U. S.) 170; *Bulkley* v. *Protection Ins. Co.*, 2 Paine (U. S.) 82. In *Power* v. *City Fire Ins. Co.*, 8 Phila. (Penn.) 566, the application which was incor-

[11] In *Jones Manuf. Co.* v. *Mut. F. Ins. Co.*, 8 Cush. Mass. 82, the application contained a notice that it was expected that the answers thereto will meet the requirements of the insurer's office, one of which requirements is that a cask of water and buckets will be kept in each story, and one of the answers stated that "casks of water and buckets are kept in each story," and it was held that the burden was upon the defendant to show the falsity of the answer.

Misrepresentation as to premiums paid for insurance on same property to other insurers.

SEC. 222. A misrepresentation as to the amount paid to other insurers for insurance upon the same property, is material to the risk, and if it is stated at a sum *less* than that actually paid, the policy is void.[1] In the language of the court in the case last cited, it induces a confidence without which the insurer would not have acted. It naturally influences both the taking of the risk, and the rate to be charged therefor. But such misrepresentation, in order to avoid the policy, *must be shown to have influenced the insurers. If, notwithstanding the representation, they acted upon their own judgment and fixed a rate of premium commensurate with the risk,* the policy is valid. Thus, where the plaintiff told the insurers that he had no doubt he could get insurance in New York at 15 per cent., when in fact he had applied to several offices there, and they rejected the risk, and the defendants took it at 20 per cent., it was held not to avoid the policy.[2] "While," said the court, "the statement could not be defended at the bar of con-

---

porated into the policy, stated that there was a watchman in the mill nights, when it was not in use. Upon the night when the fire occurred the mill was stopped at six o'clock, and the fires were put out. At ten o'clock some of the employees returned to see if everything was right, and no one was in the mill after that time. The court held that it was for the jury, and not for the court, to say whether the insured had complied with his representation. A similar view was adopted in *Parker* v. *Bridgeport Ins. Co.*, 10 Gray (Mass.) 302, in which the court held that it was for the jury to say whether a "good watch," as stipulated for by the plaintiff, had been kept. In *Percival* v. *Maine Ins. Co.*, 33 Me. 242, the insured procured insurance upon his starch factory, and stated in his application that the business of manufacturing had been completed for the season. It appeared, however, that there was then a quantity of starch in the drying room, and a fire was made in the furnace to dry it. The court held that it was for the jury to say, whether the process of *drying* the starch was a part of the process of manufacture. The court cannot say as a matter of law, that an untrue representation in reference to the title, situation or use of the property *is fraudulent;* whether it is so or not, is a question for the jury. *Cumberland, etc., Ins. Co.* v. *Mitchell*, 48 Penn. St. 374. In *Sims* v. *State Ins. Co.*, 47 Mo. 311, the application for the policy contained the question "for what purpose the building was used," and the answer was "tobacco-pressing; no manufacturing." But the evidence showed that in a shed attached to the main building tobacco hogsheads were manufactured, and the court held that the question, "whether the preparation of hogsheads was such an incident of the business as to be included in it" was for the jury. When the question as to the materiality of a statement, made by an applicant for insurance, arises upon a representation unconnected with a warranty, the materiality of the statement presents a question of fact to be submitted to the jury. But when there is a specific inquiry in regard to incumbrances by mortgage, and the answer is positive, denying the existence of any mortgage upon the premises, the question of materiality of the statement in respect to the risk is settled by the parties as matters of *contract. Shoemaker* v. *Glen's Falls Ins. Co.*, 60 Barb. (N. Y.) 284. It was stated in the application that the building was tenanted, but the application was not imported into the policy, and it was held that such statement was not a warranty, but a representation; and hence, that whether it was material to the risk, was a question for the jury. *Schultz* v. *Merchants' Ins. Co.*, 57 Mo. 331.

[1] *Sibauld* v. *Hill*, 2 Dow. 263.

[2] *Clason* v. *Smith*, 3 Wash. C. C. (U. S.) 156.

science, the misrepresentation could have had no influence affecting the rate of premium *because upon* their own judgment they demanded 20 per cent. instead of 15, nor ought it to have induced the acceptance of the risk at all, nor influenced the rate of premium, for the representation expressed nothing but an opinion that the insurance could be effected at that rate."

Fraud will not be presumed.

SEC. 223. If fraud on the part of the assured is set up in avoidance of the policy, the insurer must establish it by competent affirmative proof, as it will be presumed that the assured acted honestly and in good faith, until the contrary is satisfactorily established.[1] In order, however, to avoid a policy upon the ground of misrepresentation on the part of the assured, it is not necessary that a fraudulent purpose or intent, on the part of the assured, should be established. *It is enough if the representation was in fact false, and was material to the risk.*[2]

Misstatement to re-insurers.

SEC. 224. The same rules apply between insurance companies entering into contracts of re-insurance as between individuals and insurers. The same degree of good faith is required in the one case as in the other. Thus, where an insurer sought re-insurance for $10,000, upon sugar and molasses on the plantation of K., and in the application stated, " we have buildings," meaning that they were carrying the risk upon the buildings, which was not true, it was held that the policy was void.[3] So where re-insurance is procured under a representation that the re-insured intends to retain a part of the risk, but *before the contract of re-insurance is consummated* it determines not to do so, the contract of re-insurance is invalid.[4]

Where a risk is estimated and taken on the faith of representations made by the insured, the law requires that they shall truly and completely express his knowledge of the dangers to which the property is exposed, and the contract is avoided if they do not; but it has become so common to have the property to be insured examined and described by an agent of the insurers, that it will not be presumed that an application which merely particularizes the property is intended as a representation of the hazard to which it is exposed.

[1] *Pine* v. *Vaunxem*, 3 Yeates (Penn.) 30.
[2] STORY, J., in *Carpenter* v. *American Ins. Co.*, 1 Story (U. S.) 57.
[3] *Louisiana Mut. Ins. Co.* v. *N. O. Ins. Co.*, 13 La. An. 246.
[4] *Traill* v. *Baring*, 12 W. R. 334.

28

Insurers are not always dependent upon the representations of the insured for the character of the risk. *They may contract upon their own knowledge of it; though, even then, there might be a withholding of information of circumstances plainly tending to increase the risk, which would avoid the contract.*[1]

A statement in an application for insurance, is not to be treated as a warranty, unless clearly made so by the terms of the policy.[2] The insurer writes the contract, and if he intends to bind the assured to the strict and literal construction of the statements made by him in the application, he must do so in terms.

Insurer estopped by personal examination of insured premises.

SEC. 225. When the insurer causes the premises to be examined by an agent, he is thereby estopped from setting up an innocent misdescription, misrepresentation or concealment, on the part of the assured, in reference to any matter open to observation, and which such agent ought to have seen or might have ascertained upon reasonable inquiry. In such cases he is presumed to rely upon the knowledge acquired by the agent, and is not misled as to the nature or condition of the risk.[3]

---

[1] *Cumberland, etc., Ins. Co* v. *Schell*, 29 Penn. St. 31 ; *Continental Ins. Co.* v. *Kasey*, 25 Gratt. (Va.) 268.

[2] *Daniels* v. *Hudson R. Ins. Co.*, 12 Cush. (Mass.) 416.

[3] *Michael* v. *Mutual Ins. Co. of Nashville*, 10 La. An. 737; 4 Bennett's F. I. C. 29 ; *Benedict* v. *Ocean Ins. Co.*, 1 Daly (N. Y. C. P.) 8; 4 Bennett's F. I. C. 462. In *Continental Ins. Co.* v. *Kasey*, 25 Gratt. (Va.) 268 ; 18 Am. Rep. 681, this question was ably considered and a doctrine consonant with that stated in the text announced. STAPLES, J., in passing upon this question, said: "The second instruction presents a question of greater difficulty. It declares that although the plaintiff may have represented the premises to be frame and shingle houses, yet, if the agent of the company was present and inspected the buildings at the time of the agreement to insure, and before the policy was issued, and inserted the description in the policy based upon his own inspection as well as the plaintiff's representations, and such a description was a mistaken one, the plaintiff is entitled to recover, notwithstanding the misdescription contained in the policy. The chief difficulty in the way of maintaining this instruction is, that by the express terms of the policy, the description of the property therein contained is made an express warranty. And the doctrine is well understood that a warranty is in the nature of a condition precedent. It is a matter of no sort of importance whether in such case the condition be material or immaterial, it must be literally performed. This is the general rule. Circumstances, however, sometimes occur to prevent its application. For example, if the company, not relying upon the statements of the insured, sends its own agent to examine the property, and thereupon issues the policy upon the faith of his representations, it would seem to be clear that the insured would not be responsible for a misdescription of the property, however material, though inserted in the policy and constituting a warranty, unless, indeed, there was a withholding of information by the insured incompatible with the obligation of good faith and fair dealing. But suppose, as assumed in the instruction, the agent makes an examination of the property in behalf of the company, and inserts in the policy a misdescription, based as well upon that examination as upon the representations of the insured. What is the effect of a misdescription thus attributable to the mistake of both parties? This

The same principle applies in this case as applies in the case of facts disclosed to an agent by the assured. *Unless the insurer has been mis-*

---

will depend very much upon the circumstances. If the representation of the owner was not *bona fide,* or if its effect is to induce the company to issue a policy, which it would otherwise have rejected, it may be that the insured ought to bear the loss, notwithstanding the company, through its agent, may have contributed to the mistake. On the other hand, if the mistake was an innocent one, and the representation was in no wise material to the risk, justice and sound policy would seem to require that the company shall be held to the observance of its contract. The rule of law which invalidates an insurance, unless the warranty is strictly performed, however immaterial it may be, is an extremely technical one. Its operation is often to defeat the right of recovery contrary to the plain jus. tice of the case and the real intent of the parties. A rule thus stringent ought not to be applied to an innocent mistake, not affecting the risk, to which both parties have contributed. The company cannot justly complain that it is liable in such case ; first, because its own agent has aided in the misrepresentation ; and, secondly, because its conduct would not have been different had the fact been truly stated. In the case of *Insurance Company* v. *Wilkinson,* 16 Wall. (U. S.) 222, Mr. Justice MILLER delivered a very interesting opinion, greatly to be commended for the sound and thoughtful views therein presented. Much of it has a strong application to the present case. In the course of the opinion he said : ' It is not to be denied that the application, logically considered, is the work of the assured, and left to himself or to such assistance as he might select, the person so selected would be his agent, and he alone would be responsible. It was well known, however, so well, that no court would be justified in shutting its eyes to it, that insurance companies organized under the laws of one State and having in that State their principal business office, send their agents all over the land with directions to solicit and procure applications for policies, furnishing them with printed arguments in favor of the value and necessity of life insurance, and of the special advantages of the corporation which the agent represents. The agents are stimulated by letters and instructions to activity in procuring contracts, and the party who in this manner is induced to take out a policy rarely sees or knows anything about the company or officers by whom it is issued, but looks to and relies upon the agent who has persuaded him to effect insurance as the full and complete representative of the company in all that is said or done in making the contract.' The learned justice concedes, that, according to some of the earlier decisions, the responsibility of the companies, for the acts of their agents, was limited to the simple receipt of the premiums and delivery of the policy—a doctrine which had a reasonable foundation to rest upon at a time when insurance companies waited for parties to come to them to seek assurance, or to forward applications on their own motion. But to apply such a doctrine in its full force, to the present system of selling policies through agents, would be a snare and a delusion, leading, as it has done in numerous instances, to the grossest frauds, of which the insurance corporations receive the benefits, and the parties supposing themselves insured are the victims. An insurance company, establishing a local agency, must be held responsible to the parties with whom they transact business, for the acts and declarations of the agent, within the scope of his employment, as if they proceeded from the principal." See also, *Masters* v. *Madison Co. Mut. Ins. Co.,* 11 Barb. 634 ; *Sarsfield* v. *Metropolitan Ins. Co.,* 61 id. 479; and Am. Lead. Cas. 5th ed. p. 917. The tendency of the modern decisions is in accordance with the liberal views announced by the Supreme Court of the United States. It is a source of congratulation that the courts in construing these contracts are abandoning mere technicalities, and rendering decisions more in harmony with the general sense of mankind, and the dictates of an enlightened judicial policy. The case before us presents a striking illustration of the views here suggested. The record does not contain all the evidence adduced on the trial. It is very evident, however, that the east end of the building insured was made of logs, weather-boarded and plastered. No one could see these logs, and it is very probable their existence was unknown both to the plaintiff and the agent of the company. Both concurred in representing the building as frame, and this description was inserted in the policy. Now, conced-

led by some act of the assured, he cannot defeat his liability upon the policy. If, instead of relying upon the statements of the assured, he prefers to have the premises examined by his agent, he must himself answer for the negligence or incompetency of the agent to whom he commits the duty,[1] unless there is collusion between the agent and the assured.[2]

When the insurer *knows* the character, nature and situation of the risk *before he takes it,* he cannot complain that the assured has not told him what he already knew, or that he has made statements that the insurer *knew* to be false. In such a case, he has not been misled.[3]

---

ing this was a misdescription, which is very questionable to say the least, no one can suppose it was material to the policy, or that it had the slightest effect upon the premium. In other words the misrepresentation, if such it was, was wholly immaterial. And we are told that this constitutes a breach of warranty, and a consequent forfeiture of the policy. We cannot subscribe to this view. If any breach has occurred, we think the company is estopped, under all the circumstances, to insist upon it."

[1] *Howard F. Ins. Co.* v. *Brunner,* 24 Penn. St. 50; *Clark* v. *Manufacturers' Ins. Co.,* 8 How. (U. S.) 235; *Cumberland Valley, etc., Ins. Co.* v. *Schell,* 30 Penn. St. 31.

[2] *Smith* v. *Ins. Co.,* 25 Penn. St. 320.

[3] In *McFee* v. *S. C. Ins. Co.,* 2 McC. (S. C.) 503, the defendants *knew* that the voyage was prohibited; and the court held that, in view of that fact, they could not be heard to say that the voyage was illegal. The same rule has been held in reference to the keeping of prohibited articles. When the insurer *knew* that such articles were, and would be kept by the assured, it is held that he is estopped from setting up a breach of a condition of the policy, in that respect, to avoid liability. *Phœnix Ins. Co.* v. *Lawrence,* 4 Met. (Ky.) 9; *Allen* v. *Vt. Mut. F. Ins. Co.,* 12 Vt. 366; *McFarland* v. *Peabody Ins. Co.,* 6 W. Va. 425; *McFarland* v. *Ætna Ins. Co.,* 6 id. 437; *Clark* v. *Union, etc., Ins. Co.,* 40 N. H. 333; *Patten* v. *Merchants', etc., Ins. Co.,* 40 id. 375; *James River Ins. Co.* v. *Merritt,* 47 Ala. 387; *Beal* v. *Park F. Ins. Co.,* 16 Wis. 241.

CHAPTER VII.

ALTERATION OR CHANGE OF RISK.

Alteration or change of risk.

SEC. 226. In order to invalidate a policy upon the ground· of alterations or changes in the risk made subsequent to the insurance, they must be shown *to have materially increased the risk.* The mere fact that a change has been made, or that alterations have been effected, does not affect the validity of the policy. They must materially increase the risk, and the burden of establishing the fact is upon the insurer.[1]

---

[1] In *Jones Mfg. Co.* v. *Mut. Ins. Co.*, 8 Cush. (Mass.) 83, the policy provided that, if the situation or circumstances affecting the risk thereupon should be so altered or changed by the insured, without the consent of the insurer, or so as to increase the risk, the policy should be void. After the policy was issued, the insured changed the location of the stove and its smoke pipe, without the assent of the insurer, so that the smoke pipe, instead of passing into the chimney in that story, was carried up through the floors of the second and third stories, and, after passing around the third story, about two feet from the floor, for the purpose of drying wool, entered the chimney in that story. The Judge instructed

The change must be essential and material, and such as was not contemplated by the insurer;[1] it must change and *enhance* the risk.

Prohibited uses material, per se.

SEC. 227. When the policy stipulates against the use of the premises for certain purposes, as where a list of uses regarded as hazardous, extra hazardous or specially hazardous is annexed to the policy, unless the use for which the premises are insured, or the description of the risk imports a license to use the premises, for certain purposes named as hazardous, etc., the use of the premises for any of such purposes, or the keeping of any such hazardous, etc., articles *per se* avoids the policy, and the only question is, *whether the premises were used for such prohibited purposes, or such prohibited articles were kept,* and if so, the policy is invalidated without any reference to the question whether the risk was thereby increased or not. *The insurer has made it material by the prohibition,* and his action in that respect is conclusive,[2] and the

---

the jury that such alteration and use of the pipe in the third story would not invalidate the policy, unless the change increased the risk from fire in that story, and the ruling was sustained on appeal. In *Wood* v. *Hartford F. Ins. Co.,* 13 Conn. 533, the building was insured as a paper mill. The rag cutter and duster were taken out, and a pair of stones for grinding grain were substituted in their place. Held, that the policy was not *per se* avoided by such change, nor at all *unless* the risk was materially increased thereby. See also, *Manley* v. *Ins. Co. of N. America,* 1 Lans. (N. Y.) 20. The putting up of an additional stove in the building was held of itself, not to invalidate the policy. The court held that the insurer must, in order to avoid liability, show *that the risk was increased thereby. Newhall* v. *Union, etc., Ins. Co.,* 52 Me. 180. In *Stokes* v. *Cox,* 4 H. & N. 445, the policy covered "buildings, part of the lower story used as a stable, coach-house and boiler-house; no steam engine employed on the premises, the steam from said boiler being used for heating water and warming the shops. Melting tallow by steam in said boiler-house, and the use of two pipe-stoves in said building are allowed. Warranted that no oil be boiled nor any process of japanning leather be carried on therein, nor in any building adjoining thereto." Stipulated: "If, after the insurance shall have been effected, the risk shall be increased by any alteration of circumstances, and the same shall not be indorsed on the policy by an agent of the company, and a higher premium paid if required, such insurance shall be of no force." It was a special risk. After the policy was effected, a steam engine was put up into the stable, supplied with steam from a boiler insured by the policy, of which insurers had not any notice; but the jury found specially that the risk was not increased. Held, insured was not bound to give notice of the alteration unless the risk was increased; that as it was found that no increase of risk had occurred, the plaintiffs were entitled to judgment.

[1] In *Appleby* v. *Astor F. Ins. Co.,* 54 N. Y. 253, the respondents occupied a part of the premises for storage purposes under a lease, containing a provision against the use of the building for extra hazardous purposes. A part of the premises were subsequently leased for the purpose of finishing chairs, for which various inflammable substances were used, and the fire was occasioned by the use of an alcohol lamp in this business. Held, that, in the first class of hazards, no process of manufacture or completion of any article was contemplated, and that it had reference to articles in a finished state, also, that there was an important difference between the risk of insuring against fire any article completed and finished and the same article undergoing the process of completion.

[2] *Hervey* v. *Mutual F. Ins. Co.,* 11 U. C. (C. P.) 394; *Harris* v. *Columbian Ins. Co.,* 4 Ohio 285; *Appleby* v. *Firemen's Ins. Co.,* 45 Barb. (N. Y.) 454; *Appleby* v. *Astor Ins. Co.,* 54 N. Y. 253; *Washington F. Ins. Co.* v. *Davison,* 30 Md. 91; *Merchants', etc., Ins. Co.* v. *Washington, etc., Ins. Co.,* 1 Handy (Ohio) 181.

fact that the loss did not result from such change of risk is of no con_sequence. The change having been made contrary to prohibitory clause in the policy, is fatal to a recovery for a loss, from whatever cause it arises.[1]

Question for jury. Question for court.

SEC. 228. The question whether a change of circumstances in the situation, use or condition of property insured increases the risk is purely one of fact for the jury, and their finding is conclusive;[2] but, whether an increase of risk avoids the liability of the insurer, is a question of law for the court. Thus, a policy was issued upon a dwelling-house, upon an application which set forth that the building was a dwelling-house used and occupied for "farmer's use." The building was so used when the application was made, and when the policy was issued. But subsequently it was vacated, and remained vacant for the period of fifty-three days, when it was destroyed by fire. After the tenant left the house, the assured used reasonable efforts to secure another tenant, but unsuccessfully. The defendant insisted in defense, and requested the court to instruct the jury that there had been such a change of occupancy of the building as caused a material increase of the risk, by the advice, consent or procurement of the assured, and rendered the policy void. But the court held, and so instructed the jury, that, if they found that there was no material increase of risk, caused by the change of occupancy, or of business in said buildings, that the plaintiff was entitled to a verdict; but, if they were satisfied that a dwelling-house being unoccupied *occasioned a material increase of risk, yet, if they were satisfied that it was occupied as a dwelling-house at the time when it was insured, and that it was the intention of the assured to continue its use as a dwelling-house, and he was making reasonable efforts to get a new tenant, the fact that the house was vacant at the time of the loss would not avoid the policy;* and this ruling was sustained upon appeal.[3]

---

[1] *Jones* v. *Manufacturers' Ins. Co.*, 8 Cush. (Mass.) 82 ; *Glen* v. *Lewis*, 8 Exchq. 607; *Stetson* v. *Ins. Co.*, 4 Mass. 330 ; *Clark* v. *Manufacturers' Ins. Co.*, 2 W. & M. (U. S.) 472 ; *Allen* v. *Ins. Co.*, 2 Md. 111 ; *Grant* v. *Howard Ins. Co.*, 5 Hill (N. Y.) 10 ; *Billings* v. *Tolland, etc., Ins. Co.*, 20 Conn. 139 ; *Jefferson Ins. Co.* v. *Cotheal*, 7 Wend. (N. Y.) 72.

[2] That the jury are to determine whether the risk is increased, see *Jones* v. *Fireman's Fund Ins. Co.*, 51 N. Y. 318; *Williams* v. *People's Ins. Co.*, 57 id. 274 ; *Lyon* v. *Com'l Ins. Co.*, 2 Rob. (La.) 266; *Robinson* v. *Mercer Co. Ins. Co.*, 27 N. J. 134.

[3] *Gamwell* v. *Merchants', etc., Ins. Co.*, 12 Cush. (Mass.) 167.

Knowledge of agent excuses breach, when.

SEC. 229. In order to ascertain whether a particular use of property increases the risk, the testimony of persons skilled in insurance business is admissible upon the question whether such use occasions a material increase of risk.[1] When a policy provides that unless notice is given *of changes in the risk*, or of any other matter, if the company *knows the facts from any* source, or what is equivalent thereto, if the agent knows the facts, notice need not be given *unless the policy requires that notice shall be given to the company itself, or in a particular way*,[2] and even this condition may be waived by an agent of the company, who, *with full knowledge of the facts*, waives the condition or renews the policy.[3] But a renewal of the policy, *without full knowledge* of such changes, or breach of the conditions of the policy, does not amount to a waiver. In such a case the maxim *qui tacit consentire videtur* does not apply.[4]

Immaterial changes not within the prohibition.

SEC. 230. A provision in a policy that "any change in the risk" shall avoid the policy, applies only to such changes as are *material to the risk and increase or enhance it*, and does not apply to immaterial changes that do not produce that result. Thus, where a policy was issued upon a brick, grist and plaster mill,[5] with such a provision therein, it was held that the erection of a steam power, contiguous to the mill, to be used to operate it in times of low water, was not such a change of the risk as *per se* invalidated the policy. "If," said ANDREWS, J., "there was no increase of hazard by reason of the annexation of the steam power, *there was no change of risk within the meaning of the policy*, and no notice was required to be given. The object of the provision requiring notice where the risk has been changed, is to enable the company to act intelligently upon an application for renewal. *If the risk was not increased by the changes in the condition of the property*, the company had no interest in knowing the fact that they had been made.[6] A mere temporary use for a more hazardous purpose, does not

---

[1] *Gamwell* v. *Merchants' etc., Ins. Co.*, 12 Cush. (Mass.) 167.

Hotchkiss v. *Germania F. Ins. Co.*, 5 Hun (N. Y. S. C.) 9.

[3] *Parker* v. *Arctic Ins. Co.*, 59 N. Y. 1; *Carroll* v. *C. O. Ins. Co.*, 1 Abb. N. Y. Ct. App. Dec. 816; *Franklin F. Ins. Co.* v. *Chicago Ice Co.*, 36 Md. 446.

[4] *Carpenter* v. *Prov., etc., Ins. Co.*, 16 Pet. (U. S.) 495; *Liddle* v. *Market Ins. Co.*, 29 N. Y. 184; *Kimball* v. *Howard F. Ins. Co.*, 8 Gray (Mass.) 29; *Hope* v. *Lawrence*, 50 Barb. (N. Y.) 258.

[5] *Parker* v. *Arctic F. Ins. Co.*, 59 N. Y. 1.

[6] In *Blood* v. *Howard F. Ins. Co.*, 12 Cush. (Mass.) 472, the policy contained a clause that "if the situation or circumstances affecting the risk shall be altered

come within the prohibition.   There must be a *change of use, an increase of risk* of a *permanent*, as distinguished from a *temporary* character. Thus, the use of a building, insured as a shoe factory, for a single

or changed by the agency of the assured, so as to increase the risk, the policy shall be null and void, unless confirmed by the company." The plaintiff, in his application, stated that the building was "formerly used as a machine shop, all of which business is now stopped, and shop fastened up, and only used for the purpose of the meeting of the band during the evenings of the week, on the second floor." The application was referred to and adopted as a "part of the policy, and a warranty on the part of the assured." A loss having occurred, in an action upon the policy, the defendants offered to show that the building had been used for other purposes than that specified in the application, and during the life of the policy, *but did not attempt to show that, at the time of issuing the policy,* the representation was not correct; nor that the risk was thereby increased, but claimed that, whether the risk was or was not increased by such use, the use operated as a breach of warranty which avoided the policy. *But the court held that the warranty only applied to the use of the building when the application was made, and could not be construed as a warranty that it should continue to be so used.* BIGELOW, J., delivered a very able opinion in the case, in which he said : "It is often quite difficult to determine whether a stipulation in a policy of insurance is simply descriptive and affirmative, or whether it is executory, and relates to the future use and condition of the property insured. But in the present case, we think it clear that the answer of the assured to the third interrogatory in the application for insurance was confined solely to a description of the building, and the purpose to which it was appropriated at the time the policy was entered into. Such is the proper and literal construction of the terms of the question and answer, both of them pointing only to the condition of the property at the time of making the contract, and not to its future use or occupation. A warranty will in no case be extended by construction. It cannot include anything not fairly within its terms. It is quite true that, in many cases, stipulations in form only affirmative have been held to be in fact promissory. But, in these cases, the nature of the property insured and the subject-matter of the warranty rendered such a construction of the contract necessary to carry out the plain intent of the parties. For like reasons, we think it entirely clear that there was no design by either party to the contract in the present case to make this answer an executory stipulation. It would be unreasonable, if not absurd, to suppose that the owner of the building intended the larger portion of it should remain fastened up and unoccupied during the entire term covered by the policy, or that the defendants assumed the risk under the belief that such was the stipulation on the part of the assured. The natural and reasonable inference was, that some beneficial use was intended to be made of the whole premises, and it would require very clear and explicit language to rebut such an implication. But a more decisive and satisfactory indication of the intent of the parties to limit this warranty to a description of the property as it was at the inception of the contract, and not to extend it to the mode of its future use and occupation, is found in the fact that there was an express agreement by which the defendants protected themselves against any increase of risk in consequence of a change "in the situation or circumstances" of the property. This leaves no room for doubt that the sole object of the warranty in question was to ascertain the precise nature and condition of the property at the time the risk was proposed to the defendants in the application of the plaintiff, and enable them to judge of its extent and character, and the rate of premium at which they would insure it. But it is clear that they did not rely upon it as an executory stipulation, by which the plaintiff was to be bound after the contract was entered into. To guard against any increase of risk which might arise from any change in the structure or use of the property, they relied upon a special agreement, designed for that purpose only. If they relied on the warranty, such an agreement was superfluous and useless. In order, therefore, to give effect to both clauses in the contract, it is necessary to construe the warranty as being affirmative only, and not intended to apply to the future condition of the property." *Billings* v. *Tolland Co. Mut. F. Ins. Co.*, 20 Conn. 139 ; *O'Neil* v. *Buffalo F. Ins. Co.*, 3 Comst. 122 ; *Luce* v. *Dorchester Ins. Co.*, 110 Mass. 361.

night to draw a lottery,[1] the use of premises for a single night to shelter the crew of a wrecked vessel,[2] or temporarily permitting a granary and kiln for drying corn to be used for drying bark,[3] was held not such a violation of a condition against an increase of risk as avoided the policy.

Erection of adjoining buildings avoids policy, when.

SEC. 231. When a policy provides that "if the situation or circumstances affecting the risk shall be so altered or changed, by or with the advice, agency or consent of the assured, as to increase the risk thereupon," and "if during the insurance the risk be increased by the erection of buildings, or by the use or occupation of neighboring premises, or otherwise, or if the company shall so elect," it shall be optional with it to terminate the insurance upon refunding a rateable proportion of the insurance, any alteration materially increasing the risk, avoids the policy without any election on the part of the insurers or notice from them. Thus, where under such a policy upon a dwelling-house, the insured erected a furniture factory upon an adjoining lot, with a steam-engine and boiler, the policy was held thereby avoided.[4]

Must be a change or alteration of risk.

SEC. 232. Where a policy provides that "if the situation or circumstances affecting the risk shall be so altered or changed, as to increase the risk," the policy shall be void, the policy is not avoided by the use of the premises for any purpose, or in any mode in or for which they were used when the policy was issued. It is only an *alteration or change* in the risk that renders the policy void, and in the absence of any fraudulent concealment of the situation and character of the risk, the policy is not avoided by the use of the premises in the mode, and for the purposes existing at the time when the contract was entered into. Thus, when the insurers issued a policy upon freight buildings and freight belonging to the Fitchburgh Railroad Co., with a provision similar to that referred to, and it appeared that for some time before, as well as at the time of the insurance, a dummy-engine had been employed near the buildings. It was held that its subsequent use did not avoid the policy, and that, the policy having been made without any written application, they waived all the provisions of the policy requiring " a full, just and true statement of all matters relating to or

[1] *Boardman* v. *Merrimac Ins. Co.*, 8 Cush. (Mass.) 583.
[2] *Sand* v. *Citizens' Ins. Co.*, 2 Gray (Mass.) 221.
[3] *Shaw* v. *Robberds*, 6 Ad. & El. 75.
[4] *Allen* v. *Massasoit Ins. Co.*, 99 Mass. 160.

affecting the risk," [1] and could not set up fraudulent concealment as a ground of defense.[2] When, however, under a policy containing a provision as to change of risk similar to that previously stated, any considerable and deliberate alteration of the building, *not incidental to the ordinary use of the property*, will avoid the policy, although made by a tenant, if made with the knowledge or assent of the insured, and although such change does not materially increase the risk, and did not cause the loss.[3]

Test as to what is an increase of risk.

SEC. 233. In determining the question whether certain changes are material to the risk or not, reference should first be had to the printed lists of hazardous or extra hazardous trades or uses of premises, to ascertain whether the particular use is comprehended under the express terms of either of those heads, as, if it is, the policy is invalidated without further inquiry, because the insured has made them material by expressly excluding them, and the insured having acted *with notice* of his peril, embraced in the contract itself, cannot insist that the peril was not increased. For instance, if a person insured in a non-hazardous class, should turn his building to another non-hazardous use, tho insurer could not complain unless the risk *in fact* was thereby *materially* increased ; but, if he should convert it to a use denominated *in the policy* as hazardous, or extra hazardous, the policy would be void, whether the risk was thereby in fact *materially* increased or not, and the question of increase of risk would not arise, because the parties *have made it material* by stipulating against such use.[4] But when the use is not specially named in the policy, or when any change is effected in the use, not specially stipulated against, the question then arises, whether the change is *in fact material to the risk*, and while the testimony of experts, or persons familiar with the business of insurance is competent upon the question of materiality, their testimony is by no means conclusive. It is for the jury to say whether, in view of all

---

[1] *Commonwealth* v. *Hide and Leather Ins. Co.*, 112 Mass. 136.

[2] *Liberty Hall Association* v. *Housatonic Mut. F. Ins. Co.*, 7 Gray (Mass.) 261 ; *Hall* v. *People's Mut. F. Ins. Co.*, 6 id. 185.

[3] *Lyman* v. *State Mut. F. Ins. Co.*, 14 Allen (Mass.) 329.

[4] *Murdock* v. *Chenango Ins. Co.*, 2 N. Y. 210 ; *U. S. Ins. Co.* v. *Kimberley*, 34 Md. 224 ; *Lounsbury* v. *Protection Ins. Co.*, 9 Conn. 456 ; *Ins. Co. of N. America* v. *McDowell*, 50 Ill. 120 ; *N. E., etc., Ins. Co.* v. *Wetmore*, 32 Ill. 22 ; *Glen* v. *Lewis*, 8 Exchq. 607 ; *Joyce* v. *Maine Ins. Co.*, 45 Me. 168 ; *Diehl* v. *Adams, etc., Ins. Co.*, 59 Penn. St. 443 ; *Schmidt* v. *Peoria M. & F. Ins. Co.*, 41 Ill. 295 ; *Lee* v. *Howards' F. Ins. Co.*, 3 Gray (Mass.) 383 ; *Mead* v. *N. W. Ins. Co.*, 7 N. Y. 530 ; *New Castle F. Ins. Co.* v. *Mac Morran*, 3 Dow. 255.

the circumstances, a reasonably prudent man, under the same circumstances would have been influenced in taking or declining the risk, or would have charged a higher rate of premium therefor. And in determining this question they are to say whether, in view of the evidence, the liability of the property to a destruction from the peril insured against was essentially increased.

Condition will not be extended by implication.

SEC. 234. *Conditions in a policy will not be extended by implication to cover matters not clearly and unmistakably within the meaning of the condition according to the usual and ordinary meaning of the words used.* The insurer has a right to engraft any lawful condition he sees fit, upon the policy, *but he must do so by the use of terms that leave no doubt as to the extent and purport of the condition, and will receive no aid from forced inferences.* Thus,[1] where a policy was issued upon a dwelling-house of the plaintiff's testator, with a condition that work in altering or repairing the building would vitiate the policy, unless permission therefor was indorsed thereon, but five days, however, were allowed each year for incidental repairs, without notice or indorsement, and the plaintiff procured a carpenter's risk for two months for extensive repairs, which were not completed within the two months; and subsequently further repairs were begun by putting on new siding, and *three* days after such repairs were commenced the buildings were burned; it was held that the work being done was embraced in the term "incidental repairs," and did not avoid the policy. ALLEN, J., said: "Insurers have the right to insist upon the due observance of every condition to which the assured has assented by accepting the policy, or otherwise, and to the benefit of every restriction or limitation upon their liability provided for in the contract of insurance, * * care should be taken that a strained and unnatural effect is not given to words and terms to the prejudice of the insured, *and in no case should they be extended by implication so as to embrace cases not clearly or reasonably within the very words of the condition, as such words are ordinarily used and understood.*"

Notice need not be given except when change is material.

SEC. 235. When a policy provides that "*any* change in the risk" not made known at the time of the renewal of the policy, shall avoid it, changes *material* to the risk are intended, and the question, whether a failure to give notice of a change, avoids the renewal, depends upon

---

[1] *Rann* v. *Home Ins. Co.*, 59 N. Y. 387.

whether the risk was *increased* by such change.[1] Thus, in the case last referred to, the defendants issued a policy to the plaintiffs upon their " brick grist and plaster mill," containing such a clause. In the fall, after the policy was issued, the plaintiffs erected a steam power con_ tiguous to the mill, in such a manner *as not to increase the risk in any way.* It was held by the court that neglect to give notice of the change, *did not avoid the policy.* "If," said ANDREWS, J., " there was no increase of risk by reason of the annexation of the steam power, *there was no change of risk within the meaning of the policy*, and no notice was required to be given. * * *If the risk was not increased by changes in the condition of the property, the company had no interest in knowing the fact that they had been made.*" An *additional* risk is not the same as a material increase of risk, for there may be an *additional*, without a material increase of risk.[2]

Where, however, the risk *is* increased, and notice is not given, and the insurer does not *know* of the change or increase, notice must be given or the policy is defeated.[3]

Notice of the change or increase must be given, or knowledge thereof by the insurer or his agent, or a waiver of the breach, must be established, or the policy is void.[4]

---

[1] *Parker* v. *The Arctic F. Ins. Co.*, 59 N. Y. 1.

[2] *Allen* v. *Mutual F. Ins. Co.*, 2 Md. 111.

[3] *Jones* v. *Manufacturers' Ins. Co.*, 8 Cush. (Mass.) 82 ; *Kern* v. *St. Louis, etc., Ins. Co.*, 40 Mo. 19 ; *People's Ins. Co.* v. *Spencer*, 54 Penn. St. 353 ; *Bidwell* v. *N. W. Ins. Co.*, 24 N. Y. 302 ; *Rawley* v. *Empire Ins. Co.*, 40 id. 557. Mere casual conversations, in which the change is talked about with the insurer or his agent, do not, of themselves, establish notice or knowledge of the change, knowledge in fact, or notice of the extent of the change, must be shown. Thus, in *Sykes* v. *Perry Co., etc., Ins. Co.*, 34 Penn. St. 79, the policy provided that, "in case of any alteration, etc., to the building insured, application must be made to the secretary or any agent, who shall examine the premises, and certify his opinion whether the hazard be thereby increased." A steam-engine was put up and used in the premises for nearly a year, and for the purpose of showing notice to the company, defendant's agent testified : "Plaintiff told me, when we were fixing the papers, he contemplated putting an engine into the mill. I told him to leave notice with D., and I would come up. Some time after, D. saw a boiler passing, and supposing it was going into the mill, told the agent." Further evidence was given to show that other persons had talked with the agent about the boiler. It was held, the evidence was insufficient to establish notice ; therefore, insurers were discharged.

[4] In *Howell* v. *Baltimore Eq. Society*, 16 Md. 377, the policy provided that, "when any material alteration or repairs are about to be made in the premises, which increase or vary the risk, information shall be given in writing to the office, and permission obtained from the directors to make such alterations or repairs, and, in default thereof, any loss happening by reason of making such repairs shall not be paid or demanded. Any hazardous business, trade or occupation carried on on the premises, which shall increase the risk, shall in like manner be notified, and permission obtained to carry it on, and, in default thereof, this policy shall be void." Held, any increase of risk occasioned by an alteration

Change of use does not invalidate unless risk is increased, or the use prohibited.

SEC. 236. *The fact that the property is described as of a certain class, or as devoted to a certain use, does not amount to a warranty that such use shall continue,* but merely as a warranty that the property is devoted to such use at the time the insurance is made. Therefore, unless expressly prohibited, *a change of use* does not operate to invalidate the policy, *unless the change increases the risk.*[1]

Change of tenant. Use by tenant, insured not generally responsible for.

SEC. 237. Unless the assured contracts that the same tenants shall continue to occupy the premises during the life of the policy, or that he will give notice of any change in that respect, a change of tenants does not avoid the policy, even though the first tenant was a very prudent and careful man, and the last one *grossly careless.* The assured is not treated as guaranteeing that there will be no change or increase of risk, *as respects the habits of his tenants,* unless special conditions in

---

or occupation of the premises avoided the policy. In *Gardiner* v. *Piscataqua Ins. Co.,* 38 Me. 439, the policy stipulated that "it shall be the duty of insured to give notice to the secretary of any material and manifest increase of the risk which may have happened without his agency or consent, and insurers may agree with insured for such an increase of premium as they deem sufficient to cover such increase of risk, or they may withdraw such insurance altogether; and, if insured shall neglect to give notice, or refuse to comply with the decision of the officers of the company, this policy shall, from that time, be void." A blacksmith shop was erected on land adjoining the property insured, within ten or twelve feet of its south side, used by the owner. About six or eight months thereafter, the building insured was consumed by fire, originating in it, and the blacksmith shop was also burued by fire communicated from the store. About six months thereafter, insurers made an assessment on the policy in suit for losses occurring before the fire. It was held that erecting the blacksmith shop increased the risk and avoided the policy; making and collecting the assessment did not estop insurer from treating the policy as void, because a confirmation does not strengthen a void estate; when a lease is *ipso facto* void by the condition, no acceptance of rent afterwards can give it countenance. In *Kern* v. *St. Louis, etc., Ins. Co.,* 40 Mo. 19, the policy provided that "if the risk shall be materially increased, notice thereof shall be given to the insurer immediately, that the rate of insurance may be increased, or the policy canceled, at the option of either party." Held, if the risk was materially increased, and the insured failed to give notice of it, the policy became absolutely void. In *Harris* v. *Columbian Ins. Co.,* 4 Ohio St. 285, the policy covered a brick flouring mill, engine house, steam-engine, and machinery thereto belonging." The by-laws were made part of the contract, and they stipulated : "If insured shall alter or enlarge a building, or appropriate it to purposes other than those mentioned in the policy, so as to increase the risk, the same shall, *ipso facto,* become void, unless notice thereof shall be given insurer." Insured commenced to make repairs and continued them for about three months; but they were finished a few weeks before the fire occurred. The third story of the mill had been used, a few weeks prior to the loss, for the manufacture of tubs and churns. It was held that the insurers were released. In such cases every increase of risk within the control of the assured, not noticed to the insurer, avoids the policy. *Dodge Co. Mut. Ins. Co.* v. *Rogers,* 12 Wis. 337.

[1] *Wood* v. *Hartford F. Ins. Co.,* 13 Conn. 533 ; *Manley* v. *Ins. Co. of N. America,* 1 Lans. (N. Y.) 20.

respect thereto are incorporated into the policy.[1] In the case last cited, the application contained an inquiry, " for what purpose *and by whom* occupied ? " to which the assured replied, among other things, that the premises were occupied as a tavern stand, by Eliphalet Sears. Sears was shown to be a very careful, prudent man. Before the policy expired, Sears moved from the premises, and a tenant, who was grossly careless, went into the occupancy thereof. " There is nothing," said JEWETT, J., " indicating that Sears would or should continue the occupant during the continuance of the insurance, but on the contrary, if anything may be implied, it may, I think, be implied that a change of tenants might be made. * * It would be unreasonable to imply that the defendants entered into the contract with the expectation that the then tenant was to continue in the occupation during the period of the running of the policy, *in the absence of anything of that sort being indicated in the application, policy, or proposals*." But when the *use* of the premises is changed, by any means within the control of the assured, and the policy provides that it shall be void "if the risk is increased by any means within his control," if he lets the premises to a tenant who devotes them to a hazardous use, it is held that the policy is avoided, whether the assured *knew* that the tenant devoted them to such use or not.[2] But, it would seem that this would or rather should depend very much upon the question whether the assured had the power to prevent the hazardous use, and in Canada it is held that under such a condition the policy is not avoided, unless the assured *consented* to the use or alterations, or they were made with his knowledge, and that the mere fact that he might have entered and terminated the lease, is not decisive of the question, because he is not bound to do it.[3] And under a policy containing such a condition, the erection of a building by the assured, upon an *adjoining lot*, that increases the risk, invalidates the policy,[4] or an addition to the building.[5] But,

[1] *Gates* v. *Madison Co. Mut. Ins. Co.*, 5 N. Y. 469 ; *Joyce* v. *Maine Ins. Co.*, 45 Me. 168.

[2] *Appleby* v. *Fireman's*, etc., *Ins. Co.*, N. Y. 454 ; *Hably* v. *Dana*, 17 Barb. (N. Y.) 111 ; *Sarsfield* v. *Metropolitan Ins. Co.*, 61 id. 479 ; *Witherell* v. *Ins. Co.*, 16 Gray (Mass.) 276 ; *Shepherd* v. *Union*, etc., *Ins. Co.*, 38 N. H. 232 ; *Harvey* v. *Mut. F. Ins. Co.*, 11 U. C. (C. P.) 394. In *Lyon* v. *Commercial Ins. Co.*, the court held that if the assured was inquired of as to the occupancy of the building, and was told that the insurers would not insure if gamblers occupied any part of it, that it was for the jury to say whether gamblers did occupy any part of it, and whether the risk was thereby increased. *Robinson* v. *Mercer*, etc., *Ins. Co.*, 27 N. J. 134; *Jones* v. *Fireman's Fund Ins. Co.*, 51 N. Y. 318; *Williams* v. *People's Ins. Co.*, 57 Id. 274.

[3] *Heneker* v. *British Am. Ass. Co.*, 14 U. C. (C. P.) 57.

[4] *Allen* v. *Massasoit Ins. Co.*, 99 Mass. 160.

[5] *Francis* v. *Somerville*, etc., *Ins. Co.*, 25 N. J. 78 ; *Merriam* v. *Middlesex*, etc., *Ins. Co.*, 21 Pick. (Mass.) 162.

where the policy simply provides that "if the premises shall be used, etc., or the risk shall be increasd," it is held to relate to a use or increase of risk by the assured, *or with his assent,* and does not embrace a hazardous use or increase of risk made by a tenant.[1] Neither does it apply to an increase of risk by strangers, as by the erection of buildings upon adjoining lots,[2] or applying the premises without the consent of the assured, to a prohibited purpose, or one increasing the risk,[3] nor if the policy requires notice of any extraneous changes in the risk to be given, is the policy invalidated by any such change if notice is given. If the assured does not wish to carry the risk, in view of such changes, he must cancel the policy.[4]

Nor, will a change in the occupancy or use of the premises, even though it increases the risk, invalidate it as against a loss resulting at a time when such use has ceased,[5] or, as some of the cases *tend* to hold, *if the loss did not result from such change of the risk,*[6] unless the descrip-

---

[1] *White* v. *Ins. Co.,* 8 Gray (Mass.) 566; *Rice* v. *Tower,* 1 id. 526; *Henneker* v. *British American Ins. Co.,* 14 U. C. (C. P.) 57; *Boardman* v. *Merrimac Mut. Ins. Co.,* 8 Cush. (Mass.) 583. In *Sandford* v. *Mechanics', etc., Ins. Co.,* 12 Cush. (Mass.) 541, the court held that the insured could not be made chargeable for an increase of risk by tenants, unless expressly stipulated against. But where the policy provided that *any* alteration in the building should avoid the policy, it was held that an alteration by a tenant had that effect. *Merriam* v. *Middlesex, etc., Ins. Co.,* 21 Pick. (Mass.) 162. So where the policy stipulates that "any change by the assured, *or others,* etc.", the policy is avoided by whomsoever the change is made. *Shepherd* v. *Union, etc., Ins. Co.,* 38 N. H. 232. In *Miller* v. *Western Farmers', etc., Ins. Co.,* 1 Handy (Ohio) 208, the policy covered a brick tavern-house, with a condition that "in case the premises be altered, changed or used for the pupose of carrying on or exercising therein any trade, business or vocation in the conditions and by-laws annexed, so as to increase the hazard, so long as the same shall be appropriated, applied or used, this policy shall cease, and be of no force or effect." Insurers pleaded that the plaintiff had possession of the building next east and south, and adjoining the building insured; that the same was used by the tenants of the insured, with his consent, for the purpose of manufacturing laths and spokes, which increased the risk of loss by fire to the building insured. Held, the plea was no answer to the action, for in the absence of all stipulations in the contract on the subject, the general maxim, *sic utere tuo, ut alienum non lædas,* must govern the rights of the parties.

[2] *Southern, etc., Ins. Co.* v. *Lewis,* 42 Ga. 587.

[3] *Loud* v. *Citizens' Ins. Co., ante; Shaw* v. *Robberds, ante.* In *Rice* v. *Tower,* 1 Gray (Mass.) 566, the sheriff levied upon the goods of assured and took possession of the building, and sold goods at auction therein. Held, that although the policy prohibited the use of the building for any other purpose than that named in it, the policy was not invalidated unless the risk was increased thereby.

[4] *Commercial Ins. Co.* v. *Mehlman,* 48 Ill. 313.

[5] *New Eng. F. and M. Ins. Co.* v. *Wetmore,* 32 Ill. 245; 4 Ben. F. I. C. 656; *Joyce* v. *Maine Ins. Co.,* 45 Me. 168; 4 Ben. F. I. C. 369; *Lounsbury* v. *Protection Ins. Co.,* 8 Conn. 459; *U. S. Ins. Co.* v. *Kimberley,* 34 Md. 234; 6 Am. Rep. 325. See contra, *Harris* v. *Columbian, etc., Ins. Co.,* 4 Ohio St. 285; *Mead* v. *N. W. Ins. Co.,* 7 N. Y. 530.

[6] In *Schmidt* v. *Peoria, etc., Ins. Co.,* 41 Ill. 295; 5 Ben. F. I. C. 90, the policy covered a tannery in the city of Chicago. The policy contained these words: "No fire in or about said building, except one under kettle securely imbedded

tion of the risk amounts to a continuing warranty, or the change in
the risk has in some manner contributed to the loss. But, while it is

in masonry (used for heating water), and made perfectly secure against accidents." The policy was issued on the 16th September, 1864. It was proved that
the building was destroyed by fire in March, 1865, and that, at the time of the
fire, there were two stoves in the building, one up stairs and the other on the first
floor. It was also proved that there had been no fire in the stove on the first floor
for eight days previous to the destruction of the building. In the stove up stairs
a fire had been kindled at six o'clock in the morning and extinguished at eight or
half-past eight in the morning, and was not again rekindled. The fire occurred
about eleven o'clock the following night. "It is contended by the appellee," said
LAWRENCE, J., "that the words in the policy above quoted are to be taken as a
warranty, on the part of the assured, that there shall be no fire during the continuance of the policy, except the one under the kettle, and that a breach of the
so-called warranty avoids the policy. In behalf of the appellants, it is insisted
that these words are, what is called by some writers upon insurance, an affirmative as distinct from a promissory warranty, and are to be construed as referring
to the condition of the property at the time the policy was issued. It is a question upon which the authorities differ; but, in view of the fact that insurance
companies dictate the language of their own policies, which is, therefore, to be
most strongly construed against themselves, and can, if they wish, insert a stipulation which in terms refers to the future use of the property, and do, by an
express provision in this, as in, we presume, all policies, relieve themselves from
all liability in case the risk is actually increased, we are inclined to adopt the
ruling of those cases which hold that these words are to be construed in reference
to the then condition of the property. *Smith* v. *Mechanics' Fire Ins. Co.*, 32 N.
Y, 399; *O'Neil* v. *The Buffalo Ins. Co.*, 3 N. Y. 122; *Catlin* v. *The Springfield
Ins. Co.*, 1 Sumn. 435; *Blood* v. *Howard Fire Ins. Co.*, 12 Cush. 472; *Rafferty* v.
New Brunswick Fire Ins. Co., 3 Harrison, 480. With this construction of that
clause, no violation of it is shown. There is, however, another clause in the
policy, which the company invokes for its protection, as follows: 'If, after insurance is effected, either by the original policy or by the renewal thereof, the risk
be increased by any means, or occupied in any way so as to render the risk more
hazardous than at the time of insurance, such insurance shall be void and of none
effect.' This is a very material provision in the policy, and should not have
been omitted from the abstract furnished by counsel for appellant. This language admits of no controversy as to its meaning, and the only question under it
is, was there such increased risk in consequence of these stoves at the time of the
fire? This court held, in *New England F. & M. Ins. Co.* v. *Wetmore*, 32 Ill. 245,
that the true construction of a clause like this was, that the policy became inoperative only while the increased risk was in existence, and when it terminated
the liability of the company would recommence. The instruction asked by the
defendant on this point, and given by the court, was in harmony with this ruling;
but, on the trial, the defendant was permitted, against the objections of the plaintiffs, to call insurance agents as experts, and ask them the following question:
'Q. From your experience and knowledge of your business as an insurance
agent, and of insurance, do you think that the increase of the number of fires in
a building does or does not increase the risk of fire in that building?' Neither
this question, nor any of the evidence given under it, touched the true point in
the case.
The point for the consideration of the jury was not whether an increase of the
number of fires in a building·does or does not ordinarily increase the risk, *but
whether, in the case then before the court, the risk to the building at the time it was
destroyed, at eleven o'clock at night, was or was not increased by the two stoves, in
one of which there had been no fire for eight days, and in the other none after eight
and a half o'clock of the preceding morning.* Was the risk to this particular building at the time it was burned greater in consequence of the presence of these
stoves, placed as they were and used in the manner shown by the witnesses?
This was a question of fact to be passed upon by the jury, not in reference to the
opinions of insurance agents as to the general effect of an increase of fires, but in
reference to the facts of this particular case." See also, *Newhall* v. *Union, etc.,
Ins. Co.*, 52 Me. 180.
29

true that the tendency of the cases, and perhaps justly, is to hold *that
the policy is only suspended, and not in fact vitiated by the increase of risk
during its continuance, and that it is revived as an operative instrument
when such increase in the hazard ceases, yet it is not necessary that the loss
should have resulted from such hazardous use.* It is enough if the prem-
*ises were devoted to a more hazardous use, that materially increased the risk,
at the time of their destruction by fire, whether the fire resulted as a consequence thereof or not,*[1] *because it is a breach of a condition of the policy.*
In a New Brunswick case, previously cited,[2] in a policy upon a vessel,
there was a prohibition against carrying more than twenty-five pounds
of gunpowder, and a provision that the policy should be void if, *at any
time,* there should be more than that quantity on board. The vessel
was destroyed by fire, *and when the fire broke out* there were one hun-

---

[1]*May* v. *Buckeye, etc., Ins. Co.* In *Merriam* v. *Middlesex, etc., Ins. Co.,* 21
Pick. (Mass.) 162, the tenants of the assured put stoves in the building, *which
increased the risk, but did not cause the loss,* but the court held that the policy
was void. *Lyman* v. *State Mut. F. Ins. Co.,* 14 Allen (Mass.) 329; 5 Ben. F. I.
C. 106. In *Glen* v. *Lewis,* 8 Eng. L. & Eq. 364; 8 Exchq. 311, an insurance
against fire was effected on certain premises; the policy containing, among other
things, the following conditions: The persons making insurances to give an accurate
description of the buildings, etc., and if there should be used therein any steam
engine, stove, etc., or any description of fire-heat other than common fireplaces,
etc., or any process of fire-heat be carried on therein, the same to be noticed and
allowed in the policy, otherwise the policy to be void. In case of any circumstance happening after an insurance, whereby the risk should be increased, the
assured to give notice in writing to the insurers, and the same previous to a loss,
to be allowed by indorsement on the policy, otherwise the policy to be void. In
case of any alteration being made in a building insured, etc., or of any steam-
engine, stove, etc., or any other description of fire-heat being introduced, or of
any trade, business, process or operation being carried on, or goods deposited
therein, not comprised in the original insurance, or allowed by indorsement
thereon, etc., notice thereof must be given; and every such alteration must be
allowed by indorsement on the policy, and any further premium which the alteration may occasion must be paid; and, unless such notice be duly given, such
premium paid and such indorsement made, no benefit will arise to the assured in
case of loss. The assured, who was a cabinetmaker, placed a small engine on
the premises, with a boiler attached, and used it in a heated state for the purpose of turning a lathe, not in the course of his business, but for the purpose of
ascertaining, by experiment, whether it was worth his while to buy it, to be used
in that business. After this engine had been on the premises for several days, a
fire happened, and it was held that the policy was avoided, *and that whether the
fire was occasioned in consequence of the steam engine being worked or not was immaterial.* *Dodge Co., etc., Ins. Co.* v. *Rogers,* 12 Wis. 337; *Girard Ins. Co.* v. *Stephenson,* 37 Penn. St. 293; *Harris* v. *Columbian Ins. Co.,* 4 Ohio St. 285; *Jefferson Ins.
Co.* v. *Cotheal,* 7 Wend. (N. Y.) 72; *Howell* v. *Baltimore Eq. Soc.,* 16 Md. 377; *Appleby*
v. *Astor Ins. Co.,* 54 N. Y. 253; *Perry Co. Ins. Co.* v. *Stewart,* 20 Penn. St. 45;
Fabyan v. *Union, etc., Ins. Co.,* 33 N. H. 203; *Sarsfield* v. *Metropolitan Ins. Co.,*
61 Barb. (N. Y.) 479; *Gardinier* v. *Piscatauqua, etc., Ins. Co.,* 38 Me. 439; *Appleby*
v. *Firemans' Ins. Co.,* 45 id. 454; *Sykes* v. *Perry Co., etc., Ins. Co.,* 34 Penn. St.
79; *Allen* v. *Massasoit Ins. Co.,* 99 Mass. 160; *Kern* v. *St. Louis, etc., Ins. Co.,*
40 Mo. 19; *Shepherd* v. *Union, etc., Ins. Co.,* 38 N. H. 232; *Francis* v. *Somerville, etc., Ins. Co.,* 25 N. J. 78; *Lomas* v. *British, etc., Ass. Co.,* 22 U. C. (Q. B.)
310; *Dittmer* v. *Germania Ins. Co.,* 23 La. An. 458.

[2]*Faulkner* v. *Central F. Ins. Co.,* 1 Kerr (N. B.) 279.

dred pounds of gunpowder on board, *but it in no wise contributed to the loss, as it was thrown overboard as soon as the fire was discovered,* but the court held that the fact that it did not contribute to the loss was of no account, *as the policy was invalidated by its presence on board when the fire broke out, because it was a breach of one of the conditions of the policy, and the breach continued up to the time when the loss occurred.*[1]

The usages and incidents of the risk to be considered.

SEC. 238. In determining as to whether or not there has been an increase of risk, *it is essential to ascertain what the parties must be presumed to have contemplated when the insurance was made, and this involves a consideration of the usages and incidents of the risk, because if the change was one warranted by the usages or usual incidents of the risk, although it in fact increased the risk, it does not come within the prohibition, because it is presumed to have been contemplated by the parties.* Thus, a policy upon a dwelling-house, unoccupied when the policy was issued, would not be invalidated by its subsequent occupancy, and setting up therein stoves and other appliances usually employed to heat the building, nor by using lights therein not expressly prohibited by the policy, because such things are incident to the use of dwellings. This was well illustrated in a Maryland case,[2] in which the policy covered "a two-story brick building used as a sulphuric acid factory." The policy contained a stipulation that any alteration or change in the risk increasing the hazard should invalidate the insurance. The assured subsequently erected a shed between two buildings *for the purpose of protecting the machinery and apparatus employed in the building for the purposes specified.* The insurer defended against a loss upon the ground that the shed increased the risk and operated as a breach of the conditions of the policy; but the court held that, even though the risk thereby was increased, yet, *if the erection of the shed was necessary and proper for the protection of the machinery and apparatus,* it would not affect the liability of the insurer; thus establishing the doctrine that *that which is necessary for the protection of the property or its preservation, or which is usual or incident to it for the purposes for which it is employed when insured, must be regarded as within the contemplation of the parties and excepted from the operation of the stipulation.*[3] A build-

---

[1] See also, *Witherell* v. *City, etc., Ins. Co.,* 16 Gray (Mass.) 276.

[2] *Washington F. Ins. Co.* v. *Davidson,* 30 Md. 91.

[3] *Billings* v. *Tolland Ins. Co.,* 20 Conn. 139; *Dobson* v. *Sotheby,* 1 M. & M.; 6 Ad. & El. In *New York* v. *Hamilton Ins. Co.,* 10 Bos. (N. Y.) 537, a policy was issued upon a building known as the Crystal Palace, which, with the public exhibitions that it had been erected for and to which for a number of years it had

ing insured as a dwelling-house may be used as a *boarding-house*
without invalidating the policy, unless boarding-houses are classed as

---

been exclusively devoted, were matters of great public notoriety and interest;
and it was described in the policy as the building lately owned by the Association for the Exhibition of the Industry of all Nations, and the defendants also
insured certain property in the building as "belonging to exhibitors;" it was
held that they must be deemed to have been acquainted with the business to
which the building was appropriated, the nature of the objects exhibited, and
the means employed to exhibit them, *and to have intended to include in the risk
such business and the employment of all such usual means; and that the use of fire
and steam for the purpose of the exhibition of machinery, and the keeping of a
restaurant with liquors and cigars, and a kitchen with ovens, were all to be deemed
parts of the exhibition, and did not defeat the insurance.* Under the usual provision in a policy of insurance that the conditions annexed are "to be resorted
to in order to explain the rights and obligations of the parties thereto, in all cases
not herein otherwise specially provided for," such conditions do not define the
rights and obligations of the parties under any contingency provided for in the
body of the policy. Hence, where a clause in the body of the policy provides
that the insurance shall be suspended during any increase of the risk from specified causes, and the conditions annexed provide that the policy shall become void
by any increase of the risk, *an increase of risk, such as is specified in the
clause in the body of the policy,* does not avoid but merely suspends the policy.
"*Where,*" said ROBERTSON, J., "*a policy of insurance specifies the uses to which
the premises are applied, a mere increase of risk does not avoid the policy, unless it
arises from something else than their appropriation to the uses which are contemplated and covered by the policy.*" See also, *N. Y.* v. *Exchange Ins. Co.,* 9 Bos.
(N. Y.) 424, where it was held that where a building was constructed and used
for the purposes of an exhibition of industry or fair, *and the defendants, knowing
its use,* had several times insured its owners, or lessees, in respect to it, and the
plaintiffs, subsequently becoming its owners, procured the defendants to insure
them in respect to it, the plaintiffs had a right, after obtaining such insurance, *to
occupy and use the building for the same purposes;* but it seems that the use *must
be an incident of the building, or such as the insurer, under the circumstances, is
bound to know will be continued.* Thus, where the insurer had previously insured
a building, and knew that there were no gas fixtures in it, and that the tenant at that
time used spirit gas, it was held that they were not thereby bound to know that
another tenant would also use spirit gas, because the use was not necessarily an
incident of the risk. *Minzesheimer* v. *Continental Ins. Co.,* 5 J. & S. (N. Y.) 332.
See also, *Robinson* v. *Mercer Co., etc., Ins. Co.,* 27 N. J. 134. So, too, if there is an
application, the description of the use to which the premises are to be put, contained
therein, will prevail over a previous use. *State, etc., Ins. Co.* v. *Arthur,* 30 Penn.
St. 315. In *Lounsbury* v. *Protection Ins. Co.,* 8 Conn. 439, a policy was issued on a
building occupied as a manufactory of hat bodies, and "on the privilege for all the
process of said business." The conditions specified, among occupations denominated extra-hazardous, "carpenters, in their own shops, or in buildings erecting
or repairing." It was held that the use of a room in the building as a shop, *for
the purpose of repairing the machinery necessary for the business of making hat
bodies, was protected by the policy* In *Washington, etc., Ins. Co.,* v. *Mechanics'
etc., Ins. Co.,* 5 Ohio St. 450, it was held that where a policy of reinsurance was
on the stock of flour, grain and cooperage contained in the stone and brick steam
flouring mill, with cement roof, detached from other buildings, and the policy
prohibited the buildings or any part from being used for any trade declared
hazardous, among which were mills and manufactories and mechanical operations
requiring fire heat; and it was claimed that the use of a kiln-drying corn-meal
mill, requiring fire heat in the building, avoided the policy; it was held that,
whether a kiln-drying corn-meal mill *was an ordinary incident or usual append-
age of the business of a steam flouring mill,* was a proper question of fact for the
jury, and was not to be determined by the court, and *that if such kiln-drying
apparatus in a corn-meal mill is not a necessary incident to the ordinary mode of
carrying on a steam flouring mill, carrying on such a business in such flouring mill
would avoid the policy.* The court also held that the underwriter, in entering

hazardous;[1] and so, generally, unless the policy stipulates expressly against a certain use of the premises, if the use is a usual incident of the property for the purposes for which it was insured, or if it was necessary or proper for the protection of the property, the policy is not thereby invalidated. *If the particular use is stipulated against expressly*, of course it is prohibited.[2]

Condition an independent one.

SEC. 239. The condition in reference to an increase of risk is an independent one, and in no measure dependent upon the list of hazards annexed to the policy, or the conditions in reference thereto. *If the risk is increased in any manner*, the condition is violated. Thus, in a Louisiana case,[3] the plaintiff insured his stock of groceries, wines and liquors, and to the extent of $500 on his fixtures and furniture, all contained in a frame shingle building in the town of Carrollton. Eight months afterward the premises were entirely destroyed by fire, causing the total loss of his stock in trade, furniture, etc., which, as alleged, were worth, at the time the fire occurred, over $2,500. The

---

into a contract of insurance on a mechanical establishment, can be presumed to insure only against risks *arising from the usual mode of carrying on such establishment ;* and *if an invention materially increasing the risk* is introduced into the building, it will avoid the policy. The rule is well expressed in *Hall* v. *Ins. Co. of N. America*, 58 N. Y. 292, in which it was held that where a policy is issued upon the materials used in a business, *it includes and authorizes the use of all such materials as are in ordinary use in the business, although by the printed clauses of the policy the keeping or use thereof upon the premises is prohibited, and although other materials might be substituted therefor*. *Langdon* v. *Equitable Ins. Co.*, 1 Hall (N. Y.) 226 ; *Duncan* v. *Sun F. Ins. Co.*, 6 Wend. (N. Y.) 488 ; *Franklin, etc., Ins. Co.* v. *Brock*, 57 Penn. St. 74 ; *Stetson* v. *Mass. Ins. Co.*, 4 Mass. 330 ; *Peoria F. & M. Ins. Co.* v. *Hall*, 12 Mich. 202 ; *Harper* v. *Albany City Ins. Co.*, 17 N. Y. 194 ; *Steinback* v. *Lafayette Ins. Co.*, 54 N. Y. 90 ; *Wood* v. *Protection Ins. Co.*, 3 Conn. 533 ; 2 Ben. F. I. C. 24 ; *Moore* v. *Protection Ins. Co.*, 29 Me. 97 ; *United States Ins. Co.* v. *Kimberly*, 34 Md. 224 ; *O'Neil* v. *Buffalo F. Ins. Co.*, 3 N. Y. 122 ; *Joyce* v. *Maine Ins. Co.*, 45 Me. 168 ; *Whitmarsh* v. *Charter Oak F. Ins. Co.*, 2 Allen (Mass.) 581 ; *Delonguemare* v. *Tradesman's Ins. Co.*, 2 Hall (N. Y. S. C.) 589 ; *Leggett* v. *Ætna Ins. Co.*, 10 Rich. (S. C.) 202 ; *Phœnix Ins. Co.* v. *Taylor*, 5 Min. 492 ; *Citizens' Ins. Co.* v. *McLaughlin*, 53 Penn. St. 425 ; *Goss* v. *Citizens' Ins. Co.*, 18 La. An. 97 ; *Bryant* v. *Poughkeepsie, etc., Ins. Co.*, 17 N. Y. 200 ; *Wall* v. *Howard Ins. Co.*, 14 Barb (N. Y.) 383 ; *Franklin F. Ins. Co.* v. *Chicago Ice Co.*, 36 Md. 102 ; *Com.* v. *Hide & Leather Ins. Co.*, 112 Mass. 136 ; *Niagara F. Ins. Co.* v. *De Graff*, 12 Mich. 124 ; *Franklin F. Ins. Co.* v. *Updegraff*, 43 Penn. St. 350 ; *Pindar* v. *Kings Co. Ins. Co.*, 36 N. Y. 648 ; *Harper* v. *N. Y. City Ins. Co.*, 22 id. 441 ; *Viele* v. *Germania Ins. Co.*, 26 Iowa, 9 ; *Jackson* v. *Ætna Ins Co.*, 16 B. Mon. (Ky.) 242 ; *Archer* v. *Merchants', etc., Ins. Co.*, 43 Mo. 434. *Gates* v. *Madison, etc., Ins. Co.*, 5 N. Y. 469 ; *Stebbins* v. *Globe Ins. Co.*, 2 Hall (N. Y.) 632 ; *Stokes* v. *Cox*, 1 H. & N. 531.

[1] *New England F. & M. Ins. Co.* v. *Wetmore*, 31 Ill. 221 ; *Manley* v. *Ins. Co. of N. America*, 1 Lans. (N. Y.) 20.

[2] *Townsend* v. *N. W. Ins. Co.*, 18 N. Y. 268 ; *Appleby* v. *Astor Ins. Co.*, 54 N. Y. 253 ; *Franklin Ins. Co.* v. *Chicago Ice Co.*, 36 Md. 102.

[3] *Dettmer* v. *Germania Ins. Co.*, 23 La. An. 458 ; 8 Am. Rep. 600.

defendants, being the insurers, were sued on the policy of insurance for $2,500, with interest, etc.

The defense was, that Dittmer, after he had effected the insurance, stored in the premises a quantity of unbaled hay, and kept it there until the fire, thereby acting in bad faith, and materially increasing the risk of the defendants, in violation of the contract by which he was insured, rendering, according to its conditions, the policy null and void. The defendants had judgment in the court below, and the plaintiffs appealed. Upon appeal, the judgment was affirmed. TAL-LIAFERRO, J., saying, " It is in proof that, after the policy was taken out, Dittmer, the plaintiff, permitted one of his neighbors to store within the insured premises a large quantity of loose, unbaled hay. It seems to have been put in the upper story of the building insured, and to have been placed there about three months before the fire occurred. The witness Lieble, who owned it, says that there were about four thousand pounds of the hay in the building at the time of the fire, and that it was perfectly dry. The plaintiff contends that, as ' hay pressed in bales' is expressly named and classed as hazardous, and excepted in the conditions annexed to the policy, and unbaled or loose hay not being so classed and specified, it cannot be considered as excepted, and that the policy is not thereby void. An express condition stipulated by the insurers is, that the plaintiff should not in any manner increase the danger and risk of fire on his premises during the continuance of the policy. The insurance company was not informed of the storing of the hay in the building insured, and no application was made for the assent of the company to its being so stored, and no opportunity offered the insurers to require, as a condition for continuing the policy in force, a higher or increased premium."

Change of business.

SEC. 240. A change of business does not work a forfeiture of the policy, if the new business does not increase the risk, and is not prohibited by the terms of the policy.[1] The condition will be construed strictly, and in favor of the assured so far as the language used will warrant. This was well illustrated in an English case often cited,[2] in which a policy was issued upon some cotton mills, millwrights' works, going gear therein, engine-house adjoining, and the steam-engine

---

[1] *Reynolds* v. *Commerce Ins. Co.*, *ante; Smith* v. *Merchants', etc., Ins. Co.*, 32 N. Y. 399.

[2] *Whitehead* v. *Price*, 2 Cr. M. & R. 447.

therein.   The policy described the buildings as "brick-built and slated, warmed exclusively by steam, lighted by gas, etc., worked by the steam-engine above mentioned; in the tenure of one firm, only standing apart from all other mills, *and worked by day only*." The mills were only worked by day, but the steam-engine and some of the gear was worked by night to operate other mills, the shafting used in conveying such power passing through the plaintiff's mills.   The court held that the words "worked by day only," related to the working of the mills only, and that the fact that the engine and shafting was kept in motion, did not avoid the policy or operate as a breach of any of its conditions.

No offset of benefits against increase.

SEC. 241. If the risk is materially increased in *one* respect, the fact that it was lessened in another, does not save a forfeiture, when the policy stipulates against *any* change therein increasing the risk. There can be no offset of benefits.   This question was raised in a Canada case,[1] in which it appeared that the assured took out from the building insured a furnace that was there when the insurance was made, and built an addition to the building, and placed a boiler therein, in which steam was generated and driven into the main building.   The jury found that the *external* risk was increased by the change, but that the *internal* risk was *materially lessened* thereby, and that the changes had *diminished the risk generally*.   The court held that this was equivalent to a verdict for the defendant, *because if there was an increase of risk in any respect, the policy was invalidated, without reference to its general effect upon the risk*, and there can be no doubt of the soundness of this doctrine.[2]

Experts.

SEC. 242. The opinion of experts, as to whether the non-occupation of a building increases the risk, is not admissible, being a matter within common knowledge.[3]   But, whether such a change in the occu-

---

[1] *Lomas* v. *British American Association Co.*, 22 U. C. (Q. B.) 310; *Meacker* v. *British American Association*, 14 U. C. (C. P.) 57.

[2] In *Dale* v. *Gore District Mut. F. Ins. Co.*, 15 U. C. (C. P.) 175, an apparently contrary rule was adopted. In that case the assured erected a new chimney, which the jury found increased the risk in some respects, while in other respects it diminished the risk. The court held, that if *upon the whole* the risk was diminished, the policy was not invalidated thereby. An examination of this case, however, discloses the fact that the language of the policy differed materially from the cases cited in the last note, and was distinguished from those cases upon that ground.

[3] *Luce* v. *Dorchester Ins. Co.*, 105 Mass. 297; 7 Am. Rep. 522; *Mulvy* v. *Mohawk Valley Ins. Co.*, 5 Gray (Mass.) 541; *Hartford Protection Ins. Co.* v. *Harmer*, 2 Ohio St. 452; *Lyman* v. *State Ins. Co.*, 14 Allen (Mass.) 327.

pation is material to the risk, may sometimes be tested by the question whether underwriters generally would charge a higher premium,[1] but evidence as to *a special custom of the insurers* in reference to a given matter, is not admissible, *unless it is also shown that it was known to the assured.*[2] But evidence of a *general custom* among insurers may be shown.[3]

Rate of premium not always the test.

SEC. 243. It has sometimes been thought that the test as to whether or not an increase of risk had been effected, is, whether with the alterations alleged, a higher rate of premium would have been charged; but this is, in reality, only one of the considerations involved, and *by no means the decisive one.* It is for the jury, and not for the insurers, to say whether the risk *was really increased.* The fact that the insurer would have charged a greater rate of premium for the risk as altered, establishes the fact that *they* regarded the risk as greater, but the jury may, from the evidence, believe that the risk *was not increased,* or even that it was lessened by the change, and it is for them to find the fact, and they are to find, *not how the insurers regarded the alteration,* for if they desired to guard against the particular change they should specially have stipulated against it, *but, whether in point of fact the danger to the property insured, from destruction by the peril insured against was increased by the change.*[4] If so, the policy is void. If not, it remains operative.[5]

---

[1] GRAY, J., in *Luce* v. *Dorchester Ins. Co., ante; Merriam* v. *Middlesex Ins. Co.,* 21 Pick. (Mass.) 162; *Webber* v. *Eastern R. R. Co.,* 2 Metc. (Mass.) 147; *Howes* v. *N. E. Ins. Co.,* 2 Curtis (U. S. C. C.) 229; *Mulvy* v. *Mohawk Ins Co., ante; McLannahan* v. *Universal Ins. Co.,* 1 Pet. (U. S.) 170.

[2] *Hartford Protection Ins. Co.* v. *Harmer, ante; Berkshire Woolen Co.* v. *Proctor,* 7 Cush. (Mass.) 417.

[3] *Luce* v. *Dorchester Ins. Co., ante.*

[4] In *Williams* v. *Peoples' F. Ins. Co.,* 57 N. Y. 274, the policy covered a quantity of merchandise, and contained a condition that if the risk should be increased by any means whatever within the control of the assured, the policy should be void. It appeared that the assured, for several months before the fire, kept, in the room where the merchandise was, a jug containing crude petroleum, which he used himself for medicinal purposes; also that the petroleum was not the cause of and had nothing to do with the fire, but evidence was given tending to show that its presence was dangerous, and tended to increase the risk. The court refused to charge that if the use of the petroleum increased the risk, the plaintiff could not recover. This was held erroneous as it was a question of fact for the jury whether the risk was actually and materially increased, and if so, it avoided the policy. Another condition of the policy prohibited the keeping of petroleum for sale or storage, or its use for lighting, except by permission. It was held that, while this condition did not prohibit the keeping for the purpose for which the petroleum was used, it did not permit it, if, thereby, the risk was

[5] *Commercial Ins. Co.* v *Mohlman, ante.*

Ordinary repairs does not come within the stipulation.

Sec. 244. Ordinary repairs may be made without a builder's risk, and do not operate as a violation of a condition against an increase of the risk, and even though the policy provides that "the working of carpenters, roofers, tin-smiths, gas-fitters, plumbers, or other mechanics in buildings, altering, *or repairing* the premises named in this policy, will vitiate the same, unless permission for such work be indorsed in writing hereon," it is held not to relate to *ordinary, casual, necessary repairs, even though such repairs necessitate the keeping of carpenters constantly at work,* but as prohibiting such hazardous use of the building as arises from placing it in the possession or under the control of workmen for re-building, alterations or repairs.[1] In the case last referred to the policy contained such a provision, and the president of the plaintiff company having testified that he always kept a crew of men and a carpenter or two about the building the year round, *and was constantly making repairs,* the defendants insisted that thereby the assured had forfeited its right to recover under the policy ; but the court held otherwise. "To place upon it such a construction," said Bartol, C.J., "as contended for by the appellant, would defeat the intent of the parties, and be repugnant to the written clause of the policy *insuring the building;* which, looking at its size, structure and use, must have reasonably contemplated the necessity for such repairs as the witness described, as indispensible to the proper conduct of the appellee's business. The evidence shows that the building was two hundred and sixteen feet long and one hundred and forty feet wide ; that the height, from the top of the sill to the under sill of the plate, was twenty-six feet ; that the walls were of joists three by six inches, hollow two feet thick, filled in with tan ; the materials all wood, bound with iron. There was a balcony round the upper part of the house, and an inclined plane or tramway, fourteen feet wide, extending from the lake to the plate of the ice-house, on which the ice was dragged

---

increased, and did not, in any way, affect the condition upon that subject. The policy also contained a clause authorizing the company, in case the premises should be occupied or used so as to increase the risk, to terminate the insurance upon notice, and return of the unearned premium. It was held that this condition was intended to provide for increase of risk by the acts of third persons over whom the insured had no control, and did not affect the clause providing against increase of risk by act of the insured. *Curry* v. *Com. Ins. Co.,* 10 Pick. (Mass.) 535 ; *Jolly* v. *Ins. Co.,* 1 H. & J. (Md.) 295 ; *Schmidt* v. *Peoria, etc., Ins. Co., ante; Lyman* v. *State, etc., Ins. Co., ante; Rice* v. *Tower,* 1 Gray (Mass.) 426 ; *Curry* v. *Com. Ins. Co.,* 10 Pick. (Mass.) 535 ; *Allen* v. *Massasoit Ins. Co.,* 99 Mass. 160.

[1] Bartol, C.J., in *Franklin F. Ins. Co.* v. *Chicago Ice Co.,* 32 Md. 102 ; 11 Am. Rep. 469 ; *Barrett* v. *Jeremy,* 3 Exchq. 535.

up by horse power. The capacity of the house was *twenty-four thousand tons* of ice. It is very obvious that a building so constructed would necessarily be constantly liable to be injured and damaged by the use for which it was intended, rendering it indispensible for the prosecution of the business of the appellee, that breakages should be repaired as they occurred; all of which was known to the appellants, and will be presumed to have been in their contemplation at the time the contract was made, and permitted by the written terms of the policy insuring the premises as an ice-house." [1]

The right to repair buildings is incident to the ownership and use of the property, and alterations which do not increase the risk, as well as ordinary repairs may be made without affecting the validity of the policy.[2] House building or repairing prohibited in a policy, refers to such occupations *as a business*, and not to necessary repairs made upon the buildings insured,[3] and although in making such repairs, hazardous articles are introduced into the building, as oils, turpentine, paints, etc., the insurer is not relieved from liability if such articles are necessary incidents of the repairs in progress,[4] or even though the facilities for extinguishing fires, described in the policy, are thereby temporarily suspended.[5] Even where *alterations*, materially increasing the risk, are made, and alterations are prohibited in the policy, yet, if the insurer knew that they were in progress when the policy was made,[6] or that they were contemplated,[7] the jury may find a waiver, or assent to such alterations. Where alterations are made by a tenant, the insurance is not avoided, unless the prohibition is broad enough to cover all alterations by whomsoever made, unless they are made with the assent of the assured, and the fact that he assented to some alterations being made, does not necessarily defeat the liability of the insurer. It is for the jury to say *whether such extensive alterations as those made were contemplated by the parties*.[8] But, while it is true that trifling changes in the risk, or ordinary repairs may be made even where the policy prohibits all alterations or repairs without the assent

---

[1] *Rann* v. *Home Ins. Co.*, 59 N. Y. 387.

[2] *Dorn* v. *Germania Ins. Co.*, 8 Chicago Legal News, 156.

[3] *Grant* v. *Howard Ins. Co.*, 5 Hill (N. Y.) 10.

[4] *O'Niel* v. *Buffalo Ins. Co.*, 3 N. Y. 122; *Billings* v. *Tolland, etc., Ins. Co.*, Conn.

[5] *Townsend* v. *N. W. Ins. Co.*, 18 N. Y. 168.

[6] *Hotchkiss* v. *Germania Ins. Co*, 5 Hun (N. Y.) 90.

[7] *Perry Co. Ins. Co.* v. *Stewart*, 19 Penn. St. 45.

[8] *Paddleford* v. *Providence, etc., Ins. Co.*, 3 R. I. 102; *Sanford* v. *Mechanics, etc., Ins. Co.*, 12 Cush. (Mass.) 541.

of the company, yet *this does not cover material* alterations or *extraordi_ nary repairs.*[1]

Burden of proving increase on insurer.

SEC. 245. The insurer must prove the increase of risk,[2] and the mere fact that a change in the risk is made does not make out his defense. *He must show by a fair preponderance of proof that the change increased the risk.*[3] If the use to which the premises were being devoted when the loss occurred was prohibited, the fact that the insurer *knew* of such use does not save the forfeiture. He has a right to rely upon it that the assured will perform the conditions of the contract, or that, if he fails to do so, he waives the benefits of the policy.[4] By devoting the premises to such use, the policy is suspended during its continuance, without reference to the question whether the risk was increased or not.[5] But it must be a *change* of the risk by something permanent or habitual. *A mere temporary use does not come within the prohibition.*[6]

Material alterations or changes.

SEC. 246. When the assured devotes the premises to a use *prohibited in the policy*, or makes an alteration or change therein *classed as hazardous, it is a material alteration or change*, and *ipso facto* invalidates it. In such cases, the question of materiality or increase of risk is not involved. The insurer has made the change material by prohibiting it in the policy, and the only question involved is, whether the change comes within the prohibition.[7] But in such cases, if the *hazardous use*

---

[1] *Howell* v. *Baltimore Equitable Society*, 16 Md. 377 ; *Harris* v. *Columbian Mut. Ins. Co.*, 4 Ohio St. 285 ; *Dodge Co. Mut. Ins. Co.* v. *Rogers*, 12 Wend. (N. Y.) 337 ; *Kern* v. *South St. Louis, etc.. Ins. Co.*, 40 Mo. 19 ; *Allen* v. *Massasoit Ins. Co.*, 99 Mass. 160 ; *Rann* v. *Home Ins. Co.*, 59 N. Y. 387.

[2] *Newman* v. *Springfield F. & M. Ins. Co.*, 17 Minn. 123 ; *Ritter* v. *Sun, etc., Ins. Co.*, 40 Mo. 40.

[3] *Lattaurus* v. *Farmers' Mut. F. Ins. Co.*, 3 Houst. (Del.) 404.

[4] *Dewees* v. *Manhattan Ins. Co.*, 35 N. J. 366.

[5] *Ditmer* v. *Germania Ins. Co.*, 23 La. An. 458 ; *United States Ins. Co.* v. *Kimberley*, 34 Md. 227.

[6] *Loud* v. *Citizens' Ins. Co.*, 2 Gray (Mass.) 221 ; *Gates* v. *Madison Co. Ins. Co.*, 5 N. Y. 469 ; *Leggett* v. *Ætna Ins. Co.*, 10 Rich. (S. C.) 202 ; *Moore* v. *Protection Ins. Co.*, 31 Me. 223 ; *Shaw* v. *Robberds*, 6 Ad. & El. 75 ; *Dobson* v. *Sotheby*, M. & M. 86.

[7] In *Francis* v. *Somerville, etc., Ins. Co.*, 25 N. J. 78, the plaintiff erected a small addition to a house and store insured by the defendant, and used the same as a stable for a cow, and to keep hay in. *Hay* was one of the articles designated in the policy as "extra hazardous," and the court held that this was a material addition to the risk, and that the policy was thereby avoided. In a New Jersey case, a policy on a press in a building contained the proviso that, if the premises shall, at any time when a fire shall happen, be in whole or part occupied for purposes considered hazardous, unless liberty so to occupy them be expressly stipulated for, this policy shall be void. At the time the building was

is discontinued before the loss, the policy reattaches.[1] So, if the insurer *knew*, when the policy was issued, that the change was to be made, or *after* it was issued, that they were being made, if no objections are made, it will be treated as a waiver,[2] But, in order to establish an implied assent or waiver, knowledge of the full extent of the change involved must be established.[3] Where the policy requires that *notice* of any alterations or changes shall be given to the company, proof that the agent *knew* that such alterations were being made does not dispense with the necessity of notice.[4] *But the stipulation as to notice does not apply to changes or repairs that do not increase the risk,*[5] nor to ordinary repairs incident to the property. Thus, in a New York case,[6] the house was burned while being repaired. The policy contained a stipulation that it should be void if the building should be used for any purpose denominated hazardous. Oil and turpentine were classed as hazardous, but it was held by the court that their presence in the building *for the purpose of making of necessary repairs* did not invalidate the policy, because the insurer must be treated as having contemplated all the usual and ordinary incidents of the use of the property insured. Therefore, in interpreting a policy to ascertain whether

---

insured it contained a printing press. Afterwards, without express stipulation, a steam-engine, cupola, furnace, foundry and blacksmith's shop were added to a back building, connected with that containing the press. Held, that the policy· was thereby avoided. *Robinson* v. *Mercer Co. Mut. F. Ins. Co.*, 3 Dutch. (N. J.) 134 ; *Barrett* v. *Jeremy*, 3 Exchq. 533.

[1] In *Lounsbury* v. *Protection Ins. Co.*, 8 Conn. 459, the policy provided that, if the building should be used for any occupation, or for the purpose of storing therein any goods denominated hazardous or extra hazardous, in the conditions annexed to the policy, "then, and from thenceforth, so long as the building should be so used," the policy should be of no force. It appeared that, during the existence of the risk, the building was used for an occupation denominated extra hazardous, but that, *before the fire, it had ceased to be so used.* It was held that the insured was not thereby precluded from recovering under the policy. So, where boards and other timber, not denominated hazardous, *though of a combustible nature, were put into the building, and remained in it at the time of the fire*, it was held that the insured was not thereby precluded from recovering.

[2] Thus, in *Hotchkiss* v. *Germania F. Ins. Co.*, 5 Hun (N. Y.) 91, the policy provided that it should become void in case repairs or additions were made without the consent of the company noted on the policy. After the issuing of the policy, additions and alterations were made with the knowledge of the agent, he making no objection thereto. It was held that the condition in the policy had been waived. *Liddle* v. *Market, etc., Ins. Co.*, 4 Bos. (N. Y.) 179.

[3] *Greenfield* v. *Mass., etc., Ins. Co.*, 47 N. Y. 430 ; *Van Allen* v. *Joint Stock, etc., Ins. Co.*, 4 Hun (N. Y. S. C.) 413.

[4] *Sykes* v. *Perry, etc., Ins. Co.*, 34 Penn. St.·79.

[5] *Parker* v. *Arctic F. Ins. Co.*, 59 N. Y. 1. Putting up a frame building touching a house insured will not avoid the policy, unless the risk be thereby increased. *Stetson* v. *Mass. Ins. Co.*, 4 Mass. 330.

[6] *O'Neil* v. *Buffalo Ins. Co.*, 3 N. Y. 122 ; see also, *Billings* v. *Tolland, etc., Ins. Co.*, 20 Conn. 139 ; *Lounsbury* v. *Protection Ins. Co.*, 8 id. 459 ; *Dobson* v. *Sotheby*, M. & M. 90.

a condition has been violated, the first inquiry should be whether the use alleged as a breach was *a usual or ordinary incident of the property insured, in view of the purpose to which it is devoted.*[1]

Particularly is this the case when no increase of the risk is involved.[2]

---

[1] In *Billings* v. *Tolland Co. Mut. Ins. Co.*, ante, the policy described the buildings as barns "used for hay, straw, grain unthreshed, stabling and shelter." The court held that this was not a warranty that the barns should be used *only* for that purpose, and that the assured had a right to use them for any of the purposes for which such premises are *usually* used, and that a single use of them for an *extraordinary* purpose would not avoid the policy. *Franklin Ins. Co.* v. *Brock*, 57 Penn. St. 74 ; *Washington Ins. Co.* v. *Davidson*, 30 Md. 91 ; *Merchants'*, *etc.*, *Ins. Co.* v. *Washington, etc., Ins. Co.*, 1 Handy (Ohio) 181 ; 5 Ohio St. 450 ; *Hobson* v. *Wellington F. Ins. Co.*, 6 U. C. (Q. B.) 356. In *Dobson* v. *Sotheby*, M. & M. 90, the policy was on premises "where no fire is kept, and where no hazardous goods are deposited." These words mean the habitual use of fire and deposit of hazardous goods ; and, therefore, where a fire happened in consequence of making a fire and bringing a tar barrel on the premises to repair them. Held, the insured were entitled to recover. *Shaw* v. *Robberds*, 6 Ad. & El. 75. A policy contained the usual conditions of avoidance in case of misrepresentation, or of any alteration in the buildings insured, or in the mode of using them, without notice to the office. A kiln used for drying corn, being part of the premises insured, was used upon one occasion for drying some bark, a more dangerous process, and the premises then took fire and were burned down. Held, that the conditions had reference to some permanent alteration of the buildings, or of the mode of carrying on business, and not to a single instance like the present. In a New York case, a clause in a policy suspended its operation in case the building insured should be "appropriated, applied or used" for storing or keeping therein any article denominated hazardous, of which flax was one. It had been used for flax-dressing machinery, but before the date of the policy the machinery had been removed, and a carding machine put up, but a small quantity of unbroken flax remained piled up in a corner of a room for two days, within which the building was burnt. Held, that the facts proved did not suspend the policy, they failing to show that the building was "appropriated, applied or used" for storing. *Hynds* v. *Schenectady Ins. Co.*, 16 Barb. (N. Y.)

[2] In *Buxendale* v. *Harvey*, 4 H. & N. 445, the plaintiffs had effected, with the Norwich Union Fire Insurance Society, a policy of insurance, which contained a condition that "every policy issued by this society should be void, unless it contained a full description of the nature and condition of the property insured, in respect to matters bearing upon the question of the risk taken." The plaintiffs erected on the premises insured a steam-engine, which they used for hoisting goods. This engine was specified in the policy. The plaintiffs applied the engine to grinding provender for their horses. They attached to it a horizontal shaft, which was carried through the floor to an upper room, where they erected winnowing and grinding machines. The policy was renewed in 1857. The society had no knowledge of the erection of the *additional* machinery, or that the steam-engine was used for grinding. The premises having been destroyed by fire, it was held that the alteration did not avoid the policy, the jury having found that there was no increase of risk. See also, *Stokes* v. *Cox*, 1 H. & N. 543. In *Mayall* v. *Mitford*, 6 Ad. & El. 670, in a policy upon cotton mills, "it was warranted that the mills were brick-built, and were warmed and worked by steam, lighted by gas, worked by day only." It was held, that the stipulation that the mill should be worked by day only, meant that the usual cotton manufacture carried on by mills in the daytime should not be carried on at night, and that it was consequently no breach of this warranty, that, on one occasion, in order to turn machinery in an adjacent building, the steam-engine (which was not in the mill, but in an adjoining building) and certain perpendicular and horizontal shafts in the mill were at work ; and that a plea to a declaration on the above policy that a certain steam-engine and certain perpendicular and horizontal shafts, then being respectively parts of the said mill, were, without consent of the defendants, worked by night, was bad. In *Jefferson Ins. Co.* v. *Catheal*,

But if an increase of risk is involved, and the use is not one contemplated by the parties, and notice thereof to the insurer is required, a failure to give the notice avoids the policy; and if, after notice given, the assured declines to resume or carry the risk, the policy is inoperative. Thus, in a New Hampshire case,[1] the plaintiff, after he had effected an insurance with the defendants, having set up several additional stoves in the building in which the property insured was kept and used, notified the defendants thereof, saying that he did not consider the risk much increased thereby, and requesting them to inform how much additional premium he must pay therefor. To this the defendants replied, that his policy had erroneously been taken in the wrong class, and that they declined to continue his insurance any longer, and would surrender his premium note without charge. The

---

7 Wend. (N. Y.) 72, an insurance was effected on a "steam saw mill." Subsequently, the boiler, which was placed on the outside of the mill, was enclosed by a frame building, and covered over by a roof. Held, that evidence of the opinions of underwriters, who had not seen the premises, and had no particular science in the construction of such buildings, was not admissible to show that the risk was materially increased by such additional building; such question not being a matter of skill or science, but simply a question of fact, which the jurors were as competent to decide as the witnesses. In a leading English case, an action was brought on a policy effected by the plaintiffs, who were varnish makers, with the Norwich Union Fire Insurance Society. The declaration stated the insurance to be 100l. on the stock in trade in the oil store room marked No. 7 (and which room was warranted as having no manufacturing process carried on therein), and 50l. on the stock in trade in the open part of the yard; subject to a condition that if any alteration was made to any building insured, by which the risk of fire to the building or any insured property was increased, such alteration must be immediately notified to the society, in order tó its being allowed by indorsement on the policy, otherwise the policy would be void. The declaration then averred that certain stock in trade in the open yard was destroyed by fire, and that the defendants waived the warranty of the oil store-room No. 7, having no manufacturing process carried on therein, and permitted the plaintiffs to carry on the manufacturing process of boiling varnish; and that, after the waiver, certain stock in the oil store-room was destroyed by fire. Pleas, first, that an alteration was made in the oil store-room, by which alteration the risk of fire to the room and stock in trade therein was increased, and that the alteration was not notified to the society. Secondly, that the plaintiffs erected the two boilers, in the policy mentioned as placed outward of the oil store-room No. 7, inside that room, and used the same therein, by which the risk of fire to the room and stock in trade insured therein, and also to the stock in trade in the open yard, was increased; and that the increase in risk was not notified to the society. Thirdly, that the plaintiffs carried on in the oil store-room No. 7 the hazardous trade of a varnish maker, whereby the risk of fire to the room and the stock in trade was increased; and that the increase of risk was not notified to the society. Replications de injuria. With respect to the first issue, the judge directed the jury to consider whether the alteration increased the risk of fire in the room No. 7. Held, a misdirection; the question being, whether the use of the boilers in the ordinary way as boilers, and not for boiling varnish, would have increased the risk. Semble, that the second plea was bad for want of an averment of the perpetual use of the boilers; also that the third plea was bad, inasmuch as the declaration alleged a waiver of the warranty of the oil store room having no manufacturing process carried on therein. Barrett v. Jermy, 3 Exchq. 535.

¹ Fabyan v. Union, etc., Ins. Co., 33 N. H. 203.

plaintiff then wrote to the company, inquiring whether it would not be just to return the cash payment he had made for the insurance, as it was not good, and saying that if they would return that, he would be satified, and get insured in some other company. It was held that this was notice to the plaintiff that the company declined to assume the increased risk, and elected to terminate the insurance under the provisions of an article of the by-laws of the company, that if the risk should be increased by any change of the circumstances disclosed in the application, or by the alteration of any building, the policy thereon should be void, unless an additional premium and deposit should be settled with and paid to the company, and an assent thereto by the plaintiff, and that thereupon the policy became void.

Enlargement of building.

SEC. 247. The mere enlargement of a building *ipso facto*, does not avoid a policy upon the ground of an increase of risk. It must be found that the risk was *in fact* increased; but, even though there is no stipulation in a policy against an increase of risk, yet if the use of the building for hazardous purposes is prohibited, and the building is devoted to any of the hazardous purposes named in the policy, the policy is thereby avoided; and if no list of hazards is annexed to the policy, or if the use or change does not come within the class of hazards named, the question as to whether the premises have in fact been devoted to a hazardous use, is one of fact to be found by the jury; and if there is no stipulation against an increase of risk, if the assured devotes the property to a far more hazardous use than that for which it was insured, he is bound to notify the insurer thereof, or the policy will be avoided upon the ground of fraud.[1] An increase in the dimensions of a building does not *ipso facto* invalidate the policy upon the ground of an increase of risk. In order to have that effect the risk must be in fact increased, nor, even though the policy stipulated against any change in or alteration of the risk, would a trifling or immaterial change or alteration avoid the policy; the policy in such cases is treated as referring to a *substantial, material* change.[2]

[1] In *Robinson v. Mercer, etc., Ins. Co.*, 3 N. J. 134, it was held that the addition of a steam-engine, cupola, furnace, foundry and blacksmith's forge to a back building connected with that in which the property insured was contained, was held to be evidence of an increase of risk, such as made it obligatory upon the assured to notify the insurer of the change. "In my opinion," said ELMER, J., "the decided weight of evidence was, that the risk was so changed; * * * that good faith and fair dealing required that the company should be notified."

[2] A *reasonable* construction is to be put upon all such conditions. *Mickey v. Burlington Ins. Co.*, 35 Iowa, 174; 14 Am. Rep. 494; 5 Ben. F. I. C. 389; *Dobson v.*

Not only does the removal of the building insured, in whole or in part, and its replacement by a new one, destroy the policy, but any material alteration of the risk, whereby the risk is increased, has that effect. Thus,[1] where a building is insured as "a two story building,"

Sotheby, ante; Peterson v. Miss. Val. Ins. Co., 24 Iowa, 444; *Troy F. Ins. Co.* v. *Carpenter,* 4 Wis. 20; *Gates* v. *Madison Co., etc., Ins. Co.,* 5 N. Y. 469; *Load* v. *Citizens' Ins. Co.,* 2 Gray (Mass.) 221. In *Townsend* v. *N. W. Ins. Co.,* 18 N. Y, 168, a representation was made as part of the contract of insurance on a cotton factory, that the works were in good condition, and that there was a forcing pump therein, worked by the water-wheel, designed for use in case of fire, and kept all the time ready for use. The supply of water was interrupted for several days by the assured for the purpose of substituting a new stone bulkhead for a wooden one which had gone to decay. A wooden bulkhead might have been put in or the old one repaired in much less time, but there was no unreasonable delay in the work. Held, that the diversion of the water and disabling of the pump did not avoid the policy.

[1] *Sillem* v. *Thornton,* 3 El. & Bl. 868. In *Lyman* v. *State Mut. Ins. Co.,* 14 Allen (Mass.) 329; 5 Ben. F. I. C. 106, the policy contained a condition that "*whenever a building hereby insured shall be altered, enlarged, or appropriated to any other purpose than that herein mentioned, or the risk otherwise increased by the act, or with the knowledge or consent of the insured, etc., this policy shall be void.*" The plaintiffs let the premises by a lease which was to commence January 1st, 1865, but with liberty to make alterations in the building for the lessees and his tenants' use, before the term commenced; and on the 14th of December his workmen began to work. "The building contained an upper and a lower cellar. The first story and the upper cellar had been occupied as a gentlemen's furnishing store. The lessee intended to occupy the first story as a broker's office, and to have the upper cellar occupied as a broker's office. His workmen accordingly proceeded to take out the shelves and counters which had been used as a store, and to put in new counters. They also put in a new water closet, took out some stairs leading to the upper cellar, and put in a new flight, and also put an outside door on the side next to State street, where there had formerly been a window. Most of the work was done outside the building; but in putting up the counters and stairs in the building, some shavings were made, which were removed every night. Most of the shavings were carried off by children, who took them in baskets or bags; a fire was kept in a stove during the daytime, and sometimes during the night; but there had been a stove there before. The jury found specially that this temporarily increased the risk, and that Lyman had notice of the alterations while they were in progress; they also found that the alterations which were made *did not increase the risk permanently.*" *There was no evidence tending to show that the fire was caused by the work of the carpenters, or that the alterations were not carefully made, or were unnecessary for the new tenants.* It did not appear that the upper cellar had been fitted for occupation at the time of the fire, or that anything had been done towards fitting it for such a purpose; and the plaintiffs contended that the taking away of the fixtures, and putting in the fixtures for a broker's office, and the addition of a water-closet, stairs in place of the old stairs, outer and inner door, though these alterations created a temporary increase of risk while they were in progress, did not avoid the policy. The defendants examined several experts on the question whether the risk was increased by the alterations made in the building. Among other questions put to them was the following, which was agreed by counsel to be in substance a sufficient statement of the case: "In the case of a stone building situated in Boston, if the fixtures for a store are taken out and fixtures for a banking-house or office put up, the fixtures being prepared elsewhere, and in putting them up carpenters are occupied about three weeks, making more or less shavings nearly every day, but not a great many, such shavings being daily carried off by children; also the upper floor taken up, and a new floor of tiles laid; a staircase taken away which connected that floor with the cellar, and a new staircase made connecting that cellar with the street; a water-closet put up; the shelves and fixtures taken out from the cellar, and a partition made alongside of the new staircase; a fire being kept

the addition of a *third* story, without the consent of the insurers, vitiates the policy as to the whole.   It should be borne in mind that a

---

in the stove already in the building during the day, and sometimes during the night; whether or not, in your judgment, is the risk increased beyond that arising from the occupation of the store and cellar for a gentlemen's furnishing store?" The plaintiff's counsel objected to the question; but it was allowed by the judge to be put.   The judge had ruled, however, and it was stated to some of the witnesses, that the plaintiff had a right to occupy the building for any of the purposes mentioned in the policy, viz., for a store, offices, and printing offices; and that an increased risk must be a greater risk than such occupation would create. The case was reported for the determination of the full court.   GRAY, J., delivering the opinion of the court, said: "The defendants contend that by virtue of this condition any alteration of the building, *whether increasing the risk or not,* avoided the policy.   The plaintiffs contend that no alteration which did not permanently increase the risk would have that effect.   The court is of opinion that neither of these positions can be maintained.   This condition makes it essential, in order to avoid the policy, that 'the building shall be altered, enlarged, or appropriated to any purposes than those herein mentioned, or the risk otherwise increased.'   The words are not so arranged as to make the meaning perfectly clear; but taking them altogether, there can be no doubt that they include nothing which does not increase the risk.   If it had been intended that any alteration, or enlargement, or appropriation to new purposes, which did not increase the risk, should avoid the policy, the word 'otherwise' in the last clause above quoted, would have been superfluous.   The insertion of that word shows that the previous part of the condition also relates to changes which increase the risk. The reasonable interpretation of the condition is to read it as if the words had been transposed thus: 'Whenever the risk shall be increased by altering or enlarging the building, or appropriating it to any other purposes than those herein mentioned, or otherwise.'   The case is within the principle of *Rice* v. *Tower*, 1 Gray, 426, in which a policy which was to be void 'if the assured shall alter or enlarge a building so as to increase the risk, or appropriate it to other purposes than those mentioned in the application,' was held not to be avoided by an appropriation of the building to a new use which did not increase the risk.   See also, *Stokes* v. *Cox*, 1 Hurlst. & Norm. 533; reversing *S. C.* id. 320.   *Whether the risk was increased was a question for the jury.   Curry* v. *Commonwealth Ins. Co.*, 10 Pick. 535; *Rice* v. *Tower*, 1 Gray, 426.   But although this condition is limited to acts which increase the risk, it is in other respects very sweeping, and includes every manner of increasing the risk, whether by alteration, enlargement, appropriation to new uses, or otherwise.   We have no occasion to consider whether this policy would be avoided (as different policies have been held not to be, in cases cited for the plaintiffs) by making ordinary repairs without the consent of the insurers; or by a casual or gratuitous, though unauthorized use, for a single day or night, or a single experiment.   *The facts in this case show a deliberate and considerable alteration of the building, not incidental to the ordinary use of the property, made by the tenant with the knowledge of the assured, prolonged for three weeks. and, while it lasted, increasing the risk, as the jury have found.*   There is nothing in the words of this condition to warrant us in holding that an alteration which increased the risk for such a length of time did not avoid this policy, merely because the duration of the increase of risk would not be unlimited.   On the contrary, one probable object of the condition requiring the written consent of the president of the company in case of increase of risk seems to us to have been to enable the insurers to charge an additional premium in such a case as this.   3 Kent Com. (6th ed.) 374; *Worcester* v. *Worcester Ins. Co.*, 9 Gray, 27; *Glen* v. *Lewis*, 8 Exch. 618.   *If the risk was increased at the time of the fire. contrary to the terms of the policy, the insurers were not liable. even if the acts which increased the risk did not cause the fire.   Merriam* v. *Middlesex Ins. Co.*, 21 Pick. 162.   The only remaining question is whether the opinions of witnesses, which were admitted to prove an increase of risk, were competent evidence, and upon consideration we are unanimously of opinion that they were not.   The decision of this point, as presented by the report, requires no extended examination of authorities; for it is quite clear that no witness can be permitted to testify to his own individual

change in the risk, unless prohibited, does not *per se* avoid the policy, unless the change is such as to change the identity of the risk insured. In all other cases, proof of *increase* of risk must be shown.

---

opinion merely, upon the issue whether the risk was increased, when that depends upon facts which involve no peculiar science or information, but are within the common knowledge of men. *Mulry* v. *Mohawk Valley Ins. Co.*, 5 Gray, 541; *White* v. *Ballou*, 8 Allen, 408; *Durrell* v. *Bederly*, Holt N. P. C. 283; *Berthon* v. *Loughman*, 2 Stark. R. 258; *Campbell* v. *Rickards*, 5 B. & Ad. 840; *Hawes* v. *New England Ins. Co.*, 2 Curtis C. C. 230; 1 Arnould on Ins. 572." The case was sent back for trial upon the issue whether the risk was increased by the change.

CHAPTER VIII.

WHO MAY BE INSURED—INSURABLE INTEREST.

Insurable interest.

SEC. 248. The contract being one of indemnity, it follows, as a matter of course, that the person insured must have an *interest* in the property, and be so situated in reference to it, that an injury thereto, or its destruction, would result in pecuniary loss to him.[1]

[1] *Carter* v. *Humboldt Ins. Co.*, 12 Iowa, 287; *Rohrback* v. *Germania Ins. Co.*, 62 N. Y. 47. An executor or executrix may insure the property in her hands under the will, *Phelps* v. *Gebhard F. Ins. Co.*, 9 Bos. (N. Y.) 404; an administrator, *Herkimer* v. *Rice*, 27 N. Y. 163; heirs at law, *Wyman* v. *Wyman*, 26 N. Y. 253; trustees, *White* v. *Hudson R. Ins. Co.*, 7 How. Pr. (N. Y.) 341; common carriers, bailee, *Savage* v. *Com. Ex. Ins. Co.*, 9 Bos. (N. Y.) 1; *Stilwell* v. *Staples*, 19 N. Y. 401; a tenant, *Allen* v. *Franklin Ins. Co.*, 9 How. Pr. (N. Y.) 501; or any person having the custody of property for himself or another, and responsible for its safe keeping, has an insurable interest therein. *Redfield* v. *Holland Purchase Ins. Co.*, 56 (N. Y.) 354; *Bates* v. *Equitable Ins. Co.*, 10 Wall. (U. S.) 33; *Palmer* v. *Pratt*, 9 Moore 358; *Clark* v. *Protection Ins. Co.*, 1 Story (U. S.) 109; *Norcross* v. *Ins. Co.*, 17 Penn. St. 429; *F. & M. Ins. Co.* v. *Morrison*, 11 Leigh (Va.) 354; *Higginson* v. *Dall*, 13 Mass. 96; *Williams* v. *Ins. Co. of N. America*, 1 Hilt. (N. Y. C. P.) 345; *Crawford* v. *St. Lawrence Co. Ins. Co.*, 8 U. C. (Q. B.) 314; *Milligan* v. *Equitable Ins. Co.*, 16 U. C. (Q. B) 314; *Van Natta* v. *Sun. Mut. Ins. Co.*, 2 Sand. (N. Y.) 490; *De Forrest* v. *Fulton Ins. Co.*, 1 Hall (N. Y.) 84; *St. John* v. *Am. Mut. Ins. Co.*, 2 Duer (N. Y.) 419; *Rankin* v. *Andes Ins. Co.*, 47 Vt. 144; *Wilkes* v. *People's Ins. Co.*, 19 N. Y. 184; *Williams* v. *Smith*, 2 Caines (N. Y.) 13; *Perry Co., etc., Ins. Co.*, v. *Stewart*, 19 Penn. St. 45. *Boston, etc., Ins. Co.* v. *Royal Ins. Co.*, 12 Allen (Mass.) 381; *Gordon* v. *Mass. F. & M. Ins. Co.*, 2 Pick. (Mass.) 249; *Ins. Co.* v.

Wagering policies of fire insurance, whether upon the property of the assured or of third parties, are not permitted. They would be illegal, as contrary to public policy, not only as gambling transactions but as incentives to arson and fraud, nor, viewed in the second light, could it be otherwise than odious to any·right-minded person to speculate upon the misfortunes of another. This would, indeed, seem to follow from first principles, and without seeking for authority, but the rule which lies at the foundation of all contracts of marine insurance here meets us, and appears equally apposite—namely, that the assured, in becoming such, seeks not for gain, but strives only to guard against loss. "Assecuratus non quærit lucrum, sed agit ne in damno sit." Hence, fire insurance is, in its nature, a contract of indemnity. This definition may be considered as generally true, although like most other abstract propositions, when attempted in the law, cases may be imagined in which it may require to be received with some qualification. Such, for example, is that of a bailee not liable for loss by fire, who insures the property of his bailor, in which case the right to effect and recover upon the policy can scarcely be said to be coterminous with the beneficial ownership, so as to entitle the contract to be defined as an indemnity. It will be more correct to say that this contract, like every other which can be defined as an insurance, requires an interest in the assured to support it, or that he must possess, in insurance language, an insurable interest.[1]

Updegraff, 21 Penn. St. 513; *Fenn* v. *N. O. Ins. Co.*, 53 Ga. 578; *The Southern, etc., Ins. Co.* v. *Lewis*, 42 Ga. 587; *Oakman* v. *Dorchester, etc., Ins. Co.*, 98 Mass. 57; *Cumberland Bone Co.* v. *Andes Ins. Co.*, 64 Me. 466; *Honore* v. *Lamar F. Ins. Co.*, 51 Ill. 509; *Warren* v. *Davenport F. Ins. Co.*, 31 Iowa 464: *Tallman* v. *Atlantic, etc., Ins. Co.*, 4 Abb. Ct. of App. Cases (N. Y.) 354; *Rohrback* v. *Ætna Ins. Co.*, 1 T. & C. (N. Y. S. C.) 339; *Manley* v. *Ins. Co. of N. America*, 1 Lans. (N. Y.) 20; *Ins. Co.* v. *Chase*, 5 Wall. (U. S.) 509; *Russell* v. *Union Ins. Co.*, 4 Dall. (U. S.) 421; *Dohn* v. *Farmers' Joint Stock Ins. Co.*, 5 Lans. (N Y.) 275; *Columbian Ins. Co.* v. *Lawrence*, 2 Pet. (U. S.) 25; 10 id. 507; *Lawrence* v. *St. Marks F. Ins. Co.*, 43 Barb. (N. Y.) 479; *Ins. Co.* v. *Baring*, 20 Wall. (U. S.) 159; *Seagrave* v. *Union Marine Ins. Co.*, L. R. 1 C. P. 305; *Anderson* v. *Morice*, L. R. 10 C. P, 58; *Knox* v. *Wood*, 1 Cowp. 543; *Phillips* v. *Knox Co. Mut. Ins. Co.*, 20 Ohio 174; *Sweeney* v. *Franklin F. Ins. Co.*, 20 Penn. St. 337; *Barker* v. *Marine Ins. Co.*, 2 Mass. (U. S.) 369; *Brown* v. *Hall*, F. C. (Sc.) 560; *Ellis* v. *Safone*, 8 Exchq. 546; *Georgia Home Ins. Co.* v. *Janes*, 49 Miss. 86; *Cone* v. *Niagara Ins. Co.*, 60 N. Y. 619; *Waring* v. *Indemnity Ins. Co.*, 45 N. Y. 506; *Hill* v. *Secretan*, 1 B. & P. 315; *Goulstone* v. *Royal Ins. Co.*, 1 F. & F. 276; *Protection Ins. Co.* v. *Hall*, 15 B. Mon. (Ky.) 411; *Locke* v. *North American Ins. Co.*, 13 Mass. 61; *Converse* v. *Citizen's Ins. Co.*, 10 Cush. (Mass.) 37; *Harris* v. *York Mut. Ins. Co.*, 50 Penn. St. 641; *N. E. F. & M. Ins. Co.*, v. *Wetmore*, 32 Ill 22; *Hand* v. *Williamsburgh, etc., Ins. Co.*, 57 N. Y. 41; *Curtis* v. *Home Ins. Co.*, 1 Biss. (U. S.) 485.

[1] Straccha deAssecurationibus, pt. 20, No. 4.

Personal nature of insurance contracts.

SEC. 249. The contract is personal, and insures, not the property, but the assured against loss by its destruction, consequently, does not pass as incident to the property, therefore, *unless assigned with the consent of the insurer*, it becomes inoperative when the interest of the assured in the property ceases. From this it follows that the assured must have an interest in the property, as well *when the contract is entered into, as at the time of loss.*[1] " These policies," said Lord Chancellor KING, in a case before him,[2] " are not insurances of the specific things mentioned to be insured, nor do such insurances attach on the realty, or in any manner go with the same as incident thereto by any conveyance or agreement, but are only special agreements with the assured against such loss or damage as they may sustain. The party insuring must have a property at the time of the loss, or he can sustain no loss; and, consequently, can be entitled to no satisfaction." " These policies are not in their nature assignable, nor is the interest ever intended to be transferred from one to the other without the express consent of the office." " Besides the appellants' claim is at best founded on an assignment never agreed for until the person insured had determined his interest in the policy by parting with his whole property, and never executed until the loss had actually happened." His Lordship thereupon dismissed the bill, and his decree was affirmed in the House of Lords.[3]

In another early case, an insurance had been effected in the Hand-in-Hand Fire Office, for a term of seven years, by a person having a term of six and a-half years only then to run. The obligation was, " to raise and pay out of the contribution-stock the sum of £400 to the assured, her executors, administrators and assigns, so often as the house should be burnt down within the said term, unless the directors should build the said house, or put it in as good a plight as before the fire." Upon the back of the policy was an indorsement, that if the policy was assigned the assignment must be entered within twenty-one days after the making thereof. After the expiration of the six

[1] *Illinois Mut. F. Ins. Co.* v. *Marseilles Mfg. Co.*, 6 Ill. 236; *Murdock* v. *Chenango Ins. Co.*, 2 N. Y. 210; *Wilson* v. *Hill*, 3 Met. (Mass.) 66; *Swift* v. *Vt. Mut. Ins. Co.*, 18 Vt. 305 *n.*; 2 Bennett's F. I. C. 466; *Graham* v. *Fireman's Ins. Co.*, 2 Dis.(Ohio) 255; *Gilbert* v. *N. American Ins. Co.*, 23 Wend. (N. Y.) 43. If the insurerer *parts with his interest* before loss, and is entirely divested thereof, his insurable interest is gone and the policy is absolutely void. *Hidden* v. *Slater, etc., Ins. Co.*, 2 Cliff. (U. S. C. C.) 266.

[2] *Lynch* v. *Dalzell* 3 B. & Par. Cas. 49.

[3] *Ladd Ins. Co.* v. *Badcock*, 2 Atk. 554.

and a-half years, but before the expiration of the seventh year, the
house was burnt down. The assured then assigned the policy for a
nominal consideration to her late landlords, who tendered the policy to
the office for entry, which was refused, and who thereupon filed their
bill to recover the assurance money. The fire took place in the month
of January, the tender for entry was on the 23rd of February following.
In his judgment, Lord Chancellor HARDWICKE observed, "I am of
opinion that it is necessary that the party insured should have an
interest in the property at the time of insuring and when the fire happens. It has been said for the plaintiffs that it is in the nature of a
wager laid by the insurance company, and that it does not signify to
whom they pay, if lost. Now, these insurances from fire have been
introduced in later times, and therefore differ from insurances on ships,
because their interest or no interest is almost constantly inserted, and
if not inserted you cannot recover, unless you prove a property. By.
the first clause of the deed of their incorporation, the Society are to
make satisfaction in case of any loss by fire. To whom, and for what
loss, are they to make satisfaction? Why to the person insured, and
for the loss he may have sustained; for it cannot properly be called
insuring the thing, for there is no possibility of doing it, and therefore must mean insuring the person from damage. By the terms of
the policy the defendants might begin to build and repair within six
days after the fire happens. It has been truly said, this gives
the Society an option to pay or rebuild, and shows most manifestly
that they meant to insure upon the property of the insured, because
nobody else can give them leave to lay even a brick, for another person might fancy a house of a different kind."

When, however, a fire policy is said to be unassignable even in
equity without the consent of the insurers, this distinction must be
taken, namely, that the transfer which is prohibited *is that of the entire
ownership.* The rule does not extend to forbid the creation of a mere
lien, nor a transfer *after* a loss has occurred.[1] It might be said that if
the rule requires that the assured should have an interest in the thing
insured at the time the contract is entered into, the policy would be
inoperative in the hands of a person who subsequently acquires the
title and takes an assignment of the policy with the insurers assent.
But in this latter case, the company by its assent to the transfer, is

---

[1] *Strong* v. *Manufacturers' Ins. Co.*, 10 Pick. (Mass.) 40; *Franklin F. Ins. Co.*
v. *Findlay.* 6 Wheat. (Penn.) 483; *Allen* v. *Franklin F. Ins. Co.*, 9 How. Pr. (N. ·
Y.) 501; *Pennebaker* v. *Tomlinson* 1 Tenn. Ch. 598.

treated as entering into a new contract with the assignee, and the policy is treated as a policy made to him, and he alone can maintain an action upon it.   In England, in order to acquire an insurable interest, some title, property or interest in the property, legal or equitable, must exist in the assured, or an interest therein of a pecuniary nature. A vendee under a void sale acquires no title, either equitable or legal, and consequently has no interest that can be covered by a policy.[1] Therefore, a purchaser of personal property or real estate, who is not in possession of the same, under a contract void by the statute of frauds, has no insurable interest therein;[2] but, if he is in possession, the rule is otherwise.[3]

Some property or interest, legal or equitable, must exist in the identical property insured, and, under this rule, it has been held that a purchaser of a certain number of bushels of grain—and of course the same rule applies to all species of property—that is intermingled with other grain, and not separated therefrom, and which has not actually been delivered to him, does not acquire an insurable interest therein, *because he cannot trace the identity of the property at risk, and has acquired no such interest therein as divests the vendor of an insurable interest in it.* Thus, in a case heard before the Court of Chancery in Canada,[4] the plaintiff procured insurance upon 3,500 bushels of wheat, claiming to be the owner of the same, for $5,000.   The plaintiff's interest in the wheat was derived from one Todd, who was a wharfinger, and sold the plaintiff the 3,500 bushels of spring wheat, forming part of a much larger quantity then in store, *and from which it was not separated, or in any way ascertained as distinct from the rest*, before the destruction of the warehouse and its contents by fire.   Nor was there any delivery of the same.   The plaintiff, however, had paid for the wheat.   Todd executed a receipt for the same as follows: " Received from George Carter, owner, in store, 3,500 bushels of No. 1 spring wheat, *to be delivered*

---

[1] *Sutherland* v. *Pratt*, 11 M. & W. 296 ; *Stockdale* v. *Dunlop*, 6 id. 224 ; *Hedden* v. *West*, 9 Jur. (N. S.) 747.   A void levy of an execution does not avoid a policy, even though the policy provides that it shall be void if the premises are levied upon.   In order to have the effect to invalidate the policy it must be a levy that divests the title.   *Pennebaker* v. *Tomlinson, ante*.   In *Rice* v. *Turner*, 1 Gray (Mass.) 426, it was held that neither a mortgage or levy of execution without change of possession, amounts to an alienation.   And, unless specially provided otherwise, neither the levy of an execution, attachment, decree of foreclosure, or other seizure upon legal process, will invalidate the policy.   The alienation contemplated relates to a *voluntary* sale or gift.   *Strong* v. *Manufacturers' Ins. Co., ante.*

[2] *Stockdale* v. *Dunlop, ante.*

[3] *Hand* v. *Williamsburgh F. Ins. Co.*, 57 N. Y. 41 ; *Wood* v. *N. W. Ins. Co.*, 46 N. Y. 421.

[4] *Box* v. *Provincial Ins. Co.*, 15 Grant's Ch. (Ont.) 337 ; 5 Bennett's F. I. C. 197.

pursuant to his order to be indorsed hereon, etc." The court held that the plaintiff had no insurable interest in the wheat. VANKOUGHNET, C., in passing upon the question, said : "These 3,500 bushels of spring wheat, or any portion thereof, were not separated from the mass of which they formed part, or in any way ascertained as distinct from the rest, before the fire, by which they and more of the wheat were destroyed.[1] The plaintiff had paid Todd the full value of 3,500 bushels of wheat before insurance, *and I suppose he might maintain an action against him for non-delivery of that quantity.* The questions are : *Had he an insurable interest in an ascertained quantity of 3,500 bushels of wheat ? and if he had, was it that interest which he insured ? or did he insure as owner of a specific quantity of 3,500 bushels ? and if so insuring, can he insist that under it he had a right to protect himself to the extent of the insurance money for damage which he could have recovered from Todd for the non-delivery of the wheat when called for ? The wheat clearly remained at Todd's risk, as no property in it passed to the plaintiff.* What the plaintiff did, was to insure the 3,500 bushels of wheat *as his property. He had no such property, but he had a right to claim some, still unascertained 3,500 bushels of wheat from Todd, or damages in lieu of it. Has he covered, or could he cover this right by the insurance which the plaintiff effected ?* A fire policy naturally means an indemnity against loss by the destruction *of propety which can be consumed by fire.* He had, at most, a right to damage for breach of contract. Was that covered by his insurance against fire. * * He had no 3,500 bushels of wheat, *or any part of it as his property, and it seems to me therefore, that the insurance he effected fails, and cannot be enforced.* Had the wheat been set apart before the fire, the case would be different, as they would have something then for the policy to cover or fasten on, they having then an inchoate right, and thus, an interest at the time of insurance."[2] *If the property is set apart, or is capable of being identified specifically*, there seems to be no question that a pur-

---

[1] *Stockdale* v. *Dunlop*, 6 M. & W. 224 ; *Busk* v. *Davis*, 2 M. & S. 401 ; *Aldridge* v. *Johnson*, 7 El. & Bl. 885.

[2] It is proper to say that MOWATT, V.C., dissented from this doctrine, and that the Court of Queen's Bench of Upper Canada held a contrary doctrine upon a similar state of facts, in *Clark* v. *The Western Ins. Co.*, 25 U. C. (Q. B.) 209, and given entire by Mr. BENNETT, in vol. 5 of his Fire Insurance Cases, p. 203, as a note to the principal case. But, with proper deference to the authority of the case of *Clark* v. *Ins. Co.*, *ante*, it would seem that the principal case stands upon the only correct and tenable ground. To hold that a person, under a contract for the purchase of property, the custody or possession of which has never been delivered to him, and the subject-matter of which cannot be identified, possesses an insurable interest therein, is certainly questionable, either upon principle or policy

chaser under a valid contract, thus acquires an insurable interest therein, even though he might proceed against the vendor for damages for breach of contract in not delivering.[1]

---

[1] Vankoughnet, C., in *Box* v. *Provincial Ins. Co.*, *ante*; *Manly* v. *Ins. Co of N. America*, 1 Lans. (N. Y.) 20; *Sutherland* v. *Pratt*, *ante*. In *Stockdale* v. *Dunlop*, 6 M. & W. 223, the plaintiffs purchased, *verbally*, of some ship owners, 200 tons of oil, to arrive by vessels then at sea, 100 tons to arrive by the Antelope and 100 tons by the Maria. The Maria, having 50 tons of palm oil on board, was lost. The plaintiffs, having insured the oil on board the Maria, as well as their expected profits therefrom, brought an action upon the policy to recover the loss. It was held that they had no insurable interest therein. Lord Abinger, C.B., said: "The question is, whether the plaintiffs had any insurable interest in the goods in question, and I am of opinion that they had not. The argument of the plaintiffs' counsel rests upon an analogy drawn from the law relating to insurance on freight. It is very true, where a party is entitled to the ship, either wholly or in part, the law will allow him to make a separate insurance on the freight. If there is a charter party, and the ship is lost, he is entitled to recover for the freight. But, if a ship is sent out for goods, and none are received on board, there is no interest to maintain an insurance on the profits. Where goods are received on board of a vessel, and a contract is made to secure them, then, if a loss arises, the assured may recover, because his receipt of the goods has been prevented by perils of the sea, for he has made a contract which he had great reason to expect would be performed. But the cases of freight are not analogous to cases of insurances on the profits to arise from the sale of goods. They stand upon the assumption that the party insuring has in his own power the subject-matter upon which the insurance is effected. In this case, the plaintiffs had no present interest, and none can attach on such a contract as this. If contracts for goods to be purchased in future were allowed to be the subject of insurance, it would be allowing a wager policy to be made. But such a doctrine would defeat the legislative provisions on the subject, and create an imaginary interest, which has no foundation in law. Here there was no written contract, nor any contract which the plaintiffs could have enforced. The cases of freight suppose a contract which is capable of being enforced. Here no interest in the goods was passed to the plaintiffs. There is a contract to sell 100 tons of palm oil, to arrive by the Maria; if the vessel do not arrive, or the goods do not arrive, the contract is void. Then where is the interest? *The transaction amounts in effect to an insurance of a void contract.*" Parke, B., said: "I concur in opinion with the Lord Chief Baron, that the plaintiffs have no insurable interest. I admit that profits may be insured, but that is on the ground that they form an additional part of the value of the goods in which the party has already an interest. Thus, the owner of goods on board a vessel may insure the profits to arise from them. So may a consignee or a factor in respect of his commission. So may captors, because they have a lawful possession, coupled with a well-founded expectation that their claim to retain the goods will be allowed. So may the owners of slaves, or a captain in respect of his commission. In these cases, there is either an absolute or a special property in possession. There the profits are insured as an additional value upon the goods, in which the insurer has a present interest. Here, however, the assured are not interested at the time of the goods being put on board, but only upon their arrival. They rely upon the honor of the vendor, that the goods shall be put on board the ship specified in the contract, and that they shall be delivered to them when the ship arrives. It is an engagement of honor merely. If it is not a contract capable of being enforced at law, it is nothing. The contract is to sell the goods when they arrive, but there was no memorandum in writing, and consequently no contract which was capable of being enforced, at the time either of the insurance or the loss; and, if it ultimately did become capable of being enforced, that was only by the subsequent part delivery and acceptance, which was after the loss had occurred. *At the time of the insurance and of the loss, there was merely an expectation of possession on the part of the plaintiffs, founded on the mere promise of the vendors, but there was a total absence of interest in the subject-matter of the insurance. There was no contract which could be enforced, but a mere promise on the part of Messrs. Harrison & Co. to deliver the*

An alienation before loss, destroys the policy,[1] and it cannot be kept on foot by an indorsement "in case of loss, pay to B," the vendee.[2] A conveyance as a gift, absolute on its face, deprives the donor of all insurable interest, even though it is agreed that he shall have the rents, *and although he in fact does have them*.[3] Where lessees procure insurance, upon assignment of the lease, the policy is invalidated;[4] so, generally, when the assured parts with his interest in the property, the policy is invalidated.[5] But, whatever may formerly have been the rule, it seems to be quite well settled that, where the assured retains *the property* in the thing insured, a conveyance in trust,[6] or a mortgage,[7] or any conveyance or process that does not divest the assured of an insurable interest in the property, will not, in the absence of an express provision in the policy, invalidate it.[8] Thus, where the assured has entered into a valid contract to sell the premises, but they have not been conveyed, and he retains the legal title, until the purchase money is paid, the policy is not thereby defeated.[9] So long as *any* interest remains in the assured, the policy remains in force, and covers such interest, unless the assured has done that which is prohibited in the policy.[10] The fact that goods have been fraudulently

---

oil when it arrived. There was no interest whatever, either special or general, in the cargo. The defendant is, therefore, entitled to a verdict on the third plea."

In *Sutherland* v. *Pratt, ante,* where the assured had a title under a valid contract, it was held that he had an insurable interest; yet, however questionable the doctrine may be, it has been held. PARK, B.. distinguishing that case from *Stockdale* v. *Dunlop,* because, in the one case the contract was *verbal,* and consequently void, while in the other the contract was valid and the property specifically designated.

[1] *Fogy* v. *Middlesex, etc., Ins. Co.,* 10 Cush. (Mass.) 337.

[2] *Bates* v. *Equitable Ins. Co.,* 10 Wall. (U. S.) 33; *Hidden* v. *Slater, etc., Ins. Co.,* 2 Cliff. (U. S.) 110.

[3] *McCarty* v. *Commercial Ins. Co.,* 17 La. 365.

[4] *Kip, in re* 4 Edw. Ch. (N. Y.) 86; *Lynch* v. *Dalzell,* 4 Bro. P. C. 431.

[5] *Baltimore F. Ins. Co.* v. *McGowan,* 16 Md. 47; *Powles* v. *Innes,* 11 M. & W. 10; *Citizens' F. Ins. Co.* v. *Dall,* 35 Md. 89; *Atherton* v. *Phœnix Ins. Co.,* 109 Mass. 32; *Pike* v. *Merchants' Ins. Co.,* 26 La. An. 505.

[6] *White* v. *Hudson R. Ins. Co.,* 15 How. Pr. (N. Y.) 288; *Morrison* v. *Tenn. M. & F. Ins. Co.,* 18 Mo. 262; *Norcross* v. *Ins. Co.,* 17 Penn. St. 429; *Strong* v. *Manufacturers' Ins. Co.,* 10 Pick. (Mass.) 140.

[7] *Higginson* v. *Dall,* 13 Mass. 96; *Wilkes* v. *Peoples' F. Ins. Co.,* 19 N. Y. 184.

[8] *Rice* v. *Provincial Ins. Co.,* 7 U. C. (C. P.) 548; *Shooks* v. *Marshall,* 2 Bing. (N. C.) 761; *Ins. Co.* v. *Updegraff, ante; Strong* v. *Manufacturers' Ins. Co., ante; Cone.* v. *Niagara Ins. Co., ante.*

[9] *Ins. Co.* v. *Tyler,* 16 Wend. (N. Y.) 385; *F. & M. Ins. Co.* v. *Morrison,* 11 Leigh. (Va.) 354; *Boston and Salem Ice Co.* v. *Royal Ins. Co.,* 12 Allen (Mass.) 381; *Perry Co. Ins. Co.* v. *Stewart,* 19 Penn. St. 45; *Rice* v. *Provincial Ins. Co., ante.*

[10] *Hibbert* v. *Carter,* 1 T. R. 745.

concealed from his creditors does not deprive the owner of the benefit of insurance.[1]

Void, unless assured has an interest

SEC. 250. If the person to whom a policy is issued has no insurable interest in the property covered by it, the policy is void, and no recovery can be had thereon, either by him or his assignee, for a loss under it, and notes or other obligations given for the premium thereon, are also void.[2]

Interest must exist at time of loss.

SEC. 251. And this interest must be *an interest existing both at the time when the policy issued, and when the loss occurred,* and must be an interest in and immediately connected with the property, or the policy does not attach, and is inoperative.[3]   As to whether in *any* case where, at the time

---

[1] *Goulstone* v. *Royal Ins. Co.*, 1 F. & F. 276.

[2] *Sweeney* v. *Franklin Ins. Co.*, 20 Penn. St. 337 ; *Bersch* v. *Sinnissippi Ins. Co.*, 28 Ind. 64 ; *Freeman* v. *Fulton Ins. Co.*, 38 Barb. (N. Y.) 337 ; *Sawyer* v. *Mayhew*, 51 Me. 398 ; *Fowler* v. *N. Y. Ins. Co.*, 26 N. Y. 422. In *James* v. *Royal Ins. Co.*, 9 Ir. L. T. 194, A. agreed to enter into partnership, for which a deed was afterwards to be executed, to carry on business on certain premises with B., who had mortgaged the premises to C. No deed of partnership was executed, and C. refused to allow A. to enter into possession of the premises unless he would insure the goods thereon against fire. This A. did, and entered. The goods were destroyed by fire. Held, that A. had such an interest as entitled him to effect the policy of insurance. *Marks* v. *Hamilton*, 21 L. J. Ex. 109. A general owner, a reversioner, a mortgagee, a creditor having a lien, a consignee, factor or agent having a lien on goods for advances, an insolvent who has acquired property after he has obtained his discharge, notwithstanding the discharge is revoked. *Marks* v. *Hamilton, supra ; Gordon* v. *F. & M. Ins. Co.*, 2 Pick. 249 ; 19 id. 31. A mechanic having a lien on a building for labor and materials. *Franklin Ins. Co.* v. *Coats*, 14 Md. 285. A commission merchant entitled to commissions on sales, or any person having possession under a contract that may afford him a profit or emolument. *Liter* v. *Morris*, 1 Harris 218 ; *Robinson* v. *N. Y. Ins. Co.*, 2 Caines, 357 ; *Longhurst* v. *Star Ins. Co.*, 19 Iowa, 364. A warehouseman, wharfinger, common carrier or bailee of goods, which come into their hands from time to time in the course of trade, and may keep up a floating policy for the protection of the goods of their customers, deposited in their warehouse or upon their wharf or in their boats, barges or wagons. *London & Northwestern R. R. Co.* v. *Glyn*, 1 Ellis & Ellis, 651 ; *Crowley* v. *Cohen*, 3 B. & Ad. 478. A sheriff in goods which he seizes. *White* v. *Madison*, 26 N. Y. 117. A landlord in goods liable to a distress if rent is not paid, constitute a sufficient insurable interest. *Columbia Ins. Co.* v. *Cooper*, 50 Penn. St. 331. A qualified interest in property, or any interest which would be recognized by a court of law or equity, is an insurable interest. *Warren* v. *Fire Ins. Co.*, 31 Iowa, 464 ; 7 Am. Rep. 160. And in this case it was held that the owner of stock in a corporation organized for pecuniary profit has an insurable interest in the corporate property. But *contra* see, *Sweeney* v. *Franklin F. Ins. Co.*, 29 Penn. St. 337 ; *Phillips* v. *Knox Co. Mut. Ins. Co.*, 20 Ohio 174, in which it was held that a stockholder had no insurable interest in the corporate property. A mere agent having no lien on goods for advances, commission, or otherwise, nor the possession or custody of them as carrier or other bailee, nor any liability to account for their loss by perils insured against, has no insurable interest in them, though he is named as shipper and consignee in the bill of lading. *Seagrave* v. *Union Marine Ins. Co.*, L. R. 1 C. P. 305.

[3] *Seamans* v. *Loring*, 1 Mas. (U. S.) 127.

when the policy issued, there was no insurable interest in the assured to which it could attach, but the policy was obtained in *good faith*, and, subsequently, during the life of the policy an insurable interest, which had previously rested in expectancy, was acquired, the policy would be held operative as to the subsequently acquired interest, is an open question, but it is believed that in some cases the courts would be inclined to uphold and affectuate the contract, where there was no lack of *good faith*, and the party erroneously supposed that *at the time of the issue of the policy*, he had an insurable interest therein, by holding that the consummation of the *title had relation* back to the time when the contract therefor was made.[1] As in a case where a party has entered into a parol contract for the purchase of real estate or personal property, which, under the statute of frauds could not be enforced, but which subsequently was performed. *Where the party is in possession* under such a contract, or if the contract is capable of being enforced, no question would arise,[2] but where the whole matter rests in expectation, and no present interest attaches, it is perhaps not certain whether the policy would be upheld, as the dicta, at least, of the cases, seems to regard *some interest in the insured at the time when the policy was issued*, as essential to its validity, upon the principle that, if the contract is void in its inception, it does not become operative by any subsequent events, which do not amount to a new contract.[3]

Rule in Ætna Ins. Co. v. Miers.

SEC. 252. But in a Tennessee case,[4] it was held that where a person bid off property at a sale upon an execution (real estate), although no deed has been executed or money paid thereon, he acquired an insurable interest in the property; but in such cases the contract could be enforced, and the sheriff compelled to convey, and the purchaser could be compelled to pay the purchase-money and take a conveyance, so that the case does not aid materially in the determination of this question.

---

[1] In *McLaren* v. *Hartford Ins. Co.*, 5 N. Y. 151, where property was sold at foreclosure sale, it was held that the purchaser *instantly* acquired an insurable interest therein, although no deed had been executed, and that the subsequent execution of the deed had relation back to the time of purchase. See also, *Fuller* v. *Van Geesen*, 4 Hill (N. Y.) 173.

[2] *Swift* v. *Mut., etc., Ins. Co.*, 18 Vt. 304; *Columbian Ins. Co.* v. *Lawrence*, 2 Peters (U. S.) 25; *Shotwell* v. *Jefferson Ins. Co.*, 5 Bos. (N. Y.) 247; *McGivney* v. *Phœnix Ins. Co.*, 1 Wend. (N. Y.) 85; *Ayers* v. *Hartford Ins. Co.*, 17 Iowa, 176; *Hope, etc., Ins. Co.* v. *Bralaskey*, 35 Penn. St. 282.

[3] *Stetson* v. *Ins. Co.*, 4 Phila. (Penn.) 8.

[4] *Ætna Ins. Co.* v. *Miers*, 5 Sneed. (Tenn.) 139.

Rule in Gaylor v. Lamar F. Ins. Co.

SEC. 253. But in a Missouri case,[1] a decision, approaching more nearly to the point under discussion, was made. In that case, the plaintiffs bought the insured property at a foreclosure sale, and representing verbally that they were the owners thereof, insured it, *before the equity of redemption in the mortgagor had expired.* The policy contained a provision that "if the interest in the property to be insured be a leasehold, trustee, mortgagee, or reversionary interest, *or other interest not absolute,* it must be so represented to the company, and expressed in the policy in writing; *otherwise the insurance shall be void.*" Subsequently to the issue of the policy, *and after a loss by fire,* they obtained a deed, conveying the premises to them in fee, and the court held that the deed related back to the date of the sale, and that the plaintiffs were to be regarded as the absolute owners, *both at the date of sale, and of the loss.*

Rule in Redfield v. Holland Purchase Ins. Co.

SEC. 254. This was also held in a New York case, in which the facts as well as the principles involved were clearly stated by ANDREWS, J.,[2] who said: "It is claimed that the plaintiff, when the contract of insurance was made, had no insurable interest in the barn. He was, at that time, in possession of the land on which it stood, but his wife had the legal title. She acquired it by deed from one Jencks, dated November 25, 1868, to whom, on the same day, the plaintiff had conveyed the land without consideration, with the intent that he should immediately thereafter convey it to the wife. The real transaction was a conveyance of the land from the husband to her, and the deed to Jencks was interposed for the reason that the disability of coverture was an obstacle to a direct conveyance.

It is found by the referee, that at the time the plaintiff's deed was executed, it was verbally agreed, between him and his wife, that after she should acquire the legal title to the land, she would give him a life estate therein, and convey it by a proper instrument of conveyance, and there was no other consideration for the deed to her. No conveyance had been executed by the wife to the husband at the time the insurance was effected, but he had remained in the occupation of the farm and cultivated it on his own account as he had before the conveyance to the wife, and the proceeds had been used for the support of his family. The evidence justifies the finding of the referee, as to the

---

[1] *Gaylor* v. *Lamar Fire Ins. Co.*, 40 Mo. 13.
[2] *Redfield* v. *Holland Purchase Ins. Co.*, 56 N. Y. 354.

parol agreement made, and the intention of the husband, as disclosed by the agreement, was to vest in the wife a remainder dependent upon a precedent estate for life in him, for this would have been the legal effect of the transaction, if the parol agreement had been fully executed. The fact that this intention was not effected by a conveyance of a remainder in the first instance, would be relevant to the inquiry whether the alleged agreement was made. But the agreement having been found upon sufficient evidence, its existence is to be assumed in determining whether the husband had an insurable interest in the property when the policy was issued.

The case, then, is this: The owner of land, agrees by parol, to convey it to another in fee, upon the verbal promise of the person to whom the conveyance is to be made, on receiving it to give back a conveyance to the grantor, of a life estate in the same premises. The agreement on the part of the owner, is executed by a conveyance in pursuance of the agreement. The grantee neglects or omits to convey the life estate according to the agreement, and the grantor remains in possession. Will a court of equity enforce the performance, by the grantee, of the parol agreement, or restrain the grantee from proceeding upon his legal title to acquire the possession as against the grantor? If the plaintiff had an equitable right to the possession of the land under the agreement with his wife, at the time the contract of insurance was made, which a court of equity would protect and enforce, then it cannot be doubted that he had an insurable interest in the property.[1]

The statute of frauds is supposed to furnish an answer to the assertion by the husband of a right to the possession under the parol agreement. But part performance of contracts, in respect to lands, within the statute, supplies, in the view of courts of equity, the lack of a written agreement, where otherwise one party would be enabled to commit a fraud upon another; and this case is within the principle of the case referred to by Lord HARDWICKE,[2] where a man intended to make a mortgage of his estate by two different deeds, the one an absolute one, and the other a defeasance upon payment of the mortgage money; he executed the absolute conveyance, but when he had done so, the other party refused to execute the defeasance, but the court, Lord HARDWICKE said, without any difficulty decreed him to

---

[1] *Kirby* v. *Sisson,* 1 Wend. 83; *Tyler* v. *The Ætna Fire Ins. Co.,* 12 id. 507; 2 Am. Ldg. Cas. 809, and cases cited.

[2] *Young* v. *Peachy,* 2 Atk. 257.

do it. And in another case ' the court enforced a parol contract for the exchange of lands, where one party had executed the contract, and no conveyance had been made by the other.² The agreement in this case, contemplated a conveyance by the wife of the life estate to the husband. His rights were not to be left in parol, and the arrange-ment was not subject to the objection which applies to an attempt to create a parol and secret trust in favor of a grantor. We are of opinion that the plaintiff had an insurable interest in the barn, and it does not appear that the injury to his life estate did not equal the sum for which the property was insured.

In the conditions of insurance it is provided, that if the insured property be held in trust, or be a leasehold or other interest not abso-lute, it must be so represented to the company, and it is claimed that as the plaintiff had a life estate only at the time of the insurance, which was not referred to in the application, he cannot recover. No reference to this condition was made in the pleadings, or on the trial or in the report of the referee, and the point cannot now be taken by the defendant. If the question had been raised on the trial, we can-not say that a waiver or discharge of the condition might not have been shown, and it is not raised by the general exception to the find-ing that the plaintiff was entitled to recover."

Interest may exist without property in thing insured.

SEC. 255. But, while it is generally true that, when the assured has parted with his property in the thing insured, he has no insurable inter-est therein, yet there are instances in which this is not so. *If he has sold the property and parted with its possession*, all his insurable interest therein is obliterated;³ *but if he has sold the property and received his pay therefor, but it is left in his possession to be delivered at a future day, and he is liable to the vendee for its safe keeping, his insurable interest in the property is not defeated by the sale, nor until the property is in fact delivered*, and a policy issued to him "*upon property sold, but not delivered*," is a valid instrument, and can be enforced for the benefit of the vendees.⁴ A person who has sold property and parted with the

---

¹*Caldwell* v. *Carrington*, 9 Pet. (U. S.) 86.

²See also *Ryan* v. *Dox*, 34 N. Y. 307.

³In *Macarty* v. *Commercial Ins. Co.*, 17 La. 365 ; 3 Bennett's F. I. C. 60, the plaintiff conveyed the premises, but reserved the rents thereof for a certain period. The court held that, *by the conveyance*, all interest in the property *covered by the policy* was destroyed. He had an insurable interest upon the rent, but the rents could only be covered by a policy specifically designating them, and therefore, a policy *upon the property*, did not cover the rents reserved.

⁴*Waring* v. *Indemnity Ins. Co.*, 45 N. Y. 606.

possession, but who has not been paid therefor, and retains the legal title until paid, has an insurable interest to the extent of the unpaid balance,[1] and this is so where one partner sells to the other.[2]

Where personal property has been sold and delivered, *but anything remains to be done before the title passes*, the vendor has an insurable interest until such act is done. Thus, where A. sold a quantity of wood to a railroad company, and drew and piled it on the line of the company's road, *and when measured*, it was to be treated as delivered. It was held that the vendor had an insurable interest therein, until the wood was measured.[3]

A person having title to a part of a building, and a contract for a deed for the balance, may insure the whole.[4] It is enough if the assured has an interest, whether distinct or undivided.[5]

When a person *in possession* of goods, but without title or interest therein insures them in his own name, the real owner may, within a reasonable time, adopt the contract, and it will inure to his benefit, and by relation extend to the date when the policy issued.[6] But it seems that, in order to make a policy so obtained, operative by adoption, it must have been obtained *for the benefit* of the person adopting it.[7]

Waring v. Indemnity Ins. Co.

Sec. 256. In a New York case,[8] the plaintiffs were commission merchants and brokers in petroleum and its products. They also bought and sold on their own account. To cover all their interests, and those which they represented, they took such policies of insurance as were adapted to the exigences of their business, and the necessities of the persons with whom they dealt. A part of their business was to sell petroleum for exports, and it was an advantage to them in their business to have the property covered by insurance, during the brief time between its sale and removal from the bonded warehouse to the vessel, thus saving a new insurance, which would be needed every

---

[1] *Wood* v. *N. W. Ins. Co.*, 46 N. Y. 526 ; and the purchaser also has *Bicknell* v. *Lancaster, etc., Ins. Co.*, 1 T. & C. (N. Y.) 215 ; affi'd 58 N. Y. 677.

[2] *Phœnix Ins. Co.* v. *Hamilton*, 14 Wall. (U. S.) 504.

[3] *Home Ins. Co.* v. *Heck*, 65 Ill. 111.

[4] *Columbian Ins. Co.* v. *Lawrence*, 2 Pet. (U. S.) 25.

[5] *Kenny* v. *Clarkson*, 1 John. (N. Y.) 385 ; *Georgia Home Ins. Co.* v. *Jones*, 94 Miss. 80 ; *Carruthers* v. *Shedden*, 6 Taunt. 13.

[6] *Durand* v. *Shannan*, 1 Porter (Ala.) 238 ; *Watkins* v. *Durand*, 1 id. 251.

[7] *Seamans* v. *Loring*, 1 Mass. (U. S.) 127.

[8] *Waring* v. *The Indemnity F. Ins. Co.*, 45 N. Y. 606.

31

few days. On September 13th, 1865, the plaintiffs obtained eleven
policies, of as many different companies, amounting in all to $30,000.
The written part of the policy in suit, was as follows: "Do insure
Warren, King & Co., against loss or damage by fire, to the amount of
$3,000, on refined carbón oil, and packages containing the same, their
own, or held in trust, on commission or sold, but not removed, contained in bonded warehouse." * * Subsequently, part of the property was sold. The purchasers were informed that the oil was covered
by insurance until removed. No independent insurance was effected
upon it. October 8th following, there was a total loss by fire. The
plaintiffs brought this action upon the policy, for themselves in their
own right, as well as on account of petroleum sold to different parties,
and paid for, but not removed. The court held that they were entitled to recover the full amount of the defendants' proportion of the
entire loss.

Equitable interest. Contingent interest. Assignees.

SEC. 257. The fact that the legal title of property is in another,
does not deprive a person having an equitable interest therein, from
insuring it. Such equitable interest is recognized as a valid *insurable*
interest.[1]

Thus, a policy of insurance issued to one who is in possession of
real estate under a *defective deed, but who is so situated in reference to the
parties in whom the legal title exists, that equity would compel a valid conveyance*, has an insurable interest therein, and so also has a person
holding a mortgage upon the premises executed by him.[2] A person
who, under an erroneous idea that he has title to a piece of land, and
erects a house thereon, when, in point of fact, his deed does not cover
such land, and procures an insurance upon the house, has an insurable
interest therein, *if, as against the true owner, he is entitled to be paid for
the improvements made by him on the land*, otherwise not.[3] Indeed, it
seems that when the occupant in possession *claiming title* is a trespasser, the company cannot dispute his title. His title is good as
against everybody but the true owner.[4] So, where a person has
made a conveyance which equity will treat as a mortgage,[5] and

---

[1] *Locke* v. *N. Am. Ins. Co.*, 13 Mass. 61; *Bartlett* v. *Walter*, id. 267; *Oliver* v. *Green*, 3 Mass. 133.

[2] *Swift* v. *Vermont Mut. Fire Ins. Co.*, 18 Vt. 305; 2 Bennett's F. I. C. 465.

[3] *Stevenson* v. *The London, etc., Ass. Co.*, 26 U. C. (Q. B.) 148.

[4] *Mayor, etc.*, v. *Brooklyn Ins. Co.*, 41 Barb. (N. Y.) 231.

[5] *Holbrook* v. *American Ins. Co.*, 1 Curtis C. C. (U. S.) 193; 3 Bennett's F. I. C.
357; *Russell* v. *Southard*, 12 How. (U. S.) 139; *Tittemore* v. *Vt. Mut. F. Ins. Co.*,

this is the character of all conveyance made *to secure*, rather than *to pay* a debt, even though there is no defeasance provided for in the instrument.' A mortgagee, although having merely an equitable interest in the property, may nevertheless insure the property *to the extent of his mortgage interest.*' So a mortgagor, even after a decree of foreclosure has been entered against the property, may insure the same *to its entire value, so long as an equity of redemption remains in him.*' So a judgment debtor, whose property has been attached or levied upon, has an insurable interest therein to the extent of its value, so long as the title rests in him, even conditionally.' A vendee of real estate, in possession under a contract to purchase, has an insurable interest in the property to the extent of his interest;' and, generally, *any* person who has *any* interest in the property, *legal or equitable*, or who stands in such a relation thereto that its destruction would entail pecuniary loss upon him, has an insurable interest to the extent of his interest therein, or of the loss to which he is subjected by the casualty.'

A tenant, who by his lease is required to insure the propery, or who is liable for its safe return, has an insurable interest to the extent of the *value* of the property,' and in such case he may describe the property as his,' but otherwise his interest does not extend beyond the value of his leasehold interest.' A person liable as indorser upon a note given for certain property, or for its safe keeping, has an insurable interest therein to the extent of his liability as such indorser.'° The widow of a deceased owner of real estate in

---

20 Vt. 546; *Swift* v. *Vt. Mut. Ins. Co.*, 18 id. 305; *Higginson* v. *Dall*, 13 Mass. 96; *Gilbert* v. *N. Am. Ins. Co.*, 22 Wend. (N. Y.) 43; *Bartlett* v. *Walter*, 13 Mass. 267; *Lazarus* v. *Com. Ins. Co.*, 5 Pick. (Mass.) 76; 19 id. 81; *Gordon* v. *Mass. etc., Ins Co.*, 2 id. 249.

¹ *Holbrook* v. *American Ins. Co., ante.*

² *Cane* v. *Niagara Ins. Co., ante.*

³ *Strong* v. *Manufacturers' Ins. Co.*, 10 Pick. (Mass.) 40; 1 Ben. F. I. C. 326.

⁴ *Cone* v. *Niagara Ins. Co., ante.*

⁵ *Bicknell* v. *Lancaster, etc., Ins. Co., ante.*

⁶ *Any* interest, however slight, may be insured, as, where A. advances money to B. in any venture, and by agreement is to be paid out of the proceeds of the property purchased, he has an insurable interest in such property to the extent of his advances. *Sansom* v. *Ball*, 4 Dall. (Penn.) 459; *Ins. Co.* v. *Baring*, 20 Wall (U. S.) 159; *Fenn* v. *N. O. Mut. Ins. Co.*, 53 Ga. 578.

⁷ *Duke of Hamilton's Trustees* v. *Fleming*, C. C. S. (Sc.) 327; *Bartlett* v. *Walter*, 13 Mass. 267; *Imperial F. Ins. Co.* v. *Murray*, 73 Penn. St. 13.

⁸ *Lawrence* v. *St. Marks Ins. Co.*, 43 Barb. (N. Y.) 479; *Bartlett* v. *Walter*, *ante.*

⁹ *Georgia Home Ins. Co.* v. *Jones*, 49 Miss. 80.

¹⁰ *Ins. Co.* v. *Chase*, 5 Wall. (U. S.) 509; *Russell* v. *Union Ins. Co.*, 4 Dall. (U. S.) 421.

possession, and having a dower interest therein, has an insurable interest.[1] An agent or consignee having property of his principal in his possession *and liable for it*, may insure the same *in his own name*, and especially is this so, if he has an interest therein for commissions, advances or otherwise.[2] A husband has an insurable interest in his wife's property, of which they are in the joint possession, and which in case of her death passes to him, absolutely or as tenant by courtesy.[3] In any event, when husband and wife are living together upon the property, and he insures the property in his name, it will be presumed that she ratified the act and adopted the policy.[4] An assignee of a bond for a deed has an insurable interest in the premises, to the same extent as the obligor in the bond had.[5] A person in possession under a bond for a deed, payments to be made by installments, and the bond to be void if payments are not made when due, loses his insurable interest by a breach as to payment, unless such breach is waived.[6] An assignment of a policy to a person who has become surity for the assured, does not divest the assured of an insurable interest or defeat the policy.[7] A mortgagor whose equity of redemption, as fixed by a decree of foreclosure, has expired, still retains an insurable interest in the premises, *if a valid agreement to extend the time has been entered into between him and the mortgagee*[8]. *Prima facie*, a policy covers only the legal interest of the assured,[9] but as an equitable interest is insurable, the assured may always show that he has an equitable interest in the property.[10] It is for the jury to say whether the assured had an insurable interest.[11] A person in possession, *claiming title bona fide*, has an insurable interest,[12] even though his title was attained by fraud.[13]

---

[1] *Lingley* v. *The Queen Ins. Co.*, 1 Hannay (N. B.) 280.

[2] *Ætna Ins. Co.* v. *Jackson, Peasley & Co.*, 16 B. Mon. (Ky.) 242 ; *Putnam* v. *Ins. Co.*, 5 Met. (Mass.) 386.

[3] *Goulstone* v. *Royal Ins. Co.*, 1 F. & F. 276 ; *Mutual Ins. Co.* v. *Deale*, 18 Md. 26.

[4] *Harris* v. *York Mut. Ins. Co.*, 50 Penn. St. 341.

[5] *Ayres* v. *Hartford F. Ins. Co.*, 17 Iowa, 176.

[6] *Birmingham* v. *Empire Ins. Co.*, 42 Barb. (N. Y.) 457.

[7] *Smith* v. *Royal Ins. Co.*, 27 U. C. (Q. B.) 54.

[8] *Stephens* v. *Illinois, etc., Ins. Co.*, 43 Ill. 327.

[9] *Lancey* v. *Phœnix Ins. Co.*, 56 Me. 562.

[10] *Tuckerman* v. *Home Ins. Co.*, 9 R. I. 414. In *Columbian Ins. Co.* v. *Cooper*, 50 Penn. St. 331, it was held that, where the lessor has a right to seize all the property of the lessee upon the premises, he has an insurable interest therein to the extent of his claim for rent.

[11] *Mitchell* v. *Home Ins. Co.*, 31 Iowa 421.

[12] *Franklin Ins. Co.* v. *Chicago Ice. Co.*, 36 Md. 120.

[13] *Phœnix Ins. Co.* v. *Mitchell* 67 Ill. 362.

Rule when interest is contingent.

SEC. 258. But where the interest is contingent, as, where the title to real estate, or a vessel has been absolutely conveyed, but the conveyance is subject to a provision that the surplus above a certain sum realized therefrom shall be paid to him, the extent of the insurable interest is the actual loss that would result from a destruction of the property, consequently it is incumbent upon the insured to show, the value of his interest therein, and, unless it appears that there is some pecuniary value thereto, no recovery can be had.[1]

Thus, where the plaintiff assigned his vessel with other property for the benefit of his creditors, all surplus, if any, to be paid to him, and the creditors thereupon released him from his indebtedness to them, it was held that he could not recover unless he shew that there was a surplus. PARKER, C.J., remarking: "The transfer of this vessel with other property, was in trust to pay over the proceeds to certain creditors of the plaintiff, *had he remained indebted after the making of this assignment, and personally liable in case the property so transferred should be distroyed or lost,* then the case would be like that of Gordon v. Mass. F. & M. Ins. Co., for he would be interested in the same degree as before the assignment. But the assignment was upon the condition that the creditors for whose use it was made, should release and discharge their debts, and they were so released and discharged. This changes the nature of the transaction, and takes away from the plaintiff all interest in the property; for, whether the vessel insured, were lost or not, he was equally discharged, and therefore could not be said to suffer by the loss of the vessel. On the contrary, the whole loss would be on the creditors. But still, there *was a possibility of interest remaining in the plaintiff*, because, by the assignment, the surplus, if any, should remain after paying the debts, is to be paid to the plaintiff, and it is contended that this possibility is an insurable interest, and so seems the present action. *But we do not think such a base contingency is an insurable interest,* nor indeed can it appear that there is even a possibility, unless it be shown that the property conveyed is of greater value than the debts, and that a discreet appropriation of it will leave a surplus." This class of cases, however, differs from the interest of a mortgagee, or of a grantor who conveys the absolute title, but still has the right to a reconveyance on payment of a certain sum. In such cases his interest

---

[1] *Carroll* v. *Boston Marine Ins. Co.*, 8 Mass. 515 ; *Locke* v. *No. American Ins. Co.*, 13 Mass. 61 ; *Gordon* v. *Mass. F. & M. Ins. Co.*, 2 Pick. (Mass.) 249.

is certain and definite, and a distruction of the property lessens its value to the extent of the value of the property destroyed, while in the other case, he sustains no loss whatever, except to the extent of the market value over and above the debts. Therefore, in all cases, the question really is, whether the party sustains any pecuniary loss from the distruction of the property, and how much. And this consideration is also important in determining when he may recover the whole value of the property insured. And as a test for determining that question, the nature of the interest, and the relation in which the insured stands to the property, and the legal owner, is important. In the case last referred to, at a subsequent trial, the plaintiff showed that there was a surplus over and above his debts, and, therefore, was held entitled to recover upon the policy.[1]

Right must be definite and susceptible of enforcement.

SEC. 259. This right, however, must be definite and fixed. A mere general interest, not susceptible of enforcement, which does not specifically apply, either in terms or by operation of law, is not insurable, as the interest of a creditor under a debt or contract which has not been put in judgment;[2] or the interest of an heir, before the death of the owner, and other similar interests that do not exist, as certain definite or specific interests in the particular property. Thus, it will be seen that, in order to create an insurable interest, two things must concur. A certain, definite or specific interest in the property, either by contract or operation of law, and such an interest that an injury to, or destruction of the property, would involve the person in immediate pecuniary loss, and the absence of either element, deprives the interest of its insurable character.[3]

---

[1] See *Lazarus* v. *Ins. Co.*, 19 Pick. (Mass.) 81.

[2] *Grevemeyer* v. *So. Mut. F. Ins. Co.*, 62 Penn. St. 340; *Herkimer* v. *Rice*, 27 N. Y. 163.

[3] *Lucena* v. *Crawford*, 3 B. & P. 75; *Aldrich* v. *Equitable, etc., Ins. Co.*, 1 W. & M. (U. S.) 272; *Ætna Ins. Co.* v. *Jackson*, 16 B. Mon. (Ky.) 242; *Williams* v. *Crescent, etc., Ins. Co.*, 15 La. An. 651. If such a relation exists between the assured and the property, that injury to it will, in natural consequence, be a loss to him, he has an insurable interest therein, *Wilson* v. *Jones*, L. R. 2 Excheq. 139; *Buck* v. *Chespeake Ins. Co.*, 1 Pet. (U. S.) 151; it need not have arisen to the dignity of a *lien* even, it is sufficient if a *right* therein exists, *and a pecuniary interest in its preservation.* DENIO, C.J., in *Herkimer* v. *Rice*, 27 N. Y. 163. "An insurable interest," said ALLEN, J., in *Springfield F. & M. Ins. Co.*, 43 N. Y. 380, "may exist without any estate or interest in the *corpus* of the thing insured. It was enough that there be a pecuniary interest in the preservation and protection of the property, and that loss might result from its destruction." An *assignee* of an insurance policy cannot maintain an action thereon, unless he has an interest in the property insured. *Boyles* v. *Hillsborough Ins. Co.*, 27 N. J. 163. Executors have an insurable interest in property held by them *as such*, because accountable for its safe keeping, and also because they stand as trustees for the legatees and heirs. *Colburn* v. *Lansing*, 46 Barb. (N. Y.) 37.

Person in possession under contract to purchase.

SEC. 260. A person who is in possession under a contract to purchase, has an insurable interest to the extent of his pecuniary interest in the property,[1] but if specifically inquired of as to his title, the policy will be void if he describes it as his own.[2]

Receiptor of property attached. Mechanic having lien.

SEC. 261. Following out the principle, that whenever a person has such an interest in and connected with property, as that in case of injury to or the destruction of the property, a person would sustain a loss therefrom; although having neither a legal or equitable interest in the property itself, it has been held that, where property has been attached—as a vessel—and a third person has given a bond therefor, to secure its release, he thereby acquires an insurable interest in the property, to the extent of the loss to which he would be subjected in case of its destruction;[3] and this applies, with equal force, to the case of persons recepting property attached, to the sheriff or officer attaching it, or to any person who, at the request of the debtor, becomes responsible for its return, or being forthcoming to respond to a judgment that may be obtained in the action in which it is attached. So, too, it has been held that a mechanic, who builds a house or does work upon a building, for which he is to be paid when the building is completed, has an insurable interest therein, to the extent of the work done upon the same at the time of loss. This is predicated upon the ground that, although the mechanic has no specific lien upon the property for his work, yet, as the contract is entire, and his compensation or right thereto depends upon performance, so that he has no claim upon the owner until complete performance; he has such an interest in the property as forms a legitimate basis for protection by insurance, *until the work is completed and accepted by the owner ;*[4] but, except where a specific lien is created thereon by law, this interest ceases upon completion and acceptance of the work. That is, when the liability of the person for whom the work was done, attaches, the

[1] *Draper v. Comml. Ins. Co.*, 21 N. Y. 378 ; *Columbian Ins. Co. v. Lawrence*, 2 Pet. (U. S.) 25 ; 1 Bennett's F. I. C. 264 ; *McGivney v. Phœnix Ins. Co.*, 1 Wend. (N. Y.) 85 ; 1 Bennett's F. I. C. 211 ; *Tyler v. Ætna Ins. Co.*, 12 id. 507 ; *Ætna Ins. Co. v. Miers*, 5 Sneed. (Tenn.) 139 ; *Milligan v. Equitable Ins. Co.*, 16 U. C. Rep. 314 ; *Taynes v. Hartford F. Ins. Co.*, 17 Iowa, 176.

[2] *Draper v. Ins. Co., ante.*

[3] *Fireman's Ins. Co. v. Powell*, 13 B. Mon. (Ky.) 311.

[4] *Franklin, etc., Ins. Co. v. Coates*, 14 Md. 285 ; *Protection Ins. Co. v. Hall*, 15 B. Mon. (Ky.) 411 ; *Stout v. City F. Ins. Co.*, 12 Iowa, 371 ; *Carter v. Humboldt Ins. Co.*, 12 id. 371 ; *Merchants' Ins. Co. v. Mazange*, 22 Ala. 168.

insurable interest ceases. Thus, a material man furnishing materials, when by statute he has a lien upon the building, has an insurable interest to the extent of his lien.[1] But, unless the lien can be enforced, no insureable interest exists.[2] "A lien, or an interest in the nature of a lien," says Story, J.,[3] "is an insurable interest; and it will make no difference, if the party has a right to pursue his debtor, personally, for the debt, on account of which the lien attached."

While any interest remains, insurable interest exists. Mortgagor after decree. Re-insurer Judgment debtor after levy may insure.

Sec. 262. A decree of foreclosure upon mortgaged premises does not, of itself, divest the mortgagor of all insurable interest therein. *His interest does not cease until the title has passed under the decree,* nor even then, if there is an agreement on the part of the mortgagee, to extend the time of redemption.[4] So where a person enters into possession of property under a contract to purchase, although it has not been conveyed, and the purchase-money has not all been paid, yet he has an insurable interest in the property to the extent of his ownership.[5] So a re-insurer has an insurable interest in the property to the extent of such re-insurance,[6] or if *any* interest, even remote and contingent, remains in the policy-holder. Thus, it has been held that a judgment debtor, whose premises have been sold upon execution, has an insurable interest therein, not only so long as a right of redemption remains in himself, *but also so long as such right exists in his creditors,* upon the ground that, so long as this right exists, it is possible for him to secure a loan, and confess a judgment as security therefor, and thus create a right to redeem.[7]

---

[1] *Franklin F. Ins. Co.* v. *Coates,* 14 Md. 285.

[2] *Buchanan* v. *Ocean Ins. Co.,* 6 Cow. (N. Y.) 318.

[3] *Hancox* v. *Fishing Ins. Co.; Allen* v. *Mut. F. Ins. Co.,* 2 Md. 111.

[4] *Stephens* v. *Ill. Ins. Co.,* 43 Ill. 327.

[5] *Bonham* v. *Iowa Central Ins. Co.,* 25 Iowa, 328.

[6] *Yonkers, etc., Ins. Co.* v. *Hoffman, etc., Ins. Co.,* 6 Robt. (N. Y.) 316.

[7] In *Cone* v. *Niagara F. Ins. Co.,* 60 N. Y. 619, an action was brought to reform a policy of insurance, and to recover thereon as reformed. The policy was issued by defendant to one Palmer; loss, if any, payable to plaintiff. The period of risk was for three years from June 1st, 1870. The policy contained this clause: "If the premises are, at the time of insuring, or during the life of the policy, vacant, unoccupied, or not in use, and remain thus for over ten days, * * without the company's consent is indorsed hereon, this insurance shall be void and of no effect." The reformation sought was to have such consent indorsed upon the policy. The referee found, in substance, that it was known to the defendant and its agent, at the time of issuing the policy, that the building insured was vacant, and would probably remain so; that it was expressly understood that it would remain vacant until September, to which the agent consented; that the said condition was in fine print, and that Palmer and plaintiff were ignorant that it was contained in the

Such *rights* are recognized as of *some* value, and form, therefore, the basis for an adequate insurable interest. Such a right *might* be of

---

policy until after the loss. As a conclusion of law, he found that the condition was waived, and that defendant was estopped from setting up that the policy was void in consequence of the consent not having been indorsed, and that plaintiff was entitled to have the policy reformed as prayed for in the complaint. *Held*, no error. At the time the policy was issued, the premises upon which was the building insured was subject to two mortgages in favor of plaintiff, and to two judgments in favor of other parties. It had been sold June 9th, 1869, on execution issued upon one of the judgments, and the sheriff's certificate had been assigned by the purchaser to plaintiff. On the 22d of April, 1870, plaintiff and Palmer had entered into an agreement, under seal, which recited the sale ; that the right of redemption in Palmer would expire June 9th, 1870, and that Palmer desired to occupy a portion of the premises until April 1st, 1871 ; and it was agreed that he should occupy a house (not the one insured) and garden spot without rent, and have the use of certain other portions, with various privileges ; and to put in crops on certain other portions on shares, the residue of the premises to be surrendered to plaintiff ; and it was further agreed that, in case plaintiff got title, Palmer's wife would release her dower right, and plaintiff would discharge and release his bonds and mortgages, and one of the judgments, and indemnify Palmer against another bond outstanding against him. Under this agreement Palmer had surrendered a portion of the premises, including the building insured. The house insured was destroyed by fire August 2d, 1870. The policy contained this clause : "Any interest in the property insured not absolute, or that is less than a perfect title, or if a building is insured that is on leased ground, the same must be specifically represented to the company, and expressed in this policy, in writing, otherwise the insurance shall be void." The defendant raised these points, on appeal : First. That the policy was void by its terms, as Palmer's interest was not absolute, and the policy did not express that he had not a perfect title. Fourth. That Palmer, at the time of the fire, had no insurable interest. Seventh. That plaintiff, having realized the whole or a larger part of his interest in the property, defendant is entitled to a deduction from the sum claimed on the policy, or a subrogation to plaintiff's sureties. As to the first point, the court held that the answer did not specifically set up the defense, nor was it raised upon the trial, or by any exceptions to findings or to refusal to find, and that therefore it could not be raised on appeal. That portion of the opinion relating to the other points above stated, is as follows: " The fourth point is, that at the time of the fire Palmer had no insurable interest in the premises burned. Without stopping now to consider whether, if this were so, the interest of Cone would not sustain the policy and this action on it, we state our opinion to be, that when the policy was issued, Palmer had an insurable interest in the premises, which continued until after the fire occurred. An insurable interest is that property or right of the assured to which he is liable to loss. The assured has an insurable interest, when he has an interest in the subject insured, and the happening of the event insured against, might bring upon him pecuniary loss. *Herkimer* v. *Rice*, 27 N. Y. 163, goes as far as, or farther, than this. It is not necessary that the event would, of a certainty, inflict loss ; it is enough that it might so do. This is general language, but with limitation by the facts of this case it is sufficiently particular. Now, when the policy was contracted for and issued, insuring the interest of Palmer, his right to redeem the premises from the sale by the sheriff had not lapsed. This was a right of some value. *Stephens* v. *Ill. Mut. Ins. Co.*, 43 Ill. 327 ; *Strong* v. *M. Ins. Co.*, 10 Pick. 41. Its value was made up, in part, by the existence of the insured building upon the lands. A destruction of that building lessening the value of the premises, would lessen the value of that right to redeem. *Buffum* v. *Bowditch Mut. Ins. Co.*, 10 Cush. 540. And so when the fire came, although the right of Palmer to redeem, as owner of the fee, had gone, there was a right to redeem in subsequent judgment creditors, if any. Palmer's title had not yet been divested (2 R. S. 373, § 61), and though all the subsequent liens made known by the proofs had centered in Cone, who also held the sheriff's certificate, there was yet a possible right and power in Palmer to create other judgment creditors. It was possible for him, at any time within the fifteen months (*Cheney* v. *Woodruff*,

value to him, and an injury to the property in which the right exists, might involve him in pecuniary loss.[1]

---

45 N. Y. 98, 100, 101, and cases cited) to procure an advance or loan from some friend or speculator, and confessing to him a judgment, thereby create in him a power and right to redeem from Cone. This was an interest affected by the continuance of the insured building on the one hand, or by its loss by fire on the other. Again, by the agreement with Cone, the latter was bound, if he acquired title, to discharge Palmer from his personal liability for certain mortgage and judgment debts, by having them satisfied of record, and thus to relieve Palmer. The inducement and consideration for Cone to make perfect his inchoate title, and to carry out the other parts of his agreement, was greater or less as the premises remained unimpaired in value, or were injured by fire. All this constituted an interest in Palmer in this building, which was an insurable interest. If the loss of the building by fire should turn away Cone from the fulfillment of his agreement to effect the release of Palmer from his personal liability, then there might be, almost assuredly would be, a damage to Palmer. *Waring* v. *Loder*, 53 N. Y. 581; *Franklin Fire Ins. Co.* v. *Findlay*, 6 Whart. 483. Palmer did not, by the agreement with Cone, in terms, give up his own right to redeem, or his right and power to create a judgment creditor who might redeem. He, probably, did not have any purpose to do either, and sought, by the agreement, somewhat of an equivalent for them. But, either by the possession of this right and power, or by the benefit contracted for in the agreement, he had a beneficial interest in the preservation of the buildings, which was an insurable interest. The contingency gave him an interest in the continued existence of the buildings, which was an insurable interest. It thus appears that Palmer had not, at the time of the fire, been divested of all interest in the premises. He had an interest, similar to, if not as great and as perfect, as a possessor of the legal title to real estate who has entered into a valid contract of sale with a responsible vendee put into possession, who has not yet paid over the purchase-money. Be the vendee ever so responsible, the vendor has still an interest in the premises sold, which is the subject of insurance. Palmer had this interest certainly until the last day of the fifteen months for judgment creditors to redeem, for until the expiration of that last day it was a possibility for him to find some one who would make an advance of money, take a judgment, and make immediate redemption from Cone; and he also had the security of the additional inducement to Cone to fulfill his agreement. See *Lazarus* v. *Com. Ins. Co.*, 19 Pick. 81.

It is not sound to style the agreement between Cone and Palmer a conveyance of the title to Cone. It expressly looks to other action by Cone, or lack of action by others, by which Cone should get title, and, by the terms of the instrument, it was looked upon as a possible contingency, not an assured event, that Cone should get title. It is apparent that Palmer retained the legal title to the premises until the expiration of the fifteen months. As these did not expire until after the fire, his title continued until after the fire; and he, till after that event, had a pecuniary interest in the premises which was effected by their destruction by fire, without the indemnity of insurance. The seventh point is, that the plaintiff, having realized the whole, or a larger part, of his interest in the property, the defendants are entitled to a deduction from the sum claimed on the policy, or a subrogation to the plaintiff's securities. It is not found, specifically, that the plaintiff has realized, as is in this point assumed; on the contrary, it is found that none of the claims or liens upon the property have been paid. It is found that the plaintiff has received $3,000 of insurance money from another company. There is proof that the whole premises, before that building was burned, were worth from $14,000 to $15,000, and that the plaintiff received a sheriff's deed of them after the fire. It is found that the building destroyed was worth $8,000; and there is proof of the amount (about $7,000) of the liens held and owned by the plaintiff. So that there is matter in the proofs from which can be made an estimate whether the plaintiff, by the premises which he obtained by the sheriff's

---

[1] *Herkimer* v. *Rice*, 27 N. Y. 163; *Stephens* v. *Ill. M. Ins. Co.*, 43 Ill. 327; *Buffum* v. *Bowditch*, 10 Cush. (Mass.) 540; *Waring* v. *Loder*, 53 N. Y. 581; *Franklin Fire Ins. Co.* v. *Findlay*, 6 What. (Penn.) 483.

A destruction of the buildings lessening the value of the premises, *would lessen the value of his right to redeem*, and this right of redemption, while it exists, is " a real and proprietory interest, a *jus in re*." [1] But, when the title absolutely passes under the decree or upon sale of the premises under the decree, the mortgagor's interest in the premises is ended, and the premises, from that time, are at the risk of the purchaser. [2]

Person having legal title, has insurable interest in some cases, when he has no actual interest.

SEC. 263. A person purchasing property in his own name, *but really for the benefit of another*, has the legal title thereto, as against every one but the person for whom he purchased, and his creditors, and may insure the same in his own name. The insurer has no interest in the relation of the parties, or their rights in reference to the disposition of the insurance money. *If the insured has an insurable interest*, and the legal title imports that, the fact that some other person may be equitably entitled to the benefit of the insurance, will not affect the insurer's liability. [3]

---

deed and by the money which he obtained from the Glen's Falls Insurance Company, is more than made good for the amount of his claims against the whole property. And it would result that he is. But if it is proper for this court to enter into such an inquiry and to arrive at that conclusion, are the relations of the plaintiff, the defendants and Palmer, such as that the defendants can maintain the position assumed in this point? The policy did not insure Cone; it insured Palmer and his interest. It was the loss sustained by that interest which is to be paid to Cone, not that sustained by his own. Had he failed of a full indemnity, the defendant would not have been affected by that; that he may have obtained more than a full indemnity gives them no right to resist his claim upon them. Had they insured his interest as a lienor, independently of any consideration of the interest of Palmer as the owner, and without the aid, concurrence or acquiescence of the latter, they would be in a better position to limit the amount of his recovery against them, and to set up a right of subrogation to his claims against the property subject to them, left undestroyed by the fire. But having insured Palmer on his interest, with an agreement binding upon him and them to pay to Cone the loss which that interest should sustain, there is no equity which will permit them to succeed to the right of Cone against Palmer or the property, nor to make inquiry into the state of the debits and credits between Cone and Palmer.

[1] SHAW, C.J., in *Buffum* v. *Bowditch, ante*, and is an insurable interest. *Fletcher* v. *Commonwealth Ins. Co.*, 18 Pick. (Mass.) 419; *Strong* v. *Manufacturer's Ins. Co.*, 10 id. 46; *Cone* v. *Niagara F. Ins. Co., ante*.

[2] *McLaren* v. *Hartford Fire Ins. Co.*, 5 N. Y. 151.

[3] In *Bicknell* v. *The Lancaster, etc., Ins. Co.*, 1 T. & C. (N. Y.) 215; aff'd Ct. of Appeals, 58 N. Y. 677, an action was brought upon a policy by which the plaintiff was insured "on his plainer, matcher, shingle and stave and spout machine, edger, butting saw and belting, contained in a two-story frame, water power, saw and plaining mill, held by him under a contract of purchase from George Parish. The defense was, that the plaintiff falsely and fraudulently represented that he held the property by contract of purchase from George Parish, when, in fact, he had no title or insurable interest therein, and that he had not stated his interest in the policy, as required thereby. It appeared that in January, 1868, George Parish, being then the owner of the mill, entered into a

Legal title not always evidence of insurable interest.

SEC. 264. The fact that the legal title is in the insured, is not always
the test of an insurable interest, for the legal title may be in one who
has no interest *in fact*, and when such is the case there is no insurable
interest. An interest *in fact* must always exist. Thus, where a company [1] insured "their" buildings, the ownership of which was not
otherwise stated, by policy conditioned to be void, if the assured, not
being the sole unconditional and entire owners of the property, should
fail to state that fact, it was held that the policy was avoided by
proof that the assured had contracted to sell the property to one *who
had paid for it and taken possession of it, though he had taken no conveyance of the legal estate when the policy was made.*

Personal interest not necessary.

SEC. 265. A person need not have a *personal* interest in property
in order to have an *insurable* interest therein. It is enough if he has
an interest therein *for another*, as agent, trustee, bailee, etc., provided
the interest existed both at the time of insurance and of loss,[2] and his

contract with Thompson and Judd, by which the former agreed to sell to the latter
the mill-property, and to convey, upon payment and performance of the conditions
of the contract, by the latter. There was a clause in the contract that all tools,
implements and machinery put in said mill should become part of the free-hold; and
a condition, that if Thompson and Judd failed to pay as provided, Parish might, at
his option, declare the contract forfeited. Thompson and Judd went into possession. They bought the machinery in question, and put it in the mill. Upon this
they executed to plaintiff various chattel mortgages. In January, 1870, plaintiff
purchased Thompson and Judd's interest in the contract and property, as receiver's sale, and went into possession, and was in possession at the time of the
insurance. It was claimed by defendant that as there was no agreement on the
part of Thompson and Judd in the contract, to purchase and pay for the premises, no consideration appeared for the agreement on the part of Parish, and,
therefore, the contract was void under the statute of fraud, and conveyed no
interest. Held, that, conceding the contract gave no interest in the real estate,
it did not appear that the property insured had become so affixed as to form part
thereof, and that the evidence tended to show plaintiff was owner and had an
insurable interest therein; that, whether the contract was void or not, it was
under it, plaintiff held the premises described in the policy, as therein stated, and
in reliance upon the contract as operative. But held, that the agreement contained in the contract, that Parish should have title to the machinery, was a consideration for the agreement, on his part, to sell and to convey on payment, and
made the contract valid under the statute. Upon the trial, defendant offered to
prove that plaintiff, although he bid off the property at the receiver's sale in his
own name, in fact, bought it for Thompson and Judd. This testimony was
rejected. Held, no error; that by the sale and conveyance, that if plaintiff did
so purchase, he had the legal title as against the whole world, save, perhaps,
Thompson and Judd and their creditors, and, as the owner of the legal title, he
could insure. Nor was the evidence proper to show false representations, as the
alleged false representations, i. e., that he held the property under the Parish
contract, were not false, as above shown; and even if Thompson and Judd, or
other creditors, had an equitable interest, it was still true that plaintiff held
under the contract, and the evidence was therefore immaterial."

[1] *Clay F. & M. Ins. Co.* v. *Huron Salt, etc., Co.*, 31 Mich. 346.
[2] *Graham* v. *Fireman's Ins. Co.*, 2 Dis. (Ohio) 255.

interest as indicated by the policy is alone covered thereby. Thus, if A. and B. are joint owners of real estate and buildings, an insur_ ance taken in the name of A. will only cover his interest in the prop_ erty—one-half, one-fourth, or whatever the extent of his interest may be—and, in the absence of anything in the policy indicating an inten_ tion to extend it to cover whatever equitable interest he may have as against his partner, it cannot be so extended;[1] but where, from the policy itself, it is evident that such interest was intended to be cov_ ered, or when it appears that the agent or company issuing the policy *knew* that the property belonged to two or more persons, and that the interest of both or all was intended to be covered, and a premium for that purpose was paid, but through ignorance or mistake the policy was issued to one only, parol evidence is admissible to prove that the interest of all the owners was intended to be covered, and, upon proof of the facts, a recovery of the full amount of the loss may be had by the person to whom the policy was issued.[2] But quere? in such cases, is not the true remedy to be sought by proceedings to reform the con- tract?

Insurable interest may exist where there is neither a legal or equitable interest in the property.

SEC. 266. It is not necessary that the assured should have either a legal or equitable interest, or indeed *any* property interest in the sub- ject-matter insured. *It is enough if he holds such a relation to the prop- erty, that its destruction by the peril insured against, involves pecuniary loss to him, or those for whom he acts.* It need not be an existing *jus in re,* nor *jus ad rem.*[3]

---

[1] *Bailey* v. *Hope Ins. Co.*, 56 Me. 474.

[2] *Manhattan Ins. Co.* v. *Webster*, 59 Penn. St. 227.

[3] *Hancox* v. *Fishing Ins. Co.*, 3 Sum. (N. Y.) 132. Thus, in *Carter* v. *Humboldt Ins. Co.*, 12 Iowa, 287, a mechanic having a lien for services. In *Russell* v. *Union Ins. Co.*, 1 Wash. C. C. (U. S.) 409, a surety for captured property, restored to the owner, during the pendency of an appeal. In *Aldrich* v. *Equitable Safety Ins. Co.*, 1 W. & M. (U. S.) 272, a person who advanced money to purchase a cargo for a voyage. In *Waring* v. *Loder*, 53 N. Y. 581, a person who is personally respon- sible for a mortgage debt. In *Fireman's Ins. Co.* v. *Powell*, 16 B. Mon. (Ky.) 311, a receiptor of property attached or seized. See also, *Simmes* v. *Marine Ins. Co.*, 2 Cranch C. C. (U. S.) 618. In *Rohrbach* v. *Germania Ins. Co.*, 62 N. Y. 47, this question was ably discussed by FOLGER, J. In that case an action was brought upon a policy of insurance, by its terms insuring plaintiff upon "his two framed buildings." Prior to the 28th June, 1868, the plaintiff had been in the employ of Margaretha Hartmann, and she was indebted to him for his labor and services. On that day they intermarried. On the 30th of the same month she executed and delivered to him an instrument, in writing, of the body of which the following is a copy:

"JEFFERSONVILLE. *June* 30th, 1868.

"I do hereby certify that I owe to John Rohrbach the sum of $700; and, also, $25 for each and every month from the 14th day of July, 1863, and for every

Liability to others for destruction of property confers insurable interest.

SEC. 267. *It is necessary, however, that the assured should stand in such a relation to the property that an injury thereto or its destruction by the peril*

---

month he may live with me henceforth without any deduction whatsoever, which amount shall be a lien on my property."

She died intestate July 8, 1868, leaving personal property of the value of $600, and a lot in said village upon which were the buildings in question. The principal value of the premises was in the buildings. One Armbrust was appointed administrator of her estate. Her indebtedness, other than that to plaintiff, was from $1,200 to $1,400. Her indebtedness to him was about $2,100. Plaintiff continued in the use and occupation of the buildings. In December, 1868, plaintiff negotiated for insurance on the buildings with one Brand, who was the agent of defendant, authorized to procure and submit applications, and to issue policies furnished him by defendant, signed by its officers, which were to be countersigned by him. Plaintiff showed to Brand the said instrument, and related and explained to him all the facts and circumstances. Plaintiff was a German, he could not read or write English. Brand filled out the application, giving, as he testified, his conclusions and the facts he deemed material, and the plaintiff signed it. The material part of the application was as follows : " Application of John Rohrbach, of Jeffersonville, State of N. Y., for insurance against loss or damage by fire for the period of one year from 26th day of December, 1868, to 26th day of December, 1869, at noon, by the Germania Fire Insurance Company of the city of New York, in the sum of $1,000, upon the property specified below :

	Cash value.	Sum to be insured.
" On his frame two-story building, occupied by insured as a dwelling and saloon.....	$4,000	$1,000

"The applicant will answer fully the following questions: Title—Is your title to the above property absolute ? If not, state its nature and amount. Ans. His deceased wife held the deed. And the said applicant hereby covenants and agrees to and with the said company, that the foregoing is a just, full and true exposition of all the facts and circumstances in regard to the condition, situation and value of the property to be insured, so far as the same are known to the applicant, and the same is hereby made a condition of the insurance and a warranty on the part of the insured." The policy contained these clauses, among others : "1. If an application, survey, plan or description of the property herein insured is referred to in this policy, such application, survey, plan or description shall be considered a part of this contract, and a warranty by the assured ; and any false representation by the assured of the condition, situation or occupancy of the property, or any omission to make known every fact material to the risk, or an overvaluation, or any misrepresentation whatever, either in a written application or otherwise, * * or if the interest of the assured in the property, whether as owner, trustee, consignee, factor, agent, mortgagee, lessee, or otherwise, be not truly stated in this policy, * * and in every such case this policy shall be void. If the interest of the assured in the property be any other than the entire, unconditional and sole ownership of the property, for the use and benefit of the assured, it must be so represented to the company and so expressed in the written part of this policy, otherwise the policy shall be void." "11. It is a part of this contract, that any person, other than the assured, who may have procured this insurance to be taken by this company, shall be deemed to be the agent of the assured named in this policy, and not of this company under any circumstances whatever, or in any transaction relating to this insurance." " And it is hereby mutually understood and agreed by and between this company and the assured that this policy is made and accepted in reference to the foregoing terms and conditions, and to the classes of hazards and memoranda printed on the back of this policy, which are hereby declared to be a part of this contract, and are to be used and resorted to in order to determine the rights and obligations of the parties hereto, in all cases not herein otherwise specially provided for in writing."

FOLGER, J., said : " The plaintiff cannot maintain this action, unless he had an insurable interest in the buildings which were the subject of the risk taken by the defendants, and which were destroyed by fire. He seeks to found such an

insured against, would entail pecuniary loss upon him, or those whom he represents. Thus, a railroad company, liable for property of persons

---

interest, upon the instrument in writing, executed by his wife after her marriage to him. Without entering minutely into a consideration of the effect of the marriage upon her pre-existing obligations and liabilities to him, it is sufficient to say, that the instrument executed by her was based upon a consideration adequate to uphold her express promise; that though made by a married woman it was in due form to affect her separate estate; and that though a transaction between a wife and her husband, yet equity would have upheld and enforced it in his favor against her, had she lived, and will enforce it against her estate now that she is dead. By it, he was an equitable creditor of her estate, at the time of the insurance; but he was no more than a general creditor. Though the instrument contains the phrase, 'shall be a lien on my property,' no specific lien was thereby created, and, so far as that instrument had effect, no more than a general equitable lien, yet to be enforced and made specific by a judgment in an equitable action. The plaintiff stood thereby in no better plight, so far as having an insurable interest in the buildings, than would have stood a creditor of the deceased wife, who held a judgment only, rendered and docketed against her, which would have become a general lien upon her real property. He did not stand in so good plight, but for other facts now to be mentioned. She had died after giving the instrument, leaving personal and only this real estate; a person other than the plaintiff had taken out letters of administration thereon; the personal estate was by much insufficient to pay the debts against her; and this real estate, including the insured buildings, would, in the due course of administration, for a space of at least three years from the granting of letters of administration, be liable to sale for the purpose of meeting her liabilities, and it was the only fund to which the plaintiff could look for payment; the plaintiff was in the possession of the buildings, occupying them at the time of the fire. Judgment creditors, if any, would have had a preference in payment from the personal estate (2 R. S. 87, § 27, subs. 3, 4), and of course, the lien acquired by the docketing of their judgments could not be disturbed by the application of the administrator for leave to sell the real estate, for the payment of debts, and the obtaining of permission to do so. But yet, the plaintiff had a right to compel an accounting by the administrator (2 R. S. 92, § 52), and a sale of the real estate (id. 108, § 48), for the payment of his and other debts. Thus, the real estate was to a degree subject to the payment thereof, and was, in fact, from the slender amount of the personal property, substantially all that he could look to for payment. His position was not as good in some respects as that of a judgment creditor, but it was not unlike it; both had a right to have the real estate sold for the payment of their debts; for a certain space of time it could not escape the exercise of that right; and it cannot be said that the interest of a judgment creditor in the real estate, as an interest in property, was greater or nearer than that of the plaintiff. It was more manageable, but not more direct in the end. The general definitions of the phrase 'insurable interest,' as given in the text-books, are quite vague and not always concordant. See 1 Arnould on Mar. Ins. 229; Runyon on Life Ass. 16; Hughes on Ins. 80; 1 Marshall on Ins. 115; 1 Phillips on Ins. 2; id. 107; Sherman on Ins. 93; Parsons on Merc. Law. 507; Parsons on Cont. 438; Angell on Ins. § 56; Flanders on Fire Ins. 342; May on Ins. § 76. The last cited author says, that an insurable interest sometimes exists, where there is not any present property, any *jus in re* or *jus ad rem*, and such a connection must be established between the subject-matter insured and the party in whose behalf the insurance has been effected, as may be sufficient for deducing the existence of a loss to him, from the occurrence of an injury to it; and that the tendency of modern decisions is to admit to the protection of the contract whatever act, event or property, bears such relation to the person seeking insurance, as that it can be said, with a reasonable degree of probability, to have a bearing upon his prospective pecuniary condition. While on the other hand, the statement is, that the interest must be founded on some legal or equitable title; and if it be inconsistent with the only title which the law can recognize, it will not be deemed an insurable interest. Marshall on Ins. *supra.* But the result of a comparison of the text writers above cited, is, that there need not be a legal or equitable title to the

on its line burned by sparks from its engine, or through the acts of its employees, may protect itself therefrom by insurance, although it has no interest in the property covered.[1]

---

property insured. If there be a right in or against the property, which some court will enforce upon the property, a right so closely connected with it, and so much dependent for value upon the continued existence of it alone, as that a loss of the property will cause pecuniary damage to the holder of the right against it, he has an insurable interest. Thus, a mortgagee of real estate, though he hold also the bond of the mortgagor, has an insurable interest in the buildings; while a judgment creditor of the same mortgagor, his judgment being a lien upon the same real estate and the same buildings, is said not to have an insurable interest in them. The interest of the first is said to be specific; the interest of the latter, general. As a general rule, the distinction may be sound. But I think it would be difficult to show an appreciable practical difference in the pecuniary result of the two. If the mortgagor and judgment debtor should die leaving no personal property, and no real estate save that mortgaged, it principally valuable for the buildings upon it, and they should be burned, each must then look to the real estate, the lands alone, for a security for his debt; and if that be insufficient, each must with equal certainty, suffer a pecuniary disaster, resulting directly from the fire. What legal reason is there, why the one may not, as well as the other, protect himself by a contract of insurance? In *Grevemeyer* v. *So. Mut. Fire Ins. Co.*, 62 Penn. St. 340, it was held that a judgment creditor, whose judgment was taken for the purchase-money of the property burned, had no insurable interest. See also, *Conard* v. *At. Ins. Co.*, 1 Pet. 386. The reason given is, that his lien was general and not specific; that he was not interested in the property, but in his lien only. His judgment was distinguished from a mortgage, in that the latter is a specific pledge of definite property, and the mortgagee has necessarily an interest in it, while the judgment is a general and not a specific lien; so that if there be personal property of the debtor it is to be satisfied out of that; if there be not, then it is a lien on all his real estate without discrimination. And, citing *Cover* v. *Black*, 1 Barr, 493, it is said that a judgment creditor has neither *jus in re*, nor *jus ad rem*, as regards the judgment debtor's property. It seems to me, that the decision there goes very much upon the fact or the assumption, that the judgment debtor had other property, real and personal, to look to than the real estate damaged; and that it does not touch the case of a judgment creditor whose only or principal reliance for payment, was upon the property destroyed. That there need not be an existing *jus in re*, or *jus ad rem*, is declared by STORY, J., in *Hancox* v. *Fishing Ins. Co.*, 3 Sum. 132–140; and also, that the right to pursue the debtor personally, does not deprive the creditor of an insurable interest. Id. In *Putnam* v. *Mercantile Mar. Ins. Co.*, 5 Metc. 386, which was an insurance for a commission merchant, upon his expected commission from the sale of a cargo consigned to him to be sold, but in which cargo he had no other ownership or interest, it is said, that such an interest in property connected with its safety and its situation, as will cause the insured to sustain a direct loss from its destruction, is an insurable interest. The question is one of damages rather than title or possession; and it will be enough in general to show such a relation between the insured and the property, that injury to it will in natural consequences be loss to him; and it is not necessary to show that the insured is the legal or equitable owner. *Wilson* v. *Jones*, L. R. (2 Exch.) 139; *Buck* v. *Ches. Ins. Co.*, 1 Pet. 151, *163. It will be perceived, that between the case cited from 62 Pennsylvania State, *supra*, and the case in hand, there are some features of distinction; here the debtor was dead; there was no longer any personal liability, nor sufficient personal property to satisfy the debt; nor as may be inferred any other real estate, than that insured. A fund for the payment of the debt, was to be found only in this estate, and principally in the buildings insured. By force of these circumstances, and by operation of the statutes above referred to, this real estate was for a certain length of time, bound for the payment of this debt. As it was bound, as it alone was bound, as there was nought else, nor any person, liable for the debt, it is difficult

---

[1] *Eastern R. R. Co.* v. *Relief Ins. Co.*, 105 Mass. 570.

A commission merchant to whom the cargo of a vessel is consigned for sale, although he has made no advances thereon, and has no prop.

---

to see why, in effect, the debt was not as if a specific lien upon this real estate. A lien, in its most extensive signification, is a charge upon property, for the payment or discharge of a debt or duty. A specific lien, is a charge upon a particular piece of property, by which it is held for the payment or discharge of a particular debt or duty, in priority to the general debts or duties of the owner. It is not the name of the right, which gives or refuses an insurable interest; it is the character of the right. A specific lien gives an insurable interest, because a loss of the particular property is at once seen to affect disastrously the specific lienor. But when a right to payment of a debt exists, which can be satisfied only from a particular piece of property, is there not the same result from the same cause? If I have a debt against another, and he have but one piece of real estate from which my debt may be made, and he die leaving no personal estate, though in technical language my lien may not be specific upon that real estate, it is true in fact, that there is a specific piece of property from which alone I may hope to satisfy my lien, and which is alone legally bound to satisfy it, and I am, practically, just like one to whom that piece of real property has been specifically pledged for a specific debt. If the latter, for that he may suffer pecuniary loss by the burning of that real property, has such an interest, as that he may insure against that burning, I have such an interest also, and I too may insure. The probability, nay the possibility, of the payment of the plaintiff's debt, out of the property of the deceased debtor, rested entirely upon the contingency of this real estate remaining without serious impairment in value.

"The reports of this State are meagre upon this precise question. In *Mapes* v. *Coffin*, 5 Paige, 296, the complainant had levied upon chattels in the hands of an executor of the judgment debtor, which had been insured by the testator in his lifetime, and which were destroyed by fire after the testator's death, and after the levy. The chancellor, in a contest between judgment creditors, gave the avails of the insurance to the creditors who had made the first levy. Perhaps the levy upon the property made a specific lien upon it, and so the case does not much aid us. In *Mickles* v. *Roch. City Bk.*, 11 id. 118, the defendants were judgment creditors of a manufacturing corporation, had issued several executions, had sold and bid in personal property, and advertised for sale the real estate. Pending the advertisement, they took out insurance on the buildings and fixtures in the joint name of themselves and the corporation. A few days after, the real estate was sold and bid in by the defendants. After that occurred a fire, with damage to the buildings and fixtures. The insurers repaired the buildings, and paid for the damage by fire to the fixtures. The real estate was never redeemed. There seems to have been no doubt made of there being an insurable interest in the creditors. By advertising the premises for sale, they came nearer making their judgment a specific lien thereupon, though it was still a general lien upon all other like property. In *Springfield F. & M. Ins. Co.* v. *Allen*, 43 N. Y. 389-395, 396, it is said by ALLEN, J. : 'An insurable interest may exist, without any estate or interest in the *corpus* of the thing insured;' 'it was enough that' there be 'a pecuniary interest in the preservation and protection of the property, and' that one 'might sustain a loss by its destruction.' I know, of no decision in this State bearing more directly upon this precise question than that in *Herkimer* v. *Rice*, 27 N. Y. 163. The propositions advanced there are sufficient, if sustainable, or if to be taken as authority, to uphold an insurable interest in the plaintiff in the case in hand. DENIO, Ch.J., there says : 'It is certain that the creditors had no estate whatever in the real property. In a technical sense, they had no lien. But they had important rights connected with it, and a pecuniary interest in its preservation. * * * The law does not require that the assured shall have an estate or property in the subject of the insurance. * * * No property in the thing insured is required. It is enough, if the assured is so situated as to be liable to loss, if it be destroyed by the peril insured against. Creditors having no other means of enforcing their debts, but having a direct and certain right to subject the real estate to a sale for their benefit, have an interest as positive and absolute as one having a specific lien, or even as the owner himself. * * * The creditors, whether by simple contract or specialty,

32

erty therein, and no claim that could be enforced against the owner of the property, nevertheless has an insurable interest therein to the

---

under our laws, are parties interested in the real estate, when there is a deficiency in the personal, for they have power to subject it to the payment of their debts.' It is urged that these remarks are *obiter dicta*, and that the real question to be decided, and which was decided in the case, was whether an administrator of an insolvent estate had such an interest in the real estate of his intestate, as was insurable. *Dicta* are opinions of a judge which do not embody the resolution or determination of the court, and made without argument, or full consideration of the point, are not the professed deliberate determinations of the judge himself (4 Burr. 2064-2068); *obiter dicta* are such opinions uttered by the way, not upon the point or question pending (*Rouse* v. *Moore*, 18 J. R. 407–419), as if turning aside for the time from the main topic of the case to collateral subjects. I think that no one who reads the opinion in *Herkimer* v. *Rice* can doubt that all which was said on the subject of a creditor of an insolvent estate having an insurable interest in the real property thereof, was the professed and deliberate determination of the learned Chief Justice, not hastily formed nor carelessly expressed; not by the way nor on a collateral question to that awaiting decision, but deemed essential to lead up to the solemn judgment rendered. The direct question was, indeed, whether an administrator of an insolvent estate might insure its real property. But the reasoning of the opinion shows that this was deemed to depend upon whether the creditors of that estate had such an interest. After stating the question, he says: 'It will be convenient to consider, in the first place, *whether the creditors themselves have such an interest;* and then, whether the *administrator can he said to represent that interest,* so as *to enable him* to make the *contract for the benefit of the creditors.*' Again, * * * 'the creditors of an insolvent estate are generally numerous, and having no opportunity for concerted action, except through the executor or administrators, they could scarcely ever avail themselves of the advantage of insurance, unless by the agency of the representatives. If the administrators cannot insure, *the parties interested, the creditors,* will be excluded from a remedy which all other persons having a similar interest possess.' He then proceeds to show that an agent or trustee may insure the interest of a party beneficially interested, and that the administrator, though not the trustee of the land, is a trustee of a power over it, such as is recognized by law, and says: 'In this case it was sufficiently apparent, from the language of the receipt for the premium, that it was the interest of the creditors which was designed to be covered by the contract; the beneficiaries of the administrator were the parties intended to be protected; the insurers, therefore, must have seen and known that it was the interest of the creditors * * * which it was the object of the policy to protect, * * * and which was the subject of the contract.' There is more to the same effect; and the opinion is based upon the ground that the administrator is the representative of the creditors. Indeed, but for there being creditors, the administrator would have no concern in the land, and the concern he has with it is, that they through him may dispose of it for the payment of their debts. *Herkimer* v. *Rice* was a case in which there was full argument and consideration. I consider it gives reasons, as well as authority, for the determination of the question now in consideration. It has often been cited as an authority, and at times as authority for the power of an executor or administrator to insure, as having, or as representing, an insurable interest, holding it for the beneficiaries under the will, or in the intestate's estate. *Savage* v. *Howard Ins. Co.*, 52 N. Y. 502. In *Clinton* v. *Hope Ins. Co.*, 45 N. Y. 454, it is cited by ANDREWS, J., as holding that when the personal estate of an intestate is sufficient to pay the debts, the administrator has an insurable interest in buildings, on the ground that he is the trustee of a power to sell the land for the benefit of creditors, and that *as the interest of the creditors* is *the subject of the insurance,* the administrator may insure for their benefit. The decision is there put aside as not a precedent for that then in hand, inasmuch as in that the personal property was sufficient to pay the debts, and therefore the administrator had no insurable interest. See also, *Waring* v. *Lodger*, 53 N. Y. 581, where it is cited as authority for the proposition, that a mortgagor after he has sold the mortgaged premises has still an interest in it which is insur-

extent of his expected profits,[1] and generally, it may be said, that *the real test of insurable interest is, whether an injury thereto, or its destruction by the peril insured against, would involve the assured in pecuniary loss.*[2]

Need not be a vested interest.

SEC. 268. The interest need not be vested; *it is sufficient if it exists at the time of the insurance, and loss, although contingent, and liable never to attach, or be perfected by occupancy or possession.* Mr. Justice LAWRENCE, in a leading case,[3] well expressed the doctrine as follows: "Insurance," said he, "is a contract by which the one party, in consideration of a price paid to him, adequate to the risk, becomes security to the other, that he shall not suffer loss, damage or prejudice, by the happening of the perils specified, to certain things which may be exposed to them. If this be the general nature of the contract of insurance, it follows that it is applicable to protect men against uncertain events which may, in any wise, be of disadvantage to them; *not only those persons to whom positive loss may arise, by such events occasioning the deprivation of that which they may possess, but those also, who, in consequence of such events, may have intercepted from them the advantage or profit which, but for such events, they would acquire, according to the ordinary and probable course of things.*"[4]

When person has only quasi interest.

SEC. 269. An insurable interest in property cannot be acquired from one who, although having a *quasi* interest in the property, has no right to remove or sell it. Thus, where the lessees of a farm who were bound by the lease to feed out the hay grown upon the farm, to the stock thereon, and who covenanted that they would not sell, dispose of or carry away, or suffer to be carried away from the farm any of the

---

able, inasmuch as it stands between him and personal liability for the mortgage debt. The distinction is not perceptible, so far as this question is concerned, between a power to obtain indemnity against loss from being obliged to pay a debt owing to another, and against loss from failure to obtain payment of a debt owing to one's self. I conclude that a creditor of the estate of one deceased, whose personal property left is insufficient for the payment of his debts, has an insurable interest in the sole real estate of the deceased debtor, when it is plain that if it is damaged by fire a pecuniary loss must ensue to the creditor thereby." In *Rockford* v. *Ins. Co.*, 65 Ill. 415, the husband made a *verbal* gift of a lot to his wife, and abandoned her. It was held that she had an insurable interest therein, and might properly describe it as her property.

[1] *Putnam* v. *Mercantile, etc., Ins. Co.*, 5 Met. (Mass.) 316.

[2] *Russell* v. *Union Ins. Co.*, ante.

[3] *Lucena* v. *Crawford*, 2 Atk. 292.

[4] *Barclay* v. *Cousins*, 2 East, 543; *Grant* v. *Parkinson*, Marshall on Ins. 111; *Hendrickson* v. *Walker*, 2 East, 549, *n*; *New York Ins. Co.* v. *Robinson*, 1 John. (N. Y.) 616; *Wells* v. *Phila. Ins. Co.*, 9 S. & R. (Penn.) 103.

hay, without the consent of the lessors, gave a bill of sale of the hay to a third person, who took possession of the farm and the hay, under the lease, intending to carry on the farm and feed out the hay thereon according to the terms of the lease; it was held that such third person had no insurable interest in the hay. The title thereto was in the lessors, subject only to the use of the lessees in carrying on the farm, and no property interest existed in them which they could dispose of by sale or otherwise, than in strict conformity with the provisions of the lease.[1]

Issue of policy prima facie evidence of insurable interest.

SEC. 270. While, if denied, the plaintiff must establish an insurable interest in the property, yet, the fact that the policy describes the property as that of the insured, is *prima facie* sufficient, and casts the burden upon the company of showing that *in fact* he had no interest.[2]

Indeed, in an action upon a policy, it is not essential that the plaintiff should set forth his interest in the property.[3] The policy itself is *prima facie* sufficient proof of interest, and if the insurer seeks to avoid it upon the ground that there is in fact none, he must establish his defense by proper proof.[4] The policy may be avoided by proving that he had no such interest in the property as entitled him to insurance, but the legal presumption is that he had, the law presuming in favor of honesty, rather than fraud or dishonesty, and the insurer takes the burden of showing such fraud as renders the policy void,[5] and this applies with equal force to every species of fraud, misrepresentation, etc., which is set up to defeat the policy. Not only may the insurer avail himself of a want of insurable interest at the time when the policy was issued, but also, even though such an interest then existed, it is a good defense *that it did not exist at the time of the loss.* When the interest of the insured in the property ceases, the policy ceases to be operative.[6]

Trespasser.

SEC. 271. A trespasser, or one who has erected a building upon the premises of another without any license or authority from the owner,

---

[1] *Heald* v. *Guilder's Ins. Co.*, 111 Mass. 38.

[2] *Nichols et al.*, v. *Fayette Ins. Co.*, 1 Allen (Mass.) 63; *Fowler* v. *N. Y. Ins. Co.*, 23 Barb. (N. Y.) 150; *Franklin* v. *National Ins. Co.*, 43 Mo. 491.

[3] *Nantes* v. *Thompson*, 2 East, 386; *Goring* v. *Sweeting*, 1 Saund. 200.

[4] *Thelluson* v. *Fletcher*, Doug. 301; *Nantes* v. *Thompson, ante.*

[5] *Fowler* v. *Insurance Co., ante.*

[6] *Graham* v. *Fireman's Ins. Co.*, 2 Dis. (Ohio) 255; *Hidden* v. *Slater, etc., Ins. Co.*, 2 Cliff. (U. S.) 266.

whether the owner be an individual or the State, has no property interest therein, although he is in undisturbed possession of the prem. ises, and consequently cannot effect a valid insurance thereon.[1]

Stockholder cannot insure corporate property in his own name.

SEC. 272. A stockholder in a corporation, however large may be his interest in the stock of the corporation, has no such insurable interest in either its real or personal property as will uphold a policy as *owner* of the property;[2] but it has been held, and, we believe, with much consistency, that *a stockholder in a corporation has such a qualified inter. est in the property of the corporation, that he may, as such, insure the corporate property for his benefit, to the extent of his interest as such stockholder.*[3] In the case last cited, the question was directly raised and decided. The policy covered the private stock of Goodale & Hasford, to the extent of $2,500, in a one-story saw mill belonging to the Dubuque Lumber Company, loss, if any, payable to the plaintiffs. It appeared that by "private stock" was meant the share or interest of the assured (Goodale & Hasford) in the capital stock of the company; that the insurance was affected with the full knowledge of the company, and that their interest in the stock of said company exceeded the sum insured. The court held that this was an insurable interest, and that the policy was valid.[4]

---

[1] *Sweeney* v. *Franklin F. Ins. Co.*, 20 Penn. St. 337.

[2] *Phillips* v. *Knox Co., etc., Ins. Co.*, 20 Ohio, 174.

[3] *Warren* v. *Davenport F. Ins. Co.*, 31 Iowa, 464.

[4] MILLER, J., in discussing the question said: "Policies of insurance founded upon mere hope and expectation, and *without some interest*, are said to be objectionable as a species of *gaming*, and so have been called wager policies. These polices were expressly prohibited in England by statute of George II, ch. 37, and they have been adjudged illegal and void in this country upon the principles of that statute. Angell on Fire and Life Ins., §§ 18, 55. It is not that wager policies are without consideration or unequal between the parties that they are held void, but because they are contrary to public policy. Policies of fire insurance, without interest, are peculiarly and extremely hazardous by reason of the temptation they hold out to the commission of arson by the party assured, which is necessarily attended with peril of the most deplorable kind to a whole neighborhood. In *King* v. *State Mut. F. Ins. Co.*, 7 Cush. (Mass.) 10, Mr. Chief Justice SHAW says: ' If an insurance were made on a subject in which the assured has no pecuniary interest—although in other respects he may be *deeply concerned* in it, and on that ground be willing to pay a fair premium—made with full knowledge of all the circumstances, by both parties, without coercion or fraud, we cannot perceive why it would not be valid as between the parties. But upon the strong objections, on grounds of public policy, to all gaming contracts, and especially to contracts which would create a temptation to destroy life or property, such policies without interest are justly held void.' Upon the ground of public policy, therefore, if the assured have no interest in the thing insured, the policy must be held void. This is well settled. On the other hand, it is equally well settled that not only the absolute owner, but any one having a qualified interest in the property insured, or even any reasonable expectation of profit or advantage to be derived from it, may be the subject of insurance, and especially if it be founded

Interest under void or voidable contract.

SEC. 273. A person whose only interest in the property insured is
derived from a contract within the statute of frauds, and who is not

---

in some legal or equitable title. Id., § 56. And the general doctrine that any
interest in the subject-matter insured is sufficient to sustain an insurance upon
real property is one which has been fully sustained. Id., § 57, and notes. Several persons owning different interests in the same property may insure their
several interests. And it is not material whether the interest assured be legal or
equitable. Any interest which would be recognized by a court of law or equity
is an insurable interest. The interest of a *cestui que trust*, mortgagor, mortgagee, of a lender or borrower on bottomry, so far as regards the surplus value, or
of a captor, or of one entitled to freight or commission, is insurable. So where
a lessor on ground rent has entered for the arrears, under a covenant that he may
hold until the arrears are paid, etc., has an insurable interest. So also, in case
of one in possession of land by disseisin. Angell on Fire and Life Ins., §§ 57, 58,
59; 2 Parsons on Cont., § 2 of ch. 14, commencing on p. 438, and cases cited; 2
Greenlf. on Ev., § 379. The term *interest*, as used in application to the right to
insure, does not necessarily imply *property*, Hancox v. *Fishing Ins. Co.*, 3 Sumner's C. C. 132; Angell on Life and Fire Ins., § 56; and as the contract of insurance is one of indemnity, against losses and disadvantages, an *insurable interest*
may be proved in the assured, without the evidence of any legal or equitable title
in the property. *Putnam* v. *Mercantile Ins. Co.*, 5 Metc. 386; *Lazarus* v. *The
Commonwealth Ins. Co.*, 19 Pick. 81, 98. An 'insurable interest' is *sui generis*,
and peculiar in its texture and operation. It sometimes exists where there is not
any present property, or *jus in re* or *jus ad rem*. Yet such a connection must be
established between the subject-matter insured, and the party in whose behalf
the insurance has been effected, as may be sufficient for the purpose of deducing
the existence of a loss to him from the occurrence of the injury to it. *Buck* v.
Chespeake Ins. Co., 1 Pet. 163. In the case under consideration, the assured were
stockholders in the Dubuque Lumber Co., a corportion for pecuniary profit. The
property destroyed belonged to the corporation. The insurance was upon the
interest which the assured had in that property by virtue of the capital stock
therein owned by them. The object of the insurance was to indemnify the assured
against loss to them in the event of a destruction of the property by fire. Could
or would they sustain loss in such event? How would their interest be effected?
It seems to us to be beyond controversy, that, in case of the destruction of the
corporate property by fire, the stockholders sustain loss to a greater or less extent,
dependent on the particular circumstances. Suppose the case of a grain elevator
upon some of our numerous railroad lines, built, owned and managed by a joint-
stock corporation; that this is the only property of the corporation; that the
entire capital stock is represented in and by this property; that, in consequence
of the profitable nature of the business, large dividends are realized by the stockholders, and the stock is above par in the market. The destruction of this property by fire would at once result in the loss of dividends to the stockholders and
a destruction of the value of the stock, or at least to its reduction to a nominal
value. The entire property, representing the whole capital of the corporation,
being destroyed, it is difficult to perceive what would give any value to the stock.
It is true that, primarily, the loss is that of the corporation, and hence it may
insure, but the corporation may refuse to insure, and then the real and actual
loss falls on the stockholders. The appellee argues that shares of stock in a corporation are choses in action, and are not considered to be an interest in the real
property of the company, and cites numerous authorities to sustain this position.
This may be admitted without denying the shareholders' 'insurable interest' in
the property of the corporation. A mortgage, also, is but a chose in action. The
mortgagee acquires no right to the mortgaged property which can be attached,
levied on under a general execution, or that can be inherited. It is a mere security for a debt. *Eaton* v. *Whiting*, 3 Pick. 484; *Smith* v. *People's Bank*, 11 Shep.
(Me.) 185; *Abbott* v. *Mut. Fire Ins. Co.*, 17 id. 414; *Middleton Savings Bank* v.
Dubuque, 15 Iowa, 394; *Newman* v. *De Lorimer*, 19 id. 244; *Baldwin* v. *Thomp-
von*, 15 id. 504; *Burton* v. *Hintrager*, 18 id. 348; Hilliard on Mort. 215. And yet
the cases are uniform to the effect that a mortgagee of real property has an insur-

in possession of the same, has no insurable interest therein. In order to acquire such an interest under a contract it must be enforceable either at law or in equity.[1]

Defective title does not defeat.

SEC. 274. The fact, however, that the title of the insured to the property is defective, or invalid even, will not deprive him of his insurable interest therein, *if he is in the possession and use thereof* under a *bona fide*

---

able interest therein which he may insure on his own account, but that when he does so it is but an insurance of his debt. *Eaton* v. *Whiting, supra.* And in case of damage by fire to the premises before payment of the mortgage, his loss, if any, is that his security has been impaired or lost. His interest is but a chose in action in the nature of a security, which he may insure, so that in case of destruction of or damage to the property upon which his security rests, he will be indemnified for the loss he actually sustains. So also, it seems to us that the owner of stock in a corporation for pecuniary profit has a like interest in the corporate property. A mortgagee of real property has an insurable interest in the mortgaged premises, based upon the interest he has in the preservation of the same as security for a debt. He has a legal right to contract for indemnity against injury to the value of his security. Upon precisely the same principal a stockholder may contract for indemnity against injury to the value of his stock, for he also has an interest in the preservation of the corporate property from destruction by fire; and in its destruction he sustains loss in so far as the value of his stock is depreciated in consequence thereof, or his dividends cut off. The argument that, if this is allowed, owners of stock worth not more than ten per cent upon its nominal value may be insured at its par value, and in case of loss by fire such par value of the stock recovered from the insurer, seems to us to be unsound. Without entering into a discussion in detail of what would be the exact measure of recovery in such case, we simply answer that no more than the *actual loss sustained* is in any case recoverable. This rule is well established, and rests upon just principles. See Angell on Fire and Life Ins., ch. 11, and cases cited in notes. The question under consideration has not received direct judicial determination in any of the States, so far as we have been able to discover. The case of *Phillips* v. *Knox Co. Ins. Co.*, 20 Ohio, 174, is cited and claimed as an authority against the right of a stockholder to insure. The decision in that case, as a careful examination of the same fully shows, was made entirely upon a construction of the charter of the insurance company, which gave a lien on the insured property, including the land on which the buildings stand. By the charter a sale of the insured property rendered the policy void, and the ninth section declared, that if the insured have a less estate than an unincumbered title in fee simple to the buildings insured and the lands covered by the same, the policy shall be void, unless the true title of the insured and the incumbrances be expressed in the policy and the application therefor. The plaintiff insured *as owner* of the property, which in fact belonged to a corporation of which he was a stockholder, and the court held that, 'where a building and the land on which it stands is the property of an incorporated company, the stockholders could not, under the provisions of the defendant's charter, insure such property as their individual property in the defendant's company.' Under the charter of that company, a mortgagee, even insuring the property *as his own*, would likewise be defeated in a recovery. So the owner in fee simple could not recover if the property was incumbered and the incumbrance not set forth in the policy. And of course the same result must follow where a stockholder insures corporate property as his own individual property. The decision in that case goes no further than this, and is no authority in support of the proposition, that a stockholder has no insurable interest in the property of the company, and hence, has no bearing upon the question before us."

[1] *Stockdale* v. *Dunlap*, 6 M. & W. 224; *Redfield* v. *Holland Purchase Ins. Co.*, 56 N. Y. 356, 357.

claim of title, legal or equitable.[1] But if the insured is *not* in possession of the property, and is not so situated in reference thereto that its destruction would entail pecuniary loss upon him, he has no insurable interest. Thus, a common carrier has no insurable interest in goods to be transported by him, until the same are placed in his custody and control, and prior to that time, a policy cannot attach thereto in name of the carrier.[2]

Person liable as indorser of mortgage note.

SEC. 275. A mortgagee who has sold the mortgage and duly assigned it, still retains an insurable interest in the property, *if he is liable as indorser of the mortgage note.*[3] If a person has *any* pecuniary interest in the preservation of the property, legal or equitable, direct or contingent, connected with the property, he has an insurable interest as a

---

[1] In *The Farmers', etc., Trust Co.* v. *The Harmony, etc., Ins. Co.*, 51 Barb. (N. Y.) 284, the plaintiffs (a New York corporation), were trustees of a railroad in Wisconsin, which was covered by insurance in the defendant company. It was urged in defense to an action upon the policy for the loss of property in Wisconsin, that the plaintiff could not hold real estate in the latter State, but the court held that so long as they were allowed to remain in possession and use the railroad property conveyed to them in trust, they had such an interest as would bring all their property connected therewith under the terms of the policy. In *Redfield* v. *Holland Purchase Ins. Co.*, 56 N. Y. 354, it appeared that prior to the insurance by plaintiff, he conveyed the premises insured to his wife upon the consideration, and under a parol agreement, that upon acquiring the legal title she should grant and convey back, by a proper instrument, to the husband a life estate in the land. The husband remained in possession, and received the proceeds of the lands, but no conveyance was executed to him by the wife. Held, that the husband had an insurable interest in the property. The policy of insurance contained a condition which provided that "if the insured premises be held in trust, or be a leasehold or other interest not absolute, it must be so represented to the company." Plaintiff's application did not specify or refer to the fact that he had a leasehold interest. In the action upon the policy no reference to this condition was made in the pleadings, on the trial, or in the referee's report. Held, that the point could not be taken by defendant upon appeal to this court.

[2] In *Anderson* v. *Morice*, L. R. 10 C. P. 609, the plaintiff, a merchant in London, contracted with B. S. & Co., of Calcutta, for the purchase of rice, as follows: "Bought for account of A. of B. S. & Co., the cargo of new crop Rangoon rice, per *Sunbeam*, 707 tons register, at 9s. 1¼d. per cwt. cost and freight. Payment by sellers' draft on purchasers, at six months' sight, with documents attached." The *Sunbeam* was chartered by the sellers' agent to proceed to Rangoon to ship the cargo of rice. The plaintiff effected an insurance with the defendant as follows: "At and from Rangoon, to any port in the United Kingdom or Continent, by the *Sunbeam*, on rice, as interest may appear," etc. While loading at Rangoon, and the greater part of the cargo having been shipped, but a substantial part remaining to be shipped, the *Sunbeam* sank, and the rice already shipped was wholly lost. The captain afterward signed bills of lading for the cargo shipped, which were indorsed to the plaintiff, and the sellers drew bills of exchange for the price of such cargo, which were accepted and met by the plaintiff. Held (by BRAMWELL, B., BLACKBURN and LUSH, JJ., and POLLOCK and AMPHLETT, B.B., QUAIN, J., dissenting, reversing the decision of the court below), that the plaintiff had no insurable interest in the rice, inasmuch as it was not at his risk under the contract of sale until the loading was complete.

[3] *Williams* v. *Roger Williams' Ins. Co.*, 107 Mass. 377.

mortgagor whose equity of redemption has been seized and sold on execution, so long as the right of redemption remains in him.[1]

Contingent liability. Possible loss. Voisinage.

SEC. 276. The test is, whether the insured has such an interest in the property that he will suffer loss by its destruction.[2] Thus, a rail. road company has an insurable interest in the property of persons along the line of its road for the destruction of which by fire commu. nicated by its engines it is liable,[3] and the same rule is applicable to individuals. In France, where the law upon this subject differs but little from our common law, the risk of "voisinage" is very generally insured against,[4] and in book 3d, of the Code Napoleon, it is declared that " every one is responsible for the damage of which he is the cause, not only by his own act, but also by his negligence or by his impru. dence (§ 1383), *and a person is responsible not only for the injury caused by his own act, but also for that which is caused by the acts of persons for whom he is bound to answer, or by things which he has under his care*" (§ 1284), and a lessee "is answerable in case of fire, unless he can prove that the fire happened by accident or superior force, or by faulty construction, or that the fire was communicated from a neighboring house (§ 1733), and if there are several hirers, all are jointly and sev- erally responsible for fire, unless they can prove that the fire began in the house of one of them, in which case, the latter alone is bound therein (§ 1734)." By the common law, every master of a house or chamber was liable for a fire originating therein and doing damage to the property of others, *whether such fire originated through his negligence or not.*[5] The only defense against an action for such an injury was, that the fire was kindled by a stranger, or resulted from inevitable accident.[6] And this continued to be the law in England until the statute, 6 Anne, Cap. 31, which restricted the liability to cases *where the fire resulted from the negligence* of the master of a house or chamber, or of his servants. *This statute* is a part of the common law in the States of this country. In view of this liability, it is competent for any per-

---

[1] *Strong* v. *Manufacturers' Ins. Co.*, 10 Pick. (Mass.) 40.

[2] *Springfield Ins. Co.* v. *Brown*, 43 N. Y. 389 ; *Putnam* v. *Mercantile Ins. Co.*, 5 Met. (Mass.) 386; *Eastern R. R. Co.* v. *Relief Ins. Co.*, 98 Mass. 420.

[3] *Eastern R. R. Co.* v. *Relief Ins. Co.*, *ante.*

[4] Toullier Droit Civile Francois Tome, xi, 221 ; Code Napoleon Liv. III, §§ 1384, 1733, 1734.

[5] *Tubervil* v. *Stamp*, 1 Salk. 13.

[6] Rolles Abr. Action on the Case B. ; Comyns Dig. Action on the Case for Neg- ligence, A. 6.

son or corporation about to enter upon any undertaking, whereby the property of others is liable to be destroyed by fire from the prosecution of such undertaking, under such circumstances that liability would attach for the loss, to secure protection by insurance. In some of the States, by statute, railroad companies are liable without reference to the question of negligence, for fires set by its engines, but in all cases to which the statute does not apply, the common law rule applies, and negligence must be shown. Whether a person may insure against the consequence of his own, or his servant's negligence, is perhaps an open one. It might be regarded as impolitic to permit one to indemnify himself from the consequences of his negligence ; but this is practiced in France, and no ill results have ensued, and probably with us, if a ninsurance company saw fit to carry such risks, they would be upheld. But in such cases, of course, the injury must be shown to be one for which the assured was liable to respond in damages, *and for which he has been compelled to do so,* and thus he would be placed in the novel position of being obliged to prove his own negligence. However, this question might be determined where the liability is predicated upon the *negligence* of another, there is no question but that an insurable interest exists, where liability attaches without reference to the question of negligence.[1]

Interest need not be stated except.

SEC. 277. The insured is not required to state the nature of his interest in the property in the absence of any specific inquiries in reference thereto or express stipulation in the policy ; and in such case, if he has an *insurable* interest therein, it is enough,[2] and, even though the policy requires that the interest of the assured in the property shall be truly stated, the requirement does not call for a distinction between a legal and equitable title, but only for a true statement of the *nature* of the insurable interest.[3] If the assured has an insurable interest in the

---

[1] *Eastern R. R. Co.* v. *Relief Ins. Co.*, 105 Mass. 107 ; *Monadnock R. R. Co.* v. *Manufacturers' Ins. Co.*, 113 Mass. 77.

[2] *Williams* v. *Roger Williams Ins. Co.*, 107 Mass. 377 ; *Springfield Ins. Co* v. *Brown*, 43 N. Y. 389 ; *Strong* v. *Manufacturers' Ins. Co.*, 10 Pick. (Mass.) 40 ; *King* v. *State Ins. Co.*, 7 Cush. (Mass.) 1. Where one obtained insurance on his store, occupied by himself, without disclosing the fact that it stood on the land of another, under a verbal agreement terminable at six months' notice, no inquiry being made by the insurers as to his title, it was held that there was not a concealment of a material fact, and that the policy, therefore, was not void. *Fletcher* v. *Commonwealth Ins. Co.*, 18 Pick. (Mass.) 419 ; *Gilbert* v. *N. American Ins. Co.*, 23 Wend. (N. Y.) 43.

[3] *Swift* v. *Vermont Ins. Co.*, 18 Vt. 305 ; *Hough* v. *City Ins. Co.*, 29 Conn. 10 ; *Gaylord* v. *Lamar Ins. Co.*, 40 Mo. 13 ; *Williams* v. *Roger Williams Ins. Co., ante.*

goods, it is immaterial whether he has a distinct or a divided share. *Unless called upon to state his interest, he is not required to do so.*[1] Thus, it has been held that, where a mortgagee has assigned his interest in the mortgage, but remains liable as indorser of the mortgage note, a description of his interest in the property as that of "mortgagee" was a true statement of his interest.[2] It is enough if the description of his interest comes within the *class* named.[3]

Persons having custody of, but no property interest in, property.

SEC. 278. There would seem to be no question but that, where a person has the custody, care or possession of property for another, *although he has no pecuniary interest therein, and is not responsible for its safe keeping, he may insure it in his own name for the benefit of the owners, and the insurance will inure to the benefit of the owner of the property, upon a subsequent adaption of the insurance, even after a loss under the policy.*[4] "The right," says FOLGER, J.,[5] "is put upon the fact that, having the possession of the property, exclusive as to all but the owner, to whom they are responsible, they have the right to protect it from loss, so that it or its value may be rendered to the owner when he calls for his own." *It is essential that it should appear that the owner was the person intended to be benefited by the insurance when the contract was made,* but it is not essential that such intention at the time of entering into the contract *should fasten upon the very person who, when the contract matures, seeks to take the benefit of it,* but it is enough if the intention was to effect it for any person who, during the existence of the policy, and the custody, care or possession of the nominal assured, should have a legal title to the property.[6] Thus, in the case last referred to, the plaintiffs, commission merchants and brokers, took out policies of insurance upon "refined carbon oil and packages containing the same, their own, or

---

[1] *Lawrence v. Van Horne,* 1 Cai. (N. Y.) 276. In *Dahn v. Farmers' Ins. Co.,* 5 Lans. (N. Y.) 275, assured insured as owner. He only had an equitable title. Held sufficient, and policy valid.

[2] *Williams v. Royer Williams Ins. Co.,* 107 Mass. 377.

[3] GRAY, J., in *Williams v. Roger Williams Ins. Co., ante.*

[4] *Herkimer v. Rice,* 27 N. Y. 163 ; *De Forrest v. Fulton Ins. Co.,* 1 Hall (N. Y.) 84 ; *Mittenberger v. Beacom,* 9 Penn. St. 198 ; *Lee v. Adsit,* 37 N. Y. 86 ; *Stilwell v. Staples,* 19 id. 401.

[5] *Waring v. Indemnity Ins. Co.,* 45 N. Y. 606 ; 6 Am. Rep. 146.

[6] *Waring v. Indemnity Ins. Co., ante.* Where the assured has the possession of the property insured, *the real owner may adopt the contract* (*Durand v. Thouran,* Porter (Ala.) 238), *even after loss. Watkins v. Durand,* id. 251 ; *Waring v. Indemnity Ins. Co., ante ; Routh v. Thompson,* 13 East. 283 ; *Turner v. Burrows,* 8 Wend. (N. Y.) 144 ; *Mittenberger v. Beacom,* 9 Penn. St. 198. In such case, the rule "*quod omnis ratihabitio retrotrahitur et mandato priori aequi paratur*" applies. *Wolff v. Horncastle,* 1 B. & P. 323 ; *Stirling v. Vaughn,* 11 East. 620.

held in trust on commission, or sold, but not removed, contained in bonded warehouse." Subsequently, a part of the property was sold *and paid for*, but not removed, and a total loss occurred, and the question was, whether the plaintiffs were entitled to recover for the value of the property sold as aforesaid. The court held that they were.

Insured need not be named in the policy.

SEC. 279. A policy may be issued " to whom it may concern," [1] or to John Doe, *agent*,[2] and the name of the real party insured remain unknown to the assured, provided, *at the time of the loss*, the real party in interest must show that his interests *were intended to be covered by the policy*.[3] Mr. DUER, in his excellent treatise on insurance, says : " A positive stipulation of the underwriter to pay the loss to the agent, would never be rendered by the inability of the party really assured to sustain an action on the policy in his own name." [4] And this view is sustained by ADAMS, J., in the case of Shaw v. Ætna Ins. Co., 49 Mo. 578; 8 Am. Rep. 150. " In such a case," says he, " the policy ought to enure to the benefit of the principal, and the agent or consignee be treated as a trustee of an express trust, and the amount of the recovery would go to his principal;" and he adds, " but whether he is a trustee of an express trust or not, he is nevertheless a trustee for the consignor ; *and in a suit upon the policy in the name of the consignee, this may be shown in order to show that he had an insurable interest as trustee for his consignor*." In that case, the plaintiffs shipped a lot of ice to S. & K., to be sold on commission, and directed them to insure it, which they agreed to do. *They, however, took out a policy in their own names*, without indicating their interest therein. The plaintiffs brought an action upon the policy *in their own name*, and it was held that it could be maintained. The doctrine that a policy, taken out by an agent *in his own name, but really for the benefit of his principal*, cannot be enforced, unless *at the time* the agent had the custody of the property, does not apply to a case *where the policy is taken out by direction of the principal ;* in such a case it is presumed to be taken *for the benefit of the principal*, and may be enforced by him in his own name, or in the name of the agent.[5] Indeed, there are many cases in which it

[1] *Shawmut Co.* v. *Hampden Ins. Co.*, 12 Gray (Mass.) 540 ; *Cobb* v. *N. E. Ins. Co.*, 6 id. 192; *Sanders* v. *Hillsborough Ins. Co.*, 44 N. H. 238.

[2] *Waring* v. *Indemnity Ins. Co.*, ante.

[3] *Stillwell* v. *Staples*, 19 N. Y. 403; *Watson* v. *F. & L. Ins. Co.*, 5 El & Bl. 870 ; *Lee* v. *Adsit*, 37 N. Y. 86 ; *Herkimer* v. *Rice*, 27 id. 179.

[4] 2 Duer's Ins. 7, sec. 6.

[5] *Shaw* v. *Ætna Ins. Co., ante ;* 2 Duer on Ins. 7.

is held that a policy may be taken in the name of a person *having the custody of property insured*, but no property in the thing covered by the policy *for the benefit of the real owner, even without that person's previous sanction or authority*, and that it will enure to the ‘benefit of the real owner, upon his subsequent adoption thereof, even after the happening of a loss.[1] But I do not apprehend that a stranger to the

---

[1] *Siter* v. *Motts*, 13 Penn. St. 218 ; *De Forrest* v. *Fulton Ins. Co.*, 1 Hall (N. Y.) 84 ; 1 Bennett's F. I. C. 223 ; *Shaw* v. *Ætna Ins. Co.*, 49 Mo. 574 ; *Lee* v. *Adsit*, 37 N. Y. 86 ; *Herkimer* v. *Rice*, 27 id. 180 ; *Stillwell* v. *Staples*, 19 N. Y. 403 ; *Watson* v. *Monarch, etc., Ins. Co.*, 5 El. & Bl. 870 ; *Waring* v. *Indemnity F. Ins. Co.*, 45 N. Y. 606. In *Miltenberger* v. *Beacon*, 9 Penn. St. 198, the defendant was the lessor of ground rent, and had entered for arrears. He procured an insurance upon the buildings, and had stated an account with the sub-lessees, in which he charged him with the insurance. The premises having been burnt, and he having received the insurance, an action was brought by the sub-lessees to recover the same of him ; and the court held that they were entitled to recover. "It is very clear one may insure in his own name the property of another for the benefit of the owner, without his previous authority or sanction ; and it will enure to the party intended to be protected, upon his subsequent adoption of it, even after a loss has occurred. This doctrine was asserted in *Durand* v. *Thouron*, 1 Porter's Ala. Rep. 238, and *Watkins* v. *Durand*, ib. 251. In the first of these cases, the policy was of the goods in the defendant's store, without discrimination ; but it appeared the plaintiff's goods, which had been deposited with the defendant for sale, were included in the list of goods insured ; and the defendant, after the loss, promised to account with the plaintiff for their proportion of the subscription. On the trial, the defendant requested the court to instruct the jury, that if no instructions to insure were given by the plaintiff, when the goods were deposited or before the fire, the goods were not covered. This the court refused to do ; and on error brought, this refusal was sanctioned by the supreme court, saying, the case was properly put on the ground that the defendant's promise to account contained an admission that he had insured for and on account of the plaintiffs. In the second case, the assurance effected by the defendant was of goods belonging to himself, or held in trust or on commission. In both, the plaintiffs were allowed to recover in an action for money had, although the amount of the insurance was less than the value of the defendant's proper goods destroyed. In *Hagedorn* v. *Oliverson*, 2 Maul. & Selw. 485, a ship bound to foreign ports was insured by one having no personal interest in her, in his own name and for every person to whom the same appertained. This was done without the previous authority of the owner, for whose benefit the insurance was in fact effected. He gave it no sanction before the loss of the ship, but afterwards adopted the policy ; and it was held he was entitled to recover directly against the underwriters. This case is commented on by Hughes, in his Treatise on Insurance, p. 41. He says of it, that the insurance, being for the benefit of the owner, the reasonable presumption was, that he would adopt the act ; and although he was under no legal obligation to repay the premium to the party negotiating the policy, there was such a moral obligation as furnished a sufficient consideration to support his adoption of it, after the happening of the loss. These authorities abundantly prove that the contract of assurance, like other contracts, may be effected by the agency of a third party, without the authority of the party to be benefited, if he subsequently recognize it. It is true, that to enable the beneficiary to sue upon it directly, he must be expressly named, or the policy must be so framed as to cover, generally or specially, the interest of all concerned. But where the agent receives the fund, this, as the authorities show, is not necessary to the support of an action for money had and received. In such cases, it is sufficient to prove the defendant constituted himself the representative of the interest insured, as agent of the owner, and that the latter ratified the act before or after the loss suffered. In the present instance, the only question was, did Miltenberger act as the agent of the owner of the property in procuring the insurance? This, of course, was a question of fact for the jury, and was so submitted by the court. Was there any

property, or one holding no relation to it, eiiher as agent, consignee, carrier, commission merchant bailee or some relation that gains him a *quasi* interest therein, could effect a valid insurance thereon *for any purpose,* although Mr. Angell in his work on Fire Insurance, sec. 79, seems to incline to hold that he could, but it will be noticed that all the cases cited by him to sustain his position, are cases in which the person taking out the policy, in fact stood in one or the other of these relations to it. *A mere stranger, holding no relation to the property that would entail loss upon him in case of its destruction, and standing in no fiduciary relation thereto, cannot, whatever may be his intention, insure the same, in his own name.* A contrary doctrine, is in defiance of the principle lying at

---

evidence of it ? In the account furnished to the plaintiffs below by the defendant, showing, as he averred, the condition of their pecuniary relations, there is a charge of four years' services in collecting rents, $40, and another for premiums paid of insurance in 1845 and 1846, $22.50. In his books of account, produced on the trial, there is a similar entry, and it is conceded they relate to the subject of this contest. These certainly furnish some ground for the inference, that, when the insurance was procured, the defendant regarded himself as the representative of the owners, and acted for the protection of their interests as well as his own. Why charge them with the premium if they were to take nothing in any event under the risk? But it is said the plaintiffs repudiated the charge of the premium, and thereby, instead of adopting, disavowed the act of the defendant. Upon this point we have only the evidence of Mr. Hamilton, who simply says the account was not adopted by the plaintiff. It is asserted here, this was because the defendant charged interest on the arrears of rent, and refused to allow it on the sums collected by him. The record does not show the reason of its rejection, and as it contained several items of date and credit, we cannot take it for granted, in the absence of proof, that it was disallowed because of the charge of the premium. It is said, too, this charge was excluded from the account stated by the referees, in the action of account rendered, with the assent of the plaintiff. But the testimony of the referee examined is, that it was agreed by the parties not to introduce the subject of the insurance there, inasmuch as another suit, the present, was pending to test their rival claims to the sum received from the underwriters. These adverse allegations were legitimate subjects for the jury, and were doubtless pressed upon their attention by the counsel of the respective parties. The inference of agency is also supported, in a considerable degree, by the stipulations of the policy itself. By its terms it was left in the option of the insurance company, in case of loss. either to restore the buildings to their original condition, or pay the amount of the assessed damages. Had the company re-erected the houses, it cannot be thought they would have been the property of the defendant to the exclusion of the former owners, and it is difficult to imagine that he supposed an election to pay the damages suffered would work a change in the relative rights of the parties. A jury might, therefore, well be content with slighter proof *aliunde* than would be satisfactory in other cases to establish the conclusion that the defendant. from the beginning, regarded the sum insured as representing the property in the tenements. But it is enough here, that they have acted upon some proof in finding his receipt of it a trust. The defendant, however, principally complains of that part of the charge in which the court asserted that, having entered under the deed of perpetual lease to collect the arrears of rent, he became the agent of the plaintiff. Admitting the proposition to be incorrect, a candid examination of the whole charge will make it manifest the inaccuracy did the defendant no harm. The court expressly instructed the jury, that, under the supposed agency, he was not bound to insure for the benefit of the plaintiff, and refer them to the other proofs in the case, as furnishing the only evidence upon which the presence of an agency in the transaction of a policy can be established."

the foundation of insurance law, and is a recognition of the validity of wager policies. *An agent even having no lein on goods for advances, commission or otherwise, nor the possession, care or custody of the same as carrier or bailee, or any liability to account for their loss by the perils insured against has no insurable interest therein, although he is named as shipper and consignee in the bill of lading.*[1]

And the same rule holds good as to *consignees, carriers, factors, ware-housemen or bailees, generally, unless they have at the time of effecting the insurance, some interest therein, present or contingent, as a claim for freight advances profits or some pecuniary interest, or are liable to the owner for the safe keeping of the property; an insurance effected by them in their own name, is totally inoperative and void, even though intended for the benefit of the real owner, unless ratified by him.*[2] But where an insurable interest exists in *an agent, commission merchant or other bailee of goods having the custody thereof, and by virtue of such interest and custody of the goods, they may insure them for their entire value, and recover the same for the benefit of the owner, over and above their own interest therein, unless the owner has himself insured the goods for his own benefit.*[3] The rule is that, *when a person has the custody of the goods, coupled with any interest, he may insure the same for their entire value, for in such cases the law considers him as owner.*[4] *But his right to recover beyond the extent of his own interest, must depend upon the circumstance whether he is liable to the owner for the loss, or whether he was directed by him to insure, or whether the owner has ratified his act in procuring insurance upon his interest in the property, and whether the owner has himself insured, to the extent of his interest.*[5]

Consignee—Bailee.

SEC. 280. The consignee of goods, who is not liable for their loss to the consignor, has no insurable interest therein beyond his advances

---

[1] *Seagraves v. Union M. Ins. Co.,* L. R. 1 C. P. 305.

[2] WILLES, J., in *Seagrave v. Ins. Co., ante,* said : "We are not aware that it has ever been held that a *mere agent, without possession or lien,* has an insurable interest *to the extent of the value of the goods,* simply because his name appears in the bill of lading, instead of that of the principal ; and the general rule is clear, that *to constitute an insurable interest insurable against a peril, it must be an interest, such that the peril would, by its proximate effect, cause damage to the assured.*"

[3] In *Waters v. Monarch Ins. Co.,* 5 E. & B. 876, a warehouseman insured as trustee. In *Crowley v. Cohen,* 3 B. & Ad. 478, a carrier insuring goods as such. In *De Forest v. Fulton Ins. Co.,* 1 Hall (N. Y.) 84, a commission merchant. In *Bartlett v. Walter,* 13 Mass. 267, a charterer of a vessel who agreed to insure. Also similar in principle, *Oliver v. Green,* 3 id. 133. In *Buck v. Chespeake Ins. Co.,* 1 Peters (U. S.) 151, the master of a vessel to whom goods were consigned.

[4] Opinion of OAKLEY, J., in *De Forest v. Fulton F. Ins. Co., ante.*

[5] *Seagrave v. Union, etc., Ins. Co., ante; London, etc., Railway Co. v. Glyn,* 1 E. & E. 652.

thereon for freight, and to the consignor, and his expected profits, *unless he has agreed to insure them, or has been directed to do so by the consignor, or, unless after insurance is made thereon by him, the consignor adopts it!* [1] Nor has the consignee any insurable interest upon goods in *transit, unless he is liable for the price thereof.* [2] Thus, when A. ships goods to B., to be delivered to C., upon the performance of certain things by C; C. has no insurable interest, because he has no property therein, and sustains no loss either as to the goods, or the profits thereon. [3]

But where goods are consigned to and received by the consignee, or where the consignee becomes liable upon delivery to the carrier, or where he receives the goods in trust, he stands as a bailee and a bailment on trust implies that there is reserved to the bailor the right to claim a re-delivery of the property deposited in bailment, and property held subject to such recall in specie, the policy should describe the nature of the interest ; but wherever there is a delivery of property on a contract for an equivalent in money or some other valuable commodity, and not for a return of the identical subject-matter in its

---

[1] *Oliver* v. *Green*, 5 Mass. 133. In *Shaw* v. *Ætna Ins. Co.*, 49 Mo. 578 ; 8 Am. Rep. 150, the plaintiffs consigned five barges of ice, of which they were owners, to consignees to be sold on commission, and ordered them to have the ice insured. The consignees took the insurance in their own names, and, after the loss, assigned the policy to the plaintiffs. It was held that a consignee has an insurable interest in goods consigned to him for sale on commission, only to the extent of the commissions or profits he expects to receive from the sale ; and this he may insure regardless of instructions from the consignor. If he accepts a consignment, with instructions from his principals to insure for their benefit, it becomes his duty to insure, and if he neglects to do so, and a loss occurs, he is liable to them for that amount. If, instead of taking out a new policy in the names of their principals, they had the risk entered on their own policy, in their own names, as a convenient mode of indemnifying themselves against such damages as they might suffer in not insuring in the names of their principals, it was held that they had a right thus to protect themselves, and to this end they ought to be considered as interested to the full value of the ice. After being ordered to insure, the consignees might have considered themseves trustees for the consignors, and have insured in their own names, for them, and in such case, in a suit upon the policy in the name of the consignee, the consignee might show that he had an insurable interest as trustee for his consignor. *Bartlett* v. *Walter*, 13 Mass. 267 ; *Herkimer* v. *Rice*, 27 N. Y. 163. To the extent of his advances, he may insure. *Ellsworth* v. *Alliance Ins. Co.*, L. R., 8 C. B. 596 ; *Putnam* v. *Mercantile Ins. Co.*, 5 Met. (Mass.) 386. His insurable interest is to be measured by the extent of his lien on the goods, if they come into his possession. *Wolff* v. *Horncastle*, 1 B. & P. 316 ; and his expected profits thereon if covered by the policy. *Leamans* v. *Loring*, 1 Mass. (U. S.) 127. A person not a consignee, but who assumes to occupy that position, in the first instance without authority, and makes advances upon the goods, and his acts are subsequently ratified by the consignor, such ratification has relation to the original act, and renders all his acts in reference thereto legal and valid, and thus gives vitality and validity to an insurance effected before such ratification. A contingent interest existed before ratification, which became fixed when his acts were ratified. *Wolff* v. *Horncastle, ante.*

[2] *The Atlas*, 3 C. Rob. (Admiralty) 299 ; *Warder* v. *Horton*, 4 Binn. (Penn.) 529.

[3] *Warder* v. *Horton, ante; The Aurora*, 4 Rob. 180 ; *The Josephine*, 4 id. 21.

original or an altered form, this is a transfer of property for value—a sale, not a bailment.[1] In either case an insurable interest to the extent of the value of the goods existed; but if the title was specifically inquired about, the assured was bound to state it truly. When goods consigned to a person to be sold by h m on commission, he ceases to be a consignee thereof, upon their delivery to him, and then occupies the position of bailee. *When the goods are received, the person to whom they were consigned, even though consigned for sale by him upon commission, has by virtue of the bailment an insurable interest therein to the extent of his advances, and also to the extent of the value of the goods, as trustee for the consignor, even though no instructions from the consignor to cover his interests by insurance were given, and although he had no knowledge that such insurance had been effected until after the loss.*[2] A distinction exists between a consignee, who is in possession of the goods, to sell upon commission, and a consignee proper, to whom goods have been shipped, but who has not received them. In the former case he becomes a bailee of the goods upon their receipts, and holds them in trust, as well for himself as the consignors, and by virtue of his possession thereof, is in law treated as the owner, while in the latter case, he never having received the goods, cannot be said to hold them in trust for the owner. The distinction between the two classes is marked. A trustee has a legal interest in the property, and, therefore, may insure, while a mere consignee never having received the goods, *unless liable for their price upon delivery to the carrier*, has no interest therein

---

[1] Thus in *The South Australian Ins. Co.* v. *Randell and Randell*, P. C., 22 L. T. R. 843, respondents, who were millers, received wheat from different farmers. The wheat, on receipt, was, with the consent of the farmers, mixed with other wheat, and became part of the miller's stock. The millers could at any time grind or sell the wheat so received. The farmers could at any time claim the price of the wheat delivered by each, according to the market price for wheat of like quality, at the time of payment claimed. There was also some evidence that the farmers had the option of claiming an equal quantity of wheat of like quality, instead of the value in money. The millers often made advances to the farmers on the wheat received from them. The farmers, after a certain time, paid a storage charge to the millers. The respondents insured the current stock of wheat in their mill with the appellants. In the proposal for insurance the respondents answered the question whether the insurance was "for self or in trust, and if in trust, on account of whom?" in these words, "for selves." A condition of the policy was that goods held in trust must be insured as such, otherwise the policy would not cover them. The mill and stock were destroyed by fire. To an action on the policy, the appellants pleaded that the statement in the proposal was a misrepresentation, the stock having been held by the respondents "in trust for other persons." Held that the description of the subject of insurance was correct, for that this was not a case of possession given subject to a trust, but of property transferred for value upon special terms of settlement.

[2] *Ætna Ins. Co.* v. *Jackson*, 16 B. Mon. (Key.) 242 ; *De Forest* v. *Fulton F., etc., Ins. Co.*, 1 Hall (N. Y.) 84 ; 1 Bennett's, F. I. C. 223. •

beyond his advances made thereon, and an interest that can only be covered specifically.[1]

The cases have gone to the extreme length of holding that *any person lawfully in the possession of the property may insure the property in his own name for the benefit of the owner, when the insurance is effected with that purpose and intention, and is expressed in apt terms in the policy, and may recover, as trustee for the real owner, to the extent of the value of the property, as measured by the policy, whether he personally has any interest therein or not.* Notably, as carrying the doctrine to this extreme length, is an English case often cited.[2] In that case, wharfingers effected an insurance upon goods, " their own, in trust, or on commission," under a general floating policy, which included a warehouse of their own, which was burnt. *They were not responsible to their customers, neither were the latter aware that any insurance for their benefit existed.* The defendant insisted that, under these circumstances, the plaintiffs had no insurable interest beyond the extent of their charges for landing, wharfage and cartage, and paid that amount into court. But the court held that they were entitled to recover the full amount, *and that, as to the amount beyond their own interest, they were trustees for the parties beneficially interested,* such interest being covered by the words " in trust," and not being illegal, either at common law or by virtue of any statute. Similar views have been held by our own courts, and, in the absence of any statute requiring the names of the parties in interest to be stated in the policy—and I am aware of no such statutes in any of the States—there would seem to be no question that *a policy drawn so as to cover property held " in trust," and with the evident purpose of covering interests other than those of the assured himself, may be enforced for the benefit of the owner of the property, when the assured is lawfully in possession of the same, and holding it for the owner's benefit.* As, where the policy covers " their own, or held in trust on commission, or sold, but not removed,[3] or " on goods as well the prop-

---

[1] *Lucena* v. *Crauford,* 3 B. & P. 75 ; JONES, J., in *De Forest* v. *Fulton Ins. Co., ante.*

[2] *Waters* v. *Monarch Ins. Co.,* 5 El. & Bl. 870 ; *Shaw* v. *Ætna Ins. Co.,* 49 Mo. 578.

[3] *Stilwell* v. *Staples,* 19 N. Y. 401 ; *Siter* v. *Motts,* 13 Penn. St. 218. In *Waring* v. *Indemnity Ins. Co., ante,* the opinion of FOLGER, J., is worthy of notice. He said : " Though there was a time, after the making of the policy, at which the property was covered by it, and the plaintiffs were insured by it, it must be conceded that, when the property was destroyed by fire, the plaintiffs had no such interest in it, as that they suffered any immediate pecuniary loss. The proof is, that they had sold the oil and received their pay. The proof also is, that the oil was on store in a United States bonded warehouse, and that, by the delivery of invoices and gauger's certificates

erty of the assured as that held by them in trust or on commission. [1]" In such cases, the terms "held in trust" or "on commission,"

to vendees of the plaintiffs, there had been a complete delivery of the property to
the vendees, according to the custom of the trade. Nothing more was to be done
to it by the vendors to enable the vendees to remove it. But the place of storage
had not been changed. It remained on store, where it had been deposited by the
plaintiffs, without expense to the vendees. It was also testified (under the
defendant's objection) that the plaintiffs, according to custom in Philadelphia,
retained the possession of it. It is evident that the plaintiffs had no property in
the oil, nor any lien upon it for purchase-money, or any charges of any kind.
But they did have the possession of it by the consent of vendees, and thus the
right to possession as against all the world but the vendees. Under this state of
the facts, it is to be determined whether the contract of insurance may be so construed, either from its language, or from the surrounding circumstances, as that
it can be determined that the defendants meant to continue the risk taken upon
this oil after it was sold and delivered by the plaintiffs; and also, whether they
meant to insure the pecuniary interest in it of any other persons than the plaintiffs. We have but little difficulty in holding from the peculiar phraseology of
the policy, that something other was meant than property, of which a contract
of sale had been made, but of which no delivery had yet taken place. "Sold,
but not delivered," is a phrase common with insurance men, and has an ascertained and definite meaning. It applies to property of which a contract of sale
has been made, but of which the ownership has not been changed by a delivery
in pursuance of the contract. "Sold, but not removed," is another, and we deem
a newer form to express something else. We judge that it was meant to cover
that which had been sold, and of which a legal, binding delivery had been made,
the ownership and right of control of which had passed, but which had not been
in fact removed; of which no change of place indicated a change of ownership and
possession. It is easy to be seen that it might be an advantage and a convenience
to the plaintiffs to have a policy which would thus cover property, once theirs for
sale, but after that sold and delivered and paid for. In the great rapidity, number and value of the transactions in such a commodity, in such a market, such an
insurance would much facilitate the business of both parties, increasing that of
the vendors and making safe that of the vendees. If the plaintiffs had a shifting
policy, which would change with their daily transactions in the property, and
cover it to-day as in the ownership of the plaintiffs, the next day as that held by
them in trust or on commission, and the next as that of some complete vendee,
who had not yet had the time or the occasion to remove it, much time, trouble,
care and expense would be saved to customers, and thus would arise a persuasive
inducement for dealers to become the vendees of these plaintiffs. Thus, it is to
be seen that the adoption of this phraseology, novel, and taking in property not
theretofore or without it covered by the terms of a policy, had a purpose on the
part of the assured, one which was voluntarily and intelligently acceded to by
the insurer. For, though the use of it increased in some degree the burden upon
the company, it could not have been by the company inserted in the policy aim-
lessly, or without comprehension of its meaning. I do not, from the whole written description of the property to be covered by the policy, doubt that such was
its meaning. It comes to this by natural steps. The risk is taken 'on refined
carbon oil.' *First*, 'their own;' *i. e.*, that which the plaintiffs, during the term,
held as their own property, owned and possessed by them. *Second*, 'held in
trust;' *i. e.*, that of which they had the care and custody, intrusted to them as
representatives of others, and for which they are responsible to the owner (*Stilwell* v. *Staples*, 19 N. Y. 401); and in this term may be included that which they
had sold, but not delivered. *Third*, 'held on commission;' *i. e.*, that which they
held, coming into or continuing in their care and custody for the purpose and
with the duty of sale. *Fourth*, that which was 'sold, but not removed,' an additional phrase, not to be supposed a repetition of the meaning of the others, but
to have been used as an addition to their meaning, taking in that which, once
having been their own, or once having been held by them on commission, had

---

[1] *De Forest* v. *Fulton F. Ins. Co.*, *ante.*

and kindred terms, in a policy to an agent, factor or the like, have
been held as giving to the owner of the property the right to take the

been fully sold and technically delivered; the title and the right of possession
changed, but not yet removed from that place of storage.   The phraseology com-
prehends all this, and goes naturally and regularly, as expressive of a well-
formed intention to comprehend all, and to affix the indemnity of the contract to
the property in whatsoever of these conditions it should be, and throughout them
all. And, provided that there is some one in fact beneficially interested in the
policy as an assured, there is nothing contrary to the policy of the law in intending and effecting such an insurance, and it may be upheld. For here is an actual
subject of a risk, and the proviso being met, there is a person who has an interest
in the subject, and is himself affected by the risk. We have then here a policy
which did, in its inception, by its terms, cover this particular property, and did
designedly cover it. And we have a policy, by which it was meant by insurer
and insured that the risk taken should cover and adhere to the same property,
after it had left the ownership of the persons designated by name in it; by
which, necessarily, it was also meant to follow and to cover that property in the
ownership of the vendee of the original owner named in the policy. It is not forbidden by the law that a policy should be so framed as that the insurance shall
be inseparably attached to the property meant to be covered, so that successive
owners, during the continuance of the risks, shall become, in turn, the parties
really insured. 2 Duer on Ins. 49, Lecture 9, § 31.
  "But it remains to be seen whether this contract of insurance could be made or
continued in the name of the plaintiffs for the benefit of their vendees not especially designated. It is laid down in broad terms that one may, in his own name,
insure the property of another for the benefit of the owner without his previous
authority or sanction, and that it will inure to the benefit of the owner upon a
subsequent adoption of it, even after a loss has occurred. Angell on Ins. § 79,
cited and approved by Denio, Ch. J.; *Herkimer* v. *Rice*, 27 N. Y. 163-81. In the
edition of Angell which is before me (Boston, 184), the authorities cited to sustain
this proposition disclose some relation existing between the person who effected
the insurance and was named in the policy, and the property insured, either as
the agent for the owner or as the occupant for the property, or as having the care,
possession and control of it, as bailee. *Agents, commission merchants or others,
having the custody of, and being responsible for, property, may insure in their own
names; and they may, in their own names, recover of the insurer not only a sum
equal to their own interest in the property by reason of any lien for advances or
charges, but the full amount named in the policy up to the value of the property.*
In all such cases, the right to insure and the right to recover seem to be founded
upon the relation above adverted to. See *De Forrest* v. *Fulton Ins. Co.*, 1 Hall
Sup. Ct. Rep. 84; *Stillwell* v. *Staples*, 19 N. Y. 401; *Siter* v. *Motts*, 1 Harris
Penn. St. R. 218. The right is put upon the fact, that having the possession of
the property exclusive as to all but the owner, to whom they are responsible,
they have the right to protect from loss, so that it or its value may be rendered
to the owner when he calls for his own. Now there did in this case exist a relation between the plaintiffs and the property and its owner. Although it had been
sold and paid for, and, in legal contemplation, delivered, its place of storage had
not been changed. For the purpose of saving expense in storage, for the purpose also, it may be inferred from all the circumstances, of saving expense of a
new insurance, it was left in the same warehouse, and by the custom of the trade,
as is said, in the possession still of the plaintiffs. Thus was established that relation, which enabled the plaintiffs to prolong the defendant's risk upon the property. And although the vendees of the plaintiffs, the owners of the property, are
not by name or peculiar mention designated in the policy, there are terms there,
which have been held to bring within such a contract persons not named in it,
but yet interested in the property insured, which may be done. Phillips on Ins.
1 vol. p. 197, § 382 ; p. 202, § 388. The phrases describing property ' as held in
trust,' or ' on commission,' and kindred terms, in a policy to an agent, factor or
the like, have been held as giving to the owner of the property a right to take
the place of the insured, to adopt the contract, and to enforce it in his own name
or that of his agent. *Lee* v. *Adsit, supra; Stillwell* v. *Staples, supra.* Some

place of the assured, to adopt the contract and to enforce it, *in his own name or that of his agent.*[1]

As suggested by FOLGER, J., *ante*, this right is dependant upon the ratification of the insurance *by the party in interest. If he has effected insurance in his own name, and looks to his own policy for indemnity, the policy only covers the actual interest of the agents therein;* and in such a case, to the extent of the agent's interest therein, the policy taken by the real owner would not be double insurance, so as to avoid the policy of the agent, if it stipulated against other insurance. But as to the interest as trustee, such insurance by the owner would be other insurance, because covering the same interest.[2] Again, it must be remembered that when the agent so has an interest in the property de-

---

cases go farther than this, and hold that one may insure in his own name the property of another for the benefit of the owner, without his previous sanction or authority, and that it will enure to the party intended to be protected upon his subsequent adoption, even after a loss has occurred. *Miltonberger* v. *Beacom,* 9 Barr. (Penn. St. R.) 198. Of course it must be made to appear that the owner was in the intention of the person effecting the insurance when the contract was made. 1 Phillips on Ins. p. 198, § 383. Such intention need not have fastened at the time of entering into the contract upon the very person, who, when the contract matures, seeks to take the benefit of it. Otherwise policies to commission merchants, warehousemen, factors and persons in the position of these plaintiffs, in which are clauses of this general nature, would be of little avail. For, obviously, it cannot be foreseen who will, in the course of the term of the policy, come into such relations with them. *And it is to be assumed that every one was in the intention of the insurer, who subsequently with design takes such relations to him as brings him within the clauses of the policy.* The intention must have been to effect insurance for any person and all persons who, during the running of the policy, should have goods within its description of property insured. And such intention, we hold, appears from the phraseology of this policy. Bunker Brothers were vendees of the plaintiffs, of property 'sold but not removed.' One of that firm was a witness upon the trial of the case. Nothing shows that they repudiate the contract made or continued for their benefit. And though the action is in the name of the persons named in the policy, their recovery will be in trust for Bunker Brothers. *Stillwell* v. *Staples, supra.* The exception to the admission of testimony was not well taken. The objection was to the question put, and this called for no more than the agreement of the plaintiffs and their vendees as to storage. It was not improper or immaterial to show that they made it a part of their bargain that the oil should remain where it was, in the warehouse, without charge for storage, and that it remained in the possession of the plaintiffs. It was part of the whole arrangement between the plaintiffs and their customers, by which when oil was sold but not removed, it remained free from expense for storage, and covered by the prior policy of insurance. It could not, of course, force upon the defendants any contract different from the one which they made with the plaintiffs; but it was material to aid in showing with what purpose the peculiar phraseology of this policy was adopted. It was not in contradiction or explanation of, or addition to, a written contract. It was proof of a fact which existed after the sale and delivery, that though the sale and delivery were in legal contemplation complete, the subject of the sale remained in the vendor's possession, in accordance with a custom of the trade in that city. The judgment of the court below must be affirmed, with costs to the respondent."

[1] FOLGER, J., in *Waring* v *The Indemnity F. Ins. Co., ante; Lee* v. *Adsit,* 37 N. Y. 86 ; *Stillwell* v. *Staples, ante.*

[2] *Home Ins. Co.* v. *Balt. Warehouse Co.,* 93 U. S. 324.

stroyed, the action must be in his name, and the excess of recovery above his interest is held by him in trust for the real owner. It may sometimes be quite important in determining whether goods are held "in trust," within the meaning of the term, to look at the real understanding of the parties, and their real legal relation; in a word, *whether the assured holds the position of trustee or purchaser of the property*. This will depend upon the question, whether the owner has a right to require the re-delivery of the property itself, *or only the value of the property, upon demand, or other property of the same kind*. In the latter case, the goods are not held in trust, but are the property of the assured, and are covered by a policy which provides, that property held "in trust" must be insured as such, as where corn, wheat or other grain is delivered to a miller subject to be returned in kind, or to be paid for at the market price, the transaction amounts to a sale and purchase.[1] But where cloth is given to a tailor to be manufactured into clothing,[2] or property is delivered to one to be sold,[3] or where he holds goods on storage[4] or to be repaired,[5] and generally, in all cases where the assured has no title to the property except in a technical sense, but holds it as the property of another, it is not covered by a policy issued upon his property, where the policy requires property held in trust to be insured as such.

Nature of the relation generally the test.

SEC. 281. Generally, the measure of the insurer's liability will depend upon the nature of the relation between the assured and third persons, whose property he holds. Thus, where there is nothing in the policy to indicate that the parties intended to cover other interests than those of the assured, the question whether the policy covers property of third persons held by him in any capacity, will depend upon the question *whether he is liable to those third persons for the loss of the property by the peril insured against*. Therefore, in such cases, as well as in cases where the insurer, as it is of course competent for him to do, limits his liability in case of property held "in trust," by adding the words, "for which he is responsible," or other words that limit the liability to cases where the assured is responsible to third persons for

---

[1] *So. Australian Ins. Co.* v. *Randell*, 22 L. T. (U. S.) 843.

[2] *Stilwell* v. *Staples*, 19 N. Y. 401.

[3] *Brichta* v. *N. Y., etc., Ins. Co.*, 2 Hall (N. Y.) 372; *Phœnix Ins. Co.* v. *Favorite*, 49 Ill. 259; *Waters* v. *Monarch Ins. Co.*, *ante*.

[4] *Home Ins. Co.* v. *Favorite*, 46 Ill. 263; *Waters* v. *Monarch Ins. Co.*, *ante*; *N. British Ins. Co.* v. *Moffat*, 20 W. R. 114.

[5] *Dalglish* v. *Buchanan*, 26 Scotch Jur. 160.

their destruction,[1] the question of liability must depend upon the question whether the insured stood in such a relation to the property as to be liable to the owner for its loss *by the peril insured against, and will himself sustain a pecuniary loss in consequence thereof.* In the case last cited, the policy covered "merchandise, the insured's own, in trust or on commission, *for which they are responsible,* in or on all the warehouse vaults, cellars, sheds, cranehouses, wharves, yards," etc. A quantity of tea in chests was deposited in bond, for which the warehousemen gave wharfingers' warrants, deliverable to the persons named therein, or their assigns, by indorsement, upon payment of duty and warehouse charges. The insured purchased the teas from the importers, who indorsed the warrants in blank and delivered them to the insured, who sold the teas to different persons by sample upon a credit of three months, or cash subject to discount, the sellers to pay all warehouse charges up to the time the credit should expire, and the purchasers to be liable for all custom-house duties. Each purchaser received an invoice, stating the weights, marks and numbers of the chests, and the amount payable. The sellers retained the warrants, and were to do whatever was necessary to get the teas cleared and delivered. The wharfingers never received any notice of the sale, the insured was not bound to insure, the purchasers were not liable for any premiums paid for insurance, nor had the sellers charged the purchasers with any such premiums. *The assured voluntarily paid to the purchasers the value of the teas after they were consumed by fire.* It was held that the words, "for which they are responsible," controlled the rights of the parties; *and as the insured were not responsible to the purchasers for loss by fire, it was not a loss within the meaning of the policy.* In the New York case,[2] previously cited, the court placed the decision mainly upon the ground that the vendor of the oil, although he had sold the same and received the pay therefor, at the time of sale agreed to keep the same for the vendee, and also assured him that it was insured until removed; and while nothing is said upon that point by the court, yet it is quite evident that, under the contract disclosed between the vendor and vendee, *the vendor would have been liable for the property if destroyed by fire, and was in fact uninsured.* But in this case, the policy itself covered the vendee's interest until the goods were removed, and, so far as such interests were concerned, had all

---

[1] *N. British Ins. Co.* v. *Moffat*, L. R., 7 C. B. 25.
[2] *Waring* v. *Indemnity Ins. Co.*, *ante.*

the qualities of a policy payable to bearer, or for the benefit of whom it might concern.

So, too, the assured may himself, by the representations made by him to the insurer, restrict their liability *to his actual interest* in the property. Thus, where the plaintiff procured a policy "on goods held by him in trust," *and represented to the insurers that he was receiving goods for sale on which he made advances, and that the consignors might not be able to repay the same, and that he wished for a policy to secure himself from loss by fire thereon,* it was held that the policy only covered the assured's interest therein.[1]

Policy may be made an incident of property—Payable to bearer.

SEC. 282. There is nothing in the law that prevents an insurer from making the policy *an incident of the property covered thereby,* instead of a mère personal contract. Thus, a policy may be issued to the bearer upon certain property, either specifically designated, or in kind, insuring it against fire or any other hazard, *and the instrument will be operative in the hands of any person who is the legal bearer thereof at the time of loss, and has an insurable interest in the property covered thereby.* Of course, in such a case, the holder of the policy takes the burden of establishing his rights under the policy, and his insurable interest therein.[2] So a policy may be issued to and "for the benefit of whom it may concern,' or " as the property may appear," and any person who had an insurable interest therein at the time of the loss, *and whose interersts were intended to be covered by the policy,* may recover thereon.[3] There is no question but that an insurer may so word his policy as to make it operative in the hands of any person *who may own the property at the time of loss.* Thus, a policy to "A., *or to any person who may own the property at the time of loss, and who holds this policy by transfer from A., or any intermediate owner of the property,*" would be as valid an obligation in the hands of the person who owned the property *at the time of loss,* as in the hands of A. In such a case the insurers have waived — as they may do — the *personal* qualities of the contract, and have made it an incident of the property. Thus, a policy to A. upon "goods, his own, held in trust or on commission, *sold but not removed,*" has been held to cover the interests of the purchaser of the goods who

---

[1] *Parks* v. *General Interest Ass. Co.,* 5 Pick. (Mass.) 34.

[2] *Ellicott* v. *The U. S. Ins. Co.,* 8 G. & J. (Md.) 166; 4 Bennett's F. I. C. 610.

[3] *Turner* v. *Burrows,* 2 Duer on Ins. 49 ; *City Bank* v. *Adams,* 45 Me 455 ; *Rogers* v. *Traders' Ins Co.,* 6 Paige Ch. (N. Y.) 583; *Steele* v. *Ins. Co.,* 18 Penn. St. 200 ; *Finney* v. *New Bedford Ins. Co.,* 8 Met. (Mass.) 348.

has paid for the same, but not taken them out of the possession of the assured.[1]

When a policy upon its face does not indicate for whose benefit it was made, extrinsic evidence is admissible to show *who was in fact concerned, or whose interests were intended to be covered.*[2] In such a case, it is not necessary to show *that the particular person* who seeks to enforce the policy, was in the contemplation of the parties, *but that a person occupying the relation to the property, which such person occupied at the time of loss, whoever he might be, was within their contemplation.* In the language of FOLGER, J., in a very able opinion previously referred to, and given in a preceding note:[3] "*Such intention need not have fastened at the time of entering into the contract upon the very person, who, when the contract matures, seeks to take the benefit of it.* * * *For obviously it cannot be foreseen who will,* in the course of the lien of the policy *come into such relations with them. And,*" he adds, "*it is to be assumed that every one was in the intention of the insurer, who subsequently, with design, takes such relations to him as brings him within the clauses of the policy.*" That is, *every person is presumed to be within the contemplation of the assured, who stands, at the time when a loss occurs, in such a relation to the property and the assured, as to be entitled to avail himself of the protection afforded by the policy, and who seeks to avail himself thereof.* The party seeking to enforce the policy, need not show that the assured had him in especial contemplation, but that he occupied at the time of loss, such a relation thereto, as was intended by the assured to be protected against the peril named. In Pennsylvania,[4] it has been held that the person seeking to avail himself of the benefits of a policy "for account of whom it may concern," *must show that the person effecting it, intended to insure the claimant's interest,* or, *that the claimant directed the insurance to be made,* or as was held in another case,[5] "must prove it," and the same view seems to have been held by the Massachusetts courts,[6] and by the Supreme Court of Maine.[7] But this rule does not hold good, where, *from the nature of the property insured, and*

[1] *Waring* v. *Indemnity Ins. Co., ante.*
[2] *Newson* v. *Douglass,* 7 H. & J. (Md.) 417; *Mayor, etc.* v. *Hamilton Ins. Co.,* 10 Bos. (N. Y.) 537; *Steele* v. *Ins. Co.,* 18 Penn. St. 200; *Shaw* v. *Ætna Ins. Co., ante.*
[3] *Waring* v. *Indemnity Ins. Co., ante.*
[4] *De Balle* v. *Penn. Ins. Co.,* 4 Whart. (Penn) 68; *Steele* v. *Franklin Ins. Co.,* 290.
[5] *Steele* v. *Franklin Ins. Co., ante.*
[6] *Finney* v. *New Bedford Ins. Co., ante.*
[7] *City Bank* v. *Adams,* 45 Me. 455.

the business covered by the policy, it is evident that the interests of *any person* who might stand in the relation of owner to the property, or *any part thereof*, at the time of loss, were intended to be covered. In other words, *it is not necessary that the person, but that the interest should have been contemplated by the assured at the time of taking out the policy*.[1] Especially is this so, if the policy is made "to whom it may concern *at the time of loss*."[2] Policies "for the benefit of whom it may concern" are little used in fire insurance, and are more intimately connected with marine insurance.

When a person employs an agent who is not an agent of the company to procure insurance for him, he is bound by such agent's acts. Thus in a New York case[3] the plaintiff employed a broker to procure insurance for him upon a quantity of petroleum. Upon application made to it by the broker, the defendant company issued a policy for $5,000 to the plaintiff. By the terms of the policy the defendant reserved the right to increase the rate of premium at any time. The policy was received by the broker and delivered to the plaintiff, but for some purpose not explained, the broker subsequently procured the policy of the plaintiff. The defendant called for an additional premium, and the broker's clerk, who had the supervision of the business, by mistake and without consulting the plaintiff or the broker, or the consent or knowledge of either, marked the policy to be canceled, and another clerk, without instructions from any one, returned it to the company, or its agents from whom it was received, and it was canceled. Some time after this, the property was destroyed by fire, and an action was brought against the defendant for the loss, the plaintiff insisting that the broker had no authority to have the policy canceled, and consequently that it remained a subsisting contract in full force; but the court held otherwise, upon the general principle that an agent who has authority *to make* a contract, also has power *to cancel* it, and that his acts were obligatory upon the plaintiff.[4] "The mistake" said TAPPEN, J., "if any of the plaintiff's agent cannot be permitted to bring loss to the

[1] *Waring* v. *Indemnity Ins. Co., ante; Rogers* v. *Trader's Ins. Co.*, 6 Paige Ch. (N. Y.) 583; *Turner* v. *Burrows*, 8 Wend. (N. Y.) 144. "Such policies contain a distinct declaration to the insurers, that the insured was acting for the benefit of others, and that other interests than their own were to be protected by the policy." OAKLY, J., in *De Forest* v. *Fulton Ins. Co.*, 1 Hall (N. Y.) 84; 1 Bennett's F. I. C. 256.

[2] *Rogers* v. *Traders' Ins. Co., ante.*

[3] *Standard Oil Co* v. *Triumph Ins. Co.*, 6 T. & C. (N. Y.) 300.

[4] *Jeffrey* v. *Bigelow*, 13 Wend. (N. Y.) 518; *Anderson* v. *Coonly*, 21 id. 279; *Clark* v. *Metropolitan Bank*, 3 Duer (N. Y.) 241.

defendant in a transaction of this character with all its attendant facts, because it was in law, as regards third parties affected thereby, the mistake of the plaintiffs, and the defendants were not conscious of any such mistake, nor was there anything in the course of the business which tended to create a suspicion of error or mistake in the cancellation, but on the contrary the return of the policy to the defendants and the facts preceding it entitle the defendants to be relieved from liability."

Partners.

SEC. 283. One partner has an insurable interest in a building purchased with partnership funds, although it stands upon lands belonging to another partner.[1] So he has an insurable interest in partnership property of any kind, to the extent of his interest, but cannot insure the *whole* in his own name,[2] unless so expressed in the policy, or unless the assured intended to insure the whole, for the benefit of the other partners and they subsequently valued it and the subsequent purchase by him of the interest of the other partners, does not affect the office of the policy,[3] if the agent of the insurer *knew that the assured intended*

---

[1] *Converse* v. *Citizens' Ins. Co.*, 10 Cush. (Mass.) 37; *Peck* v. *Ins. Co.*, 22 Conn. 575.

[2] *Peoria, etc., Ins. Co.* v. *Hall*, 12 Mich.

[3] In *Peoria F. & M. Ins. Co.* v. *Hall*, ante, CHRISTIANCY, J., said: "It was proved on the trial by the plaintiff below, who was sworn as a witness in his own behalf, and the fact was undisputed, that at the time of the application for insurance of the goods, and at the date of the policy (January 13, 1860), one Helam Bennett was a partner of the plaintiff in business, and, as such, was the owner of the undivided half of the goods insured, and continued to be such partner and owner until the 14th day of March, 1860, when the plaintiff bought out his interest. There was evidence tending to show (as to the policy on the goods) that King, the agent of the company, came to the store and wanted to insure the goods; that plaintiff signed the application for the policy, which was mostly blank when signed; that some one came in, and King turned around and said plaintiff could sign it, and he (King) could fill it out; that plaintiff told King he usually sold gunpowder and everything usually sold in a country store, and that he intended to do so. And (in reference to the policy on the store), there was evidence that, at the time the insurance was taken, the keeping of gunpowder was talked over with King, the agent, and he was told they had gunpowder in the store, and was asked if it would make any difference if powder was kept for sale; to which King replied, 'No.' There was also evidence that plaintiff, at the time of the application for the insurance on the goods, told the agent he did not think he (plaintiff) had a right to insure Bennett's share, and that King replied it would make no difference; that plaintiff had a right to insure the whole. The fire occurred on the 31st day of March, 1860, by which the store building and the stock of goods were destroyed. The circuit judge charged the jury that ' if the agent, King, at the time of making the policy on the goods, knew the interest of the parties—that they were jointly owned by the plaintiff and Bennett—and insured the whole stock, the policy would be valid for the whole stock insured.' To this charge exception was taken, and this presents the first question we shall consider. It is evident from the language of this charge that it was intended to instruct the jury that if the agent, at the time of making the policy, knew the

to cover the interests of the firm, and issued the policy in the name of one partner alone, a recovery may be had for the *whole* interest, if the policy is ratified by the other partners.[1] But in order to have

---

interest of the parties, etc., the policy would be valid for the whole amount of the interest of both partners, and that the plaintiff was entitled to recover in this action the whole amount of the loss of all the goods, though his interest at the time of the insurance was but one-half, and though the insurance was in his name alone, and his declaration averred that, 'at the time of making said policy, and from thence until the loss, etc., he was the owner of said property insured by said policy, and of the value, and to the amount, by the said defendant insured thereon.' Without attempting to decide what might have been the rule of law, had it appeared from the evidence that the insurance was really intended for the benefit of the firm, the premium paid from the partnership fund, and the transaction subsequently ratified by the other partner; we think where (as in the present case) there is no evidence of this kind, and its whole tendency is the other way, the rule is well settled, in reference to a fire policy like this, that if one partner, or part owner of property held in common, insure in his own name only, the policy will cover his undivided interest, *and no more. Graves* v. *Boston Marine Ins. Co.,* 2 Cranch, 419, 440 ; 3 Kent (5th ed.) 258 ; 2 Duer's Ins. §§ 20 and 24 ; *Finney* v. *Bedford Com. Ins. Co.,* 8 Metc. 348 ; *Finney* v. *Warren Ins. Co.,* 1 Metc. 16 ; *Pearson* v. *Lord,* 6 Mass. 81 ; 1 Phil. on Ins. 219, § 391 ; 1 Arnould on Ins. 146, and note. The rule may be otherwise when the partner making the insurance has made advances to the firm, which, by agreement, are to constitute a lien on the goods insured. 2 Duer on Ins. §§ 19 and 24 ; *Milliandore* v. *Atlantic Ins. Co.,* 8 La. 557. We do not see how the agent's knowledge of the interest of the parties, nor his belief or assurance that Hall had the right to insure the whole, can affect the question, so long as the insurance was not in fact made on the account, and for the benefit, of the firm. One partner cannot, by reason alone of his interest as such, insure in his own name, and for his own benefit, the interest of his copartner in the partnership stock, and though such may have been *the intention* both of the assured and the company, on entering into the contract, the policy, in legal effect, can only operate as an indemnity against loss to the extent of the plaintiffs'. undivided half of the goods. And if the policy, when made, did not cover the other partner's undivided half, that portion would not be brought within it *by the plaintiffs subsequent acquisition of the property from the other partner.*"

[1] *Manhattan Ins. Co.* v. *Webster,* 60 Penn. St. 227 ; in *Keith* v. *Globe Ins. Co.,* 52 Ill. 518 ; 4 Am. Rep. 624, a bill in chancery was filed to reform a policy. It alleges that during the summer and autumn of 1865, the firm of Keith, Snell & Taylor purchased and placed in store at West Point, in Mississippi, a quantity of cotton, for which they paid a large sum of money. To make these purchases the firm, through Samuel S. Keith, one of the partners, procured the money on a loan from the Third National Bank of Chicago, in the name of and for the firm.
On the 6th of December, 1865, Keith applied to Ira Holmes, the cashier of the bank, who was also, with his brothers, general insurance agent at Chicago, to procure a policy of insurance on the cotton. Holmes was also the treasurer of appellees. On being spoken to on the subject, Holmes referred Keith to Holmes & Brothers, to make out the policy. Ira had previously instructed Holmes & Brothers, that when an application should amount to more than the companies which they represented wished to take, to place the amount with appellees. An agreement was made by Keith and Holmes & Brothers, they acting for various insurance companies to insure the cotton.
 A certificate of insurance was made to Keith individually. The amount of insurance applied for by Keith being larger than the companies for which Holmes & Brothers were agents were willing to take, they applied to appellees and obtained a policy from them for $7,500 on the cotton. It was burned on the 6th of January, 1866. Appellees refused to pay, on the ground that, if liable at all, they were liable to pay only one-third of the loss, because the certificate was made out to Samuel L. Keith, in his individual name, and as he owned but a third interest in the cotton, they were only liable to make good his loss, and not that of

that effect, *it must be shown that he intended to cover the interests of the other partners, rather than the whole interest for his own benefit;* [1] and that

his partners. Thereupon appellants filled this bill to reform and enforce the contract as it was made and should have been written, alleging that the insurance was made for the firm, and that he so informed the agents, and was assured by them that it should all be made right, but they had taken it in his individual name. On the hearing in the court below, the relief prayed was refused and the bill dismissed.

Keith testified that he went to Holmes & Brothers on the 6th or 7th of December, 1855, to procure an insurance on two hundred and twenty bales of cotton, worth $52,000 ; that he saw Edgar and Albert Holmes, and informed them of his business ; stated to them the quantity of cotton, and where and how it was situated, and that it was guarded night and day ; that it belonged to Keith, Snell & Taylor, and would be consigned to Keith at New York, and only awaited transportation to that point, and Albert Holmes said he would take the risk ; that the rate was agreed upon ; that he then made out a list of the companies by which the insurance would be made ; that the amount was fixed at $49,500 ; that Holmes said the companies they represented could take but $42,000 ; but he would go out and get another company to take $7,500 more, making the amount ; that on the same or next day he met Albert Holmes and he said that he had placed $7,500 in the office of appellees ; that he said to him the cotton belonged to Keith, Snell & Taylor, to be consigned to Keith at New York, and asked if it would make any difference to issue it in the name of the firm and not his ; that Holmes replied that he did not think it would, but he would make it all right ; that Ira Holmes, the treasurer of appellees, knew to whom the cotton belonged ; that before applying for the insurance he saw Ira Holmes and asked him if he wanted the risk ; that he told witness to go to the insurance office and they would fix it up, and that he went and made the arrangement ; the premium was not paid at the time, as the time the policy would run was not then fixed, as that depended upon when it would be shipped ; that the premium was paid in the latter part of January or early in February ; that after the loss he had a conversation with Ira Holmes, and he said he was treasurer of appellees, and if the loss was a straight one, their company should pay it without taking any advantage of technicalities in the policies ; that he said he knew the cotton belonged to Keith, Snell & Taylor, and if it was a fair loss no advantage would be taken by reason of its being in Keith's name ; that after the proofs were made he heard no objections by Holmes or any officer of the company in regard to the proofs ; that Holmes & Brothers held the policy at the time of the fire, and when the premium was paid ; that in the month of May he consulted Swett at his office, when the policies were sent for, and that he and Swett then went to the office of Holmes & Brothers, and asked them to change them to Keith, Snell & Taylor ; that they did not deny that the cotton belonged to or was insured for the firm, but said that as some trouble was likely to grow out of the transactions, they declined to make the change.

Holmes corroborated Keith in the material portions of his evidence, and that he took the certificate of insurance to appellees' office and requested the secretary to insert the words "loss, if any, payable to Keith, Snell & Taylor," and as a reason for the request, informed him that the cotton belonged to that firm, and he thereupon inserted the language as desired ; that appellees paid Holmes & Brothers ten per cent. of the premium for soliciting or obtaining this insurance. He said he though Ira Holmes, treasurer, knew of the insurance at the time the policy was issued ; that he paid the premium, $75, less their commissions, to appellees on the 25th of January, 1866, and after he heard of the loss.

Ira Holmes corroborated Keith's evidence in part, and did not contradict his testimony. He also said that when the insurance was taken, he, as treasurer of the company, knew the cotton belonged to Keith, Snell & Taylor ; that he thinks Bowen, the president of the bank, knew the purpose for which the money was loaned, and knew of the insurance of the cotton soon after it was effected.

"From this evidence," said WALKER, J., "it is manifest that Keith intended to insure, and supposed he had insured the entire property, and not merely his

---

[1] *Peoria, etc., Ins. Co. v. Hall, ante.*

the *contract* was for such a policy, but *by the mistake or fraud of the agent or insurers*, it was made simply to cover his own.[1] When one

---

interest in it. He expressly applied for the insurance in the name of the firm, and seeing the entry in the book in his name, asked whether it would not make a difference if it was not in the name of the firm, and at the same time stated that it belonged to his firm, when Holmes said he thought not, but would make it right. The mind can arrive at no other rational conclusion, from this evidence, than that Keith intended to insure, and supposed he had so insured the property for the firm, and not his separate interest.

Again, Holmes ascertained the amount by calculating its value by the number of bales, and not by calculating the value of Keith's interest in the cotton. Keith also paid the premium on the full amount of the cotton and not on his interest. From all of these facts we must conclude that the agents understood, and could have understood nothing else than that Keith desired to insure the entire lot of cotton in the name of his firm. And it is equally clear that the agents agreed to do so when the application was made; and we will not presume that they designed to perpetrate a fraud on Keith. That it was not so insured by the agents must have arisen from inattention or from want of knowledge that it was material that the firm name should be inserted in the policy as the assured. And we presume that it was for the latter reason, from the fact that they had inserted, 'loss, if any, payable to Keith, Snell & Taylor,' perhaps under the supposition that such a clause would have the same effect as inserting the firm name as the assured.

It, however, remains to ascertain whether the officers of the appellees' company understood and intended to insure the entire interest in the cotton held by Keith's firm. They knew they were insuring all of the cotton, and not an undivided interest. They received a full premium, and specifically state that they had insured two hundred and twenty bales. Their treasurer knew that the firm had borrowed money from their bank to purchase the cotton, and it nowhere appears that Keith ever owned any cotton in his individual right, much less this large quantity. They must, therefore, have known what Keith's interest was, and the true ownership of the property, when the policy was issued, and they must also have known that the sum at which it was valued was three-fold the value of his individual interest. This might not, of itself, be sufficient to establish a mistake requiring a reformation of the contract, but it is strong evidence when considered in connection with the other circumstances of the case.

In addition to all this, Homes & Brothers were the agents of appellees. They, it is true, were not their regular agents, but they had previously solicited insurance for them, and had been paid a percentage therefor, and were in this case paid ten per cent. of the premium received by appelees on this policy, and one or more of the members of the firm of Holmes & Brothers were stockholders in the company, and Ira was not only a stockholder, but was the treasurer of the company, and a member of the firm of Holmes & Brothers. The firm, therefore had notice of the nature of the application, and agreed to insure in the name of Keith, Snell & Taylor.

In the case of *The Atlantic Insurance Company* v. *Wright*, 22 Ill. 462, it was held, that if an agent of an insurance company is informed of all the facts connected with the interests of the assured in the property described in the policy, and does not require a statement of the same, the company will be bound by his acts and cannot avoid the policy, because the true interest was not stated, but will be estopped by the acts of their agents. And the same rule has since been repeatedly recognized and applied by this court. Then, if knowledge by the agent is sufficient to charge the company, much more, an application disclosing all the facts, and a request by the assured to have it insured according to that interest, and an agreement by the agent to do so should bind the company. Holmes & Brothers, then acting in the capacity of agents of appellees, and having been fully informed that it was the interest of the firm and not Keith's alone, that was to be insured, and having agreed to do so, when coupled with the knowledge of the circumstances of the ownership of the cotton, and their receiving a premium on the full value of all the cotton and not of Keith's interest, we think, fully

---

[1] *Keith* v. *Globe Ins. Co.*, *ante*; *Manhattan Ins. Co.*, *ante*.

partner takes out a policy in his own name, *intending* to protect the interests of the other partners, who subsequently ratify the same, he stands as a trustee for them as to the amount in excess of his own interest.[1] A surviving partner, or tenant in common, may enforce a policy issued to protect the entire interest in the property.[2]

Person liable to another for loss of property.

SEC. 284. Where a person, by statute, or by the common law, or by contract, is liable to another for an injury to, or the loss or destruction by fire, of property of another, whether in his possession or not, he may protect himself against such contingent liability by insurance, as an innkeeper,[3] a lighterman,[4] railroad companies,[5] common carriers of every kind,[6] a pawnbroker,[7] warehousemen or wharfingers,[8] a person having the goods of another in his possession to be repaired or manufactured,[9] or any person having the care or custody of the goods of another, for any purpose, who is liable for their safe keeping, either by law or contract, may protect himself from loss thereof by fire, by insurance.[10] A person who, with the consent of the owner, makes repairs upon a building, *for his own benefit*, has an insurable interest thereon to the extent of his expenditures.[11]

A general creditor has no insurable interest.

SEC. 285. A mere general creditor has no insurable interest in his debtor's property, and an insurance effected upon such an interest would be void, as insurance companies have no power or authority to insure or guarantee the payment of a debt,[12] but a surety upon a mort-

---

establishes the mistake in executing the policy, and requires that it should be reformed so as to make Keith, Snell & Taylor the assured, as was intended by the parties when it was issued."

[1] *Murray* v. *Columbian Ins. Co.*, 11 John (N. Y.) 302 ; *Graves* v. *Ins. Co.*, 2 Cr. (U. S.) 419 ; *Manhattan Ins. Co.* v. *Webster, ante ; Page* v. *Fry*, 2 B. & P. 200.

[2] *Oakman* v. *Dorchester, etc., Ins. Co.*, 98 Mass. 57.

[3] Bunyon on Ins. 24.

[4] *Achard* v. *Ring*, Q. B., Dec. 19, 1874 ; *Stewart* v. *Steamship Co.*, L. R., 8 Q. B. 362.

[5] *Eastern R. R. Co.* v. *Relief Ins. Co.*, 105 Mass.; *Mondanock R. R. Co.* v. *Manufacturers' Ins. Co.*, 113 Mass. 74.

[6] *Morewood* v. *Pollock*, 1 E. & E. 743 ; *Consuley* v. *Cohen*, 3 B. & Ad. 478 ; *Chase* v. *Washington Ins. Co.*, 12 Barb. (N. Y.) 595.

[7] *Shockell* v. *West*, 6 Jur. (N. S.) 95.

[8] *Waters* v. *Monarch Ins. Co.*, 5 El. & Bl. 870.

[9] *Getchell* v. *Ætna Ins. Co.*, 14 Allen (Mass.) 325.

[10] *Chase* v. *Washington, etc., Ins. Co.*, 12 Barb. (N. Y.) 595 ; *Getchell* v. *Ætna Ins. Co.*, 14 Allen (Mass.) 325.

[11] *Looney* v. *Looney*, 116 Mass. 283.

[12] *Foster* v. *Van Reed*, 5 Hun (N. Y.) 343.

gage debt,[1] a receiptor of property attached,[2] or any person who has a legal or equitable interest in the specific property insured, and would sustain a pecuniary loss, as an incident to the destruction of the property, may insure the same.

Fixtures.

Sec. 286. One who has permitted another to build a house upon his land, but who has given no permission for its removal, has an insurable interest therein, and this is not defeated by an agreement that such person may purchase the land, nor even by a consent, revoked, however, before sale, that the house might be sold on execution as the personal property of the person building it.[3]

One held out as, but not in fact, partner.

Sec. 287. Where one permits another to use his name in the buying and selling of goods, a policy taken out in the name of both will be good, although the property *in fact* belongs to the one purchasing it. The *liability* of the other is enough to uphold an insurable interest.[4]

Tenant by curtesy. Husband's interest in wife's property.

Sec. 288. Where the husband has an interest in the real estate of his wife as tenant by curtesy, and under his right of present occupation, that will uphold a policy thereon during the life-time of the wife. He has a right to the use and enjoyment of the premises, or their rents and profits, during the joint lives of himself and wife, and is tenant by curtesy at her decease,[5] and, where he has a right to the use of her personal property during her life, and takes it at her death, he has an insurable interest therein, as of household furniture;[6] and, in either case, he may recover the whole value, and is not restricted to his interest therein.[7]

Pawnbrokers or pledgees.

Sec. 289. A person holding goods or property as security for advances made has an insurable interest therein, and having a qualified property therein, and being bound to restore it to the owner on payment of the

---

[1] *Waring* v. *Loder*, 53 N. Y. 581.

[2] *Freeman's Ins. Co.* v. *Powell*, ante.

[3] *Oakman* v. *Dorchester Ins. Co.*, 98 Mass. 57.

[4] *Gould* v. *York, etc., Ins. Co.*, 47 Me., 403.

[5] *Franklin, etc., Ins. Co.* v. *Drake*, 2 B. Mon. (Ky.) 47; *Columbian Ins. Co.* v. *Lawrence*, 2 Peters (U. S.) 43; *Harris* v. *Ins. Co.*, 50 Penn. St. 341.

[6] *Clarke* v. *Fireman's Ins. Co.*, 18 La. 431.

[7] *Fireman's Ins. Co.* v. *Drake*, ante.

advances, he is not restricted to his advances, but may insure for the entire value of the property.

Lien for material.

SEC. 290. Where a person furnishing material for a building or vessel is given a lien thereon for the price, he has an insurable interest in the building or vessel to the extent of his lien.[2]

Trustee.

SEC. 291. A trustee is not in law *bound* to insure, but he may do so, and if he does, the insurance enures to the benefit of his *cestui que trust*, and the *cestui que trust* may insure for himself.[3] One trustee— where there are more than one—may insure for the whole; or if he insures without authority of the other trustees, the others may ratify the same, and the bringing of an action in their names is a sufficient ratification.[4] Money received by a trustee upon a policy covering the trust property, is the property of the *cestui que trust*, and cannot be attached as the money of the trustee upon his debts.[5]

Many persons may have insurable interest in same property.

SEC. 292. Many persons may have an insurable interest in the same property, arising from different sources, and standing upon entirely distinct and different grounds, as the owner in fee.[6]

Mortgagee.

SEC. 293. A mortgagee of the same premises.[7]

Assignee.

SEC. 294. The assignee of a mortgagee.[8]

Surety or indorsee.

SEC. 295. A person who is personally responsible for the mortgage debt.[9]

---

[1] *Sutherland* v. *Pratt*, 11 M. & W. 296; *Waring* v. *Indemnity F. Ins. Co.*, 45 N. Y. 607.

[2] *Franklin, etc., Ins. Co.* v. *Coates*, 14 Md. 288.

[3] *Crawford* v. *Hunter*, 8 T. R. 13; *White* v. *Hud. R. Ins. Co.*, 7 How. Pr. (N. Y.) 351.

[4] *Ins. Co.* v. *Chase*, 5 Wall. (U. S.) 509.

[5] *Lerow* v. *Welworth,* 9 Allen (Mass.) 382.

[6] *French* v. *Roberts*, 16 N. H. 177; *Allen* v. *Franklin F. Ins. Co.*, 9 How. Pr. (N. Y.) 501; *Strong* v. *Manufacturers' Ins. Co.*, 10 Pick. (Mass.) 40; *Higginson* v. *Dall*, 13 Mass. 96; *Locks* v. *N. Am. Ins. Co.*, id. 61.

[7] *Holbrook* v. *American Ins. Co.*, 1 Curtis C. C. (U. S.) 193; *Davis* v. *Quincy, etc., Ins. Co.*, 10 Allen (Mass.) 113; *Fox* v. *Phœnix Ins. Co.*, 52 Me. 333; *Traders' Ins. Co.* v. *Robert*, 9 Wend. (N. Y.) 404; *Ins. Co.* v. *Updegraff*, 21 Penn. St. 513.

[8] *Ins. Co.* v. *Woodruff*, 26 N. J. L. 541.

[9] *Waring* v. *Loder*, 58 N. Y. 581.

Mechanic having lien.

Sec. 296. A mechanic erecting buildings thereon under an entire contract, or a material-man for materials.[1]

Mortgagor.

Sec. 297. A mortgagor and mortgagee may each insure the premises for their separate benefit. The mortgagee, however, can only insure to the amount of his claim or debt; and in case of loss, the insurer is entitled to an assignment of his interest, which the mortgagor may insure to the full value, and can recover the same, notwithstanding the mortgage, and the mortgagee is entitled to no benefit therefrom.[2]

Attaching or levying creditor.

Sec. 298. An attaching or levying creditor.[3]

Sheriffs.

Sec. 299. A sheriff or his deputy has an insurable interest in the property attached or levied upon by them. In case of the deputy, however, the insurance should be in the name of the sheriff;[4] but it seems that the expense cannot be taxed against the parties.[5]

Judgment creditor, when.

Sec. 300. And where, by law, a judgment is a lien upon real estate, a judgment creditor, even though execution was not issued.[6]

Vendee of property.

Sec. 301. A person in possession under a contract to purchase,[7] or who has an equitable interest in the estate.[8]

Executors. Administrators.

Sec. 302. An executor in the estate of his intestate, even where by law the title vests in the heirs, he holding in trust for the beneficiaries

---

[1] *Franklin Ins. Co.* v. *Coates*, 14 Md. 285; *Protection Ins. Co.* v. *Hall*, 16 B. Mon. (Ky.) 411.

[2] *Carpenter* v. *Providence Wash. Ins. Co.*, 16 Pet. (U. S.) 495; *French* v. *Rogers*, 16 N. H. 177; *Allen* v. *Franklin Ins. Co.*, 9 How. Pr. (N. Y.) 501; *Strong* v. *Manufacturers' Ins. Co.*, 10 Pick. (Mass.) 40; *Curry* v. *Commonwealth Ins. Co.*, id 535.

[3] *Mickles* v. *Rochester City Bank*, 11 Paige Ch. (N. Y.) 118; *Mapes* v. *Coffin*, 5 id. 296; *Herkimer* v. *Rice*, 27 N. Y. 163; *Springfield F. & M. Ins. Co.* v. *Allen*, 43 id. 389.

[4] *White* v. *Madison*, 26 N. Y. 117.

[5] *Burke* v. *Brig M. P. Rich*, 1 Cliff. (U. S.) 509.

[6] *Rohrback* v. *Germania F. Ins. Co.*, 62 N. Y. 47.

[7] *Shotwell* v. *Jefferson Ins. Co.*, 5 Bos. (N. Y.) 247; *Ayres* v. *Hartford Ins. Co.*, 17 Iowa, 176; *M'Givney* v. *Phœnix Ins. Co.*, 1 Wend. (N. Y.) 85.

[8] *Rohrback* v. *Ætna Ins. Co.*, 1 T. & C. (N. Y.) 339; *Redfield* v. *Holland Purchase Ins. Co.*, 56 N. Y. 354.

under the will or by distribution.[1] An administrator, where the personal estate is insufficient to pay the debts,[2] but when the personality is sufficient, *quere ?* [3]

Tenants—Married women, etc.

SEC. 303. A tenant for a term has an insurable interest to the extent of the value of his leasehold interest;[4] and a tenant who erects buildings under a right to remove them, may insure them as his own.[5]

A tenant by curtesy or dower.[6]

A tenant in tail.[7]

A married woman in her own estate, and her husband, where by law he is given a present interest therein.[8]

Where the plaintiff's wife was the owner of real estate in her own right, and two days after her marriage, in consideration of her indebtedness to him before her marriage, executed to him a paper of the following tenor: "I do hereby certify that I owe to J. Rohrback (the husband) the sum of $700, and the sum of $25, for each and every month from July 14th, 1863, and for every month he may live with me henceforth, without any deduction whatever, which amount shall be a lien upon my property." And the husband procured an insur- upon the property. It was held, in an action upon the policy, that, under the statute of New York relative to married women, that this created a lien upon her property that constituted a sufficient insurable interest;[9] but if the husband, having no present legal or equitable interest therein, takes a policy in his own name, it is bad.[10] Or, indeed, any person who has a certain, definite, or fixed interest in the property, so that an injury thereto or destruction thereof would result in pecuniary loss to him as a purchaser under execution before a conveyance has been made to him.[11]

[1] *Savage* v. *Howard Ins. Co.*, 52 N. Y. 502; *Herkimer* v. *Rice, ante; Phelps* v. *Gebhard,* 9 Bos. (N. Y.) 504.

[2] *Clinton* v. *Hope Ins. Co.*, 45 N. Y. 454.

[3] *Beach* v. *Bowery Ins. Co.*, 8 Abb. Pr. (N. Y.) 261 *n.*

[4] *New York* v. *Hamilton Ins. Co.*, 10 Bos. (N. Y.) 537.

[5] *Hope, etc., Ins. Co.* v. *Brolaskey,* 35 Penn. St. 282.

[6] *Harris* v. *York, etc., Ins. Co.*, 50 Penn. St. 341; *Ins. Co.* v. *Drake,* 2 B. Mon. (Ky.) 4.

[7] *Curry* v. *Commonwealth Ins. Co.*, 10 Pick. (Mass.) 535.

[8] *Mutual Ins. Co.* v. *Deale,* 18 Md. 26.

[9] *Rohrback* v. *Ætna Ins. Co.*, 1 T. & C. (N. Y.) 339.

[10] *Eminence, etc., Ins. Co.* v. *Jesse,* 1 Met. (Ky.) 523.

[11] *Ætna, etc. Ins. Co.* v. *Miers,* 5 Sneed (Tenn.) 139; *Herkimer* v. *Rice, ante; Rohrback* v. *Germania F. Ins. Co., ante.*

Receiptor or bailee.

SEC. 304. A receiptor of property attached, or any person who, at the request of the owner, becomes security for its return to the officer seizing or attaching it.[1]

Agent, trustee, bailee.

SEC. 305. An agent, bailee, trustee or any person having the custody of property for another, who is responsible for its safe return.[2]

Each joint owner or tenant in common.

SEC. 306. One partner to the extent of his interest in the property of the firm;[3] and a policy in the name of one partner will only cover his legal interest therein,[4] unless through ignorance, fraud or mistake on the part of the insurer, the policy was issued in the name of one owner, when it should have issued in the name of all.[5] Even where the partnership is merely nominal, and the business is really carried on for the benefit of *one* of them, a policy may be taken out in the name of the firm, because in such a case, all the persons who permit their names to be used as partners are liable for the debts of the firm, and therefore have an interest in the preservation of the property.[6]

Profits.

SEC. 307. A person who has an interest in the profits of property, or in the cargo of a ship, may insure the same.[7] But when profits are insured it must be *qua profits*;[8] but the profits need not be specifically defined. It is enough if the policy covers the *profits* as "*on profits*" in connection with an insurance on a business of any kind.[9] In ascertaining the profits, they are to be treated as a mere excresence upon the value of the goods *beyond prime cost.* The gain over the cost.[10]

In personal property, the owner has an insurable interest as a mat-

---

[1] *Fireman's Ins. Co.* v. *Powell,* 16 B. Mon. (Ky.) 311.

[2] *Ætna Ins. Co.* v. *Hall,* 15 B. Mon. (Ky.) 411; *Franklin Ins. Co.* v. *Coates,* 14 Md. 285; *Graham* v. *Fireman's Ins. Co.,* 2 Dis. (Ohio) 255.

[3] *Converse* v. *Citizen's Mut. Ins. Co.,* 10 Cush. (Mass.) 37; *Ohl* v. *Eagle Ins. Co.,* 4 Mass. (U. S.) 172.

[4] *Bailey* v. *Hope Ins. Co.,* 56 Me. 474.

[5] *Manhattan Ins. Co.* v. *Webster,* 59 Penn. St. 227.

[6] *Phœnix Ins. Co.* v. *Hamilton,* 14 Wall (U. S.) 504.

[7] *Patapsio Ins. Co.* v. *Coulter,* 2 Pet. (U. S.) 222; *New York Ins. Co.* v. *Robinson,* 1 Johns. (N. Y.) 616.

[8] *Sun Fire Office* v. *Wright,* 3 N. & M. 819; Bennett's F. I. C. 449; *Leonards* v. *Phœnix Ins. Co.,* 2 Rob. (La.) 131; *Elmaker* v. *Franklin Ins. Co.,* 5 Penn. St. 183; *Niblo* v. *N. A. Ins. Co.,* 1 Sandf. (N. Y.) 551; *Menzies* v. *N. British Ins. Co.,* 9 C. C. S. (Sc.) 694.

[9] *Eyre* v. *Glover,* 16 East. 218.

[10] Lord ELLENBOROUGH in *Eyre* v. *Glover, ante.*

ter of course, so also has a consignee thereof;[1] the carrier;[2] a commission merchant;[3] both the vendor and vendee in cases where the sale is conditional, and the title is not passed absolutely.[4] Thus, the vendor in a contract of sale of a factory and machinery who retained the legal title until payment of the purchase was held to have an insurable interest both in the building and machinery, and his interest was held to be a legal and not an equitable interest;[5] but when the title absolutely passes, the interest ends;[6] an attaching creditor.[7]

Master of a vessel.

SEC. 308. So it is held that the master of a vessel who is entitled to primage on freight, has an insurable interest to the extent of such primage.[8] So, too, the master of a vessel, although in fact, having no *property* in the cargo, yet, being the legal owner of the whole cargo, and the equitable owner of a part of it, has an insurable interest in the whole.[9]

Creditors under execution levied on property.

SEC. 309. Some question has been made whether a judgment creditor has an insurable interest in the real etatse or property of his debtor. If an execution has been issued, and a levy made, there is no question but that such an interest exists in the property levied upon, at least in the sheriff or officer making the levy, where he is responsible for the safe keeping of the property, if not in the creditors themselves. But there

---

[1] *Parks* v. *General Interest Assurance Co.*, 5 Pick. (Mass.) 34. A consignee generally cannot insure beyond the extent of his personal interest, which is the probable amount of commissions that will inure to him from the sale of the goods, but if he is directed by his principals to insure the goods, he may take a policy for their value, for his own protection, he acting as trustee for the owners, and in an action upon the policy, these facts are sufficient to establish his insurable interest. *Shaw* v. *Ætna Ins. Co.*, 49 Mo. 578.

[2] *Savage* v. *Corn Exchange Ins. Co.*, 36 N. Y. 655; *Chase* v. *Washington, etc., Ins. Co.*, 4 Bos. (N. Y.) 1.

Forest v. *Fulton Ins. Co.*, 1 Hall (N. Y.) 84; *Putnam* v. *Mercantile Mut. Ins. Co.*, 5 Met. (Mass.) 386.

[4] *Tallman* v, *Atlantic F. & M. Ins. Co.*, 4 Abb. (N. Y.) App. Dec. 345; *Kenness* v. *Clarkson*, 1 John. (N. Y.) 385; *M'Gevney* v. *Phœnix Ins. Co.*, 1 Wend. (N. Y.) 85; *Rider* v. *Ocean Ins. Co.*, 20 Pick. (Mass.) 259; *Shotwell* v. *Jefferson Ins. Co.*, 5 Bos. (N. Y.) 247; *Ayers* v. *Hartford Ins. Co.*, 17 Iowa, 176.

[5] *Wood* v. *N. Western Ins. Co.*, 46 N. Y. 421.

[6] *Stuart* v. *Columbian Ins. Co.*, 2 Cr. C. C. (U. S.) 442.

[7] *Mickles* v. *Rochester City Bank, ante; Mapes* v. *Coffin, ante; Springfield F. & M. Ins. Co.* v. *Allen, ante.*

[8] *Pedrick* v. *Fisher*, 1 Sprague, 565. (*Primage* is a duty at the water side due to the master of a ship, and the mariners, for the use of his cables and ropes, to discharge the goods of the merchant, and to the mariners for lading and unlading in any port or haven. 3 Tomlin's Law Dic. 215.)

[9] *Buck* v. *Chespeake Ins. Co.*, 1 Peters (U. S) 151.

can be no question but that the creditors under such execution, as such, have an insurable interest in the property,[1] and the fact that the sheriff is liable to them for any loss that might arise from the destruction of the property, would not divest them of that right, as they have a right to rely upon the property itself to liquidate their claims, and are not compelled to pursue a personal remedy.[2]

---

[1] *Mickles* v. *Rochester City Bank*, 11 Paige Ch. (N. Y.) 118; *Mapes* v. *Coffin*, 5 id. 296; *Springfield F. & M. Ins. Co.* v. *Allen*, 43 N. Y. 389.
[2] STORY, J., in *Hancox* v. *Fishing*, 3 Sum. (U. S.) 132.

CHAPTER IX.

ALIENATION.

Contract of insurance is personal.

SEC. 310. The contract, being one of indemnity, is purely personal, and does not run with the thing insured; as if buildings are insured, it does not run with the land, and if the premises are sold, it ceases to operate as a protection, either to the vendor or vendee; and the same rule prevails in reference to mere personalty. But the contract, and consequently the indemnity, can be kept on foot and made operative in favor of a vendee by the act of the insurer; that is, by the insurer consenting to transfer its liability under the contract to the vendee, and in the case of *personal* property, it may be made operative in favor of a third person, upon property belonging to the same class, even though no part of it was originally covered by the contract. Thus, if A. is the owner of a store and the goods therein which are insured, and he sells the store and goods to B., who puts therein a stock in addition to that which he purchases of A., and the policy, *with the consent of the insurer*, is transferred to B., he may recover the sum for which such goods were originally insured, although none of the goods which he purchased of A. were in the store when the loss occurred. This was well illustrated in a case recently decided by the supreme court of New Hampshire.[1] In that case, it appeared that the company insured A. on his dwelling-house a certain sum, and "on furniture and clothing therein" a certain other sum. A. sold the real estate to B. and assigned the policy to him with the consent of the company. A. did not sell his furniture or clothing to B., but removed it. B. took possession of the house, and placed therein furniture and clothing of the same kind and value, and it was burned in the house. It was held by the court that B. could recover of the company the amount of the original insurance upon the furniture and clothing of A. This decision is based on the ground that insurance is a contract of indemnity appertaining to the person or party to the contract, and not to the thing which is subjected to the risk against which the owner is protected. It is not a contract running with the land in the case of real estate, nor running with the personalty in the case of a chattel insured.[2] The principle of indemnity is the general principle which runs through the whole contract. A contract of indemnity is given to a *person* against his sustaining loss or damage, and cannot properly be called one that insures the *thing*, it not being possible so to do, and therefore, as Lord HARDWICKE has said, it must mean *insuring the person from damage—that is, damage to the thing or to his property.*[3] They are not, in their nature, incidents of the property insured, but are mere special agreements, personal in their character, and intended merely as a protection or security to the individual named therein against such loss or damage as he may sustain from an injury to, or destruction of, the property by fire, and cannot be extended or

[1] *Cummins* v. *Cheshier Mut. F. Ins. Co.*, 55 N. H. 457.

[2] *Carpenter* v. *Ins. Co.*, 16 Pet. 495.

[3] *Lucena* v. *Crawford*, 2 Bos. & Pul. (N. R.) 300; *Saddlers' Co.* v. *Badcock*, 2 Atk. 554; *Wilson* v. *Hill*, 3 Met. (Mass.) 66; Ellis on Ins. 1; Wms. on Pers. Prop. 179; 1 Phill. on Ins. 1; *Lane* v. *Maine Mut. F. Ins. Co.*, 12 Me. 44.

construed as an indemnity to any other person having an interest in the property, even though such interest be a joint interest with the person insured.[1]

Alienation defeats policy, whether so provided or not.

SEC. 311. Therefore, it does not pass with the property to the purchaser thereof, but, upon the termination of *all* the interest of the insured therein, becomes inoperative and ceases to have any validity as an indemnifying contract;[2] but, if the insured retains *any* interest in the property, legal or equitable, it remains operative *to the extent of the interest so retained by him*.[3] Being a personal contract, and operative only as an indemnity, it follows, as a matter of course, that no person can enter into a valid contract for insurance upon property, unless he has *interest therein*, legal or equitable, so that, in case of an injury to, or destruction of the property, *he would sustain a pecuniary loss therefrom*.[4] This is a feature and quality of the contract, *that arises out of*

---

[1] *Carpenter* v. *Providence, etc., Ins. Co.*, 16 Pet. (U. S.) 495 ; *Finney* v. *Bedford Com. Ins. Co.*, 8 Met. (Mass.) 348 ; *Graves* v. *Boston Marine Ins. Co.*, 2 Cr. (U. S.) 419 ; *Pearson* v. *Lord*, 6 Mass. 81 ; 1 Arnould on Ins. 146 *n.* ; 1 Phillips on Ins. 219, sec. 391 ; 2 Duer on Ins., sec. 24 ; 3 Kent's Com. (5 ed.) 258 ; *Peoria Marine Ins. Co.* v. *Hall*, 12 Mich. 202 ; *Disbrow* v. *Jones*, Harr. (Mich.) 48.

[2] *Wilson* v. *Hill*, 3 Met. (Mass.) 66 ; *Disbrow* v. *Jones*, Harr. Ch. (Mich.) 48.

[3] *Jackson* v. *Mass. Ins. Co.*, 23 Pick. (Mass.) 418 ; *Lazarus* v. *Ins. Co.*, 5 Pick. (Mass.) 75 ; also same case, 19 Pick. (Mass.) 81 ; *Sanbron* v. *Union F. Ins. Co.*, 4 Biss. (U. S.) 511. If the property is conveyed conditionally, as, if it is agreed that it shall be reconveyed on certain conditions, an equitable, and consequently an insurable interest remains. *Holbrook* v. *American Ins. Co.*, 1 Curtis (U. S. C. C.) 193. A bill of sale, executed, but never delivered, is not an alienation. *Vogel* v. *People's, etc., Ins. Co.*, 9 Gray (Mass.) 23. A conditional sale, as a sale reserving the title until paid for, although possession is given, is not an alienation. *Bates* v. *Commercial Ins. Co.*, 1 Cin. Superior Ct. (Ohio) 523. In such a case there is not a termination of the *interest* of the assured. *Jackson* v. *Ætna Ins. Co.*, 16 B. Mon. (Ky.) 242 ; *Shephard* v. *Union, etc., Ins. Co.*, 38 N. H. 232. *The title must be absolutely divested. If any, even the smallest interest, legal or equitable, exists,* the policy is valid *to the extent of such interest*. *Van Deusen* v. *People's, etc., Ins. Co.*, 1 Rob. (N. Y.) 55 ; *Cowan* v. *Iowa State Ins. Co.*, 40 Iowa, 551. The assignment of property insured, as collateral security for a debt, the assured still retaining the title thereof, or the right of redeeming, is not such an alienation as divests the assured of his insurable interest therein, or as avoids the policy. *Ayres* v. *Hartford, etc., Ins. Co.*, 21 Iowa, 193. Such provisions are construed strictly, and nothing but an absolute transfer of the entire interest of the assured will avoid the policy. *West Branch Ins. Co.* v. *Halfstein*, 40 Penn. St. 289 ; *Lazarus* v. *Com. Ins. Co.*, 5 Pick. (Mass.) 76 ; *Courtney* v. *N. Y., etc., Ins. Co.*, 28 Barb. (N. Y.) 116 ; *Ornell* v. *Hampden, etc., Ins. Co.*, 13 Gray (Mass.) 431. And the same is true of any *conditional* transfer of either of real or personal property. *Jackson* v. *Mass. Ins. Co.*, 23 Pick. (Mass.) 418 ; *Folsom* v. *Belknap, etc., Ins. Co.*, 30 N. H. 231 ; *Washington Ins. Co.* v. *Hayes*, 17 Ohio St. 432 ; *Norcross* v. *Ins. Co.*, 17 Penn. St. 429. A mere nominal change of interest is not within the prohibition. *It must be an actual parting with the entire interest of the assured in the property. Ayres* v. *Home Ins. Co.*, 21 Iowa, 185. And, if the entire interest is passed, whether voluntarily or by legal process, the policy ceases to be operative. *Campbell* v. *Hamilton, etc., Ins. Co.*, 51 Me. 69.

[4] A mortgagor has an insurable interest, and consequently, unless specially prohibited, or prohibited by fair implication, the execution of a mortgage does not

its very nature, and is dictated by sound public policy. Contracts of
insurance in favor of persons having *no interest* in the subject-matter
of the risk, were deemed so impolitic and disastrous in their consequences that, by Stat. 14, George III, insurances in favor of parties
having *no interest* in marine risks were prohibited, the act reciting as
a reason therefor that "it had been found by experience that the
making assurances, *interest or no interest*, or without further proof of
interest than the policy had been productive of many pernicious practices, whereby great numbers of ships, with their cargoes, had either
been fraudulently lost or destroyed, or taken by the enemy in time
of war; and, by introducing a mischievous kind of gaming or wagering," etc., and provided that no such policies should be issued, and
subsequently, by another statute (14 George III), it was provided that
"no insurance shall be made by any person or persons, bodies politic
or corporate, on the life or lives of any person or persons, *or on any
event or events whatever wherein the person or persons for whose use, benefit,
or on whose account such policy or policies shall be made, shall have no
interest, or by way of gaming or wagering*." Under this statute, all policies
of insurance in favor of any person not having a *pecuniary* interest—for
this has been regarded as the species of interest intended—have been

---

defeat the policy. *Conover* v. *Ins. Co.*, 1 N. Y. 290; *Ætna Ins. Co.* v. *Tyler*, 16
Wend. (N. Y.) 385; *Wilson* v. *Hill*, 3 Met. (Mass.) 66; *Abbott* v. *Ins. Co.*, 30 Me.
414. A gift of property *inter vivas* without condition, is an alienation within the
meaning of the term. *McCarty* v. *Com. Ins. Co.*, 17 La. 365. So is a transfer of
title by operation of law as an assignment to an assignee in bankruptcy. *Adams*
v. *Rockingham, etc., Ins. Co.*, 29 Me. 292; *Young* v. *Eagle Ins. Co.*, 14 Gray
(Mass.) 150. A sale upon foreclosure proceedings, no redemption existing.
McLaren v. *Hartford Ins. Co.*, 5 N. Y. 151; *Strong* v. *Manufacturers' Ins. Co.*,
10 Pick. (Mass.) 49. The assured's rights are not lost until the full title vests in
the purchaser, without right of redemption on the part of the assured or his creditors. *Story* v. *Manf. Ins. Co.*, *ante*; *Bragg* v. *N. E. Ins. Co.*, 26 N. H. 289.
In New York, a sale under foreclosure proceedings *instanter* confers a full title,
and no right of redemption exists; but in many of the states, the right of
redemption, after decree or sale, exists for a certain stated period, and while that
right remains, an insurable interest in the mortgagor exists. An assignment for
the benefit of creditors has been held an alienation, but it would seem that this
doctrine is not applicable except in cases where, by the law under which the
assignment is made, the assured is discharged from his debts by such assignment,
so that he has really no pecuniary interest at stake after the property reaches
the possession of the assignee. *Hazard* v. *Franklin, etc., Ins. Co.*, 7 R. I. 429.
Dey v. *Poughkeepsie, etc., Ins. Co.* 23 Barb. (N. Y.) 623; *Phœnix Ins. Co.* v. *Lawrence, ante.* See *Lazarus* v. *Com. Ins. Co.*, 19 Pick. (Mass.) 81, where, what
would seem to be the more correct rule is adopted, *to wit, that if there is any
interest remaining in the assured, he may recover under the policy.* A change of
the title by descent does not amount to an alienation. *Burbank* v. *Ins. Co.*, 25
N. H. 550; nor, indeed, *any* transfer or change of *title* that does not divest the
assured of *all* interest therein. *Scanlon* v. *Union F. Ins. Co.*, 4 Biss. (U. S.) 511;
Rice v. *Tower*, 1 Gray (Mass.) 426; *Colt* v. *Phœnix Ins. Co.*, 54 N. Y. 595; *Gilbert*
v. *N. A. Ins. Co.*, 23 Wend. (N. Y.) 43; *Manley* v. *Ins. Co. of N. America*, 1
Lans. (N. Y.) 20; *Hill* v. *Cumberland, etc., Ins. Co.*, 59 Penn. St. 474.

held void, as policies insuring the sex of a certain person,[1] that certain stocks will sell at a certain sum,[2] that there will be open trade between certain ports, within a certain time,[3] and generally all policies of every species in which the holder *has no pecuniary interest* in the subject. matter of the risk which it covers.

The sale of an equity of redemption is an alienation,[4] and so is any sale, whether voluntary or by operation of law, that divests the assured of all interest in the property,[5] but a conditional transfer does not avoid the policy, because an insurable interest still remains.[6]

A mortage is not an alienation unless expressly conditioned to be,[7] because the assured still retains the legal title, and a consequent insurable interest.

An absolute assignment or sale after insurance is effected, takes away all insurable interest, and consequently creates a bar to an action upon the policy. He then stands in the same position as though he had never had any interest in the property insured. But, in the absence of special stipulations as to what alienations or changes in the title shall invalidate the policy, so long as *any* interest remains in the assured, *that is, so long as he retains an insurable interest therein*, the policy is operative to protect that interest. Therefore, although he has sold the land or goods, but retains either the possession or legal title therein as security for the purchase money,[8] an insurable inter-

---

[1] *Roebuck* v. *Hammerton*, Cowp. 737.

[2] *Paterson* v. *Powell*, 9 Bing. 320.

[3] *Mollison* v. *Staples*, Park's Ins. 640, *n.*

[4] *Campbell* v. *Hamilton, etc., Ins. Co.*, 51 Me. 69.

[5] *Edmonds* v. *Mutual, etc., Ins. Co.*, 1 Allen (Mass.) 311; *Adams* v. *Rockingham, etc., Ins. Co.*, 29 Me. 292; *Edes* v. *Hamilton Ins. Co.*, 3 Allen (Mass.) 362. In *Buckley* v. *Garrett*, 47 Penn. St. 204, a transfer from one joint owner or tenant in common to another is held an alienation. So any sale or transfer that leaves no insurable interest in the assured. *Wilson* v. *Hill*, 3 Met. (Mass.) 66. And the same is true even when the property is not sold, but the policy is assigned without the assent of the company. *Smith* v. *Saratoga Ins. Co.*, 1 Hill (N. Y.) 497.

[6] *Jackson* v. *Mass. Ins. Co.*, 23 Pick. (Mass.) 418; *Wheeling Ins. Co.* v. *Morrison*, 11 Leigh. (Va.) 354; *Trumbull* v. *Portage, etc., Ins. Co.*, 12 Ohio 305.

[7] *Holbrook* v. *The Am. Ins. Co.*, 1 Curtis C. C. (U. S.) 193; *Tettimore* v. *Vt. Mut. Ins. Co.*, 20 Vt. 546; *Swift* v. *Same*, 18 id. 305; *Higginson* v. *Dall*, 13 Mass. 96; *Gilbert* v. *N. Am. Ins. Co.*, 23 Wend. (N. Y.) 43; *Gordon* v. *Mass. F. & M. Ins. Co.*, 2 Pick. (Mass.) 249; *Aurora Ins. Co.* v. *Eddy*, 55 Ill. 213; *Rallins* v. *Columbian Ins. Co.*; *Fulsom* v. *Belknap, etc., Ins. Co.*, 31 N. H. 231; *Dutton* v. *N. E. F. Ins. Co.*, 29 N. H. 153; *contra*, see *Indiana, etc., Ins. Co.* v. *Coquillard*, 2 Ind. 645; also, *Indiana, etc., Ins. Co.* v. *Connor*, 5 Ind. 170.

[8] *Stetson* v. *Mass. etc., Ins. Co.*, 4 Mass. 330; *Trumbull* v. *Portage Ins. Co.*, 12 Ohio, 305; *Higginson* v. *Dall*, 13 Mass. 96; *Gordon* v. *Mass., etc., Ins. Co.*, 2 Pick. (Mass.) 249; *Locke* v. *N. A. Ins. Co.*, 13 Mass. 61; *Tyler* v. *Ætna Ins. Co.*, 12 Wend. (N. Y.) 507; *Columbian Ins. Co.* v. *Lawrence*, 2 Pet. (U. S.) 25; *Cone* v. *Niagara Ins. Co.*, 60 N. Y. 619; *Citizens' Ins. Co.* v. *Dall*, 35 Md. 89; *Lynch* v.

est remains in him, and the policy protects that interest;[1] but the question as to whether he can recover the entire loss, or is restricted to his actual personal interest at the time of loss, will depend upon his relation to the property, and the extent of the loss pecuniarily to him, and his contract with, or accountability to the vendor.[2]

Void sale.

Sec. 312. A sale of premises or other property that is void from any cause, is not an *alienation* within the meaning of the term as employed in the prohibitory clause of a policy;[3] but a sale that is merely voidable is an alienation, that defeats a recovery for a loss occurring before the sale has been set aside.[4]

Assignment for benefit of creditors.

Sec. 313. Where property is assigned for the benefit of creditors, and the assignor remains liable to them for any balance remaining due after the distribution of assets, he still retains an insurable interest therein, to the extent of the entire value of the property, because that would be the extent of his loss.[5] But where, by statute, by such

---

Dalzell, 4 Bro. P. C. 431 ; *McCarty* v. *Com. Ins. Co.,* 17 La. 365 ; *In re Kip* 4 Edw. Ch. (N. Y.) 86 ; *Bartey* v. *Ætna Ins. Co.,* 10 Allen (Mass.) 286 ; thus a conveyance of the property to a third person *in trust* to be sold, and the proceeds applied to the payment of the assured's debt, still leaves an insurable interest, *White* v. *Hudson River Ins. Co.,* 7 How. Pr. (N. Y.) 341 ; an *agreement* to sell does not divest the assured of his insurable interest, *Perry Co. Ins. Co.* v. *Stewart,* 19 Penn. St. 45 ; even though part of the purchase money has been paid, *Boston and Salem Ice Co.* v. *Royal Ins. Co.,* 12 Allen (Mass.) 381 ; *Ins. Co.* v. *Updegraff,* 21 Penn. St. 513 ; *Norcross* v. *Ins. Co.,* 17 Penn. St. 429 ; *Ins. Co.* v. *Morrison,* 11 Leigh (Va.) 354 ; but otherwise if the *whole* purchase money has been paid, unless the assured by contract or otherwise is liable for the loss of the property, *Wariny* v. *Indemnity Ins. Co.,* 45 N. Y. 606 ; *Wilkes* v. *People's Ins. Co.,* 19 id. 184 ; a mortgage for *more* than the property is worth, does not, *Higginson* v. *Dall, ante;* a conveyance of the property if the purchase money is not paid, and there is a mortgage back, or a deed to a third person in trust to secure the same, *Morrison* v. *Tenn., etc., Ins. Co.,* 18 Mo. 262 ; an assignor of goods under an insolvent act, although the title has vested in an assignee, still retains an insurable interest, *Marks* v. *Hamilton Ins. Co.,* 7 Exchq. 323 ; and, generally, *so long as an insurable interest remains,* the policy remains operative. Therefore, to ascertain what interest will uphold the policy, see chapter on INSURABLE INTEREST, *ante.*

[1] *Hitchcock* v. *N. W. Ins. Co.,* 26 N. Y. 68.

[2] *West Branch Ins. Co.* v. *Halfenstein,* 40 Penn. St. 289 ; *Hill* v. *Cumberland, etc., Ins. Co.,* 59 id. 474 ; *Waring* v. *Indemnity Ins. Co.,* 45 N. Y. 606 ; *Manley* v. *Ins. Co. of N. America,* 1 Lans. (N. Y.) 20 ; *People's Ins. Co.* v. *Strachle,* 2 Cin. S. C. (Ohio) 186 ; *Jackson* v. *Ætna Ins. Co.,* 16 B. Mon. (Ky.) 242.

[3] School District No. 6, in *Dresden* v. *Ætna Ins. Co.,* 62 Me. 330 ; 5 Ben. F. I. C. 524 ; *Copeland* v. *Mercantile Ins. Co.,* 6 Pick. (Mass.) 198 ; *Pitney* v. *Glens Falls Ins. Co.,* 65 N. Y. 6.

[4] *Worthington* v. *Bearse,* 12 Allen (Mass.) 382 ; *Lane* v. *Maine, etc., Ins. Co.,* 13 Me. 44 ; *Power* v. *Ocean Ins. Co.,* 19 La. 28 ; *Hooper* v. *Hudson River Ins. Co.,* 17 N. Y. 424 ; *West Branch Ins. Co.* v. *Halfenstein,* 40 Penn. St. 284.

[5] *Lazarus* v. *Com. Ins. Co.,* 19 Pick. (Mass.) 81.

assignment he is absolved from all further liability to his creditors, an assignment divests him of all interest in the property, and amounts to an absolute alienation.[1]

Does not apply when insurer knows goods are kept for sale.

SEC. 314. As in all other instances, this condition in a policy is to be construed according to the evident intention of the parties, from the language used *and the nature of the risk.* If the policy covers a stock in a store, a manufactures' stock *or other property which the insurer knows is kept for sale,* the condition has no application.[2] Consequently, a sale of an undivided interest in such property, does not invalidate the policy as to the interest remaining in the assured.[3]

Alienation; when it avoids the policy.

SEC. 315. While a sale of the property, and an assignment of the policy without notice to and the consent of the insurer, avoids the policy,[4] yet it is not essential that the consent should be given before or at the time of the sale or transfer, but consent given *afterwards* will be equally effectual to keep the policy on foot as a valid instrument.[5] No particular form of expression is essential to indicate the company's consent. It is enough if words are used that show consent to the assignment of the policy and the transfer of the property.[6] Where a policy contains a provision invalidating it in case of a transfer of the property, or any change of title therein, the policy is invalidated by *any* transfer or change of title, whether by the voluntary act of the

---

[1] *Young v. Eagle, etc., Ins. Co.,* 14 Gray (Mass.) 150; 4 Ben. F. I. C. 417; *Dey v. Poughkeepsie, etc., Ins. Co.,* 23 Barb. (N. Y.) 623; *Hazard v. Franklin F. Ins. Co.,* 7 R. I. 429.

[2] *Wolfe v. Security F. Ins. Co.,* 39 N. Y. 49; *Lane v. Maine Ins. Co., ante.*

[3] *West Branch Ins. Co., v. Halfenstein,* 40 Penn. St. 289.

[4] *Savage v. Howard Ins. Co.,* 52 N. Y. 502; *Bachanan v. The Westchester, etc., Ins. Co.,* 61 N. Y. 611; *Sinreal v. Dubuque, etc., Ins. Co.,* 18 Iowa, 319; *Hazzard v. Franklin, etc., Ins. Co.,* 7 R. I. 429; *Bell v. Firemans' Ins. Co.,* 3 Rob. (La.) 423; *Burger v. Farmers', etc., Ins. Co.,* 71 Penn. St. 422; but unless otherwise specially provided, nothing less than an absolute sale or conveyance will have that effect. *Washington, etc., Ins. Co. v. Kelly,* 32 Md. 421; 5 Ben. F. I. C. 302.

[5] In *Buchanan v. The Exchange, etc., Ins. Co.,* 61 N. Y. 26, the consent was indorsed by an agent whose authority had been revoked, but afterwards the secretary of the defendant upon being shown the indorsement upon the policy, said that the assignment and consent were all right, and it was held that this was such a notification as bound the company as to effect of acts of secretary of an insurance company. *Fish v. Cottinett,* 44 N. Y. 538; *Ellis v. Albany Ins. Co.,* N. Y. 405.

[6] *Shearman v. Niagara Ins. Co.,* 46 N. Y. 526; *Potter v. Ins. Co.,* 5 Hill (N. Y.) 149; *Hooper v. Hud. R. F. Ins. Co.,* 17 N. Y. 424; *Wolfe v. Security F. Ins. Co.,* 39 N. Y. 49.

assured,[1] or by operation of law, as by an adjudication in bankruptcy
and an assignment by the register in pursuance of the statute.[2]

---

[1] In *Savage* v. *Howard Ins. Co.*, 52 N. Y. 502, the defendant company issued a
policy to "the heirs and representatives of Andrew Kirk," upon a grist mill and
machinery. The policies were conditioned, "if the property be sold or transferred, or any change takes place in title or possession, whether by legal process
or judicial decree or voluntary transfer, or conveyance, without the consent of the
company indorsed thereon, the policy shall be void." In Feb. 9, 1870, after the
policies were issued, Marilla Kirk, as executrix, sold the grist-mill to Henry O.
Arnold without obtaining the consent of the insurance companies and without
notice to them, and did not assign the policies of insurance. The grist-mill was
sold for $8,000 in cash, Arnold giving a mortgage back for $7,000, which mortgage is still unpaid. Arnold was in possession of the mill before purchasing, and
when the policy was given, under a lease from Marilla Kirk, the executrix, and
continued in possession after the purchase. August 1, 1870, the mill was destroyed
by fire, and due notice, accompanied with proper proof of loss, was given to the
companies. ALLEN, J., said : "If the assured assented to the contract with this
condition and limitation, effect must be given to the condition according to its terms.
Davenport v. *New England Ins. Co.*, 6 Cush. 340 ; *Edmunds* v. *Mutual Safety F.
Ins. Co.*, 1 Allen, 311. As well the insured as the insurers are interested in the
faithful observance of the conditions of the contract. The premium demanded
is essentially regulated by the conditions of the contract and the risk assumed,
and if conditions deemed material by the insurers are disregarded by the insured
or nullified by the courts, the insurers will be made to suffer in the increased cost
of insurance, as all will be made to pay for absolute .and extreme risks. By the
policies, "the heirs and representatives of A. Kirk, deceased," were insured
against loss, etc. It is not disputed that they were, and are valid policies in favor
of the plaintiff as testamentary trustee of the real estate of the deceased, in whom
the title to the premises insured was vested at the time of the insurance. He
held the title in trust for the heirs of the decedent, and is entitled to the benefit
of the policy, in trust for the beneficiaries under the will, although he is not
specifically named. *Clinton* v. *Hope Ins. Co.*, 45 N. Y. 454 ; *Herkimer* v. *Rice*, 27
id. 163. Each of the insurances was upon the condition expressed in the body of
the policy, that 'if the property be sold or transferred, or any change take place
in the title or possession, whether by legal process or judicial decree or voluntary
transfer or conveyance, etc., then and in every such case this policy shall be void.'
The word 'property' was used here for the *corpus* of the thing insured, as distinguished from the interest of the insured in it; the thing owned and which
was capable of being sold or transferred, and of which possession could be had.
The word was used as it is in the division of property into real or personal, to
indicate the thing itself, and not the estate or interest in it. In other policies,
other expressions, widely different from this, have been held to mean simply the
insurable interest in the property or thing insured ; as in *Hitchcock* v. *N. W.
Ins. Co.*, 26 N. Y. 68, the polic was to become void 'in case of transfer or termination of the interest of the assured in the property insured,' and it was held
that, so long as an insurable interest remained, the policy was not avoided. An
insurable interest may exist independent of the title to the property, and, in that
case, as the property may be sold, but an insurable interest covered by the policy
may remain. That case was decided upon the peculiar phraseology of the condition. The conditions before us are broader, and intended to provide against a
transfer of title or change in the title or possession, irrespective of any insurable
interest that might arise or remain upon the change of title. In other cases cited,
the conditions of the policies have differed somewhat in words from that in *Hitchcock's Case*, but were in substance the same ; and in none of the cases upon which
the respondent relies did the condition make void the policy upon a sale or transfer of the property itself. The condition found in these policies has been held,
whenever it has come before the courts, to prohibit the sale or transfer of the
property, and a change of title has been held to work an avoidance of the policy.
It is by no means a forfeiture or penalty, or in the nature of a forfeiture. The

[2] *Perry* v. *Lorrillard Ins. Co.*, 61 N. Y. 214.

SEC. 316. An adjudication of bankruptcy terminates the interest of the bankrupt in any policy of insurance, and the policy is thenceforth

---

parties have determined, by their agreement, the conditions of the liability and the extent of the obligations of the insurers, and they can only be held liable in accordance with the terms of the agreement, and within the conditions of the obligation. In *Tittemore* v. *Vermont Mut. F. Ins. Co.*, 20 Vt. 546, the policy was to become void if the property should be alienated by sale or otherwise; and while it was held that a conveyance and a simultaneous reconveyance with the right of the original owner to continue in possession was not an alienation within the condition, although the last deed was conditioned to be void on the payment of a fixed sum within a specified time, the court was of the opinion that had the premises been conveyed, and a mortgage merely taken back for the purchase-money, it would have been an alienation avoiding the policy. There was no personal agreement by the grantor in the second deed to pay the moneys mentioned therein, so that the transaction was but a conditional sale, optional with the vendee whether he would consummate it, and the vendor retained the possession. It was in substance and effect an executory agreement to sell in the future. *Van Deusen* v. *Charter Oak F. & M. Ins. Co.*, 1 Rob. 55, was within the same principle. There was no absolute alienation or transfer of title and possession. In *Stetson* v. *Mass. Mut. F. Ins. Co.*, 4 Mass. 330, the court construed the policy as importing the continuance of the contract, notwithstanding the alienation of the premises to the extent of the insurable interest remaining. The policy gave the insured the liberty upon an alienation to surrender the policy or to transfer it. The effect of a conveyance of the property and the taking back a mortgage for the consideration upon a policy conditioned to become void upon a sale or alienation of the property insured in whole or in part, was considered in *Abbott* v. *Hampden Mut. F. Ins. Co.*, 30 Me. 414, and it was adjudged that, to constitute an alienation which would avoid the policy, it was not necessary that there should be an absolute transfer of the whole or any distinct portion of the property. If there has been a disposition of any part of it in such form that any property has passed to another, the alienation has occurred. The title was regarded as having passed to another who had become the owner, entitled to the possession, and the vendee had but a lien for the purchase-money, which would never serve to restore the title except upon the failure of the purchaser and mortgagor to perform the condition of the mortgage, and the latter could at any time discharge the lien by paying the mortgage debt. While the interests of the owner in fee and the mortgagee are both insurable, and each may have independent insurances, each covering his own interest, the interests are entirely distinct, and the rights and obligations of the parties to the contract different. Had the plaintiff been insured as mortgagee, the insurer, upon payment of a loss, would be entitled to be subrogated to the rights of the mortgagee against the mortgagor. The distinction between an issue based on a denial of an insurable interest, and the question whether there had been an alienation or change of title, was recognized in *Orrell* v. *Hampden F. Ins. Co.*, 13 Gray, 431. A change of title valid as between the parties was treated as a breach of the condition, but there no alienation was proved. A mortgage is not an alienation of the property mortgaged; but when the condition of the policy was that 'all alienations and alterations in the ownership,' etc., of the property should make void the policy, a mortgage was held to be an alteration of the ownership and to make void the insurance. *Edmunds* v. *Mut. Safety F. Ins. Co.*, 1 Allen, 311. The court thought it material to the insurer's to know who had title to or interest in the property insured. The question was directly before this court in *Springfield F. & M. Ins. Co.* v. *Allen*, 43 N. Y. 389, and it was there held without dissent, following the current of authority, and giving the policy a fair and reasonable interpretation, that, the policy providing it should be void upon 'any change of title in the property insured,' it became void by a transfer of the premises by the owner, although the interest of the assured, a mortgagee, was not changed subsequent to the date of the policy. When the insurance was to the owner of the property, loss, if any, payable to a mortgagee, with a similar condition as in this case, an alienation of the property by the mortgagor was adjudged to make void the policy. *Grosvenor* v. *Atlantic*

void and of no effect ; but an insurance company may consent to continue
their liability by the usual transfer of the policy to the register in charge
of the bankruptcy proceedings, until an assignee shall have been
appointed, and may also tranfer said policy to the assignee, when
appointed.   It is optional with the company to continue the risk by
such transfers, or to cancel the same.   The title to the property of a
bankrupt, by operation of law, vests in the register as register ;
although the property may be in the possession of the U. S. marshal
as messenger, it is still in the possession of the court, and the register
is, by the bankrupt law, the court.[1]

F. Ins. Co. of Brooklyn, 17 N. Y. 391.   The condition is not capable of two read-
ings, and the courts have no right under the pretence of interpretation to nullify
a material provision inserted for the reasonable protection of the insurers, and
thus exercise a dispensing power in favor of the insured.   It cannot be said that
a conveyance of the fee, and the taking back a mortgage for the purchase-money,
is not as well a sale or transfer as a change of title.   It is sufficient, to put an end
to the policy, that there has been a change in the title ; and no one can say that a
conveyance of the fee, and substituting the interest of a mortgagee in the insured,
is not a substantial change in the title.   But the sale or transfer of the property
was complete and absolute, and the retaining a lien for the purchase-money,
either in the form of a mortgage or otherwise, did not change the character or
effect of the conveyance.   The fact that, to preserve equities and exclude liens
which might otherwise defeat purchase-money liens, courts regard a deed of conveyance and purchase-money mortgage as simultaneous, and the rights of the
parties as if the title to the amount of the mortgage interest had never passed
out of the *grantor,* do not aid in construing this contract, or tend to establish the
claim of the respondent that there has been no transfer of the property.   Another
clause in the policy adds force to the views expressed.   It requires that if the
interest of the assured in the property be any other than the entire, unconditional and sole ownership, it shall be so represented and so expressed in the policy.
Had the plaintiff desired to be insured as mortgagee, he should have seen that
the interest was truly expressed in the contract.   Another clause, providing for
the case of the sale and delivery of property insured, is only applicable by its
very terms to personal property, and does not qualify or affect the condition which
has been considered, and which controls in these actions."

[1] *In re Carow,* 4 Bank. Reg. 178 ; in *Perry* v. *Lorillard Ins. Co., ante,* the policy
was issued to one Cochran, who was the owner and in possession of the premises
described in the policy, and the loss, if any, was made payable to the plaintiff.
The policy contained the following clause, viz. : ".That if the property shall be
sold or transferred, or any change take place in the title or possession whether by
legal process or judicial decree, or voluntary transfer or conveyance without the
consent of the company, etc., then, and in every such case, the policy shall be
void."   In January, 1870, Cochran, on the petition of his creditors, was adjudged
a bankrupt, and an assignee of all his property was duly appointed, and the said
assignee took possession.   In May, 1870, the property insured was destroyed by
fire.   Held, that the adjudication and assignment in bankruptcy changed the
title to the property insured, within the meaning of the terms of the policy, and
was, for that reason, a breach of the condition, and the policy was therefore void.
In *Adams* v. *Rockingham Ins. Co.,* 29 Mo. 292 ; 3 Bennett's F. I. C. 30, it was held
that the bankruptcy of *one* of the assured invalidates a policy that prohibits
alienation.   In that case TENNY, J., carefully reviewed the questions involved,
and his opinion will be found valuable.   A transfer by operation of law to a
trustee or assignee, is an alienation.   *Young* v. *Eagle Ins. Co.,* 14 Gray (Mass.)
150 ; *Hazard* v. *Franklin Ins. Co.,* 7 R. I. 427 ; *contra,* see Hobbs v. *Memphis Ins.
Co.,* 1 Sneed (Tenn.) 444.   A contrary doctrine has been held where the policy
simply provided that "if the title to the property is transferred or changed, this

Interest suspended, loss during, not within policy.

SEC. 317. Under such a provision, an alienation of the property *without the consent of the insurer, works a forfeiture, and the fact that the property is afterwards* in whole or in part reconveyed to the insured, does not restore its validity.[1] In such cases, the rights of the parties are suspended; and, if a loss occurs before the title re-vests in the assured, the policy is inoperative, and this is so, even though the invalidity results from a sale made under legal proceedings, which is subsequently set aside.[2] So when the policy provides that "if the title of the property shall be transferred or changed," and that the entry of a foreclosure suit upon a mortgage shall be deemed an alienation, the service of preliminary process of foreclosure avoids the policy.[3]

---

policy shall be void." In such a case it has been held *that the forfeiture only applies in case of a transfer or change made by the assured himself,* and is not applicable to a transfer effected by operation of law or judicial decree. *Starkweather* v. *Cleavland Ins. Co.,* 2 Abb. (U. S) 67. But it is hardly believed that this doctrine is tenable, and if a legal transfer is in fact effected, whether voluntary or by operation of law, the policy becomes void. *Reynolds* v. *Mut. F. Ins. Co.,* 34 Md. 280.

[1]Thus in *Home, etc., Ins. Co.* v. *Hauslein,* 1 Ins. L. J. 818 (an Illinois case) the policy contained a condition that, in case of any sale, transfer or change of title to the property insured, the insurance should be void, and cease. A section of the charter of the company—a mutual company, of which the assured became a member—printed on the back of the policy, also provided that the policy should be void upon any alienation of the property by sale or otherwise. At the time the insurance was effected, the insured was the absolute owner of the property. He afterward made an assignment of the policy to Seibert, the mortgagee, with the assent of the company, and, subsequent to this, sold and conveyed the property to three other persons, one of whom reconveyed to him, and the other two executed mortgages to secure the purchase-money. Held, "the assignee of a policy takes it subject to the conditions expressed upon its face, and his equities confer no right, if the assignor has lost all right of recovery by a violation of the terms or conditions of the policy." The assignee knew of the condition in the policy providing for forfeiture in the event of alienation, and his rights must be controlled thereby. There was a change of title in the property. The absolute ownership of the entire property is easily distinguished from the ownership of one-third, and a mortgagee of two-thirds. The assignment was made with the consent of the company, but the condition of forfeiture upon alienation, without the consent of the company, was still applicable to the assignee as well as to the insured. The company did not waive the effect of the breach of the condition. By the act of the insured the policy became void. It was contended that the memorandum, that the loss, if any, should be payable to the assignee, as his interest might appear, shows that his interest was intended to be protected; and that the change of title did not affect his interest. The insured cannot sue, because he had so acted as to forfeit the policy. The assignee cannot sue, for he was not a party to the contract originally. In its nature the policy was only assignable so as to pass an equitable interest to the assignee. Even, as in this case, where the assignment was made with the consent of the company, the assignee cannot sue for a breach in his own name.

[2]*Mt. Vernon Mfg. Co.* v. *Summit Co., etc., Ins. Co.,* 10 Ohio St. 347.

[3]Thus, in *McIntire* v. *Norwich Ins. Co.,* 102 Mass. 458, a policy of fire insurance on personal property contained a proviso that "if the title of the property is transferred or changed" "this policy shall be void; and the entry of a foreclosure of a mortgage" "shall be deemed an alienation of the property, and this company shall not be holden for loss or damage thereafter." The insured prop-

Deed and mortgage back, effect of.

SEC. 318. A conveyance of property by deed, and an execution of a mortgage back, to secure the purchase money, delivered at the same time, is a part of the same transaction, and does. not amount to an alienation.[1]

But the language of the condition must be looked to, as upon it depends the rights of the parties. The insurer may specially stipulate what shall be treated as an alienation, and when such a stipulation exists, its breach will be fatal to a recovery. So, too, it is of great importance to remember that the word *alienated* is to be construed in its ordinary sense, and may be so used as to rob all the special provisions of the policy upon this point of their force. Thus, a policy providing that, "if the property shall be alienated, mortgaged, sold, conveyed, levied upon, attached, or the title therein otherwise changed," is rendered void, if either or any of those changes in the title are effected; but, if the policy provides "*if the property shall be alienated by mortgage, sale, levy, attachment,*" etc., the mere fact that the property is levied upon, attached or mortgaged does not avoid the policy, *because there is no alienation* of the property *until the title is divested under* the mortgage, levy, attachment, etc.,[2] the courts holding very properly that the insurer must be held to the strict construction of the word alienated, and that its use in that form qualified the meaning of all the special terms employed to designate the species of alienations that should avoid the policy. Where there is a conveyance and a mortgage back to secure the purchase-money, an insurable interest still remains and the policy is valid, unless provision against such change of interest is specially made in the policy.[3]

---

perty was mortgaged at the time the insurance was effected, and notice of foreclosure had been duly served, certified and recorded when the fire occurred. Held, that the policy was avoided.

[1] *Stetson* v. *Mass. Ins. Co.*, 4 Mass. 336 ; *Hitchcock* v. *N. W. Ins. Co.*, 26 N. Y. 68 ; *Sanders* v. *Hillsboro Ins. Co.*, 44 N. H. 238 ; *Washington Ins. Co.* v. *Hayes*, 17 Ohio St. 432.

[2] *Shepherd* v. *Union, etc., Ins. Co., ante.*

[3] *Howard Ins. Co.* v. *Bruner*, 23 Penn. St. 50. Where the assured conveyed an undivided half of the premises and took a mortgage to secure the purchase-money, the policy was held not to be invalidated or the rights of the assured under it affected. *Stetson* v. *Mass. F. Ins. Co.*, 4 Mass. 330. See also, *Stetson* v. *Ins. Co.*, 8 Phila. (Penn.) 8. When *any* change of title is prohibited, the sale of an undivided interest and a mortgage back is within the prohibition. *Home, etc., Ins. Co.* v. *Hauslin*, 60 Ill. 521 ; *Bates* v. *Com. Ins. Co.*, 2 Cin. Sup. Ct. (Ohio) 195. In *Tittemore* v. *Vt. Mut. F. Ins. Co.*, 20 Vt. 540, the contract provided that it should be binding if the insured had title in fee simple unincumbered to the land upon which the buildings insured stood ; that it should be void if he had not such title, unless the title that he did have, and incumbrances, were expressed upon the policy, and in the application made for it ; also, when any house or

Death of assured avoids policy, when.

SEC. 319. Where a policy provides that, in case of any sale, transfer *or change of title* in the property insured, * * such insurance shall be void, the *death* of the assured operates such a change of title as renders the policy invalid.[1] But where the policy simply provides that the property shall not be sold or alienated, the death of the party does not operate as an alienation.[2]

Alienation in fact, must be established.

SEC. 320. In order to avoid a policy upon the ground that the property has been alienated, *an alienation in fact* must be shown by the insurers; the fact that the assured, for the purpose of preventing the attachment of the property by his creditors, ha1 represented that he had sold the property, *when in fact he had not*, will not

---

building insured shall be alienated by sale or otherwise, the policy shall be void, but that the alienee might have it transferred to him with the consent of the company. The plaintiff conveyed to P. by deed of warranty, and P. conveyed to the plaintiff at the same date by deed of warranty, conditioned to be void if P. or his representatives should pay plaintiff $2,000 within three years and allow plaintiff to hold peaceable possession until payment should be made. P. never made any payment up to the time the fire occurred, which was more than four years after the date of the transaction. Held, both deeds were to be regarded as one transaction, hence there was no alienation.

[1] In *Laffin* v. *Charter Oak Ins. Co.*, 58 Barb. 325, it was held that where a policy of insurance against loss by fire runs to the "assured, his executors, administrators and assigns," an action is properly brought, after the death of the assured, in the name of his administrators, if a right of action has accrued to any one by reason of the destruction of the property insured. The administrator, in such a case, prosecutes for the benefit of the person or persons entitled to the moneys recovered on account of such loss, provided the contract remains in force, notwithstanding the change of title to the property insured. A contract of insurance provided that the policy should not be assignable without the consent of the company manifested in writing thereon; that "in case of assignment without such consent * * * the liability of the company shall then cease;" that "in case of any sale, transfer or change of title in the property insured, * * * or of any interest therein, such insurance shall be void, and cease;" and that "in case of * * * possession by another of the subject insured, without the consent of the insurers indorsed on the policy, the same should cease." It was held that the policy, by the terms and provisions thereof became void, and ceased to have any binding force upon the death of the assured during the life of the policy, and the vesting of the title to the property insured in his heirs at law; that this was a change of title from the assured to others, which brought the case within the express terms of the policy. It was, also, that the possession of the property insured by others than the assured, without the consent of the company indorsed upon the policy, also produced the same result. It put an end to the contract, and rendered it no longer obligatory. Where the description of the property insured is made a part of the contract, and a warranty by the assured, and it is expressly provided, among other things, that in case of any misrepresentation or concealment, or omission to make known any fact which increases the hazard, the insurance shall be void; and the property is described and insured as a *dwelling-house*, when, in fact, it is used in part as a *saloon*, which increases the risk, *it seems*, the policy is void and of no effect by reason of this misrepresentation.

[2] *Burbank* v. *Rockingham, etc., Ins. Co.*, 24 N. H. 550.

avail the insurer,[1] and it seems that in all cases the burden of establishing an alienation is upon the insurer.[2]

Sale under decree of foreclosure.

SEC. 321. Where premises were sold under decree of foreclosure, and no equity of redemption remained in the mortgagor, it was held that the policy was void, even though the deed had not been enrolled;[3] and even though the assured has assigned the policy to a mortgagee with the assent of the insurer, yet a subsequent conveyance by him to the mortgagee of his equity of redemption, of which the insurer has no notice, avoids the policy.[4]

Assignment of property, effect of.

SEC. 322. When the property is assigned, and sold by the assignee to pay the debts of the assured, the policy is void,[5] even though the conveyance is fraudulent.[6] *Where a conveyance is good between the parties thereto, the fact that it is void as to third persons*, does not affect the question. The conveyance, under such circumstances, is in fact, and in law, an alienation, and avoids the policy.[7] A conveyance from the assured to a trustee *for his wife*, is an alienation that avoids the policy.

Sale and partial payment, effect of.

SEC. 323. The fact that the insured has sold his interest in the property and received a partial payment thereon, which reduces his actual pecuniary interest therein below the amount insured, does not relieve the insurer from paying the full amount of the insurance *if the title to the property has not passed*, even though the purchaser is legally bound to pay the insured the full value of the property. Thus, in a Massachusetts case,[8] the plaintiff, holding a mortgage upon a quantity of furniture to the amount of over $99,000, agreed to assign the same to a third party on payment of $62,500, divided into four payments, for which notes were given; $20,000 was paid under said agreement. The property was insured by the mortgagees for $57,000. The mort-

---

[1] *Orrell* v. *Hampden F. Ins. Co.*, 13 Gray (Mass.) 431.

[2] *Orrell* v. *Ins. Co., ante.*

[3] *McLaren* v. *Hartford F. Ins. Co.*, 5 N. Y. 151.

[4] *Hoxsie* v. *Providence, etc., Ins. Co.*, 6 R. I. 517; *Billson* v. *Manufacturers' Ins. Co.*, 7 Am. Law Reg. 661; *Loring* v. *Manufacturers' Ins. Co.*, 8 Gray (Mass.) 28; *Hazard* v. *Franklin Ins. Co.*, 7 R. I. 429.

[5] *Dadmun Mfg. Co.* v. *Worcester, etc., Ins. Co.*, 11 Met. (Mass.) 429.

[6] *Treadway* v. *Hamilton, etc., Ins. Co.*, 29 Conn. 68.

[7] *Treadway* v. *Hamilton, etc., Ins. Co.*, 29 Conn. 68.

[8] *Langdon* v. *Minn., etc., Ins. Co.*, 22 Minn. 193.

[9] *Haley* v. *Manufacturers' Ins. Co.*, 120 Mass. 292.

gage was not to be assigned until the four notes were paid. After the sum of $20,000 had been paid, the property was destroyed by fire, and the loss under the policies was $53,140.57. The insurers claimed that they were liable only for the *actual* loss to the insured; that is, the difference between the sum for which the mortgagees had agreed to assign and the sum actually paid under the agreement, to wit, $62,500 less $20,000; but the court held that they were liable for the full amount of the loss. "They held," said DEVENS, J., "the *legal* title to the mortgages, and had an interest in the property insured to the amount of the debt it was mortgaged to secure. Although they had made a contract for the sale of those mortgages, such contract was executory simply; its terms might never be complied with, or it might be abandoned by mutual agreement of the parties; no *property* had passed to Cheeny, and, although he had made no default, he had not complied with the terms upon which he was to obtain these mortgages when the loss occurred. Even if he was in possession of the mortgaged property, *he was not in possession of the mortgages* which the plaintiffs had agreed to sell;" and, consequently, the rights of the assured were not affected by any payments made under such agreement.[1]

When mortgage avoids policy.

SEC. 324. A mortgage upon land s not an *alienation* thereof, within the meaning of the term,[2] but it is such an *alteration* in the ownership as avoids a policy that provides that "all alienations and alterations

---

[1] *Davis* v. *Quincy Ins. Co.*, 10 Allen (Mass.) 113; *Suffolk Ins. Co.* v. *Boyden*, 9 id. 123; *Rider* v. *Ocean Ins. Co.*, 20 Pick (Mass.) 259.

[2] *Jackson* v. *Mass. Ins. Co.*, 23 Pick. (Mass.) 418; *Rice* v. *Tower*, 1 Gray (Mass.) 426; *Rollins* v. *Columbian, etc., Ins. Co.*, 25 N. H. 200; *Conover* v. *Ins. Co.*, 1 N. Y. 290; *Holbrook* v. *American Ins. Co.*, 1 Curtis C. C. (U. S.) 193; *Pollard* v. *Somerset Ins. Co.*, 42 Me. 221; *Ayres* v. *Hartford Ins. Co.*, 21 Iowa, 198; *Folsom* v. *Belknap, etc., Ins. Co.*, 31 N. H. 231; *Lazarus* v. *Ins. Co.*, 5 Pick. (Mass.) 81; *Shepperd* v. *Union, etc., Ins. Co.*, 38 id. 232; *Van Deusen* v. *Charter Oak Ins. Co.*, 1 Rob. (N. Y.) 55. But it must be remembered that this depends entirely upon the language of the policy. If the policy stipulates against any change of title, or alteration therein, or against an alienation *in whole or in part*, a mortgage is held within the prohibition. *Edmunds* v. *Ins. Co.*, 1 Allen (Mass.) 311; *Abbott* v. *Hampden, etc., Ins. Co.*. 30 Me. 414. But if a mortgage is not within the prohibition, and there is no clause avoiding the policy by entry of foreclosure proceedings, or levy of execution, the policy is valid *so long as a right to redeem exists*. *Clark* v. *N. E. Ins. Co.*, 6 Cush. (Mass.) 342; *Campbell* v. *Hamilton, etc., Ins. Co.*, 51 Me. 69; *Cone* v. *Niagara Ins. Co.*, 3 T. & C. (N. Y.) 33; aff'd, 60 N. Y. 619. In *Allen* v. *Franklin Ins. Co.*, 9 How. Pr. (N. Y.) 501, the assured executed a mortgage upon machinery, and afterwards procured a policy thereon without giving notice of the mortgage, and it was held that the policy was valid. In *Stetson* v. *Mass., etc., Ins. Co.*, 4 Mass. 330, the assured conveyed an undivided half of the insured premises, reserving a term of seven years, and took back a mortgage to secure the purchase-money, and the court held that this was not an alienation.

in the ownership, situation or state of the property in any material particular," shall render the policy void, unless notice is duly given to, and the assent of the company thereto is obtained.[1]

Where the policy contains a prohibition of any "*alterations*" in the title, it is held that a mortgage is such an alteration, and avoids the policy;[2] and where the policy specially provides that "*any incumbrance*" shall invalidate it, of course a mortgage operates as a breach.[3]

The sale of property and taking back a mortgage to secure the purchase money is not such a change of title, within the meaning of a condition, that, in case of any change of title, the policy shall cease to be operative; as defeats the policy,[4] and so, too, where the property has been sold, but not conveyed, and a portion of the purchase money remains unpaid, the policy remains operative to the extent of the insurable interest remaining;[5] but, if a conveyance was made and delivered, and no mortgage taken to secure the unpaid purchase money, no insurable interest remains, even though a judgment was taken for the amount.[6] But it must be remembered that this question is always to be tested by the language of the contract (policy) itself, and cannot be made the subject of a general rule applicable to all cases. Thus, where a policy provided that the entry of a foreclosure of a mortgage shall be deemed an alienation of the property such as should avoid the policy, it was held that the commencement of proceedings for foreclosure destroyed the validity of the policy, even though not consummated.[7] So, where a policy provided that, in case of any change in the title or possession of the property, whether by sale, lease, legal process, judicial decree or voluntary transfer, without the assent of the company, the policy should be void, it was held that a sale of an undivided interest in the property destroyed the policy.[8]

The company has a right to make its own contract, and specify the terms upon which it will take the risk, and the only office of the court is, to construe and give such effect to the contract *made by the parties*, as the parties, from the language used, evidently intended. The

---

[1] *Edmunds* v. *Mut. Safety F. Ins. Co.*, 1 Allen (Mass.) 311.

[2] *Hutchins* v. *Cleaveland, etc., Ins. Co.*, 11 Ohio St. 477; *Edwards* v. *Ins. Co.*, 1 Allen (Mass.) 31.

[3] *Edes* v. *Hamilton, etc., Ins. Co.*, 3 Allen (Mass.) 362.

[4] *Kitts* v. *Massasoit Ins. Co.*, 56 Barb. (N. Y.) 177.

[5] *Hill* v. *Cumberland, etc., Protection Co.*, 59 Penn. St. 474.

[6] *Grevemeyer* v. *Southern Ins. Co.*, 62 Penn. St. 340.

[7] *McIntire* v. *Norwich Ins. Co.*, 102 Mass. 230.

[8] *McEwan* v. *Fraser*, 1 Mich. (N. P.) 118; see also, as bearing upon the effect of sale, *Bates* v. *Equitable Ins. Co.*, 10 Wall (U. S.) 33.

court cannot make a contract for the parties, or give to that made any other or different effect than its just interpretation warrants, however unjust or inequitable such construction may appear. Thus, where a policy provides that, in case, at any time during the existence of the policy, the premises shall be unoccupied, the policy shall thereby become void. If the premises are vacant for *one day*, the policy becomes void, and a subsequent loss cannot be recovered.

Where a policy provides that " *any change of title*, by sale, mortgage or otherwise," etc., shall render the policy void, the execution of a mortgage *does not change the title*, hence the prohibition is held not to apply, except to an actual change of title under foreclosure proceed-ings.[1]

Effect of special conditions.

SEC. 325. "When the property shall be alienated, by sale or otherwise, the policy thereupon shall be void." Under this condition, a sale of the equity of redemption in mortgaged premises, avoids the policy;[2] so the execution of a subsequent mortgage.[3] So when *any* alienation is prohibited the execution of a deed absolute on its face, although in fact given only as a mortgage, avoids the policy, although a bond for a reconveyance on payment of the debt is given simultaneously with the deed, but is not recorded. *Quere*. Would that be the effect if the bond was recorded?[4] Of course, unless the statute so provides a bond for the conveyance of real estate, is not a proper matter of record, and in the absence of such a statute, the fact that it was recorded would not change the *status* of the parties, because it is inoperative as notice.

"If the property be sold or transferred, or *any* change in the title or possession takes place, whether by legal process, judicial decree, voluntary transfer or conveyance, without consent of this company indorsed hereon, the policy shall be void." Under such a policy, the executrix of the assured sold the property, and took a mortgage back to secure most of the purchase-money, and it was held that the insurers were discharged.[5]

"Any transfer or termination of the interest of the assured, by sale or otherwise," renders the policy void. Under such a condition while

[1] *Shepherd* v. *Union, etc., Ins. Co.*, 38 N. H., 232; *McLaren* v. *Hartford F. Ins. Co.*, 5 N. Y. 151.

[2] *Lawrence* v. *Holyoke Ins. Co.*, 11 Allen (Mass.) 387.

[3] *Edes* v. *Hamilton, etc., Ins. Co.*, 3 Allen (Mass.) 362.

[4] *Tomlinson* v. *Monmouth Mut. F. Ins. Co.*, 47 Me. 232.

[5] *Savage* v. *Howard Ins. Co.*, 52 N. Y. 502.

the execution of a mortgage does not avoid the policy, yet a conveyance to the mortgagee of the assured's equity of redemption *does* have
that effect, and that too, even though the insurer consented *after*
the conveyance, *but without knowledge thereof*, to a transfer of the policy
to the mortgagee.[1] " If the premises are *alienated* by sale, *mortgage*,
etc.," the policy shall be void. Under such a condition it is held that
the condition is not violated by a mere mortgage, but only by a divest-
ment of the title under proceedings for its enforcement.[2] Unless otherwise provided, in order to operate as an alienation, the assured must
be divested of *all* interest in the property. *So long as an insurable
interest remains in him* the policy is valid to the extent of that interest.[3]

When levy or sale under legal process does not invalidate the policy.

SEC. 326. Where the policy provides simply that " any sale or transfer
of the premises, in whole or in part," shall avoid the policy. The condition simply refers to a *voluntary* sale or conveyance by the assured, and
does not include a sale made under legal proceedings.[4] Neither does a
levy or sale under a void process, or that does not divest the assured of
his title in the property, have that effect ;[5] nor where it does not divest

---

[1] " The conveyance," said CADWALLADER, J., in *Bilson* v. *The Manufacturers'
Ins. Co.* (U. S. C. C.) 7 Am. Law. Reg. 663, " converted his " (the mortgagee's)
" interest in the subject of insurance from that of a mere security for a debt, into
an absolute, exclusive ownership, and at the same time determined entirely the
plaintiff's interest in the subject." *Hoxsie* v. *Providence Mut. Ins. Co.*, 6 R. I.
517 ; *Hazard* v. *Franklin Mut. Ins. Co.*, 7 id. 429.

[2] *Shepherd* v. *Union, etc., Ins. Co.*, 38 N. H. 232.

[3] *Scanlon* v. *Union F. Ins. Co.*, 4 Biss. (U. S.) 511 ; *Lane* v. *Maine, etc., Ins. Co.*,
12 Me. 44.

[4] *Strong* v. *Manufacturers' Ins. Co.*, 10 Pick. (Mass.) 40 ; *Franklin Ins. Co.* v.
Findlay, 6 Whart (Penn.) 483.

[5] *Pennebaker* v. *Tomlinson*, 1 Tenn. Ch. 598. In *Colt* v. *The Phœnix F. Ins.
Co.*, 54 N. Y. 595, it was held that, while an insurance company cannot be held
liable where, by the terms of its contract, it is exempted, however harsh the
result, it cannot be excused on a rigid and strict interpretation of words, without
regard to the surrounding circumstances and the apparent intent of the parties.
Thus, a policy of insurance upon a building forbade alienation, and also contained this clause, " the commencement of foreclosure proceedings or the levy of
an execution shall be deemed an alienation of the property." A mechanic's lien
was subsequently filed and perfected on the insured building, and, in proceedings to enforce the same, judgment was obtained and execution issued, under
which the premises were advertised for sale. Prior to the sale the building was
destroyed by fire. In an action upon the policy, held that, by " foreclosure proceedings," was intended only the ordinary proceedings to foreclose a mortgage,
and not exceptional statutory proceedings of the nature of those stated. That the
" levy of an execution " referred only to a levy on personal property, as a levy
upon real estate is unnecessary, and is now unknown to the law. That, therefore, the proceedings aforesaid were not within the prohibition of the policy, and
did not avoid it. In this case, it appeared that, on the 10th of July, 1868, the
defendant insured Susannah Berniz, for one year, against loss or damage by fire,
for $1,000, on her frame two-story building in Niagara City, occupied as a hotel,
and, in case of loss by fire, the amount of the insurance was to be paid to the

him of the possession of the property. The fact that the sheriff levies upon goods in a store, takes the key, and retains exclusive possession, is

---

plaintiff, Leander Colt, the mortgagee of the premises. The question arises upon a provision in the policy forbidding alienation, and that "the commencement of foreclosure proceedings or the levy of an execution shall be deemed an alienation of the property." After the policy of insurance was made, and on the 17th of July, 1868, a mechanic's lien was filed and perfected on the insured building, and lot on which it stood, against the owner in fee, Susannah Berniz. By subsequent proceedings, the claimant, Walton, in enforcement of his lien, on the 10th of February, 1869, obtained a judgment for $194.35, which, on that day, was duly docketed, and an execution thereon, in proper form and according to the statute in such case provided, was issued and delivered to the sheriff of the county of Niagara. On the 15th of February, 1869, the sheriff, under this execution, advertised the building and premises insured for sale on the 30th of March, and on that day duly adjourned the sale until the 10th of April, 1869. On the 8th of April, the insured property was totally destroyed by fire, and its value exceeded the amount of the insurance, and no further proceedings were had upon the execution. While we fully recognize the principle that insurance companies can only be held responsible upon the contracts they have made, yet the language employed must, as in all other cases, have a reasonable interpretation. The defendant must not be made liable where, by the terms of the contract, it is fairly exempted. however harsh the result may appear; nor can it be excused where the exemption is claimed upon a strict and rigid interpretation of words, without regard to the circumstances surrounding the transaction and the apparent intent of the parties. The provisions of the policy in this case, under which the exemption from liability is claimed, appear to be unlike any hitherto considered by the courts, so far as our researches have extended. The effect of an alienation of the insured property, partial or complete, has been frequently considered, but those decisions afford but little aid in the solution of the present question. We have no hesitation in holding that 'the commencement of foreclosure proceedings,' which was to be "deemed an alienation of the property,' was not intended to refer to proceedings to enforce a mechanic's lien, under the provisions of recent statutes. It doubtless was intended by the parties to refer to the ordinary proceedings for the foreclosure of a mortgage upon real estate, and not to the exceptional proceedings allowed by special statutes, differing in different localities, to aid mechanics in enforcing their claims for materials furnished and labor performed in the construction of a building. It must unquestionably be held to mean the foreclosure of a mortgage in the ordinary sense in which these terms are employed. The policy also provided that "the levy of an execution shall be deemed the alienation of the property," which rendered it void. REYNOLDS, C., said: "We may fairly assume that the policy, in this case, was the ordinary printed blank, common with insurance companies, adapted to the insurance of either real or personal property, and filled up according to the requirements of any particular application. We may also assume that the 'levy of an execution' was intended to have some intelligent reference to a fact that might possibly have some bearing upon the risk of insurance. The levy of an execution upon real estate, under an ordinary judgment (in the State of New York; not so, however, in many of the States, where a levy and set-off or sale is provided for), is at this day unnecessary. and, in fact, never is done, and it may be said is now unknown to the law. *Wood* v. *Colvin*, 5 Hill, 228; *Catlin* v. *Jackson*, 8 J. R. 546; 2 Rev. Stat., p. 359, §3; *Learned* v. *Vandenburgh*, 8 How. Pr. R. 78. In special proceedings, by attachment or otherwise, a different rule may prevail; but, where a judgment is obtained in an ordinary proceeding, which is made by law a lien on the land, no levy under an execution issued thereon is ever contemplated or necessary for any purpose. We therefore conclude that this language could not have been intended to apply to real estate, but to the levy of an execution upon personal property only, where the actual levy by the sheriff divests the personal property of the debtor, to a large extent,

---

[1] *Rice* v. *Tower*, 1 Gray (Mass.) 426; *Phœnix Ins. Co* v. *Lawrence* 4 Met. (Ky.) 9; *Lane* v. *Maine, etc., Ins. Co.*, 12 Me. 44.

not an alienation ; ¹ nor does a sale under an execution, unless otherwise stipulated, operate as an alienation under the conditions of a policy. In order to come within the prohibition there must be a *voluntary* sale.² So even when the policy expressly provides that "the levy of an execution shall be deemed an alienation," it has been held in Kentucky, *that a levy which does not divest the title* is not within the condition.³ Where proceedings for partition have been brought, the assured can recover for a loss occurring before the partition is in fact made.⁴

Conveyance must be perfected—Title must have passed

SEC. 327. The mere making of a conveyance does not avoid the policy. The conveyance must be perfected by delivery, and the mere fact that it is recorded does not necessarily establish a legal conveyance. The assured may show that it was delivered in *escrow*, and was recorded without authority.⁵

Alienation of part of insured party

SEC. 328. When a policy merely stipulated that "if the property shall be sold or transferred," it shall be void ; the sale of a *part* does not invalidate the policy, except as to the part sold.⁶ So where, under such a condition, the policy covers real estate and personal property, it has been held in Pennsylvania, that a sale of the one does not invali-

---

at least, and the sheriff takes, or is supposed to take, the actual possession and retain his dominion until the sale. Such a proceeding does, in fact, effect a sort of alienation of the debtor's title, so soon as the levy is complete ; and it may be assumed that, in many such cases, the risk of the insurer would be largely increased, which would afford a very satisfactory reason for the insertion of such a stipulation in the policy. None of these reasons can apply to a judgment and execution against real estate."

¹ *Franklin F. Ins. Co.* v. *Findlay*, 6 Whart. (Penn.) 483 ; *Rice* v. *Tower*, 1 Gray (Mass.) 426 ; *Phœnix Ins.·Co.* v. *Lawrence*, 4 Met. (Ky.) 9.

² *Strong* v. *Manufacturers' Ins. Co.*, 10 Pick. (Mass.) 40.

³ *Pennybaker* v. *Tomlinson*, 1 Tenn. Ch. 598.

⁴ *Gates* v. *Smith*, 4 Edw. Ch. (N. Y.) 702 ; *Farmer's Mut. Ins. Co.* v. *Grayhill*, 74 Penn. St. 15.

⁵ *Gilbert* v. *N. American Ins. Co.*, 23 Wend. (N. Y.) 43 ; *People's Ins. Co.* v. *Srachle*, 2 Cin. Sup. Ct. (Ohio) 186 ; *Washington Ins. Co.* v. *Kelly*, 32 Md. 421.

⁶ In *Stetson* v. *Massachusetts, etc., F. Ins. Co.*, 4 Mass. 330, under a policy containing such a condition, the assured sold an undivided half of the estate, and the grantee, *at the same time*, reconveyed by mortgage to secure the purchase money, and the court held that this was not an alienation of any part of the estate. In *Commercial Ins. Co.* v. *Spanknable*, 52 Ill. 53, the policy contained a condition that any sale, alienation, conveyance, transfer or change of title should avoid it. The policy covered a steam boiler, its connections, vats, tubs, etc., and the building. The husband of the assured sold the boiler. Held, that the policy still remained good upon the building. In *Manley* v. *Ins. Co. of N. America*, 1 Lans. (N. Y.) 20, the assured sold an undivided half of the property. Held, that the policy was operative as to the half retained ; the conveyance does not necessarily invalidate the policy, and if the vendor subsequently takes a conveyance back before a loss, the policy is operative. *Worthington* v. *Bearse*, 12 Allen (Mass.) 382.

date the policy as to the other.[1] But, generally, the rule is held otherwise, and, unless separate rates of premium are fixed, an alienation of either or a part of either is held fatal. Especially is this so, if the policy stipulates against the sale of any part of the property.[2]

An agreement to sell does not invalidate.

SEC. 329.. An agreement to sell, even though possession of the property is given under the contract, is not an alienation, unless all the requisite requirements to pass the title have been complied with.[3] The

---

[1] *West Branch Ins. Co.* v. *Halfenstein,* 40 Penn. St. 289.

[2] In the case of *Plath* v. *Minnesota Farmers' Mut. F. Ins. Co. Assoc.,* decided on the 6th of April, 1877, and not yet reported, by the Supreme Court of Minnesota, and reported in the N. W. L. Rep. of June 2, the plaintiff procured insurance upon several distinct items of property for a gross sum of $1,150, which was distributed among the several items. The consideration for the insurance was single ande ntire. The policy contained this condition among others: "In case the insured shall mortgage the property without notifying the secretary, then the insured shall not be entitled to recover from the association any loss or damage which may occur in or to the property hereby insured, or any part or portion thereof." The question was whether a mortgage of one of the items of property would invalidate the insurance as to all the property. The court said that it is well settled by a uniform current of authority, that a contract of insurance of this character is an entirety and indivisible, the sole effect of the apportionment of the amount of insurance upon the separate and distinct items of property named in the policy, being to limit the extent of the insurers' risk as to each item, to the sum so specified, and held that as the contract of insurance was entire and indivisible, the legal effect of a violation of this condition, if valid, on the part of the insured, by mortgaging any portion of the insured property, was to avoid the entire policy. The conclusion of the court is in accordance with numerous decisions. See *Gottsman* v. *Penn. Ins. Co.,* 56 Penn. St. 210; *Friesmuth* v. *A. M. F. Ins. Co.,* 10 Cush. (Mass.) 587; *Brown* v. *P. M. Ins. Co.,* 11 id. 280; *Lee* v. *Hno. Ins. Co.,* 3 Gray, 583; *Kimball* v. *How. Ins. Co.,* 8 id. 33; *Lovejoy* v. *Augusta Ins. Co..* 45 Me. 472; *Richardson* v. *Maine Ins. Co.,* 46 id. 394; *Gould* v. *York M. F. Ins. Co.,* 47 id. 403; *Barnes* v. *Union M. F. Ins. Co.,* 51 id. 110; *Day* v. *Charter Oak Ins. Co.,* 51 id. 91; *Russ* v. *Ins. Co.,* 29 U. C. (Q. B.) 73. In the same case the question arose whether the deposit by plaintiff of a notice of the mortgage in the post-office in the town where the owner of the property resided, post-paid and addressed to the secretary of the insurance company at the place of business of the company, was a sufficient compliance with the condition mentioned. The court held that the plaintiff, in sending the notice by mail, took the risk of its reaching defendant, and while the presumption would be that it did so, this might be rebutted by proof that it never was received, and, unless actually received, it would not be sufficient.

[3] In *Clinton* v. *Hope Ins. Co.,* 45 N. Y. 454, the mother and the guardian of certain infants made a contract to sell real estate and personal property belonging to them, as soon as the guardian could obtain the requisite authority from the court. This property had been insured for the benefit of the "estate." The vendee entered into possession as tenant, paying rent. Much of the property was destroyed by fire before the contract was consummated. None of the papers or orders were filed until after the fire. After that event, a new contract was entered into between the same parties, the vendee purchasing the real estate and the claims for insurance, and taking a deed. It was held that the vendee, by the first contract, acquired no title to the property, and by his second contract, the claims to recover the amount insured were not extinguished; held, further, that the destruction of the property, which fixed the liability of the insurers, at the same time discharged the vendee from his obligation to purchase; and, therefore, that the insurers could not be subrogated to that obligation to the extent of their liability for the insurance. A similar doctrine, on a similar state

title must be actually passed, or, at least, *all* the interest of the vendor in the property be divested.[1] An agreement to sell, although valid and binding, and capable of being enforced in equity, is not an alienation,[2] even though possession of the property is given to the vendee.

---

of facts, was held in *Gates* v. *Smith*, 4 Edw. Ch. (N. Y.) 702. *Ætna Ins. Co.* v. *Jackson*, 16 B. Mon. (Ky.) 242; *Masters* v. *Madison Co. Mut. Ins. Co.*, 11 Barb. (N. Y.) 624; *Phillips* v. *Merrimack, etc., Ins. Co.*, 10 Cush. (Mass.) 350; *Davis* v. *Quincy, etc., Ins. Co.*, 10 Allen (Mass.) 113; *Hitt* v. *Cumberland Valley Ins. Co.*, 59 Penn. St. 474; *Truwbull* v. *Portage, etc., Ins. Co.*, 12 Ohio St. 305; *Perry Ins. Co.* v. *Stewart* 19 Penn. St. 45; *Orrell* v. *Hartford Ins. Co.*, 13 Gray (Mass.) 431. And this is so, even though possession is given under the contract, *and after the loss* the vendee paid the entire amount due under the contract. *Shotwell* v. *Jefferson Ins. Co.*, 5 Bos. (N. Y.) 247. So too, even though the purchase money is in part paid. *Boston and Salem Ice Co.* v. *Royal Ins. Co.*, 12 Allen (Mass.) 381; *Adams* v. *Park F. Ins. Co.*, id. 381.

[1] *Pitney* v. *Glens Falls Ins. Co.*, 61 Barb (N. Y.) 335; affd., 65 N. Y. 6. A mortgage of real estate or personal property does not amount to an alienation unless so provided. *Jackson* v. *Mass., etc., Ins. Co.*, 23 Pick. (Mass.) 418; *Allen* v. *Franklin F. Ins. Co.*, 9 How. Pr. (N. Y.) 501; *Pollard* v. *Somerset, etc., Ins. Co.*, 42 Me. 221; *Washington Ins. Co.* v. *Hayes*, 17 Ohio St. 432. But where there is an absolute conveyance, and the records do not show an agreement to re-convey, it has been held that the policy is invalidated, although a bond for a re-conveyance exists, if it is not under seal. *Adams* v. *Rockingham, etc., Ins. Co.*, 29 Me. 292. Or is not recorded. *Tomlinson* v. *Monmouth, etc., Ins. Co.*, 47 Me. 232. But the doctrine of these cases is strained, and not tenable. The validity of a policy does not depend upon the state of the records. The simple question is, *whether a contract to re-convey, enforceable in equity, exists.* If so, the policy is good; if not, it is void.

[2] *Masters* v. *Madison, etc., Ins. Co.*, 11 Barb. (N. Y.) 624. In *Pitney* v. *Glens Falls Ins. Co.*, 65 N. Y. 6, the assured contracted to sell the wool covered by the policy, and to apply it on a debt due the vendee. Before the wool had been weighed, it was destroyed by fire, and the court held that the property was not alienated, and that the assured could recover upon the policy. It was shown that the assured regarded the title as being in the vendee. As to the effect of this, DWIGHT, C., said: "It is immaterial that the plaintiff *supposed* that the title was in Thayer. This was a mere mistake in law, having no influence on the rights of the parties." So, even though there is a conveyance in fact, if there is anything to be done by the vendee as a condition to the vesting of the title in him, unless he performs the stipulation. In a Massachusetts case (*Phillips* v. *Merrimac, etc., Ins. Co.*, 10 Cush. (Mass.) 350), one of the by-laws of the company required that, in case of an alienation, the assent of the directors thereto should be obtained. The assured *made a contract to sell*, assigned the policy and gave the vendee possession, *but the title still remained in the assured.* Held, that the policy was not avoided. So in a Pennsylvania case (*Hill* v. *Cumberland Mut. Pro. Ins. Co.*, 59 Penn. St. 474), the assured made a contract to sell, *and received part of the purchase-money*, but the title was retained by him, and it was held that he could recover upon the policy. See also, to same effect, *Washington F. Ins. Co.* v. *Kelly*, 32 Md. 421. In a case heard before the Supreme Court of Cincinnati, Ohio, *People's Ins. Co.* v. *Strachle*, 2 Cin. S. C. 186, one S. erected a building and procured insurance upon it. He afterwards agreed to exchange it with F. for other lands, and to give a clear title. Deeds were executed and delivered in *escrow* until F. could clear up the title on his premises. Before F. had accomplished this result, S. got possession of F.'s deed, and had it recorded, without F.'s knowledge, and returned it to the custodian. Before an exchange was *in fact effected*, F.'s premises were burned by fire, and it was held that there was no alienation of the premises, as the record of the deed was fraudulent. In a Kentucky case, a question in some respects similar to that raised in *Pitney* v. *Ins. Co., ante*, was raised. See *Phœnix Ins. Co.* v. *Lawrence*, 4 Met. (Ky.) 9, where the assured made a deed of the goods insured to certain persons, for them to sell and pay his debts. Before the goods were delivered, they were burned,

There is no alienation until the title passes.   Thus, in a New York case,[1] the guardian of some infants contracted to sell some of the property as soon as the necessary authority could be procured, and the vendee, by his permission took possession of the property.   It was held that the insurers were liable for a loss occurring before a conveyance was made.   Nor does a sale of the property made *after* a loss, but before it was known, prevent a recovery by the assured.[2]

A sale by an agent or attorney without authority or contrary to instructions, does not affect the policy, because the title never passed under the sale.[3]

---

and it was held that the delivery of the deed, without a transfer of possession, did not amount to an alienation. A similar doctrine was held in another Kentucky case, *Jackson* v. *Ætna Ins. Co.*, 16 B. Bon. (Ky.) 242, in which the assured procured insurance upon a large quantity of shoulders (bacon). They sold to certain parties 40,000 shoulders in bulk, *to be paid for in cash on delivery*. Ascertaining that they had not that number on hand smoked, they agreed that the number should be made up from shoulders then being smoked. The vendees employed an inspector, who inspected and weighed them several days before the fire, and the vendees had advanced about $17,000, on account of the purchase, which was about one-half the sum to be paid for the whole. The court held that it was competent for the assured to show that it was understood that the property was to remain at the risk of the assured, and the ownership was to remain in him, under the protection of the insurance, until delivered, and that the insurer could not claim this as an alienation, because, if they set up a contract of sale in defense, they must abide by the legal effect of the contract.

In a Louisiana case, *Power* v. *Ocean Ins. Co.*, 19 La. 28, the policy covered barroom furniture, etc., for one year. The assured sold the property, and the vendee after keeping possession six months, not having paid for it, returned it to the assured who took and kept possession of it up to the time of the fire, and the policy was held operative to cover the loss. In *Hutchinson* v. *Wright*, 25 Beav. 444, the assured transferred the vessel by a conveyance absolute in form, but which was really to secure a debt due to the grantee, *and the assured still remained personally liable for the debt*, and it was held that there was no such alienation as defeated the policy.

[1] *Hill* v. *Cumberland, etc., Ins. Co.*, 59 Penn. St. 374 ; *Clinton* v. *Hope Ins. Co.*, 45 N. Y. 454 ; *Phillips* v. *Merrimac, etc., Ins. Co.*, 10 Cush. (Mass.) 350 ; *Davis* v. *Quincy, etc., Ins. Co.*, 10 Allen (Mass.) 113.

[2] *Duncan* v. *Great Western Ins. Co.*, 3 Keyes (N. Y.) 394.

[3] *Copeland* v. *Mercantile Ins. Co.*, 6 Pick. (Mass.) 198. In *Comml. Ins. Co.* v. *Spanknable*, 52 Ill. 53 ; 4 Am. Rep. 582, this question was ably considered. In that case the policy provided that, "in case of any sale, alienation, transfer, conveyance, change of title," etc., the policy should be void. WALKER, J., said : "It was insisted that the policy was rendered void by the sale of the boiler and building to Klausen. The evidence shows that, although appellee says in her examination after the fire, by the attorney of the company, that her husband sold the property, still she, at the same time, says they owed Klausen, and the house was never moved ; and she further says, that Klausen paid no money.   *   *   * It nowhere appears that a valid sale of the house was made. It does not appear that such an instrument was executed as would pass the title, nor was it severed from the freehold, of which it was a part. Again, from an examination of the testimony of the husband, although he admitted it to be a sale, still, taking his testimony altogether, we are satisfied that the bill of sale, as he calls it, was only intended as a mere security. This is rendered more apparent because he says Klausen came to him afterward and asked him how much he must have for the boiler, and, on being informed, Klausen sold it. If it had been his, why ask the

Interest remains until title passes.

SEC. 330. A mere contract to sell property covered by insurance, even though the insured has bound himself to convey upon the performance of certain conditions, does not affect the validity of the policy, and, if a loss occurs before the conditions are performed, a recovery may be had by the insured, even though the conditions are subsequently performed, and, if it was agreed that the policy should be assigned to the purchaser, the judgment will inure to his benefit;[1] neither will a conditional transfer of property avoid the policy;[2] but, if the insured parts with *all* his interest in the property, the policy ceases to be operative.[3]

Conveyance and re-conveyance.

SEC. 331. Where a *part* only of the property is sold, the policy is only invalidated as to the part sold.[4] A sale of the property and a recon-

---

former owner how much he must have on the sale ? Again, the policy was to the appellee, and there is no pretense that she ever sold, or authorized the property to be sold. And surely a policy containing such a condition cannot be defeated by a stranger to the transaction. Nor should it be by a husband, whose right to sell and dispose of the wife's realty is not recognized. It will be observed that the various articles of property were separately insured ; and on this boiler there was $500 risk, named and separately specified. Under such a policy, even if the condition related to the personalty, it would but be a fair and reasonable construction to say that the sale named in the condition referred to each item of separate insurance, and that the sale of one class separately insured would not affect the others. But the clause under consideration obviously relates alone to the real estate. It refers to sale, conveyance, alienation, transfer or change of title in the property insured. But if such is not the true construction, as the boiler was alone sold, it only rendered the insurance on it void. If a mortgage was given on the house, that would not be a sale, alienation, conveyance, transfer or change of title, such as was prohibited by this clause. The explanatory clause would exclude such a construction. It says an entry for a foreclosure of a mortgage, or a levy on execution, or assignment for the benefit of creditors, shall be deemed an alienation of the property. But it does not say that a mortgage shall be so regarded. See *Smith* v. *Mut. F. Ins. Co.*, 50 Me. 96 ; *Masters* v. *Madison Ins. Co.*, 11 Barb. 624 ; *Rollins* v. *Columbian Ins. Co.*, 5 Foster, 204 ; *Ayres* v. *Hartford F. Ins. Co.*, 17 Iowa, 180. These authorities hold, that a mortgage does not operate as such a sale or transfer of property as to bring a policy within such a prohibitory clause. A party claiming such a forfeiture is *stricti juris*, and must bring himself strictly within the clause of forfeiture to defeat the right. See *Washington F. Ins. Co.* v. *Kelly*, 3 Am. Rep. 149."

[1] *Wheeling Ins. Co.* v. *Morrison*, 11 Leigh. (Va.) 354 ; *Trumbull* v. *Portage M. F. Ins. Co.*, 12 Ohio, 305 ; *Chandler* v. *St. Paul Ins. Co.*, 2 Minn. 85.

[2] *Jackson* v. *Mass. Ins. Co.*, 23 Pick. (Mass.) 418 ; *Trumbull* v. *Portage Ins. Co.*, 12 Ohio, 305.

[3] *Wilson* v. *Hill*, 3 Met. (Mass.) 66, and it seems that, where the policy provides that, if the property is transferred, or the interest of the insured therein is terminated, the policy shall be void, an assignment of the policy is as fatal as the sale or assignment of the property itself. *Smith* v. *Saratoga Ins. Co.*, 1 Hill (N. Y.) 497. But, where a policy has been assigned by the consent of the company, the policy remains in force, and an action may be maintained thereon by the assignee. *Mann* v. *Herkimer Ins. Co.*, 4 id. 187.

[4] *West Branch Ins. Co.* v. *Halfenstein*, 40 Penn. St. 289 ; *Rex* v. *Ins. Co.*, 2 Phila. (Penn.) 357 ; *Commercial Ins Co.* v. *Spanknable*, 52 Ill. 53.

veyance to the assured before a loss under the policy reinstates the assured to all his rights under it for the unexpired term.[1]

Alienation after loss does not avoid.

SEC. 332. An alienation *after* the loss, although neither party knew of the loss at the time, does not affect the policy.[2]

Voidable sale avoids.

SEC. 333. Where the policy prohibits *any* change of title, a sale that is voidable comes within the prohibition, but one that is absolutely void, does not, for under a *void* sale no title passes.[3] It must be a sale that terminates the interest of the assured in the property, and divests him of the title therein. A mere nominal sale, the vendor retaining the title, or a lien for the price does not avoid the policy, although "*any* change of title" is prohibited.[4] Thus, under a policy with such a condition, a mortgage is not within the prohibition.[5]

Sale by one joint owner to another.

SEC. 334. The question whether a sale by one joint owner to another is such an alienation as avoids a policy prohibiting any change in the title, is not definitely settled, and numerous authorities are to be found sustaining either view. It would seem, however, that the question must mainly depend upon the language of the policy, and the evident intention of the parties, from the language used. Where a policy is issued to *two* joint owners of property, and the policy stipulates that

---

[1] *Worthington* v. *Bearse*, 12 Allen (Mass.) 382. It is enough if the assured had an insurable interest at the time the insurance was made, *and at the time of the loss*, and the effect of these clauses are evidently intended to apply in cases where there is an absolute transfer, and no interest in the assured at the time of the loss. The policy is suspended during the interim, but revives without the consent of the assured, upon a restoration of the *status quo*. *Power* v. *Ocean Ins. Co.*, 19 La. 28. In *Lane* v. *Maine, etc., Ins. Co.*, 12 Me. 44, the assured gave an oral lease of the store and sold the goods therein to one D., but within six months thereafter, and before the loss, the assured came into the possession of the store again, and the goods were retransferred to him, and it was held that the insurers were liable for the loss. *Shearman* v. *Niagara F. Ins. Co.*, 46 N. Y. 526.

[2] *Duncan* v. *Great Western Ins. Co.*, 3 Keyes (N. Y.) 394; *Farmers' Mut. Ins. Co.* v. *Graybill*, 74 Penn. St. 17.

[3] *School District* v. *Ætna Ins. Co.*, 62 Me. 330; *Jackson* v. *Ætna Ins. Co.*, 16 B. Mon. (Ky.) 242.

[4] *Jackson* v. *Ætna Ins. Co.*, ante.

[5] *Commercial Ins. Co.* v. *Spanknable*, 52 Ill. 53; *Ayres* v. *Hartford Ins. Co.*, 17 Iowa, 176; *Hartford F. Ins. Co.* v. *Walsh*, 54 Ill. 164. But in Michigan it is held that an absolute transfer, although intended as a mortgage is, *Western Mass. Ins. Co.* v. *Riker* 20 Mich. 279; but *contra*, see *Ayres* v. *Hartford Ins. Co., ante; Aurora F. Ins. Co.* v. *Eddy*, 55 Ill. 213; and in New York it has been held by the supreme court, that a contract to sell and a receipt of part of the purchase money, *if the contract is enforceable*, is such a change of title or interest as avoids the policy, *Germond* v. *Home Ins. Co.*, 5 F. & C. (N. Y.) 120.

any sale, transfer or change of title in any property insured, etc., or
of any *undivided interest* therein shall avoid the policy, there would
seem to be no question but that a sale by one tenant in common to
another, or of one partner to another, would come within the prohibition.[1] But when the policy merely provides that " any sale transfer or change of title, etc.," shall avoid the policy, it is held by the
later, and by a very respectable class of cases, that a sale by one joint
owner to another, *does not* come within the prohibition.[2] So it has been
held that, where the policy provides that " if the said property shall
be sold or conveyed, *or the interest of the parties therein changed*," the
policy shall be void, that this does not exclude a sale by one partner
to his co-partner, of his interest in the property.[3] The court in this
case held that, inasmuch as the interest of each partner in the goods
is *per my et, per tout*, and the language used is susceptible of different
interpretations, that interpretation that is most favorable to the assured,
must be placed upon it, and the contract upheld. This case carries
the doctrine farther than was warranted by the cases to which it
referred as authority, and farther than the rules of fair construction
would permit. The *interest* of the parties in the property was clearly
changed, when a part owner became sole owner, or when one joint
owner parted with *any part* of his joint interest in the property. The
New York case to which the court referred, did not carry the doctrine
to any such length. In that case the policy simply provided that " if
the said property shall be sold or conveyed," the policy should be
void, and the court held that, a sale by one partner to another, was not
such a sale as was contemplated by the insurers. That the language
of the policy, being fairly susceptible of an interpretation *consistent
with such a sale*, that interpretation would be placed upon it that was
most favorable to the assured.[4] But when, as in the Alabama case,

---

[1] *Hartford F. Ins. Co.* v. *Ross*, 23 Ind. 179 ; *Dix* v. *Mercantile Ins. Co.*, 22 Ill.
272 ; *Keeler* v. *Niagara Ins. Co.*, 16 Wis. 523 ; *Dreher* v. *Ætna Ins. Co.*, 18 Mo.
128 ; *Tillou* v. *Kingston, etc., Ins. Co.*, 5 N. Y. 405. So where the policy stipulates
that any alienation " by sale or otherwise" shall avoid the policy, it has been held
that a sale by one partner to a co-partner was within the prohibition. *Finlay* v.
Lycoming Ins. Co., 31 Penn. St. 311 ; *Buckley* v. *Garrett*, 48 Penn. St. 204.

[2] *Hoffman* v. *Ætna Ins. Co.*, 32 N. Y. 405 ; *Wilson* v. *Genesee Mut. F. Ins. Co.*,
16 Barb. (N. Y.) 511 ; *Manley* v. *Ins. Co. of N. America*, 1 Lans. (N. Y.) 20.

[3] *Burnett* v. *Eufala Home Ins. Co.*, 46 Ala. 11.

[4] In that case (*Hoffman* v. *Ætna Ins. Co.*, 32 N. Y. 405), the action was on a
policy of insurance for $6,000. issued in February, 1861, to Hoffman, Place & Co.,
of New York, covering their stock of merchandise, including not only thair own
goods, but those held by them in trust or on commission, or sold but not delivered, in their brick and marble store in Broadway. The policy contained, among
other things, a printed proviso that it should be null and void, " if the said prop-

referred to, the policy provides that "any change of interest" shall avoid the policy, it might as fairly be held that a sale to a stranger,

---

erty shall be sold or conveyed." The insurance was renewed in February, 1862. On the 7th of March following, Silvernail, one of the partners, retired from the business, selling out his interest to Hoffman & Place, by whom the business was continued. They subsequently, with the written consent of the company, removed the business and stock to their new brick and marble store in Duane street. The loss occurred on the 9th of April, and the company declining to pay, the present action was brought. It was tried in the Superior Court before Judge MONELL, and the jury found a verdict for the plaintiffs. The judgment was affirmed on appeal, and the present appeal is from that decision. The principal questions of law raised on the trial were, whether the transfer avoided the sale, and if not, whether goods afterwards added to the stock were within the protection of the policy. PORTER, J., in delivering the opinion of the court, said: "The weight of judicial authority in this State is against the doctrine that a policy issued to a firm is forfeited by a transfer of interest as between the parties assured. As a contrary opinion has prevailed to some extent, it may be well briefly to retrace the history of this question in our courts. It first arose in 1840, on the trial of the case of *McMasters* v. *The Westchester Mut. Ins. Co.*, 25 Wend. 379. The policy was issued to McMasters & Bruce. Evidence was given tending to show that the interest of Bruce in the partnership property was assigned before the loss to McMasters. At the circuit, it was held by Judge RUGGLES, as matter of law, that such a sale by one partner to another would not relieve the insurers. The plaintiffs recovered, and a new trial was denied; but it did not become necessary to consider this question on review, the jury having found specially that the interest was not in fact transferred. The case of *Howard & Ryckman* v. *The Albany Ins. Co.* was decided in 1846, and turned on a mere question of misjoinder, arising on a demurrer to the defendants' plea that, before the loss, one of the plaintiffs transferred to the other his interest in the property insured. It was held that, under these circumstances, a *joint* action could not be maintained by the original parties; and from this decision Chief Justice BRONSON dissented. 3 Denio, 301.

The case mainly relied on by the appellants is that of *Murdock & Garrett* v. *The Chenango Mut. Ins. Co.*, decided in this court in 1849. 2 Comst. 210. It did not involve the question now under discussion. The property insured was a building, owned at the date of the policy by the plaintiffs, as tenants in common. Garrett afterwards conveyed to Murdock, the other plaintiff, his undivided half of the property. The company indorsed a consent in writing to the conveyance, with a stipulation that the policy should remain good to Murdock, as the sole owner of the property. Under a special provision in the charter of the company, this gave the grantee, as the sole party in interest, a right to maintain the action in his own name—equivalent to that now given by the general law to the real party in interest. Laws of 1836, 314; 42, sec. 7. The building was afterwards destroyed by fire, and an action was brought in the joint names of Murdock and Garrett. It was claimed by the defendants and adjudged by the court that the misjoinder of Garrett was fatal, as he had no interest in the action. Mr. Hill, who argued the cause for the defendants, insisted that, as Murdock was the sole owner at the time of the loss, the action might and should have been brought by him alone. No question was made, and, under the stipulation indorsed on the policy, none could be made, as to the liability of the company to Murdock for the entire loss, unless absolved from it on other grounds. Opinions were delivered by Judges CADY, STRONG and JEWETT, all holding the misjoinder to be fatal. The opinion of Judge STRONG was put on the specific ground that Murdock succeeded to all the rights of Garrett, and the action should, therefore, have been brought in his own name. Judge CADY conceded that it was not material to inquire whether Murdock might not have maintained an action in his own name. The observations on this question in the course of his opinion are, therefore, not to be regarded as views expressed by the court, but as the *obiter dicta* of the learned judge. They are entitled to high consideration as the views of an able and eminent jurist, but they have not the controlling force of authority. In 1850, the direct question now involved was first discussed and decided in the Supreme

36

of the interest of one partner, did not effect a change in that respect,
as that a sale to a co-partner did not. In such cases, there would

---

Court. *Tillou* v. *Kingston Mut. Ins. Co.*, 7 Barb. 570. The policy in that case
had been issued in 1842, to the firm of Tillou, Doty & Crouse. In 1844, it was
assigned by them to one Ketchum, with the written consent of the company, as
security for the payment of a mortgage on the premises. Subsequently, and
before the loss, Crouse, without the consent of the company, sold his interest in
the property to the other two partners. It was provided by law, in the act of
incorporation, that any policy issued by the company should become void, *upon
the alienation, by sale or otherwise*, of the property insured. Laws of 1836, 44;
466. The action was brought in the names of the original parties, for the benefit
not only of the assignee of the policy, but also of the then owners of the property.
The court adjudged that a sale by one joint owner to another of his interest in
the property insured was not a cause of forfeiture within the intent and import
of this provision. They also held—the decision in 2 Comstock not having then
been reported—that the recovery could be sustained, not only for the amount due
to the assignee of the policy, but also for the surplus due to the owners. When
the case came before this court on appeal, the judgment was sustained to the extent
of the interest of the assignee, who, in virtue of the consent of the company was entitled to sue in the names of the original parties, as the action was commenced before
the adoption of the Code. The judgment was, of course, modified by striking
out the excess recovered by the owners; as it had been settled in the case of
Murdock v. *The Chenaago Ins. Co.* that, to the extent of their claim, the misjoinder of Crouse as a plaintiff was a fatal ground of objection. The opinion of the
court, delivered by Judge Foot, shows the modification to have been made on
the authority of that decision. Through an oversight, such as occasionally happens in all reports, the point of the decision was misapprehended in the note of
the case on which the appellants rely. 5 N. Y. 405; 17 id. 399.
  The precise question was again presented for judgment in 1853, in the case of
Wilson v. *The Genesee Mut. Ins. Co.*, 16 Barb. 511. The insurance was on the
mercantile stock of Dixon & Co., a firm in Michigan, consisting of A. H. Dixon
and Samuel G. Goss. Shortly afterward the firm was dissolved. Dixon succeeded, by purchase, to the interest of Goss, and continued the business on his
own account down to the time of the fire. The action was brought by Wilson,
to whom Dixon subsequently assigned the claim. Two defenses were interposed.
The first was, that the policy was forfeited by the transfer from one partner to
the other, of his interest in the property insured; the other was, that it was forfeited by Dixon's afterwards obtaining a further insurance on the goods without
the written consent of the company, though such a consent was obtained from
their local agent in Michigan. The court overruled both defenses, and held that
the policy was not forfeited, either by the sale made by the retiring partner, or
by the subsequent insurance effected by his successor in interest, with the consent
of the Michigan agent. The case was heard in this court, on appeal, in 1856 (4
Kern. 418.) The counsel for the defendant insisted, as a principal point, that the
sale by one partner to the other avoided the policy, and cited the cases of *Howard*
v. *The Albany Ins. Co.*, *Murdock* v. *The Chenango Ins. Co.*, and *Tillou* v. *The
Kingston Ins. Co.*, as authorities supporting the proposition. Judge Comstock,
who delivered the opinion of the court, did not deem it worthy even of a passing
notice, but disposed of the case on a subsequent and subordinate point. He
was of opinion, and the court so held, that the consent of the Michigan agent to
the further insurance by Dixon, was not binding upon the company, as it
appeared, by his power of attorney, that his authority was limited to receiving
applications for insurance. No member of the court intimated a doubt of the
correctness of the adjudication, that the sale by one partner to the other did not
invalidate the policy; and of the seven judges who took part in the decision, two
were in favor of a general affirmance. In 1857, the supreme court had occasion
incidentally to reaffirm the proposition, that the validity of a policy is not affected
by transfers of interest as between the parties assured, in the case of *Dey* v. *The
Poughkeepsie Mut. Ins. Co.*, 23 Barb. 627. The attention of this court was drawn
the following year to the decision of the supreme court in the case of *Tillou* v.
The Kingston Ins. Co., that transfers as between the assured are not within the

seem to be no room for doubt, that the object and purpose of the insurers was, to keep the interest in the property *entirely unchanged*,

---

prohibition against alienation; and that decision was approved by Judge PRATT, who delivered the prevailing opinion. *Buffalo Steam Engine Works* v. *The Sun Mut. Ins. Co.*, 17 N. Y. 412. It is quite apparent, therefore, that, in this State, there is a decisive preponderance of judicial authority against the recognition of a sale by one to another of the assured, as cause of forfeiture within the meaning of the proviso. But if the authorities were in equipoise, and the solution of the question depended on general reasoning and the application of settled and familiar principles of law, our conclusion would be in accordance with that of the court below. The terms of the proviso are, that the policy shall be null and void 'if the said property shall be sold and conveyed.' But these words are, themselves, vague and indeterminate. Are they to be understood in their largest sense, without restriction or limitation? Clearly not; for we find, on referring to other portions of the policy, that it was issued to the assured as merchants, and that it covered a stock of goods which it was their business to sell from day to day. Is the proviso applicable to the particular goods in the store at the date of the insurance? Such a construction would not only defeat the purpose of protecting a fluctuating stock, but it would annul the policy at once, for it would bring the first mercantile sale at the counter within the terms of the co dition. What description of sales and conveyances, then did the parties contemplate when this provision was framed? Evidently such, and such only, as would transfer the proprietary interest of those with whom the insurers contracted, to others with whom they had not consented to contract. They testified their confidence in each of the assured, by issuing to them the policy; but they did not choose to repose blind confidence in others who might succeed to the ownership. If the assured parted with the possession as well as the title to the goods, the insurers knew, of course, that their liability would cease; but they were aware that, in the exigencies incident to business, parties often retain the control, possession and apparent ownership of goods, after parting with all their title. To guard against such contingencies, they choose to provide for the forfeiture of the policy on the transfer of the title to others, even though the business should continue to be conducted by the assured.

It is suggested that the proviso may have been designed to secure the continuance in the firm, of the only member in whom the insurers reposed confidence. The only evidence of their confidence in either, is the fact that they contracted with all; and the theory is rather fanciful than sound, that they may have intended to conclude a bargain with rogues, on the faith of a proviso 'that an honest man should be kept in the firm to watch them. Certainly, nothing appears in the present case to indicate that all the assured were not equally worthy of confidence; and it is not to be presumed that, in any case, underwriters would deliberately insure those whose integrity they had reason to distrust.

The policy in question having been issued to a mercantile firm, the company must be deemed to have had in view the fluctuating nature of a partnership business, and the changes of relative interest incident to that relation. These might be very important to the assured, though wholly immaterial to the risk. It is manifest that mere variations in the character and amounts of the interests of the assured as between themselves, did not constitute the mischief at which the proviso was aimed. If the applicants had originally objected to the form of the policy, on the ground that the effect of the clause might be to prevent the increase by a partner of his interest from one-fourth to one-third of the business, by purchase from the other members of the firm, the answer would undoubtedly have been that such a change was not within the operation or intent of the proviso. There is probably not a business firm in the State, which would accept at the usual rates, a policy declaring *in terms* that the premium should be forfeited and the insurance annulled, by a mere change of interest as between the partners. In this instance there is no such declaration; and an *implication* so repugnant to the evident design of the contract, is not to be deduced from the unguarded use of general words, if they can be fairly limited to the appropriate and obvious sense in which they were employed by the parties.

The design of the provision was, not to interdict all sales, but only sales of proprietary interest by parties insured to parties not insured. If the words were

both as to persons and quantity.   At least, there is a change of title,
and a change of interest.[1]   As a general rule it may be said that, the

---

taken literally, a renewal of the policy would be required at the close of each
day's sales.   Indeterminate forms of expression, in such a case, are to be understood in a sense subservient to the general purposes of the contract.   It is true
that the language of the proviso against sales, was not guarded by a special
exclusion of changes of interest as between the assured, or of the sales of merchandise in the usual course of their business; but this was for the obvious reason
that there was nothing in the tenor of the instrument to denote, that the *application* of the clause to such a case was within the contemplation of the underwriters.
'The matter in hand is always presumed to be in the mind and thoughts of the
speaker, though his words seem to admit a larger sense; and therefore the
generality of the words used, shall be restrained by the particular occasion.'
Powell on Contracts, 389; *Van Hagen* v. *Van Rensselaer*, 18 Johns. 423.   Thus,
in an action on a life policy, containing a proviso that it should be void 'in case
the assured should die by his own hands,' it was held by this court, that though
in terms it embraced all cases of suicide, it could not properly be applied to self-
destruction by a lunatic, as there was no reason to suppose that such a case was
within the purpose of the clause or the contemplation of the parties.   *Breasted*
v. *Farmers' Loan and Trust Co.*, 4 Seld. 299.   'All words,' says Lord BACON,
'whether they be in deeds or statutes, or otherwise, if they be general, and not
express and precise, shall be restrained unto the fitness of the matter and the
person.'   Bacon's Law Maxims, Reg. 10.
    Reading the proviso as it was read by the parties, it is easy to discern the pur-
pose of its insertion.   It was to protect the company from a continuing obligation
to the assured, if the title and beneficial interest should pass to others, whom they
might not be equally willing to trust.   Words should not be taken in their broad-
est import, when they are equally appropriate in a sense limited to the object the
parties had in view.   22 N. Y. 443; 4 Kernan, 615, 622; 5 Duer, 340; 7 Hill, 255;
1 Duer on Ins. 163, § 8.   The terms of the policy were not such as would naturally suggest even a query in the minds of the assured, whether a transfer of
interest as between themselves would work a forfeiture of the insurance, and
relieve the company from its promise to indemnify both—the buyer as well as the
seller—the premium being paid in advance, and the risk remaining unchanged.
One of two joint payees of a non-negotiable note would hardly be more surprised
to be met with a claim, that by buying the interest of his associate he had extinguished the obligation of the maker to both.   It is a rule of law, as well as of ethics,
that where the language of a promisor may be understood in more senses than one,
it is to be interpreted in the sense in which he had reason to suppose it was *understood* by the promisee.   *Potter* v. *Ontario Ins. Co.*, 5 Hill, 149; *Barlow* v. *Scott*, 24
N. Y. 40.   It is also a familiar rule of law, that if it be left in doubt, in view of the
general tenor of the instrument and the relations of the contracting parties,
whether given words were used in an enlarged or a restricted sense, other things
being equal, that construction should be adopted which is most *beneficial* to the
promisee.   Coke's Litt. 188; Bacon's Law Maxim's, Reg., 3; *Doe* v. *Dixon*, 9
East, 16: *Marvin* v. *Stone*, 2 Cowen, 806.   This rule has been very uniformly
applied to conditions and provisos in policies of insurance, on the ground that
though they are inserted for the benefit of the underwriters, their office is to
limit the force of the principal obligation.   *Yeaton* v. *Fry*, 5 Cranch, 341; *Palmer*
v. *Western Ins. Co.*, 1 Story's R. 364, 365; *Petty* v. *Royal Exchange Ins. Co.*, 1
Burrows, 349.   In the case first cited, the action was for a marine loss, and one
of the issues was, whether a recovery was barred by the entry of a ship into a
blockaded port, such ports being excepted by the policy.   The court held that
though the case was within the terms, it was not within the intent of the exception; and that as the risk contemplated in the clause was merely that of capture,
the rule of liberal construction must be applied in favor of the promisee.   The
reason assigned by Chief Justice MARSHALL was, that 'the words are the words

---

[1] *Barnes* v. *Union, etc.*, *Ins. Co.*, 51 Me. 110; *Dreher* v. *Ætna Ins. Co.*, 18 Mo.
128; *Hartford F. Ins. Co.* v. *Ross*, 23 Ind. 179; *Dix* v. *Mercantile Ins. Co.*, 22
Ill. 272; *Keeler* v. *Niagara Ins. Co.*, 16 Wis. 523.

tendency of the courts is to hold that, unless the language of the policy is such as clearly to prohibit a sale of the interest of one joint owner to

---

of the insurer, not of the insured; and they take a particular risk out of the policy, which but for the exception would be comprehended in the contract.' The appellants also encounter another rule equally at variance with the proposition they seek to maintain: 'Conditions providing for disabilities and forfeitures are to receive, when the intent is doubtful, a strict construction against those for whose benefit they are introduced.' *Livingston* v. *Sickles*, 7 Hill, 255; *Catlin* v. *Springfield Ins. Co.*, 1 Sumn. 434; *Brested* v. *Farmers' Loan & Trust Co.*, 4 Seld. 305. This rule, applicable to all contracts, has peculiar force in cases like the present, where the attempt is to seize upon words introduced as a safeguard against fraud, and make them available to defeat the claim of the assured on the theory of a technical forfeiture without fault. If the policy admits of such a construction, it is due to the dexterity of the draftsman, and not to a meeting of the minds of the parties. There was nothing in the tenor of the contract to indicate to the owners that under this proviso the promise of indemnity might fail, though they did not part with the property; nor to warn them that the insurance did not protect the entire stock of goods in their store, whether they bought it from each other or from third parties. Even after the transfer of interest as between themselves, there was nothing in the policy to apprise them that their rights under it were forfeited, and that without a new insurance their property was unprotected. The general words employed are too indeterminate in their import, to create a disability so profitless to the company and so injurious to the assured. It was suggested, rather than insisted, on the argument, that the company may have intended to make the proviso more stringent and comprehensive than it was assumed to be by the plaintiffs; and that they are bound by the words to which they assented, even if they did not fully apprehend their effect. The obvious answer is, that it would be just to neither party to assume that the insurers aimed at drawing customers into the payment of premiums, by holding out illusory promises, couched in vague and deceptive terms, for the very purpose of enabling them to elude liability. Nothing but the clearest expression of such a design would justify the assumption, that an executed contract was intended by either party as a snare. If technical forfeitures could be sustained by such intendments, the effect would be to weaken private confidence in commercial faith, and occasion just solicitude as to the security of important rights. The other exceptions presented in the case were argued with great ability by the respective counsel, but the disposition to be made of the more important of these is mainly dependant on our views of the principal question. They are fully considered in the opinion delivered by Judge ROBERTSON in the court below, and it is sufficient for us to express our concurrence in his conclusions. The appellants seem to suppose that there is a technical embarrassment on the question of damages, growing out of the fluctuating character of the stock, and the continuance of the business by the remaining members of the firm, who succeeded, under the transfer, to the interest of the retiring partner. Looking to the nature and design of the contract of insurance, we find no such embarrassment. The language of this court, on a former occasion, is equally appropriate in the case at bar: 'It was manifestly the intention of the parties to the policy, that it should cover, to the amount of the insurance, any goods of the character and description specified in the policy, which, from time to time during its continuation, might be in the store. A policy for a long period upon goods in a retail shop, applies to the goods successively in the shop from time to time. Any other construction of a policy of insurance, upon a stock in trade continually changing, would render it worthless as an indemnity' *Hooper* v. *Hudson F. Ins. Co.*, 17 N. Y. 425. The plaintiffs were parties to the contract made with the defendant. They were conducting the business contemplated by the terms of the policy. The insurance was intended to cover the mercantile stock of which the assured were proprietors, stored, from time to time, in the building in which that business was conducted. There was no substantial change of material to the risk, and clearly none within the intent of the proviso. Each member of a partnership firm, as Lord HARDWICKE said, is 'seized *per my et per tout*' of the common stock and effects. *West* v. *Skip*, 1 Vesey Sen. 242. This interest of each and all, the policy in question was

*another in the joint property, and the policy can fairly be upheld in the
face of such prohibition, or if there is any doubt as to whether it was
intended to apply to such a sale, the prohibition will be held not to apply in
such cases*, but will be restricted to the case of sales to a stranger.[1]
"A mere change of interest," says the court in a New Hampshire
case,[2] among partners, where no stranger is introduced, and no addition
made to the number of the insured, when there is no change in the
condition or situation of the property or risk, a mere assignment of his
interest by one partner to the other, is obviously not within the principle or motives on which the condition is founded.[3] In case of a sale
of the *property* in such cases, and a delivery of the policy, the delivery
of the policy operates as an equitable assignment and transfer of all
the other partners' interest in the insurance.[4] But, unless *after* the
assignment the insurer has promised to pay the insurance to the
assignee, the suit must be brought in the name of the assignee.[5] But
if *after* such assignment, *and with knowledge thereof*, the policy is
renewed, a new contract arises and the right of the assignee, even at
common law to maintain an action in his own name, is fixed,[6] and this

---

designed to protect; and its language, fairly construed, is in harmony with this
intent. There is no reason why the full measure of agreed indemnity should be
withheld from the plaintiffs, who were owners at the date of the insurance, and
sole owners at the time of the loss. *Hooper* v. *Hudson River Ins. Co.*, 17 N. Y.
425, 426; *Wilson* v. *Genesee Mut. Ins. Co.*, 16 Barb. 511; *Jefferson Ins. Co.* v.
Cotheal, 7 Wend. 73; Code, § 111."

[1] *Hoffman* v. *Ætna Ins. Co.*, *ante*; *Burnett* v. *Eufala Home, etc., Ins. Co.*,
ante; *Pierce* v. *Ins. Co.*, 50 N. H. 297; *West* v. *Citizens' Ins. Co.*, 27 Ohio 1;
Cowan v. *Iowa State Ins. Co.*, 40 Iowa 551; 20 Am. Rep. 583.

[2] *Pierce* v. *Nashua F. Ins. Co.*, 50 N. H. 297.

[3] *Niblo* v. *N. Am. F. Ins. Co.*, 1 Sandf. (N. Y.) 551; *Tillou* v. *Kingston, etc.*,
Ins. Co., 7 Barb. (N. Y.) 570; *Wilson* v. *Genesee, etc., Ins. Co.*, 16 id. 512. *Hoffman* v. *Ætna Ins. Co.*, 32 N. Y. 405; *West* v. *Citizens' Ins. Co.*, 27 Ohio St. 1.

[4] *Pierce* v. *Ins. Co.*, *ante*; *Thompson* v. *Emery*, 27 N. H. 269; *Shepherd* v. *Ins.
Co.*, 38 N. H. 237; *Sanders* v. *Ins. Co.*, 44 id. 243.

[5] *Pierce* v. *F. Ins. Co.*, *ante*; *Sanders* v. *Ins. Co.*, *ante*; *Foster* v. *Ins. Co.*, 2
Gray (Mass.) 216; *Hobbs* v. *Memphis Ins. Co.*, 1 Sneed. (Tenn.) 444; *Wood* v.
Rutland, etc., Ins. Co., 31 Vt. 552.

[6] In *Pierce* v. *Ins. Co.*, *ante*, an action was brought upon a policy issued to
Mower & Pierce. Subsequent to the issue of the policy, Mower sold his interest
in the property insured to Pierce. The policy was not assigned. Just before the
policy expired, Pierce carried the old policy to the agent who issued it, and told
him he wanted the mill re-insured. The agent *knew* that Pierce had bought
Mower's interest in the mill, and that the policy had not been assigned. The
agent took the policy, said he would have the property re-insured, but did not
know what the premium would be. The agent procured a *renewal* of the old
policy, instead of a new policy as requested, which was not known by Pierce
until after the fire. The receipt was a renewal of the old policy to Mower &
Pierce, and was issued to them upon this state of facts, the court held that Pierce
was entitled to recover upon the policy. "The sale of Mower's interest in the
property insured," said FOSTER, J., "and the delivery of the policy, operated as
a valid assignment, and transferred to the plaintiff all his partner's equitable

is so although the renewal is made by an agent,[1] and the fact that the receipt given by the agent for the new premium states it to have been received from the firm, is not conclusive, but the assured may show that he paid the money, and is the only party with whom the contract was made.[2]

In a Vermont case [3] it was held that, by operation of law, the surviving partner became vested with the legal title in the goods, and the legal assignee of the policy, and that in case of loss he alone could sue for a breach of the policy. "So long," said ALDIS, J., "as Wood continued in the care and disposition of these goods *as surviving part-ner*, we think the policy continued in force as to them, *notwithstanding the decease of Johnson.*" But in this case, it appeared that Wood went on after Johnson's death and sold out the goods belonging to the firm, and replenished the stock by goods purchased by himself, so that at the time of the loss but a small amount of the goods on hand at Johnson's decease were destroyed; and the question was, whether Wood could recover for the goods purchased by himself subsequent to the loss.[4]

---

interest in the insurance. 1 Phil. Ins., 80; *Thompson* v. *Emery*, 27 N. H. 269, and cases cited; *Shepherd* v. *Ins. Co.*, 38 id. 237; *Sanders* v. *Ins. Co.*, 44 id. 243. Although in such cases the equitable interests of the assignee will be protected, yet, *ordinarily*, and at common law, he cannot maintain a suit upon the original policy in his own name, but must sue in the name of the assignor. But if the insurer, upon notice of the assignment, promises the assignee to pay the insurance to him in case of loss, the assignee can, upon proper averment, maintain a suit upon the policy in his own name. *Sanders* v. *Ins. Co.*, 44 N. H. 243; SHAW, C.J., in *Wilson* v. *Hill*, 3 Met. 66; *Foster* v. *Ins. Co.*, 2 Gray, 216. The declaration, in such case, should set forth the original contract and policy, and the assignment as a consideration for the new promise, and such promise must be proved as alleged. *Shepherd* v. *Ins. Co.*, before cited; *Barns* v. *Ins. Co.*, 45 N. H. 24. The equitable interests obtained by the assignment is a sufficient consideration to sustain the subsequent express promise to pay to the assignee. *Currier* v. *Hodgdon*, 3 N. H. 82; *Thompson* v. *Emery*, before cited." See also, *Burnett* v. *Eufala Home Ins. Co.*, 46 Ala. 11; 7 Am. Rep. 581, where a similar doctrine is held.

[1] *Goodall* v. *Ins. Co.*, 25 N. H. 169; *Sanders* v. *Ins. Co.*, ante.

[2] *Pierce* v. *Ins. Co.*, ante; *Ryan* v. *Rand*, 26 N. H. 15.

[3] *Wood* v. *Rutland, etc., Ins. Co.*, 31 Vt. 552; 4 Bennett's F. I. C. 333.

[4] ALDIS, J., in passing upon this question, said: "This is not a mere change of relative interest. It is a new business, and a new party, and to make the defendants liable to Wood alone, it must be shown that they have contracted with him. A contract with Wood and Johnson cannot be transferred into a contract with Wood without their consent. Such a change in the contract and the business the defendants cannot be supposed to have contemplated when they issued the policy. They may have contemplated that if one partner should die during the term of the policy it should be kept in force while the survivor closed the business of the firm. That is reasonable. But it is unreasonable to extend it to a new business, and a new firm. Hence, when one partner sells to his associates, there can be no recovery by the old firm for a subsequent loss. *Tillou* v. *The Kingston Mut. Ins. Co.*, 1 Seld. 406; *Murdock et al.* v. *The Chen. Co. Ins. Co.*, 2 Comst. 210;

Dissolution of firm, and division of property.

SEC. 335. When a firm is dissolved, and the property divided among the partners,[1] or where proceedings for a dissolution are brought and

---

3 Denio, 301. This has sometimes been put upon the ground that, at the time of the loss, the old firm had no insurable interest in the property. But we think, where there is a voluntary change of the firm, the insurance company may also well say that the new firm is not the party with whom they contracted. They might consider the risk increased as much by the departure of one of the assured from the firm as by the introduction of a new party; and when such a change is voluntary, it is a risk which they did not contemplate. They might be willing to insure Wood while connected in business with Johnson, and wholly unwilling to insure or deal with him alone. The rights and liabilities of Wood & Johnson might be very different from those of Wood alone. They might be solvent and he insolvent. The fact that by the partnership articles the plaintiff had the right to purchase the stock and continue the business, upon the dissolution of the firm of Wood & Co. cannot alter the rights of these parties as to the extension of the insurance. The clause in the articles was not made known to the defendants, and therefore could not bind them. Even if known, we think it could have had no effect, unless it had been incorporated into the contract by express words. Without the assent or agreement of the defendants to treat the policy as a policy to Wood alone, we do not think he can recover for these subsequently purchased goods. II. The more important question next arises, as to the effect of the evidence excluded by the court. The plaintiff, in his declaration, alleges the execution of the policy, the agreement in the partnership articles, the death of Johnson, the purchase of the goods by Wood, and an agreement of the defendants with Wood, that, in consideration of his paying all subsequent calls upon the premium note, 'the policy should enure to his benefit, and stand as a policy to him for the insurance of his sole goods and property, kept in the store and employed in the prosecution of the business;' and performance by the plaintiff, relying on this promise of the defendants, whereby the defendants became liable, etc. The evidence excluded by the court tended to prove such an agreement, entered into with the plaintiff, upon full notice of all the facts, both by the agent and directors of the defendants' company. But it was not claimed that the agreement was in writing. The evidence showed that it was express, but verbal with the agent, assented to by the directors, and had been acted upon by both parties. A policy of insurance is a mere *chose in action*, and not assignable at common law so that the assignee can sue in his own name; and though, like a bond, it may be made payable to the insured and his assigns, still, if a loss happens, the equitable assignee must sue in the name of the original assured. *Skinner* v. *Somes*, 14 Mass. 107; *Jessell* v. *Williamsburg Ins. Co.*, 3 Hill, 88; 7 Wend. 72; Phil. on Ins. p. 61; 9 Wend. 404. In the charters of modern insurance companies, and usually in policies of insurance, there is a provision that a sale of the property insured shall avoid the policy; but that the vendee, having the policy assigned to him, on application to the company within some limited period of time, may have the policy ratified and confirmed to him, so that he may be substituted for the original assured, and have all his rights and liabilities In New York it has been held that the vendee and assignee, under such a policy, must sue in his own name, and not in the name of the assignor. *Mann* v. *The Herk. Co. Ins. Co.*, 4 Hill, 788; 1 Hill, 71.

As to the form of bringing this action, the question is not important in this case, for the plaintiff is both vendee and assignee, and also, as surviving partner, the only one who can sue as the original party insured. And as, under our decisions, he might join his individual claims with those as surviving partner (2 Vt. 569; 4 Vt. 26), the question as to who should sue does not arise. In the charter of this company, section 12, it is provided that, when a house or building is alienated, the policy shall be void; but that the vendee having the policy assigned him may, within thirty days, have it confirmed to him, etc. There is nothing in the charter as to the alienation of goods. Nor is there any provision in the charter or by-laws specifying how the policy shall be confirmed to the vendee, or that it shall

[1] *Dreher* v. *Ætna Ins. Co.*, 18 Mo. 128.

a receiver is appointed, and a decree dissolving the firm and directing the sale of the property is entered, the insurer is discharged under a

---

be in writing. The first and second sections of the eighth article in the by-laws enable the vendor of goods insured to have his policy cancelled in whole or in part. They have no further application. As, therefore, there is nothing in the charter, or by-laws, or policy, to determine the effect of consent by the company to an alienation of his interest in the goods by one of the assured to his associate, nor how the vendee or assignee may have the policy ratified to him so as to enure to his benefit, we are obliged to recur to the general principles of the law of insurance so as to determine the point here in issue. The general rule of the common law is, that a *chose in action* cannot be assigned so that the assignee can sue in his own name, unless there is an express promise by the debtor, upon sufficient consideration, to pay the assignee. It has been held in this State that the *bona fide* assignment of a debt and notice constitute a sufficient consideration for a promise by the debtor to pay the assignee. *Moar* v. *Wright*, 1 Vt. 57, contains an elaborate opinion of Judge ROYCE on this point. It has since been followed in this State. 7 Vt. 197; 11 Vt. 82. See also, 18 Maine, 122; 24 id. 484; 4 N. H. 69; 4 Cow. 13; 3 Hill, 88; 9 Wend. 317. In *Mowry* v. *Todd*, 12 Mass. 283, PARKER, C.J., says: 'Whatever may be the effect of handing over a written contract to a party to whom it is intended to be transferred, without a recognition of the transfer by the person bound by the contract, and a promise to pay to the holder, we are satisfied that, with such recognition and promise, the assignment is sufficient, without the name of the assignor. It amounts to the substitution of one creditor for another, by the consent of the two creditors and the debtor; and an action may be maintained by the assignee in his own name, founded on the assignment and the express promise to pay.' In England, it has been held that, to make the consideration sufficient, there must be something more than the assignment of the debt, such as release of another's liability or forbearance. 4 B. & C. 163 and 166; 8 B. & C. 402, 395.

In applying this general rule to the law of insurance, Mr. PHILLIPS, in his Treatise on Insurance, pp. 61 and 62, says: 'If the underwriter has agreed to account and make payment to an assignee, the latter may commence proceedings in his own name, where nothing remains to be done on the part of the assignor, and all his interest in the contract has ceased; and, if the assignment, taken in connection with the policy, plainly transfers the assured's whole interest, the underwriter's *assent to it is evidently equivalent to his agreement to be directly answerable to the assignee.* In such case, the suit may be in the assignee's name, and he becomes, to all intents and purposes, the substituted party to the contract.' The 8 Mass. 515 seems to recognize the rule as thus expressed. The correctness of the rule is indisputable so far as it is founded on an express promise by the insurer to pay. Nor does it seem an unreasonable conclusion, that the assent of the insurer to the assignment and continuing validity of the policy, and to the alienation of the property where alienation avoids the policy, should be held equivalent to an express promise, since, without such consent, the policy would be void. The assent of the insurer in such cases is nothing, unless it amounts to an express promise, for he knows that assent or agreement with one who has parted with all his insurable interest in the property insured would be null—a mere gaming policy. We think the rule expressed by Mr. PHILLIPS is founded upon good sense and the fair analogies of the law. The case of *Bodle* v. *The Chenango Co. Ins. Co.*, 2 Comst. 53, has been cited to show that no action at law will lie. That was a bill in equity, and the court of appeals held that it was well brought, and that the orators had no remedy at law. There, Jona Bodle sold to James Bodle an undivided interest in the goods insured, and the insurance company agreed that the policy should remain good to Jona Bodle on the store for six hundred dollars, and to Jona and James for fourteen hundred dollars on their goods. The charter of the company had the usual provision that the grantee having the policy assigned to him might, on application, have the same ratified so that he should be substituted for the original assured.

The case seems to have been considered only in the one view, whether the orators had complied with the provisions of the charter so that they might sue at law; and the court held that there was no assignment of the policy or any part

policy prohibiting "a transfer or change of title in the property insured." [1]

Recovery in such cases.

SEC. 336. When a sale by one partner to another does not invalidate the policy, the weight of authority seems to support the doctrine that a

of it by James to Jona, so as to enable them to sue as assignees under the charter. If the suit had been by James and Jona Bodle, on the express promise to pay the $1,400 to them, and had set forth their application to have the policy continued and ratified to them, and the agreement of the company to do so, and the entry of Jona Bodle's name as a member, we think a sufficient consideration and a valid contract would have been shown so as to have sustained the action at law. But this view of the case does not seem to have been presented. In the case at bar, Wood, by the decease of Johnson, became the legal assignee of the policy, and had the sole care and disposition of the property insured. He purchased the beneficial interest which Johnson's estate had in the goods, and thus became the legal owner of both the goods and the policy. Johnson's estate had nothing in either. Being thus the legal assignee of the policy and vendee of Johnson's interest in the goods, he applied to the general agent of the company to ratify and continue the policy to him alone, and for his sole goods, during the period for which the policy by its terms was to continue. The agent did expressly agree to this proposition. If he had authority to so agree, he thereby bound the company. But whether he had or had not we do not consider material, for the case states that the directors, with notice of the death of Johnson and that the plaintiff was continuing the business, assented to this agreement, and treated the policy as so continuing. The agent had authority to receive the proposal of the plaintiff, and if not authorized to accept it, it was his duty to communicate with the directors. As the plaintiff had no communication with the principals, but did the whole business through the agent, he could not be expected to have proof of an express assent by them. If they treated the agreement he had expressly made with the agent as valid, and acted upon it for more than two years and up to the time of the loss, we think such conduct a sufficient ratification of the agreement, and fully sufficient to support and confirm it, although no direct and express language of affirmance is shown. Circumstantial evidence, which establishes such assent to the agreement has all the force of a positive agreement in words. Assent that the policy should continue in force for Wood's sole benefit, excludes all idea of its continuance for the benefit of Wood & Johnson. Johnson being dead, and the policy and the goods being vested in Wood, an assent that the policy should continue in force for his sole benefit may be deemed equivalent to an express promise to pay him the insurance money in case of loss. Indeed this may be considered not so much an assignment of a *chose in action* as a ratification of the policy, upon sufficient consideration by the insurer to the plaintiff as the party insured; the plaintiff thereafter holding the policy not by assignment, but as a party substituted by contract, upon sufficient consideration, for the original party. It was not necessary that the substitution should be pursuant to the provisions of the twelfth section, for that applied only to buildings, and not to the alienation of goods. The agreement of the plaintiff to remain liable on the premium note was a sufficient consideration. It is objected also by the defendants, that such a substitution or assignment cannot be by parol, but must be in writing. Then there is nothing in the charter, by-laws, or policy, requiring the assent of the company to such substitution to be in writing. It is well settled that the promise to assume a *chose in action*, made by the debtor to the assignee, enabling the latter to sue in his own name, need not be in writing. 8 B. & C. 842; Chitty on Cont. 532, and notes. This cannot be deemed the creation of a new contract of insurance by parol evidence, but only the ratification and confirmation of an existing policy to a new party having an interest in the subject-matter of the insurance. Though such confirmations are by many insurance companies required by charter or by-laws to be in writing, yet it is obvious that in the absence of any statute requiring such act to be done only by writing, parol evidence that it has been done and acted upon is admissible. *Goodall* v. *Ins. Co.*, 38 N. H. 169; *Perch* v. *Ins. Co.*, 22 Conn. 575."

[1] *Keeney* v. *Home Ins. Co.*, 3 T. & C. (N. Y.) 478.

recovery may be had for the full amount of the insurance, and that the purchasing partner is not restricted to a recovery to the extent of his interest at the time when the insurance was made.[1]

Special provisions, and effect of.

SEC. 337. Where a policy provided that, in case of any sale, transfer or change of title in the property insured, such insurance shall be void and cease, the death of the person to whom the policy was issued, renders the policy void and inoperative, as by that circumstance the title of the property changes, and vests in the heirs at law.[2]

Where a policy provided that upon sale or transfer of the property the policy shall become void, but at the same time provides that if the policy is assigned to the grantee, he may have the same ratified and confirmed to him, etc., upon application to the directors, and *with their consent*, any time within thirty days, next after such alienation, etc., and the policy was so assigned, but before it was received by the company, and before the thirty days had elapsed, the property was destroyed by fire, and the directors refused to ratify, etc. It was held that the policy was operative during the entire thirty days, and that the company was liable to the grantee to the same extent that it would have been liable to the grantor.[3]

When the policy covers both real and personal estate, as a building and machinery, a provision, that in case of a sale or transfer without the assent of the company, the policy shall be void, relates merely to the realty, and a sale of the machinery does not avoid the policy. So held, in a case where a brewery and the machinery was covered by the policy, a sale of the boilers, vats, etc., covered by the policy, was held not to affect the validity of the policy so far as it covered the realty. The rule may be said to be, in such cases, that where the property is separately insured, although embraced in one policy, the sale of one piece of property will not avoid the policy as to the other.[4]

---

[1] *Hoffman* v. *Ætna Ins. Co., ante; West* v. *Citizens' Ins. Co., ante.*

[2] *Lappin* v. *Charter Oak Ins. Co.,* 58 Barb. (N. Y.) 325.

[3] *Boynton* v. *Farmers' etc., Ins. Co.,* 43 Vt. 256.

[4] *Com. Ins. Co.* v. *Spanknable,* 52 Ill. 53 ; *Manley* v. *Ins. Co.,* 1 Lans. (N. Y,) 20.

CHAPTER X.

Assignment of policy.

SEC. 337. As has previously been stated, a policy of fire insurance is personal, and cannot be assigned so as to enable an assignee to maintain an action thereon, unless the *consent* of the insurer is had to such transfer or assignment,[1] unless the policy on its face is made to

---

[1] *Loring* v. *Manufacturers' Ins. Co.*, 8 Gray (Mass.) 28 ; *Carroll* v. *Boston Marine Ins. Co.*, 8 Mass. 515; *Simreal* v. *Dubuque, etc., Ins. Co.*, 18 Iowa, 319 ; *Columbian Ins. Co.* v. *Lawrence*, 2 Pet. (U. S.) 25 ; *Ætna Ins. Co.* v. *Tyler*, 16 Wend. (N. Y.) 385. In *Fogg* v. *Middlesex, etc., Ins. Co.*, 10 Cush. (Mass.) 327; 3 Ben. F. I. C. 414, SHAW, C.J., in commenting upon the questions involved in an assignment of insurance policies, pertinently said : "This action is brought by the assignees of a policy of insurance against fire, for $3,000, on a stock of goods in a store at Cambridgeport, originally made to Daniel Leland and James Luke, Jr. By the original act of incorporation, March, 1826, this company was authorized to make insurance on real estate only; but by an additional act, in March, 1828, they were empowered to insure all kinds of personal property, in the same way and manner they were empowered to insure the kinds of property in said act mentioned This act. we suppose, extends to all the provisions of the charter, by-laws, and regulations of the company, made in regard to insurance on buildings and real estate, so far as applicable to insurance on personal property. The plaintiffs sue as assignees, and if they can recover at all, it must be in that capacity, and upon that title. As a policy of insurance is not a negotiable instrument, it cannot be legally transferred so as to enable the assignee to maintain a suit in his own name, without the consent of the other party. But in general, at the common-law, where one party assigns all his right and interest in the contract, and the assignee gives notice to the other party to the contract, and he agrees to it, this constitutes a new contract between one of the original parties and the assignee of the other, the terms of which are regulated and fixed by those of the original contract. This rule applies to policies as well as other contracts, and it is often convenient and desirable to apply it ; and there are two cases where this application frequently happens. The first is, when the insured property is alienated or sold by the assured. After such

cover the interest of any person who may own or have an interest in the property at the time of loss, as where the policy is "for the benefit

sale, if nothing more is done—no surrender or change of the policy—and the goods should be burnt, nobody could recover on the policy; not the original assured, for he has sustained no loss; the property was not his, and the loss of it was not his loss; not the purchaser, because he had no contract with the com_ pany. And although, in popular language, the goods are said to be insured against loss by fire, yet, in legal effect, the original assured obtains a guaranty by the contract that he shall sustain no damage by their destruction by fire. But in case of such sale or alienation of the insured property, the original assured having no longer any interest in the policy, except to claim a return of premium, if he will assign his policy, or his contract of insurance to such purchaser, and the company assent to it, here is a new and original contract, embracing all the ele_ ments of a contract of insurance between the assignee and the insurers. The property having become the purchaser's, is at his risk, and if burnt, it is his loss and he has a good original contract, upon a valid consideration, to guarantee him against such loss. Accordingly, provision is made in the charter and by-laws, and also by the terms of the policy, for an assignment of the con_ tract; the company returns no part of the premium, but the assignee has the benefit of it, upon such terms as he and his assignor may determine; the assignment is indorsed on the policy, and presented to the president of the com_ pany, who ordinarily is authorized to give the assent of the company to the assignment; the old deposit note is surrendered, and a new deposit note is given by the assignee. In the regulations of this company in a circular of instruction to agents, a form is given for such transfer, notifying the sale of the property, naming the purchaser, and assigning to such purchaser, his executors, etc., the policy of insurance, and in case of loss, directing the amount to be paid to the said purchaser, his heirs, etc. Upon such assignment perfected, there is an entire change in the contract, in the party contracted with, in the insurable inter- est in the property at risk, and it becomes an insurance on the property of the assignee, and ceases to be a contract of insurance of the property of the assignor.

But there is another species of assignment, or transfer it may be called, in the nature of an assignment of *a chose in action;* it is this: 'In case of loss, pay the amount to A. B.' It is a contingent order or assignment of the money should the event happen upon which money will become due on the contract. If the insurer assents to it, and the event happens, such assignee may maintain an action in his own name, because, upon notice of the assignment, the insurer has agreed to pay the assignee instead of the assignor. *Mowry* v. *Todd*, 12 Mass. 281. But the original contract remains; the assignment and assent to it form a new and deriva- tive contract out of the original. But the contract remains as a contract of guar- antee to the original assured; he must have an insurable interest in the property, and the property must be his at the time of the loss. The assignee has no insur- able interest, *prima facie.* in the property burnt, and does not recover as the party insured, but as the assignee of a party who has an insurable interest and a right to recover, which right he has transferred to the assignee, with the consent of the insurers.

The plaintiffs, to recover in the present case, must prove themselves assignees of the contract, because they prove an alienation of the property, and a sale to themselves, long before the fire, so that all insurable interest in the orignal assured had ceased, and no loss was sustained by them by the fire, payable to anybody. The plaintiffs having acquired the property, so that it was at their risk, the question is, whether they have proved such an assignment of the contract as to bring themselves within the provisions of the charter and by-laws, as assignees, holding in all respects the rights of the original assured.

In order to prove their title as assignees, the plaintiffs offered the original policy, made in 1845, to Leland and Luke, Jr., the subsequent transfer of Daniel Leland, Jr., who had become the assignee of the policy, and the sole owner of the stock; and a sale in March, 1847, of the whole stock to the plaintiffs. There are several indorsements on the policy, but none affecting the present case, until the one said to have been made and indorsed April 1, 1848, in the words following: 'For value received, pay the within, in case of loss, to Fogg and Hearsey.' By the

of whom it may concern,"[1] or is made transferable by statute.[2] But, although the policy is conditioned to be void in case of transfer or

---

twelfth section of the act of incorporation, the 'grantee or alienee of the property insured, having the policy assigned,' may have the same ratified, etc., to his own proper benefit, on application to the directors, and with their consent, within thirty days next after such alienation, on giving proper security, etc. Here it is manifest that no assignment to the plaintiff of any kind was made till more than a year after the time of the sale of the stock. But if the directors had been notified of such sale and alienation of the stock insured, and had been informed that a full and complete transfer of the contract, and all interests in it, had been made, although at a time more than thirty days after the sale, and had then expressed their full assent to it, it might be a waiver of the mere point of time. Waiving that point, therefore, the question is, whether the indorsement in question was an assigment of the policy, and was so understood and assented to by the company. It is in few and brief terms, and *prima facie* we should be inclined to think that it was not an assignment of the contract, but only of a right to the money in case of loss. But it was strongly urged by the plaintiffs that it was intended by one party as a transfer and assignment of the entire policy, and was so understood by the other, and that the circumstances which preceded, attended, and followed it would be sufficient to show that it was so intended and understood. When words are doubtful, it is competent for parties to go into proof of the relation in which the parties stood to each other, the acts mutually done by them, and generally the surrounding circumstances, in order the better to understand the meaning of the language used by them, and thus ascertain their intent; and under this rule the evidence was admitted. But we think the ruling was sufficiently favorable to the plaintiffs, in permitting them thus to go into evidence *aliunde*, to explain the terms of the transfer.

The plaintiffs, in order to satisfy the court and jury that their circumstances were such as usually attend a full assignment of the contract, were permitted to prove if they could, 1. That there was an actual alienation of property by the assignee of the original assured to the plaintiffs. 2. That this fact was known to the president when he gave the assent of the directors to the transfer as it was actually made and presented to the company. 3. That the plaintiffs, as assignees, filed their own deposit note in place of the deposit note originally given by the assured. 4. That this fact was known to the president and secretary of the company when they gave the assent of the company in behalf of the directors. There was some evidence tending to show that a new deposit was made by the assignees, and placed in the hands of Pond, now deceased, who had been the agent of the company for receiving proposals, through which this policy was originally made; but the evidence failed to show that he had any authority to receive deposit notes on the assignment of a policy, and the evidence was very strong that no such note was deposited with the then treasurer, or any resident agent of the company by Pond, or otherwise. We think, therefore, that the jury were rightly instructed that if such a note had been left with Pond, but he never transmitted it to the company, or notified the proper officers of the company of his having it, it could not be considered proof that the plaintiffs had complied with that requisition of the law which requires a new deposit note before the assignment is complete. Again, as to the knowledge of the president at the time he assented to the assignment as made to pay to the assignees in case of loss. The extent of a simple assent to a statement or proposition must depend on the terms of such proposition. If the most natural construction of the terms of this assignment was, that it was the assignment of a right to the assignees to recover the money in case of loss, which, but for such assignment, would be due to the origi-

---

[1] *Rogers* v. *The Howard Ins. Co.*, 6 Paige Ch. (N. Y.) 583; *Lawrence* v. *Sebor*, 2 Caines (N. Y.) 203; *Seamans* v. *Loring*, 1 Mason (U. S.) 127; *Augusta, etc., Ins. Co.* v. *Abbott*, 12 Md. 348; *Ballard* v. *Merchants' Ins. Co.*, 9 La. 258; *Bell* v. *Western M. & F. Ins. Co.*, 5 Rob. (La.) 423; *Forgay* v. *Atlantic, etc., Ins. Co.*, 2 Rob. (N. Y.) 79; *Watson* v. *Swan*, 11 C. B. (U. S.) 756.

[2] *N. Y. Life Ins. Co.* v. *Flack*, 3 Md. 341.

assignment, the company may waive the breach, even after loss, and a recognition of the claim by adjusting the loss with the assignee is such a waiver of the breach, and an assent to the transfer, as will enable the assignee to sue for and recover the loss, and hold the funds resulting therefrom against either the assignor or his creditors.[1] An assignment of a policy as collateral security vests an equitable interest in the assignee, which will be enforced against the creditors of the assured,[2] and, generally, it may be said that, in equity, an assignment of a policy will be made to inure to the benefit of the assignee, *if there is no violation of any condition in the policy by such assignment*,[3] and may be enforced by the assignee, *in the name of assured*, either at law or in equity.[4] But the assured may plead any defense, either to defeat the action or reduce the recovery, that could be set up if such assignment had not been made, except payment, after notice of assignment.[5] Where the policy prohibits an assignment, an assignment without the insurer's consent invalidates it,[6] but, in the absence of such a condition, the validity of the policy is not affected thereby, but still remains operative as to the assured;[7] nor does an assignment *after* a loss has transpired invalidate it. In such case, the insurer becomes

---

nal assured, then the conclusion would be, that they assented to that proposal. But if the plaintiffs would show that the assured had at the time sold their property to the assignees, and that the assignees had duly given a new deposit note, in order to draw the conclusion that the officers of the company knew and understood that this was an assignment of the contract, and assented to it with that understanding, the burden of proof was upon them to show that these officers had that knowledge. But Brooks and Shattuck both testified that they never knew or heard of the sale and transfer of the stock by Leland, Jr., to the plaintiffs, until the spring of 1849, which was long after their assent to the transfer; and when they heard of it, they gave notice to the plaintiffs that there was no deposit note given by them, and that the policy was void unless such note was given. These were the principal points to which the instructions of the court referred, and we think they were correct and were adapted to the state of the evidence."

[1] *Ins· Co.* v. *Trask*, 8 Phila. (Penn.) 32. So, where an assignment was made, and the agent of the insurers *knowing* the fact, renewed it, it was held a waiver of the breach and a sufficient assent to the assignment, even though knowledge thereof only came to the agent when the renewal was made. *Bilson* v. *Manuf. Ins. Co.*, 7 Am. Law Reg. 661 (U. S. C. C.), and, although the assured has parted with all his interest in the property insured to the assignee, the assignee may maintain an action against the insurer in the name of the assured for a loss occurring subsequent to the renewal.

[2] *Wakefield* v. *Martin*, 3 Mass. 558 ; *Lazarus* v. *Com. Ins. Co.*, 19 Pick. (Mass.) 81.

[3] *Carpenter* v. *Providence Ins. Co.*, 16 Pet. (U. S.) 502 ; *Traders' Ins. Co.* v. *Robert*, 9 Wend. (N. Y.) 404.

[4] *Carter* v. *U. S. Ins. Co.*, 1 John. Ch. (N. Y.) 463 ; *Jessel* v. *Williamsburgh Ins. Co.*, 3 Hill (N. Y.) 88 ; *Mann* v. *Herkimer, etc., Ins. Co.*, 4 id. 187.

[5] *Archer* v. *Merchants', etc., Ins. Co.*, 43 Mo. 434.

[6] *Smith* v. *Saratoga, etc., Ins. Co.*, 3 Hill (N. Y.) 508 ; *Ferru* v. *Oxford Ins. Co.*, 67 Penn. St. 373.

[7] *Earl* v. *Shaw*, 1 Johns. Cas. (N. Y.) 314.

absolutely a debtor to the assured for the amount of the actual loss, to the extent of the sum insured, and it may be transferred or assigned like any other debt. After a loss, the *delectus personæ* no longer becomes material,[1] and even though the policy prohibits such an assignment and provides that, if so assigned, the policy shall be void, it is held that such prohibition is void,[2] as the insurer cannot restrict the assignment of a debt. The reasons that induce the restrictive clause have no existence or application after the risk has ceased.[3] If, however, the *property* is sold *before* a loss, and the policy is assigned afterwards, it is inoperative, because *the assured must own the property at the time of loss*, or there is nothing at risk.[4] "These policies," said Lord Chancellor KING, in the case last referred to, " are not insurances of the specific things mentioned to be insured ; nor do such insurances attack on the realty, or in any manner go with the same, *as incident thereto*, by any conveyance or assignment, *but they are only special agreements with the persons insured against such loss or damage as they may sustain. The party insured must have a property at the time of the loss.* * * *These policies," said he further on in the course of his opinion, " are not in their nature assignable, nor is the interest in them ever intended to be transferable from one to another, without the express consent of the office.*"

The fact that a policy is " payable in case of loss " to A., does not make A. an assignee of the policy, so that, except in those States, where aided by statute, he can maintain an action upon the policy in his own name.[5]

---

[1] *Carter* v. *Humboldt Ins. Co.*, 12 Iowa, 287 ; *West Branch Ins. Co.* v. *Halfenstein*, 40 Penn. St. 289 ; *Brichta* v. *Lafayette Ins. Co.*, 2 Hall (N. Y.) 372.

[2] *West Branch Ins. Co.* v. *Halfenstein*, 40 Penn. St. 289 ; *Gait* v. *National Protection Ins. Co.*, 25 Barb. (N. Y.) 189 ; *Pennybaker* v. *Tomlinson*, 1 Tenn. Ch. 598 ; *Mershon* v. *National Ins. Co.*, 34 Iowa, 87 ; *Manley* v. *Ins. Co. of N. America*, 1 Lans. (N. Y.) 20 ; *Carroll* v. *Charter Oak Ins. Co.*, 1 Abb. Dec. (N. Y.) 316 ; *Courtney* v. *N. Y. City Ins. Co.*, 28 Barb. (N. Y.) 116 ; *Perry* v. *Merchants' Ins. Co.*, 25 Ala. 355 ; *Walters* v. *Washington Ins. Co.*, 1 Cole Cas. (N. Y.) 404 ; *Mellen* v. *Hamilton Ins. Co.*, 17 N. Y. 609. See contra, *Dey* v. *Poughkeepsie Ins. Co.*, 23 Barb. (N. Y.) 623 ; 4 Ben. F. I. C. 181. But the doctrine of this case was afterwards repudiated in *Courtney* v. *N. Y. City Ins. Co.*, ante, and in *Gait* v. *Ins. Co.*, ante, and is not recognized as of any validity as an authority in the New York courts. Indeed, the opinion is very loose, and cites no authorities to support it.

[3] *Brichta* v. *N. Y.*, etc., *Ins. Co.*, 2 Hall (N. Y.) 372 ; 1 Ben. F. I. C. 282.

[4] *Lynch* v. *Dalzell*, 3 B. & P. C. 431 ; 1 Ben. F. I. C. 1 ; *Sadlers' Co.* v. *Badcock*, 2 Atk. 554 ; 1 Ben. F. I. C. 7.

[5] *Hale* v. *Mechanics' Ins. Co.*, 6 Gray (Mass.) 169 ; 4 Ben. F. I. C. 59 ; *Fogg* v. *Middlesex*, etc., *Ins. Co.*, 10 Cush. (Mass.) 346 ; 3 Ben. F. I. C. 419 ; *Russ* v. *Waldo Ins. Co.*, 52 Me. 187. But see, *National Ins. Co.* v. *Crane*, 16 Md. 260, where it was held that such words written in the policy operated as an assignment.

'Attempt to assign does not defeat policy.

Sec. 338. A mere attempt to assign a policy which is not consummated, does not defeat it, and it still remains operative, unless the assured has parted with his interest in the property. Thus, where the assured wrote and signed an assignment upon the policy to A., and sent it to the insurers to obtain their consent thereto, which they refused, it was held that this was a mere attempt to assign, but not an assignment in fact that would defeat a recovery upon the policy by the assured himself.[1] The mere possession of the policy by a third person does not evidence an assignment. There must be an assignment *in fact*, or the rights of the assured or of an equitable assignee are not affected thereby.[2]

Assignment as collateral security.

Sec. 339. A mere prohibition against an *assignment* of a policy, does not prevent its being pledged as collateral security for a debt,[3] but if the policy prohibits the assignment, transfer or pledging of a policy, it cannot be used as collateral security; but the mere fact that a policy is deposited with a third person does not furnish even *prima facie* evidence that the policy was pledged, even though such person is acting as the assignee of the assured under a general assign. ent for the benefit of creditors, which includes all policies of insurance, as it will be presumed that the assured intended only to pass those policies that were susceptible of being passed under such an instrument.[4]

Assignment, what is.

Sec. 340. After loss, no particular form is necessary to constitute an assignment of the assured's interest, either in whole or in part. Any writing that directs the payment of a certain sum to the holder, operates as an assignment to that extent, as an order upon the insurers; and if, after notice thereof, they pay the whole sum to the assured, or a former assignee whose claim does not cover the whole sum, a recovery may be had against the insurer for the sum due under the order.[5] And the words, "loss, if any, payable to A.," operate as

---

[1] *Smith* v. *Monmouth Mut. F. Ins. Co.*, 50 Me. 96.

[2] *Wood* v. *Phœnix, etc., Ins. Co.*, 22 La. An. 617.

[3] *The People* v. *Beigler*, Hill & Den. N. Y. 133.

[4] *Lazarus* v. *Com. Ins. Co.*, 5 Pick. (Mass.) 76 ; *Edwards* v. *Martin*, L. R. 1, Eq. Cas. 121.

[5] *Hall* v. *Dorchester Mut. Ins. Co.*, 111 Mass. 53 ; *Norwood* v. *Guerdon*, 60 Ill. 253 ; *Chawne* v. *Baylis*, 31 Beav. 351 ; *Jones* v. *Consolidated, etc., Ass. Co.*, 26 Beav. 256.

an assignment to A. of the whole amount secured by the policy.[1] After a policy has been assigned, or after the insurers have been directed by the assured, in case of loss, to pay to a certain person the amount secured by the policy, or a part thereof, the assured cannot, if the assignment was upon a valid consideration, withdraw the same; but as long as the interest of the assignee remains, the insurer is bound to account to him under the assignment, although the assured subsequently assigned the policy to another person.[2] Thus, in the last case the assured, a clerk, robbed his employers of a considerable sum of money, and was prosecuted and convicted by them of the offense. He assigned certain fire policies to them as security for the amount stolen by him, and the insurers were notified of the assignment. Subsequently he executed another assignment to other parties. In proceedings in equity to settle the question as to who was entitled to the proceeds of the policies, it was held that the assignees, under the first assignment, were equitably entitled thereto.[3]

Merely leaving the policy in the custody of a third person to whom the assured is indebted, does not operate as an assignment to him, nor does he thereby acquire any right to the proceeds of the policy.[4]

Before a loss under a policy has transpired, the giving of an order upon the insurer to pay the loss, if any, to A., does not operate as an *assignment* of the policy within the meaning of a prohibition in the policy. The title to the policy is not thereby affected, but merely the fund that may become due thereunder.[5]

It has sometimes been stated by text writers, and apparently held by the courts, that a general assignment of all his property, made by the assured to an assignee for the benefit of his creditors, operates as an assignment of the policies covering the property assigned. But this is erroneous, and a general assignment of the assured's property, unless, by statute, upon making such assignment, he is discharged from his debts and is divested of all his title in the property, does not affect the validity of the policies covering the property, *and does not, even though the words, and " all policies of insurance," are used in the assignment, pass any policies except such as are susceptible of transfer.*[6]

---

[1] *National Ins. Co.* v. *Crane*, 16 Md. 260.

[2] *Chowne* v. *Baylis*, 31 Beav. 351.

[3] See *Dickinson* v. *Phillips*, 1 Barb. (N. Y.) 454.

[4] *Hitchcock* v. *N. W. Ins. Co.*, 26 N. Y. 68.

[5] *Russ* v. *Waldo Mut. Ins. Co.*, 52 Me. 187; *Succession of Risley*, 11 Rob. (La.) 298.

[6] *Lazarus* v. *Com. Ins. Co.*, 5 Pick. (Mass.) 76.

But where the assignment, by virtue of any statute, passes all the title of the assured in the property to the assignee, *and no interest remains in the assured*, the policies thereon are invalidated ; *not, however, because the assignment operates as an assignment of the policies, but because the assured has been divested of all interest in the property insured.*

Assignment invalidates, although property still remains in assured.

SEC. 341. The fact that the policy is assigned, contrary to the pro_ visions of the policy, invalidates it, *even though the property insured is not assigned.* The insurers are not bound to inquire whether the title to the property passes with the assignment of the policy. It is enough that the assured has violated the conditions of the policy, whether the assignee had any *interest* to sustain the assignment or not.[1]

Rights of assignee.

SEC. 342. By an assignment of the policy, with the consent of the insurer, the company is not regarded as yielding any of its rights as to the performance by the assured, of all the conditions of the policy, *and any violation by the assured of any of the conditions of the policy, is fatal to a recovery by the assignee.*[2] The same defenses may be made in an action brought by an assignee, as could be made if the action was brought by the assignor.[3]

---

[1] *Smith* v. *Saratoga, etc., Ins. Co.,* 1 Hill (N. Y.) 497.

[2] *Illinois Mut. Ins. Co.* v. *Fix,* 53 Ill. 151 ; *Birdseye* v. *City F. Ins. Co.,* 26 Conn. 165 ; *Eastman* v. *Carroll Co. Ins. Co.,* 45 Me. 307 ; *Mellen* v. *Hamilton Ins. Co.,* 17 N. Y. 609 ; *Grosvenor* v. *Atlantic F. Ins. Co.,* id. 391 ; *Archer* v. *Merchants', etc., Ins. Co.,* 43 Mo. 434 ; *Bowditch Ins. Co.* v. *Winslow,* 3 Gray (Mass.) 415 ; *Papke* v. *Resolute Ins. Co.,* 17 Wis. 378 ; *Loring* v, *Manufacturers' Ins. Co.,* 8 Gray (Mass.) 28 ; *Bergeson* v. *Builders' Ins. Co.,* 38 Cal. 541 ; *Home Mut. Ins. Co.* v. *Hauslin,* 60 Ill. 521 ; *State Mut. F. Ins. Co.* v. *Roberts,* 31 Penn. St. 438 ; *Merrill* v. *Farmers', etc., Ins. Co.,* 48 Me. 285 ; *Young* v. *Eagle Ins. Co.,* 14 Gray (Mass.) 150.

[3] *Hale* v. *Mechanics', etc., Ins. Co.,* 6 Gray (Mass.) 169 ; *Archer* v. *Merchants', etc., Ins. Co.,* 43 Mo. 434 ; *Bergeson* v. *Builders' Ins. Co.,* 38 Cal. 541 ; *Baltimore Ins. Co.* v. *McFadden,* 4 H. & J. (Md.) 31. See cases cited in the last note. In *Illinois, etc., Ins. Co.,* v. *Fix,* 53 Ill. 151 ; 5 Am. Rep. 38, it was held that the defendant might show that the assured set the building on fire. The court, through LAWRENCE, J., saying, after a careful review of the cases : "The consent of insurance companies to an assignment of the policy by a mortgagor to a mortgagee, should not be construed as imposing upon them, as a consequence of such mere naked assent, a liability which they never would intentionally assume, and against which they take all possible pains to guard themselves, and must guard themselves in order to preserve their solvency. The principle contended for by counsel for appellee, and laid down in the earlier New York cases is, that no act of the assignor done without the consent of the assignee, can invalidate the policy, so far as relates to the assignee. If this be true without limitation, then, as said by the New York court of appeals, a risk taken by a company at the lowest rates, because in the least hazardous class, might be changed, by the mortgagor remaining in possession, and without the concurrence of the mortgagee, to the class of extra-hazardous, and the liability of the company would remain the same. A detached dwelling-house might be converted into a powder magazine, or to some

A contrary doctrine has been held in some of the States, but it is now generally repudiated.[1]

---

other use which would prevent any sound insurance company from taking the risk on any terms, and still, under the rule claimed by appellee, the company would remain responsible. The mortgagor might go further, and not only convert his buildings to extra-hazardous uses, but absolutely set it on fire, with a view of defrauding the company, as the appellants offered to prove was done in the present case.

We cannot adopt a rule which would lead to such results. In analogy to the case of absolute sales by the assured, we should be much inclined to hold to the rule announced in 1 Selden, if it were possible to separate the interest of mortgagor and mortgagee. But it is not, for the mortgagor is not only interested in the payment of the mortgage, but, where he pays the premium, the fruits of the policy absolutely belong to him, subject to the lien of the mortgagee. Where there is an absolute sale, there is no difficulty in determining the measure of the assignee's rights and the company's liabilities, for he stands in the position of receiving a new policy as owner, and becomes responsible for any extra-hazardous uses to which the building may be applied, a responsibility he cannot evade on the ground that the building is not under his control. But where there is no sale, but the policy is merely assigned as security, we are obliged to hold, either that the company is bound, absolutely to the assignee, no matter how far the conditions of its contract may have been violated, which would be a very unreasonable ruling, or that there is such identity of interest in regard to both the property and the policy, that there can be no recovery, even for the use of the assignee, if the assignor fails to comply with the conditions.

The utmost that can be claimed for an assignee in such cases is, that he should stand in the same position as if he had taken out a new and independent policy to protect his own interest as mortgagee. But, admitting such claim, we have no rule to guide us. It is impossible for us to say what conditions the company would deem it necessary to insert in such a policy for its own protection. It is very certain it would stipulate that the hazard to the building should not be increased, and thus would compel the mortgagee to take upon himself the responsibility of the mortgagor's acts, from which he could not escape by saying that his rights should not be prejudiced by the acts of a third person. It would necessarily result, from the nature of the interest insured, that its owner might be damnified by the acts of the mortgagor in possession, although beyond his control. Whether a company would also stipulate, in such a policy, that neither the mortgagor nor the mortgagee should obtain further insurance, without its consent, we do not know, though it is evident such a stipulation would be a wise precaution.

The history of the *Robert case* in 9 Wend. singularly illustrates the injustice of attempting to base a judgment against an insurance company, in favor of the mortgagor, upon the equities of his assignee. In that case the judgment was rendered in favor of Robert, the mortgagor, for the use of Bolton, his assignee, on the ground that, though Robert had violated the policy, this could not prejudice Bolton. After the rendition of the judgment, and before its payment, Robert paid off the mortgage, and threatened the insurance company with an execution. The company moved the court for a perpetual stay, which was granted, the court holding, consistently with its former ruling, that Robert had no equitable rights under the policy. 9 Wend. 404, 474. From this order an appeal was taken to the court for the correction of errors, and that court held, as the original decision was unreversed, it was conclusive upon the rights of the parties, and as the mort-

[1] Holding that an assignment operated as a new contract with the assignee, see *Tillou* v. *Kingston, etc., Ins. Co.,* 5 N. Y. 405; *City F. Ins. Co.* v. *Mark,* 45 Ill. 382; *Charleston Ins. and Trust Co.* v. *Neve,* 2 McMull. (S. C.) 237; *Foster* v. *Equitable, etc., Ins. Co.,* 2 Gray (Mass.) 216; *Pollard* v. *Somerset, etc., Ins. Co.,* 12 Me. 221. Overruling the New York case, see *Grosvenor* v. *Atlantic F. Ins. Co.,* 17 N. Y. 391; the Massachusetts case, *Hale* v. *Mechanics' Mut. Ins. Co.,* 6 Gray (Mass.) 169. In Canada, it is held that the assignee may recover, notwithstanding the *laches* of the assured. *Burton* v. *Gore Dist. Ins. Co.,* 12 Grant Ch. 158; *Kreutz* v. *Niagara, etc., Ins. Co.,* 16 U. C. (C. P.) 131.

But, where the premises are sold and the policy is assigned, with the assent of the insurer, it is held that the policy becomes a contract with the assignee, and the *laches* of the assignor do not affect his rights.[1]

Equitable assignment.

SEC. 343. There may be an equitable assignment of a policy that binds the insurers *to pay the loss* to the assignee, when there is no valid, legal assignment, and, unless specially provided against, such an assignment does not operate as a breach of the prohibition against assignment; but, in such cases, the action must be in the name of the assured, and is subject to all defenses, as though no other person was interested in the fund;[2] but, in case of an equitable assignment, the insurer is bound to pay the judgment, or so much of it as is covered by the claim of the assignee, to him, and if the amount is paid to the assured, the insurer will be compelled to pay it again to the equitable assignee.[3]

Sale of property does not operate as assignment of the policy.

SEC. 344. The fact that the property is sold by the assured, as has previously been shown, does not confer upon the vendee the benefits of the policy, and this is the rule, whether the property is sold before[4]

---

gage had been paid, the benefit of the judgment reverted to Robert, the mortgagor. He thus received the full benefit of the policy, although he had forfeited all rights under it, and a judgment had been rendered in his favor only in consequence of the equities of his assignee. 17 Wend. 631.

It is, in our opinion, very clear, if we attempt to dispose of cases of this character on the theory that the assignment is to be treated as a new policy, issued directly to the mortgagee, for his exclusive benefit, and to adjust the rights of these parties in accordance with what we may suppose such a policy would contain, we shall be wandering in a labyrinth where there would be but one thing certain, and that is, that great injustice would be done these companies. We should practically be enforcing liabilities against them which they never intended to incur, and giving to the mortgagor the benefit of a policy in which he has forfeited all his rights.

We deem it safer and more just to say that, where a policy is assigned as collateral to a mortgage, though with the consent of the company, the assignee takes it subject to the conditions expressed upon tis face, or necessarily inhering in it, and that no recovery can be had merely in consequence of the equities of the assignee, if the assignor has lost the right to recover by violating the terms of the contract.

The evidence offered to show that the plaintiff set the building on fire should have been admitted, and the instruction asked for by defendants, in regard to the effect of a second insurance, should have been given."

[1]*N. E. Ins. Co.* v. *Wetmore,* 32 Ill. 221; *Foster* v. *Eq. Mut. Ins. Co.,* 2 Gray (Mass.) 216; SHAW, C.J., in *Fogg* v. *Middlesex, etc., Ins. Co.; ante.*

[2]*Rousset* v. *Ins. Co. of N. America,* 1 Binn. (Penn.) 429; *Gourdon* v. *Same,* 3 Yeates (Penn.) 327; *Baltimore Ins. Co.* v. *McFadden,* 4 H. & J. (Md.) 31.

[3]*Cromwell* v. *Brooklyn F. Ins. Co.,* 44 N. Y. 42.

[4]*Stout* v. *City F. Ins. Co.,* 12 Iowa, 371.

or *after* the loss,[1] or mortgaged,[2] or leased, or otherwise conveyed or transferred. The policy is personal, and not an incident of the property insured, and the transfer of the property does not necessarily defeat the claim of the assured under a policy, unless so specially provided, and, in the absence of such a condition, so long as he retains *any* interest therein *that is insurable*, the policy is operative to protect it.[3]

Pledging of policy avoids it, when.

SEC. 345. When it is provided that the assignment of a policy *or any interest therein* shall invalidate it, it is invalidated by any transfer, of *any* interest therein, legal or equitable, and cannot be pledged as collateral security for a debt, or for any purpose;[4] but, as has previously been stated, the mere fact that the policy is in the custody of a third person, does not, even *prima facie*, establish a pledge or transfer of the policy. The insurers, if they rely upon such a defense, must show that the policy was in fact pledged.[5]

Assignment to mortgagee.

SEC. 346. When a policy is assigned to a mortgagee, or when it is upon its face made payable to him in case of loss, the policy does not stand as a contract made with the mortgagee, and the mortgagee's right, of recovery, may be defeated by any breach of the conditions of the policy by the assured, whether such conditions are precedent or subsequent;[6] but, if there have been no breaches of conditions on the part of the assured, *after a loss*, the assured cannot defeat the rights of the mortgagee by a release of the claim against the insurers, nor by an assignment of it to another.[7] Nor can he defeat the claim or any part thereof by agreeing upon a sum as due under the policy, less than that which the insurers are legally liable to pay, unless the sum so agreed upon is sufficient to meet the claim of the mortgagee, nor can he defeat the mortgagee's claim, *or lessen it*, by a submission of the claim for loss to arbitration. In order to give validity to a settlement

---

[1] *Pierce* v. *Nashua Ins. Co.*, 50 N. H. 297; *Wheeling Ins. Co.* v. *Morrison*, 1 Leigh. (Va.) 354.

[2] *Prows* v. *Ohio Valley Ins. Co.*, 2 Cin. S. C. (Ohio) 14.

[3] *Sherman* v. *Niagara F. Ins. Co.*, 46 N. Y. 526; *Lazarus* v. *Com. Ins. Co.*, 5 Pick. (Mass.); see chap. 8 on Insurable Interest and chap. 7 on Alienation.

[4] *Ferree* v. *Oxford F. Ins. Co.*, 67 Penn. St. 373; *Lazarus* v. *Com. Ins. Co.*, 5 Pick. (Mass.) 76.

[5] *Lazarus* v. *Com. Ins. Co., ante; Ellis* v. *Krentinger*, 27 Mo. 211; *People* v. *Bigler*, Hill & D. (N. Y.) 133.

[6] *Ill. Mut. F. Ins. Co.* v. *Fix*, 53 Ill. 151.

[7] *Chowne* v. *Baylis*, 31 Beav. 351.

or arbitration, the consent of the mortgagee must be obtained.[1] The reason is evident. *After a loss*, the right of the mortgagee to have the amount secured by the policy, to the extent of his claim, and to the extent of the loss, becomes absolute, *and it is a claim against the insurers* which they have agreed to, and upon the happening of the loss *have become absolutely liable to pay to him*, and they are thereby estopped from doing anything with the assured, that will destroy or impair the claim. Of course, if the policy provides that the insurers may, if they elect to do so, rebuild the buildings destroyed, they may do so, *because this is a reservation in the contract itself*, but in the absence of such a provision in the policy, they would not have that right, even with the assent of the assured, as against the mortgagee or assignee of the policy, *because their liability to him was to pay in money*, which neither the assured or the insurer, or both, can defeat. But, in the case of a mortgagee, *where the debt secured by the mortgage is not due*, it would seem that the mortgagor may compel the expenditure of the proceeds of the policy to the re-instatement of the property destroyed.[2]

Assent to assignment. Waiver of breach.

SEC. 347. Although the policy provides that it shall be void unless assent to an assignment be expressed in writing upon the policy, yet it is well settled that a parol assent, or any act of the assured, or its duly authorized agent, that amounts to an assent or a waiver of the condition, will estop the insurer from setting up a breach of the condition in defense to an action upon the policy. As where an agent upon being informed of the assignment, assures the assured that it is all right,[3] or when a policy is renewed, the agent *knowing* that an assignment had been made,[4] or a consent written on a separate piece of paper and attached to the policy by a wafer.[5] So, where a policy upon its face is made payable to a person other than the assured, this is an assent to the assignment before the insurance is made and ratified by the insertion of the same in the contract itself.[6] So an assent given after a partial loss, as to that portion not covered by the loss, is

---

[1] *Brown* v. *Hartford F. Ins. Co.*, 5 R. I. 394; see mem. of case, 4 Ben. F. I. C. 299; also *Brown* v. *Roger Williams Ins. Co.*, 7 id. 301; mem. 4 Ben. F. I. C. 299.

[2] *Gordon* v. *Ware Savings Bank*, 115 Mass. 588.

[3] *Illinois Mut. Ins. Co.* v. *Stanton*, 2 Ins. L. J. 29 (Ill.).

[4] *Bilson* v. *Manufacturers' Ins. Co.*, 7 Am. Law. Reg. 661.

[5] *Penn. Ins. Co.* v. *Bowman*, 44 Penn. St. 89.

[6] *Aldrich* v. *Equitable Safety Ins. Co.*, 1 W. & M. (U. S.) 272; *Mershon* v. *National Ins. Co.*, 34 Iowa, 87; *Keeler* v. *Niagara F. Ins. Co.*, 16 Wis. 523.

treated as a full assent that will uphold an action.[1] But unless there is a waiver, the mode prescribed by the policy must be strictly followed.[2]

When a mortgagee procures insurance upon his mortgage interest, and subsequently becomes the purchaser of the premises at foreclosure sale, his policy is thereby avoided *by reason of the change of interest,* but if, *after the change of interest,* the insurer, by parol, *either by himself or by his agent, consents that the policy shall stand as a valid obligation,* the breach is waived, and the policy remains operative.[3] Thus, in the case last referred to, the plaintiff having a mortgage upon certain premises, applied to the defendant's agent for insurance thereon, disclosing the nature of his interest in the property. The policy was issued in form to the mortgagor, " loss, if any, payable to E. B. Pratt (plaintiff), as his interest may appear." The policy contained a condition against an assignment of the policy, and providing that it should be void in case of any change of title, *or of any change of interest,* or by the foreclosure of a mortgage, levy of execution, etc. Some time after the policy was issued, and while it was still in force, the plaintiff foreclosed his mortgage, and purchased the premises at their sale under such foreclosure proceedings. After obtaining his deed he gave notice to the defendant's agent, of the change of title and interest. The agent consented that the policy should stand as security, and stated that " the proper entries would be made in the books." No indorsement was made upon the policy, and the next night the premises were burned. The court held that the insurers were liable for the loss.[4]

---

[1] *Manley* v. *Ins. Co. of N. America,* 1 Lans. (N. Y.) 20.

[2] *Smith* v. *Saratoga, etc., Ins. Co.,* 3 Hill (N. Y.) 508.

[3] *Pratt* v. *N. Y. Central Ins. Co.,* 55 N. Y. 505.

[4] ANDREWS, J., in delivering the opinion of the court, said: " The question arises whether the parol consent of the company, after the title to the insured property vested in the plaintiff by the foreclosure, that the policy should continue in force for his benefit, confirmed it as a valid subsisting contract, notwithstanding the provision in the policy that upon a change of title to the property, by foreclosure or otherwise, the insurance should ' immediately cease.' I think that it cannot be held that the retention of the premium, paid on effecting the insurance, furnished a consideration for renewing and continuing the contract of insurance after it had been avoided by the act of the insured. The policy had attached, and the risk had been assumed by the defendant, liable to be terminated by the occurrence of certain events specified in the policy. If it was terminated pursuant to any condition in the policy, and without fault of the defendant, the whole premium was earned, and the insurer had a legal right to retain it, although the whole term fixed for the running of the policy had not elapsed. SHAW, Ch. J., *Felton* v. *Brooks,* 4 Cush. 207. It is not like the cases cited where the policy was void in its inception, and no risk had been incurred by the underwriter; nor is it the case of the modification of a contract, which at the time was

In the case of a mutual company where the charter provides the mode in which assent shall be given, assent must be procured in the mode provided, but if it is procured in any other mode, that is, if it is given by any other officer than the one designated, if it is entered in the company's books, or otherwise brought to the attention of the officer or officers authorized to assent to the transfer, it will be their duty to notify the assured of their dissent, or their silence will be taken as a ratification of the assent,[1] and it seems that, if the directors, or other officer empowered to give assent in such cases, has permitted another officer to act for him in this respect, the act of such person will be treated as the act of the proper officer.[2]

---

mutually obligatory. *Fish* v. *Cottenet*, 44 N. Y. 538; *Shearman* v. *The Niagara F. Ins. Co.*, 46 id. 526; 2 Phil. on Insurance, § 1819. But clauses of forfeiture and avoidance are for the benefit of the party in whose favor they are made, and he may assist upon them or not, at his election. 2 Am. Leadg. Cases, 306, and cases cited; *Clark* v. *Jones*, 1 Denio, 516. In many cases the party who could insist upon the forfeiture of a contract, and who could elect to abandon it, has an interest to waive the forfeiture, and treat the contract as subsisting, notwithstanding the failure of the other party. In this case, the defendant elected to continue the insurance in force for the benefit of the plaintiff, who had paid the premium, and for whose immediate benefit the policy was issued, and who was entitled to the insurance money in case of loss, and the company could not afterward, and after a loss had occurred, abandon its election, to the prejudice of the plaintiff. The plaintiff may have been, and upon the evidence it is probable that he was prevented from procuring other insurance, relying upon the assurance of the defendant that the policy should remain in force. It was the natural result of the defendant's act, and I am of opinion that the case is within the reason upon which the doctrine of equitable estoppel is founded, and that the defendant is precluded from averring the want of consideration for the agreement to continue the policy, or from insisting upon the previous forfeiture. *Frost* v. *Saratoga Mut. Ins. Co.*, 5 Den. 154, and cases cited; *Wolfe* v. *Security F. Ins. Co.*, 39 N. Y. 52; *Atlantic Ins. Co.* v. *Goodall*, 35 N. H. 328."

[1] *N. E. Ins. Co.* v. *De Wolfe*, 8 Pick. (Mass.) 56; *Durar* v. *Hudson, etc., Ins. Co.*, 24 N. J. 171.

[2] *Phillips* v. *Ins. Co.*, 10 Cush. (Mass.) 350; *Tapping* v. *Bickford*, 4 Allen (Mass.) 120.

CHAPTER XI.

OTHER INSURANCE—DOUBLE INSURANCE.

Other void insurance.

SEC. 348. A condition that, if other insurance shall be obtained without the consent of the company, the policy shall be void, only relates to other *valid* insurance, and the policy is not avoided by the procurement of other policies that, for any cause, are invalid.[1] But the entire invalidity of such other insurance must be established. The other policy or policies *must, at the time of the loss, have been inoperative, so that no action could be maintained to enforce them*.[2] It is not necessary that they should have been absolutely void; it is sufficient if they were voidable. " There is an intrinsic absurdity," says BELL,

---

[1] *Thomas v. Builders' Ins. Co.*, 119 Mass. 121; *Jackson v. Mass. Mut. F. Ins. Co.*, 28 Pick. (Mass.) 418; *Hardy v. Union Ins. Co.*, 4 Allen (Mass.) 217; *Clark v. N. E. Mut. F. Ins. Co.*, 6 Cush. (Mass.) 342; *Kimball v. Howard Ins. Co.*, 8 Gray (Mass.) 33; *Stacey v. Franklin F. Ins. Co.*, 2 W. & S. (Penn.) 506; *Gee v. Cheshire Co. Mut. Ins. Co.*, 55 N. H. 265; 20 Am. Rep. 170; *Obermeyer v. Globe Mut. Ins. Co.*, 43 Mo. 573; *Hubbard v. Hartford F. Ins. Co.*, 33 Iowa, 325; 11 Am. Rep. 125; *Forbes v. Agawam Ins. Co.*, 9 Cush. (Mass.) 470; *Philbrook v. N. E. Mut. F. Ins. Co.*, 37 Me. 187; *Gale v. Belknap*, 41 N. H. 170; *N. Y. Central Ins. Co. v. Watson*, 23 Mich. 486; *Lindley v. Union Ins. Co.*, 65 Me. 368; 20 Am. Rep. 701; *Knight v. Eureka Ins. Co.*, 26 Ohio St. 664. A policy conditioned to be void, "if any prior or subsequent insurance is made without the consent of the company indorsed thereon." is not defeated by the taking of a foreign policy, void for want of compliance with statutory regulations. *Rising, etc., Ins. Co. v. Slaughter*, 20 Ind. 520; *Philbrook v. N. E. Mut. F. Ins. Co.*, 37 Me. 137; *Lochlan v. Ætna Ins. Co.*, 4 Allen (N. B.) 173; *Allison v. Phœnix Ins. Co.*, 3 Dill (U. S. C. C.) 480. See contra, *Lackey v. Georgia, etc., Ins. Co.*, 42 Ga. 456; *Bigler v. N. Y. Central Ins. Co.*, 22 N. Y. 402; *David v. Hartford Ins. Co.*, 13 Iowa, 69; *Carpenter v. Providence Ins. Co.*, 4 How. (U. S.) 185; *Ramsay Woolen Cloth Co. v. Mut. Ins. Co.*, 11 Upper Canada (Q. B.) 516. An *interim* receipt for insurance is other insurance. *Hutton v. Beacon Ins. Co.*, 16 U. C. (Q. B.) 316. So the *renewal* of prior insurance, when the assured, at the time of obtaining additional insurance, informed the agent it *would not* be renewed. *Deitz v. Mound City Ins. Co.*, 38 Mo. 85. But the renewal of a prior outstanding policy is not. *Pitney v. Glens Falls Ins. Co.*, 65 N. Y. 1. But the procurement of new insurance to the same amount in other companies, in place of previous policies, is other insurance. *Conway Tool Co. v. Hud. R. Ins. Co.*, 12 Cush. (Mass.) 144. So other insurance, obtained without the knowledge or consent of the assured, invalidates a prior policy if the assured subsequently adopts the insurance, and this may be done by accepting the payment of a loss under it. *Dafoe v. Johnstown, etc., Ins. Co.*, 7 U. C. (C. P.) 55. But that cannot be regarded as *other* insurance that is procured by a third person, and to which the assured *has never assented*. *Burton v. Gore Dist., etc., Ins. Co.*, 14 U. C. (Q. B.) 342. Mere notice to the insurer, or his agent, of an *intention* to procure other insurance, is not enough to cause a breach of the condition. To have that effect, *it must be notice of insurance already obtained*. *Healey v. Imperial Ins. Co.*, 5 Nov. 268, Although, if the insurer, upon such notice being given, *assents to the procurement of other insurance*, it is a waiver of notice, although a contrary rule prevails in Massachusetts. *Barrett v. Un. Mut. F. Ins. Co.*, 7 Cush. (Mass.) 175; *Fox v. Phœnix Ins. Co.*, 52 Me. 333; *Mitchell v. Lycoming Ins. Co.*, 51 Penn. St. 402; *Allison v. Phœnix Ins. Co.*, Dil. (U. S. C. C.) 480. When a prior policy exists upon the property containing a condition against other insurance, and a subsequent policy is procured without notice, the first policy is thereby invalidated, and the second stands. *Duclos v. Citizens', etc., Ins. Co.*, 23 La. An. 332.

[2] *Mitchell v. Lycoming Mut. Ins. Co.*, 51 Penn. St. 402; *Jackson v. Mass. F. Ins. Co.*, 23 Pick. (Mass.) 418; *Clark v. N. E. Mut. F. Ins. Co.*, 6 Cush. (Mass.) 542; *Hardy v. Union Ins. Co.*, 4 Allen (Mass.) 217. If the policy is *prima facie* valid, the assured must show its invalidity. *Schenck v. Mercer Co. Ins. Co.*, 24 N. J. L. 447; *Bigler v. N. Y. Cent. Ins. Co.*, 20 Barb. (N. Y.) 635. But if invalid on its face, it does not avoid the other policies. *Schenck v. Mercer Co. Ins. Co., ante.*

J.,[1] "in holding that to be an insurance by which another is bound to make good another's loss, *only in case he pleases to do it.*" Therefore, if the policies at the time of the loss were only voidable by reason of the breach of some condition, and the insurer *had waived* the breach, either expressly or impliedly, *before the loss,* the policies are operative, and constitute "other insurance" within the meaning of the terms.[2]

In an Iowa case,[3] the plaintiff applied to defendant's agent for insurance on his property, on the 18th of the month, and it was agreed that the agent should issue and send to A. the policy on that day. The policy was, in fact, issued on and bore the date of that day, but was not delivered to A. nor the premium paid until the 22d of the month. The policy contained a condition that it should be void in case of prior or subsequent insurance. On the 21st of the same month A. applied to the agent of the P. company for insurance on the same property, and the terms were agreed on and the premium paid. The agent of the P. company, having no blanks for policies, agreed to send a policy to A., and gave him a receipt, specifying the property to be insured. The usual policies of the P. company contained a condition of avoidance in case of other insurance. Neither company was informed of the transaction with the other. On the 26th of the month the insured property was burned. As soon as the P. company was informed of the policy issued by defendant, it treated its contract with A. as void. In an action on the policy issued by defendant, it was held that the policy became operative and binding from the day it was issued, though not delivered, and was, therefore, prior to the P. company's contract; that the effect of the receipt given by the agent of the P. company was to bind the company the same as if a policy, with the ordinary conditions, had been issued; that the contract with the P. company being void by reason of the prior insurance, and being so treated by the company, did not amount to a breach of the condition in defendant's policy against subsequent insurance.[4]

---

[1] *Gale* v. *Belknap Co. Ins. Co.*, 41 N. H. 170; *Lindley* v. *Union Ins. Co.*, 65 Me. 368; *Lovett* v. *United States*, 9 Ct. of Claims (U. S.) 147.

[2] *Mitchell* v. *Lycoming Ins. Co.*, 51 Penn: St. 402.

[3] *Hubbard* v. *Hartford F. Ins. Co.*, 33 Iowa, 325; 11 Am. Rep. 125.

[4] BECK, J., in passing upon the question, said: "We have the case of two policies given at different dates covering the same property, each having a condition against other insurance, both prior and subsequent, and providing that a breach thereof shall avoid the respective instruments. The question for us to determine is which, if either, of these instruments is valid, and which is avoided by the operation of a breach of the condition. It will be remembered that a breach of the condition does not absolutely render void and of no effect the policy; it simply

SEC. 349. It is held that the fact that the policy *is invalid* of itself, prevents the forfeiture, and that the fact that the insurer under such invalid

---

renders it voidable—its binding force and effect being subject to be defeated at
the option of the company issuing the instruments. If no objection be made by
the company on account of the breach of the condition, the policy may be enforced
as though no forfeiture had ever happened. The act of the company, whereby
it is shown that the instrument is treated as avoided, must be shown in order to
defeat recovery thereon. If no such act or objection on the part of the company
be shown, the contract will be considered binding. It is not necessary here to
state what will amount to an act avoiding the contract, or when it must be done,
further than to observe that it must appear that the underwriter relied upon the
breach of the condition to defeat the contract. Of course, the company issuing
the subsequent policy could not rely upon the breach of the condition, in order
to avoid the instrument, until knowledge thereof was acquired, and its acts treating the policy as avoided would be sufficient, if shown to have been done after
such knowledge. The same principles will apply to the prior policy. It was
not absolutely void, on account of the subsequent insurance, but was voidable
only. It was a binding instrument when executed, and would so continue until
some act done by defendant intended to avoid it, on account of the breach of the
condition against the subsequent insurance. But it could not be avoided on
account of the Phœnix policy, unless that instrument itself was valid. If it so
happened that, when the action was brought on defendant's policy, or even at
the trial, it was made to appear that the Phœnix policy could not be enforced,
was avoided on account of the breach of a condition therein, it is obvious that the
existence of that instrument shown to be inoperative would not constitute a breach
of the condition in defendant's policy against subsequent insurance. That condition is against actual insurance to be subsequently made. The Phœnix policy
created no insurance; it was avoided by the act of the company, and therefore
did not constitute a breach of defendant's policy. The general principle of law
upon this point may be stated as follows: In order to avoid a policy on account
of a subsequent insurance against an express condition therein, it must appear
that such subsequent insurance is valid, and that the policy upon which it is
made is capable of being enforced. If it cannot be enforced, it is no breach of
the prior policy. This principle is substantially embodied in the fourteenth
instruction given by the court to the jury. The instruction could have been more
properly worded, but its import is quite clear, and to the effect that, if the Phœnix company treated its policy as avoided, after notice of the existence of defendant's policy, it constituted no such subsequent insurance as would invalidate the
policy in suit. Our conclusion upon this branch of the case is not without support of the authorities. The following cases may be cited as sustaining the principles above stated: *Jackson* v. *Mass. Mut. Ins. Co.*, 23 Pick. (Mass.) 418; *Clark*
v. *New England Ins. Co.*, 6 Cush. (Mass.) 343; *Gale* v. *Belknap Ins. Co.*, 41 N.
H. 170; *Stacy* v. *Franklin Ins. Co.*, 2 W. & S. (Penn.) 506; *Philbrook* v. *New
England Mut. Ins. Co.*, 37 Me. 137; *Schenck* v. *Mercer Co. Mut. Ins Co.*, 4 Zabr.
(N. J.) 447; *Jackson* v. *Farmers' Ins. Co.*, 5 Gray (Mass.) 52.
The doctrine which we have above announced does not go to the full extent of
some of the cases just cited. It is held in *Philbrook* v. *The New England Mut.
Ins. Co.*, *supra*, that the prior policy is valid, even though the subsequent policy
is not avoided by the underwriter issuing it, but the loss thereon is paid; and,
in others of these cases, the rule is not expressly based upon the fact that the subsequent policy was treated by the underwriter issuing it as avoided. The doctrine which we recognize here is based upon the fact that the subsequent policy
was treated and considered as avoided by the company issuing it as soon as it
had notice of the prior insurance. In our view, this is a most important consideration, for, if the underwriter in the second policy does not treat it as avoided,
it cannot so be considered by the insured or the company issuing the prior policy.
The condition against prior insurance in the subsequent policy is for the benefit
of the insurer, who may, at his option, waive it or insist upon enforcing its terms.
If he seeks to enforce the condition, and treats the policy as a void contract, it is
indeed difficult to see upon what grounds it may be regarded as valid, as an

policy sees fit, *after the loss*, to waive the invalidity and pay the loss under it, does not affect the question.[1] This question was raised in a recent case in the Supreme Court of Massachusetts.[2] In that case the plaintiff procured a policy in the defendant company upon certain property, among the conditions of which was one that "if the assured shall have made, or shall hereafter make, any other insurance upon said property, without the knowledge or consent of this company in writing, then in such case this policy shall be void." A few days subsequently another policy, *upon the same property*, was taken out by the plaintiff in the Merrimack Ins. Co., which also contained a condition "that without the consent of this company, no other insurance shall exist upon the property insured by it. No consent was given by either company. A loss occurred and the Merrimack Company settled the loss under its policy, without insisting upon the forfeiture. The defendant insisted that it was not liable, because of the breach of this condition by taking out the insurance in the Merrimack Company, and that, the plaintiff could not insist that the policy in the Merrimack Company was invalid, because the company had elected to treat it a valid obligation, and had settled the loss with him thereunder. But the court held that the question was, simply, *whether any other valid insurance had been effected upon the property*, and that if the policy in the Merrimack Company *was in fact invalid*, no other insurance within the meaning of the term employed in the policy, had been effected, and that the mere circumstance that that company had seen fit to waive the forfeiture, did not affect the question of the defendant's liability, and could not alter the rights of the parties under the policy. The test is *whether a policy exists in defiance of the condition, which is a valid outstanding legal obligation, and which can be enforced in a court of*

---

insurance that will defeat the prior policy. In this view, our conclusion is not in conflict with *David* v. *The Hartford Ins. Co.*, 13 Iowa, 69, and *Bigler* v. *The N. Y. Central Ins. Co.*, 20 Barb. 635, and same case, 22 N. Y. 402. In the first of these cases, an action was brought upon a policy containing a condition against subsequent insurance. Other insurance, taken after the date of the policy, was relied upon to defeat recovery. The plaintiff claimed that the subsequent policies, on account of certain conditions therein which were violated, were void. It is held that these policies are not void, but, on account of the breach of their conditions, might have been avoided. As they were treated as valid contracts by both of the parties thereto, the losses occurring thereon having been paid by the companies executing the subsequent policies, the breaches of the conditions were regarded as waived, and the instruments held to be binding upon the respective underwriters."

[1] *Jackson* v. *Mass. F. Ins. Co.*, 23 Pick. (Mass.) 418 ; *Hardy* v. *Union Ins. Co.*, 4 Allen (Mass.) 217 ; *Clark* v. *N. E. Mut. F. Ins. Co.*, 6 Cush. (Mass.) 342 ; *Lindley* v. *Union Ins. Co.*, *ante* ; *Lovett* v. *United States*, *ante*.

[2] *Thomas* v. *Builders' Mut. F. Ins. Co.*, 119 Mass. 122.

law. If so, the condition is broken. If not, it is not broken, and if the insurer, under such invalid policy, sees fit to pay to the holder thereof, the amount secured by it, it stands in the light of a gratuity, rather than a payment, and does not estop the plaintiff from asserting that there was no valid policy outstanding.[1] A similar question arose in a recent case decided by the Supreme Court of Maine,[2] it was held that where there is a stipulation in a policy of insurance that the policy shall be void if the insured shall subsequently make insurance on the same property, and shall not give notice thereof with all reasonable diligence to the insurers, and have the same indorsed on his policy or otherwise acknowledged by them, *if the second policy is void,* it will not defeat the first, even though the subsequent insurers, after a loss, pay to the insured a sum of money by way of compromise of his claim thereon. And in this case the court went still further, holding that, where the case finds that the loss was accidental, and there is nothing to show that the subsequent insurance materially increased the risk, the plaintiff's claim on the first policy would not be defeated even by a *valid* subsequent insurance. But it is difficult to perceive upon what principle the latter ruling was predicated, or how the question, as to whether the subsequent insurance was material to the risk or not, can be held to affect the question as to whether the condition of the policy had been broken.

Practically, the same doctrine was adopted by the New Hampshire court.[3] In that case a policy was obtained containing a condition that it should be void, if other insurance was obtained without the consent of the insurer. Subsequently a policy was obtained upon the same

---

[1] *Hardy* v. *Union Ins. Co., ante; Philbrook* v. *N. E. Ins. Co.,* 37 Me. 137; *Bardwell* v. *Conway Ins. Co.,* 118 Mass. 465. See *contra, Lindley* v. *Union Ins. Co., ante; David* v. *Hartford Ins. Co.,* 13 Iowa, 67, in which an insurance policy was conditioned to be void, in case of any further insurance being taken on the property, without notification to this company, and their written acknowledgment. Subsequent insurance was effected in two companies; but each policy was conditioned to be void, if the interest of the insured was leasehold, unless it were so expressed in the policy. Payment for loss was made to the insured under these policies without litigation, or any question as to their validity. He then sought to enforce payment upon the first policy, though he had not notified the company of the subsequent ones, on the ground that his interest in the insured property was, in fact, leasehold, and that therefore these subsequent policies were void and of no effect. Held, that though a litigation of the question might, perhaps, have resulted in the avoidance of these policies, yet this could not be absolutely certain; that certainly they were valid as against the insured, and could only be avoided at the suit of the insurers, who, on the contrary, had paid under them; that therefore they broke the condition of the first policy, and rendered it void. Also *Bigler* v. *N. Y., etc., Ins. Co.,* 22 N. Y. 402.

[2] *Lindley* v. *Union Ins. Co.,* 65 Me. 368.

[3] *Gale* v. *Belknap,* 41 N. H. 170.

property in another company containing a similar condition, and applying to prior as well as subsequent insurance. No consent was obtained from either company, and the court held that the first policy was not invalidated by the second, because the second policy being *voidable* at least, was not " other insurance." BELL, J., in a very able opinion pertinently said, " The policy *was neither utterly void, nor was it voidable*, in the sense that it was a valid and binding contract, and to be so treated for all practical purposes *until it was avoided*. On the contrary, it was an instrument invalid and inoperative, binding upon nobody, until, and unless it should be ratified and confirmed by some further act on the part of the insurers, with knowledge of the facts which cause the invalidity, either by an express assent to be bound, or by some implied waiver of the objections." [1] *A valid policy must exist at the time of the loss*, and there would seem to be no good reason for holding that a waiver of the breach, *subsequent to the loss*, could have the effect, by relation, to render the policy valid *ab initio* so as to avoid a prior policy. But a distinction is made in some states between a void, and voidable policy ; thus in a Pennsylvania case,[2] a policy issued by defendant contained a condition that "the aggregate amount insured shall not exceed two-thirds of the estimated cash value. Policies exceeding that amount were issued, but were not enforcible. The court held that policies that were void *ab initio*, did not constitute insurance, but that policies *that were at any time valid*, were to be treated as such. AGNEW, J., remarking, "The over insurance was attempted to be surmounted by the alleged invalidity of the subsequent policies. We think the court adopted the proper distinction— *if they were void at the time of the loss* they constituted no obstacle ; *but if voidable only* by reason of some breach of condition enabling the insurers to avoid them, *but which they had waived*, the over insurance

---

[1] *Hale* v. *Union Ins. Co.*, 32 N. H. 299; *Leathers* v. *Farmers' Ins. Co.*, 24 id. 262 ; see *Gee* v. *Cheshire, etc., Ins. Co.*, 55 N. H. 265, in which the doctrine of *Gale* v. *Belknap* is fully sustained.

[2] *Mitchell* v. *Lycoming Ins. Co.*, 51 Penn. St. 402. This question arose in *Hardy* v. *Union Ins. Co.*, 4 Allen (Mass.) 217. In that case a policy of insurance, which contains a provision that if the assured "shall hereafter make any other insurance on the property hereby insured, and shall not obtain the consent of this company thereto, or have such consent indorsed upon this policy, then this insurance shall be void and of no effect," is not defeated by the taking of a subsequent policy upon the same and other property, which is invalid by reason of a failure to disclose certain essential facts, although such consent is not so indorsed upon it, or obtained of the company. And the assured may set up the invalidity of the second policy, although, after the loss, they had the defendants' consent thereto indorsed upon another similar policy issued by them upon the other property which that policy covered, and although they received the full amount of it from the insurers.

doubtless exists." [1] But the doctrine that the "other insurance" must be valid, in order to operate as a forfeiture is by no means uniform or well settled, and it is very pertinently urged by the courts in several well considered cases, that this circumstance does not affect the operation of a forfeiture. That the object and purpose of the condition is to be looked to, and that obviously is, to compel the insured to carry a portion of the risk so as to induce greater care on his part in the protection of his property against loss by fire, and that this object is defeated as well by the procurement of a void policy, as by one that is valid. It is unreasonable to suppose that a person would pay for insurance which he *knew* to be void or invalid, and the mere circumstance that he has procured and paid for it, is enough to show that he supposed it was a protection, and upon the theory upon which the condition is predicated, relaxed his vigilance over the property, as much in the one case as in the other, so that the spirit, if not the exact letter of the condition is broken. [2]

But upon the other hand, it is argued, and with great consistency to principle, that the parties are at liberty to make their own terms, and when they use language to express their actual bargain, they are presumed to use it in its ordinary and usual sense, and, in the absence of anything to show the contrary, it must be construed in that sense, and that, as "insurance" in its legal sense means "indemnity," that cannot be regarded as "insurance" which affords no "indemnity" by reason of vices that destroy its legal validity; in the absence of words to show that invalid policies were to be treated as defeating the contract as well as valid, the parties must be regarded as having intended simply actual legal indemnity; and further, that all conditions or exceptions in an instrument are to be construed most strongly against those in whose favor they are made, and consequently, when "*other insurance*" is prohibited, and the procurement of it by its terms, avoids the policy, that it must be taken to mean *other insurance*, that is, other *actual indemnity* against loss or damage from the *same cause* upon the *same property*, and, that where there is no validity to a contract of that character, it is not, either in fact or in law, "*other insurance*," because it furnishes *no indemnity* to the party, and has no legal validity.

The same rules apply in case of "over insurance," as, where a policy

---

[1] In *David* v. *Hartford Ins. Co.*, 13 Iowa, 69.

[2] *Bigler* v. *N. Y. Central Ins. Co.*, 22 N. Y. 402 ; *David* v. *Hartford Ins. Co.*, 13 Iowa 69 ; *Carpenter* v. *Providence, etc., Ins. Co.*, 16 Pet. (U. S.) 49, 508 ; *Mussey* v. *Atlas Ins. Co.*, 14 N. Y. 79 ; *Lackey* v. *Georgia Ins. Co., ante.*

provides that insurance, exceeding a certain sum named in the policy, shall not be made. It is held, in such cases also, that legal, valid insurance is intended, and that, where any of the policies are void, they cannot be reckoned as *insurance*.[1] When *valid* policies are obtained, contrary to the conditions of the policy, the condition is violated, and the policies whose conditions are so broken, are void.[2]

Policy void unless notice or assent is shown.

SEC. 350. When other insurance is procured without notice or assent thereto express or implied, the prior policy is held to be void,[3] *unless the insurer in some manner waives the breach*, so that it is perhaps not quite proper to say that the policy *is void, but rather that it is voidable* at the election of the assured, and may be put on foot again as an operative instrument by any act from which a waiver can fairly be implied,[4] and if no waiver exists no recovery can be had.[5] But, as has been previously stated, such other insurance must be upon the *same property and to the same person, or his assignee*, and policies issued to other persons having an insurable interest in the property, are not a violation of the condition.[6]

---

[1] *Shurtliff* v. *Phœnix Ins. Co.*, 57 Me 137.

[2] *Burt* v. *People's Mut. F. Ins. Co.*, 2 Gray (Mass.) 397 ; *Gilbert* v. *Phœnix Ins. Co.*, 36 Barb. (N. Y.) 372 ; *Harris* v. *Ohio Ins. Co.*, 5 Ohio, 466 ; *Walton* v. *Louisiana, etc., Ins. Co.*, 2 Rob. (La.) 563 ; *Dietz* v. *Mound City, etc., Ins. Co.*, 38 Mo. 85 ; *Healey* v. *Imperial Fire Ins. Co.*, 5 Nev. 268 ; *Manhattan Ins. Co.* v. *Stein*, 5 Bush (Ky.) 652 ; *Duclos* v. *Citizen's Mut. Ins. Co.*, 23 La. An. 332.

[3] *Holbrook* v. *American Ins. Co.*, 1 Curtis (U. S. C. C.) 193 ; *Bigler* v. *Ins. Co.*, 22 N. Y. 402 ; *Mussey* v. *Atlas Ins. Co.*, 14 N. Y. 79 ; *Burche* v. *People's Ins. Co.*, 2 Gray (Mass.) 397 ; *Carpenter* v. *Providence, etc., Ins. Co.*, 16 Pet. (U. S.) 495.

[4] *Horwitz* v. *Equitable Ins. Co.*, 40 Mo. 557 ; *Carrol* v. *Charter Oak Ins. Co.*, 10 Abb. Pr. N. S. (N. Y.) 167 ; *Hubbard* v. *Hartford Ins. Co.*, 33 Iowa, 325 ; *Pechner* v. *Phœnix Ins. Co.*, 6 Lans. (N. Y.) 411 ; *Couch* v. *City F. Ins. Co.*, 37 Conn. 248 ; *Pitney* v. *Glens Falls Ins. Co.*, 65 N. Y. 1 ; *Battaile* v. *Merchant's Ins. Co.*, 3 Rob. (La.) 384 ; *Harris* v. *Ohio Ins. Co.*, 5 Ohio, 466.

[5] *N. Y. Central Ins. Co.* v. *Watson*, 23 Mich. 486.

[6] *Ætna Ins. Co.* v. *Tyler*, 16 Wend. (N. Y.) 385 ; *Mutual Safety Ins. Co.* v. *Hone*, 2 N. Y. 235. In *Whitwell* v. *Putnam F. Ins. Co.*, 6 Lans. (N. Y.) 166, defendant issued its policy to the plaintiff, insuring him against loss by fire on his stock of liquors and spirits contained in a frame building occupied by him as a rectifying establishment, in Dresden, in this State, $2,000, and on the fixtures, etc., $500, for one year. The policy contained a condition, "that if the insured shall have or shall hereafter make any other insurance on the property hereby insured, without the consent of the company written thereon, the same shall be void." Subsequently the plaintiff procured from the Security Insurance Company a policy for the term of one year, insuring him against loss by fire to the amount of $1,000 on his stock of liquors and spirits stored in the same building described in the policy of defendant. The consent of defendant to the second insurance was never written on the policy. On the trial the plaintiff gave evidence tending to prove a waiver, by the defendant's agent of the condition aforesaid. At the close of the trial this evidence was stricken out by the court and the plaintiff nonsuited. Held, that the insurer or its agent may waive conditions inserted in the policy for its benefit, and that the evidence of the waiver in this case was competent and

Policies must cover same property.

SEC. 351. Where one policy covers a building alone, and another covers the building, machinery, etc., this does not constitute double insurance within the meaning of the conditions of the policy.[1] But if another policy is issued covering a *part* only of the property, when that part of the property is separately valued in the other policy, it avoids the policy. Thus, where a policy contained a condition that if other insurance is procured without consent indorsed on the policy, upon a

---

should not have been stricken out. That in the following section of the policy, viz : "that if the assured shall have or shall hereafter make any other insurance *on the property hereby insured*, without the consent of the company written hereon, the policy shall be void," etc.; the meaning of the words "*property hereby insured*," is property of the same description stored on the same premises described in the policy, and not the same identical property. The second insurance, therefore, was upon the same property covered by defendant's policy, and therefore within the condition which required notice. Judgment reversed, and new trial ordered. *Williams v. Cincinnatti Ins. Co.*, Wright (Ohio) 542 ; *Harris v. Ohio Ins. Co.*, id. 514. Where the owner of a stock of goods sold them, and the vendee procured insurance thereon *and assigned the policy, with the insurers consent, to the vendor*, and then insured the goods for his own account, it was held that thereby avoided. *Leavitt v. Western F. & M. Ins. Co.*, 7 Rob. (La.) 351 ; *New v. Columbian Ins. Co.*, 2 McMull (S. C.) 351. A provision for apportionment of the loss, in case of other insurance, only applies to insurance covering the *same interest*. If the mortgagor and mortgagee each have separate insurance, the condition for apportionment does not apply. *Fox v. Phœnix Ins. Co.*, 52 Me. 333. A policy made by the mortgagor to cover the interest of the mortgagee, *without his knowledge or consent*, is not other insurance. *Johnson v. N. British Ins. Co.*, 1 Holmes (U. S. C. C.) 117. The assured cannot be held chargeable for the acts of a third person over whom he has no control. *Carpenter v. Prov., etc., Ins. Co.*, 16 Pet. (U. S.) 501 ; *Fox v. Phœnix Ins. Co.*, 52 Me. 133 ; *Ætna F. Ins. Co. v. Tyler*, 12 Wend. (N .Y.).

[1] *Sloat v. Royal Ins. Co.*, 49 Penn. St. 14. In *Clark v. Hamilton, etc., Ins. Co.*, 9 Gray (Mass.) 148, a policy upon "a carpenter's shop and carpenter's tools" provided that the issuing of any other policy, covering any portion of the property insured, and not disclosed to these insurers, should avoid this policy. Held, that evidence of the issuing of another policy to the same person upon " four chests of carpenter's tools in the wood shop," described as situated in the same street as in the first policy, and that there were in the shop two chests of tools belonging to the assured, and two or perhaps three belonging to the journeymen of the assured, did not show that any part of the property was covered by both policies. In *Vose v. Hamilton Ins. Co.*, 39 Barb. (N. Y.) 302, a policy of insurance was issued on stock in trade in No. 146 R. street, with a proviso that "in case any other policy has been, or shall be issued, covering the whole, or any portion " of the insured property, the policy should be void. Pending this policy, with the consent of these insurers, the insured stock was removed into No. 148 of the same street, where the insured had a large quantity of other goods insured by another company, by a policy of prior date to the one aforesaid, of which the insurers in the latter had no notice, or knowledge. Held, that this was not a double insurance, and did not work a forfeiture under the above proviso. *Vose v. Hamilton, etc., Ins. Co.*, 39 Barb. (N. Y.) 302. Where a consignor of a vessel effected an insurance on the freight, with the warranty, "no other insurance," and the consignee, who had accepted a draft against such freight, without instruction from the consignor, effected another insurance on the freight at the place of destination, it was held, that this last insurance could not be considered a violation of the warranty contained in the former. *Williams v. Crescent Mutual Ins. Co.*, 15 La. An. 851 ; *McMustin v. Ins. Co. of N. America*, 64 Barb. (N. Y.) 536 ; *Rowley v. Empire Ins. Co.*, 36 N. Y. 557 ; *Tyler v. Ætna Ins. Co.*, 16 Wend. (N. Y.) 385. So where a policy upon a store provided "that no person whose property is insured in the

stock of goods, at a certain sum, and upon the fixtures at a certain
sum, it was held that a subsequent insurance upon the fixtures alone,
avoided the first policy.[1] The insurer takes the burden of establishing
the fact that the same property covered by its policy, is covered by
the policy claimed to operate as a breach,[2] and it is a question of fact
for the jury to find and not a question for the court,[3] and the jury must
find, not only that the policies cover the same property, *but it must
also appear that the other policy is valid.*[4]

Must be other insurance by assured, or for his benefit, with his assent.

Sec. 352. In order to invalidate a policy upon the ground of a breach
of the condition against other insurance, it must be shown that such
other insurance *was obtained by the insured, or some one authorized by him
to obtain it,*[5] *or that he subsequently assented thereto.*[6] He cannot be affected
by the acts of a stranger who also has an insurable interest in the
property, and, unless it is shown that he himself procured other insurance, or *authorized* it to be procured, or assented thereto after it was
procured, the condition of the policy is not broken, although insurance
upon the property is taken by others.[7]

Thus, where the mortgagor of real estate procured an insurance upon
the property, conditioned that other insurance upon the property, without the consent of the company, it was held that the taking out of a

---

company shall be allowed to insure the same *or any other property connected with
it,* in any other company, or at any other office, and in case of any such insurance,
his policy obtained from this company, shall be void and of no effect," it was held
that this did not prevent the taking out of a policy upon the *goods in* the store,
in some other company. *Jones* v. *Maine, etc., Ins. Co.,* 18 Me. 155.

[1] *Kimball* v. *Howard Ins. Co.,* 8 Gray (Mass.) 33. But *contra,* see *Illinois, etc.,
Ins. Co.* v. *Fix,* 53 Ill. 151, where it was held that when one policy covers certain
property, and afterwards another policy is taken upon *part* of the same property,
the policy is only invalidated as to such part covered by other insurance, and a
recovery may be had *less* the value of the property doubly insured.

[2] *Clark* v. *Hamilton Ins. Co.,* 6 Gray (Mass.) 169.

[3] *Nive* v. *Columbia Ins. Co.,* 2 McMull (S. C.) 220 ; 2 Ben. F. I. C. 147.

[4] *Stacey* v. *Franklin F. Ins. Co. ; Jackson* v. *Mass. etc., Ins. Co.,* 23 Pick.
(Mass.) 423.

[5] *Ætna Ins. Co.* v. *Tyler,* 16 Wend. (N. Y.) 385 ; *Acer* v. *Merchants' Ins. Co.,*
57 Barb. (N. Y.) 68 ; *Pitney* v. *Glens Falls Ins. Co.,* 61 id. 335 ; *Nichols* v. *Fayette
Mut. F. Ins. Co.,* 1 Allen (Mass.) 63 ; *Burbanks* v. *Rockingham, etc., Ins. Co.,* 24
N. H. 550 ; *Fox* v. *Phenix Ins. Co.,* 52 Me. 333 ; *Norwich F. Ins. Co.* v. *Bonner,*
52 Ill. 442 ; *Bates* v. *Commercial Ins. Co.,* 1 Cin. (Ohio) Superior Ct. 523 ; *Marigny*
v. *Home Mut. Ins. Co.,* 13 La. An. 338 ; *Williams* v. *Crescent, etc., Ins. Co.,* 15 id.
651.

[6] In *Dafae* v. *Johnstown, etc., Ins. Co.,* 7 Upper Canada (C. P.) 55, the father
of the assured procured other insurance in the son's name, and subsequently, the
son ratified it by accepting payment of a loss under the policy. Held, that the
prior policy was thereby avoided.

[7] See Sec. 353.

policy upon the *same property* by the mortgagee, was not "other insurance" within the meaning of the condition.[1]

Identity of interest the test.

Sec. 353. *Neither identity of name or identity of property is decisive upon the question; in order to amount to other insurance, the interests covered by the policies must be identical.* If the interest is not *identical*, there is not other insurance, as if the mortgagee insures his interest in the mortgaged property, the policy is not avoided by a subsequent insurance in favor of the mortgagor;[2] or if A. hold possession under a contract for a deed, an insurance by him upon his interest in the property, will not be avoided by a policy in favor of the owner of the legal estate.[3] It is not identity of *name*, but *identity of interest* that determines whether other insurance exists. Thus, where the mortgagor authorizes the mortgagee to make subsequent insurance, and the mortgagor pays the premium, it is for the protection of his interests, as well as of those of the mortgagee, and is such "other insurance" as avoids a prior policy.[4] An insurance upon *goods* in a store does not

---

[1] In *Woodbury, etc., Bank* v. *Charter Oak Ins. Co.*, 31 Conn. 517, where a condition of the policy provided that it should become void if any further insurance was obtained on the property insured, without the consent of the insurance company indorsed on the policy, and the owner of the equity of redemption procured a later insurance of the property, of which no notice was given to the company, and of which the party originally insured had no knowledge, it was held that, as the original insurance was intended as an insurance of the mortgage interest of the insured, and was to be regarded as equitably such, the later insurance was not a further insurance of the same property, and not a breach of the condition. *Nichols* v. *Fayette, etc., Ins. Co.*, 1 Allen (Mass.) 63.
    In *Burbank* v. *Rockingham, etc., Ins. Co.*, 24 N. H. 550, the assured gave a bond for a deed of an undivided half of the premises insured. The obligee of the bond was to keep the premises in repair, and, if destroyed by fire, to rebuild. It was also agreed that the obligor should keep the property insured at the expense of all, and if burned, the insurance money was to be applied to rebuilding. It was claimed by the insurer that this bond, providing for a rebuilding in case of its loss by fire, was "other insurance," but the court held otherwise.

[2] *Nichols* v. *Fayette Ins. Co.*, 1 Allen (Mass.) 63.

[3] *Ætna Ins. Co.* v. *Tyler*, 16 Wend. (N. Y.) 507; *Acer* v. *Merchants' Ins. Co.*, 57 Barb. (N. Y.) 68; *Mut. Safety Ins. Co.* v. *Hone*, 2 N. Y. 235. In a case recently decided in the Court of Appeals of New York, *Sprague* v. *Holland Purchase Ins Co.*, decided March 20, 1877, an application for insurance upon a house, contained these questions: "What is your title to the property?" Answer. "Contract." "How much insured in other companies?" Answer. "None." Held, a statement that applicant held title under a contract of purchase and sale, and that there was no other insurance upon applicant's interest, and the fact that the vendor of the house had insurance upon it did not render the statement untrue.

[4] *Holbrook* v. *Am. Ins. Co.*, 1 Curtis C. C. (U. S.) 193; *Mussey* v. *Atlas Ins. Co.*, 14 N. Y. 79; *Carpenter* v. *Providence, etc., Ins. Co.*, 16 Pet. (U. S.) 495. In a recent case in the United States Supreme Court, *Home Ins. Co.* v. *Baltimore Warehouse Co.*, 93 U. S. 324, the defendants, as warehousemen, took out a policy on goods consigned to them, on their own account, to secure their advances and charges, and also for the protection of the consignor. The policy was conditioned to be void, if other insurance was obtained. The consignor also took out a policy

avoid a policy upon the store itself, although such policy provides that
it shall be void if the assured shall procure other insurance upon the
"store, or anything connected with it."[1]   The assignee takes a policy,
subject to all express stipulations or conditions named therein, and a
subsequent breach thereof by his assignor, avoids the policy, as if the
assignor subsequently obtains other insurance without consent.[2]   *If
the interest and the risk are the same,* the condition is broken, otherwise
not.[3]   But it was held in an early case in New York,[4] that the policies
must not only attach upon the same property, but also in the same
manner, and that if one policy covers a specific sum upon one species
of property, and a certain sum upon another, a policy for a gross sum
upon the same property is not double insurance within the meaning of
the term.   Thus, in that case, a prior policy covered $3,000 on stock
and $1,000 on fixtures.   A subsequent policy was procured for $5,000,
on stock *and* fixtures, and it was held that this did not constitute
double insurance, because the loss could not be apportioned under the
latter policy.   But this doctrine is hardly tenable.

Parol contracts—Interim receipts.

SEC. 354. It is not necessary that *another policy* should be issued.
It is enough if a valid contract *to* insure or *of* insurance exists, although

---

upon the same goods. Held that, as to all beyond the interest of the defendants
in the goods, this constituted *double insurance.* A provision in a policy, that any
other insurance which the insured had must be notified to the insurer, applies
only to insurances held by the party insured, or some one for his benefit. *Ætna
F. Ins. Co.* v. *Tyler,* 16 Wend. 385; *Mutual Safety Ins. Co.* v. *Hone,* 2 N. Y. 235.
Insurance by a mortgagor, and also by a mortgagee, for their *individual* benefit,
is not other insurance. When a policy provides that "other insurance obtained
by the assured, *or any other person or parties interested,*" etc , it is held that the
provision must be construed *as relating entirely to an interest in the assured's
insurance,* and does not apply to insurance obtained by other persons *having a
distinct interest in the property. Acer* v. *The Merchants' Ins. Co.,* 57 Barb. (N.
Y.) 68.

[1] *Jones* v. *Maine, etc., Ins. Co.,* 18 Me. 155.

[2] *State, etc., Ins. Co.* v. *Roberts,* 31 Penn. St. 438.

[3] *Mussey* v. *Atlas Ins. Co.,* 14 N. Y. 79. In *Burton* v. *Gore Dist. Ins. Co.,* 12
Grant's Ch. (Ont.) 156, the mortgagor procured a policy and assigned it to the
mortgagee, and afterwards procured another policy in his own name and for his
own benefit, and it was held *not* other insurance, and in all cases, when the mortgagee, by the assignment, becomes the assured ; that is, when he gives a premium note and becomes bound for the premium, and the assignment of the policy
is treated as a new contract with the mortgagee. See, also, *Allen* v. *Hudson R.
Ins. Co.,* 19 Barb. (N. Y.) 442; 5 Ben. F. I. C. 1, where a similar doctrine is held.
Where there is doubt as to whose interests are covered, evidence is admissible
to establish the fact. *Planters', etc., Ins. Co.* v. *Deford,* 38 Md. 382. In *Home
Ins. Co.* v. *Baltimore Warehouse Co.,* 92 U. S. 284, an insurance by the consignor,
and an insurance by the warehousemen for the benefit of the consignor or bailor,
was held double insurance.

[4] *Howard Co.* v. *Scribner,* 5 Hill (N. Y.) 298.

merely evidenced by an *interim* receipt, or resting entirely in parol.[1] It is held in New York that, when the policy provides that if any other insurance "prior or subsequent," shall exist, the policy shall be void, the policy is not defeated, because at the time when the application was made another policy was outstanding, if such other policy was sur. rendered before the policy relied upon was issued;[2] but it would seem that this should depend upon whether the defendant company *became liable as insurers at the time when the application was made*, because it would be absurd to hold, that, *if the contract was made, and the defendants liability attached under it*, the legal rights of the parties were changed by the issue of a policy. The contract was complete and operative without the policy, and all its conditions attached *instanter* when the minds of the parties met, and the policy is only the evidence of what the parties in fact agreed upon. Without knowing what the facts were, in the New York case referred to, I think it may be safe to presume that no valid contract of insurance existed until the policy issued, and in that view the decision was correct. But if an enforceable contract existed when the application was sent, the decision could hardly be regarded as consistent.[3] The fact that a third person, having an insurable interest therein, has, previously to the issue of a policy to the plaintiffs, obtained, without their knowledge, an insurance thereon, does not avoid the policy.[4]

Renewal avoids policy, when.

SEC. 355. If other insurance exists upon the property, and is referred to and stated in the application, but the assured therein states that such

---

[1] *Mason* v. *Andes Ins. Co.*, 23 U. C. (C. P.) 37.

[2] Thus in *Train* v. *Holland Purchase Ins. Co.*, decided in the Court of Appeals of New York, January 16th, 1877, and not yet reported, the plaintiff, by G., an agent of the A. insurance company, made a written application to defendant, the H. insurance company, for insurance against fire. The application stated and warranted that there was no other insurance upon the same property. There was, at the time of forwarding the application, a policy in the A. company covering the property, but this was surrendered, by plaintiff on the same or the next day, in pursuance of an agreement to that effect, to G., who had authority to and did accept the surrender. On or about the day of the surrender, defendant made out and forwarded to G., for plaintiff, a policy containing a condition making the policy void if there was other insurance. Held, that, in the absence of evidence, the fair intendment was, that the surrender of the policy in the A. company took place before the contract under the policy would, by defendant, come into force, and that there was not, at that time, any other insurance on the property avoiding the policy. It was also held that evidence that the A. Company furnished G. with blanks for accepting the surrender of policies, and had ratified his acceptance of previous surrenders, was sufficient to establish his authority to receive such surrender. *Continental Ins. Co.* v. *Horton*, 28 Mich. 173.

[3] *Inland Ins. Co.* v. *Staffer*, 33 Penn. St. 397.

[4] *Nichols et. al.* v. *Fayette Mut. Ins. Co.*, 1 Allen (Mass.) 63; *Harris* v. *Ohio Ins. Co.*, Wright (Ohio), 544; *Williams* v. *Cincinnati Ins. Co.*, id. 514.

insurance expires at a certain date, *and will not be renewed,* the renewal thereof, without notice to the company, avoids the policy as much as though new policies in other companies had been taken.[1] But if the policy simply stipulates against other insurance, it is treated as referring to other insurance to be thereafter procured, and not to insurance already obtained; consequently the *renewal* of a prior policy does not come within the stipulation.[2] "A renewal," said DWIGHT, C., in the case last cited, "is, in one sense, a new contract, but it is not other insurance within the meaning of the policy. *It is but a continuation of an existing insurance. * * * If the notice of prior insurance is given, it must be held to continue through all true renewals of it."* [3]

Other insurance without notice until required, effect of.

SEC. 356. Where the company incorporates a written clause into the policy, "other insurance permitted without notice until required," it overcomes the force of printed conditions therein repugnant thereto. Thus, where a policy contained such a written clause, and the printed conditions provided that, "in case the assured shall have already any other insurance against loss by fire on the property hereby insured, not notified to this company and mentioned in or indorsed upon the policy," the policy shall be void and of no effect, such written clause was held to have so far modified such printed condition that the policy was not invalidated by reason of other prior insurance existing upon the property.[4] "Other insurance without notice," applies to prior as well as subsequent insurance.[5] The *other insurance must exist at the time of loss.* The mere fact that it did exist some time during the life of the policy, does not prevent a recovery if it had ceased to exist before a loss occurred. The policy is not absolutely avoided, but only suspended by the other insurance.[6]

Permission indorsed on policy.

SEC. 357. Privilege for other insurance written upon the face of the policy, is a waiver of notice of such other insurance, regardless of the printed conditions therein.[7]

---

[1] *Dietz* v. *Mound City Ins. Co.,* 38 Mo. 85.

[2] *Pitney* v. *Glens Falls Ins. Co.,* 65 N. Y. 1.

[3] *Brown* v. *Cattaraugus Ins. Co.,* 18 N. Y. 391.

[4] *Blake* v. *Exchange, etc., Ins. Co.,* 12 Gray (Mass.) 265; *Kimball* v. *Howard Ins. Co.,* 8 id. 33; *Frederick, etc., Ins. Co.* v. *Deford,* 38 Md. 404.

[5] *Frederic Co., etc., Ins. Co.* v. *Deford,* 38 Md. 404.

[6] *Obermeyer* v. *Globe, etc., Ins. Co.,* 43 Mo. 573; 5 Ben. F. I. C. 235.

[7] *Benedict* v. *Ocean Ins. Co.,* 31 N. Y. 389.

Permission for other insurance indorsed upon a policy, applies to prior as well as subsequent insurance, and in either case is not a breach of the printed conditions against other insurance,[1] unless the limit fixed in the permission is exceeded. If the permission extends "until otherwise ordered," it is limited in amount; but if a certain amount is specified, such amount must not be exceeded by a single cent.[2] As if "two-thirds of the value" is the limit, and such value is fixed at a certain sum, additional insurance to cover *improvements* subsequently made, will avoid the prior policies; and the fact that the premises were greatly increased in value by the improvements, is not material. The value fixed, controls.[3]

Notice may be given to agent.

SEC. 358. An agent of an insurance company authorized to make and revoke contracts for insurance, is the proper person to give consent to additional insurance, and notice to him is notice to the company, unless there is an express provision in the policy as to whom notice shall be given, and when notice is so given the company cannot, by neglecting to assent to or dissent from such additional insurance, and thus putting the assured off his guard, subsequently set up such additional insurance as a breach of the conditions of the policy. They are treated as having assented thereto, and as having waived strict compliance with the conditions.[4]

Knowledge of agent estops company, when.

SEC. 359. *If, at the time a policy is written,* the agent writing it, *knew* that this was other insurance, the condition against other insurance does not apply to such other insurance as was *at that time known* to the agent.[5] The courts will not permit an insurer to receive the premium when they *knew* that the policy was not binding, and which they never intended to pay; and to avoid liability thereon by setting up in defense matters of the existence of which they were fully aware when

---

[1] *Blake* v. *Exchange Ins. Co.*, 12 Gray (Mass) 265 ; *Benedict* v. *Ocean Ins. Co.*, 31 N. Y. 389 ; *Warner* v. *Peoria Ins. Co.*, 14 Wis. 318.

[2] *Blake* v. *Ocean Ins. Co., ante; Lycoming Ins. Co.* v. *Stockbower*, 26 Penn. St. 119.

[3] *Elliott* v. *Lycoming Mut. Ins. Co.*, 66 Penn. St. 22.

[4] *Ins. Co.* v. *Lyons, Lindenthal & Co.*, 38 Tex. 253 ; *Ins. Co.* v. *Wilkinson*, 13 Wall. (U. S.) 222 ; *Pitney* v. *Glen's Falls Ins. Co.*, 65 N. Y. 1.

[5] *Lycoming Ins. Co.* v. *Barringer*, 73 Ill. 235 ; *Pitney* v. *Glen's Falls Ins.Co., ante ; Van Bories* v. *V. S. Ins. Co.*, 8 Bush. (Ky.) 133 ; *Carroll* v. *Charter Oak Ins. Co.*, 10 Abb. Pr. (N. Y.) U. S. 166 ; *Hubbard* v. *Hartford F. Ins. Co.*, 33 Iowa. 325 ; *Peckren* v. *Phœnix Ins. Co.*, 6 Lans. (N. Y.) 441 ; *Horwitz* v. *Equitable Ins. Co.*, 40 Mo. 557.

they entered into the contract.[1] The notice of prior or subsequent
insurances need not be in writing, unless so provided by law.[2] But
if the statute, or in case of a mutual company, the clause requires it
to be in writing, or to be given to a particular officer, it must be strictly
complied with.[3]

Where the by-laws of a mutual fire insurance company provide that
all policies shall be void unless previous insurance shall be expressed
therein, a policy not expressing previous insurance will be void, even
in the hands of an assignee, *and even though the insurers knew that
other insurance existed,* and that the assured intended that it should
remain in force, and that he supposed that the insurers would make
the policy subject to such prior insurance. The remedy, in such cases,
is to seek a reformation of the contract.[4] A court of law must act
upon the agreement as it is. It cannot add to, strike out or change
anything in it, so as in any respect to change or vary the contract as
evidenced by the writing itself.[5]

Substantial compliance.

SEC. 360. Where the charter provides that other insurance shall
be with the consent of the directors, " signified by indorsement on
the *back* of the policy," a recital of such other insurance *in the body
of the policy,* is a substantial compliance with the requirements of the
charter,[6] and the amount being assented to, and the charter not requiring the name of the company in which such other insurance exists
should be inserted in the consent, such policies may be renewed, or
insurance to the same amount obtained in other companies.[7] The
charter held that consent might be given by the secretary *and* president. Held, that consent given by the secretary or a director was not
sufficient.[8]

---

[1] BREESE, J., *Lycoming Ins. Co.* v. *Barringer,* 73 Ill. 235 ; *Com. Ins. Co.* v.
Spanknable, 52 Ill. 53 ; *Ætna Ins. Co.* v. *Maguire,* 57 id. 342 , *Reaper* v. *Ins. Co.,*
62 id. 458 ; *Schettler* v. *Ins. Co.,* 38 id. 168. No defense based upon a breach of
a condition, requiring notice and indorsement of other insurance, can be made
when the policies were all issued by the *same agent.* *Farmers' Mut. Ins. Co.* v.
Taylor, 73 Penn. St. 342 ; *Russell, etc., Co.* v. *State Ins. Co.,* 55 Mo. 585. Or even
where the agent issuing the policy had notice that other insurance had been or
would be obtained, and did not object thereto. *Planters', etc., Ins. Co.* v. *Lyons,*
38 Tex. 253.

[2] *McEwen* v. *Montgomery, etc., Ins. Co.,* 5 Hill (N. Y.) 101.

[3] *Bigler* v. *N. Y. Central Ins. Co.,* 20 Barb. (N. Y.) 635.

[4] *Barrett* v. *Union, etc., Ins. Co.,* 7 Cush. (Mass.) 175.

[5] FLETCHER, J., in *Barrett* v. *Ins. Co., ante.*

[6] *First Baptist Society* v. *Hillsborough Mut. Ins. Co.,* 19 N. H. 580.
[7] Id.

[8] *Stark, etc., Ins. Co.* v. *Hurd,* 19 Ohio 149.

A by-law of a mutual insurance company, that "persons insuring with this company may insure with other companies, with the consent of the directors indorsed on the policy," was printed on the policy, and the court held that it was to be treated as a stipulation amount. ing to a warranty, and amounted to a prohibition.[1] When the by-laws of a company provide that any insurance subsequently obtained without the consent *in writing*, of the president, and that such by-laws shall not be changed except by vote of two-thirds of the stockholders or directors, the mere verbal assent of the president to other insurance is not sufficient.[2] Where, ten days before the fire, another policy was taken out upon the property, and no notice thereof given, it was held that the insured was bound to use reasonable diligence in that respect, and that, as there was no evidence that he had given any notice or attempted to, there was no question for the jury as to diligence.[3]

Effect of charter provisions.

SEC. 361. It has been held that, when the policy requires that notice shall be given in writing, unless waived, the requirement must be complied with strictly, and, if the charter of the company requires the notice to be in writing, and consent indorsed, the company cannot waive compliance, as compliance with a provision of any condition of the contract fixed by law cannot be waived ;[4] and it would seem that, generally, notice must be given *instanter*, at the peril of the assured. He cannot avoid the effect of a breach of the condition by pleading, or showing, *that he had not had time to give the notice*. The question of diligence does not arise.[5]

Prior insurance, erroneous statement of.

SEC. 362. It is not necessary, where notice of other insurance is required, that the name of the company or the amount of the insurance should be

---

[1] *Hygum* v. *Ætna Ins. Co.*, 11 Iowa, 21.

[2] *Hall* v. *Mechanics', etc., Ins. Co.*, 6 Gray (Mass.) 169.

[3] *Inland, etc., Ins. Co.* v. *Phœnix Ins. Co.*, 31 Penn. St. 348.

[4] *Security Ins. Co.* v. *Fay*, 22 Mich. 467 ; *Coach* v. *City F. Ins. Co.*, 38 Conn. 181 ; *Gilbert* v. *Phœnix Ins. Co.*, 36 Barb. (N. Y.) 372, even though the agent makes a memorandum of, on private book of his own, which contains some entries relating to insurance, *Pender* v. *Am. Ins. Co.*, 12 Cush. (Mass.) 469 ; *Hutchinson* v. *Western Ins. Co.*, 21 Mo. 97 ; *Simpson* v. *Penn. Ins. Co.*, 38 Penn. St. 280. When required to be indorsed on policy, such indorsement is a condition precedent, and is not satisfied by a verbal notice to the insurer. *Hutchinson* v. *Ins. Co.*, 21 Mo. 97. Nor by exhibiting a memorandum thereof to the agent, who said he had entered it in his book, and it would be the same as though indorsed on the policy. *Worcester Bank* v. *Hartford Ins. Co.*, 11 Cush. (Mass.) 265. But this would hardly be regarded as the rule now, where the charter of the company provides the mode in which consent must be given ; it must be complied with, and a different mode will be inoperative. *Blanchard* v. *Atlantic Ins. Co.*, 33 N. H. 9 ; *Fabyan* v. *Am. F. Ins. Co.*, 33 id. 203.

[5] *Hendrickson* v. *The Queen's Ins. Co.*, 30 U. C. (Q. B.) 186.

correctly stated, and a mistake in either respect, if the insurance is not greater than that stated, is not material.[1] But if, at the time of taking out a policy, it is stated that prior insurance exists in certain companies for certain amounts, when, in fact, no such insurance exists, the insurer is not justified in afterwards taking out policies for that amount in other companies, and if he does so, they will render the prior policy void.[2] But, where the charter itself contains no provision in this respect, the fact that the policy expressly provides that no condition shall be waived, except in writing, signed by the secretary or other officer, will not prevent the insured from setting up a waiver by parol, especially if the acts constituting the waiver can be fairly attributed to the company, which is always the case when it is the act of an agent authorized to make or revoke contracts of insurance.[3]

In a Georgia case,[4] the company's agent, who had authority to make and revoke contracts, was notified that other insurance would be made, and he consented thereto verbally, but did not indorse consent on the policy. The policy afterwards expired, and was renewed by the same agent, and it was held that the condition was waived. McCAY, J., in passing upon this question, said: "Consent to a prior or subsequent insurance is within the scope of the agent's authority, as the every-day practice of the country proves, and, if an agent does, in fact, so consent, and the insured, in good faith, acts upon it, we think it is fraud upon the insured for the company to set up that they had stipulated this consent to be in writing.

It will be noticed that this stipulation has nothing really to do with the *contract of insurance*. Double insurances are perfectly legal. They are, in fact, an advantage to the company, since, in case of loss, they can compel a division of the loss. The only object of this clause, at least the only legitimate object, is to guard against the over insurance of the property, and the consequent temptation to crimes. But, when it affirmatively appears that the consent was given, and that the insured has *acted* upon it, we think it would but be the perpetration of fraud to permit the company to take advantage of its own wrong, and escape liability, because *its agent* has failed to do his duty to the insured. For myself, I am of opinion that such stipulations are void.

[1] *Osser* v. *Provincial Ins. Co.*, 12 U. C. (C. P.) 141.

[2] *Conway Tool Co.* v. *Hudson R. Ins. Co.*, 12 Cush. (Mass.) 144.

[3] *Pechner* v. *Phœnix Ins. Co.*, 6 Lans. (N. Y.) 411; aff'd, Ct. of App., 65 N. Y. 195.

[4] *Carrugi* v. *Atlantic Ins. Co.*, 40 Ga. 135; 2 Am. Rep. 567.

Parties may stipulate as they please, in their contracts, as to the several rights and obligations of each, but the mode by which it shall be proven, whether or not there has been a breach or performance of those stipulations, is matter to be regulated by law, and not by the stipulations of the parties. Whether parol evidence is admissible to prove the facts, or whether they can only be proven by writing, it seems to me is regulated by law, on grounds of public policy, and for the public convenience, and is not matter of stipulation. Would a promissory note from A. to B., stipulating that no proof of its discharge should be taken, unless it were proven by two witnesses, be binding? Would a contract to be performed on a certain day, and stipulating that the day should not be altered by a subsequent contract, without proof in writing, signed by the obligee, bind the obligor, if, in fact, for a new consideration, there should be a change of the day, and no writing be taken? I think not, and I think these stipulations stand on the same footing. It is an attempt to change the rules of evidence, to make a new law, to regulate the proceedings of the courts. This is not like the execution of a promise, which contains limitations as to the mode of its exercise. This is a simple attempt to change the mode by which the courts should arrive at whether there has been a performance or breach of a contract. In my judgment, parties cannot do that. Such rules and modes are regulated by law, on grounds of public policy. They might as well stipulate that the fact of consent should be proven only by personal attendance of the witness, and not by interrogatories, or that it should not be proven, as our law now permits, by the parties. The judgment of the court in this case is, however, put upon the ground that it would be a fraud upon the rights of the insured, after he has got the consent of the agent, and *acted upon it*, to insist upon the written consent. The issue before the jury, in this case, is wholly one of *bona fides*. If there was an intent on the part of Carrugi to defraud, as a matter of course the policy is void. It is the essence of these contracts that there should be the utmost good faith, and this on grounds of public policy, independent of the rights of the parties in the particular case."

Verbal notice to agent sufficient.

SEC. 363. Verbal notice to an agent is sufficient, unless written notice is required,[1] and if required to be indorsed, knowledge of the agent of

---

[1] *Planters' Mut. Ins. Co.* v. *Lyons*, 33 Tex. 253; *Schenck* v. *Mercer, etc., Ins. Co.*, 24 N. J. L. 447; *McEwen* v. *Montgomery, etc., Ins. Co.*, 5 Hill (N. Y.) 101.

other insurance is knowledge of the company, and if consent is not indorsed, the condition is waived,' and if the agent is notified of other insurance, and the policy is left with him for that purpose, and he neglects to indorse consent, the condition is waived.² Where the by-laws require that notice shall be given, and consent indorsed by the secretary, consent indorsed by a *director* is insufficient.³ The notice must be given to a person authorized to receive it, and consent to other insurance, and notice given to one having no such authority, is inoperative,⁴ as to a broker who is not an agent of the company,⁵ and it seems that the test of authority is, whether the person has authority to countersign the policy,⁶ unless some particular officer is named in

---

Notice may be given by parol, and if, after such notice is given, the company does anything that recognizes the policy as valid, it is treated as an assent to such other insurance. *The Kenton, etc., Ins. Co. v. Shaw,* 6 Bush. (Ky.) 174.

¹ *Russell* v. *State Ins. Co.,* 55 Mo. 585.

² *Cobb* v. *Ins. Co. of N. America,* 11 Kan. 98.

³ *Forbes* v. *Agawam Ins. Co.,* 9 Cush. (Mass.) 470.

⁴ *Gilbert* v. *Phœnix Ins. Co.,* 36 Barb. (N. Y.) 372. Notice of other insurance in order to be operative must be given to the insurer *or to an agent authorized to act in that respect for it,* notice given to a special agent, having no authority to consent thereto, is not sufficient. *Security Ins. Co.* v. *Fay,* 22 Mich. 467 ; *Gilbert* v. *Phœnix Ins. Co.,* 36 Barb. (N. Y.) 372 ; *Mellen* v. *Hamilton F. Ins. Co.,* 17 N. Y. 609. And the ground upon which the Massachusetts cases rest is, that the agent had no authority to waive a condition of the policy. *Barrett* v. *Mut. etc., Ins. Co.,* 7 Cush. (Mass.) 175 ; *Worcester Bank* v. *Hartford F. Ins. Co.,* 11 id. 265. When the policy provides whose consent shall be obtained, the consent of any other person is not operative, as the consent of a director, when the policy requires the consent of the secretary. *Stark, etc., Ins. Co.* v. *Hurd,* 19 Ohio, 149. The assured takes the burden of establishing the authority of the agent to receive notice of and consent to other insurance, and the mere fact that he acted as solicitor and delivered the policy, is not enough to establish it. *Mellen* v. *Hamilton F. Ins. Co., ante.* But an agent who is authorized to issue policies and make the contract therefor, is to be treated as having authority to consent to other insurance, or waive the breach of a condition of the policy relating thereto. Such an act is within the scope of his apparent authority. *Pitney* v. *Glen's Falls Ins. Co.,* 65 N. Y. 1 ; *Rowley* v. *Empire Ins. Co.,* 36 N. Y. 550. When the charter of a mutual company, or the general statute provides, the method by which the business of the company shall be done, and also provides that no waiver shall be operative unless in writing upon the policy, of course, neither an officer or agent can waive the condition. *Couch* v. *City F. Ins. Co.,* 38 Conn. 181 ; *Fabyan* v. *Union, etc., Ins. Co.,* 33 N. H. 203. A general agent, or the agent who issued the policy, or an agent appointed in place of the one who issued the policy, may generally bind the company by their consent to other insurance. But an agent in another town, who is merely a local agent, is held not authorized *prima facie* to give consent to other insurance upon a policy, issued by another local agent, and the burden is upon the plaintiff to show authority in such agent, and failing to do so, such consent will be inoperative. *Security Ins. Co.* v. *Fay,* 22 Mich. 467.

⁵ *Mellen* v. *Hamilton Ins. Co.,* 17 N. Y. 609.

⁶ *Security Ins. Co.* v. *Fay,* 22 Mich. 467. In the *Dayton Ins. Co.* v. *Kelly,* 24 Ohio St. 345, it was held toat a condition in a contract for insurance requiring notice of prior insurance is waived by accepting the risk on an application wherein the question concerning prior insurance is not answered. Where notice of additional insurance is required to be given to the insurer, it may, before the

the policy, and a notice given to a local agent neither authorized nor held out as authorized to act for the company in these respects, is not good.[1] And the same rule applies in the case of consent. It must be be given by a person *authorized* to give it, otherwise it is invalid; as, where the policy provides that consent shall only be given by the secretary; consent given by the president is not binding upon the company,[2] unless it is subsequently ratified, and the breach of the condition waived. The distinction, however, between companies whose charter limits their powers in these respects, and those whose charters impose no restrictions. In the one case, the charter mode must be literally complied with, and cannot be waived,[3] while those companies whose powers are not restricted in those respects, either by their charter or by general law, may waive strict compliance.[4]

Notice to former agent, but who was not agent when notice was given, insufficient.

SEC. 364. The fact that, through negligence on the part of the assured in making inquiry, he gave notice of other insurance to the agent of whom he procured the insurance, but whose authority to act for the company at that time had been revoked, will not screen him from the operation of the condition. He was bound, *at his peril*, to give notice to one authorized to receive it.[5] Notice to a person authorized to act upon it must be shown, and if the assured omits to testify positively that he gave notice, the inference *is warranted* that he did not give it.[6]

The mere fact that the authority of an agent has been revoked,

receipt of the policy, be given to the agent of the insurer who effected the insurance, and with whom the policy is intrusted for delivery to the assured in fulfillment of the contract; and the indorsement of such additional insurance upon the policy by such agent must be regarded as the act of the principal, thereby assenting to the additional insurance. Where the agent of an insurance company effects a contract for intermediary insurance and for a policy, and delivers a certificate of the contract to the applicant, under an agreement to give time for the payment of the premium, and the principal charges the agent with the amount of the premium, which is settled and paid after the loss, a condition that "no insurance, original or continued, shall be considered as binding until the actual payment of the premium" contained in the printed policies of the company, according to the terms of which the insurance was effected, must be deemed to have been waived, although the agent had no express authority to give time for the payment.

[1] *Security Ins. Co.* v. *Fay, ante.*
[2] *Hale* v. *Mechanics', etc., Ins. Co.,* 6 Gray (Mass.) 169.
[3] *Couch* v. *City F. Ins. Co.,* 38 Conn. 181; *Blanchard* v. *Atlantic Ins. Co.,* 33 N. H. 9; *Security Ins. Co.* v. *Fay,* 22 Mich. 467; *Hale* v. *Mechanics, etc., Ins. Co., ante; Fabyan* v. *Un. Mut. F. Ins. Co.,* 33 N. H. 203; *Forbes* v. *Aqawam Ins. Co.,* 9 Cush. (Mass.) 470.
[4] *Couch* v. *City F. Ins. Co., ante.*
[5] *Ill. Mut. Ins. Co.* v. *Malloy,* 50 Ill. 419; *Gilbert* v. *Phœnix Ins. Co.,* 36 Barb. (N. Y.) 372.
[6] *Ill., etc., Ins. Co.* v. *Malloy,* 50 Ill. 419.

does not of itself render notice to, or consent given by him inoperative. The question is whether the company took proper measures to withdraw all his apparent, as well as actual authority. Whether the assured *knew*, or might have known upon reasonable inquiry, that his agency had been revoked; and this involves the further question whether there was anything to put him on inquiry. The company cannot permit an agent whose power has been revoked, to still hold himself out as their agent when they have the power to prevent it, and then shield themselves from liability upon the ground that his authority had been revoked. In all such cases the question is, as a prudent man, ought the assured have made inquiry, and having made it, could he have ascertained the fact of want of authority in the agent?

When change in the distribution of the risk avoids.

SEC. 365. Where the policy provides that the "insured shall give notice of all additional insurance, and of all changes that may be made in such additional insurance," a change in the sums insured by each policy, although the aggregate amount of the insurance is not increased, operates as a breach of the condition. Thus, the plaintiff gave notice of additional insurance of $1,000 on the building, $2,000 on stock, and $7,000 on machinery. Subsequently one policy was renewed, but the sum insured was subdivided differently, and it was held that the change in this respect was a breach of the condition.[1]

Simultaneous policies.

SEC. 366. Of course, policies simultaneously issued by two companies, by the *same* agent, do not operate as a breach of the conditions of either policy, under the rules before stated;[2] but where two policies are issued by different companies and different agents, although the risk commenced at the same moment, yet it cannot without proof be presumed that the agents of the two different companies issued to the same assured two simultaneous policies, and the presumption, both of law and fact, is, that one was antecedent to the other, so that both companies are entitled to notice in respect to prior and additional insurance, and, unless such notice is given, both policies are void.[3]

---

[1] *Simpson* v. *Pennsylvania F. Ins. Co.*, 38 Penn. St. 250.

[2] In *Washington Ins. Co.* v. *Davison*, 30 Md. 91, a fire insurance company was applied to for a policy upon certain property, and, for its own convenience, and not at the request of the insured, it applied to another company to share the risk. The secretaries of the two companies examined the risk together, but two policies, precisely similar, were drawn, and subsequently altered in the same particulars, and the premium on both was paid at the same time. It was held that the policies were *simultaneous*, and neither required notice or consent of or for the other to be given.

[3] *Manhattan Ins. Co.* v. *Stein*, 5 Bush. (Ky.) 652.

Renewal must keep former policies on foot without change as to amount or distribution of risk.

SEC. 367. While the renewal of a prior policy existing at the time when insurance is made, and assented to, is not a breach of a condition requiring notice to be given " of any insurance already made, or which shall hereafter be made elsewhere upon the same property," yet the taking of a new policy for the same amount in another company in place of a policy expired, *is* a breach of such condition, unless notice thereof is given.[1]

Such a provision may be recinded or modified, even by parol, and may be implied from the conduct of the parties;[2] as by the renewal of the policy with notice or knowledge of other insurance.[3] The bur-

---

[1] *Healey* v. *Imperial Ins. Co.*, 5 Nev. 268.

[2] *Dearborn* v. *Cross*, 7 Cow. (N. Y.) 48 ; *Carroll* v. *Charter Oak Ins. Co.*, 38 Barb. (N. Y.) 402; 40 id. 292 ; *Carrugi* v. *The Atlantic, etc., Ins. Co.*, 40 Ga. 135. In *Pechner* v. *Phœnix Ins. Co.*, 65 N. Y. 195, it appeared on the trial that the policy in question was issued at Elmira by Thomas Perry, agent for the defendant. It was in force from the 31st day of March, 1866, to the same date in 1867, and was issued to Henry D. Straus upon a stock of goods in that city. Pechner, the plaintiff, bought the goods of Straus, who had three other policies upon them, issued by one Ayres, amounting in the aggregate to $5,500. When the sale to Pechner took place the plaintiff and Straus called at the office of Perry and stated the terms of the transaction. Scott, Perry's partner, looked at all the policies and wrote a consent to the transfer on that of the defendant, saying to the plaintiff, "you are all right, this is all you want." Afterwards, and while the policy of the defendant was in force, the plaintiff surrendered the policies issued by Ayres and took out three new policies in other companies. The amount of insurance was the same. In April the plaintiff removed to another store. He thereupon saw Scott and got his consent in writing to the removal. At the same time he exhibited to him the new policies, and Scott had them in his hands and opened them. The plaintiff then asked Scott if these insurances were good and all right, and Scott having opened and looked them over said they were all right. The renewal of the defendant's policy took place in March, and the facts just detailed occurred thereafter. Scott denied that he ever knew that the plaintiff had other insurance to the amount of $5,500, or that he was ever asked to consent to that amount, or did consent to it. He however said that he had consented to $2,000 other insurance, and that when Straus and the plaintiff called on him to get consent to the assignment they had papers in an envelope and handed him the package which was said to contain policies written by Ayres, and that he took out one policy and gave consent to the assignment. It was proved by Scott's testimony that he had been an agent for the defendant for about nine years, and was such at the time, and had issued many policies and renewals in the company, and consented to other insurance. It was held that the plaintiff was entitled to recover.

[3] *Carroll* v. *Charter Oak Ins. Co., ante.* In *Mentz* v. *Lancaster Ins. Co.*, 78 Penn. St. 475, the court held that while a general agent of an insurance company could not waive any of the conditions of the policy, yet, if an agent did any act that induced the assured to believe that a condition in reference to consent to and indorsement of other insurance upon a policy had been complied with, the company would be estopped thereby from setting up a breach of such condition. In this case Mentz procured a policy in the Lancaster Ins. Co., for $600, which contained a condition "that if the assured, or any person or parties interested, shall have existing during the existence of this policy, any other contract or agreement for insurance, whether valid or not, * * not consented to by this company in writing, and mentioned in or indorsed upon this policy, then this policy shall be of no effect. A loss having occurred, the plaintiff offered to prove that the agent who effected the policy for the Armenia Company had knowledge of the policy in the Lancaster Company, he having been the agent who procured

39

den is upon the assured to prove notice and assent,[1] but there is no question but that, if distinct notice is given to an agent that other insurance is to be obtained, *and he consents to it,* that the company will thereby be estopped from setting up a breach of this condition.[2] It is enough if the insurer has *actual knowledge* of such other insurance.[3] But, although the policies are *simultaneously* issued, yet if they are issued by different agents and in different companies, notice must be given.[4]

Where a prior policy existed, and was referred to in a later one obtained upon the same property, or where a subsequent policy has been permitted, a renewal of either policy may be made without notice.[5]

Where a policy contains a statement that other insurance to a certain amount exists upon the property, even if a warranty, it is satisfied if such insurance, *in fact,* existed *at the time* of issuing the policy, although such prior insurance became void immediately upon the issue of the subsequent policy, because assent thereto was not obtained, and the subsequent insurer will be liable for the whole loss, although the policy provides that in case of other insurance prior or subsequent, in force at the time of a loss, the company shall only be liable for a propor-

---

the policy. Also that at the time of effecting the policy in the Armenia Company, the assured called the agent's attention to the fact, and that notice ought to be given and consent indorsed, and that when the agent returned the policy to the assured, who could not read English, he told him that the proper indorsement had been made on the Lancaster policy—the agent having both policies in his possession—which was not true. This testimony was offered to excuse notice and want of indorsement. The lower court rejected the evidence and a verdict having been rendered for the defendant, upon appeal it was set aside and the evidence held admissible. SHARSWOOD, J., said: "It may be conceded that a general agent has no power to waive any express condition in the policy. But the question was not of their power to do this, *but whether their declaration of a fact, namely, that the condition had been actually complied with,* would not estop the company from controverting that fact. The evidence offered and rejected was, that the agent had told the assured that the proper indorsement had been made on the policy. Now *such a declaration made by a duly authorized agent, would operate as an estoppel.* It lulled the party to sleep by the assurance that the conditions of his policy had been complied with, and that his indemnity was secured." The court distinguished the case from that of *Worcester Bank* v. *The Hartford F. Ins. Co.,* 11 Cush. (Mass.) 265, upon the ground that in that case the agent undertook to waive performance of a condition, while in this he positively affirmed that the condition had been performed.

[1] *Healey* v. *Imperial, etc., Ins. Co.,* 5 Nev. 268.

[2] *Carrugi* v. *Atlantic F. Ins. Co.,* 40 Ga. 135.

[3] *Eureka Ins. Co.* v. *Robinson,* 56 Penn. St. 256 ; 5 Ben. F. I. C. 141.

[4] *Manhattan Ins. Co.* v. *Stein,* 5 Buch. (Ky.) 652.

[5] *Brown* v. *Cattaraugus Ins. Co.,* 18 N. Y. 385. A renewal of an outstanding policy is not other insurance. "A renewal," says DWIGHT, C., in *Pitney* v. *Glens Falls Ins. Co.,* 65 N. Y. 1, "is in one sense, a new contract, but it is not other insurance within the meaning of the policy. *It is but the continuation of an existing insurance. * * If notice of the original insurance is given, it must be held to continue through all true renewals of it.*"

tionate amount of the loss.[1] But where an application stated that there was other insurance to the amount of $8,000, on the property, $5,000 in the Ætna, and $3,000 in the Conway Mutual; and there was, in fact, at the time when the application was made, *no* insurance upon the property, but a policy was subsequently obtained for $8,000, in the Trenton and Lafayette offices, it was held that the procurement of these policies invalidated the policy in the defendant company.[2]

Assent without indorsement

SEC. 368. It has formerly been held that, not only notice of the other insurance, prior or subsequent, must be given, *but also that it must be indorsed upon the policy when so provided therein.*[3] But the tendency of the courts laterly is towards a more liberal construction in favor of the assured, *and there is now no question but that oral notice and an oral assent, or acts amounting to an assent, without an indorsement upon the policy, is sufficient;*[4] and knowledge of the existence of *prior* insurance by the agent issuing the policy, which he understands is to be retained, or, perhaps, to state it more broadly, which the insured has not promised to cancel, dispenses with the necessity of either notice or indorsement. By issuing the policy with knowledge of such prior insurance, the insurer waives compliance with the conditions of the policy in that respect, and is afterwards estopped from setting it up in defense;[5] as where the same agent procured both policies;[6] or

[1] *Forbush* v. *Western, etc., Ins. Co.*, 4 Gray (Mass.) 337.

[2] *Conway Tool Co.* v. *Hudson R. Ins. Co.*, 12 Cush. (Mass.) 144.

[3] *Carpenter* v. *Providence, etc., Ins. Co.*, 16 Pet. (U. S.) 495; 2 Ben. F. I. C. 120; *Hutchinson* v. *Western Ins. Co.*, 21 Mo. 97.

[4] *Pitney* v. *Glens Falls Ins. Co.*, 65 N. Y. 1.

[5] *Horwitz* v. *Equitable Ins. Co.*, 40 Mo. 557; *Hubbard* v. *Hartford F. Ins. Co.*, 33 Iowa, 325; *Carroll* v. *Charter Oak Ins. Co.*, 38 Barb. (N. Y.) 402; *Peckney* v. *Phœnix Ins. Co.*, 6 Lans. (N. Y.) 411; affd. 65 N. Y. 196; *Pitney* v. *Glens Falls Ins. Co.*, 65 N. Y. 1; *Geib* v. *International Ins. Co.*, 1 Dill. (U. S. C. C.) 443; *McEwen* v. *Montgomery Co. Ins. Co.*, 5 Hill (N. Y.) 101; *Sexton* v. *Montgomery, etc., Ins. Co.*, 9 Barb. (N. Y.) 191. The assured will be permitted to show the agent's knowledge of such insurance, or any acts tending to establish a waiver. *Whitwell* v. *Putnam F. Ins. Co.*, 6 Lans. (N. Y.) 166; *Potter* v. *Ontario, etc., Ins. Co.*, 5 Hill (N. Y.) 147; *McMahon* v. *Portsmouth, etc., Ins. Co.*, 22 N. H. 15; *National Ins. Co.* v. *Crane*, 16 Md. 260; *Farmers', etc., Ins. Co.* v. *Taylor*, 73 Penn. St. 342; *Schenck* v. *Mercer Co., etc., Ins. Co.*, 24 N. J. 447; *Hadley* v. *N. H. F. Ins. Co.*, 55 N. H. 110; *Goodall* v. *N. E., etc., Ins. Co.*, 25 id. 169; *Hayward* v. *National Ins. Co.*, 52 Mo. 181; *Kenton Ins. Co.* v. *Shea*, 6 Bush. (Ky.) 174; *Washington F. Ins. Co.* v. *Davison*, 30 Md. 91; *Ins. Co. of N. America* v. *McDowell*, 50 Ill. 120; *Dayton Ins. Co.* v. *Kelly*, 24 Ohio St. 345; *Cobb* v. *Ins. Co. of N. America*, 11 Kan. 93; *Osser* v. *Provincial Ins. Co.*, 12 U. C. (C. P.) 141; *Planters', etc., Ins. Co.* v. *Lyons*, 38 Texas, 253; *Webster* v. *Phœnix Ins. Co.*, 36 Wis. 67; *Carrugi* v. *Atlantic F. Ins. Co.*, 40 Ga. 135.

[6] *Russell* v. *State Ins. Co.*, 55 Mo., 585; *Kenton Ins. Co.* v. *Shea, ante; Van Bories* v. *United, etc., Ins. Co., ante; Washington F. Ins. Co.* v. *Davison, ante.*

where the policy was left with the agent for indorsement of assent, which he promised to make, but did not;[1] or where notice of such other insurance was given, and no objection made thereto.[2] In all cases the question is, whether notice was given, and assent, express or implied, on the part of the insurer or the agent, is established. If notice is given, it is the business of the company *at once* to elect whether to cancel or continue the risk; and failing to cancel, it is held to have elected to retain the risk; and the justice of this doctrine is not doubtful.[3]

Knowledge of other insurance after policy was made, effect of.

SEC. 369. But a waiver cannot be inferred from the fact that the company after its policy was issued, *knew* that other insurance had been effected upon the property, unless with such knowledge they do some act that amounts to a recognition of the policy as a valid obligation.[4] But if the assured gives notice of such other insurance, and no objection is made, and the policy is not taken up and canceled, the fact that such consent was not indorsed on the policy will not render it inoperative and void, at least in equity, when it is otherwise free from objection.[5] So, while the mere fact that the agent *knows* that other insurance exists upon the property is not evidence of notice given by the assured,[6] yet, if subsequently, with such knowledge the agent or the company do any act that recognizes the validity of the policy, it is treated as a waiver.[7]

Waiver of breach may be inferred.

SEC. 370. Where the policy stipulates that the aggregate amount of insurance in this and other companies shall not exceed two-thirds of the estimated cash value of the property, and greater insurance is made, with notice to the company, *who afterwards make and collect an assessment on the premium note*, the forfeiture is waived.[8] So if notice is given *before, or at the time* of the issue of a renewal receipt, the forfeiture is

---

[1] *Cobb* v. *Ins. Co. of N. America, ante.*

[2] *Planters' Ins. Co.* v. *Lyons, ante.*

[3] *Planters' Ins. Co.* v. *Lyons, ante.*

[4] *Simpson* v. *Penn, etc., Ins. Co.,* 38 Penn. St. 250; *Schenck* v. *Mercer County, etc., Ins. Co.,* 24 N. J. 447.

[5] *National, etc., Ins. Co.* v. *Crane,* 16 Md. 260.

[6] *Schenck* v. *Mercer, etc., Ins. Co.,* 24 N. J. 447.

[7] *Ins. Co.* v. *Stockblower,* 26 Penn. St. 199.

[8] *Lycoming Ins. Co.* v. *Stockholm,* 3 Grant (Penn.) 207.

waived, *but not* if the notice was not given until *after* the receipt was issued.[1]

Insurer, upon notice, must cancel policy, or indorse assent.

Sec. 371. Where at the time when insurance is effected the agent knows that other insurance is to be obtained, and engages to obtain it, and so notifies the company, but no indorsement is made upon the policy, unless the company objects thereto or notifies the assured of its objection thereto, it is estopped from setting up such other insurance as a breach of the conditions of the policy.[2] So where the company or its agent is notified of other subsequent insurance, it is its or his duty to indorse consent upon the policy, or to notify the assured of the company's refusal to carry the risk, and failing to do so it is estopped from setting up such other insurance as a breach of the conditions of the policy.[3] Where the plaintiff procured a policy in the defendant company, and subsequently procured other insurance, of which notice was not given, but when the policy was renewed, he informed the defendants' agent of such other insurance, and after such notice, the agent renewed the policy. The court held that the defendants were thereby estopped from setting up such other insurance as a breach of the conditions of the policy.[4] So where the policy prohibited other insurance without notice and consent, the plaintiff procured other insurance and notified the insurer, who acknowledged the receipt of the notice, but refused to give consent thereto unless the insured would consent that the sum recoverable under the policy should not, together with all other insurance thereon, exceed two-thirds the value of the property insured. In an action upon the policy, it was held that the

---

[1] *Carroll* v. *Charter Oak Ins. Co.*, 40 Barb. (N. Y.) 492. A general agent of an insurance company, may grant permission for other insurance, or waive a forfeiture for a breach of a condition against it. Thus in *Warner* v. *Peoria, etc., Ins. Co.*, 14 Wis. 318, the policy provided that it should become invalid, if further insurance should be effected without notice to the company, etc. Afterward the insured applied to the general agent of the company in another city, to procure him other insurance on the property, at the same time handing him this policy. The agent inserted in the policy, "other insurance permitted without notice till required. J. C. M." and then procured the other insurance desired. Held, that he was authorized, by his character as general agent, to insert this clause, and that the insurance, effected after he had done so, did not work a forfeiture of the policy.

[2] *Horwitz* v. *Equitable Ins. Co.*, 40 Mo. 507; *Geib* v. *International Ins. Co.*, 1 Dill. (U. S.) 443; *McEwen* v. *Montgomery, etc., Ins. Co.*, 5 Hill (N. Y.) 110; *Potter* v. *Ontario Ins. Co.*, 5 id. 147; *Pechner* v. *Phœnix Ins. Co.*, 7 Lans. (N. Y.) 411; *Carroll* v. *Charter Oak Ins. Co.*, 40 Barb. (N. Y.) 292; *Continental Ins. Co.* v. *Horton*, 28 Mich. 174.

[3] *Planters' Mut. Ins. Co.* v. *Lyons*, 38 Tex. 253.

[4] *Carroll* v. *Charter Oak Ins. Co.*, 1 Abb. Dec. (N. Y.) 316.

condition of the policy was not broken, and that the insurer had no right to impose such condition, that it should either have assented to or dissented from such other insurance.[1] So where notice of other insurance was given, and receipt thereof was acknowledged, but neither approbation of or dissent thereto was expressed, it was held that the defendants must be regarded as having assented.[2] So where notice was given to the agent who procured the policy, that other insurance existed, the court held that the company was thereby estopped from setting up such other insurance as a breach of the condition of the policy, because not indorsed thereon.[3] Merely employing the same broker who procured the original policy, to procure other insurance, is not such constructive notice to the company issuing the first policy, as to constitute a compliance with the clause requiring notice of other insurance to be given with reasonable diligence.[4] When a company upon being notified of other insurance does not signify an objection, it is treated as assenting thereto.[5] And the notice is not vitiated by an error in the name of the company.[6]

Parol contract.

SEC. 372. Where insurance is effected by parol, no policy having been issued, mere notice of additional insurance is sufficient, although the usual form of the company's policies required that it should be indorsed thereon.[7]

Breach of condition suspends policy.

SEC. 373. When a policy provides that if other insurances or insurance beyond a certain amount shall be obtained, such policy shall be *of no effect*, the policy is not rendered void by other insurance, or over insurance, but only inoperative during the period that such "other" or "over insurance" exists, and if, prior to a loss such other insurance has ceased to exist, or no over insurance exists, the policy is operative and enforcible.[8] And it has been held in Illinois,[9] that where a policy

---

[1] *Westlake* v. *St. Lawrence Ins. Co.*, 14 Barb. (N. Y.) 206.

[2] *Potter* v. *Ontario Ins. Co.*, 5 Hill (N. Y.) 147.

[3] *Sexton* v. *Montgomery, etc., Ins. Co.*, 9 Barb. (N. Y.) 191.

[4] *Mellen* v. *Hamilton F. Ins. Co.*, 5 Duer. (N. Y.) 101; Affd. 17 N. Y. 609.

[5] *Potter* v. *Ontario, etc., Ins. Co.*, 5 Hill (N. Y.) 147.

[6] *Benjamin* v. *Saratoga, etc., Ins. Co.*, 17 N. Y. 415.

[7] *Eureka Ins. Co.* v. *Robinson*, 56 Penn. St. 256.

[8] In *Obermeyer* v. *Globe, etc.. Ins. Co.*, 43 Mo. 573, one O. effected insurance upon his mill for $3,000. The policy containing the clause " $18,000 on same, insured elsewhere, and $2,000 additional to be insured, to be reported in total when

[9] *N. E. F. Ins. Co.* v. *Schettler*, 38 Ill. 166.

declared that it should be void in case other insurance should "be existing on the property during the continuance of the policy," that the fact that other insurance had existed during the time, but which *did not exist at the time of the loss*, did not defeat the insurer's liability under the policy. The condition being construed as intending merely that such policy should be inoperative only, while such other insurance existed.

Insolvency of other insurers does not prevent forfeiture.

SEC. 374. The fact that the company in which the "other insurance" was made *is insolvent*, does not prevent the operation of the forfeiture. The test is not whether the insurance in the other companies *can be collected, but whether it is enforceable as a legal claim.*[1]

Confusion of goods.

SEC. 375. In a New York case, a question arose as to the effect upon such a condition by what may be termed a confusion of the property. Thus, the plaintiff had a policy in the defendant company upon a stock of goods at 146 River street, Troy. The policy contained a condition that "in case any other policy of insurance has been or shall be issued, covering the whole or any portion of the property insured by this company, the policy shall be void, unless notice thereof be given, and the company's assent obtained thereto in writing." The defendants subsequently consented that the goods might be removed to a store adjoining, 148 River street, at which place, *at that time*, the plaintiffs had a large stock of similar goods insured in another com-

---

required," with the usual stipulations for notice and indorsement upon the policy of all previous and subsequent insurance, in default of which the policy should be of no effect. While the policy was in force, O., on the 13th of September, 1865, was insured up to $23,000, the stipulated amount, and on the 11th of November, 1865, for $2,500 additional, of which the insurance company had no notice. The agent of the company that issued the last insurance in June, 1865, told O. that he should cancel one of his old policies for the same amount, when it expired in November, which was before the new policy was taken, but did not do so until December, 1865, thus making an over insurance for more than a month. At the date of the loss the total amount of insurance was $12,000, including this policy. Held, that there was no violation of the conditions of the policy, which would discharge the insurance company. See, similar in principle, *Ins. Co. v. Coatsville Shoe Factory*, 80 Penn. St. 385.

[1] Thus, in *Ryder v. Phœnix Ins. Co.*, 98 Mass. 185, it appeared that, at the time when the plaintiffs took out the policy in the defendant company, they held policies in other companies to the full value of the property insured, covering the same risks. One of the companies, in which a policy existed, had become insolvent, and proceedings for its dissolution had been commenced in New York, but whether dissolution had actually been decreed did not appear, nor was it material, in the view that the court took of the question. The court held that the policy was void in any event, as the validity of the subsequent policy did not depend upon the question whether the prior insurance was worthless and could not be collected, but upon the question whether, in law, other insurance existed.

pany, of which fact the defendant was not aware. A loss having occurred, the defendants held that they were not liable because of the insurance upon the goods in 148, of which they had no notice. But the court held that there had been no breach of the conditions of the policy, because the two policies did not cover the same goods.[1] But a contrary doctrine is held in Louisiana.[2] In that case, the plaintiff had an insurance upon a stock of goods owned by him and kept in his store, and the policy prohibited other insurance. Subsequently he purchased another similar stock, upon which there was an insurance, and took an assignment of the policy, and the court held that this was "other insurance," and avoided the policy. It is proper to say that, where a policy of insurance exists upon a dealer's stock, the risk is not permanent, but fluctuating. It does not apply to the same property, but to property within the class insured, although purchased subsequent to the taking of the policy. The contract impliedly contemplates a changing risk. There is an implied understanding that the insured may sell and buy goods of that class, and the policy shall attach to goods similar in kind, which are in the place indicated by the policy at the time of loss; and in this view it would seem that the doctrine of the Louisiana case is clearly correct. The goods are assimilated, and each policy *covers the whole stock;* therefore there is other insurance, within the meaning and intent of the insurer. In an Ohio case,[3] a doctrine in consonance with that adopted in the Louisiana case was held. In that case, the plaintiff was the owner of two stocks of goods in different towns, which were covered by separate policies. The policy upon the goods at A. prohibited other insurance, but the company consented to their removal to B., but not to other insurance. They were moved to B. and mingled with the goods kept there by the plaintiff, which were insured by another policy. It was held that the policy upon the goods removed from A. was avoided by the insurance upon the goods at B. But if the goods are not intermingled, but are kept separate and distinct, it is not other insurance; and whether they were so intermingled as to become one common inseparable stock, is a question for the jury.[4]

In what cases evidence may be given to show that the policies do not cover same goods.

SEC. 376. Where there is a latent ambiguity in the prior policy, parol evidence is admissible to show that it was not intended to, and

[1] *Vose* v. *Hamilton Mut. Ins. Co.*, 39 Barb. (N. Y.) 302.
[2] *Walton* v. *Louisiana, etc., Ins. Co.*, 2 Rob. (La.) 263.
[3] *Washington Ins. Co.* v. *Hayes*, 17 Ohio St. 432.
[4] *Peoria, etc., Ins. Co.* v. *Anapaw*, 45 Ill. 86.

does not cover the property insured by a subsequent policy. Thus, in a Maine case,[1] a policy of insurance was obtained, from the defend. ants, upon a stock of goods and merchandise contained in a certain building designated in the policy. Subsequently another policy of insurance was obtained of the defendants, upon a stock of merchan. dise "in the chambers" of the same building. The goods in the chambers were destroyed by fire. In an action upon the latter policy, it was held, that there was a latent ambiguity in the policies, in regard to the merchandise intended by the parties to be embraced therein, properly explainable by parol testimony; and that, it being proved that the goods in the chambers were not intended to be included in the first policy, the defendants were liable for the whole loss.[2] So, where there is doubt as to whether two policies upon the same prop. erty cover the same interest, as where D. & Co. take out a policy upon certain property, conditioned to be void if other insurance exists thereon, and it appears that a policy existed in the name of D. & A., *trustees*, it is competent to show by parol whether the interest of D. & Co. is identical with that of D. & A.[3]

Notice must be given as prescribed by policy.

SEC. 377. If notice is required, unless given within a reasonable time, or within the time prescribed in the policy, in the manner required by the terms of the policy, the policy will be void,[4] and the notice must be given by the assured or some person authorized by him. The mere fact that the agent or even the secretary of the company accidentally learns that other insurances has been obtained, and takes no steps to withdraw from the risk, does not amount to a waiver. And this was held in a case where no policy had in fact been issued. Notice must be given in such a way as to show that compliance with the requirements of the policy was intended.[5] But if the insurer, or an agent of the

---

[1] *Storer* v. *Elliott, etc., Ins. Co.*, 45 Me. 175.

[2] In *Haley* v. *Dorchester Ins. Co.*, 1 Allen (Mass.) 536, it was held that where the policy provided that in case double insurance exists, the company should be liable only for such proportion of the loss as the sum insured bears to the whole amount insured. such amount not to exceed three-fourths of the value of such property, and the amount of insurance already existing was stated at a certain sum, the insured may show by parol that the policies cover but a part of the property.

[3] *Planters' Ins. Co.* v. *Deford*, 38 Md. 382; *Frederick, etc.*, v. *Deford*, 38 Md. 404.

[4] *Burt* v. *Peoples' Mut. Ins. Co.*, 2 Gray (Mass.) 397; *Bigler* v. *N. Y. Central Ins. Co.*, 22 N. Y. 402; *Forbes* v. *Agawam Ins. Co.*, 9 Cush. (Mass.) 470; *Burt* v. *Peoples' Mut. Ins. Co.*, 2 Gray (Mass.) 397; *Mellen* v. *Hamilton Ins. Co.*, 17 N. Y. 609; *Shurtleff* v. *Phœnix Ins. Co.*, 57 Me. 137; *Neve* v. *Columbian Ins. Co.*, 2 McMull (S. C.) 220; *Harris* v. *Ohio Ins. Co.*, 5 Ohio, 466; *N. Y. Central Ins. Co.* v. *Watson*, 23 Mich. 486.

[5] *Eureka Ins. Co.* v. *Robinson*, 56 Penn. St. 256.

insurer, had knowledge of prior insurance, *when the policy was issued*, no breach can be alleged, because notice is unnecessary where knowledge of the fact exists when the risk is taken, and by issuing a policy, *knowing* of outstanding insurance upon the policy, although it is not indorsed upon the policy, is yet a waiver of any objection thereto, or of any defense on that account,[1] whether he derived his knowledge from the insured himself,[2] or from any other source,[3] as to permit the insurer to issue a policy and take the premium with such knowledge, without assuming the risk, would be to encourage fraud; therefore, the insurer is estopped by such knowledge from setting up such other insurance as a breach of the conditions of the policy.[4]

The assured must use reasonable diligence in giving notice of other insurance, and the question as to whether he has used such diligence or not, is for the jury,[5] and notice of an *intention* to procure other insurance is not sufficient. It must be notice of a consummated fact.[6]

May show policy covers other property in whole or in part.

SEC. 378. A statement by the assured of the amount of previous insurance upon the property is not conclusive upon him, and he may show that, although the sum named is the amount of the previous policy, yet, that the policy in fact, in part, covers other property.[7]

Special conditions waived by parol, or waiver inferred from acts of insurer, though policy stipulates that certain matters shall not amount to waiver.

SEC. 379. Where a policy contains a prohibition of other insurance, " without the consent of the company *written* hereon," and also provides that "the use of general terms, or anything less than a distinct, specific agreement, clearly expressed or indorsed on the policy, shall not be

---

[1] *Washington Ins. Co.* v. *Davison*, 30 Md. 92; *Gale* v. *Belknap Ins. Co.*, 41 N. H. 170; *Rowley* v. *Empire Ins. Co.*, 36 N. Y. 550; *Tallman* v. *Atlantic Ins. Co.*, 40 N. Y. 87; *Kenton Ins. Co.* v. *Shea*, 6 Bush (Ky.) 174; *N. E. F. Ins. Co.* v. *Schettler*, 38 Ill. 166.

[2] *N. E. F. & M. Ins. Co.* v. *Schettler. ante; Kenton Ins. Co.* v. *Shea, ante; Van Bories* v. *United States, etc., Ins. Co.*, 8 Bush. (Ky.) 133.

[3] *Washington Ins. Co.* v. *Davison, ante; Ins. Co. of N. America* v. *McDowell* 50 Ill. 120; *Gale* v. *Belknap Ins. Co., ante.* But in *Durlas* v. *Citizens', etc., Ins. Co.*, 23 La. An. 332, the court held that a policy containing such a provision is avoided, even though the subsequent insurance is taken out in the same offices, but the doctrine of this case hardly commends it either as fair expression of law or morals.

[4] *Bidwell* v. *N. W. Ins. Co.*, 19 N. Y. 179, also 24 N. Y. 302.

[5] *Kimball* v. *Howard, etc., Ins. Co., ante.*

[6] *Kimball* v. *Howard Ins. Co., ante.* In *Healey* v. *Imperial F. Ins. Co.*, 5 Nev. 268, the plaintiff informed the defendant's agent of his intention to get another policy, and it was held that this was not such a notice as satisfied the condition.

[7] *Haley* v. *Dorchester Mut. Ins. Co.*, 1 Allen (Mass.) 536.

construed as a waiver of any printed or written condition or restriction therein," yet, if the agent who effected the insurance, and whose authority is not shown to have been restricted in any way, so conducts as to have bound himself by way of estoppel from disputing the validity of subsequent insurance on the point of consent, the company will be bound thereby. Thus, where an agent, who had issued a policy containing such conditions, was subsequently applied to for additional insurance, and undertook to procure it, but neglected or failed to do so, and the insured themselves subsequently procured it, and notified the agent thereof by mail, giving him the precise amount and stating in detail all the policies they held, and subsequently one of the plaintiffs met the agent and had a conversation with him about such additional insurance, and he made no objections thereto, it was held that this amounted to a waiver of all objections thereto, and estopped the insurer from setting up the same in avoidance of their policy.[1] "The ground upon which this case rests is, that, where an agent, by his conduct, has misled the insured and induced him to make application for insurance or accept conditions under a misapprehension as to their literal accuracy, the company is estopped by the agent's conduct from setting up, in defense, any matter which the agent has fairly waived.[2]

May be partial breach.

Sec. 380. Where the policy provides that if other insurance is obtained without the consent of the company, the policy shall be void; other insurance is held only to avoid the policy as to the property, covered by the subsequent insurance. Thus, where a policy is issued upon a store *and* fixtures, and a subsequent policy without consent is procured upon the *fixtures* only, the first policy still remains operative as to the store, but becomes void as to the fixtures.[3] Unless the policy expressly provides that the procurement of other insurance shall have the effect to destroy the validity of the contract *for the remainder of the term covered by it*, the procurement of temporary insurance without consent

---

[1] *Westchester Ins. Co.* v. *Earle,* 33 Mich. 143.

[2] *Michigan Ins. Co.* v. *Lewis,* 30 Mich. 41; *Ins. Co.* v. *Wilkinson,* 13 Wall. (U. S.) 222; *Continental Ins. Co.* v. *Horton,* 28 Mich. 173; *Ætna, etc.,* *Ins. Co.* v. *Olmstead,* 21 Mich. 246; *Ins. Co.* v. *Mahone,* 21 Wall. (U. S.) 151; *Ins. Co.* v. *Slaughter,* 12 id. 404. Thus, where an insurance company instructed its agents not to deliver a policy until the premium was paid, it was held that its delivery *without payment,* the agent giving credit to the assured, was obligatory. *Miller* v. *Brooklyn Life Ins. Co.,* 12 Wall. (U. S.) 285. The principal is bound by the acts of the agent within the scope of his authority, and this extends even to mistakes made by the agent in filling up applications made for insurance. *Hingston* v. *Ætna Ins. Co.,* 42 Iowa, 46.

[3] *Ill. Mut. Ins. Co.* v. *Fix,* 53 Ill. 151; 5 Am. Rep. 38.

only suspends the policy during the time that such temporary insur-ance exists, and when such temporary insurance terminates the policy is revived, and becomes operative, and recovery for a loss occurring *after* such temporary insurance is terminated, cannot be defeated upon the ground that the policy was thereby invalidated.[1]

Double insurance.

Sec. 381. Double insurance exists when the insurer has two or more policies upon the *same* risk and covering the *same* interest.[2] They need not necessarily be issued to the same party, but they must cover the same interest, and inure to the advantage of the same party. Thus where policies were issued to H. C. & Co., loss if any payable to B., and B. had made large advances on the property and had other policies covering goods *their own and held in trust*, it was held that all the policies—the one in suit having been made payable to B.—must be treated as covering the same interest, and consequently as consti-tuting double insurance, which bound all the insurers to contribute to the loss.[3]

Where different policies are issued upon the *same* property covering *different* interests, there is no double insurance, as, any person having an insurable interest in property, may protect it by insurance. The question as to whether[4] double insurance exists or not, only becomes material when the policy stipulates against it, or in the adjustment of losses. If there are several policies outstanding upon the same property, and the total amount of insurance is less than the amount of the loss, each insurer must pay in full.[5] But, where a subsequent policy stipulates that "if the said insured shall have made any other insurance upon the premises aforesaid prior in date, to this policy, then the insurers shall be liable only for so much as the prior insur-

---

[1] In *Obermeyer* v. *Globe Ins. Co.*, 43 Mo., the policy contained the usual stipula-tion requiring notice and indorsement upon the policy or acknowledgment in writ-ing of all previous and subsequent insurances, in default of which the policy should cease and be of no effect. The court held that a subsequent temporary insurance effected after the issuing of the policy, without notice, but not existing at the time of the loss, did not avoid the policy under this stipulation. See, to same effect, *Ins. Co.* v. *Coatsville Shoe Co.*, 80 Penn. St. 385.

[2] *Root* v. *Cincinnati Ins. Co.*, 1 Dis. (S. C. Ohio) 138; *Stout* v. *Royal Ins. Co.*, 50 Penn. St. 14; *Merrick* v. *Germania F. Ins. Co.*, 54 id. 277; *London* v. *London Ass. Co.*, 1 Burr. 492; *Baltimore F. Ins. Co.* v. *Lancy*, 20 Md. 20; *Lucas* v. *Jeffer-son Ins. Co.*, 6 Cow. (N. Y.) 635; *Peoria F. & M. Ins Co.* v. *Lewis*, 18 Ill. 553.

[3] *Haugh* v. *People's F. Ins. Co.*, 36 Md. 398; *Godin* v. *London Ass. Co.*, 1 Burr. 489; *Home Ins. Co.* v. *Baltimore Warehouse Co.*, 93 U. S. 543.

[4] *Wells* v. *Philadelphia Ins. Co.*, 9 S. & R. (Penn.) 103; *Excelsior Ins. Co.* v. *Royal Ins. Co.*, 55 N. Y. 343; 14 Am. Rep. 271.

[5] *Whiting* v. *Independent, etc., Ins. Co.*, 15 Md. 297.

ance may be deficient in covering the premises hereby insured" if the loss does not exceed the amount of the prior policy, the subsequent insurers are not liable.[1] Under such a policy, the prior policy cannot be cancelled without the consent of the subsequent insurer.[2]

In case of double insurance, the assured may sue upon all the policies and is entitled to judgment upon all, *but he is entitled to but one satisfaction;* therefore, if, during the pendency of suits on several policies covering the same risk and interest, the loss is paid in full by one company, the actions against the others must fail,[3] and the insurer paying the loss has a remedy against the other insurers for a proportionate share of the loss.[4] If there is any doubt as to whether the policies cover the same property or interest, evidence is admissible to show the fact.[5]

If a subsequent policy contains no provision in respect to prior insurance, the amount of insurable interest in it will be the same as for the first policy; for the insured may insure again and again the same property, but can recover but one indemnity, and he may proceed for that purpose against either the prior or subsequent insurers, or both, leaving the one from whom indemnity is ultimately obtained to pursue the others for contribution.[6]

Re-insurance.

SEC. 382. It is held that an insurer has an insurable interest in the property covered by its policy,[7] and consequently it may re-insure to

[1] *Peters* v. *Delaware Ins. Co.*, 5 S. & R. (Penn.) 473; *Kent* v. *Manufacturers' Ins. Co.*, 18 Pick. (Mass.) 19; *American Ins. Co.* v. *Griswold*, 14 Wend. (N. Y.) 399. In *Fairchild* v. *The London F. & M. Ins. Co.*, 51 N. Y. 65, the defendants issued a floating policy upon merchandise in any of the warehouses and while *in transitu* in any of the streets of New York, Brooklyn and Jersey city, subject to a condition, in substance, that the policy should not extend to cover goods upon which there were any specific insurances, except as far as relates to any excess of value beyond the amount of such specific insurances, which excess was declared under the protection of the policy. A fire occurred in a warehouse wherein plaintiffs had merchandise to the amount of $386,026, covered by specific insurances to the amount of $324,000; the amount of the loss was $274,192.46. Held, that the intent of the condition was to throw the loss upon the specific insurances unless it exceeded them in amount, and as the specific insurances exceeded the value of the goods destroyed, the interest insured by the policy was not affected and defendant was not liable to contribute any portion of the loss.

[2] *Marcy* v. *Whaling Ins. Co.*, 9 Met. (Mass.) 354.

[3] *Newby* v. *Reed*, 1 W. Bl. 416; *Wiggin* v. *Suffolk Ins. Co.*, 18 Pick. (Mass.) 145; *Ætna Ins. Co.* v. *Tyler*, 16 Wend. (N. Y.) 385; *Lucas* v. *Jefferson Ins. Co.*, 6 Cow. (N. Y.) 635.

[4] *Wiggin* v. *Suffolk Ins. Co.*, *ante.*

[5] *Vose* v. *Hamilton Ins. Co.*, 39 Barb. (N. Y.) 302; *Peoria F. & M. Ins. Co.* v. *Anapaw*, 45 Ill. 85.

[6] *Willardson* v. *Western M. & F. Ins. Co.*, 9 La. 27; 1 Ben. F. I. C. 562; WADD-WORTH, J., in *Lucas* v. *Jefferson Ins. Co.*, *ante.*

[7] *Yonkers, etc., Ins. Co.* v. *Hoffman*, 6 Robt. (N. Y.) 316.

the extent of the risk it holds upon the property. It cannot insure for more than it may be liable for, nor against any other or different casualty.[1] If the original insurer settles the loss for a less sum than that covered by re-insurance, the re-insurer is only liable for the sum paid.[2] Whether if the original insurer becomes insolvent before the loss, *and compromises for a less sum than is covered by the policy of re-insurance*, the re-insurers are entitled to the benefit of such compromise, is an open question. It has been held in New York,[3] and in Indiana,[4] and in Maryland,[5] and in the United States Circuit Court;[6] but this doctrine is denied in Illinois,[7] and upon the principle that a contract of insurance is merely a contract of indemnity, the doctrine of the latter State would seem to be more consistent and consonant with principle. But it must be admitted that the weight of authority is the other way. In New York[8] the court held that the insurer was not obliged, in order to maintain an action against its re-insurer, to show that it had paid the loss, but might at once bring its action, and was only obliged to show a legal liability on its part to respond for the loss upon its policy. In the Maryland case[9] the policy contained a clause "loss, if any, payable *pro rata* to them, *at the same time and in the same manner as they pay*." The policy of the original insurers covered $10,000, and the policy of re-insurance one-half the risk. It was held that the re-insurer was bound to pay one-half the loss, notwithstanding the original insurer had become bankrupt and paid only a small dividend.[10] Where the policy of re-insurance provides that the "loss, if any shall be paid *pro rata*, and re-insurance, in case of loss, to be settled in proportion as the sum re-insured shall bear to the whole sum covered by the re-insured company," the re-insurer is only liable to indemnify the re-insured in the same proportion that it is liable to indemify the assured in the original policy.[11] The re-insurer is not

[1] *Phila. Ins. Co.* v. *Washington Ins. Co.*, 23 Penn. St. 25.

[2] *Ill. Mut. Ins. Co.* v. *The Andes Ins. Co.*, 67 Ill. 362.

[3] *Howe* v. *Mut. Safety Ins. Co.*, 1 Sandf. (N. Y. S. C.) 137; Affd. 2 N. Y. 234. See Sec. 85.

[4] *Eagle Ins. Co.* v. *Lafayette Ins. Co.*, 9 Ind. 443.

[5] *Consolidated Ins. Co.* v. *Cushaw*, 41 Md. 59.

[6] *Cashaw* v. *N. W. Ins. Co.*, 5 Biss. (U. S. C. C.) 476; *ex parte* Norwood, 3 id. 504.

[7] *Illinois Mut. Ins. Co.* v. *Andes Ins. Co.*, ante.

[8] *Howe* v. *Mut. Safety Ins. Co.*, ante.

[9] *Consolidated F. Ins. Co.* v. *Cushaw*, 41 Md. 59.

[10] The same doctrine was held in *Blackstone* v. *Almenia Ins. Co.*, 56 N. Y. 105. See Sec. 85.

[11] *Norwood* v. *Resolute F. Ins. Co.*, 4 J. & Spencer (N. Y. S. C.) 552.

liable at all, if the re-insured is not liable, and may make any defense to an action brought by the original insurer against it, that the re-insured might have made in an action against it upon the original policy.[1] It may avail itself of the breach of any of the conditions of the original assured therein, for if the re-insured is not liable upon the original policy, it has no insurable interest to be covered by the re-insurer's policy. The re-insured must establish its liability upon its policy to the person originally insured, and show compliance on the part of such original assured, with all the conditions of the policy, or a waiver thereof without any fraudulent intent on its part. It must also comply with the requirements and conditions of the policy of re-insurer in all respects, as to proofs of loss,[2] and in *all* respects. The contract is personal between the companies, and the person insured under the original policy has no privity therein. He can maintain no action thereon, or claim any benefit therefrom.[3] When the insurer, at the request of the re-insurer, and for its benefit, defends against an action upon its policy, the re-insurer is bound by such judgment, although not a party to the action.[4]

---

[1] *Delaware Ins. Co. v. Quaker City, etc., Ins. Co.,* 3 Grant's Cas. (Penn.) 71; *Eagle Ins. Co. v. Lafayette Ins. Co.,* 9 Ind. 443; *New York, etc., Ins. Co. v. Protection Ins. Co.,* 1 Story (U. S.) 458; *Merchants', etc., Ins. Co. v. N. O. Ins. Co.,* 24 La. An. 305; *Carpenter v. Providence Ins. Co.,* 16 Pet. (U. S.) 495; *St. Nicholas Ins. Co. v. Merchants' Ins. Co.,* 11 Hun (N. Y.) 108.

[2] *The Yonkers, etc., Ins. Co. v. Hoffman Ins. Co.,* 6 Robt. (N. Y.) 316; *Carrington v. Com'l Ins. Co.,* 1 Bos. (N. Y.) 188; *Bowery F. Ins. Co. v. N. Y. F. Ins. Co.,* 17 Wend. (N. Y.) 359; *Alliance, etc., Ins. Co. v. La. State Ins. Co.,* 8 La. 1; 1 Ben. F. I. C. 447.

[3] *Herckenrath v. American, etc., Ins. Co.,* 3 Barb. Ch. (N. Y.) 63.

[4] *Strong v. Phœnix Ins. Co.,* 62 Mo. 289; 21 Am. Rep. 417.

CHAPTER XII.

AGENTS.

Powers and functions of.

SEC. 383. The same rules apply to insurance companies as apply in the case of individuals, and a person who is clothed with power to act for them at all, *is treated as clothed with authority to bind them as to all matters within the scope of his real or apparent authority.*[1] Persons

---

[1] *Bodine* v. *Exchange F. Ins. Co.*, 51 N. Y. 117; *Ecletic Life Ins. Co.*, v. *Fahrenkrug*, 68 Ill. 463; *Warner* v. *Peoria M. & F. Ins. Co.*, 14 Wis. 318; *Ins. Co.* v. *Wilkinson*, 13 Wall. (U. S.) 222; *Ide* v. *Phœnix Ins. Co.*, 2 Bis. (U. S.) 333; *Taylor* v. *Germania Ins Co.*, 2 Dill. (U. S. C. C.) 282; *Clark* v. *Manufacturers*

dealing with them *in that capacity* are not bound to go beyond the apparent authority conferred upon them, and inquire whether they are, *in fact*, authorized to do a particular act for the company. *It is enough if the act is within the scope of their apparent power*, and beyond this, third persons are not bound to make inquiry.

Illustration of the rule.

SEC. 384. Thus, where an insurer entrusts applications in blank for insurance to a person who forwards the same to the insurer, and is the medium through whom the insurer delivers the policy and receives the premium, the person so entrusted therewith is treated as clothed with the requisite authority to effectuate the duties confided to him, and to that extent represents the company, and can bind it. The applicant would not, upon these facts, be justified in treating him as having authority to make contracts of insurance binding upon the company, because the very fact that an application is required to be made and forwarded to the company, is notice to him that the insurer reserves the right to judge and determine for himself, whether or not the risk shall be taken, but the assured has a right to rely upon it, that the agent has authority to explain the inquiries put in the application, and to determine what facts are required to be stated, as well as *how* they shall be stated, and acting upon his direction, if any error is committed, it is chargable to the insurer, and not upon the assured,[1] and if he fills out the

---

Ins. Co., 8 How. (U. S.) 235 ; *Baubic* v. *Ætna Ins. Co.*, 2 Dill. (U. S. C. C.) 156 ; *Roth* v. *City F. Ins. Co.*, 6 McLean (U. S.) 524 ; *Goit* v. *Nat. Protection Ins. Co.*, 25 Barb. (N. Y.) 189 ; *Gloucester Mfg. Co.* v. *Howard F. Ins. Co.*, 5 Gray (Mass.) 497 ; *Baker* v. *Cutter*, 45 Me. 236 ; *Citizens' Mut. F. Ins. Co.* v. *Sartwell*, 8 Allen (Mass.) 217 ; *Union, etc., F. Ins. Co.* v. *Keyser*, 32 N. H. 313 ; *Hotchkiss* v. *Germania F. Ins. Co.*, 5 Hun (N. Y.) 90 ; *Rowley* v. *Empire Ins. Co.*, 36 N. Y. 550 ; *Perkins* v. *Washington Ins. Co.*, 4 Cow. (N. Y.) 645 ; *Peck* v. *New London, etc., Ins. Co.*, 22 Conn. 584 ; *Cabot* v. *Given*, 45 Me. 144 ; *De Groot* v. *Fulton F. Ins. Co.*, 4 Rob. (N. Y.) 504 ; *Conover* v. *Mut. Ins. Co.*, 1 N. Y. 290 ; *Bush* v. *Westchester F. Ins. Co.*, 2 T. & C. (N. Y.) 629. But it is competent for the insurer to limit the powers of an agent, and when the policy contains a notice of such limitation, it is operative as to all matters *after* notice. *Van Allen* v. *Farmers', etc., Ins. Co.*, 64 N. Y. 469.

[1] *Malleable Iron Works* v. *Phœnix Ins. Co.*, 25 Conn. 465 ; and when the agent, through fraud or mistake, misstates facts in the application which he fills up himself, and which is made a part of the policy, a court of equity will reform the instrument according to the contract. *Woodbury Savings Bank* v. *Charter Oak Ins. Co.*, 31 Conn. 519. And at law the insurer will be treated as estopped from setting up the errors or fraud of the agent in avoidance of the policy. *Com. Ins. Co.* v. *Spanknable*, 52 Ill. 53 ; *Keith* v. *Globe Ins. Co.*, id. 518 ; *Rowley* v. *Empire Ins. Co.*, 36 N. Y. 550 ; *Combs* v. *Hannibal, etc., Ins. Co.*, 43 Mo. 148 ; *Ayres* v. *Home Ins. Co.*, 21 Iowa, 185 ; *Ins. Co.* v. *Throop*, 22 Mich. 146 ; *Kelly* v. *Ins. Co.*, 3 Wis. 254. In *May* v. *Buckeye Ins. Co.*, 25 Wis. 291, the court say : "The whole truth in relation to these matters was fully disclosed to the agent of the company by the assured, and that he himself prepared the papers, filled up the application, and wrote down such portions of the answers as he considered material or important. The assured explicitly informed him that the night watch was kept

application, and being correctly informed of the facts, misstates them, or omits to state them, the consequences are not to be visited upon the assured,[1] even though a policy issued thereon, specially provides that

---

and the pump examined and kept in readiness for use only when the mill was running. This fully appears by his own testimony, and he says, probably with good reason, that he did not write that down in the answers, because he considered that the risk was much less when the factory was not running, even without any of these precautions, than it was when running with them all. The recent cases upon this subject fully sustain the position that, upon this state of facts, the company is responsible for the accuracy and omissions of its agent, even without any express undertaking to be so, and that it cannot avoid liability by reason of any discrepancy between the real facts as disclosed to him and his presentation of them in the papers. The tendency of modern decisions has been strongly to to hold these companies to that degree of responsibility for the acts of the local agents which they scatter through the country, that justice and the due protection of the people demand, without regard to private restrictions upon their authority, or to cunning provisions inserted in policies with a view to elude just responsibility. See the following authorities: *Rowley* v. *Ins. Co.*, 36 N. Y. 550; *Columbia Ins. Co.* v. *Cooper*, 50 Pa. St. 331; *Viele* v. *Germania Ins. Co.*, 26 Iowa, 9; *Franklin* v. *Atlantic F. Ins. Co.*, 42 Mo. 457; *Ins. Co.* v. *Schetteler*, 38 Ill. 166. In *N. E. Ins. Co.* v. *Schetteler*, 38 Ill. 166, the defendant company sought to avoid liability upon their policy on the ground that the plaintiff had procured other insurance without its assent. It appeared, however, that the agent making the insurance *knew* from the plaintiff that other insurance existed when he made the policy, and the court held that the defendant was estopped by the agent's knowledge. In *Moliere* v. *Penn. F. Ins. Co.*, 5 Rawle (Penn.) 342, the court say: "If he," (the agent), "acting in his capacity, undertakes to reduce the verbal particulars to writing, * * the insured has a right to expect that he will insert all that is material, and if he omits to do so, I should deem it his act and not the act of the assured, and that the company would, in equity, be precluded from setting up this omission as an objection to a recovery." *Eames* v. *Ins. Co.*, 94 U. S. 184.

[1] In *Beebe* v. *Hartford Mut. F. Ins. Co.*, 25 Conn. 51, it was held that, where a local agent of a fire insurance company, authorized to receive and forward to the company applications for insurance, and instructed by the company to consider himself in so doing the agent of the party applying rather than of the company, neglects to communicate to the company facts disclosed to him by an applicant for insurance, material to the risk, and the company in consequence issues a policy in ignorance of such facts, the neglect of such agent is not chargeable to such applicant, unless such agent be also acting as the agent of the applicant; and the instructions of the company above stated, not communicated to the applicant, do not make him such agent. The insured is bound to disclose fairly and with entire frankness, all facts known to him which are material to the risk; and the neglect to do so, even though by inadvertence and without actual fraud, will vitiate the policy. But the application of this rule does not require him, after making a general statement of such facts, to go into details about which the insurer manifests no interest and makes no inquiry. Where, on a motion for a new trial for a verdict against evidence in an action on a fire insurance policy, it appeared, that before the insurance was effected, fires had repeatedly occurred in the buildings insured, and that the plaintiff in applying for insurance omitted to state the precise number of fires which had so occurred, but from the whole evidence it did not appear that there was any neglect to communicate material facts, and especially no intentional concealment on his part; it was held that such motion ought not to be granted. In another case decided by the same court, it was held that an agent of an insurance company, authorized to procure applications for insurance, and furnished by the company with printed blanks therefor, containing interrogatories to be answered by the applicant, with regard to the condition of the property to be insured, has, as incidental to such power, authority to make all necessary explanations of the meaning and effect of the terms employed by the company in their interrogatories, and to agree with the applicant as to the terms

"if any agent in the transaction of their business shall assume to violate these conditions, such violation shall be construed to be the act of the insured, and shall render this policy void."[1]

---

which he shall employ, to express the facts stated by him, in answer to the interrogatories. Therefore, where such an agent, at the request of an applicant from whom he had solicited proposals for insurance, read to him the interrogatories and wrote in the application his answers, and while doing so, the question occurring, "Is a watch kept on the premises during the night?" the applicant answered "No," and then stated certain facts with regard to the employment of a man during part of the night, for most of the time, at an adjacent shop within the same inclosure, who would be likely to see if anything was wrong about the premises, upon which the agent remarked that he should consider the man to be a watchman till twelve o'clock, and the applicant remarking that he did not know how it would be considered, but would leave it to him, the agent wrote as the answer, "Watchman till twelve o'clock;" which application was forwarded to the insurance company by the agent without explanation, and a policy issued upon it, the company receiving no notice until after the insured property was burned, that the fact was not as stated in the application, and the insured not knowing until then that the answer was objectionable; on a petition in chancery, to procure the correction of the application in the above statement, and praying that the insurance company be ordered to pay the amount of the loss, it was held, that the relief prayed for, ought to be granted. The agent, in filling out the application, having also inserted a statement that there was a watch-clock in the building, when in fact there was none, and the applicant had not so stated, but the agent supposing that a clock which he saw in the building was a watch-clock, so entered it without inquiry, the applicant being ignorant that such statement was contained in the application, until after the fire; it was held, that the misstatement did not affect the case, having been made purely by mistake, and having become wholly unimportant in the view taken by the court of the matter of the watchman. Id. *Malleable Iron Works* v. *Phœnix Ins. Co.*, 25 Conn. 465. When an agent of the insurer fills out the application, and, although the premises are correctly described to him by the insured, he misdescribes them, the company cannot, even though such description is to be treated as a warranty, set up such misdescription as a breach. The knowledge of the agent is treated as the knowledge of the company, and his mistake is the company's mistake, and the consequences are to be visited upon it, and not upon the assured. Thus, in a Nevada case, in *Gerhauser* v. *N. British Mercantile Ins. Co.*, 7 Nev. 15, the defendant company issued a policy to the insured upon his house described as a brick building. At the time of the insurance, on account of the settling of the foundations, a portion of one of the walls had been removed and replaced by a temporary wooden substitute. One of the conditions of the contract—not a warranty—was that any misstatement in the description of the property should vitiate the policy. It was claimed that the court erred in refusing to instruct that the change was material, and in leaving it to the jury to find whether the condition of the building resulting from the change was material. The court held that the description was inserted not by way of warranty, but to identify the premises, and that, if the plaintiff told Harvey, the agent, of the wooden studding in the wall, and if that amounted to telling him that it was a wooden building, Harvey should have so described it in the policy. The company was responsible for his omissions, and cannot avoid liability by reason of any discrepancy between any facts as disclosed to him and his statement of them in the papers. It cannot saddle the blunder of its own agents on the plaintiff, and thus take advantage of its own wrong, and that, in order to make a forfeiture under the subdivision relating to the value of the property insured, the false statement must be wilfully made with respect to a material matter, and with purpose to deceive the insurer. See *Sprague* v. *Holland Purchase Ins. Co.*, decided by Court of Appeals of New York, March 20th, 1877; *Coombs* v. *Hannibal, etc., Ins. Co.*, 43 Mo. 108.

[1] *Columbia Ins. Co.* v. *Cooper*, 50 Penn. St. 331 ; *Commercial Ins. Co.* v. *Ives*, 56 Ill. 402 ; *Sprague* v. *Holland Purchase Ins. Co.* (Ct. of Appeals, N. Y., not yet reported decided February, 1877.) *Eclectic Ins. Co.* v. *Fahrenkrug*, 68 Ill. 463

Insurer cannot make its agent, agent of assured, except.

SEC. 385. If the insurer seeks to make *its* agent the agent of the assured, as to any matter within the scope of his apparent authority, *notice of the limitation upon his authority must be given to him before the assured has acted in reliance upon the apparent authority with which the agent has been invested*, and it is not competent for the principal afterwards, and without notice to the assured as stated, by a provision in the *policy* to constitute *its* agent, as to an act already done, the agent of the assured.[1]

[1]*Commercial Ins. Co.* v. *Ives*, 56 Ill. 402; *Columbia Ins. Co.* v. *Cooper, ante; Sprague* v. *Holland Purchase Ins. Co., ante; Ins. Co.* v. *Wilkinson, ante.* In *Com. Ins. Co.* v. *Ives*, 56 Ill. 402, the court, in commenting upon the effect of such a provision in the policy, very pertinently says: "The words have no magic power residing in them capable to transmute the real into the unreal, nor had they power to make the agent of the company the agent of the insured." In *Masters* v. *Madison Co. Mut. Ins. Co.*, 11 Barb. (N. Y.) 624; 3 Ben. F. I. C. 398, this question was ably discussed by CRIPPEN, J., and his remarks are so pertinent and pregnant with good sense that I give them here. He said: "The defendants also insist that they are not liable in this action to the plaintiff, for the reason that she omitted to set forth, in her application for the insurance, that the mill was incumbered by the Lucas mortgage, which was then a lien upon the property, and that she omitted to notify the defendants in writing of the same, in answer to the interrogatory upon the margin of the application, which rendered the policy void, upon the ground that it was a breach of warranty, or a concealment of important matter affecting the risk. The proof establishes that the agent of the company made out the application for the plaintiff to sign. He used the blank furnished to agents for that purpose. It is true that the by-laws of that company make the person taking the survey the agent of the applicant. Nevertheless, he is still the agent of the company. He is not divested of his office by being deemed the agent also of the person making application for a policy. I have always regarded this clause in the by-laws of these companies as a device resorted to by them for the purpose of shunning just responsibility. They employ their own agents, and send them abroad in community with their printed blanks and such instructions as the officers of the company deem proper and necessary to give them. The business of these agents is to obtain insurances for their principals, the company employing them for that purpose. The public know nothing of their by-laws or the instructions under which such agents transact their business. They are regarded as the agents of the company, and confided in as being competent to transact the business intrusted to them accurately and according to law. Gray, the surveyor and agent of the defendants, was applied to for an insurance of the plaintiff's mill. He proceeded to make a survey, and went to the mill, about seven miles from the plaintiff's residence; he then saw the property, its situation, and how bounded, the distance from other buildings. for what purpose occupied, and by whom. The plaintiff did not accompany him; being an old lady, seventy years of age, she relied upon Mr. Gray to transact the business, and do whatever was necessary to be done to insure her a valid and binding policy. It appears that Gray was informed by the son of the plaintiff, at the time he made out the application and while drawing it for the plaintiff to sign, that there was a mortgage on the premises, given by Lucas, and told him all the particulars about it. Notwithstanding such information, the agent left the application entirely a blank in relation to any incumbrance upon the property. Neither the act of incorporation, nor the by-laws, declare the policy void for the omission of the applicant to give notice of an incumbrance upon the property. Neither is it required that a written notice of such incumbrance be given. Nothing is said in the policy itself, or in the printed proposals annexed thereto, requiring a notice in writing or otherwise to be given by the applicant of a prior mortgage or incumbrance upon the property. In the printed proposals, provision is made that when buildings are mortgaged at the time they are insured

SEC. 386. In *all cases* where the agent, filling up the application, is clothed with real or apparent authority to make a contract of insurance,

---

the mortgagee may have the policy assigned to him, on his signing the premium note, or giving security for the payment of the same, and obtaining the consent of the company, which assent and assignment shall be entered on said policy. If a notice of the existence of the Lucas mortgage was necessary to be given by the applicant, I have no doubt it was sufficiently given in the case, and legally and properly established on the trial. The proof shows positive notice given to Gray, the agent of the company, and that was sufficient. His being declared by the by-laws the agent of the applicant, as above remarked, did not divest him of his attributes as an agent of the defendants. He was in the employment of the defendants, soliciting risks and making contracts for the company with anybody and everybody who might wish to insure. He also made out the applications, and prepared the necessary papers to effect insurance; and it would, in my opinion, be little less than legalized robbery to allow these insurance companies to escape from liability upon the merest technicality possible, and that, too, when created by their own by-laws, which remain a sealed book to ninety-nine out of every hundred persons insured. The authorities settle this question against the defendants, and without showing any more valid defense against the plaintiff's claim the judgment cannot be disturbed. *Sexton* v. *Montgomery Co. Mut. Ins. Co.*, 9 Barb. S. C. Rep. 191; *McEwen* v. *The Same*, 5 Hill, 101; 3 Denio, 259. See also, *Plumb* v. *Cattaraugus Ins. Co.*, 18 N. Y. 392.

In New York, however, a contrary doctrine has recently been held in *Rohrbach* v. *Germania F. Ins. Co.*, 62 N. Y. 47, but, while the opinions of that court are entitled to great respect, its vascillation upon this question, according to the admission of the learned judge who delivered the opinion, in connection with its decision in a very recent case which conflicts with this. *Train* v. *Holland Purchase Ins. Co.*, decided March 20th, 1877, leaves the whole doctrine unsettled in that court, and in a worse condition than the learned judge says the case of *Rowley* v. *Empire Ins. Co.* was left by the comments of GROVER, J., in *Owens* v. *Holland Purchase Ins. Co.*, 56 N. Y. 565. I give the portion of the opinion of FOLGER, J., in *Rohrbach* v. *Germania Ins. Co.*, *ante*, relating to this point. He said: "There is another view of the matter, however, in which the phrase and the circumstances in which it was used may be of more advantage to the defendant. By the fourth condition of the policy, it is provided 'that, if the interest of the assured in the property be any other than the entire, unconditional and sole ownership, for the use and benefit of the assured, * * * it must be so represented to the company, and so expressed in the written part of the policy, otherwise the policy shall be void.' By the first condition, it is provided 'that any omission to make known every fact material to the risk, or any misrepresentation whatever, or if the interest of the assured in the property * * * be not truly stated in the policy, * * * it shall be void.' It is plain that these conditions have not been observed and kept by the plaintiff. The nature of his interest in the property was not expressed in the policy, and it was other than the ownership of it. The application was referred to in the policy; and, by the first condition of the policy, in such case the application became a warranty. In it, it is stated that the plaintiff has disclosed all the facts in relation to the property so far as the same are known to him. But, in answer to the question, 'Is your title to the property absolute? If not, state its nature and amount,' the only answer given is, 'His deceased wife held the deed.' There is in that answer no affirmation of a falsehood, for his deceased wife did, in fact, hold the deed; but there is not a just, full and true exposition by the answer of all the facts and circumstances. The purport of the question and the answer to it would imply and convey the idea that he was in equity the owner, though the formal legal title was in the wife. The facts of his interest in or connection with the property were quite otherwise. The written application did not, by its representations, put the defendant in possession of the exact facts of the case; it did thereby tend to mislead as to the real situation of the property and the real interest of the plaintiff in it. The application, in this respect, was a warranty. *Chaffee* v. *Catt. Co. Mut. Ins. Co.* 19 N. Y. 376. The truth of that warranty became a condition pre-

or to insure, and to bind the company in that respect, *the agent, knowing the facts*, the principal is estopped from claiming that he has been misled by such omissions or misstatements.[1] But where the agent has

cedent to any liability to the plaintiff from the defendant, *Bryce* v. *Lorillard Ins. Co.*, 55 N. Y. 440 ; and it was a warranty and a condition precedent, not to be avoided by any consideration of whether it was essential to the risk or not, or whether or not it was an inducement to the defendant to enter into the contract. Id. It is very evident that the plaintiff did not intend a deception upon the defendant ; nay, it is evident that he laid open to Brand, the agent of the defendant to procure and submit applications, and to issue policies when signed by the proper officers of the defendant and transmitted to him, all the facts of his connection with and interest in the property ; and that the statements in the application were Brand's conclusions from those facts, and the omissions from it were of matters not deemed essential by Brand. It is hereupon urged by the plaintiff that the errors and omissions were those of the defendant. But the plaintiff and defendant have, in the policy, the contract between them, expressly agreed that Brand should be deemed the agent of the plaintiff, and not of the defendant, under any circumstances whatever. It is true that, in *Plumb* v. *Catt. Co. Mut. Ins. Co.*, 18 N. Y. 392, a rule is held which tends to the shielding of the plaintiff, in this case, from the effect of his contract; but since then, it is held, that under such a contract as this the knowledge of such an agent of facts not stated in the application, is immaterial in the absence of fraud, or prevention of the statement of them by the applicant. *Chase* v. *Ham. Ins. Co.*, 20 id. 52 ; where the case in 18 New York, *supra*, is considered and distinguished. As to *Rowley* v. *Empire Ins. Co.*, 36 N. Y. 550, cited in General Term opinion, it is much shaken in *Owens* v. *Holland Purchase Ins. Co.*, 56 N. Y. 565–570. (The learned judge perhaps had forgotten that every judge of the court, himself included, dissented from the views of GROVER, J., in reference to the case of *Rowley* v. *Empire Ins. Co.*, and thus left the doctrine of that case to stand as indorsed by them, not only by this dissent, but also by the actual judgment in the case of *Owens* v. *Holland Purchase Ins. Co.* The remarks of GROVER, J., were purely his own, and the court took pains to have the reporter so inform the profession.) It is to be regretted that corporations, of the power and extended business relations with all classes in the community, which insurance companies have, should prepare for illiterate and confiding men contracts so practically deceptive and nugatory ; and should, in cases as free from fraud and wrong on the part of the insured as this is, hold their customers to the letter of an agreement so entered into. I am aware that often the companies are made the victims of dishonest and designing persons, but I cannot agree that the remedy for that, is to refuse to be bound by the acts of agents of their own selection when dealing with simple and unlettered men. If there should be less greediness for business, and such care in the selection and appointment of agents as would insure the confidence of the companies in their capability, discretion and integrity, it would not need that there be laid upon unwise policyholders an agreement to take the burden of the opposite qualities in those put forward to them as actors for the insurers. But we must take the contracts of the parties as we find them, and enforce them as they read. By the one before us the plaintiff has so fettered himself as to be unable to retain, as the case now stands, the real essence of his agreement. Though he has frankly and fully laid before the actor between him and the defendant all the facts and circumstances of the case, he is made responsible for error in legal conclusions which he never formed, and which were arrived at by one in whom he trusted and whom he supposed to stand in the place of the defendant."

[1] *Beebe* v. *Hartford Ins. Co.*, 25 Conn. 51 ; 4 Bennett's F. I. C. 55 ; *Masters* v. *Madison, etc., Ins. Co.*, 11 Barb. (N. Y.) 624 ; *Ins. Co.* v. *Wilkinson, ante; Marshall* v. *Columbian Ins. Co.*, 28 N. Y. 157 ; 3 Bennett's F. I. C. 634. When the agent of the insurer *knows* that the representations made by the assured are false, *and the insurer acts with full knowledge of the facts*, the insurer will be estopped from setting up the falsity of such representations to defeat the policy. *Guardian, etc., Life Ins. Co.* v. *Hogan*, 80 Ill. 35 ; *Roberts* v. *Continental Ins. Co.*, 11 Wis. 321 ; *Ætna, etc., Ins. Co.* v. *Olmstead*, 21 Mich. 246.

neither actual or apparent authority to make a contract, but only author.
ity to receive and forward proposals for a policy, and to deliver the
same to the assured and receive the premium therefor, knowledge of
the agent cannot be imputed to the principal, because in that case the
assured has no right to regard the agent as clothed with power to do
more than the nature of the business committed to him by his principal naturally includes.[1] But even in such cases, it has been held that
the *explanation* of questions, is within the scope of the agent's authority,
and that, if through his direction or advice a question is erroneously
answered, the principal must bear the consequences and not the assured.
"It is within the sphere of his duty to explain the questions and decide
for himself and the *bona fide* applicant, *what was a satisfactory answer,
and how the answer should be applied to the subject.*"[2]

When insurer is not estopped by acts of.

SEC. 387. In all cases where the assured has notice of any limitation
upon the agent's power,[3] or where there is anything about the transaction to put him on inquiry as to the actual authority of the agent,
acts done by him in excess of his authority are not binding, as where
it is generally known that limitations are imposed in certain respects.[4]

So where direct notice, or any notice which the assured as a prudent
man is bound to regard, is brought home to the assured, limiting the
powers of the agent, he relies upon any act in excess of such limited
authority at his peril. That an insurance company has a right, in a
fair way, to limit the powers of its agents must be conceded, and
when it does impose such limitations upon his authority, in a way that
no prudent man ought to be mistaken in reference thereto, it is not
bound by an act done by its agent in contravention of such notice.
This was well illustrated in a recent and very ably considered case
before the court of appeals,[5] in which a life insurance company had

---

[1] *Mitchell* v. *Lycoming Mut. Ins. Co.*, 51 Penn. St. 402; *Wilson* v. *Conway Ins.
Co.*, 4 R. I. 141; 4 Ben. F. I. C. 113; *Sexton* v. *Montgomery Co. Mut. Ins. Co.*, 9
Barb. (N. Y.) 191; *Lowell* v. *Middlesex Mut. Ins. Co.*, 8 Cush. (Mass.) 127; 3 Ben.
F. I. C. 240.

[2] ELLSWORTH, J., in *Malleable Iron Works* v. *Phœnix Ins. Co.*, 25 Conn. 465; 4
Ben. F. I. C. 161. In this case the agent simply had power to take and forward
proposals for insurance, deliver the policy and take the premium. By his direction, an erroneous answer was *bona fide*, given to an inquiry, and the court held
that the company was bound by the agents' acts in this respect, and ordered the
policy to be reformed to accord with the facts. See also, to same principle,
Devendorf v. *Beardsley*, 23 Barb. (N. Y.) 600; *Sanford* v. *Handy*, 23 Wend. (N.
Y.) 260; *Nelson* v. *Cowing*, 6 Hill (N. Y.) 336.

[3] *Winneshiek Ins. Co.* v. *Halzgrafe*, 53 Ill. 316.

[4] *Baines* v. *Ewing*, L. R. 1 Excheq. 320.
Messereau v. *Phœnix, etc., Ins. Co.*, 66 N. Y. 274.

printed upon all its policies a notice that no agent had a right "to
receive any premium after date of its being due, without special permission from the officers of the company." The assured died Sept.
14th, 1872, and the defense was that the semi-annual premium, due
Aug. 31st, 1872, was not paid. To obviate the forfeiture it was shown
that the general agent of the company gave the assured credit for the
premium, or rather waived its payment according to the requirements
of the policy, and agreed to keep him good with the company. The
plaintiff had a verdict at circuit, but it was set aside in the court of
appeals, *upon the ground that the agent had no authority to waive payment
of the premium, and that the assured, in the face of the notice printed upon
his policy, had no right to rely upon his authority to do so.* MILLER, J.,
dissented from this doctrine, and wrote a very able dissenting opinion,
but it will be noticed that he leaves out of sight the express notice given
to the assured, that the agent had no authority to waive the payment
of the premium at the precise time when it became due, without special
permission from the officers of the company, and predicates his views
upon a class of cases *where no such limitation was noticed to the assured.*
Upon the authority of this case, and indeed without it, there is no
question but that an insurance company may lawfully limit the
authority of its agents, *and when it does so, and the assured knows, or as
a prudent man ought to know of such limitation,* he deals with him in
reference to matters in excess of his power at his peril. This has been
held in numerous cases cited elsewhere in this chapter, and is an
elementary principle in the law of agency.

Agent filling out application.

SEC. 388. Where the insured is himself required to make out his application, if he requests the agent to do it for him, there is propriety in
holding that the agent, as to that act, is the agent of the assured, because
it is done at his request, and in discharge of a duty that devolves upon
the assured ; but, when the agent voluntarily fills up the application,
or by any act of his gives the assured to understand, or leads him to
believe that it is a part of his (the agent's) duty to fill it up, it cannot
be said that he acts as the agent of the assured. The question may
fairly be said to be one of fact for the jury, to be determined from the
facts and circumstances of each case,[1] and, if there is nothing shown
to put the assured on inquiry as to the authority of the agent in this
respect, and he is not expressly required to fill up the application him-

---

[1] *Houyh v. City F. Ins. Co.,* 29 Conn. 10.

self, the jury would be justified in finding that he acted as the agent of the insurer, and not of the assured.[1] The acts and declarations of the agent will be treated as the acts and declarations of the principal,[2] particularly is this the case where the agent is required by the company to fill out the application, or where he does it voluntarily.[3] If he fills it up *at the request of the assured*, a different question is presented, and he might possibly be treated as the agent of the assured to that extent.[4] But generally, in either case, if the agent was correctly informed of all the circumstances required to be stated in the application, it would make no difference whether the agent is to be treated as the agent of the insurer or the assured, *as knowledge on his part, in reference to the risk*, is the knowledge of the company, and if the risk is taken with knowledge of all the circumstances incident to it, it cannot complain of mistatements by the assured upon which it did not rely.[5] So far as his authority extends, real or apparent, he

---

[1] *Ins. Co.* v. *Wilkinson*, 13 Wall. (U. S.) 221; *Woodbury Savings Bank* v. *Charter Oak Ins. Co.*, 31 Conn. 526; *Coombs* v. *Hannibal Savings Ins. Co.*, 43 Mo. 158; *Rowley* v. *Empire Ins. Co.*, 36 N. Y. 550; *Plumb* v. *Cattaraugus Ins. Co.*, 18 N. Y. 392; *Simmons* v. *Ins. Co.*, 8 W. Va. 493; *Howard F. Ins. Co.* v. *Brunner*, 23 Penn. St. 550; *Kingston* v. *The Ætna Ins. Co.*, 42 Iowa, 46; *Bartholomew* v. *Merchants' Ins. Co.*, 25 id. 508; *Comnr'l Ins. Co.* v. *Ives*, 56 Ill. 402; *Anson* v. *Winneshiek Ins. Co.*, 23 Iowa, 84; *Bidwell* v. *N. W. Ins. Co.*, 24 N. Y. 302; *Moliere* v. *Penn. Ins. Co.*, 5 Rawle (Penn.) 342; *Rathbone* v. *City F. Ins. Co.*, 31 Conn. 193; *Cumberland Valley, etc., Ins. Co.* v. *Schell*, 29 Penn. St. 31; *Columbia Ins. Co.* v. *Cooper*, 50 Penn. St. 331; *Witherell* v. *Maine Ins. Co.*, 49 Me. 200; *Emery* v. *Piscataqua, etc., Ins. Co.*, 52 id. 322; *Clark* v. *Union, etc., Ins. Co.*, 40 N. H. 333; *James River Ins. Co.* v. *Merritt*, 47 Ala. 387; *Patten* v. *Merchants', etc., Ins. Co.*, 40 N. H. 375; *Andes Ins. Co.* v. *Shipman*, 77 Ill. 189; *Aurora F. Ins. Co.* v. *Eddy*, 55 id. 213; *Howard, etc., Ins. Co.* v. *Cormack*, 24 id. 455; *Bartholmew* v. *Merchants' Ins. Co.*, 25 Iowa, 507; *Ætna, etc., Ins. Co.* v. *Olmstead*, 21 Mich. 246; *Ayres* v. *Hartford Ins. Co.*, 21 Iowa, 186; *American, etc., Ins. Co.* v. *McLanathan*, 11 Kan. 533; *Michigan State Ins. Co.* v. *Lewis*, 30 Mich. 41.

[2] MILLER, J., in *Ins. Co.* v. *Wilkinson*, *ante*; *Beebe* v. *Hartford Ins. Co.*, 25 Conn. 51; *Davenport* v. *Peoria Ins. Co.*, 17 Iowa, 276; *Beal* v. *The Park Ins. Co.*, 16 Wis. 241; *Lycoming Ins. Co.* v. *Schallenberger*, 44 Penn. St. 259; *Ayres* v. *Hartford Ins. Co.*, 17 Iowa, 176; *Savings Bank* v. *Charter Oak Ins. Co.*, 31 Conn. 517; *Howard Ins. Co.* v. *Brunner ante*; *Horwitz* v. *Equitable Ins. Co.*, 40 Mo. 5⃣; *Roth* v. *City Ins. Co.*, 6 McLean (U. S.) 324.

[3] *Sprague* v. *Holland Purchase Ins. Co.*, *ante*.

[4] BECK, J., in *Kingston* v. *The Ætna Ins. Co.*, 42 Iowa, 47; *Smith* v. *Empire Ins. Co.*, 25 Barb. (N. Y.) 497. This idea was repudiated in *Clark* v. *Union, etc., Ins. Co.*, 40 N. H. 333, and where the insurers was informed by the assured that he could not particularly describe the property, *and agreed to pay the agent* for going to make the necessary survey, which the agent did; it was held, that the agent should not be treated, as to this duty, the agent of the assured, *but still remained the agent of the insurer*, and this would seem to be the most consistent rule.

[5] In *Pierce* v. *Nashua Ins. Co.*, 50 N. H. 297: 9 Am. Rep, 235, it appeared that the plaintiff and another person were partners, and the policy in suit was issued to them *as* partners. Subsequently the plaintiff became sole owner by purchase from his partner, and the policy was renewed *after* such purchase by the defendant's agent, who *knew* that the plaintiff was sole owner. The *ninth* condition of

can bind the principal, and in reference to all matters in which he can
bind the principal, the principal is chargeable with his knowledge.[1]

the policy was as follows : "Policies of insurance * * shall not be assignable
without the consent of the company expressed by indorsement thereon.   In case
of assignment made without such consent, *whether of the whole policy or of any
interest therein*, the liability of the company in virtue of such policy shall thenceforth cease."   In passing upon the effect of the agent's knowledge of the change
in the title, FOSTER, J., said : "There was no misunderstanding between the con
tracting parties.   The case find that Wood, the defendant's agent, when he
received the new premium from the plaintiff and promised to re-insure the property, 'knew fully that Pierce had bought and was the sole owner of the property,
and that the policy had not been assigned.'   And his knowledge and new promise
or consent to the continuance of the policy for the benefit of the plaintiff must be
considered to be that of the company, and the authority of the agent to make such
contract must be presumed till the contrary be shown.   *Goodhall* v. *Ins. Co.*, 25
N. H. 169 ; *Sanders* v. *Ins. Co.*, 44 id. 244.   The receipt given by the agent, in
which it is stated that the new premium was received by Mower & Pierce, is not
binding and conclusive upon the plaintiff, who may show, by extrinsic evidence,
that he is the only party from whom the money was received, and with whom the
contract was made.   2 Pars. on Cont. 67 ; *Hersom* v. *Henderson*, 23 N. H. 498 ·
Ryan v. *Rand*, 26 id. 15.   But the defense to this suit rests mainly upon the inter-
position of the ninth condition. requiring the company's consent to an assignment
to be indorsed on the policy.   This indorsement has not been made ; and the
company, which has received the full consideration for the insurance, claims,
nevertheless, that, because of this informality, they shall incur no obligation to
pay the loss which the plaintiff has sustained.   The court will be reluctant to
encourage or give validity to such a defense.   The plain recital of the facts deprives it of any claim to favorable consideration.   The agent of the company
knew that Mower had sold out his interest in the property insured to the present
plaintiff.   The plaintiff, informing him of all the facts, carried the policy to the
agent and told him he wanted the mill re-insured.   The agent told him he would
have the property re-insured, but did not know what the premium would be for
the next year ; said he would get the policy, and the plaintiff might pay the
amount due when he should receive it ; and talked about a probable dividend
which might reduce the amount of the premium to be paid for the new policy.
The plaintiff paid him $10, and the agent carried off the old policy, the plaintiff
trusting him to insure him properly.   Subsequently the agent met him on the
street, told him he had got his insurance papers for him, and demanded $5 more,
which the plaintiff paid.   The plaintiff, then, placing full confidence in the agent,
incautiously put the defective papers away without looking at them, and never
discovered their imperfections till after the destruction of the mill, but always
supposed he held a new and valid policy.   The proofs of loss were made in due
form and proper time.   There is no claim by the defendants that there was over-
insurance, nor any concealment of facts, nor any fraud or misrepresentation on
the part of the plaintiff, nor that the full amount of premium for insurance has
not been received.   It would seem to be a serious defect in our jurisprudence if
courts of law could not provide a remedy for such a case, without turning a party

. [1] *Devendorf* v. *Beardsley* 23 Barb. (N. Y.) 656.   Thus, where an agent of an
insurance company is sent out to solicit risks and negotiate contracts of insurance,
notice to him of a prior insurance, while he is engaged in the business, and acting
within the scope of his authority, is notice to the company.   Whether a general
or special agent, he stands in the place of the principal, and persons dealing with
him are, for most purposes, regarded as dealing with the principal.   *McEwen* v.
Montgomery Co. Mut. Ins. Co., 5 Hill (N. Y.) 101 ; *Sexton* v. *Montgomery, etc.,
Ins.. Co.*, 9 Barb. (N. Y.) 191, where verbal notice was held sufficient.   To similar
effect, *Masters* v. *Madison Co. Mut. Ins. Co.*, 11 id. 624.   *Sheldon* v. *Atlantic
Ins. Co.*, 26 N. Y. 460 ; *Wood* v. *Poughkeepsie, etc., Ins. Co.*, 22 id. 619 ; *Post* v.
Ætna Ins. Co., 43 Barb. (N. Y.) 351 ; *Lightbody* v. *N. A. Ins. Co.*, 23 Wend. (N.
Y.) 18 ; *N. Y. Central Ins. Co.* v. *National Protection Ins Co.*, 20 Barb. (N. Y.)
468 ; *Leeds* v. *Mechanics' Ins. Co.*, 8 N. Y. 351.

In New York, it has been held that when the insured signs an application in blank, and intrusts it to the agent of the insurer to be

---

over to the equity side of the court. And we think that, under the circumstances of this case, a jury may find that the insurance company have waived their right to require an indorsement of the company's consent to the assignment upon the policy, and that they have made a new and valid contract of insurance with this plaintiff. The condition upon which the defendants rely was inserted for their benefit, and the company had the right to waive it. If the defendants themselves, knowing all the facts, might do this, so might their agent. Every agent of such company is presumed by law, and may well be presumed by all persons innocently dealing with him, to possess every power necessary, or naturally incident, to his agency. This principle of law is essential, quite as much to the successful and profitable management of the insurance company, as for the protection of the community; for it is obvious that the business and profits of the former would be most essentially diminished, if, in case of every unessential departure, for convenience, from the usual requirements of the company's rules, resort were to be had to the directors and the home office. An examination of the authorities shows us that the books are full of cases in which the doctrine now suggested has been applied. Whether there *was* such a waiver of the condition in this case is, of course, a question for the jury; and it will be for them to say whether an insurance company, systematically transacting and soliciting business at points remote from its primary location, may reasonably be presumed to have conferred upon a person held out to the world as '*the agent* of the Nashua Fire Insurance Company,' authority to act for them to the extent of dispensing with a formality the waiver of which could do the company no harm so long as they received a full consideration for their contract. And then, if they find he had authority, it will be for the jury to say whether the agent *has exercised* the power of waiving the requirements of the condition in this case; upon which question, evidence of his full knowledge of the sale to the plaintiff, of the absence and want of the written assignment, of his assurances to the plaintiff that such assignment would not be required, and of his reception of the full premium for re-insurance, would probably have quite a direct bearing. *Atlantic Ins. Co.* v. *Goodall,* 35 N. H. 328; *Barnes* v. *Ins. Co.,* 45 id. 24; *Boehm* v. *Ins. Co.,* 35 N. Y. 131; *Franklin Ins. Co.* v. *Updegraff,* 43 Penn. St. 350; *Wilson* v. *Ins. Co.,* 16 Barb. 513; *N. E. F. & M. Ins. Co.* v. *Schettler,* 38 Ill. 166; *Keenan* v. *Ins. Co.,* 13 Iowa, 375; *North Berwick Co.* v. *N. E. F. and M. Ins. Co.,* 52 Me. 336; *Lightbody* v. *Ins. Co.,* 23 Wend. 18; *Nicoll* v. *Ins. Co.,* 3 Woodb. & M. 529; *Woodbury Savings Bank* v. *Ins. Co.,* 31 Conn. 518; *Carroll* v. *Ins. Co.,* 40 Barb. 292; *Conover* v. *Ins. Co.,* 3 Denio, 254; Angell on Ins., § 217. *Rathbone* v. *Ins. Co.,* 31 Conn. 194, was the case where a policy provided that the insurance should be void if articles denominated 'hazardous' should be stored in the building without the consent of the company indorsed on the policy. The agent consented to the removal of the property insured to another building in which such hazardous articles were stored; and agreed to make whatever entry was necessary on the policy to continue it in force, notwithstanding such storage; and took and retained the policy for that purpose. It was held that the agreement of the agent was a waiver, by the company, of the condition which required such written indorsement of consent, until such indorsement should be made. Insurance companies are naturally more anxious to obtain premiums than to pay losses; but, in such a case as this, where there is no pretense of fraud or concealment, and where the company have received all the benefits of a mutual contract, contemplated and provided by their charter and by-laws, they should understand that the contract imposes mutual obligations. The defense is purely technical. 'Such defenses,' says ROOSEVELT, J., in *Wilson* v. *Ins. Co.,* before cited, 'where there has been perfect fair dealing on the part of the assured, in modern times, are not favored by either judges or jurors; nor are they in accordance with the true interests of the insurers themselves, or with the general sense of the community. That sense is usually common sense. And it cannot be too often repeated, that common sense and common honesty are the true sources of common law.'" In *Marshall* v. *Columbian Ins. Co.* it was held that, when the agent at the time of making a policy, knew the existence of certain facts, his

filled up, and correctly states the situation and condition of the property to him, and the agent omits to set forth incumbrances upon the property, of which he was informed by the insured, and a policy was issued upon the basis of such erroneous application, the company is to be treated as having issued the policy with notice of the incumbrances, and is estopped from setting up the fact that incumbrances exist, as a breach of warranty.[1] GROVER, J., in a later case,[2] severely criticises the doctrine of this case, but none of the other members of the court concurred with him in his views; and in a recent case[3] against the same defendant, the court reaffirmed the doctrine of Rowley v. Empire Ins. Co., and held that where an applicant signs an application in blank, and the agent of the company, having been correctly informed of the situation and condition of the property, erroneously fills out the application, the misstatements do not constitute a breach of warranty. In that case, the applicant signed an application in blank, which was thereafter filled up by the agent of the insurance company carelessly, and certain misstatements were made in such filling up. It was held that such erroneous statements did not constitute a breach of warranty that the statements contained in the application were true, and that a clause providing that the one who procured the insurance should be held by contract to be the agent of the applicant, taken in connection with a provision that the application must be made out by an agent of the company, did not make the agent who filled out the application, after it was signed, the agent of the applicant.

Exceptions.

SEC. 389. Where the agent has authority only to take applications and deliver policies, his knowledge of the facts are not imputable to the principal so as to estop the principal from setting up a breach of warranty expressed *upon the face of the policy*. As, where the policy is "on his two-story, shingle roof and extension, frame building, *occupied as a dwelling house*," the fact that the agent knew *that the building was unoccupied* when the policy was issued, does not estop the insurer

---

knowledge is the knowledge of the company. See also *Delathy* v. *Memphis Ins. Co.*, 8 Humph. (Tenn.) 624; *Fletcher* v. *Com. Ins. Co.*, 18 Pick. (Mass.) 563; *Strong* v. *Manufacturers' Ins. Co.*, 10 id. 44; *Franklin Ins. Co.* v. *Drake*, 2 B. Mon. (Ky.) 47.

[1] *Rowley* v. *The Empire Ins. Co.*, 36 N. Y. 550.

[2] *Owens* v. *Holland Purchase Ins. Co.*, 56 N. Y. 571.

[3] *Sprague* v. *Holland Purchase Ins. Co.*, decided March 20, 1877, and not yet reported.

from setting up such fact in avoidance of its liability.[1] But, where the agent is a general agent, and has authority to consummate the contract by the issue of a policy, and does so in the case in question, his knowledge is the knowledge of the company, and the misstatement by him of a material fact therein, is not binding upon the assured.[2]

Secret limitation of an agent's power—Waiver of forfeiture.

Sec. 390. A secret limitation of an agent's power does not prevent third persons from dealing with him to the full extent of his apparent authority. If the company sees fit to place limitations upon his authority that qualify his apparent authority, it must see to it that every person who deals with him on their behalf *has notice of such limitation*, or at least do that which will enable him to ascertain the agent's power, and which, as a prudent man, would inform him of the fact, otherwise they will be bound by all his acts within the scope of his apparent power.[3] Thus, he may waive forfeitures of any description,[4] conditions of the contract;[5] may change the contract by erasing con-

---

[1] *Alexander v. Germania F. Ins. Co.*, 66 N. Y. 464. Upon the point that the words "occupied as a dwelling," or otherwise, is a warranty that the building is *then* occupied as described. See case, *supra*, also *Parmalee v. Hoffman Ins. Co.*, 54 N. Y. 143; *Chase v. Hamilton Ins. Co.*, 20 N. Y. 52; *Wall v. The East River, etc., Ins. Co.*, 7 N. Y. 370; *Farmers' Ins. Co. v. Curry* (Ky.) 2 W. Ins. Rev. 88; *Residence F. Ins. Co. v. Hannawald* (Mich.) 2 id. 88.

[2] *Ames v. N. Y. Mut. Ins. Co.*, 14 N. Y. 253; *Meadowcraft v. Standard F. Ins. Co.*, 62 Penn. St. 91; *Combs v. Hannibal etc., Ins. Co.*, 43 Mo. 248; *Boas v. World, etc., Ins. Co.*, 6 T. & C. (N. Y.) 364; *Owens v. Holland Purchase Ins. Co.*, 56 N. Y. 565.

[3] *Com., etc., Ins. Co. v. Union Mut. Ins. Co.*, 19 How. (U. S.) 318; *Perkins v. Washington Ins. Co.*, 4 Cow. (N. Y.) 645.

[4] *Jacobs v. National Life Ins. Co.*, 1 MacArthur (U. S.) 632; *North Berwick Co. v. N. E. Ins. Co.*, 52 Me. 336; 4 Ben. F. I C. 790.

[5] *Ide v. Phœnix Ins. Co.*, 2 Biss. (U. S.) 333. In *Cone v. Niagara F. Ins. Co.*, 3 T. & C. (N. Y.) 33; affd. 60 N. Y. 619, an action was brought upon a policy of insurance for $3,000, issued to one Palmer, and loss payable to the plaintiff. The plaintiff asked to reform the policy by indorsing upon the same the consent of the company that the dwelling-house be and remain vacant in accordance with the agreement alleged to have been made at the time when the policy was taken out, between the plaintiff and the defendant's agent. It appeared, upon the trial, that Carlton G. Palmer owned the property, and the plaintiff held judgments and mortgages, which were liens upon it, to a considerable amount. On the 9th of June, 1869, the property had been sold at a sheriff's sale, and the plaintiff held an assignment of the sheriff's certificate of sale. Palmer remained on the premises, it being understood that a proper amount of insurance should be procured on the house. In May, 1870, on Palmer's application, a $3,000 policy was issued thereon by the Glens Falls Insurance Company, by Henry E. Barns, its agent, and at the same time the defendant's general agent, *and having full knowledge of all the liens and the situation of the title to the premises, and that the house was and would remain vacant until the September following*. On June 1st the policy was issued by defendant, by Barns, its regularly commissioned agent, whereby, for $18, it insured Palmer against loss or damage by fire to the amount of $3,000 on the house; loss, "if any, payable to" the plaintiff, "as his interest may appear," against all such loss, etc., "to the property specified,"

ditions therein;[1] adding provisions or exceptions thereto;[2] by issuing policies upon property upon which the company has forbidden him to

---

etc., for three years from June 1, 1870. This insurance was procured by plaintiff with Palmer's knowledge and consent; was applied for by letter to Barnes, who sent his agent, who came to see plaintiff, and Barns sent the policy afterward to plaintiff by mail. On June 4, 1870, the agent, Barns, mailed to the defendant's home office in New York his written report of this risk, which was there received on the 7th of June, answering the printed inquiry as to "occupation," as follows: "*Dwelling not occupied now, as it is just purchased, but will be soon.*" Before accepting the policy, plaintiff wrote Barns to come and see him, and, on the 14th of June, Barns went there and examined this house, *and then, as also before he sent the policy, saw and knew that it was "vacant, unoccupied and not in use," and the plaintiff then informed him fully of, and he knew the situation of the title, and all the liens thereon, including the sheriff's certificate of sale, and the contract of 22d of April, also when Palmer's time to redeem expired, and when the time the creditors had to redeem would expire, and also, that the house would probably remain "vacant," etc., till fall.* The agreement for this insurance was then fully completed, and Barns, as such agent, accepted the $18 from the plaintiff as the consideration for the policy, with full knowledge of all the facts relating to the title and liens, and the rights and interests respectively of Palmer and the plaintiff, and with the clear and expressed understanding that this house would probably remain vacant until September, he also having knowledge of all the terms and conditions of the policy. The agent, Barns, testified he did not know he had found out anything as to the situation of the premises or interests of the parties; that he did not know fully on the 14th of June, and that he had not learned anything in particular since that he did not know before. On August 2, the house insured, then of the value of $8,000, was burned, and on the next day the plaintiff, in reading the policy, discovered among the conditions, in very small type, one declaring it void if the premises were at the time of insuring, or should remain vacant, etc., for ten days without an indorsement of the company's consent; but neither the plaintiff nor Palmer had any knowledge of any such condition until then. No objection was ever made by the defendant or its agents to the house being or remaining vacant, etc., without indorsement of consent, until after the fire. Notice and proofs of loss were duly given and furnished; the proof, in which both plaintiff and Palmer joined, having been received at defendant's home office in New York, August 30, to which no objection was ever made. The plaintiff's liens by mortgages, judgments and certificate of sale, at the time of the insurance and loss, exceeded $6,000, and the only other insurance was $3,000. On September 14, 1870, the sheriff executed and delivered to the plaintiff the usual sheriff's deed of the premises in pursuance of his certificate of sale. The judge found in favor of the plaintiff, and decreed that the contract be reformed as claimed, and directed a judgment for $3,315. Exceptions were taken to various decisions made upon the trial, and, judgment having been entered, the defendant appealed; and the judgment was affirmed at general term, MILLER, P.J., saying: "The policy upon which this action was brought contained a condition which provided, 'if the premises are at the time of insuring, or during the life of this policy, become vacant, unoccupied, or not in use, and remain thus for over ten days, whether by removal of the owner or occupant, or for any cause, without this company's consent is indorsed hereon, this insurance shall be void and of no effect.' This condition was printed in very small type, and was not discovered by the plaintiff or Palmer until the next day after the house was burned. The judge very properly, I think, allowed testimony to show that the agent, at the time and before the premium was paid, knew that the house was vacant, and that it was to remain unoccupied until the 9th of September then next, unless the plaintiff should find a married man, without children, to go in as a tenant: and in accordance with the proof, also properly held that the indorsement of the consent on the policy that the premises might be and remain vacant was waived by

---

[1] *Dayton Ins. Co.* v. *Kelly,* 24 Ohio St. 345.

[2] *Gloucester Mfg. Co.* v. *Howard Ins. Co.,* 5 Gray (Mass,) 497, 4 Ben. F. I. C. 32

issue them,[1] or outside of his jurisdiction,[2] and indeed in all cases where the principal has clothed the agent with apparent authority, he

---

the defendant's agent, and that the defendant was estopped from setting up that the policy was void in consequence of such consent not being indorsed upon the policy. The authority of an agent to waive conditions of this character is established beyond any question, and the books are full of cases which sanction the principle. *Rowley* v. *Empire Ins. Co.*, 36 N. Y. 550; *Bodine* v. *Ex. F. Ins. Co.*, 51 id. 117; *Carroll* v. *Charter Oak Ins. Co.*, 10 Abb. N. S. 166; in court of appeals, 38 Barb. 302; 40 id. 292–4. The application for the policy was made by mail to the agent for three years' insurance from the 1st day of June, 1870, the day of its date. On the 4th day of June, a report of the same was mailed to the defendant by the agent, containing a statement to the effect that the dwelling was unoccupied, but would be occupied soon. The fact that the report of the agent was made on the 4th day of June does not, I think, impair the authority of the agent to make the waiver afterward. There was evidence to establish that the policy was not accepted until the agent had been written to and came and saw the plaintiff on the 14th of June, examined the house and knew that it was for some time to remain vacant and unoccupied, and also learned the situation of the title. After this the premium was paid, and the contract, which was imperfect then, became complete. It was not fully consummated antecedent to the payment of the premium, and then only became perfect. * * * Without discussing the question, how far the act of the agent in not making the proper statement in the policy, after the title had been specifically stated, may affect the omission alleged to have been made, it is a sufficient answer to this objection to say, that no such defense was set up in the answer. nor any such point made upon the trial. * * After a careful examination of the whole case, it is entirely apparent that the plaintiff and the agent of the defendant both understood that the house was to remain vacant until the 9th of September, and that the insurance was intended to cover a house which then was and afterward was to continue to remain unoccupied for the period of time named. It is also equally clear, that the plaintiff did not know of the provision in the policy on this subject, and it was an entire misapprehension and mistake on his part in taking the policy in this form. To allow it to stand under such circumstances and defeat the plaintiff's claim, would be contrary to the evidence; and I am of the opinion that the judge properly arrived at the conclusion that the plaintiff was entitled to the equitable relief suitable to the case, and to a reformation of the policy in this respect."

[1]*Citizens' Mut. F. Ins. Co.* v. *Sortwell*, 8 Allen (Mass.) 217.

[2]*Lightbody* v. *N. A. Ins. Co.*, 23 Wend. (N. Y.) 18; *Ætna Ins. Co.* v. *Maguire*, 51 Ill. 342. In *Winans* v. *Allemania F. Ins. Co.*, 38 Wis. 392, the principle that the agent of an insurance company may waive by parol a condition in the policy issued by him was affirmed. This case involved a parol agreement in reference to the use of gasoline. There was an indorsement upon the policy as follows: "Permission is granted to light the premises with gasoline gas *when the generator is removed thirty feet from the building*," but there was another clause in the policy which provided that "the generating, evaporating or using, within any building where this policy may apply, or contiguous thereto, of gasoline, benzine, naptha, or of any substance for burning gas or vapor, for lighting, other than the ordinary street gas or kerosene, is prohibited, unless permitted in writing hereon." The building had previously been lighted with gasoline gas, generated *within* thirty feet from the building, and, at the time when the policy was issued, the agent through whom it was procured *knew* the fact that the building was lighted by, and that the gasoline gas was generated within thirty feet from the building, and that the plaintiff was then engaged in removing the business and fixtures and putting lamps in their places for the purpose of burning kerosene, *and that the agent consented orally that the premises might be lighted with gasoline until the change could be effected.* The premises having been consumed before the change could be effected, the court held that the company was estopped from setting up a breach of this condition, *because of the knowledge of the agent that gasoline was used when the policy was issued, and because of his oral consent that it might be used until a change could be made.* In *Miller* v. *Phœnix Ins. Co.*, 27 Iowa, 203;

is bound by acts done by him within the scope thereof, although in
violation of the orders of the principal or in excess of the powers actually conferred upon him.[1]

---

1 Am. Rep. 262, it was held that local agents of foreign insurance companies,
appointed by a general agent, may bind the companies, though their acts may be
in violation of certain limitations on their authority, unknown to the assured. An
agent may waive forfeitures. *Bodine* v. *Exchange F. Ins. Co.*, 51 N. Y. 117; 10
Am. Rep. 566; *Shearman* v. *Niagara F. Ins. Co.*, 46 N. Y. 526; 7 Am. Rep. 380;
Miner v. *Phœnix Ins. Co.*, 27 Wis. 693; 9 Am. Rep. 429; *Walsh* v. *Ætna Life Ins.
Co.*, 30 Iowa, 133; 6 Am. Rep. 664. An agent may receive a premium, with
binding force, after the time stipulated for payment. See *Bouton* v. *American
Life Ins. Co.*, 25 Conn. 542; *Wing* v. *Harvey*, 27 Eng. L. & Eq. 140. It is no
defense to an action on an insurance policy that the agent acted beyond his
authority, unless it shall appear that the assured knew or ought to have known
the precise limits of the authority. BREESE, C.J., in *Ætna Ins. Co.* v. *Maguire*,
51 Ill. 342. See *Eastern R. R. Co.* v. *Relief Ins. Co.*, 105 Mass. 570; *Sheldon* v.
Com. Mut. Life Ins. Co., 25 Conn. 207.

[1]*Beebe* v. *Hartford Ins. Co.*, 25 Conn. 51; *N. Y. Cen. Ins. Co.* v. *National, etc.,
Ins. Co.*, 20 Barb. (N. Y.) 476; aff'd, 15 N. Y. 85; *Nicol* v. *American Ins. Co.*, 3
W. & M. (U. S.) 529; *Gloucester Mfg. Co.* v. *Howard F. Ins. Co.*, 5 Gray (Mass.)
497. In a case recently decided in the Supreme Court of Georgia, not yet
reported, *M. F. D. Ins. Co.* v. *Coleman* (decided May, 1877), the court held that
parol evidence is admissible to prove that the insurance agent knew a fact which
he ought to have stated in the policy, but did not, and that, to render a contract
of insurance void under the Code of Georgia for any matter, whether of covenant
or representation, there must be some degree of materiality in such matter; also,
that the cash value of a house is not necessarily what it cost to build it, or what
it would cost to build a similar house at the same place. In an Illinois case,
Hartford Ins. Co. v. *Farrish*, 5 Ins. L. J. 46, the agent of the defendant accepted
a risk of $5,500 in a certain warehouse. The defendant offered to prove that the
agent had authority only to take limited risks therein, and that the limitation had
been reached before this risk was taken, but the court held that the evidence was
not admissible, unless the defendant also show that the plaintiff, *before* the policy
was delivered to him, had notice of the limitation upon the agent's authority.
Imperial F. Ins. Co. v. *Thurrey*, 73 Penn. St. 13. In *Langstrap* v. *German Ins.
Co.*, 57 Mo. 107; 8 Am. Rep. 100, it was held that a person who deals with an
agent or officer of a corporation who assumes authority to act in certain matters,
when no want of authority is apparent or brought to his knowledge, and nothing
occurs which would lead the party to suppose that he is not authorized to act in
that respect, the company is bound, although the agent in fact had no power to
do the act in question. See also, *Fayles* v. *National Ins. Co.*, 49 Mo. 380; *Washington F. Ins. Co.* v. *Davidson*, 30 Mo. 91; *Ætna Ins. Co.* v. *Maguire*, 51 Ill. 342;
Eclectic Ins. Co. v. *Fahrenkrug, ante; Farmers', etc., Ins. Co.* v. *Cheshunt*, 50 Ill. 111.
In *Hotchkiss* v. *Germania F. Ins. Co.*, 5 Hun (N. Y.) 9, the agent was furnished
with blank policies signed by the president and secretary to be filled up and
delivered to persons who might wish to contract. He had the right to renew
policies, to fix the premiums, and to receive and remit them to the company. It
was held that he had authority to make a parol agreement to insure and to waive
the payment of the premium, notwithstanding the printed condition of the policies
stipulated that the risk should not commence till payment of premium. *DeGroat*
v. *Fatton F. Ins. Co.*, 4 Rob. (N. Y.) 504; *N. E. F. & M. Ins. Co.* v. *Schettler*, 38
Ill. 166; *Dayton Ins. Co.* v. *Kelly, ante*. In *Gloucester Manuf. Co.* v. *Howard F.
Ins. Co.*, 5 Gray (Mass.) 497, the defendant furnished G. & C. with policies signed
in blank, for them to write in the consideration, amount insured, and all other
matters pertaining to the contract. G. & C. issued a policy upon certain buildings in course of construction, but insured refused to receive it or to pay the premium, on the ground that the printed stipulations prevented its operation, while
the buildings were being constructed. G. & C. made an indorsement assuming
the risk while the buildings were being constructed, notwithstanding the stipulations mentioned. Insurers had not any notice of the indorsement until after the

SEC. 391. That an insurance agent authorized to make contracts of insurance and issue policies, may waive forfeitures and reinstate and restore a void policy, as a valid instrument, is held by numerous cases. Indeed, it is a power incident to the authority to make a contract of insur-ance, and the company is as much estopped from denying that he pos-sessed such power, as it is from denying his authority to make contracts when it has delegated such power to him, or permitted him to exer-cise it. Thus, in a New York case[1], the policy contained a condition that if the property insured was conveyed, without the assent of the company, it should be void. The property was conveyed to the plain-tiff *March* 4, 1867, and its renewal procured by the vendor March 21, 1867, and on *April* 15th following, the defendant's agent assented to such conveyance, and to an assignment of the policy to the plaintiff,

---

loss occurred. Before the buildings were completed they were consumed by fire. Held, insured had the right to assume that G. & C. were authorized to make the indorsement, therefore insurers were liable for the loss. It is not the real, but the apparent authority that controls, and the jury are to say whether the agent had authority in a given case. *Hough* v. *City F. Ins. Co.*, 29 Conn. 16; *Ætna Ins. Co.* v. *Maguire*, 51 Ill. 342. In *Franklin F. Ins. Co.* v. *Massey*, 33 Penn St. 221, a policy was issued to the plaintiff for one year, *and for the full term of any future time or times for which a premium shall be paid and indorsed, or otherwise acknowledged in writing* by the secretary or other authorized officer. It was renewed from year to year for about six years, when the company directed the agent who renewed it, to cancel it, of which he notified insured; but he did not pay or offer to insure the return premium. Before that was done the loss occurred. It was held that the authority of the agent did not depend on that which was actually delegated to him by the company, but on that which the plaintiff had a right to believe was given him; that the principal was bound to dissent from the act of his agent in renewing the policy, within a reasonable time after the fact of renewal was communicated, and if that was not done the company could not subse-quently repudiate his acts. Where the policy provided that it should be void if assigned without the assent of the secretary. The agent indorsed consent and reported to the company who did not dissent. Held that whether the agent had authority to assent or not, if he was in the habit of doing so, the company were bound. *Farmers', etc., Ins. Co.* v. *Taylor*, 73 Penn. St. 342. In *Baubie* v. *Ætna Ins. Co.*, 2 Dil. (U. S. C. C.) 156, the company supplied the agent with blank policies signed by the company's officers. He was authorized to fill them up and to deliver them without first consulting the company. He filled up and delivered one for $4,000, upon the property in question, insuring it for six months; renewed it in writing for six months longer, but beyond that there was no further written renewal. The insured claimed an agreement resting between the agent and himself, that the agent would keep the property constantly insured by renewing the policy every six months, and draw for the premium. It was held that the powers of an insurance agent are presumed to be coextensive with the business intrusted to his care; and his presumed powers were not to be narrowed by limitations not communicated to the person dealing with him; that if the agent did not exceed his apparent authority, the company were bound by his acts. *Palm* v. *Medina, etc., Ins. Co.*, 20 Ohio, 529; *Dayton Ins. Co.* v. *Kelly*, 24 Ohio St. 345; *Imperial F. Ins. Co.* v. *Murray*, 73 Penn. St. 13; *Hotchkiss* v. *Germania Ins. Co.*, 5 Hun (N. Y.) 90. The imposition of a duty implies a power necessary for its performance. *Baker* v. *Cotter*, 45 Me. 256; *Gloucester Manuf. Co.* v. *Howard Ins. Co.*, 5 Gray (Mass.) 497.

[1] *Shearman* v. *Niagara F. Ins. Co.*, 46 N. Y. 526; 7 Am. Rep. 380.

and the court of appeals held that the policy was thereby reinstated. The defendant insisted that the policy *was made void by the transfer, and that being void when the agents assented to the conveyance, and assignment of the policy,* they had no authority to reinstate it.   They further insisted that as the property was conveyed March 4th, *the vendor had no insurable interest on March 21st when the policy was renewed in his name,* and that the policy for *this* cause being void, the consent of their agent to its transfer to the plaintiff, *knowing the facts* when the assent was given, did not render it an operative or valid instrument.   But the court held otherwise and the opinion of CHURCH, C.J., upon this point is given in the subjoined note.[1]

---

[1] He said: "The points relied upon by the appellants in this court are the same presented upon a motion for a nonsuit, when the plaintiff rested, and again at the close of the evidence. They are, substantially : 1. That the property, having been transferred without the consent of the company, the renewal of the policy afterward without such consent was void, and rendered the policy a wager policy, void both by statute and common law ; 2. That there was no evidence of a consent on the part of the company to a transfer of the property to the plaintiff ; and 3. That there was such a change of possession of the property as to render the policy void. The property was transferred to the plaintiff on the 4th of March, 1867, the renewal was made the 21st of March, and on the 15th of April of the same year the policy was transferred to the plaintiff.   On the same day the defendant, by its agent, by an indorsement on the back, consented to such transfer of the policy.   It is well settled that the person insured must have an insurable interest in the property (*Fowler* v. *New York Ins. Co.*, 26 N. Y. 422 ; *Ruse* v. *Mutual Benefit Life Ins. Co.*, 23 id. 516); and one of the conditions of the policy is, that if any transfer of the title or possession of the property is made, without the consent of the company, the policy shall be void.   Assuming that when Lewis J. Shearman transferred the property he retained no insurable interest, I cannot assent to the position that the policy thereby became a wager policy, and void in the sense that it was an illegal contract, and that it could not be revived and restored to life by the act of the defendant.   It was void, not for any vice or illegality in the contract itself, but for the reason that there was nothing upon which it could operate. *Howard* v. *Albany Ins. Co.*, 3 Denio, 301.   The parties, it is true, agreed that in a certain contingency it should be void ; and if a loss had occurred during that period, no action could have been maintained upon the policy, but the happening of the contingency did not impress upon the contract the character of illegality, so that no subsequent agreement could restore it.   The case of *Gray* v. *Hook*, 4 N. Y. 449, cited by the learned counsel for the appellant, will serve to illustrate the distinction between a contract valid in its creation, which has become void by an act of the party so that it cannot be enforced, and one that is illegal and contrary to public policy.   In that case the cause of action grew out of an agreement between the plaintiff and defendant, by which one of them was to withdraw his application for appointment to an office by the governor in favor of the other, upon an agreement to divide the fees.   The court very properly held that this agreement was contrary to public policy and void at common law, and being thus tainted, no new agreement entered into to carry into effect any of its provisions was valid.   The same principle was decided by this court in *Woodworth* v. *Bennett*, 43 N. Y. 273. But this principle is not applicable to the present case.   Here the original contract was lawful and valid ; it was not tainted with the vice of corruption or other illegality.   It had become void according to its terms, and in that condition it could not be enforced ; but it was not beyond resurrection by the act of the parties themselves.   I am aware that there is an intimation, by BRONSON, J., in *Smith* v *Saratoga County Mutual Fire Insurance Company*, 3 Hill, 508, that a mere waiver would not revive such a policy.   He says: 'It is difficult to see how anything short of a new creation could impart vitality to this dead body.'   He did not, how-

Facit per alium, facit per se—Apparent authority the test.

SEC. 392. The rule is not a doubtful one, either in policy or principle, that in transactions of this character, where one of two persons must

---

ever, intend to decide the question of waiver, and added: 'But it is unnecessary to put this case upon the ground that the forfeiture could not be waived;' and then proceeds to show that there had been no waiver. In 7 Hill, 49, in a similar case, BEARDSLEY, J., said: 'Whether a policy, after having become void by the alienation of the property insured, can be restored to vitality by a mere act of waiver on the part of the underwriters, need not now be decided.' Precisely what is intended as a 'mere act of waiver' is not very clear; but it is probable that both of the learned judges intended to make a distinction between such an act and an act which would amount to an agreement to revive and continue the contract. I have been unable to find any adjudged case holding that such forfeiture may not be waived, and such policy revived, by an act from which the consent of the underwriters may fairly be inferred. The authorities in this State and elsewhere are quite decisive that it may be done. *Solms* v. *Rutgers' Fire Ins. Co.*, 5 Abb. (N. S.) 201; *Howell* v. *Knickerbocker Fire Ins Co.*, 44 N. Y. 276; *Wolf* v. *Security Fire Ins. Co.*, 39 id. 51; *Hooper* v. *Hudson River Fire Ins. Co.*, 17 id. 424; *Carroll* v. *Charter Oak Fire Ins. Co.*, 38 Barb. 402; *Keeler* v. *Niagara Fire Ins. Co.*, 16 Wis. 523. It is claimed, however, by the counsel for the appellant, that, when the renewal was obtained, the transfer had been made. and that this renewal constituted a new policy, which was void and illegal within the principles before stated. I do not think so. The renewal simply revived the original policy, and continued it with all the virtue which it would have had, for any purpose, if it had not expired. Besides, Lewis J. Shearman had an insurable interest remaining, as lessee and owner of the equity of redemption, which may be deemed sufficient to obviate this objection. The important question is, whether the forfeiture was waived and the policy revived by the consent of the defendant to the transfer of it to the plaintiff. In the case of an insurance upon goods, it has been held by this court, that a request that the company would consent to an assignment of the policy was sufficient notice to them that the party making it had acquired, or was about to acquire, some interest in the goods insured, and was a compliance with the condition of the policy on that subject. *Hooper* v. *Hudson River Fire Ins. Co.*, 17 N. Y. 424; *Wolf* v. *The Security Fire Ins. Co.*, 39 id. 49. An assignment of the policy would be useless for any purpose, unless the assignee had some interest in the subject insured. This interest may be as owner or incumbrancer, but whatever it is, the underwriters, by consenting to the assignment, agree to become answerable to the assignee, to the extent of whatever interest he has, and if the whole interest is transferred, the consent is equivalent to an agreement to be liable to the assignee upon the policy as a subsisting operative contract. I see no reason why the same rule should not apply to a policy upon real as well as personal property, but it is unnecessary in this case to determine that the request to assign was a sufficient notice of the transfer of the property, because it expressly appears that the agent was informed of the fact at the time the request was made. It is objected that the agent was not informed of the time of the transfer, nor that the renewal was subsequent to the transfer, but this is not material. It is enough that the plaintiff requested that he should be substituted as the insured, on the ground that the property had been transferred to him, and the company consented to it. It is of no importance whether his conveyance was recent or remote, nor whether they knew that the policy was void at the time of the renewal by reason of the transfer before that time. They might have insisted upon the forfeiture if they so elected, at whatever time it was made. They knew that the policy was void when the request was made, and they chose to revive it, and thereby consented to insure the property in the hands of the plaintiff as effectually as if they had given a new policy to him. The retention of the premium received on the renewal was a good consideration for this agreement. No other construction can be given to the transaction. The condition requiring consent is important to underwriters, to enable them to determine the character and standing of the insured; and when they agree to a transfer of a policy to a particular person, knowing that he owns the subject insured, the whole purpose of the provision is complied with, and they have no interest to know how or why he acquired it.

sustain a loss, the loss must fall upon him who has made it possible for
the other, innocently, to be placed in a position where loss might result
to him except for the application of this rule. It would be disastrous
to commercial, as well as other interests, if a person, by acting through
the agency of another, could shield himself from liability for such
person's acts, *ad libitum*. Fortunately, no such rule exists, *and he who
entrusts authority to another, in whatever department of business, is bound
by all that is done by his agent within the scope of his apparent power, and
cannot screen himself from the consequences thereof upon the ground that
no authority in fact was given him to do the particular act, unless the act
was clearly in excess of his apparent authority, or was done under such
circumstances as put the person dealing with him, upon inquiry, as to the
agent's real authority;* and no exception to this rule exists in the law
of insurance. It is always a question of fact, whether the act was
done under such circumstances that the assured had a right to believe
that the agent was clothed with authority to do the particular act in
question.

The rule may be said to be that, *unless notice is given to the assured,
that in respect of certain matters within the scope of his apparent authority,
certain limitations are imposed upon the agent, his acts within the scope of
such authority shall be treated as the acts of his principal, and not the acts
of the person with whom he deals as the representative of the principal,
even though the policy declares him the agent of the assured.*[1] The question
is not what the powers of the agent in fact were, but what power did the
company hold him out as possessing.*[2] From the business with which the
agent was entrusted, had the assured a right to understand that he
had authority to do the particular act, in reference to which the principal denies his authority.*[3] In order to charge the company, the

---

The only remaining point made is, that the possession of the premises was
changed, which rendered the policy void. Lewis J. Shearman remained the
occupant of the premises, and was temporarily absent with his family at the time
of the fire. The house was in charge of one Brown for him. This is not such a
change of possession as will avoid the policy. Brown's possession was in fact
and in law Shearman's possession. He was Shearman's servant. * * It was
never contemplated that the assured should remain *constantly* on the premises."

[1] *Commercial Ins. Co.* v. *Ives*, 56 Ill. 402; *Columbia Ins. Co.* v. *Cooper*, 50 Penn.
St. 331; *Beebe* v. *Hartford, etc., Ins. Co.*, 25 Conn. 51; *Ins. Co.* v. *Wilkinson*, 13
Wall. (U. S.)

[2] *Eclectic Life Ins. Co.* v. *Fahrenkrug*, 68 Ill. 463.

[3] *Ætna Ins. Co.* v. *Maguire*, 51 Ill. 354; *Washington F. Ins. Co.* v. *Davidson*,
30 Md. 91; *Home Life Ins. Co.* v. *Pierce*, 5 Ins. L. J. 290 (Ill.); *Farmers', etc.,
Ins. Co.* v. *Cheshunt*, 50 Ill. 111; In *Franklin F. Ins. Co.* v. *Murray*, 73 Penn. St.
13, the defendant's agent entered into a contract with the plaintiff to insure his
property from year to year, at a certain rate. After the insurance had been kept
on foot for about six years, the company directed the agent to cancel it, of

assured must, from the facts, be warranted in relying upon it that the agent had authority to do the act in question, and to bind the company in respect of the matter with which it is sought to charge it.[1]

---

which he notified the assured, but did not offer to refund the unearned premium, and a loss having occurred, the defendants denied the authority of the agent to renew the policy. The court held, however, that the derendant's liability did not depend upon what authority they had actually delegated to the agent, *but upon that which the assured had a right to believe was given him.* In *Dayton Ins. Co.* v. *Kelly, ante,* the agent erased certain conditions from the contract before its delivery to the plaintiff, and the court held that, as the insurers held the agent out as having apparent authority to deliver the contract, with or without the con_ dition ; that delivering it with the condition erased, was not notice to the assured that he exceeded his authority, because the assured had no means of knowing whether the agent exceeded his authority or not. *Keenan* v. *Missouri Ins. Co.,* 12 Iowa, 126 ; *Mound City Life Ins. Co.* v. *Heeth,* 49 Ala. 529. In *Ide* v. *Phœnix Ins. Co.,* 2 Biss. (U. S. C. C.) 333, the insurer's agent was familiar with the prop_ erty, and offered to insure $1,000 for a term of three years for a premium of $13.50, which money was paid to him. Insured called for the policy frequently, but failed to get it, and soon after he left the state. The property was burned by an accidental fire before any policy was delivered, and before the agent remitted the money to the company. It appeared that the agent had never reported the risk to the company, but had converted the premium to his own use. Prompt notice of the loss was given to the agent, who said he was satisfied that the loss was all right, and promised payment of the claim on different occasions between the autumns of 1864 and 1866. In 1866 the agent notified insured that the com_ pany would not pay the claim. It was held that the agent had authority to waive proofs of loss ; his acts and assurances in regard to the payment of the loss were also sufficient to waive the clause which required suits to be brought within one year after the loss ; and the claim could be enforced without the delivery of a policy, hence the complainant was entitled to recover the amount insured with interest and costs of suit.

[1] In *Winnesheick Ins. Co.* v. *Holzgrafe,* 53 Ill. 516 ; 5 Am. Rep. 64, the plaintiff sought to charge the insurer with liability upon a parol contract of insurance made with its agent pending an application for insurance. BREESE, C.J., said : "The appellee insists there was a contract of insurance made by the lawfully authorized agents of the company. That contract must rest in parol, for it is not found in the writings we have been considering. Taking the representations and declarations of these agents made to complainant, in connection with his written application to the company for insurance, a contract may be predicated upon them. The question then arises as to the power of these agents to make such a contract. The warrant of their authority is in the record. By that they were only authorized to receive applications for insurance in accordance with the instructions to agents, and to collect and transmit the premiums therefor. This was the extent of their authority, and no instructions have been shown from their principals authorizing them to go one step beyond this, nor is there any proof they ever did, or ever designed, to go a step beyond. They both state they never held themselves out to community as possessing authority to effect insurances, write up policies, adjust losses, or do anything more than the letter of their appointment specified. We have said, in several cases, where an agent of an insurance company shall, with the knowledge of his principal, so hold himself out to the public by receiving applications for insurance, and granting policies, to such an extent as to induce the public doing business with him to believe he is the lawfully constituted agent, the principal, having accepted the cash premium, shall not be permitted afterward, in case of loss, to repudiate the act. Such was the case of *Ætna Ins. Co.* v. *Maguire,* 51 Ill. 342. We decide this case on the ground that an application for an insurance was all that was made by complainant, and that the delay in responding to it was not of a character from which an acceptance of the proposal can be implied, and that any contract of insurance effected by the agents of appellants was not binding upon appellants, such contract not being within the scope of the authority with

False answers to questions avoid the policy, and where the agent is merely an agent to solicit risks, notice to him that certain matters stated are incorrect, is not notice to the company.[1] There are cases[2] that hold that notice to the agent is notice to the insurer, but this does not extend beyond matters within the real or apparent power of the agent. When the assured *knows* or *ought* to know the extent of the agent's authority, he cannot charge the principal for matters in excess thereof,[3] and if the assured knows the extent of the agent's power, and colludes with him for a contract in excess thereof, he can derive no benefit therefrom.[4]

Agent may waive forfeiture.

SEC. 393. That an agent may waive a forfeiture, is well established by numerous authorities.[5] *But, where a limitation is imposed upon the power of the agent upon the face of the policy, of which the assured, as a prudent man, ought to know;* and there is no evidence that the agent has been accustomed to act in excess of such power, with the express or implied assent of the insurer, the assured is not justified in dealing with him in reference to such matters, and his acts, as to the excess of authority, are not binding upon the company.[6]

---

which they were vested by the company, and which was well known. We repeat here what was said in *Ætna Ins. Co. v. Maguire, supra.* That case turned upon the question of a cancellation of the policy of insurance which had been written up by the agent, and the premium transmitted to the general agent, and retained by him, and an adjuster of the loss had been sent out to examine into the loss. There, the contract was evidenced by the policy which the agent had written, and who seemed to possess all the symbols of an unrestricted agency, and had actually issued the policy then in question. Here the application for insurance was not accepted, and the agents never, at any time, represented or intimated to any one that they had any other authority than to transmit applications and receive premiums." *Quere,* if the agent had represented that he had authority to bind the company, would that of itself, established the company's liability? The rule is that it would not.

[1] *Galbraith* v. *Arlington, etc., Ins. Co.,* 12 Bush. (Ky.) 29.

[2] *Miller* v. *Mutual Benefit Ins. Co.,* 31 Iowa, 216.

[3] *Galbraith* v. *Arlington. etc., Ins. Co.,* 12 Bush. (Ky.) 29; *Vose* v. *Eagle Ins. Co.,* 6 Bush. (Mass.) 42; *Lowell* v. *Middlesex, etc., Ins. Co.,* 8 id. 127.

[4] *Smith* v. *Ins. Co.,* 24 Penn. St. 323; *Galbraith* v. *Ins. Co., ante.*

[5] *Carroll* v. *Charter Oak Ins. Co.,* 10 Abb. (N. Y.) U. S. 166; *First Baptist Church* v. *Brooklyn F. Ins. Co.,* 19 N. Y. 305; *Goit* v. *National Protection Ins. Co.,* 25 Barb. (N. Y.) 189; *Cone* v. *Niagara Ins. Co.,* 60 N. Y. 619; *Bodine* v. *Exchange Ins. Co.,* 51 N. Y. 117; *Dohn* v. *Farmer's Joint-Stock Ins. Co.,* 5 Lans. (N. Y.) 265; *Hotchkiss* v. *Germania Ins. Co.,* 5 Hun (N. Y.) 90; *Ins. Co.* v. *Wilkinson,* 13 Wall. (U. S.) 222; *Shearman* v. *Niagara F. Ins. Co.,* 46 N. Y. 526; *Miller* v. *Phœnix Ins. Co.,* 27 Iowa, 203; *Sheldon* v. *Atlantic, etc., Ins. Co.,* 26 N. Y. 460; *Whitwell* v. *Putnam F. Ins. Co.,* 6 Lans. (N. Y.) 166; *Dean* v. *Ætna, etc., Ins Co.,* 4 T. & C. (N. Y.) 497.

[6] *Catoir* v. *American, etc., Ins. Co.,* 33 N. J. 487; *Mersereau* v. *Phœnix, etc., Ins. Co.,* 66 N. Y. 274.

In commenting upon the effect of such notice given to a policy-holder in a New York case,[1] ALLEN, J., announced what we conceive to be the rule applicable and generally held. He said : "In the face of a distinct written expression in the policy of a want of power in the agent, the party suing to recover upon such policy has no right to infer the subsequent existence of such power by any uncertain sign. *There must be evidence to justify the belief that the company by direct authority enlarged the powers of the agent, or that they knowingly permitted him to act for them beyond the scope of the powers originally conferred.*"[2]

Other insurance.

SEC. 394. When the agent of the insurer *knows* at the time when he issues a policy that there is other insurance upon the property, his failure to write the company's consent thereto in the instrument *will not defeat an action thereon, although the policy itself declares that it shall be void in case the assured* "*shall have or shall hereafter make any other insurance upon the property without the consent of the company written herein ;*" and also declares that "the use of general terms, or anything less than a distinct, specific agreement, clearly expressed and indorsed upon the policy, shall not be construed as a waiver of any printed or written restrictions therein."[3] The knowledge of the agent of such other insurance, and his failure to indorse it upon the policy, is a waiver of the condition, and estops the insurer from setting it up in avoidance of the policy.[4] Where the policy requires notice of other insurance to be given, notice to the agent is notice to the company, unless the policy expressly requires notice to be given to a certain officer, or in a certain manner.[5]

---

[1] *Mersereau* v. *Phœnix, etc., Ins. Co.,* 66 N. Y. 279.

[2] See also, *Bourton* v. *American, etc., Ins. Co.,* 25 Conn. 542.

[3] *Roberts* v. *Continental Ins. Co.,* Wisconsin Sup. Ct., March 20, 1877, not yet reported.

[4] *Kenton Ins. Co.* v. *Shea,* 6 Bush. (Ky.) 174 ; *Geib* v. *International Ins. Co.,* 1 Dill. (U. S. C. C.) 443 ; *McEwen* v. *Montgomery, etc., Ins. Co.,* 5 Hill (N. Y.) 101 ; *Carroll* v. *Charter Oak Ins. Co.,* 38 Barb. (N. Y.) 402 ; *Goodall* v. *N. E. Mut. Ins. Co.,* 25 N. H. 169 ; *Hadley* v. *N. H. F. Ins. Co.,* 55 N. H. 110 ; *Schenck* v. *Mercer, etc., Ins. Co.,* 24 N. J. L. 447 ; *National Ins Co.* v. *Crane,* 16 Md. 260 ; *Horwitz* v. *Equitable, etc., Ins. Co.,* 40 Mo. 557 ; *Van Bories* v. *United States, etc., Ins. Co.,* 8 Bush. (Ky.) 133 ; *Carrugi* v. *Atlantic F. Ins. Co.,* 40 Ga. 135.

[5] *Schenck* v. *Mercer, etc., Ins. Co., ante* ; *Sexton* v. *Montgomery, etc., Ins. Co.,* 9 Barb. (N. Y.) 191 ; *McEwen* v. *Montgomery, etc., Ins. Co., ante* ; *Ins. Co. of N. America* v. *McDowell,* 50 Ill. 120 ; *Hayward* v *National Ins. Co.,* 52 Mo. 181 ; *Cobb* v. *Ins. Co. of N. America,* 11 Kan. 93 ; *Webster* v. *Phœnix Ins. Co.,* 36 Wis. 67.

Power to waive proofs of loss.

SEC. 395. Where an agent is entrusted with policies signed in blank, and is authorized to issue them upon the application of parties seeking insurance, he is thereby clothed with apparent authority to bind the party in reference to any condition of the contract, whether precedent or subsequent, and may waive notice or proofs of loss,[1] and may bind the company by his admissions in respect thereto. Thus, where preliminary proofs were submitted to an agent, and he proceeded to ascertain the amount due thereon, and brought the money into court, it was held an admission by the insurers that the proofs were sufficient.[2] A waiver of notice, or proofs of loss, may be found from the acts or language of an agent which reasonably induced the assured to delay making them. Thus, in a New York case,[3] the policy contained a stipulation that the "insured shall, within ten days after any loss occurs, deliver a particular account thereof to the company, signed and verified by the insured." The court held that evidence that the person who solicited the insurance used language to the insured which might have induced him to postpone the making and forwarding of the proofs within the time limited, was evidence to sustain a waiver of the condition. The authority of an agent to waive these conditions in a policy is recognized, even where the policy itself provides that no waiver shall be binding unless in writing, unless actual knowledge of this condition, on the part of the assured, is shown.[4]

[1] *Imperial F. Ins. Co.* v. *Murray*, 73 Penn. St. 13; *Dean* v. *Ætna L. Ins. Co.*, 4 T. & C. (N.Y.) 497; *Ide* v. *Phœnix Ins. Co.*, 2 Biss. (U.S.) 333; *Franklin F. Ins. Co.* v. *Coates*, 14 Md. 285; *Manhattan Ins. Co.* v. *Stein*, 5 Bush. (Ky.) 652; *McBride* v. *Republic F. Ins. Co.*, 30 Wis. 562; *Parker* v. *Amazon Ins. Co.*, 34 id. 362; *Norwich, etc., Trans. Co.* v. *Western Mass. Ins. Co.*, 34 Conn. 561; *Lycoming Ins. Co.* v. *Dunmore*, 75 Ill. 14; *Warner* v. *Peoria M. & F. Ins. Co.*, 14 Wis. 318; *Bush* v. *Westchester Ins. Co.*, 2 T. & C. (N.Y.) 629; *Home Ins. Co.* v. *Cohen*, 20 Gratt. (Va.) 312; *Underwood* v. *Farmers', etc., Ins. Co.*, 57 N.Y. 500; *Hibernia Ins. Co* v. *O'Connor*, 29 Mich. 241. In *Eastern R. R. Co.* v. *Relief F. Ins. Co.*, 105 Mass. 570, the defendant's agent was supplied with policies signed in blank. He had filled out and delivered one for this risk containing a stipulation that the "insured shall forthwith give notice thereof (loss) in writing to the company, and within sixty days from the occurring of the fire, shall deliver as particular an account of the loss as the nature of the case will admit." The secretary of the insured informed him that numerous fires were occurring along the line of the road; that insured were examining carefully the claims made therefor. The agent replied: "This was satisfactory, and that when the railroad company should get through paying, to hand in a schedule of what had been paid, and it should be attended to." Neither notice nor proofs of loss were made; but about eight months after all the claims had been paid by the railroad company, the treasurer made a sworn statement of each and all the losses which had been sustained. The court held that the preliminary proofs of loss were waived, and insured entitled to judgment.

[2] *Johnson* v. *Columbian Ins. Co.*, 7 John. (N.Y.) 315; *Franklin Ins. Co.* v. *Updegraff*, 43 Penn. St. 350.

[3] *Dohn* v. *Farmers' Joint Stock Ins. Co.*, 5 Lans. (N.Y.) 27.

[4] *Pitney* v. *Glens Falls Ins. Co.*, 61 Barb. (N.Y.) 335.

SEC. 396. But the burden is upon the assured, to show that the act relied upon was within the scope of his apparent authority, and the question is not wholly one of fact, *but a mixed question of law and fact*, and if the jury find such authority upon insufficient evidence, their verdict will be set aside. Thus, in a recent case in Massachusetts,[1] the plaintiff shew that the agent received application for insurance, took risks, settled rates of premium, and issued policies, and from these facts the jury found that he had authority to waive proofs of loss ; but the court held that this finding was unwarranted, and that the plaintiff was bound to go a step farther, and show that the person was the general agent of the company, or was permitted by it to do acts that would warrant the inference that he was authorized to transact all their business at the place in question. Something more than acts amounting to proof of a *special agency* must be shown. *Authority, in fact, or apparent authority, justifying a stranger in dealing with him as their general agent, must be established*: If the evidence merely establishes a special agency, a person deals with him as to matters in excess of such apparent, special authority, at his peril. In all cases, in the absence of proof of actual authority, the question is, whether authority to do the act relied upon is fairly within the scope of the agent's apparent authority, and in determining this question, it is competent to show what acts the agent has been permitted to do by the company, and if the proof establishes nothing more than a special or limited authority, which does not fairly embrace the act in question, the assured, as to such matter, has dealt with him at his peril, and cannot charge the company beyond the scope of the agent's real or apparent power.[2] Authority *to make a contract*, does not necessarily

---

[1] *Sohnes* v. *Ins. Co. of N. America*, 121 Mass. 438 ; see also, *Bush* v. *Westchester F. Ins. Co.*, 63 N. Y. 531.

[2] In *Buch* v. *Westchester F. Ins. Co.*, *ante*, the plaintiff insisted that the condition of the policy as to proofs of loss were waived by the defendant's agents. To sustain the allegation of wavier, the acts and declarations of Mr. Straight, of the firm of Sly & Straight, local agents of the defendant for the issuing and countersigning of policies, were allowed to be proved under exceptions. The evidence, on the part of the plaintiff, showed that after the fire the agents of the other companies having policies on the property examined the store and the plaintiff's books, and estimated the damage, and agreed that the loss exceeded the amount insured. That Mr. Straight acted with them and concurred in their conclusion, and said he was satisfied that the loss was more than double what the plaintiff was insured. The defendant objected to all this evidence, on the ground that the authority of Mr. Straight was not proved. There was no direct proof of the authority of Mr. Straight, except that Sly & Straight were agents for the purpose of issuing policies, and it was not proved that they had ever acted for the company in adjusting losses or waiving conditions in other cases. Their acts and declarations in reference to this loss were allowed to be given in evidence as bind-

carry with it authority to change any of its details, or waive any of its provisions, *after* it is made and accepted by the other party. In order to establish such authority, it must be shown that he was in fact authorized to make the change, or that he has, with the knowledge of the company, held himself out and acted as their general agent, or has previously done acts for the company that warranted the assured in believing that he had authority to do the particular act.[1] If he is in fact, or apparently, the general agent of the company, whatever may formerly have been the rule, it is now well established that he stands in the place and stead of the company to the assured, and, in the absence of any limitation of his power known to the assured, any

---

ing upon the defendant, and the judge charged the jury, among other things, as follows: "It does not appear, from any evidence in the case, that the plaintiff knew or had information as to the precise extent of authority that the local agent of the company had who resided here in Elmira, hence the plaintiff, as a matter of law, had the right to infer that the agent had such authority, as he would seem to have from the way and manner that he transacted business here for the company, the same that either of you would have if you came to one of those agents there and obtained a policy of insurance upon your property, and he said nothing as to the nature and extent of his authority to do business for the company, and there was nothing in or on the policy to advise or show you precisely the nature and extent of his authority, as you would have a right to infer he possessed in doing business for the company."

This ruling was reversed by the Court of Appeals, RAPALLO, J., saying, "We think that the charge on the subject of the authority of Sly & Straight, and the effect of their acts, was erroneous. It was not proved that they had ever acted for the company in adjusting losses or waiving conditions before the occasion in question, nor that they were agents of the company for any other purpose than that of issuing and countersigning policies upon risks accepted by the company; yet, the judge who presided at the trial charged the jury, in substance, in reference to the omission of the plaintiff to furnish proofs of loss, as required by the policy, that, so far as Sly & Straight assumed to act for the defendant (the company) in waiving such proofs, the plaintiff had a right to infer that they had authority to act. That if Sly & Straight, either of them, said it was all right and the loss would be paid, of course, that would be a waiver on the part of the defendant of any thing else to be done by the plaintiff. In various forms, during the progress of the trial, the judge held that whatever Sly & Straight did in respect to the loss, the plaintiff had a right to infer they had authority to do. In one part of the charge, the judge expressly stated, in presence of the jury, that the plaintiff had the right to infer that Sly & Straight had such authority as they assumed to exercise. Their own acts were thus made the evidence of their authority, without bringing home to the defendant any recognition, or even knowledge, of such acts, or showing any previous authority for them. The case was evidently tried upon the theory that Sly & Straight having been shown to be agents for the purpose of countersigning and delivering the policy, whatever they said or did after the loss was binding upon the defendants, unless notice was given to the plaintiff that they had not authority to do such acts, or make such declarations, and this proposition was in substance enunciated by the judge. * * * *
It cannot be held that the authority of an agent to receive proposals for insurance, and countersign and deliver policies, extends to adjusting losses or waiving the stipulated proofs of loss, and binding the company to pay without them. Neither can it be held that the mere fact that such an agent, assuming in a particular case to do those acts, establishes his authority."

[1] *Shones* v. *Ins. Co. of N. America, ante.*

act done by him in reference to the contract or risk, either *before* or *after* the contract is entered into, is binding upon it.[1]

[1] Where an agent, without any written examination, but upon his own personal examination, and having free access to all parts of the building, and without any fraud on the part of the assured, issues a policy upon the property, the insurer is bound thereby, although, in fact, the risk was more hazardous than the agent supposed, and was devoted to hazardous uses that he *might* have discovered, but failed to. *Beal* v. *Park F. Ins. Co.*, 16 Wis. 241. In *Hayward* v. *National Ins. Co.*, 52 Mo. 181; 14 Am. Rep. 401, the effect of a waiver of a condition of a policy by an agent, was ably considered. Vories, J., said: "It appears from the evidence in the cause, that at and before the execution of the policy sued on to John A. Lennon, he was doing business in the city of Hannibal, as a merchant tailor, that his stock of goods amounted to from seven to eight thousand dollars, that one David S. Eby also resided in Hannibal, and followed the business of an insurance agent, that he was agent for several insurance companies in the Eastern States, as well as being agent at Hannibal for defendant. That said Lennon had taken two policies of insurance from said Eby for three thousand dollars each, one in each of two Eastern companies for which Eby was agent, and that he had transacted the business with and procured the policies from said Eby. That in the month of July, 1868, shortly before the making of the policy sued on, Eby told said Lennon that one of his policies of three thousand dollars was about to expire, and that he could not renew it at the same rates that he had been charged before. Eby testified that he was the vice-president of the defendant, and agent for several insurance companies, had his office in the same room with the president and secretary of defendant, that he was in the habit of taking risks for the defendant most generally in consultation with the other officers of the company; when the risks were out of the ordinary run of business, there was a general consultation; that he thought he was authorized by virtue of his postion as agent to take risks generally. Haynes, the president, and Meadows, the secretary of defendant, were both apprised of the issue of the policy to Lennon upon which the suit is brought, before it was issued. Eby further stated that he was carrying six thousand dollars on Lennon's stock. A short time previous to the expiration of one policy, he had a conversation with Meadows and Haynes, and told them that there was an opportunity of taking three thousand dollars on Lennon's stock, as he could not renew it in the company that it was in. After consultation with the company, they agreed to take the risk. The company knew that he was carrying six thousand dollars insurance for Lennon at the time, did not know whether he received the premium from Lennon, or whether the company received it. When Lennon was informed that one of his policies was about to expire, and that it could not be renewed at the same rate as before, he told Eby that he wanted it renewed, and requested him to continue it; said he had too much stock on hand to suffer any of his insurance to drop; he said he had about $8,000 in stock or over; that he wanted the policy continued. The evidence further shows that, after Eby had the consultation with the other officers of defendant, that he made out the policy upon which this suit was brought, and when the old policy had expired he handed it to Lennon, who objected to it; said he did not want to be put in the National, but that Eby assured him that it was a good company, and he then received it, telling him that he took it on his word; that he never examined the policy until after the fire which destroyed his goods. The evidence further tends to show that Eby continued to be agent and vice-president of the defendant until after the month of September, 1868. In September, 1868, Eby was, as agent of an eastern company, still carrying the three thousand dollar policy on Lennon's goods, in addition to the policy in suit, and that at said time said policy was about to expire, Eby told Lennon that the policy was about to expire, and that he could not renew it at the same rates paid before. Lennon said he wanted the policy renewed. Eby told him to wait a few days and he might still be able to renew it; that afterward, on the day the policy expired, Eby told Lennon that he was then prepared to renew the policy. Lennon told him he was too late; that he had just insured in another company, and thus renewed the amount of the three thousand dollar policy. Eby told him that that was all right. Eby states that he thinks he was still vice-president and acting as agent of defendant at the time of this last conversation.

Distinction between powers of general and special agents must be kept in view.

SEC. 397. But, in all cases, the distinction between the powers of special and general agents should be kept in view, and, in the case of a special

---

The foregoing is substantially the evidence in the cause in reference to the knowledge and consent of defendant as to the three thousand dollar insurance on the property, in addition to the policy sued on, either at the time of the execution of the policy by the defendant, or at the time that said insurance was changed to the Phœnix Company in September afterward. The question presented for the consideration of this court is, whether the evidence in this case or the circumstances under which the policy was sued on was executed and delivered to Lennon, were such as to amount to a waiver of the condition in the policy, that the policy should be void or no recovery had thereon, if the insured should have other insurance on the same property, which was not much known and not indorsed on the policy? And whether the condition was waived that required notice to be given and indorsement made thereof on the policy of any additional insurance being afterward made on said property? Or whether the defendant was estopped from setting up the breach of said conditions as a defense to the action? In my mind, there can be very little doubt as to the three thousand dollar policy which existed on the property at the time the policy was executed by the defendant. Eby, the agent and vice-president of the defendant, had executed and delivered to Lennon two policies, as agent for eastern companies, one of which was about to expire. Lennon wanted it renewed, but Eby could not renew it on terms to suit. This being the case, he had a consultation with the president and secretary of defendant, in which he informed them of the whole matter, and that there was a chance for the defendant to take a risk for three thousand on Lennon's goods in place of the policy about to expire. After a full consultation, they concluded to take the risk, and the policy was made out before Lennon was seen on the subject, and the same afterward handed to him. He hesitated to receive it until he was assured that the company was a good, responsible one, when he accepted the policy without ever looking at its contents, as the evidence shows. It was evidently known by all parties that the remaining three thousand dollar policy was to continue on the property insured, because Lennon had informed him that he could not afford to let any of his insurance be *dropped*. Lennon had a right to expect, under these circumstances, that defendant had indorsed on the policy its consent to this remaining policy of three thousand dollars, which good faith required it under the circumstances to have done. So far as this prior insurance is concerned, the case comes exactly within the principle laid down in the case of *Horwitz* v. *The Equitable Mut. Ins. Co.*, 40 Mo. 557. The defendant considered the whole matter in reference to the insurance already on the property and took the risk in reference thereto, and they should be estopped from setting up the breach of said condition as a defense to the action, said breach having been waived. In reference to the renewal of the insurance at a time subsequent to the execution of the policy sued on by the defendant, or the changing the same to another company, the evidence is not so clear of an intention to waive the condition requiring the defendant's knowledge and consent thereof to be indorsed on the policy. It is contented by the defendant that it was not notified of said subsequent insurance, and that it never in any way assented thereto, while, on the other hand, it is contended by the plaintiff that the evidence shows that defendant had full notice of the subsequent insurance and assented thereto, and so acted as to induce the said Lennon to rest in security in the belief that his property was fully insured. The main question in the case is, whether notice of this subsequent insurance to the agent who effected the risk for defendant will be considered as notice to the defendant. For I think that the evidence clearly shows that Eby was still vice-president and agent for the defendant at the time that this last insurance was effected. At least, if there were any doubts as to his agency at the time, that fact ought to have been submitted to the jury by a proper instruction. The authorities upon this last question are somewhat in conflict and cannot well be reconciled with each other. The cases referred to by the defendant in the Massachusetts courts, and other cases referred to, seem to accord with the views entertained by the defendant.

agent, the assured *must, at his peril, know whether the act relied on is within the scope of his real or of his apparent authority.* He is bound to

---

In the case of *The General Ins. Co.* v. *United States Ins. Co.*, 10 Md. 517, the question was as to notice by the corporation of an unrecorded deed of mortgage, so as to affect a subsequent mortgage. It is there held, that the notice in such case must be sufficient to put a party on inquiry, and that, conceding that a director of the corporation to be affected had notice of the prior mortgage, it does not appear that he had communicated the notice to the board of directors, and was therefore not sufficient; that the notice received by a director of a corporation in a private way, or which he had acquired from rumor, would not bind the institution; that the case must be so clear as to satisfy the mind that the allowance of the subsequent claim would be a fraud on the party setting up the first deed; and to the same effect is the case of *Farrell Foundry* v. *Dart*, 26 Conn. 376. The case of the *Worcester Bank* v. *Hartford Ins. Co.*, 11 Cush. 265, was a case where the policy sued on contained a clause almost precisely similar to the clause in the policy of defendant under consideration. It was held that in such case, where a subsequent insurance had been obtained and the agent of the company notified thereof, and he had promised the assured to have the consent of the subsequent insurance entered in the policy, but failed to have it done, that still the policy is avoided, the technicalities of the contract not having been complied with, and to the same effect are several other cases in Massachusetts.

It is contended by the defendant in this case that no notice to an agent of the company could operate as notice to the defendant, unless the agent received the notice at a time when said agent was engaged in the execution or performance of the business to which the notice related, unless it is shown that the agent comunicated the notice to his principal. To sustain this view of the case reference is made to several cases. In the case of *McCormick* v. *Wheeler*, 36 Ill. 114, it is held that notice to an attorney of one party which he has received while acting as the attorney of another party is not such notice as will effect his client. It is remarked by the judge delivering the opinion in the case 'that the English authorities manifest a disposition to depart from this rule, but it is deemed by the court to 'be a rule just in itself.' In the case of the *Mechanics' Bank* v. *Schaumburg*, 38 Mo. 228, Judge HOLMES delivering the opinion of the court, says, that 'knowledge acquired by the president, cashier and teller, while engaged in business of the bank in their official capacity, will be notice to the bank; so far as either has authority to act for the bank, his acts are the acts of the bank, and his official knowledge is the knowledge of the bank; but mere private information obtained beyond the range of his official functions will not be deemed notice to the bank.' It is difficult to exactly understand what is meant by the language used in these decisions. The defendant contends that it is meant by the decisions referred to as well as other decisions using similar language, that no notice served on an agent will be effectual to bind his principal, unless the agent should receive the notice while actually engaged in the transaction of the very business to which the notice relates, or unless it is shown that it was communicated to the principal. If that should be the proper construction to be given to the language, then it would become impossible that an agent of an insurance company could ever be notified of a subsequent policy of insurance being issued upon the same property before insured by said agent for his principal. Every agent as soon as he takes a risk and issues a policy therefor and delivers it to be insured, dismisses the subject of that policy from his mind. If the insured should afterward procure a subsequent insurance on the same property and go to the agent to give him notice thereof, he would be sure to find the agent in the transaction of some other business, when, according to the construction given to these cases, no notice could be given to the agent because he was not at the time engaged in the particular business to which the notice related, and this, notwithstanding the agent was the only agent of the corporation whose business it was to attend to the very matter to which the notice related. I think that this is not the proper construction to give to these cases; the meaning must be that the notice must be given to the agent while his agency exists, and it must refer to business which comes within the scope of his authority; when this is the case I think that notice to the agent is notice to the principal, in fact there is no

know when he has passed the precise limits of his power, and cannot
rely upon the assumption of authority by the agent to do an act beyond

---

other way to notify a corporation than to notify an agent. A corporation only
acts through and by agents, and the proper and only way to give notice to a corporation is to notify an agent, and generally it is sufficient to notify an agent whose
proper business is to attend to the matter in reference to which the notice is
given. In the opinion of Judge Holmes in the case of the *Bank* v. *Schaumburg*,
above referred to, Story's Agency, § 140, is referred to, from which it may be
seen what was meant by the language used in that direction. The section referred
to reads as follows: ' Upon a similar ground notice of facts to an agent is constructive notice thereof to the principal himself, where it arises from or is at the
time connected with the subject-matter of his agency ; for upon general principles
of public policy, it is presumed that the agent has communicated such facts to
the principal, and if he has not, still the principal, having intrusted the agent
with the particular business, the other party has a right to deem his acts and
knowledge obligatory on the principal, otherwise the neglect of the agent, whether
designed or undesigned, might operate most injuriously to the rights and interests of such party, but unless notice of the facts come to the agent while he is
concerned for the principal, and in the course of the very transaction, or so near
before it that the agent must be presumed to recollect it, it is not notice thereof
to the principal ; for otherwise the agent might have forgotten it, and then the
principal would be affected by his want of memory at the time of undertaking
the agency. Notice therefore to the agent before the agency is begun, or after it
has terminated, will not ordinarily affect the principal.' The quotation from
Story seems to me to solve the whole question, which is, that *notice to the agent
before his agency has begun, or after it has terminated, will not ordinarily affect
the principal.* If notice is given before the agency has begun, to affect the principal it must be so near before it that the agent must be presumed to recollect it.
This rule, as laid down by Judge Story, I think, is the correct one, and must be
the proper interpretation to be given to the language used in the cases on the
subject. Now, to return to the facts of the case under consideration we find that
Lennon in the month of July, 1868, had procured from one Eby two policies of
insurance for $3,000 each, one in each of two eastern companies for which said
Eby was agent. That said Eby was also agent for defendant, having authority to
take risks and issue policies for it. That one of the eastern policies was at said
time about to expire. That Eby informed Lennon that he could not renew the
policy on the same terms that the policy had been issued before. Lennon insisted
that he wanted the policy renewed, that he could not afford to drop any part of
his insurance, that he was not then fully insured, that his stock of goods was
heavy, etc. Under these circumstances, Eby communicated the facts in reference
to this matter to the president and secretary of defendant, telling them that one of
Lennon's policies was about to expire, and that there was a chance for defendant
to take the risk for $3,000 in place of the policy about to expire. After full con-
sultation it was concluded to take the risk for $3,000, and a policy was executed to
Lennon therefor, without any application on his part therefor, and in fact without
his knowledge, and that when it was delivered to him, he first objected to receive
it, but upon being assured by Eby that the company was a good one he received
the policy. At this time it was well known to Eby and defendant, that Lennon
intended to continue the one Eastern policy upon his goods, and that he did not
intend in any way to lessen or diminish his insurance. This being the case, some
time in the month of September or October of the same year, when the second or
last eastern policy was about to expire, Lennon was informed by Eby (who the
evidence shows was still agent of defendant) of the fact, and that he could not
renew it on the same terms that it had been originally issued. Lennon expressed
a desire to have the policy renewed and wanted to keep up his insurance. Eby
at this time told him to wait a few days, that he might yet be enabled to renew
the policy. Lennon did wait until the day that the policy expired, and then
insured in another company in the same amount, and upon meeting with Eby, he
informed him of what he had done, and was told by Eby that it was all right.
Now under the circumstances had Eby, the agent, notice at the time of the change
of the policy procured from him in the eastern company for the policy to the

the scope of his actual authority, real or apparent.[1] The declarations
of an agent are not evidence of his authority,[2] *but the scope and extent*

---

same amount in the Phœnix Company, and did he assent thereto? And did such
assent amount to a waiver on the part of the defendant of the condition in the
policy, avoiding the same where additional insurance is taken without the consent of defendant indorsed on the policy, as has been before stated? That Eby
knew of the new policy, there can be no doubt; in fact it was known by Eby and
the officers of defendant at the time of the issuing of the policy sued on, that
Lennon intended to continue the whole six thousand dollars of insurance on his
stock of goods. The policy of defendant was made with that view, and what was
afterward done was only carrying out the understanding had between the parties
at the time; hence when the policy was about to expire, Eby told Lennon that
the policy was about to expire, and that he could not then renew it on the same
terms, but to *wait* a few days, that he might still become able to renew it. Why
was it that Eby asked him to wait? It was to my mind, because it was known
and expected that if Eby did not renew the policy, the insurance would be taken
in another company, and this was only a continuation of the original understanding and was expected by Eby, and when he was told that it had been done, he
answered that it was all right. Eby was at the time still agent of the company
and notice to him was notice to the defendant. In a late case in the State of
Illinois, *Illinois Mutual Fire Ins. Co.* v. *Malloy,* 50 Ill. 419, the policy in question contained a clause to this effect: 'If the assured shall thereafter make any
other insurance on the same property, and should not with all reasonable diligence give notice thereof to the insurer, and have the same indorsed on the policy,
or otherwise acknowledged by them in writing, the policy shall . cease and be of
no further effect.' The insured in that case did effect an additional insurance on
the same property. It was held that it was not sufficient in such case to give
notice to a stranger who had long since ceased to be an agent of the company.
The court, however, in rendering the opinion says, 'Had the party notified been
the agent of the company, his failure to indorse consent on the policy would not
have prejudiced the assured; as we said in the case of *N. E. Fire and Marine
Ins. Co.* v. *Schettler,* 38 Ill. 166.' It was, however, further held, in that case,
that it was the duty of the assured to know that the party notified was agent.
This case seems to sustain the view that a notice to one who is known to be an
agent is sufficient to charge the company, and that, where notice is given of an
after insurance and no objection made at the time, the policy will not be thereby
forfeited. I do not say that the fact that Lennon told Eby after he had taken the
last policy that he had given the risk to another company would have been sufficient of itself to constitute a waiver of the condition in the policy in question; but
this fact, *taken in connection with all of the other facts connected with the transaction, I think is sufficient;* and that to permit the defendant to insist on a forfeiture
of the policy, under all of the circumstances. would be to enable it to perpetrate
a fraud on Lennon. In the investigation of the case, it has not been overlooked
that this court, in the case of *Hutchinson* v. *The West. Ins. Co.,* 21 Mo. 97, held
that a condition in a policy similar to the one under consideration was a condition
precedent to the right of the insured to recover on the policy, and that nothing
would prevent a forfeiture of the policy but the actual indorsement of the consent
of the insurer to the subsequent insurance. Subsequent cases, however, in this
court, as well as in other courts. which seem to have been well considered, have
recognized a more liberal rule in favor of the insured. In these late cases, it has
been held that the condition in the policy under consideration, as well as other
conditions of similar nature, may be waived by the company, and that the waiver
may be made as well by 'acts as by positive declarations, and that the company
may be estopped under certain circumstances, where, by a course of dealing or
its open actions, it has induced the assured to pursue a policy to his detriment.'"

---

[1] *Marvin* v. *Wilbur,* 52 N. Y. 270; *Allen* v. *Ogden,* 1 Wash. (U. S. C. C.) 174;
Adriance v. *Rowell,* 52 Barb. (N. Y.) 270; *Bush* v. *Westchester F. Ins. Co.,* 68 N.
Y. 531; *Owings* v. *Hull,* 9 Pet. (U. S.) 608.

[2] *James* v. *Stookey,* 1 Wash. (U. S. C. C.) 330; *Bush* v. *Westchester Ins. Co.,*
ante.

of his powers must be determined by his acts, and the recognition thereof by his principal.[1] The assured ·has no right to infer authority in the agent, farther than he is justified in doing so *from the nature and requirements of the business intrusted to him, and what he has previously done in the prosecution thereof, with the assent of the insurers, express or implied.*[2]

Apparent power—Instances.

SEC. 398. As has been previously stated, the assured may rely upon the authority of the agent, within the scope of his apparent authority. He may rely upon it, in the absence of any special limitations of which he has notice, that he is authorized to do any act essential to effectuate the business committed to him, or that is fairly incident thereto. Thus, if an agent is permitted to receive and remit premiums for an insurance company, *he is authorized to do so,*[3] and the company is bound by his acts within the scope of his apparent authority, even though his acts are, in fact, *in excess of his real authority, or in disobedience of private instructions given him by the company.*[4]

Horwitz v. *The Equitable Mut. Ins. Co.*, 40 Mo. 557; *Franklin* v. *The Atlantic Fire Ins. Co.*, 42 id. 456; *Coombs* v. *Hannibal Savings and Ins. Co.*, 43 id. 148; *Northrup* v. *The Miss. Val. Ins. Co.*, 47 Mo. 435; *Viele* v. *Germania Ins. Co.*, 26 Ia. 54, 55; *Walsh* v. *The Ætna Life Ins. Co.*, 30 id. 133; 6 Am. Rep. 664; *Von Bories* v. *The United Life, Fire and Marine Ins. Co.*, 8 Bush (Ky.) 133.

[1] *Nicoll* v. *American Ins. Co.*, 3 W. & M. (U. S.) 529.

[2] *Marvin* v. *Wilber*, 52 N. Y. 270; *Bush* v. *Westchester F. Ins. Co.*, 63 N. Y. 531; *Shones* v. *Ins. Co. of N. America*, *ante*.

[3] *Perkins* v. *Washington Ins. C.*, 4 Cow. (N. Y.) 645; 1 Bennett's F. I. C. 162. In *Fay* v. *Richmond*, 43 Vt. 25, the court say.: "If a person acts for and in behalf of another, it is immaterial to the question of agency so far as third persons are concerned, whether he acts by his direction and request, *or by his permission merely*, he is equally his agent in both casses."

[4] In *Perkins* v. *Washington Ins. Co.*, upon the facts stated in the next note, this doctrine was fully recognized and COLDEN, Senator, in a very able opinion, gave expression to the true rule in this respect. He said: "Russell was appointed surveyor, etc. If this were the extent of the authority given by the respondents to Russell, then, unquestionably, no act of his would be binding on the company; for I do not see that a survey made by him could be in anywise obligatory. But most certainly he exercised other powers, not only with the consent and approbation of the respondents, but by the direction of their president. These powers were such as well warranted him is assuming the title of agent, and such as leave us no reason to be surprised that the respondents should have known that he was in the habit of calling and signing himself their agent, without their objecting to his doing so until the present controversy arose. Two of the letters of Russell to the respondents, which are exhibits in the cause, are signed by him as agent. These letters relate to premiums received and transmitted by Russell. And the receipt of the letters and of the premiums are acknowledged in subsequent letters of the respondents. So little were the acts of Russell directed by the power given to him by the warrant, that it is hardly necessary to refer to that instrument in the further examination of the cause. Russell was acknowledgedly not only the agent of the respondents, to make surveys, but to agree to make insurances, to charge such premiums as he should think proper, to receive the premiums, and to remit them to the respondents at New York. That he was the agent of the

Thus,[1] where an insurance company has permitted a special agent to fix the rates of premium for risks, and to bind them for the risk

---

respondents for these purposes, appears from the letter of the president of the 27th April, 1819, which is an answer to the one from Russell of the 9th of the same month, applying for signed blank policies, which were refused. It is true that, by the same letter, it appears that the company intended to reserve a right to judge of the rate of premium and of the risk. I shall in the sequel advert to this part of the letter. I only refer to it at this time, to show that the respondents never intended to confine the powers of Russell to those of a surveyor, or supposed that they were limited to those conferred by the warrant. That Russell was the agent of the respondents, to receive premiums and to transmit them to the company, not only appears from the letters already mentioned, but is acknowledged in the answer. The words of the answer to which I now refer, are as follows: 'They permitted him as in their said answer afterwards particularly mentioned, to receive from such persons as were willing to pay the same to him, the sums which he might think fit to name as the probable premiums, and to transmit the same to the respondents in the city of New York, in order to prevent any unnecessary delay in effecting the insurance.' If they *permitted* Russell to receive and remit premiums, they *authorized* him to do so. This acknowledgment of the respondents is not qualified by any subsequent part of the answer, further than by a denial that they authorized, or intended Russell to be their agent to make insurances. But, on the contrary, they aver that they refused to give him such powers when he applied for them. This would be conclusive against the appellant, if the points were, what powers the respondents intended to give to Russell. But that is not the case. The question is, what powers were the citizens of Savannah, and the appellant, as one of them, justified from the acts of Russell, and of the respondents, in presuming he possessed. It might have been very far from the intention of the respondents to authorize their agent to bind them to an insurance at his pleasure. It might have been very imprudent in the company to have renounced the important right of deliberating on the expediency of a risk. To keep these matters under the control of the directors, may be very essential to the credit and safety of every insurance company. In all this I entirely agree with his honor the late chancellor. But if the directors have incautiously given to their agent, or suffered him to exercise too large a power, they must bear the consequences of their own imprudence. I am not disposed to sacrifice the just claims of one who confided in the respondents, to their safety or to the support of their credit. I will presume that it is established that Russell was the agent of the respondents to receive premiums, and to remit them to the company at New York. Then we are to inquire, whether the respondents were bound by the receipt, as if the payment had been made to themselves. It will not be questioned, that if the premium had been paid at the office of the company in New York, and the president or secretary had signed the receipt which was given by Russell, the insurance would have been as binding as if a policy had been executed. Receipts of this nature are in common use. Much of the insurance made in this city is done, in the first instance, by similar receipts signed by some officer of the corporation. They are intended to give immediate effect to the insurance, and supply the place of a formal policy, until one can be prepared. It has been decided that these receipts are as binding as a policy could be. In truth, the receipt answers all the use of a policy, except that the latter authorizes the assured, in case of loss, to sue in a court of law, instead of being obliged to resort, as in this case, to a court of chancery. The letter from the president of the company to Russell, which enclosed his appointment as surveyor, also covered the printed proposals of the company. From these, Russell, as he says, in his answer to the second direct interrogatory, framed an advertisement, which is one of the appellant's exhibits, inviting the citizens of Savannah to make insurance through him, with the respondents. To this advertisement he put the names of the president and secretary.

The respondents aver in their answer, and we must therefore believe, that this

---

[1] In *Perkins* v. *Washington Ins. Co.*, 4 Cow. (N. Y.) 645; 1 Ben. F. I. C. 143, this question was ably discussed. In that case a bill in equity was brought to

pending the application, it is liable for a loss sustained by a person
who, relying upon the agent's authority to do so, has applied to him

---

advertisement was unauthorized by them, and that they never had knowledge
of it till after this controversy arose.   But, although they disclaim the advertisement, yet they admit in their answer that they sent the printed proposals, which
are an exhibit, to Russell.   And he testifies that these proposals, together with
the letter, which was written on the back of them, he pasted on a piece of paste-
board, and hung it in his store for the information of those who might choose to
read it.   These proposals, after a preface which gives assurances of the solidity
of the company, and of the fairness, candor and liberality which the directors
meant to practise, proceeds to state a number of articles for the information and
government of those who meant to do business with the company.   The fifth of
these articles is in the following words: 'No insurance is to be considered as
made or binding until the premium is paid.'   It is to be observed that here is no
intimation as to where or to whom the premium is to be paid.   There is nothing
from which those who read the proposals, as they were stuck up in the office of
Russell, could understand that the payment of a premium to an agent of the company authorized to receive the same would not be as binding as if it had been
paid at the office of the respondents in New York.   I presume it will be admitted
that all persons dealing with the respondents, and who had knowledge of this
article of the proposals, would be authorized to infer from it a converse proposition, to wit, that every insurance would be considered as made and binding when
the premium *was* paid.   How then does the case stand?   The appellant found
Russell, the agent of the respondents, to accept propositions to insure his property,
and to receive payment of the premium.   He also found a declaration of the
respondents, which was in effect that, when the premium was paid, the insurance
was to be considered as binding.   I think the appellant was authorized to conclude, when he had paid the premium to the agent of the respondents in Savannah, that the respondents were bound to make good to him any loss he might
subsequently sustain.   I cannot think that anything was communicated to him
from which he was to understand that his property was to remain uninsured until
Russell should have collected so large an amount of premiums as he might think
worth while to remit to his constituents.   Russell says it was not his practice to
send on these premiums immediately; that, with respect to the premium in question, he pursued his usual course of waiting until he had got a considerable sum
of money for the purpose of purchasing a bill of exchange to make the remittance.
*In my view of the subject, it is entirely immaterial how far the respondents intended
to limit the agency of Russell.   If they meant that those who dealt with him should
understand that he had a limited agency, it was their business to have made known
the bounds which they had prescribed to him.   But, on the contrary, their authority to
him to receive premiums, and their notice that the payment of a premium should be
binding, I think, left them without the power to disavow Russell's acts.*   It appears
to me, however, that the case may be put on another footing, no less unfavorable
to the defense of the respondents.   I apprehend it is a well-settled rule of the
Court of Chancery that whatever a party was under a legal obligation to perform,
shall, as to all persons who had a right to claim the performance, be considered
as having been performed.   In other words, no person shall be allowed any
advantage from his own or his agent's laches.   As the respondents admit Russell
was authorized to receive premiums, and to remit them, it was his duty to remit
the premium he received from the appellant without delay.   If he had done so,
the respondents must have received it before they had news of the fire, which did
not happen till the 11th of January.   Had the premium been duly remitted, there
is no doubt but that the policy would have been made, because there is no intimation on the part of the respondents that there was any objection to the risk, or
to the premium.   I think, therefore, the Court of Chancery would have been well
warranted in considering the case as if the premium had been transmitted to the
respondents in due time, and had, as it must have been, received by them before
they had news of the fire.   Suppose an action had been brought against Russell

---

compel the defendants to execute a policy of insurance to the plaintiff, or pay a
loss sustained under it.   The bill alleged that the plaintiffs, on the 5th day of

for insurance, even though in fact the company, without the knowledge
of the assured, reserved the right to revise the rate of premium, and

---

for not sending the premium in due time, can there be a doubt but that the appellant would have recovered in a court of law, and that the measure of damages
would have been the amount which was to have been insured, and for which the
premium was paid? The plaintiff, in such an action, would only have had to have
shown that, if the premium had been duly forwarded, the risk would have been
taken, and he would have had the benefit of an insurance. And so in this case,
when Russell, who was the agent of the respondents to receive and remit the premium, has withheld it, I think the respondents are to be held responsible, as they
would have been if he had performed his duty. It will be seen that I take but
little notice of the correspondence between Russell and the respondents, by which
it may appear that *they intended* to limit his agency. I disregard it, because it
does not appear that the appellant ever had any knowledge of this correspondence. But, if we regard this correspondence, I confess I find myself entirely at a
loss to reconcile the defense which the respondents have made in the court below
with principles of justice and equity. In Russell's letter of the 9th April, 1819,
he applies for ready signed blank policies, or to have his receipt for premiums
made binding on the company until policies could be obtained from the office.
The answer to this letter is from the president of the company, and is dated the
28th of the same month. In this answer the president, after objecting to furnishing blank policies, says: 'The most and best that can be done, I think, is this,
that all insurances that you may agree to make, and for which such premiums as
you may think proper to charge, shall be actually paid and received here, the
office will consider as enuring at the time of the payment to you, so that, in case
of accident between such time of payment and the receipt of the money here, the
company will indemnify such loss; provided, however, the office shall recognize
the rate of premium which you shall charge, and shall be otherwise satisfied with
the risk.' Now what is the actual state of things? Russell has agreed to make
an insurance for the appellant, for which he has thought proper to charge a certain premium, which has been actually paid, and which has been *received* at the
office of the respondents. I say received there, because it has been tendered to
them. But an accident between the date of the receipt and the tender of the
money here has happened. What, then, can the defendants say, consistently with
the president's letter, why they should not make a policy which shall enure at
the time of the payment to Russell? All that this letter of the president will permit them to say is, that the office did not recognize the rate of premium, and
were not otherwise satisfied with the risk. But can they honestly and conscien-
tiously say this? Was this the truth? Was it not the truth that the loss had
intervened, and therefore they would not make the policy? If they may make
the excuse they offer in this case, then they might have made it in every case
where a loss happened between the payment of the premium to their agent and
the receipt of the money here. In other words, whenever they received an
account of a loss before the premium came into their hands, however long their
agent may have chosen to retain it, they would not make a policy; and so it will
be seen that the president's undertaking that a policy should enure from the time
of the payment to the agent, if we give to his letter the construction the respondents contend for, is a perfect fallacy. But the respondents should, in my opinion,
be *obliged* to recognize the rate of premium which was charged, and to be satisfied with the risk, unless they can show some objections to the one or the other.
This they do not pretend to do."

January, 1820, applied to one Henry P. Russell, of Savannah, Ga., the agent of
the defendants, to insure a stock of dry goods, groceries, etc., in a storehouse in
said city; that Russell, on the same day, agreed that the respondents should
become insurers on the stock, for one year from that day, for $5,000, at a premium
of 2¼ per cent., the premium to be paid on that day; and that the company should
execute a policy in the usual form; that the premium was accordingly paid to
Russell, with $3.50 for the expense of a survey and policy; that Russell gave a
receipt for these sums, declaring the object, consideration, and purpose as above
set forth, and signed the receipt, " John P. Russell, agent of said company; "

made the circumstance of their liability for a loss occurring pending the application, dependant upon their acceptance of the risk.

---

that on the morning of the 11th January, an extensive and destructive fire broke out in Savannah, and consumed the greater portion of the goods ; that the appellant gave notice to Russell of the loss, offered the usual preliminary proof, and demanded a policy of insurance ; but Russell stated that he had not forwarded the premium to the company, and had not received a policy from them, and he intimated that the company would not consider themselves bound by what had been done ; that proper notice with the usual proofs, were, in May, 1820, given to the respondents in the city of New York ; but they had refused to execute a policy or indemnify the appellant to the amount lost, although the appellant had, on the 28th of April, 1821, tendered to their president the amount of the premium. To this the respondents answered, admitting all the material facts charged, except Russell's agency. They denied that he was agent, or had power or authority to act for them otherwise than as a surveyor. They admitted that they had appointed him surveyor for them in Savannah, etc., of buildings insured, or in which goods offered for insurance were kept ; and empowered him to state to applicants of Savannah the probable rates, according to the nature of the risk at which insurance might be expected to be effected by them ; always, however, reserving to themselves the power and control to abide by, or to vary the rates so stated by him, or entirely to decline such insurance, when the proposal for such insurance and his report or survey should be presented to them for their deliberation. That they permitted him to receive the probable premiums, and transmit them to the respondents, in order to prevent unnecessary delay in effecting insurance ; but absolutely denied that they ever appointed him their agent for insuring or effecting any insurance against loss or damage by fire. Upon these facts given below, and others set forth in the opinion of Woodworth, J., Kent, Chancellor dismissed the bill, and held that the agent had no authority to bind the company, but, upon appeal, his ruling was reversed, and it was held that the company *were* bound by the agent's acts. Woodworth, J., in discussing the questions relating to the apparent authority of the agent, said : "The material question is, whether Henry P. Russell was the agent of the respondents, and in that capacity had the authority to bind them to insure the appellant's goods? and a concise view of some of the leading facts becomes necessary in order to arrive at a correct conclusion. On the 11th of December, 1818, the respondents appointed Russell surveyor. The power was limited to this object solely. On the 10th of February, 1819, Russell caused to be published in a newspaper printed at Savannah, the proposals of the company ; and added that insurance might be effected by application to him ; and that he would obtain policies from the office with the least possible delay. To this notice Russell subscribed his name as agent for the city of Savannah. It appears by the depositions, that subsequently, and previous to the 5th of January, 1820, he agreed to insure for a number of individuals, and received the premiums, which were transmitted to the respondents ; and that in every instance save one the company confirmed the insurance, and transmitted policies bearing date at the time the receipt was given to the applicant for insurance. It also appears that Russell applied to the respondents for an enlargement of his powers as agent. In his letter, dated April 9, 1819, to Mr. Hawes, the secretary, he observes, 'There is a difficulty, owing to the distance from New York, in getting along with insurances here. Unless I am furnished with blank policies ready signed, or unless my receipt for the premiums, as agent, is binding upon the company until the policies can be obtained from the office, I suspect but little can be done in the way of insuring ; for I find that applicants want the risk to commence as soon as the premium is paid.' On the 28th of April, 1819, Mr. Hawes writes in reply, that 'the directors are aware of the difficulty of making insurance at a distance, and will obviate it, as far as consistent with the principle they had adopted, which was no insurance shall be binding until the premium is received at their office in New York.' He assigned as the reason of the rule, that the company would not be responsible 'for the risk of sending the premium either by land or water ;' and that in all cases when the risk is accepted, the policy is to take effect from the time when the premium was received by the agent. On the 27th of April, 1819, Mr. Swords, president of the company, wrote

It is enough that the insurer has held him out to the world as pos. sessed of the requisite authority.[1]

---

to Russell as follows: 'All insurances that you may agree to make, and for which such premiums as you may deem proper to charge shall be actually paid, and shall be received here, the office will consider as enuring at the time of the payment to you; so that in case of accident between such time of payment, and the receipt of the money here, the company will indemnify such loss; provided, however, the office shall recognize the rate of premium which you shall charge, and shall be otherwise satisfied with the risk.' After this review we may safely dismiss the inquiry, what were the original powers conferred on the agent? It may be conceded that they were no greater than those of surveyor, strictly; and that he could not, in that capacity, bind his principal by an agreement to insure. The limited nature of such an appointment, it was soon perceived, could answer no beneficial purpose. It is to be presumed that very few, if any, would be disposed to advance the premium, and wait an indefinite period before the policy should attach. Russell communicates the difficulty to the president, who is to be considered the organ of the company communicating their assent to the enlarged powers of the agent; an particularly, as it is not pretended that his letter to Russell was unauthorized. According to the instructions thus given to the agent, when and in what cases were his agreements to insure binding on the respondents? Upon payment of the premium to the agent, the applicant for insurance was subject to the following contingencies: first, that the premium should be received at the office in New York; secondly, that the rate of premium should be recognized at the office; and lastly, that the company should be otherwise satisfied with the risk.

As to the first, no doubt can arise; for it depends on the fact whether the money has been received or tendered at the office in New York. As to the second, it was undoubtedly intended that if the rate of premium taken by the agents conformed to the rules and regulations of the company, and was not less than the uniform rate before taken in other and similar cases which had invariably received the sanction of the respondents, the applicant would be entitled to a policy of insurance, commencing on the day the premium was paid; for, although it is provided that the office shall recognize the rate of premium, it must be understood as having referred to the rules and regulations sanctioned by the board of directors, and the powers vested in the agent. The right of the company to exercise their judgment whether the agreement of the agent to insure correspond with the instructions given, cannot be questioned. But, from the nature of the case, it seems necessarily confined within such limits. It cannot be urged that the company reserved, or intended to reserve, the right of arbitrarily refusing to subscribe a policy when every prerequisite which they had themselves prescribed had been fairly and honestly complied with. It must then be confined within the bounds I have already traced; and if so, when the agent presents a case, having received the premium, the fair implication of the proviso is, that the company shall act upon it; and if they decline to act, or point out any objection, the presumption is, that none exists within the true intent of the proviso inserted in the instructions. It is very evident to my mind that the respondents did not repose themselves on any objectionable features in the conduct of the agent, but on an absolute right of refusal, which they conceived was vested in them, without assigning any cause. This is inferrible from that part of their answer wherein they state, 'that, not considering themselves bound by any such alleged agreement for insurance, they did not examine into, and, therefore, neither they nor their officers or agents did at any time object to the sufficiency of the proofs; nor did they, in any way, intimate or pretend that there had been any unfairness or fraud on the part of the appellant in obtaining the insurance.' It is also remarkable that no suggestion is made, that the rate of

---

[1] *Haughton* v. *Embark*, 4 Camp. 88; *Neal* v. *Erving*, 1 Esp. 61. Proof that the agent has performed similar acts, is enough to establish his authority. *Goodson* v. *Brooke*, 4 Camp. 163; *Newman* v. *Springfield F. & M. Ins. Co.*, 17 Minn. 123; *Viele* v. *Germania Ins. Co.*, 26 Iowa, 9; *Bush* v. *Westchester F. Ins. Co.*, 2 T. &. C. (N. Y.) 629.

If the company has recognized and adopted similar acts of the agent, it is estopped from denying his authority in that respect[1].

Even where a policy, in terms, provides that agents shall not waive forfeitures, alter or discharge contracts, it is held that the words of the policy are not conclusive, because it is within the power of the company to waive this provision. In such cases, the question is not what power the agent had, but what power did the company hold him out as possessing.[2]

---

insurance was not conformable to the general usage of the company. Can it be doubted that, had the loss not have happened previous to the time when the premium was offered to be paid in the city of New York, that this policy would have been signed as readily as others which had been transmitted by the agent? These remarks are equally applicable to the third and last proviso, 'that the company shall be otherwise satified with the risk.' The question upon this should be considered in the same manner as if application had been made for the policy before any loss sustained. What reasons could have been assigned for dissatisfaction with the risk? If any existed, it was the duty of the respondents to point them out. Not having done so, it is not uncharitable to suppose that they declined acting as in ordinary cases, in consequence of the loss, erroneously supposing that a literal adherence to the words of the instructions would shield them against the appellant's claim to compensation. It is not unnatural, in controversies between individuals, for them, however upright, to seize upon every plank that may possibly lead to safety. Hence it comes that no man is a proper judge in his own cause; and that courts are established to measure out equal and exact justice to contending parties. The only remaining inquiry is, whether the agreement to insure, between the appellant and Russell, the agent, was within the instructions given by the respondents, and agreeable to their rules and regulations. The insurance was at 2¼ per cent premium on dry goods and groceries. It does not appear whether the storehouse which contained the goods was included in the first, second or third class of hazards. Supposing it to have been the last, the rate of insurance on such buildings, not having goods hazardous therein, is stated at from 175 to 200 cents on the $100. Goods hazardous, which includes groceries, are charged with 12½ cents in addition to this premium. The rate, then, paid by the appellant was equal to the highest sum claimed by the respondents in their proposals for insurance. I apprehend, therefore, that there is no well founded objection to the rate of insurance This is evident from the acts of the respondents in uniformly accepting former risks, upon contracts of insurance made on the same, or not more favorable terms. The only risk rejected was not on the ground that the premium was too small, but that the application was for six months' insurance and the premium paid for that time only; whereas an insurance for six months is always chargeable with three-quarters of a year. If, then, we look at the instructions given, the proposals issued containing the rates of insurance, and the acts of the respondents in reference to similar cases, the conclusion seems to be irresistible, that the risk and rate of premium were entirely satisfactory. The premium was also tendered in New York and refused, which is a compliance with the first part of the proviso. This, in my view, removes every obstacle in the appellant's way. I am of opinion that the decree of his honor, the chancellor, be reversed, and that the respondents be decreed to pay to the appellant the amount agreed to be insured." See also, sustaining the doctrine of this case, *Leeds* v. *Mechanics' Ins. Co.*, 8 N. Y. 351; *Woodbury Savings Bank* v. *Charter Oak Ins. Co.*, 31 Conn. 518; *Hallock* v. *Conn. Ins. Co.*, 26 N. J. 268; *Lightbody* v. *N. American Ins. Co.*, 23 Wend. (N. Y.) 18.

[1] *Peck* v. *New London, etc., Ins. Co.*, 22 Conn. 584. In *Fayles* v. *National Ins. Co.*, 49 Mo. 380, the plaintiff brought an action upon a bill of exchange, given him by defendants' agent in settlement of a loss. The defense was want of authority. It was shown that he had done the same thing before, and the court held that this was a recognition of authority in this respect binding upon them.

[2] *Eclectic Life Ins. Co.* v. *Fahrenkrug*, 68 Ill. 463.

SEC. 399. The law makes no presumptions as to the powers of an agent. His authority must be shown; and what the agent has done for the principal, which has been ratified by him, is competent proof, in the absence of other, as to the powers of the agent.[1] And the fact that a person acts as a special agent, will not necessarily warrant the inference that he is a general agent, and whether he be so or not, is a question of fact to be found by the jury from the evidence.[2]

SEC. 400. Where the agent of the insurer knows the situation and condition of the risk, at the time when the contract is entered into, and the application is made, an unintentional misstatement or concealment of facts known to the agent, will not avoid the policy, even though the application is made a part thereof. The Supreme Court of the United States in a case[3] decided May 5th, 1877, and not yet reported, held in a case where the policy prohibited the keeping of gunpowder and petroleum, but the agent who issued the policy *knew* that the assured kept and intended to keep it as a part of his stock, that evidence of the agent's knowledge thereof was admissible, and that if the omission to insert permission therein to keep such articles *was the fault of the agent*, the policy was not avoided by reason of their being kept in the usual way,[4] but in the absence of such knowledge

---

[1] *Dickinson County* v. *Miss. Valley Ins. Co.*, 41 Iowa, 286; *Swan* v. *Liv., Lon. & Globe Ins. Co.*, 52 Miss. 704; *Fayles* v. *National Ins. Co.*, 49 Mo. 380; *Imperial Ins. Co.* v. *Murray*, 73 Penn. St. 13; *Lungstrap* v. *German Ins. Co.*, 57 Mo. 107; *Eclectic, etc., Ins. Co.* v. *Fahrenkrug*, 68 Ill. 463; *Miller* v. *Phœnix Ins. Co.*, 27 Iowa, 203.

[2] *Dickinson County* v. *Miss. Valley Ins. Co.*, ante.

[3] *Mobile F. Department Ins. Co.* v. *Miller*, partially reported in Albany Law Jour., vol. 15, p. 447.

[4] In *Campbell* v. *Merchants', etc., Ins. Co.*, 37 N. H. 41; 4 Bennett's F. I. C. 288, the applicant omitted to state the existence of a small steam-engine in the building, and by the by-laws and regulations of the company this avoided the policy. But it appeared that the agent of the insurer, who took the application, *knew* of the existence of the engine, and the court held that this estopped the company from setting up such omission to defeat the policy. EASTMAN, J., in a very able and carefully considered opinion reviewed the cases, and the principles applicable in such cases, and said, "In *Marshall* v. *The Columbian Mut. F. Ins. Co.*, 27 N. H. (7 Foster) 157, it was held that where the application is taken by an agent of the company, and he is aware of facts material to the risk, but which are not set forth in the application, the company will be charged with knowledge; and that, under such circumstances, an unintentional concealment or misrepresentation will not make void the policy. The same principle was alluded to in *Leathers* v. *Farmers' Mut. F. Ins. Co.*, 24 N. H. (4 Foster) 262. As, however, the point has not been very fully considered by the courts of this state, and the counsel for the defendants have cited several cases of high authority sustaining a different doctrine, we have thought it proper to examine the question at some length, with a view to test the accuracy of the position. So far as the insurance companies in

on the part of the agent or the insurer, a stipulation in the policy that
the keeping of such articles shall render the policy void, it will be·

---

this state are to be considered, the legislature have settled the principle by enact-
ing that applications taken by the agents of the companies shall not be void by
reason of any error, mistake, or misrepresentation, unless it shall appear to have
been intentionally and fraudulently made. But that act does not apply to corporations established by the laws of other states, and consequently not to this case.

Great strictness has always been held in contracts of marine insurance. A misrepresentation or concealment of any fact material to the risk, even though it
happen through mistake or accident, and though the loss arises from a cause
unconnected with such misrepresentation, will make void the policy. Park on
Insurance, 249, 6th ed. ; 3 Burr. 1905 ; *Fitzherbert* v. *Mather*, 1 T. R. 12 ; *McDowell*
v. *Frazer*, Doug. 260 ; *Bridges* v. *Hunter*, 1 Maule & Selw. 15. A breach of a
warranty avoids a contract *ab initio;* and it makes no difference whether the
thing warranted be material or not, or whether the loss happened by reason of a
breach of the warranty or not. A warranty differs from a representation in this
respect, that it is in the nature of a condition precedent, and requires a strict and
literal performance; but all express warranties must appear upon the face of the
policy. 3 Kent's Com. 288. There may also be implied warranties, such as necessarily result from the nature of the contract; and in every policy it is implied
that the ship is sea-worthy when the policy attaches. *Law* v. *Hollingworth*, 7 T.
R. 160 ; *Silva* v. *Low*, 1 Johns. Cases, 184. I apprehend that from this strictness
existing in the law of marine insurance have been drawn the rigid rules laid
down by many tribunals upon fire insurance policies, and that the authorities in
cases of marine insurance have been followed in actions upon policies against fire,
without perhaps sufficently adverting to the difference that exists in the knowledge of facts upon which the respective contracts are founded. Kent says that
the strictness and nicety required in the contract of marine insurance do not so
strongly apply to insurance against fire, for the risk is generally assumed upon
actual examination of the subject by skilful agents on the part of the insurance
offices. 3 Kent's Com. 873. The severity of these rules has caused courts in
many instances to endeavor to avoid their effect. Thus Lord MANSFIELD, in *Pawson*
v. *Watson*, Cowper 785, says that it is the opinion of the court that to make
written instructions valid and binding, they must be *inserted* (not referred to) in
the policy. And SUTHERLAND, J., in *Jefferson Ins. Co.* v. *Cotheal*, 7 Wendell, 80,
also says, that the doctrine of warranty in the law of insurance is one of great
rigor, and frequently operates very harshly upon the assured. And again, after
discussing an application not embraced in the policy, and holding that it shall
not be considered a warranty, he says: 'I am not disposed·to lead the way in
the extension of this harsh and rigorous doctrine.' And there are authorities
which hold that where inquiries are not put by the company or its agents, as to
the title and situation of the property, and no fraud appears, a suppression of
facts will not make void· the policy. *Strong* v. *Manufacturers' Ins. Co.*, 10 Pick.
40 ; *Fletcher* v. *Com. Ins. Co.*, 18 Pick. 419 ; *Niblo* v. *North American Fire Ins.
Co.*, 1 Sand. 551. The books abound in cases as to what are and what are not
necessary disclosures, and as to what shall be held representations and what
warranties; and the authorities not unfrequently seem confused and contradictory,
arising from the different construction which is put upon the applications for
insurance and the effect that is given to them. And there appears to be a manifest
disposition in some tribunals, which hold the rules with strictness, to bring as few
cases as possible within their range. The business of insurance against fire has
greatly increased by the incorporation and establishment of mutual companies,
and the mode of transacting the business, as well as the property insured, differs
very essentially from that of marine insurance. The method of doing the business in these companies also varies materially, in some respects, from that which
prevails in stock companies, as they are usually termed. And were the courts
now, for the first time, to lay down, without regard to authority, the rules of law
that should govern contracts made between mutual companies and their members,
I apprehend that in many jurisdictions they would differ essentially from the
rules which at present prevail. As a general practice, these companies require
all applications for insurance to be in writing, and they make the application a

avoided thereby, and evidence of a custom to keep such articles in such stores, is not admissible to save the policy. It is only when the

---

part of the policy. As a general practice, also, they send out agents appointed by themselves, who are oftentimes directors of the companies, who examine the buildings and make the surveys, and make out the applications for the insured to sign. Now, aside from authority, upon what principle of right can it be said that in regard to facts which are obvious and known to the agent and company, but which are unintentionally not communicated, a different rule of law should prevail from that which exists in the sales of property? Why should it be held that the unintentional neglect to state facts in an application for insurance, which are perfectly obvious and well known to the officers of the company, shall defeat the contract and make void the policy, while the sale of property made upon a warranty is not to be affected by any defects which are obvious to the senses? I entirely agree with the court in *Jennings* v. *The Chenango County Mutual Ins. Co.*, 2 Denio, 79, when they say that it would be difficult to assign a satifactory reason for a distinction in this respect. Why should not an insurance company be estopped from setting up defects in an application, which are known to them, as well as the owner of property who knowingly stands by and sees the property sold by a third person, without disclosing his title, be afterwards estopped from setting up that title? It appears to me that the fraud in the former case is quite equal to that in the latter.

I am aware that there are many cases, and of high authority, which lay down the rule the other way, and hold that, when the application is made a part of the policy, statements contained in it are warranties, and if untrue, the policy is void, even though the variance be not material to the risk. The same authorities also hold that the rule which prevails upon sales of property, that the warranty does not extend to defects which are known to the purchasers does not apply to warranties contained in contracts of insurance. And such is the doctrine of *Jennings* v. *The Chenango County Mut. Ins. Co.*, 2 Denio, 75, already cited, and which is an authority in point for the defendants. The authorities are examined at length in that case, and the conclusion arrived at that they show the policy to be void. In closing the opinion, however, the court say: 'At the same time, it cannot be denied that the application of these principles to the case under consideration operates with great severity upon the plaintiff, and is well calculated to lead to serious doubt whether the intention of the parties and the interests of justice were duly regarded in the establishment of the rule.' And they then add: · Here the mistake was proved to have been the consequence, either of the ignorance, carelessness or bad faith of the agent of the defendants. He filled up a printed blank application, furnished by the defendants, to be subscribed by the plaintiff, who probably neither had nor pretended to have any information or knowledge of what such a paper ought to contain in order to render the policy available, but relied in that respect implicitly upon the agent sent out by the defendants.' The defects in that application were, that the building was occupied by a further purpose than that stated in the application, and also that the surrounding buildings were not correctly given. These facts were known to the agent, who said that the risk was not increased, and that it was of no use to put them into the application. Still the court felt themselves bound by the authorities, and held that the application, taken in connection with the conditions of the policy, was a warranty, and that the policy was void.

The evident harshness and severity of this doctrine, so well shown by the court in the last case cited, has since led to a different result in some cases in the same state.

In *Masters* v. *The Madison County Mut. Ins. Co.*, 11 Barb. Sup. Ct. 624, the agent of the company, on being applied to for an insurance upon the plaintiff's mill, went to see the property, and made a survey of the same, the plaintiff not accompanying him, but leaving him to transact the business, and do whatever was necessary. The agent then made out the application for the plaintiff to sign, using the printed blank furnished to agents for that purpose. He was informed at the time by the plaintiff's son that there was a mortgage on the premises, which was a lien thereon; but the application made no mention of any incumbrance. It was held that the notice given to the agent of the incumbrance was a

written description is such as amounts to a license to keep certain prohibited goods, that the effect of a printed prohibition is overcome.
*The words used in describing the stock or business must of themselves import
the fact.*[1]

The effect of the agent's knowledge of material facts upon the

---

sufficient notice to the company, and that the omission to set forth the mortgage
in the application was not a breach of warranty, or a concealment of important
matters affecting the risk, notwithstanding the application, by a memorandum in
the margin, required the applicant to state whether the property was incumbered,
by what, and to what amount, and if not, to state it ; and although the by-laws of
the company made the person taking the application the agent of the applicant ;
and further, that notwithstanding such by-law, he was still the agent of the company, and that they were bound by his acts. See also, *New York Central Ins.
Co.* v. *National Ins. Co.*, 20 Barb. 468.

Kent says that the decisions contain strict doctrines on the subject of concealment ; but he adds that the insured is not bound to communicate any facts which
the underwriter may be presumed to know equally with himself. 3 Kent's Com.
285.

We would not relax any of the sound and wholesome rules which require integrity and good faith on the part of the insured, and would hold them to as strict a
compliance with their contracts as we would the companies ; but upon a reëxamin-
ation of the question, we think that the rule laid down in *Marshall* v. *The Columbian Mut. F. Ins. Co.*, contains the just and true doctrine.

The applicant, unused to the business of making applications, and ignorant of
what is necessary to be done, trusts to the skill, knowledge, and judgment of the
agent to fill up the application, which is usually a blank, by giving all the information that is required by the company. He puts full confidence in the agent, and
relies upon him to see that the business is done correctly, and the application
made out according to the requirements of the company ; and if he acts honestly
and in good faith, the company ought to be charged with a knowledge of all the
facts that are known to the agent. It would be unjust to the insured, after he has
made such an application, paid the premium demanded, the expenses of the
policy, and the assessments as they are made, to permit the company, upon the
destruction of the property, to say that they will not make good the loss, because
their agent, whom they have authorized to act for them and make their application, has failed to make it sufficiently full.

There are many facts which the agent may know quite as well as the applicant.
Upon an application and survey of a building, if personally made by himself, he
will ordinarily become possessed of all the material facts in this respect. The
title to the property he does not investigate, and of course relies upon the statements of the applicants. He knows the requirements of the company, and the
details that should be set forth in the application, while the insured is in most
cases entirely ignorant of these matters ; and if the application is unintentionally
defective, upon a point well known to the agent, the company and not the insured
should be the sufferers. The agents are, to this extent, and for the purpose of
taking the applications, the officers of the company.

The facts in the present case appear to come distinctly within the rule which
we have endeavored to explain, and which, we think, should prevail ; and we are
therefore of opinion that, according to the agreement of the parties, there should
be." *Malleable Iron Works* v. *Phœnix Ins. Co.*, 25 Conn. 465 ; 4 Ben. F. I. C.
161 ; *Benedict* v. *Ocean Ins. Co.*, 1 Daly (N. Y. C. P.) 8 ; 4 Ben. F. I. C. 462.

[1] In the case of *Birmingham F. Ins. Co.* v. *Kroeger*, not long since decided by
the Supreme Court of Pennsylvania (see vol. 15, p. 447, Albany Law Journal), a
policy of insurance on stock, etc., in a store, provided " that if the assured shall
keep or have in any place on premises where this policy may apply, petroleum
* * * without written permission in this policy, then, and in every such case,
this policy shall be void." The court held that if petroleum was kept on the
premises it avoided the policy, and evidence of a custom to keep petroleum in
such stores would not affect this question.

rights of the assured, when he has been guilty of no fraudulent suppression or misrepresentation of a fact material to the risk, was illustrated in a case just decided by the Court of Appeals of Virginia,[1] in which the policy contained a provision as follows : "If the inter_ est of the assured in the property be other than the entire, un_ conditional and sole ownership of the property, for the use and benefit of the assured, or if the building insured stands on leased ground, it must be so represented to the company, and so expressed in the written part of this policy, otherwise the policy shall be void." There was an incumbrance by deed of trust on the property at the time of the insurance, which was not stated, and about which no inquiries were made. And the house stood on leased ground. Which latter fact was known by the agent of the company at the time the policy was taken out, but not so represented in the written part of the policy. The court said that unless there be a *warranty*, or a representation that amounts to a *warranty* that there are no incumbrances, or unless the applicant makes a false or fraudulent representation in answer to interrogations about the same, the policy will not be avoided for them. This condition does not refer to the *legal title* but to the *interest* of the assured in the policy. And held that the knowledge of the agent that the house was built on leased ground must be imputed to the company. The court said that regarding the clause of the policy above quoted as a *warranty*, then there was a breach of it *eo instanti* that the contract was made, which the company knew of ; it was taking the premiums without incurring any risk, which they are estopped from doing. And the policy is *not void* for the failure to state facts known to the agent in the written part of the policy." And this doctrine is now generally held.[2] Thus, it has been held

---

[1] *Manhattan F. Ins. Co.* v. *Ullman*, vol. 15 Alb. Law Jour. p. 447.

[2] *Masters* v. *Madison Co. Ins. Co.*, 11 Barb. (N. Y.) 624 ; 3 Bennett's F. I. C. 398 ; *Hartford Ins. Co.* v. *Harmer*, 2 Ohio St. 452 ; 3 Bennett's F. I. C. 643 ; *Lee* v. *Howard F. Ins. Co.*, 3 Gray (Mass.) 583 ; 3 Bennett's F. I. C. 733 ; *Marshall* v. *Columbia Ins. Co.*, 28 N. H. 157 ; 3 Bennett's F. I. C. 634. But it has been held in New Jersey. *Dewees* v. *Manhattan Ins. Co.*, 35 N. J. 366, that knowledge on the part of the agent who procures the policy does not defeat a forfeiture if the insured makes out his own application and does not provide for the prohibited use, and such is the doctrine of *Roth* v. *City F. Ins. Co.*, 6 McLean (U. S.) 324. In *Rohrbach* v. *The Ætna Ins Co.*, 62 N. Y. 613, the insurance was upon certain buildings, and the question was as to the insurable interest of plaintiff. No written application appeared, and it did not appear that he made any representation save to show the agent the instrument executed by his wife under which he claimed an interest. The question as to breach of warranty, therefore, did not arise. Defendant claimed a breach of a condition subsequent. The policy provided that all persons having a claim thereunder should give immediate notice and render a particular account stating the ownership of the property insured ;

that, where the agent of the insurer *knew* of the situation and character of the property, and made the survey, a misstatement therein known by the agent to be incorrect, would not invalidate the policy.[1] As where the policy required all incumbrances to be stated, but the assured omitted to state them all, but the agent *knew* of the incumbrances, and particularly of the existence of the one not stated, it was held that such knowledge was the knowledge of the company, and, as they had not been misled by a failure on the part of the assured to state it, they could not complain.[2]

---

also that any fraud, or attempt at fraud, would forfeit all claim under the policy. In the account rendered plaintiff stated the property belonged to him as "the legal heir of his wife" and "by purchase at auction." Held, that there was no breach of the condition; that there was no designed deception, as defendant's agent was fully advised as to the facts; that the statement that he was a legal heir of his wife, although incorrect, was not of a fact so much as of a legal conclusion which did not, and could not, mislead, and that therefore plaintiff was entitled to recover.

[1] *Roth* v. *City F. Ins. Co.*, 6 McLean (U. S.) 324; *Ludwig* v. *Insurance Co.*, 48 N. Y. 379; *Hadley* v. *N. H. F. Ins. Co.*, 55 N. H. 110; *Owens* v. *Holland Purchase Ins. Co.*, 56 N. Y. 565; *Mechler* v. *Phœnix Ins. Co.*, 38 Wis. 665; *Ayres* v. *Home Ins. Co.*, 21 Iowa, 185; *Peoria F. & M. Ins. Co.* v. *Hall*, 12 Mich. 202; *In re the Universal, etc., Ins. Co.* v. *Forbes*, L. R. 19, Eq. Cas. 485; *Longhurst* v. *Star Ins. Co.*, 19 Iowa, 364; *Viele* v. *Germania Ins. Co.*, 26 id. 9; *Atlantic Ins. Co.* v. *Wright*, 22 Ill. 462; *Howard, etc., Ins. Co.* v. *Cornick*, 24 Ill. 455; *Ayres* v. *Hartford F. Ins. Co.*, 17 Iowa, 176; *Hartford Protection Ins. Co.* v. *Harmer*, 2 Ohio St. 452; *Miner* v. *Phœnix Ins. Co.*, 27 Wis. 693; *Winans* v. *Allemania Ins. Co.*, 38 id. 342; *Andes Ins. Co.* v. *Shipman*, 77 Ill. 189; *Clark* v. *Union, etc., Ins. Co.*, 40 N. H. 333; *Campbell* v. *Farmers', etc., Ins. Co.*, 37 N. H. 35; *Emery* v. *Piscataqua, etc., Ins. Co.*, 52 Me. 322; *Reaper City Ins. Co.* v. *Jones*, 62 Ill. 458; *McBride* v. *Republic Ins. Co.*, 30 Wis. 562; *Sprague* v. *Holland Purchase Ins. Co., ante; Patten* v. *Merchants', etc., Ins. Co.*, 40 N. H. 375. In a recent case in Missouri not yet reported, *Coolidge* v. *Charter Oak Ins. Co.*, vol. 2, Western Ins. Rev. 90, the court held that where an agent taking an application for an insurance upon a person's life, *knew* at the time when the application was made, that the applicant had a severe cold, the insurer was estopped from setting up the fact that the applicant did not state the fact in his application in avoidance of its liability upon the policy.

[2] *Hartford Protection Ins. Co.* v. *Harmer*, 2 Ohio St. 452. In *Emery* v. *Piscataqua, etc., Ins. Co.*, 52 Me. 322, the insurer's agent knowing that the plaintiff had only a mortgage interest in the premises, described his title in the policy as absolute, and the court held that the company was estopped from setting up such misstatement in avoidance of its liability on the policy. See also, *Hodgkins* v. *Montgomery. etc.. Ins. Co.*, 34 Barb. (N. Y.) 213; *Columbia Ins. Co.* v. *Cooper*, 50 Penn. St. 331; *Michigan State Ins. Co.* v. *Lewis*, 30 Mich. 41; *Franklin* v. *Atlantic Ins. Co.*, 42 Mo. 456; *Ayres* v. *Home Ins. Co.*, 21 Iowa, 185; *Longhurst* v. *Star Ins. Co.*, 19 Iowa, 364; *American Ins. Co.* v. *McLanathan* 11 Kan. 533. In *Greene* v. *Equitable, etc., Ins. Co.*, 28 Ohio St. 84, the defendant issued a policy to C., payable in case of loss to G., for $1,000, with permission for $6,250 other insurance, and providing that if the assured, or any other person interested, should have other insurance on the property not assented to in writing, and mentioned in or indorsed on the policy, then the policy should be void. There was $8,000 other insurance procured, and the E. Company, after loss, denied its liability for this reason. G., in an action against the E. Company, offered to prove that he gave notice to the E. Company of $8,000 other insurance; that the company consented to the amount, and thereupon wrote its policy with permission for $6,250; that neither C. nor G. noticed the variance till after the loss; and that the inser-

Insurer must have been misled.

SEC. 401. *The rule is, that in order to avoid a policy on account of a misrepresentation or concealment of a fact, the insurer must have been misled thereby, and, when the agent knew the facts, his knowledge is imputable to the principal, and consequently they could not have been misled, or influenced in reference either to the taking of the risk or fixing the premium thereon by anything said or omitted to be said by the assured.[1] In a case previously*

---

tion of $6,250, instead of $8,000, was a blunder of the E. Company. It was held that the evidence was admissible to defeat the defense of the E. Company by way of estoppel.

[1] *Rowley* v. *Empire Ins. Co.*, 36 N. Y. 550; *Aurora F. Ins. Co.* v. *Eddy*, 55 Ill. 213; *Atlantic Ins. Co.* v. *Wright*, 22 Ill. 462; *Andes Ins. Co.* v. *Shipman*, 77 Ill. 189; *Horne, etc., Ins. Co.* v. *Garfield*, 60 Ill. 124; *Miller* v. *Mut. Ben., etc., Ins. Co.*, 31 Iowa, 216; *Ætna, etc., Ins. Co.* v. *Olmstead*, 21 Mich. 246; *Guardian Life Ins. Co.* v. *Hogan*, 80 Ill. 164; *Longhurst* v. *Star Ins. Co.*, 19 Iowa, 364; *Continental Ins. Co.* v. *Roberts*, 41 Wis. 564; *Anson* v. *Winneshiek Ins. Co.*, 23 Iowa, 84; *Reaper City Ins Co.* v. *Jones*, 62 Ill. 458; *Owens* v. *Holland Purchase Ins. Co.*, 56 N. Y. 565; *Clark* v. *Union Mut. Ins. Co.*, 40 N. H. 333; *Combs* v. *Hannibal Ins. Co.*, 43 Mo. 148; *Cumberland, etc., Ins. Co.* v. *Schell*, 29 Penn. St. 31; *Southern Ins. Co.* v. *Lewis*, 42 Ga. 587; *Franklin* v. *Atlantic Ins. Co.*, 42 Mo. 456; *Ames* v. *N. Y. Union Ins. Co.*, 253; *Maher* v. *Hibernian Ins. Co.*, 6 Hun (N. Y.) 353; *Allen* v. *Vt. Mut. F. Ins. Co.*, 12 Vt. 366; *McFarland* v. *Peabody Ins. Co.*, 6 W. Va. 425; *Witherell* v. *Maine Ins. Co.*, 49 Me. 200. In *Beebe* v. *Hartford Ins. Co.*, 25 Conn. 51; 4 Bennett's F. I. C. 55, HINMAN, J., in passing upon this question, said: "This was an action on a policy of insurance against fire, in which the plaintiff recovered, and the defendants now move for a new trial, on the ground of errors in the rulings and charge of the court, and also on the ground that the verdict is against the weight of evidence in the case. The first point of law relates to the charge in respect to the agency of Lay. Lay was the local agent of the defendants at Lyme, for the purpose of receiving applications for insurance, and for other purposes, and he testified that the officers of the company had told him that he must consider himself the agent of the insured than of the company, and as it was an important inquiry in the case, whether the company was fairly apprised of certain facts material to the risk, the defendants requested the court to charge the jury that if the plaintiff did communicate those facts to Lay, yet if he neglected to communicate them to the officers of the company, and the policy was issued by those officers without a knowledge of them, then the policy ought to be deemed void. This claim was very properly rejected; and the jury were told that if Lay was the agent of the company, any neglect on his part was not chargeable to the plaintiff, unless he was also his agent. Of course the company could not make their agent also the agent of the insured, unless the insured chose to recognize him as his agent; and however desirous the defendants may have been that their agent should conduct fairly with applicants for insurance, most applicants, probably, would prefer for their own agent some one connected with the company. We have no reason to doubt that it was the object of the company that Lay should conduct fairly and honorably towards all applicants for insurance; and for the purpose of impressing his duty upon him, it was very proper for the president of the company to say to him that he must consider himself the agent of the insured as well as the agent of the company. But to attempt to dignify a caution of this sort, into a real agency for the insured is wholly unjustifiable both in law and fact, and is rather calculated to change the honorable character of the caution into a snare for the unsuspecting. Again, the charge is claimed to be erroneous in respect to the disclosure to the agent of certain unusual circumstances material to the risk. Several fires had occurred in an unusual manner, in the plaintiff's house, just previous to the application for insurance, and it was claimed that, in disclosing this circumstance to the agent, the plaintiff did not go sufficiently into detail, and did not, therefore, give a full and fair disclosure. Undoubtedly, the insurer is understood to take the risk upon the sup-

cited,[1] a distinction was made where the agent filled out the application, and where it was filled by the applicant himself. In the former

---

position that nothing material exists that is not fully disclosed. And the fact that his buildings had been on fire a number of times shortly before the insurance was effected was certainly a very material circumstance, which, if not disclosed would have rendered the policy void. Such an unusual occurrence tended to a suspicion that incendiaries had attempted and might again attempt to fire his buildings ; and this concealment—and silence on such a subject would amount to concealment—would operate as a fraud upon the insurer, and render the policy void. Pars. Mer. Law, 524 ; *Curry* v. *Commonwealth Ins. Co.*, 10 Pick. 535 ; *Clark* v. *Manufacturers' Ins. Co.*, 8 How. (U. S.) 235. We have no intention of relaxing, in the least, the rule which requires of the insured the most unreserved frankness on such a subject as this. But we think the charge required this of the plaintiff in this case. The insured is not bound to force his knowledge upon the insurer. In many cases he could not do it if he tried. 'He need not,' says Lord MANS-FIELD, 'mention what the underwriter ought to know ; what he takes on himself the knowledge of, or what he waives being informed of.' *Carter* v. *Boehm*, 3 Burr. 1905. Now it is apparent, from the evidence, that the alarm of Beebe on account of these fires was well understood by the agent. When he first applied for insurance, he told the agent that he had had some fires in his wood-house and house, and wanted his buildings insured ; and when told that he must first bring the dimensions of his buildings, he replied that he would come the next day. The agent answered immediately, 'You'll come while the fire is hot.' And when he did come with the dimensions, prepared to effect the insurance, he again told the agent he had had fires in his wood-house and house ; that the first fire was discovered in a barrel of shavings in the wood-house, and how it was put out. The agent interrupted him to ask where the fire was in the main part of the house, and he told him in the bed in the west front chamber. And when asked how much the bed was damaged, he told him it was about spoiled. Then the agent inquired if he had any enemy, or any suspicion of any one ; and he told him he could not tell anything about it, only that these fires had occurred ; he could not tell how ; it was all a mystery. To this the agent replied, that he had frequently been afraid his house would get burned, for fires frequently occurred, and no one could tell how they occurred. Then they had a conversation about slow matches, and as to who had been at the house, and whether any one had been there that the plaintiff suspected of setting fire to the premises. Now, as applicable to these facts, the jury were instructed that any suppression of material facts, though by mistake and without actual fraud, would vitiate the policy, whether the result of stupidity, mistake, or inadvertence, because it operates as a fraud upon the insurer. But that the insured was not bound to go into details as minutely as on the witness stand, but is bound to state fairly the substantial facts material to the risk. And in commenting on the facts, the court told the jury that much in respect to details which ought to be communicated would depend on the conduct of the insurer ; that a party could not be expected to go into details about which the insurer manifested no interest, and made no inquiry ; and in another part of the charge it is intimated that it was sufficient to disclose such facts as would occur to an honest man of ordinary intelligence as being material to the risk, though he may omit to go into all the details. On a point quite analogous to this, Lord MANSFIELD remarked that the underwriter, knowing the governor to be acquainted with the state of the place ; knowing that he apprehended danger, and must have some ground for his apprehension ; being told nothing of either, signed this policy without asking a question. By so doing he took the knowledge of the state of the place upon himself. With some slight variations, to adapt this language to the circumstances of the case under consideration, it seems almost as applicable to it as to the case of *Carter* v. *Boehm*. The material difference in the two cases is, that instead of being told nothing, the agent here was told all which occurred to the plaintiff as material to the risk, and he only omitted to go into a full detail of all the circumstances, because the agent not only expressed

---

[1] *Roth* v. *City F. Ins. Co.*, 6 McLean (U. S.) 324 ; *Dewees* v. *Manhattan Ins. Co.*, 35 N. J. 366.

instance the court say the insurer is estopped by the knowledge of the agent, while in the latter he is not, and perhaps this is the general doctrine, but it does not seem to accord with principle, when the misstatement or concealment relied on to defeat the policy is the result of a mistake. The whole theory upon which the doctrine proceeds is, that, where the agent is fully informed as to the risk, the insurer is not misled, and it cannot be said that the theory is strengthened at all by the fact that the agent makes out the application. The question is, and in all cases *should be, whether the insurer has been misled as to the risk by anything done or omitted by the assured.* And upon this question, under the rule, that knowledge of the agent is imputable to the principal, it would seem that the insurer can never claim that he was misled, when the agent *knew the facts.*[1]

---

no desire for more full information, but by his questions to the plaintiff, turned his attention from the subject to the point whether he suspected any one, and, if so, whom, as having caused the fires. Is it not correct then to say, on such a question, that, in respect to details, much must depend on the conduct of the insurer ? And if the plaintiff, under the circumstances, disclosed all that occurred to him, and all that would be likely to occur to an honest man of ordinary intelligence, is it not enough ? It may be that the agent did not suppose there was so much occasion for alarm as Beebe appeared to feel. But so long as he did not obtain this erroneous impression by means of anything done by Beebe to mislead him, the consequences of his error cannot be charged to the plaintiff."

[1] *Hartford Ins. Co.* v. *Harmer, ante.* When the agent of an insurance company takes an application for insurance *knowing* that certain articles are kept by the assured interdicted by the terms of the policy, usually printed in small types and difficult to read, and gives no notice to the assured of the stringent character of such conditions, but *consents* to the keeping of such articles, the company will be held to waived a forfeiture of the policy upon that ground. *Reaper City Ins. Co.* v. *Jones,* 62 Ill. 458 ; *Phœnix Ins. Co.* v. *Slaughter,* 12 Wall. (U. S.) 404 ; *Con. Ins. Co.* v. *Spankable,* 52 Ill. 53 ; *Atlantic Ins. Co.* v. *Wright,* 22 Ill. 462 ; *Handy* v. *N. H. F. Ins. Co., ante.* In *Phœnix Ins. Co.* v. *Lawrence,* 4 Met. (Ky.) 9, it was held that where the agent *knew* that certain prohibited articles were to be kept for sale, the prohibition in the policy was waived, and the insurer was estopped from setting up the same in avoidance of liability. A similar doctrine was held in *Peoria, etc., Ins. Co.* v. *Hall,* 12 Mich. 202, where the keeping of gunpowder was prohibited but which the insurer's agent *knew the assured not only did, but intended to continue to keep.* See also, *Rathbone* v. *City F. Ins. Co.,* 31 Conn. 193, where the assured *with the knowledge of the agents,* kept twenty-five barrels of wine on the premises in which the insured property was kept, and it was held that the agent's knowledge estopped the insurers from setting up this fact in avoidance of liability. So it has been held in numerous cases that a misstatement of title, *the agent knowing the facts in reference thereto,* could not be set up to defeat the policy. *American Ins. Co.* v. *McLanathan,* 11 Kan. 533 ; *Hodgkins* v. *Montgomery, etc., Ins. Co.,* 34 Barb. (N. Y.) 213 ; *Franklin* v. *Atlantic Ins. Co.,* 42 Mo. 456 ; *Maher* v. *Hibernian Ins. Co.,* 6 Hun (N. Y.) 353 ; *Home Mut. Ins. Co.* v. *Garfield,* 60 Ill. 124 ; *Southern, etc., Ins. Co. Lewis,* 42 Ga. 587. *Rowley* v. *Empire Ins. Co.,* 36 N. Y. 550 ; *Ayres* v. *Home Ins. Co.,* 21 Iowa, 185 ; *Combs Hannibal, etc., Ins. Co.,* 43 Mo. 148 ; *McBride* v. *Republic F. Ins. Co.,* 30 Wis. 562; *Bartholomew* v. *Merchants' Ins. Co.,* 25 Iowa, 507 ; *Atlantic Ins. Co.* v. *Wright,* 22 Ill. 462 ; or an omission to fully describe the risk as to matters material thereto. As, where a steam boiler was used, *as the agent knew,* but which was not referred to. *Campbell* v. *Merchants', etc., Ins. Co.,* 37 N. H. 35. So, where the assured kept benzine and paints as the agent knew, *McFarland* v.

SEC. 402. When the agent is aware of the *facts* relative to a risk before the contract is entered into, the insurer is charged with such knowledge, and is estopped from setting up an innocent mistake of the assured either in setting forth the facts in the application, or in omitting to state them. The insurer cannot be misled even by a warranty, when at the time the contract is entered into, *he knew the actual condition of the risk,*[1] as where the policy provides that it shall become void if the

---

Peabody, 6 W. Va. 425 ; so where the agent knew that there was a planing machine in the building, *James River Ins. Co.* v. *Merritt,* 47 Ala. 387 ; so where the premises, as the agent knew, were used for distilling whisky, *Peoples' Ins. Co.* v. *Spencer,* 53 Penn. St. 353 ; so where there was an oven and bakery in the building insured as the agent knew, *Cumberland, etc., Protection Co.* v. *Schell,* 29 id. 31 ; so where the building was described as " brick, slate roof," when one of them had a roof of only tar and felt, as the agent knew, *In re Universal, etc., Ins. Co.* v. *Forbes,* L. R. 19 Eq. 485 ; so in a life policy, where the assured was represented in the application as strictly temperate, when the agent knew he was addicted to habits of intemperance, *Miller* v. *Mut. Ben., etc., Ins. Co.,* 31 Iowa, 216 ; so where the agent who drew the application stated that a watch clock was kept, which he knew was false, *Andes Ins. Co.* v. *Shipman,* 77 Ill. 189. And in all these cases it was held that the agents knowledge estopped the insurer from setting up a breach arising from the falsity of any statements relating to facts, the true state of which was known to him. A contrary rule would be unjust and in aid of fraud.

[1] In *Maher* v. *Hibernian Ins. Co.,* recently decided in the Court of Appeals of New York, and not yet reported (Nov. 14th, 1876) the plaintiff applied to a local insurance agent of defendant for insurance upon a building occupied as a dwelling, grocery and saloon. *The agent knew the building, and the use which was made of it.* A policy of insurance was issued which contained a clause setting forth that the building was occupied as a dwelling. Plaintiff, doubting the validity of the policy, appealed to the agent to have it so changed that there would be no doubt as to its validity, and was told that the wording in the policy properly described the building, and the general agent afterward told plaintiff the same thing. In an action for loss, the defendant set up the misdescription in the policy as to the use of the house, as a defense, avoiding it. It was held that plaintiff having been, by the acts of defendant's agents, misled as to the effect of the provision in the policy, and prevented from changing such policy, defendant could not take advantage of such provision, or exclude evidence of the declarations of its agents. The complaint asked for a reformation of the policy to correspond with the intention of the insurer, and a judgment for plaintiff upon it as reformed. Held, that evidence of the transaction between plaintiff and the agents of defendant was admissible to establish the intention of the parties as to the terms of the contract, and also, that an action for the reformation of a contract, and a recovery thereon, can be brought, and it is not irregular to try such action before a judge and jury.

By a condition of the policy it was provided that fraud or false swearing should vitiate the policy. The plaintiff in his proof of loss, that he was required by the policy to make, swore that the insured building was occupied as a dwelling-house, and for no other purpose whatever. It was held, that the defendant knowing to the contrary, was not, and could not be deceived by the false statement, and therefore could not take advantage of the same after having received the proof of loss without question. In *Alexander* v. *Germania Ins. Co.,* 2 Hun (N. Y.) 655, a similar doctrine was held, but the judgment was overruled in the Court of Appeals, but by the above decision, the doctrine of the Supreme Court in this case, stands as correct.

In *Williamsburg City F. Ins. Co.* v. *Cary,* decided January 31, 1877, the Supreme Court of Illinois, held that it is not indispensable to a recovery for a loss of goods insured, after their removal to a different place, that consent should be first obtained for the removal ; a subsequent ratification of the act, with a full

premises shall be vacated,[1] or that the exercise of certain classes of business or the keeping of certain hazardous articles shall avoid the policy,[2] knowledge of the *actual facts* by the agent estops the principal from setting them up in avoidance of the policy.[3]

---

knowledge of all the facts, is equivalent to a precedent consent. *When the local agent of an insurance company is informed that goods insured have been removed long before any loss occurs, and the company does not elect to cancel the policy and give assured an opportunity of again insuring, it will be liable for the loss.* It would be inequitable to permit an insurance company to maintain that its policy was not binding upon it, and still retain the balance of the unearned premium, when it had positive knowledge of that which it insists effected the forfeiture. A policy of insurance does not become absolutely void on a breach of the implied warranty as to the location of the property embraced in it, as the company may waive any restriction made for its benefit; and when such waiver distinctly appears, the insurer will be estopped from insisting upon that which is inconsistent with what he has said and done, and which affects the rights of others. The court also holds that although a policy of insurance may contain a clause prohibiting a suit for a certain time after loss, yet if the company positively refuses to pay under any circumstances, claiming that it is not liable at any time or in any event, the assured may bring suit at once, as the refusal will render the limitation clause nugatory.

[1] In *Georgia Home Ins. Co.* v. *Kennier's Administratrix*, recently decided by the Supreme Court of Appeals of Virginia, not yet reported, a fire insurance policy purported to insure one Kennier and his legal representatives against loss by fire on his dwelling-house. The policy provided that if the "title of the property is transferred or changed, or the policy is assigned without written permission hereon, the policy shall be void." And also, "this policy shall be vitiated if the premises hereby insured become vacated by the removal of the owner or occupant for a period of more than twenty days, without immediate notice to the company and written consent. Any change within control of the assured, material to the risk, shall avoid this policy." And also, that the policy should not be valid until the premium should be paid. Kennier died, intestate, and his widow was appointed administratrix. Kennier did not, during his life, pay the premium, but the agent of the company kept the policy. After his death the administratrix paid the premium, and took the policy. Previous to this time she had vacated the house, and no one occupied it, though a servant occupied a tenement on the same lot within twenty feet of the house. *At the time of the payment of the premium the agent of the company was informed of all the facts, and asked if the insurance money would be paid, and he said it was "all right, and the money would be paid."* The house was subsequently burned. In an action for loss by the administratrix, the court held that the term "legal representatives" in the policy included the administratrix and the action was properly brought in her own name, and *that the stipulation against non-occupation was waived by the agent of the company when he received the premium with a knowledge of the facts; that the company were bound by the knowledge and acts of its agent, and estopped from insisting on the condition.*

[2] *Ludwig* v. *Ins. Co.*, 48 N. Y. 379; *McFarland* v. *Peabody Ins. Co.*, 6 W. Va. 425; *McFarland* v. *Ætna Ins. Co.*, 6 id. 437; *Peoria M. & F. Ins. Co.*, 12 Mich. 202; *In re Universal Non-Tariff F. Ins. Co.*, L. R. 19 Eq. 485; *Winans* v. *Allemania Ins. Co.*, 38 Wis. 342; *People's Ins. Co.* v. *Spencer*, 53 Penn. St. 353; *Phœnix Ins. Co.* v. *Lawrence*, 4 Met. (Ky.) 9; *Leggett* v. *Ætna Ins. Co.*, 10 Rich. (S. O.) 202; *Keenan* v. *Missouri. etc., Ins. Co.*, 12 Iowa, 126; *Bryant* v. *Poughkeepsie, etc., Ins. Co.*, 21 Barb. (N. Y.) 154; *Moore* v. *Protection Ins. Co.*, 29 Me. 92; *Keenan* v. *Dubuque, etc., Ins. Co.*, 13 Iowa, 375; *McFee* v. *South Carolina Ins. Co.*, 2 McCord (S. C.) 503; *Frost* v. *Saratoga Mut. Ins. Co.*, 5 Den. (N. Y.) 154.

[3] *Peoples' Ins. Co.* v. *Spencer*, 53 Penn. St. 353; *Kelly* v. *Ins. Co.*, 3 Wis. 254; *Ayres* v. *Hartford Ins. Co.*, 21 Iowa, 185; *Plumb* v. *Cattaraugus Ins. Co.*, 18 N. Y. 392; *Combs* v. *Hannibal Ins. Co.*, 43 Mo. 148; *Franklin* v. *Atlantic Ins. Co.*, 42 id. 456; *Columbia Ins. Co.* v. *Cooper*, 50 Penn. St. 331; *Hough* v. *Ins. Co.*, 29

43

The rule was well illustrated in an English case,[1] in which a person representing himself as an insurance agent, and who in fact was a solicitor for risks for several different companies, but who simply forwarded the applications, received and delivered the policies and received the premiums therefor, for which each company paid him a commission, effected an insurance upon certain premises in the Universal, etc., Ins. Co. He inspected the buildings, had free access to all parts thereof, and communicated the result of his examination to the insurer. The policy described the buildings as built of brick, and slated. In fact, *one* of the buildings was not slated, but the roof was covered with tar and felt when the insurance was effected. The insurer claimed that the agent was the agent of the assured, and that the policy was void because of this misdescription of the risk; but the court held that the agent was the agent of the insurer, *and that the company were estopped from taking advantage of the misdescription, because it was a misdescription made by their own agent.*[2]

Conn. 10; *Rath* v. *Ins. Co.*, 6 McLean (U. S.) 324; *Howard Ins. Co.* v. *Brunner*, 23 Penn. St. 50; *Harris* v. *Columbian, etc., Ins. Co.*, 18 Ohio St. 120; *Harner* v. *Hartford Ins. Co.*, 2 Ohio St. 452; *Howard F. Ins. Co.* v. *Cormack*, 24 Ill. 455. The authority of an agent cannot be questioned, when the acts of the insurer have been such as to amount to a recognition of his agency, and evidence that a person effected the insurance, paid the premium, received the policy, and generally was recognized as agent; the company is estopped from denying it. *Swan* v. *Liv., Lon. & Globe Ins. Co.*, 52 Miss. 704.

[1] *In re the Universal, etc., Ins. Co.*, L. R. 19, Eq. 485.

[2] A contrary doctrine was held in Virginia *Continental Ins. Co.* v. *Kasey*, 25 Gratt. (Va.) 268, but is virtually overruled by a later unreported case, cited page , in *Massachusetts Forbes* v. *Agawam Ins. Co.*, 9 Cush. (Mass.) 497, and *qualifiedly* in New York, *Rohrback* v. *Ins. Co.*, *ante;* *Stringham* v. *St. Nicholas Ins. Co.*, 3 Keyes (N. Y.) 280, but the later doctrine is as stated in the text, and is the doctrine supported by the weight of authority, both in this country and England, and it may be regarded as so well settled, as to be regarded as a legal rule, in the absence of express notice, to the insured, *that the agent's knowledge of the real condition and situation of a risk is imputable to the principal, and may be shown to defeat the effect of a warranty inconsistent therewith.* *Rowley* v. *Empire Ins. Co.*, *ante;* *Ames* v. *N. Y. Central Ins. Co.*, 14 N. Y. 253; *Owens* v. *Holland Purchase Ins. Co.*, 56 N. Y. 565; *Plumb* v. *Cattaraugus Ins. Co.*, 18 N. Y. 392; *Bidwell* v. *W. W. Ins. Co.*, 24 N. Y. 302. A qualification of the rule, however, exists in New York, where the agent's powers are limited to the taking of applications, when the warranty appears upon the *face* of the policy, *Chase* v. *Hamilton Ins. Co.*, 20 N. Y. 52; *Wall* v. *East River Ins. Co.*, 7 N. Y. 370; *Alexander* v. *Germania Ins. Co.*, 66 N. Y. 464; or when the *policy* expressly provides that the agent in making the application and survey, shall be treated as the agent of the assured, *Rohrbach* v. *Germinia Ins. Co.*, 62 N. Y. 47; unless the insurer *requires* its agent to fill up the application. *Sprague* v. *Holland Pur. Ins. Co.*, *ante.* But in the most of the States, the question is made to depend upon the *authority* of the agent, real or apparent. In *McFarland* v. *Peabody*, 6 W. Va. 425, the agent's knowledge that benzine and paints were to be kept, was held to be imputable to the insurer, and estopped it from setting up a breach of the policy on that account. See, to the same effect, *Peoria F. & M. Ins. Co.* v. *Hall*, 12 Mich. 168; *People's Ins. Co.* v. *Spencer*, 53 Penn. St. 353; *Southern Ins. Co.* v. *Lewis*, 42 Ga. 587; *Combs* v. *Hannibal Ins. Co.*, 43 Mo. 148;

SEC. 403. In a Connecticut case,[1] a policy was issued upon a quantity of cider stored in a certain building designated in the policy. The policy prohibited any increase of risk whatever within the control of the assured, whether as to occupancy or otherwise, and prohibited the keeping or storing of spirituous liquors upon the premises, without the consent of the company. In fact, *at the time when the insurance was effected*, there were about twenty-five barrels of native wine stored in the same building, *which fact was known to the agent of the insurers when he effected the insurance*. A loss having occurred under the policy, the defendants sought to avoid their liability under the policy, by setting up the keeping of the wine upon the premises, without their consent. But the court held that if the agent had full knowledge that the wine was stored there, and that he had possession of the policy, and an opportunity to indorse consent thereon and failed to do so, the company were thereby estopped from sitting up his *laches* in that respect, in defense. In a Pennsylvania case,[2] the defendant issued a policy to the plaintiff upon a stock of barley, malt and hops. The policy was conditioned that the risk should not be increased. The plaintiff used the premises both before and after the policy was issued, to distill whiskey, which increased the risk. The agent of the defendant examined the premises before the risk was taken, and the machinery for distilling was then in the building. A loss having occurred, the defendants set up the use of the premises for distillation of whiskey, in avoidance of the policy, but the court held that *if the agent knew, or ought to have known*, from the examination he made of the premises, that they would be used for the purposes of distilling, the defendants were estopped from setting up such use in avoidance of their liability, and that the question of such knowledge was for the jury. In a New Hampshire case,[3] the rules of the company forbade the issue of policies upon premises containing a steam boiler. The defendants' agent, *knowing* that there

---

Clark v. *Union, etc., Ins. Co.*, 40 N. H. 333 ; *Witherell* v. *Maine Ins. Co.*, 49 Me. 200 ; *Castor* v. *Monmouth Ins. Co.*, 54 Me. 170 ; *Beal* v. *Park Ins. Co.*, 16 Wis. 241 ; *Atlantic Ins. Co.* v *Wright*, 22 Ill. 462 ; *Hartford Protection Ins. Co.* v. *Harmer*, 2 Ohio St. 452 ; *Viele* v. *Germania Ins. Co.*, 26 Iowa, 9 ; *Miller* v. *Mut. Benefit Ins. Co.*, 31 Iowa, 216 ; *Michigan State Ins. Co.* v. *Lewis*, 30 Mich. 41 ; *Swan* v. *Ins. Co.*, 57 Miss. 704. In the United States courts, *Ins. Co.* v. *Wilkinson*, 13 Wall. (U. S.) 221 ; *Roth* v. *City F. Ins. Co.*, ante. In England, *In re Universal, etc., Ins. Co.* v. *Forbes*, L. R. 19 Eq. 485.

[1] *Rathbone* v. *City F. Ins. Co.*, 31 Conn. 193.

[2] *Peoples' Ins. Co.* v. *Spencer*, 53 Penn. St. 353.

[3] *Campbell* v. *Merchants', etc., Ins. Co.*, ante.

was a steam boiler upon the plaintiff's premises, wrote an application for insurance thereon, in which he omitted to state the fact. The defendants, in an action for a loss under the policy, set up the omission of the plaintiff to state the fact that a steam boiler was used, as well as the rules of the company forbidding the taking of such risks, in defense, but the court held *that the knowledge of the agent was the knowledge of the company*, and that the plaintiff was not to be affected by its rules or regulations, unless actual notice thereof to him was shown, and that the defendants were estopped by the knowledge and acts of the agent, from setting up such matters in defense.[1] In a case in West Virginia,[2] the defendants' agent, who effected the insurance, issued a policy to the plaintiff upon a "barrel factory, manufactured barrels and materials for the same, contained therein." The policy contained a stipulation that the defendants should not be "liable for damages occasioned by the use of camphene, burning fluid, etc., unless otherwise specially provided for." At the time when the contract was entered into, the plaintiff had a barrel of benzine in a building contiguous to the factory, which was used for storing and painting empty barrels, and the fire originated in that building. In an action to recover for the loss, the defendants set up the keeping of the benzine in avoidance of its liability. The court held that, while the use of benzine could not be considered *as an incident to the subject insured, yet, if the defendants' agent, at the time of entering into the contract, knew that the plaintiffs were using paints and benzine in their business in the premises insured,* the insurer must be charged with such knowledge, and would thereby be estopped from setting up such use in avoidance of liability under the policy, and that this question was for the jury. In an Alabama case,[3] the defendant company issued a policy to the plaintiffs, upon an application which described the property as being "a frame steam saw-mill, situate, etc., boiler, engine, machinery and belting contained therein." Before the policy was issued, the defendants' agent inspected the premises. There was a planeing machine upon the same floor with the machinery proper, which was plainly visible, only about twenty feet from the machinery, and attached to it by belting, *which the agent ought to have seen, if he did not.* The agent, *after he had examined the premises, wrote the application,* and the court held that, under this state

---

[1] See full statement of the case, *ante*, p.
[2] *McFarland* v. *Peabody Ins. Co.*, 6 W. Va. 625.
[3] *James River Ins. Co.* v. *Merritt*, 47 Ala. 887.

of facts, the defendants were estopped from setting up the existence and use of the planing machine to defeat their liability for the loss. In a Michigan case,[1] the question of estpppel upon the ground *of the agent's knowledge of the facts,* was very forcibly presented. In that case the defendants' agent took the plaintiff's application, signed in blank, for insurance upon a stock of goods, kept by the plaintiff for sale, to be insured in one policy, and for an insurance upon certain buildings, among which was the store in which the goods were kept, to be insured by another policy. At the time when the applications were signed, the plaintiff told the agent that he usually sold gunpowder, and everything kept in a country store, and that he intended to do so. The agent took the applications, signed in blank, and the policies were subsequently issued. The applications were referred to as the ground upon which the policies were issued, and, among other things, specially prohibited the keeping of gunpowder or fire-works, for sale or on storage, without written permission in the policy. No permission to keep gunpowder was in or indorsed upon the policies, and a loss having occurred, the defendants, among other things, set up the breach of this condition in defense, but the court held, *that notice to the agent, that the assured kept gunpowder for sale, and intended to keep it,* was notice to and the knowledge of the company, and estopped them from setting up the same in defense. "As to the condition in reference to keeping gunpowder," said CHRISTIANCY, J., "there was evidence from which the jury were justified in finding *that the agent knew it was kept at the time, and was to be kept after the insurance, and that he assented to it,* and induced the plaintiff to believe that it would make no difference upon this point, the court charged, that 'if the plaintiff informed the agent that he kept gunpowder in his store for sale, and the agent intended to insure against keeping it, but neglected to indorse permission on the back of the policy, such neglect would not make the policy invalid.' The condition did not provide for any indorsement *upon* the policy, but the keeping of gunpowder was to render the policy void, 'without written permission *in* the policy.' To this extent the charge was inaccurate, yet we do not think it can be treated as error of which the company can complain, since we think the plaintiff was entitled to a still stronger charge in his favor. *He would have been entitled to a charge that, if the agent knew it was kept and to be kept, the keeping it would not render the policy void, whether the permission was*

---

[1] *Peoria M. & F. Ins. Co.* v. *Hall,* 12 Mich. 202; 4 Bennett's F. Ins. Cas, 737.

indorsed or intended or neglected to be indorsed or not. But the counsel for the plaintiff in error insists that the printed condition *was notice to the assured of the agent's want of authority to assent to the keeping of gunpowder, etc., and that this assent would be given only by the company itself.* This, at first view, would seem plausible and might be sound, but for another principle which lies back of it, and defeats its application. The principle to which we allude is *that notice to the agent is notice to his principal. The company must be regarded as knowing what he knew. If he knew that powder was kept at the time of the insurance, or to be kept during its continuance, the company must be regarded as knowing it also. They had power to waive the condition, and by taking the premium and issuing the policy with such notice or knowledge, they must be regarded as having waived the condition that prohibited its keeping.* It would be a gross fraud in the company to receive the premium for issuing a policy on which it did not intend to be liable, and which they intended to treat as void in case of loss." [1] It may be stated as a general rule, that, *where the agent effecting the insurance knows the situation and condition of the risk, or its incidents or uses, or the existence of conditions, uses or incidents that conflict with the conditions of the policy, and fails to provide therefor, his knowledge is the knowledge of the company, and the company cannot set up such matters in avoidance of the policy,* [2] *and this applies to all matters, such as incumbrances upon the property,* [3] *the interest of the assured*

---

[1] *Bidwell* v. *N. W. Ins. Co.,* 24 N. Y. 302 ; *Frost* v. *Saratoga, etc., Ins. Co.,* 5 Den. (N. Y.) 154 ; *Masters* v. *Madison, etc., Ins. Co.,* 11 Barb. (N. Y.) 624 ; *Campbell* v. *Merchants' etc., Ins. Co., ante; Marsnall* v. *Columbian Ins. Co.,* 27 N. H. 157 ; *Hartford, etc., Ins. Co.* v. *Harmer, ante; Howard F. Ins. Co.* v. *Brunner, ante; Clark* v. *Union, etc., Ins. Co.,* 40 N. H. 333.

[2] *Ayres* v. *Home Ins. Co.,* 21 Iowa, 185 ; *Peoria, etc., Ins. Co.* v. *Hall, ante; Campbell* v. *Merchants' Ins. Co., ante; Anson* v. *Winneshiek Ins. Co.,* 23 Iowa, 84 ; *Howard F. & M. Ins. Co.* v. *Cornack,* 24 Ill. 455 ; *Aurora F. Ins. Co.* v. *Eddy,* 55 id. 213 ; *Viele* v. *Germania Ins. Co.,* 26 Iowa, 9 ; *Reaper City Ins. Co.* v. *Jones,* 62 Ill. 458 ; *Beal* v. *Park, etc., Ins. Co.,* 16 Wis. 241.

[3] *Ames* v. *N. Y. Union Ins. Co.,* 14 N. Y. 253. In *Howard F. Ins. Co.* v. *Brunner,* 23 Penn. St. 50, the policy contained, among others, a condition that a false description of the building or its contents should vitiate the policy. The description and survey were made a part of the policy, and a warranty on the part of the insured. The application failed to disclose one mortgage for $5,000, and another for $1,000. It stated the works are operated by the proprietor and lighted by closed lamps. The proof showed that an open light was generally used to light up the others, and that the works were not exclusively operated on account of the proprietor ; that he rented portions of the building, and supplied steam power to the renters ; but it was proved that a person, acting for insurers' agents, surveyed the building, knew how it was occupied, and that the insured signed the application in blank, delivered it to this person, who afterwards filled it up from memory, and it was not afterwards shown to the insured. One of the insurers' agents testified that he knew the building, and as to how it was occupied ; that he knew of the mortgage not mentioned in the policy or in the application. Held, the application was not the act of the insured, although he signed it ; that it was a description by insurers' agents, and though it were false, could

therein,[1] the value of the property,[2] the existence of other insurance,[3] and every and any matters that it would have been the duty of the insurer himself to have provided for in the policy, if the matters *known to the agent had been in fact known by him.*[4] The principle that an insurer who contracts with full knowledge of facts that constitute a breach of the conditions of the policy, is estopped from asserting them to defeat his liability thereon, is predicated upon the rules of fair dealing, sound morality, and is in consonance with requirements of the most healthful public policy.[5] It is the duty of the insurer under such circumstances *to so frame the policy as to be operative in view of the circumstances existing*

---

not affect the plaintiff's right to recover. *Maher* v. *Hibernian Ins. Co.*, 6 Hun (N. Y.) 353 ; *Rowley* v. *Empire Ins. Co.*, 36 N. Y. 550 ; *Ætna, etc., Ins. Co.* v. *Olmstead*, 21 Mich. 246. In *Columbia Ins Co.* v. *Cooper*, 50 Penn. St. 331, the policy expressly provided that, "if any agent of this company, in the transaction of their business, shall assume to violate these conditions, such violation shall be construed to be the act of the insured, and shall render this policy void." The application required the assured to state what incumbrances existed upon the property, and he stated " none." The application was made a part of the policy. In fact, there were judgments against the real estate that operated as liens and incumbrances thereon, and the defendants insisted that this was a breach of the warranty against incumbrances and avoided the policy. But the court held that it was competent for the plaintiff to show that the agent was informed of these liens before the contract was made, and he (the agent), in filling up the application, with full knowledge of the facts, wrote " none," and that these facts estopped the defendants from setting up the existence of such liens in avoidance of the policy. The doctrine of this case is similar in principle to *Malleable Iron Works* v. *Ins. Co.*, *ante.* See also, *Cumberland Valley, etc., Ins. Co.* v. *Schell*, 29 Penn. St. 31, where it was held that the omission of the agent to state in the application, which was filled up by him, the existence of an oven and bakery upon the premises, of the existence of which he knew, *and which was material to the risk*, could not be set up by the defendants to avoid the policy. See also, *Maliere* v. *Penn. Ins. Co.*, 5 Rawle (Penn.) 342, where the defendants' secretary, although correctly informed, misdescribed the property, and it was held that such misdescription could not avail the defendants in defense. As to neglect to state incumbrances *known* to agent, see *Michigan State Ins. Co.* v. *Lewis*, 30 Mich. 41 ; *Home Mut. F. Ins. Co.* v. *Garfield*, 60 Ill. 124 ; *Hartford, etc., Ins. Co.* v. *Harmer*, 2 Ohio St. 452. See statement of case, *ante ; Bidwell* v. *N. W. Ins. Co.*, 24 N. Y. 302.

[1] *Hodgkins* v. *Montgomery, etc., Ins. Co.*, 34 Barb. (N. Y.) 213 ; *Southern, etc., Ins. Co.* v. *Lewis*, 42 Ga. 587 ; *Caston* v. *Monmouth, etc., Ins. Co.*, 54 Me. 170 ; *Franklin* v. *Atlantic Ins. Co.*, 42 Mo. 456 ; *Longhurst* v. *Star Ins. Co.*, 19 Iowa, 364 ; *American Central Ins. Co.* v. *McLanathan*, 11 Kan. 533 ; *Atlantic Ins. Co.* v. *Wright*, 22 Ill. 462 ; *McBride* v. *Phœnix Ins. Co.*, 27 Wis. 693 ; *Rockford Ins. Co.* v. *Nelson*, 65 Ill. 415 ; *Coombs* v. *Hannibal Ins. Co.*, 43 Mo. 148 ; *Emery* v. *Piscataqua, etc., Ins. Co.*, 52 Me. 322 ; *Buckley* v. *Garrett*, 47 Penn. St. 204.

[2] In *Owens* v. *Holland Purchase Ins. Co.*, 56 N. Y., 565, the assured placed the valuation of the farm, buildings and personal property at $14,000. The agent wrote the valuation *of the buildings and personal property* at that sum, and the plaintiff signed the application without discovering the error. The court held that the error must be treated as the error of the insurer, and the agent being informed of the real facts, the company could not set up the misstatement in defense.

[3] *Rowley* v. *Empire Ins. Co.*, *ante ; Maher* v. *Hibernian Ins. Co.*, *ante.*

[4] *Jackson* v. *Ætna Ins. Co.*, 16 B. Mon. (Ky.) 242 ; *Gilliat* v. *Pawtucket, etc., Ins. Co.*, 8 R. I. 282 ; *Peoria M. & F. Ins. Co.* v. *Hall*, *unte.*

[5] *Mershon* v. *National Ins. Co.*, 34 Iowa, 87.

in relation to the risk and known to him,[1] and, failing to do so, the courts, *acting upon the presumption that he intends to deal honestly,* will treat him as having waived the conditions of the policy, so far as they operate to defeat liability in view of the facts known to the insurer prior to the time when it was made.[2] And in all cases the knowledge of the agent is to be imputed to the principal.[3] Thus, where the assured has, *with the knowledge of the insurer,* forfeited his rights under the policy by a breach of some of its conditions, as by increasing the hazard,[4] or exceeding the limit as to the amount of the aggregate insurance permitted;[5] or where it is known by the insurer that the policy was obtained by fraud,[6] or by misrepresentation as to the character or situation of the risk;[7] or in any respect, or for any cause, a recognition thereof by the insurer or his agent, *after such knowledge is acquired,* as a subsisting, valid obligation, by accepting the premium thereon;[8] renewing the same;[9] making an assessment when none would be permissible, if not a valid obligation;[10] or, indeed, any decisive act recognizing the validity of the contract, is treated as a waiver of the forfeiture.[11] The effect to be given to the agent's knowledge of the facts must of course be measured by his authority, apparent or real. If he is authorized to pass upon a risk without submitting it to the principal, *or if he is authorized to fill up the application and examine or survey the risk for the company,* his knowledge is the knowledge of the company, and his

---

[1] *Jackson* v. *Ætna Ins. Co.,* 16 B. Mon. (Ky.) 242.

[2] *Peoria M. & F. Ins. Co.* v. *Hall, ante.*

[3] *Witherell* v. *Maine Ins. Co.,* 49 Me. 200; *Peoria M. & F. Ins. Co.* v. *Hall, ante; Rowley* v. *Empire Ins. Co.,* 36 N. Y. 550; *Owens* v. *Holland Purchase Ins. Co.,* 56 id. 565.

[4] *Keenan* v. *Missouri, etc., Ins. Co.,* 12 Iowa, 126; *Viall* v. *Genesee, etc., Ins. Co.,* 19 Barb. (N. Y.) 440.

[5] *Lycoming Ins. Co.* v. *Stockblower,* 26 Penn. St. 199; *Handy* v. *N. H. Ins. Co., ante.*

[6] *Armstrong* v. *Turquand,* 9 I. & C. L. 32.

[7] *Frost* v. *Saratoga, etc., Ins. Co.,* 5 Den. (N. Y.) 154; *Hadley* v. *N. H. Ins. Co., ante.*

[8] *Mershan* v. *National Ins. Co.,* 34 Iowa, 87; *Armstrong* v. *Turquand, ante.* In *Washoe Tool, etc., Co.* v. *Hibernia Ins. Co.,* 66 N. Y. 613, it was held that where an agent delivers a policy containing a clause that the company should not be liable unless the premium "be actually paid," without requiring prepayment, the condition was waived, and that the fact that the premium was several times demanded, and was not paid, *and the policy was not canceled,* did not operate to defeat the waiver, but that the policy remained operative, and the original credit would continue until notice of the cancellation of the policy was given.

[9] *Miner* v. *Phœnix Ins. Co.,* 27 Wis. 693.

[10] *Frost* v. *Saratoga, etc., Ins. Co., ante; Viall* v. *Genesee, etc., Ins. Co., ante.*

[11] *Lycoming Ins. Co.* v. *Stockbower, ante.*

neglect is their neglect;[1] but if he only has authority to receive and forward applications, and does not assume to act as surveyor of the risk, and does not attempt to advise the assured what questions to answer, or how to answer them, his knowledge of the facts does not estop the insurer.[2]

In all cases the binding force of an act done or omitted by an agent, is to be measured by his apparent authority, and is to be determined by the jury,[3] and if there is any limitation placed upon the agent's authority, of which the assured has notice, he can claim no advantage from anything done by the agent in excess thereof.[4] *But, in order to estop the insurer, the act claimed as a waiver, must be shown to have been done with full knowledge of the forfeiture,*[5] and one which *necessarily* operates as a recognition of the validity of the policy.*[6]

[1] *Ayres* v. *Hartford Ins. Co.*, 17 Iowa, 176; *Plumb* v. *Cattaraugus, etc., Ins. Co.*, 18 N. Y. 392; *Miller* v. *Mut. Benefit Life Ins. Co.*, 31 Iowa, 216.

[2] *Ayres* v. *Hartford Ins. Co., ante; Malleable Iron Works* v. *Phœnix Ins. Co., ante; Smith* v. *Cash. Mut., etc., Ins. Co.*, 24 Penn. St. 320; *Bartholomew* v. *Merchants' Ins. Co.*, 25 Iowa, 507. The doctrine of this case, however, has been virtually denied in the case cited *ante, Miller* v. *Mut. Ben. Life Ins. Co.*

[3] In *Carrugi* v. *Atlantic Ins. Co.*, 40 Ga. 135, the defendant's agent was authorized to take and revoke risks. It was held that this gave him authority to consent to other insurance, either in writing or by parol. In *Neal* v. *Irving*, 1 C. & P. 61, the person who signed the plaintiff's policy had been in the habit of signing the defendant's name to policies, and it was held that this was sufficient to show that the defendant had authorized him to do so. *Brocklebank* v. *Sugrell*, 5 C. & P. 21. In *Miller* v. *Phœnix Ins. Co.*, 27 Iowa, 203, the agent of the defendant issued a circular, stating that all losses under policies issued at his office would be paid through him; and also another circular, stating that they would be paid in bankable funds. This was held proper evidence for the jury, from which they might find that he had authority to accept an order drawn by the assured upon the insurer in favor of a third person, for the amount of a loss. See also, *Fayles* v. *National Ins. Co.*, 49 Mo. 380. In *Veile* v. *Germania Ins. Co.*, 26 Iowa, 9, it was held that where an agent had authority to cancel policies because of an increase of risk, he also had authority to waive breaches of conditions in the policy. In *Ætna Ins. Co.* v. *Maguire*, 51 Ill. 342, the agent was authorized to issue policies in Nebraska city. He issued a policy upon property in an other county, and the insurers defended against a loss under the policy, upon the ground that he had no authority to issue policies there, but the court held that this defense could not be available unless they show that the plaintiff *knew* that he was acting in access of his authority. The question is not what power the agent had, *but what power did the insurers hold him out as having. Lungstrap* v. *German Ins. Co.*, 57 Mo. 107; *Eclectic, etc., Ins. Co.* v. *Fahrenkrug*, 68 Ill. 463; *Goit* v. *National Protection Ins. Co.*, 25 Barb. (N. Y.) 189; *Keenan* v. *Missouri State Ins. Co.*, 12 Iowa, 126; *McCullough* v. *Talladega Ins. Co.*, 46 Ala. 376; *Wilson* v. *Genessee Ins. Co.*, 14 N. Y. 418; *Warner* v. *Peoria, etc., Ins. Co.*, 14 Wis. 318; *Bodine* v. *Exchange Ins. Co.*, 51 N. Y. 117; *Malleable Iron Works* v. *Phœnix Ins. Co.*, 25 Conn. 465; *Gale* v. *Lewis*, L. R. 9 Q. B. 730; *Goodson* v. *Brooke*, 4 Camp. 163; *Com'l Ins. Co.* v. *Ives*, 56 Ill. 402; *Grady* v. *American, etc., Ins. Co.*, 60 Mo. 116.

[4] *Thayer* v. *Agricultural Ins. Co.*, 5 Hun (N. Y.) 566.

[5] *State, etc., Ins. Co.* v. *Arthur*, 30 Penn. St. 315; *Finley* v. *Lycoming Ins. Co.*, 30 id. 311; *Hazard* v. *Franklin Mut. F. Ins. Co.*, 7 R. I. 429; *Diehl* v. *Adams Co. Mut. Ins. Co.*, 58 Penn. St. 443; *Allen* v. *Vermont Mut. F. Ins. Co.*, 12 Vt. 366.

[6] *Neeley* v. *Onondaga, etc., Ins. Co.*, 7 Hill (N. Y.) 49.

Mere rumors, known to agent, not imputable to principal.

SEC. 404. While the knowledge of the agent is imputable to the principal, yet, this holds only as to knowledge acquired in his capacity as agent, and mere rumors, or matters coming to his knowledge in his individual capacity, are not imputable to the principal.[1] Neither is the insurer affected by knowledge as to the risk or any changes therein that come to the agent in his individual capacity, *after* the contract is made.[2] But knowledge of matters brought to his attention by the assured or his agent, concerning the risk, is imputable to the insurer and binding upon him.[3] The agent, in filling up the application, is not necessarily the agent of the assured, although the company has expressly directed him to so consider himself.[4]

No power implied to settle loss, from fact of agency.

SEC. 405. The mere fact that an agent is shown to have authority to issue policies and countersign the same, does not warrant an inference that he has authority to adjust and settle losses, or waive the performance of conditions in the policy, and the fact that he *assumes* to do so does not even tend to establish his authority. *Authority in fact, or a usage that warrants such an inference, or a ratification of his acts must be shown.*[5] The principal is only liable for acts done by the agent *within the scope of his real or apparent authority*, and no amount of assumption of authority by him, not within the scope of such real or apparent authority, will confer power upon him to bind his principal.[6]

Notice to agent, notice to principal.

SEC. 406. In all cases where notice is required to be given, *unless some special officer is named* to whom it shall be given, notice to an agent of the company, is notice to the company. Thus when notice of other

---

[1] *Keenan* v. *Dubuque, etc., Ins. Co.*, 13 Iowa. 375.

[2] *Ayres* v. *Hartford Ins. Co.*, 17 Iowa, 176.

[3] In *Hadley* v. *N. H. F. Ins. Co.*, 55 N. H. 110; 5 Ben. F. I. C. 700, it was held that the agent's knowledge of other insurance was imputable to the company; also that where the agent insured the plaintiff's building, which was used as a *summer hotel*, as a *dwelling-house*, concealing the fact from the company, but knowing it himself, there being no collusion or fraud on the part of the assured, his knowledge was imputable to the plaintiff, and estopped the defendant from setting up such matters in defense.

[4] *Beebe* v. *Hartford Ins. Co.*, 25 Conn. 51; 4 Ben. F. I. C. 55.

[5] *Bush* v. *Westchester Ins. Co.*, 63 N. Y. 531. An agency cannot be created by the representation of an assumed agent. *Marvin* v. *Wilbur*, 52 N. Y. 270; *Lightbody* v. *N. American Ins. Co.*, 23 Wend. (N. Y.) 22; *Plumb* v. *Cattaraugus Ins. Co.*, 18 N. Y. 392; *Adriance* v. *Rowe*, 52 Barb. (N. Y.) 399.

[6] PECKHAM, J., in *Marvin* v. *Wilbur, ante; Post* v. *Ætna Ins. Co.*, 43 Barb. (N. Y.) 361; *Ins. Co.* v. *Wilkinson*, 13 Wall. (U. S.) 222; *Bush* v. *Westchester Ins. Co., ante.*

insurance is required to be given, notice given to the agent is sufficient,[1] and if no special mode in which it shall be given is provided, any notice conveying the requisite information, wr tten or verbal, is sufficient,[2] or if the agent *knew* of the other insurance when the contract was entered into, it is not only a waiver of notice, but also of a forfeit. ure on that ground.[3] It is not necessarily essential that the agent should be clothed with authority to issue policies. It is enough if he is authorized to receive applications, make surveys, deliver policies and receive the premiums therefor, and is in any measure held out by the insurer as having authority to act for it in any or all of these respects.[4]

Mistake of agent imputable to insurer.

SEC. 407. There seems to be no question but that, *in all cases where the mistake is the fault of the agent it may be shown, and when established, the insurer is bound to respond upon the contract actually made,*[5] and this extends not merely *to mistakes in the policy, but also to mistakes arising from mis-advice of the agent, or his misconception of the legal effect of certain conditions.*[6]

---

[1] *McEwen* v. *Montgomery, etc., Ins. Co.,* 5 Hill (N. Y.) 101; 3 Bennett's F. I. C. 208.

[2] *McEwen* v. *Montgomery, etc.. Ins. Co.,* 5 Hill (N. Y.) 101; Bennett's F. I. C. 269; *Sexton* v. *Montgomery, etc., Ins. Co.,* 9 Barb. (N. Y.) 191; *Carroll* v. *Charter Oak Ins. Co.,* 38 id. 402; *Schenck* v. *Mercer, etc., Ins. Co.,* 24 N. J. 447; *National Ins. Co.* v. *Crane,* 16 Md. 260; *Dayton Ins. Co.* v. *Kelly,* 24 Ohio St., 345; *Hayward* v. *National Ins. Co.,* 52 Mo. 181; *Ins. Co. of N. America* v. *McDowell,* 50 Ill. 120; *Russell* v. *State Ins. Co.,* 55 Mo. 585; *Hardy* v. *N. H. F. Ins. Co., ante.*

[3] *Getb* v. *International Ins. Co.,* 1 Dill. (U. S.) 443; *Carroll* v. *Charter Oak Ins. Co., ante; Hadley* v. *N. H. F. Ins. Co ,* 55 N. H. 110; *National Ins. Co.* v. *Crane, ante; Van Bories* v. *United Life and Fire, etc., Ins. Co.,* 8 Bush (Ky.) 133; *Hayward* v. *National Ins. Co., ante; Cobb* v. *Ins. Co. of N. America,* 11 Kan. 93; *Webster* v. *Phœnix Ins. Co.,* 36 Wis. 67; *Horwitz* v. *Equitable Ins. Co.,* 40 Mo, 157. In *Kenton Ins. Co.* v. *Shea,* 6 Bush. (Ky.) 174, the agent *knew* of other insurance obtained subsequently through him. It was not indorsed on the policy issued by defendants. But it was held that the acts of the agent amounted to a waiver of the condition. The same doctrine was held in *Horwitz* v. *Equitable Ins. Co., ante,* under a similar state of facts. In *Dayton Ins. Co.* v. *Kelly, ante,* it was held, that where the agent contracted to deliver "*a regular policy,*" it must be construed to mean a *valid* policy, and as a permission for all prior insurance. When notice of other insurance is given to an agent or to the company, they are bound either to indorse consent thereon or cancel the policy, and failing to cancel, they are treated as consenting. *Planters', etc., Ins. Co.* v. *Lyons,* 38 Tex. 253; *National Ins. Co.* v. *Crane, ante.*

[4] *McEwen* v. *Montgomery. etc., Ins. Co., ante.*

[5] *Hadley* v. *N. H. Ins. Co.,* 55 N. H. 110; 5 Ben. F. I. C. 700; *Marshall* v. *Columbian Ins. Co.,* 27 id. 164; *Ins. Co.* v. *Wilkinson,* 13 Wall. (U. S.) 222; *Rowley* v. *Empire Ins. Co.,* 36 N. Y. 550; *Union, etc., Ins. Co.* v. *Keyser,* 32 N. H. 313; *Guardian Life Ins. Co.* v. *Hogan,* 80 Ill. 35; *Roberts* v. *Continental Ins. Co.,* 41 Wis. 321; *Franklin* v. *Atlantic Ins. Co.,* 42 Mo. 456; *American Ins. Co.* v. *McLanathan,* 11 Kan. 549; *Campbell* v. *Ins. Co.,* 37 N. H. 35.

[6] In *Ætna, etc., Ins. Co.* v. *Olmstead,* 21 Mich. 246; 4 Am. Rep. 483, this question was carefully discussed by COOLEY, J. The facts appear in the opinion, and I

Thus, where the assured held a mechanic's lien upon premises, and the agent described it in the policy as a mortgage interest, and the

---

give it entire. He said: "Olmstead recovered judgment in the court below upon a policy of insurance issued by the plaintiff in error, and by which they insured him against loss by fire on his hotel and the furniture therein, and hotel-barn, in the village of Lyons. A loss having occurred, the insurers refused to pay on the ground of a breach of warranty by the insured, which, by the terms of the policy, rendered that instrument void. It appears that, by the policy, it was expressly provided that 'if an application, survey, plan or description of the property herein insured is referred to in this policy, such application, survey, plan or description shall be considered a part of this policy, and a warranty by the insured.' The policy was based upon an application, which contained questions and answers, and the ninth question, with the answer thereto, was as follows: '9. Incumbrance; if any, state the amount. Is there any insurance by the mortgagees? State the amount. 9. No.' The breach of warranty relied upon was, that at this time there were two mortgages upon the insured property; and this fact was not disputed. To avoid the force of this objection, Olmstead, the plaintiff (below), called the agent of the insurance company, and proved by him that at the time of taking the application he knew of the existence of the two mortgages; that the witness drew the application, and asked Olmstead to look at and sign it; that the question of incumbrances was talked over between them at the time, and whether the mortgages should be mentioned in the application was fully discussed; that the witness advised Olmstead that he did not think it would make any difference whether the mortgages were mentioned in the application or not, as there was no insurance by the mortgagees; that the witness expressed the opinion to Olmstead that he could answer the ninth interrogatory 'No,' and that Olmstead would not have signed it if the witness had not told him he had better. If we recur again to the ninth interrogatory we shall perceive that in fact it embraces a number of questions, only one of which can be answered by a distinct affirmative or negative. The only answer given to all these questions is 'No;' and this is a proper reply only to the question 'Is there any insurance by the mortgagees?' It does not answer the request to state the amount of incumbrance, if any. The interrogatory and the answer taken together are ambiguous, and we cannot feel assured that the applicant, in signing this paper, understood his reply as asserting any thing more than that there was no insurance on behalf of mortgagees on the same property. The parol evidence tends to show that that was his understanding; that he was led to believe that it was to the point of other insurance that the interrogatory was directed, and consequently he had given the insurers all the information their blank application called for. And we think it becomes pertinent to inquire who impressed him with this belief? Had it been some one of whom he sought information and counsel on his own behalf, or had it even been a mere stranger, the insured must have acted upon his belief at his peril. Such, however, was not the case here. The agent of the insurance company assumed to have all the requisite knowledge for preparing the proper papers, and volunteered to make them out. He had all the necessary information for that purpose, and nothing was concealed from him. If the application is not in due form, and if it fails to give all the information called for, it must be either because the agent was too ignorant of the business to be properly intrusted with the agency, or because he was so negligent or reckless that he did not trouble himself to draft them correctly; or lastly, because he was disposed to take Olmstead's money on the fraudulent pretense of giving him indemnity when he knew he was giving none whatever. The general rule undoubtedly is, that, in the absence of fraud, accident or mistake, a party must be conclusively presumed to understand the force of his contracts, and to be bound by their terms. But it cannot be tolerated that one party shall draft the contract for the other, and receive the consideration, and then repudiate his obligation on the ground that he had induced the other party to sign an untrue representation which was, by the very terms of the contract, to render it void. Still less can this be allowed when the representation itself is so ambiguously worded as to be well calculated to conceal its real meaning, and to deceive the party signing it. It is true that in this case the paper in question was drawn by an agent; but we do not think that, in a legal point of view, the rights

agent, upon having his attention called to the error, said that a mort-gage and a mechanic's lien were the same thing in the law of insur-ance, and thereupon the assured paid the premium and took the policy, it was held that the company were bound to respond to the contract *as made*, and that the fact that the assured accepted it with full knowledge of the error, did not, in view of the acts of the agent, estop him from seeking a reformation thereof.[1] So where the assured, in answer to an inquiry as to the value of the premises, stated that the land, buildings *and personal property* were worth $14,000, and the agent wrote the answer "farm and buildings $14,000," it was held that the mistake was the defendants, and they were estopped from setting it up in avoidance of the policy.[2]

Revocation of authority.

SEC. 408. Of course it is competent for the insurer at any time to revoke the authority of an agent, and a person dealing with him after

---

of the parties are any different from what they would be had the agent himself been insurer. The insurance business of the world is done through agents almost exclusively, and the maxim *qui facit per alium facit per se* applies with special force to their acts. These agents assume to have, and generally do have, much more intimate knowledge of the business than those with whom they deal. They may also be fairly presumed to understand the requirements of their prin-cipals, and how properly and legally to fill up the blank applications and other papers with which their principals intrust them. The community in general do not assume to be familiar with these matters, and would not venture in any case to set up their own view of what was or was not the proper form of an application, against the positive assertion of an expert. The forms and requirements of dif-ferent insurers are different; and when an agent, who at the time and place is the sole representative of the principal, assumes to know what information the prin-cipal requires, and after being furnished with all the facts, drafts a paper which he declares satisfactory, induces the other party to sign it, receives and retains the premium moneys, and then delivers a contract which the other party is led to believe, and has a right to believe, gives him the indemnity for which he paid his money, we do not think the insurer can be heard in repudiation of the indemnity, on the ground of his agent's unskillfulness, carelessness or fraud. If this can be done it is easy to see that the community is at the mercy of these insurance agents, who will have little difficulty in a large proportion of the cases, in giving a worth-less policy for the money they receive. We have never seen reason to doubt the correctness of the decision in *Peoria Marine and Fire Ins. Co.* v. *Hall*, 12 Mich. 203, the principle of which governs the present case. Without undertaking to say that the answer to the ninth interrogatory as above given can be declared untrue, we think if it is so, and the policy for that reason, according to its terms, made void at its delivery, the agent, who had knowledge of all the facts, was chargeable also with knowledge of this invalidity; that the insurers are also chargeable with the knowledge possessed by their agent, and that consequently it was a fraud on their part to receive the premium moneys and deliver the policy without intending it should have effect under such circumstances. Such a fraud the law will not permit to be consummated, *but on the contrary will hold that when they delivered the policy, it was with the intention that it should take effect and that the insured should have the benefit from it for which he paid, and if there was any error or ambiguity in the application which their agent prepared, they must be held to have waived it."*[*]

[1] *Longhurst* v. *Star Ins. Co.*, 19 Iowa, 364.

[2] *Owens* v. *Holland Purchase Ins. Co.*, 56 N. Y. 565.

his authority is revoked, *who knows, or ought to know* the fact, derives no advantage therefrom; but in all cases it is a question of fact for the jury, whether the assured knew, or *ought* to have known, that the agent's authority had been revoked;[1] and if it is claimed that notice of the revocation was given, it must be such notice as clearly brings the fact to the mind of the assured. A simple direction, "remit (premiums) direct to home office," does not serve as notice that the agent's authority to receive premiums has been withdrawn.[2]

"A person," says ANDREWS, J., in the case last referred to, "who has dealt with an agent in a matter within his authority, has a right to assume, *if not otherwise informed*, that the authority continues; and when the dealing continues after the authority is revoked, the principal is nevertheless bound, *unless notice of the revocation is brought home to the other party ;*" and if the agent remains an agent for *any* purpose, the assured has a right to presume that he remains agent, with power to do all acts that he has previously been accustomed to do: and if his authority has been curtailed in *any* respect, the insurer must bring notice of the curtailment of authority home to the assured.[3]

In no case, *after* a loss, can a foreign insurance company revoke the authority of an agent so as to defeat the service of process upon it.[4]

Agent's clerk.

SEC. 409. Not only is the insurer responsible for the acts of its agent, but also for the acts of the agent's clerks, or any person to whom he delegates authority to discharge his functions for him.[5] Of course, the act must be done by some person authorized expressly, or impliedly by the agent, and under such circumstances that the insurer knew, or ought to have known that other persons would be employed by, and to act for the agent. In a New York case,[6] the question was whether the policy was renewed. The original policy was issued to the plaintiffs through John Whelp, who had been agent for the defendant for several years, and his name was indorsed upon the policy as such agent. His son, Charles Whelp, had, for three or four years, acted as his clerk and assistant in the business of his

---

[1] *McNeilley* v. *Continental, etc., Ins. Co.*, 66 N. Y. 23.

[2] *McNeilley* v. *Ins. Co., ante.*

[3] *McNeilley* v. *Ins. Co., ante.*

[4] *Michael* v. *Ins. Co. of Nashville*, 10 La. An. 737; 4 Ben. F. I. C. 29.

[5] *Houghton* v. *Ewbank*, 4 Camp. 88; *Niel* v. *Erving*, I Esp. 61; *Mound City Life Ins. Co.* v. *Heeth*, 49 Ala. 529.

[6] *Bodine* v. *Exchange Ins. Co.*, 51 N. Y. 566; 10 Am. Rep. 666.

agency. On the 10th of January, 1863, the day after the policy expired, Charles, acting for his father, called upon the company and obtained a renewal certificate for the plaintiffs for one year from January 18, 1863. He had been in the habit for three or four years of receiving such renewals from the company for a similar purpose, and frequently, with the knowledge of his father, delivered them to the parties for whom they were intended, without exacting payment of the premiums. There was a conflict of evidence as to what occurred at the time the renewal certificate in question was taken to the plaintiffs by Charles. Bodine, one of the plaintiffs, testified that Charles said he had brought to him (Bodine), a renewal of the exchange policy, and that the Excelsior company had refused to renew. The witness said he did not know about taking the renewal; if they did not renew, he would prefer putting it all into one company, as the plaintiffs had had some trouble in getting companies to take general policies. Charles said, "you had better take this." The witness said, "I will not decide now; I will think over it; I think I had better get into one company." "Well," said he, "will you remain uninsured?" The witness said, "I think I will for the present, at least, until I decide this question in my own mind." And he promised that if Charles would call the next day he would decide. He did call, and the witness decided. He told Charles he would take the renewal, and Charles should go on and get him a policy for the like amount, and bearing even date with the policy. Charles said, "Then you will take this?" The witness said, "Certainly." At another interview, Charles called for the Excelsior policy, and the witness gave it to him. He then tendered the witness the renewal in question, saying: "You had better take this renewal." The witness said, "It makes no difference Charles, you may as well keep it; it is just as safe in your custody as in mine; go on and get the other as soon as you can; bring it to me and I will pay you for them both together." Charles said, "The money makes no difference." The witness replied, "It is not for the want of money; it is a matter of no consequence; it is just as safe with you; when you get them both, bring them to me and I will pay you for them." He said, "Very well." This last conversation was on Saturday, and the fire occurred on the following Tuesday. After the fire, Charles Whelp delivered the certificate to his father, and the latter delivered it to the company.

Prior to the commencement of the suit, the plaintiffs tendered the amount of the premiums, claiming that the policy had been renewed.

At the close of the plaintiff's evidence, the defendant moved to dismiss the complaint, on the grounds : 1. That Charles Whelp was not the agent of the defendant; 2. That, if such agent, he was not authorized to deliver the renewal certificate without payment, or to make the arrangement claimed by the plaintiffs ; 3. That on the evidence, the defendant could not maintain an action against the plaintiffs for the premiums ; 4. That the evidence was insufficient to sustain the plaintiffs' alleged cause of action.

The court denied the motion, and the defendant excepted.

The judge charged the jury, among other things, as follows: " If you find that Mr. Whelp was agent of the defendant in this matter, and that he did agree with Mr. Bodine, at the third interview, that he would trust him for the amount of the premium * * until a future period; and if you find, also, that there was nothing said at that time about Bodine being his own insurer, then, so far as that part of the case is concerned, the plaintiffs would be entitled to your verdict in this action, if the other facts necessary to entitle them to recover are made out. (Exception.) If the company, through their agent, so conducted .the transaction that Mr. Bodine thought himself insured on the property to the amount of $3,000, and you believe Mr. Whelp was agent of the company, then the plaintiffs, if the other necessary facts as I have before charged are proved to your satisfaction, would be entitled to recover $3,000 at your hands, with interest after the expiration of sixty days, less $37.50, the amount of the premium. (Exception.) In order to make out the insurance, they must show that Whelp was agent of the company, acting for them, and that he waived the present payment of $37.50 premium. If they fail to establish that, the plaintiffs are not entitled to recover. If Mr. Whelp was an agent of this company, he was authorized to make the arrangement with the plaintiffs, which they say he did make; he had a right to trust the plaintiffs for $37.50, if he thought fit to do so. If he was not their agent, he had no right to do anything about the transaction." (Exception by the defendant.) The jury found a verdict for the plaintiffs.

EARL, C., said: " Notwithstanding the condition in the original policy, that no insurance, whether original or continued, should be considered binding until the actual payment of the premium, it was still competent for the insurance company to disregard this condition, and upon any renewal of the policy to waive by parol the payment in cash of the premium, and this waiver of payment could be shown by direct proof that credit was given or could be inferred from circumstances,

and the waiver could be by the company or any of its authorized
agents. This is too well settled to be longer the subject of discussion
or dispute. Goit v. The Nat. Protection Ins. Co., 25 Barb. 189; The
Trustees of First Bap. Church v. The Brooklyn F. Ins. Co., 19 N. Y.
305; Sheldon v. The Atlantic F. & M. Ins. Co., 26 id. 460; Wood v.
Poughkeepsie Mut. Ins. Co., 32 id. 619; Boehen v. Williamsburgh Ins.
Co., 35 id. 131. In the case from 19 N. Y., Judge COMSTOCK said: ' A
provision in a policy already executed and delivered, so as to bind the
company, declaratory of a condition that premiums must be paid in
advance, manifestly has no effect, except to impart convenient information to persons who may wish to be insured. As such a provision
in the policy in question could have no effect upon the delivered and
perfect contract in which it was contained, so it could have none to
prevent the same parties from making such future contract as they
pleased. In any subsequent agreement for a renewal or continuation
of the risk, it was competent for the parties to contract by parol and to
waive the payment in cash of the premium, substituting therefor a
promise to pay on demand or at a future day. Proof of such an agreement would have no tendency to contradict or to change the written
policy already in force between the parties, and which would be wholly
spent before the new agreement could take its place.' We must infer
that John Whelp had all the power of ordinary insurance agents. He
had acted for this company for nine or ten years in procuring risks for
it and in delivering policies and renewal certificates. His name was
indorsed upon the original policy as the company's agent. It was,
therefore, according to the decisions above cited, as competent for him
to waive the condition of prepayment as for any other officer or agent
of the company. But conceding this, it is claimed on the part of the
appellant that his son, Charles Whelp, had no authority to waive the
prepayment of the premium so as to bind the company. Charles had
been the clerk and assistant of his father for three or four years. He
had procured policies and renewal certificates from the company and
frequently delivered them to the persons insured, waiving prepayment
of the premiums. All this he did with the knowledge and assent of
his father, and hence we must infer that he was authorized by his
father to do it. The agency of John Whelp was not such as to require
his personal attention to all the details of the business intrusted to him.
We know, according to the ordinary course of business, that insurance
agents frequently have clerks to assist them; and that they could not
transact their business if obliged to attend to all the details in person,

44

and these clerks can bind their principals in any of the business which they are authorized to transact. An insurance agent can authorize his clerk to contract for risks, to deliver policies, to collect premiums and to take payment of premiums in cash or securities, and to give credit for premiums, or to demand cash; and the act of the clerk in all such cases is the act of the agent, and binds the company just as effectually as if it were done by the agent in person. The maxim of *delegatus non potest delegare* does not apply in such a case. Story on Agency, § 14. If the agent or his clerk waive the prepayment of premiums without authority from the company, it can lose nothing, as the agent becomes responsible for the amount of the premiums, as if the same had been paid to him in cash.

There is another reason for holding the company bound by the act of Charles Whelp in waiving prepayment of the premium. It delivered to him the renewal certificate, and thus clothed him with apparent authority to deliver the same to the assured. If he had delivered it to them without exacting payment of the premium, or saying anything about it, according to the cases above cited, it would have been inferred that prepayment was waived, and the company would have been bound. If his mere silent delivery would have had this effect, much more will his express waiver make the renewal effectual to bind the company.

There was some evidence tending to show that the plaintiffs accepted the certificate, and that it was arranged that Charles Whelp should hold it for them until a future day, when they would pay the premium. Hence the court committed no error in the refusal to dismiss the complaint, and in the charge to the jury."

In any event, it is within the power of the agent or the insurer, or both, to ratify the act of any person who assumes to act for them, and it is for the jury to say whether they have done so in such a manner as to bind them.[1]

A firm of two or more may be agents.—Effect of death of one.

Sec. 410. Where the agency of a company has been given to a firm, the death of one partner dissolves the agency, and when the assured *knows* the fact of such partner's death, he is bound at his peril to ascertain the powers of the surviving partner, before relying upon his acts,[2] and the same rule exists when the firm is dissolved.[3]

---

[1] *Buchanan* v. *Western Ins. Co.*, 5 Alb. L. J. 334; *Bently* v. *Columbian Ins. Co.*, 17 N. Y. 421; *Neal* v. *Irving*, 1 Esp. 61; *Richardson* v. *Anderson*, 1 Camp. 43 *n.*
[2] *Martine* v. *International, etc., Ins. Co.*, 62 Barb. (N. Y.) 181.
[3] *Green* v. *Miller*, 6 John. (N. Y.) 39; Story on Agency, Sec. 42.

CHAPTER XIII.

NOTICE AND PROOFS OF LOSS.

Compliance with requirements of contract must be shown.

Sec. 411. When the policy requires that certain proofs shall be made and conditions complied with, to establish a legal claim upon the company for a loss, all the conditions must be *substantially*, if not *strictly*, complied with, or no recovery can be had,[1] and this extends to furnishing

---

[1] Where a statement of loss declares, in accordance with the provisions of the insurance policy, the manner in which the building insured was occupied at the time of the loss, and it appears from such statement that the occupation was illegal, and, therefore, by the terms of the policy void, no action can be maintained upon such policy. If the statement is made under a mistake of fact, it may, *it seems*, be amended, but the action cannot be maintained until the amendatory statement is made. *Campbell* v. *Charter Oak, etc., Ins. Co.*, 10 Allen (Mass.) 213. A policy of insurance against fire provided that in case of loss the assured should

notice and proofs of loss in the manner, and specifically as provided. Thus, if the policy requires that proofs of loss shall be furnished, and that they shall contain certain specific information, as, a statement of the interest of the assured in the property;[1] the certificate of the nearest magistrate;[2] of a builder as to the value of the building, at the time of loss, or as to the cost of reinstatement, or both,[3] or any other specific information, it must be complied with fully, or, unless waived, no recovery can be had. In this connection it is proper to say that it is highly important that the provisions of a policy in this respect should be carefully examined, as, although it is much to be regretted, and probably does not materially aid insurance companies in securing strict justice at all times, yet they often insert useless and utterly impracticable conditions as to proofs of loss, and sometimes in such a manner and in such a place in the policy that the assured might think that certain of the conditions were not to be complied with, unless the company called for the information designated, when, *in fact,* the requirement is absolute, and a condition precedent to a recovery. This is quite often the case as to the clause requiring a builder's certificate. Generally, the insurer would not profit by such an omission

give immediate notice, and as soon as possible render, under oath, a particular account of such loss, "stating whether any and what other insurance has been made on the said property, giving copies of the written portions of all policies thereon." It was held that the furnishing of such copies was a condition precedent, without the performance of which (if not waived by the company) no recovery could be had on the policy. The affidavit of loss in this case showed that "there were three hundred dollars additional insurance made on the property: viz., a policy believed to be dated January 27, 1863, and numbered 6736, in the Mechanics' Mutual of Milwaukee, Wis., on the building;" and that the assured was unable to furnish a written copy thereof, because the policy had been mislaid, and the company had no record of the written part of it. Held, that this was not such a compliance with the condition precedent above stated, as to render the defendant liable. *Blakeley v. Phenix Ins. Co.,* 20 Wis. 205.

[1] *Shawmut Sugar, etc., Co.* v. *Peoples' Ins. Co.,* 12 Gray (Mass.) 535; 4 Ben. F. I. C. 357; *Edgerley* v. *Farmers' Ins. Co.,* 43 Iowa, 587.

[2] *Phœnix Ins. Co.* v. *Taylor,* 5 Minn. 492; *Mann* v. *Western Ins. Co.,* 19 U. C. (Q. B.) 190; *Germania F. Ins. Co.* v. *Curran,* 8 Kan. 9; *McMasters* v. *Westchester Ins. Co.,* 25 Wend. (N. Y.) 379; *Wright* v. *Hartford Ins. Co.,* 36 Wis. 522; *Columbian Ins. Co.* v. *Lawrence,* 10 Pet. (U. S.) 507; *Billbrough* v. *Metropolis Ins. Co.,* 5 Duer. (N. Y.) 587; *Bryne* v. *Rising Sun Ins. Co.,* 20 Ind. 103; *Basch* v. *Humboldt, etc., Ins. Co.,* 35 N. Y. 429; *Johnson* v. *Phœnix Ins. Co.,* 112 Mass. 47; *Moody* v. *Ætna Ins. Co.,* 2 Thomp. (N. S.) 173; *Langel* v. *Mut. Ins. Co.,* 17 U. C. (Q. B.) 524; *Oldman* v. *Berwicke,* 2 H. Bl. 577 n; *Protection Ins. Co.* v. *McPherson,* 5 Ind. 417; *Worsley* v. *Wood,* 6 T. R. 710; *Ætna Ins. Co.* v. *Tyler,* 16 Wend. (N. Y.) 385; *Cornell* v. *Hope Ins. Co.,* 15 Martin (La.) 223; *Mason* v. *Harvey,* 8 Excheq. 819; *Routledge* v. *Burrell,* 1 H. Bl. 254; *Roumage* v. *Mechanics' Ins. Co.,* 13 N. J. 110; *Noonan* v. *Hartford Ins. Co.,* 21 Mo. 81; *Fireman's Ins. Co.* v. *Crandall,* 33 Ala. 9; *Turly* v. *N. A. Ins. Co.,* 25 Wend. (N. Y.) 374; *Killips* v. *Putnam F. Ins. Co.,* 28 Wis. 472; *Van Deusen* v. *Charter Oak Ins. Co.,* 1 Rob. (N. Y.) 55; *Bailey* v. *Hope Ins. Co.,* 56 Me. 474; *O'Neil* v. *Buffalo F. Ins. Co.,* 3 N. Y. 122.

[3] *Fawcett* v. *Liverpool, etc., Ins. Co.,* 27 U. C. (Q. B.) 225.

on the part of the assured, as, unless the proofs were objected to upon that ground, the defect would be treated as waived, but instances might arise where the defect would be fatal, and great care should be used to comply substantially with the requirements of the policy in this respect, in the first instance.

As to time.

SEC. 412. When the policy requires that the proofs shall be made out and forwarded to the company within a certain specified time, as ten days,[1] thirty days,[2] sixty days,[3] three months,[4] or any other specified time, unless such proof is made within that time, or facts shown that establish a waiver of strict compliance, no recovery can be had. As to whether the requirements of the policy as to time, have been complied with, is, in cases where there is no dispute as to the fact, a question of law for the court, but in cases where the fact is in dispute, it is a question for the jury; and in all cases, as to whether or not the company has waived strict compliance with the conditions as to the time within which proof is to be made, is a mixed question of law and fact, of law, as to what amounts to a waiver, and of fact, as to whether the facts shown bring the plaintiff within its beneficial operation. When the policy requires that notice of loss shall be given within a reasonable time, the question as to what is a reasonable time, and as to whether the insured has complied with the provision of the policy, is a question for the jury in view of all the circumstances attending the loss, the facilities for communication, and all facts that tend to excuse delay or to fix *laches* in this respect upon the insured. But when notice of loss is required to be given *forthwith* or *at once*, these terms are not to be construed with absolute strictness, so as to require a literal compliance, but, reasonably, in view of the loss and the circumstances surrounding it.[5]

Who may make.

SEC. 413. Proofs of loss should be made as required by the policy, both as to substance and time, or a legal excuse shown therefor.[6] They

---

[1] *Dohn* v. *Farmers' Joint Stock Ins. Co.*, 5 Lans. (N. Y.) 275.

[2] *Planters' Mut. Ins. Co.* v. *Deford*, 38 Md. 382; *Troy Fire Ins. Co.* v. *Carpenter*, 4 Wis. 20.

[3] *Eastern R. R. Co.* v. *Relief Fire Ins. Co.*, 105 Mass. 170.

[4] *Cumberland Valley Mut. Protection Co.* v. *Schell*, 29 Penn. St. 31.

[5] *Edwards* v. *Baltimore Ins. Co.*, 3 Gill. (Md.) 176; 2 Ben. F. I. C. 405; *Wightman* v. *Western, etc., Ins. Co.*, 8 Rob. (La.) 432; 2 Ben. F. I. C. 330; *St. Louis Ins. Co.* v. *Kyle*, 11 Mo. 278; 2 Ben. F. I. C. 641.

[6] *Smith* v. *Haverhill, etc., Ins. Co.*, 1 Allen (Mass.) 297. In an action upon a policy the declaration or complaint must allege that all conditions precedent to

should be made either by the assured himself, his agent, or the
party in interest. If the assured himself does not make the proofs, a
valid reason therefor should be shown ;[1] and it is sufficient to show that
he is a non-resident,[2] dead,[3] or was absent or insane at the time when the
loss occurred, and did not return in season to make the proofs;[4] or
that he did not possess the necessary information in reference to
the matters required to be stated to make the proofs;[5] or that the

a right of recovery have been complied with, or an excuse therefor; and where
a policy requires that proofs of loss must be made in thirty days after the loss,
unless the declaration or complaint alleges a performance of such condition, or a
waiver thereof, it is bad, on demurrer. *Home Ins. Co.* v. *Lindsey*, 26 Ohio St. 74.

[1] *Kernochan* v. *New York Bowery Ins. Co.*, 17 N. Y. 428 ; *Barnes* v. *Union, etc.,
Ins. Co.*, 45 N. H. 21.

[2] *Ayres* v. *Hartford Ins. Co.*, 17 Iowa, 176.

[3] *Farmers' Mut. Ins. Co.* v. *Grayhill*, 74 Penn. St. 17.

[4] *O'Connor* v. *Hartford F. Ins. Co.*, 31 Wis. 160 ; *N. W. Ins. Co.* v. *Atkins*, 3
Bush. (Ky.) 328 ; *Sims* v. *State Ins. Co.*, 47 Mo. 54.

[5] In *Sims* v. *State Ins. Co.*, 47 Mo. 54 ; 4 Am. Rep. 312, BLISS, J., in commenting
upon this matter, said : "The assured was required by the policy to give notice
forthwith, and within three days to send to the office of the company a particular account of the loss, signed and sworn to by the assured. Notice was at
once given, and an agent of the company appeared upon the ground, produced
the usual blank for making the proofs, and giving the "particular account" of
the loss, which was filled up under his directions, and sworn to by E. W. Sims, as
agent for the insured. This, it was claimed, was not a compliance with this
requirement of the policy, but the court held otherwise. There is no doubt that,
under policies with such a requirement, it is the duty of the assured to furnish a
sworn certificate of loss ; and the performance of such a duty is a condition precedent to a recovery. *Col. Ins. Co.* v. *Lawrence*, 10 Pet. 507; *Noonan* v. *Hartford Ins. Co.*, 21 Mo. 81. The special objection to the certificate, as furnished,
arises from the fact that it was sworn to by his agent, and not by the assured
himself. Under ordinary circumstances, I should deem this a fatal objection, for
it may with propriety be said that the owner is supposed to know not only his
own loss, but also any secret reason why he should not be paid. The company
contracted that he should take the responsibility of the oath, and if he was the
one with whom they had personally dealt, who had knowledge of the matter, he
would be bound to assume such responsibility. But to insist on it in this case,
would involve a defeat of the policy altogether. The insured was a resident of
St. Louis, and the property was in Carroll county, under the exclusive management and control of the agent. The policy was obtained by the agent, the application was made and signed by him, the premium note was executed by him ; he
had other policies in the same company, obtained also as agent; in his whole
correspondence with the company at their home office, and in his interviews with
their agents, he acted as agent for the insured, and it does not appear that the
latter was known to the officers of the company, or knew anything about the
policies, or whether he had any. Under these circumstances, if the proof is not
to be made by this agent it cannot be made at all ; and the position assumed by
counsel places the officers of the company in the attitude of issuing policies and
receiving premiums, knowing, from the nature of the case, that no legal proof
could be made of the losses if they should occur. We will not place them in that
position, but, on the other hand, hold that proof and certificate made by the man
with whom they had all their dealings, who was in sole possession of the property insured, and who alone knew the facts necessary to be embodied in the
paper—who, in fact, was, as it were, insured as agent—is a compliance with this
requirement of the policy. *Ayres* v. *Hartford Ins. Co.*, 17 Iowa, 176. If we
thought otherwise, we could not hold the policy forfeited for that defect, for the
reason that the company received the certificate, made no objection to it upon

person making the proofs is the party in interest, to whom the loss, with the assent of the insurers, is made payable;[1] or is the real party is interest, and that the assured refused to execute them;[2] or that they were made as directed by the insurers' agent;[3] or that the objection as to their being made by the wrong person, has been waived.[4] Thus, it will be seen that even when the policy requires that "all persons sustaining loss by fire are forthwith to give notice thereof to the company, and as soon after as possible to give a particular account of it, *signed and verified by insured*," the proofs may be made by an agent,[5] by an executor,[6] by the real party in interest,[7] or even by a creditor of the assured, under certain circumstances;[8] but proofs signed by a person who has no authority from the assured, express or implied. are not sufficient, unless adopted by him;[9] but a person who has the custody of the property and the entire management, is a proper person, in the absence of the assured, to make such proofs,[10] as the wife, when the husband is absent, when she has been left in charge of the same;[11] but where the assured himself can make the necessary proofs he should do so, or a sufficient excuse for the failure must be given.

Notice of loss—to whom may be given—by whom—when in time—waiver of.

SEC. 414. Notice of loss, when required to be given "forthwith," "immediately," etc., is in time, *if given with due diligence in view of all the circumstances.*[12]

---

that account until the case came on to trial, long after the thirty days had expired; and, when payment was refused, placed the refusal upon other grounds. *St. Louis Ins. Co.* v. *Kyle*, 11 Mo. 278; *Phillips* v. *Protective Ins. Co.*, 14 id. 220; *Ayres* v. *Hartford Ins. Co., supra; Taylor* v. *Merchants' F. Ins. Co.*, 9 How. (U. S.) 300."

[1] *Keeler* v. *Niagara F. Ins. Co.*, 16 Wis. 532; *Barnes* v. *Union Ins. Co.*, 45 N. H. 21.

[2] *Pratt* v. *N. Y. Cent. Ins. Co.*. 55 N. Y. 505.

[3] *Pratt* v. *N. Y. Cent. Ins. Co., ante; Frost* v. *Saratoga, etc., Ins. Co.*, 5 Den. (N. Y.) 54; *Sims* v. *State Ins. Co.*, 47 Mo. 54.

[4] *Kernochan* v. *N. Y. Bowery Ins. Co., ante; Walker* v. *Met. Ins. Co.*, 57 Me. 281; *Bailey* v. *Hope Ins. Co.*, 56 id. 474.

[5] *Sims* v. *State Ins. Co., ante; O'Connor* v. *Hartford Ins. Co., ante; Ayres* v. *Hartford Ins. Co., ante.*

[6] *Farmers' Ins. Co.* v. *Graybill, ante.*

[7] *Keeler* v. *Niagara F. Ins. Co., ante; Pratt* v. *N. Y. Cent. Ins. Co.*

[8] *N. W. Ins. Co.* v. *Atkins,* 3 Bush. (Ky.) 328.

[9] *Ayres* v. *Hartford Ins. Co.*, 17 Iowa, 176.

[10] *Sims* v. *State Ins. Co., ante.*

[11] *O'Connor* v. *Hartford Ins. Co., ante.*

[12] *Edwards* v. *Lycoming Ins. Co.*, 78 Penn. St. 378; *Cashaw* v. *N. W. Ins. Co.*, 5 Biss. (U. S.) 476; *St. Louis Ins. Co.* v. *Kyle*, 11 Mo. 278; *Beatty* v. *Lycoming Ins. Co.*, 66 Penn. St. 9; *Peoria M. & F. Ins. Co.* v. *Lewis*, 18 Ill. 553. In *New*

Where a policy requires that notice of a loss shall be given *to the secretary* " forthwith," *due diligence under all the circumstances* is meant, and notice given to *an agent* is not a compliance with the condition.[1] And eleven days has been held not in time;[2] eighteen days,[3] fifteen days,[4] four months,[5] thirty-eight days,[6] one month,[7] twenty days,[8] eleven days.[9] But, where notice is simply required to be given to the company, notice to an agent is sufficient.[10] What might be deemed

---

York Central Ins. Co. v. *National Protection Ins. Co.*, 20 Barb. (N. Y.) 468, the fire occurred on the 15th day of June, and was not known to the assured until the 18th. Upon the 23d he notified the defendant insurer by mail. The policy required the notice to be given *forthwith*, and this was held a compliance therewith. The only question is, in such cases, whether there is a *reasonable excuse* for delay, and in all cases where the delay is *prima facie* unreasonable, the assured must show a proper excuse for delay, and the jury are to say whether such excuse is reasonable. *Edwards* v. *Baltimore Ins. Co.*, 3 Gill. (Md.) 176; *St. Louis Ins. Co.* v. *Kyle*, 11 Mo. 278. In *Kingsley* v. *N. E. Mut. F. Ins. Co.*, 8 Cush. (Mass.) 393, the loss occurred on the 5th day of August, 1849. On the 8th of August, notice of loss was sent by mail, and the president of the defendant company visited the ruins. On the 19th of February, 1850, more than *six months* after the loss, proofs of loss, including the magistrate's certificate, were sent. The by-laws required that notice of loss should be given "forthwith," and, as soon thereafter as practicable, that the assured should furnish the office with a particular account of the loss. In *West Branch Ins. Co.* v. *Halfenstein*, 40 Penn. St. 289, the fire occurred October 4th. The insured went the next day to see. The local agent was absent, but notice was given as soon as he returned on the 8th of October, the agent sending notice by mail, and the court held this to be a compliance with the condition requiring notice to be given forthwith. The defendants claimed that the conditions of the policy in this respect had not been complied with, and the plaintiff offered no proof to excuse delay. A verdict was rendered for the plaintiff, which was sustained upon appeal, it appearing that the by-laws were not made a part of the policy, and the court holding that the furnishing of proofs of loss, was not, therefore, a condition precedent to recovery. In *Providence Life Ins. Co.* v. *Martin*, 32 Md. 310, the policy required notice to be given as soon as possible in writing. The assured was killed July 21, and within a week thereafter his wife reported the death to the agent, who, at the time of the death, was absent from home, and made the necessary proof. Held, a compliance with the policy. In *Provident Ins. Co.* v. *Baum*, 29 Md. 236, the policy stipulated for notice of death "as soon thereafter as possible." The assured died of a gunshot wound, and notice might have been given the next day, but it was shown that the policy was in the assured's trunk, and was not seen till eight days after his death, when proofs were duly made and sent to the insurer. It was held a substantial compliance.

[1] *Edwards* v. *Lycoming Ins. Co.*, 75 Penn. St. 378. A condition that notice of loss be given "forthwith," is satisfied by due diligence. Notice mailed on the 23d, of a fire on the 15th, of which the insured knew on the 18th—held sufficient. *N. Y. Central Ins. Co.*, v. *National Protection Ins. Co.*, 20 Barb. (N. Y.) 468; *Inman* v. *Western F. Ins. Co.*, 12 Wend. (N. Y.) 452.

[2] *Trask* v. *Ins. Co.*, 29 Penn. St. 198.

[3] *Edwards* v. *Lycoming, etc., Ins. Co., ante.*

[4] *Roper* v. *Lendon*, 1 El. & El. 825.

[5] *McEvers* v. *Lawrence*, Hoff. Ch. (N. Y.) 172.

[6] *Inman* v. *Western F. Ins. Co.*, 12 Wend. (N. Y.) 452.

[7] *Cornell* v. *Milwaukee, etc., Ins. Co.*, 18 Wis. 387.

[8] *Whitehurst* v. *N. C. Mut. Ins. Co.*, 7 Jones (N. C.) 433.

[9] *Trask* v. *State F. & M. Ins. Co.*, 29 Penn. St. 198.

[10] *People's Ins. Co.* v. *Spencer*, 53 Penn. St. 353; *Kendall* v. *Holland Purchase Ins. Co.*, 2 T. & C. (N. Y.) 375; *Newman* v. *Springfield F. & M. Ins. Co.*, 17 Minn. 123; *Marsden* v. *City, etc., Ins. Co.*, L. R., 1 C. P. 232.

sufficient or reasonable notice of loss in one case might not be so regarded in another. In every case, the conditions of the policy and the circumstances that tend to excuse delay are to be considered, and the jury are to say from the facts established whether there was a sub. stantial compliance with the conditions of the policy; and, in determining this question, the facilities for communication, the presence or absence of the assured at the place where the fire occurred at the time when it occurred, the time when he became aware of the loss, etc., are all important elements. Thus, where the policy required that notice be given forthwith, and the fire occurred on Saturday, and notice thereof was given to the agent of the assured, twelve miles distant, the same day, and by him sent to the company, seventy miles away, reaching the insurer in five days after the fire, it was held a *substantial* compliance.[1] So, where notice was given within forty-eight hours.[2] The particular circumstances of each case are to be considered, and the jury are to say whether there has been a substantial compliance.[3] Thus, where the assured, a day or two after the loss,

---

[1] *West Branch Ins. Co.* v. *Halfenstein*, 40 Penn. St. 289 ; *Continental Ins. Co.* v. *Lippold*, 3 Neb 391 ; *Ward* v. *Law Property Assurance, etc., Co.;* 4 W. R. 605.

[2] *Germania Ins. Co.* v. *Curran*, 8 Kan. 9.

[3] It is a question for the jury whether a waiver has been shown, and, unless their verdict is clearly against the evidence, it will be upheld. *Swan* v. *Liverpool, London & Globe Ins. Co.*, 52 Miss. 704 ; *Edwards* v. *Baltimore F. Ins. Co.*, 3 Gill (Md.) 176 ; *Davis* v. *Western Mass. Ins. Co.*, 8 R. I. 277. This rule was forcibly illustrated in *Charleston Ins. Co.* v. *Neve*, 2 McMull. (S. C.) 237 ; 2 Ben. F. I. C. 154, in which an action of assumpsit was brought on a policy made by the Charleston Ins. and Trust Co. The amount insured was $2,000, and the property insured was described in the policy as " stock groceries and liquors, contained in the two story wooden house, with shingle roof, situated at No. 31 State street, and occupied by the assured in the grocery business, as described in the offer, No. 1983, filed in this office." It appeared that this store, which was a grocery and liquor store, had belonged to C. F. Kohnke ; that in May, 1839 (the precise day was not fixed in evidence), Kohnke had sold out the stock to William Neve for the sum of $2,200, and of this sum $1,200 were paid in cash, and to secure the balance Neve confessed a judgment in favor of C. F. Kohnke for $1,000. The confession of judgment appears to have been entered up in the office of the clerk of the court of common pleas for Charleston district, the same day that the policy was executed. At the time of the execution of the policy by the defendant, permission was granted to Neve to assign the policy to C. F. Kohnke. A day or two after the date of the policy, Kohnke, being about to leave this country, placed the policy in the hands of John Klinck, who seems to have been his agent. There was no assignment of the policy, in writing, from Neve to Kohnke, at the time it was delivered to Kohnke. The assignment which is now on the policy was written subsequently to the commencement of the suit. The sale from Kohnke to Neve was an absolute sale, and Kohnke seems to have retained no interest in the stock, except through his confession of judgment. In November, 1840, Neve applied for insurance on the stock in the same store, to Alexander Robinson, agent for the Columbia Insurance Company. They could not agree as to the rate of premium, and no insurance was at that time effected. The first day of January, 1841, Neve again applied to Mr. Robinson for insurance. Mr. Robinson exhibited some surprise, and asked him if he had been his own underwriter, and asked him, also, if there was any other insurance on the property ? Neve told Robinson that there

called at the defendants' office and told them that he had been burned
out, and the agent of the insurer was seen examining the ruins before

---

was no other insurance on the property, and after an examination of the premises,
Robinson, as the agent of the Columbia Company, insured the stock. The policy
of the Columbia Insurance Company described the property insured as follows:
"A stock of groceries, liquors, wines, etc., contained in the two story wooden
building, with shingle roof, and in the cellar, No. 31 State street, Charleston,
occupied by him (William Neve) in the grocery business and as a residence." On
the night of the 25 h of April, 1840, the building and entire stock was consumed
by fire, and on the 28th, the next day, Neve rendered in a statement to the
defendants of his loss, amounting in the aggregate to $6,500. The same day on
which Neve rendered his statement to the defendants, or soon after, Mr. Moise,
who was the legal advisor of Kohnke, and in whose possession the policy had
been placed by Mr. Klinck the day after the fire, went to the office of the defendants, and gave to the president, Mr. Street, notice of the claim of Kohnke, and
seemed to have inquired as to the intention of the company, for Mr. Street
informed him that he would prefer to submit the matter to the board of directors
before he would give an answer. The next day, or soon after, Mr. Moise called
again, and Mr. Street then informed him that the company declined paying the
amount, because Neve had effected a second insurance, and because the directors
believed thrt the premises had been fired by Neve, or some objection similar in
substance, and manifesting that they supposed Neve had not acted fairly in the
matter. Nothing further passed between the parties, and soon after this action
was commenced for the present plaintiff.

For the defendants, several objections were urged; among others, that there
had been no compliance with the eleventh condition of the policy; that no certificate, as is required by the terms of that condition, had been proved to have
been submitted to the defendants; that a strict compliance with this was in the
nature of a condition precedent, and without proving performance, there could
be no cause of action. BUTLER, J., before whom the cause was tried at circuit,
said: "I regarded a compliance on the part of the plaintiff with the eleventh condition in the policy as a condition precedent, and that the defendants had a right
to require a certificate from a clergyman or justice of the quorum, stating that
he believed the property insured had been destroyed accidentally or without
criminal design by the plaintiff. No such certificate was produced on the trial.
The certificate of one Jeffries was produced, who was not proved to be, nor was
he, I believe, either a clergyman or justice of the quorum. From the fact that
plaintiff was advertised by plea of the defendant that such certificate was required,
it might be inferred that he could not produce one, for I am inclined to think
that he would have regarded it as a sufficient compliance with the condition if the
proper certificate had been produced at the trial. Although this preliminary
proof was necessary to subject the insurance company to liability, it was, nevertheless, in their power to waive it, and to rely exclusively on other grounds of
defense; and it was contended, on the part of the plaintiff, that such evidence
had been waived when the policy was presented for payment. This depended
entirely upon what Mr. Street said to Mr. Moise. Mr. Moise seemed to have
regarded it as a waiver, as the proof was not insisted on at the time, and it may
have been so. *When, however, the agent of the company said that his refusal to
pay was founded on the belief that Neve had fired his own house as well as that
he had effected a double insurance, it seemed to me* (and I said so the jury) *it was
not a waiver of any evidence that was requisite to satisfy the company that the
house was not burnt by design.* As I observed by adjudicated cases that *this is
always a question of fact to be submitted to a jury,* I submitted this to the finding of the Jury. *What is, or is not a waiver of preliminary proof, must depend
on circumstances and the language used at the time.* In general, I think it is right
that the company should insist on the proof at the time the policy is presented
for payment after the loss." The jury found for the plaintiff, and upon this point
the verdict was sustained. It will be noticed that, in this instance, the finding of
the jury was contrary to the views of the court as to the legal effect of the evidence. But the supreme court held that their verdict was conclusive, and also
that the facts proved established a waiver.

the fire was completely extinguished, and notice *in writing*, as required by the policy, was not given for twenty days after the loss, it was held that, under the circumstances, the assured had exercised due diligence.[1]

When the policy requires notice of the loss to be given *in writing*, it is not necessary that it should be given by the insured himself. *It is sufficient if the notice is given by the agent of the insurer even, if it is given at the request of the assured*, although the insurer does not know that it was given *for* the insured.[2] Thus, where the policy required that notice of loss should be given in writing by the assured, it was held that written notice from the local agent of the insurers, from information communicated to him by the assured, was a sufficient compliance with the terms of the policy.[3]

The fact that the company *knows* of the loss does not excuse the giving of notice. The conditions must be strictly complied with, unless waived;[4] but the fact of its knowledge of the loss may tend to excuse *delay* in the giving of the notice, but not in giving notice in the form stipulated for.[5] *Unless notice is waived by the insurer, it must be given;* and, if *written* notice is called for by the policy, *verbal* notice is not a compliance, unless this special requirement has been waived.[6]

---

[1] *Phillips* v. *Protection Ins. Co.*, 14 Mo. 220.

[2] *Stimpson* v. *Monmouth, etc., Ins. Co.*, 47 Me. 379.

[3] *West Branch Ins. Co.* v. *Halfenstein*, 40 Penn. St. 289.

[4] *Woodfin* v. *Asheville, etc., Ins. Co.*, 9 Jones (N. C.) 558; *Edwards* v. *Lycoming Ins. Co.*, 75 Penn. St 378.

[5] *Cornell* v. *Milwaukee, etc., Ins. Co., ante.* An insurance company, after notice of the fire, by letter from the insured, five or six days after it had occurred, sent an agent to investigate the loss, etc., who was authorized by them to offer a compromise, which he did. Another agent, by authority of the company, offered to settle the loss. Afterwards, upon the trial, the defense was set up that the notice was not sent " forthwith," as required by the policy. Held, that the company had, by their acts, waived the objection, and were estopped from setting it up on the trust. *Lycoming Ins. Co.* v. *Schreffler*, 42 Penn. St. 188.

[6] *Boyle* v. *N. C. Ins. Co.*, 7 Jones (N. C.) 373; *Cornell* v. *Milwaukee, etc., Ins. Co., ante.* In *Eastern R. R.* v. *Relief, etc., Ins. Co.*, 98 Mass. 420, the plaintiffs were insured "on their liability for loss and damage by fire, occasioned by sparks of locomotives, to property of others, situate on lands not owned or occupied by assured," and, by the printed clauses in the policy, the insurance company agreed to make good "all such loss, not exceeding the sum insured, as shall happen by fire to the property as above specified, during one year, the said loss to be estimated according to the actual cash value of said property at the time the same shall happen, and to be paid within sixty days after due notice and proof thereof, in conformity with conditions annexed to the policy." One of the conditions required notice to the company within sixty days after the loss. It was held that the railroad company could not await the result of suits and claims against the company by the owners of property lost or destroyed, but must furnish, within sixty days, notice and proof of loss to the company. But, in this case, it was also held that compliance with the conditions of the policy might be waived, even by an agent of the company, and the treasurer of the plaintiff having informed the

But, when the assured has *attempted* to comply with the requirement as to notice, and the insurer examines the loss and refuses
to pay *upon other grounds*, and does not object to the sufficiency of
the notice, strict compliance is waived.[1] So, when the insurer sends
an agent to examine the loss, and he says or does anything that indicates that notice is unnecessary, it is a waiver of notice.[2] *Any notice
that induces the company to examine the loss* is enough,[3] but, when the
notice is *in fact* too late, and compliance is not waived, it is fatal to a
recovery.[4] In a recent case in New York,[5] the policy provided that

defendant's agent that they were having numerous fires, and were investigating
the losses, and the agent having replied, "All right; when you get them all in,
send them in and they shall be attended to," or words to that effect, it was held a
waiver.

[1] *Clark* v. *N. E. Mut. Ins. Co.*, 6 Cush. (Mass.) 342 ; *Lumpkin* v. *Ontario, etc.,
Ins. Co.*, 12 U. C. (Q. B.) 578.

[2] *Schenck* v. *Mercer Co. Mut. Ins. Co.*, 24 N. J. 447. In *Lycoming Ins. Co.* v.
Schreffler, 42 Penn. St. 188, the policy required notice to be given *forthwith*. The
insured did not give notice of the loss until six days after. The insurers then
sent an agent to examine the loss and offer a compromise, and it was held that
this was a waiver of the breach as to notice, if any existed. In *Clark* v. *N. E.
Mut. Ins. Co.*, 6 Cush. (Mass.) 342, the insured was required to give notice in
writing within thirty days. Notice was not given at all by the insured, but the
agent of the company notified it the next day, and the president came on and
examined the loss and refused to pay at all, but making no question as to notice.
This was held a waiver of notice, FLETCHER, J., saying: "The refusal to pay the
loss was not put on the ground of any defect or insufficiency in the notice. No
objection was taken at that time to the form of the notice, no further or more
particular information was requested, but the defendants declined to pay the loss
altogether, and that, within the thirty days after the loss, and of course before
the expiration of the time allowed the plaintiff to give notice. This conduct on
the part of the defendants, upon any sound and just principle of fair dealing,
must be regarded as a waiver of any further or different notice. *Heath* v. *Franklin Ins. Co.*, 1 Cush. (Mass.) 257 ; *Vose* v. *Robinson*, 9 John. (N. Y.) 192 ; *McMasters* v. *Westchester County Mut. Ins. Co.*, 25 Wend. 379 ; *Ætna F. Ins. Co.* v.
Tyler, 16 Wend. (N. Y.) 385. The principle of waiver is a recognized and well-
settled principle, and applies with much force to the present case." *Underhill* v.
Agawam Ins. Co., 6 Cush. (Mass.) 440 ; *Inland Ins. Co.* v. *Stauffer*, 33 Penn. St.
397 ; *Com. Ins. Co.* v. *Sennett*, 41 id. 161. In *Drake* v. *Farmers' Union Ins. Co.*,
3 Grant's Cas. (Penn.) 325, notice was required to be given forthwith in writing.
No written notice was given, but an agent of the company residing near the fire
had immediate notice thereof. The president of the company and one of the
directors visited the place a few days after the fire and examined the loss. Afterwards, the claim was rejected for want of written notice, but the court held that
it was for the jury to say whether there had been a waiver.

[3] *Ins. Co. of N. America* v. *McDowell*, 50 Ill. 120. In *West Rockingham, etc.,
Ins. Co.* v. *Sheets*, 26 Gratt. (Va.) 854, one of the members of a firm wrote the
president of the company two days after the fire, informing him of the loss, and
what would have to be done by the company, and the company proceeded to act
upon it, and it was held that the fact that the notice was not signed by the firm,
or sent to the company as required by the rules of the company, did not operate
to defeat the plaintiff's claim, upon the ground that no notice of loss had been
given, as, by acting upon the letter *as* a notice, and treating it as such, the company waived formal notice.

[4] *Patrick* v. *Farmers' Ins. Co.*, 43 N. H. 621 ; *Beatty* v. *Lycoming Ins. Co.*, 66
Penn. St. 9.

[5] *Brink* v. *Hanover F. Ins. Co.*, decided by Ct. of Appeals, June 5th, 1877, and
not yet reported.

the assured should furnish proofs of loss as soon after the loss "*as pos-sible.*" The court held that this required *reasonable diligence* on the part of the assured, and a loss occurring, November 23d, and the assured being, in the exercise of reasonable diligence, able to complete his proofs upon the 8th of January, *that he was bound, upon their com-pletion, to send them at once,* and having withheld them until February 16th, it was held that he had failed to comply with the conditions of the policy, and could not recover. The court also held that, as to what is "a reasonable time" in which to send proofs, the facts being admit-ted, is a question of law, and only becomes a question for the jury, *when the facts are disputed, or there is evidence tending to excuse delay.*

Where the policy required notice of loss to be given *forthwith,* it has been held that the examination of the assured the next morning after the fire and taking his statement, by the agent of the assured, who transmitted it to the secretary, was sufficient.[1]

When the time limited in the policy for making proof of loss has elapsed, nothing short of *an express agreement* on the part of the insurer will renew or revivify the contract,[2] but where the company's agent has notice of the loss within the time, and upon being informed that proofs of loss may not be made within the time, and he says it will make no difference, and subsequently, but long after the time limited for making them has expired, but within a *reasonable* time, in view of the circumstances, they are made and forwarded to the com-pany, who, after keeping them for ten days, returned them, it was held that strict compliance with the requirements of the policy was waived, and the proofs having been made *within a reasonable time,* in view of the facts, a recovery could be had.[3] So, generally, when the delay in making proofs is due to the acts of the company or its agent, strict compliance as to time is waived.[4]

Notice should be given by the assured, his agent, or the person to whom, *by the consent of the company,* the loss is payable,[5] and must be

---

[1] *Beatty* v. *Lycoming, etc., Ins. Co.,* 66 Penn. St. 9.

[2] *Beatty* v. *Lycoming Ins. Co.,* 66 Penn. St. 9. A waiver cannot be predicated when a statement made to the assured long after the time for filing proofs of loss had elapsed, that the company would do what was right about it, that they knew at the time of the fire that it was their loss, etc. *Smith* v. *Haverhill, etc., Ins. Co.,* 1 Allen (Mass.) 297.

[3] *Owen* v. *Farmers' Ins. Co.,* 57 Barb. (N. Y.) 518.

[4] *Dohn* v. *Farmers' Ins. Co.,* 5 Lans. (N. Y.) 275.

[5] *Cornell* v. *LeRoy,* 9 Wend. (N. Y.) 163; *Sims* v. *State Ins. Co., ante; Barnes* v. *Union Mut. F. Ins. Co.,* 45 N. H. 21; *Stimpson* y. *Monmouth Mut. F. Ins. Co.,* 47 Me. 379.

such as apprises the company of the loss and gives it an opportunity of examining the same if desired.[1]

It has been held in one case that where the policy requires that the assured shall "*deliver in*" to the company a particular account of the loss, proof that such proof was deposited in the post-office properly directed and postpaid, was not a compliance with the conditions of the policy, although the policy elsewhere provided that "all communications must be postpaid, and directed to the secretary."[2] But it is hardly believed that this would be now held, as, in the construction of the policy and its various conditions, the evident *intent and purpose* of the parties is to be looked to, and, as is the case with insurance companies, that they are generally located at a great distance from the insured, frequently doing business in all the States as well as in foreign countries, hundreds and often thousands of miles away from the home office, it cannot reasonably be supposed that they expected or intended that the assured should, in person, or even by an agent, *deliver in* the proofs of loss, but that he should execute them with due diligence and with equal diligence send them to the company by mail, which is now the principal medium through which the commercial business of the world is transacted. A contrary rule gives undue force to arbitrary conditions and jeopardizes too seriously the interests of the assured.[3]

The waiver must either be express, or must result from such acts and conduct, on the part of the insurer, as operate as an estoppel against a defense predicated upon the ground of a failure to comply with the condition on the part of the assured, and in *all cases* the question is for the jury whether compliance was waived, and must result from acts done *before* the forfeiture, because of such breach attached.[4]

---

[1] *Rix* v. *Mutual Ins. Co.*, 20 N. H. 198.

[2] *Hodgkins* v. *Montgomery County, etc., Ins. Co.*, 34 Barb. (N. Y.) 213.

[3] *Stimpson* v. *Monmouth Ins. Co.*, 47 Me. 379; *Caston* v. *Monmouth, etc., Ins. Co.*, 54 id. 176; *Bartlett* v. *Union M. F. Ins. Co.*, 49 Me. 500; *Bunstead* v. *Dividend Mut. Ins. Co.*, 12 N. Y. 81; *Lycoming, etc., Ins. Co.* v. *Updegraff*, 40 Penn. St. 311.

[4] In *Underwood* v. *Farmers', etc., Ins. Co.*, 57 N. Y. 500, EARL, C., very ably elucidated the doctrine and the rule applicable in such cases. He said: "Upon the trial, the judge submitted to the jury but one question of fact, to wit: whether the plaintiff himself set fire to the barn insured; and charged them to render a verdict for the plaintiff if they found that question in his favor. To this portion of the charge defendant's counsel excepted. It is not disputed that it was, by the policy, a condition precedent to plaintiff's right of recovery that he should deliver to the company a verified account, in writing, of his loss, within ten days after the loss. This condition was part of the contract of insurance; and effect should be fairly given to it as to every other part of the contract. It is undisputed that no account of the loss was delivered to the defendant or any of its agents until about one month after the loss. But the judge, at the trial,

When the insurer has done nothing to induce delay on the part of
assured in complying with the condition, the policy is invalidated, and

---

held, as matter of law, upon the evidence, that this condition had been waived
by the defendant, and hence, that non-compliance with it on the part of the
plaintiff did not defeat the action. It therefore becomes necessary to examine
the evidence upon the question. The plaintiff testified that, on Monday after the
fire, which was on Friday night, he called upon one Selover, who was the agent
of the defendant by whom the insurance was effected, and informed him of the
fire, and asked him what he should do ; and he told him to wait until the general
agent came, and said that he would write to the general agent, and promised
that he and the general agent would, in a few days, call upon him and make
affidavits and straighten the matter up; that in about a month they came to
him, and the general agent drew up an affidavit, which he verified, giving an
account of the loss, and they took it ; that they then left him, saying that, upon
their return, they would straighten the matter up; that they returned in the
afternoon of the same day and talked with the plaintiff, but did not adjust or pay
the loss. The plaintiff also proved that, about three weeks after this interview
with the general agent, he caused another account of the loss to be drawn up
and verified and sent to the secretary of the company, by whom it was returned
with a notification that it was rejected, because it was not made and delivered
within the time required by the policy. This was the first notification received
by the plaintiff that he was in default for not delivering the verified account of
his loss in time. Such is the case made by plaintiff upon this question; and if
this had been all the evidence I think the judge might well have held, as matter
of law, that the condition in question had been waived. Selover was the local
agent of the company who effected the insurance. The proof does not show what
his precise powers were, but he testified that he had been allowed to adjust and
pay losses without first consulting the company, and that he had taken a large
amount of insurance for it; and he seems to have acted for the company in reference to this loss, with its knowledge and sanction. It is proper, therefore, to
hold that the company would be bound by what he said and did in reference to
settling and paying this loss, as detailed in the evidence of the plaintiff. This
agent. when informed of the fire and asked by the plaintiff what to do, told him
to wait until the general agent came, and that he and the general agent would
be along in a few days and draw the affidavit and straighten the matter up. The
plaintiff had the right to infer from this that he had nothing more to do until the
general agent came, and that his affidavit giving an account of his loss would
then be drawn, and be in time. But the most material part of this evidence is
contradicted. Selover testified that plaintiff called upon him at the time mentioned, and notified him of the fire; that after inquiring as to the circumstances
of the fire and expressing his suspicions about it, he told him that he would call
and look the matter over during the week, and if he found it fair and square the
company would pay; if otherwise, not. He denied that he said a word about
the general agent, or about making out the papers, or that he promised to make
them out. He testified that on the Thursday following—less than a week from
the time of the fire—he did call upon the plaintiff in reference thereto ; told him
that the matter looked bad; that he was accused of burning the barn, and that
he must accout for his whereabouts on the night of the fire, before the company
would pay ; that, in about four weeks after this, he and the general agent called
upon the plaintiff and asked him to go to a justice of the peace and make an
affidavit, as the matter looked suspicious, and they wanted to pry into it; that
he went with them and made the affidavit, which, although not literally, was
substantially, except as to time, a compliance with the condition annexed to the
policy ; that they then told him that they did not feel safe in paying him a dollar,
and could not do it with propriety, but that they would pay him $200 rather than
go to law about it. The judge was asked to charge the jury, substantially, if
they believed this evidence of Selover, that the action was successfully defended ;
and he refused, and to his refusal, defendant's counsel excepted. I think the
learned judge erred in refusing this charge. There was conflict in the evidence,
and as the judge disposed of the question as one of law, and refused to submit the
evidence to the jury, we are bound to take that view of the evidence most favor-

if the insurer objects to the proofs because unseasonable, the fact that
other objections are also taken does not warrant the jury in finding a

---

able to the defendant which the jury might have taken. Taking the evidence
of Selover, then, there was no compliance with the condition, and no waiver of it.
He did nothing within the ten days to induce the plaintiff to believe that he was
not bound to deliver the verified account of his loss within the time specified in
the policy. What he did and said, on the contrary, showed that the company
would scrutinize the loss, and, probably, contest it, and should have made the
plaintiff scrupulous in a strict compliance with all the requirements of his policy.
Instead of delivering his affidavit within the ten days, he waited about a month,
until the local and general agents called upon him. They then drew an affidavit,
not for the purpose of a compliance with the condition, but to enable them to pry
into the cause of the fire, which they regarded as suspicious; and they then
informed him that they could not pay the loss, except upon the compromise which
they proposed. In drawing and keeping this affidavit there certainly was no
waiver of the condition. The doctrine of estoppel lays at the foundation of the
law, as to waiver. While one party has time and opportunity to comply with a
condition precedent, if the other party does or says anything to put him off from
his guard, and to induce him to believe that the condition is waived. or that a
strict compliance with it will not be insisted on, he is afterward estopped from
claiming non-performance of the condition. Unless there is some consideration
for a waiver or some valid modification of the agreement between the parties
which contains the condition, I think there can be no waiver of a condition precedent, except there be in the case an element of estoppel. At the time when the
affidavit was drawn the plaintiff had forfeited his rights under his policy.
Nothing that was then said or done induced him in any way to forego any of
his rights, or to omit the performance, on his part, of anything required
by his policy; and, hence, furnished no estoppel against the defendant. In
Clark v. *The New England Fire Ins. Co.*, 6 Cush. 342; *Underhill* v. *The Agawam M. F. Ins. Co.*, id. 440; *Bunstead* v. *The Dividend Mut. Ins. Co.*, 12 N. Y.
81; *Post* v. *Ætna Ins. Co.*, 43 Barb. 351; *Ames* v. *The N. Y. Union Ins. Co.*, 14
N. Y. 253; *Trustees First Baptist Church* v. *Brooklyn F. Ins. Co.*, 19 id. 305, and
all the other similar cases that have fallen under my observation, with one exception which will be hereafter noticed, the waiver claimed was based upon the conduct of the defendant or its agents, at a time when the plaintiff could have complied with the conditions. The true rule, I think, is laid down by MULLIN, J., in
Ripley v. *The Ætna Ins. Co.*, 30 N. Y., 136, as follows: 'It seems to me that a
waiver, to be operative, must be supported by an agreement founded on a valuable consideration; or, the act relied on as a waiver must be such as to estop a
party from insisting on performance of the contract or forfeiture of the condition;'
and, in that case, there was held to be no waiver upon facts fully as significant as
the undisputed facts in this case. The case of *Owen* v. *Farmers' Joint Stock Ins.
Co.*, 57 Barb. 518, is apparently in conflict with the views above expressed. That
was an action against this same company, and the policy sued on contained the
same condition as the one under consideration. In that case, the plaintiff was
absent from home at the time of the fire, and the proof of loss was not delivered
to the company within the ten days But, more than a month after the fire, the
agent of the company stated to a party interested in the policy that, it made no
difference, and that the proofs could be sent in after the return of the plaintiff;
and they were sent in after his return, after a further delay of about six weeks.
It was held, upon these facts, that the condition was waived. If all the facts in
that case appear in the opinion, I cannot doubt that the court fell into error by
not noticing the distinction between a waiver before forfeiture and one made afterward. In that case, there was no estoppel as the plaintiff did not delay until
after the ten days in consequence of anything said or done by defendant's agent.
There was no consideration for the waiver, and no valid agreement to waive the
condition. Although that case is said to have been affirmed in the Court of
Appeals, the opinion of that court is not furnished, and we are unable to see the
precise ground upon which the affirmance was based. In this case, the facts
should have have been submitted to the jury, with proper instructions; and if
they had found that, in consequence of what the defendant's agent said or did

waiver. A waiver does not exist when the party sought to be estopped gives the other party to distinctly understand that he does not waive any rights incident to the matter against which the estoppel is sought to be set up.[1]

---

before the expiration of the ten days, as testified to by the plaintiff, he was induced to delay compliance with the condition until after that time, then there would have been a waiver of the condition, and non-compliance with it would have furnished no defense to the action. But my brethren are unwilling to express an opinion upon the doctrine of waiver as I have stated it, but concur with me in reversing the judgment, upon the ground that the judge erred in holding as a matter of law that the condition was waived, and that the evidence in reference thereto should have been submitted to the jury." *Ames* v. *N. Y. U. Ins. Co.*, 14 N. Y. 253; *Trustees First Bap. Ch.* v. *Bklyn F. Ins. Co.*, 19 id. 305; *Goit* v. *Nat. Pro. Ins. Co.*, 25 Barb. (N. Y.) 189; *Owen* v. *Farmers' J. S. Ins. Co.*, 57 id. 518; *Sheldon* v. *At. F. & M. Ins Co.*, 26 N. Y. 460; *Boehen* v. *Winsburg Ins. Co.*, 35 id. 131; *Bodle* v. *Chenango Co. M. Ins. Co.*, 2 N. Y. 53; *Wood* v. *Pough. Ins. Co*, 32 N. Y. 619; *Bumstead* v. *Mut. Ins. Co.*, 12 N. Y. 81; *Post* v. *Ætna Ins. Co.*, 43 Barb. (N. Y.) 351; *Francis* v. *Ocean Ins. Co.*, 6 Cow. (N. Y.) 404; *Ætna Ins. Co.* v. *Tyler*, 16 Wend. (N. Y.) 402; *O'Neil* v. *Buff. F. Ins. Co.*, 3 Comst. 122; *Underhill* v. *Agawam F. Ins. Co.*, 6 Cush. (Mass.) 440; *Vos* v. *Robinson*, 9 John. (N. Y.) 192; *Ripley* v. *Ætna Ins. Co.*, 30 N. Y. 164; *Savage* v. *Ins. Co.*, 4 Bosw. (N. Y.) 1; *Bk. of U. S.* v. *Davis*, 2 Hill (N. Y.) 451–461; *Ingalls* v. *Morgan*, 10 N. Y. 178–184; *McLaughlin* v. *Wash. Ins. Co.*, 23 Wend. (N. Y.) 525; *Norton* v. *R. & S. Ins. Co.*, 7 Cow. (N. Y.) 645; *Gilbert* v. *N. S. Ins. Co.*, 23 Wend. (N. Y.) 43.

[1] In a recent case before the Court of Appeals of New York, *Blossom* v. *Lycoming Ins. Co.*, 64 N. Y. 162, this question arose in this form : The policy contained a clause requiring the assured in case of loss or damage by fire to deliver to defendant's secretary, within thirty days after such loss, a particular account thereof under oath. The building insured was destroyed by fire on the 29th November, 1870. No proofs of the loss were furnished until March 29, 1871 ; these were sent by plaintiff's attorney ; defendant sent a letter in reply containing the following : "The proof of loss is too late. It should have been made within thirty days after loss ; besides, after a careful investigation of the matter, we have become satisfied that it is a clear case of fraud. The company have, therefore, rejected the claim." Plaintiff gave evidence upon the trial to the effect that one Krouse, an adjuster for defendant, having learned of the fire and being near the premises, went to and examined them, and made inquiries as to the fire. He had received no instructions from the defendant to adjust the loss, and what he did was without plaintiff's knowledge ; that he reported his action to the company, but no action was taken by it until receipt of proofs of loss. At the close of the evidence defendant's counsel moved for a nonsuit on the ground, among others, that proofs of the loss were not furnished within thirty days thereafter, as required by the policy, and that there had been no waiver shown. The court denied the motion, holding that the question as to waiver was one of fact for the jury. Upon appeal, ALLEN, J., in passing upon this question, said : "The failure of the plaintiff to furnish proof of loss within thirty days after the fire, entitled the defendant to a nonsuit upon the evidence as it stood at the close of the trial. That the condition was not complied with was conceded ; that a substantial compliance with that condition, unless waived by the insurers, was necessary to enable the plaintiff to recover, is well established. *Savage* v. *The Howard Ins. Co.*, 52 N. Y. 502; *Underwood* v. *Farmers' J. S. Ins. Co.*, 57 id. 500. Upon a careful review of the case we can find no evidence of a waiver of this condition by the defendant ; there was no communication, direct or indirect, between the plaintiff and defendant, or its agents, in respect to it, or any negotiations between them from which the plaintiff had a right to infer that a strict compliance with every condition of the policy would not be insisted upon. Neither was there proof of any act by the defendant or its agents which could have led the plaintiff to believe that the proofs of loss prescribed by the policy would not be required. The action of Krouse, the adjuster, in visiting the premises and making inquiry into the circumstances of the fire, were not known either to the plaintiff or any agent of his ; so that his

45

The question, as to whether a failure on the part of the insurer to object to the unseasonableness of the proofs of loss, furnished *after the forfeiture has attached,* can be set up as a waiver, does not seem to be free from doubt. It has been held that such failure operates as a waiver,[1] but generally it will be found that the delay has been induced by such acts and conduct on the part of the insurer or his agents as amounts to an estoppel, rather than a waiver, and the better doctrine seems to be, and that more consistent with principle, *that, when the failure to comply with the condition is due wholly to the fault of the insured, the policy is dead, and cannot be revived by anything short of a new consideration or an express waiver on the part of the insurer.*[2]   In a New York case,[3] it was held that *a failure to object to proofs because they were too late, does not operate as a waiver of that ground of defense, even though the objection stated is, that the claim is fraudulent.   It is only when the proofs are in season, but are defective,* that a failure to object thereto is

---

omission to furnish the proofs was not induced by such action. Had the plaintiff known of the doings of Krouse they could not legitimately have influenced his action or omission to act in respect to the proof. The visit of Krouse was without authority or direction from the defendant, and was rather casual than otherwise, and precautionary, that he might be better able to act understandingly should occasion require. He neither by act or by declaration intimated that the defendant would, or was liable to, pay the loss ; or that the loss was recognized as a valid claim against the company. In truth there was no communication or negotiation between the plaintiff and the defendant, or its agents, after the notice of the loss, if such notice was ever given, until the forwarding of the proof of loss in April, after the fire, which occurred in November. But stress was laid by the learned judge, in his charge to the jury, upon the letter from the defendant to the attorney for the plaintiff, upon the receipt of the proof of loss, some four months after it occurred. In that letter the defendant takes two objections to its liability: First, that the proof of loss was too late, and that it should have been made within thirty days after loss ; and second, that the claim was fraudulent. Distinctly taking the ground that the condition as to the proof of loss had not been complied with. The taking of another and distinct objection was not a waiver of the first. The entire letter was a distinct intimation that the company would rely upon both the objections stated. Had the defendant omitted to notice the omission to furnish proof of loss within the time prescribed, that time having long elapsed, it is questionable whether it would have been deemed a waiver, for the reason that it was then too late to supply the omission ; and the plaintiff would have lost nothing by the omission of the company to call his attention to it. The defendant was at liberty, in response to the claim then made for the first time, by the plaintiff, to take every objection which was open to it. The objections did not annul or destroy or operate as a waiver of each other. It is difficult to see how a party waives or is estopped from taking an objection which he distinctly asserts and makes at the very first opportunity. There was no evidence of waiver ; and it was error for the learned judge to submit the question to the jury. The result was, as may be expected in every like case, the jury sympathizing with the insured, and thinking lightly of conditions which are really of the essence of the contract, and regarding them rather as technicalities than matters of substance, have given their verdict against the insurers."   *Edwards* v. *Baltimore Ins. Co.,* 3 Gill. (Md.) 370.

[1] *Hibernian Ins. Co.* v. *O'Connor,* 29 Mich. 241.

[2] *St. Louis Ins. Co.* v. *Kyle,* 11 Mo. 278 ; *Blossom* v. *Lycoming Ins. Co., ante ; Hobson* v. *Western Ass. Co.,* 19 U. C. Q. B. 314.

[3] *Brink* v. *Hanover F. Ins. Co.,* decided in Ct. of App. Jan. 5, 1877, not yet reported.

treated as a waiver. "If," said the court, "no proofs are served in time, *and the insurer has done nothing to induce the omission,* the insured has lost all rights under the policy, and the insurer is not bound to specify its defenses, nor does it waive those not specified." A promise to pay a loss after a forfeiture for a breach of the condition, the company having full knowledge of the breach, is a waiver of non-compliance,[1] but a mere failure to object to paying upon that ground, cannot be treated as a waiver. The insurer, by the *laches* of the assured, is absolved from all liability, and he may well refuse to take any notice whatever of proofs furnished out of time, and cannot thereby be said to have waived compliance on the part of the assured. But when an action is brought to recover a loss under such circumstances, and the insurer does not avail himself of this breach of the conditions of the policy, either by setting it forth specially in his answer or pleadings, or insisting upon it at the trial, he cannot afterwards avail himself thereof in a hearing upon an appeal. The defense is thereby waived, and its benefits lost to him.[2] When timely notice and proofs of loss are averred by the insurer, and not denied by the pleadings filed by the defendant, the plaintiff is not called upon to prove the fact, as it is thereby admitted.[3]

What should be stated in the proofs of loss.

SEC. 415. The requirements of the policy should be strictly followed unless compliance is waived, or is impossible. Thus, where the policy provides that the preliminary proofs shall contain "a par-

---

[1] *Greenfield* v. *Mass. Mut. Life Ins. Co.,* 47 N. Y. 430. It is only when a positive act is done *with full knowledge of the facts,* that a waiver can be predicated thereon, therefore no act done *in ignorance* of the facts can be construed as a waiver. Thus, where a policy of insurance, executed by a mutual fire insurance company, is obtained upon the suppression of a fact in the application, which was material to the risk, a subsequent reception, by the company, of an instalment on the premium note of the insured, can have no effect to render the policy binding on the company, in a case where neither the company nor their agent had notice of the existence of the fact suppressed. *Alllen* v. *Fire Ins. Co.,* 12 Vt. 366.

[2] *Martin* v. *Fishing Ins. Co.,* 20 Pick. (Mass.) 389; *Thwing* v. *Gt. Western Ins. Co.,* 111 Mass. 93; *Vos* v. *Robinson,* 9 John. (N. Y.) 192; *Lycoming Ins. Co.* v. *Dunmore,* 75 Ill. 14. In *Columbian Ins. Co.* v. *Lawrence,* 10 Pet. (U. S.) 25, the court very justly say: "If the company had contemplated the objection *it would have been but ordinary fair dealing to have apprized the plaintiff of it; for it was then obvious that the defect might have been immediately supplied;* as it was, the company *unintentionally,* as it may be, *by their silence misled him.*" See also, *Tayloe* v. *Merchants' F. Ins. Co.,* 9 How. (U. S.) 390. Good faith on the part of the insurers requires that if they mean to insist upon a merely formal defect in the preliminary proofs, they should apprise the insured of the nature of the objection, so as to give him an opportunity of supplying the defect; *and if they neglect to do so, their silence should be held a waiver of the defect.* *O'Niel* v. *Buffalo F. Ins. Co.,* 3 N. Y. 122; *Kernochan* v. *N. Y. Bowery Ins. Co.,* 17 N. Y. 348.

[3] *Fox* v. *Conway Ins. Co.,* 53 Me. 107.

ticular account of the loss in writing, under oath, stating the *value* of the property lost, the *nature and value* of the insured's interest in the property," the requirement must be complied with, and, even though the loss is total, proofs omitting to state the *nature and value* of the interest of the assured in the property destroyed are defective.[1] But, unless the policy requires that the nature of the interest of the assured in the property should be stated, a statement giving an account thereof and the value of the property destroyed is enough, as, if the loss is total, a simple statement to that effect, in the form required by the policy.   Thus, when the policy is valued and the loss total, and the policy requires a particular statement thereof, it is enough to state, " My dwelling-house insured by you for $2,500, by policy 46842, was burned down this morning."[2] If required to be signed by the assured, it must be so signed, unless a good reason for its not being so signed is shown, in which case it may be signed by an agent,[3] and must also be under oath if so required by the policy.[4]

---

[1] *Wellcome* v. *People's, etc., Ins. Co.*, 2 Gray (Mass.) 480. Where the policy requires that the proofs of loss shall contain " a particular account of the loss," a statement merely reiterating the language of the policy as " household furniture $367, groceries $233," although the loss is total, is not a compliance with the condition. A particular statement, itemizing the articles as far as possible, should be given. *Beatty* v. *Lycoming. etc., Ins. Co.*, 66 Penn. St. 9. By a condition in the policy, the insured were bound, in case of loss by fire, to forthwith give notice to the secretary, and within thirty days after loss to deliver to the secretary a particular account of such loss or damage. An account was sent by mail to the secretary, setting out the names of the partners, the number of their policy and amount insured therein, the value of their stock in the store, as estimated from their books, and reciting insurances in two companies (the store in front and its brick extension having been insured by another company), giving an account of an entire undivided loss, and claiming it to be embraced in the policies of the two companies, *but without stating the amount of the loss or damage upon the policy of the insurance company defendant, nor that the loss was upon goods insured under that policy, nor in what way that loss was ascertained.* It was held that the account sent was not such a particular account of the loss and damage as was required by the policy. *Lycoming, etc., Ins. Co.* v. *Updegraff*, 40 Penn. St. R. 311. And it was also held that the fact that the president of the company, when examining the books of the plaintiffs, to ascertain the loss of goods in the store, was applied to by them for instruction how to make out their statement, and gave a memorandum in pencil, without date or signature, of what it should contain, neither the examination of the books nor the memorandum were held evidence that the requirements of the policy in relation to a particular account of the loss had been waived by the company. Id.

[2] *Lycoming Ins. Co.* v. *Schalenberger*, 44 Penn. St. 259 ; *Gilbert* v. *N. American Ins. Co.*, 23 Wend. (N. Y.) 43.

[3] *Sims* v. *State Ins. Co.*, 47 Mo. 54 ; 4 Am. Rep. 53; *Ayres* v. *Hartford Ins. Co.*, 17 Iowa, 176.

[4] Where the conditions of the policy require the statement of loss to be sworn to, a neglect to do so, unless waived, is fatal to a recovery. *Sims* v. *State, etc., Ins. Co.* 47 Mo. 9. So where a policy calls for a *particular* account of the loss, a general statement, as " household furniture, $367; groceries, $233, is not a compliance. *Beatty* v. *Lycoming Ins. Co.*, 66 Penn. St. 9. But if the insurer was unable to give any more definite statement because of the destruction of his books,

Indeed, all the requirements of the policy in this respect must be observed, if possible.[1] If the manner of the occupancy of the building at the time of the loss, is required to be stated, the condition must be fully and fairly complied with, and if, from such statement, it appears that the occupancy was in violation of the provisions of the policy or unlawful, no action can be maintained for the loss.[2] The proofs of loss are not evidence of the amount or value of the loss, but they may be used by the insurers to show fraud on the part of the assured, or the valuation that he placed upon the property,[3] and for this purpose the defendant may read them to the jury, and then introduce evidence to show their falsity.[4] They are evidence for the plaintiff *only to the extent of showing compliance with the requirements of the policy*, and cannot be used to show the amount or value of the loss,[5] and, if admitted generally as evidence for the plaintiff, and read to the jury, it is error, even though the judge directs them to regard them only as proof of compliance with the conditions of the policy,[6] but, if they are admitted without objection on the part of the defendant, they are treated as evidence for all purposes.[7]

All that can be required of the insured is to render as full and particular account of his loss as the nature of the case will admit of, and if all his books and papers are destroyed, so that he cannot itemize it, a general statement of the gross amount of his loss, and of the nature, character and value of the property destroyed, is a compliance with the terms of the policy.[8] Thus, when the policy required that the assured " shall, within thirty days, deliver to the insurer a particular account of loss, verified by oath, and, if required, by his books

invoices, etc., the rule might be different, but it would be incumbent upon the assured to establish the excuse. *Hoffman* v. *Ætna Ins. Co.*, 32 N. Y. 405. The insured is only required to furnish reasonable information to the insurer, *and if he furnishes the best evidence possessed by him at the time*, he has done all that can be required of him.   *Child* v. *Sun Mut. Ins. Co.*, 3 Sandf. (N. Y.) 26 ; *Barker* v. *Phœnix Ins. Co.*, 8 John. (N. Y.) 307 ; *Lawrence* v. *Ocean Ins. Co.*, 11 id. 241.

[1] *Sims* v. *State Ins. Co.*, *ante; O'Brien* v. *Com. Ins. Co.*, 63 N. Y. 113.

[2] *Campbell* v. *Charter Oak Ins. Co.*, 10 Allen (Mass.) 213.

[3] *Phœnix Ins. Co.* v. *Munday*, 5 Cald. (Tenn.) 547 ; *Southern Ins., etc., Co.* v. *Lewis*, 42 Ga. 587.

[4] *Howard* v. *City F. Ins. Co.*, 4 Den. (N. Y.) 502.

[5] *Com. Ins. Co.* v. *Sennett*, 41 Penn. St. 161 ; *Newmark* v. *Liverpool, etc., Ins. Co.*, 30 Mo. 160 ; *Lycoming Ins. Co.* v. *Rabin*, 8 Chicago Leg. News, 150 ; *Lafayette, etc., Ins. Co.* v. *Winslow*, 66 Ill. 219.

[6] *Lafayette, etc., Ins. Co.* v. *Winslow*, 66 Ill. 219 ; *Lycoming Ins. Co.* v. *Rubin*, 8 Chicago Leg. News, 150 ; *Phœnix Ins. Co.* v. *Lawrence*, 4 Met. (Ky.) 9.

[7] *Moore* v. *Protection Ins., Co.*, 29 Me. 97 ; *Jones* v. *Mechanics' Ins. Co.*, 36 N. J. 29 ; *N. American Ins. Co.* v. *Zaengar*, 63 Ill. 464.

[8] *Norton* v. *Rensselaer Ins. Co.*, 7 Cow. (N. Y.) 645.

and papers," and the books, papers and inventories were consumed,
it was held that the conditions of the policy were met by as full and
accurate an account as the plaintiff, without fraud on his part, was
able to furnish.[1]

Magistrate's certificate.

SEC. 416. A provision in a policy that in case of loss the insured
shall procure the certificate of the nearest magistrate, must be *strictly
complied with*, and in case of two magistrates near the fire, *any distance between them is material.*[2]

---

[1]*Hynds* v. *Schenectady Ins. Co.*, 11 N. Y. 554 ; *McLaughlin* v. *Washington, etc.,
Ins. Co.*, 23 Wend. (N. Y.) 525 ; *Harkins* v. *Quincy Mut. F. Ins. Co.*, 16 Gray
(Mass.) 591. The proofs need not follow the exact words of the policy. *Tyler* v.
Ætna F. Ins. Co., 16 Wend. (N. Y.) 385 ; *Turley* v. *N. A. Fire Ins. Co.*, 25 id.
374, and when they are presented, if the insurer does not object to their suffi-
ciency, but places his refusal specifically on some other ground, it is an admission
of their sufficiency, or a waiver of proof. *Vos* v. *Robinson*, 9 Johns. (N. Y.) 192 ;
McMasters v. *Westchester Co. Mut. Ins. Co.*, 25 Wend. (N. Y.) 379 ; *Miller* v.
Eagle Life & Health Ins. Co., 2 E. D. Smith (N. Y.) 268 ; *Peacock* v. *N. Y. Life
Ins. Co.*, 1 Bos. (N. Y.) 338. And it is well settled that where a refusal to pay the
loss is put upon grounds other than the insufficiency or defectiveness of the notice
or proofs furnished, the company will be held to have waived objections of that
character. And the reason upon which the principle is founded, equally justifies
its extension, in a proper case, to the waiver of proof altogether. When the
underwriter refuses to pay because no valid contract has been entered into, the
impression is necessarily conveyed, and the claimant has reason to believe, that
the refusal is made solely and exclusively on that account. The company has the
same power to waive the condition entirely, as it has to accept an imperfect or
merely colorable performance of it. Conditions precedent are waived by such
conduct, on the part of the party entitled to insist upon them, as is inconsistent
with the purpose to require the performance of them. And contracts of insurance constitute no exception to the rule. *Post* v. *Ætna Ins. Co.*, 43 Barb. (N.
Y.) 351.

[2]Thus in *Leadbetter* v. *Ætna Ins. Co.*, 13 Me. 265, it was one of the conditions
annexed to the policy, that in case of loss the assured should procure from a magistrate or notary public most contiguous to the place of the fire, not concerned in
interest, or related to the insured, a certificate, certifying to such matters as the
policy provided. After the property was destroyed, the plaintiff applied to the
nearest magistrate for such a certificate, but he refused to give it, and he then
applied to and secured the certificate of the next nearest. The court held that the
procurement of such a certificate, was a condition precedent to the plaintiff's right
of recovery. *Worsley* v. *Wood*, 6 T. R. 710 ; 7 Cow. (N. Y.) 462. In *Johnson* v.
Phœnix Ins. Co., 112 Mass. 49, an action was brought on a policy of insurance on
a house against fire. The policy required the assured to "produce a certificate,
under the hand and seal of a magistrate, notary public or commissioner of deeds
(nearest to the place of the fire not concerned in the loss as a creditor or otherwise,
nor related to the assured), stating that he has examined the circumstances
attending the loss, knows the character and circumstances of the assured, and
verily believes that the assured has without fraud sustained loss on the property
insured, to the amount which such magistrate, notary public or commissioner of
deeds shall certify ;" and provided that until such certificate was produced, the
loss should not be payable. At the close of the evidence it was conceded by both
parties that the plaintiff did not furnish the certificate of a magistrate, notary
public or commissioner, as required in the policy ; and that before the suit was
brought the plaintiff applied to two magistrates for such a certificate, but did not
get one, and thereupon did not furnish any certificate. The defendant's counsel
requested the presiding judge to rule that. if no certificate was furnished, the
plaintiff could not maintain his action, unless the company had waived the right

It seems however that this condition may be waived, and such waiver may be implied. Thus when a certificate was procured from a magistrate,

---

to a certificate ; and that there was no sufficient evidence to warrant the jury in finding that the company had waived its right to such a certificate. The presiding judge granted the second prayer, that there was no evidence of a waiver, and refused the first, to which refusal exception was taken by the defendant. The presiding judge ruled, for the purposes of the trial, that if the plaintiff, in good faith, applied to the proper magistrate for such a certificate, with a real desire to get one, and the magistrate refused, this excused the plaintiff from furnishing such a certificate, and the plaintiff could then maintain the action without having furnished a certificate; to which ruling the defendant excepted. The verdict was for the plaintiff, and the defendant alleged exceptions. Upon appeal, the ruling, the *nisi prius* judge reversed. GRAY, J., saying : "The position of the defendant in this case is sustained by a uniform current of authorities, beginning with a series of decisions made upon full argument in England soon after policies of fire insurance first came into common use. The earliest case in the reports was decided in 1785. The condition of the policy there sued on required the assured to 'procure a certificate, under the hands of the minister and churchwardens, together with some other reputable inhabitants of the parish not concerned in such loss,' to substantially the same facts as are specified in the conditions now before us, and provided that until such certificate should be made and produced, the loss money should not be payable : The declaration, besides averring compliance with the condition in other respects, alleged that the minister of the parish, at the time of the loss and long before, resided at a distance from and out of the parish, and was wholly unacquainted with the character and circumstances of the assured, and wholly unable to make such a certificate as the policy required. After verdict for the plaintiff, judgment was arrested by the court of common bench, on the ground that the stipulation to produce the specified certificate was a condition precedent to the right to sue upon the policy. *Oldman v. Bewicke,* 2 H. Bl. 577, note. In 1789, in an action on a policy containing the same words, the declaration alleged that the assured applied to the minister and churchwardens, and to many respectable inhabitants for the certificate required, but that the defendants, by false insinuations and promises of identity, prevailed upon them to refuse to sign it. The defendants pleaded that they did not do so, and that the plaintiff had not procured the certificate required by the policy. The plaintiff demurred to the plea. After an able argument in support of the demurrer, the same court, stopping the opposing counsel, 'said the matter was too clear to admit of a doubt, and accordingly gave judgment for the defendants.' *Routledge v. Burrell,* 1 H. Bl. 254. In another case, in 1795, in which the clause in question differed only in omitting to declare that the loss should not be paid until the certificate was produced ; and the declaration alleged, and the jury found, that the minister and churchwardens refused to sign a certificate wrongly and unjustly, and without any reasonable or probable cause, the Court of Common Bench (a majority of the members of which had been changed since the decision last mentioned), being divided in opinion, gave judgment *pro forma* for the plaintiff, in order that a writ of error might be brought. *Wood v. Worsley,* 2 H. Bl. 574. And that judgment was unanimously reversed in the King's Bench, after thorough discussion at the bar and by all judges. *Worsley v. Wood,* 6 T. R. 710. The reasons for the decision were in brief, that the insurers, in order to protect themselves against fraud, had the right to say, and by the terms of the policy had said, that they would pay no loss except upon the certificate of the persons specified ; and that the assured by accepting the policy, assented to the condition, and came within the rule by which one who engages for the act of a stranger must procure the act to be done, and the refusal of the stranger, without the interference of the other party, is no excuse. In a case in the Privy Council in 1829, upon an appeal from Canada, these cases were considered to have settled the law upon the subject. *Scott v. Phœnix Ins. Co.,* Stuart, 354. And it was admitted at the argument of the present case that they have never been denied or doubted in England. See also, *Mason v. Harvey,* 8 Excheq. 819; *Langell v. Mut. Ins. Co.,* 17 Upper Canada, Q. B. 524. The American decisions upon the question are to the same effect. The Supreme Court of the United States has held that where a policy provided that

but he was not the *nearest* magistrate, and it, with the other proofs, was given to the agent of the defendants, who made no objection to the instru-

---

until the production of a certificate of a magistrate or notary of the town or county in which the fire happened, to the same facts which are specified in the condition now before us, the loss should not be payable; and the assured obtained a certificate from such a magistrate, which did not fully comply with the requirements of the condition; no action could be maintained upon the policy, unless the want of a certificate in the requisite form had been waived by the defendant. *Columbian Ins. Co.* v. *Lawrence,* 2 Pet. 25, and 10 id. 507. The courts of several States have held a stipulation like that in the present case, requiring a certificate from the nearest magistrate, to be a condition precedent, which must be complied with according to its terms before an action can be brought upon the policy. *Leadbetter* v. *Ætna Ins. Co.,* 13 Me. 265 ; *Inman* v. *Western Ins. Co.,* 12 Wend. 452, 456, *et seq.* ; *Ætna Ins. Co.* v. *Tyler,* 16 id. 385, 391, 401 ; *Turley* v. *North American Ins. Co.,* 25 id. 374 ; *Roumage* v. *Mechanics' Ins. Co.,* 1 Green (N. J.) 110 ; *Protection Ins. Co.* v. *Pherson,* 5 Ind. 417 ; *Noonan* v. *Hartford Ins. Co.,* 21 Miss. 81 ; *Cornell* v. *Hope Ins. Co.,* 3 Martin (N. S.) 223. The exact question has never been decided in this commonwealth. But it has been held by this court that compliance with the condition as to proof of loss in other respects is essential, unless waived by the insurers, and that an error in the statement cannot be cured by evidence at the trial. *Wellcome* v. *People's Ins. Co.,* 2 Gray, 480 ; *Shawmut Sugar Refining Co.* v. *People's Ins. Co.,* 12 id. 535 ; *Campbell* v. *Charter Oak Ins. Co.,* 10 All. 213. And in the last case, the court referred to *Worsley* v. *Wood,* above cited, as laying down the true rule. At the trial of the present case, it was admitted that the plaintiff did not furnish the certificate required by the policy, and there was no evidence that the defendant did anything to prevent his getting a certificate or to waive the want of one. His application in good faith to the proper magistrate for the requisite certificate could not enable him to maintain the action ; for the condition precedent to his right to sue was not that he should use his best efforts to procure, but that he should procure, the certificate. He has not, therefore, proved the case upon which the defendant promised to indemnify him." In *Protection Ins. Co.* v. *Pherson,* 5 Ind. 417, a policy was issued to the plaintiff with a provision similar to that embraced in the previous case, and the plaintiff after a loss under his policy applied to the nearest magistrate for a certificate, which was refused, and he then applied to the next nearest magistrate who resided over a mile farther from the fire than the magistrate first applied to. Held that no recovery could be had. The compliance must be literal. *Worsley* v. *Wood,* 6 T. R. 710 ; *Dawes* v. *N. R. Ins. Co.,* 7 Cow. (N. Y.) 462 ; *Columbian Ins Co.* v. *Lawrence,* 2 Pet. (U. S.) 25. In *Turley* v. *The North American F. Ins. Co.,* 25 Wend. (N. Y.) 374, it was held that a strict *literal* compliance with such a provision is not required, but that a substantial compliance is sufficient. In that case it appeared that the certificate of a magistrate or notary public most contiguous to the place of the fire, should be produced. The plaintiff procured the certificate of a magistrate three or four blocks from the fire, but it appeared that there was a notary public who resided across the street a few feet nearer, and the company among other things objected to the insufficiency of the certificate. NELSON, J., in commenting upon this point, said : "It seems that the *residence* of a notary happens to be a few feet nearer the fire, than the *office* of the judge, and we are asked to go into a nice calculation of distances, and settle the point upon the law of measurement. *De minimis,* etc., is a sufficient answer to the objection. *The spirit of the condition* requires no such mathematical precision from the assured. Its object is completely secured by the proximity of the certifying magistrate." But in this case there was really another ground upon which the case could have been placed. It seems that, unless the policy requires that the certificate shall be procured from the magistrate *residing* nearest the fire, the *office* is to be regarded in ascertaining the place most contiguous, and in this case while it was shown that the notary *resided* nearest the fire, it did not appear that *his office* was nearest. A policy required, in case of loss, a certificate of certain facts from the nearest magistrate or notary public. On the 22d of March following a loss in January, a certificate of a notary public was sent and was not objected to by the company until the day of trial, when they set up that another

ment on that account, and promised to pay the loss, and no objection was made until the trial, it was held that the defect, if any, was waived by the company.[1] Where the policy required a certificate of the nearest magistrate, but instead of furnishing that, the insured furnished the certificate of a reputable citizen, and no objection was made thereto by the insurers, the court left it for the jury to say whether the production of the certificate was waived, and they having found that it was, the verdict was sustained.[2] And where a *defective* certificate is served, and no objections are made thereto, the defects are waived.[3] Where performance of this condition is rendered impossible, because of the refusal of the nearest magistrate to give a certificate, no recovery can be had. The assured is bound absolutely to comply with the requirement, and, unless the insurer has been instrumental in procuring the magistrate to refuse to give the certificate, the insurer is discharged,[4] or unless the magistrate is disqualified because of relationship, or because of the pendency of proceedings before him against the assured for arson in burning the premises, in which case it is regarded as the intention of the parties that the certificate shall be given by the next nearest magistrate who is not disqualified *by interest or prejudice*.[5] Where the statute prescribes the manner in which

notary public lived about one square nearer to the property lost. One witness positively testified to a promise by the company's agent to pay the loss. Held that the company had waived their right to object to the certificate. *Byrne* v. *Rising Sun Ins. Co.*, 20 Ind. 103, and in the same case it was held that it need not be averred, in pleading, that the notary, whose certificates formed a part of the preliminary proof of loss, was the nearest notary to the place of the fire, if the certificate is received without objection; if there is a formal defect in the proof, exception should be taken in time for the assured to correct it, and the defendant takes the burden of establishing it.

[1] *Byrne* v. *Rising Sun Ins. Co.*, 20 Ind. 103; See *Peoria M. & F. Ins. Co.* v. *Walsner*, 22 Ind. 73; *Franklin Fire Ins. Co.* v. *Chicago Ice Co.*, 36 Md. 102; 11 Am. Rep. 469. So where the insurer does not object on the ground that no certificate has been furnished, but refuses upon other grounds. *Bilbrough* v. *Metropolis Ins. Co.*, 5 Duer. (N. Y.) 587; *Bailey* v. *Hope Ins. Co.*, 56 Me. 474; *O'Niell* v. *Buffalo F. Ins. Co.*, 3 N. Y. 122; *Brown* v. *Kings Co. Ins. Co.*, 31 How. Pr. (N. Y.) 508. Where no objection is made, the production of the certificate is waived. Thus, where the certificate was required by the policy to be under seal, but was not, and no objection was made, the defect was held to have been waived. *McMasters* v. *Westchester, etc., Ins. Co.*, 25 Wend. (N. Y.) 375; *Van Deusen* v. *Charter Oak Ins. Co.*, 1 Robt. (N. Y.) 55.

[2] *Taylor* v. *Roger Williams Ins. Co.*, 51 N. H. 50. Where a certificate was furnished, but not of the *nearest* magistrate, and no objection was made upon that ground, it was held that the insurer was estopped from proving that the magistrate was not the nearest. *Byrne* v. *Rising Sun Ins. Co.*, 20 Ind. 103; *Phœnix Ins. Co.* v. *Taylor*, 5 Minn. 492; *Germania Ins. Co.* v. *Curran*, 8 Kan. 9; *Wright* v. *Hartford Ins. Co.*, 36 Wis. 522; *Killips* v. *Putnam Ins. Co.*, 28 id. 472.

[3] *Turley* v. *N. American Ins. Co.*, 25 Wend. (N. Y.) 374.

[4] *Johnson* v. *Phœnix Ins. Co.*, *ante*; *Ætna Ins. Co.* v. *Tyler*, *ante*; *Moody* v *Ætna Ins. Co.*, *ante*; *Protection Ins. Co.* v. *Pherson*, *ante*; *Roumage* v. *Mechanics' Ins. Co.*

[5] *Wright* v. *Hartford F. Ins. Co.*, 36 Wis. 522.

proofs of loss shall be made, the mode prescribed by statute prevail over the conditions of the policy. Thus, where the policy required the assured to procure a certificate from the *nearest* magistrate, while the statute provided that he should procure the certificate of a magistrate, it was held that if a magistrate's certificate was procured, it was sufficient, whether it was the certificate of the *nearest* magistrate or not.[1] Where the nearest magistrate is related to the assured, or interested or concerned in the loss *in any way*, the certificate of the next nearest magistrate is sufficient. The condition, in this respect, being interpreted as though it read, " the certificate of the nearest magistrate not concerned in the loss." Thus, where the assured applied to the *nearest* magistrate for a certificate, and he refused to give it, and made a complaint against the assured for arson, charging him with setting fire to the property embraced in the loss, and the insured procured the certificate of the next nearest magistrate, the court held that it was a compliance with the terms of the policy, as the nearest magistrate *was concerned in the loss* to such an extent as to excuse the assured from procuring his certificate.[2] If the magistrate's certificate is defective in form,[3] or in substance,[4] the insurer must seasonably object thereto, specifically designating the ground of objection, or the defects will be treated as waived. So, too, where no certificate is furnished, unless called for by the assured, or the proofs are objected to upon that ground, within a reasonable time, the defect is waived, and cannot afterwards be set up by the insurer to defeat its liability upon the policy.[5] And this is so, even though the insured is, before proofs of loss are furnished, informed by the insurer that compliance with the requirements of the policy as to proofs of loss, *to the very letter*, will be insisted on. It is not what a person does or says *before* an act is done by another, that determines their legal status, *but what is said or done, or omitted to be done, after the act is consummated.*[6] If the insured neglects to procure the certificate of the *nearest* magistrate, and no objection is made to the proof upon that ground, the defect is waived.[7]

---

[1] *Bailey* v. *Hope Ins. Co.*, 56 Me. 474.

[2] *Wright* v. *Atlantic Ins. Co.*, 36 Wis. 522.

[3] *McMasters* v. *Westchester, etc., Ins. Co.*, 25 Wend. (N. Y.) 379.

[4] *Turley* v. *N. American Ins. Co.*, *ante;* *Germania F. Ins. Co.* v. *Curran,* 8 Kan. 9.

[5] *Taylor* v. *Roger Williams Ins. Co.,* 51 N. H. 50 ; *Fireman's Ins. Co.* v. *Crandall,* 33 Ala. 9.

[6] *Fireman's Ins. Co.* v. *Crandall, ante.*

[7] *Killips* v. *Putnam Ins. Co.,* 28 Wis. 472; *O'Neil* v. *Buffalo Ins. Co.,* 3 N. Y. 122; *Bryne* v. *Rising Sun Ins. Co.,* 20 Ind. 103.

Where the insurer specifically objects to the certificate upon *one* ground, as, that it was not given by the *nearest magistrate*, he is precluded from setting up an objection thereto upon any other ground, at the trial ; as, that it is informal, or does not comply with the policy as to what should be stated, etc.[1] As to whether the production of a certificate, or the defects therein have been waived by the insurer, as well as whether the certificate was furnished in a reasonable time, are questions for the jury.[2]

The same rules apply where the policy requires the certificate of a minister, two reputable citizens, a builder, etc., and strict compliance in these respects must be observed. Whether, where the policy requires the certificate of one or more reputable citizens, the assured takes the burden of proving their respectability, does not seem to have ever been passed upon. But, there is probably no question but that the production of a certificate of any person is, *prima facie*, a compliance, as the law will presume every person to be reputable until proved to be otherwise. But the insurer may prove *that they are not reputable citizens*, and, in that event, the assured must fail in his action. So, in reference to the certificate of the nearest magistrate, etc., the condition being a condition precedent, the assured takes the burden of showing full compliance, consequently, must show that the certificate was given by the *nearest* magistrate, or a valid excuse for the failure. In determining the question, the office of the magistrate, if he has one, is presumed to be intended, rather than his place of residence.[3]

Defective proofs.

SEC. 417. Where defective proofs have been made, *a refusal to pay upon special grounds, or a denial of liability unless specially predicated upon the defects in the preliminary proofs, is a waiver of all defects therein, and estops the insurer from insisting upon them to defeat his liability.*[4]

---

[1] *Bailey* v. *Hope Ins. Co.*, ante.

[2] *Columbian Ins. Co.* v. *Lawrence*, 10 Pet. (U. S.) 507 ; *Taylor* v. *Rogers Williams' Ins. Co.*, ante.

[3] *Turley* v. *N. A. Ins. Co.*, 25 Wend. (N. Y.) 374 ; 2 Ben. F. I. C. 50.

[4] *Rogers* v. *Trader's Ins. Co.*, 6 Paige Ch. (N. Y.) 583 ; *Ayres* v. *Hartford Ins. Co.*, 17 Iowa, 176 ; *Frances* v. *Somerville, etc., Ins. Co.*, 25 N. J. L. 78 ; *Franklin, etc., Ins. Co.* v. *Coates*, 14 Md. 285 ; *Post* v. *Ætna Ins. Co.*, 43 Barb. (N. Y.) 351 ; *Franklin, etc., Ins. Co.* v. *Updegraff*, 43 Penn. St. 350 ; *Fireman's Ins. Co.* v. *Crandall*, 33 Ala. 9 ; *Lewis* v. *Monmouth, etc., Ins. Co.*, 52 Me. 492 ; *Hartford, etc., Ins. Co.* v. *Harmer*, 2 Ohio St. 45 ; *Gt. Western, etc., Ins. Co.* v. *Staaden*, 26 Ill. 360 ; *Bailey* v. *Hope Ins. Co.*, 56 Me. 474 ; *Frances* v. *Ocean Ins. Co.*, 6 Can. 404. When the requirements of the policy have not been complied with as to proofs of loss, and payment is declined upon other grounds, all defects are waived. *Underhill* v. *Agawam Ins. Co.*, 6 Cush. (Mass.) 440 ; *Clark* v. *N. E.*

It seems to be settled beyond dispute, that, where there are defects in the proofs of loss, whether formal, substantial, or indeed in *any* respect, which could have been supplied if specific objections had been made thereto by the underwriters, a failure on their part to object to the proofs upon that ground, or to point out the specific defect, or to call for the information omitted within a reasonable time, is considered a waiver, however defective, informal or insufficient such proofs may be.[1]

Mut. F. Ins. Co., 6 id. 342; *Ætna Ins. Co.* v. *Tyler*, 16 Wend. (N. Y.) 385; *Heath* v. *Franklin Ins. Co.*, 1 Cush. (Mass.) 257; *Vos* v. *Robinson*, 9 John. (N. Y.) 192; *McMasters* v. *Westchester. etc., Ins. Co.*, 25 Wend. (N. Y.) 379. Failure to object to the proofs of loss furnished within a reasonable time, and a refusal to pay *upon other grounds*, is a waiver of defect in the proofs. *Graves* v. *Washington, etc., Ins. Co.*, 12 Allen (Mass.) 391; *Martin* v. *Fishing Ins. Co.*, 20 Pick. (Mass.) 389; *Heath* v. *Franklin Ins. Co.*, 1 Cush. (Mass.) 257; *Rathbone* v. *City etc., Ins. Co.*, 31 Conn. 193; *Bartlett* v. *Union Mut. Ins. Co.*, 46 Me. 500; *Dean* v. *Ætna Life Ins. Co.*, 4 T. & C. (N. Y.) 497; *Parker* v. *Amazon Ins. Co.*, 34 Wis. 363. In *Unthank* v. *Travelers' Ins. Co.*, 4 Biss. (U. S.) 357, the policy required *immediate* notice of the injury to be given, none was given; but subsequently the assured made proofs of the injury, and the company after examining the proofs, *refused to pay upon other grounds*, and it was held that this was a waiver of notice. *Manhattan Ins. Co.* v. *Stein*, 5 Bush. (Ky.) 652; *Norwich, etc., Transportation Co.* v. *Western Mass. Ins. Co.*, 6 Blatch. (U. S.) 241. If, after the preliminary proofs of a loss by fire under a policy of insurance, the officers of an insurance company visit the premises and converse with the insured, make no reference to the preliminary proofs, and raise no objection to them, while any defect therein may be remedied, and refuse to pay on other and distinct grounds, the insurance company will be estopped to set up any defect in the preliminary proof, although the conditions, made part of the policy, give explicit directions about proofs of loss, and the policy provides that no condition, stipulation, covenant, or clause in the policy shall be altered, annulled, or waived, except by writing indorsed on or annexed to the policy, and signed by the president or secretary. *Blake* v. *Exchange, etc., Ins. Co.*, 12 Gray (Mass.) 265. Notice of loss will not be rendered ineffectual by the omission to mention that the debt of the assignee, as mortgagee, was also secured on other property. *Barnes* v. *Union, etc., Ins. Co.*, 45 N. H. 21. The officers of a mutual insurance company have power to waive any preliminary proof of loss, and if the directors are dissatisfied with the notice or proof of loss, they should notify the assured, and when they fail to do so, and put their objection on entirely different grounds, they will be held to have waived any non-compliance with the law in regard to such notice and proof. *Lewis* v. *Monmouth, etc., Ins. Co.*, 52 Me. 492. In case of loss by the terms of a policy of insurance, formal proof of loss was required. It was held, that the absolute denial of any liability on the part of the company after notice of the loss, and after an examination of the property insured, waived the right to formal proof of loss. *Norwich, etc., Trans. Co.* v. *Western Mass. Ins. Co.*, 34 Conn. 561; but a waiver of notice of loss, is not a waiver of *proofs of loss*. *Desilver* v. *State, etc., Ins. Co.*, 38 Penn. St. 130.

[1] *McMasters* v. *Western Mut. Ins. Co.*, 25 Wend. (N. Y.) 382; *Ocean Ins. Co.* v. *Francis*, 2 Wend. (N. Y.) 71; *Ætna Ins. Co.* v. *Tyler*, 16 id. 401; *Edwards* v. *Baltimore F. Ins. Co.*, 3 Gill. (Md.) 176; 2 Ben. F. I. C. 406; *Warner* v. *Peoria, etc., Ins. Co.*, 14 Wis. 318; *Hartford Protection Ins. Co.* v. *Harmer*, 2 Ohio St. 452; *Ins. Co. of N. America* v. *McDowell*, 50 Ill. 120; *Peoria, etc., Ins. Co.* v. *Lewis*, 18 id. 553; *St. Louis Ins. Co.* v. *Kyle*, 11 Mo. 278; *N. A., etc., Ins. Co.* v. *Burroughs*, 69 Penn. St. 43; *Great Western Ins. Co.* v. *Staaden*, 26 Ill. 360; *Allegre* v. *Maryland Ins. Co.*, 6 H. & J. (Md.) 136; *Imperial F. Ins. Co.* v. *Murray*, 13 Penn. St. 13; *Home Ins. Co.* v. *Cohen*, 20 Gratt. (Va.) 312; *Atlantic Ins. Co.* v. *Wright*, 22 Ill. 462; *Globe Ins. Co.* v. *Boyle*, 21 Ohio St. 419; *Franklin F. Ins.*

Thus. if the insurer objects to paying the loss upon the ground that
no contract of insurance was ever made; [1] or if the insurer's examiner
makes an examination of the loss, and denies all liability under the
policy; [2] or if a portion of the claim is paid; [3] or if the defendant's
agent, upon proofs of loss being submitted to him, proceeds to ascertain the loss; [4] or if, after proofs have been made, defective in fact,
the insurer negotiates for a settlement without objecting to the sufficiency of the proofs; [5] or if the proofs are correct in some respects,
but defective in others, and the objections thereto are to the parts that
are correct; [6] or if the insurers absolutely and unqualifiedly refuse to
pay the loss; [7] or where no objection is made to the proofs; [8] or where

Co. v. Chicago Ice Co., 36 Md. 102 ; 11 Am. Rep. 469; Patterson v. Triumph Ins.
Co., 64 Me. 500 ; Phillips v. Protection Ins. Co., 14 Mo. 220 ; Lycoming Ins. Co.
v. Dunmore, 75 Ill. 14; Johnson v. Columbian Ins. Co., 7 John. (N. Y.) 315;
Blake v. Exchange Ins. Co., 12 Gray (Mass.) 265 ; Heath v. Franklin Ins. Co., 1
Cush. (Mass.) 257 ; Bumstead v. Dividend Ins. Co., 12 N. Y. 81 ; Rathbone v.
City F. Ins. Co., 31 Conn. 193 ; Thwing v. Gt. Western Ins. Co., 111 Mass. 93;
Hynds v. Schenectady, etc., Ins. Co., 11 N. Y. 554 ; Vos v. Robinson, 9 John.
(N. Y.) 192 ; Peoria, etc., Ins. Co. v. Whitehill, 25 Ill. 466 ; Basch v. Humboldt,
etc., Ins. Co., 33 N. J. 429 ; Walker v. Metropolitan Ins. Co., 56 Me. 371 ; Under-
hill v. Agawam, etc., Ins. Co., 6 Cush. (Mass.) 440 ; Boynton v. Clinton, etc., Ins.
Co., 16 Barb. N. Y. 254 ; Badle v. Chenango, etc., Ins. Co., 2 N. Y. 53 ; Sexton v.
Montgomery, etc., Ins. Co., 9 Barb. (N. Y.) 191 ; Nuthank v. Travelers' Ins. Co.,
4 Biss. (U. S. C. C.) 357 ; Planters', etc., Ins. Co. v. Deford, 38 Md. 382 ; Under-
wood v. Farmers', etc., Ins. Co., 57 N. Y. 500 ; Cumberland, etc., Ins. Co. v.
Schell, 29 Penn. St. 31 ; Columbian Ins. Co. v. Lawrence, 10 Pet. (U. S.) 507 ;
Bailey v. Hope Ins. Co., 56 Me. 474 ; Brown v. Kings Co., etc., Ins. Co., 31 How.
Pr. N. Y.) 508 ; O'Neil v. Buffalo Ins. Co., 3 N. Y. 122 ; Fireman's Ins. Co. v.
Crandall, 33 Ala. 9 ; Bryne v. Rising Sun Ins. Co., 20 Ind. 103 ; Ketchum v. Protection Ins. Co., 1 Allen (N. B.) 136 ; Van Deusen v. Charter Oak Ins. Co., 1 Rob.
(N. Y.) 57; Taylor v. Roger Williams Ins. Co., 51 N. H. 50 ; Germania Ins. Co.
v. Curran, 8 Kan. 9.
[1] Tayloe v. Merchants' Ins. Co., 9 How. (U. S.) 330.
[2] McBride v. Republic Ins. Co., 30 Wis. 562.
[3] Westlake v. St. Lawrence, etc., Ins. Co., 14 Barb. (N. Y.) 206.
[4] Johnson v. Columbia Ins. Co., 7 Johns. (N. Y.) 315.
[5] Graves v. Washington Mar. Ins. Co., 12 Allen (Mass.) 391.
[6] Rathbone v. City F. Ins. Co., 31 Conn. 193.
[7] Francis v. Ocean Ins. Co., 6 Cow. (N. Y.) 404 ; Hynds v. Schenectady, etc.,
Ins. Co., 11 N. Y. 554 ; Thwing v. Gt. Western Ins. Co., 111 Mass. 93. Where
the insurers declared "they would not settle the claim in any way," it was held
a waiver of any imperfection in the preliminary proofs. Francis v. Ocean Ins.
Co., 6 Cow. 404 ; Rogers v. Traders' Ins. Co., 6 Paige, 583. So where they
answered that they were not liable for the loss under the policy. O'Neil v. Buffalo F. Ins. Co., 3 N. Y. 122. Where the insurers received insufficient preliminary proofs, and without notice to the insured of the defect, procured additional
affidavits, it was held that a verdict treating such affidavits as completing the
preliminary proofs should be sustained. Sexton v. Montgomery Co. Mut. Ins.
Co., 9 Barb. (N. Y.) 191. In Bodle v. Chenango Co., etc., Ins. Co., 2 N. Y. 53,
the policy required the insured, within thirty days after loss, to transmit a particular account thereof. The insured, within that time, furnished a statement of

[8] Globe Ins. Co. v. Boyle, 21 Ohio St. 119 ; Franklin F. Ins. Co. v. Chicago Ice
Co., 36 Md. 102.

the insurer retains them for an unreasonable time, without objections as to their sufficiency;' or where the proofs are made out by the insurer or its agent '—the insurer is treated as waiving all defects in the preliminary proofs, and will not be heard to object thereto. The insurer must seasonably object. He must make his objections known within a reasonable time; and whether he has done so or not in a given case, is a question for the jury.'

Perfect good faith is required on the part of both the insurer and assured, and it is presumed that all conditions imposed upon the assured, are imposed in good faith and to protect the insurer from fraud and imposition or loss. Therefore, proofs of loss are presumed to be required as a means of enabling the insurer to determine whether there has been a loss, whether the insured had the requisite insurable

loss, made out in a manner directed by an agent of the company, at the request of the company, and produced his books for further explanation. The company made no objection to the account, and offered to pay a large portion of the loss. Held, that they could not subsequently object to the sufficiency of the account. Part payment of the loss is a waiver of preliminary proofs. *Westlake* v. *St. Lawrence Co. Mut. Ins. Co.*, 14 Barb. (N. Y.) 206. Where a statement of the amount of the loss in the preliminary proofs is definite, sworn, and certified by two appraisers, the insurers cannot object at the first time, at the trial, that it had not the certificate of a magistrate. *Bilborough* v. *Metropolis Ins. Co.*, 5 Duer (N. Y.) 587.

¹ *Madsden* v. *Phœnix Ins. Co.*, 1 S. C. 24.

² *Warner* v. *Peoria, etc., Ins. Co.*, 14 Wis. 318.

³ *Swan* v. *Liv., Lon. & Globe Ins. Co.*, 52 Miss. 704; *Gt. Western Ins. Co.* v. *Staaden*, 26 Ill. 365; *Peacock* v. *N. Y. Life Ins. Co.*, 20 N. Y. 293; *Herron* v. *Peoria Ins. Co.*, 38 Ill. 238; *Ætna Ins. Co.* v. *Tyler*, 16 Wend. (N. Y.) 358; *Bryne* v. *Rising Sun Ins. Co.*, 20 Ind. 103. In *Van Deusen* v. *Charter Oak Ins. Co.*, 6 Rob. (N. Y.) 55, the insurers received and examined the proofs of loss presented by the insured, and in answer to subsequent inquiries on his part, whether there were any further proofs that he could show, or anything further was wanted of him, answered that there was not, and afterwards offered to compromise the claim, but without making any objection to the proofs. Held, that they could not defeat his action on the policy by objecting that the magistrate's certificate, which the policy required should accompany the proofs of loss, was never served on them. Where papers containing preliminary proofs of loss by fire are served on, and received by the insurance company without objection, it is too late for the company to object on the trial that these proofs were insufficient and defective, especially so where the refusal to pay the loss, when payable, was placed on the ground alone that the risk had been increased. *Brown* v. *Kings Co. F. Ins. Co.*, 31 How. 508. Where proofs of loss are furnished, if they are defective or unsatisfactory, the company should give notice *within a few days, or they will be bound by them. Savage* v. *Corn Exchange Fire & Inland Nav. Ins. Co.*, 4 Bosw. 1. In *Van Deusen* v. *Charter Oak Ins. Co.*, 1 Rob. (N. Y.) 55, the insured, after a loss by fire, presented to the insurers proofs of their loss, which were received and examined by them. The insured afterward inquired of the insurers if he could show any further proofs that they needed, and was answered that if there was anything more needed they would let him know. The insurers afterward offered to compromise the loss, and never until the trial objected that the proofs of loss were insufficient. Held, that on the trial a motion to dismiss the complaint, on the ground that the proofs as served did not comply with the terms and conditions of the policy, should be denied.

interest on the property, and whether it was lost by any of the perils insured against, and the nature and extent of the loss, rather than as a means of enabling the insurer by sharp practices and knavish tricks, to defeat its liability for the loss. Therefore, when the insured has attempted, in *good faith*, to conform to this requirement of the policy, if he fails to meet it, or if the insurer desires further information, common honesty, and the rules of fair dealing require that he should point out the defects, or call for the additional information, and failing to do so, he is treated as being satisfied with the performance of the condition by the assured, and is estopped from afterwards setting up any objection thereto. *But when no attempt to comply with the conditions of the policy in this respect, in the mode required thereby,* has been made ; as where verbal notice is given to an agent of the insurer, and by him verbally given to the company, when the policy requires the notice to be given in writing, the failure of the company to object, will not be treated as a waiver of the defect ; for, *where the insurer has done nothing to mislead the assured, he is not bound to object, until there has, at least, been an attempt to comply with the plain requirements of the policy.*[1]

When, however, the assured has attempted to comply with the requirements of the policy, but the proofs furnished are defective, *it is the duty of the company specifically to point out the defects,* and failing to do so, the retention of the proofs without making specific objections thereto, is in law a waiver of all defects.[2] General objections, as " the

---

[1] *Cornell* v. *Milwaukie, etc., Ins. Co.,* 18 Wis. 387 ; *Franklin Ins. Co.* v. *Chicago Ice Co.,* 36 Md. 102.

[2] *McMasters* v. *Westchester, etc., Ins. Co.,* 25 Wend. (N. Y.) 379 ; *Boynton* v. *Clinton, etc., Ins. Co.,* 16 Barb (N. Y.) 254 ; *Walker* v. *Metropolitan Ins. Co.,* 56 Me. 371 ; *Graves* v. *Washington, etc., Ins. Co.,* 12 Allen (Mass.) 391 ; *Hynds* v. *Schenectady, etc., Ins. Co.,* 11 N. Y. 554 ; *Hartford Protection Ins. Co.* v. *Harmer,* 2 Ohio St. 452 ; *Warner* v. *Peoria, etc., Ins. Co.,* 14 Wis. 318 ; *Home Ins. Co.* v. *Cohen,* 20 Gratt. (Va.) 312 ; *Winnesheik Ins. Co.* v. *Schueller,* 60 Ill. 465 ; *Peoria M. & F. Ins. Co.* v. *Lewis,* 18 id. 583 ; *Ins. Co.* v. *McDowell,* 50 Ill. 120 ; *Marks* v. *Farmers' Ins. Co.,* 57 Me. 281. 'Good faith," says Chancellor WALWORTH, in *Ætna F. Ins. Co.* v. *Tyler,* 16 Wend (N. Y.) 401. " on the part of undewriters, requires that if they mean to insist upon a mere formal defect in the preliminary proofs, they should apprise the assured that they consider the same defective in that particular, or to put their refusal to pay upon that ground as well as others, so as to give him an opportunity to supply the defect before it should be too late, or if he neglects so to do, then silence should be held a waiver of such defect." In *Peacock* v. *N. Y. Ins. Co.,* 1 Bos. (N. Y.) 338, the court say : "The defendants are allowed sixty days after the preliminary proofs are furnished before they can be required to pay. When, therefore, what are in good faith presented to them as preliminary proofs *are in any respect* defective, common fairness requires that such defects be suggested." *Frederick, etc., Ins. Co.* v. *Derford,* 38 Md. 404 ; *Priest* v. *Citizens' Ins. Co.,* 3 Allen (Mass.) 604 ; *McLoughlin* v. *Mut. Ins. Co.,* 23 Wend. (N. Y.) 525 ; *Underhill* v. *Agawam Ins. Co.,* 6 Cush. (Mass.) 440 ; *Jones* v. *Mechanics' Ins. Co.,* 36 N. J. 29 ; 13 Am. Rep. 405 ; *Gilbert* v. *N. American Ins. Co.,* 23 Wend. (N. Y.) 43. In *Kimball* v. *Hamilton Ins. Co.,* 8 Bos. (N. Y.) 495,

proofs are defective," are not enough; good faith requires that the insurers *should point out the defects and inform the assured in what respects additional or different proof is required;* and, failing to do so, the law will assume that the proofs were correct, and will not permit the insurer to prove the contrary.[1] Thus, where proofs were furnished

---

the general doctrine is recognized, although held not applicable in that case, because the president looked over the papers and told the insured they were defective, and referred him to the policy for information. *Bush* v. *Westchester Ins. Co.*, 4 T. & C. (N. Y.) 497; *Francis* v. *Ocean Ins. Co.*, 6 Cow. (N. Y.) 404; *Brewer* v. *Chelsea Ins. Co.*, 14 Gray (Mass.) 203; *Bumstead* v. *Dividend Ins. Co.*, 12 N. Y. 81; *O'Neil* v. *Buffalo Ins. Co.*, 3 id. 122; *Bodle* v. *Chenango Ins. Co.*, 2 id. 53; *Norton* v. *R. & S. Ins. Co.*, 7 Cow. (N. Y.) 645; *Planters', etc., Ins. Co.* v. *Derford*, 38 Md. 382; *Winnesheik Ins. Co.* v. *Schueller*, 60 Ill. 465. A contrary doctrine has been held in several cases, which have been regarded as so authoritative as to leave this question open as debatable ground, notwithstanding the very large number of cases in which a contrary doctrine was held. Principal among these is *Columbian Ins. Co.* v. *Lawrence*, 2 Peters (U. S.) 25, in which Chief Justice MARSHALL held a contrary doctrine. But it should be remembered that although the opinions of that eminent jurist are entitled to great weight, yet this case cannot be regarded as authoritative, for the doctrine was virtually overruled upon a re-hearing (see S. C., 10 Pet. [U. S.] 507), and was directly repudiated by the United States Supreme Court in *Taylor* v. *Merchants' Ins. Co.*, 9 How. (U. S.) 404, and the question is, by that court, now regarded as settled beyond dispute, that *silence* on the part of the assurer is to be treated as a waiver. The main case falling to the ground, those cases that have followed it, citing it as authority, fall with it. Among these are *Shawmut Co.* v. *Peoples' Ins. Co.*, 12 Gray (Mass.) 535; *Beatty* v. *Lycoming Ins. Co.*, 66 Penn. St. 9; *Keenan* v. *Missouri Ins. Co.*, 12 Iowa, 26; *Schenck* v. *Mercer Ins. Co.*, — N. J. 447; all of which, as will be seen by later cases cited elsewhere, have been repudiated by later decisions in the states in which they were rendered. *The waiver extends not only to defects in form, but also to defects in substance.* Thus, it has been held that the substitution of the certificate of a reputable citizen in place of that of the nearest magistrate, unless objected to, is to be treated as a waiver of compliance in this respect. *Taylor* v. *Roger Williams Ins. Co.*, 51 N. H. 50.* So, where no certificate of any kind was furnished and no objection was made on that account, it was held a waiver of compliance with this condition. *Franklin Ins. Co.* v. *Chicago Ice Co.*, 36 Md. 102; 11 Am. Rep. 467. And generally it may be said that a waiver may be predicated upon the *silence* of the assured where there has been *an attempt* at compliance, of any defects in the proofs, *whether of form or substance*, and the courts have gone so far as to hold *that where the insurer relies upon defects in the proofs of loss in defense to an action upon the policy, he must show that he notified the assured of the defects in season for him to have corrected them,* and failing in such proof that they were estopped from setting up the defects in avoidance of their liability. *Killips* v. *Putnam Ins. Co.*, 28 Wis. 472; *McBride* v. *Republic Ins. Co.*, 30 Wis. 502.

[1] *Blake* v. *Exchange, etc., Ins. Co.*, 12 Gray (Mass.) 265; *Vose* v. *Robinson*, 9 John. (N. Y.) 192; *Clarke* v. *N. E., etc., Ins. Co.*, 6 Cush. (Mass.) 324; *Ætna F. Ins. Co.* v. *Tyler*, 16 Wend. (N. Y.) 401; *Bumstead* v. *Dividend Mut. Ins. Co.*, 12 N. Y. 81; *McMasters* v. *Westchester Co. Ins. Co.*, 25 Wend. (N. Y.) 379; *Underhill* v. *Agawam Mut. F. Ins. Co.*, 6 Cush. (Mass.) 440; *Patterson* v. *Triumph Ins. Co.*, 64 Me. 500; *Ocean Ins. Co.* v. *Francis*, 2 Wend. (N. Y.) 64; *Imperial F. Ins. Co.* v. *Murray*, 73 Penn. St. 13. In *Van Allen* v. *Farmers' Joint-Stock Ins. Co.*, 6 T. & C. (N. Y.) 501, a fire insurance policy contained a provision that, in case of loss, notice to the company should be forthwith given, and, "within twenty days after the loss," a particular statement, etc., should be delivered; and another provision that nothing less than a written agreement, signed by an officer of the company, should operate as a waiver of any condition. The holder of the policy, before the expiration of twenty days after a loss, went to a local agent of the company, who had pre-

that were in fact defective, but the insurer subsequently negotiated for a settlement of the loss, and made no objections to the proofs;[1] so where proofs were sent that did not comply with all the provisions of the policy in not stating the interest of the assured in the property, whether or not it was encumbered, or whether there was other insurance, but the objection was not taken until the trial;[2] so where the policy required a certificate of the nearest magistrate, but none was sent, and no objection was made on that account;[3] so where proofs were made and signed by the plaintiff's agent, no other defects being pointed out or insisted on, and they were returned because not signed by the assured himself, and they were subsequently seasonably sworn to by the assured;[4] in all these instances it was held that all other defects in the proofs were waived, and could not be insisted upon in defense.

Mere delay on the part of the company in objecting to proofs of loss, does not amount to a waiver of defects therein;[5] but their retention without objection for an unreasonable time will be treated as a waiver of defects, and estop the insurer from setting them up as a defense;[6]

---

viously been permitted by the company to receive proofs of loss, for the purpose of furnishing the particular statement, etc., required, and was told by such agent to wait until the adjuster of the company came around, in consequence of which the policy-holder did not furnish the statement within the twenty days. It was held that the agent had authority to waive the condition of the policy, and that his direction to the policy-holder constituted a waiver which bound the insurance company. In *Franklin F. Ins. Co.* v. *Chicago Ice Co.*, 36 Md. 102; 11 Am. Rep. 469, the policy contained a clause: "*Nothing but a distinct, specific agreement, clearly expressed and indorsed on this policy shall operate as a waiver of any written or printed condition thereon.*" It was held that this did not relate to proofs of loss, and that their production might be waived by a agent orally, or by his conduct, precisely the same as though the condition did not exist.

[1] *Graves* v. *Washington, etc., Ins. Co., ante; Hibernian Ins. Co.* v. *O'Connor*, 29 Mich. 241.

[2] *Underhill* v. *Agawam Ins. Co., ante; Patterson* v. *Triumph Ins. Co., ante; Bush* v. *Humboldt, etc., Ins. Co.*, 35 N. J. L. 429.

[3] *Franklin Ins. Co.* v. *Chicago Ice Co.*, 36 Md. 102; 11 Am. Rep. 649; *Taylor* v. *Roger Williams Ins. Co.*, 51 N. H. 50.

[4] *Home Ins. Co.* v. *Cohen*, 20 Gratt. (Va.) 312.

[5] *Savage* v. *Corn Exchange Ins. Co.*, 4 Bos. (N. Y.) 1; *O'Neil* v. *Buffalo Ins. Co.*, 3 N. Y. 122; *Cohen* v. *Home Ins. Co.*, 20 Gratt. (Va.) 312; *Walsh* v. *Hartford Ins. Co.*, 54 Ill. 164; *McLaughlin* v. *Washington, etc., Ins. Co.*, 28 Wend. (N. Y.) 525.

[6] *Walsh* v. *Hartford Ins. Co., ante.* In *Globe Ins. Co.* v. *Boyle*, 21 Ohio St. 119, it was held that it is the insurer's duty to object to the preliminary proofs when presented, or they will be treated as waived; but this was probably not intended to deprive them of a *reasonable* time in which to examine and ascertain the defects. Where an insurance company has, by its own conduct, been instrumental in producing a non-compliance with certain stipulations in the policy, thus, where a policy provides that an action shall be commenced thereon within a certain time after the loss, if the company, by holding out hopes of a settle-

objections thereto, should be made promtly ' and rejected *in toto*,' or
the defects relied on should be specifically pointed out, and all others
will be treated as waived,' and if they are returned *without specific
objections thereto*, all existing objections are waived.' When the insurer
intends to insist upon any defects in proofs of loss, he must apprise

---

ment, has induced the assured to delay bringing his action until after the time
has elapsed, they are thereby estopped from setting up such non-compliance as a
bar to the action. *Grant v. Lexington, etc., Ins. Co.*, 5 Ind. 23. Where the policy
requires notice of the loss, which is given, a mere withholding of the necessary
information, invoices, documents and proofs, unless specially called for by the
policy within a certain time, will not bar a recovery, unless it is done with a fraudulent intent. *Betts v. Franklin, etc., Ins. Co.*, Taney's Dec. (U. S.) 171. Where the
policy requires that reasonable notice of loss shall be given, the question as to
what is a reasonable notice, is for the jury, and all the attendant circumstances
are proper to be shown. *Provident, etc., Ins. Co. v. Baum*, 22 Ind. 236.

¹ *Franklin Fire Ins. Co. v. Chicago Ice Co.*, 36 Md. 102 ; 11 Am. Rep. 469 ; *Patterson v. Triumph Ins. Co.*, 64 Me. 500 ; *Boyntom v. Clinton & Essex, etc., Ins. Co.*,
16 Barb. (N. Y.) 254 ; *Hartford Protection Ins. Co. v. Harmer*, 2 Ohio St. 452 ;
Globe Ins. Co. v. Boyle, 21 Ohio St. 119. Where the insurers received and kept
the proofs nearly two months and then returned them, stating generally that they
were not in accordance with the requirements of the policy, and that until such
conditions were complied with, no answer would be given as to what the company
would do, it was held that the company could not remain silent for that length of
time and then object in general terms. That by its delay and failure to point out
specifically the defects relied on, it was estopped from setting up the defects
by way of defense. *Imperial F. Ins. Co. v. Murray*, 73 Penn. St. 13 ; *Peoria F
& M. Ins. Co. v. Whitehill*, 25 Ill. 466. In *St. Louis Ins. Co. v. Kyle*, 11 Mo. 278,
the court very pertinently said : "If the formal proofs of interest and loss are
defective the insurer must apprise the assured of their objections. If insurers
receive the proof without objection, and refuse to pay the claim upon other
grounds, they cannot be permitted to avoid liability by showing technical objections to proofs furnished." In *Franklin Fire Ins. Co. v. Chicago Ice Co.*, 36 Md.
102 ; 11 Am. Rep. 469, the policy, among other things, required that a certificate
of a magistrate, notary public, or commissioner of deeds, most contiguous to the
fire, should be forwarded, etc. The proofs were furnished but the certificate was
not. The insurer kept the proofs two months without objecting to their form or
sufficiency. Held, that they thereby waived all objection to the non-production
of the certificate. Where defects in the proofs exist, which have not been pointed
out or objected to by the insurer, they are waived ; but the assured *may* amend
his proofs on trial to meet the defendant's objections, *when the objection is then
made for the first time*, or even supply new and complete proofs to meet the objection, and their reception by the court is not a good ground of exception. *Works
v. Farmers' etc., Ins. Co.*, 57 Me. 281 ; *Post v. Ætna Ins. Co.*, 43 Barb. (N. Y.) 351.

² *Citizens' Ins. Co. v. Doll*, 35 Md. 89 ; 6 Am. Rep. 360 ; *Edwards v. The Balt.
Ins. Co.*, 3 Gill. (Md.) 176.

³ *Hartford Protection Ins. Co. v. Harmer*, 2 Ohio St. 452 ; *Globe Ins. Co. v. Boyle*,
21 Ohio St. 119 ; *Vose v. Robinson*, 9 John. (N. Y.) 192 ; *Peoria M. & F. Ins. Co.
v. Lewis*, 18 Ill. 553 ; *Warner v. Peoria M. & F. Ins. Co.*, 14 Wis. 318 ; *Imperial
F. Ins. Co. v. Murray*, 73 Penn. St. 13. In *Winnesheik Ins. Co. v. Schueller*, 60
Ill. 465, the policy required the proofs to be made within thirty days after the loss.
The proofs were made and delivered to the company, but were not correct in form.
The insured called at the office several times, but no objections were made to the
proofs. It was held that all objections were waived, and could not afterwards be
set up as a defense to an action upon the policy. In *Basch v. Humboldt, etc., Ins.
Co.*, 35 N. J. L. 429, the proofs were seasonably furnished, and no objections were
made thereto until the time of trial. It was held that they were waived.

⁴ *Ins. Co. of N. America v. McDowell*, 50 Ill. 120 ; *Imperial F. Ins. Co. v. Murray*, 73 Penn. St. 13.

the assured of the defects, so that he may know what is essential in order to perfect his claim, and a mere general objection to their sufficiency does not exclude the idea of a waiver of strict prooof.[1]

But, it is held in Maryland that when the insurer, after receiving the proofs, wrote the insured that the proofs of loss furnished by him were totally unsatisfactory, as to the amount of his claim, and that, while the company denied all responsibility, by reason of misrepresentations as to title and property they reserved *all* objections to his right to recover, *in any form*, it was held that the insurer could not be said to have waived *any* of the defects in the preliminary proofs.[2] Where the proofs are made out by the insurer's agent, or according to his direction, the company cannot by a general notice, without specifying in what respects the proofs are defective, require the assured to furnish additional proofs.[3]

A waiver of *notice of loss* does not operate as a waiver of preliminary

[1] *Home Ins. Co.* v. *Cohen*, 20 Gratt. (Va.) 312; *Madsden* v. *Phœnix, etc., Ins. Co.*, 1 S. C. 24.

[2] *Citizens' Ins. Co.* v. *Doll*, 35 Md. 89; 6 Am. Rep. 360; *Edwards* v. *Balt. F. Ins. Co.*, 3 Gill (Md.) 176. But the doctrine of these cases rests upon the ground that the proofs were stated to be insufficient, and the act of the insurer was such as to put the insured upon his diligence in conforming to the requirements of the policy, all idea of a waiver was excluded. In *Phillips* v. *Protection Ins. Co.*, 14 Mo. 220, the insurers placed their refusal upon other grounds than defects in the proofs of loss, and did not object to the proofs as defective, but stated generally, " *we waive nothing.*" The court very properly held that the plaintiff could not affect the legal rights of the insured by any such general reservation, and that the question was whether there was a *waiver in fact.*

[3] In *Pratt* v. *N. Y. Central Ins. Co.*, 55 N. Y. 505; 14 Am. Rep. 304, the plaintiff having a mortgage on certain property applied to defendant's agent for an insurance upon his interest. The form of the policy was left to the judgment of the agent, who made out the policy in form to the owners of the property, " loss, if any, payable to E. B. Pratt, as his interest may appear." The premium was paid by plaintiff. The policy contained a clause, that if there was any change of title or foreclosure of a mortgage, without the consent of the company indorsed thereon, the insurance should immediately cease. In case of claim for loss made payable to another party as collateral security, proof of loss was to be made by the party originally insured. The mortgage was afterward foreclosed and plaintiff became the purchaser of the mortgaged premises. He then gave notice of the change in title to defendant's agent, who said the policy might stand as security for plaintiff's interests, and that the proper entries would be made in the books. The next night the insured property was burned. The mortgagors declined to furnish proofs of loss; plaintiff procured a blank of the agent, and under his instructions made out the proofs. These proofs were received by defendant May 26, 1871, and retained by it. On June 6, 1871, defendant notified plaintiff that the proofs were not in conformity with the policy and would not be recognized as proofs. No additional proofs were made. The trial was without a jury and plaintiff obtained judgment, which was affirmed at general term. Defendant appealed. Upon this point, ANDREWS, J., said: " The proofs of loss were prepared in conformity with the direction of the defendant's agent and secretary, and were retained by the defendant; and under the circumstances the plaintiff was not bound to furnish additional proofs upon a general notice by the company, without specification of the points in respect to which they were deemed defective ."

proofs,[1] and the fact that the insurer sends an agent to examine the premises, is not, of itself, a waiver of such proofs.[2] The insurer, either through its officers or agents must say or do that which fairly induces a belief that proofs of loss are not required, and whether they have done that in a given case, is purely a question for the jury,[3] and it is also for the jury to say whether they contain an as particular account of the loss as the circumstances of the case admit of,[4] but it is for the court to determine their sufficiency.[5]

Approval cannot be withdrawn.

SEC. 418. Where the insurer has once signified his satisfaction with the proofs, he cannot subsequently withdraw such approval, and set up objections thereto.[6] In the proofs of loss, an *honest*, although *erroneous* statement, will not defeat the insurer's liability. Thus, where the policy provided that all persons having a claim under the policy should give immediate notice and render a particular account, stating the ownership of the property insured; and that any fraud or attempt at fraud should forfeit all claim under the policy, and the plaintiff stated that the property belonged to him as "the legal heir of his wife," and by "purchase at auction" it was held, that the statement that he was the legal heir of his wife, although incorrect, there being no designed deception, and the defendant's agent being aware of all the facts, was not the statement of a fact calculated to mislead, and did not destroy the plaintiff's rights under the policy.[7]

When proofs of loss need not be made.

SEC. 419. There would seem to be no doubt that, *whenever the insurer has done or said that which is calculated to mislead the insured, or induce him to believe that proofs of loss would be of no avail, and are not required, such acts operate as a waiver of the presentation of preliminary proofs.* Thus, in a case recently decided by the Supreme Court of Illinois, but

---

[1] *Desilver* v. *State, etc., Ins. Co.*, 38 Penn. St. 13.

[2] *Busch* v. *Ins. Co.*, 6 Phila. (Penn.) 252.

[3] *Todd* v. *Ætna Ins. Co.*, 1 W. N. C. 227 (Penn.); *Franklin F. Ins. Co.* v. *Updegraff*, 43 Penn. St. 350; *Lycoming, etc., Ins. Co.* v. *Schollenberger*, 44 Penn. St. 259; *Farmers', etc., Ins. Co.* v. *Taylor*, 73 id. 342; *Greenwald* v. *Ins. Co.*, 3 Phila. (Penn.) 323; *Lycoming Ins. Co.* v. *Schreffler*, 42 id. 188.

[4] See first two cases in preceding note.

[5] *Com. Ins. Co.* v. *Sennett*, 41 Penn. St. 161.

[6] In *Atlantic Ins. Co.* v. *Wright*, 22 Ill. 462, the agent of the insurer expressed satisfaction with the proofs of loss furnished, but subsequently the secretary objected thereto, and required new proofs without specifying the defects in those furnished. The court held, that having once expressed its satisfaction therewith, they were estopped from objecting thereto.

[7] *Rohrbach* v. *The Ætna Ins. Co.*, 62 N. Y. 613.

not yet reported,[1] the insurer, before proofs of loss had been made, *denied all liability under the policy, and absolutely refused to pay anything thereon*, in consequence of which the insured neglected to make any preliminary proofs. The insurer, however, upon the trial of an action upon the policy to recover the loss, set up the failure of the plaintiff to make the preliminary proofs of loss as required by the policy. But the court held that the defendant, by his acts, had led the plaintiff to believe that such proofs were not required and would be of no avail, and was thereby estopped from setting up the breach of such condition in defense, and that his acts were such as operated as a waiver, and this seems to be consistent with the doctrine generally held by the courts, although, in most of the cases, defective proofs had been furnished, while in this, *none whatever* were made, the court holding that a person is not compelled to do that which the act of the other party has led him to suppose was unnecessary.[2]

There would seem to be no good reason why the acts of the insurer might not be treated *as a waiver of the production of any proofs whatever*, as well as of a failure in particular respects, and, in cases where the question depends upon oral proof, it is for the jury to say whether a waiver of *any* proofs of loss is established, or whether all objections to defects in those furnished, were waived by the insurer.[3]

A refusal to pay, and an absolute denial of all liability for the loss, before any preliminary proofs have been made, and while there is yet time for the insured to comply with the conditions of the policy in that respect,

---

[1] *Williamsburgh City F. Ins. Co.* v. *Cary.*

[2] *Norwich and New York Trans. Co.* v. *Western Mass. Ins. Co.*, 34 Conn. 561, aff'd in U. S. Sup. Ct., 12 Wall. 194; *Schenck* v. *Mercer Co., etc., Ins. Co.*, 24 N. J. 447; *Tayloe* v. *Merchants', etc., Ins. Co.*, 9 How. (U. S.) 396; *Maryland Ins. Co.* v. *Bathurst*, 5 G. & J. (Md.) 159; *Allegre* v. *Maryland Ins. Co.*, 6 H. & J. (Md.) 408; *Graves* v. *Washington, etc., Ins. Co.*, 12 Allen (Mass.) 391; *Francis* v. *Somerville Ins. Co.*, 25 N. J. 78; *Noyes* v. *Washington, etc., Ins. Co.*, 30 Vt. 680.

[3] *Norwich and New York Trans. Co.* v. *Western Mass. Ins. Co.*, ante; *Graves* v. *Washington, etc., Ins. Co.*, 12 Allen (Mass.) 391; *Martin* v. *Fishing Ins. Co.*, 20 Pick. (Mass.) 389; *Francis* v. *Ocean Ins. Co.*, 6 Cow. (N. Y.) 404; *Heath* v. *Franklin Ins. Co.*; *O'Neill* v. *Buffalo Ins. Co.*, 3 N. Y. 122; *Drake* v. *Farmers' Ins. Co.*, 3 Grant's Cas. (Penn.) 325. It is true that, in some cases, a contrary doctrine has *seemingly* been established, but it will be found that generally the distinction arises because the requirement as to preliminary proofs is contained in the charter or by-laws of the company, so that the officers of the company could not waive compliance. In *Patrick* v. *Farmers' Ins. Co.*, 43 N. H. 621, it was held that a vote of the directors not to pay anything on the policy was held not a waiver of proofs of loss, and that, in order to perfect his claim, the assured must comply with the policy in that respect. In *Pettengill* v. *Hinks*, 9 Gray (Mass.) 169, the assured and an agent of the assured submitted the questions at issue under the policy to arbitration. The court held that, where the insurer in his answer denied that he had ever waived the conditions of the policy, the submission cannot be regarded as proof of a waiver of preliminary proofs. But the doctrine of these cases is not generally accepted.

is in law a waiver of the conditions of the policy requiring such proofs to be made. By an absolute denial of all liability, the insurer admits the loss, and such denial operates as a notice to the assured that payment will not be made, in any event, upon grounds other than a failure to comply with the conditions as to proofs of loss, and thus renders them wholly unnecessary, as the law does not require that a person shall perform an act which the act of the other party has rendered unnecessary, or a mere idle formality,[1] and, where the insurer denies all liability for the loss, before preliminary proofs have been made, the insurer may commence his action *at once* without making such proofs, and even though the policy provides that an action shall not be brought within a certain time, which has not expired.[2] The payment of a part of the loss before preliminary proofs have been furnished, is a waiver of their production.[3]

The entire incapacity of the assured to make proofs of loss, as, if he is incapacitated by severe illness, or by reason of having become insane, or from any cause that operates as an absolute incapacity, performance of the condition is excused.[4]

When defense is put on other grounds.

SEC. 420. When an insurer, *with knowledge of a claim made under a policy*, rests his defense exclusively on other grounds, he is treated as

---

[1] *Norwich, etc., Trans. Co.* v. *Western Mass. Ins. Co., ante; Williamsburgh City F. Ins. Co.* v. *Cary, ante; Tayloe* v. *Merchants' Ins. Co., ante.* In *Post* v. *Ætna Ins. Co.*, 43 Barb. (N. Y.) 351, the defendants denied all liability, upon the ground that no contract of insurance existed, the insurer claiming that the policy had not been renewed. No proofs of loss were furnished, and, upon trial of the action to recover for the loss, the defendant set up the plaintiff's failure to make preliminary proofs in defense. The court held that, if the defendant intended to resist payment upon that ground, they should have so stated, because the plaintiff had then ample time to have supplied them, and that, not having done so until it was too late for the plaintiff to furnish them, they might be treated as having waived their production. In *Dean* v. *Ætna Life Ins. Co.*, 4 T. & C. (N. Y.) 497, the insured applied to the insurer's agent for blanks to make preliminary proofs, who refused to furnish them. *because the defendants did not recognize any liability.* The court held that this was a waiver of preliminary proofs, and that none were necessary. See also, *McBride* v. *Republic F. Ins. Co.*, 80 Wis. 562 ; *Parker* v. *Amazon Ins. Co.*, 34 id. 363 ; *La Societe, etc.,* v. *Morris*, 24 La. An. 347 ; *N. E. F. & M. Ins. Co.* v. *Robinson*, 25 Ind. 536 ; *Manhattan Ins. Co.* v. *Stein*, 5 Bush (Ky.) 652 ; *Stetson* v. *Ins. Co.*, 4 Phila. (Penn.) 8 ; *Martin* v. *Fishing Co.*, 20 Pick. (Mass.) 389 ; *McComas* v. *Covenant, etc., Ins. Co.*, 56 Mo. 573 ; *Lewis* v. *Monmouth, etc., Ins. Co.*, 52 Me. 492 ; *Priest* v. *Citizens, etc., Ins. Co.*, 3 Allen (Mass.) 602 ; *Noyes* v. *Washington Ins. Co.*, 30 Vt. 659 ; *Rippstein* v. *St. Louis, etc., Life Ins. Co.*, 57 Mo. 86 ; *Spratley* v. *Hartford Ins. Co.*, 1 Dill. (U. S. C. C.) 392.

[2] *Warren* v. *Peoria, etc., Ins. Co.*, 14 Wis. 318 ; *Norwich, etc., Ins. Co.* v. *Western, etc., Ins. Co.*, 24 Conn. 561 ; *Phoenix Ins. Co.* v. *Taylor*, 5 Minn. 492.

[3] *Westlake* v. *St. Lawrence Ins. Co.*, 14 Barb. (N. Y.) 206 ; *Parker* v. *Amazon Ins. Co.*, 34 Wis. 363.

[4] *Ins. Companies* v. *Boykin*, 12 Wall. (U. S.) 433.

having waived all objections to the *seasonableness or sufficiency* of notice or proofs of loss, and cannot afterwards avail himself of defects therein.[1]

When the policy requires that, in case of loss, the assured shall deliver to the company a particular account, in writing, under oath, stating the value and nature of his interest therein, such condition must be strictly complied with; and an account which *does not* state the nature and value of his interest in the property is insufficient, although the loss is total, and the value of the property, as well as the nature of the assured's interest in the property, is stated in the application, which was expressly made a part of the policy.[2] "Whatever," said MERRICK, J., in the case last referred to, "may be the extent or the degree of its importance to the defendants, the parties, by an express stipulation have made the rendition of such an account an essential pre-requisite to the right to recover any part of the insurance. The plaintiff having failed to comply with this indispensable condition, can maintain no action against the defendant upon the policy."

When the insurer is informed of a loss by the insured, and without saying anything about preliminary proofs, proceeds to inquire whether the insurance is valid, upon a specific ground independent of those required to be stated in the proofs, and declines to pay the loss upon a specific ground, this operates as a waiver of all objection to the insufficiency, or even the entire absence of preliminary proofs.[3] All that can be required of the insurer is a reasonable and substantial compliance with the conditions of the policy. Thus where proofs of loss, really informal or insufficient, have been made,

---

[1] *Martin* v. *Fishing Ins. Co.*, 20 Pick. (Mass.) 389; *Vos* v. *Robinson*, 9 John. (N. Y.) 192; *Tayloe* v. *Merchants' Ins. Co.*, 9 How. (U. S.) 390; *Thwing* v. *Gt. Western Ins. Co.*, 111 Mass 110. In *Peoria M. & F. Ins. Co.* v. *Whitehill*, 25 Ill. 466, the plaintiff sent his proofs to the company, and subsequently asked the defendant's secretary if he should make further proofs. The secretary replied that "he could do so if he pleased." The court held that the failure of the defendant to point out the defects in the proofs, and resting his defense on *other* grounds, had waived all defects in the preliminary proofs. *Gt. Western Ins. Co.* v. *Staaden*, 26 Ill. 360; *Globe Ins. Co.* v. *Boyle*, 21 Ohio St. 119; *Allegre* v. *Maryland Ins. Co.*, 6 H. & J. (Md.) 408; *Catlett* v. *Pacific Ins. Co.*, 4 Wend. (N. Y.) 75; *Bumstead* v. *Dividend Mut. Ins. Co.*, 12 N. Y. 81; *Ocean Ins. Co.* v. *Francis*, 2 Wend. (N. Y.) 64. Where the defendant's agent informed the plaintiff that the company objected to paying on account of the quantity, quality and value of the loss, it was held that this amounted to a waiver of defects in preliminary proofs. *Phillips* v. *Protection Ins. Co.*, 14 Mo. 220; *Lycoming Ins. Co.* v. *Dunmore*, 75 Ill. 14.

[2] *Wellcome* v. *People's, etc., Ins. Co.*, 2 Allen (Mass.) 480.

[3] *West Rockingham, etc.,* v. *Sheets & Co.*, 26 Gratt. (Va.) 854.

and the company return them for correction in a *particular* respect, they thereby waive all other informalities or insufficiencies.[1]   Thus, in the last named case one of the conditions of the policy required that the insured should forwith give notice of his loss, and as soon as possible deliver in a particular statement of such loss, *signed with his own hand* and verified by his oath or affirmation; and also, if required, to produce his books of account, etc., and exhibit the same for examination to any person named by the company; and that, until such proofs were furnished the loss should not be deemed payable. The account was first furnished under the oath of an agent, and being objected to was then furnished under the oath of the principal.   No other proofs were called for by the insurer, and no person was named to examine the books of the insured, and the court held that this constituted a waiver of all other proofs, and of an examination of the books.   In a recent case in Illinois,[2] it was held that, where goods are insured and are afterwards removed to another place, where they are lost, and the company having been notified of the removal, had not canceled the policy, their failure to so cancel will be taken as a ratification of the act of removal, and they will be held liable for the loss.   And where it is evident that, in any event, the company intend to dispute the claim, the insured is not bound to make a proof of loss which he has every reason to believe will be wholly useless by the rejection of the company.   And, in case of refusal, an insured is at liberty to bring suit at once, and is not bound to await the expiration of the time given the company in the policy to pay any loss.

Where the policy requires that the insured shall, as preliminary to payment of the loss, submit himself to examination upon oath, by the insurer, as to the loss and the claim therefor, and after it has been reduced to writing shall subscribe the same, the insurer is bound to comply with the provision, and upon failure to do so, cannot recover upon the policy.[3]

Agent may waive.

SEC. 421. Although the policy specially provides that preliminary proof of loss shall be made in a particular mode, and within a certain limited time, yet the company may, *through its agents, even,* waive the benefit of the provisions, and a waiver may be implied from the

---

[1] *Home Ins. Co.* v. *Cohen,* 20 Gratt. (Va.) 30.

[2] *Williamsburgh F. Ins. Co.* v. *Cary.*   (Not yet reported.)

[3] *Bonner* v. *Home Ins. Co.,* 13 Wis. 677.

manner in which the company or its agents have dealt with the policy-holder subsequent to the loss; and where there is no dispute as to the facts, the question as to whether compliance with such preliminaries has been waived, is one of law for the court. It is not essential that the company should, in express terms, have waived compliance; it is sufficient if it, or its agents, have done that which was calculated to induce the policy-holder to so believe, or that its acts have been such as to lessen his diligence in the matter, or as led him to suppose that such preliminaries were not required.[1]

---

[1] *Eastern R. R. Co. v. Relief Ins. Co.*, 98 Mass. 420; *Ames v. N. Y. Union Ins. Co.*, 14 N. Y. 253; *Phœnix Ins. Co. v. Taylor*, 5 Minn. 402; *Madsden v. Phœnix Ins. Co.*, 1 S. C. 24; *Warner v. Peoria, etc., Ins. Co.*, 14 Wis. 318; *Ide v. Phœnix Ins. Co.*, 2 Biss. (U. S.) 333; *Ins. Co of N. America v. Hope*, 58 Ill. 75; 11 Am. Rep. 48. A particular statement of the loss may be waived by the company, and if there be any evidence from which such a waiver may be inferred, it is for the jury. Where the agent of the company had agreed with the assured to ascertain the amount of their loss from their books, and in the answer sent by the company in reply to the statement of the loss, refusing payment "on account of circumstances connected with the insurance," there was no objection to the statement sent, the evidence of waiver was held sufficient to justify a submission to the jury; and the jury must determine from the evidence what degree of particularity in the account of the loss sent to the insurance company the nature of the case admitted of. *Franklin, etc., Ins. Co. v. Updegraff*, 43 Penn. St. 350. If the company, on notice of loss, refer the insured to their resident agent for settlement, and instruct the agent to procure a statement of the loss, he is thereby invested with full authority to receive, and extend the time for furnishing it; and if given within the time required by the agent, *though after thirty days from the fire*, the condition in the policy requiring it to be made within that time is not broken. Where there is any evidence as to the authority given to the agent by the company to act in the premises, and of an actual waiver of condition on the part of the agent, it is for the jury; and though a waiver must be intentional and clearly proven, the sufficiency of the evidence relating thereto is for the jury, whose error in judgment thereon can be corrected only by motion for a new trial. In an insurance of a single property (a coal-breaker) under a valued policy, where the insured, immediately after its destruction by fire, wrote to the company, stating that his "coal-breaker burnt down this morning," giving the number of his policy and the amount of his insurance, such a statement of loss, though in the preliminary notice, was held substantially a partular statement, and a compliance with the condition requiring it. *Lycoming, etc., Ins. Co. v. Schollenberger*, 44 Penn. St. 259. The waiver by the insurer of a written notice of loss by fire, as required by the conditions of a policy of insurance, is a question for the jury. *Drake v. Farmers' Union Ins. Co.*, 3 Grant (Penn.) 325; *Witherell v. Maine Ins. Co.*, 49 Me. 200. *Where the general agent of an insurance company, acting in the matter of his agency, and in relation to the particular loss and controversy in question, stated to an agent of the plaintiff, who had prepared and forwarded the preliminary proofs, that it was only the quantity and value of the property that the company disputed, it was held that the evidence was both admissible and important, as going to prove a waiver by the company of all objection to the preliminary proofs on accounts of defects in them.* *Rathbone v. City, etc., Ins. Co.*, 31 Conn. 193. If the insured complies with the instructions of the agent of the insurer in making his preliminary proofs, either as to form, substance or time, all defects in those respects are waived. *Security Ins. Co. v. Foy*, 22 Mich. 467; *Sims v. State Ins. Co.*, 47 Mo. 54; *Atlantic Ins. Co. v. Wright*, 24 Ill. 462. The question of waiver is for the jury. *Davis v. Western Mass. Ins. Co.*, 8 R. I. 277; *Franklin, etc., Ins. Co. v. Updegraff, ante: Edwards v. Baltimore F. Ins. Co.*, 3 Gill. (Md.) 176; *Noonan v. Hartford Ins. Co.*, 21 Mo. 81. And it seems that an agent, whose power has been revoked, may bind the com-

But, in the case of a mutual company, the charter must be looked to, to determine the powers of officers and agents. If the charter in any wise restricts the powers of officers, the restriction is complete. Thus, where the charter provided that the president, with one-third of the directors, shall be competent to transact all business of the corporation, neither the president alone, or the directors alone, have power to waive the preliminary proofs ;[1] but, where the matter rests simply in contract, as, where the policy provides that " no act or omission of any officer or agent shall be deemed a waiver of a full and strict compliance with the conditions concerning preliminary proofs, except it shall be in writing, signed by the secretary or president," the production of such proofs may, nevertheless, be shown to have been waived by any acts or omissions of the officers or agents of the insurer, that in fact or in law amount to a waiver.[2] The authority of the agent of an insurance company to receive proposals for insurance, and to countersign and deliver policies upon risks accepted by the company, does not extend to adjusting losses, nor empower him to waive the stipulated conditions as to proofs of loss, and to bind the company to pay without them ; nor does the fact that such agent assumes in a particular case to do those acts establish such authority.[3]

---

pany when the assured has no knowledge of the revocation of his power. Thus, an insurance policy on plate-glass windows, effected through L., the local agent of the defendant company, was subject to a condition, that, in case of loss, notice must be given to some known agent of the company. After the making of the policy, but before loss, the defendants transferred this branch of business to another company. It was held that notice of loss by the plaintiff (who did not know of this transfer) to L., who made his report thereon to the latter company, was sufficient. *Marsden* v. *City, etc., Assurance Co.,* L. R., 1 C. P. 232.

[1] *Dawes* v. *No. River Ins. Co.,* 7 Cow. (N. Y.) 462.

[2] *Pitney* v. *Glen's Falls Ins Co.,* 61 Barb. (N. Y.) 335.

[3] Thus, in *Bush* v. *Westchester Ins. Co.,* 2 T. & C. (N. Y.) 629, an action was brought upon a policy of insurance containing a condition that in case of loss the assured would render a particular account of the loss, would cause the property insured to be put in order, and an inventory to be made and furnished to the company, and would have the amount of damage ascertained by appraisal. This condition was not complied with, but plaintiff claimed that it had been waived by the defendant. To sustain the allegation of waiver, evidence was admitted, showing that after the fire, agents of other companies having policies on the property, estimated the damages, and agreed that the loss exceeded the whole amount of insurance, and that S., defendant's local agent for countersigning and issuing policies who had acted with the other agents, concurred in their conclusion, and said that he was satisfied the loss was more than double what the plaintiff was insured. The defendant objected to the evidence on the ground that S.'s authority was not proved. The judge at the trial charged the jury in substance that, so far as S. assumed to act for the defendant in waiving the proofs of loss required by the policy, the plaintiff had a right to infer that he had authority to act; that if S. said it was all right, the loss would be paid, that would amount to a waiver. It was held, that the admission of the evidence of the acts and declarations of S., and the charge as to the effect thereof, were error.

Other proof than that required by policy need not be given.   Reasonable proof.

SEC. 422. Where the policy requires proofs of loss to the satisfaction of
the company, *reasonable* proof only is required.   The company cannot
capriciously demand proof that is unreasonable.[1]   It is only required
in such cases, that such proof of the loss and its extent, from some one
of the perils insured against, should be given, *as ought to satisfy a
reasonable man.*[2]   If the policy provides the manner and extent, of
proof to be given, proofs in a different form or of other matters cannot
be required.[3]   The contract is the measure of the parties rights.`

Where the policy provides that the assured shall furnish a particular account of the loss, "and shall produce such other evidence
as the company may reasonably require," it is for the jury to say
whether certain evidence required was reasonable; and where the
company required the assured to furnish a builder's certificate, setting
forth the cost of reinstatement, or the value of the building, at the time
of loss, the failure of the assured to do so was held fatal to a recovery.[5]

Copies of invoices, books, vouchers, etc.

SEC. 423. *Full compliance with the conditions of a policy are indispensable to the insurer's right to recover, unless compliance is shown to be impossible, without the fault of the insurer, or has been waived by the insurer,*[6]
therefore, where the policy provides how, when and in what manner
proof of loss shall be made, and also provides that unless proof is made
in that way the insurer shall not be liable for the loss, the conditions
must be strictly performed, or a legal excuse therefor alleged and proved
by the assured.[7]   Thus, where the policy contains a clause requiring
the insured to produce " certified copies of all bills and invoices, the
originals of which have been lost," the condition must be complied
with, *or it must be shown that it was impossible for the insured to do so, or
that performance of the condition was waived by the insurer,* or no recovery
can be had, and the fact that the bills and invoices were all destroyed
by the fire does not of itself excuse full compliance with the condition.

[1] *Lawrence* v. *Ocean Ins. Co.,* 11 John (N. Y.) 240 ; *Braunstein* v. *Accidental
Death Ins. Co.,* 1 B. & S. 782 ; *Talcot* v. *Marine Ins. Co.,* 2 Johns. (N. Y.) 130.
[2] *Moore* v. *Woolsey,* 4 El. & Bl. 243 ; *Taylor* v. *Ætna Life Ins. Co.,* 13 Gray
(Mass.) 434.
[3] *Taylor* v. *Ætna Ins. Co., ante.*
[4] *Fox* v. *Conway F. Ins. Co.,* 53 Me. 107.
[5] *Fawcett* v. *Liverpool, etc., Ins. Co.,* 27 U. C. (Q. B.) 225.
[6] *Jennings* v. *Chenango Ins. Co.,* 2 Den. (N. Y.) 75 ; *Savage* v. *Howard Ins. Co.,*
52 N. Y. 502 ; *Jube* v. *Brooklyn Ins. Co.,* 28 Barb. (N. Y.) 412 ; *Columbian Ins.
Co.* v. *Lawrence,* 2 Pet. (U. S.) 52.
[7] *Bumstead* v. *Div. Mut. Ins. Co.,* 12 N. Y. 81 ; ALLEN, J., in *O'Brien* v. *Commercial Ins. Co.,* 63 N. Y. 111-113.

A reasonable attempt to perform it and a failure without the fault of the insured, must, at least, be shown.' Thus, in the case last referred to, the plaintiff, as sheriff of New York county, claimed to recover, by virtue of attachments in his hands against one Candler, the amount of a policy of insurance issued to Candler upon a stock of goods owned by him in Florida, and which had been destroyed by fire. The policy contained a provision identical with that referred to *supra.* The lower court instructed the jury, virtually, that if the invoices and bills were destroyed by fire, the insured was excused from compliance therewith. The portion of the charge covering this point was as follows: " I say, as matter of law, he was not bound to send off to persons of whom he was in the habit of purchasing, and require a new statement of the items; but if the facts of the case show that he could reasonably procure them, he was bound so to do." This ruling was held erroneous by the Court of Appeals, and the rule established that *compliance with the condition, or a reasonable effort, and a failure to do so without fault on his part, must be shown.*[2]

---

[1] *O'Brien* v. *Commercial Ins. Co.*, ante.

[2] *O'Brien* v. *Commercial Ins. Co.*, ante. The opinion of ALLEN, J., will be useful upon this point, and as it is not voluminous, I will give it entire. He said: " In addition to the more usual and ordinary preliminary proofs required to be furnished as a condition precedent to the right of the insured to indemnity against loss, the policy upon which this action is brought provides that the insured shall, if required, produce copies of all bills and invoices, the originals of which have been lost. The defendant's undertaking is to pay the loss or damage occasioned by the perils insured against, within sixty days after due proof thereof, in conformity to the conditions annexed to the policy. A full compliance with this condition was indispensable to a right of action upon the policy unless a compliance was impossible or was waived by the insurers. *Worsley* v. *Wood*, 6 T. R. 710; *Columbian Ins. Co.* v. *Lawrence*, 2 Pet. 52, 53; *Jube* v. *Brooklyn Fire Ins. Co.*, 28 Barb. 412; *Jennings* v. *Chen. Co. Mut. Ins. Co.*, 2 Den. 75; *Savage* v. *Howard Ins. Co.*, 52 N. Y. 502.

The books and papers of the insured, including the original invoices and bills of purchase, were destroyed by fire, and this gave to the insurer the right to certified copies. They were distinctly and specifically called by the letter of the agent of the defendant, and the other insurers of December 31, 1868, the insured having on the 9th of the same month, been formally advised that 'complete proofs of loss, as required by said policies,' must be made. They were not furnished, and on the 12th of January, in reply to an evasive letter from the insured, he was referred to the requirements of the letter of the 31st December, and told that the whole would be required under oath; and upon the 5th of February he was again called upon by letter for duplicate copies of all invoices of goods purchased in 1867 and 1868. The request was not complied with, nor was compliance shown to be impossible. No attempt to supply these proofs were shown. It will not be assumed that the merchants, of whom goods had been bought for the twenty months preceding the fire, were not known, could not be found, or would be unable to furnish duplicates of the bills of goods sold the insured during these months. There was no claim upon the trial that this condition had been complied with, that compliance was impossible, or that the defendant had waived it. The counsel for the respondent contended on the argument in this part of the condition had been waived; but had that been the contention at the trial it would have been a question of fact for the jury. The cause was not tried upon that

SEC. 424. Where an insurance company after a loss, has adjusted the claim therefor, and has agreed to pay a certain sum in liquidation of the claim, it cannot, in an action setting forth such facts, object that the action was not brought within the time limited in the policy. In such a case, the action is not upon the policy, but upon the agreement to pay. Neither, in such a case can it set up a breach of warranty, or of any of the conditions of the policy in defense, for *adjusting the loss and promising to pay it* is a waiver of all breaches on the part of the assured, and of all defenses which might have been made, except for such waiver.[1] A breach of any warranty or of any condition in the policy must be insisted upon when the claim is made, and before an agreement to pay the loss has been made, and even ignorance of the breach until after the agreement to pay was made, will not operate to lessen the force of the waiver. Nothing short of *fraud* on the part of the assured will have that effect.[2] In the language of CHURCH, C.J., in the case first referred to in the note, " If they saw fit to pay the claim, or compromise it, or to make a new contract without examination, it must be deemed to have waived it, *and in the absence of fraud, it cannot afterwards avail itself of such breach.* It cannot urge payment or settlement by mistake, on account of want of knowledge of

---

theory. The judge at circuit instructed the jury that the insured was not bound, as a condition precedent to a right of action upon the policy, and as a part of preliminary proofs, to furnish certified or duplicate copies of the bills of purchase, but was only bound to furnish such as he had in his possession, and left it to the jury to say whether he had given the insurers all the information he had, and the jury were told that if he had done so he had complied with the condition and was entitled to recover so far as that objection was concerned. It is not a question whether the condition is reasonable or unreasonable. It is lawful, the assured has assented to it, and we cannot dispense with it and make a new contract for the parties. Had the insured been unable from any cause fully to comply with the condition, and the inability had been shown to exist, and without his fault probably, a failure literally to comply with it might not have been fatal to the action. *Bunstead* v. *Div. Mut. Ins. Co.*, 2 Ker. 81. The difficulty is that the condition was ignored and set aside by the judge in his instructions to the jury, and the defendant deprived of the benefit of a material clause and condition of the contract. The intent and meaning of the clause is neither ambiguous nor obscure, and upon the most favorable interpretation for the insured, exacts from him upon the requisition of the insurers, duplicates of his invoices of purchases certified by the merchants from whom the purchases were made. The condition is reasonable and not difficult of performance, and the defendant has a right to insist upon a compliance. The court below seems to have regarded the certified copies called for by the condition as copies of originals in the actual possession having been destroyed, that the condition had become impossible of performance. They overlooked the fact that it was only in case of loss of the originals that certified copies could be required necessarily imposing the duty upon the insured to supplement his proofs by copies to be obtained from other sources, the sellers of the goods."

[1] *Smith* v. *Glen's Falls Ins. Co.*, 62 N. Y. 85.

[2] *Smith* v. *Glen's Falls Ins. Co.*, *ante; National Life Ins. Co.* v. *Minch.* 53 N. Y. 144.

such breach. *The time for investigation as to breaches of warranty, is when a claim is made for payment, and if the company elects to pay the claim, or what is equivalent, to adjust it by independent contract, it cannot afterwards, in the absence of fraud, fall back upon an alleged breach of warranty.*" The mere fixing of the amount of a loss under a policy, or an agreement that the loss amounts to a certain sum, is not of itself an admission on the part of the insurer that any liability exists against it upon the policy, but is a mere admission that a certain sum is due, if any liability exists. Thus, in a Rhode Island case,[1] the parties in interest fixed the amount of loss and damage, "subject to the terms and conditions of several policies." In an action against the insurers, it was held that this adjustment meant "subject to" *all the* "terms and conditions of the policies" not superseded by the agreement. Also, that the question of liability was not affected by this adjustment, which only determined to amount due in case of liability.

The burden of proving a loss from the cause, and to an amount for which insurers are liable, is upon the assured,[2] and notice to the company of the loss, and proper proofs thereof in conformity with the requirements of the policy, or a legal excuse for not making them, is a condition precedent to his right of recovery.[3] The assured takes the burden of proving the waiver of any condition of the policy, performance of which is a condition precedent to a recovery, and which has not been strictly performed.[4]

The proofs of loss filed by the assured are admissible as *prima facie* evidence of the facts stated therein, in favor of the insurer,[5] but they are not admissible as proof of the facts stated therein, in favor of the assured. A party cannot thus make evidence for himself.[6] Where the defects in proofs of loss are due to the agent of the insurers, or where the delay in sending them is due to such agent, the insurer cannot avail himself of such objection in defense.[7]

Waiver by mutual companies.

Sec. 425. Proofs of loss, not being of the substance of the contract, may be waived even by the officers of a mutual insurance company, and such

---

[1] *Whipple* v. *N. British, etc., Ins. Co.*, 11 R. I. 84 ; 5 Ins. L. J. 71.
[2] *Cory* v. *Boylston, etc., Ins. Co.*, 107 Mass. 140.
[3] *Mitchell* v. *Home Ins. Co.*, 32 Iowa, 421 ; *Commonwealth Ins. Co.* v. *Sennett*, 41 Penn. St. 161 ; *Citizen's F. Ins. Co.* v. *Dall*, 35 Md. 89 ; 6 Am. Rep. 360.
[4] *West Rockingham, etc., Ins. Co.* v. *Sheets*, 26 Gratt. (Va.) 854.
[5] *Ins. Co.* v. *Newton*, 22 Wall. (U. S.) 32.
[6] *Lycoming Ins. Co.* v. *Schreffler*, 44 Penn. St. 259 ; *Commonwealth Ins. Co.* v. *Sennett*, 41 id. 181.
[7] *Ins. Co. of N. America* v. *Hope*, 58 Ill. 75 ; 11 Am. Rep. 48 ; *Eastern R. R. Co.* v. *Relief Ins. Co.*, ante.

waiver may be proved by any act that shows that such preliminaries
are not required. Thus, where after a loss one of the officers made a
personal examination of the premises, and afterwards within the time
limited for making the proof, the secretary told the plaintiff that no
further proof of loss was necessary, and the company subsequently
voted not to pay the loss, basing their refusal on other grounds, it was
held that the plaintiff was thereby excused from making formal proof
of loss as required in the policy.[1]

Notice of a loss is unnecessary when the officers of the company the
next day after the fire are present to inspect the premises.[2]

Estoppel.

SEC. 426. In all cases where a party has an election, he will be bound
by the course he first adopts, with full knowledge of all the facts, and
any act that indicates that an election has been made, and that in any
respect affects the rights of the other party, estops him from afterwards
doing anything inconsistent with such election. Therefore, where an
insurance company is in a position where it may be liable upon a policy
or not, at its election, whenever it does an act that indicates that it
has elected to treat the policy as the basis of a legal claim against it,
it cannot afterwards recede, if anything has been done of a decisive
character, indicating its election. Thus, in a Wisconsin case,[3] the
plaintiff took out a policy of insurance upon his dwelling-house in the
defendant's company, conditioned that " if the assured shall have, or
shall hereafter make any other insurance on the property hereby
insured, or any part thereof, without the consent of the company,
written hereon," the policy should be void ; subsequently, without
consent, he procured other insurance. After a loss under the policy,

---

[1] *Priest* v. *Citizen's, etc., F. Ins. Co.*, 3 Allen (Mass.) 602 ; *Underhill* v. *Agawam
Ins. Co.*, 6 Cush. (Mass.) 440 ; *Brewer* v. *Chelsea Ins. Co.*, 14 Gray (Mass.) 203 ;
Blake v. *Exchange Ins. Co.*, 12 Gray (Mass.) 265 ; *Hale* v. *Mechanics' Ins. Co.*, 6
id. 169. In *Eastern R. R. Co.* v. *Relief Ins. Co.*, 105 Mass. 570, the effect of a
waiver of a strict compliance with the conditions of a policy was well illustrated.
The plaintiff had a policy against loss by fire occasioned by sparks from its
engine to property of others on lands not occupied by it. The policy provided
that notice of such loss should forthwith be given to the company in writing by
the parties interested, and that within sixty days from the time of the happening
of the fire, as particular an account of the loss should be given as the case would
admit of. Several fires had occurred, of which no notice was given. The treasurer
of the plaintiff, after several fires had occurred, informed the agent that a good
many fires were occurring the claims for which they were examining carefully.
The agent said this was satisfactory and when they got through paying to hand
in a schedule and it should be attended to. The court held that this amounted to
a waiver of the condition of the policy in reference to proofs.

[2] *Rowmage* v. *Ins. Co.*, 1 Green (N. J.) 110.

[3] *Webster* v. *Phœnix Ins. Co.*, 36 Wis. 67 ; 17 Am. Rep. 479.

the defendant *knowing* that the plaintiff had procured such other insurance, required him to furnish plans and specifications of the building,
which was done *at great expense*, and the court held that this was such
a decisive act as indicated the defendant's election, and estopped it
from afterwards setting up the breach of the condition of the policy,
in avoidance of liability. But acts that merely indicate that the
defendant is gathering information to enable it to make an election,
and which do not change the *status* of the parties, or involve any
expense on the part of the assured, are not sufficient to indicate a
waiver. As where after a loss the insurer appoints an appraiser to
ascertain the loss,[1] and it has been held that where a mutual company,
after a loss under a policy, in issuing a notice of assessment indorsed
in a printed form, a printed schedule of losses *claimed* of the company,
among which was that of the plaintiff, but marked " unadjusted."
This is not evidence of a waiver, of a breach of the condition of the
policy, because it does not indicate that an election has been made,
but is a mere notice that such a loss is claimed. Acts relied upon by
way of estoppel, must clearly indicate an *election made*, and must be
such as are inconsistent with a purpose on the part of the insurer to
rely upon the breach of the conditions of the policy, and such as have,
in some manner, changed the *status* of the parties.

The assured may show errors in, in certain cases.

Sec. 427. When the assured has erroneously stated certain facts in
his proofs of loss *without any fraudulent intent* as to the quantity of
property destroyed,[2] or their value, when the *cost* thereof was only
stated in the proofs, as required by the insurer,[3] or as to the occupancy
of the property at the time of the loss, or in reference to other insurance, he may show that the proofs are erroneous, and what the facts
really are.[4]

---

[1] *Jewett* v. *Home Ins. Co.*, 29 Iowa, 562.

[2] *Ætna Ins. Co.* v. *Stevens*, 48 Ill. 31 ; *Commercial Ins. Co.* v. *Huchberger*, 52 id·
464.

[3] *Hoffman* v. *Ætna Ins. Co.*, 32 N. Y. 405.

[4] *Parmalee* v. *Hoffman F. Ins. Co.*, 54 N. Y. 193. In *McMasters* v. *Ins. Co. of
N. America*, 55 N. Y. 222, Folger, J., in a very able opinion covering this question, said : "The other branch of the objection is, that the assured, having made
his verified proofs of loss with this statement in it, had led them into a particular
defense, and is estopped to deny it. The fact that there is a verification does not
of itself conclude the assured. It has been repeatedly held to the contrary.
Smith v. *Ferris*, 1 Daly, 18–20, and cases there cited. If by this objection is
meant, that the plaintiff is estopped to show the existence of a contract of insurance, and the circumstances which have created a liability to him on the part of
the defendants, and that this rests upon the established doctrine of an *estoppel in
pais*, we cannot so hold. The proofs of loss do not create the liability to pay the

But in Massachusetts, the courts, relying upon the *dicta* of a case[1] heard in the superior court of New York city, have held that if a

---

loss. They do no more in this aspect than to set running the time at the end of which the amount contracted for shall become payable, and at which action may be brought to enforce the liability. All the elements of an *estoppel in pais* are lacking. It arises from an act or declaration of a person, intended or calculated to mislead another, on which that other has relied, and has so acted or refrained from action, as that injury will befall him if the truth of the act or declaration be denied. Now the declaration of the assured in the proofs of loss was not intended nor calculated to mislead the defendants into any change of their situation, by which they assumed a liability to him or assented to the existence of one. Its natural effect if it is to be interpreted as the defendants claim that it should be, is to prevent an assent to the existence of a liability; and it had no effect, if thus interpreted, to create one. Nor did the defendants rely upon this declaration, and thereupon change their situation so as to contract or incur a liability. Before it was made they had done that from which their liability took its rise. Nor does the exhibition of the truth, though at enmity with the declaration, create or increase or change the situation. The case differs from two of those cited by the defendants, *The Trustees, etc.*, v. *Williams*, 9 Wend. 147, and *Sheppard* v. *Hamilton*, 29 Barb. 156, for in each of those the plaintiff, having an option of two courses of action in which to enforce a claim against the defendant, was led by the declaration of the latter, calculated to mislead, to take one which he could not afterward forsake without injury, but which he must be defeated in and forsake, if the defendant was permitted to falsify his declaration. And the fact stated there, in the declaration of the defendant, was the sole fact material in affecting the action of the plaintiff. Those cases do not go upon the ground that the declaration of the defendant led the plaintiff to sue; but on this, that he having a valid claim which might be sued in one form or another, or upon one instrument or another, dependent upon the existence of a certain fact; the statement of the defendant averring the existence of that fact, led to the adoption by the plaintiff of one of those courses, to abandon which or be driven from it afterward would have been of injury to the plaintiff; therefore the defendant was held to be estopped from denying the truth of that statement. If, notwithstanding the statement of the existence of that fact, the plaintiff had still been obliged to inquire for the existence of other facts, and to rely upon them also to sustain the course of action adopted, those decisions would have been different. The plaintiff's situation there, was changed after the declaration and by reason of it. Here the defendant's situation, as to its liability, is not changed thereby. It does not appear that, relying upon the defense supposed to be furnished by the statement in the proofs of loss, any other tenable defense had the go-by. It is suggested, that the plaintiff claimed on the trial that the other insurance was not on the same property, by reason of the words "on storage" in these policies, and that these words meant that the subject insured was the property of some one other than the insured, and, that, if this had been revealed by the proofs of loss, another defense would have been opened to the defendants; that then they would have insisted that the assured had no insurable interest, or that he had avoided the policy by omitting to state that his interest was not absolute. We do not understand that the plaintiff claimed on trial that the words mentioned meant that the property was not his. Indeed the witness, Lake, did not quote or refer to these words. The learned justice who tried the cause does, indeed, refer to them in his opinion, but only to enforce his position that the defendants, having the burden of proof upon them, did not give to the court all the light they should have done, if they would bring the court to see the case as they did. It is not perceived that this phrase was of such vitality in the case, as that the plaintiff's right of action hinged upon it, or that the true interpretation of it depended upon any fact, which would have afforded to the defendants another tenable defense. The decision in *N. Y. Central Ins. Co.* v. *Watson*, 23 Mich. 486, does not conflict with these views; while that of *Commerce Ins. Co.* v. *Huckberger*, 52 Ill. 464, and of *Huffman* v. *Ætna F. Ins. Co.*, 1 Robt. 601, aff'd 32 N. Y. 405–415, aid it. *Irving* v. *Excelsior F. Ins.*

---

[1] *Irving* v. *Excelsior Ins. Co.*, 1 Bos. (N. Y.) 507.

47

material statement in a notice and proofs of loss is erroneously made, and no amended statement is furnished before trial of an action upon

---

Co., 1 Bos. 507, is also cited by defendants. With respect for the considerate views of the learned judge who delivered the opinion in that case, we are bound to say that the utterance relied upon is *obiter*. Though it is said there that the plaintiff was concluded by the statement in his proofs of loss, and could not be heard to controvert it, yet the testimony which was objected to on that ground, and was received at trial notwithstanding objection, is considered on review, is given weight to as harmonizing with and confirming the statement, and judgment is given for the plaintiff, the statement being held to be substantially true. It is plain that the view taken of this point did not conduce to the judgment, and was not necessary to the judgment arrived at. So far as the *dictum* in that case is put upon the rendition of the proofs of loss being a condition precedent to a recovery, we shall allude to it further on. The case of *Campbell v. Charter Oak Ins. Co.*, 10 Allen. 213, went mainly upon that ground. Says DEWEY, J., delivering the opinion of the court : 'A true statement was called for by the conditions of the policy. It was a condition precedent to the liability to be called upon to pay the loss. If this be rejected as being a false statement, then no statement has been filed, and for that reason the plaintiff cannot recover. If allowed to stand as part of the statement, the policy has been avoided. It is difficult to perceive how the dilemma can be avoided while this statement remains as the only one filed with the company.' There are some observations of the learned judge, which look toward a recognition of the applicability, of the doctrine of an *estoppel in pais*, to the facts of the case. But there is nothing putting it squarely on that ground; and if there was, we should be compelled to differ for the reasons above stated. And, indeed, we may say that it seems to be with hesitation that the learned judge comes to the result, on any ground, that the assured was concluded by the statements in his proofs of loss. There is nothing in the case in hand which compels us to express an opinion upon the soundness of the view contained in the passage, which we have quoted from the opinion in the case last cited, and which is, to some extent, put forth in 1 Rosworth, *supra*. The conditions of the policies in the case here, require that the assured shall render a particular account of his claim, with an affidavit stating the time and circumstances of the fire, the other insurance, if any, and a copy of all policies, etc. ; and it is declared that until such proofs are rendered the loss shall not become payable. The current of the decisions runs to this : That courts will not be astute to find ways to work the forfeiture of a contract of insurance ; rather they will strive to uphold it, and will construe conditions and provisions in a policy strictly against an underwriter, and will incline to uphold the agreement. The terms of the condition will not be enlarged by construction to include what is not within its letter. With this in view, what is the claim of the defendants ? This : That the conditions of the policy are, that 'if the *assured* shall have any other insurance on the property therein insured, or any part thereof, without notice to and consent of the defendants in writing, the policy shall be null and void ;' that the proofs of loss do state that 'there was other insurance on the same property,' and give copies of the written parts of the policies ; that this shows that the assured has violated the condition against *his* having other insurance ; that thus the proofs of loss do declare to the defendants that the policies issued by them to him are · null and void ;' and that, relying upon that, they may make that defense and need make no other, for the plaintiff is concluded from denying the existence of the facts which he thus averred. This chain has one imperfect link. The assured does not declare, in his proofs of loss, that *he* had other insurance on the property. He declares only that there was other insurance upon it, which he is required to do by the terms of the clause in the policy which provides for the rendition of proofs of loss. The two things, other insurance had by the assured, and other insurance on the property, are not the same. *Ætna F. Ins. Co. v. Tyler*, 16 Wend. 385 ; *Rowley v. Empire Ins. Co.*, 3 Keyes, 557. He has not then, stated in his proofs of loss that which shows that he has made null and void his policies, and has not thus furnished to the defendants a defense upon which they may rely. Hence the plaintiff is not estopped by the statement of that as a fact. He has declared to them only that there was other insurance, it may be of him or

the policy, the assured will be held to the truth of his statement, and will not be permitted to show that the facts were otherwise than as stated therein.[1] "We do not mean," said DEWEY, J.,[2] "to say that the party may not correct mistakes of facts in his original statement, *but such corrections are not for the first time to be made known to the insurers at the trial of the action to recover for the loss by the introduction of evidence showing that the statements filed were not true in a material fact, which, if it existed as stated, was fatal to the right of the insured to recover.*" But the doctrine of the Massachusetts case is not generally recognized, and there would seem to be no doubt that the assured may, without filing an amended statement, show upon the trial that his proofs of loss are erroneous, *when the error is in fact a mistake, and not an attempt upon the part of the assured to defraud or mislead the insurer.* The justice of this rule is not doubtful. It often occurs that the assured is compelled, in order to comply with the conditions of the policy as to the time in which proofs are to be made, to make them

---

of some other man. They still are without the material for a perfect defense, and remain so until they learn and are able to show that such other insurance, was insurance had by the assured. Though they did at the trial show this fact, by the stipulation read, as to one of the policies of the other insurance, that was proof *aliunde* the proofs of loss. The plaintiff had a right to combat it, and, in view of the trial court, he combated it successfully, by proving to its satisfaction that it was not on the same property. It is contended that no inference can possibly be made, from the statements in the proofs of loss, save that the assured in these policies did have the other insurance. The defendants thus ask, in effect, that setting up a technical defense, they shall be sustained in it, in the absence of express showing, by an inference; and thus there be wrought a forfeiture of a contract, which the law looks upon with disfavor, solely upon the ground of an *estoppel in pais*, which the law equally disrelishes. For the law loves that the truth comes to light; but an estoppel hides it. It is permitted to do so only that a fraud shall not be wrought. We are not inclined to go the length that is demanded in such a case as this. There was one other objection made at the trial, which is referred to in the points in this court, and should be noticed. To the witness, Lake, was put the question: 'The buggy, chariotees, lumber-wagon, and other vehicles—was that the same property as mentioned in either of the policies sued upon?' It was objected that it was incompetent for the witness to state whether it was or not—the description should control. We understand this objection to raise the point that Lake, being a party to the contract of insurance containing this description, could not contradict it by parol. The rule that parol testimony may not be given to contradict a written contract, is applied only in suits between the parties to the instruments or their privies. The parties to a written instrument have made it the authentic memorial of their agreement, and for them it speaks the whole truth upon the subject-matter. It does not apply to third persons, who are not precluded from proving the truth, however contradictory to the written statements of others. Strangers to the instrument, not having come into this agreement, are not bound by it, and may show that it does not disclose the very truth of the matter. And as, in a contention between a party to an instrument and a stranger to it, the stranger may give testimony by parol differing from the contents of the instrument, so the party to it is not to be at a disadvantage with his opponent, and he, too, in such case, may give the same kind of testimony. *Badger* v. *Jones*, 12 Pick. 371; *Reynolds* v. *Magness*, 3 Iredell, 26."

[1] *Campbell* v. *Charter Oak Ins. Co.*, 10 Allen (Mass.) 213.
[2] *Campbell* v. *Charter Oak Ins. Co.*, *ante*.

up from mere recollection, without any data to guide him, and without time or opportunity to verify the absolute truth of his statements. Under such circumstances, it would be an exceedingly harsh and unjust rule that held the assured up to the strict truth of his statement, and denied him the privilege of showing that he had made an innocent mistake. Insurers have no right, under such circumstances, to exact *absolute* certainty, but only approximate, according to the means at hand, and the honest judgment, knowledge and understanding of the assured. "The proofs of loss," said FOLGER, J., in a very able opinion,[1] "are not a part of the contract of insurance, *nor a part of any contract. They are the act or declaration of one of the parties to a pre-existing contract in attempted compliance with its conditions.* The other party to the contract is not a party to this act or declaration, takes no part in making it, does not assert that it is a true statement, and is not bound thereby. The instrument which makes the proofs of loss may be amended at his will, subject always to the necessity that it be furnised to the insurer in such reasonable time as meets the requirements of the conditions of the policy." In the case last referred to, an action was brought upon two policies of insurance, issued by the defendants to one Lake. The policies containod a provision, that, in case other insurance upon the property was obtained without the consent of the insurer, the policy should be void. Lake had a policy in another company upon *other* property, in the same building, but had, in fact, no other insurance upon the *same* property covered by the defendant's policies. In the proofs, Lake stated that there was *other* insurance on the same property, setting forth the policy in the other company. Upon the trial, the defendant claimed exemption from liability upon the ground that other insurance existed without its consent, and relied upon the proofs of loss made by Lake to establish the fact. The plaintiff offered to prove by Lake that this was a mistake, and that, *in fact*, the other policy *did not* cover the property insured by the defendant. The evidence was admitted, and, upon appeal, the ruling of the court was sustained.

Notice of total loss does not dispense with proofs of loss.

SEC. 428. The fact that the loss is total, and that a notice of that fact, fixing the value at the sum for which it is insured in the policy, does not dispense with preliminary proofs, nor a particular statement of the loss if required by the terms of the policy, and this is not dispensed with because the insurer's agent examines the premises, and

---

[1] *McMasters* v. *N. American Ins. Co., ante.*

takes the sworn statement of the insured immediately after the loss. Thus in a Pennsylvania case,[1] the policy was, "on household furni. ture, $367, and upon groceries, $233." The policy provided that "the insured shall forthwith give notice thereof to the secretary, and within thirty days after said loss shall deliver to the secretary a particular account of such loss or damage, signed by his or her or their own hand or hands, or by their guardian, attorney or agent." A loss by fire occurred on the 31st day of August, 1858, and the next morning the local agent of the company, in company with counsel, visited the premises and made an examination of the circumstances attending the fire. The insured was examined under oath, and his testimony was reduced to writing, signed by him, and, the following day, sent by the agent to the secretary of the company. On the 20th of September, the insured sent the following notice to the secretary of the company :

"One frame house, insured in the Lycoming County Mutual Insurance Company, etc., was, on the 31st day of August, 1858, completely destroyed by fire and entirely lost.

"You are also hereby notified that, at the same time and place, the household furniture and groceries of the undersigned, insured by policy of insurance, dated the 29th day of July, 1854, and numbered 37,775, as follows, viz., household furniture, $367, groceries, $233, making together the sum of $600, were also lost and destroyed by fire aforesaid ; the whole property of undersigned in the house at the time being destroyed, with the exception only of a few articles of household furniture.

"You will take notice further, that the said the Lycoming County Mutual Insurance Company will be looked to by me for payment in full of the amount and sum insured by the policies aforesaid, and payment in full hereof will be required and demanded from them.

"DANIEL BEATTY.

"Duncansville, Blair Co., Pa."

No notice of insufficiency in the statement was given to the insured before the expiration of the "thirty days" mentioned in the policy. Under the instructions of the court, the insured recovered on the policy on the dwelling-house, but not on that on the furniture and groceries. The points made by counsel and the rulings of the court are stated sufficiently in the opinion. Both parties appealed.

---

[1] Beatty v. Lycoming Ins. Co., 66 Penn. St. 9; 5 Am. Rep. 318.

SHARSWOOD, J., in passing upon the question, said : "The learned judge instructed the jury that there was sufficient evidence of notice forthwith given by the assured of the occurrence of the fire to fulfill the requirement of the policies in that respect. It appears that the fire occurred August 31, 1858, and that the morning after, the local agent of the company, in company with counsel, visited the premises and made an examination of the circumstances attending it. Daniel Beatty, the insured, was himself examined as a witness under oath, his testimony or statement reduced to writing and signed by him. It was forwarded by the agent to the secretary of the insurance company on the following day, and was received by him. We think the learned judge was perfectly right in holding this a sufficient notice of the loss within the terms of the policy. In was held in The West Branch Insurance Company v. Helfenstein,[1] in cases in which the policy contained a condition expressed in the same words as this, that a written notice to the secretary from the local agent, upon information conveyed to him by the assured, is sufficient. There is nothing to prevent the assured from constituting the agent of the company his attorney to give the notice, and if he does not give the notice accordingly, the company cannot object, without a rule or condition prohibiting the agent from being employed for such purpose. But this case is stronger than that. The statement of the fact and circumstances of the fire was signed by the assured himself, and transmitted through the local agent to the secretary of the company. How it reached the proper destination is entirely immaterial, provided it was forwarded in due and reasonable time, which in this instance is not denied. This disposes of the writ of error of the insurance company.

The second question which is raised by the first assignment of error of the plaintiff below is, whether there was any evidence of such a particular statement of the loss under the policy upon household furniture and groceries as was required by its terms. The learned judge instructed the jury that there was not. The plaintiff maintains that the sufficiency of the statement was for the jury, upon the authority of The Franklin Ins. Co. v. Updegraff.[2] The report of that case does not furnish us with the statement. It is said in the charge of the court below to have been general, not particular ; that it did not specify the different articles consumed. We must assume, however, that some information was given of the character and extent of the loss.

[1] 37 Penn. St. 289.
[2] 44 id. 350.

It was then for the jury to say whether it was as particular as it should have been. But in this case there was no statement at all. The paper given in evidence as such is a mere reiteration of the description in the policy, namely: " Household furniture, $367 ; groceries, $233, making together the sum of $600, were also lost and destroyed by fire afore. said, the whole property of undersigned in the house at the time being destroyed, with the exception only of a few articles of household fur. niture." It is certainly not necessary in every case to report all the items in detail which constitute the loss. It may be entirely out of the power of the assured to do so. His books and papers may have been destroyed by the fire. But every person assured must be presumed to know enough to be able to remember some particulars, or to give a description, if it do not descend to details of the different kinds and value of the articles. There are few men who, with assistance of the members of their family, could not give some description of their house. hold furniture. In The Lycoming Co. Ins. Co. v. Updegraff,[1] an instruction to the jury that a statement of this character was not such a particular account of the loss as was required by the policy, was approved and affirmed by this court. The assignment of error, there. fore, is not sustained.

The only remaining question which is raised by the plaintiffs' second assignment is, whether there was any evidence of waiver by the company of the condition requiring a particular statement. The learned judge held that there was not, and we think rightly. It was required to be within thirty days after the fire. Now, to constitute a waiver, there should be shown some official act or dec. laration by the company during the currency of the time, dispens. ing with it; something from which the assured might reasonably infer that the underwriters did not mean to insist upon it. As is remarked by the present chief justice in Diehl v. Adams County Insurance Company,[2] " this never occurs unless intended or where the act relied on ought in equity to estop the party from denying it." Mere silence is not enough. After the thirty days had expired without any statement, nothing but the express agreement of the company could renew or revivify the contract. Had a statement been furnished, within the time it might have been the duty of the insurers to notify the assured of any merely formal defect, so that it might be remedied. If the paper, dated September 20th, 1858, was

---

[1] 41 Penn. St. 311.
[2] 59 Penn. St. 452.

to be regarded as a statement and not a mere notice of the loss, the defects of it were substantial, not formal merely. The case of The Inland Insurance Company v. Stauffer, 3 Penn. St. 397, was where a notice of loss was given to a director and not to the secretary. A few days afterward the president of the company and another director came out to view the ruins, meeting there committees from other insurance companies, and avowing that they came on the business of the insurers. These facts it was held might be submitted with others to the jury as evidence of a waiver, of a strict and formal compliance with the condition. That case is in none of its circumstances parallel with this."

False swearing, or attempt at fraud.

Sec. 429. Where the policy provides that any "false swearing, or attempt at fraud," or "if there shall appear any fraud in the claim by false swearing or otherwise," or "any attempt at fraud," etc., shall avoid the policy, in order to avail itself of the defense, the insurer must show that the assured *knowingly* and *intentionally* swore falsely, or said or did that which is claimed to be fraudulent.[1] *There must be a wilful intent to defraud,*[2] rather than an innocent mistake.[3] This condition in the policy extends to every matter material to be stated, or which the policy in terms requires to be stated. Thus, a false statement as to the title of the property, as to the existence of other insurance, as to the cause of the loss, or the amount thereof, or as to any matter, information in reference to which is called for in the proofs of loss, or as a condition precedent to a right of recovery.

Where the assured was required to state whether he was absolute owner of the premises, and he stated that he was, and that there was no incumbrance, and it appeared that he owned the property as tenant, in common with his wife, and had given a bond for the support of the granter during life, it was held that his statement was not false.[4] Upon

---

[1] *Rice* v. *Provincial Ins. Co.,* 7 U. C. (C. P.) 548; *Huchberger* v. *Merchants' F. Ins. Co.,* 4 Biss. (U. S. C. C.) 265; *Gerhauser* v. *North British, etc., Ins. Co.,* 7 Nev. 174; *Hickman* v. *Long Island Ins. Co.,* Edm. Sel. Cas. (N. Y.) 374.

[2] *Gerhauser* v. *North British Ins. Co.,* 7 Nev. 174; *Clark* v. *Phœnix Ins. Co.,* 36 Cal. 168; *Wolff* v. *Goodhue F. Ins. Co.,* 43 Barb. (N. Y.) 400; *Marion* v. *Great Republic Ins. Co.,* 35 Mo. 148; *Franklin F. Ins. Co.* v. *Updegraff,* 43 Penn. St. 350; *Parker* v. *Amazon Ins. Co.,* 34 Wis. 363; *Jones* v. *Mechanics' F. Ins. Co.,* 36 N. J. 29.

[3] *Planters' Mut. Ins. Co.* v. *Deford,* 38 Md. 382; *Parker* v. *Amazon Ins. Co.,* 34 Wis. 363; *Wolff* v. *Goodhue F. Ins. Co.,* 43 Barb. (N. Y.) 400; *Beek* v. *Germania Ins. Co.,* 23 La. An. 510; *Unger* v. *People's F. Ins. Co.,* 4 Daly (N. Y. C. P.) 96; *Clark* v. *Phœnix Ins. Co., ante.*

[4] *Mason* v. *Agl., etc., Ins. Co.,* 18 U. C. (C. P.) 84. But, see *Security Ins. Co.* v. *Bronger,* 6 Bush. (Ky.) 146, where the assured stated that he was absolute

the other hand where the assured, in swearing in reference to his ignorance of the cause of the fire, swears that he was at a place so far distant from the place of the fire, at the time when it broke out, that he could not have any knowledge of the circumstances, when he, in fact, was not at such place, but left the place of the fire for such place only two hours before the fire occurred, the policy is avoided by such false swearing.[1] If there is any evidence to show that the assured, by not complying with the conditions of the policy, *attempted to defraud the insurers*, the policy is invalidated, and this is a question of fact for the jury;[2] as, if it is shown that the assured *knowingly and falsely* stated his loss to be much greater than it is.[3] If he makes a fraudulent claim against the insurer, the policy is void.[4]

The mere fact that the plaintiff swears to a state of facts that he believes to be true, but does not *know.* to be, although false in fact, does not avoid a policy.[5]

owner, and that the premises were unincumbered, when, in fact, there was a lien for the whole consideration which he had bid for them at a decretal sale, and also by his wife's dower, and it was held that he was guilty of such fraud and false swearing as avoided the policy.

[1] In *Smith* v. *The Queen Ins. Co.*, 1 Hannay (N. B.) 311, the assured swore that when the fire broke out, he was in the county of Sunbury. It appeared that he left the place where the property burned was situated, by stage, for Sunbury, at 7 P. M. The fire broke out at 9 P. M., at which time he would have been only a few miles away. It was held fatal to a recovery.

[2] *Security Ins. Co.* v. *Fay*, 22 Mich. 467.

[3] *Gieb.* v. *International Ins. Co.*, 1 Del. (U. S. C. C.) 443 ; *Grenier* v. *Monarch F. Ins. Co.*, 7 L. C. Jur. 100 ; *Haigh* v. *De La Cour*, 3 Camp. 319 ; *Hersey* v. *Merrimack Co., etc., Ins. Co.*, 27 N. H. 149 ; *Hercules Ins. Co.* v. *Hunter*, 15 C. C. (Sc.) 800 ; *Britton* v. *Royal Ins. Co.*, 4 F. & F. 905.

[4] *Chapman* v. *Pole*, 22 L. T. (N. S.) 306.

[5] In *Marion* v. *The Gt. Republic Ins. Co.*, 35 Mo. 148 ; 4 Ben. F. I. C. 744, BATES, J., said : "This is a suit upon a policy of insurance of a stock of goods in a store in St. Louis. The policy required the assured on sustaining loss or damage by fire, forthwith to give notice thereof to the company, and as soon after as possible to deliver in a particular account of his loss or damage, signed with his own hand, and verified by his oath or affirmation. The policy also provided, that if there appear any fraud or false swearing, the insured shall forfeit all claim under this policy. The answer set up, that after the loss the plaintiff had given the defendant a false and fraudulent account of his loss and damage, whereby the defendant was discharged from liability. At the trial, evidence was given tending to prove that the statement of loss made to the defendant by the plaintiff, and sworn to by him, was false in material matters. At the instance of the defendants, the court gave the following instruction : 'If the Jury believe from the evidence that the plaintiff made and subscribed the affidavit dated April 10, 1860, read in evidence, and delivered the same to the defendant as containing a statement of his actual loss and damagd by the fire in question ; and if they further believe from the evidence that his said loss and damage was materially less than would appear by said statement, and that plaintiff knew this fact when he made and subscribed said affidavit, then the plaintiff cannot recover.' And the court refused the following instruction : 'If the jury believe from the evidence that the plaintiff made the affidavit of 10th April, 1860, and that at the time he made it he did not know the amount of stock on the first floor and cellar of the store therein

The fact that the value of the property *is largely overstated* by the assured, does not avoid the policy. The fact that the jury do not find the property to be half as valuable as the assured · states it to be in his proofs of loss, does not even amount to presumptive evidence of fraud. In order to prevail on this ground, the insurer must show that the assured *knew* that it was worth much less than he swore them to be.[1] There may be an honest difference of opinion as to the

---

mentioned ; if at said time plaintiff knew that he did not know such amount, then he has been guilty of false swearing, within the intent and meaning of the policy, and in that case plaintiff cannot recover.' There was verdict and judgment for the plaintiff, and the defendant appealed. The only error complained of is the refusal to give the instruction above copied. The affidavit referred to stated that the value of his stock of groceries, produce, and merchandise, contained in first floor and cellar of store No. 89 South Main street, in the city of St. Louis, and which were on hand the day previous, and at the time of the fire, was $7,180.22. The counsel for the appellant treats the instruction which was refused as if it differed from that given in one respect only ; that is, in that the statement was of a matter of which the affiant was ignorant ; while in the instruction given, the statement was of a matter which the affiant knew to be false. If that were so, I would have no hesitation in reversing the judgment ; but the instruction is fatally defective in another respect ; that is, that it does not require that the false swearing should have been done with an intention to deceive the defendant, or get an advantage of it. The clause in the policy in respect to false swearing is to be viewed in connection with all the other parts of the policy, and the general nature of the contract ; and so viewing it, it is obvious that it was intended thereby to require the insured to give the insurer real and reliable information as to the amount of the loss, and that a mistake or unintentional error, or misstatement of an immaterial matter in the sworn statement, would not avoid the policy ; but the false statement must be wilfully made in respect to a material matter, and with the purpose to deceive the insurer. Now this instruction requires that the false statement (that is, the statement made in ignorance of its truth) shall have been knowingly made, but does not require that the jury shall find that it was in respect to a material matter, or made with an intention to deceive the defendant. It might probably be inferred that the matter was material ; but under that instruction, if given, the jury would have been required to find for the defendant, notwithstanding that the false statement was not intended to deceive the defendant, and did not deceive it, and that the plaintiff derived, and could derive, no advantage from it ; and the defendant received, and could receive, no detriment from it. *Hoffman* v. *Western Marine & Fire Ins. Co.*, 1 La. 216. No doubt an indictment for perjury might be supported by proof of a swearing to the truth of matters of which the accused was ignorant (and which might, in fact, be true), but the prosecution for perjury is distinctly for the offense of false swearing, irrespective of the effect of the falsehood ; whilst here, the clause as to false swearing is a part of a contract between two persons, and is important only in its effect, actual, presumed, or intended. It is no part of the intention of the parties to punish one of them for an immoral or illegal act ; but the provisions of the contract have reference only to their interests in respect to the subject matter of the contract. And if it be true that the plaintiff had on the first floor and cellar of his store the precise amount of merchandise, groceries, and produce so particularly mentioned in his statement, the defendant could not have been injured by the statement, notwithstanding the plaintiff was wholly ignorant of the amount of merchandize, etc., which he had, and was guilty of the moral offense of false swearing."

[1] *Unger* v. *People's Ins. Co.*, 4 Daly (N. Y. C. P.) 96 ; *Beck* v. *Germania Ins. Co.*, 23 La. An. 510 ; *Franklin Ins. Co.* v. *Culver*, 6 Ind. 137 ; 4 Ben. F. I. C. 13 ; *Marion* v. *Gt. Republic Ins. Co.*, 35 Mo. 148 ; 4 Ben. F. I. C. 744 ; *The Planters', etc., Ins. Co.* v. *Deford*, 38 Md. 382. In *Rice* v. *Provincial Ins. Co.*, ante, the assured swore that the value of the goods was £600. The jury found the value

real value of property; and if the jury find, that, although the valuation *was largely excessive*, yet it was made by the assured in good faith, his statement in that respect cannot be held to amount to false swearing or fraud, within the meaning of the policy.[1]

In all cases, it is a question of fact for the jury to find whether the assured willfully and intentionally swore falsely with intent to defraud the insurers, and their finding is conclusive.[2] The fact that a great disparity exists between the value of the property as sworn to by the assured as having been destroyed and the real value as found by the jury, of itself does not furnish evidence of fraud;[3] but it is a circumstance from which, taken in connection with other facts or circumstances, fraud may be found.[4]

Arbitration clause not obligatory—Except.

SEC. 430. A condition in a policy, that in case of disagreement *as to the amount of the loss*, the question shall be submitted to arbitration, is held to be a valid and operative condition. It is revocable by either party, and does not operate to oust the courts of their jurisdiction over contracts.[5] In a case recently heard before

---

to be £200, but also found that no fraud was intended by the assured; and it was held that the policy was not avoided.

[1] *Ins. Co.* v. *Wiedes*, 14 Wall. (U. S.) 375; *M'Quaig* v. *Unity Ins. Co.*, 9 U. C. (C. P.) 85. In *Marchesson* v. *Merchants' Ins. Co.*, 1 Rob. (La.) 438, the assured swore the property to be worth $15,549. The jury found it worth $8,000. So in *Gerhauser* v. *N. B. Mercantile Ins. Co.*, 7 Nev. 174, assured swore the value to be $6,000. The jury found it to be $3,000. In *Wolf* v. *Goodhue Ins. Co.*, 43 Barb. (N. Y.) 400, assured swore value to be $2,933.34 of those destroyed, and damages to those saved $107.42, making $3,100.76 in all. There were two policies for $1,000 each. The jury found the defendant's half of the loss to be $412.27. In *Williams* v. *Phœnix Ins. Co.*, 61 Me. 67, the plaintiff swore value at $2,500; jury found value to be $1,750. In *Unger* v. *People's Ins. Co.*, *ante*, the plaintiff swore value of property destroyed to be $9,989.93; jury found it to be $6,500 only; and in all these cases it was held that the disparity between the value as sworn to by the assured and as found by the jury, did not furnish evidence of fraud within the meaning of the conditions in the policies.

[2] *Wolf* v. *Goodhue Ins. Co.*, *ante*.

[3] *Beck* v. *Germania Ins. Co.*, 23 La. An. 310; *Unger* v. *People's Ins. Co.*, *ante*; *Protection Ins. Co.* v. *Hall*, 16 B. Mon. (Ky.) 411.

[4] *Marchesson* v. *Merchants' Ins. Co.*, *ante*; *Hoffman* v. *Western M. & F. Ins. Co.*, 1 La. An. 216.

[5] *Mentz* v. *Armenia Ins. Co.*, 78 Penn. St. 478; *Snodgrass* v. *Gavit*, 28 Penn. St. 224; *Gray* v. *Wilson*, 4 Watts (Penn.) 41; *Lanman* v. *Young*, 31 Penn. St. 306; *Wright* v. *Ward*, 24 L. T. (N. S.) 430; *Insurance Co.* v. *Morse*, 20 Wall. (U. S.) 445; *Scott* v. *Avery*, 5 H. L. Cas. 827; *Furnivall* v. *Coombs*, 5 M. & G. 786; *Trott* v. *City Ins. Co.*, 1 Cliff. (U. S.) 439; *Braunstein* v. *Accidental Ass. Co.* 1 B. & S. 782. In an action on a policy of insurance, the defendants cannot, by way of defense, avail themselves of the condition in the policy that, "no holder of a policy shall be entitled to maintain any action thereon against the company, until he shall have offered to submit his claim to a reference," unless that defense has been set up in their specifications. *Dyer* v. *Piscataqua Fire and Marine Ins. Co.*,

the Supreme Court of Pennsylvania,[1] the policy contained a clause as follows: "In case any difference or dispute shall arise between the assured and this company, *touching the amount* of any loss or damage sustained by him, such difference shall be submitted to the judgment of arbitrators, one to be appointed by each party, with power to select a third, in case of disagreement, whose decision thereupon shall be final and conclusive ; and no action, suit or proceedings at law or in equity shall be maintained on this policy, unless the amount of loss or damage, in case of difference or dispute, shall be first thus ascertained." In an action for a loss, under the policy, the defendant, in the lower court, moved for a non-suit, upon the ground that the plaintiff had not complied with this condition of the policy, which was granted. Upon appeal, however, the non-suit was set aside ; the court holding that, before the company could insist upon any such condition, they must show *that they admitted the validity of the policy and their liability under it, and that the only question open between the parties, was the question of damages.* But, where the policy provides that the whole matter in controversy between the parties, including the right of recovery at all, shall be submitted to arbitration, the condition is void.[2] Because, in such a case, the effect of the provision is to oust the courts of their legitimate jurisdiction, which the parties cannot contract to do.

Where the policy stipulates that, "in case of loss or damage, it shall be sumitted to arbitrators, whose award shall be binding," it is held to relate only to the adjustment of the loss, the ascertainment of the damages, and, to that extent, is a condition precedent.[3] But the insurer cannot claim the benefit of this clause when he denies all liability under the policy.[4] In order to avail itself of the benefit of this provision, it must admit its liability to pay something.[5] Where,

---

53 Me. 547. *Stephenson* v. *Piscataqua F. & M. Ins. Co.*, 54 Me. 55 ; *Liverpool, etc., Ins. Co. Creighton*, 51 Ga. 95 ; *Cobb* v. *N. E. Mut., etc., Ins. Co.*, 6 Gray (Mass.) 192 ; *Tredwen* v. *Holman*, 1 H. & C. 72 ; *Ins. Co.* v, *Creighton*, 51 Ga. 95 ; 5 Ben. F. I. C. 622.

[1] *Mentz* v. *Armenia F. Ins. Co.*, 78 Penn. St. 478 ; 21 Am. Rep. 80.

[2] *Gray* v. *Wilson.* 4 Watts (Penn.) 41 ; *Lanman* v. *Young*, 32 Penn. St. 310 ; *Ins. Co.* v. *Morse*, 20 Wall (U. S.) 445 ; *Scott* v. *Avery*, 4 H. L. Cas. 827 ; *Kill* v. *Hollister.* 1 Wilson, 129 ; *Trott* v. *City Ins. Co.*, 1 Cliff. (U. S. C. C.) 437 ; *Cobb* v. *N. E. Mut. Ins. Co.*, 6 Gray (Mass.) 192 ; *Roper* v. *London*, 1 El. & El. 825 ; *Tredwen* v. *Holman*, 1 H. & C. 72 ; *Braunstein* v. *Accidantal, etc., Ass. Co.*, 1 B. & S. 782 ; *Lowndes* v. *Lord Stanford*, 18 Q. B. 425 ; *Rowe* v. *Williams*, 97 Mass. 163. See cases cited in note.

[3] *Elliott* v. *Royal Ex. Ass. Co.*, L. R. 2 Exchq. 237 ; *Scott* v. *Avery, ante.*

[4] *Robinson* v. *Georgia Ins. Co.*, 17 Me. 131 ; *Mentz* v. *Ins. Co., ante ; Millandon* v. *Atlantic Ins. Co.*, 8 La. 568 ; *Gouldstone* v. *Overton*, 2 C. & P. 55.

[5] *Mentz* v. *Ins. Co., ante.* See cases cited in last note.

however, *after* a loss, the parties in interest submit all questions to arbitration, and there is no fraud, the award is binding; [1] but if there is fraud,[2] or if the submission is made by the insured *without the assent of the assignee*,[3] or if the arbitrators are not selected in the manner provided in the policy,[4] the award is not binding; and if the award is void for any cause, it cannot be set up to defeat an action for the loss.[5] The courts will not interfere if the parties see fit to resort to such a tribunal voluntarily, but it will not compel them to do so.

In one case,[6] it is intimated that *if there had been a reference depending*, or the matter had proceeded to final termination, it might have been a bar to the action.   It can hardly be held, however, that the fact that an arbitration was depending would operate as a bar, because it is always competent for either party to revoke the submission by submitting to an action for the damages resulting therefrom; and there would seem to be no question that the bringing of an action for the same matters embraced in the submission is a complete and effectual revocation of the submission.   But where an award has been made, it is an effectual bar to an action, in the absence of fraud, because all the rights of the parties are merged in the award as effectually as though it was the judgment of a court of competent jurisdiction.[7] Where, by the act of incorporation or general law, provision is made for the settlement of differences in this mode, the courts could not interfere, unless there is some constitutional provision militating against the establishment of such tribunals.[8]

The doctrine of our courts upon this question has sometimes been regarded as inconsistent with the doctrine of a large number of analogous cases that have arisen under building contracts,[9] where the right of the builder is made dependent upon the production of the

---

[1] *Kyanston* v. *Liddell*, 8 Moore, 223 ; *Hamilton* v. *Phœnix Ins. Co.*, 106 Mass. 395 ; *Zallee* v. *Laclede, etc., Ins. Co.*, 44 Mo. 530 ; *McDermott* v. *U. S. Ins. Co.*, 3 S. & R. (Penn.) 604.

[2] *Hercules Ins. Co.* v. *Hunter*, 14 C. C. (Sc.) 147.

[3] *Brown* v. *Roger Williams Ins. Co.*, 5 R. I. 394.

[4] *Ætna Ins. Co.* v. *Stevens*, 48 Ill. 31.

[5] *Patterson* v. *Triumph Ins. Co.*, 64 Me. 500.

[6] *Kill* v. *Hollister*, 1 Wils. 129.

[7] *Burchell* v. *Marsh*, 17 How. (U. S.) 344 ; *Hughes* v. *F. Ins. Co.*, 9 U. C. (Q. B.) 387 ; *Richardson* v. *Suffolk Ins. Co.*, 3 Met. (Mass.) 573.

[8] *Elliot* v. *Royal Ex. Ins. Co.*, L. R. 2 Exchq. 237 ; *Zallee* v. *Laclede, etc., Ins. Co.*, 44 Mo. 530.

[9] *Herrick* v. *Belknap*, 27 Vt. 673 ; *R. R. Co.* v. *McGrann*, 33 Penn St. 530 ; *O'Reilly* v. *Kerns*, 52 Penn. St. 224 ; *Condon* v. *R. R. Co.*, 14 Gratt. 302.

certificate of an architect, or of a railroad contractor whose right of
recovery is made dependent upon the production of the certificate of
an engineer, and with that class of insurance cases that require the
production of a certificate of a certain officer, as in one case the certificate of a surgeon in chief of the company, that in his judgment
the assured did not die of intemperance,[1] or of the nearest magistrate,
notary, minister, etc., that in his opinion the loss occurred without
fraud on the part of the assured, and amounts to a certain sum.[2] It
is true that in this class of cases, the production of these certificates
is held to be a condition precedent to a right of recovery, and nothing
short of fraud and collusion between the insurer and the person or
officer named, will excuse the assured from producing it, and failing
to do so, his right of recovery is lost, and the courts are powerless to
compel the person named to give the certificate.[3] But there is really
no analogy of principle between the cases.   In the one case, the jurisdiction of the courts for every or any purpose is ousted, and a tribunal
is established that takes the place of the courts, and adjudicates all the
rights of the parties ; while in the other, the person whose certificate is
required, is merely to give or withhold it, as the facts may appear to
him.   The certificate, when given, does not conclude either party.   It
does not settle the rights either of the assured or the insurer, as to any
matter contained in it, but leaves all questions open to investigation and
determination, precisely the same as though no certificate had been
given.   It is a mere precautionary provision on the part of the insurer,
to enable it to have the judgment of the person designated as to whether
the assured has, in good faith, sustained a loss, and its *prima facie*
extent.   It is a reasonable condition precedent, with which the assured
has contracted to comply, and is as vaild and binding as a provision
in the contract that no recovery shall be had until the contract is fully
completed, or that any other lawful act shall be done by the party
contracting to perform.   It cannot be said to interfere with the jurisdiction of the court, any more than a provision in a contract, that a
builder shall complete a building in a certain mode, or by a certain
time, or be entitled to no recovery for the labor performed by him.
In either case, if there is a valid excuse for the failure to fully perform, a recovery may be had ; otherwise not.   It does not go to the
remedy, but to the right of recovery itself.

---

[1] *Campbell* v. *American Popular Life Ins. Co.*, 1 McArthur, 246.
[2] See *ante*, sec. 416.
[3] *Nightingale* v. *Worcester, etc., Ins. Co.*, 5 R. I. 38 ; *Manby* v. *Gresham*, 29
Beav. 420.

When submission is a condition precedent.

SEC. 431. Whether submission to arbitration is a condition precedent or not, will depend upon the language employed. A clause, simply providing that "in case of difference of opinion as to the amount of loss or damage, such difference shall be submitted," etc., is not a condition precedent, because the parties, by the terms of their contract, have not made it so,[1] but, where the parties have stipulated that a submission *shall precede the right to sue upon the policy*, it is — if valid at all — a condition precedent, performance of which, or an offer to perform, by the assured, or a waiver thereof by the insurer, must be shown. Thus in an English case,[2] the plaintiff and the defendant were members of an insurance association, and by one of the rules of that society it was provided (interalia) that the sum to be paid by the association to any suffering member for any loss or damage should, in the first instance, be ascertained and settled by the committee ; and the suffering member, if he agreed to accept such sum in full satisfaction of his claim, should be entitled to demand and sue for the same as soon as the amount to be paid has been ascertained and settled, but not before, which could only be claimed according to the customary mode of payment in use by the society ; and if a difference should arise between the committee and any suffering member relative to the settling of any loss or damage, or to a claim for average, or any other matter relating to the insurance, that arbitrators should be selected out of certain persons mamed in the rule, and that they should settle the claims and matters in dispute according to the rules and customs of the club. *The rule also provided, that no member, who refused to accept the amount of any loss as settled by the committee in manner specified in full satisfaction of such loss, should be entitled to maintain any action at law or suit in equity on his policy, until the matters in dispute should have been referred to and decided by arbitrators appointed as therein specified, and then only for such sum as the arbitrators should award ; and that the obtaining the decision of such arbitrators on the matters and claim in dispute was thereby declared to be a condition precedent to the right of any member to maintain any such action or suit.* The plaintiff effected an insurance upon a ship in which he was interested with the association, and by the policy it was expressly stated that all rules and regulations of the association should be binding upon the assured and

---

[1] *Liv. Lon. & Globe Ins. Co.* v. *Creighton.* 51 Ga. 95 ; 5 Ben. F. I. C. 573; *Robinson* v. *Georgia Ins. Co.,* 17 Me. 131 ; *Millandon* v. *Atlantic Ins. Co.,* 8 La. 558.

[2] *Scott* v. *Avery,* 8 Exq. 487 ; Affirmed 5 H. L. Cas. 811.

assurers as effectively as if such rules were inserted in the policy. To an action by the plaintiff against the defendant, as one of the underwriters, to recover from him compensation for the loss of the vessel, which took place during the period covered by the policy, the defendant pleaded, setting out the above rule of the association, and alleging that before action brought, the committee ascertained and settled the sum to be paid to the plaintiff for the loss; that the plaintiff was dissatisfied with the settlement, and that the defendant and the committee had always been ready and willing to refer the matters in difference to arbitration, but that the plaintiff was not ready and willing so to do. It was held in Exchequer Chamber, reversing the judgement of the Court of Exchequer, that the condition, not divesting the courts of their jurisdiction, was valid, and a condition precedent to the plaintiff's right to sue, and this judgement was sustained and affirmed in the House of Lords.[1] But although this is the fixed doctrine of the English courts, there is no American case going to the same length, neither have I been able to find any where the question, under such a clause in the policy as referred to, ante, existed. But, upon principle, there would seem to be no question but that, if the condition to arbitrate is valid, the parties may, by express stipulation, make it a condition precedent, like any other condition of the policy. As has heretofore been stated, it may be waived by the insurers, and a refusal to pay the loss, without offering to submit the question as to the amount thereof to arbitration, is held to amount to a waiver.[2]

Where the policy does not, in express terms, make the submission a condition precedent to the right to sue, it is treated as a collateral agreement, which does not bind the assured to await a reference.[3] So where *the dispute is one of law purely*, the assured is not bound to submit to arbitration before bringing his action;[4] and where the condition is in such terms as leaves it optional with the parties whether they will submit the questions; as, where the word "*may*" is employed instead of "*shall*"; as, "the parties *may* refer," etc., it is held that submission is optional, and the bringing of an action sufficiently indicates the purpose of the assured not to submit the questions.[5]

---

[1] To the same effect, see *Tredwen* v. *Holman*, 1 H. & C. 72; *Elliott* v. *Royal Ins. Co.*, L. R. 2 Excq. 237; *Wright* v. *Ward*, 24 L. T. (U. S.) 439.

[2] *Millaudon* v. *Atlantic Ins. Co.*, 8 La. 558; *Robinson* v. *Georgia Ins. Co.*, 17 Me. 131.

[3] *Roper* v. *London Ass. Co.*, 1 El. & El. 825.

[4] *Alexander* v. *Campbell*, 27 L. T. (N. S.) 417.

[5] *Scott* v. *Phœnix Ins. Co.*, 1 Stuart (Sc.) 152.

SEC. 432. When the insurer or its agent, having authority to make a submission, enters into a submission with the assured, before notice or proofs of loss have been served, of the matters involved, there can be no question but that the submission operates as a waiver of both, but, where the agent has no such authority, and the insurers, in their answer, deny that they ever waived the service of notice and proofs, it has been held that the submission does not of itself amount to a waiver.[1] If the insurers rely upon the breach of this condition, they must set it up in their answer, or it is waived.[2]

When arbitrators exceed their jurisdiction.

SEC. 433. Of course, an award of arbitrators, in order to be valid, must only cover the matters submitted. If they travel beyond the limits of the submission, their award is void. This was well illustrated in an English case,[3] where the question was as to what amount of damage had been sustained by the plaintiff under three several policies upon the same property. The submission was "to award what was the total sum of money which ought to be paid to the plaintiff under or by virtue of the said policies, or any of them, in respect of loss or damage occasioned by the said fire to or in the said chattels particularized as aforesaid," in three certain schedules referred to in the submission, and the proportion thereof that each insurer ought to pay. The arbitrators, by their award, found that £8,288 0s. 7d. was the total sum that ought to be paid by all the insurers, and fixed the proportions that each insurer should pay. They then found *that the whole loss exceeded the insurance, and that the whole salvage belonged to the plaintiff absolutely.* It appeared that the salvage arose upon the goods embraced in one schedule alone. The court held that, in awarding that the salvage belonged to the plaintiff alone, the arbitrators had exceeded their jurisdiction, and, consequently, that their award was void.

[1]*Pettengill* v. *Hanks,* 9 Gray (Mass.) 169.
[2]*Dyer* v. *Piscataqua Ins. Co.,* 54 Me. 457.
[3]*Skipper* v. *Grant,* 10 C. B. (N. S.) 237.

CHAPTER XIV.

LIMITATION OF ACTION.

Contracts limiting time, within which actions shall be brought, are valid.

SEC. 434. While the parties cannot contract so as to oust the *jurisdiction* of the courts, yet they may lawfully contract to limit the time within which an action shall be brought upon a contract. Therefore, a provision that no action shall lay upon a policy, unless brought within six months, one year, or any other stated period after the loss, is valid and binding upon the parties.[1]

The provisions of a policy in reference to proofs of loss, as well as for enforcing a claim therefor, must be complied with, unless the insurer has

---

[1] *Peoria Ins. Co.* v. *Whitehill*, 25 Ill. 466; *Ames* v. *N. Y. Ins. Co.*, 14 N. Y. 253; *Wilson* v. *Ætna Ins. Co.*, 27 Vt. 99; *Carter* v. *Humboldt Ins. Co.*, 12 Iowa, 287; *Crary* v. *Hartford Ins. Co.*, 1 Blatch. (U. S. C. C.) 280; *Brown* v. *Savannah Ins. Co.*, 24 Ga. 101; *Brown* v. *Hartford Ins. Co.*, 5 R. I. 394; *Brown* v. *Roger Williams Ins. Co.*, 5 R. I. 394; *N. W. Ins. Co.* v. *Phœnix Oil Co.*, 31 Penn. St. 449; *Edwards* v. *Lycoming Ins. Co.*, 75 Penn. St. 378; *Amesbury* v. *Bowditch Ins. Co.*, 6 Gray (Mass.) 603; *Merchants' Ins. Co.* v. *La Croix*, 35 Tex. 249; *Goodwin* v. *Amoskeag Co.*, 20 N. H. 73; *Ripley* v. *Ætna Ins. Co.*, 29 Barb. (N. Y.) 552; *Fullam* v. *N. Y. Ins. Co.*, 7 Gray (Mass.) 161; *Woodbury Savings Bank* v. *Charter Oak Ins. Co.*, 31 Conn. 518; *Ins. Co.* v. *La Croix*, 35 Tex. 263; *McFarland* v. *Peabody Ins. Co.*, 6 W. Va. 425; *Riddlesberger* v. *Hartford Ins. Co.*, 7 Wall. (U. S.) 386; *Williams* v. *Vt. Mut. Ins. Co.*, 20 Vt. 222; *McFarland* v. *Peabody Ins. Co.*, 6 W. Va. 425; *Carraway* v. *Merchants'*, etc. *Ins. Co.*, 26 La. An. 268; *Roach* v. *N. Y. and Erie Ins. Co.*, 30 N. Y. 546; *Portage Co. Ins. Co.* v. *West*, 6 Ohio St. 599; *Portage Co. Ins. Co.* v. *Stukey*, 18 Ohio, 455; *Keim* v. *Home Mut. Ins. Co.*, 42 Mo. 88; *Patrick* v. *Farmers' Ins. Co.*, 43 N. H. 621; *Brown* v. *Savannah Ins. Co.*, 24 Ga. 97; *Trask* v. *State F. Ins. Co.*, 29 Penn. St. 198; *Beatty* v. *Lycoming Ins. Co.*, 66 id. 9; *Franklin F. Ins. Co.* v. *Updegraff*, 43 id. 350; *Inland*, etc., *Ins. Co.* v. *Stauffer*, 33 id. 397. *Contra*, see *French* v. *La Fayette Ins. Co.*, 5 McLean (U. S.) 46; *Eagle Ins. Co.* v. *La Fayette Ins. Co.*, 9 Ind. 443. But is proper to say that the doctrine of these two cases is generally repudiated.

done that which amounts to a waiver of compliance ; and in order to amount to a waiver, the insurer must have done that which justified the assured in remaining inactive. The mere pendency of negotiations between the parties, or the fact that occasional interviews have been had between them, in regard to the adjustment of the loss, has been held not to amount to a waiver.[1] The conduct of the insurer must be such as to amount to an agreement, express or implied, to suspend the legal remedies,[2] or as would operate as a fraud upon the insured. Thus, if an insurance company holds out hopes of an adjustment, and thereby induces delay, it is estopped from setting it up in bar of the action.[3]

The condition being a mere matter of contract, may be waived, either expressly or by implication, and when the insurer, by any act of his, causes the delay, or prevents the bringing of the action within the time, strict compliance is not necessary.[4] Thus, in the case last referred to, the defendant was a foreign corporation, and no agent upon whom process could be served could be found within the time limited, and this was held a sufficient excuse for not bringing the action within the period limited. The assured is not bound to pursue the company in its own domicile, but may wait until process can be served upon it in the state where he resides, and if delay is thus entailed, it is excused, as it is the duty of the insurer, if it means to insist upon the condition to render it possible for the insurer to comply with the condition, to have a known agent, upon whom process may be served, in the state where the insurance is made. So it seems that compliance as to time may be excused when the nature of the loss and the interest of the assured therein is such that its extent or value cannot be determined within the time limited. Thus it has been held that a condition that an action must be brought within a certain time after the loss, will not bar an action, brought after the time had elapsed, upon a policy in which the interest insured was a mechanic's lien, *when it was impossible to fix the value of the lien within the prescribed time.*[5]

---

[1] *McFarland* v. *Peabody Ins. Co.*, 6 W. Va. 425 ; *Gooden* v. *Amoskeag Ins. Co.*, 20 N. H. 73.

[2] GILCHRIST, J., in *Gooden* v. *Amoskeag Ins. Co.*, ante.

[3] *Grant* v. *Lexington, etc., Ins. Co.*, 5 Ind. 23.

[4] *Peoria Ins. Co.* v. *Hull*, 12 Mich 202.

[5] *Longhurst* v. *Star Ins. Co.*, 19 Iowa, 364. But opposed to this doctrine, see *Eastern R. R. Co.* v. *Relief Ins. Co.*, ante, where it was held that a railroad company insured against losses from the destruction of the property of people along its line by sparks, etc., from its engines, which, by the terms of the policy, was required to make proofs in sixty days, could not wait until such claims were adjusted and their amount ascertained.

Thus, in a New York case,[1] by the terms of the policy, losses were to be paid within ninety days after proofs should be completed and filed, and a suit not commenced within six months after the loss was to be barred. The loss occurred July 5th, and proofs of loss were duly filed, but being defective, the company suggested the defects, and amended proofs were filed seven days afterwards (Oct. 14th), and it was then stated by the secretary, in a letter to the assured, that the loss would be paid January 15th, and, in consequence of this statement, an action was not brought until *after the lapse of six months.* The loss not being paid January 14th, an action was brought, and the company set up the breach of the condition of the policy as to the *time* of bringing an action thereon in defense. The court held that, by the letter of the secretary promising to pay January 14th, the stipulation was suspended and strict compliance waived. It is more than likely that the action would have been upheld upon the *promise to pay*, as a new contract, and, in such cases, it is often expedient to declare upon the policy, and also upon the *promise to pay*, if there has been one.[2]

A condition that no suit shall be sustainable, unless commenced within six months after a loss occurs, and also that the payment of losses shall be made in sixty days from the date of the adjustment of preliminary proofs of loss by the parties, must be so construed as not to conflict unnecessarily with each other, and where the parties, in good faith, and without any objection that unnecessary time is taken for the purpose, are occupied so long in adjusting proofs that sixty days from the date of adjustment does not expire within the six months, the policy does not become forfeited merely because the suit is not brought within six months and before the loss is payable. An action brought promptly upon the expiration of sixty days from the adjustment of loss, is not barred because commenced more than six months after the loss occurred. *Where objections are made by the insurers to the preliminary proofs of loss, the sixty days are not to be deemed to commence until after a reasonable time for the insured to examine the objections.*[3]

Where the policy stipulates or the charter of the company that, unless the insured is satisfied with the decision of the company in reference to the settlement of the loss, action shall be brought in the next court to be held in the county, if one is to be held within sixty

[1] *Ames* v. *N. Y. Union Ins. Co.*, 14 N. Y. 253.
[2] *Amesbury* v. *Mutual F. Ins. Co.*, 6 Gray (Mass.) 596.
[3] *New York* v. *Hamilton, etc., Ins. Co.*, 10 Bos. (N. Y.) 537.

days, otherwise before the next court, the condition must be complied with, or the insurer is relieved from liability.[1] And the same is true where any condition as to the *time* of bringing an action upon the policy is violated.[2]

Effect of war upon the condition.

SEC. 435. Where, by the policy, right to sue on it ceased within twelve months after loss, and the plaintiff was prevented from suing by reason of the war, and did not actually sue until more than twelve months after loss, exclusive of the time of the war, it was held that, although the statute of limitations is capable of enlargement to accommodate a precise number of days of disability, yet the contract in a policy of insurance is not; and that this clause of the contract is rebutted by the state of war, and is not presumed to revive when the war ceases.[3]

Premature actions.

SEC. 436. Where the policy provides that the loss shall be payable within sixty days, ninety days, or any other period after proof of loss is made, an action brought inside of the period limited is premature.[4]

---

[1]*Portage Ins. Co.* v. *West*, 6 Ohio St. 599; *Dutton* v. *Ins. Co.*, 17 Vt. 369. One of the conditions of a policy provided that no suit should be begun more than six months after any loss or damage. A subsequent condition provided that payment of losses should be made in sixty days after the adjustment of the preliminary proofs of loss. It was held that these two provisions should be construed together, and that the six months did not begin to run until the expiration of the sixty days. *Mayor of New York* v. *Hamilton, etc., Ins. Co.*, 39 N. Y. 45. The policy contained a condition that a party dissatisfied with the refusal of the company to pay the insurance should bring an action at the next term of court to be held in the county, unless such court should sit within sixty days after the refusal to pay, and in that case at the next term after the sixty days; and, unless suit was so brought, all claim under the policy should be forfeited. It was held that an insured who failed to bring his action at the first term, held more than sixty days after the refusal to pay the insurance, was precluded from subsequently maintaining his action. *Keim* v. *Home, etc., Ins. Co.*, 42 Mo. 38. By the terms of a policy, the insurers, in case of loss, were allowed sixty days in which to pay the loss. It was held that a general denial of any liability on the part of the company enabled the insured to bring an action at once. *Norwich, etc., Trans. Co.* v. *Western Mass. Ins. Co.*, 34 Conn. 561. An insurance policy stipulated that the company should not be liable to pay until after the sixty days from the loss. Pending these sixty days a petition was filed. It was held that the irregularity could be cured by a supplemental petition. The want of validity in the notice upon the agent of an insurance company is waived by their subsequent appearance and pleading. *Franklin Ins. Co.* v. *McCrea*, 4 Iowa, 229.

[2]*Ripley* v. *Ætna Ins. Co.*, 30 N. Y. 136; *Roach* v. *N. Y. Ins. Co.*, 30 id. 546; *Brown* v. *Savannah Mut. Ins. Co.*, 24 Ga. 97.

[3]*Semmes* v. *City F. Ins. Co.*, 13 Wall. (U. S.) 158.

[4]*Cumberling* v. *McCall*, 2 Dall. (Penn.) 280; *Davis* v. *Davis*, 49 Me. 282; *Kimball* v. *Hamilton F. Ins. Co.*, 8 Bos. (N. Y.) 495. Where the policy provides that no action shall be brought within twelve months, or any other period after the loss, an action brought *before* the period named has elapsed, will be dismissed. *Riddlesberger* v. *Hartford F. Ins. Co.*, 7 Wall. (U. S.) 386.

Clause restricting the insured to bring action in certain county not valid.

SEC. 437. It is not competent for a party to a contract to stipulate that an action to enforce it shall be brought in a certain court or county only. The jurisdiction of the courts can only be ousted by law; hence, unless the charter of the company provides that actions upon policies shall only be brought in certain courts or counties, the parties themselves cannot affect the general jurisdiction of the courts by any restrictions thereon in the contract.[1] They may contract to waive the statute of limitations, or any other statute merely affecting the contract, but they cannot contract to change, control or restrict the jurisdiction of courts of law or equity. But, where the charter provides that the action shall be brought in a certain county, the provision must be complied with, because it is competent for the legislature, in the absence of constitutional limitations in that respect, to limit or fix the jurisdiction of the courts, or to determine before what tribunal certain questions shall be determined.[2]

When adjustment is essential.

SEC. 438. When the policy provides that, if the assured is not satisfied with the adjustment of the loss by the insurer, action must be brought within a certain time, the insurer is not bound to bring his action except within that time *after the loss is adjusted.*[3]

Effect of appointment of receiver.

SEC. 439. Where the company is dissolved, and its property placed in the hands of a receiver, the limitation is dispensed with, as every person insured in the company is treated as a party to the suit for the winding up of the company, although not named as a party thereto.[4]

Parol contracts.

SEC. 440. Where the contract rests in parol, and no policy is issued, the conditions of the policies of the company do not apply. Thus, where the assured took a binding receipt from the insurer's agent, and paid the premium, conditioned that a policy should be issued within twenty-one days, or the money be refunded, and thirty-three days thereafter, no policy having been issued, and the premium not refunded, and the company refused to make one, it was held that a condition of the policies issued by the company, requiring actions for

---

[1] *Richard* v. *Manhattan Ins. Co.,* 31 Mo. 518; *Amesbury* v. *Bowditch Ins. Co.,* 6 Gray (Mass.) 596; *Nute* v. *Hamilton, etc., Ins. Co.,* 6 id. 174.

[2] *Portage County, etc., Ins. Co.* v. *West,* 6 Ohio St. 599.

[3] *Landis* v. *Home Mut. Ins. Co.,* 50 Mo. 591.

[4] *Pennell* v. *Chandler,* 7 Chicago Leg. News, 227.

losses to be brought within six months, did not apply, for the reason that the action was not founded on the policy, but upon the contract to insure.[1]

Commencement of action—what is.

SEC. 441. An action is deemed to be commenced when the summons or writ is issued; consequently, if an action is *commenced* within the time limited, the assured's rights are preserved, even though, by reasonable diligence, the assured fails to obtain service thereof upon the insurer. In a Michigan case,[2] this question was directly passed upon, and, as the facts relating to this point, as well as the rule applicable in such cases, are embraced in the opinion of CHRISTIANCY, J., I give that portion of it relating to this question. He said : " It was objected by the defendant below that the action was not brought within the period of twelve months after the loss, according to the seventeenth condition attached to the policy. It appears from the bill of exceptions that a summons was issued in the cause March 18, 1861 (thirteen days before the expiration of the twelve months), returnable on the 2d day of April, 1861; that, on the 3d day of April, 1861, the sheriff made a return upon the said summons that defendant could not be found in his bailiwick ; that, on the next day, another summons was issued, with which defendant was served, nothing appearing on this summons showing it to be a continuation of the first, except the word ' *alias*,' written by the clerk upon the face of the seal.

We do not deem it necessary to discuss the question whether this second summons, as an ' *alias*,' operated strictly as a continuation of the first, so as to save a right of action against a statute of limitations which had run upon it in the meantime ; nor do we think it necessary to determine the validity of this species of limitation by contract. If valid at all, it was valid *as a contract*, and *not* as a *statute*. A limitation fixed by statute is arbitrary and peremptory, admitting of no excuse for delay beyond the period fixed, unless such excuse be recognized by the statute itself. But a limitation by contract (if valid) must, upon the principles governing contracts, be more flexible in its nature, and liable to be defeated or extended by any act of the defendant which has prevented the plaintiff from bringing his action within the prescribed period. The plaintiff had the whole of the twelve months in which to bring his suit; and it was as competent for him

---

[1] *Penly* v. *Beacon Ins. Co.*, 7 Grant's Ch. (Ont.) 130.
[2] *Peoria F. & M. Ins. Co.* v. *Hall*, 12 Mich. 202 ; 4 Ben. F I. C. 737.

to institute it on the last as the first, or any intervening day. And the fundamental idea, the tacit condition upon which such a limitation must rest, and without which it could not be tolerated for a moment, is, that the defendant should be accessible to the service of process by which suit may be commenced against him, if not for the whole period, at least for a sufficient time immediately preceding its close, to enable the plaintiff to commence his suit against him, by the service of process in the ordinary legal mode; otherwise, the defendant would be enabled to take advantage of his own wrong, and, by absenting himself entirely, to defeat the plaintiff's right of action.

The defendant in the present case was a foreign corporation, doing insurance business in this State. By the act of February 15, 1859, full provision was made for bringing the action within the State; and the company, before doing any business in the State, were required to file, in the office of the Secretary of State, a resolution consenting that service of process may be made upon any agent of the company. Nothing is said in the case upon what agent the service of the second summons was made; but it must have been made upon some agent of the company. It does not appear whether there was an agent in the county of Jackson, or in any other particular county. It appears that S. S. Brown was the general agent of the company for this State, and that Knight was also an agent, but neither their residence nor place of business is stated. From anything which appears in the case, the plaintiff was as much at liberty to bring his action in Jackson as in any other county, so far as the residence of an agent could have any bearing, if, indeed, it could have any under the law; and if an agent of the company resided in Jackson county, the action was certainly very properly brought there.

All that was necessary for the plaintiff to do, to excuse the delay beyond the twelve months, was to take the proper and usual means for instituting his suit and getting service of process within the limited period, which he did by issuing a summons thirteen days before the expiration of that period, returnable two days after it had expired. The return shows that no service could be had during that time. We can see no possible ground for imputing any want of good faith to the plaintiff in his endeavor to get the process served in time. Upon the facts stated in the case, therefore, it appears to have been the fault of the defendant—the absence of the agent—that the first summons was not served and the action commenced within twelve months; and this is sufficient to defeat the limitation or extend it till the service was made under the second summons, which was issued immediately on the return of the first."

It is held, however, in Vermont, that, where an action is commenced within the period limited, but for any reason the plaintiff is compelled to become nonsuit, or the action fails, a new action, commenced after the limitation has expired, will be defeated by the limitation in the policy,[1] but this is not believed to be sound doctrine, either upon the score of morality, justice, or fair construction, and the doctrine of the Michigan case commends itself most favorably, and expresses the best and soundest rule, and in an case in Ohio, involving similar questions, the doctrine of the Vermont case is repudiated,[2] and it was held that, where a suit is. commenced within the time, but which is dismissed, or for any cause is not carried to final judgment, another action may be brought, although the limitation has expired.

Delay induced by insurer.

SEC. 442. Where the insurer or its agent does or says anything to warrant the assured in believing that his claim will be settled, and which induces him to delay bringing an action within the time limited, the insurer cannot allege a breach in that respect.[3] But the circumstances must have been such as fairly to induce delay, and as would operate as a fraud upon the part of the insurer to set up such delay in avoidance of liability.[4] Forfeitures are not favored by the law, and slight evidence of a waiver will be deemed sufficient.[5]

When the insurer adjusts the loss, *and promises to pay it* within a specified time, the period covered by the promise is excluded from the limitation. Thus, where a loss occurred Oct. 17th, 1869, and was adjusted Nov. 6th, 1869, and the insurer agreed to pay it on or before Feb. 6th, 1870, and the action was not brought until Nov. 7th, 1870, it was held that it was brought in time, as the period of time between Nov. 6th, 1869, and Feb. 6th, 1870, must be excluded from the limitation.[6] So where the insurer or its agent has induced the assured to delay bringing an action, if the circumstances are such as fairly warranted the delay, it will be excused. Thus, where the

---

[1] *Wilson* v. *Ætna Ins. Co.,* 27 Vt. 99.

[2] *Madison Ins. Co.* v. *Fellows,* 1 Dis. (Ohio Sup. Ct. of Cin.) 217.

[3] *Mickey* v. *Burlington Ins. Co.,* 35 Iowa, 174; *Curtis* v. *Home Ins. Co.,* 1 Biss. (U. S.) 485; *Brady* v. *Western Ass. Co.,* 17 U. C. (C. P.) 597; *Ripley* v. *Astor Ins. Co.,* 17 How. Pr. (N. Y.) 444; *Coursin* v. *Penn. Ins. Co.,* 46 Penn. St. 323.

[4] *Brady* v. *Western Ass. Co.,* ante.

[5] *Ripley* v. *Astor Ins. Co.,* ante.

[6] *Black* v. *Winnesheik Ins. Co.,* 31 Wis. 472.

insurer's general agent objected generally to the proofs of loss, and wrote the assured that he would call upon him, and the assured having waited five months without hearing from or seeing the agent, wrote him, and then was for the first time informed that the insurers would insist upon a strict compliance with the conditions of the policy as to proofs of loss, and the assured within four months' afterwards made his proofs and sent them to the insurer, it was held that the five months during which the insurer had delayed the making of corrected proofs must be excluded from the limitation, and an action brought within one year from the time when he was informed that strict compliance as to proofs was required, was seasonable.[1]

When claim is regarded as arising.

Sec. 443. When a policy stipulates that no action shall be brought, unless commenced within a certain time after loss or damage shall accrue, and there is a provision in the policy that the company will pay in thirty, sixty, ninety, or any other number of days after proofs of loss have been served, *the limitation does not attach until after the period which the company has in which to pay the loss has expired.*[2] *The limitation cannot apply until a right of action has accrued*, and until the period has expired which the company has to pay the loss in, has expired, no right of action exists.

Waiver of limitation.

Sec. 444. The forfeiture arising under the limitation clause, may be waived by the company, and a waiver may be found from the fact that, *after* the time within which the action should have been brought, the company acted and promised as if it did not intend to rely upon the limitation,[3] or from its conduct *before* the limitation has expired, which fairly induces a confidence that the loss will be paid without action, as the fact that negotiations for a settlement are pending, and other facts and circumstances calculated to induce delay.[4]

---

[1] *Killip* v. *Putnam Ins. Co.*, 28 Wis. 47. See also, similar in its facts and doctrine, *Ames* v. *N. Y. Central Ins. Co.*, 14 N. Y. 253 ; *Mayor, etc.*, v. *Hamilton Ins. Co.*, 39 N. Y. 45.

[2] *Mayor of New York* v. *Hamilton Ins. Co.*, 39 N. Y. 45.

[3] *Coursin* v. *Penn. Ins. Co.*, 46 Penn. St. 323.

[4] *Mickey* v. *Burlington Ins. Co.*, 35 Iowa, 174 ; *Ripley* v. *Astor Ins. Co.*, 17 How. Pr. (N. Y.) 444 ; *Curtis* v. *Home Ins. Co.*, 1 Biss. (U. S. C. C.) 485.

CHAPTER XV.

ADJUSTMENT OF THE LOSS.

How ascertained.

SEC. 445 Except in cases where the policy is valued, the right of the assured to a recovery upon his policy is only commensurate with his *actual loss*, within the limits of the sum insured. If the loss is total, and the sum insured is less than the value of the property, the insurer must pay the full amount insured; but if the loss is total, or partial, and the insurance exceeds the loss, the sum insured is to be reduced by such an amount as represents the excess of insurance over the value. To illustrate: If a policy is issued to A. upon his dwelling-house for $1,000, which, at the time of the issue of the policy, fairly represents its insurable value, if no depreciation or deterioration of the property transpires between the issue of the policy and the loss, the amount insured would be a fair measure of recovery, *but not necessarily the legal measure.* The contract is one of indemnity, and the assured's right of recovery *must be measured by the actual loss. The value of the property at the time of loss, and not its value at the time of the issue of the policy, is to be taken;* and this applies as well in favor of the assured as of the insurer. Thus, B. takes out a policy upon a stock of dry goods for $10,000, which, at the time of insurance, fairly represents his usual line of stock; but, before any loss transpires, a decline in prices of that class of goods occurs, and by such decline the value of his stock is reduced one-third, one-half, or to *any* extent. B. cannot recover the amount insured, although his stock remains the same in quantity, nor, although the goods in fact *cost him* the amount insured, but only such a sum as the goods were actually worth *at the time of loss.* Not what they cost him,[1] not necessarily what it would cost him to replace the goods, *but the sum which the goods were worth when they were destroyed by the casualty insured against. It is their value at that time,* and not at any prior or subsequent time, that indicates the extent and measure of his loss, and, consequently, the measure of his recovery.[2] Therefore it is competent for the insurer, on the one hand, to show a *deterioration* in the value of the property, arising from *any* cause, for which the insurer is not responsible, in reduction of the claim of the assured, as a depreciation in prices and values of that species of property; that it was damaged or diminished in value by age, or any other cause; and, on the other hand, the assured may show that the value of the property was largely increased; that prices rule higher than when the property was insured; that it has been improved and increased in value, or any fact that tends to show what the value of the property, *at the time of loss,* actually was.

If, however, the change in values arises from *temporary* causes, not likely to be permanent, or to affect the intrinsic or market value of the goods for any considerable period, such circumstances may be shown, and, if established, the value of the property is to be ascertained irrespective of such temporary change.[3]

[1] *Snell* v. *Del. Ins. Co.,* 4 Dall. (U. S.) 430; *Carson* v. *Marine Ins. Co.,* 2 Wash. C. C. (U. S.) 468.

[2] *Hoffman* v. *Western M. & F. Ins. Co.,* 1 La. An. 216; *Hercules Ins. Co.* v. *Hunter,* 14 C. C. S. (Sc.) 1137; *Ellmaker* v. *Franklin F. Ins. Co.,* 5 Penn. St. 183; *Conn. Ins. Co.* v. *Sennett,* 37 id. 205; *Equitable F. Ins. Co.* v. *Quin,* 11 L. C. 170; *Savage* v. *Corn Exchange Ins. Co.,* 36 N. Y. 655; *Atwood* v. *Union, etc., Ins. Co.,* 23 N. H. 234; *Ela* v. *French,* 11 N. H. 356; *Douglass* v. *Murphy,* 16 U. C. (Q. B.) 113; *American Ins. Co.* v. *Griswold,* 14 Wend. (N. Y.) 399; *Wills* v. *Wells,* 8 Taunt. 264; *Wolfe* v. *Howard Ins. Co.,* 7 N. Y. 583.

[3] In *McQuaig* v. *Quaker City Ins. Co.,* 18 U. C. (Q. B.) 130.

If the property is damaged, the difference between the value of the property in its damaged condition, and its value before it was injured, is the measure of recovery. This leaves the insurer at liberty to show, if he can, that the property *at the time of the fire*, was worth less than new property of the same class; that it had been damaged by causes other than those insured against, or any facts that show or tend to show that the property was deteriorated in value ; and on the other hand, the assured may show that the property was not damaged, or any fact that shows or tends to show what its real value was.[1]

In a Pennsylvania case,[2] the policy provided that the loss or damage should be estimated according to the true actual cash value of the property at the time of the happening of the loss. The policy covered agricultural implements, and the assured sought to recover their value as estimated in the manufacture of each machine before it had been tested in the field. But the court held that this was not the fair criterion, but that the recovery must be limited to what *they were actually worth at the time when the fire happened*, and that this must be ascertained by testimony. This rule, while permitting the *cost* of the property to be shown, as one of the elements of value, yet very properly ignores it as the true test. The actual cost of production may largely exceed the price for which the property can be sold, and consequently its *actual value*, and that would be a harsh, as well as a dangerous rule, that compelled the insurer to pay more than the property could be sold for in the ordinary course of business.

Buildings.

SEC. 446. In the case of buildings, it would seem that the measure of recovery should be *the actual value of the property in the condition it was in at the time of loss, taking into consideration its age and condition, and not necessarily what it would cost to erect a new building.* The assured should be allowed *the value of his building at the time of loss, and if, by reason of age or use, it is less valuable than a new building, erected upon the same plan, of similar materials, and of the same dimensions, the insurer should be allowed for such difference arising from deterioration.*[3] This rule, however, does not apply where the insurer elects to rebuild. In that case, he is to be allowed nothing for the differ-

---

[1] *Hoffman* v. *Western, etc., Ins. Co.,* 1 La. An. 216 ; *Western, etc., Ins. Co.* v. *Transportation Co.,* 12 Wall. (U. S.) 201 ; *Hercules Ins. Co.* v. *Hunter,* 14 C. C. (Sc.) 1137.

[2] *Com. Ins. Co.* v. *Sennett,* 37 Penn. St. 205.

[3] *Ætna Ins. Co.* v. *Johnson,* 11 Bush. (Ky.) 587 ; 5 Ben. F. I. C. 798.

ence between the value of an old and a new building. If he would avail himself of the advantages of deterioration, he must pay in cash. He cannot charge the insured with the burden of paying or allowing to him the difference arising in consequence of his election to erect a new building. That would permit a person to make another his debtor against his will, which the law does not permit. It is for the jury to say what the actual value of the building was, in view of all the facts, and their finding is conclusive.[1] Where there is unreasonable delay in repairing, after notice is given of its intention to do so by the insurer, the assured is entitled to damages for the building by the action of the weather,[2] and for the rent of the premises during such delay.[3] The rule is, applicable alike to buildings, machinery, or other property, that the value is to be determined by the condition the property was in at the time of loss, and in arriving at the measure of loss, it is proper to show what the expense of similar new buildings, machinery, or property would be, and then ascertain what the difference in value is between the new and that which was destroyed, and the difference, if any, is to be allowed to the insurer.[4]

The value of the building *as such,* and not what the assured loses by way of interruption to his business, loss of profits, etc., is the measure of recovery,[5] but if the value of the building is put in issue by the pleadings, the rental of the buildings may be shown.[6] When the loss is total, and exceeds the sum insured, the whole sum named in the policy is due.[7]

Extent of insurable interest cannot be exceeded—Mortgagee, etc.

SEC. 447. This rule is extended to mortgagees or any other persons holding an interest in the property as security for a debt, or against

---

[1] *Brinley* v. *National Ins. Co.,* 11 Met. (Mass.) 195.

[2] *American Central Ins. Co.* v. *McLanathan,* 11 Kan. 533; 5 Ben. F. I. C. 471.

[3] *Home Mut. Ins. Co.* v. *Garfield,* 60 Ill. 124; 14 Am. Rep.; see sec. 130.

[4] In *Vance* v. *Forster,* 2 Can. & D. 118, the policy covered machinery, and in an action for the loss, the court held that the state and condition of the property, *at the time of loss,* must be considered by the jury, *and what it would cost to replace it,* and that they might ascertain what would be the entire cost of new machinery, and then, whether the mill would be better, and how much, with *new* machinery, than with that destroyed, and that the difference between the value of *new machinery and that which was destroyed* should be deducted from the entire expense of the new, and the remainder would express the measure of recovery.

[5] *Willis* v. *Boston Ins. Co.,* 6 Pick. (Mass.) 182; *Menzies* v. *N. British Ins. Co.,* 9 C. C. (Sc.) 694; *Niblo* v. *N. A. Ins. Co.,* 1 Sandf. (N. Y.) 551; *Wright* v. *Sun F. Ins. Co.,* 1 Ad. & El. 621.

[6] *Cumberland, etc., Ins. Co.* v. *Schell,* 30 Penn. St. 31.

[7] *Miss. Mut. Ins. Co.* v. *Ingram,* 34 Miss. 215; *Peddie* v. *Quebec F. Ass. Co.,* Stuart (Sc.) 174; *Phillips* v. *Perry Co. Ins. Co.,* 7 Phila. (Penn.) 673; *Ætna Ins. Co.* v. *Tyler,* 16 Wend. (N. Y.) 385; *Richmondville Seminary, etc.,* v. *Hamilton Ins. Co.,* 14 Gray (Mass.) 459; *Nicolet* v. *Ins. Co.,* 3 La. 366.

loss to themselves. Their *actual* loss is the measure of recovery. If the mortgage debt, or other claim has been paid in full or quieted, nothing is due upon the policy, because all insurable interest is gone. If it has been paid in part, or in anywise been partially satisfied, *only the balance remaining due*, can be recovered, for that is the limit of the insurable interest.[1] But, it is only when payments have been actually made *before* loss, that any deductions can be made. The fact that the mortgage debt was paid, or assigned to a third person, *after* a loss under the policy, does not benefit the insurer, and cannot be set-off, against the insurance.[2] Nor can the insurer avail himself of the fact, that the property covered by the mortage, even after the loss, is ample security for the debt, or that it is worth partly as much as the debt. The loss must be paid to the extent of the mortgagee's interest, covered by the policy, irrespective of the value of the security.[3] So where goods are insured by a carrier, bailee, commission merchant, agent or other person insuring for himself, the measure of recovery *is his interest* in the goods, which is represented by his charges paid thereon, or to be paid, and his expected profits therefrom,[4] unless by law or general usage he is liable to the bailor for the full value of the goods, in which case he would be entitled to recover the value of the goods at the time of loss,[5] and the same is true, where the policy covers " goods his own, or held in trust or on commission."[6]

Re-insurers.

SEC. 448. As between re-insurers, the same rule prevails. The re-insurer is entitled to the benefit of any settlement made by the original insurer with the original assured, and cannot be called upon to pay more than the original insurer pays,[7] except, possibly, in cases

---

[1] *Hadley* v. *N. H. F. Ins. Co.*, 55 N. H. 110 ; 5 Ben. F. I. C. 700 ; *S. P. Ill. Mut. Ins. Co.* v. *Andes Ins. Co.*, ante.

[2] *Davis* v. *Quincy, etc., Ins. Co.*, 10 Allen (Mass.) 113 ; 5 Ben. F. I. C. 35.

[3] *Strong* v. *Manufacturers' Ins. Co.*, 10 Pick. (Mass.) 40 ; *Ins. Co.* v. *Updegraff*, 21 Penn. St. 513 ; *Carpenter* v. *Washington Ins. Co.* 16 Pet. (U. S.) 496 ; *Kernochan* v. *Bowery Ins. Co.*, 17 N. Y. 428 ; *Sussex, etc., Ins. Co.* v. *Woodruff*, 26 N. J. 541 ; *Foster* v. *Equitable Ins. Co.*, 2 Gray (Mass.) 216 ; *Boston & Salem Ice Co.* v. *Royal Ins. Co.*, 12 Allen (Mass.) 381 ; *Clark* v. *Wilson*, 103 Mass. 221 ; *King State, etc., Ins. Co.*, 7 Cush. (Mass.) 1.

[4] *Putnam* v. *Mercantile Ins. Co.*, 5 Met. (Mass.) 386 ; *Savage* v. *Corn Ex. Ins. Co.*, 36 N. Y. 655 ; Field on Damages, 447, *et seq.*

[5] *DeForest* v. *Fulton Ins. Co.*, ante.

[6] *Waring* v. *Indemnity Ins. Co.*, ante ; *Turner* v. *Stetts*, 28 Ala. 420 ; *Waters* v. *Monarch Ins. Co.*, 5 El. & Bl. 80 ; *Ayres* v. *Hartford Ins. Co.*, 17 Iowa, 176 ; *Hough* v. *Peoples' Ins. Co.*, 36 Md. 398 ; *DeForest* v. *Fulton Ins. Co.*, 1 Hall (N. Y.) 84 ; *Lee* v. *Howard Ins. Co.*, 11 Cush. (Mass.) 324.

[7] In *Ill. Mut. Ins. Co.* v. *The Andes Ins. Co.*, 67 Ill. 362 ; 5 Ben. F. I. C. 456, the original insurer's policy covered $6,000 ; the re-insurer covered $2,000 of the risk. The original insurer settled the loss for $600. Held, that he could recover no more than that of the re-insurer.

where the orignal insurer has become insolvent, although upon what ground, or upon what principle a different rule prevails in such cases, it is difficult to see or understand. That any distinction should be made between a solvent or insolvent company in this respect, is not warranted by principle or the rules of fairdealing, and is wholly repugnant to the rules ordinarily prevailing as to insurable interest or adjustment of losses.[1]

Shifting risks—Substituted property.

SEC. 449. Where a policy is issued for a term upon goods in a store, manufacturer's stock, or other property which the insurer knows or ought to know the assured does not intend to keep constantly on hand, but simply desires and expects the policy to cover goods of the same class, the assured is entitled to recover for any goods of the same class, although none of them were on hand when the policy was issued. This rule applies to household furniture, and, in case the policy is assigned with the consent of the insurer, the policy will be operative to cover the furniture of the assignee in the same building and for the same sum.[2]

Rule when several policies in part cover the same property.

SEC. 450. Where several policies cover, in part, the same property, as where one policy covers stock manufactured and unmanufactured, and and another covers manufactured stock simply, the rule of adjustment, as stated by THOMAS, J.,[3] is "ascertain the amount of manufactured and unmanufactured stock, separately. Then, as the value of the entire stock is to the sum insured, so would be the amount of the unmanufactured stock to the result sought. For example: The entire stock is, say $2,100, of this the manufactured is $1,500, the unmanufactured $600. The amount insured on both, is $700. Then, as $2,100 is to $700, so is $600 to the result sought."

Rule where there is other insurance, and a limitation as to liability to three-fourths or any other portion of actual value.

SEC. 451. When there are two or more policies upon the same property, and one of them contains a provision that "when property is insured by this company solely, three-fourths only of the value will be taken, and in case of loss will pay only three-fourths the value at the time of loss," and that "in case of loss or damage of property, upon which double insurance exists, the company shall be liable to

---

[1] See Sec. 382.

[2] *Cummings* v. *Cheshire, etc., Ins. Co.*, 55 N. H. 457; 5 Ben. F. I. C. 769.

[3] *Blake* v. *Exchange, etc., Ins. Co.*, 12 Gray (Mass.) 265; 4 Ben. F. I. C. 306.

pay only such proportion thereof, as the sum insured by this company bears to the whole amount insured thereon, such amount not to exceed three-fourths the actual value of the property at the time of loss." The rule of adjustment is, first to ascertain the *actual* value of the property at the time of loss, from which deduct one-fourth the amount. Then ascertain the total amount of insurance, and divide the amount of loss by the amount of insurance, and multiply the quotient by the amount of the policy, and the product will be the amount for such insurer to pay, if no more than the amount of the policy. If it exceeds the amount of the policy the loss is total, and the full amount covered by the policy is due. If less than the amount of the policy, only such proportional part is due. Thus, where under such a policy $2,000 is insured, and there is other insurance to the amount of $3,000, the insurer is liable only for two-fifths of three-fourths of the actual loss.[1] If, however, the other policy or policies do not cover all the property covered by such policy, the value of the property not covered by the other policies, is not subject to such proportionate assessment, and the policy must bear that portion of the loss alone. Thus, where a policy with such provisions as were stated, supra, covered $2,000, "on his stock in trade, being mostly chamber furniture in sets, *and other articles usually kept by furniture dealers*," and there were two other policies of $1,500 each, covering simply the assured's "stock of furniture," and which did not embrace articles usually kept by furniture dealers, such as paints, oils, varnish, etc., and there was a loss, which the jury found amounted to $5,917.50, and the value of the paints, oils and varnish was $826.84—the court held that the value of those articles should be deducted from the total loss, and two-fifths of the remainder added to three-fourths of $826.84, would give the amount for which the defendant company was liable.[2] Where there are no such limitations upon liability, and there are several policies covering the same property, and the loss is less than the insurance, the amount of the loss divided by the whole amount of insurance, and the quotient multiplied by the amount of each policy, gives the proportion that each is to pay. Where, as in the case previously cited, the policies do not all attach alike, if the property destroyed is covered by *all* the policies, and the property also covered by one or more of the other policies is *not* destroyed, the value thereof

---

[1] *Haley* v. *Dorchester*, etc., *Ins. Co.*, 12 Gray (Mass.) 349 ; 4 Ben. F. I. C. 348.
[2] *Haley* v. *Dorchester*, etc., *Ins. Co.*, 1 Allen (Mass.) 536.

is not to be deducted, because each policy-holder is liable for the destruction of *any* of the property, to the extent of the sum insured by it.[1]

Rule when insured bears proportion of loss.

SEC. 452. Where, as is sometimes the case, a policy contains a condition that "where property is damaged by removal from a building which is exposed to fire, said damage shall be borne by the assured and insurers in such proportion as the whole sum insured bears to the whole value of the property insured, of which proof in due form shall be made by the claimant," in case of a destruction of a part of the property by fire, and an injury to a part by removal, the rule for ascertaining what proportion of such damage each should bear, is to ascertain the total value of the property at risk, the damage by removal, and this each party must pay in proportion to their respective interests. To illustrate: The total value of the stock is $20,000; the loss by removal is $1,000, and the amount of insurance is $1,000. The interest of the assured is $\frac{19}{20}$ths of $1,000, and the interest of the insurer $\frac{1}{20}$th, leaving $50 of such loss for the insurer to pay, and the balance of $950 to be borne by the insured himself.[2]

Assured, unless stipulating to do so, not bound to keep up other insurance.

SEC. 453. Unless the insurers, in their policies, stipulate that other prior or subsequent insurance shall be kept on foot during the life of their respective policies, the assured may cancel either or any of them, and the insurer is entitled to no deduction of a proportional part which such insurance would have borne if kept on foot. If the insurers desire to avail themselves of such relief, they must stipulate therefor in their policies, and the fact that the policy, on its face, states "other insurance exists upon the property to the amount of $5,000," is not a warranty that such other insurance shall continue to exist for a single hour even after the policy is issued. It is enough, if true when the policy was made.[3]

Partial loss—Subsequent total loss.

SEC. 454. Where there has been a partial loss paid under a policy, and subsequently there is a total loss of the same property, the assured is only liable *for the difference between the sum insured and the amount paid under the partial loss*. Thus, if a policy covers a building for $500, and there is a partial loss of $50, which is paid, the sum insured

---

[1] *Com.* v. *Hide & Leather Ins. Co.*, 112 Mass. 436.

[2] *Peoria M. & F. Ins. Co.* v. *Wilson*, 5 Minn. 53; 4 Ben. F. I. C. 497.

[3] *Forbush* v. *Western Ins. Co.*, 4 Gray (Mass.) 337; *Haley* v. *Dorchester, etc., Ins. Co.*, 12 Gray (Mass.) 349.

is thereby reduced to $450, and if subsequently there is a total loss, $450 is the maximum limit of the insurer's liability.[1]

Leasehold interest.

SEC. 455. Where the policy simply covers the interest of the assured under a lease, the limit of recovery *is the value of the unexpired term.* Nothing can be recovered for damages by the interruption of the business, or for loss of profits. If the assured desires to have those interests covered, the policy must expressly and specifically cover them.[2]

Where a policy covers a building upon leased land, the lease of which is about to expire, the measure of recovery is the *intrinsic value of the building*, and not what it is worth to remove to another lot.[3]

Effect of adjustment.

SEC. 456. The fact that the loss has been adjusted by the insurers, does not necessarily entitle the assured to recover that amount. The adjustment, of itself, merely amounts to an admission on the part of the insurer that the sum fixed, is due, *if the insured is entitled to have anything under the policy,*[4] and does not estop the insurer from setting up fraud upon the part of the assured, or a breach of any of the conditions of the policy that operate to defeat the insurer's liability.[5]

Contract for purchase.

SEC. 457. The fact that the assured does not hold the absolute title to the property insured, does not necessarily prevent him from recovering the full value of the property insured. Thus, a person who has gone into possession of premises under a contract to purchase, but who has not paid all the purchase-money, nevertheless has an insurable interest to the extent of the full value, and may recover the same upon the policy.[6] But where the assured has contracted to sell the property, and has given possession under the contract, and received a part of the purchase money, although the title has not passed, he cannot recover beyond the unpaid purchase-money.[7]

[1] *Curry* v. *Com. Ins. Co.*, 10 Pick. (Mass.) 535.

[2] *Niblo* v. *N. American F. Ins. Co.*, 1 Sandf. (N. Y.) 551; *Menzies* v. *N. British Ins. Co.*, 9 C. C. (Sc.) 694; *Laurent* v. *Chatham Ins. Co.*, 1 Hall (N. Y.) 41.

[3] *Laurent* v. *Chatham Ins. Co.*, 1 Hall (N. Y.) 40.

[4] *Whipple* v. *North British, etc., Ins. Co.*, 5 Ins. L. J. 71.

[5] *Herbert* v. *Champion*, 1 Camp. 134; *Gammon* v. *Beverly*, 1 Taunt. 119; *Matthews* v. *General, etc., Ins. Co.*, 9 La. An. 590; *Lash* v. *Martin*, 19 C. C. (Sc.) 101; *Russell* v. *Dunskey*, 6 Moore, 233.

[6] *Ætna Ins. Co.* v. *Tyler*, 16 Wend. (N. Y.) 385.

[7] *Shotwell* v. *Jefferson Ins. Co.*, 5 Bos. (N. Y.) 247.

Goods in the hands of a manufacturer.

SEC. 458. The measure of recovery upon stock wrought and unwrought and in process of manufacture being the actual loss, the value of each is to be ascertained, to wit: the value of the raw material; then to that in process of manufacture, the cost of labor and materials employed as far as the process of manufacture has advanced, is to be added to the value of the raw materials employed, and nothing can be claimed for interest on capital, either in plant or machinery, or for prospective profits; and it would seem that where a policy covers property in the hands of a manufacturer, as stated *supra*, that his recovery for the loss of *manufactured* stock, in the absence of any provision covering profits, should be restricted to the value of raw materials with the cost of manufacture added. I have found no case in which this question has been directly raised or passed upon, and merely put forward the idea as a suggestion. There are many difficulties in the way of the rule, and many serious objections to it, that would seem to render it impracticable; but the result attained is far more just, both to the assured and the insurer, than that which virtually permits the manufacturer to recover profits upon his manufactured goods by recovering their market value. In the case of manufactured goods in the hands of a dealer who has purchased them in market, of course *the value* of the goods upon the day of loss is the measure. In such cases the value of raw material and the cost of production are of no account, and is not admissible in evidence upon the question of value, neither is the cost of the goods to the dealer determinate of the question, although proper to be shown in the process of adjustment; but the real limit of recovery *is the value of the goods at the time and place of loss*, which the assured must establish.

Total and partial loss—The salvage.

SEC. 459. Mr. Bunyon, in a recent English work upon Fire Insurance, p. 115, *et seq.*, in treating upon the subject of adjustment, says: "A total loss, in the language of fire insurance, does not mean, as in marine insurance, the total destruction of the property, but its destruction or injury to such an extent as to render the insurer liable to pay the total sum insured. A ship may be, and perhaps often is, caught by a hurricane and lost, with all hands on board, but a fire rarely totally destroys the insured property. The residue remaining after the fire is termed the salvage. Upon the settlement of a loss it is always an important consideration to decide to whom the salvage belongs. It will be remembered that, when the policy, as is usually the case, contains no conditions of average, the assured is entitled to recover in case of fire for any damage up to the amount insured, without reference to any proportion between the sum insured and the value of the property. When, therefore, the owner is insufficiently insured upon an ordinary policy, and the insurance money, together with the value of the salvage, does not make up more than the value of the property immediately before the fire, the salvage will always belong to him. When the owner is insured up to the full value, and the claim is admitted as a total loss, any salvage belongs to the insurers.[1]

When the policy contains conditions of average.

SEC. 460. When conditions of average are added, the assured can only recover such proportion of the loss as the sum insured shall bear to the whole value of the property immediately before the fire. If the property is fully insured, these conditions are inoperative ; but if this is not the case, the assured, in the settlement, takes the position of an insurer for the proportion uncovered by the policy, and is entitled to share in the salvage precisely as if, instead of being the assured, he had been an underwriter for an amount equal to the uninsured proportion. The expenses of putting out the fire are, as we have seen, provided for by the conditions, and form a separate and distinct item, involving a liability in addition to the risk of paying the sum assured ; but if any expenses have been incurred in preserving the salvage these will fall primarily upon the salvage, and must be borne by the persons benefiting by it in proportion to their respective interests.

When the insurers have paid the full value.

SEC. 461. When, as sometimes happens, the insurers pay to the assured the full value of a parcel of goods which have been damaged, leaving the property in the hands of an auctioneer to dispose of, in such a case, and whenever the assured receives the full value of his property, and his claim is so discharged, the salvage, as we have seen, belongs to the insurers; and should it eventually, upon a rise in the markets, fetch more money than they have paid to the insured, they will be entitled to retain the whole as purchasers of the goods. Such cases have, it is understood, actually occurred in practice.

Unauthorized detention of salvage by third parties.

SEC. 462. An interesting case upon the subject of salvage, arose out of the great fire of June, 1861, at London Bridge.[2] A quantity of

---

[1] *Da Costa* v. *Firth,* 4 Burr., 1966.
[2] *Buckley* v. *Gross,* 3 B. & S. 566, Q. B.

tallow, the property of various persons, was melted by the fire, and flowed through the sewers into the river. When floating down the Thames, a portion was taken possession of by unauthorized persons, and sold to the plaintiff, who was, of course, aware of all the circumstances relating to it. The police took the plaintiff with his purchase into custody, and charged him with unlawful possession of the tallow. The magistrate dismissed the charge, but ordered the tallow to be detained under the provisions of the Police Regulation Act.[1] This was done, but becoming a nuisance, it was sold by the direction of the Commissioner of Police before the expiration of the 12 months limited by sec. 30 of the Act. Under these circumstances, the plaintiff brought an action against the purchaser to recover the value of the tallow taken from him, contending that the tallow had been abandoned by the owners and was vested in the finder, in whom the property had beed revested by the unlawful sale. The court held otherwise, considering that there was no evidence that the tallow had been abandoned, and inclining to think that the possession of the plaintiff had been felonious; that, as regards the original owners, the legal effect of the mixture of the tallow was probably to make them tenants in common in equal portions of the mass; also, that without resorting to the Police Acts at all, the constable was justified in seizing the tallow, and that thereupon the possesion of the police was that of the true owners.

The assured cannot abandon without the consent of the insurer.

SEC. 463. On another occasion, where there was a considerable damage done to a large and varied stock of goods, a claim was made by the assured, upon proving that the value of the stock as it stood upon his books was fully equal to the amount of the insurances, to abandon it to the offices, and to have immediate payment made to him in full of the insurance money. It was argued that the right to abandon was good by a forced analogy to the right to abandon in marine cases, where there is a constructive total loss, and that to deny it would be a great hardship upon the assured, whose credit and even solvency might depend upon the possession of the stock in an undamaged state. This latter argument, which is based upon a consideration of general convenience rather than of law, appears to be met by observing, that the credit which may be obtained either through the ordinary banking channels or elsewhere upon policies on which serious claims have

---

[1] 2 & 3 Vict. c. 71, s. 29.

arisen, can scarcely be said to be less available than the power of obtaining advances upon or realising by sale the goods themselves. A careful consideration of the contract of fire insurance will, however, at once prove that the contention thus raised could not be sustained. The terms in which the contract is couched, which are, by the way, much more limited than those of a marine policy, negative the claim, for the obligation is to make good to the assured 'such loss or damage by fire as may happen to the property, not in the event of damage to purchase it at the price of the day of the fire; neither have the insurers any right to compel the assured to hand the property over to them. The right of abandonment as exercised under a marine policy is, moreover, inapplicable, since it does not arise where the goods insured come into the possession of the assured, although in a damaged state, yet still marketable at a proportionate price;[1] but only when there is a total loss either absolutely or constructive; no amount of damage, however great, which does not threaten the entire destruction of the thing insured, justifying an abandonment;[2] and further, since even in the case of a marine insurance, if the facts were such as to justify a notice of abandonment, yet if at the time an action is brought, what had antecedently been a constructive total loss, has, by subsequent events, ceased to be so, and become an average loss merely, a compensation for an average less can alone be recovered.[3] Thus, in a recent case in the House of Lords, upon a marine policy, where the opinion of the judges was called for, BLACKBURN, J., observed: There is no notice of abandonment in cases of fire insurance, .but the salvage is transferred upon the principle of equity, expressed by Lord HARDWICKE, in *Randal* v. *Cockran*, 1 Ves. 98, that the person who originally sustains the loss, is the owner, but after satisfaction made to him the insurer.[4]

Ascertainment of damage by sale.

SEC. 464. The usual practice, when a loss has happened and the goods are materially injured, is to ascertain the amount of the damage by a sale by auction with the consent and for the benefit of all parties. The damaged goods are placed in the hands of the auction-

[1] *Thompson* v. *The Royal Exchange Assurance Company*, 10 East. 214; *Navone* v. *Haddon*, 9 C. B. 30; *Rosetto* v. *Gurney*, 11 C. B. 176.

[2] *Cazalet* v. *St. Barbe*, 1 T. R. 187; *Furneaux* v. *Bradley*, Parke on Insurance, 365 8th Ed.; *Anderson* v. *Wallis*, 2 M. & Sel. 240; *McAndrew* v. *Vaughan*, Parke on Insurance, 252; Arnould on Marine Insurance, 919, 968, *et seq.*, Ed. 1866.

[3] *McIver* v. *Henderson*, 4 M. & Sel. 584.

[4] *Rankin* v. *Potter*, L. R. 6 Eng. & Ir. Ap. 118.

eer, who accounts to the insured or the insurers, as the case may be,
for the proceeds of the sale less the expenses, the difference between
the value of the goods at the time of the fire and the proceeds of the
sale being made good by the insurers. In such a case, it is essential
to their interests that undamaged goods should not be included, since
the loss by a forced sale may be very great, and a responsibility
thereby thrown upon them, which can, in no case, be fairly entitled a
damage by fire. And it is here that the importance of the question
of abandonment arises. It is one thing for the insurers to pay for the
injury actually occasioned, and another to be compelled to become the
immediate purchasers of a vast amount of merchandise, which they
may only be able to realize on terms far below its value. If, however, the insured and the insurers cannot agree as to the mode of dis-
posing of the salvage, the former may be entitled to test the amount
of his loss by a sale, without their concurrence, but he will be responsible in such a case for the propriety of his proceedings.

Sound goods not to be sold.

SEC. 465. It is also important to observe that the rule which holds
good in marine insurance, that the insurers *'are not liable to loss,
owing io the assortment being broken,'* is equally applicable here, and
that, therefore, if out of whole packages or bales of manufactured
goods only a few articles are damaged, the assured will not be entitled to have the sound and damaged goods sold together, since the
insurers are not liable for loss to the sound portion, being accountable
only for the actual injury done to the things insured, by the direct
operation of the peril insured against, and not for consequential
damages.[1]

The assured is bound to exert himself to save the property, and protect the salvage.

SEC. 466. When a fire occurs, the assured is bound to do all in his
power to save the property, and so to deal with the salvage that the
least possible injury may eventually happen ; *a fortiori*, he cannot be
justified in standing by, and, relying for his protection upon his
policy, suffering others to misuse the damaged goods. It speaks well
for the good feeling usually displayed on such occasions, that no case
has been reported in which this question has arisen upon a fire insurance. It cannot, however, be doubted but that this rule, which
applies in marine insurance in the case of abandonment, is here

---

[1] Arnould on Marine Insurance, 836, ed. 1866, citing Stevens on Average, 155-
158, 5th ed. ; Benecké, Pr. of Indem. 437, 438.

equally applicable. It is thus stated by Mr. ARNOULD:[1] 'By the general law maritime, as recognized alike in this country and foreign states, the assured is bound, on the occurrence of any casualty which authorizes an abandonment, to use his utmost endeavors to rescue from destruction, or to reclaim from capture, the property insured, so as to lighten, as far as possible, the burden which is to fall on the underwriters. In so doing, he is considered to be their agent, and the exertions which he makes in that capacity do not at all prejudice his right to insist on his abandonment.' This generally recognized right is expressly conferred on the assured in our English (marine) policies, by a special clause, to the following effect: 'And in case of any loss or misfortune, it shall be lawful to the assured, their factors, servants and assigns, to sue, labor and travail for, in or about, the defense, safeguard or recovery of the said goods and merchandises, or any part thereof, without prejudice to the insurance,' etc. The clause only says, ' it shall be lawful' for the assured to do so ; but the law and practice of this and almost all other countries *impose it upon him as his 'bounden duty,'*[2] and, of course, the same principle would apply in a partial as in a constructive total loss.

Arbitration.

SEC. 467. When the parties are unable to agree as to the amount of the loss, and no fraud is imputed, this question is usually settled by arbitration, and it will be found that all policies contain conditions to this effect. The form of the condition is important, although not so much so as formerly. It was long considered that such conditions could not be framed in such a manner as to make them compulsory on both parties, on the ground that courts of law will not permit their jurisdiction to be ousted by previous agreement ; but although this proposition is true, it was afterwards shown that the agreement of the parties might make it a condition precedent to the right to bring an action, that the amount of damages, or the time of paying them, or any other matter which does not go to the root of the action, should be settled by arbitration. Such a condition reduces the policy from a contract to pay the amount of damage absolutely, to one to pay such a sum as the damage shall be ascertained to amount to by a third party, and operates as the substitution of the arbitrator for the jury to ascertain the amount of the damage, which is a very different thing

---

[1] Law of Marine Insurance, 875 ; Marshall, Law of Marine Insurance, p. 497.
[2] *Mitchell* v. *Edie,* 1 T. R. 609.

from an agreement to refer every question or matter of dispute to arbitration.[1]

When the condition consisted of an agreement in general terms, that, 'in case any difference or dispute shall arise between the insured and the company touching any loss or damage, or otherwise in respect of any insurance, such difference shall be submitted to two indifferent persons as arbitrators,' one chosen by each party, and with liberty to choose an umpire, and whose award, in writing, 'shall be conclusive and binding upon all parties;' it was held that the agreement to refer was collateral, and not a condition precedent, which could be pleaded in bar to the action.' Although there is no doubt as to the general principle of the law on this subject, the question whether the true construction of any policy brings it within the rule of Scott v. Avery, and makes the ascertainment of the damage by arbitration a condition precedent or not, may be one of some nicety. In a late case,[2] the contract in the policy was to satisfy the loss according to the exact tenor of the articles subjoined. One of the articles provided that persons assured should prove their loss by oath or affirmation, and the production of their books and other proper vouchers, 'which loss, *after the same shall be adjusted*, shall immediately be paid in money by the said corporation,' with power of reinstatement added; and then went on to say, 'in case any difference shall arise touching any loss or damage, such difference shall be submitted to the judgment and determination of arbitrators, indifferently chosen, whose award shall be conclusive on all parties.' Here the question was, whether the words '*after the same shall be adjusted*,' coupled with the arbitration clause, made the adjustment by arbitrators a condition precedent, and it was held (BRAMWELL, B., dissenting) that it did so. Some doubt was thrown upon the correctness of the preceding decision of Roper v. Lendon, but the doubt was as to the true construction of the contract in that case, and the application of the law—not as to the law itself.

In Roper v. Lendon, it was held that the arbitration clauses in the common law procedure act[4] made no difference, and that the eleventh section of that act does not operate as a bar to an action, but only lays

---

[1] *Scott* v. *Avery*, 5 H. L. C. 811; 2 Jur. N. S. 815; *Braunstein* v. *Accidental Death Assurance Co.*, 1 B. & S. 782; *Lowndes* v. *Lord Stamford*, 18 Q. B. 425; *Tredwen* v. *Holman*, 1 H. & C. 72.

[2] *Roper* v. *Lendon*, 5 Jur. N. S. 491; 1 E. & E. 825.

[3] L. R. 2 Exch. 237.

[4] 17 and 18 Vict. c. 125.

the foundation for a summary application to the court or a judge to stay proceedings. On these clauses, it is to be observed that the latter section includes courts of equity as well as courts of law, and although there is a discretien reposed in the court, the tendency of modern practice is to consider the arbitration clause binding, and to give effect to it as a substantial term of the agreement between the parties.[1] These clauses are as follows: ' That if it be made to appear, at any time after the issuing of the writ, to the satisfaction of the court or a judge, upon the application of either party, that the matter in dispute consists wholly or in part of matters of mere account, which cannot conveniently be tried in the ordinary way, it shall be lawful for such court or judge, upon such application, if they or he think fit, to decide such matter in a summary way, or to order that such matter, either wholly or in part, be referred to an arbitrator to be appointed by the parties, or to an officer of the court, or, in county causes, to the judge of any county court, upon such terms as to costs or otherwise as such court or judge shall think reasonable; and the decision or order of such court or judge, or the award or certificate of such referee, shall be enforceable by the same process as the finding of a jury upon the matter referred' (sec. 3); and further, where parties to any instrument executed after the act, 'shall agree that any then existing or future differences shall be referred to arbitration,' and an action at law or suit in equity shall have nevertheless been commenced, it shall be lawful for the court in which the action or suit is brought, or a judge thereof, on the application of the defendant, after appearance and before plea or answer, upon being satisfied that no sufficient reason exists why such matters should not be referred to arbitration, and that the defendant was, at the time of the bringing of such action or suit and is still, willing to concur in all necessary acts proper for causing such matters to be so decided by arbitration, to make a rule or order, staying all proceedings, on such terms as to costs or otherwise as to such court or judge may seem fit, with power to discharge or vary such order (sec. 11).

In the ordinary case, when the question is one of amount on a fire loss, this enactment renders the application of the principle in Scott v. Avery far less important than formerly, since all fire policies contain conditions for reference.

---

[1] *Plews* v. *Baker*, L. R. 16 Eq. 564; *Willesford* v. *Watson*, L. R. 8 C. P. 473, 480.

Sec. 468. When a fire has taken place, and the liability is disputed by the insurers, the assured will be driven to enforce his claim by an action at law.

When a claim has been adjusted, and the amount of loss agreed between the assured and the insurers, or their agents, disputes may arise how far the adjustment is binding upon the insurers before payment. This question has been the subject of numerous cases in marine insurances, in which it has been held that the adjustment is nothing more than a promise to pay, which is only binding when founded on the consideration of a previous liability. 'What,' it is said, 'is an adjustment?' 'An admission on the supposition of certain facts stated that the assured are entitled to recover on the policy. An underwriter must make a strong case after admitting his liability, but until he has paid the money he is at liberty to avail himself of any defense which the facts or the law of the case will furnish.' [1]

In like manner, if after the assured has put in and proved his claim, and agreed to its amount, which would be an adjustment, if he clearly proved that he had omitted some article, he would not be concluded by such adjustment.[2]

But after the loss has been paid, when the insurers knew, or might have learnt upon inquiry, all the circumstances upon which they might have resisted the claim, they cannot recover the money in the absence of actual fraud; and a mistake or ignorance of law is no excuse.[3] This rule is adopted as one of general convenience, and for the prevention of endless litigation, and expressly applies where the payment is made under the compulsion of legal process, or as the compromise of a suit.[4]

If, however, after the settlement, the insurers discover that there was fraud, misrepresentation, or concealment in the original contract, or circumstances transpire which would have justified their resisting the claim, but which they had no means of ascertaining at the time of payment, they may recover the money paid to the assured.[5] The only exception being, when in the absence of actual fraud, the payment has been made under the pressure of legal proceedings.

[1] *Herbert* v. *Champion*, 1 Camp. 133; *Shepherd* v. *Chewter*, 1 Camp. 274; *Gammon* v. *Beverley*, 1 B. Moore, 563.

[2] *Elliott* v. *Royal Exchange Assurance Company*, L. R., 2 Exch. 240.

[3] *Bilbie* v. *Lumley*, 2 East. 469; *Shepherd* v. *Chewter*, 4 Camp. 274.

[4] *Marriot* v. *Hampton*, 7 T. R. 269; see 2 Smith's Lead. Cas., p. 237.

[5] Arnould, Marine Insurance, 1003, citing *Buller* v. *Harrison*, Cowp. 565.

If no cause is shown for rejecting the claim after adjustment, nothing remains for the insurers but to pay the money. When the policy is granted in the names of several persons any one of them can give a legal discharge and release the debt, but it is usual and proper to require the receipt of all the assured.

When the assured is compelled to have recourse to a court of law, he may recover interest on the amount of the loss during the delay, juries being empowered, if they think fit, to allow interest in the nature of damages thereon.

The assured, under a fire policy, cannot recover for successive losses occurring within the term of the insurance for which the premium is paid more than the amount insured." [1]

---

[1] *Cromlie* v. *Portsmouth Ins. Co.*, 26 N. H., 389.

CHAPTER XVI.

SUBROGATION.

Subrogation, right of insurer to. Mortgagee.

SEC. 469. Where a policy is held by a mortgagee in his own name, the insurer becomes liable to pay him in case of loss, *notwithstanding the premises have been fully repaired.*[1] As to whether in case of loss, the insurer has a right to be subrogated to the rights of the mortgagee, proportionally, under the mortgage, was at one time regarded as open, and some text-writers[2] upon this subject announced the rule broadly, that under such circumstances the underwriters, upon payment of the loss thereby became entitled to a *proportional* interest in the mortgage debt. But, even if the cases referred to in support of this position, can be said to have warranted this statement, which is doubted, such can hardly be said to be the recognized doctrine at the present time, and the author himself in a later edition of his work,[3] suggests a different rule, and one more in accordance with the doctrine now held. In Massachusetts it has been held that, *a payment of a total loss under a policy to a mortgagee upon mortgaged property, and a tender of the amount remaining unpaid upon the mortgage, over the loss, does not entitle the insurer, either in law or equity, to an assignment of the mortgage debt,*[4] and in this case it was held that the fact that the policy provided· that, in case of loss the insurer will assign " all his rights to recover

---

[1] *Foster* v. *Equitable Ins. Co.*, 2 Gray (Mass.) 221.
[2] 2 Phillips on Insurance, 419, 2d ed.
[3] 5th ed., Sec. 1512, 1712.
[4] *Suffolk, etc., Ins. Co.* v. *Boyden*, 9 Allen (Mass.) 123.

satisfaction therefor from any other person or corporation," did not affect the question. But this was put upon the ground that the mortgage debt *was not, in " any sense a right to recover satisfaction for the loss by fire.*" Where the policy in express terms provides for an assignment of the mortgage debt, the courts will enforce its performance, but the better doctrine seems to be, *that in the absence of such a provision the right dose not exist.* The doctrine seems to be that the mortgagee is entitled to have both the amount of the loss under the policy, and the amount of the mortgage debt, and that the payment of a loss under the policy does not apply *pro tanto* upon the mortgage debt,[1] *nor does a payment of the mortgage after a loss* destroy the mortgagee's right to recover the amount of the loss under the policy.[2] But otherwise if the mortgage debt is paid *before* loss, as in such case the insurable interest of the mortgagee, in the property covered by the policy, is destroyed, and the validity of the policy is destroyed thereby.[3]

Right of insurer when loss is less than the mortgage debt.

SEC. 470. But, while it is true that the insurer is not entitled to be subrogated to the rights of the mortgagee under the mortgage to the extent of the amount of the loss paid under a policy, yet it is held in New York, as well as many other States, that *the insurer may, by paying to the mortgagee the loss under the policy, and the balance due upon the mortgage above the loss, be subrogated to the rights of the mortgagee, and is entitled to, and may enforce, an assignment of the mortgage debt to it,* and this, *whether the policy provides for such assignment or not,*[4] and the amount due under such mortgage, or under a lien upon the property, may be recovered in the name of the insured for the benefit of the insurer,[5] and this is applicable to a lien which the mortgagee may have upon any property of the mortgager, for the payment of the debt secured by the mortgage,[6] and if

---

[1] In *King* v. *The Sun Mut. F. Ins. Co.*, 7 Cush. (Mass.) 1. In *Honore* v. *Lamar F. Ins. Co.*, 51 Ill. 409, the defendant executed two notes to a firm for a certain sum, and deposited with them 74 barrels of whiskey as security. The firm insured it without the knowledge of the defendant on their own account. It being destroyed by fire, the plaintiff (insurer) paid the loss, first requiring an assignment of the note. In an action thereon by the insurers, the court held that the receipt of the amount of the insurance, under the circumstances, did not extinguish the debt, and that the plaintiffs were entitled to recover.

[2] *Robert* v. *Traders' Ins. Co.*, 17 Wend. (N. Y.) 631.

[3] *King* v. *Sun Mut. F. Ins. Co.*, *ante.*

[4] *Kernochan* v. *N. Y. Bowery, etc., Ins. Co.*, 17 N. Y. 428; *Springfield F. & Mut. Ins. Co.* v. *Allen*, 43 N. Y. 389.

[5] *The Ætna Ins. Co.* v. *Tyler*, 16 Wend. (N. Y.) 385; *Hall* v. *R. R. Companies* 13 Wall (U. S.) 367; *Harp* v. *Western R. R. Co.*, 13 Met. 99.

[6] *Sussex Co. Mut. Ins. Co.* v. *Woodruff*, 26 N. J. 541.

such lien is discharged by the insured, he will be liable to the insurers for the value of the property covered by the lien. Or if any of the mortgaged property is saved, the insurer will be entitled to have its value deducted from the policy, particularly if it has been sold, will the insurer be entitled to have the amount received therefor deducted.[1]

Right does not exist when policy inures to benefit of mortgagor.

SEC. 471. Where, however, the mortgagor is entitled to have the money received from the insurance go in liquidation of the mortgage debt, the right of subrogation does not exist. This right, however, on the part of the mortgagor, never exists, *where the insurance is effected by the mortgagee himself, in his own name, and paid for by himself with his own funds. But if the policy is in the name of the mortgagor, and assigned by to him the mortgagee ; or if it is in the name of the mortgagee, and paid for by the mortgagor, or if, by virtue of an arrangement between the mortgagor and mortgagee, the mortgagor is liable for the premium paid by the mortgagee,* the insurance, while primarily for the benefit of the mortgagee, is for the ultimate benefit of the mortgagor, and goes in liquidation of the mortgage debt, *pro rata,* and a right of subrogation does not exist on the part of the insurer.[2] This was well illustrated in the New York case last cited. The mortgage contained a condition that the mortgagor should keep the premises insured, and that in case of failure on her part to do so, the mortgagee might procure them to be insured, *and the premium should be a lien upon the mortgaged premises.* The mortgagor failed to comply with the condition, and the mortgagee procured a policy in his own name, and paid the premium therefor. The policy contained a stipulation that, in case of loss, the assured should assign to the company an interest in the mortgage equal to the amount of loss paid. The policy was for $4,000. The amount of the mortgage debt was $7,044. A total loss having occurred, the insurers paid the mortgagee the amount of his claim, and took an assignment of the mortgage. The court correctly held that the mortgagor was entitled to the benefit of the insurance, *being liable for the premium paid therefor by the mortgagor,* and that the assignment was inoperative,

---

[1] *Harris* v. *Gaspee, etc., Ins. Co.,* 9 R. I. 207.

[2] *Springfield F. & M. Ins. Co.* v. *Allen,* 43 N. Y. 389.

[3] *Foster* v. *Van Reed,* 5 Hun (N. Y.) 321. In *Holland* v. *Smith,* 6 Esp. 11, a policy was taken out upon the life of the debtor. By an arrangement between them, the creditor always paid the premiums, and charged them to the debtor in account, and he had paid all of them except the last. The court held that the representatives of the deceased were entitled to the amount of the insurance, less the last premium. In *In re Kerr's Policy,* L. R. 8 Eq. Cas. 331, under similar circumstances a similar rule was adopted. See also, *Simpson* v. *Walker,* 2 L. J. (U. S.) Ch. 55 ; *Coon* v. *Swan,* 30 Vt. 6 ; *Stokes* v. *Coffey,* 8 Bush. (N. Y.) 533.

except as to the balance remaining unpaid above the loss.' The fact that there is no stipulation in the mortgage itself, that the mortgagor shall pay the mortgagee any sum that he may pay for premiums, does not defeat the right of the mortgagor, *if there is any arrangement between them, whether verbal or written, by which the mortgagor becomes liable to pay for the insurance he is entitled to the benefit thereof*, by having it applied in liquidation of the mortgage debt, *pro rata, and the simple test of his right in this respect, is, not whether he has paid for the insurance, nor whether the mortgagee procured the insurance, intending to look to him for a re-imbursement of the premium, but whether he is liable to the mortgagee therefor, under any agreement, express or implied.*²

The fact that the policy stipulates for an assignment of the mortgage upon payment of a loss under it, to the mortgagee, does not affect the rights of the mortgagor in this respect, as the insurers can impose no stipulations in their policy that defeat the legal or equitable rights of the mortgagor in this respect;³ but, when the mortgagor has done that which releases the insurer from liability to him, it may, when the policy so provides, elect to pay the mortgagee the amount of the mortgage debt, and take an assignment thereof, and in such case the mortgage will remain a valid security in its hands.⁴

---

¹ It is proper to say that the court of appeals has recently reversed the judgment in this case (*Foster* v. *Van Reed*), but upon what ground I have not been able to ascertain, as the case has not yet been reported. Probably the general doctrine, as announced in the text, has not been disturbed, but the reversal placed upon technical grounds, *or* placed upon the ground that the insurer was an assignee of the mortgage for value, and stood as a *purchaser* thereof—as the loss was not paid, but the mortgage purchased—or, possibly, that the insurer was entitled to recover the *balance* of the mortgage over the amount of the loss, but that the general doctrine has not been disturbed I feel quite confident.

² In *Kernochan* v. *N. Y. Bowery Ins. Co.*, 17 N. Y. 428, the court held that evidence of an agreement, by the mortgagor, to pay the premiums, was admissible for the purpose of showing who was entitled to the benefit of the policy, and that such an agreement is not obnoxious to the objection that it varies the written contract of the parties. The court also held that if any such agreement existed, the insurers had no right of subrogation.

³ *Foster* v. *Van Reed, ante.*

⁴ In *The Springfield F. & M. Ins. Co.* v. *Allen*, 43 N. Y. 389, the plaintiff company insured the buildings upon mortgaged premises by a policy issued to the mortgagor, containing a clause, "the loss, if any, is payable to the mortgagee," and also a condition that in case of any change of title in the property insured, the policy should be void, the interest of the mortgagee however being excepted from the provisions of the condition, and also a condition that in case of a payment to the mortgagee for a loss for which the insurer would not have been liable to the mortgagor, the insurer should be subrogated to the rights of the mortgagee and to an assignment of the mortgage, and the mortgaged premises having been sold prior to the loss, it was held that the amount of the loss paid to the mortgagee did inure to the benefit of the mortgagor, or go in liquidation of the mortgaged debt, and that the mortgage having been assigned to the insurer upon payment of the entire amount thereof, was a valid security in its hands. The opinion of ALLEN, J., covers the rights of the parties under such circumstances so

Right does not exist when only part of the mortgage debt is met by the insurance.

SEC. 472. A very important question is, whether, when an insurer has paid a loss to the mortgagee that covers only a part of the mortgage

---

completely, and is such an able review of the principles involved, that I give it entire. He said: "The parties to the policies of insurance have, by the terms of their contract, avoided some of the questions which have embarrassed the courts, and led, in some instances, to an apparent conflict of opinion if not of decision. The rights of the mortgagees are protected against the effect of certain acts of the mortgagor in derogation of the policies, by an agreement that the policies, as to the interest of the mortgagee, with the qualification, however, that if the mortgagee fail to notify the insurers of any change of ownership after the same shall have come to his knowledge, the policies shall be void. They have definitely determined the question, perhaps not definitely settled by adjudication as to the right of subrogation, by an agreement making part of the contract of insurance that, whenever the insurer shall pay to the mortgagee any sum for loss, for which loss the company would not have been liable to the mortgagor or owner, the insurers shall be subrogated to the rights of the mortgagee and entitled to an assignment of the mortgage. This provision is probably in accordance with the legal and equitable rights of the parties, regarding the policy from the time it might become void as to the mortgagor as an insurance, existing only in favor and for the benefit of the mortgagee, and as an insurance upon his interest as mortgagee, and not as an insurance upon the property generally, although the doctrine has been question in *King* v. *State Mut. Ins. Co.*, 7 Cush. 1 ; *Kernochan* v. *N. Y. Bowery F. Ins. Co.*, 17 N. Y. 428 ; *Roberts* v. *Traders' Ins. Co.*, 17 W. R. 631 ; *Carpenter* v. *Washington Ins. Co.*, 16 Pet. 495 ; *Tyler* v. *Ætna Ins. Co.*, 12 W. R. 507 ; and S. C. 16 W. R. 385, per CHANCELLOR. If then, the mortgagor, who was the party primarily insured, could not for any reason have enforced the policies, and recovered thereon for his own benefit, either as owner or as having an insurable interest as the mortgagor, personally liable for the payment of the mortgage debt, he is precluded by the terms of the policies, from claiming the benefit of the insurance in satisfaction of the mortgage debt, and the insurers are entitled to be subrogated to the rights of the mortgagee. The mortgagee was equitable assignee of the policies, containing a provision, which upon the happening of certain events, should absolutely vacate and avoid the insurance, as of the property generally, and as a contract of indemnity to the mortgagor, and resolve it into an insurance of the interest of the mortgagee as such, and make it a personal contract with her, in which the mortgagor would have an interest. Per SHAW, C.J., *King* v. *State Mut. F. Hand vol. 4, Ins. Co.*, 7 Met. 1 ; per STORY, J., *Columbia Ins. Co.* v. *Lawrence*, 10 Pet. 507. Ferris, the grantee of the premises and owner of the equity of redemption, can, as the representative and equitable assignee of Allen, claim no greater rights under the policies than his grantor and assignor Allen could have claimed. *Grosvenor* v. *Atlantic F. Ins. Co.*, 17 N. Y. R. 391. The policies were made and accepted by Allen, the insured, with full knowledge of and subject to all the terms and condition expressed therein, and he had personal knowledge of every fact and circumstance effecting their validity existing at the time they were made, and was a party and assenting to every act which has been alleged as breaches of the conditions of the policies, and avoiding them as to him, and all (except mortgagees) claiming under him. One of the conditions of each of the policies was, that in case of any change or transfer of title of the property insured, the policy should be void and cease.

A contract of insurance, like every other contract, must be so construed as to give effect to the intent and understanding of the parties; and the language employed must be taken in its popular sense, unless it appears to have been used in a technical sense, or custom or usage has impressed a different meaning upon it. *Whiton* v. *Old Colony Ins. Co.*, 2 Met. 1 ; *Mutual Safety Ins. Co.* v. *Hone*, 2 Comst. 235. Every part of a policy should be read and construed in obedience to this rule. There was a change and transfer of the title of the property, which was the subject of the insurance, after the insurance was effected and before the loss. If the words employed were used in their popular sense, this condition of the policy was violated, and the policy, as an insurance of the property generally

debt he acquires, *as against the mortgagee*, a right to reimbursement of
the amount so paid, *when the mortgage debt is paid to him, or when it is*

---

and for the benefit of the mortgagor and owner, ceased. Had the parties
intended only to provide for a change in, or transfer of the interest of the assured,
which, in one sense, is. 'the property assured,' it may be assumed that language
more appropriate to express the idea would have been chosen. An insurable
interest may exist without any estate or interest in the corpus of the thing
insured. As guarantor of the mortgage debt, personally liable for its payment,
Allen probably had an insurable interest in the buildings upon the mortgaged
premises. *Gordon* v. *Massachusetts F. & M. Ins. Co.*, 2 Pick. 249. But it was
an interest that would not ordinarily and popularly be classified as 'property,'
and any change in such insurable interest would not be spoken of as a change in,
or transfer of title. The insurable interest would cease by a discharge of liability for the mortgage debt. 'Title' has respect to that which is the subject of
ownership, and with a change of title, the right of property, the ownership
passes. 'Property' is a thing owned; that to which a person has, or may have
a legal title. Both words are inappropriate to describe the insurable interest,
which exists solely by reason of the personal liability of the insured for the payment of a sum of money charged upon the building of goods insured. The word
'property' may have different meanings, depending upon the connection in
which, and the purposes for which, it is used, as indicating the intention of the
parties. In *Whiton* v. *Old Colony Ins. Co.*, 2 Met. 1, it was used as a part of
the description of the subject-matter of the insurance, and was held to include
current bank bills as within the intention of the parties, as manifested by the
contract and the circumstances under which it was made. Acting upon the same
principle of interpretation, it was held that an insurance of property did not
cover freight, except it was to be paid by a specific portion of lumber which was
on board the vessel, and which the assured, as carrier, was to receive for freight.
It was held that the contract gave the insured an interest in that part of the cargo
coming within the term property, but that the freight upon the other parts of the
cargo was not within the term as used. *Wiggin* v. *Mercantile Ins. Co.*, 7 Pick.
271. To the same effect, in *Holbrook* v. *Brown*, 2 Mass. 280. In the clause
prohibiting double insurance, the prohibition is generally in terms so restricted
in it application that 'property' can mean nothing else but the interest of the
assured, whatever that may be. As in the Massasoit policy before us, the condition is, 'if the *insured* or his assigns shall hereafter make any other insurance
on the *same property*,' etc., thus preventing a double and possibly fraudulently
excessive insurance of the same interest. Neither the policy of the law or the
contracts of insurance forbidding, but permitting as many several insurances
upon the same property as there are separate insurable interests. As mortgagor
and mortgagee have several interests in the same property, and each may insure
to the extent of his interest, the insurance will not be double, and neither will be
in violation of the clause forbidding other insurance. Both will be valid. The
policy of the law is to prevent insurances in excess of the value of the thing
insured in favor of the same party and against the same risks; and hence the
restrictive clause, whatever its form, unless its language clearly demands a different interpretation, should be held as operative to this extent only, and the
term *property* in such clause means the interest of the assured. *The Traders'
Ins. Co.* v. *Robert*, 17 W. R. 631; *Godin* v. *London Assurance Co.*, 1 Burr, 489;
Mutual Safety Ins. Co. v. *Hone*, 2 Comst. 233. The interest of Allen, by reason
of his personal liability for the mortgage debt. was properly insured by an insurance of the property, and it was not necessary that the particular interest should
be specified. It was enough that he had a pecuniary interest in the preservation
and protection of the property, and might sustain a loss by its destruction.
Neither was it necessary that the nature of the interest should be disclosed to the
insurers. *Tyler* v. *Ætna Ins. Co.*, 12 Wend. (N. Y.) 507. When the word 'property'
is used in the clause forbidding alienation, it is used to designate the thing insured,
and not the interest of the insured. Where a special interest, rather than the
general property, is the subject of insurance, no such condition is necessary to the
protection of the insurer, for the reason that with a loss of interest the insurance
ceases, *Carpenter* v. *Washington Ins. Co.*, *supra*, and an interest in the policy

sold or transferred by him. Of course no equities could be created that would be operative against a *bona fide* assignee of the mortgage debt, but, the question whether as against the mortgagee himself *to whom the loss has been paid,* such equities exist, is one of somewhat difficult to answer consistently with the principles upon which the doctrine of subrogation has been applied in insurance cases. But the question has been settled by the courts, so far as it has been raised *against* the right of the insurer in such cases, although the *reason* therefore is not quite convincing,[1] and it would seem that the only really tenable ground is, that where the insurer has at his election the right to be subrogated to the rights of the mortgagee by paying the *entire* amount of his mortgage, by neglecting or refusing to do so, he is treated in law as waiving the right, and cannot afterwards enforce it.[2]

As to wrong-doers.

SEC. 473. Where the property insured is dertroyed by the negligence of a third person, so that the assured has a remedy against him there-

does not pass by a transfer of the interest insured. *Columbia Ins. Co.* v. *Lawrence,* 10 Pet. 507. But, if the owner is insured generally, and transfers the property, retaining a lien for the purchase-money or other special interest, the insurance will continue to the extent of the interest remaining in the insured, if it does not contravene some condition of the policy. As some evidence of the sense in which the term 'property' is used in the clause under consideration, it is worthy of remark that, when the policy is upon a special interest, as in favor of a mortgagee, and it is designed to save the policy from the effect of a breach of the condition forbidding a change of title, it is done by a special clause of exception, as in this case, and in *Graves* v. *Hampden F. Ins. Co.,* 10 Allen, 281. The policies before us are, in form, upon the property generally, and in favor of Allen as owner. In one of the policies, the insurance is in his favor 'as owner,' and in both it is 'upon *his* two four-story brick stores,' etc., and the insurers had, as found by the judge on the trial, no notice or knowledge of any conveyance of the property by Allen. The insurers only knew Allen as owner, and the policies must be interpreted as if they were upon the interest of Allen as owner, and upon the property generally in fact as they were in form. They were then insurers of Allen as owner and Miss Williams, a mortgagee, to the extent of her mortgage debt, and both interests are represented and cared for in the policies. The change or transfer of title in the property insured, intended in the clause under consideration, was the title, the ownership of the thing insured, and upon such transfer or change the policy ceased and became void as to the principal party insured, and, but for the saving clause in favor of the mortgagee, would have been void as to her. *Grosvenor* v. *Atlantic F. Ins. Co.,* 67 N. Y. 391; and see *Jackson* v. *Mass. Mut. F. Ins. Co.,* 23 Pick. 418; *Tillou* v. *The Kingston Mut. Ins. Co.,* 1 Seld. 405. The case last cited may he regarded as greatly shaken, if not overruled, by *Grosvenor* v. *Atlantic F. Ins. Co., supra,* so far as it sustained a policy in favor of the mortgagee and equitable assignee, which could not have been enforced by the mortgagor or assignor, but, upon the other points decided, it has not been questioned. In the elementary treatises, this clause is treated as relating to a transfer or alienation of the insured subject, the thing insured, and the question has been as to what has constituted an alienation. The change of title to the property by the conveyance to Ferris was a breach of the condition which avoided the policies as to Allen, the mortgagor. It is first provided that, upon an assign-

[1] *Norwich F. Ins. Co.* v. *Boomer,* 52 Ill. 442; 4 Am. Rep. 618.
[2] *Newcomb* v. *Cincinnati Ins. Co.,* 20 Ohio St. 382.

for, the insurer, by payment of the loss, becomes subrogated to the rights of the assured *to the extent of the sum paid under the policy.*[1] An assignment of the claim cannot be enforced, but *the assured becomes trustee for the insurer* and by necessary implication the payment of the loss operates as an equitable assignment to the insurer to the extent of the sum paid under the policy.[2]

Insurer may sue in name of assured.

SEC. 474. If the assured receives full indemnity from the insurer, and does not choose to bring an action against the third person, *the insurer may bring the action in the name of the assured,*[3] but if a recovery is had for

ment, without consent, of the whole policies, or of any interest in them, the liability of the insurer shall cease, and then follows the very general clause prohibiting 'any sale, transfer or change of title in the property;' and, by another clause in the policies, it is provided that, if the mortgagee should neglect to notify the insurers of any *change of ownership of the property insured* after the same should come to their knowledge, the policy should be void; all indicating clearly that the parties used the term ' property' in its popular sense, and that the change of title referred to was of the thing insured, of which the mortgagee might have no knowledge, and not of the mortgage interest, of which she would necessarily have knowledge. The mortgagor could not have recovered upon the policies, and it follows that he is not entitled to have the moneys paid under the policies to the mortgagee applied to the satisfaction of the mortgage."

[1] *Hart* v. *Western R. R. Co., ante.* But this doctrine is denied in Maine in *Rockingham, etc., Ins. Co.* v. *Bosher,* 39 Me. 253, and in Connecticut in *Conn. Mut. Life Ins Co.* v. *N. Y. & N. H. R. R. Co.,* 25 Conn. 265. In *Carroll* v. *New Orleans, etc., R. R. Co.,* 26 La. An. 447, where goods were insured and destroyed by fire while in the hands of the carrier and in transit, and the insurer paid the loss and brought suit in the name of the insured; it was held by a divided court (three for and two against) that no right of subrogation existed in the absence of a conventional subrogation from the insured to the insurer.

[2] KENT, C., in *Gracie* v. *N. Y. Ins. Co.,* 8 John. (N. Y.) 245. This principle has long been recognized and is predicated upon the equitable rights of the parties. Thus, in *Mason* v. *Sainsbury,* 3 Doug. 61, the defendants paid a loss occasioned by rioters, and it was held that they thereby became subrogated to the rights of the assured against the hundred. In *Clark* v. *The Hundred of Blything,* 2 B. & C. 254, the same principle was applied. See also, *Yates* v. *Whyte,* 4 Bing. (N. C.) 272; *Randall* v. *Cockran,* 1 Vis. Sr. 98; *Gracie* v. *N. Y. Ins. Co.,* 8 John. (N. Y.) 245; *Cullen* v. *Butler,* 5 M. & I. 466; *Monticello* v. *Mollison,* 17 How. (U. S.) 152; *Monmouth Co. Ins. Co.* v. *Hutchinson et al.,* 21 N. J. Eq. 107. In *Atlantic Ins. Co.* v. *Storran,* 5 Paige Ch. (N. Y.) 285, the defendant, a common carrier, became liable to the person insured under a policy issued by the plaintiffs for a total loss of the goods by theft. The insured procured judgment against the plaintiff upon the policy therefor. The assured assigned the policy and all claims thereunder to the defendant, and delivered the bill of lading to him. It was held that the insurers were entitled to have the amount paid by the carriers to the assured, deducted from the amount of the judgment against them on the policy,

[3] *Hart* v. *Western Ins. Co., ante; Simon* v. *Leland,* 6 Hill (N. Y.) 237; *Whitehead* v. *Hughes,* 2 Cr. & M. 318; *Phillips* v. *Claggett,* 11 M. & W. 84. This principle has been recognized in numerous cases, and perhaps is no where better illustrated than in *Payne* v. *Rogers,* 1 Doug. 407. In that case, the plaintiff was tenant of a commonable tenement, and his landlord brought an action on the case, in the name of the tenant, for an encroachment on the common, by inclosure, and offered to indemnify him against all costs, charges and expenses in the action. While the action was pending, the defendant procured a release from the tenant (the nominal plaintiff), whereupon the landlord procured an order upon the defendant to show cause why the release should not be given up and cancelled.

an amount in excess of the policy, the balance must be paid to the
assured.[1]

---

and he be permitted to proceed in the cause in the name of the tenant. The rule
was opposed on the ground that the court could not interfere, as the landlord was
not a party on the record; that he had not been under any necessity of using the
tenant's name, but might have sued in his own, and that the defendant could not,
with safety, go on in this action, because the tenant was not able to pay the costs,
if there should be a verdict against him. The report of the case says that the
court expressed great indignation at this attempt of the defendant to prevent a
landlord from trying a right in the name of his tenant, and ordered the release to
be delivered up and cancelled. In this country, the right of an insurance company to maintain an action, *in spite* of the assured, against a third person, for
negligence in causing the loss, was first raised and decided in *Hart v. The Western
R. R. Co.*, 13 Met. (Mass.) 99. In that case, it appeared that on the 9th of July,
1845, a carpenter's shop, owned by William W. Boyington, adjoining the railroad
track of the defendants, near their passenger depot, in Springfield, was destroyed
by fire, communicated by the locomotive engine of the defendants. There was a
high wind, which wafted sparks from this shop while it was burning, over Lyn-
nan street, sixty feet, upon the dwelling-house of the plaintiffs, and set it on fire,
whereby it was partly consumed. The plaintiffs were insured by the Springfield
Mutual Fire Insurance Company, who requested the plaintiffs to commence a suit
against the defendants, to compel payment by them of the plaintiff's loss, and
offered to indemnify the plaintiffs from costs, and to save them harmless, in reference to said suit. The plaintiffs refused to commence a suit as requested, but
demanded the amount of their loss of the said insurance company, who paid the
same, first notifying to the defendants that they did not intend thereby to relinquish any claim which they might have against the defendants for the amount in
their own or in the plaintiffs' names. The insurance company, in the name of the
plaintiffs, then brought this action to recover the amount paid by said company
to the plaintiffs. After the action was commenced, and before the entry of the
writ, the plaintiffs executed an instrument, declaring they had received payment
of their loss of the insurance company; that they had no claim against the
defendants; that they (the plaintiffs) had not authorized the commencement of
this action against the defendants, and did not wish to have it prosecuted; and
fully releasing any claim which they might have against the defendants on account
of said loss. At the May term of this court, in 1847, the case was opened to the
jury, and the defendants presented the aforesaid release from the plaintiffs, and
contended that the insurance company, in consequence of this release, could not
maintain this action.

The court ruled, that receiving payment of the loss by the plaintffs of the insurance company, constituted an equitable assignment by the plaintiffs to the company of any claim they might have had. When the owner, who, *prima facie*,
stands to the whole risk and suffers the whole loss, has engaged another person
to be at that particular risk for him, in whole or in part, the owner and insurer
are, in respect to that ownership and the risk incident to it, in effect, one person,
having together the beneficial right to an indemnity, provided by law for those
who sustain a loss by that particular cause. If, therefore, the owner demands
and receives payment of that very loss from the insurer, as he may by virtue of
his contract, there is a manifest equity in transferring the right to indemnity,
which he holds for the common benefit, to the assurer. It is one and the same
loss, for which he has a claim of indemnity, and he can equitably receive but one
satisfaction. So that if the assured first applies to the railroad company and
receives the damages provided, it diminishes his loss *protanto* by a reduction
from, and growing out of, a legal provision attached to, and intrinsic in, the subject insured. The liability of the railroad is, in legal effect, first and principal,
and that of the insurer secondary; not in order of time, but in order of ultimate
liability. The assured may first apply to which ever of these parties he pleases;

---

[1] This principle is illustrated in *Coon v. Swan*, 30 Vt. 6; also in *Stokes v. Coffey*,
8 Bush. (Ky.) 533; *Morland v. Isaac*, 20 Beav. 389; *Holland v. Smith*, 6 Esp.
11; *Simpson v. Walker*, 2 L. J. (N. S.) Ch. 55; *In re* Kerr's Policy, L. R., 8 Eq.
Cas. 331.

In cases where the amount paid under the policy is only a partial amount of the actual loss, *the assured stands in the relation of a trustee to the assurer, to the extent of the amount paid under the policy*, and an action will lie against him therefor in the name of the insurer, or a court of equity will, in certain cases, direct payment to be made to the insurer direct.[1] Or an action at law will lie against the wrong-doer in the name of the assured, even after the damages have been paid to him.

Settlement with assured after payment of loss by insurer.

SEC. 475. When such wrong-doer, *knowing* that the insurer has paid the whole or a part of the loss under a policy of insurance upon the property, settles with the insured and takes a release from him, such settlement and payment is treated as a fraud in law, and he will still remain liable to the insured in an action, in the name of the insured, for the amount paid by him under its policy.[2]

Assured can have but one satisfaction.

SEC. 476. Therefore, it follows that, in cases where the insured has also a remedy for his loss against a third person, he may pursue either the insurer or the wrong-doer, or both at the same time, but he can have but one satisfaction for the loss. If he pursues the wrong-doer, and collects the amount of his loss against him, *he cannot also pursue the insurer. Thereby the insurer is discharged.* If he pursues the insurer, and secures satisfaction for his loss, *in whole or in part*, from him, while his remedy against the wrong-doer is not thereby defeated,[3] yet

---

to the railroad company, by his right at law, or to the insurance company, in virtue of his contract. But if he first applies to the railroad company, who pay him, he thereby diminishes his loss by the application of a sum arising out of the subject of the insurance, to wit, the building insured, and his claim is for the balance. And it follows, as a necessary consequence, that if he first applies to the insurer and receives his whole loss, he holds the claim against the railroad company in trust for the insurers. Where such an equity exists, the party holding the legal right is legally bound to make an assignment, in equity, to the person entitled to the benefit; and if he fails to do so, the *cestui que trust* may sue in the name of the trustee, and in *Allison* v. *Ins. Co.* 3 Dill. (U. S. C. C.) 478, his equitable interest will be protected."

[1]*Robert* v. *Traders' Ins. Co.*, *ante*.

[2] In *Monmouth Co. F. Ins. Co.* v. *Hutchinson et al.*, 21 N. J. Eq. 107, the plaintiff issued to one Hutchinson a policy upon his dwelling-house, which was worth much more than the amount of the insurance. The house was destroyed by the negligence of the Camden and Amboy R. R. Co., and the insurer paid the loss. The railroad company paid Hutchinson $2,000, in full satisfaction of the damages, and took a release from him therefor. This action was brought jointly against Hutchinson and the railroad company by the insurer. The court held that the plaintiff was entitled to recover against the railroad company, and that the release was no bar thereto; that the settlement made with the assured by the railroad company, *knowing* that he had been paid the amount insured by the plaintiff, was fraudulent and void.

[3]*Collins* v. *N. Y. C. R. R. Co.*, 5 Hun (N. Y.) 503; *Merrick* v. *Brainard*, 34 N. Y. 208; *Weber* v. *Morris & Essex R. R. Co.*, 35 N. J. 409; *Hayward* v. *Cain*, 105 Mass. 213; *Perrat* v. *Sheaver*, 17 Mich. 48. Insurance is personal, and does not

he stands to the insurer in the relation of a trustee to the extent of the
amount paid under the policy, and cannot release the right of action,
nor the action itself, if one has been commenced, so as to defeat the
rights of the insurer to reimbursement from any recovery from such
wrong-doer for the injury producing the loss.[1]

When insurer is estopped from recovering against the wrong-doer.

SEC. 477. But if the insurer pays the loss *knowing* that the insured
has released the wrong-doer, and takes an assignment of the insurer's
claim against the wrong-doer "remaining to him after such settlement," it is a recognition of the settlement and release, and the
insurer takes no rights under it against the wrong-doer. Thus, in a
New York case,[2] one John Martin was the owner of certain buildings
and premises in Orange county in the year 1872, and on the 20th day
of December in that year he procured them to be insured against fire,
by the plaintiff, for the sum of $1,500. The property adjoined the
railroad of the defendant, and on the 13th day of May, 1873, the
buildings were destroyed by a fire, which had its origin in sparks
which were emitted from one of the locomotive engines running on
the defendant's road. On the 10th day of September, 1873, Martin
effected a settlement with the defendant for the damages he claimed
to have sustained by reason of negligence in setting fire to, and
destroying his buildings, and received from the defendant the sum of
$2,100 in money, and gave a full receipt and discharge to the company
for all his loss and damage by the fire which destroyed his buildings.
In August, 1873, an action was commenced by Martin against the
plaintiff to recover the amount of his insurance, which resulted in a
judgment in favor of the plaintiff for the full amount of the claim.
This judgment was paid by the plaintiff on the 11th day of February, 1874, and on that day Martin executed and delivered to the
Plaintiff an assignment which contained this clause: "The said John
Martin hereby sells, assigns, transfers and sets over to the said insurance company all claim, demand and right of action against the said

---

inure to the benefit of one not a party thereto. *Disbrow* v. *Jones,* Harring (Mich.)
Ch. 48; *Merrick* v. *Brainard,* 38 Barb. (N. Y.) 574; *Hart* v. *Western R. R. Co.,*
ante; Mason v. *Sainsburry, ante; Morrison* v. *Bartholomeo,* 5 C. C. S. (Sc.) 3d
Series, 848.

[1] *Yates* v. *Whyte,* 4 Bing. (N. C.) 272; *Honore* v. *Lamar F. Ins. Co.,* 51 Ill. 409;
Mason v. *Sainsbury,* 3 Doug. 61; *Randall* v. *Cockran,* 1 Ves. Sr. 98; *Hart* v. *West-*
ern R. R. Co., ante; Payne v. *Rogers, ante; Quebec F. Ass. Co.* v. *St. Louis,* 7
Moore P. C. C. 286. But it is held in Ohio, that, where the insurer refuses to
prosecute the action, it can claim no part of, nor benefit from, the recovery. *New-*
comb v. *Cincinnati Ins. Co.,* 22 Ohio St. 382.

[2] *Connecticut Ins. Co.* v. *Erie R. R. Co.,* 10 Hun. (N. Y.) 59.

Erie Railway Company arising out of the fire aforesaid, which he now has, or which may have remained to him after the settlement of the claim made by him against said Erie Railway Company as aforesaid." The plaintiff brought an action to recover the sum of $1,500, the amount of the insurance paid by the plaintiff. The case was tried at the circuit, where a verdict was rendered for the plaintiff, which was set aside by the court, and the action of the court in setting aside the verdict was sustained by the general term.[1]

[1] DYKMAN, J., in rendering the judgment of the court, said: "The right of the plaintiff to recover in this action is vested on the principle of equitable subrogation, a doctrine which had its origin and much of its growth in the Roman civil law, under the name of substitution; and it is one of the many illustrations of the enlightened policy of that people, that a doctrine so much in accordance with the principle of natural justice should have early found a place in that splendid system of Roman law. It has been transplanted from the civil law into our system of equity jurisprudence, and is very useful in bringing about just results in a great variety of cases. Concisely stated, it means that where one person discharges an obligation which primarily rests upon another, he shall be substituted to the place of a creditor in respect to the party who is primarily liable. and shall have the benefit of all securities or claims which are held by the creditor. The doctrine may be applied to cases of insurance as well as any others, as the chancellor said in the case of *The Etna F. Ins. Co.* v. *Tyler*, 16 Wend. 397. This principle of equitable subrogation, or substitution of the underwriters in the place of the assured, is recognized by every writer on the subject of insurance, and is constantly acted upon in courts of law as well as in equity ; so that where the assured has any claim to indemnity for his loss against a third person who is primarily liable for the same, if the assured discharges such third person from his liability before the payment of the loss by the underwriters, he discharges his claim against them for such loss *pro tanto ;* or, if he obtain payment from such third person afterwards, it is in the nature of salvage, which he holds as trustee for the underwriters who had paid the loss. So in the case of *Gracie* v. *The New York Ins. Co.*, 8 Johns. R. 246, where there was a recovery by the assured for the full amount of the policy, upon the condemnation of a vessel and cargo under ther the Berlin and Milan decrees, Chief Justice KENT said that if the French government should at any time make compensation for the capture and condemnation, the United States would receive and hold the money as the trustee of the underwriters, who would clearly be entitled to be paid the same. If this case is to be determined in accordance with the principles enunciated in the foregoing extracts, then there is very little trouble in reaching a satisfactory conclusion. At the time Martin made his assignment to the plaintiff he had settled with the defendant; had been paid the full amount of his damages, and had given a full discharge of all claim against the company; he therefore had no claim against the defendant at that time, in relation to which the plaintiff could be substituted and put in his place. The doctrine of subrogation can have no application where there is no person who is primarily liable to discharge the claim which is paid and discharged by the party seeking to be subrogated. Here the defendant, the party primarily liable to pay for the loss, had done so—had discharged the obligation. Certainly there was no further claim of Martin against it, and there was therefore, no claim of his to which the plaintiff could be substituted. The plaintiff cannot get, through him, what he cannot get himself. This seems to go to the very foundation of the plaintiff's claim, and must defeat a recovery. After the destruction of the buildings, Martin had two remedies for the recovery of his loss : one against the defendant. given to him by law, and one against the plaintiff, by virtue of his contract of insurance. He had the right to pursue whichever of these remedies he chose in the first instance. If he had applied to plaintiff and been paid the amount of his policy, he might still have brought an action against the defendant for the recovery of his damages resulting from the negligence which caused the fire, and in such an action his recovery would not

SEC. 478. When the mortgagor procures the mortgaged premises to be insured, and assigns the policy to the mortgagee, the mortgagee takes the policy subject to all the defenses thereto that can be made against the mortgagor, and if he violates any condition of the poilcy, it is fatal to the right of recovery of the mortgagee thereon.[1] But if the mortgagee procures the property to be insured in his own name, and on his own account, the rule is otherwise, and the mortgagee will not be responsible for the acts of the mortgagor in the use of the premises,[2] and it seems that such is the case when the policy is *assigned* to the mortgagee, with the consent of the insurer, under such circumstances that the transfer can be said to create a new contract between the mortgagee and the insurer, as when, in the case of insurance in a mutual company, he is required to, and does, execute a new premium note.[3]

As the mortgagor has no interest in an insurance effected upon the mortgaged premises exclusively by the mortgagee, neither has the mortgagee any interest in an insurance effected by the mortgagor, *and cannot, under any circumstances,* compel payment thereof to himself in discharge of the mortgage. If he would be protected in that respect, he must provide therefor by taking an assignment of a policy from the mortgagor, or take a policy in his own name.[4]

---

have been diminished by any amount received from the insurance company. *Merrick* v. *Brainard,* 38 Barb. 589; 34 N. Y. 208. We are not now called upon to determine what rights the plaintiff would have acquired by such payment to Martin. As the liability of the defendant to Martin was primary, it may be that the plaintiff, in that event, might have had a right of substitution; or, in an action against the plaintiff by Martin to recover this insurance, after having been paid by the defendant, he might have been limited in his recovery to an amount that would make good his loss. But we have no such case. Instead of applying to the plaintiff, he applied the defendant, and was paid a sum of money in full discharge of its liability. No fraud or collusion is alleged, and he had no further claim against the defendant, and it follows that the plaintiff had none."

[1] *Franklin Savings Institution* v. *Central, etc., Ins. Co.,* 119 Mass. 240; *Fogg* v. *Middlesex, etc., Ins. Co.,* 10 Cush. (Mass.) 337; *Loring* v. *Manufacturers', etc., Ins. Co.,* 8 Gray (Mass.) 28; *Hale* v. *Mechanics', etc., Ins. Co.,* 6 Gray (Mass.) 169. But *contra,* see *Charleston Ins. Co.* v. *Neve,* 2 M'Mullan (S. C.) 237, where a party took a policy of insurance upon liquors, groceries, etc., and the same day on which the policy was executed, permission was given to assign the policy to a third person, it was held, that the party to whom the assignment was made was entitled to recover, to the amount of the interest he had in the policy, notwithstanding the party to whom the policy was granted had deprived himself of his right to recover by acts of fraud.

[2] *Foster* v. *Equitable Ins. Co.,* 2 Gray (Mass.) 241.

[3] *Foster* v. *Equitable Ins. Co., ante; Tillou* v. *Kingston, etc., Ins. Co.,* 5 N. Y. 405.

[4] *McDonald* v. *Black,* 20 Ohio, 185; *Wilson* v. *Hill,* 3 Met. (Mass.) 66; *Hancox* v. *Fishing Ins. Co.,* 3 Sum. (U. S.) 132; *Columbia Ins. Co.* v. *Carpenter,* 10 Pet. (U. S.) 507; *Powell* v. *Innes,* 11 M. & W. 10; *Carpenter* v. *Providence, etc., Ins. Co.,* 16 Pet. (U. S.) 495; *Concord, etc., Ins. Co.,* v. *Woodbury,* 45 Me. 447; *White* v. *Brown,* 2 Cush. (Mass.) 413; *Cushing* v. *Thompson,* 34 Me. 496.

It is a conceded principle of law that the underwriter, in a policy of marine insurance, who has paid a loss, is entitled to recover what he has paid of the carrier who caused the loss, and in a case involving this question decided in. the Supreme Court of the United States, it was held that this doctrine is applicable to a case of fire insurance on land; or, that where goods are lost in the hands of a carrier, the insurer of them who pays to the assured the amount of the policy, may recover in the name of the assured the amount of the carrier; and this, even though the carrier was guilty of no actual fault or negligence. This right does not depend at all upon the privity of contract, but is in accordance with the principles of equity.[1] As between the insurer and carrier, in such case, the liability to the owner is primarily upon the carrier, while the liability of the insurer is only secondary. The insurer stands to the owner practically in the position of a surety, and, when he has indemnified the owner for loss, he is entitled to be subrogated to all the means of indemnity which the owner had against the party primarily liable.[2] The underwriter cannot maintain the action in his own name. Being dependant upon the the doctrine of subrogation, the action must be in the name of the assured. In a Vermont case,[3] an attempt was made to establish a converse of the rule before stated, by deducting from the amount of a recovery against a town for injuries received on one of its highways, the proceeds of an accident insurance policy held by the injured party. But the court held, that the liability of the town was primary, and that it was therefore not entitled to the reduction.[4]

---

[1] *Hall* v. *Nashville, etc., R. R. Co.*, 13 Wall (U. S.) 367.
[2] *Randall* v. *Cochran*, 1 Ves. Sr. 98; *Clark* v. *Blything*, 2 B. & C. 254; *Yates* v. *Whyte*, 4 Bing. (N. C.) 272; *Mason* v. *Sainsbury*, 3 Doug. 60; *Rockingham Mut. F. Ins. Co.* v. *Bosher*, 39 Me. 253; *Peoria Ins. Co.* v. *Frost*, 37 Ill. 333; *Conn. Mut. Life Ins. Co.* v. *N. Y. & N. H. R. R. Co.*, 25 Conn. 265.
[3] *Harding* v. *Townsend*, 43 Vt. 435.
[4] *Plympton* v. *Ins. Co.*, 43 Vt. 497; *Mason* v. *Sainsbury*, 3 Doug. 61; *Clark* v. *The Inhabitants of the Hundred of Blything*, Q. B. & C. 254, 9 Eng. Com. L. 77; *Yates* v. *Whyte et. al.*, 4 Bing. (N. C.) 272; *The Propeller Monticello* v. *Mollison*, 17 How. (U. S.) 152; but see *Pym Admr* v. *The Great Northern Railway Co.*, 4 B. & S. 396, where one of the counsel referred to *Hicks* v. *The Newport, etc., R. R. Co.*, a *nisi prius case* where a contrary rule was adopted by Lord CAMPBELL.

CHAPTER XVII.

REFORMATION OF POLICIES.

Sec. 479. When policy will be reformed.
Sec. 480. Must be shown not to embody the contract made.
Sec. 481. Acceptance does not of itself estop assured.
Sec. 482. Must be mutual mistake.
Sec. 483. Remedy must be sought before final judgment.
Sec. 484. Application may be made after loss.

When policy will be reformed.

Sec. 479. Where the terms of the contract are plain and distinct, and the actual intention of the insurer and insured is not doubtful, a policy issued, either by fraud or mistake, that does not comply with the terms of the order therefor, or embody the real intention of the parties thereto, may be reformed in equity, or in those States where the court is permitted to exercise the functions of a court of law and equity, *instanter*, upon trial.[1] But, in order to entitle the party to this relief, the policy must materially vary from the real contract of the parties,[2] and the variance must be fully made out by the clearest evi-

---

[1] *Delaware Ins. Co.* v. *Hogan*, 2 Wash. C. C. (U. S.) 4; *Motteaux* v. *The London Assurance Co.*, 1 Atk. 545; *Collett* v. *Morrison*, 9 Hare, 162; *Henkle* v. *Royal L. Ins. Co.*, 1 Ves. Sr. 317; *Cone* v. *Niagara F. Ins. Co.*, 62 N. Y. 619; *Equitable Ins. Co.* v. *Hearne*, 20 Wall (U. S.) 494; *Phœnix Ins. Co.* v. *Gurnee*, 1 Paige (N. Y.) Ch. 278. In *Equitable Ins. Co.* v. *Hearne*, 20 Wall (U. S.) 494, the plaintiff applied for insurance upon his vessel for a voyage from Liverpool to Cuba and to Europe *via* Falmouth, at a rate named, and the company offered to insure at a somewhat higher rate, saying: "It is worth something, you know, to cover the risk at the port of loading in Cuba." It was held that, under an insurance issued at such higher rates, it must be implied that the port of loading might be different from the port of discharge, and where the assured accepted this offer, and told the insurer to insure at and from Liverpool to Cuba and to Europe *via* a market port, etc., a policy which insured to port of discharge in Cuba and Europe *via* market port, etc., did not conform to the contract, and was reformed accordingly.

[2] *Delaware Ins. Co.* v. *Hogan, ante; Ionides* v. *Pacific F. & M. Ins. Co.*, L. R. 6 Q. B. 674. The rule applicable to this class of cases is well illustrated in the following case. Thus, in *Hearne* v. *New England Mut. Ins. Co.*, 10 Albany Law Jour. 348, the United States Supreme Court considered the questions involved in reference to the powers and duties of courts in reformation of a contract of marine insurance, which was entered into under the following circumstances: On the 7th of May, 1866, Hearne made his application by letter to the company for insurance. He said: "The bark Maria Henry is chartered to go from Liverpool to Cuba and load for Europe, *via* Falmouth for orders where to discharge. Please insure $5,000 on this charter, valued at $16,000, provided you will not charge over four per cent. premium." On the 9th of that month, the company, through its president, replied: "Your favor of the 7th is at hand. As requested, we have

dence.[1]   The real intention of the parties, at the time when the policy was made, will control, and, as it *prima facie* is presumed to

---

entered $5,000 on charter of bark Maria Henry, Liverpool to port in Cuba, and thence to port of advice and discharge in Europe, at four per cent." The policy was made out on the same day, and described the voyage as follows: "At and from Liverpool to port in Cuba, and at and thence to port of advice and discharge in Europe." Thereafter the policy was delivered to the assured and received without objection. The vessel was loaded with coal at Liverpool, and proceeded thence to St. Iago de Cuba. There she discharged her outward cargo. She went thence to Manzanillo, another port in Cuba, where she took on board a cargo of native woods. On the 17th of September, 1866, she sailed thence for Europe, intending to go by Falmouth for orders Upon the 10th of that month, on her homeward voyage, she was lost by perils of the sea. Due notice was given of the loss, and it is admitted to have occurred as alleged in the bill. The company refused to pay, upon the ground that the voyage from St. Iago de Cuba to Manzanillo was a deviation from the voyage described in the policy, and therefore put an end to the liability of the assured. On the 7th of December, 1868, two years after the loss occurred, Hearne brought an action at law against the company. The court held that he was not entitled to recover by reason of the deviation before stated. He failed in the suit. On the 16th of January, 1871, he filed his bill, and prayed therein to have the contract reformed so as to cover the elongated voyage from St. Iago to Manzanillo. The court held that the contract was not entitled to be reformed to meet the complainant's demand. SWAYNE, J., who delivered the opinion, said: "The correspondence between the parties constituted a preliminary agreement. The answer to Hearne's proposal was plain and explicit. It admitted but of one construction. He was bound carefully to read it, and it is presumed he did so. In that event there was as little room for misapprehension on his part as on the part of the company. Such a result was hardly possible. There is nothing in the evidence which tends to show that any occurred. The inferrence of full and correct knowledge is inevitable. It is as satisfactory to the judicial mind as direct evidence to the same effect would be."   *   *   * "The party alleging the mistake must show exactly in what it consists, and the correction that should be made. The evidence must be such as to leave no reasonable doubt upon the mind of the court as to either of these points. *Beaumont* v. *Bramley*, 1 F. & R. 41–50; *Marquis of Broadalbane* v. *Marquis of Chandos*, 2 M. & C. 711; *Fowler* v. *Fowler*, 4 D. G. & Jones, 255; *Sells* v. *Sells*, 1 Dr. & S. 42; *Loyd* v. *Crocker*, 19 Beav. 144. The mistake must be mutual and common to both parties to the instrument. It must appear that both have done what neither intended. *Rook* v. *Lord Kensington*, 2 K. & I. 753; *Eaton* v. *Bennet*, 34 Beav. 196. A mistake on one side may be a ground for rescinding, but not for reforming, a contract. *Mortimer* v. *Shortal*, 2 Dr. & War. 572; *Sells* v. *Sells, supra*." The complainant claimed that there was a usage that vessels going to Cuba might visit at least two ports, one for discharge and the other for reloading. But it appeared that, in such cases, the contract of insurance was expressed so as to allow such a course. A reformation on this ground was, therefore, denied. The court also refused to decree a return of the premium. In *Equitable Safety Ins. Co.* v. *Hearne*, 20 Wall (U. S.) 474, a reformation of the contract of insurance was allowed on the following state of facts: "Hearne's proposition to the company was by the letter, to insure the bark Maria Henry, "voyage from Liverpool to Cuba, and to Europe *via* Falmouth." The company's response was in effect: ' We will insure as proposed by you—Europe to Cuba—at three and one-half per cent. It is worth something, you know, to cover the risk at port of loading in Cuba.' But the contract, as expressed in the policy, was "four thousand dollars on charter of bark Maria Henry, at and from Liverpool to port of discharge in Cuba, and at and hence to port of advice and discharge in Europe." The court was of opinion that the true contract was: "This company hereby insures $4,000 upon the charter of the bark Maria Henry, as proposed by the assured, from Europe to Cuba and back to Europe, at three and one-half per cent. net, the pre-

---

[1] *Head* v. *Providence Ins. Co.*, 2 Cranch (U. S.) 127; 2 John. Ch. (N. Y.) 630; 2 Cranch (U. S.) 419; *Andrews* v. *Essex F. & M. Ins. Co.*, 3 Mas. (U. S.) 6.

embody the real understanding of the parties, the evidence to overcome it must be clear, direct and conclusive.[1] In all cases where the
variance is material, and seriously affects either the party's remedy,
or measure of recovery, application to reform the policy should be
made, as, except it be reformed, except in exceptional cases hereafter
enumerated, the contract as expressed therein, will control. The real
intention of the parties may be arrived at, as well by showing that
the agent or company issuing the policy *knew* that the plaintiff did
not intend to have certain provisions in the policy apply in a given
case, as by a contract actually expressed. Thus, where a policy was
issued upon a building, with a provision that "if the premises are at

---

mium enhanced to cover the risk at port of loading in Cuba." SWAYNE, J., who
delivered the opinion, said: "The intent of the parties, as manifested, is the contract. Upon any other construction, the important language as to 'the port of
loading' would be insensible and without effect. No other interpretation, we
think, can reasonably be given to it. In *Dickey* v. *The Balt. Ins. Co.*, 7 Cr. 327,
the policy insured the vessel upon a voyage 'from New York to Barbadoes, and
at and from thence to the Island of Trinadad, *and at and from Trinidad* back to
New York.' This court held that the words, 'at and from' protected the vessel
in sailing from one port to another in Trinidad to take in a part of her cargo.
MARSHALL, C.J., said: 'It is the settled doctrine of the courts of England that
insurance *at and from an island*, such as those in the West Indies, generally
insures the vessel while coasting from port to port for the purpose of the voyage
insured.' He refers to *Bond* v. *Nutt*, 2 Cow. 601, and to *Thelluson* v. *Ferguson*,
1 Doug. 360. The case of *Cruikshank* v. *Jansen*, 2 Taunt. 310, is to the same
effect. These authorities fully sustain the proposition laid down. We are not
aware that their authority has been questioned. They show the just liberality of
construction which obtains where contracts of insurance are involved. In this
controversy, the clear terms of the preliminary agreement warranted the court
below in overruling the departure from it found in the policy."
[1]*Head* v. *Prov. Ins. Co., ante.* In *Mead* v. *The Westchester F. Ins. Co.*, 64 N. Y.
454, it was held that to justify a court of equity in changing the language of a
written instrument sought to be reformed, in the absence of fraud, it must be
established that both parties agreed to something different from what is expressed
in the writing, and the proof should be so clear and convincing as to leave no
room for doubt. In an action to reform a policy of fire insurance upon a dwelling-
house, the alleged mistake was that an adjoining building was intended to be
insured instead of the dwelling described. It appeared that the applicant had
owned both buildings and had lived in the one described; that defendant's agent
had insured the furniture therein; that he had insured the building claimed to
have been intended and the policy was then outstanding. He had the description of both buildings upon his books. The applicant had removed from the
dwelling to the adjoining building, which was occupied as a dwelling and paint
shop, and did not, in fact, own the former. The agent, however, testified that he
supposed that he did. The premium upon the dwelling was one and one-half per
cent. upon the building it was two and one-half. The application was by letter
for a policy on "my house." The agent, thereupon, made out the policy in question upon the dwelling, charging one and one-half per cent. The building was
burned. The only direct evidence to establish that defendant intended to insure
the building was that of the agent who, in answer to the question, "To what property *do* you understand this letter * * referred?" answered, to the property
burned. Upon his cross-examination he testified, in substance, that at the time
and before the policy was issued he was in doubt, but his idea was it was on the
dwelling and he so made out the policy. It was held that the facts did not show
an intent, on the part of defendant, to insure the building burned, and did not
justify a reformation of the policy.

the time of insuring, or during the life of this policy, vacant, unoccupied, or not in use, and remain thus for over ten days, without the company's consent is indorsed hereon, this insurance shall be void and of no effect." In an action to reform the policy, it was shown that the agent, *at the time of issuing the policy, knew that the building was vacant and would probably remain so*, and that it was expressly understood that it would remain vacant until September, to which the agent consented, it was held that this amounted to a waiver of the provision, and that the plaintiff was entitled to have his policy reformed, by having the company's consent indorsed thereon, according to the real understanding and intention of the parties.[1] Without a reformation of the policy, however, the provision under the decisions of the New York courts would have applied and been a bar to a recovery. Thus, where commission merchants applied for insurance upon property in their warehouse, and the company issuing the policy *knew* that they were engaged in commission business, and the policy issued contained a provision that "goods held in trust or on commission are to be declared as such, otherwise the policy will not extend to cover such property," and the policy was not reformed, or any application for that purpose made, it was held that the policy must be construed according to its terms, and that, being plain and unambiguous, parol evidence was not admissible to vary its import or meaning. COCHRAN, J., in passing upon this point, said: "The appellees contended, on the hypothesis that the appellant *knew* that their application was to be for insurance on all the goods destroyed, both their own and those held on commission, that the policy should be so construed as to give effect to that intention, or in other words, that the extent of the risk underwritten should be ascertained from the fact stated, and not from the terms of the policy. The rule presented in this proposition we think cannot be applied here. The authorites referred to sustain the construction sought, present facts so far different from those in this case, as to involve other principles. In all of them the construction turned, either upon the meaning of terms, which by usage or custom had acquired a particular sense, or on evidence that the insurer, after a full disclosure of facts material to the risk *and in violation of an obligation implied therefrom*, neglected to insert in the policy such a reference to those facts as was essential to its validity as a contract of insurance. Parol evidence was admitted in

---

[1] *Cone* v. *Niagara Ins. Co.*, 62 N. Y. 619.

one class not to change or vary the contract, but to explain the meaning of the terms used, and in the other to prevent the insurer from obtaining the 'advantage of a contract which, through his fault, would otherwise have been without obligation, and void. The policy in this case is entirely consistent with the terms of the application, free from ambiguity and susceptible of a consistent construction in all its parts, and if there was mistake or error in the insurance effected, it does not appear to be one attributable to the appellant, nor such as to authorize us to look beyond the terms of the policy in ascertaining its meaning and legal effect. We think it cannot be excepted from the operation of the general rule requiring written contracts to be interpreted by their own terms, without regard to extrinsic facts.[1]

The appellees appear to have obtained this insurance without making any specific statement of the nature of their interest in the goods destroyed, and had there been no express condition to the contrary, their interest in the goods held on commission might have been covered by the policy, for upon that state of fact, the material question would have been, whether the failure to inform the insured that the goods were held on commission would have affected the risk, and the admission that the communication of that fact would not have changed the rate of premium, might have been relied on as concluding it. But that is not the question here. This policy expressly provides that it was not to cover goods held on commission unless they were so declared, or as we understand it, so expressed as to appear, in some form, in the description of the goods intended to be covered by it. The right of the insurer to limit the extent of the risk by that condition cannot be doubted.[2] And as we must presume, from the acceptance of the policy by the appellees, that they had knowledge of that condition, we think it should have the contemplated effect of limiting the risk to the goods which belonged to them."[3]

Must be shown not to express the contract made.

Sec. 480. The same rules prevail in reference to the reformation of a policy of insurance as to any other contract. *The court cannot make a new contract for the parties, but only compel such a change therein as makes the*

---

[1] *Mumford* v. *Hallet,* 1 Johns. 439 ; *Mellen & Nesmith,* v. *National Ins. Co.,* 1 Hall, 452 ; Phil. Ins. 47, 319.

[2] *Phillips* v. *Knox Co. Ins. Co.,* 20 Ohio, 174; *Briehta* v. *Lafayette Ins. Co.,* 2 Hall, 372 ; 2 Am. Lead. Cas. 642.

[3] *Baltimore Fire Ins. Co.* v. *Loney et al.* 20 (Md.), 3 Am. Law Reg. (U. S.) 651 ; see also, *Peoria M. & F. Ins. Co.* v. *Hall,* Mich. 3 id. 417.

instrument express the contract actually made by the parties,[1] and conform to their actual intention [2]—in a word, to make it speak and set forth the real agreement and contract of the parties.[3] The jurisdiction will not be exercised, except when, through, accident, fraud or mistake, the contract has been erroneously set forth. If it embodies the contract actually made, the fact that the parties acted under a mistaken idea of law or equity, or even of facts, will not entitle a party to this relief. It can never be exercised *to change the contract actually made.* Therefore, in all cases, the question is, does the instrument embody the actual agreement and intention of the parties?[4] and in all cases, the mistake or error must be evidenced by undoubted proof. It must be clearly and unmistakably established, and not be left doubtful or uncertain.[5] It will not relieve against mere carelessness on the part of

[1]*Dinman* v. *Providence, etc., R. R. Co.,* 5 R. I. 130; *Cassady* v. *Woodbury,* 13 Iowa, 113; *Vallette* v. *White Water Valley Canal Co.,* 5 McLean (U. S.) 192.

[2]*Wyche* v. *Greene,* 11 Ga. 159; *Clapton* v. *Martin,* 11 Ala. 187; *Fowler* v. *Adams,* 13 Wis. 355; *Lockport* v. *Cameron,* 29 Ala. 355; *N. Y. Ice Co.* v. *N. Western, etc., Ins. Co.,* 31 Barb. (N. Y.) 72; *Clearey* v. *Babcock,* 41 Ill. 271; *Shirley* v. *Witch,* 2 Oregon, 288; *Hall* v. *Claggett,* 2 Md. Ch. 151; *City R. R. Co.* v. *Veeder,* 17 Ohio, 385; *Longhurst* v. *Star Ins. Co.,* 19 Iowa, 364.

[3]*Ward* v. *Camp,* 28 Ga. 74; *Nixon* v. *Careo,* 28 Miss. 414; *Lesson* v. *Atlantic Mut. Ins. Co.,* 40 Mo. 33; *Oliver* v. *Commercial, etc., Ins. Co.,* 2 Curtis C. C. (U. S.) 277.

[4]*Kent* v. *Mahchester,* 29 Barb. (N. Y.) 595; *Leavitt* v. *Palmer,* 3 N. Y. 19; *Dinman* v. *R. R. Co.,* ante.

[5] In *Mackenzie* v. *Coulson,* L. R., 8 Eq. Cas. 368, the defendants, who were iron merchants, had to provide for the carriage of some iron which they wanted to transport by water, and desired to have it insured as well from rust as from perils of the sea, etc. They communicated to their carriers their desire to have such a policy effected, and the carriers communicated with an insurance broker, who again communicated with some other persons, who were intermediate agents between the insurance broker and the plaintiffs, who were underwriters. They (the underwriters) had several clerks in their employ, one of whom entered upon a slip of paper the details of the kind of insurance wanted, as follows:

"Fleming, Seymour & Co. 28 Oct., 1867.
Cash.
Thomas and John, Gloucester.
£890 on 501 bundles hoops—Plymouth.
£40 r. freight—H. M. Dockyard.
So valued;"

and took the slip to an underwriting agent, who asked what kind of hoops they were, and declined to underwrite the same unless the insurance was made free from particular average. The clerk then wrote upon the slip "f. p. a." and took it away, and the underwriters put their names upon the slip, each for a certain amount. The slip was taken back to the office of his employers, by the clerk, and another clerk filled out a policy in the common form, which was presented to the underwriters, who signed it, without noticing that it did not conform to the provisions of the slip. The policy was sent to the defendants, who paid the premium thereon. There was a loss under the policy, and an action having been brought upon the policy, they filed a bill to restrain the action, setting forth that it was not the contract they entered into, and asking to have the policy corrected so as to set forth the provision "free from particular average." The relief was refused by the court, upon the ground that the policy alone, and not the slip, embraced the contract of the parties. Sir W. M. JAMES, V.C., said: "If this

51

either party, or set aside or change a policy which has been accepted in good faith *after a loss* has been sustained upon it,[1] but, while the parties remain *in statu quo*, it will, upon a proper case, where it appears that no contract *has in fact been made*—that is, that the minds of the parties have never met upon the terms of the policy, direct its surrender upon repayment of the premium.[2]

Acceptance of policy does not of itself estop the assured.

SEC. 401. When it appears that the policy does not embody or express the contract of the parties, and the party seeking the relief has not understandingly accepted it as written, it may be reformed;[3] and in order

---

contract be a good contract in law, what is there to vary it in equity? If all that the plaintiff can say is, ' we have been careless, *whereas the defendants have not been careless,*" it is useless for them to apply to this course for relief. The defendants positively say they would not have accepted the policy on any other terms. It is too late, now that the loss has been incurred, for the plaintiffs to set aside the policy on the terms of paying back the premium. *Courts of equity do not rectify contracts;* they may and do *rectify instruments purporting to have been made in pursuance of the terms of contracts, but it is always necessary for a plaintiff to show that there was an actual, concluded contract, antecedent to the instrument which is sought to be rectified, and that such contract is inaccurately expressed in the instrument.* In this instance, there never was any contract other than this policy which the plaintiffs have signed. I certainly will not be the first judge to extend the jurisdiction of this court in the way which is sought by the prayer of this bill. There is no class of documents as to which the strictest good faith is more rigidly required in courts of law than policies of insurance, and a court of law may safely be left to deal with the circumstances of this particular policy. *It is impossible for the court to rescind or alter a contract with reference to the terms of negotiation which preceded it.* The plaintiff cannot escape from the obligation of the contract on the ground that they verbally informed the clerk of the defendant's agent something different from what they afterwards, in writing, acceded to. *Men must be careful if they wish to protect themselves; and it is not for this court to relieve them from the consequences of their own carelessness.*" See also, *Ionides Pacific F. & M. Ins. Co.,* L. R., 6 Q. B. 674; *Parsons* v. *Bignold,* 15 L. J. Ch. 379. Where an agent, without any fraudulent design, declares the interest on whose account it is obtained in the wrong person, equity will correct the mistake; but, if made with a fraudulent purpose, no relief can be had in equity by the principal. *Oliver* v. *Mut. Com. Ins. Co.,* 2 Curtis C.C. (U. S.) 277.

[1] *Mackenzie* v. *Coulson, ante.*

[2] *Fowler* v. *The Scottish Equitable Ins. Co.,* 4 Jur. N. S. 1169.

[3] In *Bennett* v. *City Ins. Co.,* 115 Mass. 241. In *Phœnix Ins. Co.* v, *Hoffeheimer,* 46 Miss. 645, a bill was brought to reform a policy of insurance under the following circumstances: Sartorius, the agent of the plaintiffs, doing business both by publication and sign, stated to the agent of the company, at the time of taking out a former policy in another company, of which he was also agent, that he was doing business as agent of the appellees, and the policy was issued to him as such agent. Afterward, he requested the same agent to make out another policy in this company, as the first was made out, and took it for granted the agent had done so. By accident or mistake, the agent omitted or neglected to insert in said policy that said Sartorius was insured as agent. The court held that "a court of equity has authority to reform a contract, where there has been an omission of a material word or stipulation by mistake, and a policy of insurance is within the principle. But a court ought to be extremely cautious in the exercise of such an authority. It ought to withhold its aid where the mistake is not made out by the clearest evidence." And that a court of equity will grant relief in cases of mistake in written agreements, not only when the fact of the mistake is

to arrive at the real intention and contract of the parties, parol evidence is admissible of all that was said and done by the parties during the progress of the negotiations.[1]

If a person accepts a policy of insurance without dissent, the law presumes that he knows its contents,[2] but this is a mere presumption that may be overcome by proof that he did not in fact know the contents of the instrument.[3], but the evidence must be such as shows that he did not understandingly accept the policy, as that he did not compare it with the application or other papers from which it was drawn,[4] or that it was received by a third person,[5] or by himself and put away without examination,[6] or that he relied upon the knowledge of the insurer and supposed he had correctly drawn it.[7] Thus it has been held that a policy should be reformed when there was a mistake in the duration of the risk,[8] or in reference to the risk itself, as, when it does not cover the risk contracted for,[9] or as to the person or persons to whom the policy should be issued, or misdescribes the interest of the assured,[10] or when the premises or property is wrongly described as where application was made for insurance " on a two story and a half

---

expressly established but is fairly implied from the nature of the transaction." Also, that " parol evidence is admissible to prove the mistake, though it is denied in the answer, and this, either when the plaintiff seeks relief affirmatively, on the ground of mistake, or when the defendants sets it up as a defense, or to rebut an equity." So in *Keith et al.* v. *Globe Ins. Co.*, 52 Ill. 518, a bill was brought to reform a policy that had by mistake been issued to *one* partner when it should have been made to all. The bill was not brought until after a loss under the policy. The court decreed its reformation upon the ground that the defendants intended to insure and the partner intended to have insurance upon the entire interest of the property.

[1] *Moliere* v. *Pennsylvania F. Ins. Co.*, 5 Rawle (Penn.) 342 ; *National Traders' Bank* v. *Ocean Ins. Co.*, 62 Me. 519 ; *Motteaux* v. *London Assurance Co.*, 1 Atk. 545 ; *Woodbury Savings Bank* v. *Charter Oak Ins. Co.* 31 Conn. 517; *North America Ins. Co.* v. *Whipple*, 2 Biss. (U. S.) 418; *Malleable Iron Works* v. *Phœnix Ins. Co.*, 25 Conn. 465 ; *Bennett* v. *City Ins. Co.*, 115 Mass. 241.

[2] *Monitor Mut. F. Ins. Co.* v. *Buffum*, 115 Mass. 343.

[3] *Motteaux* v. *London Assurance Co.*, 1 Atk. 545.

[4] *Motteaux* v. *London Ass. Co.*, *ante*.

[5] *Bennett* v. *City Ins. Co.*, 115 Mass. 241.

[6] *Motteaux* v. *London Ass. Co.*, *ante*.

[7] *Brioso* v. *Pacific Mut. Ins. Co.*, 4 Daly (N. Y.) 246 ; *Van Tuyl* v. *Westchester Ins. Co.*, 55 N. Y. 657 ; *Weed* v. *Schenectady Ins. Co.*, 7 Lans. (N. Y.) 452.

[8] *North American Ins. Co.* v. *Whipple*, 2 Biss. (U. S.) 418.

[9] *Bates* v. *Grabham*, 2 Salk. 441 ; *Equitable Ins. Co.* v. *Hearne*, 20 Wall. (U. S.) 494 ; *Lippincott* v. *Ins. Co.*, 3 La. 546 ; *Delaware Ins. Co.* v. *Hogan*, 2 Wash. C. C. (U. S.) 4 ; *Motteaux* v. *London Ass. Co.*, *ante*; *National Traders' Bank* v. *Ocean Ins. Co.*, 62 Me. 519.

[10] *Oliver* v. *Mut. Com. Ins. Co.*, 2 Curtis (U. S.) 277 ; *Keith* v. *Globe Ins. Co.*, 52 Ill. 518 ; 4 Am. Rep. 624 ; *Woodbury Savings Bank* v. *Charter Oak Ins. Co.*, 31 Conn. 517; *Phœnix Ins. Co.* v. *Hoffeheimer*, 46 Miss. 645 ; *Franklin Ins. Co.* v. *Hewitt*, 3 B. Mon. (Ky.) 231.

grist mill," and the policy described it as " a frame mill house two and
a half stories high, privileged as a grist mill only,"[1] or where the
amount of the insurance is not as agreed,[2] or where conditions not
agreed upon, and inconsistent with the business are imposed,[3] or any
error, mistake or condition exists in the policy that does not express the
real contract made by the parties. The fact that the policy has been
for a long time in the plaintiff's possession, and that a loss has occurred
before any move for a change therein was made, is a strong circumstance to establish the assent of the insured to the policy as received,[4]
and sometimes will estop him from the benefits of this remedy, yet if
the laches are satisfactorily explained, the policy will be reformed and
made to accord with the real contract and intent of the parties,[5] and the
remedy is open to either party.[6] The party seeking relief takes the

---

[1] *Phœnix Fire Ins. Co.* v. *Gurnee,* 1 Paige Ch. (N. Y.) 278; *S. P. Moliere* v.
Penn. F. Ins. Co., 5 Rawle (Penn.) 342.

[2] *Bidwell* v. *Astor Mut. Ins. Co.*, 16 N. Y. 263.

[3] *Van Tuyl* v. *Westchester F. Ins. Co.*, 55 N. Y. 657; *Malleable Iron Works* v.
Phœnix Ins. Co.. 25 Conn. 465.

[4] *Bidwell* v. *Astor Mut. Ins. Co.*, 16 N. Y. 263.

[5] *Woodbury Savings Bank* v. *Charter Oak Ins. Co.*, 31 Conn. 517; *Malleable Iron
Works* v. *Phœnix Ins. Co.*, 25 Conn. 465; *Law* v. *Warren,* 6 Ir. Eq. 299; *Bates* v.
Grabham, 2 Salk. 444.

[6] *Woodruff* v. *Columbus Ins. Co.*, 5 La. An. 697; *No. American Ins. Co.* v. *Whipple, ante.* In *Woobury Savings Bank* v. *Charter Oak Ins. Co.*, 31 Conn. 517, P.
was the agent of the defendant at New Haven, and B. was agent there for several
other insurance companies. The practice between P. and B. was, if B. met with
property which would not be insured by any of the companies he represented, to
make application through P. to some company for which P. was agent, and when
the policy was issued P. and B. divided the commissions. This was a general
custom among insurance agents well known to the officers of insurance companies
generally, and to this company in particular. P.'s companies furnished him with
applications, renewals, and policies signed in blank, some of which he delivered
to B., who represented that he was the agent of P., and as proof thereof exhibited the blank renewals, policies, and applications. W. was mortgagee of certain
property, and the mortgagors had become insolvent. S. was directed by W. to
procure insurance to protect the mortgagee's interest. He stated his object to B. ;
said that he did not know the situation of the property; that he understood the
title of it was in dispute; requested him to examine it and to procure for the
mortgagee a policy in proper form to insure and protect the mortgage, of which
he (S.) was no judge himself. B. undertook to do so, and stated to P. the substance of what S. had communicated to him. P. and B. examined the property,
took measurements of it, and made inquiries of persons whom they found on the
premises. B. delivered to S. a blank application for him to sign. the heading was
filled in with the names of S. B. and B. (the mortgagors), the amount to be
insured, premium, and the amount of the mortgage ; after the name S. B. and B.,
the words " or assigns " were added by S., who signed it and delivered it to B.,
who carried it to P., and together they completed the application. P. made a
policy insuring S. B. and B., loss, if any, payable to W., and delivered it to S.,
who took it, supposing that it would insure the mortgagee's interest. Before the
policy was made, S. B. and B. made another mortgage to another person. which
was foreclosed, and S. B. and B. conveyed all their equity of redemption to a
third person. Held, public policy and the protection of the community require
that local agents of insurance companies, in giving aid to applicants for insurance,

burden of establishing not only the error, but the real nature of the contract,[1] and he must show this by clear and conclusive evidence,[2] and it must also appear that the contract, as proved, was understood by both parties,[3] as if it is shown that both parties were laboring under a mistake as to the matter, there is no contract to reform, as the minds of the parties never met.[4] The fact that the assured made a mistake, that led to the issue of the policy in an erroneous form, will not warrant its reformation, because the policy is as the insurer supposed it was to be, and he has never contracted for anything different, and as the court has no power to compel a change in the *real* contract, but only to correct the written evidence of it so as to embody the real contract made, it has no power under such circumstances to compel a change.[5]

It must appear that the policy does not embody the contract as made, and if both parties were laboring under a mistake, there is, of course, no contract to reform. Thus, where a policy was made to cover goods in buildings Nos. 189 and 191 Water street, and the goods were destroyed in 187, same street, the court refused to reform the policy, because it did not appear that the insurer at any time knew or understood that the property was in 187.[6] So in a case where the application called for insur-

shall be deemed the agents of the insurance companies, and not agents of the applicants, and therefore the companies are bound by the acts of local agents whenever that can be done consistently with the evidence and the rules of law; that P. and B. were to be regarded as agents of the insurer in making the preliminary contract to insure; that B. was the agent of the company, for he was employed by P. in pursuance of a general custom which prevailed among local agents, which was known and approved by companies in general, and this one in particular; that the case was to be regarded as one where there was an agreement to insure the mortgagees on their interest as mortgagees in the property in question; that it was a case of mutual mistake as to the proper mode of filling out the papers, for the application was made in the wrong name and the policy issued to the wrong person; they would have been made out right if the agents had known how to make them, and it was immaterial whether the mistake was one of fact or of law; hence the complainants were entitled to a decree correcting the mistakes and prohibiting the insurer from producing evidence to show that the property described in the policy was not the property of the complainants.

[1] *Woodruff* v. *Columbus Ins. Co., ante.*
[2] *Carpenter* v. *Providence, etc., Ins. Co.,* 16 Pet. (U. S.) 495.
[3] *N. Y. Ice Co.* v. *N. West'n Ins. Co.,* 31 Barb. (N. Y.) 72.
[4] *N. Y. Ice Co.* v. *N. West'n Ins. Co., ante; Guernsey* v. *American Ins. Co.,* 17 Minn. 104.
[5] *N. Y. Ice Co.* v. *N. W. Ins. Co.,* 31 Barb. (N. Y.) 72; *Cooper* v. *Farmers' Ins Co.,* 50 Penn. St. 299.
[6] *Severance* v. *Continental Ins. Co.,* 5 Biss. (U. S.) 156. In *Cooper* v. *Farmers' Ins. Co.,* 50 Penn. St. 299, the assured incorrectly stated the incumbrances, and upon application to reform the contract upon the ground that the assured made a *mistake* in that respect, the court denied the relief, although the agent, *who only had authority to take applications,* filled out the application, and, knowing the facts, erroneously stated the incumbrances. In order to entitle a party to have a policy or any other contract reformed upon the ground of mistake, it must be mutual, *and violate the understanding of both parties;* and the evidence to establish it must be clear and unequivocal. *Daneger* v. *Crescent, etc., Ins. Co.,* 7 La. An. 228.

ance " on his dwelling house, household furniture therein, barn and shed adjoining, grain therein, on his hay and other fodder therein, live stock and farming utensils therein," and the policy followed the application, the court, upon proof that the application was made through an agent to agree with the terms of another policy, exhibited to the agent, which covered property anywhere on the farm, and that the application was made by the agent, and signed by the plaintiff without reading, and that the policy was received and not read until after the fire, the court refused to reform the policy, because it did not appear that the insurer understood the contract in the same way that the insured did.[1] So where a policy previously existing had permission endorsed thereon for other insurance, and before its expiration, application was made for its renewal, but instead of renewing it by renewal receipt, a new policy was issued, and the permission for other insurance omitted by the direction of the company, and the assured accepted the policy, and on two or three occasions had presented it to the company for changes in certain respects, but never had called attention to this omission, but, after a loss, applied for a reformation of the policy by the insertion of permission for other insurance, the court refused to reform it, as no contract for such permission appeared to have been made,[2] but if such omission is the mistake or fault of the insurer, and no laches are shown on the part of the assured, amounting to an acceptance, the court will reform the policy, and it would seem in the case last referred to, that the plaintiff had a right to expect that, as he applied for *a renewal* of a policy containing such permission, if a new policy was issued, it would contain the same matter that was contained in the other, and that if the assured neglected to notify the assured of such omission, and he innocently accepted the policy, relying upon the insurer's good faith that it would be made as applied for, he *was* entitled to a reformation of the contract, and a refusal to direct it was inequitable and unjust.[3]

Must be mutual mistake ;—mistake on one side not enough.—Illustrations.

SEC. 482. Thus it will be seen, that policies of insurance cannot be reformed except *to express the contract really made.* And if the parties mutually misunderstood each other, it cannot be reformed to accord with the understanding of either, because no contract was, in fact, made. The fact that the assured made a mistake does not entitle him

---

[1] *Guernsey* v. *American Ins. Co.*, 17 Minn. 104.

[2] *McHugh* v. *Imperial F. Ins. Co.*, 48 How. Pr. (N. Y.) 230.

[3] *Barrett* v. *Union Ins. Co.*, 7 Cush. (Mass.) 175.

to relief, because the insurer made the contract as the insurer represented matters to be, and there *is no mistake in the contract.* So relief
will be denied after the statute of limitations has run upon the policy,
or if the limitation fixed by the policy for the bringing of an action
thereon has expired, or when, by the exercise of due diligence, the
mistake ought to have been discovered.[1]

If a person accepts a policy, which was obtained upon an application made by a third person, without his knowledge, which misdescribes the use to which the property is devoted, although he is
ignorant of the misdescription so made by such person, and that the
insurers were misled thereby, yet the policy is inoperative and void,
although such misrepresentation was accidental, unintentional and
without fraudulent intent. The insurers, being misled thereby, are
not bound. In the language of AMES, J.,[2] "The misrepresentation
takes away the foundation of the policy, and, as it was an affirmation
of a fact as then existing, it is enough to prevent the policy from
taking effect as a contract. The minds of the parties have not met."
Thus, in the case referred to, an insurance broker solicited insurance
upon the plaintiff's organ factory. He was told that insurance was
desired, but that no more than a certain rate named would be paid
therfor. The broker afterwards partially filled up an application and
took it to one Mowry, an agent for the defendant, and, in answer to
the question, "what is manufactured, and of what material; are wood
shavings made on the premises?" he told Mowry that it was used as
an organ and melodeon factory, but he believed that a small part of it
was sometimes to be used as a machine-shop. Mowry answered the
question by writing "machinery," and the policy was issued as upon
"a machine-shop," and was accepted and paid by the plaintiff, without objection or notice to the defendants of the error. A loss happening under the policy, it was held that no recovery could be had, for
the reasons previously stated. But it should be stated that, in this
case, Mowry, who wrote the reply to the question relative to the purposes to which the building was devoted, had no authority to countersign or issue policies for the defendant, but referred all applications
directly *to* the company, who accepted or rejected the risk, and issued
its policies from the office direct. If Mowry had been authorized to
issue policies, and had stood in the place of the company in that

---

[1] *Dodge* v. *Essex Ins. Co.*, 12 Gray (Mass.) 65; *Hough* v. *Richardson*, 3 Story
(U. S.) 369; *Brooksbank* v. *Smith*, 2 Y. & Call. 58.

[2] *Goddard* v. *Monitor Ins. Co.*, 108 Mass. 57.

respect, a different rule would doubtless have been enforced, *unless the plaintiff had seen the error and failed to notify the company thereoj.* In such a case, the agent being notified that the building was used as an "organ and melodeon factory," would have been notice to the company, and the plaintiff could have secured redress by proceedings to reform the policy, so as to cover the risk as represented. But in order to secure that result, the plaintiff would have been required to show, not only that the company was fully acquainted with the character of the risk, but also that he himself had been guilty of no *laches* that estopped him from securing that species of relief. In a recent case in the court of appeals, in New York,[1] an action was brought to reform a policy, and to recover the loss thereunder when reformed, under the following circumstances: The policy was issued to one Palmer, loss, if any, payable to the plaintiff. The period of risk was for three years from June 1st, 1870. The policy contained this clause: "If the premises are, at the time of insuring or during the life of the policy, vacant, unoccupied or not in use, and remain thus for over ten days * * without the company's consent is indorsed hereon, this insurance shall be void and of no effect. The reformation sought was to have such consent indorsed upon the policy. The referee found, in substance, *that it was known to the defendant and its agent,* at the time of issuing the policy, that the building insured was vacant, and would probably remain so; that it was expressly understood that it would remain vacant until September, to which the agent consented; that the condition was in fine print, *and that Palmer and the plaintiff were ignorant that it was contained in the policy until after the loss.* As a conclusion of law, the referee found that the condition was waived, and that the defendants were estopped from setting up that the policy was void in consequence of the consent not having been indorsed thereon, and that the plaintiff was entitled to have the policy reformed. And the court held that this conclusion was not erroneous.

Proceedings must be commenced before final judgment in action on the policy.

SEC 483. When a party has brought an action at law and prosecuted it to judgment, and a judgment is rendered against him thereon, he cannot subsequently bring proceedings in equity to reform the contract. Having elected to pursue his remedy upon the policy at law, he thereby elects to treat it as embodying the contract, and cannot subsequently deny the fact.[2]

---

[1] *Cone* v. *Niagara F. Ins. Co.,* 60 N. Y. 619.
[2] *Washburn* v. *Gt. Western Ins. Co.,* 114 Mass. 175.

Where the assured brings an action to reform a policy, and subse-quently, but before the action for the reformation of the policy has been heard, brings an action at law upon the policy, and is defeated thereon, he cannot afterwards pursue his action for the reformation of the instrument.[1]

Where a party has his election of two remedies, when an election is made, he is bound thereby, *and any decisive act of the party with knowledge of his rights, and of the fact, determines his election in the case of conflicting and inconsistent remedies.*[2]

Application may be made after loss.

SEC. 484. When an application for insurance is made and accepted, and a policy is issued which, either by mistake or fraud on the part of the insurer, essentially varies from the contract made, *and the policy is not seen or examined by the assured until after a loss thereunder occurs*, he is not estopped from seeking a reformation of the contract, upon the ground that *he accepted the policy*. Thus, where the plaintiffs entered into a contract for insurance with the defendant's agent, and paid him the premium, and took from him a receipt, stating that the insurance was for $10,000, upon " merchandise, generally contained in their three-story brick building, metal roof, etc., *and occupied by them as a commission house*," and a policy was issued containing all the provisions of the contract, except the words " *as a commission house*," and the policy was received by a clerk of the plaintiffs, and its terms were not known to the assured until after the loss, it was held that, inasmuch as the insurers refused to pay the loss upon goods held by commission, the assured were entitled to have the policy made to conform to the agreement, and could not be said to have accepted the change in the contract, as indicated by the policy.[3] The fact that proceedings are not instituted for its reformation until after a loss, does not of itself bar the remedy. It is a circumstance to be taken into consideration in connection with other circumstances in determining whether the plaintiff waived the variance, but, if the delay is excused, the remedy remains.[4]

---

[1] *Washburn* v. *Great Western Ins. Co.*, 114 Mass. 175.

[2] *Sanger* v. *Wood*, 3 John. Ch. (N. Y.) 416; *Thwing* v. *Great Western Ins. Co.*, 111 Mass. 93. If the insured has been guilty of *laches* or delay in seeking a correction of the error—that is, if, after knowledge of the mistake, he takes no steps to secure its correction, he is treated as having waived the error, and cannot invoke the aid of a court of equity to reform it. *Paddock* v. *Com. Ins. Co.*, 104 Mass. 521; *Ryder* v. *Phœnix Ins. Co.*, 10 id. 548; *Thwing* v. *Great Western Ins. Co.*, 111 id. 110; *Conant* v. *Perkins*, 107 id. 79.

[3] *Franklin F. Ins. Co.* v. *Hewitt*, 3 B. Mon. (Ky.) 202; 2 Ben. F. I. C. 202.

[4] In *Van Tuyl* v. *The Westchester F. Ins. Co.*, 55 N. Y. 657, the plaintiff procured insurance upon his stock and materials in his manufactory. One of the

When the policy is inconsistent with the risk and the facts, which were *known* to the insurer or his agent when the policy issued, a reformation is not necessary, as the doctrine of waiver and estoppel comes in aid of the assured. For instances in which an action at law will lie when the risk is inconsistent with the policy, see chapter 20.

---

printed conditions declared it void in case of the establishment running, in whole or in part, over or extra time, or running at night, without special agreement. The plaintiffs gave evidence to show that they previously insured with defendant, but had the policy canceled because of the condition above mentioned being in the policy ; that plaintiffs' agent informed defendant that the United States Insurance Company of Baltimore was writing on the property, and that their policy did not contain that clause ; that defendant thereupon agreed to write as the other companies did, and to follow the form of the United States policy, which plaintiffs were to and did furnish for defendant to copy. Plaintiffs thereupon produced a blank form, which the witness testified was a blank policy of the latter company. This was offered in evidence, and was objected to upon the ground that the copy shown defendant should·be produced, and that a blank form not filled up was not proper evidence. The objection was overruled, and defendant excepted. Plaintiffs also gave evidence tending to show that they did not discover that the permission required was not in the policy until after the fire. The evidence, as to the agreement, was denied by defendant's agent who effected the insurance. It was held that the plaintiffs were entitled to have the policy reformed. See also, *Phenix F. Ins. Co.* v. *Gurnee,* 1 Paige Ch. (N. Y.) 278 ; 1 Ben. F I.-C. 257 ; *N. Y. Ice Co.* v. *N. Western Ins. Co.,* 23 N. Y. 357 ; *National F. Ins. Co.* v. *Crane,* 16 Md. 260 ; *Harris* v. *Columbia, etc., Ins. Co.,* 18 Ohio, 116 ; *Weed* v. *Schenectady, etc., Ins. Co.,* 7 Lans. (N. Y.) 452 ; *Bidwell* v. *Astor, etc., Ins. Co.,* 16 N. Y. 263 ; *Brioso* v. *Pacific Mut. Ins. Co.,* 4 Daly (N. Y. C. P.) 246 ; *Bunten* v. *Orient, etc., Ins. Co.,* 2 Keyes (N. Y.) 667 ; *N. American Ins. Co.* v. *Whipple,* 2 Biss. (U. S.) 418 ; *Malleable Iron Works* v. *Phenix Ins. Co.,* 25 Conn. 465 ; *Bennett* v. *City Ins. Co.,* 115 Mass. 241 ; *Oliver* v. *Mut. Com. Ins. Co.,* 2 Curtis (U. S.) 277 ; *Moliere* v. *Penn. F. Ins. Co.,* 5 Rawle (Penn.) 342 ; *National Traders' Bank* v. *Ocean Ins. Co.,* 62 Me. 519 ; *Lippincott* v. *Ins. Co.,* 3 La. 546 ; *Law* v. *Warren,* 6 Irish Eq. 299. A policy existing upon the property, by its terms, permitted other insurance. Plaintiff's agent, before it expired, applied for renewal, and defendant made a new policy, but omitted to indorse permission to make other insurance. This omission was not discovered by insured till after the fire occurred. The defendant's clerk testified that he was instructed by his superior not to insert the clause giving permission to make other insurance. It also appeared that the plaintiff presented the policy for material changes to be made in it on two different occasions before the fire occurred. It was held that it could not be reformed for the purpose of inserting permission to make other insurance, that to do so would be to impose upon the defendants, conditions and terms to which they never assented. *McHugh* v. *Imperial Fire Ins. Co.,* 48 How. Pr. (N. Y.) 230.

CHAPTER XVIII.

COURT AND JURY — QUESTIONS FOR.

SEC. 485. Questions for court.
SEC. 486. Questions for jury.

Questions for the court.

SEC. 485. It is the province of the court to construe contracts, and determine their legal effect, and to pass upon all questions of law arising under them. It is for the court to determine from the context and an inspection of the instrument, *what* words are used therein and to decipher illegible words, and it is error for it to leave it to the jury to say what an illegible word was intended to be. Thus where the word "six" was illegibly written, the "s" having the appearance of an "o," and the court left it for the jury to say whether it was "six" or "oix," it was held error, and that it was the province and duty of the court to determine that question.[1] So it is for the court to determine whether the facts proved will warrant a verdict for the plaintiff,[2] or to say, when certain facts are admitted, what their legal effect is. Thus, it is for the jury to say whether a fact concealed is material, but when the facts are agreed upon, it is a question for the court to determine whether as a matter of law it was material,[3] and in all cases it is for the court to say what is the legal effect of a certain state of facts,[4] and if the facts are admitted, it is for the court to apply the law thereto, and there is nothing for the jury to pass upon.[5] So, too, it is for the court to say whether the contract is executed in proper form, or as required by law, but, whether a contract was in fact made is a question for the jury.[6] So it is for the court to say what forms a

---

[1] *Lapeer, etc., Ins. Co.* v. *Dagss*, 30 Mich. 159; *Crafts* v. *Marshall*, 7 C. & P. 597.

[2] *Ins. Co.* v. *Folsom*, 18 Wall. (U. S.) 237; *Fay* v. *Alliance Ins. Co.*, 16 Gray (Mass.) 455.

[3] *Fletcher* v. *Commonwealth Ins. Co.*, 18 Pick. (Mass.) 419; *Clark* v. *Union Mut. F. Ins. Co.*, 40 N. H. 333; *Lyon* v. *Commercial Ins. Co.*, 2 Rob. (La.) 266; 2 Ben. F. I. C. 192; *Appleby* v. *The Astor F. Ins. Co.*, 54 N. Y. 253.

[4] *Winnesheik Ins. Co.* v. *Schueller*, 60 Ill. 465; *Riggin* v. *Patapsco Ins. Co.*, 7 H. & J. (Md.) 279.

[5] *Wood* v. *Atlantic, etc., Ins. Co.*, 50 Mo. 112; *Smith* v. *Newburyport, etc., Ins. Co.*, 4 Mass. 668; *Winnesheik Ins. Co.* v. *Scheuller*, *ante*; *Appleby* v. *Astor F. Ins. Co.*, *ante*.

[6] *Vatton* v. *National Ass. Co.*, 22 Barb. (N. Y.) 9.

part of the contract, as whether the application, by-laws, etc., are so far incorporated into as to become a part of it. But, where a paper on its face does not purport to have been made by him, or on his behalf, it is for the jury to say whether he in fact executed it, or authorized its execution, and the mere fact that it is referred to and made a part of the policy, does not tend even *prima facie* to establish the fact.[1] It is for the court, in the first instance, to construe the meaning of common words used in a policy, and it is presumed that they were used in their common or ordinary sense,[2] but it may be shown that the words have, by usage, acquired a local or peculiar meaning, and in that case, evidence is admissible to show what peculiar meaning the words have acquired, and it then becomes the province of the jury to define their meaning, and such also is the case in reference to words not belonging to the common vernacular,[3] and it may be said that, in all cases, when extrinsic evidence must be resorted to to determine the meaning of a word or phrase, it is the province of the jury to determine the sense in which it was used.[4]

Thus, it has been held competent to introduce evidence of an usage among insurers to regard a building filled in with brick in front and rear and supported by brick buildings on both sides, as a building "filled in with brick ;" and in such case, it is for the jury to find whether such was the usage ;[5] and, generally, when, by usage, a word has acquired a signification *different* from that ordinarily attached to it, it is for the jury to determine whether such usage exists, and what

---

[1] *Witherell* v. *Maine Ins. Co.*, 49 Me. 200 ; *Denny* v. *Conway, etc., Ins. Co.*, 13 Gray (Mass.) 492.

[2] *Wall* v. *Howard Ins. Co.*, 14 Barb. (N. Y.) 383.

[3] *Sleight* v. *Rheinlander*, 1 John. (N. Y.) 192 ; *Smith* v. *Wilson,* 3 B. & Ad. 728 ; *Allegre's Admrs.* v. *Maryland Ins. Co.*, 6 H. & J. (Md.) 408 ; *Dow* v. *Whetton*, 8 Wend. (N. Y.) 160 ; *Taylor* v. *Briggs*, 2 C. & P. 525 ; *Macey* v. *Whaling Ins. Co.*, 9 Met. (Mass.) 354 ; *Locke* v. *Rowell*, 47 N. H. 46 ; *Wait* v. *Fairbanks*, Brayt. (Vt.) 77 ; *Noyes* v. *Canfield*, 27 Vt. 76 ; *Stewart* v. *Smith*, 28 Ill. 397.

[4] *Harb* v. *Hammett*, 18 Vt. 127 ; *Reynolds* v. *Jourdan*, 6 Cal. 108 ; *Williams* v. *Wood*, 16 Md. 220 ; *Brown* v. *Brooks*, 25 Penn. St. 210 ; *Myers* v. *Walker*, 24 Ill. 133 ; *Ganson* v. *Madigan*, 15 Wis. 144 ; *Baron* v. *Placide*, 7 La. An. 229 ; *Hite* v. *State*, 9 Yerg. (Tenn.) 357 ; *Fitch* v. *Carpenter*, 43 Barb. (N. Y.) 40 ; *Carey* v. *Bright*, 58 Penn. St., 70 ; *Jenny Lind Co.* v. *Bower*, 11 Cal. 194 ; *Eaton* v. *Smith*, 20 Pick. (Mass.) 150 ; *Sleight* v. *Hartshorne*, 2 John. (N. Y.) 531 ; *Home* v. *Mut. Saftey Ins. Co.*, 1 Sandf. (N. Y.) 137 ; *Spicer* v. *Cooper*, 1 Q. B. 424. In *Houghton* v. *Gilbert*, 7 C. & P. 701, a question arose as to the meaning of the word "cargo." Erle, counsel for the defendant, was referring to *Entick's Dictionary* to ascertain the meaning, when he was stopped by Tindal, C.J., who said, "It is a question of mercantile construction. You had better lay aside your dictionary and appeal to the knowledge of the jury, for, after all, the dictionary is not authority."

[5] *Fowler* v. *Ætna Ins. Co.*, 7 Wend. (N. Y.) 270.

meaning, by such usage, the words or phrase have acquired;[1] and, generally, it may be said that *in all cases* where extrinsic evidence is resorted to, to ascertain the peculiar sense of words or phrases, it is the province of the jury to determine whether, by usage, they have acquired a peculiar sense, and what sense they have acquired, and then it is for the court to construe the policy according to the sense of the words or phrases as found by the jury. But when words have received a judicial interpretation;[2] or when the language of the policy is plain and explicit;[3] or the usage is not communicated to the party sought to be affected by it, or of such notoriety that it must be presumed that the parties knew of, and contracted in reference to it, it cannot be permitted to affect the interpretation to be placed upon the policy.[4] Nor can a new or independent stipulation or condition be incorporated into a policy by proof of a usage. Thus, it is not competent to show that it is the usage for the insured to give notice of the erection of a new building,[5] or that the insurer is not regarded as liable for a loss, unless it is ascertained in a certain manner,[6] nor, indeed, of any usage contravening the express provisions of the policy;[7] and in all such cases, the court is to construe the words or phrases employed, according to their ordinary and usual signification.[8]

Proof of a custom or usage is never admissible when it has been expressly excluded by the parties, nor when it is excluded by necessary implication. When it is opposed to the clear intention of the parties, to admit it, would permit the making of another and different contract from that made by the parties.[9]

[1] *Scott* v. *Bourdillou*, 5 B. & P. 213; *Hancox* v. *Fishing Ins. Co.*, 3 Sum. (U. S.) 132; *Eyre* v. *Marine Ins. Co.*, 5 W. & S. (Penn.) 116; *Hartshorn* v. *Union, etc., Ins. Co.*, 36 N. Y. 172; *Marcy* v. *Whaling Ins. Co.*, 9 Met. (Mass.) 354; *Union Bank* v. *Union Ins. Co.*, Dudley (S. C.) 171; *Coit* v. *Commercial Ins. Co.*, 7 John. (N. Y.) 385; *Dow* v. *Whitton*, 8 Wend. (N. Y.) 160; *May* v. *Buckeye Ins. Co.*, ante.

[2] *Barget* v. *Orient, etc., Ins. Co.*, 3 Bos. (N. Y.) 385.

[3] *Lattomus* v. *Farmers' Mut. F. Ins. Co.*, 3 Houst. (Del.) 254; *Smith* v. *Mobile, etc., Ins. Co.*, 30 Ala. 167; *Hare* v. *Barstow*, 8 Jurist, 928; *Hall* v. *Janson*, 4 El. & Bl. 500; *Hone* v. *Mut. Safety Ins. Co.*, 2 N. Y. 235; *Winthrop* v. *Union Ins. Co.*, 2 Wash. C. C. (U. S.) 7.

[4] *Protection Ins. Co.* v. *Harmer*, 2 Ohio St. 452.

[5] *Stebbins* v. *Globe Ins. Co.*, 2 Hall (N. Y.) 632.

[6] *Rankin* v. *American Ins. Co.*, 1 Hall (N. Y.) 619.

[7] *Turner* v. *Burrows*, 8 Wend. (N. Y.) 144; *Parkinson* v. *Collier*, Park. on Ins. 470; *Pawson* v. *Barnvelt*, 1 Doug. 12.

[8] *Harmer* v. *Protection Ins. Co.*, ante; *King* v. *Enterprise Ins. Co.*, 45 Ind. 43; *Cobb* v. *Little Rock, etc., Ins. Co.*, 58 Me. 326; *St. Nicholas Ins. Co.* v. *Mercantile, etc., Ins. Co.*, 5 Bos. (N. Y.) 238; *Hearne* v. *Marine Ins. Co.*, 20 Wall. (U. S.) 488; *Warner* v. *Franklin Ins. Co.*, 104 Mass. 518.

[9] *Insurance Co.* v. *Wright*, 1 Wall. (U. S.) 471; *Allegre* v. *Ins. Co.*, ante.

As to what constitutes a warranty, is a question for the court, but whether there has been a breach thereof, is a question for the jury.[1] So as to what facts establish a waiver of a condition in a policy, is a question for the court, but as to whether there were facts amounting to a waiver, is for the jury.[2] So as to whether notice or proofs of loss were in time, or whether the proofs are sufficient, is for the court, but the question whether there are facts excusing delay, or whether delay or defects have been waived, is for the jury.[3] So whether a loss is within the perils insured against, the facts being found or admitted, is for the court, but it is for the jury to say what peril caused the loss.[4] So, too, it is for the jury to say whether the assured rendered as full an account of the loss as the circumstances would permit.[5]

Jury

SEC. 486. It is the peculiar province of the jury to determine all questions of fact in a case. Thus, it is for the court to say what amounts to a misdescription of premises, but it is for the jury to say whether or not a misdescription was material to the risk,[6] so as to misrepresentation or concealment,[7] so it is for the jury to say whether there has been a breach of warranty, and, in a case where the warranty is dependent upon a matter of fact whether a warranty in fact exists.[8] It is for the jury to say whether there has been a *material* alteration or increase of the risk;[9] whether a certain usage exists;[10] whether a

---

[1] *Gates* v. *Madison Co., etc,, Ins. Co.*, 2 N. Y. 43; 2 Bennett's F. I. C. 785.

[2] *Bodle* v. *Chenango, etc., Ins. Co.*, 2 N. Y. 53; 2 Bennett's F. I. C. 794; *Noonan* v. *Hartford F. Ins. Co.*, 21 Mo. 81; *Charleston, etc., Ins. Co.* v. *Neve*, 2 McMull, (S. C.) 237.

[3] *Edwards* v. *Baltimore Ins. Co.*, 3 Gill. (Md.) 176.

[4] *Kenniston* v. *Merrimack, etc., Ins. Co.*, 14 N. H. 341; 2 Bennett's F. I. C. 288;. *Merchants', etc.. Ins. Co.* v. *Tucker*, 3 Cr. (U. S.) 357; *Abithal* v. *Bristow*, 6 Taunt. 464; *Miles* v. *Fletcher*, Doug. 230.

[5] *Franklin F. Ins. Co.* v. *Updegraff*, 43 Penn. St. 350.

[6] *Columbian Ins. Co.* v. *Lawrence*, 10 Pet. (U. S.) 507.

[7] *Sexton* v. *Montgomery Mut. Ins. Co.*, 9 Barb. (N. Y.) 191; *Clark* v. *Union Ins. Co.*, 40 N. H. 333; *Lyon* v. *Com'l Ins. Co.*, 2 Rob. (La.) 266; *Cumberland Valley Ins. Co.* v. *Mitchell*, 48 Penn. St. 374; *Protection Ins. Co.* v. *Harmer, ante; Masters* v, *Madison, etc., Ins. Co.*, 11 Barb. (N. Y.) 624; *Seminary* v. *Hamilton Ins. Co.,* 14 Gray (Mass.) 459; *Mutual Ins. Co.* v. *Deale*, 18 Md. 26; *N. Y. F. Ins. Co.* v. *Walden*, 12 John. (N. Y.) 513; *Bans* v. *World, etc., Ins. Co.*, 6 T. & C. (N. Y.) 364.

[8] *Curry* v. *Com'l Ins. Co.*, 10 Pick. (Mass.) 535; 1 Ben. F. I. C. 333; *Denis* v. *Ludlow*, 2 Cai. (N. Y.) 111; *Percival* v. *Maine Mut. Ins. Co.*, 33 Me. 242.

[9] *Richards* v. *Protection Ins. Co.*, 30 Me. 273; *Curry* v. *Com'l Ins. Co.*, 10 Pick. (Mass.) 535; *Gammell* v. *Merchants', etc., Ins. Co.*, 12 Cush. (Mass.) 167; *Jolly* v. *Baltimore Eq. Society*, 1 H. & G. (Md.) 295; *Schenck* v. *Mercer Co. Mut. F. Ins. Co.*, 24 N. J. 447; *Perry, etc., Ins. Co.* v. *Stewart*, 19 Penn. St. 115.

[10] *Daniels* v. *Hud. Riv. Ins. Co.*, 12 Cush. (Mass.) 416; *Palmer* v. *Blackburn*, 1 Bing. 62.

word has acquired a peculiar meaning, and what that meaning is;[1] whether the assured has an insurable interest in the property insured;[2] whether a notice required by the policy to be given was given within a reasonable time;[3] whether performance of a condition has been waived;[4] whether the assured has been guilty of fraud[5] or false swearing;[6] whether a misdescription is material;[7] whether a certain usage exists;[8] *and indeed, all questions of fact arising under the issues made, are exclusively for the jury,* and it is error for the court to trench upon their province.[9]

Thus it will be seen that nearly all questions arising outside the actual construction of the contract, and the legal effect of facts found or admitted, are mixed questions of law and fact, and which it is not competent for the court to decide without the aid of the jury. If the facts are admitted, or there is no dispute thereto, it is for the court alone to apply them and determine their legal effect,[10] but in all cases where the facts are in dispute, it is exclusively for the jury to find what the real facts are, and it is error for the court to withdraw the question from the jury, or to direct a verdict, even though the facts are uncontradicted; for, although the facts are not denied, yet, unless admitted, it is competent for the jury to refuse to find a fact from the testimony of a witness whose credibility they doubt.[11]

---

[1] *Evans* v. *Com'l, etc., Ins. Co.*, 6 R. I. 47.

[2] *Mitchell* v. *Home Ins. Co.*, 32 Iowa, 421; *Mowry* v. *Home, etc.*, 9 R. I. 346.

[3] *Davis* v. *Western Mass. Ins. Co.*, 8 R. I. 277.

[4] *Lycoming, etc., Ins. Co.* v. *Schollenberger*, 44 Penn. St. 259.

[5] *McLaws* v. *United, etc., Institution*, 33 Scot. Jur. 286.

[6] *McKurdy* v. *N. British Ins. Co.*, 20 C. C. (Sc.) 463.

[7] *Columbian Ins. Co.* v. *Lawrence*, 2 Pet. (U. S.) 25; S. C., 10 id. 507.

[8] *Palmer* v. *Blackburn*, 1 Bing. 62.

[9] *Charleston, etc., Ins. Co.* v. *Corner*, 2 Gill. (Md.) 410; *Field* v. *Ins. Co. of N. America*, 3 Md. 244.

[10] *Winneshiek Ins. Co.* v. *Schueller, ante; Smith* v. *Newburyport, etc., Ins. Co., ante; Fletcher* v. *Commonwealth Ins. Co., ante; Woods* v. *Atlantic Ins. Co.*, 50 Mo. 112.

[11] *Charleston Ins. Co.* v. *Carver*, 2 Gill. (Md.) 410; *Field* v. *Insurance Co. of N. America*, 3 Md. 244.

CHAPTER XIX.

REMEDIES UPON POLICIES.

Form of action.

SEC. 487. When the policy is under seal, which is seldom the case in this country, an action of debt[1] or covenant[2] should be brought thereon, and assumpsit will not lie,[3] and if assumpsit is brought upon a sealed policy, and a verdict for the plaintiff is rendered thereon, it will be arrested on motion,[4] but where, under Codes or Practice acts all distinctions between remedies upon specialties and simple contracts is abolished, assumpsit will lie upon a sealed policy.[5] So if the policy is renewed by a receipt, *not* under seal, the character of the instrument is changed from a specialty to a simple contract, and assumpsit is the proper remedy.[6] And upon all policies, not under seal, assumpsit is the proper form of action. It is held, however, that where a policy under seal contains a provision for its being kept in force for any future time, by payment of the premium, which is indorsed thereon, the instrument does not lose its character as a specialty, and the remedy is in debt or covenant.[7] And it seems that an action of debt cannot be maintained upon a sealed policy, where the

---

[1] *People's Ins. Co.* v. *Spencer*, 53 Penn. St. 353 ; *Sunderland, etc., Marine Ins. Co.* v. *Kearney*, 16 Q. B. 925 ; *Peoria Marine, etc., Ins. Co.* v. *Whitemill*, 25 Ill. 466.

[2] *Luciani* v. *American F. Ins. Co.*, 2 Whart. (Penn.) 167.

[3] *Marine Ins. Co.* v. *Young*, 1 Cr. C. C. (U. S.) 332.

[4] *Marine Ins. Co.* v. *Young*, ante.

[5] *Protection L. Ins. Co.* v. *Palmer*, 81 Ill. 88.

[6] *Flannagan* v. *Camden, etc., Ins. Co.*, 25 N. J. 506 ; *Aurora Fire Ins. Co.* v. *Eddy*, 55 Ill. 213 ; *Mutual Ins. Co.* v. *Deale*, 18 Md. 26 ; *Luciani* v. *American F. Ins. Co.*, 2 Whart. (Penn.) 167.

[7] *Franklin F. Ins. Co.* v. *Massey*, 33 Penn. St. 221.

insurer has the right to pay in money or rebuild. In such case, covenant is the proper remedy.[1] Where a person agrees to procure insurance for another, and fails to do so, or does it so negligently that the policy does not benefit the assured, an action on the case is the proper remedy.[2] Where a parol contract to insure, or of insurance, is entered into, and no policy is issued, an action of assumpsit upon the contract made is the proper remedy, and in such a case, the assured may recover the amount of his loss, not exceeding the sum agreed to be insured,[3] or he may resort to a court of equity, to compel the issue of a policy according to the terms of the contract, and the court will not only direct specific performance, by the issue of a policy, but will also compel the payment of a loss sustained under it.[4] In an action upon a policy, the declaration or complaint must set forth the contract, substantially, a loss under it by the peril insured against, and must also aver performance, on the part of the assured, of all conditions precedent contained in the contract, and when the application is made a part of the policy, it must be set forth, or so much of it as is of the essence of the contract.[5]

Who may sue.

SEC. 488. In the absence of a statute authorizing an assignee of a chose in action to bring suit thereon in his name, an action upon a policy, although upon its face made payable to a third person in case of loss, or assigned, with the consent of the assured, as collateral security, *must* be brought in the name of the assured,[6] and the rule is not changed by the fact that the policy is made payable to the assured "or his assigns."[7] But when the property is sold, and the policy is assigned, with the consent of the insurer, *knowing* that the entire insurable interest is vested in the assignee, the assignment, and assent

---

[1] *Flanagan* v. *Camden, etc., Ins. Co.,* 25 N. J. 506.

[2] *Wilkinson* v. *Caverdale,* 1 Esp. 75.

[3] *Angel* v. *Hartford Ins. Co.,* 59 N. Y. 171.

[4] See page 32 *et seq. ante.*

[5] *Bobbitt* v. *Liverpool, etc., Ins. Co.,* 66 N. C. 70.

[6] *Jessel* v. *Williamsburgh F. Ins. Co.,* 3 Hill (N. Y.) 88; *Gourdan* v. *Ins. Co. of N. America,* 3 Yeates (Penn.) 327; *Bayles* v. *Hillsborough Ins. Co.,* 27 N. J. 163; *Woodbury Savings Bank* v. *Charter Oak Ins. Co.,* 29 Conn. 874; *Flynn* v. *N. American L. Ins. Co.,* 115 Mass. 449; *Blanchard* v. *Atlantic Mut. Ins. Co.,* 33 N. H. 9; *Folsom* v. *Belknap, etc., Ins. Co.,* 30 id. 231; *Conover* v. *Mutual Ins. Co.,* 1 N. Y. 296; *Rollins* v. *Ins. Co.,* 26 N. H. 22; 3 Ben. F. I. C. 377; *Conover* v. *Mutual Ins. Co.,* 1 N. Y. 290; 2 Ben. F. I. C. 677; *Exchange Bank* v. *Rice,* 107 Mass. 37.

[7] *Beemer* v. *Anchor Ins. Co.,* 16 U. C. (Q. B.) 485; *Orchard* v. *Ætna Ins. Co.,* 5 U. C. (C. P.) 445.

52

thereto, is held to operate as a new contract with the assignee, and he may maintain an action thereon in his own name, and an action in the name of the assignor will not lie.[1] But when the assured conveys the property, and takes a mortgage back to secure the payment of the purchase money, and he assigns the policy to the purchaser, who re-assigns it to the assured, with the consent of the insurer, the assured may still sue thereon in his own name.[2] Where the policy is open, and payable " to whom it may concern," an action may be maintained in the name of any person, having an insurable interest in the property, whose interest and relation to the property is such that he can be said to have been within the contemplation of the parties, and the declaration must show such interest and relation;[3] or the person interested may maintain an action in the name of the assured, for his benefit, and such is the better practice.[4] Where a policy is taken out by an agent, in his own name, for his principal, the insurer being aware of the facts, the principal may sue in his own name,[5] or in the name of the agent.[6]

When a policy is issued to a carrier, he may maintain an action to recover the entire loss, he standing as trustee for the owner, for all the amount recovered in excess of his own interest.[7] In such cases, however, when the assured brings the action, he should set forth the interests in respect of which he sues, and it should also be shown, or at least appear, that he had authority to cover such interest. This may be done by proof of express authority, or an usage,[8] or by the ratification of the act by the party in interest, at any time before judgment.[9] A policy under seal, although professedly made for the benefit of third

---

[1] *Mann* v. *Herkimer, etc., Ins. Co.*, 4 Hill (N. Y.) 187; *Summers* v. *U. S. Ins. Co.*, 13 La. An. 504.

[2] *Kingsley* v. *N. E., etc., Ins. Co.*, 8 Cush. (Mass.) 393; *Sanders* v. *Hillsborough, etc., Ins. Co.*, 44 N. H. 238.

[3] *Fleming* v. *Ins. Co.*, 12 Penn. St. 391; *Anonymous*, Skinner, 327; *Waring* v. *Indemnity Ins. Co.*, 45 N. Y. 606; *Williams* v. *Ocean Ins. Co.*, 2 Met. (Mass.) 203; *Adrich* v. *Equitable Ins. Co.*, 1 A. & M. (U. S.) 272; *Strahn* v. *Hartford Ins. Co.*, 33 Wis. 648.

[4] *Illinois F. Ins. Co.* v. *Stanton*, 57 Ill. 354; *Protection Ins. Co.* v. *Wilson*, 6 Ohio St. 553; *Walsh* v. *Washington Ins. Co.*, 32 N. Y. 427; *Waring* v. *Indemnity Ins. Co.*, 45 N. Y. 606; *Sturm* v. *Atlantic Ins. Co.*, 6 J. & S. (N. Y.) 281.

[5] *Stillwell* v. *Staples*, 19 N. Y. 401; *Seamans* v. *Loring*, 1 Mass. (U. S.) 127; *Solmes* v. *Rutgers F. Ins. Co.*, 3 Keyes (N. Y.) 416; *Mattey* v. *Manufacturer's Ins. Co.*, 29 Me. 337.

[6] *Goodall* v. *N. E. Mut. F. Ins. Co.*, 25 N. H. 169.

[7] See Chap. 8.

[8] *DeForest* v. *Fulton Ins. Co.*, 1 Hall (N. Y.) 84.

[9] *Bridge* v. *Niagara Ins. Co.*, 1 Hall (N. Y.) 247; *Jefferson Ins. Co.* v. *Cotheal*, 7 Wend. (N. Y.) 72.

persons not named, *must* be sued in the name of the assured,[1] but if the person for whose benefit the policy is made, is named in the policy, as, if it is issued to "A., on account of B.," B. may maintain an action thereon, in his own name.[2]

Where a policy is made, "loss, if any, payable to A. *and the insured, as their interest shall appear*," the action must be in the name of the insured.[3] Generally, when the policy, upon its face, shows that it was made for the benefit of third persons, exclusively, the beneficiaries may maintain an action in their own name, or in the name of the assured, for their benefit. Thus, the *cestui que trust* may maintain an action upon a policy issued to A., as trustee of B.[4] The assignee may bring an action upon the policy in the name of the assured, and the assignment is ample evidence to establish his authority to do so. The assignor cannot prevent him from doing so, and cannot release, discharge or control the action.[5] But in such cases, the assured may show that the interest of the assignee has been quieted.[6]

When, by statute, the assignee may maintain an action upon a chose in action assigned to him, the assignee not only *may* maintain an action upon the policy in his own name, but he *must* thus bring the action,[7] unless his interest has been quieted. So, too, the assignee may sue when the insurer, either before or after the loss, upon a sufficient consideration, has promised to give him the benefit of the policy.[8]

When a policy, assigned to a third person, is renewed *in his name*, and the premium is paid by him, he may maintain an action for a loss in his own name.[9] So, where a policy in a mutual company is assigned with the consent of the company, and the assignee gives a new premium note, the policy becomes a new contract with him, and he may sue thereon in his own name.[10] If the policy is under seal, unless the assignment is also under seal, the action must be in the name of the

---

[1]*American Ins. Co.* v. *Insley*, 7 Penn. St. 233; *DeBalle* v. *Penn. Ins. Co.*, 4 Whart. (Penn.) 68.

[2]*Maryland Ins. Co.* v. *Graham*, 3 H. & J. (Md.) 62.

[3]*Owens* v. *Farmers' J. S. Ins. Co.*, 57 Barb. (N. Y.) 518.

[4]*Hillyard* v. *Mut. Ben. Ins. Co.*, 35 N. J. 415.

[5]*Nevins* v. *Rockingham, etc., Ins. Co.*, 25 N. H. 22.

[6]*Summers* v. *U. S. Ins. and Trust Co.*, 13 La. An. 504.

[7]*Grosvenor* v. *Atlantic Ins. Co.*, 17 N. Y. 391; *Cone* v. *Niagara Ins. Co.*, 60 N. Y. 619; aff'd, S. C., 3 T. & C. 33; *Clinton* v. *Hope Ins. Co.*, 45 N. Y. 544; *Frink* v. *Hampden Ins. Co.*, 45 Barb. (N. Y.) 384; *Ripley* v. *Astor Ins. Co.*

[8]*Demill* v. *Hartford Ins. Co.*, 4 Allen (N. B.) 341.

[9]*Peoria, etc., Ins. Co.* v. *Harvey*, 34 Ill. 46.

[10]*Stimpson* v. *Monmouth, etc., Ins. Co.*, 47 Me. 379; *Shepherd* v. *Union, etc., Ins. Co.*, 38 N. H. 232.

assured.[1] In all cases, the assignee, in order to maintain the action, must show that he had an insurable interest in the property at the time of loss.[2]

When a policy is made payable to two or more persons, the action should be in the name of all.[3] When, however, a policy issues to two or more joint owners, and one has sold his interest to his co-owner, in those States where, by statute, the assignee of a chose in action may maintain an action in his own name, an action will lie only in favor of the joint owner or owners to whom the policy has been assigned, or in whom the entire title vests.[4] Where a sale by one joint owner to another is held not to amount to an alienation, within the meaning of the term as employed in policies, it would seem that, to recover a loss *after* such sale, the action must, in the absence of the assent of the insurer to such sale, or of a statute authorizing an action in the name of an assignee, be brought in the name of the persons named in the policy as the assured, setting forth the facts as to the transfer, and the interest of the real owner in the loss.[5] But if, after notice of such sale or transfer, the insurer promises the assignee to pay the loss to him, the assignee may, upon proper averment of the facts, maintain an action in his own name.[6] The doctrine stated, *ante*, that the action may be brought in the name of *both* joint owners, after one has parted with all his interest therein, militates seriously against the rule that a policy is void as to one who has no insurable interest therein at the time of loss, and has been denied in several cases;[7] and in a New York case,[8] it was held that no recovery could be had at law upon the policy in such a case, and that the only remedy of the party in interest was by bill in equity; and this would seem to be the most consistent doctrine. But whatever may be the rule in such cases, it is settled that when a policy is issued to partners, upon the death of one

---

[1] *Bayles* v. *Hillsborough, etc., Ins. Co.*, 23 N. J. 163.

[2] *Bayles* v. *Hillsborough Ins. Co., ante; Graham* v. *Fireman's Ins. Co.*, 2 Dis. (Ohio) 255.

[3] *Marsh* v. *Robinson*, 4 Esp. 98.

[4] *Murdock et al.* v. *Chenango Ins. Co.*, 2 N. Y. 210; see statement of case, p. 561, n.; *Hoffman* v. *Ætna Ins. Co.*, 32 N. Y. 405; see statement of case, p. 560, n. 4.

[5] *Pierce* v. *Nashua F. Ins. Co.*, 50 N. H. 297; see statement of case, p. 566, n. 6; *Tate* v. *Citizen's, etc., Ins. Co.*, 13 Gray (Mass.) 79.

[6] *Pierce* v. *Nashua Ins. Co., ante; Wood* v. *Rutland Co. Ins. Co.*, 31 Vt. 552; see statement of case, p. 567, n. 4.

[7] See opinion of ALPIS, J., in *Wood* v. *Rutland, etc., Ins. Co., ante;* also, *Hoffman* v. *Ætna Ins. Co., ante,* and the cases referred to therein.

[8] *Bodle* v. *Chenango Mut. Ins. Co.*, 2 N. Y. 53.

the survivor may sue thereon alone, as surviving partner,[1] and neither the executor, administrator or heirs of such deceased partner can be joined in the action. The surviving partner alone must sue.[2]

Trover lies when policy has been executed and delivery refused.

SEC. 489. When the contract is complete, and the policy has been in fact executed, but is wrongfully withheld, an action of trover will lie against the insurer therefor;[3] but in order to sustain such an action, it must be shown that the contract is complete, and not inchoate only. That is, the terms of the contract must not only have been agreed upon, but the policy must also have in fact been executed, although it seems that it is not necessary that the premium should have been paid, provided it is tendered and the policy demanded within a reasonable time after its execution.[4] But while this remedy exists and *may* be resorted to, yet it is never desirable to resort to it *after* a loss, as the remedy in equity is much more efficacious, besides being safer. In an action of trover, the assured is compelled to prove not only that the contract was complete and the policy executed, but also that the policy embodies the contract; while in equity, he is only compelled to prove the contract, and the court, upon such proof, will decree not only the execution of a policy in conformity therewith, but also the payment of the loss, if any, under it.[5]

Remedy of insurer against wrong-doer negligently causing the loss.

SEC. 490. Where the insurer is entitled to be subrogated to the rights of the assured against third persons for a negligent burning of the premises, the action can only be maintained in the name of the assured.[6]

Remedies in equity.

SEC. 491. When a policy has been fraudulently obtained, a court of equity will compel its surrender to the insurer for cancellation, particularly where no provision authorizing its cancellation is incorporated

---

[1] *Wood* v. *Rutland, etc., Ins. Co., ante.*

[2] *Work* v. *Merchants', etc., Ins. Co.,* 11 Cush. (Mass.) 271.

[3] Marshall on Insurance, 303.

[4] In *Kohne* v. *Ins. Co. of N. America,* 1 Wash. C. C. (U. S.) 93.

[5] *Andrews* v. *Essex Ins. Co.,* 3 Mass. (U. S.) 6 ; *Angell* v. *Hartford F. Ins. Co.,* 59 N. Y. 171.

[6] *Allison* v. *Ins. Co.,* 3 Dill. (U. S. C. C.) 81 ; *London Ass. Co.* v *Sainbury,* 3 Doug. 245 ; *Peoria Ins. Co.* v. *Frost,* 37 Ill. 333 ; *Hart* v. *Western R. R. Co.,* 13 Met. (Mass.) 101 ; *Clark* v. *Wilson,* 103 Mass. 219 ; *Weber* v. *Morris, etc., R. R. Co.,* 35 N. J. 409 ; *Rockingham F. Ins. Co.* v. *Bosher,* 39 Me. 253 ; *Perrot* v. *Shearer,* 17 Mich. 48.

into the policy.[1]   Where, however, an action at law is pending upon the policy, or a loss has transpired under it, and the facts alleged, if true, operate as a complete legal defense, the bill will not be entertained.[2]   As where it is claimed that the assured misrepresented the risk, or concealed material facts,[3] or was guilty of other fraud in obtaining the policy,[4] and even when the bill is brought before a loss under the policy to compel its surrender, the relief will be denied, unless the proof of fraud is full and conclusive.[5]

So where the insurer has fraudulently or by mistake issued a policy to the assured that does not embrace the contract made, or cover the property contracted to be insured, proceedings in equity may be brought for its reformation, so as to embrace the real contract.[6]   So where a contract to insure has been entered into, but the insurer refuses to deliver a policy, although an action at law might be brought upon the contract, yet, as the remedy for a specific performance of the contract is an appropriate remedy, a court of equity will not refuse to entertain jurisdiction because a remedy at law may also exist, but will entertain the suit, and decree not only specific performance by a delivery of a policy, but will also ascertain and compel payment of a loss under the contract.[7]   So where proceedings are properly brought in a court of equity *after* a loss, as for the correction of an error in the policy, if no action thereon is pending in a court of law, the court having acquired jurisdiction for one purpose, will, if the bill prays therefor, retain the matter for all purposes, and will ascertain and decree payment of the loss, if the assured is entitled to recover at law upon the policy.[8]   So where a policy is lost or has been destroyed,

---

[1] *McEvens* v. *Lawrence*, Hoffman's Ch. (N. Y.) 172; *French* v. *Connelly*, 2 Austruther, 454; *Fenn* v. *Craig*, 3 Y. & C. 216; *Godart* v. *Garrett*, 2 Vern. 269; *Globe Mut. Ins. Co.* v. *Reals*, 48 How. Pr. (N. Y.) 502.

[2] *Hoare* v. *Bremridge*, L. R. 8 Ct. App. 22.

[3] *Hoare* v. *Bremridge, ante; Marine Ins. Co.* v. *Hodgson,* 7 Cr. (U. S.) 332; *Ins. Co.* v. *Bailey,* 13 Wall. (U. S.) 616.

[4] *Home Ins. Co.* v. *Stanchfield,* 1 Dill. (U. S. C. C.) 424; *Ins. Co.* v. *Bailey,* 13 Wall. (U. S.) 616; *Charleston Ins. Co.* v. *Potter,* 3 Dess. (S. C.) 6.

[5] *Koowles* v. *Haughton,* 11 Ves. Jr. 168.

[6] *Harris* v. *Columbian Ins. Co.,* 18 Ohio, 116.   See chapter on REFORMATION OF CONTRACTS.

[7] *Tayloe* v. *Merchants' Ins. Co.,* 9 How. (U. S.) 390; *Palm* v. *Medina, etc., Ins. Co.,* 20 Ohio, 529; *Carpenter* v. *Mut. Safety Ins. Co.,* 4 Sandf. Ch. (N. Y.) 408; *Post* v. *Ætna Ins. Co.,* 43 Barb. (N. Y.) 351; *Gerrish* v. *German Ins. Co.,* 55 N. H. 355; see *ante,* pp. 32–34.

[8] *Harvey* v. *Beckwith,* 12 Weekly Rep. 819; *Franklin Ins. Co.* v. *McCrea,* 5 Iowa, 229; *Phœnix Ins. Co.* v. *Hoffheimer,* 46 Miss. 645; *Fireman's Ins. Co.* v. *Powell,* 13 B. Mon. (Ky.) 311.

if the insurer refuses to give a duplicate, the assured may resort to a court of equity for full relief.[1]

When the officers of a mutual insurance company have funds in their hands with which to pay a loss under a policy, but neglect or refuse to do so, and have fraudulently applied the funds to other purposes, or threaten to do so, a court of equity will compel the application of the funds to the payment of the loss, but the company must be joined as a party defendant.[2]

Where a judgment has been obtained against an insurer by fraud, or where the insurer after judgment, for the first time becomes aware of fraudulent acts on the part of the assured that would have defeated a recovery, and the insurer has been guilty of no laches in ascertaining the facts, a court of equity will, if the facts are such as to warrant it, enjoin the assured from enforcing the judgment, and will set it aside.[3] Generally, where the parties have a complete and full remedy at law, a court of equity will not interfere. But, if action is brought upon a policy, and the assured threatens to proceed to trial without giving the insurer a proper opportunity to prepare his defense; as, where the loss occurred in a foreign country, and the insurer desires to, and must have the testimony of witnesses there, a court of equity will, when the court of law has not the requisite power to give relief, enjoin the action, and issue a commission for the taking of such evidence;[4] but if the court of law in which the proceedings are pending, has ample jurisdiction and power to give relief, even though it has refused it, a court of equity will not interfere.

What must be set forth in the complaint or declaration.

Sec. 492. The declaration, in an action upon a policy of insurance, must set forth an insurable interest in the plaintiff at the time of loss,[5] but it is sufficient if language is used that clearly imports such an interest, although not in express or direct terms, as that the policy was issued to the plaintiff upon certain property, as, the issue of the policy, upon the property to the plaintiff, is an admission by the insurer that the assured had an insurable interest in the property, *when it issued*, and, it is unnecessary for the plaintiff to aver that such

---

[1] *Chase* v. *Washington Ins. Co.*, 12 Barb. (N. Y.) 565.

[2] *Lyman* v. *Bonney*, 100 Mass. 562; see also *Scott* v. *Eagle F. Ins. Co.*, 7 Paige Ch. (N. Y.) 198; *Curran* v. *Arkansas*, 15 How. (U. S.) 304; *Robinson* v. *Smith*, 3 Paige Ch. (N. Y.) 222; *Cunningham* v. *Pell*, 5 id. 607.

[3] *Ocean Ins. Co.* v. *Field*, 2 Story (U. S.) 59.

[4] *Chitty* v. *Selwyn*, 2 Atk. 359.

[5] *Henshaw* v. *Mutual Safety Ins. Co.*, 2 Blatchf. (U. S.) 99.

interest continued to the time of loss, as that fact will be presumed, and if not a fact, must be set up and proved by the insurer in avoidance of liability.[1] If the action is predicated upon a written policy, it must be alleged to be in writing, otherwise it will be presumed that it was by parol, unless it is one that the statute requires to be in writing, in which case it will be presumed that the statutory provisions were complied with.[2] The complaint must set forth a loss, arising from the peril insured against,[3] and if the policy excepts against a loss occasioned by a fire arising from an explosion, or from lightning, or from the falling of a building, or from any other special cause, although not necessary, it is proper to aver that the loss resulted from a fire not arising from any of the excepted causes. Thus, if the policy provides that the insurer shall not be liable for a fire resulting from the falling of a building, it has been held sufficient to aver that the loss was caused by fire, and not by the falling of any building.[4] No particular form of words are necessary; it is enough if the averment is of a loss covered by the policy, in whatever way expressed. It is not indispensibly necessary that the declaration should negative the exceptions contained in the policy, as that the loss did not result from an invasion,[5] as such matters are exclusively for the benefit of the inurer and are strictly matters of defense, and not conditions precedent.[6] The declaration must not only aver a loss, arising from a peril insured against, but must also aver that the property destroyed was insured by the policy.[7] Fire must appear to be the proximate cause of the loss, although it is not essential that the complaint should show that the goods were burned. It is enough if a loss, not excepted against, of which fire is the proximate cause, is set forth as, that the goods were injured by water in attempts to extin_ guish a fire in the adjoining building, or that they were injured or stolen while being removed from a building in imminent danger of destruction by fire, and indeed in all cases the occasion and the man_ ner of the loss must be set forth according to the facts.[8]

---

[1] *Rising Sun Ins. Co.* v. *Slaughter*, 20 Ind. 520.

[2] *Kine* v. *Enterprise Ins. Co.*, 45 Ind. 43.

[3] *Ferrer* v. *Home Ins. Co.*, 47 Cal. 416.

[4] *Ferrer* v. *Home Ins. Co.*, *ante*.

[5] *Lounsbury* v. *Protection Ins. Co.*, 8 Conn. 459 ; *Forbes* v. *American, etc., Ins. Co.*, 15 Gray (Mass.) 249 ; *Catlin* v. *Sprinfield F. & M. Ins. Co.*, 1 Sum. (U. S.) 434

[6] *Lounsbury* v. *Protection Ins. Co.*, *ante*.

[7] *Rodi* v. *Rutgers F. Ins Co.*, 6 Bos. (N. Y.) 23.

[8] ROBINSON, C. J., in *Thompson* v. *Montreal Ins. Co.*, 6 U. C. (Q. B.) 319.

If the action is in the name of an assignee, or any other person than the assured, and is predicated upon an interest in the policy, acquired before a loss under it, the declaration must aver an insurable interest in the plaintiff *at the time of loss*, or it will be held bad on demurrer.[1] Thus, where an action is brought upon a policy, for account of whom it may concern, the plaintiff must aver an interest in the subject insured, *and his relation thereto*, in order that it may be determined from an inspection of the declaration whether, if the facts averred are true, he had an insurable interest in the property; and a declaration that merely states that the plaintiff " was, at the time of the making of the policy, and at the time of the loss, the person for whom the insurance was effected, and whom it concerned, and his interest therein, at the time of loss, exceeded the sum insured," is demurrable, because the interest may not have been an insurable interest, and he should have set forth his relation to the property, and the nature of his interest.[2]

Performance on his part, of all conditions precedent, or facts that excuse performance, must be averred by the plaintiff,[3] as, where the policy provides that notice shall be given, and proofs of loss shall be furnished forthwith, or within a stated time; compliance with the condition, or facts that excuse compliance, must be set forth, or no recovery can be had, and, if the condition was complied with, but the declaration does not aver compliance, it has been held that the proofs of loss are not admissible in evidence.[4] And if properly averred, unless admitted, compliance must be proved, or the action will fail.[5] It can readily be determined of what matters performance should be averred, by ascertaining what, under the policy, the assured has stipulated to do, and what he must do, in order to recover, and he must aver performance of all such conditions, as where he stipulates to erect a chimney; to keep a watchman; to put in a force pump; to keep water in certain quantities, and in certain places;[6] or any other matter or thing which the insurer has contracted to do, whether the same relates

---

[1] *Fowler* v. *N. Y. Ins. Co.*, 26 N. Y. 422; *Freeman* v. *Fulton Ins. Co.*, 38 Barb. (N. Y.) 247.

[2] *Freeman* v. *Fulton F. Ins. Co.*, ante.

[3] *Edgerly* v. *Farmers' Ins. Co.*, 43 Iowa, 587; *St. Louis Ins. Co.* v. *Glasgow*, 8 Mo. 713.

[4] *Edgerly* v. *Farmers' Ins. Co.*, ante.

[5] *Washington Ins. Co.* v. *Herckenrath*, 3 Rob. (N. Y.) 325; *Battaite* v. *Merchants' Ins. Co.*, 3 Rob. (La.) 384.

[6] *Glendale Woolen Co.* v. *Protection Ins. Co.*, 21 Conn. 19.

or is material to the risk, or not. The question is not, whether such matter is material to the risk, but whether the assured has contracted to do it, and if so, he must aver performance, even though it is entirely foreign to the risk, or any of its incidents. But, as to all other matters, which are in the nature of exceptions,[1] or which are merely prohibitory, and provide that the assured *shall not* do certain things, the plaintiff need not make any special averments, as they are merely matters of defense, which, if relied upon by the insurer, must be plead and proved by him;[2] and if nothing is said in the declaration, as to whether such conditions have been broken or not, the declaration will not be defective,[3] yet, it is proper to aver, and a finished pleader always would aver, that the plaintiff has " duly performed and kept all the conditions " of the policy. When the *application* is made a part of the policy, it must be declared on as a part of the contract, and performance of all the conditions precedent therein, must be averred, or the declaration will be bad upon demurrer.[4]

The declaration must set forth the contract substantially, at least, and the practice is to set it out in *hæc verba*, although it is proper to set it out in substance. But where such a practice is permitted, it is the better plan to annex a copy of the policy to the complaint, and make it a part thereof by proper reference. The declaration must allege that the period *after* notice and proof of loss has elapsed, within which, by the terms of the policy, an action cannot be brought. In other words, that the plaintiff's action is not premature, and a mere general allegation that "the sum is now due," is insufficient.[5] A statement of evidence is not equivalent to the averment of a fact. The fact itself must be averred, and a declaration merely containing averments from which the jury might possibly be induced to find the fact, is not enough. Thus, in an English case,[6] the declaration stated, that the plaintiff made a policy of insurance with an assurance company, upon the goods, body, tackle,

---

[1] *Lounsbury* v. *Protection Ins. Co., ante.*

[2] *Henshaw* v. *Mut. Safety Ins. Co.,* 2 Blatch. (U. S.) 99 ; *Catlin* v. *Springfield Ins. Co., ante.*

[3] *Hunt* v. *Hudson River Ins. Co.,* 2 Duer (N. Y.) 481.

[4] *Bobbitt* v, *Liverpool Ins. Co.,* 66 N. C. 70 ; *Ripley* v. *Ætna Ins. Co.,* 30 N. Y. 136 ; *Glendale Woolen Co.* v. *Protection Ins. Co.,* 21 Conn. 19 ; *Murdock* v. *Chenango Ins. Co.,* 2 N. Y. 210 ; *Chaffee* v. *Cattaraugus Ins. Co.,* 18 N. Y. 376 ; *Worsley* v. *Wood,* 6 T. R. 710 ; *Tebbetts* v. *Hamilton Ins. Co.,* 1 Allen (Mass.) 305 ; but see *contra: Throop* v. *N. A. Ins. Co.,* 19 Mich. 423.

[5] *Doyle* v. *Phœnix Ins. Co.,* 44 Cal. 264.

[6] *Dawson* v. *Wrench,* 3 Exchq. 359.

apparel, etc., of a ship valued at £5,000; that the ship and freight were warranted free from average under £3 per cent., unless general, or the ship were stranded; that the capital stock and funds of the company should alone be liable to make good all claims and demands under that policy; and that no proprietor of the company should be charged, by reason of that policy, beyond the amount of his share in the stock of the company; that the company became insurers to the plaintiff for £1,500, and the policy was signed by the defendants, as directors of the company; and, in consideration of the payment of the premium at their request, the defendants undertook that the company should perform all things contained in the policy to be performed by them. The declaration then alleged, that the ship ran aground; that it was necessary for her safety to let go the larboard bower anchor and kedge anchor, and to cut away the cables from the anchors; that the anchors and cables were left in the sea, and lost to the plaintiff; that afterwards the ship was further strained, damaged, and broken, whereby the plaintiff sustained a general average loss. Second breach, that, the ship being strained and damaged, the plaintiff sustained an average loss on the ship, her masts, ropes, and cables, to a larger amount than £3 per cent. on all the moneys insured thereon, to wit, to the amount of £50 by the hundred for each and every hundred insured thereon, whereby the company became liable to pay to the plaintiff a certain sum of money, to wit, £200, being their proportion of the average loss in respect of the said sum of £1,500; and that, though the funds of the company were sufficient, the defendants had not paid the said losses. The defendants pleaded, that the anchors and cables were not left in the sea and lost; also, that the plaintiff had not suffered an average loss on the said ship or vessel, her masts, ropes, and cables, to the amount of £3 per cent. on all the moneys insured thereon. On special demurrer to the pleas: it was held, first, that the pleas were bad, the the traverses being too large.

Secondly, that the defendants were personally responsible, it being averred, that the funds were sufficient, and that it was not necessary to allege notice to them of the loss.

Thirdly, that the stipulation, that the ship and freight should be free from average under £3 per cent., was not a proviso which required to be pleaded; and that the second breach was bad, as it did not distinctly aver that the loss was more than £3 per cent. on the value of the ship.

Lastly, that the defendants were entitled to judgment on the second breach, notwithstanding the plea was bad.

Where a waiver is relied upon, it need not be alleged. It is sufficient to allege performance, and the waiver may be proved, although it is proper to allege the waiver, if it does not involve a ‑statement of evidence, but is not generally the practice.[1] An averment of a total loss includes a partial loss, upon the principle that the greater includes the less.[2]

Rule when there is other insurance and loss is less than entire insurance.

SEC. 493. When several policies are outstanding upon the same property, and the loss is less than the amount of the insurance, in the absence of any provision in the policy restricting the liability of the insurers, the assured may sue either or all of them, and recover the actual amount of his loss. If he elects to sue one or more of them he may recover the full amount of the loss of them to the extent of the sum insured, leaving them to seek such redress as the law affords from the other insurers;[3] but if he sues *all* of them, in several actions, he can recover no more than the actual loss; and if his claim is satisfied in an action against *one*, his suits against the others will fail.[4] But the fact that he has obtained a judgment for the full amount of his loss against other insurers, will not bar a recovery against the other insurers, *unless such judgment is also shown to be satisfied.*[5] He is entitled to judgment against *all* the insurers, unless the claim has been previously satisfied, but he can have but one satisfaction.[6]

If the policy expressly provides, or in the case of a mutual company, if the by-laws provide, that, in case of other insurance, the defendant insurer shall not be required to pay more than "such a proportion of the insurance as the sum insured" under such policy

---

[1] *Schultz* v. *Merchants' Ins. Co.*, 57 Mo. 331 ; *Ketcham* v. *Protection Ins. Co.*, 1 Allen (N. B.) 136.

[2] *Devaux* v. *Artell*, 4 Jur. 1135 ; *Gardiner* v. *Crossedale*, 2 Burr. 904.

[3] *Wiggin* v. *Suffolk Ins. Co.*, 18 Pick. (Mass.) 145 ; *Lucas* v. *Jefferson Ins. Co.*, 6 Cow. (N. Y.) 635. In case of double insurance, where there is a partial loss, the second insurers are liable for all that is not covered by *prior* insurance. *Watson* v. *Ins. Co. of N. America*, 3 Wash. (U. S.) 661 ; *Murray* v. *Ins. Co. of Penn.*, 3 id. 186. And the assured may elect to sue either underwriter, and upon recovery by him the other insurer is bound to contribute. *Potter* v. *Marine Ins. Co.*, 2 Mass. (U. S.) 475 ; *Thurston* v. *Koch*, 4 Dall. (U. S.) 348.

[4] *Ætna Ins. Co.* v. *Tyler*, 16 Wend. (N. Y.) 385 ; *Lucas* v. *Jefferson Ins. Co.*, ante.

[5] *Newby* v. *Reed*, 1 W. Bl. 416.

[6] In *Newby* v. *Reed*, ante.

"bears to the whole amount insured," the recovery is restricted to a proportional amount of the loss, according to the terms of the policy.[1]

Where the loss exceeds the insurance, the total sum insured is due and payable, without any reference to the value of the property saved,[2] but the declaration must set out the contract, and the recovery will be limited by its provisions.

Jurisdiction.

SEC. 494. While it is true that a corporation is merely the creature of the law, and in this country, except in very rare and exceptional instances of legislative enactment, State or National, has no recognized powers outside the jurisdiction creating it, except such as is conceded to it by the *lex loci* of such foreign jurisdiction;[3] yet, if it, through its agents, enters into contracts in such foreign jurisdiction, that are fully executed by the other party, it cannot avoid liability under the contract, even though its charter expressly provides that it shall do no business except in the State of its creation, upon the ground that its acts are *ultra vires*.[4]

The courts will not lend their aid to a corporation in thus imposing upon its customers, but will compel a performance on its part so far as it has become liable to perform under the contract.[5] Whether a court of equity would, upon proper bill for that purpose, brought by a stockholder, annul the contract as to any future liability, is, perhaps, an open question. The insurer, domiciled in one jurisdiction, cannot defend against a loss taken in another State, upon the ground that it has failed to comply with certain statutory regulations, which are made preliminary to its right to do business in such State,[6] as, that it has not taken out a license,[7] or complied with the statute as to the

---

[1] *Haley* v. *Dorchester Mut. F. Ins. Co.*, 12 Gray (Mass.) 545; also later, under new phase of the case, 1 Allen (Mass.) 536; 4 Bennett's F. I. C. 348.

[2] *Underhill* v. *Agawam Mut. F. Ins. Co.*, 6 Cush. (Mass.) 446; *Post* v. *Hampshire Mut. F. Ins. Co.*, 12 Met. (Mass.) 555; *Liscom* v. *Boston Mut. F. Ins. Co.*, 9 id. 205.

[3] *Liverpool Ins. Co.* v. *Massachusetts*, 10 Wall (U. S.) 566; *Ducat* v. *Chicago*, 10 id. 410; *Paul* v. *Virginia*, 8 id. 168.

[4] *Fane* v. *Ins. Co.*, 83 Penn. St. 396.

[5] In *Western* v. *General Ins. Co.*, 12 N. Y. 258, the defendant, a mutual company, established under the laws of New York, was held liable upon a policy issued upon property in Canada. *Korn* v. *Mut. Ass. Soc.*, 6 Cr. (U. S.) 192.

[6] *Union, etc., Life Ins. Co.* v. *McNillen*, 24 Ohio St. 67; *Hartford Live Stock Ins. Co.* v. *Matthews*, 102 Mass. 221; *Provincial Ins. Co.* v. *Lapeley*, 15 Gray (Mass.) 262; *The Manister*, 5 Biss (U. S.) 381; *Harp* v. *Goodnow*, 3 N. Y. 266; *Clay F. Ins. Co.* v. *Huron Salt and Lumber Co.*, 31 Mich. 346; *Columbus Ins. Co.* v. *Walsh*, 18 Mo. 220.

[7] *Columbus Ins. Co.* v. *Walsh, ante.*

appointment of agents,[1] or any other requirement, unless contracts made in defiance of the statute are declared void. But in Pennsylvania,[2] Indiana,[3] and in Kentucky,[4] it is held, that *where the statute is prohibitory*, the contract is illegal, and not enforceable by either party, and such is doubtless the rule everywhere. But where the statute is not prohibitory, such contracts are enforceable, if a loss ensues under them. But even in Massachusetts,[5] where it is held that a loss sustained under a policy issued by a company, before it has complied with the requirements of a statute, may be recovered, it is held that the company cannot maintain an action for the premium, or to enforce a premium note.[6]

Pleas.

SEC. 495. The insurer, if it relies upon special matter in defense, must set it forth by proper pleas, as such matter cannot be shown or relied upon under the general issue, as, when fraud is relied upon,[7] or a breach of any of the conditions of the policy, as a refusal to arbitrate.[8] The insurer must specially plead it in defense,[9] and, failing to do so, evidence of such special matter is not admissible. The special matter must be set forth with such certainty and particularity, as that the plea, on its face, *prima facie* constitutes a defense,[10] and the insurer can only defend as to the matter set up,[11] and the fact that evidence was admitted without objection, not warranted by the pleadings, will not defeat the plaintiff's claim. The plaintiff is entitled to have all such evidence stricken out of the case.[12] When, however, the plea or answer *denies* the matter set forth in the complaint, either generally or specifically,

---

[1] *Thornton* v. *Western Reserve Ins. Co.*, 31 Penn. St. 529; *Atlantic, etc., Ins. Co.* v. *Conclin*, 6 Gray (Mass.) 73; *Hartford, etc., Ins. Co.* v. *Matthews, ante.*

[2] *Thorne* v. *Travelers' Ins. Co.*, 5 Ins. L. J. 169.

[3] *Rising Sun Ins. Co.* v. *Slaughter*, 20 Ind. 520.

[4] *Franklin Ins. Co.* v. *Packet Co.*, 9 Bush (Ky.) 590.

[5] *Washington, etc., Ins. Co.* v. *Dawes*, 5 Gray (Mass.) 376.

[6] *Cincinnati Mut. Ass. Co.* v. *Rosenthal*, 55 Ill. 85; *Hoffman* v. *Banks*, 41 Ind. 1; *Ford* v. *Buckeye Ins. Co.*, 6 Bush (Ky.) 133; *Thorne* v. *Travelers' Ins. Co.*, (Penn. S. C.) Ins. L. J. 169.

[7] *Sterling* v. *Mercantile Ins. Co.*, 32 Penn. St. 75.

[8] *Dyer* v. *Piscatiqua Ins. Co.*, 53 Me. 118; *Dewees* v. *Manhattan Ins. Co.*, 34 N. Y. 244; *Caston* v. *Monmouth Ins. Co.*, 54 Me. 170.

[9] *Pino* v. *Merchants' Mut. Ins. Co.*, 19 La. An. 214; *Flynn* v. *Merchants', etc., Ins. Co.*, 17 id. 135; *Sussex Co. Mut. Ins. Co.* v. *Woodruff*, 26 N. J. 541; *Haskins* v. *Hamilton Ins. Co.*, 5 Gray (Mass.) 342; *Feeney* v. *People's Ins. Co.*, 2 Rob. (N. Y.) 599; *Fox* v. *Conway F. Ins. Co.*, 53 Me. 107.

[10] *Fogg* v. *Griffin*, 2 Allen (Mass.) 1.

[11] *Mayor, etc.,* v. *Brooklyn Ins. Co.*, 4 Keyes (N. Y.) 465.

[12] *Williams* v. *Mechanics', etc., Ins. Co.*, 54 N. Y. 577.

evidence is admissible to disprove any of the allegations so denied,[1] and, in Tennessee, it has been held that, under the plea of *nil debet*, evidence of fraud or false swearing, or any matter that goes to entirely defeat the defendant's liability, is admissible.[2] But, generally, the rule is, that the defendant must spread the matter of his defense upon the record, that the plaintiff may be informed of the matters which he intends to litigate.[3] If the defendant demurs to the declaration, he admits the truth of all matters stated therein, but, where a plea is filed setting up fraud on the part of the assured, the plea is not be taken as an admission of all the allegations of the complaint;[4] thus where the plaintiff sued for a loss, and the defendant denied that the plaintiff had any insurable interest in the property, it was held that the plea did not operate as an admission of the truth of the plaintiff's allegations as to the extent or value of the loss.[5] If the answer or plea merely denies the allegations of the plaintiff's complaint, no reply is necessary, but if special matter in defense is set up, a replication should be filed;[6] and if the plea is traversed, the defendant will be permitted to prove the allegations therein, even though such evidence would not have been admissible if the plea had not been traversed.[7] The plea of *nul tul corporation* cannot be plead except as to misnomer, or unless the corporation has been dissolved, as such a plea is absurd when the corporation appears, and yet pleads its non-existence.[8]

---

[1] *Greenfield* v. *Mass., etc., Ins. Co.*, 47 N. Y. 430; *Bruynot* v. *Louisiana, etc., Ins. Co.*, 12 La. 326.

[2] *Phœnix Ins. Co.* v. *Munday*, 5 Cold. (Tenn.) 547.

[3] *Weed* v. *Schenectady Ins. Co.*, 7 Lans. (N. Y.) 452; *Maher* v. *Hibernia Ins. Co.*, 6 Hun (N. Y.) 353; *Cassacia* v. *Phœnix Ins. Co.*, 28 Cal. 628.

[4] *King* v. *Walker*. 2 H. & C. 384.

[5] *Clark* v. *Western Ass. Co.*, 25 N. C. (Q, B.) 209.

[6] *Dayton Ins. Co.* v. *Kelly*, 24 Ohio St. 345.

[7] *Home Ins. Co.* v. *Favorite*, 46 Ill. 263.

[8] *McCullough* v. *Talledge Ins. Co.*, 46 Ala. 376.

CHAPTER XX.

WAIVER

Waiver implied, when.

SEC. 496. When the insurer, knowing the facts, does that which is inconsistent with its intention to insist upon a strict compliance with the conditions precedent of the contract, it is treated as having waived their performance, and the assured may recover without proving performance,[1] and that too, even though the policy provides that none of its conditions shall be waived except by written agreement.[2] Thus, in a recent Pennsylvania case,[3] where the policy provided that proofs of loss should be furnished within thirty days, and also that no condition of the policy should be waived, except by a general officer, it was held that, where, soon after the loss the secretary of the company notified the assured of its intention to rebuild, and interfered with the agent of the assured in making proofs, and told him not to make them, whereby they were not made within the time limited, the condition was waived and the company was estopped from setting up strict compliance as to time in avoidance of its liability. So where the by-laws of the company, or the policy, require that a written application shall be made, the company may waive the condition, and the issue of a policy, without a written application, is sufficient to establish a waiver.[4] So, where the policy or by-laws require that all questions in the application shall be truly answered, if a policy is issued upon an application in which any of the questions are left unanswered, it is not only treated as waiving the provisions of the policy or by-laws in this respect, but also the information which an answer to such inquiry should have imparted.[5] So, too, the production of proofs of loss, or defects therein, may be waived, and such

---

[1] *Greenfield* v. *Mass. Mut. Ins. Co.*, 47 N. Y. 430 ; *Merchants', etc., Ins. Co.* v. *Curran*, 45 Mo. 142 ; *Buffum* v. *Bowditch, etc., Ins. Co.*, 10 Cush. (Mass.) 540.

[2] *Van Allen* v. *Farmers' J. S. Co.*, 4 Hun (N. Y.) 413.

[3] *Ins. Co.* v. *Todd*, 83 Penn. St. 272.

[4] *Bahringer* v. *Empire, etc., Ins. Co.*, 3 T. & C. (N. Y.) 610.

[5] *Haley* v. *Dorchester Ins. Co.*, 12 Gray (Mass.) 545 ; *Com.* v. *Hide & Leather Ins. Co.*, 112 Mass. 136 ; *Dodge, etc., Mut. Ins. Co.* v. *Rogers*, 12 Wis. 337 ; *Dayton Ins. Co.* v. *Kelly*, 24 Ohio St. 345.

waiver may be implied from what is said or done by the insurer.[1] So the breach of any condition in the policy, as against an increase of risk,[2] or the keeping of certain hazardous goods,[3] or the prosecution of a certain hazardous trade,[4] or indeed the violation of *any* of the conditions of the policy may be waived by the insurer, and a waiver may be implied from the acts and conduct of the insurer *after* knowledge that such conditions have been broken.[5] Generally in order to establish a waiver by the insurer, its actual knowledge of the breach waived must be established, or proof of such a state of facts that it may fairly be said that it ought to have known thereof.[6] Thus, an insurer may waive the condition as to the time within which an action for a loss shall be brought, and this may be established by proof of anything said or done by it fairly inducing delay on the part of the assured.[7]

---

[1] See chapter 13, *Lycoming Ins. Co.* v. *Dunmore*, 75 Ill. 14 ; *Patterson* v. *Triumph Ins. Co.*, 64 Me. 500.

[2] *Viele* v. *Germania Ins. Co.*, 26 Iowa, 9.

[3] *Reaper City Ins. Co.* v. *Jones*, 62 Ill. 458.

[4] *Conn.* v. *Hide & Leather Ins. Co.*, 112 Mass. 136.

[5] *Planters' Ins. Co.* v. *Cowfont*, 50 Miss. 562; *Smith* v. *Glens Falls Ins. Co.*, 62 N. Y. 85 ; *Joliffe* v. *Madison Mut. Ins. Co.*, 39 Wis. 111; *Sherman* v. *Madison Ins. Co.*, 39 id. 104; as the payment of assessments upon premium notes, *Vial* v. *Genessee, etc., Ins. Co.*, 19 Barb. (N. Y.) 440; the prepayment of premiums, *Baehen* v. *Williamsburgh F. Ins. Co.*, 35 N. Y. 131 ; *Pino* v. *Merchants' Ins. Co.*, 19 La. An. 214; *Ide* v. *Phœnix Ins. Co.*, 2 Biss. (U. S.) 333 ; *Washoe Tool Co.* v. *Hibernia F. Ins. Co.*, 66 N. Y. 613 ; *Hambleton* v. *Home Ins. Co.*, 6 Biss. (U. S. C. C.) 91 ; written assent to assignment of policy, *Gilliat* v. *Pawtucket, etc., Ins. Co.*, 8 R. I. 282; service of notice of loss, *Beatty* v. *Lycoming F. Ins. Co.*, 52 Penn. St. 456; *Imperial Ins. Co.* v. *Murray*, 73 Penn. St. 13; of proofs of loss, *Owens* v. *Farmers' J. S. Ins. Co.*, 57 Barb. (N. Y.) 518; *Security Ins. Co.* v. *Fay*, 22 Mich. 467 ; *Dohn* v. *Farmers' J. S. Co.*, 5 Lans. (N. Y.) 275 ; *Cobb* v. *Ins. Co.*, 11 Kan. 93 ; *Globe Ins. Co.* v. *Boyle*, 21 Ohio St. 119 ; *O'Connor* v. *Hartford Ins. Co.*, 31 Wis. 160; written assent to other insurance ; *Carroll* v. *Charter Oak Ins. Co.*, Abb. Ct. App. Dec. (N. Y.) 316 ; *Baer* v. *Phœnix Ins. Co.*, 4 Bush (Ky.) 242 ; *Shurtliff* v. *Phœnix Ins. Co.*, 57 Me. 137 ; *Jewett* v. *Home Ins. Co.*, 29 Iowa, 562 ; *Peekington* v. *National Ins. Co.*, 55 Mo. 172 ; *Benedict* v. *Ocean Ins. Co.*, 1 Daly (N. Y. C. P.) 8 ; defects in application, *Farmers', etc., Ins. Co.* v. *Chestnut* 50 Ill. 111 ; in certificate of magistrate whether of form or substance, *Bailey* v. *Hope Ins. Co.*, 56 Me. 474 ; *Taylor* v. *Roger Williams Ins. Co.*, 51 N. H. 50 ; *Herron* v. *Peoria, etc., Ins. Co.*, 28 Ill. 235; alienation without consent, *Illinois, etc., Ins. Co.* v. *Stanton*, 57 Ill. 354 ; *Bachelor* v. *Peoples' F. Ins. Co.*, 40 Conn. 56 ; of condition as to countersigning of policy, *U. S. L. F. & M. Ins. Co.* v. *Ins. Co. of N. America*, 42 Ind. 588 ; *Hibernia Ins. Co.* v. *O'Connor*, 29 Mich. 241 ; or any condition of the policy, *Webster* v. *Phœnix Ins. Co.*, 36 Wis. 67.

[6] *Finley* v. *Lycoming Ins. Co.*, 31 Penn. St. 311 ; *Allen* v. *Vermont Mut. F. Ins. Co.*, 12 Vt. 366.

[7] In *Brady* v. *Western Ins. Co.*, 17 U. C. (C. P.) 597 ; 5 Ben. F. I. C. 132, WILSON, J., in passing upon this question, said : "The pleas to the court on the policy are : 1. That the policy is not the policy of the defendants. 2. A denial of the waiver before mentioned. 3. That the property in the policy mentioned was not burned and destroyed by fire. It will be better to consider whether a waiver or dispensation of the condition relating to the limitation of action has in law and in fact been proved, before considering it as a question of pleading. The policy is not under seal ; the evidence sustains a waiver in fact ; it remains, then, to con-

53

But a waiver cannot be implied unless the language or act of the insurer is such as fairly leaves the assured to understand that nothing

---

sider whether the waiver was or was not valid in law. It is said not to be valid, because, firstly, it was the mere saying or act of an unauthorized person; and, secondly, because it was by word only. What did take place amounts to this: Before the six months' limitation had expired, and while the plaintiff had a complete cause of action, it was agreed (and for the present we make no distinction between the company and Mr. De Grassi) that if the plaintiff would not prosecute his right at law until Mr. Scott returned from England, the defendants would pay the claim, and would take no advantage of the limitation clause in case the six months expired before the payment was made. If an action were brought upon this special agreement, the evidence would, I think, maintain it just as stated. There was no breach of the condition of the policy at that time; there was nothing, therefore, to prevent such an alteration of it as above stated, by the assent of both parties. *Goss* v. *Lord Nugent*, 5 B. & Ad. 58. The defendants would be liable to an action for breach of it. *Nash* v. *Armstrong*, 10 C. B. N. S. 259. But it is also available to the plaintiff as an answer to their plea. In *Pinn* v. *Reid*, 6 M. & G. 1, the judge at *nisi prius* held, in an action on a policy not by deed, that the not furnishing a particular statement of loss according to the policy might be dispensed with. In *Wing* v. *Hervey*, 23 L. T. 120, in appeal in chancery, it was held that, although the life policy not under seal was liable to be forfeited by reason of the person whose life was insured having gone to a foreign country, contrary to the condition of the policy, that this breach was waived by the company because after the breach the local agent of the company, at the place where the policy was effected, had notice of the breach and received the premiums as before the breach, stating that the policy would be perfectly good providing the premiums were regularly paid, and the company must be deemed to have had constructive notice by the express notice to their agent. In *Supple* v. *Cann*, 9 Ir. C. L. Rep. 1, to an action on a policy not under seal, the statute of limitations was pleaded, and the plaintiff replied, on equitable grounds, that a suit was commenced in chancery before the expiry of the six years; and the question arose there whether the premiums had been regularly paid, upon which the court ordered an issue at law to try the question, and that it would be inequitable to permit this defense under the statute not to be set up, and it was held to be a good equitable answer to the plea. In this same case another point arose which is very applicable. The plaintiff in his summons and plaint admitted the non-payment of certain premiums within the required period, and he relied upon the subsequent receipt by the agent of the company as amounting to a new contract for the revival of the policy, or to a waiver of the default. The company pleaded a specific mode contained in the policy, by which within a limited period after default the policy could be set up again. *Held*, that the parties were not precluded from waiving the lapse in any other mode they might agree upon. In *Armstrong* v. *Turquand*, 9 Ir. C. L. Rep. 32, on a plea of fraud to an action on a policy under seal, the plaintiff replied waiver by subsequent receipts of premium after knowledge of the fraud. *Held*, the policy was not absolutely void by the fraud, but only at the election of the company, and that, like a lease under seal, they might elect not to create a forfeiture, and that the replication was good. The case of *Lambkin* v. *The Western Assurance Co.*, 13 U. C. 237, does not apply, because the policy there was under seal, and the condition as to bringing the action within twelve months could not therefore have been dispensed with at law except by deed, and the dispensations relied on were by parol only. I think this waiver a valid answer to the defense which is opposed to it. If the plaintiff had not stated the waiver in his declaration, but had replied it as an equitable answer to a plea setting up the limitation, then, according to the case in 9 Ir. C. L. Rep. 1, it would have been a good replication. The ordinary defense which may be made to an action to enforce a claim forms no part of the contract between the parties. The agreement that it does, as Lord BROUGHAM said, in *Don* v. *Lippman*, 5 C. & F. 1, 'supposes that the parties look only to the breach of it. Nothing is more contrary to good faith than such a supposition, that the contracting party looks only to the period at which the statute of limitation will begin to run; it will sanction a wrong course of conduct, and will turn a protection against

further is required to be done by him. Thus, where the assignee of a
policy who had purchased the property insured, called upon the agent

laches into a premium for evasiveness.' In this particular case the parties did
contract expressly with respect to the period of limitation; but not more in this
case than in any ordinary case can it be said that the defendants looked only to
the breach, and not to the performance of the contract, as the substance of the
agreement between them and the plaintiff. I see no reason why the statutory
defense by lapse of time might not be expressly agreed to be waived for forbearance, or for any other good consideration, nor why such waiver might not be
replied to a plea setting up the defense; and I see no reason why it may not
equally be relied on against any conventional period of limitation. I think, then,
the waiver, if made by a competent person to bind the company, valid in law.
The further question is, whether the agent of the company had power to bind the
company. The contract of insurance was made by and through him; the premiums were paid to him, or to Mr. Scott, whose name is mentioned in the evidence, and who was acting in cooperation with him; the adjustment of the claim
was made, and the payment would also be made by or through him, for he is
named in the policy expressly as 'manager for the said company in Upper
Canada,' the company itself having its principal office in London, England; the
company have got the benefit of the forbearance which he bargained for, and
they are enabled to set up this condition only by reason of his bargain and conduct. If, therefore, there be no positive rule of law against such an agent having
power by his conduct and bargain to bind the company, we should hold the company to be bound. In some of the cases before mentioned the company was held
responsible by their agent's receipt of premiums after the defaults had happened; these were acts, as distinguished from a mere bargain and the agent's conduct in this case. The *nisi prius* decision in *Pim* v. *Reid* was not, however, an
act, but a course of correspondence by letter, and there a waiver was held to have
taken place. In the present case, too, it must also be considered that there was
something more than a bargain. there was a tender of payment made by the
agent of the company, and made without any qualification or reserve after the
six months had expired. We pass no opinion upon the evidence. We are obliged
to take it as it was given; nor can we tell what reason may have influenced the
company in setting up this defense. In actions on policies there are often reasons,
actual or supposed, which induce companies to claim a rigid compliance with their
conditions; and to jurors and judges who do not know the secret causes of such
resistance, the conduct of the companies appears to be somewhat 'iniquitously
legal.' However the real facts may be it is impossible for us to tell, but the company does appear to be in the unfortunate position we have referred to. Any
person would think that it would be better for the company to rely upon their
actual defense, such as fraud or arson, than seek shelter under a class of conditions which places their conduct in the worst possible light before the public.
It may be that fraud or arson is a serious charge, and that the setting of it up
might be prejudicial to the defense, if not well maintained by the evidence; but
how can such a plea, if pleaded upon reasonable grounds, be anything like so
hurtful to the credit of a company as the evasion of what seems to be a just
claim, upon the pretext of *ultra vires*, or upon any other of the many frivolous
defenses put forward so frequently by such companies. The argument for the
defendants, to be available, must be capable of being pressed to this extent, that
the company could equally claim the right to be acquitted from the payment of
this policy, if on the last day of the six months the agent had induced the plaintiff to stay his suit until the following day, on a promise that the claim would be
paid, and having thus put him over the six months, the agent then claimed to be
exempted altogether, because the action was not commenced within the six
months. It would require a strong argument to establish in such a case as the
present that such is the law. I think this agent, the manager for the company in
Upper Canada, had the power to stipulate for the indulgence which he got, and
to bind the company not to take any advantage of the plaintiff for the indulgence
which he gave to them." In *Walker* v. *Metropolitan Ins. Co.*, 56 Me. 371; 5 Ben.
F. I. C. 707, it was held that failure to require fuller proofs after defective proofs
had been severed, operated as a waiver of defects. *Monk* v. *Farmers', etc., Ins.
Co.*, 57 id. 281; 5 Ben. F. I. C. 288; *Pitney* v. *Glens Falls Ins. Co.*, 66 N. Y. 6.

and informed him of that fact, and the agent told him *to bring the policy and he would indorse consent to the transfer thereon,* which the plaintiff failed to do, it was held there was no waiver, because what the agent said was merely confirmatory of the condition, and required the assignee to do precisely what the policy required.[1] But if, instead of saying what he did, the agent had said " it is all right," or made use of any expression that indicated satisfaction with the change, without requiring compliance on the part of the plaintiff, a waiver would have been established.[2]

---

[1] *Equitable Ins. Co.* v. *Cooper,* 60 Ill. 507; *Lycoming Ins. Co.* v. *Updegraff,* 40 Penn. St. 311.

[2] *American Ins. Co.* v. *McLanathan,* 11 Kan. 533; *Hambleton* v. *Home Ins. Co.,* 6 Biss. (U. S. C. C.) 91.

CHAPTER XXI.

ESTOPPEL.

When insurer is estopped from setting up breach of condition.

SEC. 497. The insurer is estopped from setting up the breach of any condition of the policy, when, at the time of its issue, it knew that the condition was inconsistent with the facts, and the assured has been guilty of no fraud; or the breach of any condition *after* the policy was issued, if it has induced the assured to believe or rely upon it, that such breach was waived, whereby he has been induced to do any act at the request, or by the direction of the company, which he otherwise would not have done.[1] Thus, in the case last cited, the policy prohibited other insurance without notice and consent endorsed upon the policy, and the plaintiff procured other insurance, which was not endorsed. Whether the defendant's agent knew of such other insurance or not, *before* the loss, did not clearly appear, but *after* the loss, the agent informed the defendant of it, and, *knowing of the breach*, the defendant required the plaintiff to furnish plans and specifications of the building destroyed, which he did, at considerable expense, and it was held that this operated as a waiver of the breach, and estopped the defendant from setting it up in avoidance of its liability. "A party," said LYON, J., "cannot occupy inconsistent positions; and where one has an election between inconsistent courses of action, he will be confined to that which he first adopts. Any decisive act of the party, done with knowledge of his rights and of the fact, determines his election, and works an estoppel.

In the present case the defendant had an election between two courses of action, each entirely inconsistent with the other. It could have declared the policy void because of the additional insurance effected without its consent, or it could treat the policy as valid, and pursuant to stipulations therein, could require the plaintiff to furnish, in addition to the usual proofs of loss, plans and specifications of the building destroyed. With full knowledge of all the facts, it chose the latter course; and the plaintiff, at great expense to herself, complied

---

[1] *Webster* v. *Phœnix Ins. Co.*, 36 Wis. 67; 17 Am. Rep. 481.

with its requirements. This was a most decisive act on the part of the defendant—an act utterly inconsistent with an election to consider the policy void for a breach of any of the conditions thereof; and it seems very clear to us that the defendant is estopped thereby from insisting on a forfeiture of the policy.

It is quite immaterial that the plaintiff was also required by another insurance company, having a risk on her house, to furnish such plans and specifications. The requirement of this defendant in that behalf, as evidenced by the letter of February 7, 1873, written by its general agent, is entirely independent of any similar requirement by any other insurance company. But we do not see that the principle of the transaction would be any different, had the defendant joined with some other company in requiring the plans, etc., and had the same been furnished to such companies jointly. The act of the defendant would still be an election to treat the policy as a valid and subsisting contract."

So, where other insurance is required to be endorsed upon the policy, if notice thereof is given to the insurer or its agent, and consent is not endorsed, nor the policy canceled, further compliance is treated as waived, and the insurer is estopped from setting up such other insurance to defeat its liability upon the policy,[1] and the same is true where the *same* agent issues both policies; although consent is not endorsed upon either policy, yet, being issued with knowledge of the facts, the insurer is treated as having waived compliance, and is estopped from setting up non-endorsement in defense.[2] In all cases when the insurer, at the time when the policy is issued, *knew* of other insurance, and there is no agreement for its cancellation or non-renewal, or when notice is given that other insurance has been obtained, *it is bound either to endorse consent upon the policy, or cancel it*, or, failing to do either, it will be treated as having assented thereto.[3]

When the insurer issues a policy to the assured without any written

---

[1] *Planters' Ins. Co.* v. *Lyons*, 38 Tex. 253; *Osser* v. *Provincial Ins. Co.*, 12 U. C. (C. P.) 141; *Cobb* v. *Ins. Co. of N. America*, 11 Kan. 93.

[2] *Carrugi* v. *Atlantic Ins. Co.*, 40 Ga. 135.

[3] *Planters' Ins. Co.* v. *Lyon*, ante; *Hadley* v. *N. H. Ins. Co.*, 55 N. H. 110; *Westlake* v. *St. Lawrence, etc., Ins. Co.*, 14 Barb. (N. Y.) 406; *Potter* v. *Ontario, etc., Ins. Co.*, 5 Hill (N. Y.) 147; *National Ins. Co.* v. *Crane*, 16 Md. 260; *Farmers', etc., Ins. Co.* v. *Taylor*, 73 Penn. St. 342; *Goodall* v. *N. E., etc., Ins. Co.*, 25 N. H. 169; *Dayton Ins. Co.* v. *Kelly*, 24 Ohio St. 345; *Horwitz* v. *Equitable, etc., Ins. Co.*, 40 Me. 557; *Ins. Co. of N. America* v. *McDowell*, 50 Ill. 120; *N. E. F. & M. Ins. Co.* v. *Schettler*, 38 Ill. 166; *Van Bories* v. *U. S. L. F. & M. Ins. Co.*, 8 Bush. (Ky.) 133; *Washington F. Ins. Co.* v. *Davison*, 30 Md. 91; *Geib* v. *International Ins. Co.*, 1 Dill (U. S. C. C.) 443.

application, containing conditions inconsistent with the risk; or, if *after* the policy is issued it *knows* that its conditions have been broken, and afterwards it renews the policy or makes an assessment for a subsequent loss, *the insurer knowing the facts*, it is estopped from setting up a breach of such conditions in defense to an action upon the policy, and the assured may maintain an action for a loss under the policy, without seeking its reformation, as the doctrine of estoppel and waiver comes in aid of the assured.[1]

And the same rule prevails when the insurer *ought* to have known the facts constituting the alleged breach,[2] as, where the insurer sends its agent to examine the risk, and he, without fraud on the part of the assured, and having opportunity to ascertain the real character of the risk, failed to do so,[3] or where from the *nature* of the risk, or the usages incident thereto, the insurer was bound to know that certain things would be done, or articles kept, that were prohibited by the policy,[4]

---

[1] *Plumb* v. *Cattaraugus Ins. Co.*, 18 N. Y. 392; *Moliere* v. *Pennsylvania Ins. Co.*, 5 Rawle (Penn.) 342; *Rowley* v. *Empire Ins. Co.*, 36 N. Y. 550; *Mershon* v. *National Ins. Co.*, 34 Iowa, 87. "If." say the court in the case last cited, "the insurer receives the premiums *with full knowledge of facts* constituting a breach of one of the conditions of the policy, the right to insist that the policy is forfeited for that cause is gone." In *Viall* v. *Genesee, etc., Ins. Co.*, 19 Barb. (N. Y.) 440, the insurer made an assessment upon a premium note for general losses, after it had become aware of the fact that the risk had been changed and increased. It was held that the plaintiff might recover, notwithstanding the breach, the court remarking, "The insurer is estopped to say the contract is void, for they are not at liberty to *enforce the plaintiff's part of the contract* and then insist that the contract was void, immediately after it was made. Having taken its fruits, they must not be relieved from its obligations." *Carroll* v. *Charter Oak Ins. Co.*, 40 Barb. (N. Y.) 292; *Allen* v. *Vermont Mut. Ins. Co.*, 12 Vt. 366; *Phenix Ins. Co.* v. *Lawrence*, 4 Met. (Ky.) 9; *Kruger* v. *Birmingham F. Ins. Co.*, 83 Penn. St. 64; *Bryant* v. *Poughkeepsie, etc., Ins. Co.*, 21 Barb. (N. Y.) 154; *Ames* v. *N. Y. Union Ins. Co.*, 14 N. Y. 253; *Hodgkins* v. *Montgomery, etc., Ins. Co.*, 34 Barb. (N. Y.) 213; *Hibernian Ins. Co.* v. *Mahar*, 6 Hun (N. Y.) 353; *Guardian Life Ins. Co.* v. *Hogan*, 80 Ill. 35; *Roberts* v. *Continental Ins. Co.*, 41 Wis. 321; *Ætna Ins Co.* v. *Olmstead*, 21 Mich. 246; *Hough* v. *City F. Ins. Co.*, 29 Conn. 10; *Ins. Co.* v. *Wilkinson*, 13 Wall. (U. S.) 221; *Pierce* v. *Nashua F. Ins. Co.*, 50 N. H. 297; 9 Am. Rep. 235; *Andes Ins. Co.* v. *Shipman*, 77 Ill. 187; *Owens* v. *Holland Purchase Ins. Co.*, 56 N. Y. 571; *Sprague* v. *Holland Purchase Ins. Co.*, Ct. of Appeals (N. Y.) March 20, 1877, not yet reported; *Marshall* v. *Columbian Ins. Co.*, 37 N. H. 41; 4 Ben. F. I. C. 288; *American, etc., Ins. Co.* v. *McLanathan*, 11 Kan. 533; *Rathbone* v. *City F. Ins. Co.*, 31 Conn. 193; *McFarland* v. *Peabody Ins. Co.*, 6 W. Va. 425; *Withwell* v. *Maine Ins. Co.*, 49 Me. 200; *Columbia Ins. Co.* v. *Cooper*, 50 Penn. St. 331; *Franklin* v. *Atlantic Ins. Co.*, 42 Mo. 456; *Caston* v. *Monmouth, etc., Ins. Co.*, 54 Me. 170; *James River Ins. Co.* v. *Merritt*, 47 Ala. 387; *Ayres* v. *Hartford Ins. Co.*, 17 Iowa, 176; *Hartford Protection Ins. Co.* v. *Harmer*, 2 Ohio St. 452; *Southern Ins. Co.* v. *Lewis*, 42 Ga. 587; *Miner* v. *Phenix Ins. Co.*, 27 Wis. 193; *Winans* v. *Allemania Ins. Co.*, 38 id. 342.

[2] *People's Ins. Co.* v. *Spencer*, 53 Penn. St. 353; *Allen* v. *Vermont Mut. Ins. Co.*, *ante*; *Continental Ins. Co.* v. *Kasey*, 25 Gratt. (Va.) 268.

[3] *James River Ins. Co.* v. *Merritt*, *ante*; see cases cited in last note.

[4] *May* v. *Buckeye Ins. Co.*, 25 Wis. 291; *Citizens' Ins. Co.* v. *McLaughlin*, 53 Penn. St. 485; *Fowler* v. *Ætna Ins. Co.*, 7 Wend. (N. Y.) 270; *Hancox* v. *Fishing Ins. Co.*, 3 Sum. (U. S.) 132; *Fulton Ins. Co.* v. *Milner*, 23 Ala. 420.

as where the policy covers a shop, stock therein, or manufactory or
stock therein, that all articles necessary or usually employed in the
prosecution of such business will be used.[1] Thus, where a policy is
issued upon a stock of goods "such as are usually kept in a country
store," it is held that all such goods as usually form a part 'of such a
stock may be kept, although prohibited by the printed terms of the
policy,[2] and there seems to be no good reason why, if the store is *in
fact* a country store, and the insurer knows the fact, or knows that the
assured keeps certain prohibited articles, and no objection is made
thereto, or if he knows that, as a part of such a stock as the policy
covers, certain prohibited articles are *usually* kept, he is estopped from
setting up the fact that such articles are kept in avoidance of liability
under the policy, even though the words, "such as are usually kept in
a country store," are not used ; and in a recent case in Pennsylvania,[3]
it has been held—and we can but commend the court for the sensible
doctrine it has enunciated—that when a policy covers a stock of merchandise, which is in fact kept in a country store, although the words,
"*such as are usually kept in a country store*," are not employed, the
policy will *not* be invalidated by the keeping of articles embraced
under the list of hazards, *if the articles so kept are usually kept in such
stores*, nor by the keeping of an article *usually* kept in such stores,
although in the printed provisions of such policy, the keeping of such
article is specially prohibited.

---

[1] *Daniels* v. *Hudson River Ins. Co.*, 12 Cush. (Mass.) 416 ; *Mayor of N. Y.* v.
Exchange Ins. Co., 3 Keyes (N. Y.) 436 ; *Lubenstein* v. *Baltic Ins. Co.*, 45 Ill. 301 ;
Leavey v. *Central, etc., Ins. Co.*, 111 Mass. 540 ; *Haley* v. *Dorchester Ins. Co.*, 12
Gray (Mass.) 545 ; *Kreuger* v. *Birmingham Ins. Co.*, 83 Penn. St. 64 ; *Sprately* v.
Hartford Ins. Co., 1 Dil. (U. S. C. C.) 392 ; *Moadinger* v. *Mechanics' F. Ins. Co.*,
2 Hall (N. Y.) 490.

[2] See Sec. 63 and notes thereto.

[3] *Kreuger* v. *Birmingham F. Ins. Co.*, 83 Penn. St. 64.

CHAPTER XXII.

EVIDENCE.

Waiver may be shown.

SEC.. 498. When a policy has been issued, with conditions incon-sistent with the risk, it is competent for the assured to show that the insurer or his agent *knew* the facts, and issued the policy without any promise or understanding that the condition of the risk would be changed;[1] as, that other insurance existed upon the property,[2] that certain hazardous and prohibited articles were kept or used by the assured,[3] that the premises were devoted to certain prohibited uses,[4] that the title to the property was incorrectly stated by the defendant's agent in the application, or by the insurer in the policy, when the true state of the title was known to the insurer;[5] and in all cases, when

---

[1] *Roth* v. *City F. Ins. Co.*, 6 McLean (U. S.) 324; *Kreuger* v. *Birmingham F. Ins. Co.*, 83 Penn. St. 64; *Ins. Co.* v. *Mahone*, 21 Wall. (U. S.) 152; *Howard Ins. Co.* v. *Bruner*, 33 Penn. St. 50; *May* v. *Buckeye Ins. Co.*, 25 Wis. 291; *Hough* v. *City F. Ins. Co.*, 29 Conn. 10; *Geib* v. *International Ins. Co.*, 1 Dill. (U. S. C. C.) 443.

[2] *Planters' Mut. Ins. Co.* v. *Deford*, 38 Md. 382.

[3] *Peoria, etc., Ins. Co.* v. *Hull*, 12 Mich.; *McFarland* v. *Peabody Ins. Co.*, 6 W. Va. 625; *Reaper City Ins. Co.* v. *Jones*, 62 Ill. 458; *Winnans* v. *Allemania Ins. Co.*, 38 Wis. 342.

[4] *James River Ins. Co.* v. *Merritt*, 47 Ala. 387; *Harper* v. *Albany City Ins. Co.*, *ante;* *Campbell* v. *Merchants', etc., Ins. Co.*, 37 N. H. 35.

[5] *McBride* v. *Republic Ins. Co.*, 30 Wis. 562; *Caston* v. *Monmouth Ins. Co.*, 54 Me. 170; *Southern Ins. Co.* v. *Lewis*, 42 Ga. 587; *Hartford Protection Ins. Co.* v. *Harmer*, 2 Ohio St. 452; *Cone* v. *Niagara Ins. Co.*, *ante;* *Home Mut. F. Ins. Co.* v. *Garfield*, 60 Ill. 124; *Combs* v. *Hannibal Ins. Co.*, 43 Mo. 148; *Franklin* v. *Atlantic Ins. Co.*, 42 id. 456; *Rockford Ins. Co.* v. *Nelson*, 65 Ill. 415; *Atlantic Ins. Co.* v. *Wright*, 22 id. 462.

the policy contains conditions inconsistent with the risk, and the
insurer *knew*, or *ought* to have known the facts, it may be shown, not
to alter or vary the contract, but to show a waiver of those conditions
as applied to the risk.[1] In order to establish *knowledge* on the part of
the insurer or its agent, of the real facts, and a consequent waiver of
inconsistent conditions, it may be shown that the agent examined the
risk and *might have ascertained*, if he did not, its real condition;[2] that
the assured *told* the insurer or its agent, facts in relation thereto,[3] or
that the usages of the business involved the matters set up as a breach
of the condition,[4] or that the matters set up in defense, are usual incidents of such risks.[5] To avoid the effect of this evidence, the insurer
may show, if he can, that the matters alleged in defense were not
usual incidents of the risk, and were not discoverable upon an ordinary
examination of the risk, and that the insurer did not point them out

---

[1] *Witherell* v. *Maine Ins. Co.*, 49 Me. 200; *Aurora F. Ins. Co.* v. *Eddy*, 55 Ill.
213; *Ayres* v. *Hartford F. Ins. Co.*, 17 Iowa, 176.

[2] *Continental Ins. Co.*, v. *Kasey*, 25 Gratt. (Va.) 268; *Allen* v. *Vt. Mut. Ins. Co.*,
ante; *Michael* v. *Mutual Ins. Co.*, 10 La. An. 737; *Benedict* v. *Ocean Ins. Co.*, 1
Daly (N. Y. C. P.) 8; *Howard F. Ins. Co.* v. *Bruner*, *ante;* *Clark* v. *Manufacturer's Ins. Co.*, 8 How. (U. S.) 235; *Cumberland, etc., Ins. Co.* v. *Schell*, 25 Penn.
St., 320. In *People's Ins. Co.* v. *Spencer*, 53 Penn. St. 353, the policy covered a
stock of barley, malt and hops; stipulated: " The risk shall not be increased
without consent of the insurers." Insured used the premises for the purpose of
distilling whisky, which was an increase of risk. Insurers' agent examined the
premises before the contract was made. It was held a question of fact for the
jury to determine whether the agent ought to have known from the examintion he
made, or was told, that the premises would be used for distilling, and if he did
know it, the company must be held to have taken the risk with their eyes open to
the fact that distilling whisky, as well as brewing ale would be carried on in the
premises.

[3] *Moliere* v. *Penn. Ins. Co.*, 5 Rawle (Penn.) 342. In *Michigan State Ins. Co.*
v. *Lewis*, 30 Mich. 41, the assured was required to state the amount of incumbrances on the property. The defendant's agent drew up the application, and
although he was told by the assured that the mortgage was for $5,325, and
about seven years interest, he wrote, mortgage *about* $5,300. The court held
that the assured might show that the agent knew the facts, and if established,
the defendants were estopped from setting up such misstatement in defense.
The same rule was adopted in *Peoria, etc., Ins. Co.* v. *Hall*, 12 Mich. 202, where
the policy prohibited the keeping of gunpowder, but the agent issuing it knew
that it was kept by the assured. In Iowa, in numerous cases, the courts have
held that knowledge of the facts by the insurer or its agent, at the time when the
risk was taken, estopped it from setting up a misstatement in reference thereto,
without fraud on the part of the assured, in defense, and such is the doctrine
generally held. *Ayres* v. *Home Ins. Co.*, 21 Iowa, 185; *Merchon* v. *National Ins.
Co.*, 34 Iowa, 87; *McFee* v. *S. C. Ins. Co.*, 2 McCord (S. C.) 503; *Phenix Ins. Co.*
v. *Lawrence*, 4 Met. (Ky.) 9; *Viall* v. *Genessee, etc., Ins. Co.*, 19 Barb. (N. Y.)
440; *Rowley* v. *Empire Ins. Co.*, 36 N. Y. 556; *McFarland* v. *Peabody Ins. Co.*, 6
W. Va 425; *Campbell* v. *Merchants', etc., Ins. Co.*, 37 N. H. 35; *Witherell* v.
Maine Ins. Co., 49 Me. 200; *Franklin* v. *Atlantic Ins. Co.*, 42 Mo. 486; *McBride*
y. *Republic Ins. Co.*, 30 Wis. 562; *Rockford Ins. Co.* v. *Nelson*, 65 Ill. 415; *American Cent'l Ins. Co.* v. *McLanathan*, 11 Kan. 533.

[4] *May* v. *Buckeye Ins. Co.*, *ante*.

[5] *Peoria, etc., Ins. Co.* v. *Hall*.

to the examiner,[1] or that the insured did not describe the true condi_
tion of the risk, and that the description given by him did not neces_
sarily involve a breach of the conditions of the policy. Whether, when
the insurer knows, or *ought* to know the true state of the risk, the fact
that the assured himself made out the application and *misdescribed* it,
operates to overcome the effect of the insurer's knowledge of the facts
is not free from doubt. Many respectable authorities can be found to
sustain either position. Thus, in New York, the negative of the propo_
sition seems to be established,[2] and nearly *all* the cases seem to lay
stress upon the fact that the application was made by the agent of the
insurer, who, knowing the facts, misstated them,[3] and, by inference, at
least, to hold that if the application had been made by the assured
himself, knowledge of the real condition of the risk would not estop
the insurer from setting up such matters in defense.[4] But, upon prin_
ciple, it would seem that a person, in law, cannot rely upon a warranty
that he *knows* to be false, nor upon a statement that *he knows to be a lie.*[5]
Under such circumstances the insurer cannot claim that he has been
misled, and to permit him to issue a policy, and take the benefits of
the contract, *knowing* that he is not bound thereby, and with a precon-
ceived intention of disputing his liability, is aiding a fraud on his
part, generally, upon a person who intended no fraud upon him, and
who has innocently been led into making the misstatement. Such a
doctrine is at variance with the principles that underlie the doctrine of
warranty, of which the sale of a *blind horse* is an apt illustration, and
is repugnant to that sense of justice and morality that should underlie
the law, and in several cases a contrary doctrine has in effect been
held.[6] But the practitioner must remember that the great weight of

---

[1] *Allen* v. *Vt. Mut. Ins. Co., ante.*

[2] *Rohrback* v. *Germania F. Ins. Co., ante; Sprague* v. *Holland Purchase Ins.
Co., ante.*

[3] *Roth* v. *City F. Ins. Co., ante; McFarland* v. *Peabody Ins. Co.,* 6 W. Va. 425 ;
Campbell v. *Merchants', etc., Ins. Co.,* 37 N. H. 35 ; *Hodgkins* v. *Montgomery, etc.,
Ins. Co.,* 34 Barb. (N. Y.) 213 ; *Cane* v. *Niagara Ins. Co., ante; Sprague* v. *Holland Purchase Ins. Co., ante; Kreuger* v. *Birmingham Ins. Co., ante; James
River Ins. Co.* v. *Merritt, ante; Cumberland, etc., Ins. Co.* v. *Schell, ante; Plumb*
v. *Cattaraugus, etc., Ins. Co.,* 18 N. Y. 392 ; *Rowley* v. *Empire Ins. Co.,* 36 N. Y.
550 ; *Carroll* v. *Charter Oak Ins. Co.,* 40 Barb. (N. Y.) 292 ; *Ayres* v. *Hartford F.
Ins. Co.,* 17 Iowa, 176 ; *Atlantic Ins. Co* v. *Wright,* 22 Ill. 462 ; *Hartford Protection Ins. Co.* v. *Harmer,* 2 Ohio St. 452 ; *Mechler* v. *Phœnix Ins. Co.,* 38 Wis. 665.

[4] *Roth* v. *City F. Ins. Co.,* 6 McLean (U. S.) 324 ; *Continental Ins. Co.* v. *Kasey,
ante.*

[5] *Cole* v. *Boland,* 22 Penn. St. 431.

[6] *M$_c$Fee* v. *U. S. Ins. Co.,* 2 McCord (S. C.) 503 ; *Beal* v. *Park F. Ins. Co.,* 16
Wis. 241 ; *Phœnix Ins. Co.* v. *Lawrence,* 4 Met. (Ky.) 9 ; *Patton* v. *Manuf. Ins.
Co.,* 40 N. H. 375 ; *Kreuger* v. *Birmingham F. Ins. Co,* 83 Penn. St. 64 ; *With-*

authority sustains the negative of the proposition, but gradually the courts are approaching a more equitable position.

Value of property.

SEC. 499. Witnesses may be called, in the absence of other trust-worthy sources of information, who are engaged in the same business, and who keep similar stocks of goods, at the same place, to show the average amount of stock, kept by merchants in that place, previous to and at the time of the loss, as tending to establish the value of the stock lost.[1] So, too, it has been held competent to show by a person engaged in a store adjoining the one in which the loss occurred, which was of equal size with the other, and in which a similar stock was kept, what the value of the stock kept in such other store was, as tending to establish the value of the stock destroyed.[2] So, where the assured has attempted to establish the value of the goods destroyed, by the amount for which he sold similar goods just prior to the fire, it is competent for the insurer to show that they were sold on a long credit, or to be paid for in other property, and that, on that account, a greater price was charged therefor.[3] So, the failure of the assured to call his clerks to testify as to the value of the stock, is proper to be considered by the jury, unless satisfactorily explained.[4]

In order to establish the damage to property, it is proper to show the nature, character, quality and purposes thereof, and to show that the goods, although left intact, and apparently not seriously injured, are, nevertheless, rendered worthless for the purposes for which they were designed, either by the action of heat, smoke, water, or other cause, of which fire is the proximate cause.[5] If the insurer, previously to the fire, offered to sell the property, it is competent to show the *price* at which he offered to sell it, and if the articles are merchandise, it is competent either for the assured or the insurer to show the price at which the assured was selling the goods just previous to the fire.[6] So it is competent to prove the *cost* of the goods, either by the assured or

---

erell v. *Maine Ins. Co.*, 49 Me. 200 ; *Carroll* v. *Charter Oak Ins. Co.*, 40 Barb. (N. Y.) 392 ; *Columbia Ins. Co.* v. *Cooper*, 50 Penn. St. 331 ; *Winans* v. *Allemania Ins. Co.*, 38 Wis. 342.

[1] *Ins. Co.* v. *Weedes*, 11 Wall (U. S.) 439 ; *Howard* v. *City F. Ins. Co.*, 4 Den. (N. Y.) 502.

[2] *Howard* v. *City F. Ins. Co.*, *ante.*

[3] *Sturm* v. *Williams*. 6 J. & S. (N. Y.) 325.

[4] *Fowler* v. *Old North State Ins. Co.*, 74 N. C. 89.

[5] *Bradford* v. *Boylston F. Ins. Co.*, 11 Peck. (Mass.) 162.

[6] *Hersey* v. *Merrimac, etc., Ins. Co.*, 27 N. H. 149.

any person knowing the facts;[1] and their condition and value may be shown by any person having the means of knowing.[2] So it may be shown that the price of such goods has materially diminished since their purchase, or that it has materially increased, and, as a means of settling their value, the market price of such goods in the markets where the assured usually purchases, or within a reasonable distance of the place of loss, may be shown, as well as the cost of transportation and other expenses that properly form an element of value at the place of loss, and, in view of all the evidence, it is for the jury to say what the loss in fact is.[3]

It is the *value* of the goods at the time and place of loss, that determines the measure of recovery, and it is not competent to show that the goods have not been paid for, that the duties are unpaid, etc., with a view to a reduction of the value. These facts do not affect the value of the goods.[4]

In reference to building, it is proper to show its age and condition, the purposes to which it was devoted, its rental value, and as an element in arriving at its value,[5] the cost of a new building of the same class, dimensions and style. It is then for the jury to say whether the old building was worth less than a new one, and if so, how much, and the difference deducted from the cost of the new, gives the value of the loss.

Damages resulting from non-occupancy, while the building is being reinstated or repaired, or for extra wages paid during non-occupancy, are not recoverable, and cannot be shown, unless the policy expressly covers such losses.[6] If the assured owns the building, but not the land on which it stands, the *intrinsic* value of the building is the measure of recovery.[7] If the policy covers a leasehold interest, the value of the unexpired term may be shown, and is the measure of recovery.[8] If a building is injured, but not totally destroyed, the test

---

[1] *Continental Ins. Co.* v. *Horton,* 28 Mich. 173.

[2] *City F. Ins. Co.* v. *Carrugi,* 41 Ga. 660.

[3] *Rogers* v. *Mechanics' Ins. Co.,* 2 Story (U. S.) 173.

[4] *Wolfe* v. *Howard Ins. Co.,* 7 N. Y. 583 ; *Equitable Ins. Co.* v. *Quinn,* 11 L. C. 170 ; *Savage* v. *Com. Ins. Co.,* 36 N. Y. 655. A purchaser of personal property, although he has not paid the price thereof, and has left them in the hands of the vender to be sold for him, has an insurable interest therein. *Franklin F. Ins. Co.* v. *Vaughan,* 92 U. S. 516.

[5] *Hotchkiss* v. *Germania Ins. Co.,* 5 Hun (N. Y. S. C.) 776.

[6] *Menzies* v. *North British Ins. Co.,* 9 C. C. (Sc.) 694. See *Niblo* v. *N. American Ins. Co.,* 1 Sand. (N. Y.) 551.

[7] *Laurent* v. *Chatham Ins. Co.,* 1 Hall (N. Y.) 40.

[8] *Niblo* v. *N. American Ins. Co., ante.*

of loss is the cost of repair;[1] and in the case of goods, the difference between the value of the goods, sound and injured, is the measure,[2] and in the case of machinery, it may be shown what new machinery would cost, whether the injured machinery is of any value as such, the actual age and condition of the machinery at the time of loss, and from this evidence the jury are to say whether new machinery would be worth more to the assured for the purposes of his business than the old, and if so, how much, and the difference deducted from the expense of the new gives the cash value of the loss.[3]

In an action in the name of the assignee of a policy, neither his declarations nor those of his assignor, as to the contents of the building, or the cause of the fire, are admissible in evidence against him.[4]

How powers of agent may be shown.

SEC. 500. Of course where the assured relies upon the knowledge of the agent of the true condition of the risk, as amounting to a waiver of inconsistent conditions, the burden is upon him to show that the agent had real or apparent authority to waive the conditions. In order to establish his authority, it is proper to show what his real authority is, but this is by no means the test. The assured has a right to rely upon his apparent authority, and, unless the circumstances are such as to put him upon inquiry, he is not bound to enquire as to his special powers. It is sufficient, without other proof, to show that he was a general agent of the company, and in a recent case in Pennsylvania,[5] it was held that proof that a person has been appointed "agent and surveyor," is sufficient to show him a general agent, and that the word surveyor cannot be regarded as limiting the word agent. The fact that a person is appointed "agent," *prima facie* at least, establishes his authority to act for and in the place of the principal in reference to all matters usually entrusted to agents. But, if there is anything calculated to put the assured upon inquiry, as to his powers, he is bound to make inquiry at his peril. Thus, it is competent for the insurer to show that the assured knew, or ought to have known, that the agent was only invested with special powers, as to take applications and forward them to his principal for acceptance or rejection,[6] and had no

---

[1] *Western Mass. Ins. Co.* v. *Transportation Co.*, 12 Wall. (U. S.) 201.

[2] *Hoffman* v. *Western, etc., Ins Co.*, 1 La. An. 216.

[3] *Vance* v. *Forster*, 2 Craw. & D. (Ir.) 118.

[4] *Kingsley* v. *N. E. Mut. F. Ins. Co.*, 8 Cush. (Mass.) 404.

[5] *Lycoming Ins. Co.* v. *Woodworth*, 81 Penn. St. 223.

[6] *Ayres* v. *Hartford Ins. Co.*, 17 Iowa, 176.

authority to make a final contract. On the other hand, it is competent for the assured to show what the agent did, or claimed to be authorized to do, and, if the insurer ever adopted similar acts, or if they were not beyond the scope of his *apparent* authority, the insurer is bound thereby.[1] Thus, where an agent is authorized to take risks in one place, it is presumed that he had authority to take them anywhere, and a risk taken by him outside his real jurisdiction, will be binding upon the company.[2] So, where it is shown that an agent had authority to make a contract of insurance, it is presumed that he had authority to make such a contract as he chose, hence that he might waive any conditions of the policy, or add new ones thereto.[3]

Limitations upon the authority of an agent have no effect upon the rights of the assured, unless he knew, or ought to have known thereof,[4] and, if the act relied upon by the assured is within the scope of the agent's apparent authority, the insurer will not be permitted to show that he had not authority in fact, as, where an agent has authority to take risks and issue policies, that he is limited to a certain amount on certain classes of risks,[5] or was not authorized to consent to other insurances,[6] or to an alienation of the property and assignment of the policy,[7] or to an increase of risks,[8] or any other act that is an incident to the power to contract, or within the scope of his apparent authority, or that is usually intrusted to agents in that business.[9] The assured may also show that the assured has, in other instances permitted the agent to exercise extraordinary powers, as to settle losses and draw drafts upon it therefor,[10] or to alter policies,[11] or do any other act or

---

[1] The authority of an agent cannot be questioned when the acts of the company have been such as to amount to a recognition of his agency; and evidence that a person effected the insurance, paid the premium, received the policy, and generally was recognized as agent, the company is estopped from denying it. *Swan* v. *Liv., Lon. & Globe Ins. Co.*, 52 Miss. 704.

[2] *Lightbody* v. *N. America Ins. Co.*, 23 Wend. (N. Y.) 18; *Ætna Ins. Co.* v. *Maguire*, 51 Ill. 342.

[3] *Washington Ins. Co.* v. *Davidson*, 30 Md. 91; *Geib* v. *International Ins. Co.*, 25 Barb. (N. Y.) 189.

[4] *Keenan* v. *Missouri Ins. Co.*, 12 Iowa, 126; *Ætna Ins. Co.* v. *Maguire, ante; Lightbody* v. *N. America Ins. Co., ante.*

[5] *Hartford F. Ins. Co.* v. *Farrish*, 5 Ins. L. J. 46.

[6] *Carrugi* v. *Atlantic Ins. Co.*, 40 Ga. 135.

[7] *Illinois Ins. Co.* v. *Stanton*, 57 Ill. 354.

[8] *Viele* v. *Germania F. Ins. Co.*, 26 Iowa, 9.

[9] *Frazer* v. *Gallway*, F. D. (Sc.) 298; *Farmers' Ins. Co.* v. *Taylor*, 73 Penn. St. 342; *Fayles* v. *National Ins. Co.*, 49 Mo. 380.

[10] *Fayles* v. *National Ins. Co.. ante.*

[11] *Washington Ins. Co.* v. *Davidson, ante.*

thing relating to the business, and acquiescence by the insurer in these. acts, sufficiently establishes the agent's authority to warrant the assured in relying upon the agent's authority to do them again.[1]

Usage and Custom.

SEC. 501. Not only is the insurer bound by all customs, prevailing in reference either to the business or property insured, or in reference to the construction or conditions of the contract itself,[2] but also by all general or *special* usages incident to the risk,[3] or as to the methods and incidents of a certain trade or business, as that certain hazards are incident thereto,[4] or that certain practices exist among those engaged in a certain trade.[5]

If the policy is ambiguous, evidence is admissible to explain it, and this may be done, when necessary, by proving the course of business and the incidents thereof,[6] even though it does not establish or amount to a general usage,[7] for a contract may be established either by proof of *general usage*, or by similar acts of the parties in like cases.[8] But, neither custom nor usage can be set up to overcome a plain provision of a contract, as where the contract provides the mode of payment and delivery, a custom to pay and deliver in a different mode cannot be shown,[9] nor can it be shown to put an interpretation on a contract inconsistent with its language,[10] nor to vary it.[11] But, even though inconsistent with the *printed* conditions of a policy, an usage or custom may be shown, not to alter or vary the contract, but to show that such

---

[1] *Lungstrass* v. *German Ins. Co*, 57 Mo. 107; *Eclectic Life Ins. Co.* v. *Fuhrenkrug*, 68 Ill. 463; *Lightbody* v. *N. A. Ins. Co., ante.*

[2] Thus, it is competent to show that among insurers and owners of whaling ships, an insurance upon an *outfit* covers one quarter of the catchings. *Macy* v. *Whaling Ins. Co.*, 9 Met. (Mass.) 354. So, to show a custom in case of re-insurance to confine the warranty to the condition of the risk at the date of the original insurance. *Foster* v. *Mentor Life Ass'n Co.*, 3 El. & Bl. 48. The usages of a trade must be considered a part of the contract, and must be considered in construing it. *Hancox* v. *Fishing Ins. Co.*, 3 Sum. (U. S.) 132.

[3] The insurer is presumed to know what the incidents of a risk are, as what is commonly embraced as a part of "a stock in a country store."

[4] *Harper* v. *Albany, etc., Ins. Co.*

[5] *May* v. *Buckeye Ins. Co., ante.*

[6] *Fabri* v. *Phœnix Ins. Co.*, 55 N. Y. 133.

[7] 1 Duer on Insurance, 57; *Black* v. *Cal. Ins. Co.*, 42 N. Y. 393; *Bourne,* v. *Gatliff*, 11 Cl. & F. 45; *Clinton* v. *Hope Ins. Co.*, 45 N. Y. 460; *Rushforth* v. *Hadfield*, 6 East. 619.

[8] *Green* v. *Farmer Burr,* 2221; *Rushforth* v. *Hadfield, ante;* Backus' Abr. Trover, 663.

[9] *Duncan* v. *Green*, 43 Iowa, 679.

[10] *Marks* v. *Elevator Co.*, 43 Iowa, 337.

[11] *Partridge* v. *Ins. Co.*, 15 Wall (U. S.) 373; *Ins. Co.* v. *Wright*, 1 id. 456; *Cash* v. *Hinkle*, 36 Iowa, 623; *Barnard* v. *Kellogg*, 10 Wall (U. S.) 383.

conditions were waived, because, when an usage or custom, or an incident of a business is established, the insurer is presumed to know of, and to contract in reference to it.[1] It need not be shown that the insurer knew of the usage, but its existence must be established to such an extent that he *ought* to, and by the exercise of ordinary prudence would have known of it.[2]

Effect of printed rules, advertisements, etc.

SEC. 502. Where the company has issued printed rules in reference to the methods of its business, they may be admitted in evidence *against* the company without preliminary proof that the assured had ever seen them.[3] So where it has issued printed advertisements, prospectuses, etc., they may be introduced in evidence to show a waiver of certain conditions of the policy.[4]

---

[1] Insurers are presumed to know the incidents and usages of a business insured by them, and cannot be heard to deny their knowledge thereof. The law imputes such knowledge to them. *Hazard* v. *N. E., etc., Ins. Co.*, 8 Pet. (U. S.) 557; *Buck* v. *Chepeake, etc., Ins. Co.*, 1 id. 151.

[2] *May* v. *Buckeye Ins. Co., ante.*

[3] *Walsh* v. *Ætna Ins. Co.*, 30 Iowa, 133. In *Wood* v. *Dwarris*, 11 Echq. 493, the defendants plead that the policy was made upon the terms of a previous proposal and upon the express condition, that, if any statement in the proposal was untrue, the policy should be void; and that a particular statement was untrue. Replication on equitable grounds: that, before the policy was made, the defendants issued a prospectus containing a statement, that all policies effected by them should be indisputable, except in cases of fraud; and that the plaintiff effected the policy on the faith of such representation. Rejoinder: that the policy was made on the basis of the proposal; and that there was not, before or at the time of the making of the policy, any promise by the defendants that the policy should be indisputable except in cases of fraud, except that, before the proposal, the defendants issued the prospectus containing such statement. Held, that the rejoinder was bad; and that the replication was, on equitable grounds, a good avoidance of the plea.

[4] In *Steel* v. *St. Louis Mut. Life Ins. Co.*, recently decided by the St. Louis Court of Appeals, and reported 5 Cent. L. Jour. 158, the action was on a policy of life insurance. The policy contained a clause rendering it void if there should be a failure to pay any premium upon the day it was due. There had been such a failure, but to excuse it the plaintiff relied upon a clause in an advertisement which had been, during several years previous to its occurrence, issued by the defendant, and very extensively circulated, which clause read thus: "This company, having no desire to reap an advantage from the misfortunes of such of its members as may, through adverse circumstances, be unable to meet promptly their annual premiums, has made its annual life-policies, now in force and hereafter to be issued, non-forfeiting, by extending the full amount of the insurance over such period of time as the 'premium reserve' or 'value of the policy' will pay for, applied as a single premium for temporary insurance." This statement was followed by a table illustrating the plan. *The court held that the advertisement was admissible in evidence, and could not be excluded on the ground that it tended to vary by parol a written contract, and that, if brought to the knowledge of the insured, and he, in reliance upon it, failed to pay his premium when due, the defendant was estopped from setting up such failure as a defense to the policy.* It has been held in several cases that the terms of a prospectus could not be introduced to vary those of a policy issued after the prospectus had been published. In *Insurance Co.* v. *Rose*, 8 Ga. 534[?] a prospectus stated that failure to pay a pre-

Effect of acceptance of policy.

SEC. 503. A person receiving a policy of insurance is presumed to know its contents, and if through negligence, inadvertence or other cause, he omits to inform himself as to its provisions, he cannot thereby excuse himself for the violation of its conditions.[1] Thus in a New York case,[2] the plaintiff applied to an agent of defendant, for insurance upon a tenant-house owned by plaintiff, and situated on his farm, in Chautanqua county. The agent knew the house, its situation and value, having spent a night therein previous to the receipt of the application. The amount of insurance asked for was $1,200, and a three years' policy was issued by defendant for this amount.

Among the provisions of this policy was the following: "This company will not be liable for more than two-thirds the cash value of any building hereby insured." This provision was in very fine print, and in the same paragraph with a number of other provisions of various kinds. It was not noticed by plaintiff at the time, and did not come to his knowledge until after the destruction of the building insured, which happened October 4, 1871. Proofs of loss were forwarded, and the defendant refusing to pay the full amount of insurance, this action was brought, and a verdict for the full value of the building was rendered. Upon appeal the General Term reversed this judgment, holding that the plaintiff was bound by the conditions of the policy, and could not overcome their force by proving his ignorance thereof. "The omission to ascertain its contents," said MULLIN, P.J., in delivering the opinion of the court, "is gross negligence that cannot be allowed as

---

mium for thirty days after it was due would forfeit a policy. A policy taken out contained no reference to the prospectus, and the court held that the time to pay the premium was not extended thereby so as to render the contract enforceable when the insured had died, four days after the payment was due. See also, *Tarleton* v. *Stainforth*, 5 T. R. 695; *Galvin* v. *Jones*, 6 East, 571; *Rose* v. *Mut. Benefit Life Ins Co.*, 23 N. Y. 578. The decision in the latter case was shaken by an opinion delivered upon a motion for a rehearing. 24 N. Y. 653. The following cases will be found fully to sustain the doctrine of *Steel* v. *St. Louis*, etc., *Ins. Co.*, *ante*; *Wood* v. *Dwaris*, 11 Exch. 493; *Collett* v. *Morrison*, 9 Ware, 173; *Wheelton* v. *Hardisty*, 8 El. & B. 232; *Viele* v. *Germania Ins. Co.*, 25 Iowa, 1; *Henning* v. *United States Ins. Co.*, 47 Mo. 425; 4 Am. Rep. 232 (see, however, S. C., 2 Dill. 26); *Horwetz* v. *Equitable Ins. Co.*, 40 id. 360; *Thompson* v. *St. Louis Life Ins. Co.*, 52 id. 478. And the doctrine is certainly equitable and consistent with the principles applicable to estoppel. In the case of a waiver of a condition of a policy by a person having authority to waive it, it is held that a parol waiver is sufficient, and that a waiver may even be implied from the acts and conduct of such person. If, then, a waiver may be established by parol, why may it not be established by a written or printed circular issued by the insurer? Such evidence does not tend to alter or vary a written contract, but simply to show that the insurer has done or said something that estops him from enforcing certain of its conditions.

[1] *Pindar* v. *Resolute Ins. Co.*, 47 N. Y. 114.

[2] *Ervin* v. *N. Y. Central Ins. Co.*, 2 T. & C. (N. Y.) 213.

an excuse for a violation of its provisions by the one party, or to deprive the other of the full benefit of them."

Where a policy contains a condition that "nothing but a distinct specific agreement clearly expressed and indorsed on the policy, shall operate as a waiver of any printed or written condition therein," it is held to relate only to those conditions and provisions of the policy *which enter into and form a part of the contract between the parties, and does not include those stipulations that are to be performed after a loss has occurred.* Therefore, notwithstanding such a condition in a policy, notice and proofs of loss, or any informality therein, may be waived by parol, or a waiver may be established by the acts of the company or its agent [1] from the same class of evidence by which a waiver may be established in a case where no such condition exists.[2]

Defense of wilful burning.

SEC. 504. When the defense of wilful burning is set up to defeat an action upon a policy, the weight of authority, English [3] and American,[4]

---

[1] *Franklin F. Ins. Co.* v. *Chicago Ice Co.*, 32 Md. 191; 11 Am. Rep. 469. In a case recently decided in Pennsylvania, and not yet reported, *State Ins. Co.* v. *Todd*, it was held that a condition contained in an insurance policy, that no officer could waive the performance of a condition except by indorsement on the policy, will not prevent a general officer of the company from waiving a condition by parol, and the question is one of fact for the jury. By the terms of the policy "no agent or other person, excepting one of the general officers of the company (and then only by indorsement hereon made and signed by said officer) is authorized to waive, change, alter, or amend any condition or provision of this policy." The secretary having requested the plaintiff's adjuster to delay making out proofs of loss, pending estimates for rebuilding, thereby leading the insured to believe that proofs of loss would not be required within the time specified in the conditions. It was held that it was a question of fact for the jury whether there was a waiver or not. The terms of a policy stipulated that "if any incumbrance exists on the insured property at the date of this policy * * * and the insured shall fail to notify the secretary of this company thereof in writing * * * this company shall not be liable for loss or damage under this policy." An undisclosed mortgage existed at the time of issuing the policy; subsequently, through the same agents, the mortgagee's interest was insured under another policy, and eight months after a renewal certificate of the first policy was issued. Both policies were signed by the president and secretary of the company, and countersigned by the agents. It was held that the above facts, if not conclusive, were yet sufficient to warrant the jury in finding that the defendant had knowledge of the incumbrance. Pennsylvania, Jan. 12, 1877.

[2] *Taylor* v. *Merchants' F. Ins. Co.*, 9 How. (U. S.) 403; *Allegre* v. *Ins. Co.*, 6 H. & J. (Md.) 408; *Franklin F. Ins. Co.* v. *Coates*, 14 Md. 294; *Edwards* v. *Baltimore F. Ins. Co.*, 3 Gill. (Md.) 68.

[3] *Thunlétt* v. *Beaumont*, 1 Bing. 339; *Willmett* v. *Harmer*, 8 C. & P. 695; *Chalmers* v. *Schackell*, 6 id. 475.

[4] *Shultz* v. *Pacific Ins. Co.*, 2 Ins. L. J. 495, (Fla.); *Kane* v. *Hibernia, etc., Ins. Co.*, 28 N. J. 441; 20 Am. Rep. 409; *Huchberger* v. *Merchants' etc., Ins. Co.*, 4 Biss. (U. S.) 265. In *Butman* v. *Hobbs*, 45 Me. 227, the defendant set up in defense that the premises were burned either through the gross carelessness of the person insured, or fraudulently by design on his part. The court instructed the jury that the defendant was bound to prove beyond a reasonable doubt the allegation

favors the doctrine, that it must be established by the same class of
evidence as to quantity and quality required to convict the assured of

---

stated in the plea, and defined such doubt to be: "That if felt by an intelligent,
concientious and reasonable man would occasion mental distress if disregarded
by him, or such a substantial doubt as would hold in suspense the judgment of
an intelligent, reasonable, concientious man." The jury returned into court, saying that there was some doubt in the minds of the jurers whether this was
to be treated as a civil or criminal matter; whereupon the court instructed
them : "You must be satisfied of the truth of the matter alleged in the plea,
beyond any reasonable doubt." It was held the instruction was correct. But in
a late case decided by the supreme court of Maine, *Ellis* v. *Buzzell*, 60 Me. 209 ; in
11 Am. Rep. 204, the court held that in civil actions where a criminal act is set up in
defense, a preponderance of evidence is sufficient to establish it, BURROWS, J., saying:
  "We see no good reason for thus confounding the distinction which is made by
the best text-writers on evidence, between civil and criminal cases with regard to
the degree of assurance which must be given to the jury as the basis of a verdict. Greenl. on Ev. vol 3, § 29 ; Roscoe's Crim. Ev. p. 15 ; Best on Presumptions, § 190 ; Starkie on Ev. 1st Am. ed. Part 3, § 52, vol. 2, pp. 450, 451. It is
true, that this distinction has heretofore been carried into civil cases and applied
to suits in which it incidentally became necessary to determine, in order to settle
the issue which the parties were litigating, whether one of the parties had committed an offense against the criminal law. Hence have arisen in these actions
for defamation among others, a series of decisions which, if juries had acted
according to their tenor, would have been productive not unfrequently of very
unjust results. Practically we do not consider the form of expression used in the
instructions to juries in cases of this description as very likely to change the
result. We do not believe, if the jury in the present case found themselves
inclined to believe upon the whole evidence that the plaintiff was verily guilty, as
the defendant hath said, that they would have proceeded to assess damages in
his favor, because he might have started a reasonable doubt in their minds
whether he ought to be convicted of the crime and sent to the State prison, upon
that evidence, even had they been so instructed. The practical effect of such an
instruction would probably have been to eliminate the doubt from the minds of
the jury, not to change the result at which they arrived. But we think it best to
recognize what has been justly said to be 'well understood, that a jury will not
require so strong proof to maintain a civil action as to convict of a crime;' and
to draw the line between the cases where full proof beyond a reasonable doubt
shall be required, and those where a less degree of assurance may serve as the
basis of a verdict, where the juror instinctively places it, making it to depend
rather upon the results which are to follow the decision, than upon a philosophical
analysis of the character of the issue. We must remember, as remarked by
Roscoe, *ubi supra* that 'in civil cases it is always necessary for a jury to decide
the question at issue between the parties; however much, therefore, they may
be perplexed, they cannot escape from giving a verdict founded upon one view
or the other of the conflicting facts before them; presumptions, therefore, are
necessarily made upon comparatively weak grounds. But in criminal cases there
is always a result open to the jury which is practically looked upon as merely
negative, namely, that which declares the accused to be not guilty.' This is often
substantially deemed equivalent only to 'not proven,' and in cases of doubt it is
to this view that juries are taught to lean. *A greater degree of caution in coming
to a conclusion should be practiced to guard life or liberty against the consequences
of a mistake always painful, and possibly irreparable, than is necessary in civil
cases, where, as above remarked, the issue must be settled in accordance with one
view or the other, and the verdict is followed with positive results to one party or the
other, but not of so serious a nature.* In England there was a reason for carrying
the distinction thus made between civil and criminal cases, into suits of this
description—which never existed here—because there, as Lord KENYON remarked,
in *Cook* v. *Field*, 3 Esp. 133, 'where a defendant justifies words which amount to
a charge of felony, and proves his justification, the plaintiff may be put upon his
trial by that verdict without the intervention of a grand jury;' and so penal consequences might in some sort be said to follow the verdict in a civil cause. See

arson. That is, that the defense must be established beyond a reasonable doubt. But there is a growing tendency on the part of courts to adopt a more sensible rule so far as defenses to civil actions are concerned, by setting up matters of a criminal nature in avoidance of a claim. There would certainly seem to be no good reason why the same degree of rigor should be observed, as is essential in criminal cases. The reason for the rule in criminal cases grew out of the fact that the accused was not allowed to be heard in his own defense, and because either his life or his personal liberty was involved. In civil cases the *reasons* for the rule do not exist, and there would seem to be no good reason why the rule itself should be retained, and as pre-

---

note (a) to *Willmett* v. *Harmer*, 8 Car. & P. 695, in E. C. L. R. vol. 34, p. 590, and the cases there cited. Considering the universal presumption in favor of innocence, and the fact that whether it is presented directly, on the criminal side, or arises incidentally on the civil side, it is still the same question—guilty or not guilty—which is to be determined, it is not at all strange that those English decisions should have been followed in this country, though the reasons that operated there were wanting. *But we think it time to limit the application of a rule which was originally adopted in favorem vitiæ in the days of a sanguinary penal code, to cases arising on the criminal docket, and no longer to suffer it to obstruct or incumber the action of juries in civil suits sounding only in damages.* Nor in so doing do we deprive the plaintiff in an action of this sort of any substantial right. It is doubtless incumbent upon the defendant to 'make out' (as the phrase was in the ruling here complained of), *i. e.*, to satisfy the minds of the jury by a preponderance of evidence of the strict truth of the words he uttered. And the plaintiff is entitled to the full benefit of the presumption of innocence; for as was justly suggested by WALTON, J., in *Knowles* v. *Scribner*, 57 Me. 497 (where we held the complainant in a bastardy process against a married man not bound to furnish the same amount of proof of the defendant's guilt, as would be necessary to convict him if he were on trial for adultery, in order to entitle herself to a verdict and contribution from the father of her bastard child), 'it is more accurate to say that there is no preponderance unless the evidence is sufficient to overcome the opposing presumptions as well as the opposing evidence.' If the words said to be slanderous impute to the plaintiff the commission of a crime, the defendant must fasten upon the plaintiff all the elements of the crime, both in act and intent, and to do this he must furnish evidence enough to overcome, in the minds of the jury, the natural presumption of innocence, as well as the opposing testimony. But to go further, and say that this shall be done by such a degree and quantity of proof as shall suffice to remove from their minds every reasonable doubt that might be suggested, is to import into the trial of civil causes between party and party a rule which is appropriate only in the trial of an issue between the State and a person charged with crime and exposed to penal consequences if the verdict is against him. The doctrine contended for by the plaintiff did not prevail in the courts of New Hampshire or North Carolina. *Matthews* v. *Huntley*, 9 N. H. 150, per PARKER, C.J. ; *Folsom* v. *Brawn*, 5 Foster, 122 ; *Kincade* v. *Bradshaw*, 3 Hawks. 63. It is worthy of remark, that, with a very few unimportant exceptions, the cases in which it has been held, that to sustain a plea of justification the defendant in an action of slander must adduce such proof as would suffice for the conviction of the plaintiff upon an indictment, have been cases in which words used imputed perjury to the plaintiff, and in most of them, the matter more directly under consideration has been the propriety of regarding the plaintiff's testimony upon the occasion referred to, as evidence in the case, to be overcome by the production of more than one witness to prove its falsity—the necessity of showing that his testimony was false in intent as well as in fact—its materiality or some point affecting the truth of the charge, and not the necessity of proving the commission of the crime beyond a reasonable doubt."

viously stated, the tendency of the courts is to place this class of
actions and defenses upon the same ground as other defenses in civil
actions, and leave the jury to predicate their verdict upon a fair preponderance of evidence.[1]

Experts—testimony of, when admissible.

SEC. 505. The testimony of experts, or persons skilled in the business of insurance, is not admissible as to any matters of common
knowledge or observation, and of which the jury are as competent to
judge as the witnesses. It is only in reference to matters, a knowledge of which is alone acquired by a peculiar training, or by a peculiar
experience or knowledge, that experts can be admitted to testify.[2] Thus

---

[1] *Hoffman* v. *West. M. & F. Ins. Co.*, 1 La. An. 216; *Washington Union Ins.
Co.* v. *Wilson*, 7 Wis. 169; *Qualifiedly Schmidt* v. *N. Y. Union, etc., Ins. Co.*, 1
Gray (Mass.) 529; *Ætna Ins. Co.* v. *Johnson*, 11 Bush. (Ky.) 587; *Simmons* v.
Ins. Co., 8 W. Va. 474; see 2 Wharton on Evidence, Sec. 1245, 1246; *Wightman*
v *Western Marine Ins. Co.*, 8 Rob. (La.) 216; *Scott* v. *Home Ins. Co.*, 1 Dill. C. C.
(U. S.) 115; *Blaiser* v, *Milwaukee. etc., Ins. Co.*, 37 Wis. 31; *Regnier* v. *Louisi-
ana, etc., Ins. Co.*, 12 La. 336; *Matthews* v. *Huntly*, 9 N. H. 150; *Kincade* v.
Bradshaw, 3 Hawk. (N. C.) 63.

[2] In a case recently decided in the United States Supreme Court, and not yet
reported (see Albany Law Journal, Vol. 15, p. 407), the court, in *Milwaukee & St.
Paul Railway Co.* v. *Kellogg*, considered the question of "proximate cause." In
that an action was brought to recover compensation for the destruction by fire of
the saw mill of the plaintiff below, and a quantity of lumber, situated and lying
in the State of Iowa, and on the banks of the river Mississippi. That the property
was destroyed by fire was uncontroverted. From the bill of exceptions it appears
that the "plaintiff alleged the fire was negligently communicated from the
defendants' steamboat 'Jennie Brown,'" to an elevator built of pine lumber, and
hundred and twenty feet high, owned by the defendants, and standing on the
bank of the river, and from the elevator to the plaintiff's saw-mill and lumber
piles, while an unusually strong wind was blowing from the elevator toward the
mill and lumber. On the trial it was admitted that the defendants below owned
the steamboat and elevator; and that the mill was five hundred and thirty-eight
feet from the elevator, and that the nearest of plaintiff's piles of lumber was three
hundred and eighty-eight feet distant from it. Among the exceptions taken by
the defendants in the court below was that the court refused to permit the defendants to prove by witnesses who were experts, experienced in the business of fire
insurance, and accustomed by their profession to estimating and calculating the
hazard and exposures to fire from one building to another, and to fixing rates of
insurance, that owing to the distance between the elevator and the mill, and the
distance between the elevator and the lumber piles, the elevator would not be
considered as an exposure to the mill or lumber, and would not be considered in
fixing a rate thereon, or in measuring the hazard of mill or lumber. The court
said: "This exception is quite unsustainable. The subject of proposed inquiry
was a matter of common observation, upon which the lay or uneducated mind is
capable of forming a judgment. In regard to such matters experts are not permitted to state their conclusions. In questions of science their opinions are
received, for in such questions scientific men have superior knowledge and generally think alike. Not so in matters of common knowledge. Thus it has been
held that an expert cannot be asked whether the time during which a railroad
train stopped was sufficient to enable the passengers to get off (*Keller* v. *R. R. Co.*,
2 Abb. N. Y. App. 480), or whether it was prudent to blow a whistle at a particular time. *Hill* v. *R. R. Co.*, 55 Me. 438. Nor can a person conversant with real
estate be asked respecting the peculiar liability of unoccupied buildings to fire
Muloy v. *Ins. Co.*, 2 Gray, 241. In *Durell* v. *Bederley*, Chief Justice GIBBS said:

it is not competent to inquire of a witness what the effect is upon a
risk, by leaving a house unoccupied,[1] or whether a risk has been

---

'The opinion of the underwriters on the materiality of facts, and the effect they
would have had upon the premium, is not admissible in evidence.' Powell's Ev.
(4th ed.) 103. And in *Campbell* v. *Richards*, 5 Barn. & Adol. 846, Lord DENMAN
said: 'Witnesses are not receivable to state their views on matters of legal or
moral obligation, nor on the manner in which others would probably be influenced
if the parties had acted in one way rather than in another.' See also, Lord MANS-
FIELD'S opinion in *Carter* v. *Boehm*, 3 Burr. 1905, 1913, 1914, and *Norman* v. *Higgins*, 107 Mass. 494, in which it was ruled that in an action for kindling a fire on
the defendant's land so negligently that it spread to the plaintiff's land and
burned his timber, the opinion of a person experienced in clearing land by fire,
that there was no probability that a fire set under the circumstances described by
the witnesses would have spread to the plaintiff's land was inadmissible." Another
exception was the refusal of the court to instruct the jury as requested, that "if
they believed the sparks from the 'Jennie Brown' set fire to the elevator through
the negligence of the defendants, and the distance of the elevator from the nearest
lumber pile was three hundred and eighty-eight feet, and from the mill five hundred and twenty-eight feet, then the proximate cause of the burning of the mill
and lumber was the burning of the elevator, and the injury was too remote from
the negligence to afford a ground for a recovery." This proposition the court
below declined to affirm, and in lieu thereof submitted to the jury to find whether
the burning of the mill and lumber was the result naturally and reasonably to be
expected from the burning of the elevator ; whether it was a result which, under
the circumstances, would naturally follow from the burning of the elevator ; and
whether it was the result of the continued effect of the sparks from the steamboat, without the aid of other causes not reasonably to be expected. All this is
alleged to have been erroneous. The court said : " The assignment presents the
oft-embarrassing question, what is and what is not the proximate cause of an
injury. The point propounded to the court assumed that it was a question of law
in this case, and in its support the two cases of *Ryan* v. *The New York Central R.
R.*, 35 N. Y. 210, and *Kerr* v. *Penn. R. R. Co.*, 62 Penn. St. 353, are relied upon.
Those cases have been the subject of much criticism since they were decided, and
it may perhaps be doubted whether they have always been quite understood. If
they were intended to assert the doctrine that when a building has been set on
fire through the negligence of a party, and a second building has been fired from
the first, it is a conclusion of law that the owner of the second has no recourse to
the negligent wrong-doer, they have not been accepted as authority for such a
doctrine even in the States where the decisions were made. *Webb* v. *The Rome,
Watertown and Ogdensburg Railroad Co.*, 49 N. Y. 420, and *Pennsylvania Railroad Co.* v. *Hope*, 80 Penn. St. 373. And certainly they are in conflict with
numerous other decided cases. *Kellogg* v. *The Chicago and Northwestern Railroad Co.*, 26 Wis. 224 ; *Perley* v. *The Eastern R. R. Co.*, 98 Mass. 414 ; *Higgins* v.
Dewey, 107 id. 494 ; *Tent* v. *The Toledo, Peoria and Warsaw Railroad Co.*, 49 Ill.
349. *The true rule is that what is the proximate cause of an injury is ordinarily a
question for the jury. It is not a question of science or of legal knowledge. It is
to be determined as a fact, in view of the circumstances of fact attending it. The
primary cause may be the proximate cause of a disaster, though it may operate
through successive instruments*, as an article at the end of a chain may be moved
by a force applied to the other end, that force being the proximate cause of the
movement, or as in the oft-cited case of the squib thrown in the market-place. 2
Blacks. Rep. 892. The question always is, was there an unbroken connection
between the wrongful act and the injury, a continuous operation? Did the facts
constitute a continuous succession of events, so linked together as to make a natural whole, or was there some new and independent cause intervening between
the wrong and the injury? It is admitted the rule is difficult of application. But
it is generally held that, in order to warrant a finding, that negligence, or an act
not amounting to wanton wrong, is the proximate cause of an injury, it must

---

[1] *Joyce* v. *Maine Ins. Co.*, 45 Me. 168. "None of the inquiries," said TENNY.
J., "related to matters of science or skill. A witness cannot give his views on

increased by a certain alteration therein,[1] nor whether certain facts would have influenced the rate of premium,[2] or were material to the

appear that the injury was the natural and probable consequence of the negligence or wrongful act, and that it ought to have been foreseen in the light of the attending circumstances. These circumstances, in a case like the present, are the strength and direction of the wind, the combustible character of the elevator, its great height, and the proximity and combustible nature of the saw-mill and the piles of lumber. Most of these circumstances were ignored in the request for instruction to the jury. Yet it is obvious the immediate and inseparable consequences of negligently firing the elevator would have been very different if the wind had been less, if the elevator had been a low building constructed of stone, if the season had been wet, or if the lumber and the mill had been less combustible. And the defendants might well have anticipated or regarded the probable consequences of their negligence as much more far-reaching than would have been natural or probable in other circumstances. We do not say that even the natural and probable consequences of a wrongful act or omission are in all cases to be chargeable to the misfeasance or non-feasance.. They are not when there is a sufficient and independent cause operating between the wrong and the injury. In such a case the resort of the sufferer must be to the originator of the intermediate cause. But when there is no intermediate efficient cause, the orignal wrong must be considered as reaching to the effect, and proximate to it. The inquiry must, therefore, always be whether there was any intermediate cause disconnected from the primary fault, and self-operating, which produced the injury. Here lies the difficulty. But the inquiry must be answered in accordance with common understanding. In a succession of dependent events an interval may always be seen by an acute mind between a cause and its effect, though it may be so imperceptible as to be overlooked by a common mind. Thus, if a building be set on fire by negligence, and an adjoining building be destroyed without any negligence of the occupants of the first, no one would doubt that the destruction of the second was due to the negligence that caused the burning of the first. Yet it in truth, in a very legitimate sense, the immediate cause of the burning of the second was the burning of the first. The same might be said of the burning of the furniture in the first. Such refinements are too minute for rules of social conduct. In the nature of things there is in every transaction a succession of events, more or less dependent upon those preceding, and it is the province of a jury to look at this succession of events or facts, and ascertain whether they are naturally and probably connected with each other by a continuous sequence, or are dissevered by new and independent agencies, and this must be determined in view of the circumstances existing at the time. If we are not mistaken in these opinions, the Circuit Court was correct in refusing to affirm the defendants' proposition, and in submitting to the jury to find whether the burning of the mill and lumber was a result naturally and reasonably to be expected from the burning of the elevator under the circumstances, and whether it was the result of the continued influence or effect of the sparks from the boat, without the aid or concurrence of other causes not reasonably to have been expected. The jury found in substance that the burning of the mill and lumber was caused by the negligent burning of the elevator, and that it was the unavoidable consequence of that burning. This, in effect, was finding that there was no intervening and independent cause between the negligent conduct of the defendants and the injury to the plaintiff.

the manner in which others would probably be influenced, if the parties acted one way or the other. Therefore the opinion of a witness conversant with the business of insurance, upon a question whether a premium would have been increased by the communication of certain specified facts, has been held inadmissable." *Connell* v. *Phenix Ins. Co.,* 59 Me. 582; *Luce* v. *Dorchester, etc., Ins. Co.,* 105 Mass. 297; *Maloy* v. *Ins. Co.,* 5 Gray (Mass.) 541.

[1] *Jefferson Ins. Co.* v. *Cotheal,* 7 Wend. (N. Y.) 72. "Whether the risk was increased by the supposed alteration in the former construction of the mill," said

[2] *Joyce* v. *Maine Ins. Co., ante;* but *contra* see *Hawes* v. *N. E., etc., Ins. Co.,* 2 Curtis C. C. (U. S.) 220; see *Luce* v. *Dorchester, etc., Ins. Co., ante; Korn* v. *South St. Louis, etc., Ins. Co., ante.*

risk.[1] It is not competent to show what is generally understood among insurance men respecting the hazardous or non-hazardous character of

SUTHERLAND, J., "was not a matter of skill or science, so as to justify this description of evidence. * * * The witness was no more competent to judge upon that matter than the jurors were. The map of the premises was exhibited to the jury, and they heard the testimony of witnesses who had seen the mill and were acquainted with the usual and proper manner of erecting steam saw-mills. What was there in the supposed skill of the witnesses, acquired as president of an insurance company, to enable him to judge more accurately than the jurors whether the mill was more exposed to conflagration than it would have been if the boiler and boiler-house had been differently located? In my opinion there was nothing; the question was properly overruled. He was then asked whether, *from his own knowledge and experience*, the erection of the boiler-house increased the risk; this was also properly excluded, because the witness had already admitted that he had no knowledge or experience upon the subject. The secretary of the defendants, John Guion, was then called, and the counsel proposed to ask him whether the last renewal of the policy would have been made by him, if he had known of the change in the building by the erection of the boiler-house. It is obvious that this was merely asking him whether in his opinion the risk was increased by such erection. His opinion upon that subject was not legal evidence. On questions of science, or skill or trade, persons of skill in those particular departments are allowed to give their opinions in evidence; but the rule is confined to cases in which, from the very nature of the subject, facts disconnected from such opinions cannot be so presented to a jury as to enable them to pass upon the question with the requisite knowledge and judgment. Thus a physician in many cases cannot so explain to a jury the cause of the death, or other serious injury of an individual, as to make the jury distinctly perceive the connection between the cause and the effect. He may therefore express an opinion that the wound given, or the poison administered, produced the death of the deceased; but in such a case, the physician must state the facts on which his opinion is founded. 1 McNally, 329, 335; 8 Mass. R. 371; 9 id. 225. So ship builders may give their opinions as to the seaworthiness of a ship, from examining a survey or description of the vessel made by others, when they were not present. This is evidently a matter of mechanical skill. Peake's N. P. C. 25, 43; 1 Campb. 117. So an engineer or engraver may give his opinion on matters belonging to his particular science or art. 4 T. R. 498; 1 Phil. Ev. 227. The cases of *Durrell* v. *Bederly*, 1 Holt's N. P. C. 283, and *Berthon* v. *Loughman*, 2 Stark. N. P. R. 258, are more immediately applicable to this case, and are in direct conflict with each other. In the first case it was held that the opinion of underwriters, whether, upon certain facts being communicated to them, they would or would not have insured the particular voyage, could not be received as evidence; that the materiality of the intelligence or rumors which the assured was charged with having suppressed, was a question for the jury, under the circumstances of the case, and ought not to rest upon the opinions of mercantile men. This was ruled by Chief Justice GIBBS, before whom the cause was tried. In the case of *Berthon* v. *Loughman*, HOLROYD, J., permitted a witness, who was conversant with the business of insurance, to give his opinion as a matter of judgment, whether the communication of particular facts would have enhanced the premium. The cases are irreconcilable in principle, and I have no hesitation in expressing my concurrence in the opinion of Chief Justice GIBBS. It supports what I understand to be the true rule on this subject. 3 Stark. Ev. 1176, note; 4 id. 1737, 1738. The Chief Justice says: 'I am of opinion that the evidence of the underwriters who were called to give their opinion of the materiality of the rumors, and of the effect they would have had upon the premium, is not admissible evidence. Lord MANSFIELD and Lord KENYON discountenanced this evidence of opinion, and I think it ought not to be received. It is the province of a jury, and not of individual underwriters, to decide what facts ought to be communicated. It is not a question of science in which scientific men will mostly

[1] *Scottish Mut. Ins. Co.* v. *Turner*, 15 C. C. (Sc.) 33; *Lyman* v. *Ins. Co.*, 14 Allen (Mass.) 329.

a certain trade or business,[1] or whether a loss resulted from negligence,[2] or whether if certain facts had been known to the witness he would have taken the risk,[3] or whether he would under a certain state of facts have consented to additional insurance,[4] whether putting an additional number of stoves into a building increased the risk;[5] whether if certain facts had been known to the agent he would have issued a policy,[6] or would have communicated them to his principal.[7] And in all cases it may be said that unless the matters to which the witness is called

---

think alike, but a question of opinion liable to be governed by fancy, and in which the diversity might be endless.' In the case at bar, whatever might have been the opinion of underwriters, it was shown conclusively by witnesses acquainted with the mode of constructing steam saw-mills, and with this mill in particular, that the boilers were located, not only in the place where they were usually located in such buildings, but where the hazard of fire was much less than though they had been within the body of the mill. Against this evidence the bare opinions of all the underwriters in the city of New York, if they had been admitted, ought not to have prevailed with the jury." *Luce* v. *Dorchester Ins. Co.*, 105 Mass. 297; *Schmidt* v. *Peoria, etc., Ins. Co.*, 41 Ill. 295; *Lyman* v. *Ins. Co.*, 14 Allen (Mass.) 327; *Washington, etc., Ins. Co.* v. *Davidson*, 30 Md. 91; *Joyce* v. *Maine Ins. Co.*, 45 Me. 168. Upon this question there is some conflict, and there are cases in which it is held that the opinions of persons shown to be competent to do so, may be given, as to whether a certain state of facts, or rather condition of things, increased the risk. But generally it will, *Mitchell* v. *Home Ins. Co.*, 32 Iowa, 421; *Schenck* v. *Mercer Co. Ins. Co.*, 24 N. J. 447; *Kern* v. *South St. Louis, etc., Ins. Co.*, 40 Mo. 19; *Daniels* v. *Hudson River Ins. Co.*, 12 Cush. (Mass.) 416, be found that the instances in which such evidence was admitted, a peculiar state of facts existed, rendering it impossible for a jury to determine with accuracy whether the risk was increased or not. Generally it is required that the witness state *facts*, leaving the jury to draw the inferences therefrom, and, even though a witness is permitted to give an opinion, the jury are not bound to accept, but, from the facts, may find contrary thereto. In *Daniels* v. *Ins. Co., ante,* a witness was permitted to testify whether in his opinion a risk was increased by a partition erected in the building, and whether the erection of such partition created a necessity for keeping another cask of water in the room. In *Kern* v. *Ins. Co., ante,* whether the erection of a boiler, the location of the engines, and the erection of a wooden shed over the boiler, increased the risk, and required an enhanced premium. And upon the latter question, as to the admissibility of the evidence of experts as to whether the non-occupancy of a house involved an increase of the rate of premium, the case of *Luce* v. *Dorchester Ins. Co., ante,* holds that it is, and in *Mitchell* v. *Home Ins. Co., ante,* an insurance agent was permitted to testify whether in his opinion a certain change in the occupancy of a building increased the risk, and it may be said that the tendency of the later cases is towards the admission of such evidence *in all cases* where the question cannot, from the facts stated, be as well solved by a person not experienced in such matters, as by one who is, and perhaps the relaxation of the rule is not unwise, as the jury may, after all, act upon their own impressions, entirely ignoring the opinions of experts.

[1] *Washington F. Ins. Co.* v. *Davidson*, 30 Md. 91.

[2] *Ins. Co.* v. *May*, 20 Ohio, 211.

[3] *Sturm* v. *Williams*, 6 Jones & Spencer (N. Y.) 325; *Baker* v. *Scottish, etc., Ins. Co.* 28 Scot. Jour. 293; but *contra* see *Quin* v. *National Assurance Co.*, 1 J. & C. (Irish) 316.

[4] *Eureka Ins. Co.* v. *Robinson*, 56 Penn. St. 256.

[5] *Schmidt* v. *Peoria F. & M. Ins. Co.*, 41 Ill. 295.

[6] *Washington Life Ins. Co.* v. *Haney*, 10 Kan. 525.

[7] *Baker* v. *Scottish, etc., Ins. Co.*, 18 C. C. (Sc.) 691.

to give his opinion are properly matters of skill or science, the *facts* must be shown and the jury determine the result from them.[1] A witness, in order to be permitted to testify as to the value of property, must be shown to be competent to speak upon the subject. In estimating a loss under a policy of insurance, he cannot be permitted to state what in his opinion the value of the property destroyed was, from the mere fact that he has frequently seen it. He must be shown to be familiar with the value of such property, and his facilities for estimating its value must be shown,[2] and then he must state *facts*, leaving the jury to draw conclusions therefrom,[3] and the opinion of a witness as to value can only be permitted when he is shown to have peculiar knowledge thereof.[4]

Thus, a farmer, who testified that he had been in the store quite frequently, and was in there the day before the fire, from these facts alone, was held not competent, as an expert, to testify as to the *value* of the stock,[5] nor can a witness be permitted to state what his *impressions* were from a given state of facts;[6] as whether a claim is a legal one,[7] or whether the assured must have known of a certain condition of things,[8] or how certain matters are usually understood by insurers.[9]

The evidence of experts as to the meaning of terms employed in a policy must be confined to their meaning at the place where the risk is located; thus, where the policy covered " dry goods and groceries " the terms must be construed according to the sense of the words at the *situs* of the property, and not according to their meaning elsewhere.[10] In the absence of a stipulation as to occupancy, it is held in Mississppi that the evidence of an expert as to whether the risk is increased by being left vacant, is not admissible.[11]

It is competent for any person, whether an expert or not, to testify as

[1] *Mobile, etc., Ins. Co.* v. *McMillan*; 31 Ala. 711 ; *Washington, etc., Ins. Co.* v. *Haney*, 10 Kan. 525 ; *Lindaver* v. *Delaware, etc., Ins. Co.*, 13 Ark. 461 ; *Reid* v. *Piedmont, etc., Ins. Co.*, 58 Mo. 421 ; *Kendall* v *Holland Purchase Ins. Co.*, 2 T. & C. (N. Y.) 375 ; *Rider* v. *Ocean Ins. Co.*, 20 Pick. (Mass.) 259 ; *Van Zandt* v. *Ins. Co.*, 55 N. Y. 169 ; *Rawle* v. *Ins. Co.*, 27 N. Y. 282.

[2] *Terpenning* v. *The Corn Exchange Ins. Co.*, 43 N. Y. 279 ; *Norman* v. *Wells*, 17 Wend. (N. Y.) 136 ; *Lincoln* v. *R. R. Co.*, 23 id. 433.

[3] *Morehouse* v. *Matthews*, 2 N. Y. 514.

[4] *Clark* v. *Baird*, 9 N. Y. 183 ; ALLEN, J., *Terpenning* v. *Ins. Co., ante.*

[5] *Terpenning* v. *Corn Ex. Ins. Co.*, 43 N. Y. 279.

[6] *Higbie* v. *Guardian, etc., Ins. Co.*, 53 N. Y. 603.

[7] *Rider* v. *Ocean Ins. Co.*, 20 Pick. (Mass.) 259.

[8] *Perkins* v. *Augusta, etc., Ins. Co.*, 10 Gray (Mass.) 312.

[9] *Washington Ins. Co.* v. *Davidson, ante.*

[10] *Germania F. Ins. Co.* v. *Francis*, 52 Miss. 457.

[11] *Liv., Lon. & Globe Ins. Co.* v. *McGuire*, 52 Miss. 227.

to *facts*, relating to a material matter, leaving the jury to draw their own conclusions from the facts. Thus, it is competent for an insurer to testify what rates of premium are charged for certain classes of risks, but not whether a certain rate would have been charged for the risk in question.[1] So it is competent for a person not shown to be versed in the value of certain classes of property to testify as to its condition, the amount of it, and similar matters, but not to testify as to what, in his opinion, its value was.[2] It is not enough that the witness states that he had sufficient knowledge of the matter to satisfy his own mind in reference to it. It must appear that he had such knowledge of the matter as to enable him to give an opinion as an expert. His opinion must be based upon *facts*, and not upon mere conjecture,[3] and it is for the court, in the first instance, to determine whether the witness has such knowledge of the matter as to constitute him an expert, but his competency may be tested upon cross-examination, and it is for the jury, ultimately, to say whether they will credit his evidence.[4] A person who is not an expert cannot be permitted to testify as such, and even though the court decides that he is competent, yet, if the decision was not warranted by the facts, it is error.[5] If improper evidence is admitted, the error is not cured by afterwards instructing the jury to disregard it.[6] When the question calls for an inference from a supposed fact, it is not admissible, because it is the province of the jury to draw inferences from facts. In order to make the evidence of an expert admissible it must relate to facts or information peculiarly within the knowledge of an expert.[7]

General matters.

SEC. 506. Proofs of loss are admissible to prove the making and delivery thereof, but not for the purpose of showing the extent of the loss.[8] They do not form a part of the contract; therefore, where the assured has made a mistake therein he may show the mistake, so far as is essential to maintain the validity of his policy and of his claim. As, where the assured has made a mistake in his proofs as to the occu-

[1] *Joyce* v. *Maine Ins. Co.*, *ante*.
[2] *Terpenning* v. *Ins. Co.*, *ante*.
[3] *Higbie* v. *The Guardian Life Ins. Co.*, 53 N. Y. 603.
[4] *Gulf City Ins. Co.* v. *Stephens*, 51 Ala. 121.
[5] *Southern Life Ins. Co.* v. *Wilkinson*, 53 Ga. 535.
[6] *Lycoming F. Ins. Co.* v. *Rubin*, 79 Ill. 402.
[7] *Van Zandt* v. *Mut. Ben. Ins. Co.*, 55 N. Y. 169.
[8] *Knickerbocker Ins. Co.* v. *Gould*, 80 Ill. 388.

pancy of the premises insured.[1] When a party who has an insurable interest takes out a policy largely in excess thereof, it tends to show that the policy was taken for speculative purposes, and to render it void,[2] as a mere wager.[3]

When there is no dispute as to the facts, it is a question of law whether proofs have been seasonably served, but if there is a dispute as to the facts, it is for the jury to say whether the condition has been substantially complied with,[4] and evidence is admissible that tends to excuse delay, as that the insurer retained the notice and proofs of loss and made no objection thereto.[5] A liberal construction is given to all such provisions, and if there is any thing in the facts or circumstances surrounding the transaction that serves to excuse delay, it will be given due effect. Thus where the policy required notice of loss to be given forthwith, and the office of the insurers was destroyed so that the assured did not know where to find the officers, and the fire was of such extent as to suspend all general business, it was held that notice given in thirty-seven days, after the fire, was in time.[6]

If the insurer, after a risk becomes hazardous, knowing the facts, permits the policy to stand, when the increase of hazard does not result from the agency of the assured, the policy remains operative as an indemnity.[7]

If a person who has an insurable interest in property, takes out a policy in the name of the person having the legal title, and upon the happening of a loss, receives the amount as the agent of such person, he is liable to such person for the amount so received by him, and cannot be permitted to show that he took the insurance for his own benefit.[8] But if he takes the policy in his own name, he is not in the first instance called upon to prove his interest in the property, as the issue of the policy to him is an admission of his title, and *prima facie* establishes it, leaving the insurer the burden of showing that in fact, he had no insurable interest.[9]

As to whether or not, there is *double insurance*, depends entirely

---

[1] In *Parmalee* v. *Hoffman F. Ins. Co.*, 54 N. Y. 193.

[2] *Guardian, etc., Ins. Co.* v. *Hagan*, 80 Ill. 35.

[3] *Cumma* v. *Lewis*, 15 Wall. (U. S.) 643.

[4] *Knickerbocker Ins. Co.* v. *Gould*, 80 Ill. 388.

[5] *Knickerbocker Ins. Co.* v. *Gould*, 80 Ill. 388.

[6] *Knickerbocker Ins. Co.* v. *Gould*, 80 Ill. 388.

[7] *Fireman's, etc., Ins. Co.* v. *Congregation of Rodlph Shalom*, 80 Ill. 558.

[8] *Looney* v. *Looney*, 116 Mass. 283.

[9] *Nichols* v. *Fayette Ins. Co.*, *ante*.

upon the circumstance of *identity of property and interest.* If the policies cover the *same property and protect the same interest,* although issued to different persons, there is double insurance, and the restriction as to recovery applies.[1] But, although policies cover the same property, yet, *if they do not cover the same interest,* there is no double insurance, and each of the assured may recover his loss without reference to the other.[2]

The burden of establishing the existence of other insurance, is upon the insurer, and this extends to all the details, as identity of risk, interest, etc., and the same is true as to any matter that is not in the nature of a condition precedent, but rather a matter of defense.[3]

The question as to whether a credit was given,. or a condition waived, is for the jury, and may be established either by an express waiver, or may be implied from circumstances, as that the policy was delivered without requiring prepayment,[4] or that the premium was subsequently received,[5] or that it was subsequently demanded by the insurer and he treated it as a debt against the assured, or any act or circumstance that tends to show that there was an assent on the part of the insurer to a non-compliance with the condition.[6]

It seems now to be well established that, when a credit has in fact been given, the policy remains in force until canceled for non-payment of the premium,[7] and the issue and delivery of a policy without requiring pre-payment of the premium, *prima facie* establishes the fact that credit was given therefor.[8] In order that a misrepresentation should render the policy void, it is immaterial whether it is fraudulent or unintentional. It is enough if it amounts to a misrepresentation *material* to the risk, whether made through mistake or design.[9] It is the duty of the assured to state all the facts known to him *material* to the risk, and whether facts known to him, but not disclosed,

[1] *Hough* v. *People's Ins. Co.,* 36 Md. 378.

[2] *Wells* v. *Phila. Ins. Co.,* 9 S. & R. (Penn.) 103.

[3] *Catlin* v. *Springfield F. & M. Ins. Co.,* 1 Sum. (U. S.) 434; *Lounsbury* v. *Protection Ins. Co.,* 8 Conn. 459.

[4] *Bowman* v. *Agricultural Ins. Co.,* 59 N. Y. 521; *Washoe Tool Co.* v. *Hibernia Ins. Co.,* 66 N. Y. 613.

[5] *Young* v. *Mut. Life Ins. Co.,* 2 Sawyer (U. S.) 325.

[6] *Washoe Tool Co.* v. *Hibernia Ins. Co.,* ante.

[7] *Washoe Tool Co.* v. *Hibernia Ins. Co.,* 66 N. Y. 613.

[8] *Latoix* v. *Germania, etc., Ins. Co.,* 27 La. An. 113.

[9] *Carpenter* v. *American Ins. Co.,* 1 Story (U. S.) 57; *Wilson* v. *Herkimer Ins. Co.,* 6 N. Y. 53; *Day* v. *Conway Ins. Co.,* 52 Me. 60; *Mutual Ins. Co.* v. *Mahon,* 5 Call (Va.) 517.

were material to the risk, is a question for the jury, and the burden of establishing their materiality is upon the insurer.

When a mortgagor procures a policy and assigns the same to the mortgagee, or has the same made payable to him " as his interest may appear," a conveyance of his equity of redemption in the premises is such an alienation as avoids the policy, as to the mortgagee, when the policy provides that " an alienation of the property by sale or otherwise, shall avoid the policy," [1] even though the conveyance is made to the mortgagee.[2] But where the mortgagee takes out a policy in his own name, *as mortgagee,* a conveyance by the mortgagor would not invalidate the policy, unless so specially provided in the policy.

The right of a mortgagee to insure the premises to the amount of his debt, *is the lien given upon the property by the conveyance, as security for the payment of the debt,* yet the insurance is in no sense *an insurance of the debt,* but of the mortgagee's interest in the property *as security for the debt.* Except where the insurance is effected by the mortgagor, or under an arrangement with him, or he pays for the same, or agrees to do so, *payment of a loss under the policy does not operate as a payment of the debt, or relieve the mortgaged premises from the lien, or the mortgagor from liability for the whole sum payable by the terms of the contract,* nor does it estop the mortgagee from recovering *both the insurance and the debt.*[3]

It is true that the insurer's liability ceases when the *debt* is paid, but it ceases only because, by payment of the debt, the *interest* of the mortgagee is extinguished. The fact that the mortgagee has received from another source a sum equal to the amount of the debt, but which the mortgagor is not equitably entitled to have applied to its discharge, does not destroy the interest. *It must be a payment of the debt, as such, and by a party who is lawfully authorized to pay it.* It may, perhaps, be true, as stated by GIBSON, J., in a Pennsylvania case,[4] that it is, *in effect,* an insurance of the debt, but it is not so in fact. The right of the mortgagee to recover under the policy is not dependent upon the question whether the security for his debt is thereby impaired, but, *if there is a loss, however small,* his right to recover therefor attaches, and the

---

[1] *Lawrence* v. *Holyoke Ins. Co.,* 11 Allen (Mass.) 365 ; *Hazard* v. *Franklin, etc., Ins. Co.,* 11 Allen (Mass.) 385 ; 5 Bennett's F. I. C. 65 ; *Loring* v. *Manuf. Ins. Co.,* 8 Gray (Mass.) 28.

[2] *Hazard* v. *Franklin Ins. Co., ante ; Hoxie* v. *Providence Mut. Ins. Co.,* 6 R. I. 517.

[3] *Hancox* v. *Fishing Ins. Co.,* 3 Sum. (U. S.) 132.

[4] *Smith* v. *Columbia Ins. Co.,* 17 Penn. St. 253.

amount received does not apply upon the debt to extinguish it *pro tanto*, except as previously stated.[1] Thus it will be seen, that the

---

[1] FOLGER, J., in a very able opinion in *Excelsior F. Ins. Co.* v. *Royal Ins. Co.*, 55 N. Y. 343, reviews the cases, and eliminates the doctrine applicable in such cases thus: " But," said he, " when this case is closely scanned, it is this: that an insurance of a mortgage interest is an indemnity against a loss of that debt by a loss or damage to the property mortgaged; that if the mortgaged property is, after the loss occurs to it, still enough in value to pay the debt, there has been, in effect, no loss; that the insurer, having paid the mortgage, is entitled to have recourse to the mortgaged property, and, therefore (and this is the point made on the argument of that case and the point decided), that any concealment of the facts which affects the value of the property is an injury to the insurer and a material concealment which avoids the contract, inasmuch as thereby the insurer is misled as to the value of the property on which he relies for ultimate security and reimbursement. The insuree, having several mortgages upon the same property, insured his interest as mortgagee, disclosing the existence of but one, which was the last. This it was which was held to be a material concealment, and injurious to the insurer for the reason stated. . We do not understand the learned judge to maintain that an insured mortgagee may not call upon the insurer to pay the loss upon the property, so long as the property remaining is enough to satisfy the debt. It is true that there are to be found *dicta* of learned and eminent judges which it is claimed go the length of the proposition of the defendants. See *Ætna F. Ins. Co.* v. *Tyler*, 16 Wend. (N. Y.) 385-397, where Chancellor WALWORTH says: 'In the present case all the insurable interest which Schaeffer had in the property * * * * was the amount of his unpaid purchase-money, so far as the land upon which the house stood was insufficient to protect him from loss, and provided the purchaser was unable to pay the same.' See also, *Carpenter* v. *Roc. Ins. Co.*, 16 Pet. (U. S.) 495-501, per STORY, J.: It is not in either of these cases declared that the mortgagee can claim no more of the insurer than what the security for his debt fails to yield. And if that should be held to be the rational sequence from what is stated, it is certainly to be said, as is said by SHAW, Ch.J., in *King* v. *State Mut. F. Ins. Co.*, 7 Cush. (Mass.) 1-11, 12, that a principle is stated not necessary to the decision of the cases. *Kernochan* v. *Bowery Ins. Co.*, 17 N. Y. 428, is cited also, in which T. R. STRONG, J., says: 'If the insurance was of the debt, there should, to warrant a recovery, be a loss as to the debt, which has not occurred and cannot take place, as the mortgaged property still far exceeds in value the sum unpaid and the debtors are solvent.' We do not think that this is a statement of a principle, but an argumentative statement of what would be the result of a suppositious case, did it in fact exist, though neither its existence nor indeed the possibility of its existence. under like circumstances, is admitted. Moreover, it was not necessary to the decision of that case, even if it is taken as the statement of a principle. Mr. PARSONS, in his book on Marine Insurance (vol. 1, p. 229), though inclining to the proposition presented by the defendants here, yet says: 'We are not prepared to say that, whenever the insured interest is a lien, the insurer may interpose as a bar to a claim for a loss the remaining sufficiency of the property to pay the debt.' And in his work on Contracts, 6th edition, 2d vol., pp. 339, 340, though he says: 'There is both reason and authority for saying that in such case he has no claim on the insurer;' yet he adds: 'This may not be regarded as an established rule.' There are some authorities which tend to the contrary. It is apparent that if it is the debt only of the mortgagee which is insured, and that he has no claim against the insurer until the mortgaged property is exhausted, that the same rule will apply as to the obligation of the mortgage debtor, and that the remedy against him must also be first exhausted. Yet this proposition does not seem to receive sanction. In *Hancox* v. *Fish Ins. Co.*, 3 Sumner, 132, the same eminent jurist who pronounced the opinion in 16 Peters, *supra*, said: 'It has been suggested that the plaintiff has in fact sustained no loss, because, for anything that appears, he may still recover the debts due to him from the seamen, and if so he has sustained no loss. * * * .The question is not, in cases of this sort, whether the party has actually lost his debt, * * * but is, whether he has lost the security for the debt. * * *" In *Russell* v. *Un. Ins. Co.*, 1 Wash.

question, whether the acts of the mortgagor are admissible in evidence
to avoid a policy in the hands of the mortgagee, will depend upon the

---

C. C. (U. S.) 409, it was contended by the defendants, as it is by the defendant
here, that the insurer might still resort elsewhere than to the insured, and that,
therefore, there was no loss. The court did not sustain the position, saying that
a loss had actually happened, and that, though the lien was not destroyed, yet it
was such a loss as that the insured might, by an abandonment, throw it upon the
underwriter. And see *Godin* v. *Lond. Ass. Co.*, 1 Burr. 489. In the absence of
direct authority, how is the reason of this matter? Can it be said, in any strict
or legal sense, that the defendants have contracted to indemnify Mrs. Connelly
for a loss of her mortgaged debt? Whence is their power to guarantee the payment or collection of a debt? Fire underwriters in these days, in this State, are
the creatures of statute, and have no rights, save such as the State gives to them.
They may agree that they will pay such loss or damage as happens by fire to
property. They are limited to this. It was not readily that it was first held that
they could agree, with a mortgagee or lienor of property, to reimburse to him
the loss caused to him by fire. He is not the owner of it; how, then, can he
insure it, was the query. And the effort was not to enlarge the power of the
insurer so that it might insure a debt, but to bring the lienor within the scope of
that power, so that the property might be insured for his benefit. And it was
done by holding that, as his security did depend upon the safety of the property,
he had an interest in its preservation, and so had such interest as that he might
take out a policy upon it against loss by fire, without meeting the objection that
it was a wagering policy. The policy did not, therefore, become one upon the
debt, and for indemnification against its loss, but still remained one upon the
property and against loss or damage to it. It is doubtless, true, as is said by
GIBSON, J., in 17 Penn. *supra*, that in *effect* it is the debt which is insured. It is
only as an effect, however; an effect resulting from the primary act of insurance
of the property which is the security for the debt. It is the interest in the property which gives the right to obtain insurance, and the ownership of the debt, a
lien upon the property, creates that interest. The agreement is usually, as it is
in fact in this case, for insuring, from loss or damage by fire, the property. The
interest of the mortgagor is in the whole property, just as it exists, undamaged
by fire at the date of the policy. If that property is consumed in part, though
what there be left of it is equal in value to the amount of the mortgage debt, the
mortgage interest is affected. It is not so great, or so safe, or so valuable, as it
was before. It was for indemnity against this very detriment, this very decrease
in value, that the mortgagee sought insurance and paid his premium.
    To say that it is the debt which is insured against loss, is to give to most, if not
all, fire insurance companies a power to do a kind of business which the law and
their charter do not confer. They are privileged to insure property against loss
or damage by fire. They are not privileged to guarantee the collection of debts.
If they are, they may insure against the insolvency of the debtor. No one will
contend this; and, it will be said, it is not by a guaranty of the debt, but an
indemnity is given against the loss of the debt by an insurance against the perils
to the property by fire. This is but coming to our position; that it is the property which is insured against the loss by fire, and the protection to the debt is the
sequence thereof. As the property it is which is insured against loss, it is the
loss which occurs to it which the insurer contracts to pay, and for such loss he is
to pay within the limit of his liability, irrespective of the value of the property
undestroyed. So as to the remark, that it is the capacity of the property to pay
the debt which is insured. This is true in a certain sense; but it is as a result
and not as a primary undertaking. The undertaking is that the property shall
not suffer loss by fire; that is, in effect, that its capacity to pay the mortgaged
debt shall not be diminished. When an appreciable loss has occurred to the
property from fire, its capacity to pay the mortgaged debt has been affected; it
is not so well able to pay the debt which is upon it. The mortgage interest, the
insurable interest, is lessened in value, and the mortgagee, the insuree, is
affected, and may call upon the insurer to make him as good again as he was
when he effected his insurance. Another consideration: It is settled that when a
mortgagee, or one in like position toward property, is insured thereon at his own

circumstance whether, by arrangement between the parties, the mortgagor has the ultimate benefit of the policy. In the latter case, his acts, violating the conditions of the policy—unless otherwise provided —will defeat the mortgagee's rights under it, consequently may be shown ; but when the mortgagee's interests alone are affected thereby, he is not held chargable for the acts or *laches* of the mortgagor, and his acts cannot be given in evidence to defeat the rights of the mortgagee.

Burden of proof.

SEC. 507. The insured is charged with the burden of proving all matters that stand as a condition precedent to his recovery, and this imposes upon him the burden of proving a literal compliance on his part with all the express warranties in the policy.[1] Thus, where in an insurance upon a ship there was a warranty " not to carry coolie passengers or petroleum," and the vessel had on board 2,000 gallons of kerosene illuminating oil, it was held that the burden was upon the assured to show that the article carried was known in commerce as a different article from that bought and sold as petroleum.[2] So where a policy contained a warranty in these words, " warranted by the assured that the vessel be commanded by a captain holding a certificate from the American Shipmasters' Assocation," it was held that the burden of proving compliance with this warranty was upon the assured.[3] The rule applies with equal force, whether the warranty is promissory, or

---

expense, upon his own motion and for his sole benefit, and a loss happens to it, the insurer, on making compensation, is entitled to an assignment of the rights of the insured. This is put upon the analogy of the situation of the insurer to that of a surety. If this analogy be made complete, then has the insurer no more right to refuse payment of the loss, so long as the insured has other remedy for his debt, than has the surety. One as well as the other, as soon as the creditor's right to make demand is fixed, must respond to it and seek his reimbursement through his right of subrogation ; and, indeed, the application of this equitable right of subrogation makes our view of this subject harmonious and consistent with all the rights and interests of all the parties."

[1] *McLoon* v. *Comrl. Ins. Co.*, 100 Mass. 472; *Craig* v. *United States Ins. Co.*, Pet. C. C. (U. S.) 416 ; *Campbell* v. *N. E. Ins. Co.*, 98 Mass. 390. Where a policy provided that it should not cover any loss or damage by fire which shall originate in the theater proper, it was held incumbent upon the plaintiff to negative the exception. *Lobier* v. *Norwich City Ins. Co.*, 11 Allen (Mass.) 336. " Warranted against seizure." *Held* that the assured must show a loss from a cause other than by seizure. *Bradhurst* v. *Columbian Ins. Co.*, 9 John. (N. Y.) 18. " Not liable for any derangement of machinery or bursting of boilers, unless occasioned by stranding." *Held* that the assured must show a loss from causes other than those excepted against. *Hebdon* v. *Eagle Ins. Co.*, 10 Gray (Mass.) 131.

[2] *McLoon* v. *Mercantile, etc., Ins. Co.*, 100 Mass. 474, *n.*

[3] *McLoon* v. *Comr'l., etc., Ins. Co.*, 100 Mass. 472. But general evidence of compliance is enough, when a *prima facie* compliance is established the insurer must falsify it. *Ludlow* v. *Union Ins. Co* , 2 S. & R. (Penn.) 119. The insured is required merely to prove *prima facie* compliance. If a breach is relied on, the insurer must establish it. *Swick* v. *Home Life Ins. Co.*, 2 Dill. (U. S. C. C.) 160 ; *Halbraid* v. *Ins. Co.*, 2 id. 166, *n.*

relates to things past, present or future. The insured must aver performance on his part, and consequently must prove performance.[1] And the rule also applies as to all exceptions or conditions in the nature of warranties or that are prohibitory contained in the policy. Thus, where the policy provided that the insurers should not be liable, unless the loss amounted to seven and a half per cent. on the property insured, it was held that the burden was upon the plaintiff to show that it amounted to that sum.[2] So, when a policy upon a vessel contained a clause "prohibited from all guano islands except Chinchas," it was held that the assured must show that there had been no breach of the warranty on his part.[3] But, as to representations merely, the burden is upon the insurer, not only to prove their *falsity*, but also their materiality.[4]

Some apparent conflict exists in the cases, but it will be found that really there is none, as in the cases where it is seemingly held that the burden is upon the insurer to prove a breach of the warranty, the rule applied to representations and not to warranties,[5] or that the cases were decided in inferior courts, and have not been sustained by the higher courts.[6] It is not only the duty of the assured to show performance of all conditions precedent, but he also takes the burden of proving a loss by some one of the perils insured against.[7] If the

---

[1] *Wilson* v. *Hampden F. Ins. Co.*, 4 R. I. 159. The party who holds the affirmative of the issue must sustain it. *Rogers* v. *Traders' Ins. Co.*, 6 Paige's Ch. (N. Y.) 583.

[2] *Merchants' Ins. Co.* v. *Wilson*, 2 Md. 217.

[3] *Wheton* v. *Albany City Ins. Co.*, 109 Mass. 24. See also, on general question, *Hoffman* v. *Western M. & F. Ins. Co.*, 1 La. An. 216; *Young* v. *Pacific Mut. Ins. Co.*, 2 Jones & Spencer (N. Y. Sup. Ct.) 321; *Mallory* v. *Conrl. Ins. Co.*, 9 Bos. (N. Y.) 101; *Lea Ins. Co.* v. *Fowler*, 21 Wend. (N. Y.) 600; *Cory* v. *Boylston Ins. Co.*, 107 Mass. 140.

[4] *Campbell* v. *N. E. Mut. Life Ins. Co.*, *ante*; *Catlin* v. *Springfield F. Ins. Co.*, 1 Sum. (U. S.) 435; *Clark* v. *Hamilton Ins. Co.*, 9 Gray (Mass.) 148; *Hollonun* v. *Life Ins. Co.*, 1 Woods (C. C. U. S.) 674; *Wilson* v. *Hampden Ins. Co.*, 4 R. I. 151; *N. Y. Life Ins. Co.* v. *Grahan* 2 Dav. (Ky.) 506; *Lenon* v. *Peoria M. & F. Ins. Co.*, 28 Ill. 235; *Jones' Manufg. Co.* v. *Manuf.*, *etc.*, *Ins. Co.*, 8 Cush. (Mass.) 82. Fraud must be proved by him who alleges it *Oliver* v. *Mut. Conrl. Ins. Co.*, 2 Curtis (U. S.) 277. Therefore if fraudulent concealment of material facts is relied on, the insurer must establish the defense. *Ins. Co.* v. *Folsom*, 18 Wall. (U. S) 237; *Franco* v. *Natusch*, 6 Tryw. 401; and the same is true as to misrepresentations. *Kingsley* v. *N. E. Mut. F. Ins. Co.*, 8 Cush. (Mass.) 392; *Tidmarsh* v. *Washington, etc., Ins. Co.*, 4 Mass. (U. S.) 439; *Clark* v. *Hamilton Mut. Ins. Co.*, 9 Gray (Mass.) 148; *Trenton Mut. Life Ins. Co.* v. *Johnson*, 24 N. J. L. 576; *Ross* v. *Hunter*, 4 T. R. 33.

[5] *Underhill* v. *Agawam Ins. Co.*, 6 Cush. (Mass.) 441; *Catlin* v. *Springfield F. Ins. Co.*, 1 Sum. (U. S.) 435; *Ritter* v. *Sun Mut. Ins. Co.*, 40 Mo. 40; *Sheldon* v. *Logan*, Fac. Dec. (Sc.) 520.

[6] *Swick* v. *Honne Life Ins. Co.*, 2 Dill. C. C. (U. S.) 160; *Holloman* v. *Life Ins. Co.*, 1 Wood° (U. S.) 674.

[7] *Hebdon* v. *Eagle Ins. Co.*, 10 Gray (Mass.) 131; *Tobin* v. *Norwich City Ins. Co.*, *ante*.

policy is "on account of whom it may concern," he must also show that it was intended to cover his property, and that he had an insurable interest therein.[1]

To explain ambiguities.

SEC. 508. Whenever there is a latent ambiguity in the policy, so that the instrument cannot be construed from anything contained therein, parol evidence is admisable to explain the same, as, where the policy applies equally well to either of two subjects, to show which was intended to be covered by the parties;[2] so where the term of insurance is indefinite, what term was intended;[3] so where a policy covers a stock of merchandise, whether it is usual in connection with such stocks, to keep certain prohibited articles;[4] or that the insurer knew that certain prohibited articles were kept by the assured;[5] or what was intended by certain words used in the policy, where their meaning, as applied to the subject-matter, is doubtful, as, where a policy covers a dwelling-house and *wood shed*, that a certain building, in part used for a carriage house, and in part for storing wood, was

---

[1] *Steele* v. *Franklin Ins. Co.*, 17 Penn. St. 290; *De Bolle* v. *Penn. Ins. Co.*, 4 Whart. (Penn.) 68.

[2] *Beatty* v. *Lycoming Ins. Co.*, 52 Penn. St. 456; *Lycoming, etc., Ins. Co.* v. *Sailer*, 67 id. 108. In *Burr* v. *Broadway Ins. Co.*, 16 N. Y. 267, a policy covered a three and a half story brick building, slate roof, coped, occupied as a patent cordage manufactory, situate No. west corner of First and South Eighth streets, Williamsburgh, etc., and on main shafting and fixtures, $1,000; and on lignum vitæ in the cellar of said building, $1,000. The evidence showed, that at the time the insurance was made, insured owned two brick buildings, each on the opposite corners of South Eighth and First streets, one of which was occupied as a patent cordage factory, the other as a block factory. Both were on westerly corners of South Eighth and First streets. The cordage factory was the southwesterly corner, the blockfactory on the northwesterly corner. The building which contained the lingum vitæ and shafting was burned; the block factory was saved. The defendant contended that the two letters "No.," preceding the words "West corner of First and South Eighth streets," were an abbreviation of the word *north*, and being so read, the block factory was the building insured. *Held*, a latent ambiguity raised by extrinsic evidence, presented by the fact that there were two buildings on west corners of First and South Eighth streets, alike in every respect except the cellars, both the property of the insured; hence, extrinsic evidence was admissible to remove the ambiguity, and for that purpose it was proper to prove what took place between the person who made the application and took the answers; that the word "No." could not be regarded as an abbreviation for either number or north. See also, *Storer* v. *Elliott F. Ins. Co.*, 45 Me. 175.

[3] *Lancey* v. *Phenix Ins. Co.*, 56 Me. 562.

[4] *Steinback* v. *LaFayette F. Ins. Co.*, 54 N. Y. 90.

[5] *Mayor of N. Y.* v. *N. Y. Exchange F. Ins. Co.*, 3 Keyes (N. Y.) 436; *Viele* v. *Germania Ins. Co.*, 26 Iowa, 9. In *Somers* v. *Atheneum Ins. Co.*. 9 L. C. 61, the defendant's agent sent a diagram of the premises to the office, in which the buildings were represented as detached. It was held admissible to show that the defendant's agent visited the premises before the risk was taken, and knew the real situation of the buildings.

known as the "wood shed."[1] So where the policy is issued to an agent, in favor of an unnamed principal, or to whom it may concern, to show who was intended as the assured.[2]

Where a defense is set up that other insurance has been made, contrary to the conditions of the policy, that the policies, although apparently covering the same risk and interest, in fact cover different risks, or different interests. Thus, where a policy covered *bulk sides* belonging to M. & L., in a certain pork house, and another bulk meat, hams, lard and mess pork, in the same building. Subsequently, while both policies were in force, an indorsement was made upon upon the latter policy: "The above risk is transferred to sides and shoulders belonging to J." It was held that evidence was admissible to show that the two policies did not cover the same risk.[3]

When a policy is issued in a wrong name, that the assured is also known by that name,[4] or that a policy issued to a certain firm, was intended to cover the interests of all persons interested in the firm.[5] So parol evidence is admissible to show that the premium has been paid, or that credit therefor has been given,[6] or that pre-payment was waived,[7] and in order to establish a waiver, by showing that the company *usually* delivered policies without requiring the premium to be pre-paid,[8] and generally, where there is any ambiguity, to discover the real intention of the parties.[9]

When an insurer accepts an application to renew a policy, and

---

[1] *White* v. *Mutual F. Ins. Co.*, 8 Gray (Mass.) 566. It has been held proper to show that a whole story of a building, applied to a particular purpose, although divided by partitions, is commonly called a room. *Daniels* v. *Hudson River Ins. Co.*, 12 Cush. (Mass.) 416; *Storer* v. *Elliott Ins. Co.*, 45 Me. 175.

[2] *Callett* v. *Pacific Ins. Co.*, 1 Wend. (N. Y.) 561; *Stephenson* v. *Piscataqua F. & M. Ins. Co.*, 54 Me. 55; *Bell* v. *Western, etc., Ins. Co.*, 5 Rob. (La.) 423. So where a contract to insure certain property held by the plaintiff "in store" was made, but no policy was issued, it was held competent to show for whose benefit the insurance was made. *Strohn* v. *Hartford F. Ins. Co.*, 33 Wis. 648.

[3] *Roots* v. *Cincinatti Ins. Co.*, 1 Dis. (Ohio) 138; *Planters' Ins. Co.* v. *Deford*, 38 Md. 382.

[4] *Dickson* v. *Lodge*, 1 Starkie, 226; *Carruthers* v. *Shedden*, 6 Taunt. 13.

[5] *Carruthers* v. *Shedden, ante.*

[6] *Pino* y. *Merchants' Mut. Ins. Co.*, 19 La. An. 214; *Miss. Valley L. Ins. Co.* v. *Neyland*, 9 Bush. (Ky.) 430; *La. Societe* v. *Morris*, 24 La. An. 347; *Heaton* v. *Manhattan F. Ins. Co.*, 7 R. I. 502; *Ins. Co.* v. *Colt*, 20 Wall. (U. S.) 560.

[7] *Sims* v. *State Ins. Co.*, 47 Mo. 54; *Jalippe* v. *Madison, etc., Ins. Co.*, 39 Wis. 14; *Dayton Ins. Co.* v. *Kelly*, 24 Ohio St. 345; *Lycoming Ins. Co.* v. *Schallenberger*, 44 Penn. St. 259; *Bowman* v. *Agricultural Ins. Co.*, 2 T. & C. (N. Y.) 261; *Sheldon* v. *Atlantic Ins. Co.*, 26 N. Y. 460.

[8] *Pino* v. *Ins. Co., ante; Baxter* v. *Massasoit Ins. Co.*, 13 Allen (Mass.) 820.

[9] *Stacey* v. *Franklin Ins. Co.*, 2 W. & S. (Penn.) 506; *Lawrence* v. *Sebor*, 2 Caines (N. Y.) 203.

issues a receipt without payment of the premium, relying upon the representations of the agent that the assured is responsible, and sends it to the agent, holding him responsible for the premium, it is a waiver of pre-payment, and a valid contract to insure is thereby created.[1]

---

[1] *Planters' Ins.* v. *Ray*, 52 Miss. 325.

CHAPTER XXIII.

MUTUAL INSURANCE.

Peculiar features of.

SEC. 509. The distinction between mutual and stock insurance is, that in the former the assured become members of the company, and stand in the relation of assured and insurers to each other, and liable to contribute to the loss of each member, as well as to their own, to the extent of the premium note given by them, while in stock companies, upon payment of the sum named as the premium, the company alone assumes the risk. It often happens that mutual companies combine both features, and give their customers the choice of becoming members of the company, or of paying a gross sum for insurance, without assuming any further liability. In the latter case, the assured does not become a member of the company, and is not liable to contribute to the losses of others.[1] When a premium note is given, and the assured becomes a member of the company, he is held chargable with notice and knowledge of the provisions of the charter and by-laws of the company, and is bound thereby,[2] but he is not affected by by-laws subsequently adopted, particularly if they conflict with the charter or the policy.[3]

Liability beyond amount of note.

SEC. 510. Whether the members of a mutual company are liable *beyond* the amount of their premium notes, for losses, will depend upon the provisions of the charter, but, in any event, there is no such liability until the premium notes are exhausted.[4]

---

[1] *Illinois F. Ins. Co.* v. *Stanton,* 57 Ill. 354.
[2] *Mutual Ass'n* v. *Korn,* 7 Cr. (U. S.) 396.
[3] *N. H. Mut. Ins. Co.* v. *Road,* 45 N. H. 292.
[4] *Com.* v. *Monitor Mut. F. Ins. Co.,* 112 Mass. 150.

SEC. 511. Whether a premium note is valid or not, will depend upon the question whether the policy ever attached, or whether the company or its agent were guilty of fraud in procuring it,[1] as a policy that *is invalid* does not furnish a legal consideration for the note. But the fact that the company was in fact insolvent when the policy issued, does not invalidate the note, if the officers and agents were ignorant of the fact.[2] *If the policy ever attached, the note is valid,*[3] but the fact that a note was given, and a policy made, does not fix the liability of the maker, the policy must have been delivered, *or at least accepted*, or the note is inoperative.[4] The policy must have attached, and if it never became operative as an indemity, no portion of the premium is collectable.[5]

SEC. 512. Stock notes; that is, notes given to assist in the formation of the company, and as capital, as well as notes given for premiums, that are not subject to assessments, are absolute obligations and negotiable, and may be sued in the name of any *bona fide* holder.[6] In all cases where the notes are subject to assessments, the assured is liable upon the notes in the manner and to the extent provided by the charter, or, in the absence of charter provisions, by the by-laws, *and in no other way*. If the charter provides that the insurer may, at its option, collect the entire amount of the premium note, of course it may do so, but if it makes the note payable by way of assessments, that is the only mode in which payments can be required, and only in that way, when assessments are necessary to meet actual losses,[7] and the assessments must be restricted to losses occurring *after* the premium note was given, and if it includes prior losses, it is void.[8] The liability of the assured is not absolute, but contingent upon losses, to which he is liable to contribute; therefore, in order to recover an assessment, the company takes the burden of

---

[1] *Lynn v. Burgoyne*, 13 B. Mon. (Ky.) 400; *Russell v. De Grand*, 15 Mass. 35.

[2] *Lester v. Webb*, 5 Allen (Mass.) 569; *Alliance Ins. Co. v. Swift*, 10 Cush. (Mass.) 433; *Sterling v. Mercantile Ins. Co.*, 32 Penn. St. 75.

[3] *Atlantic Ins. Co. v. Goodall*, 25 N. H. 369.

[4] *Real Estate Ins. Co. v. Roessle*, 1 Gray (Mass.) 336.

[5] *Homer v. Dorr*, 10 Mass. 26; *Merchants' Ins. Co. v. Clapp*, 11 Pick. (Mass.) 56.

[6] *Rhinehart v. Alleghany Ins. Co.*, 1 Penn. St. 389; *Dana v. Munro*, 38 Barb (N. Y.) 528; *White v. Haight*, 16 N. Y. 310; *Tuckerman v. Brown*, 38 N. Y. 297

[7] *Sumissippi Ins. Co. v. Taft*, 26 Ind. 240.

[8] *Long Pond Mut. Ins. Co. v. Houghton*, 6 Gray (Mass.) 177.

establishing losses to which the assured is bound to contribute, and the necessity of such assessment, to meet such losses.[1]

In order to establish losses, as a basis of assessments, the company need not prove *losses in fact*, in the first instance, but its record book of losses, in the first instance, is sufficient for that purpose, and if not contradicted is sufficient for all purposes.[2]

The company is bound to regulate its assessments by the losses actually due, and must impose them upon *all* the premium notes. If any are *intentionally* omitted from its operation, the assessment is void.[3]

Unless so provided in the charter, the premium note does not become inoperative upon a cessation of the risk; but the assured remains liable thereon during the entire period covered by his policy,[4] even though the company declares the policy void for non-payment of assessments, or other breach of conditions.[5] All assessments must be paid within the time prescribed by the charter or by-laws, or the policy becomes void, if so provided in the charter, by-laws or policy.[6] In all cases, the charter, by-laws and policy must be looked to, and the rights of the parties will depend upon the provisions or conditions thereof, and no general rules can be given applicable in all cases. Necessarily the measure of liability is to be determined by the charter and by the contract.

In a recent Pennsylvania case[7] it was held that where a person is induced to insure in a mutual company through fraudulent representations of the agent, such fraud is a complete defense to an action upon the premium note or for assessments made on it.

---

[1] *Pacific Mut. Ins. Co.* v. *Guse*, 40 Mo. 329; *American Ins. Co.* v. *Schmidt*, 19 Iowa, 502; *Savage* v. *Midbury*, 19 N. Y. 32; *Atlantic Ins. Co.* v. *Fitzpatrick*, 2 Gray (Mass.) 279; *Bangs* v. *Gray*, 12 N. Y. 477; *Stair* v. *Wadleigh*, 8 John. (N. Y.) 124; *Bangs* v. *Duckingfield*, 18 N. Y. 592.

[2] *People's Ins. Co.* v. *Allen*, 10 Gray (Mass.) 297.

[3] *Marblehead, etc., Ins. Co.* v. *Hayward*, 3 Gray (Mass.) 208.

[4] *Marblehead Ins. Co.* v. *Underwood*, 3 Gray (Mass.) 210; *Iowa, etc., Ins. Co.* v. *Prossee*, 11 Iowa, 115.

[5] *Marblehead Ins. Co.* v. *Underwood, ante.*

[6] *Blanchard* v. *Atlantic, etc., Ins. Co.*, 3 N. H. 9; *Hale* v. *Union Mut. F. Ins. Co.* 32 id. 295.

[7] *Lycoming Ins. Co.* v. *Woodworth*, 83 Penn. St. 223.

INDEX.

A.

B.

BLANKET POLICIES (see OPEN POLICIES—POLICY).

    when the risk is shifting, varying, 91, 92.

BREACHES :

    of contract of insurance must be pleaded, 378.

BRICK BUILDING:

    is within meaning of term, though outside is partly wood, 413 *n*, 4.

BUILDER'S CERTIFICATE (see PROOF OF LOSS—MAGISTRATE'S CERTIFICATE).

    when required, doctrine relating to, 715.

    production of, when may be required, 731.

BUILDINGS (see POLICY—DWELLINGS).

    effect of use of, for unlawful purpose, 187, 245, 353.

    new building erected in place of one insured, not covered, 464.

    contingent interest in, not covered unless expressed, 188.

    materials of, not insured as such, 239.

    distance from others, stated in application, effect of, 240.

        misstatement as to, 240-242, 243.

    enlargement of does not necessarily avoid policy, 463.

    removal of, does, 464.

    addition to, avoids policy, when, 463 *n*.

BURDEN OF PROOF :

    upon insurer to establish matters of defense, 862.

        as double insurance, 862.

        fraud, 233.

        material misrepresentation, 862, 867.

        concealment of material facts, 379-436.

        assured bound to establish compliance with all conditions precedent, 866.

        must show that he has not broken warranty, 866.

        must show loss not excepted against, 866.

        within the peril insured against, 192.

BY-LAWS :

    assured bound to know provisions of, when, 3, 871.

C.

CANCELLATION (see POLICY).

    of policy, right to, 231.

    reservation of, 231.

    when it takes effect, 231-233.

    cannot exercise right if property is threatened at the time, 233.

    assured may cancel previous policies, although subsequent ones provide for *pro rata* payment in cases of loss, 247.

    without authority, 266.

CONCEALMENT—*Continued.*
> as to facts inquired about, 423.
> as to proximity of buildings, 423.
> as to title, 423.
> of matters incident to risk, 424.
> question for jury, 431.
> fraud not presumed in case of, 433.
> effect of examination of risk by insurer, 434.

CONDITIONS (see POLICY—APPLICATION—WARRANTY).
> all conditions or stipulations in policies are warranties, 37, 130, 234 n, 313–316, 335.
> of policy, language of the condition, 132.
> cannot affect rights incident to business, 135.
> ambiguous, rule in case of, 140–147.
>> repugnant, rule in case of, 140–147.
>>> effect of, 142–147.
>> must be clearly set forth, 147.
>> must be in the proper place, and not obscure, 147, 148.
>> construction of in favor of assured, 147.
>> effect of written, upon printed, 148.
>> repugnant, as to the subject-matter of the risk, 149–155.
>> when the insurers are estopped from setting up breach of, 179.
>> relating to vacant or unoccupied premises, 180–184.
>> prohibiting use of building for certain purposes, 244.
>> must be strictly complied with, 270.
>> precedent, in case of warranty, 130, 234 n, 313–316, 335.
>> relating to sale, effect of, 551.
>> new conditions cannot be imported into contract, 291.
>>> to alienation, 535–571.
>>> other insurance, 586–623.
>>> hazardous uses, 130, 149–155, 244, 362, 368–372.
>>> change of risk, 437–463.
>>> alteration of risk, 437–463.
>>> increase of risk, 437–463.
>>> notice and proofs of loss, 537–571.
>>> time of bringing action, 754–762.
>>> arbitration, 747–753.
>>> keeping watchman, 321–334.
>>> keeping force pump, 334, 335.
>>> keeping water on premises, 321, 335.

CONDITIONS SUBSEQUENT:
> must be complied with, 244.

CONFUSION OF GOODS:
> when covered by two policies, operates as other insurance, when, 615–617.
> cases illustrating, 615.

CONTRACT—*Continued.*

must be proved by plaintiff, 38–40.

may be renewed by parol, 41.

when plaintiff must show authority of agent, 42, 649, 663.

application for, and acceptance by mail, 43.

liability where policy is ante-dated, and both parties ignorant of a loss at the time, 45.

when acceptance binds the company, 46.

notice of acceptance is sent by mail, 49–55.

policy conditionally delivered, 56.

when it takes effect, 56.

issued but not delivered, 56–61.

where the agent is to select the company, 61.

presumption in case of, when rate not agreed on, 64.

effect of acknowledgement of premium in policy, 65.

prepayment of premium for, 66.

may be waived, 66–72.

credit for, effect of usage, 72.

not always essential, 73–79.

not due till policy issues, 74.

when application for, will bind the company, 76–79.

agent bound to deliver policy, 82.

stipulations of application may affect, if not delivered, 82.

should conform to agreement, 82, 83.

when enforceable, although insurers mistaken as to value, 84.

validity of, not affected by omission of formal matters, 84–86.

equity will compel specific performance, 29.

contract, personal, 535.

alienation of property usually avoids, 535–571.

where sale is void, 540, 541, 559.

in case of assignment for benefit of creditors, 540.

rule as to property kept for sale, 541.

bankruptcy, when it avoids, 543.

suspended, loss during, 545.

deed of property, and mortgage back, 546.

death of assured, 547.

alienation, must be in fact, 547.

sale under a decree, 548.

assignment of property, 548.

sale and partial payment of, 548.

mortgage of property, 549.

effect of conditions, 551.

in case of levy and sale under legal process, 552.

contract of sale of property, it must be perfected to avoid, 554, 555.

alienation of part of property, 554.

interest remains until title passes, 558.

FIRE INSURANCE—*Continued.*

parol evidence not generally admissible to contradict or vary, 11.
construction of, 12.
conditions of, may be waived, 13.
requisites of valid, 13–16.
elements of, 18.
must be complete, 19–21.
in case of failure to notify the applicant of rejection, 24.
in case of discretion given to the agent as to the company, 25.
power of agents to bind the company, 25.
distinction between executory and executed, 29.
parol, when enforced in equity, 29–34.
how proved, 35–37.
conditions precedent, 37.
plaintiff must establish, 38–40.
may be renewed by parol, 41.
plaintiff must establish authority of agent, 42.
policy, application for and acceptance by mail, 43.
where both parties are ignorant at the time of the destruction of the property, and policy is ante-dated, 45.
acceptance of, binds the company, 46.
when sent by mail, 49–55.
policy, when conditionally delivered, 56.
where the agent is to select the company, 61.
presumptions, in certain cases, 63.
may be complete, when rate not agreed on, 64.
in case of acknowledgment of receipt of premium in the policy, 65.
prepayment of premium, 66.
may be waived, 66–72.
premium, effect of usage, 72.
not always essential, 78–79.
payable until the policy issues, 74.
when binding on the company, 76–78.
when agent bound to deliver, 80–82.
when affected by provisions of the application, if not delivered, 82.
should conform to agreement of the parties, 82, 83.
not affected by mistake in the value of the property, on the part of the insurer, 84.
neglect of formalities will not affect, 84–86.

FORCE PUMP:

condition relating to, 334.
what is included under term, 334, 335.
power to operate included, 334, 335.

FOREIGN COMPANIES:

liable for risks taken outside their jurisdiction, 829.
contracts made by, by what law governed, 189.

FORFEITURE (see INSURANCE—POLICY).
    when waived, 66, 608, 612, 715, 728.

FORTHWITH:
    what is, within meaning of policy, 161, 693, 696,

FRAUD:
    not presumed, 233.
    in securing policy, effect of, 146.
    attempt at, avoids policy, when, 744, 747.
    wilful, must be established to avoid, 744.
    large over-valuation, does not establish, 746.
    question for jury, 747.
    in case of, when insurers may recover back money paid, 780.

FURNITURE DEALERS:
    stock, policy on, embraces what, 125.

G.

GASOLINE:
    when use of, does not avoid, 165.

GERMAN JOBBER:
    policy covering stock of, includes fire-works, 150 *n.*

GOODS:
    intermingling of, operates to avoid policy, when, 615.
    "kept in country store," 149–155.

GOODS IN COUNTRY STORE (see COUNTRY STORES).

GROSS NEGLIGENCE (see NEGLIGENCE—POLICY—EVIDENCE).
    may furnish evidence of corrupt design, 224, 229.

GUNPOWDER:
    keeping of, does not avoid policy, when, 149.

H.

HAZARDOUS ARTICLES:
    keeping or use of, does not avoid policy, when, 149–155.
        when does, 130, 244, 362, 368–376.

HEAT (see POLICY—RISKS—LOSS).
    injury by, not within risk, 192.

HOTEL:
    building insured as, need not be used as, for whole term, 351.

HOUSE (see DWELLINGS).
    what is embraced in policy upon, 165.

HUSBAND (see INTEREST),
    has insurable interest in property of wife, when, **528.**

I.

IMMEDIATE :
    what is, within meaning of policy, 161.

IMPLIED LICENSE :
    what is, from what implied, 362–366, 368, 378.

INCIDENTS OF RISK (see EVIDENCE—POLICY).
    insurer bound to know, 314–316, 457, 461 *n.*
    presumed to insure with reference to, 358, 382, 461 *n.*
    policy not avoided by matters regarded as, 457.

INCREASE OF RISK (see RISK—ALTERATION—WARRANTY).
    when material *per se*, 438, 439, 459.
        question for jury, 439.
            for court, 439.
    test as to what is, 443.
    effect of knowledge by agent, 440.
    in case of erection of adjoining buildings, 442.
    conditions relating to, not extended by implication, 444.
    notice of, not required unless by stipulation, 446.
    change of tenant not, 446.
    usuages affecting, 451.
    in case of change of business, 454.
    stoves, use of additional, is not, 462.
    experts when admissible to prove, 455.
    burden of proof on insurer, 459.
    in case of enlargement of building, 463.
    by tenant or third persons does not invalidate policy, 446, 451.
    can be no offset of benefits, 454.
    ordinary repairs not within condition, 457.
    enlargement of building, effect of, 463.
    burden of proving increase on insurer, 459.
    when results from ordinary use, or incidents of property, not within condition, 451.
    condition as to, independent, and if certain use is prohibited, policy void, whether material or not, 453.
    any increase avoids, 453.

INCUMBRANCES :
    what are, 542–571.
    must be stated, when, 301.
    avoid policy when, 237.
    mis-statements as to, avoid policy, when, 237, 293, 301.

INSURANCE—*Continued.*

conditions precedent as to assured, 56.

takes effect, when, 56

where policy is issued, but not delivered, 56–61.

where the agent is to select the company, and makes an entry in
their books, 61.

presumptions in case of, 63.

may be complete when rate not agreed on, 64.

in case of acknowledgment of receipt of premium in the policy, 65.

prepayment of premium, 66.

may be waived, 66–72.

premium, effect of usuage, 72.

payment of not always essential, 73–79.

not payable until the policy issues, 74.

when application for policy will bind the company, 76–78.

when agent bound to deliver policy, 80–82.

when policy affected by the application, if not delivered, 82.

policy should conform to agreement, 82, 83.

when may be enforced though the insurers were mistaken as
to the value of the property, 84.

when the omission of a mere formality will not affect, 84–86.

who may be insured, 497–534.

interest of, required in the property, 468.

contract of, void unless interest exists, 476.

assured must have at the time of loss, 476.

illustrations, 477–480.

Ætna Ins. Co. v. Miers, 477.

Redfield v. Holland Purchase Ins. Co., 478.

may exist without property in, 480.

cases illustrating, 481.

equitable interest, 482–484, 522.

contingent, 482–484.

in case of assignees, 482–484.

rights insurable, must be susceptible of enforcement, 486.

in case of attachment, 487.

in case of mechanic's lien, 487, 488.

in case of mortgage, after decree, 488–491.

legal title, in the insurer, where he has no actual interest, 491.

legal title not always evidence of insurable interest, 492.

personal not necessary, 492.

may exist, without being legal or equitable title, 493.

in case of liability of assured, if the property is destroyed, 494–499.

need not be vested, 499.

only quasi, 499.

policy prima facie evidence of, 500.

in case of a trespasser, 500.

INTEREST—*Continued.*
>trustee, 532.
>joint owners and tenants in common, 532.
>master of vessel, 533.
>party in profits of business, 532.
>>contingent, 539.
>need not be described in the policy, 508.

INTEREST POLICIES (see POLICY).
>all fire insurance policies are, 91.

J.

JEWELRY :
>not wearing apparel, 127.

JOINT OWNERS (see POLICY).
>rights of, in case of loss, 252.
>sale of interest of one to the other, does not avoid policy, 559-567.

JUDGMENT DEBTOR (see INTEREST—INSURED).
>right of, to insure after levy, 488.

JURY (see EVIDENCE—ACTIONS—TRIAL).
>questions for, 814, 815.

JURISDICTION :
>condition of policy ousting courts of, invalid, 747-753.
>>requiring action in particular court, invalid, 758.
>>>exceptions where the provision is in the charter, 758.
>when acts outside the limits of legislature creating it, are valid, 829.

K.

KEROSENE :
>keeping of, does not avoid policy, when, 150 *n*, 151-155.

L.

LEGAL INTEREST (see INTEREST—INSURER).
>not necessary to constitute insurable interest, 493.

LEGAL TITLE (see TITLE—INTEREST—INSURED).

LICENSE :
>effect of, 131-139.
>may be implied, 362-366, 368-378.
>from what, how and when, 131-139.

LIGHTS :
>kerosene used as, does not avoid policy, when, 150-155.
>when use of lights prohibited, avoids, 344 *n*, 357.

57

M.

MORTGAGOR—*Continued.*

 right to have insurance money paid to assignee before debt is due applied to restore property destroyed, 236.

 breach of condition by, avoids policy in hands of mortgagee, 245, 574, 863.

    ....

MORTGAGEE (see POLICY—INSURER—INTEREST).

 rights under assigned policy, 236.

 when, may insure, 529.

 has insurable interest, when, 530.

 rights of insurer to be subrogated under, 782.

  when loss is less than mortgage debt, 783.

 when only part of debt is due, 786.

 payment of mortgage debt after loss does not relieve insurer, 863.

 when breach of conditions of policy by mortgagor defeats policy, 579, 863.

 when not, 863.

 will be compelled to apply money received from policy assigned by mortgagor, before debt is due, to restore property destroyed, 236.

 not obliged to look to property for indemnity, 863, 864 *n.*

MUTUAL INSURANCE:

 peculiar features of, 871.

 distinction between, and stock, 871.

 persons insured in, bound to know conditions of charter and by-laws, 871.

 exception, 871.

 liability of assured on premium note, 871.

 test for determining validity of premium note, 872.

 liability for assessments on, 872, 873.

N.

NEGLIGENCE (see POLICY—EVIDENCE—GROSS NEGLIGENCE).

 of assured, no defense against, 221-229.

  though gross, 221-229.

NOTICE (see POLICY—PROOFS OF LOSS—DOUBLE INSURANCE).

 requirements of policy relating to, must be complied with, 191.

 where policy requires notice of facts after the issue of policy, 244.

 of other insurance, 594.

 of change of risk, 191, 444.

 of incumbrances, 168.

NOTICE OF LOSS (see PROOF OF LOSS—POLICY).

 conditions of policy in regard to, must be complied with, 691.

  time of, 692.

  compliance with terms of policy as to, question for jury, 693.

  how "forthwith" "immediately," etc., are construed, 693, 695.

  notice of loss, 695.

  who may give, 695-705.

PROOF OF LOSS—*Continued.*

what is reasonable proof, is question for jury, 731.
in case of invoices, 731.
books, 731.
vouchers, 731.
when production of, excused, 731.
waiver by mutual companies, 734.
when insurer is estopped from setting up breach of, 735.
assured may show proofs of loss erroneous, when, 736.
waiver of notice, not waiver of proofs of, 740.
what should be stated in, 707.
magistrates' certificate, 710.
defective, 715-730.
implied waiver of, 715-724.
approval of binding, 724.
defense on other grounds, effect of, 726.
agent may waive, 728.
other proof not required, 731.
reasonable proof required by issuer, what is, 731.

PROPERTY (see Policy).

location of, 116.
when within description, 116.
change of location does not affect, 117.
not belonging to the class insured, 118.
concealed, not covered, 118.
when covered, though not in use, 119.
covered by implication, 119.
stock in trade, 119-126.
tools, machinery, fixtures, 119-126.
keeping, storing, meaning of, in policy, 164.
merchandise, what is covered by, 166.
described, without limiting risk to a locality, 248.
persons having custody of, 507.
policy may be, 520.

PROXIMATE CAUSE:

fire must be, 119-229.
illustrations, 119-229.

R.

REASONABLE NOTICE:

of loss, what is, 693, 696.

REBUILD (see Policy).

right of insurer to, 253-264.
effect of notice of intention to, 257, 264.

SURETY (see INTEREST).
　　may have insurable interest, 529.

SURRENDER :
　　of policy, when may be made, 231.

SURVEY (see POLICY).
　　meaning of, 162.

T.

TENANTS (see INTEREST—INSURER), 528.
　　have insurable interests, 531.
　　increase of risk by does not avoid policy, when, 446.
　　　　when does, 245.

THEFT (see POLICY—LOSS).
　　in case of fire, 215.

TITLE (see INTEREST—INSURED).
　　who has sufficient to insure, 467-534.
　　legal, not always evidence of insurable interest, 492.
　　defective, does not defeat, 503.

TRESPASSER :
　　has not generally an insurable interest in, 500.

TRUST :
　　goods held in, may be insured by trustee, 529.

TRUSTEES (see INSURANCE—INTEREST—POLICY).
　　have insurable interest, when, 529.

U.

USAGES (see EVIDENCE—POLICY).
　　insurer bound to know, 129, 314-316, 327, 451, 457, 461 n.
　　　　presumed to insure with reference to, 129, 358, 382, 451, 457, 461.

USE (see WARRANTY—APPLICATION).
　　as to occupancy, 180, 350.
　　as to method of, 351.
　　fluctuating, 355-358.
　　permanent, 355, 358.
　　unlawful, 245, 353.
　　incidental, 358.
　　ordinary, 358-361.
　　prohibited, avoids policy *per se*, 362-366, 438.
　　change of, 366.
　　description of, warranty, 367.

WATCH:
    not wearing apparel, 327.

WATCHMAN:
    condition relating to, in policy, 321–334.
    what is compliance with, 321.
    what is not, 321–334.
    relating to keeping on Sunday, 326.

WATER:
    condition requiring to be kept, what is compliance with, 321, 335.

WIFE:
    has insurable interest in husband's property, when, 528.

WILFUL BURNING:
    what must be shown to establish, 228, 851, 861.

WORDS:
    used in policy, how construed as, detached, 159.
    machinery, 160.
    in trust, 160.
    occupied, 164.
    vacant, 164.
    from—until, 161.
    contiguous, 161.
    immediate, 161.
    forthwith, 161.
    contained in, 110, 162.
    deliver in, 162.
    survey, 162.
    hazardous, 149–155.
    keeping—storing, 164.
    room, meaning of, may be established by usage, 125, *n.* 1, 283.
    factory, meaning of term may be shown by usage, 125, *n.* 1.
    ship-yard, 120.
    "stock of goods such as are usually kept in country store," 131–139, 149–
        155, 317–341, 839.
    merchandise, 104, 122.
    stock in trade, 123.
    groceries, 119–124 *n.*
    "including," used in describing property insured, enlarges risk, 124.
    "consisting of," effect of, 123.
    "used in," effect of, 125, also *n.* 1.

WRONG-DOERS (see SUBROGATION).
    doctrine as to liability of, to insurer, 788.